HOLYOAK AND TORREMANS
INTELLECTUAL PROPERTY LAW

HOLYOAK AND TORREMANS INTELLECTUAL PROPERTY LAW

Fifth Edition

PAUL TORREMANS

Licentiaat in de Rechten (KU Leuven)
Licentiaat in het Notariaat (Examencommissie van de Staat, Leuven)
Geaggregeerde voor het HSO en het HOKT in de Rechten (KU Lueven)
LLM (Leicester)
PhD (Leicester)
City Solicitors' Educational Trust Professor of Intellectual Property Law,
University of Nottingham
Professor of Private International Law, University of Ghent

OXFORD

UNIVERSITY PRESS

OXFORD
UNIVERSITY PRESS

Great Clarendon Street, Oxford OX2 6DP

Oxford University Press is a department of the University of Oxford.
It furthers the University's objective of excellence in research, scholarship,
and education by publishing worldwide in

Oxford New York

Auckland Cape Town Dar es Salaam Hong Kong Karachi
Kuala Lumpur Madrid Melbourne Mexico City Nairobi
New Delhi Shanghai Taipei Toronto

With offices in

Argentina Austria Brazil Chile Czech Republic France Greece
Guatemala Hungary Italy Japan Poland Portugal Singapore
South Korea Switzerland Thailand Turkey Ukraine Vietnam

Oxford is a registered trade mark of Oxford University Press
in the UK and in certain other countries

Published in the United States
by Oxford University Press Inc., New York

British Library Cataloguing in Publication Data

Data available

Library of Congress Cataloging in Publication Data

Torremans, Paul.
Holyoak and Torremans intellectual property law / Paul Torremans.—
5th ed.
    p. cm.
Includes index.
ISBN 978–0–19–921785–4
1. Intellectual property—Great Britain.   2. Intellectual property.
I. Title.   II. Title: Intellectual property law.
KD1269.T67 2008
346.4104'8—dc22   2008000744

Typeset by Newgen Imaging Systems (P) Ltd., Chennai, India
Printed in Great Britain
on acid-free paper by
Ashford Colour Press Ltd, Gosport, Hampshire

ISBN 978–0–19–921785–4

1 3 5 7 9 10 8 6 4 2

Outline contents

Detailed contents

Preface to the fifth edition

In the course of revising the previous editions of this book, lots of material was added to its various paragraphs and chapters; on this occasion, even more material had to be inserted. I have therefore tried to make the ever-longer chapters more readable by introducing further headings and subheadings. This improved structure should help to make the pages look clearer and should make the content even easier to read.

Its different look is clearly one of the major changes in this new edition. The new look is also part of an effort to make the book a better study-tool. In that context, each chapter now ends with a short overview section in order to provide critical focus and some suggestions for further reading have also been added. All of this should increase the pedagogic qualities of the book and make it more pleasant to work with.

There is also more in-depth analysis of the international and European framework that supports our intellectual property system, and more attention has been devoted to issues related to new technologies and biotechnologies. Above all, the book has been thoroughly updated to take account of the continuing flow of new legislation and case law, at both domestic and European levels.

We have also attempted to reflect this approach to intellectual property law in the cover and text design. At times, intellectual property law is an attempt to capture something intangible and difficult to grasp—almost like chasing a butterfly. At the same time, a butterfly is utterly likeable, and so the scene in the cover and text design reflects the aspiration of this book to make intellectual property law understandable and interesting, at the same time as it is challenging.

I would like to take this opportunity to thank a couple of people that mean a lot to me, who have provided me with a lot of support in the preparation of this new edition and all of the work that has gone into the book over the years. My sincere thanks and appreciation go, therefore, to Maria and Leo Torremans-Sleeckx. My thanks also go to Simon Baker for his work as research assistant on this project.

This fifth edition also reflects the efforts of my team at Oxford University Press. In particular, I would like to thank Ruth Ballantyne, Matt Baldwin, and Vanessa Plaister for making this a smooth experience, as well as for the outstanding quality of their work.

I have attempted to state the law as it stands on 1 November 2007.

Paul Torremans
1 November 2007

Table of statutes

UK Secondary legislation

Table of cases

Van Bennekom, Re: 227/82 [1983] ECR 3883 . . .
442
Van Der Lely NV v Bamfords Ltd [1963] RPC 61
(HL) . . . 56, 60, 137, 140
Van Doren + Q GmbH v Lifestyle sports +
sportswear Handelsgesellschaft mbH and
Michael Orth, T-244/00 [2003] ECR I-3051
. . . 451
Van Oppen & Co Ltd v Van Oppen (1903) 20
RPC 617 . . . 179
Van Zuylen Frères v Hag AG: 192/73 [1974] ECR
731; [1974] 2 CMLR 127 . . . 452
Vanacker and Lesage, criminal proceedings
against, T-37/92 [1993] ECR I-4947 . . . 442
Vane v Famous Players Film Co Ltd (1928–35)
Macq Cop Cas 394 . . . 237
Velcro/Aplix, Re (EC Commission Decision
85/410) [1989] 4 CMLR 157; OJ L 233/22 . . .
117, 118
Venables v News Group Newspapers Ltd [2001]
EMLR 10 . . . 506
Verband Sozialer Wettbewerb eV v Clinique
Laboratories SNC and Estée Lauder
Cosmetics GmbH, T-315/92 [1994] ECR I-317
. . . 441
Vermaat and Powell v Boncrest Ltd [2001] FSR
43 . . . 191, 192
Vermaat (t/a Cotton Productions) v Boncrest Ltd
(No. 2) [2001] FSR 21 . . . 244
Vicom Systems Inc's Application, T-208/84
(1987) 2 EPOR 74 . . . 528, 531
Vine Products Ltd v Mackenzie & Co Ltd [1969]
RPC 1 . . . 459, 470, 471
Virgin Enterprises Ltd v One in a Million Ltd
[1998] FSR 265 . . . 414, 478
Vodafone Group plc v Orange Personal
Communications Services Ltd [1997] FSR 34
. . . 419, 420, 487, 489
Vokes Ltd v Heather (1945) 62 RPC 135 . . . 496
Vollers The Corset Company Ltd v Cook and
other [2004] ECDR 288 . . . 584
Volvo (AB) v Erik Veng, 238/87 [1988] ECR 6211;
[1989] 4 CMLR 122 . . . 125, 126, 297–9
Volvo (AB) see also Aktiebolaget Volvo

W v Egdell [1990] Ch 359; [1989] 1 All ER 1089
(CA) . . . 501, 502, 503–4
Wagamama Ltd v City Centre Restaurants
[1995] FSR 713 . . . 408
Walker (John) & Sons Ltd v Henry Ost & Co Ltd
[1970] 2 All ER 106; [1970] 1 WLR 917 . . . 470
Walter v Ashton [1902] 2 Ch 282 . . . 465
Walter v Lane [1900] AC 539 (HL) . . . 175, 176,
177, 178, 212
Walter v Steinkopff (1892) 3 Ch 489 . . . 263
Wardle Fabrics v Myristis Ltd [1984] FSR 263
. . . 589
WARF/Stem Cells case, T-1374/04 [2006] EPOR
31 . . . 92
Warner Bros Inc v Christiansen: 158/86 [1988]
ECR 2605; [1990] 3 CMLR 684 . . . 290, 291
Warner v Gestetner Ltd [1988] EIPR D-89 . . .
215, 252, 282

Warner-Jenkinson v Hilton Davis (1997) 117 SCt
1040, US Supreme Court . . . 147
Warnink (Erven) BV v J Townend & Sons (Hull)
Ltd [1979] AC 731; [1979] 2 All ER 927 (HL)
. . . 457, 459, 464, 470, 471, 480
Warwick Film Productions Ltd v Eisinger [1969]
1 Ch 508; [1967] 3 All ER 367 . . . 180, 216, 239
Waterford Wedgwood plc v Nagli [1998] FSR 92
. . . 386
Waterlow Directories Ltd v Reed Information
Services Ltd [1992] FSR 409 . . . 542
Weatherby & Sons v International Horse Agency
and Exchange Ltd [1910] 2 Ch 297 . . . 257
WebSphere Trade Mark [2004] FSR 39 . . . 487,
490
West (t/a Eastenders) v Fuller Smith & Turner
plc [2003] FSR 816 . . . 379, 381, 383
Western Counties Manure Co v Lawes Chemical
Manure Co (1874) LR 9 Exch 218 . . . 486
Wham-O Manufacturing Co v Lincoln
Industries Ltd [1985] RPC 127 . . . 188
Wheatley (Davina) v Drillsafe Ltd [2001] RPC
133 (CA) . . . 145
Whelan Associates Inc v Jaslow Dental
Laboratory Inc [1987] FSR 1 (CA) . . .
533, 534
White v Mellin [1895] AC 154 (HL) . . . 487, 488
Wild Child Trade Mark, Re [1998] RPC 455 . . .
393, 394
Wilkinson (Mark) Furniture Ltd v Woodcraft
Designs (Radcliffe) Ltd [1998] FSR 63 . . . 347,
349, 352
Williams v Nye (1890) 7 RPC 62 . . . 74, 75
Williams (J B) Co v H Bronnley Co Ltd (1909) 26
RPC 765 (CA) . . . 474
Windsurfing Chiemsee Produktions und
Vertriebs GmbH v Attenberger, C-109/97
[1999] ECR I-2779 . . . 386
Windsurfing Chiemsee Produktions und
Vertriebs GmbH v Boots- und Segelzubehör
Walter Huber, C-108/97 [1999] ECR I-2779
. . . 386
Windsurfing International Inc v EC
Commission, 193/83 [1986] ECR 611; [1986] 3
CMLR 489 (ECJ) . . . 116, 117, 118
Windsurfing International Inc v Tabur Marine
(Great Britain) Ltd [1985] RPC 59 (CA) . . . 57,
59, 64–7
Windsurfing International, Re (EC Commission
Decision 83/400) [1983] OJ L 229/1 . . . 117
Wiseman v Weidenfeld & Nicolson Ltd [1985]
FSR 525 . . . 184
Wm Wrigley Jr Co v OHIM, T-193/99 [2001]
ECR II-417 . . . 384
Wolters Kluwer (UK) Ltd v Reed Elsevier (UK)
Ltd [2006] FSR 28 . . . 419
Wombles Ltd v Wombles Skips Ltd [1977] RPC
99 . . . 465, 467
Wood v Boosey (1868) LR 3 QB 223 . . . 185
Woodhouse v Architectural Lighting [2006]
RPC 1 . . . 332
Woodman v French Connection Ltd [2007] RPC
1 . . . 390

Table of EU legislation

Directives

Table of international agreements, conventions, and treaties

SECTION A

INTRODUCTION

1
Themes in intellectual property

Preliminary thoughts

This book is not only about ideas: it is about ideas skilfully expressed in writing, in music, or in a sculpture. It is about the bright idea for an invention, the details of which have been worked out and which takes the form of a product or a process that can be applied industrially. It is also about a logo or name applied to products in order to distinguish them from other products in the same category and to indicate their origin. It is also about clothes and exhaust pipes made to a new design. Intellectual property is more than a reward for inventors and creators on the basis of a bright idea.

We will investigate this further on all other pages of this book, but let us start with a down-to-earth overview of the plot of our story. The background is a concert given by a famous opera singer. His performance consists of songs taken from various operas. The lyrics and music of each of these songs can attract copyright protection for its author; the opera singer will have a right in his performance of them. A live recording is made and published on compact disc (CD), and the concert is beamed around the world as a satellite broadcast—two further occasions on which copyright interests arise. Satellite technology involves various patented inventions both in relation to the missile technology and in relation to the transmission of broadcasts. The CD will bear the logo of the record company, which allows customers to distinguish the CD from that of another record company. It is most likely that the record company will have secured a trade mark for its logo to guarantee its exclusive right to use it. The CD's accompanying booklet raises copyright issues, because it contains a photograph in which the star is pictured standing next to a sculpture made by his wife. The photograph, the sculpture, and the text of the booklet can all be protected by copyright. T-shirts bearing the star's picture are of a different style, but allow him to merchandise his image and to benefit from his celebrity status.

By the time we will have unravelled all of the intellectual property aspects of this concert—or at least the legal provisions underlying them—we will have reached the final page of our book. This example provides, however, a first impression of what intellectual property means in practice and alerts the reader to the intellectual property aspects of many elements of our everyday lives.

Introduction

In recent years, intellectual property has attracted a lot of attention. Its importance for international trading relations was emphasized during the negotiations that led to the

successful conclusion of the General Agreement on Tariffs and Trade (GATT)[1] Uruguay
Round on the world trading system. The GATT Trade-Related Aspects of Intellectual
Property Rights (TRIPS) initiative, which led eventually to the Agreement on Trade-
Related Aspects of Intellectual Property Rights 1994 that was signed in Marrakesh,[2]
was sparked off by a strong desire to eradicate international counterfeiting and piracy.
It became clear at a very early stage, however, that the cure for the fake Gucci or Cartier
watch, Lacoste shirt or even counterfeited fire extinguishing system in a jet engine for a
passenger plane[3]—or for what is often described as a plague threatening (among other
things) the worldwide exploitation of intellectual property—also required a harmonization of national intellectual property laws.[4] It is much easier to eradicate counterfeits at
source, with a common set of minimum protection rules, than afterwards, at a national
border once they are in circulation.[5]

At European level, the realization of the single market gave rise to a series of initiatives in the intellectual property area. Harmonization Directives—for example, that on
the harmonization of the duration of the term of copyright protection[6] and the Trade
Mark Directive[7]—were coupled with moves towards a set of truly European intellectual
property rights[8] and Community responses to the computer industry's perceived need for
adequate protection.[9] UK legislation was updated as a result of a number of these developments and we have also seen the further development of, for example, the tort of passing
off, and the protection offered to the merchandising activities involving real and fictitious
characters, to fill the gaps not covered internationally—for example, goodwill, characters,
and information.

Due in part to these developments, the various intellectual property rights have become
relatively well known:

(a) trade marks;

(b) patents;

(c) copyright;

[1] The General Agreement on Tariffs and Trade—basically, the world free-trading system—which, as
a structure and organization, was succeeded by the World Trade Organization (WTO) as a result of the
Uruguay Round of trade negotiations.
[2] The final text of the TRIPS Agreement was published in (1994) 33 ILM 1197 and in (1994) 25 IIC 209.
The agreement is administered by the WTO, which succeeded to GATT. See D. Gervais (2003) *The TRIPS
Agreement: Drafting History and Analysis*, 2nd edn, London: Sweet and Maxwell; C. Correa (2007) *Trade-
Related Aspects of Intellectual Property Rights: A Commentary on the TRIPS Agreement*, Oxford: Oxford
University Press.
[3] See M.-C. Piatti, 'Measures to combat international piracy' [1989] 7 EIPR 239 at 239–40.
[4] See K. Thomas (2007) 'The fight against piracy: working within the administrative enforcement system
in China', in P. Torremans, H. Shan and J. Erauw, *Intellectual Property and TRIPS Compliance in China:
Chinese and European Perspectives*, Cheltenham/Northampton, MA: Edward Elgar, pp. 85–106.
[5] See the comments on the current debate between Europe and China in P. Torremans et al. (2007),
especially: G. Shoukang and Z. Xiaodong, 'Are Chinese intellectual property laws consistent with the TRIPS
Agreement?', pp. 11–28; P. Torremans, 'Substantive law issues in Europe a decade after TRIPS', pp. 29–61.
[6] Directive 93/98 harmonizing the term of protection of copyright and certain related rights (1993)
OJ L 290/9.
[7] Directive 89/104 on the approximation of the laws of member States relating to trade marks (1989) OJ
L40/1.
[8] For example, the Community Trade Mark—see Council Regulation 40/94 on the Community Trade
Mark (1994) OJ L11/1—and the Community Design—see Council Regulation 6/2002 on Community
Designs (2002) OJ L3/1.
[9] See, e.g., Directive 91/250 on the legal protection of computer programs (1991) OJ L122/42 and Directive
96/9 on the legal protection of databases (1996) OJ L77/20.

(d) rights in performances;

(e) registered designs;

(f) design rights.

Let us add some more examples to our concert example discussed above. Intellectual property addresses problems such as how the CD system, as a technological invention, is temporarily protected by patents, how the aesthetic appearance of a telephone in the shape of a golf caddy can be protected as a registered design, and whether the functional design of kitchen utensils can attract (unregistered) design protection. We could also use intellectual property laws to examine how the registration of the trade mark 'Sprite' by the Coca-Cola Company for its lemon-taste soft drink is linked to the fact that it allows consumers to identify the drink and to distinguish it from similar soft drinks, and how such a trade mark is protected against imitation, how copyright grants and protects certain rights in literary, artistic, and musical creations, and which rights exist in performances. Other related areas that we will equally have to consider include the laws of confidence and passing off. These form an essential national addition to the types and level of protection provided on the basis of international conventions.

A brief historical overview—the origins

When we refer to 'intellectual property rights', we do not wish to make the distinction between industrial intellectual property rights—such as patents and trade marks—and artistic intellectual property rights—such as copyright. This distinction appears no longer to be valid, because copyright is now used in such a flexible way—for example, to protect computer programs—that it can no longer be called an exclusively artistic right. The same concepts underlie each type of intellectual property. A strong form of unity exists between all types of intellectual property and the common law concepts in use in this area. But this dichotomy between 'industrial' patents and 'artistic' copyright has been an essential element in the historical development of the protection of what we call 'intellectual property'. Before we try to define this term and to justify the continuing existence of intellectual property rights, let us have a brief look at the historical roots of our topic.

The origin and the evolution of the patent system

Patents can be traced back as far as the end of the Middle Ages.[10] Inventor privileges—which, in England, took the form of royal grants under the royal prerogative—were granted all over Europe. Although not altogether absent, the idea of the promotion of inventive activity through the grant of a market monopoly was strongly overshadowed by the idea that these privileges were the perfect tool with which to reward political creditors and to give them a trading monopoly granted by letters patent.

In England, Parliament reacted against this practice and, in 1624, the Statute of Monopolies was issued. It was primarily a response to the existing practice and the trading monopolies to which this practice gave rise, but it was also influenced by the idea that, in certain circumstances, a market monopoly would be necessary as an incentive to innovate. The result of this influence is found in s. 6 of the Statute of Monopolies: the

---

[10] See also S. Thorley, R. Miller, G. Burkill, C. Birss and D. Campbell (2006) *Terrell on the Law of Patents*, 16th edn, London: Sweet and Maxwell, pp. 1–7.

'*true and first inventor*' was granted a patent monopoly for 14 years upon '*any manner of new manufacture*'.

Because England felt that France and Holland were further advanced in their technical development, any person who imported new technologies with a view to establishing an advanced domestic industry was equally considered to be an inventor. The flexibility on this point emphasizes that this new patent system should be seen as a deliberate act of economic policy.[11] By rewarding, eventually, both devisors and importers of new technologies, the development of industrial activity, growth, and employment emerges as the primary aim of the legislation; gratitude towards the inventor is only of secondary importance. The policy aspect is reinforced by the provision that manufactures that are '*contrary to the law or mischievous to the state, by raising prices of commodities at home, or hurt trade, or generally inconvenient*'[12] would not be protected. Only those manufactures that fit in with the policy would be protected, because the realization of the aims of the policy were the ultimate reason for the existence of the patents.

These early developments represent only the start of a long development process wherein the Industrial Revolution in Europe was the key element. The eighteenth century saw the development of the patent specification, first, as a tool with which to define the content of the protected invention against infringers by means of a statement enrolled with the Court of Chancery and, later, in the modern sense, as a source of technical information provided by the patentee as consideration for the monopoly granted to him by the patent. The novelty concept, which corresponded previously to the fact that the invention was not yet practised in the country, was enlarged to incorporate also the question of whether the trading community already knew of the invention through publication.

The Patent Law Amendment Act 1852 removed the inefficiencies and uncertainties in the procedures for securing a patent. The applicant could register his specification with the Commissioners of Patents, with an option to file a provisional application up to one year, before the complete specification was worked out and filed. Patents were granted simply upon registration and at a reasonable fee. This led to an increase in the number of patents, some of which were of dubious value, due to the absence of any examination of the applications.

The Patents, Designs and Trade Marks Act 1883 addressed the problems arising from the inadequacy of the patent litigation procedures. A single judge replaced the juries and patentees were obliged to delineate the scope of their monopoly in at least one of their claims; even more important, however, was the replacement of the Commissioners by the Patent Office, charged with the examination of the patent applications. In a first stage, the Office examined whether the formal requirements and the requirement that the patentee should provide a proper description of the patent had been observed. An examination of the novelty of the application, based on a search of previous British specifications, was added to the examination process from 1905 onwards.[13] This change clearly demonstrates how strongly the origins of intellectual property are linked with—and their evolution is a response to—commercial necessities.

All over Europe and in North America, specific patent legislation was introduced at national level in the course of the nineteenth century. As a similar evolution took place in all of these countries and because the technology that was being developed was not only to be used in the country in which it was developed, a need for international cooperation

---

[11] See B. Dölemeyer, 'Einführungsprivilegien und Einführungspatente als historische Mittel des Technologietransfers' [1985] GRUR 735. This German article is the best source for this view.

[12] See Statute of Monopolies 1624, s. 6.

[13] See Patents Act 1902.

arose. In 1883, the Paris Convention for the Protection of Industrial Property was created as the basic instrument for international patent protection.[14] It provides minimal rules of protection, which were translated into the national patent legislation. In addition, it contains a rule of national treatment that provides that foreign inventors shall be treated in the same way as their domestic counterparts and that their inventions shall be granted the same level of protection.[15]

The development of the first half of the twentieth century can be characterized as a consolidation effort at legal and organizational levels. The new phenomenon of the vast number of newly independent states created a crisis in the patent system in the early 1960s: a flood of patent applications had to be dealt with independently by an ever-growing number of national patent offices; international and regional cooperation was seen as the solution. Attempts to arrive at regional patent systems,[16] and treaties providing assistance and combating the seemingly endless duplication of the examination procedures (such as the global Patent Co-operation Treaty)[17] were established during this period. Another problem that newly independent states faced—especially in the developing world—was the inappropriateness for their purposes of the existing patent legislation. The adoption of new patent laws in these countries and the reform of the international patent system to this new environment are processes that have not yet been concluded.[18]

The origin and evolution of trade marks

The use of marks that are added to goods to distinguish them from similar goods has a history of at least two thousand years: the Romans embossed their pottery, or impressed it with a mark, and merchants have used marks ever since to distinguish their goods. Although the courts became involved in the actions against infringers,[19] no proper trade mark legislation was enacted and the system was, for a long time, based purely on common law principles. The main problem that traders faced was that, each time they brought an infringement action, they had to prove their title to the mark. This depended on the existence of an established reputation associated with the mark.

In France, this problem had been solved by the introduction of a registration system and a similar registration system was introduced in England, in 1875, under the Trade Marks Registration Act.[20] UK trade mark legislation was consolidated by the Patents, Designs and Trade Marks Act 1883—the same year in which the Paris Convention was signed. The principles contained in this Convention apply to trade marks as well as to patents.[21]

The next step in the consolidation process was the statutory definition of the term 'trade mark' in the Trade Marks Act 1905. This was followed, in the Trade Marks Act 1919, by

---

[14] See F. K. Beier, 'The significance of the patent system for technical, economic and social progress' [1980] IIC 563 at 570.

[15] Article 2 of the Paris Convention.

[16] For example, the Nordic Patent System and the European Patent Convention.

[17] See Chapter 2.

[18] See, most recently, the Patent Law Treaty (Geneva, 2000) as an attempt to harmonize procedures before the national patent offices. The UK has signed the Treaty and, in relation to the UK, it entered into force on 22 March 2006. As yet, only a limited number of states have ratified the Treaty (17 at the time of writing).

[19] See *Sykes v. Sykes* (1824) 3 B & C 541, a case that contains some basic principles: e.g. damages at common law; deceit.

[20] For a comprehensive overview of the historical development of the law of trade marks (and passing off), see C. Morcom, A. Roughton and J. Graham (2005) *The Modern Law of Trade Marks*, 2nd edn, London: Lexis Nexis Butterworths, pp. 5–12.

[21] See n. 15.

the division of the register into Part A—within which stringent requirements were coupled with better protection in terms of remedies—and Part B. The Trade Marks Act 1938 was based on the same principles, but the drafting was more detailed. It was amended by the Trade Marks (Amendment) Act 1984 to also include service marks. Although the division of the register into two parts was abolished by the Trade Marks Act 1994, the UK system still retains an examination stage before the mark is registered.

The origin and the evolution of the copyright system

We have seen that, at international level, many of the principles applied to patents are equally applied to trade marks.[22] This is not always the case for copyright, however.

Copyright is historically linked to written literary works. Because handwritten copies were such a formidable investment of time and effort, few copies were made available and plagiarism was not a problem. All this changed when Gutenberg invented movable type and Caxton developed the printing press in the second half of the fifteenth century. The arrival of this technology made the printing of multiple copies possible, quickly and at relatively little expense.[23]

Stationers acquired the works from their authors, and organized the printing and the sale of these works. These entrepreneurs took the commercial risks involved in exploiting the works of the authors and they wanted exclusive rights in the publication of the works to protect them against copiers. They found an ally in the Crown, which wanted to control the importation and circulation of books. The stationers organized themselves into a guild and the Crown granted the Stationers' Company a charter in 1556. Lawfully printed books were entered in the Company's register and, because the right to make an entry in the register was reserved for the stationers, this system effectively amounted to a licensing system and secured a printing monopoly for the Company members. On top of that, members were granted powers to act against infringing copies.

This system remained in place until the end of the seventeenth century, at which point there was a brief period of anarchy. This period was, however, followed by the first real copyright statute: the Statute of Anne 1709. It gave the '*sole right and liberty of printing books*' to authors and their assignees. There was, however, no shift from an entrepreneurial copyright to an author's right, with emphasis exclusively on literary creation and its creators: under the Statute of Anne, the emphasis remained focused on the commercial exploitation of books. Printers and booksellers were explicitly named among the author's assigns.[24] Their right started from first publication and lasted for 14 years, but it was only enforceable by seizure and penalties if the title of the book had been registered with the Stationers' Company before publication.[25] Before publication, the author could rely on certain common law rights of literary property to obtain protection against unauthorized copying[26] and, if the author was still alive on expiry of the term of protection of 14 years, the right was 'returned' to him for another 14 years.

At the end of the eighteenth and during the nineteenth centuries, the duration of the term of copyright protection was gradually increased; simultaneously, the scope of copyright

---

[22] Industrial designs are also found in this category.

[23] The history of copyright has recently been analysed in detail by R. Deazley (2004) *On the Origin of the Right to Copy: Charting the Movement of Copyright Law in Eighteenth-Century Britain (1695–1775)*, Oxford: Hart; R. Deazley (2006) *Re-Thinking Copyright: History, Theory, Language*, Cheltenham/Northampton, MA: Edward Elgar.

[24] See Statute of Anne 1709, s. 1.

[25] See ibid., ss. 1 and 2.

[26] *Donaldson v. Beckett* (1774) 2 Bro P C 129, 4 Burr 2408.

was widened to include types of work other than literary works. Engravings, prints, lithographs, sculptures, dramatic, and musical works all received copyright protection during that period. But drama and music did not fit in well with the existing 'copy-right'—that is, the right to produce copies of the work and to prevent others from doing so—because their exploitation was more likely to involve performances, rather than the sale of printed copies. As a consequence, playwrights and composers sought a 'use' right, and a performing right for dramatic works was created in 1833[27] and extended to musical works in 1842.[28]

The British emphasis on the entrepreneurial exploitation aspect of copyright was not shared by those who saw copyright almost exclusively as the expression of reverence for the creating artist and his act of artistic creation. The latter tendency was particularly strong in France and Belgium, as illustrated by the use of the term *droit d'auteur*—that is, 'author's right'—rather than a 'copy' right. As a major exporter of copyright material, Britain had an important interest in a compromise that secured at least some form of copyright protection abroad. The approach taken bears strong similarities to the contemporary evolution regarding patents: the Convention for the Protection of Literary and Artistic Works was signed in Berne in 1886.[29] From that moment on, a personal connection between the author and a member State of the Berne Union, or first publication of the work in a member State of the Union, was sufficient for protection in all member States on a national treatment basis.

When the Convention was revised in 1908, it was felt that there was a need to agree on further minimal rules. Copyright protection was no longer to depend upon registration or any other formality, but upon the act of creation of the work, and the term of copyright protection would last for at least the author's life plus 50 years. When these changes were incorporated into the Copyright Act 1911, it signalled the end for the Stationers' Company. The 1911 Act also widened the scope of copyright further. The producers of sound recordings were granted the exclusive right to prevent unauthorized reproductions of their recordings.[30] Significantly, this right was not given to the performing artist, but to the entrepreneur involved. The right was also labelled 'copyright', but the *droit d'auteur* tradition would instead distinguish it as a neighbouring right, because it does not directly protect the original artistic creation of the author; the work protected is derived only from the author's original artistic creation.

This right in sound recordings was an important precedent. It indicated that copyright would be flexible enough to offer protection to all works in whose creation new technical possibilities for artistic expression had been used. The Copyright Act 1956 granted protection on a similar basis in cinematograph films, broadcasts, and the typographical format of published editions.

At international level, the developing countries advocated major changes to the Berne Convention during the 1960s. The Stockholm 1967 and Paris 1971 Revisions of the Berne Convention granted, in the end, only minimal concessions with a lot of strings attached: they allow only certain translations and publications of foreign works if these are not otherwise made available.[31] In a separate development, performing artists have been

---

[27] Dramatic Copyright Act 1833.

[28] Literary Copyright Act 1842, s. 20.

[29] For a full account of the history of the Berne Convention and the Berne Union, see S. Ricketson (1987) *The Berne Convention for the Protection of Literary and Artistic Works: 1886–1986*, London: Kluwer Law International, ch. 1; S. Ricketson and J. C. Ginsburg (2006) *International Copyright and Neighbouring Rights: The Berne Convention and Beyond*, vol. 1, Oxford: Oxford University Press, ch. 1.

[30] Copyright Act 1911, s. 19(1). The courts later held that the producers could also prevent public performances of their recordings: *Gramophone Co. v. Cawardine* [1934] Ch 450.

[31] For more details, see the appendix to the Berne Convention upon which agreement was reached at the Paris revision conference (1971), reproduced in J. Phillips (ed.) (2007) *Butterworths Intellectual Property Law Handbook*, 8th edn, London: Butterworths Law.

granted certain rights. The Convention on the Protection of Performers, Producers of Phonograms and Broadcasting Organizations was signed in Rome in 1961. Under the provisions of this Convention, performers have the right to prevent the fixation or the broadcasting of their live performances.[32] The makers of records can prevent the reproduction of their records,[33] and broadcasting organizations can control the re-broadcasting and the public performance for an entrance fee of their broadcasts.[34] The Rome Convention has, unfortunately, never reached the same level of adherence between nations as did the Berne Convention.[35] A second Phonograms Convention, which deals with mutual protection against the unauthorized commercial copying of sound recordings, was signed in 1971. In the UK, these international provisions have been translated into the Copyright, Designs and Patents Act 1988, mainly as Part II: Rights in Performances.[36]

No absolute divide between patents and copyright

This brief historical overview of the development of patent and copyright law[37] clearly demonstrates that the divide between patents—as purely industrial rights—and copyright—as a purely artistic right—was never absolute in nature. Especially in the UK, copyright always had an entrepreneurial, almost industrial, orientation. Copyright was never an exclusively artistic right, as opposed to the other industrial property rights. In recent years, this tendency has been emphasized by the use of copyright to protect computer programs. It is, however, true that copyright is different from the other rights: patents protect the invention, while copyright protects not only the creation, but also grants some strong, additional, personal rights to the creator.

These moral rights have always been an essential aspect of the French *droit d'auteur* and, in the UK, they were incorporated in their own right for the first time in the Copyright, Designs and Patents Act 1988.[38] Each right is an intellectual property right, but each right has its own characteristics. Before examining each right in detail, we will try to define the term 'intellectual property' and we will also examine whether the continued existence of 'intellectual property rights' can be justified.

A definition and a justification of intellectual property

Intellectual property rights are, firstly, property rights—but, secondly, they are property rights in something intangible; finally, they protect innovations and creations, and reward innovative and creative activity.[39]

---

[32] See Rome Convention, Arts 7–9. The same right does not exist in relation to recorded performances.

[33] See ibid., Arts 10–12.

[34] See ibid, Art 13. They cannot, however, control the diffusion by wire or by cable of their broadcasts.

[35] Hopefully, the World Intellectual Property Organization (WIPO) Performances and Phonograms Treaty that was signed in Geneva in 1996, and entered into force in May 2002, will be more successful. The text of this Treaty is reproduced in Phillips (2007).

[36] Before the Copyright, Designs and Patents Act 1988 came into force, the Performers' Protection Acts 1958–72 offered some protection to performing artists, but the level and the type of that protection were unsatisfactory.

[37] More details can be found in K. Garnett, G. Davies and G. Harbottle (2005) *Copinger and Skone James on Copyright*, 15th edn, London: Sweet and Maxwell, pp. 30–47.

[38] Copyright, Designs and Patents Act 1988, Pt I, ch. 4, ss. 77–89.

[39] US Council for International Business (1985) *A New MTN: Priorities for Intellectual Property*, at 3.

Property rights

The essential characteristic of property rights is that they are exclusionary rights through which third parties are prohibited from the use and exploitation of the subject precluded by these rights.[40] Through property rights, externalities can be internalized[41]—that is, the subject of the right is brought under the control of the owner of the property right. These rights will only develop when the cost of this internalization is smaller than the gains to which it leads.[42]

If we take a bicycle as an example of an item of tangible property, it is immediately clear that the owner of the bicycle has the exclusive right to use the bicycle, and that such a monopolistic right in real and personal property is conceded almost naturally. Property rights in items such as our bicycle developed because nobody would be prepared to invest time, materials, and skills in designing and producing bicycles[43] if he or she would have no right in the result of the process that would enable him or her to benefit from that work. The most obvious way in which to do so is to sell the bicycle—but few would wish to acquire the bicycle should they be unable to acquire the exclusive right to its use. The nature of the object gives this right a monopolistic character: if someone uses the bicycle, no one else can use it. The physical nature of the unique embodiment of certain limited resources in the bicycle automatically leads to a particular competitive[44] exclusionary effect.[45]

Intangible property rights

In this respect, intellectual property rights are fundamentally different from rights in tangible property. The nature of the property that is the subject of the right and which is protected does not necessarily lead to competitive exclusionary effects. Concurrent uses of inventions by a number of manufacturers, including the patentee, or simultaneous performances of a musical are possible.[46] The invention and the musical will not perish, nor will any use or performance lessen their value.

The subject matter of intellectual property rights—that is, inventions or creations—has a link with knowledge and ideas. In economic terms, this subject matter constitutes a public asset and its use is not, by its nature, individually appropriable.[47] In many cases, imitation is even cheaper than invention or creation.[48] The competitive exclusion only arises artificially when a legally binding intellectual 'property' right is created as

---

[40] See M. Lehmann, 'The theory of property rights and the protection of intellectual and industrial property' [1985] IIC 525 at 530.

[41] An externality is an economic situation in which an individual's pursuit of his or her self-interest has positive or negative spillover effects on the utility or welfare of others. It can be seen as a market failure and, in this context, a property right is a tool used to correct such a market failure: see R. Ekelund and R. Tollison (1986) *Economics*, Boston, MA: Little, Brown and Co., pp. 404–5.

[42] H. Demsetz, 'Toward a theory of property rights' (1967) 57 American Economy Review 347 at 350; for an overview of the property rights theory, see R. Cooter and T. Ulen (1988) *Law and Economics*, New York: HarperCollins, esp ch. 4, but also ch. 5.

[43] At most, they would design and produce one bicycle to get from A to B themselves, but even that cannot be taken for granted in a situation in which no property rights exist.

[44] The difference is that between 'my bicycle' and 'bicycles as a concept'.

[45] Lehmann [1985] at 531.

[46] Ibid.

[47] H. Ullrich, 'The importance of industrial property law and other legal measures in the promotion of technological innovation' [1989] Industrial Property 102 at 103.

[48] See E. Mansfield, M. Schwartz and S. Wagner, 'Imitation costs and patents: an empirical study' [1981] Economic Journal 907.

an intangible property right. This gives the inventor or the creator—the owners of the intangible property right—the exclusive use of the invention or the creation.

An economic justification[49]

Market failure and free riders

So why are these intangible property rights created? Economists argue that, if everyone were to be allowed to use the results of innovative and creative activity freely, the problem of the 'freerider'[50] would arise.[51] No one would invest in innovation or creation, except in a couple of cases in which no other solution were available,[52] because to do so would put them at a competitive disadvantage.[53] All competitors would simply wait until someone else made the investment, because they would then be able to use the results without having invested that money in innovation and creation, and without having taken the risk that the investment might not result in the innovative or creative breakthrough at which it aimed.[54] The cost of the distribution of the knowledge is relatively insignificant.[55]

As a result, it is argued, the economy would not function adequately, because innovation and creation are essential elements in a competitive free market economy. From this perspective, innovation and creation are required for economic growth and prosperity.[56] Property rights should be created if goods and services are to be produced, and used, as efficiently as possible in such an economy.[57] The knowledge that they will have a property right in the results of their investment will stimulate individuals and enterprises to invest in research and development,[58] and these property rights should be granted to those who will economically maximize profits.[59] It is assumed that the creator or inventor will have been motivated by the desire to maximize profits—either by exploiting the invention

---

[49] We will approach the justification issue from the point of view of the developed countries. The international transfer of technology and the different level of development in developing countries present additional problems: see, e.g., P. Braga 'The economics of intellectual property rights and the GATT: a view from the south' [1989] Vand J Transnat'l L 243.

[50] See R. Benko (1987) *Protecting Intellectual Property Rights: Issues and Controversies*, Washington DC: American Enterprise Institute, p. 17.

[51] Inappropriability—the lack of the opportunity to become the proprietor of the results of innovative and creative activity—causes an underallocation of resources to research activity, innovation, and creation: see K. Arrow (1962) 'Economic welfare and the allocation of resources for invention', in National Bureau for Economic Research, *The Rate and Direction of Inventive Activity: Economic and Social Factors*, Princeton, NJ: Princeton University Press, pp. 609–25.

[52] For example, a case in which the existing technology is completely incapable of providing any form of solution to a new technical problem that has arisen.

[53] See Ullrich [1989] at 103.

[54] One might advance the counter-argument that inventions and creations will give the innovator an amount of lead time and that the fact that it will take imitators some time to catch up would allow the innovator to recuperate his or her investment during the interim period. In many cases, however, this amount of lead time will only be a short period—too short to allow the innovator to recuperate the investment in full and make a profit. See also Mansfield et al. [1981] at 915 *et seq.*

[55] See Benko (1987) p. 17.

[56] Ibid., ch. 4, p. 15; US Council for International Business (1985) at 3.

[57] See B. Pretnar, 'The economic impact of patents in a knowledge-based market economy' (2003) 34 IIC 887; E. Mackaay (2007) 'The economics of intellectual property rights in civil law systems', working paper received from the author.

[58] P. Lunn, 'The roles of property rights and market power in appropriating innovative output' [1985] J Legal Stud 423 at 425.

[59] M. Lehmann, 'Property and intellectual property: property rights as restrictions on competition in furtherance of competition' [1989] IIC 1 at 11.

or creation him or herself, or by having it exploited by a third party—so the creator or inventor is granted the rights.[60]

This argument applies as well to intangible property rights such as patents, which determine the value of an item in a direct way, as it does to rights such as trade marks, which do so only indirectly through their use as a means of communication.[61]

Exclusivity and perfect competition

But how does such a legally created, monopolistic, exclusive property right fit in with the free market ideal of perfect competition? At first sight, every form of a monopoly might seem to be incompatible with free competition, but we have already demonstrated that some form of property right is required to enhance economic development: competition can only play its role as market regulator if the products of human labour are protected by property rights.[62] In this respect, the exclusive monopolistic character of the property rights is coupled with the fact that these rights are transferable. These rights are marketable: they can, for example, be sold as an individual item. It is also necessary to distinguish between various levels of economic activity, as far as economic development and competition are concerned. The market mechanism is more sophisticated than the competition–monopoly dichotomy. Competitive restrictions at one level may be necessary to promote competition at another level.

Three levels can be distinguished: production, consumption, and innovation. Property rights in goods enhance competition on the production level, but this form of ownership restricts competition on the consumption level. One has to acquire the ownership of the goods before one is allowed to consume them and goods owned by other economic players are not directly available for one's consumption. In turn, intellectual property imposes competitive restrictions on the production level: only the owner of the patent in an invention may use the invention and only the owner of the copyright in a literary work may produce additional copies of that work. These restrictions benefit competition on the innovative level. The availability of property rights on each level guarantees the development of competition on the next level.

Property rights are a prerequisite for the normal functioning of the market mechanism.[63] To take the example of patents: '*patents explicitly prevent the diffusion of new technology to guarantee the existence of technology to diffuse in the future.*'[64] Trade marks, meanwhile, distinguish identical goods or services of different sources. They therefore allow the consumer to distinguish between such products and services, and grant the right holder the exclusive right to apply the mark to the goods and services for which it has been registered. In doing so, trade marks enable competition between producers of identical goods or services. They therefore encourage the availability of a wider variety of goods and services between which the consumer can distinguish, by means of the trade mark, in terms of quality, price, etc.

This clearly demonstrates that it is not correct to see intellectual property rights as monopolies that are in permanent conflict with the fundamental rule of free competition. Free competition can only exist, and a market economy can only flourish, when certain restrictions in furtherance of competition are accepted. Intellectual property

---

[60] For an economic–philosophical approach, see also E. Mackaay (1991) 'Economic and philosophical aspects of intellectual property rights', in M. Van Hoecke (ed.) *The Socio-Economic Role of Intellectual Property Rights*, Brussels: Story-Scientia, pp. 1–30.

[61] See Lehmann [1985] at 531.

[62] Lehmann [1989] at 12.

[63] Lehmann [1985] at 539.

[64] Benko (1987) ch. 4, p. 19.

rights are necessary to achieve this. The main problem is that this only justifies the exist-ence of exclusive property rights as the result of innovative activity. The particular form that intellectual property rights have taken in a particular national intellectual property statute—and, even more, the way in which these rights are used and exercised—are not automatically justified by this theory. The restrictions on competition are only justified in so far as they are restrictions in furtherance of competition on the next level, which is either the production level or the innovation level; any restriction that goes further hinders the optimal functioning of the market economy. It is the task of the provisions on competition law to regulate this system in such a way that this optimal level of function-ing is achieved and maintained. This coexistence of intellectual property and the rules on free competition is a permanent balancing act, and one of the most challenging and interesting parts of the study of intellectual property.

If we focus on patents for a moment, in order to go into a bit more detail, we have to start from the above premise that the economic justification does not give us ready-made rules on every aspect of patent law. Instead, we are confronted with a constant, built-in dialectic tension between the protection of the patented—that is, already realized—inno-vation and the promotion of subsequent innovation.[65] The strongest possible protection is therefore not only not a logical consequence of the economic justification, but would also unduly focus on one aspect of that tension. The promotion of subsequent innovation that builds on what has already been achieved would be harmed—and this would be all the more serious, because the tension is not restricted to the relationship between the paten-tee and its competitors. It does, indeed, influence the overall market's actual and potential competitive dynamics. What is needed, therefore, is a set of rules for a patent system that respects and enhances a rich dialectic interrelationship between the need to guarantee a differential return on activities and investments in research and development, on the one hand, and the need to safeguard the actual chance of third parties' subsequent innova-tion and the competitive fabric of the market as a whole, on the other. This balance will be struck in the rules on patentability—that is, that certain thresholds need to be passed before a patent is warranted—and in the scope of the patent and the limitations to the exclusive right, among others.[66]

An ideal patent system that can be fully justified will, therefore, not simply involve rewarding inventors in order to stimulate them to invent more, or stimulating them to achieve, in turn, inventive steps. The finer points of the system set out here require that such a patent system will more specifically reward:

> the innovation already developed in such a way that the reward granted to the current inventor stimulates both the inventor to continue and third parties to develop a subsequent innovation which might compete with the preceding one, thus also spurring on the first innovator, in a virtuous pro-innovation and pro-competition dynamic process.[67]

Goods perish through use, while intangible property is—at least in theory—perpetual.[68] But the socio-economic value of these rights is not so important that a perpetual restric-tion on competition is necessary and justifiable to enhance competition on other lev-els. Innovative activity will be sufficiently enhanced, without restrictions of competition

[65] See G. Ghidini (2006) *Intellectual Property and Competition Law: The Innovation Nexus*, Cheltenham/ Northampton, MA: Edward Elgar, p. 14.

[66] Ibid.

[67] Ibid., p. 24.

[68] It may, however, lose its economic value after a number of years: e.g. an inventive production process protected by a patent can be applied indefinitely, but will, after a number of years, be overtaken by new tech-nological developments and so lose its economic value.

on the production level that are too far-reaching, when the intellectual property right is restricted in time. For patents, which grant the patentee extensive restrictive powers and whose protection is wide in scope, the term of protection is relatively short (20 years). From now on, literary works are to be protected under copyright for a period of the life of the author plus 70 years, but the protection granted is weaker than that offered under patents: only the particular expression of an idea is protected; the idea as such is left unprotected. This attempt to get the balance between restriction on, and freedom of competition right through, the use of a fixed term can be seen as lacking precision and potentially unjust, but introducing a sliding scale would require the determination of the term of protection on the basis of the merits of each individual invention or creation. This would create massive administrative costs that outweigh the benefits derived from the system and, on top of this, it would create an undesirable climate of legal uncertainty.[69]

A duty to exercise

Another way of getting the balance right is the duty to exercise and use, which is linked to patent and trade mark rights. Compulsory use and compulsory licences are an integral component of most intellectual property legislations. The idea behind this is, first of all, that use of the intellectual property right will provide an income to its owner and that this profit will encourage him to continue his innovative work. The only reason why a restriction of competition at the level of production is acceptable is the enhancement of competition on the innovative level, through the possibility for the owner of the right to realize a profit. This justification collapses if this right is not used, a defect that is remedied by the introduction of the duty to exercise and use.[70] The weaker protection accorded under copyright law renders this restriction superfluous in that area; neither does such a duty exist for real and personal property. This can be seen as an important difference between intangible industrial property, and real and personal property.

A second reason for the obligation to use is the feeling that the grant of an exclusive right should be counterbalanced by the fact that the previously unavailable subject matter of the right is made available to society. The obligation to use is necessary because, due to the exclusive right, the owner of the intellectual property right is the only one who makes it available. More specifically, for patents, there is the additional requirement to reveal the technical details and specifications of the invention, in order to bring them into the public domain. In exchange for the exclusive right, society has the right to share the development of technical knowledge, and, eventually, to use it for further research and further developments.

This represents an additional advantage of the patent system, because the alternative is to be found in the use of the secrecy system. Technological developments are, in the absence of a patent system,[71] kept secret. Society is unable to share this new knowledge and the inventor can only use the invention in a way that does not reveal the technical functioning of it, because, once in the public domain, it can be used freely by all of the competitors. In that instance, the inventor is put in a very weak position. It has been demonstrated that a patent system that grants the inventor adequate property rights fulfils the task reserved for such a system in a market economy in a better way. The law of secrecy cannot replace the patent system fully; it can only be a useful addition to it.[72]

---

[69] For more details, see Lehmann [1985] at 535–6.

[70] Ibid. at 532–3.

[71] This technique can also be used as an alternative in a particular case for a patent application if the costs of revealing the technical detail of the invention and the other costs linked to such an application are perceived to be higher than the benefits of the stronger protection offered by the patent system. Potentially, the duration of the secrecy is endless, which is also an advantage over the patent system.

[72] See Lunn [1985] at 423.

Copyright involves other factors too

To this point, we have mainly been concerned with patents and trade marks. Historically, copyright developed on a very different basis, with a lot of emphasis on the link between the author and his or her work. An attempt was made to make sure that it was the author, rather than someone else, who would secure the benefits resulting from the work and its exploitation.

Over the years, however, copyright has increasingly been used to protect the commercial exploitation of the work and new, more technologically orientated, types of work have been protected by copyright.[73] It is therefore submitted that the same economic justification theory can now be applied to copyright.[74] Protection against the copying of the work, for example, will restrict competition between the right holder and his or her exploitation of the work, on the one hand, and copyists, on the other. Such a restriction will encourage the right holder to create more works, thus enhancing competition at the higher, creative level, because there is now more of a prospect of securing a return. This is no doubt not the only motivation for authors, but it is clearly an important factor.

But one additional problem arises in relation to the economic analysis of copyright. Copyright has to strike a balance between providing the incentives for authors, on the one hand, and the right of access to information of the public, on the other. In the words of the famous study by Landes and Posner:

> Copyright protection—the right of the copyright's owner to prevent others from making copies—trades off the costs of limiting access to a work against the benefits of providing incentives to create the work in the first place. Striking the correct balance between access and incentives is the central problem in copyright law.[75]

Cooter and Ulen focus on the same issue when they argue that: '*Put succinctly, the dilemma is that without a legal monopoly too little of the information will be produced but with the legal monopoly too little of the information will be used.*'[76]

Let us analyse the implications of these specificities of copyright in a little more detail. The innovation and creation level interacts with the production level; this is a given. In the copyright sphere, we are dealing with works that are the expression of ideas. Starting from these ideas, one has to recognize that they are, by their nature, public goods, and can therefore freely be accessed and used by anyone. The way in which these ideas enter the public domain is through their expression by an individual author, because such expression is required for the transmission of the idea. From an economic point of view, it is also important to keep in mind that such access is non-exhaustive in nature: the consumption of the expression does not necessarily make the expression and its material support unsuitable or unavailable for further consumption. It is also the case that, in the light of modern (digital) technological advances, the costs of reproduction and distribution of the expression of the idea have become marginal, and that such reproduction and distribution is easily achievable, and can be done in a minimum amount of time. There is therefore plenty of room for freeriders. The situation is therefore entirely in favour of competition at the production level; at the innovation and creation level, there is very little in terms of incentive to create. The creator may not be able to recoup the cost of production, because the cost of copying is lower and there is no tool to reap any substantial

---

[73] J. Reichman, 'Charting the collapse of the patent-copyright dichotomy: premises for a restructured international intellectual property system' (1995) 13 Cardozo Arts and Ent LJ 475.

[74] See R. Watt (2000) *Copyright and Economic Theory: Friends or Foes?*, Cheltenham/Northampton, MA: Edward Elgar.

[75] W. Landes and R. Posner, 'An economic analysis of copyright law' (1989) 18 J Legal Stud 325 at 326.

[76] Cooter and Ulen (1988) p. 145.

benefit from such creative activity. In economic terms, then, there is no efficient market of the authors' expression of ideas.[77]

Copyright, therefore, is the tool that is created to give authors a right in their expression of ideas, hence securing appropriate profits deriving from the act of their creation for them. Copyright will lead to the creation of an immaterial property right in the expression of an idea by the author, a right that the author can use to secure appropriate profit from that act of creation on the market.[78] This will enhance creation by providing an incentive, and therefore competition on the innovation and creation level will be stimulated, while any such right will inevitably limit competition at the production level, because competitors are no longer free to copy the copyright work. A restriction on competition is put in place in furtherance of competition.[79]

Copyright fulfils here the 'pro-competitive' regulating role filled by the property right when it comes to the consumption and the production level—but an important distinction must be drawn. Property rights are a legal recognition of a situation—that is, of the physical possession of and control over the goods—whereas copyright is not based on a de facto situation at all: it is rather an artificially created right, put in place by the legislator to regulate competition at the innovation and creation level, and to provide the much needed incentive to create. This difference gives copyright a different standing. The legislator created it specifically as a tool through which to enhance competition.

Copyright plays therefore, *mutatis mutandis*, the same pro-competitive role in relation to literary and artistic works that patents play in relation to inventions. An important additional factor in the context of copyright, however, is the need to safeguard access to information and freedom of expression. This reflects itself in the basic rule that copyright will not protect ideas, but only their expression. The threshold for that expression to be protected will be the fact that it satisfies the originality expression that allows one to distinguish it from the mere idea. It has been said that copyright therefore protects '*independently achieved expressive results*',[80] which applies both in a *droit d'auteur* tradition, with its 'subjective' notion of originality, and in an Anglo-Saxon copyright environment. In the *droit d'auteur* tradition, the author's personal expression is therefore protected as a creative work, irrespective of the mediocrity or otherwise, of the expressive results; copyright systems focus instead on the concept of independent creation. Protection by means of copyright, therefore, depends on the objective attainment of a result—again, irrespective of its mediocrity or otherwise in terms of creative effort—that arises from a contribution that is neither copied from anyone else, nor reproduced using known standard models.[81]

Up until now, we have looked at 'traditional' copyright in literary and artistic works, such as books and sculptures. It is however necessary to add that copyright has developed in two ways in recent years that may have influenced the position: on the one hand, copyright has been expanded to protect the results of technological evolutions; on the other, we have seen an increasing emphasis on the economic interests of those who exploit copyright works, such as producers and publishers. It is important to note that, as a result, copyright is increasingly used to protect information goods and the investment needed for the creation of these goods. It is clear that, in these circumstances, the level

---

[77] G. Ramello (2002) 'Copyright and antitrust issues', available online at www.serci.org/2002/ramello. pdf, p. 8.

[78] K. Maskus (2000) *Intellectual Property Rights in the Global Economy*, Washington DC: Institute for International Economics, pp. 28–32.

[79] See Lehmann [1989] at 1–15.

[80] Ghidini (2006) p. 54.

[81] Ibid.

of originality involved in the creation of such information goods is lower, and that the link with the author and his or her creativity, which makes the work his or her own individual creation, is weaker. This must also weaken the justification for strong copyright protection for these information works, because these elements were described above as the basis for the economic justification of copyright.[82] Another important element is the fact that, by their nature, information goods have a poor substitutability.[83] This applies, to some extent, to all copyright works: for example we are interested in a novel because of the way in which the author has expressed the idea and therefore the novel cannot be easily substituted by another novel in which another author expresses the same idea in his or her different own way. This factor is, however, more strongly present in relation to information goods.

A special type of monopoly

It may well be that some additional remarks on the type of monopoly that is granted by intellectual property rights are appropriate. That monopoly is, in no way, absolute and it is limited in time; it is also subject to competition with similar products, similar trade marks, etc. Inventions compete with substitute technologies, so that the profits based on the exclusive use of the invention are rarely monopolistic rents.[84] The latter situation only arises in those rare situations in which an invention is such a radical step forward that there is a (temporary) absolute lack of substitutability.[85] In copyright, meanwhile, only one particular expression of an otherwise unprotected idea is granted copyright protection.

Intellectual property rights do not give their owners an automatic profit: they are directly oriented towards demand. The reward that they provide for innovative activity depends upon the competitive structure of the market concerned. Only when the market appreciates the innovation on its merits will the owner be rewarded and make a profit:[86] 'The ownership of intangibles in the sense of abstract property rights ... is therefore limited to a temporary, ephemeral competitive restriction.'[87] Intellectual property rights confer exclusive rights, but they hardly ever confer a real monopoly, in the sense that the monopolist can act in an arbitrary way without being influenced by his or her competitors.

Those in favour and those against

It has to be added that a number of economists have argued against the existence of intellectual property rights and especially against the existence of patents. In their view, patents do not promote technological innovation—or there are more effective ways in which to do so.[88] These critics are, however, unable to provide clear evidence that intellectual property rights do not fulfil a useful economical function and none of their alternatives has ever been tested successfully in practice.[89] All they can demonstrate is that some features of the existing patent system cannot be justified economically and that the existing

---

[82] S. Lemarchand, O. Fréget and F. Sardain, 'Biens informationnels: entre droits intellectuels et droit de la concurrence', [2003] Propriétés Intellectuelles 6, 11 at 18.

[83] Ramello (2002) p. 8.

[84] Ullrich [1989] at 105.

[85] Lehmann [1985] at 537.

[86] See Ullrich [1989] at 112.

[87] Lehmann [1985] at 537.

[88] See, e.g., F. Machlup (1957) *An Economic Review of the Patent System*, Study No 15 of the Senate Judiciary Subcommittee on Patents, Trademarks and Copyrights, Washington DC: US Congress; E. Penrose (1951) *The Economics of the International Patent System*, Baltimore, MD: Johns Hopkins University Press; see also F. Machlup and E. Penrose, 'The patent controversy in the nineteenth century' (1950) 10 J Econ Hist 1.

[89] This is admitted by Machlup (1957) at the end of his study.

system does not always achieve a perfect balance between the various levels of competition. This is undoubtedly true, but the solution is not the abolition of the whole system. What is required might rather be described as 'fine-tuning' of the system.[90]

There is also a substantial amount of empirical economic evidence that supports the economic justification for the existence of intellectual property rights. Most of these studies deal with patents, and the causal relationship between the availability of patent protection and investment in research and development, and in innovation.[91]

Who gets the right?

Thus economic theory provides a justification for the existence of intellectual property rights. A related point is the issue of who gets these intellectual property rights. It has been suggested that the economic theory proves that it is valuable to have intellectual property rights, but is unable to guarantee that the enforcement of these rights will have valuable results in each individual case. The author and the inventor must obtain these rights to secure the best possible system—and this can only be accepted if one uses labour theory to justify the allocation of the property rights whose existence the economic theory justifies.[92]

Labour theory was formulated by John Locke[93] and is the combination of two concepts: the first is that everyone has a property right in the labour of his own body and brain; the second adds that the application of human labour to an unowned object gives you a property right in it. When applied to intellectual property rights,[94] this might explain why it is the author who gets the copyright in the book and why it is the inventor who gets the patent in the invention.

The combination of the economic theory and the labour theory provides a full justification for the system of intellectual property rights.[95] This reference to the labour theory explicitly justifies the fact that it is the author or the inventor who should own the intellectual property right—but it is submitted here that this is already implicit in the economic theory. An intellectual property right, as a restriction on competition at production level (because not everyone can produce the goods protected by the right), will not stimulate competition on the innovation level if the right is not given to the innovator, whether an author or an inventor. One will only be stimulated to innovate when one gets the intellectual property rights in the innovation. This effect, which is the key element in the economic justification theory for intellectual property, disappears when someone else gets the intellectual property rights in the innovation. The actual exploitation of the right can be undertaken by the right holder or by a licensee—this does not affect the justification at all.

[90] See Beier [1980] at 572.
[91] For example, C. T. Taylor and A. Silberston (1973) *The Economic Impact of the Patent System*, Cambridge: Cambridge University Press; the 1973–74 study of the Ifo-Institut für Wirtschaftsforschung in Munich concerning the relationship between the Patent System and Technical Progress, which is discussed in K. H. Oppenlander, 'Patent policies and technical progress in the Federal Republic of Germany' [1977] IIC 97; A. Silberston (1987) *The Economic Importance of Patents*, Cambridge: Cambridge University Press. An overview of older studies can be found in J. Schmookler (1966) *Invention and Economic Growth*, Cambridge, MA: Harvard University Press; see also Lunn [1985] at 423.
[92] H. Spector, 'An outline of a theory justifying intellectual and industrial property rights' [1989] 8 EIPR 270 at 272–3.
[93] J. Locke (1690) *The Second Treatise of Government*, Pt 27, reproduced in P. Laslett (ed.) (1970) *Two Treaties of Government*, Cambridge: Cambridge University Press.
[94] See R. Nozick (1974) *Anarchy, State and Utopia*, Oxford: Blackwell, pp. 181–2.
[95] Spector [1989] at 273.

Other ways of justifying intellectual property

Thus economic analysis justifies the continued existence of intellectual property rights and economic history confirms the correctness of the analysis.[96] One also finds a series of other elements of justification in an historical analysis and in a socio-economic analysis (reward theory).[97]

While these two theses, based on natural rights and rewards, are no longer fashionable as justifications for the existence of intellectual property rights,[98] the possibility to reward the inventor is still rightfully considered to be a positive side effect of the patent system.

A historical analysis

There seems to be a need for a system protecting innovation once a country starts to develop its industry. This becomes especially clear when one considers the example of patents. There is a correlation between industrialization and patent protection: patents are introduced when the process of industrialization starts and each increase in the level of patent protection corresponds to progress in the industrialization process. This evolution is visible in most European countries from the fifteenth century onwards, but it becomes very prominent in the nineteenth century, as a result of the Industrial Revolution.

It has to be added that this link between patents and industrialization is based on the idea that a country will not be able to benefit from the industrialization process in Europe if it does not introduce a system of patent protection—a conclusion that was reached as a result of an active debate in which both the advantages and disadvantages of the introduction of a system of patent protection were fully taken into account.[99]

Apart from this historical correlation, we should turn our attention also to the evolution of economic output. The introduction of a system of patent protection in a country's legal system goes together with a clear increase in the industrial production of that country. We can refer here to the English example in the eighteenth century, but all other industrialized countries might equally serve as examples. Another striking feature is the high level of industrialization in all countries with a high level of patent protection. It might even be demonstrated that their level of industrialization is higher than the level reached by countries that refuse to grant patent protection or which only grant a weak form of patent protection. The successes of the Spanish and Italian pharmaceutical industries, and the Swiss chemical industry, at times when patent protection was not available do not prove the contrary: no new product emerged and success was based purely on imitation. This situation only improved with the introduction of a system of patent protection.[100] It is not, however, possible to establish a causal link between these two facts in a conclusive manner. Factors other than the patent system may be responsible for the higher level of industrialization.[101]

These historical elements provide additional arguments in favour of the patent system and a system of intellectual property rights in general, but, taken in isolation, they do not provide a complete and convincing justification for the existence of intellectual property rights. Other theses that have been suggested as justification for the existence of patents

---

[96] See Lehmann [1989] at 11.
[97] Beier [1980] at 563.
[98] Benko (1987) ch. 4, p. 17.
[99] Ibid. at 571–2.
[100] Ibid. at 573–4.
[101] Ibid.

rely on natural rights, rewards for the inventor, and disclosure.[102] Immediately after the French Revolution, a tendency to explain and justify individual property rights as natural rights, on the basis of a series of moral and philosophical arguments, became fashionable and was extended to intangible property, such as patents and other intellectual property rights[103]—but this theory never found much support outside France.

The reward theory

Similar arguments are found in the reward theory, which sees patents as a reward owed by society to inventors in return for their creativity and their services to society[104]—that is, that society has a moral obligation to compensate and to reward the inventors.[105] But this argument cannot justify the existence of the patent system, even if one agrees that the inventor should be rewarded.

We demonstrated above that a patent offers only a potential monopoly—that is, a potential reward to the inventor. Only those patents that are commercially attractive and the commercial exploitation of which is successful offer a reward to the inventor. Furthermore, this is an indirect reward. A direct reward—such as a lump sum, a decoration, or a title—would be a better idea if the aim of the measure is to reward the inventor.[106] The inventor would be assured of a reward and would be able to assess the nature or amount of the reward in advance.

Encouraging disclosure

A further thesis that is worth mentioning emphasizes the role that the patent system plays in encouraging inventors to disclose their secrets to society. Diffusion of technology, which is considered to be desirable for society, will only take place when inventors make the technical details of their inventions public. If, as explained above, there is no protection for the invention and everyone can use the technology freely, the inventor will rely on secrecy for protection, because imitation of the invention entails only minimal costs when compared to those of the inventor. The technical details of new inventions will not be disclosed in such a system and society will not benefit to the same extent.[107]

Although this theory is helpful and the disclosure of technical knowledge is a very positive aspect of the patent system, it has to be said that its value is, in part, undermined by two important details. The inventor without patent protection would have some lead time during which he or she would enjoy a kind of market monopoly and during which he or she could collect a reward for the work, because it would take the imitator some time before being ready to produce and to enter the market.[108] This is reinforced by the fact that the exploitation of a patent quite often requires a substantial amount of secret know-how, which the imitator will have to acquire if it is to exploit the invention successfully.[109] In

---

[102] Benko (1987) ch. 4, p. 16.

[103] This theory was endorsed by the French National Assembly and became part of the Preamble to the patent law of that period: see the quotation in Machlup and Penrose (1950) at 11.

[104] This theory applies also to the other intellectual property rights.

[105] Machlup and Penrose (1950) at 17 quoted, in this respect, J. S. Mill's statement: '*That he, the inventor, ought to be compensated and rewarded ... will not be denied ... it would be a gross immorality of the law to set everybody free to use a person's work without his consent, and without giving him an equivalent.*'

[106] See M. Blakeney (1989) *Legal Aspects of the Transfer of Technology to Developing Countries*, Oxford: ESC, pp. 51–3.

[107] See Blakeney (1989) p. 53; Benko (1987) ch. 4, pp. 16–17.

[108] See M. Braunstein, W. J. Baumol and J. W. Mansfield (1980) 'The economics of R&D', in B. V. Dean and J. C. Goldhar (eds) *Management of Research and Innovation*, New York: John Wiley and Sons, pp. 19–32.

[109] See F. M. Scherer (1980) *Industrial Market Structure and Economic Performance*, Chicago, IL: University of Chicago Press, p. 447.

many cases, however, that lead time may not be long enough for the inventor to recover all costs and to make a profit.[110]

The special position of copyright

The last paragraphs have focused extensively on patents. Many of the arguments can also be used for trade marks, but are there perhaps other additional elements that can justify the existence of copyright? Originally, copyright dealt with literary and artistic works. It could be argued that the author was given certain property rights in these works to reward his or her artistic performance, or that the author's claims were based on a natural or moral right. Specifically, in the *droit d'auteur* system, a lot of emphasis is placed on the fact that the work involves an expression of the personality of the author. Copyright is then also given certain aspects of a personality right (cf moral rights) and does not remain a pure property right.

This was perfectly acceptable for works, such as novels, songs, and poems, but it becomes increasingly difficult to justify copyright exclusively on this basis. Clearly, this theory does not suit computer programs and other highly technological works, which are now equally protected by copyright. As copyright has entered the technological field, it has becomes clear that its real justification is equally to be found in the economic justification theory.[111] Works protected by copyright are knowledge goods; they are concerned with creativity and innovation, and present, in this respect, the same characteristics as inventions. They too need to be protected as economic rights, if artistic, creative, and innovative activity in this area is to be promoted.

There is, however, one essential difference when it comes to inventions and trade marks. The right involved here is a copyright, the subject matter of which is the particular expression in a literary work, in a piece of music, in a sculpture, etc., by the author of an idea. There is no direct link between the copyright and the idea embodied in the work. One can distinguish between a book and the ideas expressed in it, whereas an invention and the novel idea involved are one and the same inseparable concept.[112] The ideas contained in a work protected under copyright are, on top of that, not necessarily novel. It would not be possible to justify the protection of these ideas under the economic justification theory. Fortunately, this is not necessary, because copyright only protects the expression by the author of a certain set of ideas. These ideas themselves are not protected by copyright.

But let us come back briefly to the link between the author and the work. This special aspect of copyright does not only refer to a personality right as seen above, but also incorporates an important link with human rights. René Cassin, one of the architects of the current human rights framework, has emphasized the importance of the act of creation and the link with the creator in relation to rights that may flow from it. In his view, the ability and the desire to develop intellectual and creative activities from which copyright works may result is potentially found in all human beings. As such, it deserves respect and protection in the same way as do all other basic faculties that are common to all human beings. This would mean that creators can claim rights by the very fact of their creation.

---

[110] Reichman (1995) argues, in this respect, that patents and copyright should be restricted to the really desirable highly creative or innovative cases; anything else in between should be protected only by lead time. When necessary—because of the speed at which copying or reverse engineering takes place in the new digital environment—that lead time can be created artificially.

[111] See, in M. Van Hoecke (1991), W. Grosheide, 'Economic aspects of intellectual property rights, especially of copyright', pp. 65–72, and A. Strowel, 'An appraisal of the economic analysis of copyright law', pp. 103–35; Watt (2000).

[112] See Benko (1987) ch. 4, pp. 21 and 23.

This is a broad statement and it is by no means clear that such rights are, by definition, human rights, or that they must cover all creations and necessarily take the format of an exclusive right in such creations.[113] Further analysis is therefore warranted.

The first key provision in an international instrument that identifies copyright as a human right is found in Art. 27 of the Universal Declaration of Human Rights.[114] According to that Article, everyone has first of all *'the right to the protection of the moral and material interests resulting from scientific, literary or artistic production of which he is the author'*. But it is equally important to note another element stated in Art. 27(1): that *'everyone has the right freely to participate in the cultural life of the community, to enjoy the arts and to share in scientific advancement and its benefits'*. Copyright will therefore have to strike a balance somewhere in the middle.

The second key provision in an international instrument that identifies copyright as a human right is found in the International Covenant on Economic, Social and Cultural Rights.[115] This Covenant can be seen as a follow-up action on the Universal Declaration of Human Rights—but it is important to note that this follow-up action took the form of a Treaty and that, as such, it can impose legally binding obligations to implement its provisions on states that became contracting parties to it. Article 15 of the Covenant is very clear in this respect, and imposes a number of responsibilities and steps to be taken on contracting states in the following way:

...

(2) The steps to be taken by the States Parties to the present Covenant to achieve the full realization of this right shall include those necessary for the conservation, development and the diffusion of science and culture.

(3) The States Parties to the present Covenant undertake to respect the freedom indispensable for scientific research and creative activity.

(4) The States Parties to the Present Covenant recognize the benefits to be derived from the encouragement and development of international contacts and cooperation in the scientific and cultural fields.

These obligations apply to the substantive rights granted in Art. 15(1) of the Covenant, which is very much based on Art. 27 of the Universal Declaration of Human Rights, comprising the rights of everyone:

(a) to take part in cultural life;

(b) to enjoy the benefits of scientific progress and its applications;

(c) to benefit from the protection of the moral and the material interests resulting from any scientific, literary, or artistic production of which he is the author.

Once more, the need for copyright to strike a balance emerges, but the identification of copyright—or at least certain aspects of it—as a human right is an additional justification for the existence of copyright.[116] But it is not a complete justification, because it does not

---

[113] R. Cassin (1959) 'L'intégration, parmi les droits fondamentaux de l'homme, des droits des créateurs des oeuvres de l'esprit', in M. Mélanges Plaisant, *Etudes sur la Propriété Industrielle, Littéraire et Artistique*, Paris: Sirey, p. 229; M. Vivant, 'Le droit d'auteur: un droit de l'homme?' (1997) 174 RIDA 60 at 87.

[114] Adopted and proclaimed by the United Nations in 1948 as General Assembly Resolution 217A(III) of 10 December 1948, specifically in relation to copyright: see J. A. L. Sterling (2003) *World Copyright Law*, 2nd edn, London: Sweet and Maxwell, p. 43.

[115] The International Covenant on Economic, Social and Cultural Rights, 993 UNTS 3, GA Res 2200(XXI) 21 UN GAOR Supp (No 16), 49, UN Doc A/6316 (1966), adopted on 16 December 1966.

[116] For a complete analysis on this point, see P. Torremans (2004) 'Copyright as a human right', in P. Torremans (ed.) *Copyright and Human Rights*, London: Kluwer Law International.

indicate where the balance lies, and, as such, it is not able to justify each and every aspect of the current shape of copyright law.

The current economic importance of intellectual property

Our historical overview demonstrated that intellectual property rights were introduced because they were thought to be essential for further industrial and economic development. We will now try to analyse the current economic importance of intellectual property rights. It is submitted, on the basis of indirect evidence, that this importance is huge.

The recent GATT–World Trade Organization (WTO) agreement contained the TRIPS initiative on intellectual property. This initiative was a reaction by the governments that were concerned by the complaints of industry. Figures pointing to multimillion-dollar losses in royalties due to the counterfeiting of famous trade marks in countries that offered a low level of protection for intellectual property rights were published by industrial sources. One can understand and accept these figures on the basis that almost every product, and almost every service, now bears a trade mark. In 1974, the World Intellectual Property Organization (WIPO) estimated that four million trade marks were in use in the world[117] and there is every reason to believe that there are more trade marks in use now than there were in 1974. The recent GATT–WTO agreement attaches great importance to the strengthening of the protection for trade marks and the other intellectual property rights, which clearly emphasizes their tremendous economic value.

The evolution to an economic system based on high technological developments has resulted in the proliferation of patents. Many of these patents have an enormous commercial value.[118] Just think about the whole evolution in the field of genetic engineering: these disease-resistant plants, purified seeds, and drugs produced by genetically engineered bacteria—all protected by patents—are the products of the future and the patent holders are cashing in. It is clear that, if patent protection were not available, there would be no incentive to invest huge resources in high technology research and developments, because there would be no prospect of recuperating, and obtaining a fair return on, the investment—especially when one takes into account that not every research programme will lead to success.[119] One should also not forget the vast number of patents granted for relatively slight improvements upon the existing technology. They may not grab the headlines, but they have a tremendous importance in industry, because they allow the improver to appropriate the results of his or her work and gain a competitive edge over his or her competitors, who would otherwise, in a majority of cases, be able to reverse engineer the improvement at a fraction of the original cost.

What about the economic importance of copyright? Just imagine the range of products covered: books; CDs; movies; television broadcasts; computer programs; multimedia products, etc. Copyright has become very wide in scope and a number of the new technological developments protected under copyright are of enormous commercial

---

[117] This figure is quoted by Blakeney (1989) p. 113, with a reference to the United Nations Conference on Trade and Development (UNCTAD) 1981 report *The Role of Trade Marks in the Promotion of Exports from Developing Countries.*

[118] See also G. Parchomovsky and S. Wagner (2004) 'Patent portfolios', Scholarship Paper 51, University of Pennsylvania Law School, available online at www.lsr.nellco.org/upenn/wps/papers/51.

[119] See B. Pretnar, 'The economic impact of patents in a knowledge-based market economy' [2003] IIC 887.

importance. Add to that the business generated by the phenomenon of character mer-chandising, which allows goods featuring real and fictitious characters—such as pop stars, Popeye, or Mickey Mouse—to be marketed more easily by those who will earn more through this link than they do through their normal activities, and you will begin to per-ceive that the current economic importance of intellectual property is, indeed, huge.

Intellectual property is now involved in almost every aspect of our highly developed economic life, with its strong emphasis on technological progress and brand names. Intellectual property is pushed by market forces. The Marrakesh Agreement of the GATT, taken over by the WTO, led to many developing countries adopting stricter intellectual property protection regimes and saw an important expansion of the international intel-lectual property regime. Now, attention at WTO level is turning to a next step, in the direction of even stronger intellectual property protection, even if the economic impact of these current reforms is still the subject of a lively discussion.[120]

One might even argue that the original presumption in favour of free competition and the perception of intellectual property rights as exceptional rights, the grant of which was only appropriate in cases of exceptional, innovative, and creative activity, no longer exists. This point of view accepts that industry now presumes that intellectual property protec-tion will be available for every new product and every new development, and sees full-scale free competition as the exception.[121] It is clear that such a reversal of attitude cannot be encouraged unconditionally. Indeed, serious consideration should be given to the ques-tions of overlap between intellectual property rights, in the sense that recent expansion of rights has given rise, on many occasions, to several rights protecting the same thing.

This aspect of convergence of rights aggravates the existing inflation of rights. Innovators and creators are increasingly unable to go about their business without taking out a whole raft of licences in advance. Is this not an aberration? Has the time not come to start thinking about cutting back the, sometimes excessive, scope of intellectual property rights and about reducing the overlap between the various rights? Maybe the Doha Round of WTO negotiations and its demands to reduce, rather than expand on, the impact of TRIPS in certain areas is a sign that this is, indeed, the case, and that continued and almost unlimited expansion of intellectual property rights is not the way forward.[122] It is indeed clear, on the basis of the analysis in this chapter, that intellectual property rights should play a pro-competitive role if their existence is to be justified. Unduly wide and overlapping rights may well fail the test, and therefore endanger the survival of the whole system of intellectual property and the beneficial role it plays in our economy.

An overview

Intellectual property rights play an important role in economic life in this age of tech-nological innovation. Their existence can be justified on an economic basis, with other

---

[120] See, in general, Maskus (2000) and, for a practical example in one particular country and industry, I. M. Azmi and R. Alavi, 'TRIPS, patents, technology transfer, foreign direct investment and the pharmaceu-tical industry in Malaysia' [2001] JWIP 947.

[121] R. Merges (1994) 'The economic impact of intellectual property rights: an overview and guide', Paper delivered at the International Center for Art Economics (ICARE) international conference on The Economics of Intellectual Property Rights, 6–8 October, Venice; see also Reichman (1995).

[122] See, already, in Reichman (1995). Now, even the judiciary starts to make comments in that sense: see *MGM v. Grokster Ltd* 380 F.3d 1154 (9th Cir. 2004)—relating to copyright infringement in a US context—and *Lambretta Clothing Co. Ltd v. Teddy Smith (UK) Ltd & anor* [2005] RPC 6, *per* Jacob LJ at [101]—relating to unregistered design right overlap in a UK context.

factors offering further support. Intellectual property rights are also international in character and, in that respect, they fit in rather well with the economic reality of the global economy.

Further reading

DEAZLEY, R. (2004) *On the Origin of the Right to Copy: Charting the Movement of Copyright Law in Eighteenth-Century Britain (1695–1775)*, Oxford: Hart.

DEAZLEY, R. (2006) *Re-Thinking Copyright: History, Theory, Language*, Cheltenham/ Northampton, MA: Edward Elgar.

GHIDINI, G. (2006) *Intellectual Property and Competition Law: The Innovation Nexus*, Cheltenham/Northampton, MA: Edward Elgar.

RICKETSON, S. and GINSBURG, J. C. (2006) *International Copyright and Neighbouring Rights: The Berne Convention and Beyond*, Oxford: Oxford University Press.

2
The international and European framework

Introduction

It has become clear, in the course of this introduction, that intellectual property is not necessarily exploited at a national level;[1] it is, in fact, exploited at a global level. Video cassettes and compact discs (CDs) containing materials protected by copyright are marketed in an increasing number of countries; patents in CD technology were exploited wherever a CD-pressing plant was built, until these rights recently expired; the 'Coca-Cola' trade mark is found on cans and bottles all over the world.

Inventors and creators would, under these circumstances, lose out if intellectual property regimes were to be completely different in each country. They would not get adequate protection and they would not be adequately rewarded for their work if intellectual property rights—based on the same principles, and equally applicable to inventions and creations made abroad—were not available in each country in which the patent, trade mark, or copyright is exploited. If this were the case, the whole economic justification theory would also collapse. A global economy, therefore, presupposes a global intellectual property system.

International intellectual property conventions

Two types of international cooperation can be distinguished in this respect. First, there are the treaties and conventions that lay down minimum uniform provisions and standards of protection.[2] These recognize that each country will have its own intellectual property laws, but they harmonize the minimum standards and the basis that underlies all these laws, and they also secure protection under these laws for works of foreign inventors and creators or for works created abroad. Anti-counterfeiting initiatives are also part of this category, because they link in with global minimum standards of protection and their effective enforcement.

These treaties and conventions still require an inventor or creator to register in each country in which protection is sought; only copyright—which, as we shall see, does not have a registration requirement—is an exception to this rule. Thus the second category of treaties and conventions operates at this level. Many of these treaties and conventions

---

[1] All historical arguments refer to more than one country and the economic justification theory is not restricted to a particular national market.

[2] This is, of course, a second-best solution, but the best solution—uniform intellectual property laws—is clearly not available in practice.

involve a single application and examination procedure, or at least a certain level of coop-eration between the national intellectual property authorities. The more advanced types of measure provide for uniform provisions in the various national intellectual property laws, or at least for a thorough harmonization of these provisions. Many of these more advanced measures are found in Europe.[3]

All of the conventions, treaties, agreements, and protocols that will be summarized shortly are administered by the World Intellectual Property Organization (WIPO), which has headquarters in Geneva.[4] Its international bureau deals with international registra-tions; the Universal Copyright Convention (UCC) is an exception to this system.

As part of the Uruguay Round of world trade negotiations, the states contracting to the General Agreement of Tariffs and Trade (GATT)—taken over by the World Trade Organization (WTO)—reached an agreement on the Trade-Related Aspects of Intellectual Property Rights (TRIPS) initiative. The aim of the initiative was to impose worldwide minimum terms for the protection of intellectual property. This system does not replace the existing conventions, but it works in addition to them. It obliges those countries that do not yet protect intellectual property to introduce that protection if they do not want to be excluded from the world free-trading system and from membership of WTO. In comparison, the old system had worked on an entirely voluntary basis; the standards of protection introduced by the TRIPS initiative are also slightly higher than the minimum standards under the old conventions, at which we will look now.

The various treaties, conventions, and other measures that are in place can be sum-marized as follows.[5]

Patents

In the area of patents, the minimum international rules are found in the Paris Convention for the Protection of Industrial Property, which was signed in 1883, but which has been updated by later Acts. The Convention has been implemented in the states adhering to the Convention by means of national Patent Acts and 173 states now adhere to the Paris Convention.[6]

It is important to realize what the Paris Convention does and does not do: it *does* try to enable the protection abroad of inventions, but it *does not* create a proper international patent system. Article 1 of the Convention states that it deals with the protection of indus-trial property, which is said to include patents and is to be understood in the broadest sense. But the closest that Art. 1 comes to a definition of a patent—let alone of any condi-tions for the grant of a patent—is at Art. 1(4):

> Patents shall include the various kinds of industrial patents recognized by the laws of the countries of the Union, such as patents of importation, patents of improvement, patents and certificates of addition, etc.

---

[3] It is also worth mentioning that there have been initiatives taken by a large group of South American countries—that is, by the Andean Group. It would, however, lead us too far to discuss these measures in this book, in which we are primarily concerned with UK and European law.

[4] We do not discuss plant variety rights in this book, for further information on which, please see the International Convention for the Protection of New Varieties of Plants (the UPOV Convention), adopted in Paris in 1961; in the biotechnology area, the Budapest Treaty on the International Recognition of the Deposit of Micro-Organisms for the Purpose of Patent Procedure, in force since 1980, is also relevant.

[5] For the text of these instruments, see J. Phillips (ed.) (2007) *Butterworths Intellectual Property Law Handbook*, 8th edn, London: Butterworths Law.

[6] Figure correct as at 20 January 2008.

What the Paris Convention certainly does establish is a right to national treatment. Nationals of member States will, in all other member States, be treated as home applicants. At the time of drafting, this was an important step: it allowed inventors to apply for patent protection abroad. They would then be treated in the same way as would native applicants. It did mean, however, that one had to apply country by country and, in each country, the local law applied not only in terms of procedure, but also in terms of substantive requirements for patentability, etc. National treatment was also granted to whoever was domiciled, or had a real and effective business establishment, in a member State.[7]

The other core provision is Art. 4, which grants the priority right. National patent laws require, in one way or another, that an invention is new—but can it be 'new', when applying in a second member State, if it has already been revealed earlier in an application to a first member State? Any such revelation might also prompt a less scrupulous entrepreneur to apply in a second or third member State before the inventor has time to do so. It is these problems that the priority right addresses. Starting from the date of the first application, the applicant has a twelve-month period during which that application will be taken, in all member States to which he or she applies, to have been filed on the date of the first application. Novelty is therefore preserved and the application will have priority over any other application that has been filed in that member State the meantime.

Apart from these provisions, the Convention offers very little in terms of the harmonization of national patent laws. Additionally, it specifically states that national patents remain independent.[8] The refusal to grant or revocation in one country, for example, will therefore have no influence on parallel proceedings or on patents in another member State.

The impact of the Paris Convention was enlarged even further by the TRIPS Agreement. Article 2 of that Agreement obliges all contracting states to comply with the main substantive provisions of the Paris Convention, even if they are not members of it. This guarantees a coverage that is virtually worldwide in scope, because very few countries will be able to afford staying outside the WTO-administered system, of which TRIPS forms part. On top of that, the Agreement contains, in Arts 27–34, further and tighter substantive minimum rules in relation to patents. This is a key step. While national patent laws did already contain similar principles, important differences had remained. TRIPS introduces a first definition of the requirements for patentability—that is, novelty, inventive step and industrial applicability. It also properly defines, in a broad sense, the types of invention that can be patentable and it obliges member States to grant patents in every field of technology.

Normally, an applicant files a separate patent application in each country in which he or she intends to work the invention or desires protection. This was felt to be a complicated procedure, because the details are different in each country, and a waste of time and effort. The Patent Cooperation Treaty (PCT), signed in Washington in 1970, provides for the filing of a single application and also provides a facility for a preliminary international search for the requirements for patentability. At present, 139 states[9] adhere to the PCT. In the end, however, the application is handed over to national patent offices and they grant the national patents.

Patents are also an important source of technological information. It might be argued that the most valuable aspect of the PCT is the central publication of the applications and, hence, an extremely valuable database to search for all involved. If the patent system is

---

[7] Paris Convention, Arts 2 and 3.
[8] Ibid., Art. 4bis.
[9] Figure as at 20 January 2008.

to fulfil this role adequately at an international level, a uniform system of classification is necessary. An invention must also be new if a patent is to be granted—and this can only be tested by means of a well-structured patent register. This classification system is contained in the Strasbourg Convention on the International Classification of Patents (IPC), signed in Strasbourg in 1971.[10]

Finally, an attempt has been made to streamline national patent procedures by means of the Patent Law Treaty, signed in Geneva in 2000, which has only just come into force.[11]

Trade marks

The minimum rules for trade marks are also contained in the Paris Convention. Again, the main achievement has been national treatment in combination with a right of priority—of six months, in the UK. The rule on the independence of national rights also applies and, at a later stage, a rule on transborder protection for well-known marks was added as Art. 6bis. The TRIPS Agreement has added to that protection: most notably, by providing a definition of what can be registered as a trade mark, under which conditions, and with which rights resulting from registration,[12] as well as requiring all its contracting states to comply with the substantive provisions of the Paris Convention.

The international exploitation of a trade mark is facilitated by the Madrid Agreement concerning the International Registration of Marks, signed in Madrid in 1892. Registration in one state that is a signatory to the Madrid Agreement gives a person the right to file a single application for registration in any other signatory country designated in the application; a separate application in each state is no longer required. But some states—including the UK—could not accept some of the provisions of the Madrid Agreement. They joined the system only through the Protocol to the Madrid Agreement, signed in Madrid in 1989.[13] There are a number of differences on substance between the Agreement and the Protocol,[14] but, again, the outcome is a series of national trade marks. A further attempt to harmonize the procedural aspects of a trade mark application is made in the Trade Mark Law Treaty, signed in Geneva in 1994.[15]

A uniform classification system for trade marks—based on classes for goods and services, and lists of goods and services that fall into each of the classes—is provided by two agreements:

(i) the Nice Agreement concerning the International Classification of Goods and Services for the Purposes of the Registration of Marks, which was signed in Nice in 1861 and was last revised in Geneva in 1977;[16]

(ii) the Vienna Agreement establishing an International Classification of the Figurative Elements of Marks, signed in Vienna in 1985.[17]

---

[10] On 27 September 2007, 58 states had signed up to the Convention.
[11] From 1 April 2008, the Treaty will be in force between 17 member states. In the UK, the Treaty entered into force on 22 March 2006.
[12] Articles 15–21.
[13] On 27 September 2007, 80 states adhered to the Madrid system, 57 of them have ratified the Agreement, and 74 the Protocol. The European Union and its Community trade mark system have now also adhered to the system.
[14] See Section E of this book; see also G. Kunze, 'The Protocol relating to the Madrid Agreement concerning the international registration of marks' [1992] 82 The Trademark Reporter 1; G. Kunze, 'The Madrid system for the international registration of marks as applied under the Protocol' [1994] 6 EIPR 223–6.
[15] On 27 September 2007, 39 states adhered to this Agreement.
[16] On 31 October 2007, 81 states adhered to this Agreement.
[17] On 27 September 2007, 24 states adhered to this Agreement.

The latter also deals with device marks.

As in the area of patent law, there is also a treaty harmonizing the procedures before the national trade mark registries. The Trade Mark Law Treaty was signed in Geneva in 1994 and has been ratified by 39 states.[18]

Design rights

This is the third area covered by the Paris Convention and the TRIPS Agreement, and in relation to this area, both play similar roles as they do in relation to patents and trade marks.

An industrial design can be deposited internationally and will attract protection in all member States of the 1925 Hague Agreement concerning the Deposit of Industrial Designs, to which 47 states now[19] adhere. The provisions of this Agreement have recently been updated by the 1999 Geneva Act of the Hague Agreement concerning the Deposit of Industrial Designs, which entered into force on 23 December 2003 and currently attracts 51 contracting states, taking into account the decision of the European Union (EU) to join the system on 1 January 2008.[20]

An international uniform classification for industrial designs was established in the Locarno Agreement Establishing an International Classification for Industrial Designs, which has been in force since 1970.[21]

Copyright

The most important international convention in the copyright area is the 1886 Berne Convention for the Protection of Literary and Artistic Works (the latest Act of which is the Paris Act). This Convention is to copyright what the Paris Convention is to industrial property rights. As with the Paris Convention, the aim was not to create a supranational copyright system; the focus is once more on national treatment. Foreign authors—at least those with a link to member States—will get the same protection as national authors in any member State.

But, unlike the Paris Convention, the Berne Convention at least attempts to define the object of copyright protection—that is, literary and artistic works, and the list of examples in Art. 2. The focus is on a reproduction right that is given to right holders, but public performance rights and communication to the public eventually make their appearance. The most important point to note, however, is that there is a proper attempt to achieve at least a minimalist harmonization of the protection and the rights that are granted. The Berne Convention establishes further provisions on limitations, term of protection, and moral rights, and 163 states are now members of the Berne Union.[22]

A competing Universal Copyright Convention (UCC), signed in Geneva in 1952 and revised at Paris in 1971, was promoted by the United Nations Educational, Scientific and Cultural Organization (UNESCO), but lost most of its importance when its most influential member State, the USA, joined the Berne Convention. This effect is now reinforced

---

[18] Figure as at 27 September 2007.

[19] Figure as at 27 September 2007; EU is counted as one state by WIPO on top of member States that ratified individually.

[20] See European Commission (2007) 'Industrial property: EU joins international designs treaty', Press release, 25 September, available online at europa.eu/rapid/pressReleasesAction.do?reference=IP/07/1388&format=HTML&aged=0&language=EN&guiLanguage=fr (EU states counted individually).

[21] On 27 September 2007, there were 49 member States.

[22] Figure as at 27 September 2007.

by the fact that the TRIPS Agreement requires its contracting states to comply with most of the provisions of the Berne Convention.[23] Further substantive provisions are found in Arts 9–14 of the TRIPS Agreement and yet further measures to take account of the new developments in copyright are found in the WIPO Copyright Treaty, signed in Geneva in 1996),[24] which is closely linked to the Berne Convention as a special treaty under Art. 20 of that Convention.

TRIPS plays a somewhat different role in relation to copyright. The idea–expression dichotomy is spelled out *expressis verbis*, but otherwise there is modernization, rather the first harmonization of basic principles of substantive law. Hence, we see provisions on computer programs and databases, and rental rights, before we return to Art. 13, and its limitations and exceptions (the famous three-step-test). The WIPO Copyright Treaty, meanwhile, continues that trend and might be seen as an Internet treaty. The right of communication to the public is enshrined as the equivalent in the digital era of the right of reproduction and technical protection measure make their first appearance at international treaty level.

The rights of performers, recorders, and broadcasting organizations required supplementary protection. In this respect, the most important Convention is the 1961 Rome Convention for the Protection of Performers, Producers of Phonograms and Broadcasting Organizations.[25] The Rome Convention did not, however, achieve the number of ratifications that the Berne Convention did and proper international harmonization was never achieved. It did not come as a surprise, therefore, when Art. 14 of TRIPS started again from scratch, and introduced basic harmonized rules for the protection of performers, producers of phonograms, and broadcasting organizations.

The WIPO Performances and Phonograms Treaty, signed in Geneva in 1996,[26] provides major improvements in this area and entered into force on 20 May 2002. Broadcasting organizations were left out, however, and reaching a deal on this point proved to be extremely difficult. At the time of writing, there was some optimism that a treaty on the protection of broadcasting organizations could be reached—that is, that a diplomatic conference to agree a treaty formally could be convened in the near future—but there is clearly some distance to go.[27]

European initiatives

The creation of a single European market, based on the principle of free competition, required a further substantial harmonization of intellectual property provisions—what had previously been rather loose international cooperation on a standard basis of minimal rules was no longer sufficient.

Patents

In Europe, cooperation in the patent area was taken further than it was on an international level. The European Patent Convention (EPC), signed in Munich in 1973, provides

---

[23] But not with those on moral rights: see Art. 9.

[24] This Treaty entered into force on 6 March 2002 and, as at 27 September 2007, there are 64 contracting states.

[25] On 27 September 2007, 86 states had adopted this Convention.

[26] On 27 September 2007, there were 62 contracting states.

[27] See T. Rivers (2007) 'A broadcasters' treaty?', in P. Torremans (ed.), *Handbook of Contemporary Copyright Research*, Cheltenham: Edward Elgar, pp. 483–513.

a system comprising a single patent application and search. The EPC effectively contains a harmonized patent law for its member States, which cover the core elements such as patentability and patent infringements. The European Patent Office in Munich, which started working on 1 June 1978, carries out this search. At the end of the procedure, the applicant is granted a bundle of national patents: one for each member State indicated in the application. The EPC is not an initiative of the European Union: it is adhered to be other European countries, such as Switzerland, Turkey, and Liechtenstein.[28]

The European Community wanted to go further and replace the bundle of national patents at the end of the granting procedure by a single Community patent. This was the aim of the Community Patent Convention signed at Luxemburg in 1975,[29] but the Convention never entered into force. At present, attempts are under way to revive the project as an EU Regulation that would be administered by the European Patent Office—but a final agreement is held up by issues relating to the use of languages and litigation.[30]

Other initiatives of the Community relate to pharmaceutical inventions and inventions relating to plant protection products—for which the term of protection was extended by means of the introduction of supplementary protection certificates (SPCs) for pharmaceutical products[31] and for plant protection products[32]—and to biotechnological inventions.[33] At the lower end of the innovation scale, some form of protection is planned for inventions that do not qualify for full patent protection. The utility model that was proposed some years ago should provide that protection.[34] The European Union has also adopted a special registration system for plant varieties, which operates separately from the patent system and which is in line with the International Convention for the Protection of New Varieties of Plants (the UPOV Convention).[35]

Discussions relating to a Directive on the patentability of computer-implemented inventions, however, eventually came to nothing.[36]

Trade marks

In relation to trade marks, the Community acted on two levels: the national trade mark laws of the member States have been harmonized by means of the First Council Directive

[28] At the time of writing, there were 32 member States, and a revised version of the EPC had been agreed on 29 November 2000 and entered into force at the end of 2007.

[29] See Convention for the European Patent for the Common Market (Community Patent Convention) (1989) OJ L 401/10.

[30] See the Commission Proposal for a Council Regulation on the Community Patent (2000) OJ C 337/278, COM (00) 412 final. The most recent draft, dated 8 March 2004, is available online at www.europa.eu.int/comm/internal_market/en/indprop/patent/index.htm.

[31] EC Council Regulation 1768/92 concerning the creation of a supplementary protection certificate for medicinal products (1992) OJ L 182/1.

[32] EC Parliament and Council Regulation 1610/96 concerning the creation of a supplementary protection certificate for plant protection products (1996) OJ L 198/30.

[33] After a first attempt to get a Directive approved failed, the Commission made a second attempt, which led eventually to the adoption of the EC Parliament and Council Directive 98/44/EC on the legal protection of biotechnological inventions (1998) OJ L 213/13.

[34] See, now, the Amended Proposal for a European Parliament and Council Directive approximating the legal arrangements for the protection of inventions by utility model (2000) OJ C 248/56, COM (99) 309 final; see also Chapter 7. This proposal is now likely to be linked to that on the Community patent, if it is ever to be revived at all. (Strong opposition remains against any form of utility model at EU level.)

[35] Council Regulation (EC) 2100/94 on Community plant variety rights (1994) OJ L 227/1, as amended.

[36] Proposal for a Directive of the European Parliament and of the Council on the patentability of computer-implemented inventions COM (2002) 92 final, dated 20 February 2002 (2002) OJ C 151/129.

to approximate the laws of the member States relating to trade marks[37] and a Community trade mark has been created by means of a Council Regulation on the Community Trade Mark.[38] This latter system has been in force since 1996, with far greater success than expected, and provides a single trade mark for the Community as a whole. The Community Trade Mark Office—which is officially called the Office for Harmonization in the Internal Market (trade marks and designs), or OHIM—is located in Alicante, Spain.

The Community has also joined the Madrid System.

Industrial designs

The Community undertook the same action in this area as that taken in relation to trade marks—that is, the harmonization of the national design laws by means of a Directive and the creation of a single Community design right by means of a Regulation. The difficult issue of spare parts and a repair clause made negotiations very cumbersome, but, eventually, a Directive on the legal protection of designs was agreed in October 1998.[39] Shortly afterwards, agreement on a Council Regulation on community design[40] was reached and, in January 2003, the OHIM was able to extend its role from that relating only to Community trade marks to become a Community trade mark and design office.

The EU has now also joined the Geneva Act of the Hague Agreement, with effect from 1 January 2008.

Copyright

The Community has, up to now, refrained from making an attempt to harmonize copyright as a whole. Only certain aspects of copyright—such as the term of copyright protection—have been harmonized.[41]

A number of areas have received special attention: computer programs;[42] rental rights and lending rights;[43] satellite broadcasting and cable retransmission;[44] databases.[45] A new Copyright Directive now harmonizes certain aspects of copyright and related rights in the information society.[46] The implementation of that Directive should enable the EU to accede to the WIPO Copyright Treaty and the WIPO Performances and Phonograms Treaty soon, especially because member States have undertaken to legislate in a timely way to meet the provisions on moral rights for performers that are not retained in the Directive.[47] Although not of the same importance and dealing with a small point in copyright law, agreement on the Directive to harmonize the provisions on *droit de suite*

---

[37] (1989) OJ L 40/1.

[38] (EC) 40/94 (1994) OJ L 11/1.

[39] EC Parliament and Council Directive 98/71/EC (1998) OJ L 289/28.

[40] Council Regulation 6/2002 (2002) OJ L 3/1.

[41] EC Council Directive 93/98 harmonizing the terms of protection of copyright and certain related rights (1993) OJ L 290/9.

[42] EC Council Directive 91/250 on the legal protection of computer programs (1991) OJ L 122/42.

[43] EC Council Directive 92/100 on rental rights and lending rights related to copyright in the field of intellectual property (1992) OJ L 346/61.

[44] EC Council Directive 93/83 on the coordination of certain rules concerning copyright and rights related to copyright applicable to satellite broadcasting and cable retransmission (1993) OJ L 248/15.

[45] EC Parliament and Council Directive 96/9 on the legal protection of databases (1996) OJ L 77/20.

[46] EC Parliament and Council Directive 2001/29/EC on the harmonisation of certain aspects of copyright and related rights in the information society (2001) OJ L 167/10.

[47] See COM (97) 193.

(meaning literally 'right to follow' and referring to a right granted to artists to receive a fee on the resale of their works of art) was only reached after heated debates.[48]

At the time of writing, the Commission was focusing its attention on the management of copyright and related rights, on the one hand, and on a review of the *acquis communautaire* in the area of copyright and related rights. Both are the subject of consultation procedures, but no new legislative initiatives have yet emerged.

Other European initiatives

The Intellectual Property (IP) Enforcement Directive[49] attempts to streamline the enforcement mechanisms of the member States and to achieve a common minimum standard. The Directive covers all intellectual property rights and has now been transposed into the national laws of the member States.[50]

The Community has also adopted measures in the areas of counterfeiting,[51] topographies of semiconductor chips,[52] comparative advertising,[53] and electronic commerce.[54] A short Directive dealing with the legal protection of conditional access services was also adopted on 20 November 1998.[55]

An overview

This chapter highlights the international context in which the UK intellectual property system operates. Starting from the founding treaties—that is, the Paris Convention and the Berne Convention—and their principle of national treatment, we have come a long way. Gradually, there has been a push to harmonize the substantive intellectual property law provisions; at the same time, application procedure and procedures in front of the national intellectual property offices have also be streamlined and harmonized. The TRIPS Agreement also greatly expanded the territorial scope of the intellectual property treaties, without overlooking its massive harmonization effort.

At a European level, we have seen even further integration in order to cope with the single market. A Community trade mark and a Community design right are now in place

---

[48] EC Parliament and Council Directive 2001/84/EC on the resale right for the benefit of the author of an original work of art (2001)OJ L 272/32.

[49] EC Parliament and Council Directive 2004/48/EC on the enforcement of intellectual property rights (2004) OJ L 195/16.

[50] For a critical view of the original Commission proposal, see W. R. Cornish, J. Drexl, R. Hilty and A. Kur, 'Procedures and remedies for enforcing IPRS: the European Commission's proposed Directive' [2003] EIPR 447 (supported by a large number of academics, including this author).

[51] Council Regulation 3842/86 laying down measures to prohibit the release for free circulation of counterfeit goods (1986) OJ L 357/1, now replaced by Council Regulation 3295/94 laying down measures to prohibit the release for free circulation, export, re-export or entry for a suspensive procedure of counterfeit and pirated goods (1994) OJ L 341/8.

[52] EC Parliament and Council Directive 87/54 on the legal protection of topographies of semiconductor products (1987) OJ L 24/36.

[53] EC Parliament and Council 97/55 amending Directive 84/450 on misleading advertising (1997) OJ L 290/18.

[54] EC Parliament and Council Directive 2000/31/EC on certain legal aspects of information society services, in particular electronic commerce, in the Internal Market (2000) OJ L 178/1.

[55] EC Parliament and Council Directive 98/84/EC on the legal protection of services based on, or consisting of, conditional access (1998) OJ L 320/54. Conditional access services are typically only available through the use of a decoder or upon payment of a fee. The number of these services that is available on the Internet is increasing rapidly.

as single rights for the whole of the Community; parallel Directives have harmonized national trade mark and design laws to a large extent. The Community patent is still on the drawing board, but, in the meanwhile, the European Patent Convention allows the EPO to turn around several thousands of applications each year—and, at the end of the process, bundles of national patents are often granted. Copyright has seen a different evolution, but it is fair to say that the various Directives have, in their own piecemeal way, achieved a fair degree of harmonization.

All of this corresponds to the needs of international business that are ever increasing as intellectual property is increasingly exploited in a global market. No doubt this pressure will guarantee a further flood of initiatives and developments in this area.

Further reading

GERVAIS, D. (2003) *The TRIPS Agreement: Drafting History and Analysis*, 2nd edn, London: Sweet and Maxwell.

RICKETSON, S. and GINSBURG, J. C. (2006) *International Copyright and Neighbouring Rights: The Berne Convention and Beyond*, Oxford: Oxford University Press.

ec.europa.eu/internal_market/copyright/index_en.htm For EU copyright instruments.

ec.europa.eu/internal_market/indprop/index_en.htm For EU instruments relating to industrial property.

www.epo.org/patents.html For the text of the EPC.

www.wipo.int/treaties/en For the text of the treaties administered by WIPO.

SECTION B

PATENTS

3

Origin, background, and international aspects of the patent system

The longest standing, best known, and, arguably, economically most valuable form of protection of rights provided by the law of intellectual property comes in the form of the patent. A patent is, in essence, the grant of a monopoly to an inventor who has used his or her skill to invent something new. The monopoly is not absolute; patents are only granted for a limited period and are accompanied by public disclosure enabling others in the field to consider, and perhaps subsequently improve on, it. Each year, tens of thousands of patents are granted creating a monopoly right within the UK alone and they may cover a whole range of different types of subject matter, although it is fair to note that the level of patenting activity in the UK seems much greater than that in many major industrial nations.

Patents may cover entirely new products or, more often, enhancements to pre-existing products, or they may cover a new or improved process for performing an activity. A legal structure has been created to cover all of these variants that is elegant in its simplicity, but complex in its operation. Before we explore the detail of its ramifications, however, we must explore its origins and purpose, along with the background to, and sources of, the modern law of patents.

History

It will be seen shortly that patent law has a very distinct European dimension; consequently, it is appropriate to begin by considering the origins of patent law that are found in Europe. The German miners of the Alps seem to have been first to develop the notion of monopoly rights in their new processes as far back as the thirteenth century,[1] but the first more universal patent scheme evolved in Venice—which was then at the height of its international power—in a Decree of 1474, which rewarded inventors of new objects with a limited monopoly on condition that the invention was disclosed to the state. This is a model that, in its essentials, is still followed by the patent system five centuries later. It has been argued[2] that the earliest example of a patent being granted to an inventor in England was that granted by Queen Elizabeth I to one Acontius, an inventor from Italy who had been granted one of the earliest Venetian patents, but had fled to England for religious reasons.

Patents at this period were often not a reward for invention, but a reward for royal supporters, and patents were granted simply so as to reward loyalty with monopoly. Such

---

[1] H. Wegner (1993) *Patent Harmonization*, London: Sweet and Maxwell, pp. 2–3.
[2] J. Phillips, 'The English patent as a reward for invention: the importation of an idea' (1982) 3 J Leg Hist 71.

abuses of power could not be countenanced by the courts, however, as was finally shown in the case of *Darcy v. Allin*.[3] In this case, a patent had been granted conferring a 14-year monopoly in the entire trade in playing cards and was not upheld on the grounds that it conferred an unreasonable monopoly. While it was accepted that patents could be granted for new trades and inventions, on the grounds that there was a public benefit in the form of whatever advantages the new development conferred;[4] there was no such benefit on the facts of this case.

Against the background of the changing roles of the monarch and legislature at this period in history, Parliament also decided to flex its muscles in relation to the grant of monopolies. It passed the Statute of Monopolies 1624, which, while seeking generally to stamp out monopolies, expressly allowed their retention in favour of inventors of new methods of manufacture, who were allowed a 14-year maximum period in which to exploit their creation, subject to certain protections for the public interest.

It may be that the essence of the modern patent can be traced back to this law, but this cannot be said of the system for gaining a patent. The grant remained an exercise of the royal prerogative and it was only as the number of patents sought increased against the background of the developing Industrial Revolution that clear rules and formalities very slowly began to make their appearance. It was in the eighteenth century, therefore, that the requirement of a written specification was established.

From the chaos of informality, the burgeoning bureaucracy and ever greater demand for patents produced a different chaos—the chaos of sclerosis—and it became clear, eventually, that steps had to be taken to reform and regularize the system lest it threaten the dominance in world trade then enjoyed by Britain. The Patent Law Amendment Act 1852 greatly simplified the system—the existence of the Patent Office dates from the appointment of Patent Commissioners at this time—but also liberalized the criteria for patentability and perhaps made obtaining a patent too easy. The next landmark, therefore, was the Patents, Designs and Trade Marks Act 1883, which established the Patent Office and empowered it to investigate applications in order both to weed out those that did not meet the official criteria and—after the Patents Act 1902—to investigate whether the subject matter of the patent was truly novel. Despite tinkering by Parliament over the years, the basic system then in place continued until the Patents Act 1977, which made significant changes to the system that reflected the growing internationalization of the world of patents—as will be noted later.

Purpose

The long history of patents and the remarkable consistency that has lain as a strand through that history, from the earliest times to the present day of common ideas and principles, suggests that strong forces led to the creation of the law and that those forces have remained in place ever since. What, then, are the factors that have shaped the law of patents? And what purposes does it fulfil?

To answer these questions, it is best to consider the often-competing interests of those involved with the patent system. Looked at, first, from the standpoint of the actual inventor, the traditional assumption is that a patent is the grant of a reward for all of the skill and hard work that has been put into the invention. There is much to be said for this perspective: undoubtedly, some inventors carry out their work with the future benefits

[3] (1602) Noy 173, 74 ER 1131.
[4] Ibid. at 183 and 1139.

that it will confer on them very much in mind; large firms can justify their research and development (R&D) staff to their accountants, and thus to their shareholders, by reference to the future rewards that will be gained.

This is, however, too simplistic a notion to be regarded as an acceptable universal solution. Some inventors receive no reward, because their invention is not a commercial success or because they do not have the resources to exploit it effectively. Little commercial benefit is likely to have flowed from the invention of jet engines for aeroplanes, for example, because years were to pass before aircraft construction technology caught up. Indeed, the number of successful applications for patents that give rise to a fully exploitable commercial product or process is believed to be a small fraction of the total amount, although this may be a consequence of the ethos and financial structure of the industrial sector generally, rather than a criticism of the patent system as such. Does industry generally want to take what is inevitably a risk when failure might be at the expense of shareholders' dividends and—for a cynical perspective—directors' fees? The relationship between small-scale inventors, who cannot afford to exploit an invention themselves, and other larger firms, who may be rivals in the same trade or companies primarily interested in providing venture capital in the expectation of a return, is bound in either case to be fraught. Many inventors receive no reward, because they lose the race to patent their product. This is often the case in respect of pharmaceutical products, in which sector a new problem will be seized upon by all of the major firms, each of which will race to reach an answer—in the form of a new or improved drug on to the market—but in which race there will only be one winner. The quest for an effective viable drug to combat the HIV virus is a classic example.

The link between invention and reward has, in fact, always seemed tenuous. Arkwright's important 'Spinning Jenny' may have been a key ingredient in the Industrial Revolution, but it was refused a patent,[5] while Watt's steam engine needed special legislation before it was regarded as patentable. Other inventors are not even in the game to seek a reward. The public image of the typical inventor as a bumbling pseudoscientist working away in his potting shed in an attempt to create a perpetual motion machine may be far from the reality of most companies' R&D divisions, but such individuals do exist and are clearly not in the game for the money. Significant inventions—such as the 'cats' eyes', which enhance road safety by marking the middle of the road—are, from time to time, created by enthusiastic individuals rather than by businesses. It even appears that the ubiquitous 'Post-it' type of gummed message label was devised by a choir member who was exasperated at the way in which traditional bookmarks fell out of his hymn book. More significantly, much research is carried out by people motivated by a love of the subject, a quest for knowledge, and a desire to push back the proverbial frontiers: academics in universities, for example.

Perhaps a more appropriate refinement is to suggest that at least the patent system offers an incentive to invent. If reward is not guaranteed, at least there is a chance of it—even for the lone inventor and for the university professor too, if they choose to avail themselves of it (as they usually will). But it may be best to regard that chance as, relatively speaking, not a great one: if the risk of unexploited or unexploitable inventions is added to the problems created by the limited time during which the reward can be enjoyed and the loss of secrecy when the patent application is made, the grant of a patent is a distinctly double-edged reward.

In looking at the patent system from other standpoints, the state, or society—as grantor of the patent—emerges as the other key player. The grant is not a generous act, in that the state is not giving up anything of its own; rather, it simply sacrifices the interests of

---

[5] *R v. Arkwright* (1785) 1 Web Pat Cas 64.

other traders. In so doing, however, the state makes major gains. Clearly, society benefits from improvements in transport, industry, health care, or whatever other improvement is conferred by the patent and, more intangibly, by the increase in knowledge created by the inventive process. Sometimes, the state even benefits more directly: for example, by its ability to take over an invention and prevent its use by others.[6] In a capitalist society, the increase in trade and wealth generated by the advances of the patent system are also important justifications for that system. It may be queried—in the light of all of the developments of the Industrial Revolution, which occurred when patent protection was minimal, as the fates of Arkwright and Watt demonstrate—just how significant a role the patent system plays in the expansion of new industries, but this is perhaps a weaker argument now than then, given the need to provide legal protection for the huge investments many companies make in their R&D activity. All of the factors clearly justify the state's involvement in the patent system and go far towards explaining the presence of a system in all developed and developing countries.

Taken on their own, however, such factors would suggest a trend towards the overgenerous grant of many patents, as in the UK after the 1852 legislation, which is not the norm in most patent systems today. The reason for this lies in the interests of other parties: parties who are not directly involved in the grant of a patent, but who are closely and directly affected by it, and whose interests require a more cautious approach to the patentability question. The two obvious groups concerned here are consumers and trade rivals. The interest of consumers as a class is, of course, served by the invention of new products and processes, but not if their inventor is able to take advantage of his or her monopoly position by its abuse in terms, for example, of restricting supply or inflating prices. We have already argued that such potential rewards are not always there for the enjoyment of the inventor, but the possibility clearly exists. Thus the monopoly is limited only to a set period and, should the inventor refuse to share the benefits thereof with society, the compulsory licensing system comes into play.[7]

Similar factors arise in relation to rival traders. Clearly, a permanent monopoly granted to an inventor would unduly distort the market; even a time-restricted monopoly distorts the market for the restriction period, but the harm that may be caused thereby is diminished by the disclosure requirement, giving the rival trader the chance to experiment and develop the original concept into a patentable improvement.

Clearly, therefore, no single interest group can shape the patent system. If there is a single justification or common purpose that underpins the system, it must be the attainment of a balance between the different interests involved. The consumer wants new products—so grants patents readily—but not at any price—so restricts the scope of the monopoly. A business wants the advantage of monopoly as a reward—but not at any price—so insists on public disclosure as its price. Society wants increased trade and wealth—but not at any price—hence the various restrictions and limitations. In assessing the detail of the patent system, in due course, it will be useful to reflect on which interests are being harmed or promoted by different aspects of the law and their contemporary interpretation.

The international dimension

It is self-evident that trade between nations can be affected by the existence in each nation of differing intellectual property regimes. If I develop a new product in the UK and gain

---

[6] Patents Act 1977, ss. 22, 55–59. See Chapter 5.
[7] Ibid., s. 48. See Chapter 5.

patent protection for it, at the very least, it will be inconvenient if I cannot extend my business into France because someone else has succeeded in gaining a monopoly there. It will be equally awkward for my French counterpart, of course, if he or she seeks to expand into my market. The more international trade there is, the more of a problem this becomes—especially when that trade is taking place in what purports to be a common market, such as that created between the members of the European Union (EU), with free trade without any national interference as its core.

The Paris Convention

Inevitably, cries have long been heard clamouring for greater levels of harmonization in domestic patent law (and other aspects of the law relating to intellectual property) between trading nations. Such cries long predate the Treaty of Rome, but have tended to emanate from Europe.

The culmination of the first round of patent harmonization came with the agreement known as the Paris Convention for the Protection of Industrial Property 1883, the main feature of which was that each signatory state had to offer the same treatment to all within that jurisdiction irrespective of nationality. To revert to the earlier example, under this Convention, I might file my patent application in France knowing that the dispute between my French counterpart and myself will be dealt with fairly on a footing of equal treatment. A common priority date—that is, the date from when protection runs—also applied as between all signatory states.

Slowly, the web of cooperation broadened: the USA did not initially accept the 1883 Convention, not least because of different approaches to the priority date, but after the Convention was amended in 1890 in Brussels, the USA became a signatory to it.[8] But while further conventions and revisions extended the scope of cooperation and the numbers of countries involved in the Paris Convention, it would be wrong to see it as a harmonizer of substantive law; rather, it is best seen as a way of facilitating procedural compatibility between the patent systems of signatory nations.

The Patent Cooperation Treaty

The next level of international agreement saw an attempt to ease the burden placed on a patentee by having to claim patent protection separately in each jurisdiction. This came to fruition in the form of the Washington Patent Cooperation Treaty 1970 (PCT), which sets up a system of international patent applications, overseen by the World Intellectual Property Organization (WIPO), an international body. The system allows for a single application to be made that, if successful, will give patent protection in those signatory states in relation to which the applicant seeks protection. There is provision for either, or both, an international search of other patents and a preliminary examination of the claim made; there is not, however, an international definition of patentability, which remains a domestic matter in terms of whether an application meets the criteria of patentability. This scheme is not without its value and it facilitates thousands of applications each year, but its main problem—and the problem with much else in patent law—originates in the limited basis of both its accessibility and acceptability.

Over the last few years, the PCT system has seen a rapid expansion, both in terms of member States—numbering 137 at the last count in August 2007, compared to 111 in

---

[8] Wegner (1993) p. 22.

April 2001, for example—and in terms of applications. Now, more than half of the world's countries and territories participate in the scheme. Under the rules of the scheme, the applicant, first of all, files a single application. The treatment of that application can be subdivided into international and national phases.

In the international phase, the starting point is the filing of the application under the PCT rules with the national patent office of a member State or with the WIPO International Bureau in Geneva. The applicant designates in the application the member States that are of interest and in relation to which he or she would like to obtain a patent. In a second stage of the international phase, an international search is carried out by one of nine selected national patent offices. This search aims to throw up any relevant pre-existing materials. In a third step, the International Bureau will publish the application, which international publication is one of the main advantages of the PCT system. It provides a single and complete source of information for any innovator, rather than the pre-existing multiple national patent registers, and this greatly enhances the effective dissemination of the technical knowledge contained in patent applications. In the light of the results of the international search, the applicant has to decide whether or not to request that the fourth step of the international phase be carried out: an international preliminary examination of the application by one of the nine selected patent offices. In practice, 80 per cent of all applicants take advantage of this option. It is important to stress, however, that this examination is preliminary and that no patent is granted at the end of the international phase. It is up to the applicant to decide whether he or she still wishes to pursue the application and to move on to the national phase. This national phase will take place in front of every national patent office in the countries that are still of interest to the applicant and it is only at the end of that national phase that each country involved will decide, according to its own rules, whether or not to grant a national patent.

This scheme is, therefore, nowhere near to a global patent system: not all countries participate in the system and there is no harmonization of substantive patent law; there is really only a streamlined application procedure. This may sound more damaging than it actually is, given that most major developed countries that are active in world trade and in innovation, and which have a developed patent system, are among the member States— but it raises the problem of whether worldwide patent law is ever likely to be feasible, given the different levels of development, innovatory capacity, and legal systems that are found around the world. What is appropriate for France or Germany, for example, may not play well in Burkina Faso or Papua New Guinea, or, in more significant cases, countries in the Far East—such as Thailand—which have, until recently, taken a distinctly relaxed view of their international obligations in respect of intellectual property rights.

The TRIPS Agreement

This lack of universality remains an important issue. Extensive discussion took place, as part of the Uruguay Round of General Agreement of Tariffs and Trade (GATT) negotiations, with a view to creating a broader international level of protection for patents and other intellectual property rights. This eventually led to the signing of the Trade-Related Aspects of Intellectual Property Rights (TRIPS) Agreement and the establishment of the World Trade Organization (WTO), the competence of which includes aspects of intellectual property.

But this trend towards broader protection for intellectual property has been a path paved with difficulty, especially for countries such as India, which have consciously developed patent law to reflect local, rather than Western, conditions and which have been faced with the need to return to a more mainstream approach to patent law as a result of the GATT negotiations. In some instances, this prospect has led to violent demonstrations in the streets—a rare case of public disorder being occasioned by patent law reform—justified by the alleged effect on India's burgeoning industrial sector.

The TRIPS Agreement imposes, for the first time, substantive minimum standards in patent law with which all WTO member States eventually have to comply. Apart from national treatment and a most favourite nation clause, there are substantive provisions covering points such as patentable subject matter, the rights that are conferred by a patent, exceptions, and the right to use the patent without the consent of the right holder. The latter points are dealt with in a very restrictive way and many conditions are imposed, while the concept of patentable subject matter is defined broadly on the basis that patents should be available for any inventions in any field of technology, as long as the invention is new, involves an inventive step, and is capable of industrial application.[9]

The European Patent Convention

In the light of all of this, it is perhaps unsurprising that the most successful and, in terms of its impact on domestic patent law, the most significant move towards the integration of patent law has been achieved among the relatively homogeneous nations of Europe.[10] It is significant to note at the outset that these developments fall outside the ambit of the EU, although they closely associated with it, dating from the time at which the UK was a major trading country outside the Treaty of Rome.

The search for a common European concept of the patent led to the signing in Munich in 1973 of the European Patent Convention (EPC), which established the European Patent Office (EPO) that has, since 1978, effectively offered to applicants a European patent. This is achieved by signatory states agreeing to harmonize their own patent law with the definition in the European Patent Convention—hence the 1977 Patents Act in the UK—and the European Patent Office then awarding patents in all member States in relation to which the applicant has sought to acquire patent protection. The advantage of the system is that, on top of the harmonization of national patent laws, a single application now also leads to a single examination procedure. The downside of the system is that, at the end of the day, no single European patent is delivered: the applicant instead receives a bundle of national patents, one relating to each of the member States covered by the application.

This system has proved to be a considerable success. Applicants have shown a marked trend to seek the broader protection provided by the EPO to the extent that over 70 per cent of all applications seeking patent protection in the UK are now routed via the EPO in Munich, rather than through the domestic Patent Office, graphically reflecting the international nature of both trade in general and innovation in particular. The system slowly extends its ambit; all of the EU member States are now within the scheme, along with other states such as Switzerland. A revised version of the EPC was agreed on 29 November 2000 and entered into force at the end of 2007.

The significance and far-reaching impact of the EPC system on the law of the UK is perhaps best shown by s. 130(7) of the Patents Act 1977. This declares that most key sections of the legislation are framed so as to have '*the same effect in the UK as the corresponding provisions of the European Patent Convention, the Community Patent Convention and the Patent Co-operation Treaty*'. In the light of this, it is clearly appropriate for the courts to consider not only those agreements, but also their interpretations. In practice, this means

---

[9] For more details, see Arts 27–34.
[10] Although the homogeny can be exaggerated: the Netherlands, for example, had no patent system whatsoever between 1869 and 1912—Wegner (1993) p. 17.

that domestic litigation can, and does, make use of decisions of the EPO as to interpretation of key phrases that are common to the Convention and the 1977 legislation.

The Community patent

There is, however, one further level of cooperation. Following the 1973 European Patent Convention, further discussion took place with a view to setting up a single European Community patent. This was separate from the EPO's harmonization work, because differences between member States at that time meant that it was easier to offer a measure of harmonization of the law between those countries prepared to proceed than to impose a single patent law on all member States. As far back as 1975, however, the Community Patent Convention[11] was agreed, although agreement on its implementation has never been reached.

After a long period of difficult additional negotiations, the Commission decided to revive the project in the form of an EU Regulation[12] and the Council made it one of its priorities. It is understood that agreement has been reached on most substantive points, but that the language regime proposed clashes with the desires of a number of member States to see all languages treated equally: hence proposals such as that of adding a requirement that the claims of the patent be translated into all official Community languages unless the member State(s) concerned expressly give up that right. There is also a strongly felt need to have a centralized patent litigation system. Some member States proposed a European Patent Litigation Agreement (EPLA) in the context of the European Patent Convention, but other member States favour the establishment of a specific Community jurisdiction for patent litigation on European and Community patents that is based on the EC Treaty. The Commission is trying to draft a compromise that includes the strengths of both approaches and which might be part of a final compromise on the Community patent.[13]

If, or when, such an agreement is reached, there will be one clear benefit in making an application for the Community patent—namely, that a single application (made to the EPO, which will, it is proposed, administer the scheme) will result in a single patent conferring protection throughout the member States. Whether this is a benefit worth the expenditure of so much time, heat, and energy is perhaps questionable given the two alternative systems already in existence, but a lot will depend on the final drafting of the provisions of the Community Patent Regulation. Suffice it to say, at this stage, that a single application leading to a single patent will only be advantageous to most inventors if there is a balance between the administrative gains, in terms of obtaining and maintaining in force such a patent, and the costs of doing so. The language regime and the translations involved are an important aspect in this respect: the use of too many languages is bound to push up costs to such an extent that interested parties may well prefer to use the existing EPC system for those member States in relation to which they wish to obtain protection. But, in time, a clear picture will emerge that enables the patentee to select whichever option is appropriate to his or her resources and trading pattern.

[11] (1976) OJ L 17/1.

[12] See the Commission Proposal for a Council Regulation on the Community Patent (2000) OJ C 337/278, COM (00) 412 final. The March 2004 version of the proposal, as well as the state of play before the Council in May 2004, is available online at ec.europa.eu/internal_market/indprop/patent/index_en.htm#patent.

[13] See European Commission (2007) 'Patents: Commission sets out vision for improving patent system in Europe', Press release, 3 April, available online at europa.eu/rapid/pressReleasesAction.do?reference=IP/07/463&format=HTML&aged=1&language=EN&guiLanguage=fr, for details of the Commission's latest attempts.

The domestic system will remain and will provide domestic protection; the EPO's present system will remain if protection is sought either in a limited number of EU member States—with applicants selecting in relation to which countries they wish to have protection—and/or in relation to those states who are signatories to the Convention, but not EU members. The Community patent will, eventually, automatically confer protection in all EU member States. For the sake of completeness, it should also be remembered that the WIPO procedures established under the Washington Patent Cooperation Treaty also remain, allowing an application for patents protection more widely again, beyond the frontiers of geographical or united Europe.

The Patent Law Treaty

Despite the existence of the Patent Cooperation Treaty and its current success, the lack of international harmonization in terms of the procedures operated by the various national patent offices still represents a major hurdle for patent applicants. WIPO member States have therefore negotiated the Patent Law Treaty (PLT), which was signed by 53 states on 1 July 2000 and which, in most cases, is currently still awaiting ratification. The UK has already ratified the PLT, which has been in force between the UK and the other countries that ratified it since 22 March 2006.

The PLT does not deal with substantive law, but rather acts at procedural level and aims at harmonizing national patent formalities throughout the world. Even before ratification, however, this Treaty can be seen to be an impact, because national patent offices and legislators already use its provisions as a model for the updating of their own procedures.

Our discussion will be focused on the UK Patents Act 1977, but it will be appreciated that, due to the EPO's harmonization requirement that was the *raison d'être* for the legislation, the same principles govern the application for a domestic patent, an EPO patent, or the future Community patent, and the same very broad principles will be significant features in an application made under the provisions of the Washington Treaty.

Obtaining a patent

This is not a book that is designed to give full instructions on the practicalities of applying for a patent. The substantive law and, in particular, some of the problems it poses for applicants are, however, shaped by the way in which the procedures operate, so it is appropriate to begin our survey of the substantive law by providing an outline of the key steps to be taken in pursuit of a domestic patent.

The priority date

In relation to any patent application, the first vital point to establish is the priority date of the applicant's invention. The essence of a patent is that it is something new that has not previously existed and so it is vital to establish a priority date ahead of anyone else in the field—particularly in a typical patent race, in which rival firms are pursuing the same, or a similar, line of research.

The relevant date is the date of filing the application for a patent;[14] the only exception is if an earlier date is claimed, being a previous application within the past year that

---

[14] Patents Act 1977, s. 5(1).

discloses matter in support of the subsequent application.[15] This priority date is important not only because it establishes priority over any rival applications from the date, but also because it sets the clock running for the period of validity of the patent itself.

The priority date works internationally. Under the provisions of the Paris Convention 1883, the applicant who files in one of the member States then has 12 months from the priority date to file in any other member State. During that period, the applicant will be able to benefit from the priority date of the original first application. For various, often procedural, reasons, not all of these applications are identical: it is therefore important to ascertain whether the document that is relied on in terms of priority covers the whole content of the application that claims the benefit of the earlier priority date. The Court of Appeal recently held[16] that there should be sufficient in the priority document that is being relied on to give the 'skilled man' essentially the same information as that which formed the subject of the claim in the application for the benefit of which priority is claimed and which would enable him to work the invention in accordance with the claim. The priority document as a whole, therefore, must both disclose and enable the invention.

The filing of an application

Given that the priority date is the date on which the application is filed, the next issue to consider is what acts amount to a filing. This is defined in the UK Patents Act 1977, s. 15(1): the vital elements that are needed are the presentation to the Patent Office of documents that indicate that a patent is being sought, which identify the applicant for the patent, which contain a description of the invention, and which, naturally, are accompanied by the appropriate fee. In order to obtain an effective priority date, there has to be an enabling disclosure of the invention. The skilled person to whom the description of the invention is addressed must be able to reproduce it without engaging in inventive activity.[17] That issue is decided at the priority date, rather than at the time of the publication of the specification.[18]

These acts together create the filing date, but beg a vital question: when should an inventor time his or her filing date? On the one hand, if the inventor files at too early a stage of development, there is a risk that, in subsequent examination by the Patent Office or later revocation proceedings instigated by a rival, the invention will be found not to fulfil the precise requirements of the law for patentability. On the other hand, the earlier that a claim is filed, the better placed the inventor is as against his or her rivals in a patent race, especially because the state of the art against which the novelty of the invention is judged is that pertaining at the date of filing the application.[19]

The law gives some assistance that helps to support a decision to apply earlier rather than later. The requirements of Patents Act 1977, s. 15, are really very minimal and considerably understate the true amount of documentation that will be required by the Patent Office. Indeed, the section hints at this by stating that, after a period of 12 months,[20] the application will be deemed to have been withdrawn unless the claims and abstract have

---

[15] Ibid., (2).

[16] In *Unilin Beheer BV v. Berry Floor NV & ors* [2004] All ER (D) 603; see also the decision of the Enlarged Board of Appeal of the EPO in Case G02/98, *In re Same Invention* [2001] OJ EPO 11, *sub nom. R v. X/Same invention* [2002] EPOR 167.

[17] See *Asahi Kasei Kogyo's Application* [1991] RPC 485.

[18] See *Biogen v. Medeva* [1997] RPC 1.

[19] Patents Act 1977, s. 2(2). See Chapter 4.

[20] Under r. 22 of The Patents Rules 2007, SI 2007/3291.

already been submitted.[21] This, in effect, gives the applicant a year's leeway to get from the minimalist position at the date of filing to finalizing the detail of the application before it is formally examined, during which period it is protected by having a priority date to use against other subsequent applications.

What, then, are these all-important 'claims' and 'abstract' that must form part of the application? A starting point is s. 14 of the Act, which states that every application shall contain a request for a patent to be granted, a specification containing a description of the invention, a claim, and an abstract of it (although the position of other documents that still comply with s. 15(1) is reserved and these may also initiate an application). The vital elements are the specification and claim—the abstract simply being a help to later searchers through the files of the Patent Office—with the claim being supported by the description.

The reason why these documents are vital is that the specification and claim form the basis of the invention applied for and thus delimit its scope. The claim is part of the patent specification and will effectively delimit the scope of the monopoly. Precise drafting of the specification and claim is, therefore, important, because any subsequent litigation— whether in relation to patentability, infringement, or revocation—is bound to be very closely concerned with what is the true basis of the invention.

Statutory guidance is given as to the broad nature of these two crucial components in a patent application. Section 14(3) provides that:

> The specification of an application shall disclose the invention in a manner which is clear enough and complete enough for the invention to be performed by a person skilled in the art.

Section 14(5), meanwhile, establishes that the claim must define the matter for which patent protection is sought, must be clear and concise, must be supported by the description, and must relate either to one invention, or to a related group of inventions.

In practice, the level of detail that goes into these documents—particularly the specification—is quite significant. The specification must, in effect, contain instructions by which someone other than the inventor—albeit someone who is skilled in the relevant art—might reproduce the invention and so the fullest information should be given for this purpose: if the specification were to be found to be unworkable, no patent would be granted. Likewise, the claims are so called because they delimit the extent of the monopoly that is being claimed, so it is essential to include as many different aspects of the new invention as possible. These documents are easier to read than to describe; extensive extracts appear in many reports of patent litigation. Two examples that have the added advantage of being in relation to ordinary—that is, non-scientific—subject matter are *Procter & Gamble Co. v. Peaudouce (UK) Ltd*[22] (relating to nappies) and *AC Edwards Ltd v. Acme Signs & Displays Ltd*[23] (relating to petrol price indicators).

Again, in this area, practical difficulties are quickly placed in the way of the applicant. It is apparent from the foregoing that, in terms of gaining and retaining patent protection, the fullest information possible should be provided for the specification and claims. For other reasons, however, it is tempting to provide as little information as possible. Remember that a key aspect of the patent system is public disclosure of the patent, so the more information provided to the Patent Office, the more information is also provided to trade rivals. Also, the longer the time spent in checking and testing that procedures work, or in adding additional claims, the greater the likelihood is that a trade rival may

---

[21] Patents Act 1977, s. 15(10).
[22] [1989] FSR 180.
[23] [1992] RPC 131.

jump in first and claim patent protection for itself. In fairness, the latter point is somewhat tempered by the fact that amendments may be allowed during the application procedure, although not so as to extend the protection of the patent.[24] Typically, an amendment may consist either of a refinement of an aspect of the specification or claim within its terms as research work continues, or may be a withdrawal of some aspect of the protection sought, in the light, perhaps, of new evidence of the prior state of the art becoming available. It is even possible to seek an amendment of the patent after its grant,[25] which may be useful to pre-empt a threat of revocation by another. But it is important to note that such an amendment may never expand the claim to exclusivity of the patent;[26] only a reduction in scope is permissible.

The examination process

Returning to the steps necessary to be taken in order to gain a patent, on receipt of all of the information furnished by the applicant, the Patent Office will conduct a search among other patents—records of all patents are held—with a particular view to a provisional assessment of the application's novelty and obviousness, which are two vital factors in deciding whether it is patentable. After this takes place and assuming, of course, that the applicant has not been deterred by the experience, publication of the application then takes place no more than 18 months after the priority date.

This is another important juncture in the tactics of patent application and opposition. From the time of publication, the information in the application is obviously in the public domain, which is good for the applicant in that he or she will now be able to establish clearly that he or she has won any race to patent the invention and can claim damages for infringement from this time onwards, but bad news in that rivals are now able to find out about the invention and so can, variously, seek to develop it further, consider issues of revocation and/or infringement, or, most immediately, decide to register an objection to the grant of a patent. Interested parties have a right under the Patent Act, s. 21, to submit observations as to patentability during the next stage of the patent procedure.

The Patent Office will now proceed to a full examination of all aspects of the patent application, offering ample opportunity for the applicant to contribute his or her own observations to the process. Obviously, the time that this will take can vary enormously from case to case, depending on the problems that arise and including possible s. 21 representations by third parties. The UK Act does, however, stipulate a maximum period of four-and-a-half years from the filing date (or any earlier appropriate priority date).[27] It may seem harsh that, if the application has not been completed by that time, it will be deemed to have been refused unless an appeal is pending,[28] but, because an appeal may be lodged against the deemed refusal itself,[29] that hardship is mitigated.

After that time—and the Patent Office claims that most applications take between two and three years—a patent can be granted by the relevant Patent Office. This has the effect of creating a proprietary right in the patentee,[30] one that exists for 20 years, subject to the payment of a fee for renewal after the first five years have passed.[31] It is significant to

[24] Patents Act 1977, ss. 19 and 76(2)(b).
[25] Ibid., s. 27; see also s. 75.
[26] See *Baker Hughes Inc. v. Halliburton Energy Services Inc.* (2003) 26(1) IPD 26003.
[27] Patents Act 1977, s. 20; Patents Rules 2007, r. 30.
[28] Patents Act 1977, s. 20(1).
[29] Ibid., s. 97.
[30] Ibid., s. 30.
[31] Ibid., s. 25.

note that the 20-year period is calculated not from the grant of the patent itself, but from the date on which the application is filed, which we have just seen can be up to four-and-a-half years earlier—and this represents around a 20 per cent loss of usable exploitation time for the patent. The trend has, however, been towards lengthening the term of patent protection. The 1883 Act offered only 14 years from the date of filing, while the 1939 Act stretched this to 16 years; the current period stems from the EPC and the 1977 legislation. It is also true that, during the period between filing and grant, much preparatory work can be done to get the patent ready for the market and that there is protection against exploitation by others during this period.

There may, however, be some substance to complaints from industries such as the pharmaceutical trade who can point to the fact that, even after the grant of a patent, more time will be lost not only by the usual final preparations for marketing the launch of a new product that are common to all industries, but also the further delays that result from the need to comply with the rigorous testing requirements that have to be undergone by new products in such specific industries. It seems unlikely that the 20-year period will be extended any further for now, except in relation to specific areas such as pharmaceuticals, for which the EPC was amended in 1991 to permit such extensions, following the lead already set by the USA and Japan, and subject to the ratification of the amendment by EPC signatories. It may, however, be doubted whether this ratification will occur in the near future[32] and, besides, this problem has, to an extent, been alleviated by the idea of the supplementary protection certificate (SPC), which can, in limited circumstances, extend the period of protection for medical products and which is considered separately in Chapter 7. This point is, of course, relevant to the discussions in Chapter 1 about the incentive to invent that is provided by the patent system: until the argument of the drug firms was accepted, it might be argued that the battle to gain a monopoly would have born a result for only a little over a decade, which suggests that general profits from sales, rather than the extra profits from monopoly sales, may be just as much of an inducement.

Whether it is actually a valuable asset or not, the volume of litigation arising from the process of awarding a patent suggests that it is seen to be such and the way in which the law has created such a thorough system—some may even call it an ordeal—through which applicants must pass before a patent is granted tends to support such as perception. The fact that a proprietary right is being created is perhaps some justification for the elaborate procedures involved, but it hardly reflects the relative ease with which trade marks and copyright can be acquired. Perhaps a better justification is that the criteria issued by the law in deciding the issue of patentability are not easy to use, reflecting the difficulty encountered in translating an abstract concept, such as an invention, into black-and-white legal principles. These are, however, issues that need to be considered in the light of the substantive rules that the following chapters will consider and the whole area can be overviewed in Chapter 8. The next chapter, then, will consider the criteria used in the patentability assessment.

An overview

The patent system originated as a system of privileges that were granted to attract foreign technologies to the country. Gradually, it became a system with set benchmarks and criteria under which any inventor could apply, which is very much in line with its main

---

[32] J. N. Adams, 'Supplementary protection certificates: the challenge to EC Regulation 1768/92' [1994] 8 EIPR 323 at 326.

purpose to reward the inventor in order to encourage R&D and innovation. Newer and better products and processes are seen to be desirable, and the patent system offers incentives in this respect.

At the international level, the Paris Convention set out the basic principle of national treatment. Further harmonization and cooperation was achieved by means of the Patent Cooperation Treaty, the Patent Law Treaty, and the TRIPS Agreement. In Europe, the European Patent Convention even provided an integrated patent system of sorts.

In order to obtain a patent in the UK, an application needs to be filed. The priority date is vital in this respect, because we are dealing with a 'first to file' system. The claims and specification are also extremely important, but the application can be completed after the initial filing of a skeleton application. The Patent Office then examines the claim and, usually between two and three years after the initial filing, a patent will be granted in appropriate cases.

Further reading

Nuyts, A. (ed.) (2008) *International Litigation in Intellectual Property*, London: Kluwer Law International.

Phillips, J. 'The English patent as a reward for invention: the importation of an idea' (1982) 3 J Leg Hist 71.

Wegner, H. (1993) *Patent Harmonization*, London: Sweet and Maxwell.

4

Patentability

Few things appear simpler in patent law than the basic definition of patentability. According to s. 1(1) of the UK Patents Act 1977, which is based on Art. 52 of the European Patent Convention (EPC):

> A patent may be granted only for an invention in respect of which the following conditions are satisfied, that is to say—
>
> (a) the invention is new;
>
> (b) it involves an inventive step;
>
> (c) it is capable of industrial application;
>
> (d) the grant of a patent for it is not excluded by subsections (2) and (3) below;
>
> and references in this Act to a patentable invention shall be construed accordingly.

Section 1(2) goes on to make clear that discoveries, scientific theories, and mathematical methods cannot be regarded as inventions and are thus not patentable; likewise barred from this status are works properly found within copyright, schemes for performing a mental act, playing a game, or doing business and computer programs, and also the presentation of information. Section 1(3) also limits the role of patents by denying their protection to offensive, immoral, or antisocial inventions. So the discovery in a tropical jungle of a new curative drug, or the development of a new, but unlawful, relaxant cannot be patented even if all of the s. 1(1) requirements are met.

All of these different points will require clarification and elucidation; many have been the subject of extensive litigation and resultant case law. Our methodology will be simply to examine each aspect in turn so as to build up an overall picture of what the law will regard as matter appropriate for a successful patent application—what, in other words, will come within the legal definition of the concept of an invention. As will be seen later, the meaning of 'invention' itself has to be given some consideration, but, initially, we will approach the issue of patentability through the elements declared by s. 1(1). Note, however, that these key concepts tend to overlap in practice and that discussion in many leading cases covers more than one closely related aspect.

Traditionally, a distinction is made between patents for inventions that relate to new products—that is, product patents—and patents for inventions that relate to new processes—that is, process patents. Some discussion has arisen in relation to patents containing a claim to products produced by a process. In some decisions, the European Patents Office (EPO) seems to suggest that the limitation of a claim to such products produced by a process could not impart novelty on the claim.[1] The Court of Appeal rejected

---

[1] Decision T150/82 *International Flavors & Fragrances Inc/Claim Categories* [1984] OJ EPO 309.

that approach under UK law, only for the House of Lords to align itself with the EPO.[2] Any categorization of patents is without legal meaning on this point and one should instead focus on whether the application—and, in particular, the claims (to exclusivity)—meet the requirements for patentability to which we will now turn.

Novelty

Most laymen would understand that an invention is something new and the law reflects this. The way in which s. 2(1) of the 1977 Act expresses this is that *'an invention shall be new if it does not form part of the state of the art'*, so the reward (if such it be) of a patent goes to those who have gone beyond pre-existing knowledge, whether by creating a new product that was not previously available on the market or by developing a process not hitherto available. (The Act, for the most part, does not distinguish between patents for products and those for processes.)

The basic definition of novelty obviously begs the question of what matter is regarded as forming part of the 'state of the art'. Section 2(2) helps:

> The state of the art in the case of an invention shall be taken to comprise all matter (whether a product, a process, information about either, or anything else) which has at any time before the priority date of that invention been made available to the public (whether in the United Kingdom or elsewhere) by written or oral description, by use or in any other way.

The state of the art

Clearly, the 'state of the art' is broadly defined and represents a major hurdle for the patent applicant.[3] Several points need to be emphasized in considering what information forms part of the state of the art and what effect it has on the later patent application. An obvious point is that the key date is the priority date and applications made after that date cannot form part of the state of the art by definition, because they do not anticipate the plaintiff's application. Particular problems arise, however, in relation to patents for which applications were received on an earlier date, but which have not yet been published. It may seem harsh for something that is inherently not yet available to the public to be regarded as part of the state of the art, but to allow the later applicant to proceed would lead to a very high risk of 'double patenting'—that is, of two people having exclusive patent rights in respect of the same thing, which is, of course, a complete contradiction in terms. Accordingly, s. 2(3) establishes that, for the purpose of assessing the state of the art for an invention, material in subsequently published patent applications is included, as long as the priority date of that application is earlier than the priority date of the invention in question—and this is so even if the actual material in the subsequently published specification was not filed until after the priority date of the invention in question. In applying this rule, the EPO will only consider those applications that have been made in respect of the same states.[4] So while it is a harsh rule, perhaps, it is a clear rule that promotes certainty and, in a patent race, a rule that is an inducement to make an application sooner rather than later. The only potential dent in the rule comes from *Asahi Kasei Kogyo KK's Application*,[5] which will be considered later in this chapter.

---

[2] *Kirin-Amgen Inc. v. Transkaryotic Therapies Inc.* [2003] RPC 31 (CA); [2005] 1 All ER 667 (HL).
[3] For a good example, see *Smithkline Beecham plc v. Apotex Europe Ltd* [2005] FSR 23.
[4] EPC, Art. 54.
[5] [1991] RPC 485.

Available to the public

The widening of the relevant prior information that makes up the state of the art to include any material available to the public anywhere creates the next problem. Availability to the public is not too difficult an issue, at least in the sense that a clear line can usually be drawn between public and private circulation of information: an internal company document is clearly private, but publication of a research paper in a learned journal—even one of some obscurity—clearly places its contents into the public domain. This is particularly so in respect of any publication in the UK, copies of which must be sent to the British Library and normally to the other five so-called 'copyright libraries', in Oxford, Cambridge, Edinburgh, Aberystwyth, and Dublin.[6]

Borderline cases on the public–private divide have been the subject of some litigation. It is clear that internal documentation may become public by its subsequent use, as in *Monsanto Co. (Brignac's) Application*,[7] in which a patent was being sought for a process for colouring nylon. This was successfully opposed on the grounds that around thirty or forty copies of a brochure giving information about the process had been given out to salesmen employed by the patentees and that it was expected that these, in turn, would be passed on to potential customers. This, then, amounted to prior publication. This decision may seem to make advance publicity and prior contact with potential customers a risky business, and it is clearly safer to wait until after the priority date. But this is not essential, as was shown in the case of *Pall Corp. v. Commercial Hydraulics (Bedford) Ltd*,[8] in which a new membrane could be patented in spite of an earlier demonstration to a potential customer and others. That demonstration had been undertaken at a private gathering, under what all present understood to be circumstances of confidentiality, and also was such that vital information about the nature of the new product was not disclosed and could not be deduced. Not only was it not a disclosure to the public, neither was it an enabling disclosure: it did not allow any witnesses to gain enough information to make a similar membrane themselves. Thus it was not relevant. This concept of the 'enabling disclosure' is important and will be considered later in this chapter.

Greater problems arise not so much with the 'public' aspect of public availability, but in considering what is meant by 'availability'. Copyright libraries may resolve the problem domestically, but, on the face of it, a literal interpretation of s. 2(2) means that anything anywhere in the public domain will form part of the state of the art. Revelations made in Mongolia's press, for example, while unknown to anyone in the West, might render an invention unpatentable and liable to revocation when uncovered. This may seem unlikely, but major and growing trading nations pose similar problems of accessibility of information: Japan, China, or Thailand are all obvious examples. One argument would be to give the word 'available' a broad interpretation, in the spirit of the European origin of this part of patent law,[9] and exclude matters in the Thai technical press as not being de facto available to the public, because, in practice, the public would have no access to it. Indeed, it is a fair point that searches by the Patent Office are also unlikely to discover such obscure items of information, whether at the domestic, EPO, or Washington Patent Cooperation Treaty level of search. But this approach might lead back to the menace of double patenting and it is suggested that the better view is that, as a bar to patentability, the existence of material publicly available anywhere—even if available only after the most extensive

[6] Legal Deposit Libraries Act 2003, ss. 1 and 14.
[7] [1971] RPC 153.
[8] [1990] FSR 329. See also *Strix Ltd v. Otter Controls Ltd* [1995] RPC 607.
[9] See Chapter 6 for discussion on interpretation after the *Catnic* case.

searches—best reflects the interests of the international trading community. This has the support of the decision in *Woven Plastic Products Ltd v. British Ropes Ltd*,[10] which is to be considered later in this chapter.

The six-month grace period

One type of information that is available to the public is expressly excluded from any consideration when the state of the art is being assessed: any information that has been disclosed from six months prior to the filing date onwards, which is information that has been obtained either unlawfully or in breach of confidence, or, alternatively, if it has been divulged in breach of confidence. The protection also extends to disclosure resulting from the display of the invention at an international exhibition,[11] this being a limited category of events such as world fairs and international 'expos'. This subsection will often confer a double benefit on the inventor who, in an appropriate case, can not only exclude the revealed information from the state of the art, but also, in appropriate cases, bring an action against the confider for breach of confidence. This is a most useful reminder that actions for breach of confidence often arise from situations in which patents are being discussed and developed, and form a useful supplement to the remedies of the patentee even if—or especially if—no patent is awarded (as seen in Chapter 29).

Anticipation

So far, we have concentrated on what information forms part of the state of the art. Now we must investigate more carefully the nature of that information and, in particular, whether it actually does anticipate the patent for which an application is subsequently received. 'Anticipation' is the word commonly used to assess the impact of the prior state of the art on the later invention and the question is whether the operation of the prior product or process forestalls the later patent.[12]

A first example can be found in *Van Der Lely (C) NV v. Bamfords*,[13] in which a photograph of a hayrake machine, the rake-wheels of which were turned by contact with the ground rather than by an engine, anticipated the patent application for a hayrake machine with the same feature. It was no longer new once the courts had accepted that the photograph was sufficiently clear to reveal the intention of the photographed object to an informed person.

An equally simple example is provided by *Windsurfing International Inc v. Tabur Marine (Great Britain) Ltd*.[14] In this case, a patent had been granted in 1968 to the plaintiffs for the invention of the windsurfing board and other related forms of propulsion. On finding that the defendants were also selling such equipment, they sought to take action for infringement of their patent. The defendants, in turn, objected to the initial validity of the patent and sought to have it revoked. It should be noted that this is a very common method of raising the patentability question as a counterclaim to an allegation of infringement. The acts that were put forward as evidence of anticipation were those of a boy aged 12 back in 1958, who, while on holiday at Hayling Island in Hampshire, made and used a primitive sailboard for his own amusement. The temporary, personal, and little-known character of the user were all regarded as irrelevant,[15] and, although the

---

[10] [1970] FSR 47.
[11] Patents Act 1977, s. 2(4).
[12] *General Tire & Rubber Co. v. Firestone Tyre & Rubber Co.* [1972] RPC 457, *per* Sachs LJ at 485.
[13] [1963] RPC 61.
[14] [1985] RPC 59.
[15] Ibid. at 77–8, *per* Oliver LJ.

patented device had a more sophisticated control mechanism than that of the boy's, this apparatus was irrelevant for the purposes of anticipation given that the same basic control principles were used. (Whether the improvements were obvious is reviewed later in this chapter.) Likewise, the existence of an article featuring the excitement of the new sport of 'sailboarding', which appeared in 1966, also anticipated the patent by demonstrating something similar to the patented boards, again adopting the same basic principles of construction. Prior use can destroy novelty if it releases information in the same way that a publication would do—that is, a skilled worker must be able to discover and reproduce the invention through observation and analysis of the use.[16]

It is clear from the case law that relatively minor acts are sufficient to anticipate, but more may be needed because the anticipation has to be of the invention itself. *Fomento Industrial SA Biro Swan Ltd v. Mentmore Manufacturing Co.*[17] illustrates both points. The plaintiffs had a 1945 patent for the manufacture of a particular type of improved ballpoint pen and its revocation was sought on the basis of prior use, in the form of the limited availability of pilot models of the new pen in the 1944–45 period. There was enough non-private use that these events could, and did, amount to anticipation, but now we must consider if what was revealed by these events was the subsequently patented invention. Mere use of a biro may well not disclose anything about its workings—the patent was specifically for a method of producing the more regular flow of ink—but of greater significance was an earlier patent application by a group related to the plaintiffs for a broadly similar pen. This, however, did not amount to anticipation, because the best that could be said for it was that it 'might well' achieve the result of the later patent, whereas the effect of the later patent was effectively to ensure that the desired result *was* achieved. Thus the prior use, but not the prior patent application, was a ground for revocation.

Since 1977, public availability has been the sole test and it would therefore have to be asked whether the use of the pen disclosed the inventive concept. This will be a question of fact: in *Windsurfing*—although also under the pre-1977 law—there was a clear visible relationship between the anticipating use and the later patent, but in a case such as *Fomento*, it is less obvious that mere use will reveal the inventive concept of the improved operation of the ball point, which is almost always firmly encased in plastic, and it may be unlikely that there would be any anticipation on the facts of *Fomento* today.

Here too, though, further refinements are needed before the law can be fully appreciated. One interesting problem is that provided by the facts that underlie the decision in *Merrell Dow Pharmaceuticals Inc v. H N Norton & Co. Ltd.*[18] The fundamental issue in relation to this case is whether the availability of a product to the public necessarily carries with it all of the relevant knowledge and information that lies behind that product. In *Merrell Dow*, litigation arose in relation to an antihistamine drug including the ingredient terfenadine. The problem was that it was 'available to the public', in the sense that it was known to exist under a patent from 1972 onwards, but that research, including clinical trials, continued into how precisely it worked for some years thereafter, until fuller understanding was reached as to its workings. As a result of this research, the vital by-product that resulted from its use—the acid metabolite—was identified and itself patented in 1980. So, did the use of terfenadine, inevitably producing the acid metabolite, after 1992 infringe Merrell Dow's earlier patent or did the company's rights survive until 2000?[19] The House of Lords took the view that the earlier patent, which—albeit

---

[16] See *Stahlwerk Becker's Patent* (1919) 36 RPC 13.
[17] [1956] RPC 87.
[18] [1996] RPC 76.
[19] In each case, 20 years from the original patent's priority date.

unknowingly—produced the acid metabolite, was the relevant patent; accordingly, rivals were free to use this drug from 1992 onwards. Anticipation had occurred by disclosure and the creation of the acid metabolite had been occurring since 1972 as an inevitable consequence of following the specification of the oldest patent; the specific 1980 patent for the acid metabolite was therefore revocable.

Lest the complexities of antihistamine drugs are less than clear, Lord Hoffmann, in the sole speech in the case,[20] uses an example that is perhaps clearer. For centuries, Amazonian Indians have used a powdered tree bark to treat malaria. In 1820, it was discovered by French scientists that the active ingredient within the particular bark in question was quinine and, by 1944, its precise chemical composition had been worked out, meaning that it could be made synthetically. Lord Hoffmann argued cogently that the centuries of past history would anticipate any post-1944 attempt to patent the creation of quinine:

> The Amazonian Indian who treats himself with powdered bark for fever is using quinine, even if he thinks that the reason why the treatment is effective is that the tree is favoured by the Gods. The teachings of his traditional medicine contain enough information to enable him to do exactly what a scientist in the forest would have done if he wanted to treat a fever but had no supplies of quinine sulphate.[21]

So even ignorant use may anticipate, with the result in this case—which is one with wide implications—that the years of subsequent research into the precise working of terfenadine would be pointless in terms of patentability,[22] at least for the purposes for which the drug was used.[23]

This issue has been further considered in *Chiron Corp. v. Evans Medical Ltd.*[24] Applying *Merrell Dow*, it was found that, for the purposes of anticipation, there was no need to know that a product was being created by a process, but that anticipation would occur if there was a conscious decision to engage in a process rather than if the product was created unintentionally and, perhaps, unexpectedly.

The notional 'skilled reader'

The notion of ignorant use of a product or process begs a further question: we need to know whose use is under consideration. To revert to the *Fomento* example, we all pick up ballpoint pens continually without (until now) considering how they work; to a ballpoint expert, however, much would be clear very quickly even from mere use, let alone a quick examination. We therefore need to consider the issue of whose eyes should be used in assessing whether the anticipatory event reveals the actual inventive concept or, to put it another way, whether the prior disclosure is an 'enabling disclosure'.

Clear guidance on this issue is provided by *General Tire & Rubber Co. v. Firestone Tyre & Rubber Co.*[25] The plaintiffs had a patent for making tyres from a mixture of synthetic rubber, oil, and carbon black. The defendants attacked it on various grounds, including anticipation of the patent by three earlier specifications for similar products and an article in the journal *Rubber Age*. The Court of Appeal approached the issue by comparing the patentee's claim and the earlier documents, and construing them at the respective relevant dates by a reader skilled in the art to which they relate having regard

---

[20] [1996] RPC 76 at 88.
[21] Ibid. at 91.
[22] See I. Karet, 'A question of epistemology' [1996] 2 EIPR 97.
[23] *Per* Lord Hoffmann in *Merrell Dow* [1996] RPC 76 at 91.
[24] [1998] RPC 517.
[25] [1972] RPC 457.

to the state of knowledge in such art at the relevant date.[26] This creates the idea of the Court placing itself in the position of the 'notional skilled reader', an upmarket version of tort law's 'reasonable man', blessed with reasonable knowledge, but not, in this case, universal knowledge appropriate to the area in which the patent applies. Further, the notional skilled reader should, in an area of high technology, be replaced by a team of readers whose collective skills would be those employed in making the comparison. It was also established that it is the result of the alleged anticipatory process or product that is vital, not the expression or intention of the author, thus enabling anticipation to occur by virtue of the inadvertent qualities of the earlier activity.[27] It was found by the Court of Appeal that use of none of the alleged anticipations would have been likely to achieve the particular benefits of General Tire's new method of manufacture.

Union Carbide Corp. v. BP Chemicals[28] provides a different slant on this by noting, appropriately, that doing something that, although recognized in the prior art, was regarded as something that should not be done was clearly novel, because it would go against the perceptions of the normal skilled man.

Anticipation requires an enabling disclosure

A useful application of the 'enabling disclosure' approach is to be found in *Quantel Ltd v. Spaceward Microsystems Ltd.*[29] This concerned computer-based videographic systems, the plaintiffs owning the patents of their 'Paintbox' system for producing graphics, which was a popular system, numbering the UK's British Broadcasting Corporation (BBC) and the US National Broadcasting Company (NBC) among its users. In considering whether four other earlier videographic systems anticipated the plaintiffs' system, it was emphasized by Falconer J,[30] following *General Tire*, that the prior publication had to provide clear and unmistakable directions to its addressee before it would count as an enabling disclosure.

The use of stored data in the graphics of the plaintiffs' system was not present in those of the first rival, Levoy, so that did not anticipate. Those of the second, Paint, had many similarities, but again did not go as far as the plaintiffs' in that they did not have processing means and variants of it also did not anticipate. Two systems devised at the New York Institute of Technology (NYIT) were not seen as being properly regarded as video image creation systems. Finally, the demonstration by the plaintiffs of a prototype of their system did not anticipate, because key features had not, at that stage, been invented and a demonstration that allowed use, but provided no inspection or explanation of the equipment used, was not to be regarded as an enabling disclosure.

This area has now been considered at the highest level in *Asahi Kasei Kogyo KK's Application*,[31] in which a patent was sought for a genetically engineered polypeptide, a product useful for treating tumours. The problem was that an earlier application had claimed the existence of the polypeptide, but had not gone so far as to describe how it may be produced. The House of Lords held that this did not count as an anticipation: the indication of the existence of the polypeptide did not itself show how it could be produced, nor was it so self-evident how it may be produced that it would be regarded as an enabling disclosure. For there to be anticipation, the common general knowledge in this industry—which can be added to the material contained in the allegedly anticipating

---

[26] Ibid., *per* Sachs LJ at 485.
[27] For example, *Molins v. Industrial Machinery Co. Ltd* (1937) 55 RPC 31.
[28] [1998] RPC 1.
[29] [1990] RPC 83.
[30] Ibid. at 112.
[31] [1991] RPC 485, approved in *Biogen Inc. v. Medeva plc* [1997] RPC 1.

disclosure—should have allowed the skilled person to select or secure the starting material, or to make intermediate products.

The problem with the case is that, by interpreting s. 2(3) of the 1977 Act as only applying to enabling disclosures in earlier applications, it dents the force of that subsection by creating cases in which there is a risk of double patenting of the same invention. In this case, different patents could exist for the polypeptide and for its use, which seems unproductive. This issue was recognized by the House of Lords, but was thought to be something that would only happen rarely,[32] and, in any event, appeared to accord with the approach of both the 1977 Act and Art. 54 of the EPC.

A recent case[33] suggested an alternative approach when anticipation was claimed on the back of an application with an earlier priority date that had not yet been published when the allegedly anticipated second application was filed. The judge had suggested that the better approach in such a case was to ask whether the two inventors had, in substance, reached the same invention. If so, the application with the earlier priority date would anticipate the other application. The Court of Appeal explicitly overruled that decision,[34] however, and reiterated the test laid down in *General Tire* and *Asahi*. The *Synthon* case eventually went all the way to the House of Lords and provided a seminal judgment on what are the requirements for an enabling disclosure that leads to anticipation. The House of Lords reversed the judgment of the Court of Appeal and held that, in the context of s. 2 of the 1977 Act, 'disclosure' and 'enablement' are distinct concepts, each of which has to be satisfied for there to be anticipation.

The House defined the concept of disclosure along the following lines: the matter relied upon as prior art must disclose subject matter that, if performed, would necessarily result in an infringement of the patent. That may be because the prior art disclosed the same invention, but patent infringement does not require that one should be aware that one is infringing. From this, it follows that—whether or not it would be apparent to anyone at the time—whenever subject matter described in the prior disclosure is capable of being performed and is such that, if performed, it must result in the patent being infringed, the disclosure requirement is satisfied. This is so even if a person who reads the patent and sets out to make what is described in the application thinks that he or she is making something different because of an error in the application, as long as a skilled person would inevitably produce that which is described.

The second concept that is required in the context of s. 2—the enablement concept—was defined as follows. In *Synthon*, the applicant's application disclosed the use of a solvent that, in fact, proved to be unsuitable for crystallization, but the trial judge was correct in his view that the skilled man would have sought to try some other solvent that either was mentioned in the application or which formed part of his general knowledge. It is therefore not necessary that the disclosure enabled the invention to be performed for the first time without any trial and error on the part of the skilled person or team; enablement requires only that the skilled man or team is able to perform the disclosed invention by using the disclosure and common general knowledge.

In essence, this judgment reformulates the *General Tire* test somewhat by stressing the presence of two requirements, but it does not significantly change it. Anticipation can therefore be summed up as follows when the claims in the patent are for a process or a method of use.

---

[32] Ibid. at 542.

[33] *Synthon BV v. Smithkline Beecham plc* [2005] All ER (D) 235, [2006] RPC 10.

[34] *Synthon BV v. Smithkline Beecham plc (No. 2)* [2003] RPC 43 (CA), overruling *Synthon BV v. Smithkline Beecham plc* [2003] RPC 6.

Anything that is to anticipate the patent and remove its novelty is to give clear and unmistakable directions to what the patentee claims to have invented[35]—that is, anticipation will only occur and the novelty of the application in respect of an invention will only be destroyed if the anticipating information made the invention available to the public, which means that it must have contained clear and unmistakable directions to make the invention (making allowances for the general knowledge of the skilled person).[36] If the claims in the patent refer to a product, the anticipating item must enable the skilled reader to perceive the discovery at once, and to understand and be able to apply it practically without the necessity for further experiments.[37] Nevertheless, the anticipating information must not be so detailed that it could support a valid patent.[38]

Selection patents

It should be noted that the jurisprudence on the nature of the addressee in patent cases is more extensive and more developed in the context of obviousness, but care must be taken in applying that law here, because there are clear differences in the law relating, for example, to the mosaicking—that is, the combining of potentially anticipating documents that is only possible if they cross-refer to one another—of two separate aspects of the state of the art. In any event, a different question is being asked: the novelty of an invention is easier to assess than its obviousness and, arguably, it is for this reason that the law in the latter areas has had no option but to become more developed.

The areas in which the characteristics of the notional addressee of the patent claim and the anticipatory material are particularly important is when the patent claim is, as is quite usual, not a bolt from an otherwise clear blue sky, but rather a development of some pre-existing product or process. In this case, it is easy for an objector to say that the pre-existing product in its claims or by its working was an anticipation—*Quantel* is perhaps a good example. The problem is heightened in cases in which all that is being sought in the subsequent patent is a new method of using pre-existing matter.

Sometimes, it is easy to see that there is novelty even in such a case. This problem can particularly arise in selection patents—that is, in patents that select one particular category from a more general group that is already known. A good example of this is *Beecham Group's (Amoxycillin) Application*,[39] in which Beechams had been granted a patent for a large class of various penicillins for use as antibiotics and had then, in a further patent, singled out nine of them as being especially effective. At issue was a further application for a patent for one type of one of those nine penicillins that was especially amenable to absorption into the blood, the question being whether the naming of this sort of penicillin in the earlier patent was an anticipation. The Court of Appeal denied that it was such: the earlier patent simply showed that this sort of penicillin appeared to be effective in mice, whereas the patent in suit was for a developed, tested, and workable application of one type of that particular penicillin. It could not be anticipated by an earlier patent that gave no hint of whether or how its subject matter might be used for human consumption, even to its skilled addressees.

---

[35] *Chiron Corp. v. Evans Medical Ltd* [1998] RPC 517 at 560–1, with reference to *Flour Oxidising v. Carr* (1908) 25 RPC 428, *per* Parker J at 457; see also *Beecham Group's (Amoxycillin) Application* [1980] RPC 261 and *General Tire & Rubber Co. v. Firestone* [1972] RPC 457.

[36] *Synthon BV v. Smithkline Beecham plc (No 2)* [2003] RPC 43.

[37] *Van Der Lely (L) NV v. Bamfords* [1963] RPC 61 at 71, with reference to *Hill v. Evans* (1862) 4 De G F & J 288, *per* Lord Westbury at 300.

[38] *Ransburg v. Aerostyle* [1968] RPC 287 at 299, with reference to *King Brown v. Anglo American Brush* (1892) 9 RPC 313, *per* Lord Watson at 320.

[39] [1980] RPC 261.

The essence of this type of case is to emphasize the advantage and/or difference that the selection makes so as to create a clear gap between the earlier and later matters. In *Re Shell Refining & Marketing Co. Ltd's Patent*,[40] therefore, Esso had made a 1940 patent application relating to improved fuel consumption, which referred to the use of a particular chemical additive to fuel as being of benefit to combat corrosion in fuel tanks; Shell had subsequently obtained a patent for the use of several additives, including a small proportion of that used by Esso, for various purposes including the prevention of engine knock, of the fouling of spark plugs, and of exhaust valve corrosion. It was held that Esso's application did not anticipate the final version of Shell's patent, amended to emphasize the small amount of additive and its effectiveness in dealing with the problems that Shell sought to counteract. A more broadly drafted claim that did not emphasize the precise amount of the additive to be used by Shell was, however, anticipated—because it was, after all, the same additive in the same fuel.

The *Shell* case is also useful in giving more general guidelines on the correct approach to selection patents. Lord Evershed MR starts with the obvious basic proposition that a man who merely picks out a number of items from an already disclosed group or series has not 'invented' anything, [41] but argues that this would not be the case should later research reveal '*that certain items in the group or series possess qualities or characteristics peculiar to themselves and hitherto unknown*'.[42] He adopts the approach of Maugham J to selection patents in an earlier case,[43] identifying them as being grantable if there is a substantial advantage associated with the selected group, if that advantage is common to all of the selected group, and if that advantage is peculiar to that group.

This approach has the approval of the House of Lords in two more recent cases: *Beecham Group Ltd v. Bristol Laboratories International SA*[44] and *E I Du Pont de Nemours & Co. (Witsiepe's) Application*.[45] In *Du Pont*, Lord Wilberforce points to the need to protect the original inventor, while encouraging others to improve and enhance that invention by the discovery of fresh advantages in the selected class. On the facts, this was reflected by the finding that a previous disclosure by ICI that the use of nine glycols would produce a particular result in no way anticipated the discovery by Du Pont, after extensive research, that one of the glycols had particular benefits in a different field; this was clearly the fresh advantage of the selected class.

In a sense, these patents are not best served by being described as 'selection' patents; what signifies them and justifies their patentability is not the mere fact of selection, but the uniqueness of what is selected and the development or advantage that the selection represents. As such, their recognition is entirely justified as a reward for the work that will go into making the selection, as both *Beecham* and *Shell* demonstrate, and in recognizing them, the law reflects the commercial reality of the nature of much of the inventive work that goes on in the pharmaceutical and other chemical industries.

The first medical use exception

In one respect, the 1977 Act makes specific provisions for particular patents of this type: s. 2(6) expressly permits the patenting of a substance used in medical treatment, even if the substance itself is already part of the state of the art, as long as the use of the substance in medical treatment is not part thereof. It is clear that this only applies to first use as a

---

[40] [1960] RPC 35.
[41] Ibid. at 53.
[42] Ibid. at 55.
[43] *Re I G Farbenindustrie AG's Patent* (1930) 47 RPC 289 at 322–3.
[44] [1978] RPC 521 at 579.
[45] [1982] FSR 303 at 310.

medicine, and not to second and subsequent medical uses, even if these are completely distinct.

This exception arises from the interpretation of s. 2(6) by the Court in *John Wyeth & Brother Ltd's Application; Schering AG's Application*,[46] in which two appeals were heard together: Wyeth found that compounds called guanidines used to lower blood pressure were also valuable in combating diarrhoea, while Schering sought a patent for its research finding that substances used for the treatment of breast cancer could also be used against prostatic hyperlasia. The Patent Court *en banc* interpreted s. 2(6) as described above on the grounds that the precise wording of the legislation is that medical use of a known substance is allowed as long as its use *'in any such method does not form part of the state of the art'* and a prior medical use would be *'any such method'*. But the matter did not end there: amended claims were also considered that sought a patent for the use of a known subject in the manufacture of a new drug, thus emphasizing not the use of, for example, the guanidines as a treatment for diarrhoea, but their use in a new drug (which by coincidence, of course, would be used in the treatment of diarrhoea). Claims in this form had been allowed by the EPO on the grounds that the use in manufacture of the new drug could provide the necessary element of novelty.[47] Because judicial notice has to be taken of appellate decisions within the EPO under s. 91(1) of the 1977 Act, the court was obliged to follow this lead and allowed the subtly amended claims.

As a result of the decision of the EPO's Enlarged Board of Appeal in *Eisai*,[48] claims in a patent application that are directed to the use of a product for the manufacture of a medicament for a specified new therapeutic use do not lack novelty.[49] On that basis, a new, second, pharmaceutical use for compounds that have previously been recognized as having a different pharmaceutical use can be patented. This type of claim is called a 'Swiss-type' claim. The Court of Appeal recently had the opportunity to consider such claims.[50] The outcome of that analysis is that, apart from being inventive, the new therapeutic application also has to be new. There must be use for a new and completely different purpose, and novelty must lie in the therapeutic purpose for which the substance was used, rather than in the method of use.[51] The compounds—the second medical use of which is patented[52]—must also be effective to achieve the new treatment; it must be suitable for that purpose.[53]

A constructive approach

In making this point on a narrow issue, a broader point also becomes relevant and is an appropriate note on which to end this section. The proper approach to issues of patentability, in general, and of novelty, in particular, is a constructive one; the proper question is not 'Is this patentable?', but rather 'What parts of this are patentable?' Given that the

---

[46] [1985] RPC 545.

[47] *Re Eisai Co Ltd*, Decision Gr 05/83 (1985) OJ EPO 64.

[48] Ibid.

[49] In the same decision, it was held that, on the other hand, claims for the use of a product for the treatment of an illness are not patentable, because they come under the exclusion for methods of treatment of the human or animal body.

[50] *Bristol-Myers Squibb Corp. v. Baker Norton Pharmaceuticals Inc.* [2001] RPC 1.

[51] Ibid. at 25–7. See also *American Home Products Co. v. Novartis Pharmaceuticals UK Ltd* [2001] RPC 159.

[52] Such a patent is to be treated as a process patent: see *Monsanto & Co. v. Merck & Co. Inc.* [2000] RPC 77.

[53] See also *Pfizer Ltd's Patent* [2001] FSR 16 at 219–20. If more than one compound is used in a combination, each of them is used for the treatment (ibid.).

courts are prepared to allow quite fine adjustments as being patentable, as in *Quantel*, it will often be possible to find some part of the product or process that is novel, even if other aspects are not. This care in identifying the true novelty must then be matched by equal care in drafting the application for a patent, particularly in emphasizing those elements that have been identified as being novel. *Wyeth & Schering* stands as a monument to careful drafting, even in the post-1977 era of broader attitudes to the interpretation of patents.

Overall, with the courts taking a fairly positive attitude both to what information is in the public domain and whether that information, as properly understood, does amount to an enabling disclosure, this is an area of law that appears to be working with reasonable effectiveness.[54] The obstacle presented by novelty will be resolved, either way, at an early stage of most applications, although the interpretation of s. 2(2) may occasionally lead to disruption when a patent's revocation is sought on the grounds of the discovery of a long-standing, but previously unknown, article in the trade press in Japan, for example. A more typical problem—that of prior use—has been resolved by the 1977 Act and the fact that such use now has to be an enabling disclosure revealing its inventive concept should minimize the kind of problem epitomized by the *Fomento* decision. *Merrell Dow*, however, while probably correct in its conclusion, does create an additional doubt in cases in which ignorant prior use has taken place and will therefore stop a later patent application in its tracks—but at least this might stop the disagreeable habit of some multinationals of acquiring sundry secrets of indigenous peoples and then gaining their own monopoly by patenting them.[55] Overall, then, the sensible attitude of the law towards selection patents better exemplifies the general workability of this aspect of patent law, and shows that a reasonable balance is maintained between patentees and their rivals in trade.

Inventive step

The principle

Not everything that is new is patentable. The next requirement imposed by the law is that the invention contains an inventive step, a leap forward by the inventor that puts him or her ahead of the pack and, it may be said, justifies the reward of a patent. Section 3 of the 1977 Act states:

> An invention shall be taken to involve an inventive step if it is not obvious to a person skilled in the art, having regard to any matter which forms part of the state of the art by virtue only of section 2(2) above (and disregarding section 2(3) above).

So that which is obvious does not gain patent protection; only that which is inventive. Note also that, by excluding s. 2(3) from the definition of state of the art for the purposes of this section, the discussion of obviousness ignores patent applications that have already been filed, but which are yet to be published.

A good example of the concepts of inventiveness and obviousness in operation is provided, once again, by *Windsurfing International Inc. v. Tabur Marine (Great Britain) Ltd.*[56] We have already seen, in the context of the discussion of novelty, that the plaintiffs'

---

[54] For a good example, see *Smithkline Beecham plc v. Apotex Europe Ltd* [2005] FSR 23.

[55] On this see, inter alia, M. Blakeney, 'Bioprospecting and the protection of traditional medical knowledge of indigenous peoples: an Australian perspective' [1997] 6 EIPR 298.

[56] [1985] RPC 59.

1968 patent for windsurfing equipment had been anticipated a decade previously by a boy on holiday. The two boards were, however, by no means identical: the boy used a simple straight boom with which to hold the sail taut and provide a handhold for the rider, while the patented boom was a more sophisticated arc-shaped model, which helped the sail to assume an aerofoil shape and thus attain greater speed. This difference was held to be insignificant; the use of the boom was common and the arc-shaped design was an obvious improvement on the boy's design, because, when in use, even his boom began to assume an arc shape. Thus the admitted improvement carried out by the patentee was not sufficient to gain the protection of a patent, because there was no inventive step in making an improvement that was regarded as obvious.

In discussing what is, or is not, obvious, great care needs to be taken. What is an obvious improvement to all in an ordinary common-sense situation such as that in the *Windsurfing* case may be much less clear in a high technological field. In particular, in such a case, what may seem to the ordinary citizen to be a dazzling miracle of invention may be routine or commonplace to the person who is expert in that particular field. It is thus necessary to take care in formulating an approach to the obviousness question that is appropriate to all cases. It is also important to note, from the start, the significance of the obviousness question. Even where, as in the *Windsurfing* case, an advance is said to be obvious and thus non-patentable, it is still likely that the disappointed applicant will have put a significant amount of work into the development and perfection of the product. If patents are intended to reward the efforts of inventors, or if, more generally, intellectual property rights are expected to match up with activity of value in the commercial sector, the failure to protect such activity by the grant of the patent is a significant failing in the system. Obviously, the more often that the law depicts an advance as being obvious, the greater that this failing will be, and any willingness to expand the notion of obviousness will clearly go against the interests of new inventors and favour the interests of those already in the game, whose activities will already form part of the state of the art.

The *Windsurfing* test

How then is obviousness approached? The starting point is clearly that, in an objective test and without taking account of the views of the inventor, the invention is to be compared to the existing state of the art. The basic test is clearly outlined by Oliver LJ in the *Windsurfing* case[57] as a four-fold approach. But because obviousness has always been considered something of a jury-type issue,[58] all that is really provided is a procedure and a vague, qualitative yardstick. The Court of Appeal added, in *Dyson Appliances Ltd v. Hoover Ltd*,[59] that it was useful, but not essential, to use the four-step approach when assessing obviousness. The ultimate criterion is, indeed, still the statutory provision itself.

First, it is necessary to '*identify the inventive concept embodied in the patent in suit*'.[60] This is the problem that fell to be considered in *Biogen Inc. v. Medeva plc*,[61] in which it was made clear that the inventive concept was neither the identification of the problem, nor the general approach to be taken to it, but rather the problem and its precise resolution.

---

[57] Ibid. at 73–4. This approach is confirmed by *Mölnlycke AB v. Procter & Gamble Ltd (No. 5)* [1994] RPC 49, *per* Sir Donald Nicholls VC at 115, and—more significantly, but not uncritically—by Lord Hoffmann in *Biogen Inc. v. Medeva plc* [1997] RPC 1.

[58] See, e.g., *John Mansville's Patent* [1967] RPC 479 at 491.

[59] [2002] RPC 465.

[60] *Windsurfing International Inc. v. Tabur Marine (Great Britain) Ltd* [1985] RPC 59, *per* Oliver LJ at 73.

[61] [1997] RPC 1.

To adopt an analogy employed by Lord Hoffmann,[62] people ruminated for centuries on the problem of flying machines, so this could not be, on its own, an inventive concept; later, more precise thought was given to matters such as wing shape and engine type, but, again, mere thought is not enough. It was only when the Wright brothers succeeded in making a machine that was actually capable of powered flight that it could be said that the 'inventive concept' had come into existence. In *Biogen*, the House of Lords assumed, without deciding, that the genetic engineering techniques employed to resolve a known problem in a new way were not obvious.

In assessing the inventive concept as the problem and its precise solution, care needs to be taken to avoid an over-analytical approach. Often several events or elements are involved and these are often related. One needs to look at the combination of these events and elements, and they should not necessarily be seen as unrelated events and elements.[63] It is also important to keep in mind that the test for inventive step is to be applied for each single inventive concept. What seems to be one invention may, indeed, be a juxtaposition of more than one invention and one needs to decide whether there is one or more inventions before applying the test for inventiveness under s. 3. This is, in a sense, a preliminary point.[64]

Oliver LJ's second point is that:

> Thereafter, the court has to assume the mantle of the normally skilled but unimaginative addressee in the art at the priority date and to impute to him what was, at that date, common general knowledge in the art in question.[65]

This second stage is vital and will be considered in detail shortly. The Court of Appeal has now suggested that it is better to reverse the order of the first two stages of the test.[65a]

The third stage is to identify the differences that exist between the generally known matter and the subject matter of the patent for which the application is being made, after which:

> the court has to ask itself whether, viewed without any knowledge of the alleged invention, those differences constitute steps which would have been obvious to the skilled man or whether they require any degree of invention.[66]

In *Dyson Appliances Ltd v. Hoover Ltd*, this fourth step was held to require a technical comparison of the technical differences between the claims and the prior art. Proof of commercial obviousness was neither here nor there.

On the facts of the *Windsurfing* case, as we have seen, the development was obvious.[67] The essential inventive concept in the patent was the free-sail concept, as opposed to the rigid masts of rigging of conventional yachts—but the state of the art included the 1966 article describing sailboarding and that revealed the essence of the later invention to an audience who were, given the specialist nature of the publication, almost by definition going to be knowledgeable in the art. The only differences were in the shape of the boom and the shape of sail used, and these differences would be obvious, in the view of

---

[62] *Biogen v, Medeva* [1997] RPC 1 at 43.

[63] *Rockwater Ltd v. Technip France SA (formerly Coflexip SA) & Technip Offshore UK Ltd (formerly Coflexip Stena Offshore Ltd)*, judgment of the Court of Appeal of 1 April 2004, unreported.

[64] *SABAF v. Menghetti* [2005] RPC 10, (2004) 148 SJLB 1217 (HL).

[65] *Windsurfing International Inc. v. Tabur Marine (Great Britain) Ltd* [1985] RPC 59, *per* Oliver LJ at 73.

[65a] *Gozzoli v. BDMD* [2007] FSR 37 (CA).

[66] Ibid. at 73–4.

[67] For two recent examples based on rather straightforward facts, see *Rocky Mountain Traders Ltd v. Hewlett Packard GmbH, Westcoast Ltd & Fellowes Manufacturing (UK) Ltd* [2000] FSR 411 (confirmed on appeal, 12 December 2000, unreported) and *Minnesota Mining & Manufacturing Co. v. ATI Atlas Ltd & North American Science Associates Inc.* [2001] FSR 31.

the Court of Appeal, to the informed reader who would use his or her own knowledge to make the same adjustments him or herself, thus depriving the holders of the patent from legitimately claiming that they had made an inventive step. Often, the informed reader will combine general common knowledge in a particular field—for example, information contained in standard texts—with a specific document—such as the 1966 article in this case—to make a decision on the obviousness point.

In applying the *Windsurfing* test, then, it is of vital important to avoid hindsight. The Court is confronted with the question at a later stage, but the question needs to be answered as at the time at which the application was examined. Later scientific and technical evolutions should neither be taken into account, nor influence a decision on obviousness.[68]

The addressee of the test

It is apparent that it is at the second stage of this process that the key feature arises, because, in deciding through whose eyes the question of the inventive step should be viewed, the law is able to set the level at which the dividing line between obviousness and inventiveness is to be drawn. The classic formulation of this test is provided by Lord Reid in *Technograph Printed Circuits Ltd v. Mills & Rockley (Electronics) Ltd*,[69] when, in discussing obviousness, he described the notional addressee in the following terms:

> It is not disputed that the hypothetical addressee is a skilled technician who is well acquainted with workshop technique and has carefully read the relevant literature. He is supposed to have an unlimited capacity to assimilate the contents of, it may be, scores of specifications but to be incapable of a scintilla of invention.[70]

On the facts, the House of Lords found that the jump from a pre-existing US electrostatic shield to the patentee's printed circuits was an inventive one, in the light of expert evidence that the necessary adaptations and the alterations were far from obvious. It is clear that such expert evidence will often be of the utmost value in deciding the obviousness question.

This particular variant of the reasonable man is not, however, without its critics. His character would seem to be unrealistic: like a sponge, he apparently soaks up all known facts from, since 1977, all over the world. Yet, although he understands all this—which demonstrates a brain of great understanding power—he has no idea what to do with it and sits, bloated with facts but bereft of ideas, incapable of developing ideas from all that he knows. (Leading comedy actors must yearn to play his part.) The courts themselves have expressed occasional concern as to whether such characters hinder, rather than help, the law's development. In the *Windsurfing* case, Oliver LJ notes that such figures must not be permitted to obscure the basic statutory terminology in the objective quest as to whether an invention is obvious or not, and that the temptation to add various human qualities to this non-existent entity may well lead to confusion in the view of the judge.[71] Hoffmann LJ has also been critical of the way in which this distended version of the reasonable man has come to be utilized, noting that what may be '*a folksy way of explaining the law to a jury*' is no substitute for an analysis of the actual statutory language.[72]

It has become quite clear now that no real character is involved.[73] If there is more than one route to the desired goal, the notional person will, by definition, see all of them, whereas a real person might, out of personal experience, focus on one route and might not

---

[68] *Ferag AG v. Muller Martini Ltd* (2007) 151 SJLB 163 (CA).
[69] [1972] RPC 346.
[70] Ibid. at 355.
[71] [1985] RPC 59 at 71.
[72] *Société Technique de Pulvérisation Step v. Emson Europe Ltd* [1993] RPC 513 at 519.
[73] See, e.g., *Pfizer Ltd's Patent* [2001] FSR 16.

even see some of the others. The notional skilled person never misses the obvious, but also never sees the inventive. Evidence from real persons working in the field is, therefore, not necessarily conclusive and has to be assessed in that light by the court. But also, the fact that alternative routes are available is, therefore, not evidence of the fact that the invention is not obvious; rather, whether something was obvious depends, to a large extent, on balancing the expected rewards in the case of a successful attempt against the risks of failure.[74] In making such an evaluation, the notional skilled person will take any piece of prior art and put it in the context of the common general knowledge.[75]

The Court of Appeal emphasized the importance of the concept of common general knowledge that the notional addressee brings to the test in *Angiotech v. Conor*.[76] It is a broad concept and includes, for example, all steps that a skilled person would try without additional external intervention on the basis of his or her knowledge of the area concerned. It also includes any prior art described in documents, even if the approach described is subjected to technical prejudice. The latter will not remove the conclusion of obviousness.[77]

In contrast with the position on mosaicking in relation to novelty, in relation to the inventive step, the notional skilled person may supplement any information by consulting other readily accessible public information and sources,[78] as long as it is obvious to someone with an uninventive mind to do so.[79] In addition, when, in a particular context, it would be obvious to call in special expertise, the notional skilled person is supposed to have done so.[80] Equally, in areas in which inventive work is now regularly based on teamwork, the notional skilled team replaces the notional skilled person.[81]

In any event, it may be that the character used to test for obviousness is due for change. The German equivalent is far from being a mere technician and is found to possess imagination;[82] clearly, it is important to harmonize these approaches and, in due course, the EPO will have to consider this issue. Meanwhile, the courts have, in one significant decision, already moved away from the traditional approach to one that more closely reflects the German picture. It is to this decision that we will now turn.

The *Genentech* case

The case of *Genentech Inc's Patent*[83] is of great significance. It is also of great length—the report extends to 140 pages—and complexity. Nevertheless, careful analysis of the case and its implications is essential.

The case arose in relation to the area of genetic engineering. A patent had been granted to Genentech, in respect of various claims relating to the production of human plasminogen activator by the use of recombinant DNA technology in workable quantities. The

---

[74] Laddie J, in *Pfizer Ltd's Patent* [2001] FSR 16, refers in this respect to Decision T379/96 of the EPO's Technical Board of Appeal in *Minnesota Mining/Aerosol Propellants*.

[75] For a good example, see *Burnden Group plc v. Ultraframe (UK) Ltd* (2005) EWCA Civ 867.

[76] [2007] RPC 20 (CA).

[77] Case T-882/03 *Du Pont Teijin Films/Polyester Film*, Technical Board of Appeal of the EPO [2006] EPOR 48.

[78] *Pfizer Ltd's Patent* [2001] FSR 16.

[79] It may, therefore, still be inventive to put information from unrelated sources together.

[80] *NI Industries/Filler Mass* [1992] OJ EPO 725 and see also *Richardson-Vick's Patent* [1997] RPC 888.

[81] *Boehringer Mannheim v. Genzyme* [1993] FSR 716 at 727.

[82] E. Pakuscher, 'Examination for non-obviousness: a response' [1981] 12 IIC 816. See also J. Schmidt-Szalewski, 'Non-obviousness as a requirement of patentability in French law' (1992) IIC 725 for the position in France, where the average person skilled in the art is the test. Presumably, such a person has an average amount of imagination.

[83] [1989] RPC 147.

relevant technology had been used previously in synthesizing a number of other sub-stances, but this was the first time that it had been employed to synthesize a particular activator known as t-PA, which was of great value in combating blood clotting and thus of importance in treating thrombosis. The production of quantities of t-PA was clearly of great medical and commercial value; it was also the result of much work. Genentech took over a year to achieve the production of enough t-PA and many skilled scientists were involved. At the same time, other teams elsewhere were racing towards the same approach, but lost the race to Genentech.

In effect, Genentech were then the holders of a patent for a new application of pre-existing technology and the nub of the dispute—when others in the field sought a revoca-tion of the Genentech patent—was whether what had been achieved by Genentech was a breakthrough permitting the synthesis of the valuable t-PA for the first time and thus deserving of patent protection, or whether the discovery was simply part of the ordinary process of development of the pre-existing recombinant DNA technology, and thus did not amount to an inventive step.

The Court of Appeal found that the patent had been wrongly granted and ordered that it should be revoked. A key issue was how the hypothetical addressee concept could cope with an area of such intellectual complexity as this and the Court recognized that the traditional model was unworkable in these exceptional circumstances. As Purchas LJ recognized in relation to this type of situation:

> the artisan has receded into the role of the laboratory assistant and the others have become segregated into groups of highly qualified specialists in their own spheres of all whom must possess a degree of inventiveness.[84]

In other words, because there is no one working in the field who is incapable of invention, the 'person skilled in the art' must have inventive capacity.

Mustill LJ noted that it was wrong to assume that the person skilled in the art for the purposes of s. 3 was the same person as that envisaged in considering the information in the specification and its use by the person skilled in the art envisaged by s. 14(3).[85] The lat-ter character could be realistically seen as non-inventive in the context of having merely to read and understand a specification, but for the purposes of s. 3:

> where one is looking at the research team one cannot treat them as dull plodders, for such people would not be members of the team at all, except as laboratory assistants.[86]

Later, he comments that, in a case of this type, '*some substantial measure of ingenuity is an essential qualification for being engaged in the enterprise*'.[87]

In the light of these views—which were not, apparently, shared by the third member of the Court, Dillon LJ[88]—it became clear that Genentech should not be allowed any patent protection. The problems faced by the firm were the problems to be expected out at the cutting edge of genetic engineering and, as such, were capable of being surmounted by others skilled in the arts, with their inevitable high intellectual and inventive qualities. As Mustill LJ expresses it:

> it is inventiveness which counts, and I cannot find it here in any degree which exceeds the amount of resource expected of a group mustering the skills, remarkable as they seem

---

[84] Ibid at 214.
[85] Ibid at 279.
[86] Ibid.
[87] Ibid at 280.
[88] Ibid at 241.

to the layman, ordinarily to be expected of persons skilled in this most difficult array of arts.[89]

Purchas LJ, however, found that some of the steps taken along the way were inventive steps even by the high standards expected in this field, but found against Genentech on other grounds. Dillon LJ found it relevant, in the establishing of obviousness, that the other participants in the patent race were following the same track as Genentech, confirming his view that the steps being taken were obvious to those skilled in the art.[90]

There is much more to *Genentech*, but this is an appropriate moment to make some comments on this core part of the decision. It is unfortunate that such a range of judicial opinion exists on the obviousness point and this merely adds to the problems of the complex subject matter—but the confusion should not mask the result. In this case, the company spent substantial amounts of time and money, using its resources and those represented by its highly qualified staff (almost all of whom had a PhD), in devising a workable method of making a pharmaceutical product of great potential benefit to society. This sounds exactly the sort of scenario in which, on a traditional analysis of the rationale of the patent system, the endeavour and beneficial result to society should be rewarded by the grant of a patent; yet the patent was revoked. So no incentive or reward for the patentee exists, other than in the form of short-term, market-leading profits. Of course, society and consumers benefit in the short term from the freer availability of this type of treatment, as do the rival firms, which are freely able to market their rival treatments. In the longer term, however, Genentech gets no high-yield return on its investment in the absence of a patent and may, as a result, not be able to work towards the next step forward in the—far from cheap—advance in scientific technique. In the absence of reward or incentive, it may also simply determine it to be unwise to devote resources to research and development (R&D) in situations in which the chance of a patentable result being reached has been substantially diminished by this decision. Thus society and the customers may, in the future, be less likely to gain any benefit from future advances in genetic engineering technology.

The effect of the *Genentech* decision is not, of course, confined to that one particular field. It would seem logical to assume that it will apply to any field of scientific activity in which the players in the field are all working at a high doctoral or post-doctoral level. This is the norm in most major industries—such as electronics or telecommunications, for example—and means that the impact of *Genentech* is of great significance in reducing the availability of patents by raising the standard of inventiveness in a potentially significant range of commercially important activities. On the other hand, *Genentech* has not been widely used in the decade since the decision and it may increasingly come to be regarded as a decision made very much on its own facts—which is, of course, the common lawyer's classic method of marginalizing, or even ignoring, unhelpful decisions.

Either way, it should be made clear that the problem raised by *Genentech* exists only in a small minority of patent applications in relation to which protection is sought for an advance in an area of high technology. At lower levels, the traditional approach to obviousness still makes sense: for example, in a typical patent application for a relatively routine development or extension of a previous patent, such as a minor, but new improvement in the way in which the ink flows in the operation of a ballpoint pen. In such a case, invention and obviousness are genuine alternatives, but, unfortunately, *Genentech* reveals that this cannot always be the case.

---

[89] Ibid at 286–7.
[90] [1989] RPC 147 at 243.

So why has this come about? The key problem is alluded to in the judgment of Mustill LJ,[91] and is simply that the definition in s. 3 of the 1977 Act and in EPC, Art. 56, does not make universal sense. It makes the assumption that 'inventiveness' and 'obviousness' are but two sides of the same coin, but the facts of a case such as *Genentech* explode that assumption with a violent blast. Simply, in high-tech areas—such as genetic engineering, with its teams of highly qualified and experienced scientists—the process of invention is the norm; invention is an obvious thing for its skilled proponents to undertake. To deny invention its legal protection and economic reward in relation to the very kinds of activities for which inventiveness is most common and from which, arguably, society gains some of the greatest rewards is regrettable, to say the least. To have standards of inventiveness that vary so greatly from industry to industry also, arguably, runs contrary to the traditional idea that the inquiry into inventiveness was to be an objective one. By changing the nature of the hypothetical addressee to one who, in certain cases, is possessed with the facility of invention, the decision also changes the availability of patents for the worse. If nothing else, the case shows the vital importance of determining the true character of the hypothetical addressee and warns of the immense significance of changes to those characteristics—a lesson that should be borne in mind if the superficially more attractive Continental models are ever to be adopted.

This is not necessarily a criticism of the judgments in the case; rather, it suggests that the legal definition of inventiveness needs to be reconsidered fundamentally in the light of the high-tech times in which we live. The fact that Purchas LJ was able to find some inventive steps, even on the basis that the hypothetical addressee had some inventive capacity, also gives some ground for hope: perhaps we should now be looking for a new category of 'super-inventiveness' in businesses such as genetic engineering, or else still finding that there is inventiveness on quite narrow grounds in such a context.[92]

Equally, there are many points raised in the judgments that go some way to resolving arguments from the past. It is clear that the focus of the obviousness question should be asked in the context not of each individual, but by looking at the overall team, with all of the varying specialities that would be typical in such cases,[93] and with all of the appropriate time and equipment at its disposal.

There was particular discussion of some factors that have, from time to time, been found significant in determining the obviousness question. The fact that Genentech had won a patent race did not help that company, but neither did the fact that there was such a race in the first place. Dillon LJ was quite clear that the fact that the competing research teams were all following the same path tended to show that their activities were obvious and that the position may very well have been different if Genentech were out on its own pursuing a novel idea to a successful conclusion,[94] while Mustill LJ commented to similar effect[95] and also, in the context, made the telling remark that *'first to the post is the test of novelty, but novelty is not enough'*.[96]

Also canvassed was the idea that an inventive step is one that will often be signified by the heavy expenditure of time, skill, money, and energy. Again, the words of Mustill LJ summarize the position: '[I]*t may be that (diligent and skilled) labour and the resulting*

---

[91] Ibid. at 274.

[92] For example, *Chiron Corp. v. Murex Diagnostics Ltd & Organon Teknika Ltd* [1996] RPC 535, *per* Aldous J at 574; cf Morritt L J at 608.

[93] *Genentech Inc's Patent* [1989] RPC 147, 203, *per* Dillon LJ at 247 and *per* Mustill LJ at 278.

[94] Ibid. at 243.

[95] Ibid. at 277.

[96] Ibid. at 278.

success deserve a prize, but the law, as I read it, calls for something more.'[97] This must be
right: the time and energy may be being expended because of the inefficiency or stupid-
ity of the workers involved, who are perhaps engaged in no more than honest plodding,
although Purchas LJ takes a contrary view, suggesting that the time taken on the project
suggested that there was something non-obvious present.[98]

Maybe there is a clearer way forward from *Genentech* if one puts the focus on the outcome of the case. *Genentech* was special in terms of its facts: the substance that was to be
made was known and occurred in the human body; the relevant procedures of recombinant DNA technology that were to be used to produce it outside the body in larger
amounts were also known. Hence, both the starting point and the outcome were known,
as was the route to get there. Actually doing it involved working through the relevant procedures, solving specific problems arising from their application to this substance, and a
lot of hard labour by specialists in the field. Winning that race down the established track
to a known goal may not involve any inventive activity and anything involved, even if it
remained a long and difficult exercise, may therefore be seen as obvious. This depended,
in part, on the special nature of the area involved, in which major breakthroughs are followed by periods of consolidation during which small steps are taken to apply the newly
acquired insight to all kinds of subject matter. The latter steps may involve a lot of work,
but the outcome and the way to get there are known, rendering the process obvious.

What remains, however, is that this approach to obviousness, although in line with the
traditional approach, is very harsh in its effects on industries in which research is carried
out in circumstances similar to the biotechnology example in *Genentech*. The criticisms
raised above remain applicable—especially in the light of the terms of the judgment—
but, in recent cases, the courts seemed to have backed away somewhat from the radical
view that *Genentech* might be seen as putting forward. In those cases in which there was
nothing to highlight the particular line of research actually pursued by the patentee as
the first thing to try to reach the (known) goal and in which the notional research group
(or person) would not immediately be led to that line of research as a first thing to try, the
courts have been willing to accept that an inventive step might well be involved.[99] Lord
Hoffmann has also argued, in *Biogen v. Medeva*,[100] that an inventive step can be present
when the patentee attempts something that a person who is somewhat less skilled in the
art might regard as obvious, if the real expert in that particular field would have argued
that it was not even worth trying as a result of the many formidable obstacles involved.

It may be, therefore, that *Genentech* is nothing more than a reflection of the problems
that are associated with the traditional approach to obviousness. The EPO instructs its
examiners to consider whether the skilled person 'would' use the approach suggested in
the patent application, rather than 'could' use such an approach: only in the former scenario is the approach obvious.[101] In those cases in which the skilled person 'would' use the
approach, the use of the approach is dictated by the expectation of achieving a good result.
This is to be distinguished from the scenario in which the skilled person 'could' use the
approach, because he or she acknowledges that there is a hope of success: that, on its own,
is not sufficient to demonstrate obviousness.[102] This is an approach that pre-dates the biotech era. Its use in an era of, and in relation to, technologies that move forward with small
steps, on the basis that the art has a well-defined problem, and with most elements of a

[97] Ibid. at 280.
[98] Ibid. at 221.
[99] See *Brugger v. Medic-Aid* [1996] RPC 635 and *Hoechst Celanese v. BP Chemicals* [1997] FSR 547.
[100] [1997] RPC 1.
[101] *Japan Styrene/Foam Articles* [1994] OJ EPO 154.
[102] *Lilly Icos v. Pfizer* [2002] FSR 809 (CA); see also *Pharmacia v. Merck* [2002] RPC 775 (CA).

possible solution in mind can lead to an increasing number of cases in which obviousness is established. That is a problem that comes on top of the traditional problem that, while the approach works particularly well in cases in which the art has a particular problem in mind, there are also other cases in which the art has no problem in mind, but in relation to which a certain solution is nevertheless obvious. Despite these problems, the approach may be helpful in a large number of cases when applying the inventive step, or obviousness, test set out in the Act.

Commercial success

One further factor in dealing with inventiveness may conveniently be dealt with here, although it does not arise in *Genentech*. A further argument that has been said to favour a finding of inventiveness is the subsequent commercial success of the invention. The argument appears to be based on the idea that the popularity and utility of a new device indicates that it fills, for the first time, a long-standing want, and that this commercial success shows that there must have been an inventive step in the process of thinking up something new that users have greeted with such acclaim.[103] This is evident nonsense. All manner of factors go towards explaining the success of a new product, with the marketing effort being often of as much significance as the qualities of the product itself; the award of a patent—unless solely seen as the conferral of a reward by grateful society—can hardly be denied to a product that is only of use in a small number of, perhaps highly technical, situations.

The view of Mummery J expressed in *Mölnlycke AB v. Procter & Gamble Ltd (No. 3)*,[104] that obviousness is a technical question and not a commercial one, is therefore to be preferred. This view was followed by Jacob J, in *Beloit Technologies Inc. v. Valmet Paper Machinery Inc.*,[105] in which commercial success was no more than a matter of some evidential value in considering the issue of obviousness. Laddie J goes further in *Brugger v. Medic-Aid Ltd*,[106] suggesting that commercial factors may disguise the issue of the obviousness of, for example, a development that, though obvious, has not occurred for purely commercial, rather than technical, reasons. This is further confirmed by the judgment of Laddie J in *Raychem Corp's Patent*,[107] in which, again, novelty alone is not enough. In *Biogen Inc. v. Medeva plc*,[108] Lord Hoffmann also took the view that commercial factors were irrelevant, in so far as a commercially motivated decision to research in the area did not stop the research strategy and its consequences from being an inventive step.

The inventiveness of further developments

Just as is the case with the issue of novelty, problems arise in relation to the inventive step when a patent is being sought not for some entirely new product or process, but for something that is only a relatively minor advance on what has gone before. It therefore becomes very important to consider whether the step forward that has been made is an inventive one.

---

[103] The classic formulation is by Tomlin J in *Samuel Parkes & Co. Ltd v. Cocker Brothers Ltd* (1929) 46 RPC 241 at 248. A more recent example of this approach is *Fichera v. Flogates Ltd* [1983] FSR 198.
[104] [1990] RPC 498 at 503.
[105] [1995] RPC 705.
[106] [1996] RPC 635.
[107] [1998] RPC 31 at 66.
[108] [1997] RPC 1.

This was a problem in the *Genentech* case: at the beginning of its research, DNA technology existed and, at least in theory, could be adapted to produce t-PA, because it already had been to produce growth hormones, insulin, and other valuable products of a broadly similar nature. The production of t-PA was a natural challenge, in view of the known value of the substance. In the light of these factors, and bearing in mind the high level of the hypothetical addressee's knowledge and inventiveness, it was obvious to try to match the DNA technology to the challenge of t-PA production.[109] Dillon LJ adopted the notion that it was an obvious development for which the materials were '*lying in the road*' and available for the research worker to pick up.[110]

What *Genentech* is less clear on is what type of work is necessary to allow the steps being taken to transcend into inventive ones. We have already seen that hard work alone does not confer inventiveness and there is also discussion about the type of work. Mere trial and error experimentation is not sufficient, because such work is an obvious way for the uninventive to proceed, according to Mustill LJ.[111] In the view of Dillon LJ, however, '*empirical research industriously pursued may lead to a patentable invention*';[112] he cites House of Lords' dicta in support of the view.[113] It is suggested that this latter approach is incorrect in so far as it begs the question of why the industrious work was being carried out and whether the decision to embark on the work was obvious or not; it is also necessary to consider the inventiveness, or obviousness, issue at each stage of the research programme.[114] In so doing, the focus should be on the process and materials employed, and their obviousness (or otherwise), rather than on their use and its consequence.[115]

The quest for inventiveness at the beginning, and at each stage, of the development of the product or process is obviously important to the writer of the specification, enabling him or her to focus on those aspects in which inventiveness is most clearly to be found. It is also a helpful way of approaching the question of whether a minor step forward from what has gone before is inventive or obvious. A good example is the idea of mosaicking, which refers to the practice of taking two or more pre-existing products or processes and combining them together. Whether this combination is then able to gain patent protection will depend on whether the decision to combine is one that is inventive. The classic example is *Williams v. Nye*,[116] in which a patent was obtained for a combination of the previously separate mincing and filling machines used in the manufacture of sausages into one machine that was able to perform both functions. The Court of Appeal ruled that the patent was invalid, because the only step taken by the patentee was an obvious one; it was not inventive to combine two machines performing closely related functions into one, with no real alteration to the operation of either of the two machines. A more recent case[117] concerned the combination in one pill of two known therapeutic substances: neither interaction between the substances, nor any heightened effect due to the substances being taken together could be shown, which led to the logical conclusion that there was no inventive step.

It would be easy, however, to think of slight changes to the facts whereby it would be possible to claim inventiveness: for example, in the *Williams v. Nye* scenario, if one machine

[109] [1989] RPC 147, *per* Dillon LJ at 243 and *per* Mustill LJ at 276.
[110] Ibid. at 243.
[111] Ibid. at 274.
[112] Ibid. at 241.
[113] Lord Simonds in *May & Baker Ltd v. Boots Pure Drug Co.* (1950) 67 RPC 23 at 34.
[114] See Mustill LJ in *Genentech* at 275–6.
[115] *Per* Laddie J in *Raychem Corp's Patents* [1998] RPC 31 at 41–2.
[116] (1890) 7 RPC 62.
[117] *Ancare NZ v. Fort Dodge* [2003] RPC 8, [2002] UKPC 8. See also *SABAF v. Menghetti* (2004) 148 SJLB 1217 (HL).

were to originate in a completely unrelated field of activity in relation to recognizing the transferability of which the patentee would have made an inventive step, or if the combined machine were to offer enormous savings in time or cost that it was not obvious to seek. In cases in which the two previously separate objects are, as is likely, in some way related to a common field, however, it is likely that the courts will expect the hypothetical addressee to make the obvious connection between them.[118]

Similar issues arise in cases in which the patent is sought for a new use of a pre-existing product or process. On the one hand, if the pre-existing item is unchanged, then the same objection as that in *Williams v. Nye* will be appropriate; if, on the other hand, some adaptation of the earlier item is necessary, the patent application should focus on this and the question will be whether inventiveness was present in the decision to make the adaptation and/or during its exercise. It is the combination of the inventive idea and the inventive method of putting it into operation that seems to give the best chance of securing patent protection.[119] This approach is also applicable to selection patents: if the selection and development of one from a larger class is obvious, that will be fatal to any patent claim; it must be shown that the decision to make the selection was itself an inventive step.[120]

Limitless knowledge—how broad is the art?

In all of the discussion of the hypothetical addressee, one important factor has, until now, been avoided: the question of how much he knows—that is, of how limitless is his limitless capacity for knowledge. The theory is clear that in the area of inventiveness, as in relation to that of novelty, the state of the art encompasses all material that is available to the public at any time, anywhere (the definition provided by s. 2(2) of the 1977 Act appears equally applicable here). A clear illustration of this point is provided in the context of both novelty and obviousness by *Woven Plastic Products Ltd v. British Ropes Ltd*.[121] With evident regret, the Court of Appeal found that apparently unworked patent applications made some years earlier in Japan, not unreasonably in Japanese, had to be regarded as part of the state of the art, thus rendering the patent being worked by the plaintiffs as being invalid on the grounds that the use of polyvinyl chloride as the basis of a floor covering was not novel, and that the difference between the Japanese proposal and the English product was too minor to be regarded as anything other than an obvious variation.

A more difficult problem is in identifying the relevant art: the hypothetical addressee in, for example, a medical case will be expected to know all that there is to know about matters medical and, possibly—after *Genentech*—may even have to think about these matters. But what happens if there is a development in a very different field that may, in fact, be relevant to him, but of which, in practice, he is likely to know nothing? A possible example might be developments in metallurgy, which produce a new and lighter alloy. Once our hypothetical medical addressee learns of this, it may well be obvious to consider using it in the making of artificial limbs, but it being a development in a very different art, he may never learn of it.

---

[118] See, e.g., *Allamanna Svenska Elekriska A/B v. Burntisland Shipping Co. Ltd* (1951) 69 RPC 63.

[119] *Burrough's Application* [1974] RPC 147 at 158.

[120] *Du Pont de Nemours & Co. (Witsiepe) Application* [1982] FSR 303. See also *Hallen Co. v. Brabantia (UK) Ltd* [1991] RPC 195, in which a combination of known technologies—self-pulling corkscrew and friction-reducing coating material—was obvious and not patentable even as a selection patent; but cf *Mölnlycke AB v. Procter & Gamble Ltd (No. 5)* [1994] RPC 49.

[121] [1970] FSR 47.

Guidance in relation to this problem is provided by *Johns-Manville Corp's Patent*.[122] The patent in this case had been granted for the use of a flocculating agent—that is, an agent that causes particles of solutions to adhere to one another, thus assisting the separation of the solids from the liquids in a solution—in the manufacture of shaped asbestos cement articles, which are made from a slurry-like solution. In seeking revocation of the patent, it was argued that all that the patentee had done was obvious in the light of two previously published documents relating to the use of such flocculating agents in two other industries: mining and paper manufacture. Both of these industries, although very different from that of the patentee, can readily be imagined to find flocculating agents valuable. The Court of Appeal agreed to revoke the patent; the common factor of flocculation was sufficient for the Court to say that the patentee's knowledge should extend to what were effectively applications of the same art in different circumstances. This finding was easy to reach in the light of evidence that one of the patentee's employees had investigated (and rejected) the use of the agent in question some time previously, on hearing of its use in other industries. A similar decision was reached in the recent case of *Buhler AG v. Satake Ltd*,[123] in which the use of a milling machine for milling grain when a machine had been used in a similar way in the paint and chocolate industries was held to be obvious to the skilled expert in the construction of machines of that type, even though it was accepted that the particular use was novel.

It appears from these cases that the courts will interpret the 'art' in question broadly, to include related matters in other areas of activity. The transplanting of ideas from those related areas to that of the patentee will be regarded as obvious—but the corollary of this would appear to be that it is not obvious for the patentee to have considered apparently unrelated fields that do not form part of the state of his art and that, to do so, will represent an inventive step. It has also been held recently[124] that a team member whose expertise was in the field of obtaining regulatory approval for a new drug was not the notional addressee in question, because his expertise lay in the regulation of drugs rather than in the drug's creation.

A difficult key step

The quest for the inventive step is, perhaps, the most difficult aspect of the patent application procedure. It involves the Patent Office, on application, or the court, in subsequent revocation proceedings, in forming a qualitative judgment about the work of the patentee. Difficulties abound at every stage in relation to what was known originally, what is the patent's role in relation to the original matter, and what not the patentee himself, but the hypothetical addressee in his place would have known and deduced from that knowledge. The value judgment is then made as to whether the deduction of that hypothetical addressee—often in a highly technical field—was one that was obvious and thus not worthy of patent protection, or one that can be described by the magic word 'inventive' and thus secure the coveted reward.

This has always been an onerous burden on the applicant, but the *Genentech* decision has made it harder in raising the standard of inventiveness to be expected from the hypothetical addressee in certain industries employing the highest levels of modern technology, so that some developments that are accepted as being an inventive step are nonetheless damned by obviousness. The realization stemming from *Genentech* that there is such a concept as the 'obvious invention' reveals a fatal flaw in the approach of the law, because s. 3

---

[122] [1967] RPC 479.
[123] [1997] RPC 232.
[124] *Richardson-Vicks Inc's Patent* [1997] RPC 888.

declares obviousness and inventiveness to be incompatible opposites. Until this paradox is resolved, the inventive step cannot be lauded as an effective legislative approach and a resolution of the problem. Either *Genentech* must be accepted, with its common ground with some European jurisdictions that some inventions may be obvious and its serious adverse implications for inventors in high-tech industries—and, subsequently, for the broader interests of society—or inventiveness will have to be redefined in new terms, perhaps by demoting obviousness to being merely a factor to be considered, and/or by equating inventiveness with that which the reasonable exponent of the art in question would regard as an inventive step worthy of patent protection. The only alternative is for a court to cast around to find something that is inventive, even in the post-*Genentech* era, as in the *Chiron* case at first instance,[125] while at the same time interpreting *Genentech* in a restrictive way.

Certainly, the difficulty of defining—let alone proving the existence of—the inventive step must be the largest single contributor to the time and expense involved in making a patent application, whether successful in the end or (disastrously in economic terms) ultimately unsuccessful. It may be that the whole area needs to be reconsidered,[126] but that time has yet to come and the current patchwork is the only picture that we presently have.

Industrial application

The third key requirement of the 1977 Patents Act is that, in order to be patented, an invention must be capable of 'industrial application'. This phrase is new to the 1977 Act—previously, the invention had had to represent '*a new manner of manufacture*'[127]—and this clearly shows that a broader approach, more favourable to patentees, is now being taken and also that previous case law is not now of great assistance. This part of the law casts a useful shaft of light on the aims and purposes of the patent system: only that which is usable—or, to be precise, capable of industrial use—is regarded as deserving of the protection afforded by the grant of a patent. It also poses an important practical barrier to a patentee deciding at what stage of the inventive process an application for a patent should be sought; clearly, if the invention is still at a theoretical stage, no matter how advanced, it will be premature to make an application if its potential industrial applicability is yet to be demonstrated.

Section 4(1) of the 1977 Act is of little assistance in explaining the new terminology, simply informing the reader that '*an invention shall be capable of industrial application if it can be made or used in any kind of industry, including agriculture*'. This broad approach does seem to signify that it will be no ground for objection to a patent that it is found to work in a different field of industry from that which the inventor originally had in mind.

Methods of treatment and pharmaceutical products

More significant than s. 4(1) is the remainder of s. 4, which states:

...

(2) An invention of a method of treatment of the human or animal body by surgery or therapy or of diagnosis practised on the human or animal body shall not be taken to be capable of industrial application.

---

[125] [1998] RPC 517.

[126] See P. Cole, 'Inventive step: meaning of the EPO problem and solution approach and implications for the United Kingdom' [1998] EIPR 214 and 267.

[127] Patents Act 1949, s. 101(1).

(3) Subsection (2) above shall not prevent a product consisting of a substance or composition being treated as capable of industrial application merely because it is invented for use in any such method.

The basic effect of these two subsections is clear. Section 4(2) disallows the creation of a patent monopoly on a method of treatment. This is best explained on policy grounds: it is not in society's interests for one doctor to be able to rely on a monopoly to deny the use of a method of treatment to other doctors and, of course, to their patients. The benefits of a new treatment should be available to all.

Section 4(3), however, takes the opposite approach to pharmaceutical products, which, in many cases, will form a vital part of the treatment method and it is seen as entirely appropriate to permit a monopoly over the supply of drugs for the lifetime of the patent. This might be thought by cynics to be a reflection of the respective lobbying strengths of the medical profession and the drugs industry, but it can be justified to an extent. Precise methods of treatment will vary from surgeon to surgeon and would be hard to define accurately for the purposes of a patent specification; it is also fair to note that doctors have duties towards their profession that have no parallel in the case of a researcher employed by a pharmaceutical company. The Court of Appeal has held[128] that a patent containing a claim that a (known) product called taxol could be used with sufficient medication to prevent severe anaphylactic reactions for the purposes of producing a medicament fell foul of s. 4(2), because, as a result of the use of premedication and the selection by the doctor of the amount of taxol in each case, the real medicament was produced in the patient out of these two ingredients. The patent therefore did not explain how to manufacture the medicament, but instead explained how to treat the patient—hence the court's conclusion that the invention was not capable of industrial application.[129] Similarly, a claim to a particular regime for the administration of a drug to treat osteoporosis was rejected on the grounds that it was, in reality, a method of treatment.[130]

This area must also be considered alongside s. 2(6) of the 1977 Act, which has already been noted. It will be recalled that this allows the patenting of a pre-existing product only for the first occasion on which it is found to have a medical or related use. In extending the definition of novelty, this provides further assistance to an applicant for a patent in the area of pharmaceutical products and the circumvention of the ban on patents for a second or subsequent medical use,[131] by focusing on the manufacturing process used for that drug with a view to that use, only confirms that there is ample scope for patenting the drugs used in treatment and confirms the contrast in the approach to the two aspects of medical care. The latter is in line with the EPO's approach that allows so called 'Swiss' claims—that is, claims to the use of a substance for making it up into a medicament for pharmaceutical administration in pursuit of a subsequently discovered use.[132]

These rules have very little to do with industrial application and, instead, reflect policy considerations as to what should be patentable. The different nature and the exact impact

[128] *Bristol-Myers Squibb Co. v. Baker Norton* [2001] RPC 1.
[129] Ibid. at 21.
[130] *Teva Pharmaceutical Industries Ltd v. Instituto Gentili SpA & ors* [2004] FSR 330 (CA).
[131] *John Wyeth & Brother Ltd's Application; Schering AG's Application* [1985] RPC 545. For a case that shows the limitations of these widening attempts, see *Teva Pharmaceutical Industries Ltd v. Instituto Gentili SpA & ors* [2004] FSR 330 (CA).
[132] *Eisai's & other Applications* [1985] OJ EPO 64.

of these rules are reflected in s. 4A of the Patents Act 1977, which was inserted into the Act by s. 1 of the Patents Act 2004. It summarizes the position as follows:

4A   Methods of treatment or diagnosis

(1) A patent shall not be granted for the invention of—

   (a) a method of treatment of the human or animal body by surgery or therapy, or

   (b) a method of diagnosis practised on the human or animal body.

(2) Subsection (1) above does not apply to an invention consisting of a substance or composition for use in any such method.

(3) In the case of an invention consisting of a substance or composition for use in any such method, the fact that the substance or composition forms part of the state of the art shall not prevent the invention from being taken to be new if the use of the substance or composition in any such method does not form part of the state of the art.

(4) In the case of an invention consisting of a substance or composition for a specific use in any such method, the fact that the substance or composition forms part of the state of the art shall not prevent the invention from being taken to be new if that specific use does not form part of the state of the art.

This area creates problems: the intelligent applicant will make use of this area of the law to seek backdoor protection by patent of the inherently unpatentable. Careful drafting of a patent claim can give a monopoly on the drugs used in a method of treatment and thus confers a de facto monopoly on the treatment itself. An extreme example of this arose recently, under the admittedly different provisions of US law, when a child was born with leukaemia and its placenta was preserved for use in future medical treatment. When the time for treatment arose, it could not occur without payment of a substantial royalty to the owner of the patent in respect of that kind of treatment.[133] This sad tale explains why s. 4(2) is so important, but equally demonstrates the potentially alarming consequences of its circumvention.

The main area of concern in this part of the law has traditionally been with the establishment of the boundaries of the medical treatment exception. The proper approach to be taken is spelt out in *Unilever Ltd (Davis's) Application*.[134] In this case, a patent was sought for a method of immunizing poultry against the disease coccidiosis by using certain microorganisms as food additives. Such immunization has the effect not of curing the animals of disease, but rather of preventing them from catching the disease in the first place. The question arose whether this was a therapy for the purposes of s. 4(2). After extensive consideration of both general and medical dictionaries, Falconer J found that therapy had a broader meaning than that only of curing diseases and covered any form of medical treatment of disease;[135] this broad interpretation, albeit the result of classic common lawyers' pedantry, appears to fit well with the new era of purposive construction of the patent legislation.

Still, however, the frontiers of the s. 4(2) exception have to be delimited. The connection with disease seems to be an important feature of the exception in the *Unilever* case and this is reflected in *Stafford-Miller's Applications*,[136] in which patents were sought for a method of chemical treatment of head lice. Whitford J refused to throw out the application on s. 4(2) grounds: regarding the case as 'on the absolute frontier',[137] he held that it was arguable that an infestation of head lice, while an undoubted irritant, may very well not be

[133] BBC 2 *Newsnight*, 22 July 1998.
[134] [1983] RPC 219.
[135] Ibid. at 228.
[136] [1984] FSR 258.
[137] Ibid. at 261.

regarded as disease and thus its treatment is potentially patentable. Likewise, the view has been taken by the EPO that medical tests that may be carried out in order to see whether a disease is present do not fall within this exception and that thus, in an appropriate case, patent protection may be secured.[138]

Particular problems have been generated by contraception, which, in the form of birth control pills, involves the use of chemicals on the body. In a decision on the then common law-based exception, which appears to be equally applicable in the current statutory regime, it was held, in *Schering AG's Application*,[139] that it was acceptable to patent contraceptives. This decision is, again, consistent with the need for there to be some connection with a disease for the s. 4(2) exception to be applicable and represents a significant advance on the previous refusal to grant patents for contraception.[140] An alternative method of securing patent protection for contraception without getting entangled with the medical treatment exception is illustrated by *Organon Laboratories Ltd's Application*,[141] in which a patent was permitted for a pack containing two different types of contraceptive pill, with clear indications of the dates on which each should be taken and with the pills presented in an appropriate order. Taken together, these elements amounted to what was then a new and more effective method of contraception—but it seems that the novelty of the combination of the pills was of the essence in this case; merely making an improvement in the packaging or presentation of a product to improve its use is not sufficient to gain a patent, according to *Ciba-Geigy AB (Durr's Application)*.[142]

In general, the requirement that patents must be capable of industrial application adds little to the general picture, although it represents bad news for the ever-optimistic designers of perpetual motion machines. Its only significance lies in the associated refusal to allow medical treatment, but not the drugs used therein, to become the subject of a successful patent application.

Non-patentable matter

Even if the requirements of novelty, inventive step, and industrial application are satisfied by an applicant for a patent, there is one further group of hurdles placed in his or her way—namely, the deliberate exclusion of various matters from the ambit of patentability by s. 1(2) and (3) of the 1977 Act.

It will be recalled that the excluded matter under s. 1(2) is:

(a) a discovery, scientific theory or mathematical method;

(b) a literary, dramatic, musical or artistic work or any other aesthetic creation whatsoever;

(c) a scheme, rule or method for performing a mental act, playing a game or doing business, or a program for a computer;

(d) the presentation of information.

Non-patentable matter, but only 'as such'

It is vital at the outset to establish one important restriction on the ban in s. 1(2): it is only applicable to the prohibited matter 'as such' and the effect of these two vital words is that,

---

[138] *Bruker's Application* [1988] OJ EPO 308.
[139] [1971] RPC 337.
[140] *Riddlesbarger's Application* (1936) 53 RPC 57.
[141] [1970] RPC 574.   [142] [1977] RPC 83.

while it is not possible to patent, for example, a discovery on its own, it is quite appropriate to patent some process embodying the discovery, or a product in which the discovery has been transformed into a product of practical value. This means that, in this area too, the drafting of the specification and the claims is of vital significance. A scientist may discover a new source of energy, but it is highly likely that much work will need to be done to harness and control the new energy source, and to create the necessary technology that will embody it—and it is all of this kind of work that should be the focus of the application for the grant of a patent.

The classic example of this is provided by *Otto v. Linford*,[143] in which patent protection was sought for an internal combustion engine at the very early stages of the development of the motor car—the engine introducing, for the first time, air into the combustion process to enhance its effectiveness. The claim was found to be valid not as a discovery of the role of air, which, as a discovery would not be patentable, but as a machine that embodied and gave practical effect to that discovery. A more recent example is provided by *Rhodes' Application*,[144] in which a patent was successfully sought for a new speedometer that informed the driver both of his or her road speed and of the square of that figure, which represented kinetic energy and thus, as it was termed, the 'impact speed' of the car. The application did not founder on the rock of being merely a presentation of information, because there was, in the then statutory phrase, '*a manner of new manufacture*'[145] in the form of a working machine that combined the idea of providing a driver with an indication of his or her impact speed with a workable method of so doing. Today, this remains more than only a presentation of information 'as such'.

The precise relationship between non-patentable matter, such as a discovery, and an attempt to gain patent protection for a product or process closely connected with it was subject to further review in *Genentech*.[146] Remember that this case concerned the use of known DNA technology to produce quantities of a potentially valuable activator, t-PA, for use against blood clots. Purchas LJ expressed the view that '*a claim to a method embracing a discovery which may well be an invention…is patentable*',[147] rejecting the view previously expressed in *Merrill Lynch Inc's Application*[148] that the method of using the discovery must be novel, over and beyond the novelty of the discovery. In *Genentech*,[149] Dillon LJ made clear his view that a patent could be sought even though, once the discovery is made, the way forward to the application of it is an obvious one. The additional albeit obvious work to harness the discovery provides the additional element that means that the patent is not just for a discovery 'as such'.[150] It was clear that Mustill LJ was unhappy with the reasoning at this point, although not with the ultimate conclusion reached.[151] This did not avail Genentech, however, because the court found that some of its claims were for pure discoveries and were non-patentable, and, as we have seen, the steps that it had taken to isolate the t-PA were obvious to people of its team's expertise.

To an extent, it is appropriate to share the doubts expressed by Mustill LJ: a combination of a non-patentable discovery with its obvious application does not seem to provide the strongest of bases for the grant of a patent. The wording of s. 2 appears, however, to

---

[143] (1882) 46 LT 35.
[144] [1973] RPC 243.
[145] Patents Act 1949, s. 101.
[146] [1989] RPC 147.
[147] Ibid. at 208.
[148] [1988] RPC 1 (but see [1989] RPC 561 on appeal).
[149] [1989] RPC 147 at 240.
[150] Ibid.
[151] Ibid. at 269–70.

lead inexorably to that result, with a very fine line emerging between the non-patentable discovery of something without more, which is not patentable even if inventive, and the inventive discovery of something that is then obvious in its application, which is. The user of the discovery is protected, while the discoverer is not, which might again be said to reflect a function of patent law as the conferral of a reward on the inventor of something useful that benefits society. Also, given earlier criticisms of other aspects of *Genentech*, it may seem churlish to object to what appears to be one of its more generous aspects. The approach has been confirmed by the Court of Appeal in *Chiron Corp. v. Murex Diagnostics Ltd & Organon Teknika Ltd*,[152] in which it was held that the patent claim was for the polypeptide that resulted from the genetic sequence that had been discovered.

There is also a broader aspect to this part of *Genentech*. Mustill LJ points out the importance of identifying that there be an invention in the first place, before proceeding to consider the three legal elements that make it patentable.[153] He is fortified in this view by EPO Guidelines,[154] which make clear that this is a question that is separate and distinct from the other elements. Actions that may fall foul of s. 1(2) as being non-patentable are in some cases, he argues, not going to pass the first test of there being an invention in any event. Purchas LJ took the same view.[155]

This argument has, however, been somewhat dented by the approach adopted by Lord Hoffmann in *Biogen Inc. v. Medeva plc*.[156] He doubts whether the question of whether there is an invention or not is one of any practical importance, on the basis that the requirements in the legislation for patentability have the effect of restricting claims within the general category of 'inventions'. Lord Hoffmann claims that the drafters of the EPC and the Patents Act 1977, and even the learned counsel in *Biogen*, were unable to think of any examples of something that would be unpatentable purely because it was not an invention. So while it is, to an extent, useful to check that there is an invention, the check is unlikely to add anything to the consideration of patentability.

From these matters relevant to the whole of s. 1(2), we can now move on to consider the specific exclusions.

Section 1(2)(a)

The first exclusions in s. 1(2)(a) are self-evident in their character, but what may be less clear is the rationale for their exclusion, especially because, for example, the development of scientific theory is much more likely to be as a result of years of effort than the product of a shriek of 'Eureka!' while idling in the bathtub. The explanation is, however, that what these exclusions have in common is that they do not advance progress in the sense of creating something new, but merely reveal the existence of something that has always been there, but is only now revealed. The application of science is thus much better rewarded than its pure form; research is not enough—there must also be development.[157]

Section 1(2)(b)

The second group of exclusions—that of matter more at home in the field of copyright—is easier to explain, in so far as it is clearly convenient to have a clear dividing line between

[152] [1996] RPC 535, *per* Morritt LJ at 605–6.
[153] [1989] RPC 147 at 263–4.
[154] Guidelines for Examination in the EPO, ch. 4, paras 1.1 and 2.2.
[155] [1989] RPC 147 at 224.
[156] [1997] RPC 1.
[157] [1989] RPC 147 at 228.

the law of patents and that relating to copyright. Section 1(2)(b) appears to achieve this: a new method of painting may be the subject of patent, but the painting itself will only qualify for copyright. It may be, however, that the electronic creation of music, or the making of technical and similar drawings, may push the intended division closer to the limit, as would a novel work of art capable of an industrial application. In this case, the approach of s. 1(2) in allowing patents for excluded matter not used 'as such' would seem to give rise to a potential clash with both patent and copyright protection being secured, contrary to the assumed intention that lies behind paragraph (b).

Section 1(2)(c) and (d)

The next category—those in s. 1(2)(c) and (d)—gives rise to the usual need for careful reading of the patent application to see whether it covers the excluded material 'as such': if it goes beyond the excluded material, it will be able to get a patent, but it would be prudent to emphasize the matter over and beyond, for example, the presentation of information at the drafting stage.

A useful set of facts with which to illustrate this simply is that of *ITS Rubber Ltd's Application*,[158] in which a patent application was made for a squash ball coloured blue in order that its location could be detected more readily by players. At the time, it was found by Whitford J to be potentially patentable as a manner of new manufacture,[159] but now it would appear likely to fall within paragraphs (c) or (d) as being the presentation of information as to the location of the ball. Because this would make no change to the method of playing squash, it would seem to be claimed 'as such' and thus non-patentable, whereas the dual speedometer noted above in the *Rhodes* case was incorporated into something new and would still be awarded a patent, if drafted appropriately. The concept of presentation of information was recently held to include providing information. It is indeed difficult to see what sense the provision would still have if this were not the case, but the decision assists in focusing on the meaning of presentation of information.[160]

A recent case that illustrates the key distinction at issue well is *Lux Traffic Controls Ltd v. Pike Signals & Faronwise Ltd.*[161] The patents in this case were for traffic light control systems, one of which extended the green period by an additional period if it detected a vehicle crossing, thus ensuring that opposing traffic was held by a red light, and the other of which gave a pause on each change of lights during which no one had a green light for a time. Aldous J found that a method of regulating traffic as such would not be patentable, because it was not an invention, but rather merely an abstract plan, which at best presented information, following the EPO's decision in the *Christian Franceries* case.[162] The patent claimed was, however, for the device that, by detecting both the movement and non-movement of traffic in a novel way, created a new form of technological contribution to traffic management; it is the technical character of the improvement made that is vital[163] and that was found to be present in the first patent. Likewise, in the second patent, a known type of traffic regulation was in consideration, so, on the face of it, both non-patentability and anticipation applied; again, however, what was, in fact, being created was a new device to control this type of traffic

---

[158] [1979] RPC 318.

[159] Ibid. at 325.

[160] *In the Matter of Patent Application No. GB0301172.3, sub nom Stephen Townsend* [2004] EWHC 482.

[161] [1993] RPC 107.

[162] Ibid. at 138; *Christian Franceries/Traffic Regulation*, T16/83, 1998 EPOR 65, 69 (Technical Bd. App. 1985).

[163] Guidelines for Examination in the EPO, ch. 4, para. 1.2(ii).

regulation centrally, with the maximum ease, and that was sufficient to justify the grant of a patent in that instance too.

The decision in *Raytheon Co's Application*[164] provides a contrast with this. It was concerned with a system for improving ship recognition by creating a digital record of known ships that could then be compared with the digital silhouette of an unknown ship. This was seen as non-patentable: its two sole features were that it was a system for performing a mental act and non-patentable as such, and its other feature was a computer program and also non-patentable. There was nothing that amounted to a technical advantage here: it was the obvious mosaicking of two non-patentable items.

More detail on the computer element that is intrinsic to *Raytheon* is to be found in Chapter 30; it is appropriate to note briefly here a particular point that arises in relation to computer programs, but which also casts light on the preceding area. In *Merrill Lynch's Application*,[165] the Court of Appeal was faced with the issue of patentability of a program drawn up by the applicants for a data processing system for making a trading market in securities. In the post-*Genentech* world, it was clear that the applicants were under an obligation to prove that what they had done was to create something more than a computer program 'as such', so they pointed to the programming of the computer by the program as being the necessary extra element.

This was rejected by Fox LJ:

> it cannot be permissible to patent an item excluded under section 1(2) under the guise of an article which contains that item—that is to say in the case of a computer program, the patenting of a conventional computer containing that program.[166]

There must once again be technical advance in the form of a new result and this was a requirement that had not been satisfied in *Merrill Lynch*. This was a standard computer program and thus non-patentable, and its application was to do no more than create a method of doing business, which is also non-patentable.

A similar decision was also reached in *Gale's Application*,[167] in which an inventor created a program on a disc that gave an easier method of calculating the square roots of numbers. No patent was allowed: all that the computer did was to generate a program; placing it on the disc was, as in *Merrill Lynch*, not a technical advance and, in any event, it was only a discovery of a mathematical method and thus fell foul of s. 1(2) (a) as well. The fact that the retired plaintiff appeared in person probably explains why this matter had to go up as far as the Court of Appeal for its ultimate, and obvious, disposition.

A contested approach

The Court of Appeal reviewed this area of the law in the *Aerotel* case.[168] The Court found the current situation to be unsatisfactory, because different approaches emerge from the case law of the UK courts and that of the EPO. The Court suggested that the EPO should convene an Enlarged Board of Appeal to clarify the law; in the meantime, it found itself bound by the cases that require there to be a technical effect to bring the subject matter outside the scope of s. 1(2). Nevertheless, the Court suggested a new

[164] [1993] RPC 427.
[165] [1989] RPC 561.
[166] Ibid. at 569.
[167] [1991] RPC 305.
[168] *Aerotel Ltd v. Tesco Holdings Ltd; Macrossan's Patent Application* [2007] RPC 7.

four-stage approach to apply s. 1(2) and to bring the technical effect requirement into practice.

1. It is necessary properly to construe the claim: what exactly is claimed?
2. The contribution made by the invention is identified.
3. It is then asked whether that contribution falls solely within the excluded subject matter.
4. Finally, it is checked whether the contribution is technical in nature.

Biotechnology[169]

Two distinct types of matter that are of fundamental importance as biotechnology develops apace were excluded by the original text of s. 1(3) of the 1977 Act, which stated:

A patent shall not be granted—

(a) for an invention the publication or exploitation of which would be generally expected to encourage offensive, immoral or anti-social behaviour;

(b) for any variety of animal or plant or any essentially biological process for the production of animals or plants, not being a micro-biological process or the product of such a process.

These matters were, and are, not exclusive to issues of biotechnology, but impact more in this area than any other. Likewise, in considering this topic, regard should, of course, be had to important cases considered elsewhere, such as *Biogen*, *Chiron*, and *Genentech*.[170]

The wording of s. 1(3) has now been amended[171] and brought into line with that used in the Trade-Related Aspects of Intellectual Property Rights (TRIPS) Agreement 1994, but no change in the substantive law was envisaged. The new text stipulates that: '*A patent shall not be granted for an invention the commercial exploitation of which would be contrary to public policy or morality.*' Section 1(4) adds that:

For the purposes of subsection (3) above exploitation shall not be regarded as contrary to public policy or morality only because it is prohibited by any law in force in the United Kingdom or any part of it.

It is appropriate, though, before we look at the detailed implications of the morality clause, to have a closer look at the relationship between biotechnology and patent law in order to understand how certain issues arise, and why the situation is somewhat different from that relating, for example, to mechanical engineering.

Biotechnology and biotechnological techniques

In essence, biotechnology is concerned with the application of scientific techniques to living organisms. These living organisms are manipulated in one way or another—such as through the insertion of another gene, for example. According to the EPO Guidelines, biotechnological inventions are inventions that '*concern a product consisting of or containing biological material or a process by means of which biological material is produced,*

---

[169] See, generally, M. Llewelyn, 'The legal protection of biotechnical inventions: an alternative approach' [1997] 3 EIPR 115.

[170] See N. Jones and I. Britton, 'Biotech patents: the trend reversed again' [1996] 3 EIPR 171.

[171] The Patents Regulations 2000, SI 2000/2037, r. 2.

processed or used' and biological material is '*any material containing genetic information and capable of reproducing itself or being reproduced in a biological system*'.[172]

There have been significant developments in biotechnology over the last decades, and the area is now seen as an important potential source of new medical treatments and drugs, and plants that are disease-resistant. This explains the massive investments in the area and hence also the attempts to patent the outcome of the research to secure a return on the huge investments made.

There are several techniques that are frequently used in the field of biotechnology. We will briefly describe them here, because a minimal insight is required to understand the specific aspects of patent applications that flow from the use or development of these techniques. The first of these is tissue and cell culture technology, which essentially involves the production of cell lines. This is a vital research tool, because these cell lines are self-replicating samples of cells that are grown outside the original host, and, in principle, these lines are immortal and constitute a constant supply of the relevant cells. The original host might be a bacterium or a plant, but might also be an animal, or even a human being. The most advanced cell lines are arguably those involving human embryonic stem cell.[173]

The use of human material, in particular, can make this technique controversial. The most important aspect of cell lines is their uniformity: all of the cells share identical characteristics and genetic-make up. Accurate comparative tests therefore become possible, for example, in relation to the effect of drugs on living matter or the study of biological processes.

'Hybridoma' technology deals with the human immune response and involves two of its key players: white blood cells and antibodies. At its most basic, antibody-producing white blood cells are fused with tumour cells, which have the advantage that they produce indefinitely, and when such a hybridized cell is injected into an antigen—that is, a foreign body that will provoke an antibody response—an indefinite supply of antibodies is produced. This technique is invaluable for the research into the operation of the immune system, and has been used in the production of diagnostic and other testing kits.[174]

In silico techniques, meanwhile, search and compare databases of gene sequences using a combination of genetic and bioinformatic knowledge. The aim is to attribute a function to gene sequences on the basis of matches with already known proteins that have a similar function.

Genetic engineering is probably the most well-known, or at least well-publicized, technique. Its full name is 'recombinant DNA technology' and it involves the manipulation of matter at a sub-cellular level. DNA strings are contained in the nucleus of almost all living cells; it is DNA that is being manipulated. DNA stands for 'deoxyribonucleic acid'. It appears in strings and dictates the function of the cell in which it exists through genes, which are essentially sequences of DNA that activate the production of proteins (also known as polypeptides). They do this by bringing together different combinations of amino acids, which will, in turn, produce the proteins. Scientists talk about coding for proteins and the different proteins make cells function in different ways. By interfering with the DNA—for example, by removing fragments or inserting bits that are alien to the cell—one can influence the production of proteins and the function that is fulfilled by the cell.

---

[172] EPO Guidelines, Pt C, ch. IV, para. 2a.

[173] A. Plomer, P. Torremans, B. Knoppers, C. Denning, J. Sinden and M. Levin (2006) *Stem Cell Patents: European Patent Law and Ethics Report*, Report for the European Commission, available online at www.nottingham.ac.uk/law/StemCellProject/project.report.pdf. See also S. Crespi, 'The human embryo and patent law: a major challenge ahead?' (2006) 28 EIPR 11, 569–75.

[174] See G. Van Overwalle (ed.) (2007) *Gene Patents and Public Health*, Brussels: Bruylant.

Biotechnology patent applications

All of these techniques have developed rapidly over the last decades and some of these developments have been the object of patent applications. The knowledge, modified cells, gene sequences, and proteins, etc. that have resulted from the use of these techniques have also been the object of patent applications. A first idea of the problems that arise in this area can be gained from the basic proposition that a large part of what is being done involves unravelling the biological and genetic structure of living material. That living material was, naturally, already in existence and, apart from the morality issue, one might also question whether an inventive activity is involved when a gene is isolated and its function is discovered, for example.

Discoveries and inventions

This brings us back to the discussion of the relationship between a 'discovery' and an 'invention'. As we have seen before, patent law sees an invention as an inventive concept that brings about a technical solution for a pre-existing problem that had not yet been solved. A patentable invention involves, therefore, the application of knowledge; a mere discovery does not have that added aspect of the application of knowledge in a problem-solving context.

From a legal point of view, the conclusion is therefore, at least in theory, rather simple. The mere discovery of a gene sequence is not patentable, but locating a previously unknown gene, determining its function, and making it accessible for further exploitation brings about the required application of knowledge: the problem of the inaccessibility of the genetic problem has been solved. Patent law only excludes a mere discovery 'as such' as we have seen earlier in this chapter. The fact that the invention involves also biological or genetic material does not, therefore, stand in the way of patentability. On that basis, patents have been granted for DNA sequences, protein molecules, and recombinant DNA molecules that are used as research tools, as well as for purified forms of bacteria, vitamins, and viruses.

Novelty and inventive step

But there remains a need to look at the requirements for patentability, even if one assumes that we are in the presence of an invention. The earlier discussion of the *Genentech* case[175] allowed us to focus on the problems raised in this area in terms of inventive step; here, we would like to touch briefly on the question of novelty. In this respect, the argument that most of what is applied for in biotechnology patent applications already exists in nature is often raised. But, especially if we keep in mind the discussion about the techniques involved and the fact that we are not dealing with mere discoveries, it becomes clear that what is applied for is 'as such' not available to the public—and that is, after all, the key test for novelty. Knowing that something exists in nature is not enough to anticipate the invention: if human beings cannot access the existing material, it is not available to the public. One simply needs to recall the facts in the House of Lord decision in *Asahi*.[176] The fact that the protein was known could not anticipate a patent for the genetically engineered version of the protein—that is, a patent involving how to make the product.

Patents also often claim artificially manufactured versions of the product. Protection is even more widely available, especially if one takes into account Art. 5(2) of the Directive

[175] *Genentech Inc's Patent* [1989] RPC 147.
[176] *Asahi Kasei Kogyo KK's Application* [1991] RPC 485 (HL); see also *Kirin-Amgen Inc. v. Transkaryotic Therapies Inc.* [2003] RPC 31 (CA); [2005] 1 All ER 667 (HL).

on the protection of biotechnological inventions,[177] in which one finds the confirmation that patents are available for:

> elements that are isolated from the human body or otherwise produced by means of a technical process, including the sequence or partial sequence of a gene, even if the structure of that element is identical to that of a natural element.

The restriction in Art. 5(1) of the Directive, that patents are not available for '*the human body or its parts in their natural state or for the simple discovery of one of its elements*', is, in that respect, little more than a restatement of an obvious conclusion that only marginally reduces the scope for patentability in this area.

Overall, therefore, there is plenty of scope for patentability in this area.

The current situation

One of the perceived problems has been that a huge number of patents have been granted in the field of biotechnology, many of which have been for fundamental research tools that are needed for most forms of future research or for small incremental improvements only. The latter type of patent is due to the nature of the research in the area. Further research is therefore necessarily happening in a sea of patents, which is a complicating factor, and licensing strategies and policies are therefore becoming vital,[178] as is the control—by means of competition law, for example—of any abusive practices.

Morality and ordre public

The historical first group of exclusions that has now been retained in the new version of s. 1(3) is the UK's response to the requirement under Art. 53(a) of the EPC that no patent should be granted if so to do would be contrary to 'ordre public *or morality*'.[179] There is little jurisprudence on this section, but the key issue would appear to be whether the Patent Office and the courts are prepared to recognize personal views—which are genuinely held, but controversial—as a reason for invoking s. 1(3) of the 1977 Act. A patent that, in some way, made abortion easier would be deeply repugnant to many people, but greatly welcomed by many others; given that, as has been seen, patents are granted for methods of contraception to which significant minority groups in society are opposed, it would seem unlikely that the section would be invoked in such a case.

The legislation refers to matters 'generally' regarded as objectionable and this, it is suggested, appropriately reflects the universal, rather than personal, ideals that make up the notion of *ordre public*. So a patent that is designed to assist in some action that is universally regarded as wrong—such as safe-blowing—would be unlikely to secure patent protection; this is so, it is suggested, notwithstanding s. 1(4), which ordains that the mere fact that an act is contrary to the law does not, of itself, translate that act into one within the ban on patent protection within s. 1(3). Thus a patent for something that enables cars to travel at speeds above the current statutory limits may be patentable if it is felt that the attainment of such speeds is not contrary to the *ordre public*. A harder case that might fall either side of the boundary would be weapons or explosives, the existence of which may benefit a state's military power, but the use of which in the

---

[177] European Parliament and Council Directive 98/44/EC on the legal protection of biotechnological inventions (1998) OJ L 213/13.
[178] See Van Overwalle (2007).
[179] See P. Ford, 'The morality of biotech patents: differing legal obligations in Europe?' [1997] 6 EIPR 315.

wrong hands may be against the public interest: an undetectable explosive, such as Semtex, is a case in point.

A real-life example of a finely balanced decision would be the objections to the patenting of the genetically engineered 'OncoMouse', which offered potential benefits to cancer victims. These objections were made under Art. 53(a) of the EPC and were ultimately rejected, on the basis that the suffering of the animal, which was intended to develop cancers, nonetheless conferred benefits on humanity and were unavoidable at this stage of our scientific development.

Plant and animal varieties

The other exclusion in the old s. 1(3)(b) meant that a patent could not be granted for animal or plant varieties, or for a biological process for the production of animals or plants; microbiological processes were, however, patentable. It is submitted that this is still the case and that the change in wording has no impact on the substantive law—but the reasons for excluding animals and plants are, in many ways, very different.

Plant varieties are appropriately excluded from the realm of patent law, because there is a separate intellectual property regime in their respect. This is now provided in the form of the Plant Varieties Act 1997,[180] which develops the pre-existing law[181] by incorporating into domestic law an implementation of the 1991 revisions of the International Convention for the Protection of New Varieties of Plants (the UPOV Convention), and also fulfils the obligations created by European Regulations[182] and the TRIPs Agreement.[183] The basic principles remain, however—namely, that the plant variety must be distinct, uniform, stable,[184] and new[185] in order to secure patent-style protection.[186] Unlike patents, however,, the protection extends not only to the plant breeder, but also to anyone who discovers the new variety. It should be noted that entirely new plants appear to fall within the traditional patent sector.[187]

The period of protection varies: for example new types of roses acquire a 15-year term of right,[188] while developments in rhubarb gain a 20-year period[189] and potatoes enjoy a 30-year period of protection.[190]

The ban on patents for animal varieties creates more problems, because there is no separate system for granting intellectual property rights in their respect. The basis for the exclusion of animal varieties seems to be based on moral grounds, the law viewing with disfavour Frankenstein-like experiments on living things. This is now covered by the general provision in s. 1(3). The problem is nevertheless that such a model is quite inappropriate in modern times: the law clearly allows patents to be granted in respect of living matter through its recognition of microbiological processes, and the distinction between a biological, and thus non-patentable, process and one that is patentable as a

---

[180] See also The Plant Breeders' Rights Regulations 1998, SI 1998/1027. The Act came into force on 8 May 1998 (SI 1998/1028).
[181] Plant Varieties and Seeds Act 1964.
[182] Regulation (EC) 2100/94.
[183] See P. Torremans (2001) 'Plant varieties in the TRIPS Agreement: time for reform?', in J. McMahon (ed.) *Trade and Agriculture: Negotiating a New Agreement?*, London: Cameron May, pp. 381–402.
[184] Plant Varieties Act 1997, Sch. 2, Pt 1.
[185] Ibid., paras 4–7.
[186] Plant Varieties Act 1997, s. 6 expands the scope of protection.
[187] See T. Roberts 'Patenting plants around the world' [1996] 10 EIPR 531.
[188] SI 1965/725.
[189] SI 1966/644.
[190] SI 1992/454.

microbiological process is very fine, and even rather artificial. The circumstances under which a new animal may be created are, in reality, likely to involve highly controlled laboratory conditions with the purpose being an advance in medical science and thus a benefit to society. Whether patents are seen as a reward for the conferring of benefits on society or whether they are seen as a recompense for hard work and energy is immaterial here: both factors separately suggest that the refusal of the law to give patent protection to animals is now anomalous. In any case, the exclusion is limited to animal varieties and does not affect individual animals.

This was once thought to be an entirely academic issue—but it is no longer so. Experimentation has created the famous 'Dolly', a cloned sheep, and a substantial number of mice have also been created in the same way. Meanwhile, Europe has been struggling to find an acceptable answer to the problem of legal control of biotechnology, as will be seen.

There are several ways in which rights in new or cloned animals may be considered. The issue might be considered as an issue of *ordre public* or it might be argued that a separate *sui generis* right should be created,[191] by analogy with plants. The law has already had to consider the moral issues involved in the famous OncoMouse litigation. Following the lead from the USA, the EPO has granted a patent for the so-called OncoMouse, which is a live mouse genetically adapted to develop cancers as part of a new approach to the treatment of cancer and which, as such, is clearly is deserving of some form of legal protection. But such a conclusion can only be reached via a very narrow interpretation of Art. 53 of the EPC, which is the counterpart to the UK's Patent Act 1977, s. 1(3). The decision distinguishes new animals, which are not patentable, from new animal varieties, which, as a result of their not being expressly mentioned in the relevant Article, can be granted patent protection. The OncoMouse was merely a variation on a pre-existing species and could be the subject matter of a patent.

This is an area that now calls for reform to allow the patentability of animals without recourse to artificially and atypically narrow interpretations of the law, and the EPO is in the process of reviewing its policy in this regard. After all, the more general ban on the patenting of that which is generally offensive remains and would be appropriate to control undesirable animal experimentation; whether it is more appropriate to allow patent protection for the creation of new animals or whether it is better to create a new animal variety right by analogy with the law relating to plant patents is debatable. Certainly, an independent right would need an *ordre public* provision to protect society from undesirable or dangerous attempts at genetic manipulation, but it now looks increasingly unlikely that a *sui generis* approach will be developed. Patent law seems bound to become the general tool in this area. Thus moves are being taken, but—inevitably in this legal, moral, and scientific minefield—they are being taken slowly and cautiously.

The Biotechnology Directive

Years of discussion have finally led to advance on the European front in the form of a Directive on the legal protection of biotechnological inventions.[192] On the one hand, this provides for the protection of such biotechnological inventions through the patent law

[191] See N. Peace and A. Christie, 'Intellectual property protection for the products of animal breeding' [1996] 4 EIPR 213.

[192] European Parliament and Council Directive 98/44/EC on the legal protection of biotechnological inventions (1998) OJ L 213/13.

of member States,[193] but does not extend to plant or animal varieties, or to essentially biological processes for their creation. On the other:

> Biological material which is isolated from its natural environment or produced by means of a technical process may be the subject of an invention even if it previously occurred in nature.[194]

There is also a specific exclusion within a general *ordre public* exception that prevents the registration of processes for human cloning and related activities, including the use of human embryos for industrial or commercial purposes.[195] The human body, unlike genes isolated from it, cannot constitute a patentable invention;[196] likewise excluded is the genetic modification of animals that causes suffering and which is not conferring any substantial medical benefit.[197] Thus the OncoMouse would still be patentable, but more experimental variation would not be. There are also further detailed provisions on the scope of protection to be awarded to biotechnological inventions and provisions concerning the deposit of biotechnological material.[198]

It is clear that the European art of compromise was instrumental in securing the safe passage of the Directive, but the consequence of this is that it fails to address the most pressing concerns in this controversial area: science presses ahead, while the law lags behind. The creation of new animals and the cloning of pre-existing animals—including, in theory, humans—is taking place and the law must, therefore, have a response. The Directive is not the full answer to the problems that remain in this ethical minefield; it merely confirms that biotechnological inventions are patentable. The positive side of it is that it clarifies the law on this point, but, on the negative side, one can only conclude that the Directive did not really cover a lot of new ground. The UK has implemented the Directive by means of the Patents Regulations 2000,[199] as a result of which a series of minor changes were made to the Patents Act 1977.[200]

Recently, a debate has been sparked by inventions that involve (potentially) human embryonic stem cells: are they patentable under the terms of the Directive or do they fall foul of the morality clause? Could it be that they are necessarily caught by Art. 6 of the Directive—that is, the specific exclusion relating to the registration of processes for human cloning and related activities? National patent offices have expressed different views and, in society, there is a clear split of opinion—but some questions can no longer be avoided. What is meant by 'morality' under Art. 53 of the EPC? There is no indication as to how a common concept of morality is to be identified or created. Are we to refer back to the national situation in each member State in the absence of a common approach? What exactly is the link between Arts 5 and 6 of the Biotech Directive? Article 5 talks in broad terms about the human body and what is patentable; Art. 6 then talks about morality and gives examples of what is not patentable: is Art. 5 the principle and Art. 6 the exception? Or does Art. 6 reduce the scope of Art. 5? And how broadly or narrowly do we need to define the unpatentable examples in Art. 6 of the Directive?

. . .

(a) processes for cloning human beings;

(b) processes for modifying the germ line genetic identity of human beings;

---

[193] Articles 1 and 3(1).
[194] Article 3(2).
[195] Article 6.
[196] Article 5.   [197] Article 6.
[198] Articles 8–12 and 13–14, respectively.
[199] SI 2000/2037.
[200] See also Patents (Amendment) Rules 2001, SI 2001/1412.

    (c) uses of human embryos for industrial or commercial purposes;

    (d) processes for modifying the genetic identity of animals which are likely to cause them suffering without any substantial medical benefit to man or animal, and also animals resulting from such processes.

These are fundamental questions and a careful answer is needed. The EPO is currently considering these in the reference to the Enlarged Board of Appeal in the *WARF/Stem Cells* case.[201]

An overview

It is appropriate to step back at this juncture and assess the way in which the law has approached the overall question of patentability. The obstacles placed in the way of an applicant are quite considerable, particularly when viewed in the light of the result achieved: a monopoly right only over the matters directly claimed for a *de jure* 20-year period that will, in actual fact, only allow commercial exploitation for a lesser period, while all the time rivals are free to experiment on producing a better product at any time, or a rival imitation as soon as the 20 years are over.

    There are essentially three requirements for patentability. Novelty requires the invention to be new—that is, that the prior art must not anticipate the invention. Anticipation requires there to be an enabling disclosure, which means that the requirements of both disclosure and enablement must be satisfied. The 'new' invention must also involve an inventive step: 'inventiveness' is defined as non-obviousness by the Act. Finally the invention must be capable of industrial application.

    In order to win this somewhat less-than-glittering prize, novelty is a reasonable requirement for the applicant to have to satisfy, but this cannot always be said in relation to inventive steps, in relation to which the convolutions of the judges in the Court of Appeal in the *Genentech* saga stand as a pointer to the fact that it may not, in all cases, be sensible to define an inventive step as one that it is not obvious to take. More generally, the case indicates the difficulties that will inevitably attend any tribunal that seeks to locate itself as a notional, highly knowledgeable, but profoundly uninventive, reasonable man and then attempts to make the qualitative judgment of whether a inventive step made was, at that time, obvious or not. It is a question asked by the ill equipped, which is close to unanswerable.

    Reviewing what a court will regard as non-patentable matter also shows that this area is not without its problems. Section 1(2) of the Patents Act 1977 excludes much that may be the subject of prolonged research work, although careful drafting and the generosity of the courts in allowing inventive non-patentable matter to provide the element of inventiveness in a broader patent both go some way to limiting the difficulty for patentees. The law also seems reluctant to invoke s. 1(3) to stop patents being granted even in cases in which, as in the case of the OncoMouse, to do so would, on the face of it, be contrary to the words of the legislation.

    If a patent is a reward, it is one that is not readily gained. The need for the applicant to satisfy the various requirements, coupled with the years that the process will take, suggest

---

[201] For the referral, see Case T-1374/04 *WARF/Stem Cells* [2006] EPOR 31. An academic study has already examined this area: A. Plomer et al (2006). See also Crespi (2006) and A. Warren-Jones, 'Identifying European moral consensus: why are the patent courts reticent to accept empirical evidence in resolving biotechnological cases? (2006) 28 EIPR 1, 26–37.

that the law regards the grant of a monopoly as a matter of the utmost seriousness and gravity. Whether the consequences of being granted a patent are so wondrous as to justify the application of so much seriousness and gravity is more questionable, especially when evidence indicates that many patents are granted for inventions that do not lead to commercially successful exploitation and when the 'cutting edge' of biotechnology is not well protected by the patent system. It may be that a lifetime obligation of confidentiality *inter partes* may increasingly be seen to be a better answer.

Further reading

COOK, W. and LEES, G. 'Test clarified for UK software and business method patents: but what about the EPO?' (2007) 29 EIPR 3, 115–88.

CRESPI, S. 'The human embryo and patent law: a major challenge ahead?' (2006) 28 EIPR 11, 569–75.

FREELAND, R., 'Disclosure and enablement: the House of Lords clarifies the law on novelty' (2006) 1 JIPLP 3, 163–5.

GRANT, G. and GIBBINS, D. '"Inventive concept": is it a good idea?' (2007) 27 EIPR 5, 170–5.

PLOMER, A., TORREMANS, P., KNOPPERS, B., DENNING, C., SINDEN, J. and LEVIN, M. (2006) *Stem Cell Patents: European Patent Law and Ethics Report*, Report for the European Commission, available online at www.nottingham.ac.uk/law/StemCellProject/project.report.pdf.

SHARPLES, A. and CURLEY, D. 'Experimental novelty: *Synthon v. Smithkline Beecham*' (2006) 28 EIPR 5, 308–11.

SIMS, A. 'The case against patenting methods of medical treatment' (2007) 29 EIPR 2, 43–51.

WARREN-JONES, A. 'Identifying European moral consensus: why are the patent courts reticent to accept empirical evidence in resolving biotechnological cases?' (2006) 28 EIPR 1, 26–37.

5

Use and grant in the UK and Europe

Whose patent is it anyway?[1]

Entitlement

We have so far referred generally to applicants for patents without examining who is, in fact, entitled to be granted a patent. Section 7 of the 1977 Act is the starting point for this enquiry. Under s. 7(1), any person may make an application either alone or jointly; under s. 13(2), however, the applicant must include in the application a statement of who the inventor is, in case the inventor him or herself is not applying, and, if others are involved, an indication of what right the applicant has to be granted the patent, so that there is no danger of a patent being granted to a usurper.

This is borne out by s. 7(2) of the 1977 Act, which states that a patent may be granted:

(a) primarily to the inventor or joint inventors;

(b) in preference to the foregoing, to any person or persons who, by virtue of any enactment or rule of law, or any foreign law or treaty or international convention, or by virtue of an enforceable term of any agreement entered into with the inventor before the making of the invention, was or were at the time of the making of the invention entitled to the whole of the property in it (other than equitable interests) in the United Kingdom;

(c) in any event, to the successor or successors in title of any person or persons mentioned in paragraph (a) or (b) above or any person so mentioned and the successor or successors in title of another person so mentioned; and to no other person.

The words 'primarily' and 'in preference' simply indicate that the inventor is, first and foremost, the normal patentee, but will sometimes have lost that right: for example, to an employer under a contract of employment, as will be seen later in the chapter. Under s. 7(3), an inventor is simply defined as *'the actual deviser of the invention'*.

The House of Lords dealt with the issue of entitlement and clarified s. 7 in *Yeda v. Rhone-Poulenc*.[2] It was held that s. 7(2) and the definition in s. 7(3) form an exhaustive code for determining who is entitled to the grant of a patent. Primarily, we are talking about the inventor, but legal or treaty provisions, as well as agreements, can also give

---

[1] With apologies to television star and patent expert Clive Anderson, as in The Patent Office's Laser Disc Patent Training Package (Patent Office, 1992). It was held, in *IDA Ltd v. University of Southampton* [2005] RPC 11, that the inventor is the person who came up with the inventive concept and that other contributions do not count.

[2] *Yeda Research & Development Co. Ltd v. Rhone-Poulenc Rorer International Holdings Inc. & ors* [2007] UKHL 43.

someone else that entitlement. Successor in title can also be entitled to a patent. There is no need to cross-refer to other provisions in the Act, or to prove entitlement by virtue of a contract or a breach of confidence, as the Court of Appeal had held in *Markem*.[3] Section 7(3) then adds a definition of the inventor and s. 7(4) deals with the burden of proof of the person who wants to be added as joint inventor. That person needs to prove that he or she contributed to the inventive concept, bringing him or her within the scope of the definition in s. 7(3).

Another key decision in this area dealing with the key point of that definition was the appeal in *University of Southampton's Applications*,[4] which the Court allowed. The judgment clearly establishes that, in entitlement proceedings, the court had to identify who, in substance, had made the invention—that is, who had been responsible for the inventive concept—who had contributed what and what rights, if any. The Court had to look for the 'heart' of the invention. The House of Lords confirmed this in *Yeda v. Rhone-Poulenc*, in which it was held that s. 7(3) defined the inventor as the '*actual deviser of the invention*' and that the word 'actual' needed to be contrasted with the deemed, or pretended, deviser of the invention: hence the emphasis on the person that came up with the inventive concept. A mere contribution to the claims is not sufficient, because these may include non-patentable integers derived from prior art.[5] This point had also been made in *Markem*.[6]

The case at issue in *University of Southampton* dealt with insect traps, and there was an exact parallel between the application at issue and a patent filed in 1994. In the 1994 patent, the exposure of the insect was '*to particles carrying an electrostatic charge*', while in the patent in suit, the exposure was '*to a composition comprising particles containing or consisting of at least one magnetic material*'. The change from electrostatic particles to magnetic particles was the only new and inventive element; it was the sole key to the information in the patent in suit, and that key had been provided solely by the appellant and not by the University or its staff. The appellant did not know whether the idea would work and the University's staff did all of the testing work—but the latter was, in essence, only a matter of simple and routine experimentation, and was mere verification. All that the University staff added was the common general knowledge of those in the art. The appellant therefore provided the 'heart' of the invention and was entitled to the patent.

In cases in which a patent is awarded jointly to more than one inventor, it is important to establish the respective entitlements of the holders. Section 36 of the 1977 Act does this by establishing that each joint patentee is entitled to an equal undivided share of the patent, although this may be varied by agreement between the joint patentees. The obvious analogy is with the position of tenants in common of real property. Joint patentees have the right to do anything with the invention without having to consult their fellow patentees, with some exceptions: most significantly, that the consent of the others is required to any licensing or assignment of the patent.[7] Thus one joint patentee could exploit the invention on his or her own and pocket the proceeds without any obligation to account in any way to his or her fellow patentees in the absence of any agreement to the contrary.

---

[3] *Markem Corp. v. Zipher Ltd* [2005] RPC 31 (CA), overruled in *Yeda Research & Development Co. Ltd v. Rhone-Poulenc Rorer International Holdings Inc. & ors* (see n. 2), despite the fact that the House of Lords agreed that the case had been correctly decided, but because the House disapproved of some of its reasoning.

[4] [2006] RPC 21.

[5] *Yeda Research & Development Co. Ltd v. Rhone-Poulenc Rorer International Holdings Inc. & ors* (see n. 2).

[6] *Markem Corp. v. Zipher Ltd* (see n. 3).

[7] Patents Act 1977, s. 36(2) and (3).

Disposal of the patent can give rise to problems, especially if the need for disposal arises from a dispute between the joint patentees—if, for example, one is opposed to, and thus blocks, a proposed licensing arrangement. In *Florey's Patent*,[8] the Patent Office was faced with a dispute between a group of medical researchers who had jointly secured a patent for a new form of penicillin. All but one then wished to assign the patent to the National Research Development Council for further development and ultimate exploitation; the objector, while not opposing the assignment as such, held out for a half-share of the proceeds to which he felt entitled. Under what is now the power granted to the Patent Office to determine disputes between joint patentees under s. 37(1)(b) of the 1977 Act, the Office ordered that the assignment proceed with an equal distribution of the proceeds being made as is the normal route when, as in this case, no contrary agreement could be proven. The Court of Appeal has also held that s. 37 and the power contained therein for the Comptroller to determine the transfer of rights in the patent does include the power for the Comptroller to order the grant of a licence against the will of one of the owners of the patent in a case in which exploitation of the patent has effectively been blocked.[9]

Section 37(5) of the Patents Act 1977 allows orders to be made in relation to entitlement. *Rhone-Poulenc Rorer International Holdings Inc v. Yeda Research & Development Co Ltd*[10] is an interesting case in this respect. The grant of the patent in suit was mentioned in the European Patent Bulletin on 27 March 2002 and, on 26 March 2004, the respondent filed a reference under s. 37 claiming joint entitlement to the patent. On 29 June 2005, the respondent filed an amended statement of case, in which it claimed sole ownership of the patent. If the latter statement were a new claim, the limitation period contained in s. 37(5) would potentially apply and, in this case, only the first claim would have been made validly. The clear intention of the legislator was to avoid that entitlement claims were made a long period into the life of the patent. At such a late stage, third parties—such as licensees—may already have acquired rights and a change in ownership could then complicate things unduly. Alternatively, one could hold that, as long as a claim was brought within the two-year period, s. 37 allowed the Comptroller to decide who was entitled to the patent, irrespective almost of the exact content of the claim.

Lewison J emphatically rejected the latter interpretation, as did the Court of Appeal, but the House of Lords overturned their decisions. It was held that the claim needs to be made within the two-year period by submitting the form stipulated in the Patent Rules.[11] Once that has been done, it is up to the Comptroller to make a decision. In the course of that process, the requesting party is free to file evidence and amended statements. The limitation period only applies to bringing the case in front of the Comptroller in the first place.[12]

Employee inventions

The main area in which disputes arise over entitlement to the grant of a patent is between employers and employees. Many inventions will be made by employees, such as university professors or research and development (R&D) staff in private industry; in making their inventions, these people will, in all probability, be using the facilities and resources of their employer, and this has led the law to declare—in s. 39 of the 1977 Act—that, in many instances, the employer, rather than the employee, will be the person entitled to the grant

[8] [1962] RPC 186.
[9] *Derek Hughes v. Neil Paxman* [2007] RPC 2.
[10] [2006] RPC 24.
[11] The Patents Rules 1995, SI 1995/2093.
[12] *Yeda Research & Development Co. Ltd v. Rhone-Poulenc Rorer International Holdings Inc. & ors* [2007] UKHL 43.

of a patent. Alhough the current appearance of the law dates from the 1977 Act, there were earlier common law rules covering the same ground and decisions from those cases are said to offer guidance in the interpretation of the statutory rules.[13] Unusually, this is purely domestic law; there is no equivalent provision in the European Patent Convention (EPC).

There are two categories of situation in which the Act envisages that a grant to the employer is appropriate. First, s. 39(1)(a) of the Act provides that the employer gains the patent if the employee is in the course of his or her duties and if the circumstances are such that an invention might reasonably be expected to result. Put simply, if an employee is paid to research, he or she gains a reward in the form of his or her salary cheque and the employer gains the patent as a reward for its foresight in hiring the researcher in the first place.

The second situation in which the employer is entitled to the patent is that in which the invention is made in the course of duties by an employee who has a *'special obligation to further the interests of the employer's undertaking'*[14] by virtue of his or her duties and responsibilities. So, for example, the head of a company's R&D division would fit within this category; indeed, such a person may fall into both situations. The test in s. 39 is an objective one, but it has to be applied to the circumstances of the particular case and this includes the specific job that the employee was asked to do and the fact that it was this specific employee carrying them out. The question was therefore held to be whether *'an invention might reasonably be expected to result from the carrying out of his* [the appellant's] *duties'*.[15]

The first situation is well illustrated by the pre-1977 Act case of *Electrolux Ltd v. Hudson*.[16] The defendant was employed as a storeman by the plaintiffs, who were manufacturers of electrical goods. In the evenings, at home, the defendant and his wife amused themselves by considering possible inventions and, one night, devised a new kind of adaptor to facilitate more easily the connection of the dust bag to a vacuum cleaner. The plaintiffs claimed that they were entitled to this invention by reference to a very broad term in their contract of employment, which appeared to permit the employer to reap the benefits of all inventive activity. In striking down this clause as being too broad and thus in restraint of trade, Whitford J pointed out that Hudson earned a low salary (£1,302 per annum in 1971) and commented: *'It is not the sort of salary that is paid to a research worker. He was not employed to do research or to make inventions.'*[17] It would seem sensible, in the light of this, for employers in an appropriate case to stipulate that research and invention is part of the duties of a particular employee.

More problems have arisen in deciding just who comes into the other category of employees with a special obligation to the company. Clearly, directors and other senior managers who owe a fiduciary duty to the company must come within this category,[18] but precisely where the line is to be drawn is not an easy question. The courts have provided some guidance in *Harris' Patent*.[19] Harris was an employee of a company selling valves under licence from a Swiss firm. He was the manager of the sales department, which involved advising potential customers and also providing after-sales service. After learning that he was to be made redundant in five months' time, Harris designed a new valve, which was an improvement on the valves sold by his firm, and sought the grant of a patent for it. His employer claimed ownership of the patent, but was unsuccessful in

13 *Harris' Patent* [1985] RPC 19, *per* Falconer J at 28.
14 Patents Act 1977, s. 39(1)(b).
15 *LIFFE Administration & Management v. Pavel Pinkava* [2007] RPC 30 (CA).
16 [1977] FSR 312.
17 Ibid. at 323.
18 *Worthington Pumping Engine Co. v. Moore* (1903) 20 RPC 41.
19 [1985] RPC 19.

this argument. Falconer J found that Harris' normal duties did not include invention, but were concerned with sales and after-sales service, thus putting the case outside s. 39(1)(a). He had to be highly knowledgeable about valves and their use, but that is not the same as saying that he was under a duty to invent. An alternative argument based on his position within the company also failed: his title as a manager was not enough in itself, and examination of his powers and status in the firm—and especially the lack of discretion that he could exercise—showed that he did not owe a special obligation to the firm, and thus could retain the patent for his own benefit. This leaves open the question of where, above Harris' position as manager and below board level, the line will be drawn; the presence of a broad duty to the company over and above the day-to-day performance of the duties assigned to an employee seems necessary as an implication of *Harris*.

Harris was also referred to in the more recent case of *Staeng Ltd's Patents*,[20] in which an employee, whose primary role was in the field of marketing, was nevertheless expected to generate new ideas for new products as part of his job. This is sensible: marketing and product development are very closely related concepts and it is clear that a senior marketing executive will be expected to participate in product development activity. The senior status of the employee was also seen as relevant: as a senior executive, it was held that he had an obligation towards his employer's business and its development within the terms of s. 39(1)(b) of the Patents Act 1977.

The relationship between ordinary work and innovation remains less clear. In *Greater Glasgow Health Board's Application*,[21] a doctor employed by the Health Board had created a new type of ophthalmoscope on his own initiative and in his own time. The view was taken that the doctor's duty was to treat patients and, although the device in question would improve treatment and diagnosis, it was no part of his duties as an employee to invent such a device.

Compensation

If this appears to be harsh on employees whose vital inventions are promptly taken over by their employers, some relief is at hand in the form of the provisions that were new to the law in 1977, and which can be found in ss. 40 and 41 of the Patents Act. These entitle an employee to apply for an award of compensation by the employer if

> having regard among other things to the size and nature of the employer's undertaking, the invention or the patent for it (or the combination of both) is of outstanding benefit[22] to the employer...[23]

A similar provision applies in cases in which the employee has formally assigned the invention or the patent for it (or both)[24] to the employer for an inadequate sum,[25] although these rights do not exist if a collective agreement provides for the payment of compensation to employees,[26] as is quite common.

Under s. 41, the compensation payable by the employer should represent a fair share of the benefit to the employer of the invention, the patent, or an assignment thereof.[27]

---

[20] [1996] RPC 183.

[21] [1996] RPC 207.

[22] A new s. 43(5A), has been added by s. 10(7) of the Patents Act 2004, which limits the benefit by excluding any benefit derived from the invention after the patent has expired, been surrendered, or been revoked.

[23] Patents Act 1977, s. 40(1)(b).

[24] Patents Act 2004, s. 10(2).

[25] Patents Act 1977, s. 40(2).

[26] Ibid. (3).

[27] As amended by Patents Act 2004, s. 10(3).

The fairness of the share will depend on various factors established by s. 41(4) as including the nature of the employee's duties, pay, the effort and skill used, and the contribution of the employer and of other employees to the invention. It should also be noted that no contract term may diminish these rights[28] and that, for obvious reasons, they only apply to employees mainly employed in the UK.[29]

Before employees emboldened by these provisions rush out to buy a new Daimler or two, however, it is clear that this legislation is not designed to produce a bonanza of payments. Outstanding benefits to the employer are one of many obstacles placed in the way of an applicant and recent case law confirms that it will be an uphill struggle to take advantage of these provisions. All three reported cases on this area have resulted in failure by the plaintiff. In *GEC Avionics Ltd's Patent*,[30] the inventor of a new method of displaying information to the pilots of aircraft made a claim. This invention resulted in sales valued at US$72m, as well as other related contracts and the chance of further future sales. This was not regarded as outstanding in the context of the real profit being around US$10m and of that profit being part of the turnover of a major international firm regularly making multimillion-dollar deals. This also shows up the problem of assessing fair compensation: what is fair to the inventor, in relation to his or her salary, and to the employer, in relation to its (perhaps vast) turnover, will always be very different.

In *British Steel plc's Patent*,[31] the decision against the inventor is perhaps more understandable. The claim was made by the inventor of a new type of valve that would be of great value in controlling the flow of molten steel. The benefit was regarded as marginal: partly because the valve was only used in one steelworks; partly because the company had to spend much time and money perfecting the invention into a working product; partly because the size of British Steel meant that the proven benefits of the invention represented only 0.01 per cent of turnover and 0.08 per cent of profits. It was emphasized that the word 'outstanding' is a superlative and hard to prove, especially in the case of an application for payment that was made only seven months after the grant of the patent.

Both of these decisions were Patent Office hearings; a similar tale is told by the first case to reach the courts: *Memco-Med Ltd's Patent*.[32] The patent in this case was for a new door detector unit for passenger lifts and the applicant was a director of the company at the time of the invention. Aldous J found that the employee had the onus of proof in making the application; in this case, it was unclear even that there was a benefit created by the patent, because sales of the patented product were all to the Otis Co., with whom Memco-Med had a long-standing record of sales. Although the patented product was, in some years, responsible for 80 per cent of the sales of the company, there was no proof of the profitability of those sales and thus it was impossible to say that it was an outstanding benefit.

In themselves, these decisions are not too surprising. The claim in *Memco-Med* really came to grief for evidential reasons; in *British Steel*, the benefits of the invention appeared limited, and, in any event, the applicant had received an *ex gratia* payment at the time and had also been appointed a Member of the British Empire (MBE). But *GEC* is a reminder that almost anyone working in a large firm, in which it is reasonable to assume that the bulk of R&D work goes on, is going to find it next to impossible to make a successful claim under s. 40. This suggests, therefore, that the section was the product of the politics of gesture, rather than of substance.

---

[28] Patents Act 1977, s. 42.
[29] Ibid., s. 43.
[30] [1992] RPC 107.
[31] Ibid. at 117.
[32] [1992] RPC 403.

Grant and dealing

Let us assume that the requirements of patentability have been met and an appropriate patentee is in place. The Comptroller of Patents waves a magic wand and a patent comes into existence for a period of 20 years, normally from the date of filing the application.[33] The principal implication of this is that the patent—as well the related application—is deemed to be an item of personal property[34] and, subject to what follows, can be dealt with by its owner just like any other item of personal property.

In at least one respect, it is a somewhat odd example of personal property, because it may change its form: there is a process for the amendment of the specification even after grant[35] and this may be a useful way of pre-empting an attack on the validity of the patent. The owner of the patent may wish to deal with the valuable commodity that is his or her patent in various ways. He or she may wish to assign it to another—perhaps to someone better able than him or herself to exploit it commercially—and this is allowed by the 1977 Act, as long as the assignment is in writing and is signed by the parties to the transaction.[36] The drafting of such an assignment contract is of vital importance, especially when it comes to determining the ownership of future improvements to the invention and any rights in them.[37] Similarly, the owner of the patent may wish to use it as part of a mortgage transaction, perhaps to raise funds with which to develop the patent into a commercial success in his or her own right; this is permitted subject to the same conditions.[38]

All such transactions can, and should, be registered with the Patent Office, because registered transactions in relation to patents take priority over those that have not been registered.[39]

Licensing in UK law

The most likely form of dealing by the patentee is that he or she will seek to license out the patent by a formal agreement that allows another party to work the patent without fear of an infringement action. The virtue of this method of exploiting a patent is the flexibility that it allows: the patentee may not wish, or be able, to develop his or her invention into a perfected commercial product, for example, but by licensing it out to someone else, this can happen without the patentee losing control as would be the case in an assignment of the patent. The patent licensing agreement determines the precise extent of control retained. These agreements are documents that merit careful drafting, and are often extremely long and complex.

Another common reason for licensing is that it is easier, when developing the market for a product in another jurisdiction, to use a local firm—with its plant, distribution network, customers, and contacts—rather than to seek to create the entire necessary infrastructure to one's own account. Licensing of the product or process to a local firm is a sensible way of proceeding.

Another possible reason for using a licence is as part of a collaboration between two firms working in the same field, who may cross-license each other's patents.

[33] Patents Act 1977, s. 25(1).
[34] Ibid., s. 30(1).
[35] Ibid., s. 27.
[36] Ibid., s. 30(3) and (6).
[37] *Buchanan v. Alba Diagnostics Ltd* [2004] RPC 681 (HL).
[38] For an example, see *Buchanan*, ibid.
[39] Patents Act 1977, s. 33.

The alert reader may already have picked up on some of the major potential problems with licensing: cross-licensing between collaborators immediately evokes a picture of monopoly, while the creation of subsidiaries of other licensees in other jurisdictions reveals that this is an issue that may have international implications. Add to this the fact that many licences are exclusive licences—in other words, A only licenses B to work the patent in a given area—and it becomes clear that the creation of exclusive monopolies in an international setting is bound to attract the wrath of the European Union (EU), which is devoted to the pursuit of free trade and free competition throughout its member States.

It is this aspect that will form the major part of this section, but we will proceed by first looking at some of the different types of licence that exist.

Licences as of right

Section 46 of the Patents Act 1977 provides that the patentee may apply to the Patent Office to enter into the register of patents a statement that licences for a patent are available 'as of right'. But why should a patentee declare 'open house', and allow anyone to come in and work the patent? A typical reason would be if the patentee him or herself is unable to work up the invention into a viable product or process in the commercial marketplace, but is keen nonetheless that the patent should be exploited. Of course, the real likelihood of this occurring if the patent is truly of value is low, because, in such a case, an assignment or licensing agreement would already be likely to have been made. Thus those licences that are of right are rarely of the highest value.

A minor incentive to use the process is that patent renewal fees are halved if a licence as of right exists. The only other incentive is that the licensee has to agree terms—or have them imposed by the Comptroller in the event of a failure to agree—and this will give the patentee an opportunity to secure an appropriate fee or royalty for the licence; this will, in reality, only reflect the dubious value of a patent that is subject to this procedure.

Compulsory licences

Whereas the patentee initiates the demand for the licence as of right, it is the Patent Office itself that imposes the availability of compulsory licences. This seems totally contrary to the picture of the patentee's ownership of a piece of personal property: it is up to the owner to decide whether to use a bicycle or not—surely the same should apply to a patent? That this is not the case in relation to a patent relates to the interests of society, which, in this part of the law, are deemed to take priority over those of the patentee in certain limited circumstances.

Some examples of potential problems that can be resolved by compulsory licensing will be helpful before looking at the detailed legislation. If a monopoly represents power, and all power can be abused, while a company that has produced a new drug of great value is entitled to due reward, it might also seek artificially to push up the price by closely limiting the amount of the drug that is put on the market. Alternatively, the inadequacies of the patentee may mean that, having revealed the existence of a new process through the application process, he or she is unable to develop it properly him or herself and hence frustrates those of greater ability and/or resources. A new product might even be withheld from the market to protect pre-existing trade: the existence of, for example, a reusable condom or a light bulb of infinite duration might be concealed from the public by an established manufacturer who, having invented it, realizes that it will drastically restrict trade. (Of course, a sensible manufacturer would recognize the problem at an early stage and would not apply for the patent.) The legislation thus has to balance the interests of society and inventor.

Overall, a cautious approach is taken. After three years of a patent's life, application can be made for an individual licence, or a licence as of right, on various grounds.[40] At first, the 1977 Act stated that, if the patent is capable of being commercially worked in the UK, but is not, or is not fully, so worked, that could ground an application, as could the failure to meet the demand for a product on reasonable terms or by domestic production as opposed to imports. The failure to work an invention domestically and the use of imports instead is a further ground to the application, under the UK legislation, as is the refusal to grant a licence on reasonable terms, which refusal acts to the detriment of the export or domestic market, or the working of another related invention. The imposition of unreasonable conditions attached to licences is a final ground for objection. From 29 July 1999 onwards,[41] the relevant original text of s. 48 relating to these grounds for the grant of a compulsory licence became s. 48B and now applies only to those patents the proprietor of which is not a World Trade Organization (WTO) proprietor—that is, a proprietor who is not a national of, or domiciled in, a country that is a WTO member State, or who has no real and effective industrial or commercial establishment in such a country.[42]

This group of non-WTO proprietors is becoming increasingly narrow. In relation to patents the owner of which is a WTO proprietor, different grounds for the grant of a compulsory licence apply from 29 July 1999 onwards. A first ground is that, in the case of a product patent, the demand for the product in the UK has not been met on reasonable terms (in any way). Another ground is the refusal to grant a licence on reasonable terms as a result of which another important and valuable patent cannot be exploited, or which leads to the establishment and development of commercial or industrial activities being unfairly prejudiced. Finally, a compulsory licence can be granted if the patentee imposes conditions on the grant of a licence that are such that a form of unfair prejudice results.[43]

Even in the presence of any of these grounds, further restrictions apply to the grant of a compulsory licence. These restrictions reflect the provisions of the TRIPS Agreement on this point.[44] Prior to any grant, the applicant must, firstly, have made unsuccessful attempts to secure a normal licence on reasonable commercial terms and conditions. Secondly, any compulsory licence that is granted must be non-exclusive in nature, must be predominantly for the supply of the local UK market, must be limited in scope and duration to the purpose for which it was granted, and must be subject to the payment of an adequate remuneration to the patentee in the light of the economic value of the licence. A compulsory licence can also only be assigned in combination with the part of the business of the licensee that enjoys the use of the patent or in combination with the goodwill that relates to that part of the business.[45]

The grounds appear fairly wide and, as such, may be thought to permit frequent intervention against the interests of the inventor—but this impression would be misleading. The decision to grant a compulsory licence is entirely discretionary and s. 50 of the 1977 Act guides the exercise of that discretion. In relation to patents, the proprietor of which is a non-WTO proprietor, consideration must be given to the need to work inventions as much as possible, but only in so far as it is reasonably practicable to do so and also reflecting the need for the inventor to receive reasonable remuneration. In relation to all patents, regard should be had to the nature of the invention—some may take years to perfect in

[40] Ibid., s. 48(1) and (3). See the full analysis of this area in *Therma-Tru Corp's Patent* [1997] RPC 777.
[41] Patents and Trade Marks (World Trade Organization) Regulations 1999, SI 1999/1899, reg. 3.
[42] Patents Act 1977, s. 48(5).
[43] Ibid., s. 48A(1).
[44] TRIPS Agreement, Art. 31.
[45] Patents Act 1977, s. 48A(2)–(6).

the light of their complexity—and to the abilities and resources of the proposed licensee seeking to work the unworked invention.

The reality is that few people who go to all of the time and effort of obtaining a patent will then ignore it. Even if they do so, because of their own ignorance or lack of resources, the patent, if of value, is likely to be the subject of an assignment or licensing deal. If the difficulties of working a patent are genuine, it is not likely that an applicant can clearly show that his or her ability and resources will crack problems in relation to which the patentee has failed. Such relatively few cases that arise in the first place, in which someone might want to seek a compulsory licence, will then have to be decided against the broad discretion imposed by the law.

It may be thought that some aspects of this part of the law have a somewhat protectionist tone, but s. 53(5) of the 1977 Act makes clear that no order may be made contrary to international obligation, thus including the Treaty of Rome and the European Patent Convention. It was argued, in *Extrude Hone Corp's Patent*,[46] that to impose a compulsory licence in the UK was wrong, because demand was being met by imports from Ireland— but this argument was rejected on the grounds that the licence had not imposed a restriction on imports, but had, on the contrary, promoted free competition. Hoffmann J took a different view in *Research Corp's (Carboplatin) Patent*.[47] In this case, a licence of right had arisen under transitional provisions connected with the extension of the patent period from 16 to 20 years in the 1977 Act[48] and the licence was drafted in terms of preventing importation of carboplatin from outside the Community. Hoffmann J pointed out that it would not be possible to prevent imports from within the Community.[49] This does not, as such, contradict *Extrude Hone*, but it is a reminder of the single market in which we live.

Confirmation of this in the context of compulsory licences now comes from the European Court of Justice. In *Re Compulsory Patent Licences, EC Commission v. UK & Italy*,[50] the Commission objected to the original version of the text of s. 48 of the 1977 Act as permitting compulsory licences to be granted in the UK where provision of the product was taking place by importation from elsewhere in the EC, this being contrary to Art. 28 of the Treaty of Rome. The Court rejected the UK's arguments and found that s. 48 of the 1977 Act did run contrary to that Article. The threat of a compulsory licence was capable of hindering intra-Community trade by persuading the patentee to make its product in the UK, rather than in other member States;[51] the reduction in imports that would be consequent upon a licence being granted further contravened Art. 28[52] and thus the Court contradicted the *Extrude Hone* decision. It was therefore clear that any compulsory licence issued, in situations under which demand is met by imports from the EU, would be ineffective and, as was argued in the previous edition of this book, s. 48 of the 1977 Act should be amended to take this into account. Exercise of an invention anywhere in the EU, and not only domestically, was to be the test. The 1999 reforms do not refer to the EU, but all of its member States are also members of the WTO. The relevant section is, therefore, now s. 48A of the Patents Act 1977, and any reference to importation and local exploitation has disappeared from that section. The new section meets the requirements set out by the European Court of Justice.

---

[46] [1982] RPC 361.

[47] [1990] RPC 663.

[48] Patents Act 1977, Sch. 1, paras 3 and 4.

[49] [1990] RPC 663 at 694.

[50] [1993] RPC 283. If the importation is prohibited from outside the EU, there is no such restriction: see *Generics (UK) Ltd v. Smith Kline & French Laboratories (UK) Ltd* [1993] RPC 333.

[51] Ibid. at 328.

[52] Ibid. at 329.

A final point to note is that the terms of the compulsory licence will include appropriate compensation for the patentee, even if only the new s. 48A explicitly refers to this point; this will normally be on a royalty basis.[53] By way of general summary, then, it is clear that compulsory patent licensing is not the threat to the interests of patentees that it may at first appear to be: such licences are rarely sought, more rarely granted, and, in the future, will be even more rarely available after the decision of the European Court of Justice.

Crown rights

In one further respect, the patentee may find him or herself forced to share the benefits of the patent with another. Although it is not technically licensing, this is a convenient moment at which to consider the extent to which the Crown can intervene and exploit the patent itself. The fact that the Crown has any such rights is a useful reminder that the grant of a patent is—and has been since its earliest days—an act of the Crown; this area of the law is also significant in showing a very direct way in which the state, and thus society, can gain an undoubted advantage from inventive activity.

It is s. 55 of the 1977 Act that establishes the basic rights of the Crown in respect of patents. It empowers any government department, or person authorized thereby, to do various acts in relation to a patent without the consent of the owner, if acting for the services of the Crown. This latter aspect is interpreted broadly and includes the activities of health authorities.[54]

The acts that are authorized by the section include use or sale of either a product or a process, or the offer to another of an essential element of the invention with a view to putting the invention into effect. All of the actions listed by the section would normally count as infringements of the patent, but do not so count as a result of that section.

In so far as these provisions may be seen as draconian in their potential impact on patentees, this impression may be tempered by the obligation of the Crown to pay compensation to the patentee on either agreed, or court-imposed, terms in most instances.[55] This obligation does not arise in the cases of any invention tried or recorded by the Crown before the priority date of the invention and not as a result of information provided by the inventor. So if a private inventor and the Army are simultaneously working on the same invention, the private inventor could be forced to allow the Army to go ahead using the invention without the payment of any compensation. This is, however, clearly a narrow exception and, in the normal run of events, the inventor will receive compensation. Indeed, it is easy to envisage a situation in which the inventor will be happy for the Crown to intervene, because it will in effect guarantee that there is a market for the invention, thus removing many of the risks inherent in the decision to exploit an invention.

The provisions of s. 57 emphasize the priority enjoyed by the Crown and override third-party rights already created in respect of the patent, such as licences in favour of the Crown, although there is, again, provision for the payment of compensation to those affected.[56] During an official state of emergency, the powers of the Crown are increased by s. 59 of the 1977 Act and this allows the Crown to exercise its powers to use an invention for a range of reasons, from the efficient prosecution of a war, to the promotion of industrial productivity.

The Crown enjoys further privileges by virtue of s. 22 of the 1977 Act, under which any information in a patent application that may be prejudicial to the defence of the realm or

---

[53] *Smith Kline & French Laboratories Ltd's (Cimetidine) Patent* [1990] RPC 203, *per* Lloyd LJ at 245.
[54] *Dory v. Sheffield Health Authority* [1991] FSR 221.
[55] Patents Act 1977, s. 55(4).
[56] Patents Act 1977, s. 57A (added by the Copyright, Designs and Patents Act 1988, Sch. 5, para. 16(1)).

to the safety of the public may be prohibited from publication, or be restricted in terms of circulation. The practical effect of this is that any information in a patent application that is, for example, of military significance can be withheld from the documentation that is available to the public, but can still be disseminated to relevant official bodies.

The powers of the Crown in relation to patents are far-reaching, particularly when compared with the less draconian powers in most other jurisdictions. While it is true that due compensation is, in most cases, payable, this does not wholly meet the objection that the interests of the patentee are given short shrift across the many areas of activity in which the Crown may have an interest in the exploitation of an invention.

Exclusive licences

In many cases, the licensing of a patent will be on a basis of exclusivity. This is of benefit to the licensor, who will thus only have to make one agreement and deal with one partner, and it is of particular benefit to the licensee, who thus acquires the monopoly power inherent in the grant of a patent. The law reflects this reality by giving to the holder of an exclusive patent licence the same rights as the original patentee in relation to the bringing of infringement proceedings.[57]

As a consequence of the evident power that resides in an exclusive licence, controls have been placed on the contents of all licensing agreements, originally by s. 44 of the 1977 Act. These controls meant that any agreement tying further terms to the licence that obliged the licensee to acquire other things from the licensor, or which prevented the licensee from using the technology of others, would be void in respect of such terms. Any agreement of this type, which gave the licensee an alternative without such a tie and which was terminable on three months' written notice, was, however, acceptable.[58] That section was repealed by the Competition Act 1998—but instead of weakening the control exercised by competition law, this Act reinforced these controls and modelled them on the existing EU competition law framework.[59] Any EU block exemption, for example, will also be deemed to be applicable locally at the UK level.[60]

Indeed, the principal implication of the widespread use of exclusive licences is that their monopoly implications trigger off the interest of the EU. This is, therefore, an appropriate time to consider the range of issues that this invokes, not only in patent licences, but also across the board of intellectual property law, because its propensity towards monopoly clashes with basic principles of EU law.

Commercial exploitation in European law

We can see in the text of the chapters of this book that European intellectual property law has a great influence on the substantial provisions of that of the UK. This does not give us the complete picture, however, because the free movement and competition law provisions of the Treaty of Rome also exert influence[61]—and it is to this influence that we now turn.

---

[57] Patents Act 1977, s. 67.

[58] Ibid., s. 44(4).

[59] See Competition Act 1998, Pt I, Chs I and II.

[60] The rest of our analysis will focus on the relevant provisions of EU law. These now have mirroring provisions under the Competition Act 1998, but a full discussion of the latter would be duplication and is therefore not proposed.

[61] See, in general, A. Jones and B. Sufrin (2001) *EC Competition Law: Text, Cases and Materials*, Oxford: Oxford University Press, ch. 10.

The founding fathers of the EU clearly did not believe that intellectual property was very relevant for their purposes when they negotiated the Treaty of Rome. They therefore did not find it necessary to include a chapter on intellectual property in the Treaty of Rome and, during its first ten years, virtually no problem related to intellectual property arose. Indeed, the most important obstacles to the creation of the European Economic Community and, gradually, that of a single market were the existence of internal custom tariffs and quantitative restrictions on importations from other member States. The Treaty dutifully set out to remove these obstacles and it was only when a certain level of success had been achieved in this area that intellectual property became a problem.

In the absence of European intellectual property provisions, it was left to the member States to legislate in this area and to grant intellectual property rights on a national basis. But when they were no longer protected by custom tariffs or quantitative restrictions placed on foreign imports, certain competitors turned to intellectual property rights to protect their market share or the higher price that they could charge in the absence of competition. They tried to invoke infringement of their national intellectual property rights by the importation of the goods, or to use their intellectual property right to prevent competition. Infringement of a patent for a pharmaceutical product in member State A was, for example, invoked to prevent importation of the same drug from member State B—or one company might apply for parallel patents in all member States and use its one patent per member State to grant one exclusive licence for each, and to exclude all competition as a result. The Community felt that it had to react, to prevent the use of intellectual property rights to partition the market and to exclude competition. The European Court of Justice summarized the situation in *Parke, Davis v. Centrafarm*,[62] when it stated:

> The national rules relating to the protection of industrial property have not yet been unified within the Community. In the absence of such unification, the national character of the protection of industrial property and the variations between the different legislative systems on this subject are capable of creating obstacles both to the free movement of the patented products and to the competition within the Common Market.[63]

This absence of Community intellectual property provisions does not mean, however, that intellectual property law is not subject to the general provisions of the Treaty of Rome. The provisions on free movement and competition law apply to all areas, and, therefore, one has to start from the presumption that they also apply to intellectual property rights. Each of these provisions requires specific comments and we will consequently discuss them separately. For each, a patent-specific section will follow a general introduction— and it is self-evident that we will come back to these issues when discussing trade marks, copyright, and design.

Free movement of goods

The Treaty provisions
The general rule on the free movement of goods is found in Art. 28 of the Treaty, which sets out to eliminate all quantitative restrictions that hinder the free movement of goods by stating that '*Quantitative restrictions on imports and all measures having equivalent*

[62] Case 24/67 *Parke, Davis & Co v. Probel, Reese, Beintema-Interpharm & Centrafarm* [1968] ECR 55.
[63] Ibid. at 71.

effect shall be prohibited between member states'. This provision is qualified by the first sentence of Art. 30, which contains certain exceptions:

> The provisions of Articles 28 to 30 shall not preclude prohibitions or restrictions on imports, exports or goods in transit justified on the grounds of…the protection of industrial and commercial property.

At first sight, this would render Art. 28 inapplicable in relation to intellectual property—but this cannot be a correct conclusion, because the second sentence of Art. 30 limits the exception to the rule in Art. 28: *'Such prohibitions or restrictions shall not, however, constitute a means of arbitrary discrimination or a disguised restriction on trade between member states.'*

There must therefore be cases in which Art. 28 applies to intellectual property. Before we attempt to clarify this situation, two details need to be mentioned. Firstly, European law should not be interpreted in the same way as an English statute is interpreted. A teleological or purposive interpretation, rather than a purely literal interpretation, should be given to the provisions of the Treaty and it should therefore be specifically kept in mind that the free movement provisions had as their purpose the creation of a single market within the Community. On the issue of interpretation, it is also important to note that exceptions such as those contained in Art. 30 should be interpreted restrictively.[64]

Secondly, it has been suggested that Art. 295 of the Treaty plays, or should play, an important role in relation to intellectual property: *'This Treaty shall in no way prejudice the rules in member states governing the system of property ownership.'* If this really means that the Treaty of Rome does not interfere with intellectual property rights,[65] we can stop struggling with Arts 28 and 30—but this is clearly not the case. Article 30 would not provide for a partial exception for intellectual property rights if the Treaty were not applicable to them in the first place; additionally, Art. 295 is a final provision, rather than a principle, of the Treaty. The Treaty principles are contained in Arts 1–16 and have to be interpreted broadly, and the Articles implementing them—such as Art. 28—also have to be interpreted broadly. The final provisions in Arts 281–312, however, do not override the principles: that much is clear from their place in the structure of the Treaty and from their heading. Most importantly, Art. 295 has a very different purpose from that of Arts 28 and 30: it was derived from Art. 83 of the European Coal and Steel Community Treaty and both Articles have no purpose other than to emphasize the freedom of the member States to allow companies to be privately or publicly owned.[66] This detail was particularly important, because many governments wanted to preserve the possibility of nationalizing certain companies, even in a free competition European environment. It is thus impossible to interpret Art. 295 teleologically and arrive at the conclusion that it has no role whatsoever in relation to intellectual property, leaving only Arts 28 and 30 as the only relevant provisions of the Treaty.

Article 28 lays down the rule that quantitative restrictions are not acceptable. These are defined by the Court as *'measures which amount to a total or partial restraint of, according to the circumstances, imports, exports or goods in transit',*[67] but the text of Art. 28 makes

---

[64] See D. Pollard and M. Ross (1994) *European Community Law: Text and Materials*, London: Butterworths, pp. 218–19.

[65] Supported wrongly by C. Miller, *'Magill*: time to abandon the "specific subject-matter" concept' [1994] 10 EIPR 415 at 421.

[66] See C. Tritton, 'Articles 30 to 36 and intellectual property: is the jurisprudence of the ECJ now of an ideal standard?' [1994] 10 EIPR 422 at 423; and T. Vinje, *'Magill*: its impact on the information technology industry' [1992] 11 EIPR 397 at 398.

[67] Case 2/73 *Geddo v. Ente* [1974] ECR 865, [1974] 1 CMLR 13.

it clear that this does not necessarily have to be the aim of the measure. Measures that simply have the same effect are also struck down.

The effect of Art. 30 is to add a further requirement for measures relating to intellectual property and to raise the threshold in Art. 28 by requiring that the measure should amount to a means of arbitrary discrimination or a disguised restriction on trade between member States. Only measures that amount to a total or partial restraint of imports, exports, or goods in transit, and which also constitute a means of arbitrary discrimination or a disguised restriction of trade, will fall foul of the Treaty obligations. One should thus distinguish between intellectual property measures that are legitimate under the provisions of the Treaty and those measures that go too far, and fall foul of the threshold of Arts 28 and 30.

Further evaluation

This system provided by the Treaty is logical. The Treaty set out to create a single market based on free competition and, as we discussed in Section A of this book, intellectual property rights are justified as restrictions on competition in furtherance of competition in such a system, because competition takes place at more than one level and intellectual property rights, while restricting competition on one level, enhance competition on another level. Intellectual property rights have, as a result, a place in a European free single market, but only in so far as they fulfil this task. When they are abused to do more than that, they will lead to arbitrary discrimination or to disguised restrictions on trade between member States, and will fall foul of Arts 28 and 30.

It is clear therefore that, in such a system, the existence of intellectual property rights is a positive element,[68] but that the use that is made of them—that is, the way in which they are exercised—can either be lawful or can constitute an abuse. The European Court of Justice has summarized the position as follows:

> whilst the Treaty does not affect the existence of rights recognised by the legislation of a member state in matters of industrial and commercial property, yet the exercise of those rights may nevertheless, depending on the circumstances, be restricted by the prohibitions in the Treaty. Inasmuch as it provides an exception to one of the fundamental principles of the Common Market, Article [30] in fact admits exceptions to the free movement of goods only to the extent to which such exceptions are justified for the purposes of safeguarding the rights which constitute the specific subject-matter of that property.[69]

In the last sentence of this quotation, the Court hints at the tool that will be used to distinguish legitimate forms of exercising intellectual property rights from those that are abusive. We will have to define what is required for each intellectual property right in order for it to fulfil its task in a system of free competition: the Court calls this the 'specific subject-matter' of an intellectual property right. Once that is done, it will be possible to hold that any other use of an intellectual property right that goes further is an abuse, falling foul of Arts 28 and 30, because restrictions on competition through the use of intellectual property rights are only acceptable in so far as they are necessary to maintain an optimal level of competition within the various levels at which competition takes place.

Logically speaking, and subject to the analysis that will follow, such a specific subject matter will necessarily include the exclusive right to use, or exploit, the intellectual

---

[68] The Court explicitly stated that Arts 28 and 30 do not affect the existence of intellectual property rights, and leaves the determination of the existence of these rights to the member States in the absence of Community harmonization. See Case 35/87 *Thetford Corp. v. Fiamma SpA* [1990] Ch 339 [1989] 2 All ER 801.

[69] Case 119/75 *Terrapin (Overseas) Ltd v. Terranova Industria CA Kapferer* [1976] ECR 1039, [1976] 2 CMLR 482 at 1061 and 505.

property right and to oppose infringements. To hold otherwise would render the existence of intellectual property rights meaningless: a theoretical right that cannot be exercised would, indeed, be absurd. The exploitation of the right must allow the inventor or creator to be rewarded for his or her work and must stimulate him or her to go on inventing or creating. This is, however, only one essential element of the economic justification theory that is applicable to intellectual property in a free competition environment; the other essential element is the beneficial effect on society of making the invention or creation available. The European Court of Justice strikes the balance between the two elements by including, in the specific subject matter of each intellectual property right, that the right will be exhausted through first use by, or with, the consent of the right holder. This is often referred to as the 'exhaustion' doctrine.[70]

The Court also includes the 'essential function' of the intellectual property right in the definition of its specific subject matter,[71] because, from the point of view of the economic justification theory, the exercise of intellectual property rights is only tolerated in a free competition economic model to perform a specific function. In turn, the performance of that function is required to maintain an optimal level of competition in the various levels at which competition takes place. To use the patent law example, the essential function is to reward the inventor, because that is necessary to stimulate further inventions, and to create an adequate level of competition on the level of invention and innovation. The economic model on which the justification of patents is based would be distorted and the free competition market would no longer operate adequately if the essential function of patents were not to be fulfilled. We will further clarify these principles when applying them to patents.

A last general point relates, once more, to the teleological interpretation of the relevant Treaty provisions. The interpretation given above is only valid if the provisions are seen as a tool with which to reach the ultimate goal of the creation of the single market;[72] the Court may not interpret the same provisions in the same way in a context in which the goal of the creation of a single market is absent. This has its practical importance, because the literal text of Arts 28 and 30 is often included in treaties that the EU concludes with third-party countries. This situation arose in *Polydor v. Harlequin*[73] and, on that occasion, the Court did indeed refuse to interpret these provisions in the way it would have interpreted them in an intra-Community case. Particular caution has to be exercised in relation to the European Economic Area (EEA) Agreement,[74] because this includes the aim of the creation of a single market and, to a large extent, the interpretation that the Court gave to the relevant provision in intra-Community cases.[75]

It is submitted that the principle laid down in the *Polydor* case does not apply in relation to the EEA countries,[76] which appears now to have been confirmed by both Advocate General Jacobs and the European Court of Justice in *Silhouette v. Harlauer*.[77] The EEA Agreement has effectively made the full exhaustion doctrine applicable to the whole of the EEA.

---

[70] See, e.g., Case 15/74 *Centrafarm BV v. Sterling Drug Inc.* [1974] ECR 1147 at 1162.

[71] See, e.g., ibid.

[72] Case 270/80 *Polydor Ltd v. Harlequin Record Shops* [1982] ECR 329 at 349.

[73] Ibid., [1982] 1 CMLR 677.

[74] (1994) OJ L 1/3, in force since 1 January 1994 (1 May 1995 for Liechtenstein).

[75] See S. Von Lewinski, 'Copyright within the external relations of the European Union and the EFTA countries' [1994] 10 EIPR 429 at 433.

[76] The European Economic Area is comprised of the EU, Iceland, Liechtenstein, and Norway.

[77] Opinion of Advocate General Jacobs in Case C-355/96 *Silhouette International Schmied GmbH & Co. KG v. Hartlauer Handelsgesellschaft mbH* [1998] 2 CMLR 953, at [2] and [3].

Free movement of goods and patents

The starting point

Many of these criteria were laid down and applied in relation to patents in the *Centrafarm v. Sterling Drug* case.[78] This case involved a drug used for the treatment of urinary infections, for which Sterling Drug held parallel patents in the UK and the Netherlands. Due to the tight regulation of drug prices in the UK, the drug was sold there at approximately half the price at which it was sold in the Netherlands. Centrafarm specialized in the parallel import of drugs, and bought a large quantity of the drug in the UK and imported it into the Netherlands for resale purposes. Sterling Drug brought a case alleging infringement of its Dutch patent by the importation of the drug.

The European Court of Justice ruled that the essential function of a patent was '*to reward the creative effort of the inventor*'.[79] Although it can be argued that the patent system has many other functions—such as making the technological information available to the public—this must, indeed, be the essential one. Without reward, many inventors will, or will have to, stop their activity and their creative efforts must necessarily precede anything else, because without creation, there is no technological information to be passed on. With that essential function in mind, it was necessary to define the specific subject matter in such a way that that function was fulfilled by the patent system and an adequate level of competition was created on the innovation level, while not unduly compromising the adequate levels of competition on the other levels at which competition takes place.

The Court defined the specific subject matter of a patent as follows:

> the guarantee that the patentee, to reward the creative effort of the inventor, has the exclusive right to use an invention with a view to manufacturing industrial products and putting them into circulation for the first time, either directly or by the grant of licences to third parties as well as the right to oppose infringements.[80]

The patentee has the exclusive right to use the invention to manufacture industrial products and, obviously, he or she also has the right to oppose infringement. This is the hard core of the patent. If the function of it all is to reward the inventor, this has to be achieved through the commercial exploitation of the monopoly created by the exclusive right—that is, by allowing the patentee the exclusive right to put the product on the single market for the first time, because that will bring in the profit. But it was felt that this was sufficient to fulfil the function of rewarding the inventor and that allowing the inventor to control further transactions concerning the industrial product would unduly distort competition at other levels.

Sterling Drug had been rewarded when it got its profit when putting the drugs on the market in the UK; it was the only company that was allowed to use the patent to produce the drug and it could act against any infringing use of the patent. If it was allowed to interfere with the further commercial life of the drug, that would unduly distort competition. It would then be able to partition the single market by relying on its relevant national parallel patent in the importing country each time the drug was imported in another member State, '*where no such restriction was necessary to guarantee the essence of the exclusive rights flowing from the parallel patents*'.[81] Not only was this not necessary to reward the inventor; it went straight against the major aim of the Community. The Court

[78] Case 15/74 *Centrafarm BV v. Sterling Drug Inc.* [1974] ECR 1147, [1974] 2 CMLR 480.
[79] Ibid. at 1162.
[80] Ibid.
[81] Ibid. at 1163.

therefore limited the exploitation right that forms part of the specific subject matter to the first marketing of the drug and held that, by putting the drug on the single market for the first time, all rights under all parallel patents would be exhausted. By putting the drug on the single market through marketing it in the UK, Sterling had exhausted all of its rights under the parallel patents and could no longer use any right under its Dutch parallel patent to oppose the subsequent importation into the Netherlands of the drugs it had put on the market in the UK. It is also important to note that the essential function is an integral part of the specific subject matter, which stresses the fact that the specific subject matter is defined in such a way that the essential function will be fulfilled.

An important point is that the patentee can undertake the first exploitation him or herself or can grant a licence to a third party to undertake the first exploitation. The crucial element is that the first exploitation needs to be undertaken with the consent of the patentee.[82] The first exploitation will only lead to the exhaustion of the rights under all parallel patents if the patentee has consented to the first exploitation. This means, in practical terms, that a patentee will still be able to block the importation of goods by relying on the patent if these goods have been manufactured by a third party without the consent of the patentee. In such a situation, the third party is legally and economically independent, and owns the patent in the member States in which its manufacturing activities are based.

It is also important to clarify what are 'parallel patents'. As long as national patent legislation is not fully harmonized, it may lead to slightly different patents, because the claims are worded differently, for example. The European Court of Justice therefore adopted the only workable approach. All patents that protect the same invention are held to be parallel patents.[83]

On the basis of this analysis, the conclusion on the facts of *Centrafarm v. Sterling Drug* was that:

> the exercise, by a patentee, of the right which he enjoys under the legislation of a member state to prohibit the sale, in that State, of a product protected by the patent which has been marketed in another member state by the patentee or with his consent is incompatible with the rules of the EEC Treaty concerning the free movement of goods within the Common Market.[84]

Only those ways of exercising the patent right that stay within the specific subject matter of the right are compatible with the Treaty. Because the Treaty has an overriding effect on national law, the national provisions that allow more extensive use of the patent right can no longer be applied in a Community context.

Essential function and consent developed further

The Court had to analyse the essential function and consent ideas further in *Merck & Co. Inc. v. Stephar*.[85] This case again involved a patent for a drug, which, this time, was used to treat high blood pressure. Merck held patents relating to the drug in the Netherlands, while Stephar was importing the drug into the Netherlands from Italy. The interesting aspect of the case was the fact that, at the time, there was no patent protection for pharmaceutical products under Italian law. Merck had put the drug on the market in Italy, but argued that to hold that it had thereby exhausted its rights and could no longer rely on its Dutch patent would go against the essential function of the patent, because, due to

---

[82] Ibid. at 1162–3.
[83] Ibid. at 1163.
[84] Ibid.
[85] Case 187/80 *Merck & Co. Inc. v. Stephar BV* [1981] ECR 2063, [1981] 3 CMLR 463.

the impossibility of patenting the drug in Italy, the sale there had not taken place under monopolistic conditions, and thus the lower price and profit had not fully rewarded its creative efforts.

The Court rejected this interpretation. Firstly, no specific reward is guaranteed, because the exact amount of the reward depends, in all cases, on the market conditions. Secondly, if, in these circumstances, a choice to put the product on the market without the benefit of a patent is made, the inventor accepts the reward that the market will offer. This means that the essential function is fulfilled and that the specific subject matter will indicate the limit of the exercise of the patent rights. In other words, by marketing the drug in Italy, Merck had exhausted all rights under the existing parallel patents within the Community and the fact that no patent could exist in Italy did not influence that conclusion. It is up to the patentee to decide whether or not to market the product in a market within which a weaker form of protection, or no protection at all, is available. Needless to say, the conclusion would have been the same had Merck decided not to market the drug in Italy itself, but to have it marketed there with its consent by a third party.

The Court expressed the conclusion as follows:

> That the right of first placing a product on the market enables the inventor, by allowing him a monopoly in exploiting his product, to obtain the reward for his creative effort without, however, guaranteeing that he will obtain such a reward in all circumstances. It is for the proprietor of the patent to decide, in the light of all the circumstances, under what conditions he will market his product, including the possibility of marketing it in a member state where the law does not provide patent protection for the product in question. If he decides to do so he must accept the consequences of his choice as regards the free movement of the product within the Common Market, which is a fundamental principle forming part of the legal and economic circumstances which must be taken into account by the proprietor of the patent in determining the manner in which his exclusive right will be exercised.[86]

Merck had been rewarded for its creative activity and the patent rights had been exhausted by the marketing of the drug in Italy. It could not block the importation of the drug into the Netherlands by Stephar, because that exercise of the patent rights would go beyond the specific subject matter of the patent.

Recently, the Court was given an opportunity to overturn its *Merck v. Stephar* ruling in a case relating to the parallel importation of drugs from Spain and Portugal. Its judgment in *Merck v. Primecrown*[87] makes it clear, though, that *Merck v. Stephar* remains good law. The Court specifically rejected the argument that the manufacturers of a drug were under a moral obligation to market their products even in countries in relation to which no patent protection was available and any suggestion that this took away the free consent of the manufacturers to the marketing of the drugs was rejected.

Consent and elements of compulsion

The consent idea also needs to be applied to compulsory licence cases. The issue is, then, whether the exploitation and first marketing by the licensee amount to putting the product on the market for the first time with the consent of the patentee, and therefore exhaust the rights under all parallel patents.

---

[86] Ibid. at 2081–2.

[87] Joined Cases C-267/95 and 268/95 *Merck & Co. Inc., Merck Sharp & Dohme Ltd, Merck Sharp & Dohme International Services BV v. Primecrown Ltd, Ketan Himatlal Mehta, Necessity Supplies Ltd; Beecham Group plc v. Europharm of Worthing Ltd* [1996] ECR I-6285 and [1997] 1 CMLR 83; see P. Torremans and I. Stamatoudi, '*Merck v. Stephar* survives the test' (1997) 22 EL Rev 248; P. Torremans and I. Stamatoudi, '*Merck* is back to stay: the Court of Justice's judgment in *Merck v. Primecrown*' [1997] 9 EIPR 545.

This situation arose in *Pharmon BV v. Hoechst*.[88] Hoechst owned parallel patents in a drug in the UK, Germany, and the Netherlands, and a compulsory licence had been granted to a third party in the UK. The Court held that *'such a (compulsory licence) meas-ure deprives the patent proprietor of his right to determine freely the conditions under which he markets his products'*.[89] As a result, the product was not put on the market with the consent of the patentee in case this was done on the basis of a compulsory licence and the rights under all parallel patents were not exhausted. Hoechst could rely on the Dutch parallel patent to prevent importation into the Netherlands by Pharmon of the drugs it had bought in the UK from the licensee who had produced these under a compulsory licence.

Similarly, there was no consent in a case in which the patent holder took six weeks before bringing an infringement action after having been served with an *ex parte* injunc-tion that the defendant's product did not infringe. The six weeks' delay did not demon-strate consent.[90]

In *Merck v. Primecrown*,[91] the Court clarified the consent issue further by ruling that there is also no consent if the holder of a patent is under a genuine, existing legal obliga-tion to market its product, or to allow marketing by a third party under a compulsory licence. It is clear from the reasoning of the Court that such a legal obligation is highly unlikely to exist and that it will be difficult to prove. The presence of a legal obligation to market distinguishes the rule in *Pharmon v. Hoechst*[92] from that in *Merck v. Stephar*.[93] The two rules do not contradict each other.[94]

Articles 28 and 30 were subsequently raised on a couple of occasions in relation to compulsory licences and licences of right. Section 46 of the UK Patents Act 1977 allowed for licences of right as licences available upon application. As such, this does not create a problem, but the law clearly envisaged production only in the UK under such a licence of right. In case the holder of a licence of right imported the product from another member State, rather than produced it in the UK, an injunction could still be granted. This was exactly what Allen and Hanbury's were asking for when Generics intended to import the products for which it had obtained a licence of right from Italy, rather than produce them itself in the UK.[95] In that case, the European Court of Justice held that this was a restriction on the free movement of goods in the Community, because it blocked certain forms of importation from a member State and encouraged local production, rather than importation from within the single market. If all countries were to adopt this measure, national markets would, in the cases concerned, once again replace the single market. This measure amounted to an arbitrary discrimination under Art. 30 and could there-fore no longer be applied within the Community. Similarly, the provision in s. 48 of the Patents Act 1977 that allows for the grant of a compulsory licence if the patent is exploited by importing the products from another member State, rather than by producing the products in the UK, fell foul of Arts 28 and 30 because it is an arbitrary discrimination.[96]

---

[88] Case 19/84 *Pharmon BV v. Hoechst AG* [1985] ECR 2281.

[89] Ibid. at 2298.

[90] See the English case *Sandvik Aktiebolag v. K R Pfiffner (UK) Ltd* [2000] FSR 17.

[91] Joined Cases C-267/95 and 268/95 *Merck & Co. Inc., Merck Sharp & Dohme Ltd, Merck Sharp & Dohme International Services BV v. Primecrown Ltd, Ketan Himatlal Mehta, Necessity Supplies Ltd; Beecham Group plc v. Europharm of Worthing Ltd* [1996] ECR I-6285 and [1997] 1 CMLR 83.

[92] Case 19/84 *Pharmon v. Hoechst* [1985] ECR 2281.

[93] Case 187/80 *Merck & Co. Inc. v. Stephar* [1981] ECR 2063, [1981] 3 CMLR 463.

[94] See Joined Cases C-267/95 and 268/95 (see n. 91) at [40] and [41].

[95] Case 434/85 *Allen & Hanbury's Ltd v. Generics (UK) Ltd* [1988] ECR 1245, [1988] 1 CMLR 701.

[96] Joined Cases C-30/90 and C-235/89 *EC Commission v. UK; EC Commission v. Italy* [1992] ECR I-829, [1992] 2 CMLR 709.

It encouraged local production, rather than importation from within the single market, and therefore hindered the free movement of goods.[97] In neither of these cases were these provisions necessary to safeguard the specific subject matter of the patent.

It has also been argued that Art. 28 stands in the way of the requirement that local patent protection depends on the filing of a translation of the patent in the local language if the patent was originally filed and granted—for example, by the European Patent Office—in a foreign language. The European Court of Justice rejected this argument and upheld the provisions of national law that require the filing of a translation on sanction of the patent being declared void *ab initio*. The Court held that, even if, in certain circumstances, the translation requirement may have restrictive effects on the free movement of goods, these effects were too uncertain and too indirect to be considered an obstacle as referred to in Art. 28.[98]

Patents and competition law

Articles 81 and 82 of the Treaty of Rome deal with competition law, and neither of these Articles contains an exception for a specific area. Intellectual property must thus be subject to the EU rules on competition. We will first discuss the impact of Art. 81 on intellectual property and we will then turn our attention to Art. 82.

Article 81

Article 81 of the Treaty consists of three paragraphs:

(1) The following shall be prohibited as incompatible with the Common Market: all agreements between undertakings, decisions by associations of undertakings and concerted practices which may affect trade between member states and which have as their object or effect the prevention, restriction or distortion of competition within the Common Market, and in particular those which:

   (a) directly or indirectly fix purchase or selling prices or any other trading conditions;

   (b) limit or control production, markets, technical development, or investment;

   (c) share markets or sources of supply;

   (d) apply dissimilar conditions to equivalent transactions with other trading parties, thereby placing them at a competitive disadvantage;

   (e) make the conclusion of contracts subject to acceptance by the other parties of supplementary obligations which, by their nature or according to commercial usage, have no connection with the subject of such contracts.

(2) Any agreements or decisions prohibited pursuant to this Article shall be automatically void.

(3) The provisions of paragraph 1 may, however, be declared inapplicable in the case of:

   (a) any agreement or category of agreements between undertakings;

   (b) any decision or category of decisions by associations of undertakings;

   (c) any concerted practice or category of concerted practices;

---

[97] The provision can still be used if the patent is not exploited by local production and if the goods are instead imported from a non-member State, because, in these cases, the creation of a single market is not affected: see Case C-191/90 *Generics (UK) Ltd v. Smith Kline & French Laboratories Ltd* [1993] RPC 333.

[98] Case C-44/98 *BASF AG v. Präsident des Deutschen Patentamts* [1999] ECR I-6269.

which contributes to improving the production or distribution of goods or to promoting technical or economic progress, while allowing consumers a fair share of the resulting benefit, and which does not:

    (a) impose on the undertakings concerned restrictions which are not indispensable to the attainment of these objectives;

    (b) afford such undertakings the possibility of eliminating competition in respect of a substantial part of the products in question.

We shall start by analysing this provision briefly.[99] Article 81(1) outlaws a number of deals because they are anti-competitive, while Art. 81(2) sanctions that by declaring them void; Art. 81(3) contains an exception clause. When a number of requirements are met, a deal that would normally fall foul of Art. 81(1) will be exempted and neither that paragraph, nor Art. 81(2), will be applied to it.

So with which deals is Art. 81(1) concerned? The obvious category consists of the agreements concluded between undertakings. These will be affected if they have as their object, or simply as their effect, the prevention of competition, the restriction of competition, or the distortion of competition within the Common Market. This provision might easily be circumvented, however, if it were to stand on its own by avoiding a formal agreement. Competition could nevertheless be affected if the parties were to coordinate their actions and replace competition by coordination. The same effect might also be reached by replacing an agreement with a decision of an association of undertakings. The drafters of the Treaty avoided this risk, however, by including both concerted practices and decisions of associations of undertakings as separate categories that are covered by Art. 81. A last additional requirement is that trade between member States must be affected for Art. 81 to operate. Small deals that do not affect trade between member States are not important enough, because they will not have a substantial influence on competition at Community level. National competition authorities may nevertheless decide to pick up these deals and scrutinize them under national competition law.

When a deal is caught by Art. 81(1), the sanction provided by Art. 81(2) is that it is automatically void. No declaratory decision by a court or competition authority is necessary and, in law, we act as if the deal never existed. The deal will not bind anyone and no one will be able to rely upon it.

Exemptions that effectively place the deal outside the scope of Art. 81(1) can be granted under the authority of Art. 81(3) if four conditions—two that are positive and two that are negative—are met. These conditions are applied cumulatively—that is, all four need to be met at any one time. The anti-competitive deal must:

- provide a contribution to the improvement of the production or distribution of goods, or to promoting technical or economic progress;
- allow consumers a fair share of the resulting benefit;
- impose no restrictions that are not indispensable to the attainment of these objectives;
- allow no possibility of eliminating competition in respect of a substantial part of the products in question.

---

[99] For a full analysis from a competition law perspective, see R. Whish (1993) *Competition Law*, 3rd edn, London: Butterworths, ch. 7. For a recent application, see Case T-168/01 *GlaxoSmithKline Services v. EC Commission*, judgment of 27 September 2006 (at the time of writing, under appeal to the European Court of Justice as Case C-501/06P).

If these four requirements are met, an individual exemption can be granted. In practice, this is done by submitting the deal to the Commission, which implements and polices the Community's competition law, as an application for an individual exemption. This individual process is a fairly lengthy process and it causes a lack of legal certainty, because the parties to a deal do not know in advance which restrictive clauses will be acceptable to the Commission. In order to solve these problems and to avoid being unable to cope with a flood of applications, the Commission issues block exemptions, in the form of a Regulation containing lists of acceptable and non-acceptable clauses. Agreements that stay within the limits set out by the block exemption are automatically exempted and no further application or other procedure is required.

The next issue to address now that we know what Art. 81 is all about is whether agreements concerning intellectual property are caught by it. On the one hand, licence contracts, or eventually assignments, can restrict competition between the licensor and the licensee, or between licensees, to a considerable extent. Exclusive licences are prime examples of this. On the other hand, there is no provision in the Treaty that provides an exception for the intellectual property area. The conclusion must accordingly be that Art. 81 applies unreservedly to intellectual property agreements.[100]

Patent licences—general comments and individual exemptions

The Commission has applied Art. 81 to patent licence contracts on several occasions, and important guidance can also be derived from the *Windsurfing* case[101] and, on the point of exclusivity, from the *Maize Seeds* case.[102] Before we look at some clauses, some preliminary points need to be made. Article 81 does not apply to agreements of minor importance. The problem with this provision is that it is difficult to predict the success of certain licences and certain products, and so a licence agreement that is originally not covered may become such a success that it becomes important enough to be considered under that Article[103]—and this may have very undesirable consequences. Article 81 will also not apply if trade between member States is not affected.[104]

A normal exercise of the patent will not infringe Art. 81(1). Accordingly, the licensor may charge royalties[105] and may try to ensure that his or her licensee exploits the patent adequately. The latter element implies that minimum royalty clauses,[106] under which the licensee is obliged to pay a minimum amount in royalties even if the frequency of its use of the patented technology does not mathematically justify this, and clauses that require a licensee to produce minimum quantities of the patented product or to carry out a minimum number of operations using the patented process are acceptable, and do not restrict competition.[107] Clauses that go further than that, however, may restrict competition and have been held to infringe Art. 81(1): for example, clauses that require the licensee to pay royalties for non-patented products[108] and clauses that require the licensee to continue paying royalties after the patent has expired.[109] It is not, however, an infringement to

---

[100] See Cases 56 and 58/64 *Consten & Grundig v. EC Commission* [1966] ECR 299, [1966] CMLR 418; Case 24/67 *Parke, Davis & Co. Ltd v. Probel* [1968] ECR 55, [1968] CMLR 47.
[101] Case 193/83 *Windsurfing International Inc. v. EC Commission* [1986] ECR 611, [1986] 3 CMLR 489.
[102] Case 258/78 *LC Nungesser KG v. EC Commission* [1982] ECR 2015, [1983] 1 CMLR 278.
[103] *Burroughs/Deplanque* (1972) OJ L 13/50 and *Burroughs/Geha-Werke* (1972) OJ L 13/53.
[104] *Raymond/Nagoya* (1972) OJ L 143/39.
[105] Fourth Annual Report on Competition Policy, s. 20.
[106] See *AOIP/Beyrard* (1976) OJ L 6/8, in which such a clause was not condemned.
[107] See the old Patent Licence Block Exemption (1984) OJ L 219/15, Art. 2(1)(2).
[108] See *AOIP/Beyrard* (n. 106).
[109] Ibid.

require the licensee to keep paying royalties for know-how that the licensee continues to use after the patent has expired if that know-how is still secret and has not yet fallen in the public domain.[110]

The term of the licence agreement may be shorter than the remaining life of the patent,[111] but tie-up clauses,[112] which bind the licensee to the licensor once the patent has expired by obliging him or her to take out further licences for other technology, do infringe Art. 81(1). A licensor may also want to restrict the use that the licensee can make of the licensed technology to a certain field of application, particularly if the technology can be used in very different areas—such as, for example, a drug that can be used both in human and in veterinary medicine. These 'field of use' restrictions will fall outside Art. 81(1) if they restrict the use of the licensee to one or more specific and identifiable fields of application,[113] in line with the Commission's view that a clause prohibiting the licensee to compete with the licensor or with any connected undertakings in respect of research and development—that is, the so-called 'no competition' clause[114]—or a 'no challenge' clause,[115] which prevents the licensee—who is, in this respect, particularly well placed as user of the technology—from challenging the validity of the patent are, generally speaking,[116] bound to infringe Art. 81(1).

Clauses that equally infringe Art. 81(1) are exclusive grant-back clauses,[117] which oblige the licensee to grant an exclusive licence to the licensor in relation to all improvements of the technology, or to all new and related technology that it may develop, or, even worse, to assign these improvements or this technology outright to the licensor. This would deprive the licensee of any incentive to develop its own technology, which it will need to compete on the market and give the licensor an unwarranted permanent technological advantage. Only exclusive licences are banned; non-exclusive grant-back clauses are acceptable.[118]

The licensor has a legitimate interest in the protection of its brand image and the quality of the products. As a result, clauses requiring the licensee to promote the product, to label the product—but not non-patented items as well[119]—in a particular way and to comply with certain quality standards fall outside the scope of Art. 81(1).[120] A difficult borderline case is presented by a clause obliging a licensee to use the patentee's trade mark and get-up. This type of clause will make it difficult for the licensee to be identified as a separate entity and may make competition unworkable. It is only acceptable if it is combined with a right for the licensee to identify itself while using the patentee's trade mark and get-up.[121] The Commission's approach is that the latter clause may be caught, but may qualify for an exemption.

Tie-in clauses that, for example, oblige the licensee to buy raw materials from the licensor will only avoid being caught by Art. 81(1) if they are really indispensable for the

---

[110] *Kabel- und Metallwerke/Etablissements Luchaire SA* (1975) OJ L 222/34.

[111] Fourth Annual Report on Competition Policy, s. 29.

[112] See *AOIP/Beyrard* (1978) OJ L 6/8 and *Velcro/Aplix* [1989] 4 CMLR 157, OJ L 233/22.

[113] Fourth Annual Report on Competition Policy, s. 28.

[114] See n. 112.

[115] *Windsurfing International* (1983) OJ L 229/1 and on appeal from the Commission decision, Case 193/83 *Windsurfing International Inc. v. EC Commission* [1986] ECR 611, [1986] 3 CMLR 489.

[116] The conclusion may be different in exceptional circumstances: see Case 65/86 *Bayer AG & Maschinenfabriek Hennecke GmbH v. Sullhöfer* [1988] ECR 5249, [1990] 4 CMLR 182.

[117] See *Kabel- und Metallwerke/Etablissements Luchaire SA* (1975) OJ L 222/34; *AOIP/Beyrard* (1976) OJ L 6/8; *Velcro/Aplix* [1989] 4 CMLR 157, OJ L 233/22; *Roses* (1985) OJ L 369/9.

[118] *Re Davidson Rubber Co. Agreements* [1972] CMLR D52, OJ L 143/31.

[119] Case 193/83 *Windsurfing International Inc. v. Commission* (see n. 115).

[120] See the old Patent Licence Block Exemption (see n. 107), Arts 2(6) and 2(9).

[121] Ibid., Art. 1(1)(7).

successful exploitation of the patent.[122] Any other tie-in clause will not even be granted an exemption, because this is a perfect tool with which to control the price at which the licensee can sell and thus restrict competition.[123] Customer allocation clauses,[124] export bans,[125] vertical price fixing,[126] and obligations only to sell the patented product as part of a package[127] will also be caught by Art. 81(1).

A number of other clauses are, on the other hand, considered to fall outside the scope of Art. 81(1). Examples of these clauses are obligations of secrecy,[128] 'most-favoured licensee' clauses,[129] obligations to prevent infringement of the patent,[130] and restrictions on the assignment and the sub-licensing by the licensee.[131]

Exclusivity is the most difficult issue, because it can be used easily to stop intra-brand competition between the licensor and the licensee, and between the various licensees; it can also lead to a compartmentalization of the market. The bottom line of the debate is that the European Commission and the European Court of Justice will never tolerate absolute closed exclusivity, which would oblige the licensor and the licensee not to compete, through an active or even through a passive sales policy, in each other's area and this in combination with a similar obligation between licensees, coupled with an obligation not to deal with parallel importers.[132]

All other forms of exclusivity also fall within the scope of Art. 81(1), but may be exempted.[133] The Community is particularly keen to keep the parallel import option open, and normally requires the licensee to be free to have a passive sales policy in the territories of the licensor and other licensees. The latter means, in practice, that the licensee, while based in its own territory, can respond to unsolicited orders from these territories. In circumstances under which the licensee would not have been prepared to take the risk of taking out a licence and incurring expense in producing the patented goods if it were not given some protection against intra-brand competition at the production level in the allocated territory, an open exclusive licence exceptionally does not infringe Art. 81(1).[134] In practice, this means that no one else will be allowed to work the patent in the allocated territory, while leaving unaffected the parallel import route, whereby an importer buys the patented goods from the licensor or another licensee to import them into the allocated territory.[135] The Commission has, however, interpreted this exception restrictively.[136]

---

[122] Ibid., Art. 2(1)(1).

[123] See *Vaessen/Moris* (1979) OJ L19/32.

[124] See the old Patent Licence Block Exemption (see n. 107), Art. 3(7).

[125] *AOIP/Beyrard* (1976) OJ L 6/8; *Velcro/Aplix* [1989] 4 CMLR 157, OJ L 233/22.

[126] See the old Patent Licence Block Exemption (see n. 107), Art. 3(6).

[127] See Case 193/83 *Windsurfing International Inc. v. EC Commission* [1986] ECR 611, [1986] 3 CMLR 489, in which the Court upheld the Commission's objections against the obligation to sell the patented rig only as part of a complete sailboard.

[128] See the old Patent Licence Block Exemption (see n. 107), Art. 2(1)(7).

[129] Ibid., Art. 2(1)(11).

[130] Ibid., Art. 2(1)(8).

[131] Ibid., Art. 2(1)(5).

[132] Case 258/78 *LC Nungesser KG v. EC Commission* [1982] ECR 2015, [1983] 1 CMLR 278.

[133] See *AOIP/Beyrard* (1976) OJ L 6/8.

[134] Case 258/78 *LC Nungesser KG v. EC Commission* [1982] ECR 2015, [1983] 1 CMLR 278.

[135] See D. Hoffmann and O. O'Farrell, 'The "open exclusive licence": scope and consequences' [1984] 4 EIPR 104.

[136] See *Velcro/Aplix* [1989] 4 CMLR 157, OJ L 233/22; *Tetra Pak I* (1988) OJ L 272/27 (upheld on appeal: Case T-51/89 *Tetra Pak Rausing SA v. Commission* [1990] ECR II-309, [1991] 4 CMLR 334); *Delta Chemie/ DDD* [1989] 4 CMLR 157, OJ L 309/34; but see also Case 27/87 *Erauw-Jacquery SPrl v. La Hesbignonne Société* [1988] ECR 1919, [1988] 4 CMLR 576.

The patent licence block exemption[137]

As we discussed earlier, the Commission has not restricted itself to granting individual exemptions; it has also drafted block exemptions. The patent licence block exemption was issued in 1984, entered into force in 1985 and was bound to expire on 31 December 1994, but its life was extended until 30 June 1995.[138] It applied to patent licences, and to combined patent and know-how licences, as long as only two undertakings were parties to such an agreement.[139] Patent pool agreements and, to a more limited extent after the 1993 amendments, licence agreements between partners in a joint venture were excluded from its scope, as were reciprocal licence agreements.[140]

The block exemption introduced a standard format. Article 1 contained a list of clauses that did not come within the scope of Art. 81(1) of the Treaty of Rome altogether, while exemption Art. 2 contained a list of clauses that were exempted in case they came within the scope of Treaty Art. 81(1). These permitted clauses were called the 'white list'. Finally, Art. 3 of the patent licence block exemption contained a list of clauses that were not exempted and the presence of one of these clauses in a licence agreement meant that it could not benefit from the block exemption.

The know-how block exemption[141]

The know-how block exemption was issued in 1988, came into force in 1989, and would normally have been in force until the very end of the century.[142] In both form and substance, it was clearly modelled on the patent licence block exemption and we will therefore only highlight some differences.

The exemption covered know-how agreements and mixed know-how patent agreements, and thus a choice between two block exemptions was offered for the latter category.[143] It required 'know-how' to be a body of technical information that is secret, substantial, and identified in any appropriate form.[144] The most obvious example is the know-how that goes with the patent: all that is explained in the patent application is the invention itself. There is, of course, a most appropriate way to exploit the invention and the patent holder often keeps that knowledge secret. That body of technical information is quite substantial, and can be identified and separated from other general knowledge.

The general impression was that the know-how block exemption was slightly more flexible and that it was more advantageous to the licensor.

The first technology transfer block exemption[145]

Rather than replace the old patent licence block exemption with a new one, the Commission preferred, at the time, to repeal the know-how licence block exemption and to replace

---

[137] Commission Regulation 2349/84 of 23 July 1984 on the application of Art. 85(3) of the Treaty to certain categories of patent licensing agreements (1984) OJ L 219/15, as amended by (1985) OJ L 113/34 and (1993) OJ L 21/8; see V. Korah (1985) *Patent Licensing and EEC Competition Rules: Regulation 2349/84 ESC*, Oxford: ESC.

[138] Article 14.

[139] Article 1(1).

[140] Article 5.

[141] Commission Regulation 556/89 of 30 November 1988 on the application of Art. 85(3) of the Treaty to certain categories of know-how licensing agreements (1989) OJ L 61/1, as amended by (1993) OJ L 21/8; see Korah (1985).

[142] Article 12.

[143] Article 1(1).

[144] Article 7(1)–(4).

[145] Commission Regulation (EEC) 240/96 on the application of Art. 85(3) to certain categories of technology transfer agreements (1996) OJ L 31/2.

both block exemptions at the same time. The technology transfer block exemption[146] that took over covered all patent licences, know-how licences, and mixed patent and know-how licences to which there are only two parties.[147] As with its predecessors, the block exemption did not cover reciprocal licences, patent or know-how pools, and most licences between competing undertakings in the context of a joint venture.[148] In case other intellectual property rights were involved, the block exemption would only operate as long as these other intellectual property rights were ancillary.[149]

The technology transfer block exemption entered into force on 1 April 1996 and was to remain in force for a period of ten years.[150]

The second technology transfer block exemption[151]

Five years into the life of the first technology transfer block exemption, the Commission published an evaluation report and the public debate that followed resulted in the early withdrawal of the first technology transfer block exemption.[152] It was replaced, from 1 May 2004 onwards, by a new technology transfer block exemption.[153] The new block exemption adopts a radically different format and moves away from the lists of permitted or non-permitted clauses, towards a more economics-based approach.

The block exemption applies to technology transfer agreements, but the term 'agreement' is defined widely and includes decisions of an association of undertakings, along with concerted practices.[154] The concept of a technology transfer agreement that is used is also wider than ever before: software copyright licensing agreements have now been included, along with mixed patent, know-how, and software copyright licensing agreements, and any such agreements that include the sale and purchase of products, or which relate to the licensing of other intellectual property rights if those additional provisions do not constitute the primary object of the agreement and if they are directly related to the production of the contract products. Even assignments of patents, know-how, software copyright or a combination thereof are included in the scope of application of the block exemption, in so far as a part of the risk of the economic exploitation of the technology remains with the assignor. This is, for example, the case when part of the sum payable to the assignor in consideration of the assignment is dependent on the turnover achieved by the assignee in exploiting the technology.[155]

Article 2 of the block exemption contains its main principle. Transfer of technology agreements between two undertakings permitting the production of contract products are, in application of Treaty Art. 81(3), exempted from the application of Treaty Art. 81(1) in so far as any of their provisions fall within the scope of the latter Article. Two restrictions are to be noted immediately: firstly, the block exemption only exempts agreements

---

[146] See A. Robertson, 'Technology transfer agreements: an overview of how Regulation 240/96 changes the law' [1996] 3 ECLR 157; C. Kerse, 'Block exemptions under Article 85(3): the Technology Transfer Regulation—procedural issues' [1996] 6 ECLR 331.

[147] Article 1(1).

[148] Article 5(1).

[149] Article 5(1)(4).

[150] Article 13.

[151] Commission Regulation (EC) 772/2004 on the application of Art. 81(3) to certain categories of technology transfer agreements (2004) OJ L 123/11.

[152] Regulation 772/2004, reg. 9.

[153] This new block exemption will also remain in force for ten years. Agreements that were covered by the first TOT block exemption and that would not be covered by the exemption in the new TOT block exemption remained exempted until 31 March 2006 according to Regulation 772/2004, reg. 10.

[154] Regulation 772/2004, reg. 1(a).

[155] Ibid., reg. 1(b).

between two undertakings—agreements between more than two undertakings fall outside the scope of the block exemption and will require an individual exemption; secondly,
the exemption will only apply for as long as the intellectual property right in the licensed
technology has not expired, lapsed, or been declared invalid. In the case of know-how, the
exemption only applies for as long as the know-how remains secret, but the exemption
will continue to apply for the duration of the agreement if the know-how becomes known
as a result of an action by the licensee.

One of the main innovations in the new block exemption is the fact that the exemption provided for in its Art. 2 is linked to market share thresholds.[156] In this respect,
a distinction needs to be made between competing and non-competing undertakings.
Competing undertakings are undertakings that, in relation to the relevant technology
or on the relevant product market, license out competing technologies that are regarded
as interchangeable with, or substitutable for, the licensed technology by the licensees,
or that are active on the relevant product and geographic markets in which the contract
products are sold (or which might, realistically, be expected to undertake the necessary investment to enter that market). The relevant product market includes products
that are regarded as interchangeable with, or substitutable for, the contract products by
buyers.[157]

In case the undertakings that are party to the agreement are competing undertakings, the exemption will only apply on condition that their combined market share on
the affected relevant technology and product market does not exceed 20 per cent.[158] In
case the undertakings that are party to the agreement are *not* competing undertakings,
the exemption will only apply on condition that the market share of each of the parties
does not exceed 30 per cent in relation to the affected relevant technology and product
market.[159]

The market share of a party on the relevant technology market is determined in terms
of the presence of the licensed technology on the relevant product market; the licensor's
market share on the relevant market for the contract products is deemed to include both
the licensor's market share and that of its licensees.[160] The main problems with market
shares are, on the one hand, the way in which they are to be calculated and, on the other,
the fact that they vary—that is, that companies may meet the requirements set out in
Art. 3 of the exemption at the conclusion of their agreement, but they may exceed the
permitted market share levels at a later date.

The block exemption deals with these problems in Art. 8. The basis for the calculation
of market shares will be market sales value data and only if these are not available can
estimates based on other reliable market information be used. The data used will refer to
the preceding calendar year.[161] In case the market share goes above the 20 per cent threshold, the exemption will continue to apply for another two calendar years following that in
which the 20 per cent threshold was first exceeded. In relation to the 30 per cent threshold,
that extension will last for three calendar years.[162]

It is, however, self-evident that the market share mechanism is not sufficient to weed
out any agreement that may seriously harm levels of competition. The block exemption
therefore rules out its own application to agreements that have certain undesirable objects.
Once more, a distinction is made between agreements between competing undertakings
and agreements between not competing undertakings.[163]

---

[156] Ibid., reg. 3.   [157] Ibid., reg. 1(j).
[158] Ibid., reg. 3(1).   [159] Ibid., reg. 3(2).
[160] Ibid., reg. 3(3).   [161] Ibid., reg. 8(1).
[162] Ibid., reg. 8(2).   [163] Ibid., reg. 4.

Let us deal with agreements between competing undertakings first. The exemption does not apply to agreements between competing undertakings that have either directly, or indirectly, in isolation from, or in combination with, other factors under the control of the parties, one of the following four goals as their object.

1. An agreement should not have as its object the restriction of a party's ability to determine its prices when selling products to third parties.[164]

2. An agreement cannot, in principle, have as its object the limitation of output. It is, however, acceptable to set limitations on the output of contract products by the licensee in non-reciprocal agreements or to impose limitations on one of the licensees in reciprocal agreements.[165]

3. An agreement cannot, in principle, have the allocation of markets or customers as its object.[166] This exclusion, in principle, is, however, subject to seven exceptions. Field of use restrictions can be imposed on the licensee, as can a restriction to one or more product markets.[167] In non-reciprocal agreements, such field of use restrictions can be imposed on both licensor and licensee, and restrictions can also be placed on either party in terms of product markets or in terms of territories exclusively reserved for the other party.[168] The licence can also be exclusive in nature—that is, the licensor can agree not to appoint another licensee in a particular territory.[169] Similarly, in a non-reciprocal agreement, the licensor and/or the licensee can agree not to engage in active and/or passive sales into the exclusive territory, or to the exclusive customer group reserved to the other party.[170] And again, in a non-reciprocal agreement, active sales by the licensee into the exclusive territory or to the exclusive customer group allocated by the licensor to another licensee can also be ruled out on the condition that the other licensee was not a competing undertaking of the licensor at the time of the conclusion of its own licence.[171] Any licensee can also be obliged only to produce the contract products for its own use, as long as the licensee is not restricted in selling the contract goods actively or passively as spare parts for its own products.[172] The final exception allows the imposition on the licensee in a non-reciprocal agreement of an obligation to produce the contract goods only for a particular customer in cases in which the licence was granted in order to create an alternative source of supply for that customer.[173]

4. An agreement should not have as its object the restriction of the licensee's ability to exploit its own technology or the restriction of the ability of any of the parties to carry out research and development activities, unless that restriction is necessary to prevent the disclosure of licensed know-how to third parties.[174]

We now turn to agreements between non-competing parties. The exemption does not apply to agreements between non-competing undertakings that have either directly, or

---

[164] Ibid., reg. 4(1)(a).
[165] Ibid., reg. 4(1)(b). The terms reciprocal and non-reciprocal agreements are defined in reg. 1(c) and (d), respectively.
[166] Ibid., reg. 4(1)(c).
[167] Ibid., reg. 4(1)(c)(i).
[168] Ibid., reg. 4(1)(c)(ii).
[169] Ibid., reg. 4(1)(c)(iii).
[170] Ibid., reg. 4(1)(c)(iv).
[171] Ibid., reg. 4(1)(c)(v).
[172] Ibid., reg. 4(1)(c)(vi).
[173] Ibid., reg. 4(1)(c)(vii).
[174] Ibid., reg. 4(1)(d).

indirectly, in isolation from, or in combination with, other factors under the control of the parties one of the following three goals as their object.[175]

1. Such an agreement should not have as its object the restriction of the ability of any party to determine its own prices when selling to third parties. It is, however, permitted to set a maximum or a recommended sale price as long as, in practice, this does not amount to a fixed or minimum sale price.[176]

2. There should not be a restriction on the territory into which, or the customers to whom, the licensee may passively sell the contract products. This restriction is, however, subject to six exceptions. A territory or customer group can be reserved exclusively for the licensor[177] and the same can be done for a licensee for the first two years during which that licensee is selling the contract products in a territory or to a customer group.[178] Any licensee can also be obliged only to produce the contract products for its own use, as long as the licensee is not restricted in selling the contract goods actively or passively as spare parts for its own products.[179] Another exception allows the imposition on the licensee in a non-reciprocal agreement of an obligation to produce the contract goods only for a particular customer in cases in which the licence was granted in order to create an alternative source of supply for that customer.[180] A licensee that operates at wholesale level can be restricted from selling to end-users[181] and the final exception allows a restriction on sales to unauthorized distributors by members of an exclusive distribution system.[182]

3. A licensee that is a member of a selective distribution system and that operates at retail level should not be restricted in terms of active or passive sales to end-users, without prejudice to the possibility of prohibiting a member of such a system from operating out of an unauthorized place of establishment.[183]

Finally, the rules for non-competing undertakings will continue to apply on this point for the life of the agreement if those undertakings become competing undertakings at a later stage, unless the agreement is amended in any material aspect.[184]

Up to now, we have dealt with restrictions that exclude an agreement altogether from the scope of the block exemption. Now we turn to restrictions that are, themselves, not covered by the exemption, but the presence of which does not take the whole agreement outside the scope of the block exemption. According to Art. 5 of the exemption, it does not apply to the following obligations in technology transfer agreements:

(a) any direct or indirect obligation on the licensee to grant an exclusive licence to the licensor or to a third party designated by the licensor in respect of its own severable improvements to or its own new applications of the licensed technology;

(b) any direct or indirect obligation on the licensee to assign, in whole or in part, to the licensor or to a third party designated by the licensor, rights to its own severable improvements to or its own new applications of the licensed technology;

(c) any direct or indirect obligation on the licensee not to challenge the validity of intellectual property rights which the licensor holds in the Common Market, without prejudice to the possibility of providing for termination of the technology transfer

---

[175] Ibid., reg. 4(2).
[176] Ibid., reg. 4(2)(a).
[177] Ibid., reg. 4(2)(b)(i).
[178] Ibid., reg. 4(2)(b)(ii).
[179] Ibid., reg. 4(2)(b)(iii).
[180] Ibid., reg. 4(2)(b)(iv).
[181] Ibid., reg. 4(2)(b)(v).
[182] Ibid., reg. 4(2)(b)(vi).
[183] Ibid., reg. 4(2)(c).
[184] Ibid., reg. 4(3).

agreement in the event that the licensee challenges the validity of one or more of the licensed intellectual property rights.[185]

In addition:

> Where the undertakings party to the agreement are not competing undertakings, the exemption provided for in Article 2 shall not apply to any direct or indirect obligation limiting the licensee's ability to exploit its own technology or limiting the ability of any of the parties to the agreement to carry out research and development, unless such latter restriction is indispensable to prevent the disclosure of the licensed know-how to third parties.[186]

The block exemption contains two emergency measures to balance the increased flexibility it offers to undertakings. Indeed, the Commission, firstly, reserves for itself the right to withdraw any exemption granted under the terms of the block exemption if it thinks that an agreement nevertheless has, or has started to have, certain effects that are incompatible with the requirements of Art. 81(3) of the Treaty of Rome.[187] National competition authorities can do the same in respect of a member State, if the effects are limited to the market of that member State.[188]

The block exemption gives three examples of circumstances that may prompt a withdrawal of its benefit. These circumstances will arise if access of third parties' technologies to the market is restricted, if access of potential licensees to the market is restricted, or if, without any objectively valid reason, the parties do not exploit the licensed technology.[189]

Secondly, the Commission may declare, by Regulation, that the block exemption does not apply to certain agreements if parallel networks of similar technology transfer agreements cover more than 50 per cent of a relevant market. Such a Regulation will, at the earliest, come into force six months after being adopted.[190]

It remains to be seen whether this new block exemption, with its radically new approach, will work effectively in practice. In drafting it, the Commission has at least attempted to address the concerns raised by those involved in the licensing business, whie at the same time addressing its competition concerns.

Article 82

Article 82 of the Treaty of Rome prohibits the abuse of a dominant position. We will first examine what constitutes a dominant position for the purposes of the Treaty, but i would lead us too far to discuss all of the issues related to the technical application of Art. 82 in detail and we will need to restrict our comments to a couple of essential points.[191]

'Dominance', then, should not exist in an abstract way, but in the context of a market, and three aspects are important: a position needs to be dominant in the relevant product market, it needs to be dominant in the relevant geographical market, and the market is also restricted in time when considering the issue of dominance. The determination of the relevant product market raises issues such as the interchangeability and substitutability of products, while, in many cases, the relevant geographical and temporal markets are more obvious to determine. Once a dominant position has been established,

---

[185] Ibid., reg. 5(1).
[186] Ibid., reg. 5(2).
[187] Ibid., reg. 6(1).
[188] Ibid., reg. 6(2).
[189] Ibid., reg. 6(1).
[190] Ibid., reg. 7.
[191] For more details, see Whish (1993) ch. 8.

Art. 82 requires that that dominant position be held in a substantial part of the Common Market.[192]

But dominance, as such, is not sufficient for the purposes of Art. 82, because there also needs to be an abuse of that dominant position. Article 82 does not contain an exhaustive list of what would amount to an 'abuse', but it offers as obvious examples the charging of unfair prices, the limiting of production, and discrimination. We will have to discuss the case law in detail to discover what may amount to an abuse of a dominant position in the context of intellectual property: while it is clear that monopoly rights, such as intellectual property rights, can lead to a dominant position, an abuse of a dominant position involves a certain action and a certain use of rights. It is therefore correct to assume that, as in relation to the free movement of goods, the existence of intellectual property rights as such cannot amount to an abuse of a dominant position[193] and neither can certain uses of these rights. We will have to focus our attention on what constitutes an abusive use or exercise of an intellectual property right.

As with the free movement of goods, the existence and the normal use of intellectual property rights will not be affected, because only the abusive use of intellectual property rights for a purpose that is unrelated to intellectual property—namely, the distortion of competition and the distortion of the free movement of goods—will be targeted by the Treaty provisions. In fact, many of these elements transpire already from one of the earliest intellectual property judgments of the European Court of Justice.

The Court indicated, for the first time, that Art. 82 could interfere with intellectual property rights in its *Parke, Davis* judgment of 1968,[194] when it ruled that the existence of the intellectual property rights granted by a member State is not affected by the prohibition contained in Art. 82 of the EC Treaty and that, in the absence of any abuse of a dominant position, the exercise of such rights cannot of itself fall under that Article:

> Although a patent confers on its holder a special protection within the framework of a State, it does not follow that the exercise of the rights so conferred implies the existence of the three elements mentioned (the existence of a dominant position on the single market or on a substantial part thereof, abuse of that dominant position and a negative effect on trade between member states). It could only do so if the utilisation of the patent could degenerate into an improper exploitation of the protection.[195]

In this first case, the Court found that a higher sale price for the patented product, as compared with that of the unpatented product coming from another member State, does not necessarily constitute an abuse of a dominant position. The possibility of asking a higher price for the product as a result of the patent protection was seen as being the normal result of the existence of that patent protection and, even if—in this first case—no abuse of a dominant position was found, it opened the way for a series of other cases.

A last important preliminary point in relation to Art. 82 is that it will only apply if there is an effect on interstate trade.[196] The Court has held that this requirement will be satisfied

---

[192] Ibid.

[193] See Case 238/87 *Volvo (AB) v. Erik Veng (UK) Ltd* [1988] ECR 6211 at [8], [1989] 4 CMLR 122.

[194] Case 24/67 *Parke, Davis & Co. v. Probel, Reese, Beintema-Interpharm & Centrapharm* [1968] ECR 55, [1968] CMLR 47.

[195] Ibid. at [1968] ECR 72; in relation to copyright, see Case 78/70 *Deutsche Grammophon GmbH v. Metro-SB-Grossmarkte GmbH & Co. KG* [1971] ECR 487, [1971] CMLR 631; in relation to trade marks, see Case 51/75 *EMI Records Ltd v. CBS United Kingdom Ltd* [1976] ECR 811, [1976] 2 CMLR 235.

[196] See Whish (1993) ch. 8.

if conduct brought about an alteration in the structure of competition in the Common Market.[197]

Article 82 applied to patents

So far, only one case[198]—and a rather peculiar case, at that—has arisen at the European level, when Tetra Pak, which occupies a dominant position in the market for cartons and machines for packaging milk, took over Liquipak. Liquipak had previously obtained an exclusive licence for technology that related to a new method of sterilizing cartons that were suitable for long-life milk and Tetra Pak gained access to that technology by taking over Liquipak. The Commission held that it was an abuse for Tetra Pak to take over this company and the exclusive licence. The Commission had particular difficulties in accepting that Tetra Pak held onto the licence and did not attempt to turn it into a non-exclusive licence.

On appeal, the decision was upheld by the Court of First Instance.[199] The abuse in this case seems to be situated in the reinforcement of an already dominant position and on the basis of the acquisition of an exclusive licence. It is submitted that a non-exclusive licence would not have had the same effect. It must also be remembered that this was a very extreme case, because Tetra Pak's position was an extremely dominant one and the supplementary exclusive licence concerning a new technology would prevent every new competitor from getting into the market. It would almost eliminate any competition on the relevant market. These extreme factors were clearly important for the Commission and the Court of First Instance in reaching their decision and judgment, respectively.[200]

As a result of the European Court of Justice's decision in the *Magill* case,[201] in relation to the area of copyright, a few English cases have been brought in which an attempt was made to apply the reasoning in *Magill* to the area of patent law.[202] It has been argued in these cases that the exercise of a patent can amount to an abuse of a dominant position. The courts made it clear that *Magill* was an exceptional case and that exceptional features, such as those in *Magill*, will have to be demonstrated before the courts will be willing to refuse to assist in the enforcement of a patent on grounds of an abuse of dominant position.[203] The courts will therefore only in very exceptional circumstances—such as the abuse of the patent to reserve a secondary market for the patentee or to refuse to supply (certain) independent repairers—depart from the basic position that the patent, as such, does not amount to an abuse of a dominant position and that neither does the exercise by the patentee of his or her basic right to grant, or to refuse to grant, a licence.[204] Objectively, unreasonably high royalties, for example, did not amount to an abuse in this respect, because they were the mere equivalent of the exercise of the right to refuse to grant a licence.[205] And even in those cases in which an abuse was found, there needed to be a

[197] Cases 6/73 and 7/73 *Instituto Chemioterapica Italiano SpA & Commercial Solvents Corp. v. EC Commission* [1974] ECR 223, [1974] 1 CMLR 309.

[198] *Tetra Pak I (BTG Licence) Decision* [1990] 4 CMLR 47, OJ L 272/27.

[199] Case T-51/89 *Tetra Pak Rausing v. EC Commission* [1990] ECR II-309, [1991] 4 CMLR 334.

[200] See now also the Commission's decision in Case COMP/A.37.507/F3, *Astra Zeneca* [2006] OJ L 332/24.

[201] Joined cases C-241/91 P and C-242/91 P *Radio Telefis Éireann & Independent Television Publications Ltd v. EC Commission* [1995] ECR I-743, [1995] All ER (EC) 416; see Chapter 18 for a full analysis.

[202] *Philips Electronics NV v. Ingman Ltd & the Video Duplicating Co. Ltd* [1999] FSR 112; *Sandvik Aktiebolag v. K R Pfiffner (UK) Ltd* [2000] FSR 17.

[203] In a UK context, see *Sandisk v. Philips Electronics* [2007] I L Pr 22.

[204] See also Case 238/87 *AB Volvo v. Erik Veng (UK) Ltd* [1988] ECR 6211, [1989] 4 CMLR 122; Case 53/87 *Consorzio Italiano della Componentistica di Ricambio per Autoveicoli & Maxicar v. Régie nationale des Usines Renault* [1988] ECR 6039, [1990] 4 CMLR 265.

[205] *Philips Electronics NV v. Ingman Ltd & the Video Duplicating Co. Ltd* [1999] FSR 112; see also Case 238/87 *AB Volvo v. Erik Veng (UK) Ltd* [1988] ECR 6211, [1989] 4 CMLR 122.

nexus between the alleged unlawfulness under Art. 82 and the relief that was claimed: for example, the grant of a compulsory licence in the case of an arbitrary refusal to supply repairers with spare parts.[206]

An overview

Patent law operates a 'first to file' system and the presumption is that the person filing the application is entitled to the patent. Section 7 of the UK Patents Act 1977 nevertheless brings the inventor into the picture as the person who is logically entitled to the patent. There is also room for contractual transactions in this area.

A key problem is the ownership issue between employer and employee. Section 39 determines when inventions made in the course of duty will belong to the employer. This can depend on the inventive activity falling with the normal duties of, or duties specifically assigned to, the employee or on the employee having a special duty to further the interest of the employer's undertaking. In practice, this section gives rise to complex evaluations. Employees may also be granted compensation for inventions owned by the employer in exceptional circumstances.

The importance of that section goes far beyond the specific issue of the grant of, and dealing in, patents. That there is an inherent contradiction between the EU's ideals of free trade and free competition, and intellectual property law's blasé creation of monopoly rights is self-evident, but much of the potential force of the clash between these two fundamental principles is tempered by the (inevitable) compromise position adopted. Legitimate use of property rights for their true purpose is condoned and appropriate exemptions are given to reflect this.

The general approach is well embodied in this area of patent law, whereby a patent will be upheld unless its use is for unjustifiable purposes, as shown by such cases as *Centrafarm*. Equally, its exclusive licensing—potentially likely to fall foul of anti-trust rules—will be permitted by the sensibly pragmatic block exemption approach.

If nothing else, all of this shows that, in the context of what is intended to be a free, single market, the fact that such concessions are made in favour of intellectual property rights confirms that they are of fundamental economic importance to the effective functioning of a modern capitalist economy.

Further reading

ANDERMAN, S. (1998) *EC Competition Law and Intellectual Property Rights: The Regulation of Innovation*, Oxford: Oxford wUniversity Press.

GHIDINI, G. (2006) *Intellectual Property and Competition Law: The Innovation Nexus*, Cheltenham/Northampton, MA: Edward Elgar.

THORLEY, S., MILLER, R., BURKILL, G. and BIRSS, C. (eds) (2006) *Terrell on the Law of Patents*, 16th edn, London: Sweet and Maxwell, ch. 10.

TORREMANS, P. and STAMATOUDI, I., '*Merck* is back to stay: the Court of Justice's judgment in *Merck v. Primecrown*' [1997] 9 EIPR 545.

TORREMANS, P. and STAMATOUDI, I., '*Merck v. Stephar* survives the test' (1997) 22 EL Rev 248.

---

[206] *Sandvik Aktiebolag v. K R Pfiffner (UK) Ltd* [2000] FSR 17, applying *Philips Electronics NV v. Ingman Ltd & the Video Duplicating Co. Ltd* [1999] FSR 112.

6

Infringement and revocation

As will already have been apparent from discussion of many of the leading cases on patentability, the topics of infringement and revocation are inextricably interlinked. The standard counter-attack of an alleged infringer is to question the validity of the patent itself and to seek its revocation, while the initiation of a revocation claim may well be an attempt to clear an inconvenient patent out of the way, thus avoiding any threat of claims of infringement. In either event, the action will focus sharply on what has been actually claimed for the invention by the patentee in his or her specification and claims. It will be recalled that the specification must, under s. 14(3) of the UK Patents Act 1977, disclose the invention sufficiently that it enables the person skilled in the art to make the invention him or herself, while s. 14(5) insists that the claims clearly and concisely define the subject matter of the patent. Consideration of these documents lies at the heart of all infringement and revocation disputes. It is logical to proceed first to consider revocation, because, if no patent exists, it makes little sense to discuss an infringement of it.

Revocation

The grounds on which a patent may be revoked are clearly established by s. 72 of the 1977 Act. Any person may bring an application for the revocation of a patent; his or her motives and whether or not he or she is bringing the application at the instigation of another are irrelevant.[1] No additional requirements are imposed on this point by the Act.

The only grounds for revocation now permitted are:

(a) the invention is not a patentable invention;

(b) that the patent was granted to a person who was not entitled to be granted that patent;

(c) the specification of the patent does not disclose the invention clearly enough and completely enough for it to be performed by a person skilled in the art;

(d) the matter disclosed in the specification of the patent extends beyond that disclosed in the application for the patent, as filed, or, if the patent was granted on a new application filed under sections 8(3), 12 or 37(4) above or as mentioned in section 15(9) above, in the earlier application, as filed;

(e) the protection conferred by the patent has been extended by an amendment which should not have been allowed.[2]

---

[1] *In the Matter of an Application by Edward Evans Barker for Revocation of UK Patent No. 2314392 in the Name of Oystertec plc; sub nom. Oystertec plc v. Edward Evans Barker* [2003] RPC 559.

[2] Patents Act 1977, s. 72(1).

This is a shorter list than in earlier legislation; former objections on grounds of inutility, inadequate description, failure to claim clearly, falsity, or illegality, which were permitted grounds for revocation under the 1949 Act,[3] are no longer so, at least as such.

Patentability and entitlement

These first two of the grounds for revocation under the 1977 Act are straightforward; many of the cases that we have already considered on patentability[4] and on patent rights have arisen in the context of revocation.

Insufficiency

The third ground, however, raises issues that relate directly to the wording of the specification itself and to s. 14(3) of the Act, and poses a further burden on the patent applicant trying to resolve the perpetual dilemma of how much or how little to disclose in the application. Under s. 72(1)(c), there is now the added risk that, if insufficient disclosure occurs, the threat of revocation will loom. Note that it is only the specification and its shortcomings that give rise to this threat; there is no comparable provision to ensure the clarity of the claims made for an invention. Insufficiency is therefore a serious risk to a patent applicant who is naturally inclined to disclose as little as possible, making the issue of sufficiency a key issue in many patent cases, especially as a counter-attack argument in many infringement cases.[5]

This requirement begs several questions, not least what degree of detail is, in fact, going to be necessary. Obviously, this will ultimately depend on the facts of each case, but some guidance is given by *No-Fume Ltd v. Frank Pitchford & Co. Ltd.*[6] The subject of this dispute was an ashtray designed to retain the smoke inside itself. Romer LJ, in the Court of Appeal, upheld the validity of the patent, even though the application—in describing the various features of the ashtray—failed to indicate the size and relative proportions of the various parts of the ashtray. He stated that it was not necessary that the specification had all the detail in it that might be expected in the detailed specification given to a workman in order to make such an item; rather it was sufficient if the workman could reach the desired result through a combination of the information in the specification and the common knowledge of his or her trade, using trial and error if necessary to achieve the desired result.[7]

The next question to be faced is that of the character of the notional person skilled in the art. Once again, the law has to try and put some flesh on the dry bones of this artificial character. The leading case in this context is *Valensi v. British Radio Corp.*,[8] a case concerned with the invention of colour television. On the one hand, the Court of Appeal summarized the character of the hypothetical addressee as '*not a person of exceptional skill*

---

[3] Patents Act 1949, s. 32(1).

[4] For example, patents were revoked on grounds of obviousness in *Rocky Mountain Traders Ltd v. Hewlett Packard GmbH, Westcoast Ltd & Fellowes Manufacturing (UK) Ltd* [2000] FSR 411 (confirmed on appeal on 20 December 2000, unreported); *Minnesota Mining & Manufacturing Co. v. ATI Atlas Ltd & North American Science Associates Inc.* [2001] FSR 31; *Pfizer Ltd's Patent* [2001] FSR 202.

[5] See, e.g., *Kirin-Amgen Inc. v. Transkaryotic Therapies Inc.* [2003] RPC 31 (CA), [2005] 1 All ER 667, [2005] RPC 9 (HL).

[6] (1935) 52 RPC 231.

[7] Ibid. at 243 and 245.

[8] [1972] FSR 273, [1973] RPC 337.

and knowledge... not to be expected to exercise any invention nor any prolonged research, inquiry or experiment'.[9] On the other hand, that person must:

> be prepared to display a reasonable degree of skill and common knowledge in making trials and to correct *obvious* errors in the specification if a means of correcting them can readily be found.[10]

Applying these principles to the case, the problem was that the difficulties faced by the pioneers of colour television were highly technical and it was accepted that an ordinary shopfloor workman was not the appropriate model to consider. Equally, however, the specialist researchers in the field, who the trial judge had used as his model, were also inappropriate. Rather, between the two models were the skilled technicians, who were knowledgeable in their own right, but who would equally be reliant on the guidance provided by the specification, and they were the best model to use in considering the question of insufficiency of the information in the specification.

That the *Valensi* test remains good law under the 1977 Act is not in doubt: this has been confirmed by *Mentor Corp. v. Hollister Inc.*,[11] a decision of the Court of Appeal concerning a patent for a male incontinence device. The Court took note of the European Patent Convention (EPC) Rules,[12] which, by r. 27, state that the description *'shall disclose the invention, as claimed, in such terms that the technical problem... and its solution can be understood'*. Lloyd LJ considered that it was reasonable to expect the addressee to perform routine trials in using the specification to follow and perform the invention, and, in the light of that, the specification disclosed sufficiently the manner of manufacture and should not therefore be revoked.[13]

Put simply, the specification should be looked at to see what it teaches the *Valensi* type of reasonable man, who can be expected to carry out at the very least routine trials of this character. In doing so, the specification should be looked at as of the date of the patent application to avoid any risk of hindsight and it should be kept in mind that the skilled man is seeking success, rather than failure. The skilled man with a positive mind is also concerned with practicalities, rather than with any legal puzzles thrown up by lawyers.[14] As the Technical Board of Appeal of the European Patent Office (EPO) put it recently, the requirements of sufficiency of disclosure will be satisfied only if the invention can be performed by a person skilled in the art using common general knowledge and having regard to further information given in the patent.[15]

While the skilled person can put in some work on the back of his or her common knowledge, and engage in trial-and-error experimentation, however, the amount of work to be put in cannot be unreasonable in the circumstances. The skilled person will try to make the invention work. Insufficiency will therefore not follow if, for example, the skilled person realizes that one method would work and another would fail if the claim is broad enough to include both methods;[16] he cannot, however, engage in inventive activity to fill gaps in the common general knowledge that he possesses, augmented by the

[9] [1972] FSR 273 at 311.

[10] [1973] RPC 337 at 377.

[11] [1993] RPC 7.

[12] See www.european-patent-office.org/legal/epc/e/r27.html.

[13] Ibid. at 14. See also *Mölnlycke AB v. Procter & Gamble Ltd (No. 5)* [1992] FSR 549 at 594–602.

[14] *Kirin-Amgen Inc. v. Transkaryotic Therapies Inc.* [2003] RPC 31 (CA), applying *British Thomson-Houston Co. Ltd v. Corona Lamp Works Ltd* (1922) 39 RPC 49 (HL).

[15] Case T-1121/03 *Union Carbide/Indicator Ligands* [2006] EPOR 49.

[16] *Kirin-Amgen Inc. v. Transkaryotic Therapies Inc.* [2005] 1 All ER 667, [2005] RPC 9 (HL).

information given in the patent.[17] Despite all of this, the question of whether or not the specification was sufficient remains highly sensitive to the nature of the invention. It is therefore important to identify the invention in a first stage and to decide what it claims to enable the skilled man to do. That simplifies the further question of whether the specification enables the skilled man to do that.[18]

One helpful aspect of the current law is that the applicant does not have to put in his or her specification the best possible method of carrying out the invention. This was necessary prior to the 1977 Act; the removal of this requirement aids the inventor by enabling him or her to keep secret the best method and thus retain an additional advantage over rivals, unless and until, of course, they derive the best method themselves, in which case the tables of advantage are turned.

The Court of Appeal in *Kirin-Amgen*[19] added another point to the position on sufficiency. There will be no lack of sufficiency simply because the claims covered inventive improvements, otherwise patents that disclose a principle of general application would become impossible.[20] The specification must, however, enable the invention to be performed and this requirement covers not just a single embodiment. *Biogen v. Medeva*[21] teaches that the specification must enable the invention to be performed to the full extent of the monopoly claimed. In this sense, there is a complete parallelism between s. 14(3), which requires the specification of an application to disclose the invention in a manner that is clear and complete enough for the invention to be performed by the skilled man, and the requirements for sufficiency in s. 72(1)(c). But that parallelism does not extend to the requirement in s. 14(5) that the claims be clear and concise, and supported by the description. The latter requirements are no ground for a finding insufficiency or for revocation on any other basis. In practice, then, it might be hard to establish infringement of unclear claims, but there is no link with revocation.

Grounds for invalidity that relate to the EPC and the role of the EPO

The final two grounds for revocation in s. 72 can be dealt with speedily and were new to the law in 1977, corresponding as they do to EPC provisions.[22] They ensure that no new matter is unfairly added to broaden the scope of the patent, as is forbidden by s. 76 of the 1977 Act, by allowing revocation if such addition has occurred. This upholds the importance of the application date as the starting point of all rights in relation to patents.

Section 76, taken on its own, establishes the broad principle that amendments should not include added matter. 'Added matter' is to be understood as matter extending beyond the matter disclosed in the original application or the original patent. One might, for example, extract a feature that was not remarked upon in the specification and which was not of significance to the person skilled in the art of one of the preferred embodiments of the invention, and insert it in a claim by way of amendment. But to do so will fall foul of s. 76—especially if one then also ignores the other features of the embodiment.[23]

[17] *Halliburton Energy Services Inc. v. Smith International (North Sea) Ltd* (2007) 30 (2) IPD 30009 (CA).
[18] *Biogen v. Medeva* [1997] RPC 1 (HL).
[19] *Kirin-Amgen Inc. v. Transkaryotic Therapies Inc.* [2003] RPC 31 (CA). See also [2005] 1 All ER 667, [2005] RPC 9 (HL).
[20] In *Kirin-Amgen Inc. v. Transkaryotic Therapies Inc.* [2003] RPC 31 (CA), all 26 million products covered by the claim would be suitable, hence the finding of sufficiency. This is to be contrasted with *American Home Products Corp. v. Novartis Pharmaceuticals UK Ltd* [2001] RPC 8, in which the fact that some products were not suitable led to a different conclusion.
[21] [1997] RPC 1 (HL), *per* Lord Hoffmann.
[22] Articles 100(c) and 138(1)(c).
[23] *LG Philips LCD Co. Ltd v. Tatung (UK) Ltd* [2007] RPC 21; *Palmaz v. Boston Scientific BV* [19999] RPC 47.

A European patent is, in the nine months after its grant, also subject to opposition proceedings in the EPO. This affects the European patent for each member State in relation to which it was granted and, if the opposition is successful, the outcome is similar to the revocation of the European patent. After grant, national proceedings can be brought, because, in each country in relation to which it was granted, the European patent becomes the equivalent of a national patent. It is therefore possible that national infringement or invalidity proceedings may be brought while the opposition proceedings are still pending.

This is what happened in *Unilin Beheer BV v. Berry Floor NV & ors.*[24] The English courts had held the patent to be valid and infringed; at the same time, the opposition proceedings were still pending in the EPO. The English court then held that it could not award a stay in the proceedings concerning damages until the opposition proceedings were completed, because the matter was *res judicata* and the defendants would be estopped from challenging the claimant's entitlement if the patent were to be revoked by the EPO.

Infringement

Patents Act 1977, s. 60—the principle

We now turn to the heart of the matter in considering the grounds for, and the general approach to, the issue of infringement. Section 60 of the 1977 Act is the key provision and unusually makes separate, although not dissimilar, provisions for patents that are for products and those that are for processes.

Section 60(1) states that the following actions are infringements if they occur without the permission of the patentee:

(a) where the invention is a product, he makes, disposes of, offers to dispose of, uses or imports the product or keeps it whether for disposal or otherwise;

(b) where the invention is a process, he uses the process or he offers it for use in the United Kingdom when he knows, or it is obvious to a reasonable person in the circumstances, that its use there without the consent of the proprietor would be an infringement of the patent;

(c) where the invention is a process, he disposes of, offers to dispose of, uses or imports any product obtained directly by means of that process or keeps any such product whether for disposal or otherwise.

Under s. 60(2), it is also an infringement if unauthorized disclosure takes place of an essential element of the invention such that the recipient of that disclosure will be able to put the invention into effect. This applies to all inventions, whether products or processes, but does not apply to the supply of a staple commercial product unless it is supplied with a view to inducing an infringement under the section.[25] These provisions relate to what is commonly described as 'indirect infringement'—that is, when the act of infringement consists of enabling another to infringe.

It is clear that s. 60 covers a very wide range of activities in relation to a patented product or process. Activity before, during, or after the unauthorized manufacture of a patented item can count as infringement, and actions as diverse as importing and disposing of an item will both fall within the definition. The most significant gap in the law is that it only applies to actions within the UK and thus a sale that takes place abroad of an infringing

---

[24] [2007] FSR 25 (CA).
[25] Patents Act 1977, s. 60(3).

item does not fall within the provisions—and even an offer made within the jurisdiction to dispose of an item outside of it does not fall within s. 60.[26]

An action will lie under what are likely to be similar rules in that other jurisdiction, of course, because the subsections under consideration equate to EPC, Arts 29 and 30. But the impact of the provision becomes clear in a case in which the product is made lawfully abroad and title to the goods is transferred abroad. The manufacturer does not, in that case, infringe the patent even if it arranges the contract of carriage on behalf of the buyer: that does not amount to importation into the jurisdiction.[27] In more general terms, s. 60(2) is concerned with the means to implement the invention in the UK, such as the apparatus needed to put the invention into effect in the UK. In *Menashe Business Mercantile Ltd v. William Hill Organisation Ltd*,[28] the Court of Appeal held that a patent for a gaming system was therefore infringed through the use of a computer program supplied by the defendant on CD-ROM, which turned its customers' computers into terminals in the defendant's system despite the fact that the host computer in the latter system was located outside the UK. The input and output of the host computer was essential, but the supply of the CD-ROM and of access in the UK amounted to use in the UK.

A further, and sensible, gap in liability arises from a decision that is of assistance to those who find themselves at risk of liability under these broad provisions while acting in all innocence. In *Smith Kline amd French Laboratories Ltd v. RD Harbottle (Mercantile) Ltd*,[29] the first defendants sought to export the drug cimetidine from Italy to Nigeria. The consignment was routed via London and, while it was in storage in a British Airways cargo warehouse, became the subject of a patent infringement claim by the plaintiffs, to which the airline were joined as 'keepers' of the offending consignment. Oliver J found in favour of the airline.[30] In his view, it was appropriate to consider Art. 29 of the Community Patent Convention, which speaks of '*making, offering, putting on the market, or using*' a product, and, in the light of that, it was clearly some form of positive action that was envisaged as amounting to an infringement; the passive warehousing or transporting of an item does not count as positive action in relation to the item. Clearly, the commercial implications of any other decision would have been significant and adverse.

Defences

The courts generally seem to take a generous view of legitimate activity, even though there is no general defence of innocence. A useful pre-Act case, which would appear to be consistent with the statutory approach, is *Solar Thomson Engineering Co. Ltd v. Barton*.[31] In this case, the plaintiffs sold a conveyor system, the pulleys of which were the subjects of a patent. After some years of use, the pulleys began to wear out and the defendants repaired them by replacing a vital part with one of their own manufacture—although, of course, because it was part of a broader system, it had to be identical to the design of the plaintiffs. It was held by the Court of Appeal that it was quite in order to carry out repairs to an item without this infringing any relevant patents, as long as the work of repair could not be said to amount to the manufacture of a new item.

---

[26] *Kalman v. PCL Packaging* [1982] FSR 406.

[27] *Sabaf SpA v. MFI Furniture Centres Ltd* [2003] RPC 14 (CA); (2004) 148 SJLB 1217 (HL).

[28] [2003] 1 All ER 279, [2003] 1 WLR 1462, affirming the first instance decision reported at [2002] RPC 950 on different grounds.

[29] [1980] RPC 363.

[30] Ibid. at 373.

[31] [1977] RPC 537.

The House of Lords has now confirmed this approach in *United Wire v. Screen Repair Services*,[32] in which it was held that the notions of repair and of making are mutually exclusive for the purposes of the 1977 Act. Repair can therefore not amount to an infringement, because s. 60 requires the making of the patented item. There is also no need to confer an implied licence on the repairer, because he or she is free to do whatever is not covered by the concept of making the product.

The provisions relating to indirect infringement are not, however, without their problems. The essential concept of 'essential element' goes undefined and is bound, at some stage, to give rise to difficulties in litigation. The exception for the supply of a staple commercial product is also shrouded in uncertainty, at least to UK and European lawyers, but appears to protect the innocent seller of a common product that has obvious non-infringing uses. If A supplies water to B, for example, this may enable B to infringe C's water-powered invention, but it would clearly be unfair to burden A with any liability in the absence of any knowledge of the offending use.

There are also statutory defences provided by the 1977 Act in s. 60(5), under which acts that would otherwise count as infringements do not do so if they are done privately for non-commercial purposes. This points to the patent as an item of industrial property: it is only protected in the field of commercial exploitation. Also outside the scope of the infringement provisions are acts done by others for experimental purposes relating to the invention.[33] This is also significant in giving others trading in the same field the right to carry out experiments using the public information made available via the Patent Office as a result of the application procedure, thus ensuring the high likelihood of a further patent race hotting up as the patentee's 20-year period of protection draws to a close.

One case in particular has had to consider the experimental purposes defence. In *Monsanto Co. v. Stauffer Chemical Co.*,[34] the plaintiffs owned the patent for a herbicide and claimed infringement by the defendants, who had carried out some trials of their allegedly infringing product with a view to obtaining official product safety clearances. It was held by the Court of Appeal that experiments permitted by the Act were only those carried out for scientific purposes: for example, to test a hypothesis or to discover something unknown about the subject matter of the invention.[35] The tests in question, however, were of a very different kind and tests that were carried out for commercial, rather than scientific, purposes would not be exempt from the threat of an infringement action.

Other defences also arise from s. 60(5) and can be recorded briefly. The extemporaneous preparation in a pharmacy of a medicine under the terms of a prescription is outside s. 60; this is again directed to what, in fact, would be likely to be an innocent infringement. Also outside s. 60 are various uses of patented equipment in ships, aircraft, and even hovercraft, temporarily or accidentally in UK waters or airspace. The Court of Appeal held that, in those cases, the term 'temporarily' should be construed as 'transient', or 'for a limited period of time'.[36] The frequency with which such vessels or aircraft entered UK territorial waters or airspace was not relevant in this respect; neither was the regular and repeated nature of such presence. For example, an Irish registered ferry that made three

[32] *United Wire Ltd v. Screen Repair Services (Scotland) Ltd* [2001] RPC 439, [2001] FSR 24, [2000] 4 All ER 353.
[33] See T. Cook, 'Responding to concerns about the scope of the defence from patent infringement for acts done for experimental purposes relating to the subject matter of the invention' [2006] 3 IPQ 193–222.
[34] [1985] RPC 515.
[35] Ibid., *per* Dillon LJ at 542.
[36] *Stena Rederi AB v. Irish Ferries Ltd* [2003] RPC 37 (CA). at 676.

to four trips a day and spent about three to four hours in UK territorial waters on each trip was only entering these territorial waters 'temporarily'.[37]

A more significant exception relates to prior use—that is, to use of a product or process without patent protection by A and the impact upon it of a grant of a patent for such a product or process to B. It may seem harsh to penalize A in this example by making his or her acts into infringements of B's later patent if he or she continues with his pre-existing use. Section 64 of the 1977 Act deals with this type of situation by allowing the prior user to continue that use after the grant of a patent to another without it being an infringement, as long as the user is in good faith. The problem will only arise in cases in which the prior use was secret; if it were not, the later actions would not be novel and thus not patentable. The relatively rare instances in which the section is thus likely to be invoked mean that it may be some time before the courts have an opportunity to sort out the obvious problem that it creates—namely, whether the later act, to be permitted to continue, has to be exactly, or merely substantially, identical to the prior user. Given the steady evolution likely to occur in the history of the development of a product or process, to permit only exact replication would deprive s. 64 of much of its already limited value.

Procedural elements

The right to take action against an infringer is, under s. 66, conferred on any one among a group of joint proprietors, although the others must be joined to the action. As has been seen already, s. 67 gives exclusive licensees (but no other licensee) the right to take action against infringers, thus contributing to the popularity of this type of licence.

The legislation also sets out the remedies available to anyone who has rights against an infringer. Section 61 confers an exciting choice of any, or all, of an injunction, an order to deliver up infringing items, damages, an account of profits (these two are alternatives), and a declaration. It should be noted that both account of profits and delivery up are equitable remedies, and thus, by definition, discretionary in their approach.

The choice between account of profits and damages, meanwhile, is not easy. It is clearly good news for the plaintiff that he or she is entitled to ask for an account of all the profits and not only that proportion which is due to infringement,[38] but, equally, it is a laborious process to prove the profit actually engendered by one product that may be among many produced by a large firm.[39] Seeking damages seems simpler, but, in a competitive trading environment, precise assessment of the loss caused to the plaintiff by the infringement, rather than by any other of a myriad of factors, may also prove troublesome. By s. 62, damages and account of profits are not available as against an infringer who can prove that they were, and should have been, unaware of the existence of the relevant patent at the time of the infringing act. Damages in these cases are generally on a royalty basis: the question is what royalties or licensing fees would have been earned by a lawful licensing of the patent.

Patent infringement actions have a reputation for being long and costly, and the breadth of the different activities that can amount to an infringement means that trade in a product even threatened with an infringement action is likely to be suspended for the often considerable period of time that lapses while the litigation takes its course. In a legitimate

---

[37] Ibid.

[38] *Peter Pan Manufacturing Corp. v. Corsets Silhouette Ltd* [1963] 3 All ER 402, [1964] 1 WLR 96 (a breach of confidence case).

[39] See *Gerber Garment Technology Inc. v. Lectra Systems Ltd* [1997] RPC 443, noted by S. Moss and D. Rogers, 'Damages for loss of profits in intellectual property litigation' [1997] 8 EIPR 425.

case, this is acceptable, but a more cynical trader may recognize the disruptive effect of launching an infringement action against a rival and do so simply to achieve that effect. Section 70 of the 1977 Act does, however, provide protection against this possibility. The section creates a right for anyone aggrieved to take to court anyone who threatens an action against either the applicant or anyone else for infringement of a patent. Letters claiming infringement and demanding payment under threat of legal proceedings sent to the alleged infringer, as well as letters sent to potential customers of the latter, are covered, but a letter to a customer informing him or her that proceedings in another jurisdiction have effectively been brought does not equal a threat.[40] A declaration, injunction, or damages may be granted unless the defendant can establish that the threats are justifiable. This protection does not, however, extend to a threat of bringing proceedings for an infringement in the form of making or importing a product for disposal or of using a process.[41] This is a valuable provision and it is prudent for the plaintiff in an infringement action to bear it in mind before proceeding too far. The law has recognized the adverse effect of even the threat of an infringement action on a wide range of business dealings.

Overall, the statutory provisions on infringement appear, for the most part, to be straightforward and workable, which may make somewhat surprising the assertion that such proceedings may well be long and complex. The problem is that the statute somehow seems to assume that it will be easy to look at the patent and see what it covers, and then place that alongside the allegedly infringing act and make a comparison. Section 125 of the 1977 Act makes clear that the definition of the invention is that which is:

> specified in a claim of the specification or the application, as the case may be, as interpreted by the description and any drawings contained in that specification, and the extent of the protection conferred by a patent or application of a patent shall be construed accordingly.

It tells us, then, in a moderately clear way, what the court should be looking at in deciding what the invention is for the purpose of an infringement action; it still does not tell us, though, *how* it should be looked at—and here a clash arises between the scientist and the lawyer. The scientist may be caricatured as a bluff, commonsensical character, who is skilled in his trade and who will use his expertise to discern the inventive notion. The lawyer, however, may be caricatured as a wordsmith, rather than a blacksmith, who will use his interpretative skills—or pedantic ones, if preferred—to understand the words that define the inventive notion. Whether the specification should be read with the scientist's purposive outlook or the lawyer's literal one has been the subject of a major battle in recent years, which the scientists have won with, as will be seen, more than a little assistance from their European friends.

The Court of Appeal has summarized the position by arguing that the invention of a patent is to be taken to be that specified in the claims.[42] These claims have to be interpreted with the aid of the description and, in doing so, the court should adopt a middle way between literal construction and taking the claims as mere guidelines.

Interpretation of specifications and claims

The historical background
It should be made clear at the outset that the first part of this section describes the law as what it was and not as it is now. It is, however, valuable, for the purposes of contrasting

---

[40] *Cintec International Ltd v. Parkes & anor* (2004) 27(2) IPD 27011.

[41] Patents Act 1977, s. 70(4). See *Bowden Controls Ltd v. Acco Cable Controls Ltd* [1990] RPC 427.

[42] *BASF AG v. Smithkline Beecham plc* [2003] All ER (D) 327, [2003] RPC 49 (CA).

the old and new positions, to start with the earlier approach and a good starting point is *C Van der Lely NV v. Bamfords Ltd.*[43]

In this case, the House of Lords was faced with a claim against the patentee of a hay rake seeking revocation of that patent, with a cross-claim by the patentee alleging infringement by the claimant. The key part of the litigation centred on a claim that one of the rows of wheels on which the patented hay rake was driven could be removed for different aspects of the haymaker's art. The claim specifically referred to the removal of the hindmost wheels, while the allegedly infringing device for the same reason removed wheels, but removed the front ones instead. At this time, courts claimed to study the 'pith and marrow' of the invention to see what the true inventive step was, but the decision of the House of Lords shows the ambiguity of this phrase. It may be thought to involve a purposive type of inquiry, but this was not so. Speaking as one of the majority of the Law Lords who found that there was no infringement, Lord Jenkins stated that the patentee had deliberately claimed only the hindmost wheels and that this left it open for the rivals to arrange their wheels in any other way, even though the two machines were both achieving the same result by using the same principle.[44] Viscount Radcliffe, too, said that the words used delimit what the applicant has claimed.[45] Lord Reid dissented on the issue, however, taking the view that the precise wheels involved were not essential integers of the invention and that there was therefore no infringement.[46]

Then, in *Rodi & Wienenberger AG v. Henri Showell Ltd,*[47] the issue returned to the House of Lords. This time, the issue related to expandable watch straps and, in particular, the connections between the bands in them. The patented straps were linked together by U-shaped connecting bows; the allegedly infringing straps used C-shaped bows instead. Notwithstanding the obvious point that a 'U' shape and a 'C' shape are not exactly dissimilar, the House of Lords found, once again, that there was no infringement here. Even adopting the essential integers approach, the majority found that those were defined in the terms of the words of the specification and claim, and that therefore the 'U' shape defined itself, in effect, as an essential integer. Lord Reid, this time, was joined by Lord Pearce in dissent, seeking to look at the self-evidently similar way in which the two shapes functioned.[48]

Inexorably, at the pace of a constipated tortoise, the House of Lords inched away from the hardest of hard-line literal approaches to patent specifications. In *Beecham Group Ltd v. Bristol Laboratories Ltd,*[49] Beechams had patent rights in a type of penicillin called ampicillin, while Bristol was importing into the UK hetacillin, which was similar, but not identical to ampicillin. It was derived from it and, once in the bloodstream, it reacted with water and became ampicillin, and thus worked as an antibiotic in precisely the same way. The House of Lords found that this was an infringement by applying the 'pith and marrow' test in the broader way that we have suggested the phrase properly implies. Lord Diplock accepted that, on the most literal approach, the two products were different, but that, in their actual use, they worked in precisely the same way. The variation, he said, was '*evanescent and reversible*' and the actual use in hetacillin was a use of ampicillin.[50]

---

[43] [1963] RPC 61.

[44] Ibid. at 80.

[45] Ibid. at 78.

[46] Ibid. at 71.

[47] [1969] RPC 367, [1968] FSR 100.

[48] [1968] FSR 100, at 102 and 115 respectively.

[49] [1978] RPC 153.

[50] Ibid. at 202.

The EPC and the Protocol on the interpretation of Article 69

This welcome outbreak of common sense is perhaps better seen as a surrender to the inevitable, because, while the *Beecham* case was being argued in the Lords, Parliament was considering the new Patents Act—and that legislation, with its tie-in to the EPC, betokened a very different approach. The way in which this arises is as follows.

We have already seen that s. 125 of the 1977 Act provides that the documents at the heart of the application procedure define the invention and that s. 125(3) goes on to say that the Protocol on the Interpretation of Article 69 of the EPC should apply to the interpretation of that section of the domestic legislation. Turning, then, to Art. 69 itself, we find that it says simply that the extent of protection given by a European patent shall be determined by '*the claims*'.[51] This seems to advance us little until we find that the Protocol to it states as follows:

> Article 69 should not be interpreted in the sense that the extent of the protection conferred by a European patent is to be understood as that defined by the strict, literal meaning of the wording used in the claims, the description and drawings being employed only for the purpose of resolving an ambiguity found in the claims. Neither should it be interpreted in the sense that the claims serve only as guideline and that the actual protection conferred may extend to what, from a consideration of the description and drawings by a person skilled in the art, the patentee has contemplated. On the contrary, it is to be interpreted as defining a position between these extremes which combines a fair protection for the patentee with a reasonable degree of certainty for third parties.[52]

The background to the Protocol merits some explanation. In harmonizing any law—let alone an area of law as complex as that of patent law—compromises have to be reached and the Protocol is that compromise. It sets out two extremes of interpretation—the mindless literalism, typified by cases such as *Rodi & Wienenberger*, and the 'broad guideline' approach, which could be taken to typify the practice at this time in Germany and elsewhere—and requires a court to eschew them both, and instead to seek a compromise that balances protection for the patentee's interest in preserving a broad monopoly and regard for the need for others—subsequent inventors, users and other infringers—to know where they stand in a way that, for all its other faults, the literal approach does allow them.

It is important to emphasize the significance of this change. The old UK literal approach gave a narrow protection to the patentee, particularly if he or she was cautious in his or her claims (a caution encouraged by the need to ensure that all of the claims made for a patent are justified during the application procedure). By moving, as we clearly are, towards a looser approach with broader methods of interpretation in use, we are moving towards greater protection for the patentee. Equally, more risk of infringement is placed on others who are now to be offered only a 'reasonable degree of certainty', as opposed to the utter—if, at times, unpalatable—certainty of the former literal approach.

Catnic—*the principle of purposive interpretation in the UK*

The problem with all of this, however, is that the Protocol is keener to tell us what *not* to do than what *to* do in interpreting patents. Thus it fell to the House of Lords to consider, yet again, the appropriate approach to interpretation in the new era of patent law and the opportunity to do so arose in *Catnic Components Ltd v. Hill & Smith Ltd.*[53] It must be

---

[51] This is the wording put in place by the revised version of the EPC (dated 29 November 2000), whereas the original version used the words '*by the terms of the claims*'. No substantive change was intended and the change was seen simply as a matter of clarifying the language used even further.

[52] Article 1 of the Protocol.

[53] [1982] RPC 183.

emphasized that this was a case under the 1949 Act and that no express mention is made of the 1977 Act, the EPC, or of the Protocol. But it would be naive to see the developments in *Catnic* as solely the continuing evolution of the UK approach to the issue.[54] The *Catnic* approach represents the first UK answer to the conundrum posed by the Protocol to Art. 69 and it provides an answer that, it is suggested, is entirely compatible with European approaches.

The facts of *Catnic* were simple enough. The plaintiffs had a patent for a type of steel lintel (a load-bearing beam), which specified in its wording that the rear side of the lintel should be vertical. The defendants produced a similar lintel, but—presumably in the hope of avoiding an infringement action—made the rear side of their lintel at an angle of 6° from the vertical, which reduced its load-bearing powers by 0.6 per cent. Did this minor variation avoid the infringement danger?

Lord Diplock gave the sole substantive judgment.[55] He found that there was an infringement on the facts. The key passage makes clear that it is the purposive approach of the scientists and Europeans that should take precedence over the old approach of the common lawyers, because the patent specification is aimed at other workers in the field:

> My Lords, a patent specification is a unilateral statement by the patentee, in words of his own choosing, addressed to those likely to have a practical interest in the subject matter of his invention (ie 'skilled in the art'), by which he informs them of what he claims to be the essential features of the new product or process for which the letters patent grant him a monopoly. It is those novel features only that he claims to be essential that constitute the so-called 'pith and marrow' of the claim. A patent specification should be given a purposive construction rather than a purely literal one derived from applying to it the kind of meticulous verbal analysis in which lawyers are too often tempted by their training to indulge. The question in each case is: whether persons with practical knowledge and experience of the kind of work in which the invention was intended to be used, would understand that strict compliance with a particular descriptive word or phrase appearing in a claim was intended by the patentee to be an essential requirement of the invention so that any variant would fall outside the monopoly claimed, even though it could have no material effect upon the way the invention worked.[56]

This being the test, it then becomes very easy to conclude that no lintel manufacturer could be imagined to have thought that the vertical rear side was, in literal terms, essential, because this would enable anyone else to use the idea of the patent, but, by varying it by a degree or two, avoid an infringement action with impunity. Why bother with a patent if that were so? Of course, such arguments will depend very much on the facts of each case. It is easy to imagine a patent in which the description of something as being vertical is of great importance: for example, in some form of new guillotine, in relation to which a much cleaner cut would be best achieved by a precisely vertical drop.

It is important to put the new purposive test of interpretation derived from *Catnic* in its context. Although new to patent infringement in the UK, purposive methods of interpretation are becoming more and more important; this is because the European influence of the law is also becoming more and more important, both in patents and elsewhere. To a Continental lawyer, purposive or teleological approaches to interpretation are the norm. Within the context of the EU, the European Court of Justice takes such a course in its approach to the legal rules of the Union, prefaced as they

---

[54] *Cornish & Victoria* [1981] JBL 136. Cf Jacob J, 'The Herchel Smith Lecture 1993' [1993] 9 EIPR 312.

[55] *Catnic Components Ltd v. Hill & Smith Ltd* [1982] RPC 183 at 239.

[56] [1982] RPC 183 at 244. See also *Improver Corp. v. Remington Consumer Products Ltd* [1990] FSR 181, *per* Hoffmann J at 190.

are by extensive Preambles spelling out the purposes for which the legislation is being passed.[57]

Of course, we do not suggest that the *Catnic* test is, of itself, perfect: it will still leave some inevitable uncertainty. The volume of litigation and the different approaches taken by the courts in the years since *Catnic* speak eloquently about the difficulties facing common lawyers let loose on Continental approaches to statutory interpretation. These cases will be considered shortly, but, if we look at *Catnic* in its own terms, significant changes clearly have occurred to pre-existing case law. *Rodi & Wienenberger* would surely now be decided the other way, in accordance with the approach of the dissenting minority, but *Van der Lely* poses a problem. On the one hand, the removal of either set of wheels served the same purpose and this factor suggests a different decision post-*Catnic*; on the other hand, however, it is surely going further than *Catnic* to move from saying 'vertical equals almost vertical' to saying 'back means front'. The logic of *Catnic* does, however, suggest that, in cases in which, in terms of purpose, it is immaterial whether it is the back or front wheels that are removable, 'back' means nothing at all and might thus be ignored.

The struggle to put Catnic into practice

Further discussion of the impact and importance of *Catnic* is best postponed, to be resumed in the light of the development and application of the law since that decision. A key moment in its acceptance and use came quickly in *Codex Corp. v. Racal-Milgo Ltd.*[58] In this case, the Court of Appeal was faced with a patent relating to a method of high-speed data transmission through a modem. The alleged infringement was by a system of broadly the same type, but which was much faster and more complex in its operation. The Court adopted the *Catnic* approach without reservation and consigned previous case law to the outer darkness. It was at pains to point out, however, that the *Catnic* approach was not as radical a change as some had argued, emphasizing that the investigation is not of the principle of the patent itself, but of the purposive construction of the relevant documents.[59] This must be right: Art. 69, it will be recalled, talks of the '*terms of the claim*'.

In the light of this, the Court of Appeal was able to identify three key features in the patented system—namely, that it took in a particular sequence of signals, identified that sequence, and signalled that information onwards. Although each of these aspects was carried out in subtly different ways in the other system, the same key features were present, carrying out the same sort of functions, and thus there was an infringement.

It is not our intention to look at every case decided on the subject—but the acceptance of the *Catnic* approach meant that, as one would expect, minor variations were now no longer enough to save a later product or process from being an infringing one. So an improved method of loading skips into lorries was still an infringement, because it used the same basic idea as the earlier patent,[60] while a dental pin made out of two parts that were put together for use, but which could be separated with difficulty, infringed an earlier patent for a dental pin made in one piece, given that both pins operated in exactly the same way.[61]

Two important post-*Catnic* cases show that the law could function well, finding that there was an infringement where the old law would not. In *AC Edwards Ltd v. Acme Signs*

[57] See, inter alia, L. Neville Brown and T. Kennedy (1994) *The Court of Justice of the European Communities*, 4th edn, London: Sweet and Maxwell, ch. 14, esp. pp. 311–14 and cases cited therein.

[58] [1983] RPC 369.

[59] Ibid. at 381.

[60] *Société Nouvelle des Bennes Saphem v. Edbro Ltd* [1983] RPC 345.

[61] *Fairfax (Dental Equipment) Ltd v. S J Filhol Ltd* [1986] RPC 499.

& *Displays Ltd,*[62] the Court of Appeal had to consider the familiar digital price display panels that are typically found outside petrol stations, which work by providing seven lines that make up a rectangular figure eight, but which, by masking one or more of the lines, can make up any figure, as prices fluctuate. It is obviously important that the masked lines stay masked, and this is where conflict arose between the plaintiffs' patented product and the defendants' allegedly infringing one. The plaintiffs used springs to hold the lines in their required position, while the defendants employed a flexible piece of plastic for the same task. It was held that this did infringe: the essential idea of the use of a flexible piece of apparatus to hold lines in place was the same in both products and whether this was done by a spring, as in the patent specification, or by a piece of the plastic that, though not a spring, acted in the same way as one was immaterial. The use of the word 'spring' by the plaintiff was not a use of any particular significance.

In *Minnesota Mining & Manufacturing Co. v. Rennicks (UK) Ltd,*[63] the dispute was in connection with reflective sheeting of the kind used in road signs. The patented product was stated to have particularly effective adhesion between its different layers of plastic materials by reason of the layers having undergone a process of curing. The allegedly infringing product also claimed increased adhesion and achieved this by a different method of curing. Again, this was found to amount to an infringement, because the different methods of curing did not disguise the fact that the essential elements of the two methods were the same.[64]

The cases so far considered exemplify well what the *Catnic* approach is intended to achieve. The more flexible approach that it embodies and which is demanded by the EPC means that it will be easier for patentees to secure protection against later infringers, thus increasing the value of their patents; the infringer, in turn, will not be able to rely on purely literal interpretations of the specification and claims to disguise the fact that he or she has stolen the essential idea at the heart of the patented invention. The two cases just described show precisely this pattern—but, unfortunately, they do not represent an invariable approach and some more restrictive decisions need to be considered. It is therefore important to consider a second group of such cases, to see whether the courts are using *Catnic* properly or whether they are slipping back into older, and more literal, methods of construction.

In *Harrison v. Project & Design Co. (Redcar) Ltd,*[65] the dispute was between a private individual who devised a chair lift to enable his invalid wife to get upstairs, which he subsequently patented, and the defendants, a commercial firm that, after dealings with Harrison, began to make its own chair lifts. The case ultimately hinged on whether earlier proceedings were *res judicata*, but there was discussion of infringement too. The main difference between the two lifts was that the plaintiff used a weight to balance the progress of the chair lift and ensure the smooth running of the chain mechanism, while the defendants had abandoned this approach at an early stage and used an additional length of chain in place of the weight primarily as a safety device. The Court of Appeal found that this did not infringe: this was a different method of achieving the same overall purpose and, given that the plaintiff had specified the use of a weight and the defendants' chain did not operate as a weight, there was no clash between them. This seems sensible: in purely functional or purposive terms, there was a significant difference and no problem arises from the case.

---

62 [1992] RPC 131.
63 [1992] RPC 331.
64 Ibid., *per* Aldous J at 346.
65 [1987] RPC 151.

Improver *and what became the Protocol questions*

More problematic, perhaps, is the decision of Hoffmann J in *Improver Corp. v. Remington Consumer Products Ltd.*[66] The plaintiffs had a European patent for an electronic hair-removing device known as the 'Epilady'. The defendants had placed on the market a similar device called 'Smooth & Silky'. The principal difference between them was that the plaintiffs' device plucked hairs from the skin by capturing the hairs in a high-speed rotating arc-shaped spring, while that of the defendants employed a high-speed rotating arc-shaped synthetic rubber rod with slits cut in it to capture the hairs.

Hoffmann J summarized the *Catnic* approach in clear terms:[67]

> The proper approach to the interpretation of English patents registered under the Patents Act 1949 was explained by Lord Diplock in *Catnic Components Ltd v. Hill & Smith Ltd*. The language should be given a 'purposive' and not necessarily a literal construction. If the issue was whether a feature embodied in an alleged infringement which fell outside the primary, literal or a contextual meaning of a descriptive word or phrase in the claim ('a variant') was nevertheless within its language as properly interpreted, the court should ask itself the following three questions:
>
> (1) Does the variant have a material effect upon the way the invention works? If yes, the variant is outside the claim.[68] If no—
>
> (2) Would this (ie that the variant had no material effect) have been obvious at the date of publication of the patent to a reader skilled in the art. If no, the variant is outside the claim. If yes—
>
> (3) Would the reader skilled in the art nevertheless have understood from the language of the claim that the patentee intended that strict compliance with the primary meaning was an essential requirement of the invention. If yes, the variant is outside the claim.
>
> On the other hand, a negative answer to the last question would lead to the conclusion that the patentee was intending the word or phrase to have not a literal but a figurative meaning (the figure being a form of synecdoche or metonymy) denoting a class of things which included the variant and the literal meaning, the latter being perhaps the most perfect, best-known or striking example of the class.

Applying these criteria, the judge found that the variant had no material effect on the way in which the invention worked and that to adopt a rubber rod was obvious to the notional skilled man.[69] On the vital third question, however, he found that the claim, in specifically referring to a helical spring, could not be interpreted so broadly as to extend to a rubber rod, which presented many different problems and on which the plaintiff had done no work.[70]

Certainly, this promotes the actual words of the patent to a high level. The fact that the patent only used the helical spring, with no alternatives, was also regarded as significant in adding to the impression that the skilled reader would not think of going beyond it. Given that both products employed a high-speed rotating arc-shaped object with gaps in the outer edge, it may be thought that the defendants had hijacked the basic inventive concept and that the demand of the Protocol to Art. 69 for a balance to be achieved between fair protection for the patentee and reasonable certainty for third parties had not been met, with undue respect still being paid to the form of the words used.

---

[66] [1990] FSR 181.
[67] Ibid. at 189.
[68] For an example, see *Rohm & Haas Co. v. Collag Ltd* [2001] FSR 28.
[69] [1990] FSR 181 at 192.
[70] Ibid. at 197.

What is more worrying is that parallel litigation in Germany came to the opposite conclusion. Hoffmann J described and referred to this in his judgment,[71] and took consolation
from the fact that, at an earlier stage of the litigation there, a view similar to his own had
been taken. This is frankly shoddy: in this case, we see a European patent that is designed to
provide Europe-wide protection and yet two courts in different states come to opposite conclusions. The German court found no reason to ask the third question asked by Hoffmann J,
because the way in which the device functioned was clear and its implications obvious in
suggesting that any kind of arc-shaped slitted part would achieve the same result.

The question is, then, do we need to ask the third question? It is tentatively suggested that
the outcome of the *Improver* case suggests that we should not. The defendants' 'Smooth &
Silky' was designed by an engineer whose wife claimed that her 'Epilady' hurt her, and he
directly adapted the 'Epilady' design to give fewer slits and thus less pain. He thus altered
one minor aspect of the 'Epilady' in such a way that would make it unlikely that he could
gain patent protection for himself, it being an obvious variation. Yet, by focusing on the
words used by the patentee, the *Improver* decision allows an admitted adoption of the patented product with an obvious variant to go unpunished. If this is the effect of the third
question, it is suggested it is a bad effect—and thus a bad question.

Still struggling with Catnic—what about the language of the claim?

A further emphasis on the language of the claim was offered by the Court of Appeal in *PLG
Research v. Ardon International Ltd.*[72] This case concerned an invention of plastic netting
for use in civil engineering projects, which was described in the patent specification as being
'substantially uniplanar', while the allegedly infringing product was different in appearance, but functionally equivalent to the original patented product. In holding that both
patents were sustainable, Millett LJ referred to the Protocol to Art. 69, and claimed that the
German courts were at one with domestic jurisprudence in insisting that the scope of the
patent has to be determined with direct reference to the language employed in the patent
claim and specification.[73] The claim should not be permitted to go beyond those functional
equivalents, which are deductible from the wording used in the claim. This approach arguably represents a variation from the *Catnic* test, but only a minor one affording slightly more
protection for the patentee, despite the suggestion in the course of the proceedings that
the *Catnic* test should altogether be left to legal historians. The *PLG* decision is at least an
advance in one respect, with the decision being based on an interpretation of the Protocol to
Art. 69 rather than by reference to the pre-existing common law approach.

Other cases also seemed to concentrate unduly on the precise language employed in
the patent claim and/or specification. In *Southco Inc. v. Dzus Fastener Europe Ltd,*[74] the
Court of Appeal was faced with a patented latch mechanism and an allegedly infringing
product, which had many similarities. The key distinction was that the plaintiffs' mechanism worked in a way that was foolproof, whereas the other, at one point in its operation,
was not. This appears to be a reasonable decision, with both the words used and the overall purpose being considered by the Court. It was also argued by the plaintiffs that the
defendants had deliberately designed their product 'down' just so as to achieve that result.
Nicholls LJ came to no conclusion on the fact, but warned that the Court would take care
to ensure that any such attempt would not be rewarded.[75]

---

[71] Ibid. at 197–8. See also Jacob J, 'The Herchel Smith Lecture 1993' [1993] 9 EIPR 312 at 313.
[72] [1995] RPC 287.
[73] Ibid. at 309.
[74] [1992] RPC 299.
[75] Ibid. at 323.

A less attractive decision—or rather, approach—is that in *Daily v. Etablissements Fernand Berchet.*[76] In this case, an English inventor of an unworked patent for a walking aid that, as a safety feature, had a pressure-operated '*braking arrangement associated with the rear wheels*' (the words of the claim) sought to claim against the French manufacturers of a toy train called the 'Locopousse', which was designed to help young children to walk. This also contained a safety feature—a downward extension of the side at the rear of the toy—that slight pressure would bring to contact with the ground, thus braking the vehicle's progress without using the wheels. The Court of Appeal briefly overturned the trial judge's finding that there was an infringement. Nourse LJ referred to no cases and simply relied on the words of the plaintiffs' claim.[77] Balcombe LJ noted that he should proceed in a purposive way, but then declared that the ordinary rules of construction should be applied, evidencing some confusion, to say the least, before again relying on the words used.[78] Sir Michael Kerr at least considered the post-*Catnic* threefold test, and concluded that there were problems for the plaintiff at every stage and terminal ones at the third stage.[79]

On the facts, the decision seems fair enough. Brakes linked to wheels and brakes that act directly on to the ground are tolerably different enough to justify the view that there was no infringement. But the approach of the Court has a smack of older (some might say Luddite) approaches about it and contrasts adversely with the other cases.

Happily, a gradual consensus has evolved in the most recent cases, which show that the judges are grappling valiantly with the new European-based approach, and are concentrating more on purpose and less on the precise language employed. Thus, in *Glaverbel SA v. British Coal Corp.*,[80] the Court of Appeal stressed the importance of the purposive approach in patent litigation, but, equally, emphasized that examination of the patent claimed should concentrate on the claim, rather than on extrinsic evidence of the patentee's intention and his or her subsequent behaviour. On the facts of the case, it was held that the reasonable skilled man would not have been able to deduce from the earlier patent the solution to the same problem in the allegedly—but, in fact, not—infringing subsequent activity.

Aldous J encountered the same issue in *Assidoman Multipack Ltd v. Mead Corp.*[81] In this case, litigation concerned different types of packaging and, in finding that there was an infringement in spite of the different phraseology employed in the applications in question, the judge made clear the point that the Protocol to Art. 69 was the proper basis on which to proceed, as a middle way between '*Scylla, the rock of liberal construction, and Charybdis, the whirlpool of guided freedom*'.[82]

So, that's clear then.

Jacob J also waded into these murky waters in *Beloit Technologies Inc. v. Valmet Paper Machinery Inc.*[83] and described the *Catnic* approach as a *via media*—that is, the middle way between the two approaches discredited by the Protocol.

At around the same time, further support was given to this method of approach by the Court of Appeal in *Kastner v. Rizla Ltd.*[84] This dispute arose in relation to two inventions

---

[76] [1993] RPC 357. See P. Cole, 'Purposive construction under English law' [1994] 10 EIPR 455.
[77] [1993] RPC 357 at 358–60.
[78] Ibid. at 361.
[79] Ibid. at 362–64.
[80] [1995] RPC 255. See S. Conroy, 'The construction of claims in UK patent litigation' [1995] 4 EIPR 199.
[81] [1995] RPC 321.
[82] Ibid. at 336.
[83] [1995] RPC 705, esp. at 721.
[84] [1995] RPC 585, followed by Laddie J in *Brugger v. Medic-Aid Ltd* [1996] RPC 635.

for interleaving the cigarette papers used by connoisseurs of self-rolling cigarettes, who need the papers to contain the tobacco and any other material in the cigarette. It was held that there was an infringement in this case and Aldous LJ, perhaps unsurprisingly, followed his view in *Assidoman* and sidestepped the narrower view in *PLG* by expressing it as being obiter, and pointing out that *Catnic*, as a House of Lords decision, was to be followed in all cases.[85]

Another recent approach to this area has come in *Auchinloss v. Agricultural & Veterinary Supplies Ltd*,[86] in which emphasis was placed on the need for fairness to third parties. Thus, on the one hand, a precise claim that a new product claims benefits A, B, and C would enable another party using the same product to achieve benefit D, to avoid allegations of infringement. On the other hand, a more vaguely or broadly worded claim might extend to cover the notional benefit D and would protect the patentee, albeit at risk of the patent being regarded as initially unregistered.

Catnic *as the* via media *and a structured approach*

So where are we now? The answer is that the attempt to construe the *Catnic* approach so narrowly as effectively to overrule it has not succeeded. The recent case law suggests that *Catnic* remains the *via media*, with all of the uncertainties that such an approach inherently provides. A good recent example is the decision of Jacob J in *Impro Ltd's Patent*,[87] in which a patent for an invalid-lifting hoist was held to be infringed by a laser device, with the decision being made with reference both to the purposive interpretation of the claims and, in the light thereof, to the wording used in the claims. Final confirmation of this approach seems to have come in the form of two recent decisions of the Court of Appeal: *Wheatley v. Drillsafe*[88] and *American Home Products v. Novartis Pharmaceuticals*.[89] We will now consider these cases in more detail, while adding some further cases, in order to clarify the current position under UK law.

Wheatley v. Drillsafe confirms that the test set out in *Catnic* and reformulated in *Improver* remains the standard test for infringement. The three questions were rebaptized 'the Protocol questions', because, in the view of the court, they aimed simply as assisting in arriving at the proper purposive construction and contextual interpretation—and they were no more than aids for doing so.[90] One should, however, keep in mind that a purposive construction is only possible if the inventive purpose of the patent is clear. This requires that the meaning of the patent and the claims, in particular, should be discernible from the face of the patent documents.[91] A proper, and somewhat wider, scope of protection presupposes, therefore, the proper drafting of the patent and its claims.

The first 'Protocol question' envisages that the claim has an ambit wider than the literal meaning of the words, so as to give fair protection to the patentee. This is achieved by including all variants that do not have a material effect on how the invention works within the scope of the claim and hence potentially within the exclusive right of the patentee. The effect of this question became very clear in *American Home Products v. Novartis Pharmaceuticals*,[92] which was concerned with a claim for the '*use of rapamycin for the preparation of a medicament for inhibiting organ or tissue transplant rejection in a*

[85] [1995] RPC 585 at 594.

[86] [1997] RPC 649.

[87] [1998] FSR 299.

[88] *Wheatley (Davina) v. Drillsafe Ltd* [2001] RPC 133.

[89] *American Home Products Corp. v. Novartis Pharmaceuticals UK Ltd* [2001] RPC 159.

[90] *Wheatley (Davina) v. Drillsafe Ltd* (see n. 88), at 134–5.

[91] *Rohm & Haas Co. v. Collag Ltd (No. 1)* [2002] FSR 28 (CA).

[92] *American Home Products Corp. v. Novartis Pharmaceuticals UK Ltd* [2001] RPC 159.

mammal in need thereof. The alleged infringement was a derivative of rapamycin with a slightly different peripheral chemical structure, known as 'SDZ RAD'. The Court of Appeal ruled, firstly, that the variant for the purposes of this question was either SDZ RAD or all potential derivates of rapamycin. It did so after concluding that the reference to any derivatives in the title of the patent was not backed up by a reference to anything other than rapamycin, as a single molecule, in the claims. The claim therefore had to be construed as excluding any derivatives, especially because the specification did not identify a single derivative that had been shown to work. The patent only taught something about rapamycin itself.

The Court then went on to hold that there was no evidence that the use of the variant SDZ RAD would materially affect the way in which the invention worked. This negative answer to the first Protocol question went, therefore, in favour of the patentee and left open the possibility that the variant would infringe. At a more general level, it is worth keeping in mind that the issue of whether a variant has a material effect on the way in which the invention works depends upon the level of generality that is used to describe how the invention works.[93] The wider the description is, the easier it also is to fit the variant within the description. The correct approach to construing the way in which the invention works is therefore to describe its working at the level of generality with which it was described in the claim of the patent. This is the best way to secure a reasonable amount of certainty and predictability for third parties, which is one of the aims built into the first Protocol question.

One should also not exclude any differences between the invention and variant from consideration by defining the way in which the invention worked unduly broadly. For example, a variant was concerned with an endogenous DNA sequence that needed the introduction of a construct in order to be activated and be able to express erythropoietin, while the patent claimed an exogenous DNA sequence that was suitable to express erythropoietin when introduced to a host cell. The need for activation in case of the variant, especially, led to the conclusion that it was different and that it had a material effect on the way in which the invention worked.[94]

The second Protocol question builds in a safeguard and takes into account the interests of third parties, as different from those of the patentee. It does so by excluding any variants from the scope of the exclusive right that is enjoyed by the patentee unless the third parties should have realized that they were immaterial. Reasonable certainty on this point is achieved by excluding only those variants that are obviously or clearly immaterial. In the circumstances of *American Home Products v. Novartis Pharmaceuticals*, all that could be said was that it was likely that some derivatives of rapamycin might work, while it was impossible to predict whether a particular variant would work. It was therefore not obvious at the relevant time that SDZ RAD would obviously or clearly have no material effect. That meant, in this case, that the variant did not infringe. The Court of Appeal interprets the second Protocol question as asking whether an inventive step was involved in reaching the variant, given the teaching disclosed in the patent that it allegedly infringes. If that is, indeed, the case and if the skilled person would have concluded so at the time of publication of the patent, then the variant does not infringe the patent.[95]

---

[93] *Kirin-Amgen Inc. v. Transkaryotic Therapies Inc.* [2003] RPC 31. In the House of Lords, the approach of asking whether the variant solves the underlying problem by means that have the same technical effect was preferred: [2005] 1 All ER 667, [2005] RPC 9 (HL).

[94] Ibid.

[95] Ibid.; *American Home Products Corp. v. Novartis Pharmaceuticals UK Ltd* [2001] RPC 159.

The Court of Appeal nevertheless went on to consider the third Protocol question. The Court decided that the third question should have received a positive answer, because the word 'rapamycin' was clearly used throughout the specification to indicate a single molecule, rapamycin itself.[96] A distinction can be made in relation to the third question between the situation in which the limitations expressed in the exact wording of the claim have a technical justification and the situation in which the limitations appear to be arbitrary to the skilled man. The latter can be the case, for example, when the claim refers to a circular rod, in line with the example given in the specifications, whereas, from a technical point of view such limitation was not required and other shapes of rod were also suitable. In such a situation, the skilled man is entitled to arrive at the conclusion that such an arbitrary limitation is intended by the patentee and that, as a result, in our example, protection is limited to circular rods and other shapes of rod will therefore not infringe the patent.[97]

Returning to *American Home Products v. Novartis Pharmaceuticals*, the exclusive right was therefore limited to rapamycin, because the Court held that the skilled person would have to engage in proper research, going beyond the level of his skill and application to perform the invention, when finding out whether a particular variant had certain properties. In relation to the latter point, the specification and the claims were insufficient, and would therefore, in any case, have been invalid.[98]

Equivalents

The first instance decision in *American Home Products* had come to a different conclusion by construing the word 'rapamycin' in the claim as including any derivatives. That led to a finding of infringement, which brings up the difficult point of equivalents. The USA[99] and many European countries[100] also grant the patentee a certain level of protection for equivalents. In this case, it would be possible to argue that the derivatives of rapamycin were equivalents.

From a theoretical point of view, one can either argue that the UK does not have an equivalents doctrine and the slightly more restrictive decision of the Court of Appeal in *American Home Products* seems to point in that direction. Alternatively, one could argue that what the UK calls purposive interpretation and what occurs in the Protocol questions test equals an equivalents approach. Suffice it to say that the doctrine of equivalents does not excel by its clarity. Without wishing to analyse this issue under any national law in particular, it can be said that there are a number of facets to equivalents. Firstly, equivalent elements replace or substitute elements of a claim, but they must perform the same function as the elements that they replace or substitute. Secondly, the equivalents must be able to achieve the same result and do so in the same manner, and thirdly, the equivalent must somehow have been obvious or readily at the disposal of the skilled person. This is perfectly logical, because an inventive equivalent might be more deserving of protection in its own right, rather than of consideration as an infringement. In most legal systems,

---

[96] *American Home Products Corp. v. Novartis Pharmaceuticals UK Ltd* [2001] RPC 159.

[97] *Russell Finex Ltd v. Telesonic AG* [2004] RPC 744, applying *Société Technique de Pulvérisation Step v. Emson Europe Ltd* [1993] RPC 513 (CA), *per* Hoffmann LJ at 522.

[98] *American Home Products Corp. v. Novartis Pharmaceuticals UK Ltd* [2001] RPC 159.

[99] See *Warner-Jenkinson v. Hilton Davis*, 117 SCt 1040 (1997); the recent controversial decision in *Festo Corp. v. Shoketsu Kinzokukogyo Kabushiki Co. Ltd* 234 F 3d 558 (2000) (Fed Cir); *Festo Corp. v. Shoketsu Kinzokukogyo Kabushiki Co. Ltd* 122 SCt 1831 (2002) (Supreme Court); M. Adelman 'Festo and the doctrine of equivalents: implications for patent infringement litigation' (2002) 7 IIPLP 9, 1–16.

[100] On the German evolution, see F.-W. Engel, 'The "*Wortsinn*" of patent claims in German case law on patent infringement disputes' (2003) 34 IIC 233.

the doctrine of equivalents is excluded in those cases in which the patentee amended his or her application as a result of concerns about novelty or obviousness. This involves making reference to the prosecution history of the patent, which is not always a straightforward process leading to clear answers. Overall, the doctrine of equivalents seems to create almost more problems than it solves.

Why does all of this matter as far as the UK is concerned? The simple answer to this question is that the revised version of the EPC of 29 November 2000, which is now in force, explicitly refers to 'equivalents' in the new Art. 2 of the Protocol on the Interpretation of Art. 69, whereas the original version did not. The text that was finally agreed simply says that:

> for the purpose of determining the extent of protection conferred by a European Patent, due account shall be taken of any element which is equivalent to an element specified in the claims.

This therefore does not give a lot of additional information on how, and to what extent, these equivalents—however they are defined—are to be taken into account. One might argue that the UK already takes due account of equivalents in the first two Protocol questions and that no change is therefore needed—but one might also focus on the third question and argue that this has now become completely untenable in the light of the further increased emphasis on purposive interpretation. It is submitted that the truth may be somewhere in the middle. The recent trend in the UK towards a full purposive interpretation, and the emphasis on the first two Protocol questions, need to be encouraged and strengthened. In that context, the third Protocol question is only a marginal check that looks at what the national addressee would have understood the author to mean by using those words.[101]

The doctrine of equivalents should not allow the patentee to get away with shoddily drafted claims. The primary focus should remain on careful and accurate drafting of the claims, which also gives third parties more legal certainty. It is submitted that this approach is to be favoured. Alternatively, however, one might consider getting rid of the third Protocol question altogether, especially in the light of the revision of the EPC. But in that scenario, one needs to replace it by a protection against badly drafted claims resulting in unduly broad protection and being rescued by the courts. It has been suggested, by Professor Adelman[102] among others, that one could limit the additional protection offered by equivalents to those equivalent elements that were not reasonably foreseeable at the time that the claims were drafted.[103] But in the light of what we said earlier, this would probably also cover inventive equivalents,[104] when it might be more just to exclude them and, eventually, to grant rights to the inventor of the non-obvious equivalent.

Maybe, then, one ought to distinguish on this point between what was not reasonably foreseeable and what requires inventive activity: the patentee cannot be blamed for overlooking the former and may be entitled to protection as an equivalent,[105] but the latter would involve such an effort on the part of the alleged infringer that he or she, rather than the patentee, should own any potential right in the variant. Ultimately, this is a debate about the correct scope of protection for the patentee, and the balance between the rights of the patentee and third parties. The debate will therefore probably go on for some time

---

[101] *Kirin-Amgen v. Transkaryotic Therapies* [2005] 1 All ER 667, [2005] RPC 9 (HL).

[102] Adelman (2002).

[103] See J Brinkhof, 'Is there a European doctrine of equivalence?' (2002) 33 IIC 911.

[104] Some German decisions seem to have accepted this. See, e.g., the decision of the German *Bundesgerichtshof* (Federal Supreme Court) in *Fixing Device II (Befestigungsvorrichtung II)* 1992 IIC 111.

[105] See Brinkhof (2002) at 923.

to come, especially because the minimalist agreed text in the revised EPC was the result of a failure to agree on any more specific and detailed proposal.

As if all this were not yet complex enough, we need to add one more layer of complications. One should indeed keep in mind that the Protocol questions are nothing more than a test in order to facilitate the implementation under UK patent law of EPC, Art. 69, and the Protocol to that Article; in other words, it is ultimately the Protocol that takes precedence. This is not to say that the Protocol questions have become useless and can be set aside easily—they remain the test in the vast majority of cases—but there will be a small number of cases in which the judge will find it impossible to apply them and to come to a logical conclusion on their basis. The Court of Appeal has recognized that, in those cases, the Protocol questions can be set aside and that direct reference can be made to the Protocol in order to resolve the case, and to strike a fair balance between the interests of the patentee, who is entitled to certainty and fairness in relation to the degree of protection, and the interest of third parties, so as not to stifle competition and to allow for a healthy degree of competition.[106]

Purposive interpretation and the Protocol questions, as the key tool when equivalents become involved, therefore emerged clearly as the cornerstones of the law in this area, but, in the light of all of the complications that went before, some uncertainty remained. When given the welcome opportunity to do so in the *Kirin-Amgen* case, the House of Lords seized the opportunity to restate the position with authority.

The House of Lords provides a summary

One might summarize the UK position,[107] when the courts had to construe a patent and interpret the claims, as follows. When confronted with claims that have a plain meaning in themselves, the courts will not have recourse to the body of the patent or the specification to make the claims mean something different. The context only needs to be looked at if the language of the claim is ambiguous and capable of more than one meaning. One needs to keep in mind, however, that the author of the patent is using language to make a communication for a practical purpose: the meaning that the language has for the person for whom it was intended needs to be taken into account. In patent cases, this must include the person skilled in the art.

Hence we arrive at purposive interpretation. This does not involve extending or going beyond the definition of the technical matters for which the patentee sought protection in the claims; the question was, instead, what a person skilled in the art would have understood the patentee to mean by the language used. The choice of language is therefore of critical importance. One should recognize, however, that the patentee was describing something new and for which there might not yet be a generally accepted definition. There are, therefore, rare situations in which it is obvious to the skilled person that the patentee has departed from the conventional use of language or that non-essential elements have been included. That purposive approach is found in the Protocol to Art. 69 and it is also the approach set out in *Catnic*. It gives the patentee the full extent—but no more than that—of the monopoly that a reasonable person skilled in the art would think the patentee was claiming when he read the claims in their context.

The main problem in the context of this purposive approach is how to deal with equivalents. They clearly do not correspond to the exact language of the claim, but they fulfil an

---

[106] *Pharmacia Corp. v. Merck & Co. Inc.* [2002] RPC 775, approved by the House of Lords in *Kirin-Amgen v. Transkaryotic Therapies* [2005] 1 All ER 667, [2005] RPC 9 (HL), which also approved the approach to equivalents that we suggested above.

[107] As did the House of Lords in *Kirin-Amgen v. Transkaryotic Therapies Inc.* [2005] 1 All ER 667, [2005] RPC 9.

equivalent purpose, which makes it difficult to determine whether or not they fall within the scope of the claims. While it is important to distinguish between the core *Catnic* principle of purposive interpretation—which implements the Protocol—on the one hand, and guidance on the application of that very principle to equivalents, on the other, this is where the Protocol questions come in. They allow the court to apply the principle of purposive interpretation to equivalents—but, as such, they are only guidance and there will be cases in which they will not be useful. In those cases, one has to fall back on the Protocol and the principle of purposive interpretation itself.

The *Kirin-Amgen* facts show an example. There was, indeed, no suggestion that the term '*an exogenous DNA sequence coding for erythropoietin*' could have a loose meaning including '*an endogenous DNA sequence coding for erythropoietin*'. In this context, there is a clear equivalent, but the Protocol questions make no sense. Instead, the essential question was whether the person skilled in the art would have understood the invention to operate at such a level of generality that it was irrelevant whether the DNA that coded for erythropoietin was exogenous or not. The answer depends entirely on what that person thinks the invention is and, once that answer is in place, the rest follows automatically.

An overview

Infringement is, perhaps, the area of patent law that has been most radically transformed by the 1977 legislation. A statutory framework replaced the old common law rules and this appears to have worked well. The case law in relation to that framework suggests, however, that there remain a few problems, with the potential differences of language between the UK legislation and the European patent approach being at the heart of the difficulty.

The all-important issue is how the courts will approach the interpretation of specifications and claims. *Catnic* clearly represents the dawning of a new era, in which the patentee is treated more generously and his or her rivals are more likely to be ensnared in the web of infringement. In so far as it is appropriate to rely on the tip of reported cases that are part of the iceberg of litigation, it seems that, for the most part, the courts have understood the import of what was intended in *Catnic*.

The *Improver* litigation is, however, a sorry tale and suggests that the UK courts are yet to fully embrace a Continental approach to interpretation, being held back by the third of the three questions that now have to be asked—namely, whether the skilled reader, having seen that a variant was obvious, would then still consider that the words of the specification required strict compliance. Thus expressed, the bizarre nature of the question becomes clear: it requires the skilled reader consciously to ignore that which is obvious to him—which is quite a mental feat. Imposing this bizarre question then leads to the unacceptable situation in which, in a case such as *Improver*, a European patent has differing effects in different member States, quite contrary to the whole rationale and purpose of international patent cooperation. The *Improver* saga and the *PLG* case seem now to represent a low water mark, however, with the *Catnic* approach restored—however uncertainly—to its central position.

It could be concluded from this that *Catnic* did not intend to go as far as is required by the EPC, which, as has been noted, was not, on the face of it, in the minds of the Law Lords at the time. The better view is that, like children on new bicycles, judges asked to give purposive interpretations to specifications and claims will be inevitably cautious at first, may make the odd mistake or two, but will, as time passes and the unfamiliar becomes the familiar, grow in confidence and eventually disappear those mistakes. With more and more European legislation coming to the courts to be considered, it seems likely that the necessary confidence and accuracy will evolve sooner, rather than later, and that judges, deprived as they now are of what has been described by Professor Cornish as the rigid 'fenceposts' of literally interpreted patents,[108] will be equally able to gain as much assistance from the guidance of the 'signposts' that represent the results of the new purposive approach.

This evolution simply has to occur: if it does not, there is an obvious danger that UK patent law will start to become isolated from the mainstream international approach. Luckily, there is increasing evidence that can be derived from the judgments of the Court of Appeal that we are getting there. The House of Lords seems to have finalized developments in this area in *Kirin-Amgen*; purposive interpretation and *Catnic* are the norm, and that puts us in line with the EPC and the Protocol to Art. 69. And when it comes to equivalents, the Protocol questions offer guidance as to how to apply the principle of purposive interpretation.

All we now need to do is to continue to put it into practice...

Further reading

BRINKHOF, J., 'Is there a European doctrine of equivalence?' (2002) 33 IIC 911.

COLE, P., 'Purposive construction under English law' [1994] 10 EIPR 455.

COOK, T. 'Responding to concerns about the scope of the defence from patent infringement for acts done for experimental purposes relating to the subject matter of the invention', [2006] 3 IPQ 193–222.

CURLEY, D. and SHERATON, H., 'The Lords rule in *Amgen v. TKT*', 27(4) (2005) 27 EIPR 4, 154–8.

THORLEY, S., MILLER, R., BURKILL, G. and BIRSS, C. (eds) (2006) *Terrell on the Law of Patents*, 16th edn, London: Sweet and Maxwell, chs 6, 7, and 8.

---

[108] See W. R. Cornish and D. Llewelyn (2003) *Intellectual Property*, 5th edn, London: Sweet and Maxwell, ch. 6, p. 236.

7

Supplementary protection certificates, the proposed utility model, and the Community patent

In this chapter, we are concerned with certain aspects of the involvement of the European Union (EU) with patent law. These aspects all represent add-ons to a traditional patent system that is based on national patents. The first—supplementary protection certificates (SPCs)—is already in place; the two others—the utility model and the Community patent—are still on the drawing board.

Supplementary protection certificates

Background

Pharmaceutical products can attract patent protection just as any other product that satisfies the requirements for patentability. The complicating factor, however, is that new pharmaceutical products need testing and government authorization before they can be marketed. All of this generally takes place after the patent application has been filed and the whole process may take years, rather than months or weeks. Because the term of a patent is calculated on the basis of the filing date, patent protection for research and development-based products[1] is, in practice, eroded. The period between the first marketing of the drug and the expiry of the patent was shortened, and there have been cases in which the patent had expired before marketing authorization was obtained. Because the copying of drugs is, in addition, rather easy—especially when compared with the independent development process—this phenomenon was seriously damaging the pharmaceutical industry.[2]

The situation became particularly pressing when the USA and Japan introduced measures to restore the term of patent protection for pharmaceutical products.[3] When France and Italy started introducing national measures aiming to produce a similar effect, the European Community took over the initiative and introduced supplementary protection certificates (SPCs) as a *sui generis* intellectual property right for medicinal products.[4]

---

[1] Generic drugs are not faced with the same problem, because they do not need the extensive testing, etc., and rely, to a great extent, on the work done in respect of the original drug of which they are a copy.

[2] J. N. Adams, 'Supplementary protection certificates: the challenge to EC Regulation 1768/92' [1994] 8 EIPR 323.

[3] Two Japanese laws—one dated 1980 and the other dated 1987—address the problem and the USA introduced the Drug Price Competition and Patent Term Restoration Act of 1984 (informally known as the Waxman-Hatch Act).

[4] Regulation 1768/92 concerning the creation of a supplementary protection certificate for medicinal products [1992] OJ L 182/1.

EC Regulation 1768/92

In Europe, an extension of the patent term required the amendment of Art. 63 of the European Patent Convention (EPC). Because a number of the contracting parties have a pharmaceutical industry that is almost exclusively based on generics, it was felt that the required unanimous vote was out of reach.[5] The Convention does allow for the introduction by the contracting states of other *sui generis* rights, although only in so far as they grant new and different kinds of industrial property protection. Because the extension of the patent term was not an option, therefore, the Community took the route of the *sui generis* right and called it the 'supplementary protection certificate'.[6]

The Regulation provides that any product that is protected by a patent in a member State and which is as a medicinal product subject to an authorization procedure can be the subject of a certificate.[7] A 'product' is defined widely as the active ingredient, or the combination of active ingredients, of a medicinal product and the latter category comprises substances or combinations of substances that are used to prevent, diagnose, or treat a disease, or to restore, correct, or modify physiological functions in humans or in animals.[8] This wide definition does, however, have its limitations. Only active ingredients are covered as products and a combination of active ingredients does not include a combination of one active ingredient and another ingredient that is simply there to make a certain pharmaceutical form possible.[9] For the purposes of the definition of the concept of a 'product' in Art. 1 of the Regulations, the intended use is not decisive, but, in any case, a second medical use of an active ingredient is not part of that concept.[10] Protection is only granted for the product covered by the original authorization or by any subsequent authorization that takes place before the expiry of the patent.[11] This is particularly important in cases in which the scope of the patent is wider than that of the authorization. The various ways in which the active ingredient can be formulated are, arguably, all covered.[12] It has, indeed, now been held that the product, as a medicinal product, for the purposes of Art. 3 of the Regulation, includes all forms of it that enjoy protection under the basic patent[13]—but no supplementary protection certificate will be available for products that are not protected by the basic patent in force. For example, no certificate can be granted for the combination of an anti-ulcer agent with two specific antibiotics if the patent only refers to the anti-ulcer agent.[14]

---

[5] An amendment to Art. 63, EPC, which would allow the term of protection for pharmaceutical products to be extended awaits ratification, but which is not likely to be ratified and come into force in the near future.

[6] H. P. Kunz-Hallstein, 'The compatibility of a Community "certificate for the restoration of protection" with the European Patent Convention' [1990] 6 EIPR 209.

[7] Article 2.

[8] Article 1.

[9] Case C-431/04 *Massachusetts Institute of Technology* [2006] ECR I-4089. See N. Klix and B. Hermann, 'Bitter pill for the pharmaceutical industry' (2006) 1 JIPLP 10, 639–42.

[10] Case C-202/05 *Yissum Research & Development Co. of the Hebrew University of Jerusalem v. Comptroller-General of Patents* [2007] OJ C 96/19 (ECJ).

[11] Article 4.

[12] This is logical for anyone familiar with chemistry and the pharmaceutical industry. The *travaux préparatoires* of the Regulation seem to spell this out by referring to salts and esters of acids as coming under one product definition. See R. Whaite and N. Jones, 'Pharmaceutical patent term restoration: the European Commission's Regulation' [1992] 9 EIPR 324 at 325.

[13] Case C-392/97 *Farmitalia Carlo Erba Srl* [1999] ECR I-5553, [2000] 2 CMLR 253.

[14] *Takeda Chemical Industries Ltd's Applications (No. 3)* [2004] RPC 37.

Only the patentee of the original patent[15] or any successor in title can file an application for a certificate.[16] Licensees are excluded from this procedure, which has to take place at the national patent office that granted the patent. The whole granting procedure takes place at national level.[17] Two statutory instruments translate this into UK intellectual property law and allow the Patent Office to issue the certificate: the Patents (Compulsory Licensing and Supplementary Protection Certificates) Regulations 2007 and the Patents Rules 2007.[18]

An application for a certificate must be filed within six months of the date on which the marketing authorization for the medicinal product was granted. The one exception to this rule is the situation in which the authorization is granted before the patent is granted. In that case, the application for the certificate must be lodged with the national patent office within six months of the date of the grant of the patent.[19]

If at the date of the application the patent covering the medicinal product[20] is in force and the marketing authorization is valid, a single certificate[21] can be granted for the medicinal product.[22] It should be noted that the Regulation refers to the first marketing authorization—whether that is a medicinal product for human use or a medicinal product for veterinary use[23]—in relation to the application for, and the grant of, the certificate,[24] but that any therapeutic use that is authorized before the expiry of the certificate comes within the scope of the protection offered by the certificate.[25] A certificate confers the same rights as the basic patent and is subject to the same limitations.[26] These are granted for a period that runs from the end of the patent term and the length of that period is calculated in relation to the period for which protection was lost due to the authorization process. The starting point is the period that lapsed between the date on which the patent application was lodged and that on which the marketing authorization was granted; this

[15] A product may be covered by more than one patent. In such a case, a supplementary protection certificate can be granted for each basic patent (one basic patent and certificate per holder). For further details on this point, and on the problems that arise when patents and marketing authorization are owned by different companies, see Case C-181/95 *Biogen Inc. v. Smithkline Biologicals SA* [1996] ECR I-717, [1997] 1 CMLR 704.

[16] Article 6.

[17] Article 9.

[18] SI 2007/3293, which inserts a new s. 128B and a Sch. 4A in the Patents Act 1977, and SI 2007/3291, which deals with the procedural and formal issues in reg. 116, respectively.

[19] Article 7.

[20] The aim of Art. 3(c) is to preclude the grant of successive certificates for one and the same product, and hence the strong link with the patent. But different patents protecting the same product can be in different hands and, then, the grant of a supplementary protection certificate for a product to a holder of a basic patent before an application was lodged, in relation to the same product by a different holder of a different patent on the basis of a common marketing authorization, does not provide a ground for rejecting the latter application: *Chiron Corp's & Novo Nordisk A/S's Application* [2005] RPC 24 (Patent Office).

[21] No second certificate covering the same member State can be granted according to Art. 3(c).

[22] Article 3.

[23] Case C-31/03 *Pharmacia Italia SpA, formerly Pharmacia & Upjohn SpA* [2004] ECR I-10001.

[24] Ibid.

[25] Article 4, subject to the general limitation of the protection to anything coming within the scope of the basic patent. See also Whaite and Jones [1992] at 325.

[26] Article 5. Interesting and outstanding questions are whether, and to what extent, certificates and patents will be treated in an identical way under national law, and how certificates will relate to Art. 85 of the EC Treaty and to the block exemptions: see Whaite and Jones [1992] at 236. The High Court decided, some time ago, that the limitations to which both the patent and the certificate are subject must include compulsory licences and licences of right under the Patents Act 1977. (The case is reported as *In the matter of an application by Faulding Pharmaceuticals plc to settle the terms of a licence of right under Supplementary Protection Certificate SPC/GB93/032, in the name of Research Corporation Technologies Inc.* [1995] 1 EIPR D-16 and 17.)

period is reduced by five years. A final restriction is that the resulting term of protection offered by the certificate cannot exceed five years.[27]

Once granted, the continued existence of the certificate is subject to the payment of an annual fee[28] and the certificate will also expire if the marketing authorization for that medicinal product is withdrawn.[29] A certificate becomes invalid if the basic patent is revoked or limited to the extent that the product for which the certificate was granted would no longer be protected by the claims of the basic patent. Once the basic patent has expired, the certificate becomes invalid and anyone has the right to submit an application or to bring an action in this respect if grounds exist that would have justified the revocation or limitation of the patent.[30]

Clearly, the certificate is very closely linked to the patent covering the medicinal product that is the subject of the certificate. One might even argue that it is, in reality, more than an extension of the patent term for pharmaceutical products. There are, however, differences[31]—although one has to admit that the *sui generis* right was moulded along the lines of the patent model. The certificate is only available for products that are subject to an authorization procedure and there is no link to any disclosure. The scope of protection is in no way determined by the patent claims; the patent is only the precondition for the grant of the certificate and it is the authorization that defines the real scope of the certificate. It is submitted that the certificate constitutes a genuine *sui generis* right.[32] But the argument that it is different from the patent system only because it protects successful inventions[33] cannot be endorsed: a patented invention is successful in the sense that it fulfils the requirements for patentability and the pharmaceutical industry often finds very lucrative exploitation opportunities even for those patented products that are not granted a marketing authorization as medicinal products. The real tests for success are the sales figures for the drugs and these will only be known after the deadline for the filing of an application for a certificate—that is, in general, six months after the first authorization to market the product was obtained.

The Regulation came into force on 2 January 1993. All products that were, at that date, covered by a patent and for which the first marketing authorization within the Community was granted after 1 January 1985, qualified for a certificate. A number of other member States were allowed to use another authorization date and, accordingly, Spain, Greece, and Portugal only made certificates available from 1 January 1998 onwards.[34]

The extension of the system

Industry has lobbied hard to see the system of supplementary protection certificates extended to other products. The argument is that the system should be applied to all products that are subject to a marketing authorization. The Commission has now recognized this argument and has extended the system of supplementary protection certificates to plant protection products.[35] These products are subject to an authorization procedure

---

[27] Article 13.

[28] Articles 12 and 14.

[29] Article 14(d).

[30] Article 15.

[31] Kunz-Hallstein [1990] at 209.

[32] Ibid.; see also report of the European Max-Planck Group for Conflict of Laws in Intellectual Property (CLIP) (1991) *Supplementary Protection Certificates*, Hamburg: Max Planck Institute, pp. 16 *et seq.*

[33] Ibid.

[34] Articles 19, 21, and 23.

[35] European Parliament and Council Regulation 1610/96 concerning the creation of a supplementary protection certificate for plant protection products [1996] OJ L 198/30.

under Directive 91/414[36] and first marketing of these products can only take place once the marketing authorization has been obtained.

The new Regulation defines plant protection products as '*active substances and preparations containing one or more active substances, put up in the form in which they are supplied to the user*',[37] which have a number of intended uses: firstly, they can '*protect plants or plant products against all harmful organisms or prevent the action of such organisms*';[38] secondly, they can be used to influence the life processes of plants, in so far as they do not do that as a nutrient. They can also be used to preserve plant products, to destroy undesirable plants, to destroy parts of plants, or to check or prevent undesirable growth of plants.[39] This is followed, in Art. 1 of the Regulation, by further definitions of 'substances', 'preparations', 'plants', and 'plant products'. The rest of the provisions of the Regulation are almost exact copies of the provisions in the Regulation on pharmaceutical products: the same rules apply as if one were simply to replace the words 'pharmaceutical product' with 'plant protection product'. But it is important to emphasize that the existence of a patent for the product is, once again, a prerequisite[40] and that only the first marketing authorization for the product—to be taken in the sense of its active ingredient—counts.[41] If more than one patent exists for one product, only one certificate shall be granted in case the same holder owns the patents. More than one certificate can only be granted in respect of the same product if there are multiple patents owned by different holders, who each apply separately for the certificates.[42]

The Regulation entered into force on 9 January 1997,[43] but it only applies from 2 January 1998 onwards for those member States whose national law did not provide for the patentability of plant protection products on 1 January 1990.[44] The Patents (Supplementary Protection Certificates) Rules 1997[45] provide the procedure under which these certificates will be granted in the UK.

The challenge to the Regulation

Spain has a pharmaceutical industry that relies heavily on generic drugs and which is affected negatively by the Regulation. It brought an action in the European Court of Justice to annul Regulation 1768/92.[46] The main argument that Spain used was that the Regulation is ultra vires, in that the Community did not have the competence to create the certificate.[47] This argument was based on Arts 30 and 295 of the EC Treaty. Specifically, Art. 295 provides that the Treaty shall not interfere with the system of property ownership,[48] while Art. 30 could be said to deal only with the exercise of existing

---

[36] [1991] OJ L 230/1, as amended by Directive 95/36 [1995] OJ L 172/8.

[37] Article 1 of the Regulation.

[38] Ibid.

[39] Ibid.

[40] Article 3(1).

[41] A subsequent authorization for the active ingredient produced by a patented improved manufacturing process cannot be the basis for the grant of a supplementary protection certificate: see *BASF AG's SPC Application* [2000] RPC 1.

[42] Article 3(2).

[43] Article 21.

[44] Article 20.

[45] SI 1997/64.

[46] Case C-350/92 *Spain v. EU Council* [1995] ECR I-1985, [1996] 1 CMLR 415.

[47] See also Adams [1994] at 323.

[48] This argument attacks the validity of almost all intellectual property initiatives taken by the Community.

rights and the extent to which such exercise is acceptable. The arguments come down to the point that these provisions reserve the power to regulate substantive intellectual property law for the member States and exclude Community action in this area.

The Court flatly rejected this argument.[49] It repeated its ruling that Art. 295:

> cannot be interpreted as reserving to the national legislature, in relation to industrial and commercial property, the power to adopt measures which would adversely affect the principle of free movement of goods within the common market.[50]

It can be derived from this ruling that the argument that rules concerning the very existence of industrial property rights fall within the sole jurisdiction of the national legislature cannot be endorsed;[51] the rules of the Treaty must be allowed to interfere in appropriate cases. In relation to Art. 30, the Court referred to its judgment in *Simmenthal SpA v. Italian Minister for Finance*[52] and repeated the part of that judgment within which it ruled that '*Article* [30] *is not designed to reserve certain matters to the exclusive jurisdiction of member states*'.[53]

Having rejected Spain's main argument, the Court turned to Spain's second argument, which concerned the legal basis for the Regulation. The Council had used Art. 95 of the EC Treaty as a legal basis for the Regulation. This meant that the Regulation must pursue the objective of the creation of the single market, as set out in Art. 18 of the Treaty. It might be argued that the Regulation does not pursue that objective, because:

> as far as the free movement of goods is concerned, the certificate, by its very nature, tends to extend the compartmentalization of the market beyond the duration of the basic patent, and thus adds to the exceptions provided for in Article 30 of the Treaty, without the extension of the scope of that provision being justified by the Community objective.[54]

Thus, Spain concluded that the introduction of the certificate would create obstacles to the free movement of goods: because the creation of a single market with a free flow of goods was one of the principal aims of the Treaty, such a measure must be ultra vires.

This argument cannot, however, be accepted and it was also rejected by the Court.[55] The Court first stated that Art. 18 allows the Community to take harmonization measures to achieve its objective. Such harmonization measures may be necessary to deal with disparities between the laws of the member States, if, and in so far as, these are hindering the free movement of goods. In this particular case, Italy and France had already been creating their own national certificates, and so the only way to avoid the partitioning of the market was the creation of a measure at Community level. Indeed, differences in protection given to one and the same medicine would fragment the Common Market. The situation in which a product would still be protected in some national markets, but not in others, would give rise to different market conditions in different parts of the Common Market. The Court thus agreed with the drafters of the Regulation, who argued, in the sixth Recital, that:

> The regulation thus aims to prevent the heterogeneous development of national laws leading to further disparities which would be likely to create obstacles to the free movement of

---

[49] Case C-350/92 *Spain v. EU Council* [1995] ECR I-1985 at 2009–12.
[50] Ibid. at 2010–11.
[51] Ibid. at 2011.
[52] Case 35/76 [1976] ECR 1871, [1977] 2 CMLR 1.
[53] Case C-350/92 *Spain v. EU Council* [1995] ECR I-1985 at 2011.
[54] Ibid. at 2013.
[55] Ibid. at 2012–16.

medicinal products within the Community and thus directly affect the establishment and the functioning of the internal market.[56]

In conclusion, the Court rejected all arguments that had been put forward by Spain and its challenge to the Regulation failed.

Another approach that leads to the same conclusion is that taken by Jean-François Verstrynghe:

> The Court has already given some hint of its thinking in its recent judgment in the Article [226] infringement procedure as applied to compulsory licenses for non-use of patents in the UK. In this judgment of 18 February 1992, it declared a particular feature of the British law to be illegal under Article [28].[57] If this is so, it must then also be accepted that this feature concerning the scope and conditions of patent protection in the UK might affect the establishment and functioning of the internal market under Article [95], and that therefore the European Community could have harmonised this detail of patent protection—and by implication many other details of national IPR laws [and thus also the certificate]—which affect the establishment and functioning of the internal market.[58]

The importance of this case is not limited to the issue of supplementary protection certificates. It gives clear guidance in relation to the way in which the Community can operate in the area of intellectual property rights. As we have demonstrated in previous chapters, Community law will interfere with the exercise of intellectual property rights whenever that exercise conflicts with the Community's principles of free movement and free competition. But the role of the Community is not a purely negative one based on Arts 28–30 and 81–82 of the Treaty. This case shows clearly that Art. 18 allows the Community to create new rights and harmonize the existing national provisions, in so far as this is necessary for the creation of the single market; Art. 95 will provide a legal basis for such measures. Further measures—such as the creation of new supranational rights that are superimposed on national rights[59]—which fall outside the scope of Arts 18 and 95, can be based on Arts 94 and 308 of the Treaty.[60]

In the case at issue, the measure did, indeed, have as its object the establishment and the functioning of the internal market, because it was introduced as a measure to replace national measures that would have partitioned the internal market. The use of Art. 95 is particularly helpful in such circumstances, because it only requires a qualified majority; Arts 94 and 308 require unanimity. One can easily see the political background to the Spanish challenge on these grounds. If its arguments had succeeded, the Council would have been obliged to use Arts 94 and 308 as a legal basis, and Spain would have been able to veto any supplementary protection certificate scheme that it, and its generics-based pharmaceutical industry, did not like.

Utility models

Against the background of the complexity of, and the costs involved in, the patent system, some felt that the balancing of interests left valuable smaller inventions unprotected.

---

[56] Ibid. at 2014–15.

[57] Case C-30/90 *Commission of the European Communities v. UK* [1992] ECR I-829, [1992] 2 CMLR 709.

[58] J.-F. Verstrynghe, 'The Spring 1993 Horace S Manges Lecture: the European Commission's Direction on copyright and neighbouring rights—towards the regime of the twenty-first century' [1993] 17 Colum-VLA JL & Arts 187 at 194.

[59] For example, the Community trade mark: see Regulation 40/94 [1994] OJ L 11/1.

[60] See also Opinion 1/94 [1994] ECR I-5267 (concerning the Community's competence to sign the TRIPA Agreement).

Perhaps a new balance might be struck between, on the one hand, a weaker system of protection and exclusivity for less important innovations, and, on the other hand, some restrictions on competition that society is prepared to accept in order to get hold of the full benefit of these innovations. Consequently, there is now a further area of patent-related intellectual property activity that needs to be created. The utility model is perhaps best regarded as a 'baby patent'. It is a concept familiar across much of Europe and the EU Commission has proposed[61] that we would all benefit from the introduction—in relation to the UK, Sweden, and Luxembourg—and harmonization—in relation to the other 12 member States, which have widely differing provisions in relation to basic definitions of their domestic utility models—of laws relating to utility models.

It must be emphasized that this proposal, while part of the general drive towards the protection of the principle of free movement of goods by rationalizing intellectual property law, is highly controversial and it is not obvious whether or when the UK will enjoy the provision of a utility model. In 1999, an Amended Proposal[62] was produced, but even apart from the discussion on the merits of the proposal itself, there now seems to be a link with the introduction of the Community patent. It has become unlikely that an agreement on the utility model proposal will be reached and implemented before the Community Patent Regulation goes ahead. And even after that stage, reaching an agreement will not be obvious, despite the existence of the political will to keep the proposal on the agenda at present. All that can really be said at present is that there is a lot of opposition and doubt surrounding the proposal, and that its further development has been stalled since 2001.

The brief discussion of the proposal that follows is therefore not intended as an analysis of legislation that will be implemented at some stage. Instead, it is an attempt to highlight some of the problems of the current patent system, while, at the same time, making the point that there is no straightforward solution and that potential solutions also have their drawbacks.

Definition

As its bland name implies, the utility model is not easy to define. It may be most easily described as a form of right that is similar to a patent in that the usual requirements of novelty, inventive step, and industrial applicability need to be present;[63] the key difference is that the level of inventiveness is lower than in the case of a 'full patent'. The EU Commission propose[64] that the inventor needs to show that the invention exhibits an advantage that is not very obvious for a person skilled in the art having regard to the state of the art. Such advantage can either be of a practical, or of a technical, nature for the use or manufacture of the product or process concerned, or it can offer another benefit to the user in fields such as entertainment and education. Clearly, this may well not amount to what seems like the giant leap into the unknown that, at times, seems necessary for the purposes of the patent legislation—especially if the (vague) reference to the concept of something that is 'very obvious' is taken into account. So if the invention is a better way of doing something, rather than a radically different way, or an improvement

---

[61] COM (97) 691, 97/0356 (COD). See U. Suthersanen, 'A brief tour of utility model law' [1998] EIPR 45 and Proposal for a European Parliament and Council Directive approximating (1998) OJ C36 the legal arrangements for the protection of inventions by utility model.

[62] Amended Proposal for a European Parliament and Council Directive approximating the legal arrangements for the protection of inventions by utility model (2000) OJ C 248/56, COM (99) 309 final. The amended proposal is referred to below as the 'draft Directive'.

[63] Draft Directive, Art. 1(1).

[64] Ibid., Art. 6.

whereby the same process works in the same general way, but with greater efficiency and/ or profitability, then it is the utility model that offers a way forward in the future, assuming its introduction into UK law.

All inventions must be new, must involve such an inventive step, and must be susceptible to industrial application. But aesthetic creations, presentations of information, discoveries, scientific theories, and mathematical methods, as well as schemes, rules, and methods for performing mental acts or doing business, are considered to fall outside the scope of the concept of 'inventions', to the extent that an application refers to them as such.[65] An invention that can be made or used in any kind of industry—including agriculture—will be considered as susceptible to industrial application.[66]

Rationale

Let us say, by way of analogy, that we all fantasize about travelling by sea for leisure: what could be better than a cruise around the world on the liner *Queen Elizabeth II*? Reality will soon rear its ugly head: examinations of bank balance and diary alike rapidly demonstrate that this will only ever be an ambition. There might, however, remains a hope of pleasure on the sea, if time and money permit a day cruise from Glasgow down the Firth of Clyde instead. Likewise, the patent system is not for all. The cost of obtaining a suitable patent and the time it takes to register it from the initial priority date render this 'luxury' intellectual property right inappropriate in many cases, especially for small businesses. Thus there is a clear need to have a lesser right—hence, the Commission's proposal, based on a middle way through the different domestic approaches.

If implemented the idea would be that, with an investigation of only the formalities of the application for a utility model, the right should be conferred within six months of the initial application. Equally, this protection would then only last for six years, although with the possibility of two short extensions, if a search report is applied for.[67] Within this restricted period, similar protection would be enjoyed by the right holder to that given to the patentee. Utility models that cover a product will confer the exclusive right to make, use, sell, offer for sale, or import for these purposes the product on the proprietor of the right. Utility models that cover a process will confer on their proprietor the exclusive right to use the process and to use, offer for sale, sell, or import for these purposes at least the product directly obtained by that process. Acts done for private and non-commercial purposes, as well as acts done for experimental purposes, relating to the subject matter of the protected invention will not, however, infringe.[68]

It is easy to overestimate the apparent disadvantage of the short term of protection. Whereas the motivation behind the supplementary protection certificate is to extend protection in particular cases, the utility model may have particular value in instances in which the present patent term is unnecessarily long and the long wait for registration is potentially detrimental. The 'shelf life' of many inventions is now much less than 20 years, especially, perhaps, in relation to the kinds of relatively minor improvement under consideration here. The Commission refers to the toy industry, watch manufacture, optics, and microtechnology as areas in which it is feels that there is demand for the utility model. Overall, it claims, the average lifetime of an invention in these areas is less than six years.

---

[65] Ibid., Art. 3.
[66] Ibid., Art. 7.
[67] Ibid., Art. 19.
[68] Ibid., Art. 20.

There may also be an overlap between patents and utility models: '*The same invention may form the subject matter, simultaneously or successively, of a patent application and a utility model application.*'[69]

Do we need it?[70]

In answer to the question of necessity, a simply 'Yes' will suffice. The arguments above demonstrate a clear niche in which utility models provide a cheap and cheerful form of protection in relation to which the full patent would be uneconomic. It is also clear, from figures in the Commission's report,[71] that, in some countries, utility model applications are as numerous as patent applications, although it must be said that the precise proportion varies from state to state depending on the relative level of protection afforded by the two rights. A final argument in favour of protection of rights via the utility model route in the UK is simply that this route is available almost everywhere else in Europe and that, as a result of its absence, UK industry is therefore at a relative disadvantage.

The joys of utility model protection are not, however, unalloyed. The cost argument is perhaps overplayed, because the main cost incurred by the rights seeker remains that of professional advice, whether a patent or a utility model right is sought.[72] The definitional problem of what is meant by the 'lower level of inventiveness required' remains, at present, vague and will, in all probability, only be resolved in due course by expensive litigation. There is also a risk that this low-level protection of patent-type rights will cut across separate provisions protecting know-how or information rights, and, conceivably, even trade marks and other image rights.

Finally, there is a risk that large companies will apply for large numbers of utility models and, in the absence of a proper examination, will do so even in those cases in relation to which their validity is dubious. This could lead to a situation in which any competitor—including small and medium-sized companies—would be threatened with infringement proceedings almost every time it engages in a new development and in which the only way out would be by means of expensive litigation. This would clearly be a sharp contrast with the stated intentions of the draft Directive, which portray utility models very much as a tool *for* small and medium-sized companies.

These are all issues that will need to be considered before utility model protection is taken on board. So, although there is no UK utility model protection at present, there may well be at some stage: market forces—or, perhaps more precisely, single market forces—may well see to that. But while the value of the proposed right is self-evident, so are the serious problems that remain to be resolved.

The Community patent

It will be remembered here that the main aim of the establishment of a Community patent is to build upon the achievements of the EPC by adding the grant of a unitary patent for the whole of the Community to the single application and single examination

---

[69] Ibid., Art. 22.

[70] M. Llewelyn, 'Is there a need for a European utility model? A view from the UK' (1997) 31 Annales de la Faculté de Droit d'Istanbul 1.

[71] That is attached to the draft Directive.

[72] Llewelyn (1997).

system. As far back as 1975, the Community Patent Convention was agreed,[73] although agreement on its implementation was never reached. What followed was a long period of difficult negotiations without real progress, until the Commission decided to revive the project in the form of an EU Regulation[74] and the Council made it one of its priorities. It is understood that agreement has been reached on most substantive points, but that the language regime that was proposed—that is, adherence to the current European Patent Office (EPO) practice under which applications are filed and examined in a limited number of languages—could not overcome the desire of a number of member States to see all languages treated equally.

In the latest version of the document that is currently on the negotiating table, a requirement has been added to file, within a two-year period from grant, a translation of the claims of any Community patent that is granted. Such a translation needs to be provided for each official EU language unless the member State concerned has formally declared that it renounces the right to have the claims translated into its own language.[75] Failure to supply translation will result in the Community patent being void.[76]

Problems also arose in the past in relation to the suggestion to set up a single European patent court system that would deal with infringement and validity issues that arise in relation to Community patents. That issue seems to have been resolved by now and the draft provides for a special patent court to be set up inside the framework of the European Court of Justice. That Court will have exclusive jurisdiction to deal with infringement and validity issues, as well as with revocation issues. The Court of First Instance will hear appeals.[77] Until this system is put into place (by a tentative deadline of 1 January 2010), the national courts will stand in and each member State will nominate the smallest possible number of courts, both at first instance and on appeal, to carry out this task.[78]

The draft Regulation further contains detailed rules concerning a large number of issues and, because the scheme will be administered by the EPO and because the Community will adhere to the European Patent Convention, additional guidance can be derived from that Convention. In a sense, the draft Regulation would become the unitary patent law of the Community in relation to Community patents and would be in line with the requirements of the European Patent Convention.[79] But there are those member States that prefer the litigation system to be outside the EU system: such states support the European Patent Litigation Agreement (EPLA) that finds its roots in the EPC tradition and to which member States were able to sign up voluntarily.[80] Again, the aim of this instrument was to centralize patent litigation in Europe—and it still provides no final agreement on the language regime or the other substantial provisions.[81]

One therefore had the impression that, politically speaking, the Community patent was again shelved at the end of 2004.[82] Since that time, the Commission has sounded

---

[73] (1976) OJ L 17/1.

[74] See the Commission Proposal for a Council Regulation on the Community Patent (2000) OJ C 337/278, COM (00) 412 final. The latest full text version is available as Council document 8539/03, dated 16 April 2003, online at ec.europa.eu/internal_market/indprop/patent/index_en.htm.

[75] Ibid., Art. 24bis.

[76] Ibid., Art. 24ter.

[77] Ibid., Art. 30.

[78] Ibid., Arts 53bis and ter.

[79] The revised version of the EPC, which entered into force in 2007, makes this cooperation possible.

[80] Details are available online at www.epo.org/patents/law/legislative-initiatives/epla.html.

[81] H. Ullrich, 'National, European and Community patent protection: time for reconsideration', Law Working Paper No. 2006/41, Florence: European University Institute, available online at cadmus.iue.it/dspace/bitstream/1814/6421/1/LAW-%202006-41.pdf.

[82] Ibid.

out industry, only to find strong support for an efficient Community patent system. The Commission seems, therefore, once again determined to pick up the pieces. In a first stage, attempts have been made to reconcile the two different approaches to litigation; there may even be room for mediation in the final compromise. We understand that, at the time of writing, the Commission has agreed a proposal, which is now under consideration by the member States.[83]

If, or when, such an agreement is reached, a single application will result in a single patent conferring protection throughout the member States and this will be one clear benefit in making an application for the Community patent. Be that as it may, whether this is a benefit worth the expenditure is perhaps more questionable given the two alternative systems already in existence. A lot will depend on the final drafting of the provisions of the Community Patent Regulation. Suffice it to say, at this stage, that a single application leading to a single patent will only be advantageous to most inventors if there is a balance between the administrative gains, in terms of obtaining and maintaining in force such a patent, and the cost of doing so. The language regime and the translations involved are key elements. The use of too many languages is bound to push up costs to such an extent that interested parties may well prefer to use the existing EPC system for those member States in relation to which they wish to obtain protection.

At the time of writing, negotiations are still ongoing and it is not yet possible to speculate, with any accuracy, when they will be completed. Our optimism in the previous edition has proved to be unfounded: technically speaking, the need identified by the industry survey can be met, but there remains an urgent need to find the political will to finish this seemingly never-ending saga.

An overview

This chapter went beyond the traditional boundaries of patent law in the UK. The first transgression is caused by the fact that certain inventions, such as pharmaceutical products, also need marketing authorization before they can be marketed; a patent on its own is not sufficient. This may involve a shortening of the period during which commercial exploitation can take place under conditions of exclusivity put in place by the patent. Supplementary protection certificates have therefore been established in relation to these specific categories of invention. They are strongly linked to the patent and, in a sense, extend the protection for the invention. The loss of exclusivity for reasons that are not linked to the patent system is undone.

The second transgression is that which is caused by the consideration of utility models. UK law does not know this concept, but there is, nevertheless, a real problem in patent law. Certain small inventions do not meet the criteria for patentability, while there is still a lack of lead time in the market and a need to protect them. Small and medium-sized companies may also find that the patent system is too complex and costly for them. As 'baby patents', utility models might become the safety net that addresses these shortcomings—but

---

[83] See the European Commission (2007) 'Patents: Commission sets out vision for improving patent system in Europe', Press release, 3 April, available online at europa.eu/rapid/pressReleasesAction.do?reference=IP/07/463&type=HTML&aged=0&language=EN&guiLanguage=fr; European Commission (2007) 'Communication from the Commission to the European Parliament and the Council: enhancing the patent system in Europe', COM (2007) 165 final, available online at eur-lex.europa.eu/LexUriServ/LexUriServ.do?uri=CELEX:52007DC0165:EN:NOT.

getting the utility model right is, in its own right, a difficult exercise. At present, we are no further than a stalled draft for a Directive.

The final transgression is the saga of the Community patent. It goes beyond the UK, in the sense that it would create a single unitary patent for the whole of the EU. Decades of negotiations have yielded draft after draft, but the language regime and the substantive provisions, as well as the unified litigation system, still have not been settled completely. Recent surveys show industry support for a Community patent, but the political will to reach a final agreement remains elusive.

Further reading

ADAMS, J. N., 'Supplementary protection certificates: the challenge to EC Regulation 1768/92' [1994] 8 EIPR 323.

KLIX, N. and HERMANN, B., 'Bitter pill for the pharmaceutical industry' (2006) 1 JIPLP 10, 639–42.

THORLEY, S., MILLER, R., BURKILL, G. and BIRSS, C. (eds) (2006) *Terrell on the Law of Patents*, 16th edn, London: Sweet and Maxwell, pp. 88–91.

TILMANN, W., 'Community patent and European Patent Agreement' (2005) 27 EIPR 5, 65–7.

ULLRICH, H. (2006) 'National, European and Community patent protection: time for reconsideration', Law Working Paper No. 2006/41, Florence: European University Institute, available online at cadmus.iue.it/dspace/bitstream/1814/6421/1/LAW-%202006-41.pdf.

8
Patents—an overview

Critics of the patent system have ample ammunition at their disposal. To get a patent, much time and energy have to be expended in pursuit of an uncertain outcome—particularly if others are active in the field—that is, at best, a limited period monopoly. Within the law itself, are some real horror stories, such as the exposure in *Genentech*[1] of the falsity of the obviousness–inventiveness dichotomy and the inherent uncertainty of the purposive approach to patents being compounded by the additional uncertainty created by common law judges having to learn Continental approaches to issues of interpretation. Add to this the uncertainty that attends the basic question of the proper purpose of the patent system, and the practical problem of how much and when to claim in an application for a patent, and despair may seem an appropriate response.

Yet thousands of patents are granted annually. This fact alone may be thought to suggest that all is not lost in the patent system. Much of the law functions well and the time taken to grant a patent is a result of painstaking examination to ensure that the invention fits in with the legal criteria. Remember, too, what the thousands of applicants get from the time and effort of application. It is the triumph of the patent system that the nebulous concept of invention is translated by the law into an item of personal property that can be assigned or licensed to others and used to prevent others from infringing the monopoly it confers. Requiring change to mend some damaged parts of the law does not, in any way, prevent the conclusion that the patent system works well, on both national and international levels, balancing as it does, in different ways at different times, the competing interests of all of those affected by the law in this area: inventors, their rivals, consumers, and society itself.

In so far as the patent system may be criticized, it is clearly having trouble getting to grips with 'cutting edge' issues, such as biotechnology. The extent to which the numbers successfully worked does not match the number of patents granted also suggests that there are imperfections in the system. But the bottom line must be that the—albeit imperfect—patent system is a high-quality system involving detailed claims and their full examination. Critics of the time and cost involved in a patent application forget that these problems arise from the quality of the system: the system is neither fast nor cheap, but it generally succeeds in its aims. It would be equally churlish to criticize a Rolls-Royce motor car for being large and expensive: how else could its qualities thrive, uncompromised? It is significant that a government that is especially keen to promote business efficiency and to remove restrictions on commerce failed signally, at the height of its power in the mid 1980s, to implement proposals made for lower levels of patent protection[2] so as to suit business interests.

Further reading

GHIDINI, G. (2006) *Intellectual Property and Competition Law: The Innovation Nexus*, Cheltenham/Northampton, MA: Edward Elgar, ch. 2.

---

[1] *Genentech Inc's Patent* [1989] RPC 147.
[2] Cmnd 9117, 1983, esp. paras 4.7–4.13.

SECTION C

COPYRIGHT AND RELATED ISSUES

9

An introduction to copyright

The roots of copyright

Copyright has two types of root. On the one hand, it started as an exclusive right to make copies—that is, to reproduce the work of an author. This entrepreneurial side of copyright is linked in tightly with the invention of the printing press, which made it much easier to copy a literary work and, for the first time, permitted the entrepreneur to make multiple identical copies. On the other hand, it became vital to protect the author now that his or her work could be copied much more easily and in much higher numbers. It was felt that the author should share in the profits of this new exploitation of the work, although this feeling was much stronger in Continental Europe than it was in the UK.

Before the arrival of the printing press, many original literary or musical works were commissioned. One copy was written and the commissioner paid the author for that copy. The printing technology resulted in the production of multiple copies and it was almost naturally felt that the author should be paid for each copy that was made. Because the technique also reduced the possibility of the author controlling the format and contents of the various copies, and because the entrepreneur now undertook the reproduction work, it became necessary to think about minimum guarantees for the author in this area. This resulted in the creation of certain so-called 'moral rights', which protected the author against unfair use of his or her work. This double set of roots is still reflected in modern copyright law.

Ever since it was created, copyright was directed towards the protection of a reproduction of the work. It was, first of all, a right in the production of printed copies of the work, which means that it is exclusively concerned with the material expression of the ideas on which the work is based. Copyright is not about ideas, but about the way in which they are expressed.

Copyright has nonetheless proven to be a valuable and flexible tool. It could be used to protect various works, because it was merely a reproduction right that could be applied to very different forms of expression of ideas. At various moments in time, literary works, musical works, artistic works—such as sculptures and paintings—works of architecture, computer programs, etc. all started to attract copyright protection. A similar expansion of copyright can be seen in relation to the carriers of the various works, as sound recordings, tapes, broadcasts, films, video, etc. all entered the copyright arena.

It is, however, to the essential elements of copyright that we will turn first.

Essential elements

The Copyright, Designs and Patents Act 1988 characterizes copyright as a property right. As we saw in Chapter 1, there are many types of copyright. First of all, we will have to distinguish them, and find out which requirements should be fulfilled by the various works and materials to attract copyright protection.

In the next stage, we will have to consider who becomes the owner of the property right, what will be the duration of the right, and what constitutes infringement of this intangible property right.

A copyright work

Does a work attract copyright? This will depend upon the nature of the material involved, produced through intellectual or entrepreneurial activity, and upon the qualification issue. The latter element is more international in scope.

The copyright and related rights conventions[1] contain minimum provisions that are translated and implemented by the national copyright Acts. The provisions also require that authors and works linked in a certain way to one of the adherents to the conventions will be treated by national copyright legislation in the same way as will national authors and works. On the one hand, this link or qualification issue constitutes a separate hurdle and only those works that pass it will attract copyright protection; on the other, no formalities—such as registration—are required to secure copyright protection.[2]

The idea–expression dichotomy

A further key preliminary point is that ideas are not protected—that is, that only the particular expression of an idea is protected. The dichotomy between 'idea' and 'expression' is a key element in copyright law, but its real meaning, as well as its application in practice, raises difficult issues.

Lord Hoffmann offered the following explanation in *Designers Guild v. Russell Williams Textiles Ltd:*[3]

> My Lords, if one examines the cases in which the distinction between ideas and the expression of ideas has been given effect, I think it will be found that they support two quite distinct propositions. The first is that a copyright work may express certain ideas which are not protected because they have no connection with the literary, dramatic, musical or artistic nature of the work. It is on this ground that, for example, a literary work which describes a system or invention does not entitle the author to claim protection for his system or invention as such. The same is true of an inventive concept expressed in an artistic work. However striking or original it may be, others are (in the absence of patent protection) free to express it in works of their own: see *Kleeneze Ltd v. DRG (UK) Ltd* [1984] FSR 399. The other proposition is that certain ideas expressed by a copyright work may not be protected because, although they are ideas of a literary, dramatic or artistic nature, they are not original, or so commonplace as not to form a substantial part of the work. *Kenrick & Co. v. Lawrence & Co.* (1890) 25 QBD 99 is a well-known example. It is on this ground that the mere notion of combining stripes and flowers would not have amounted to a substantial part of the plaintiff's work. At that level of abstraction, the idea, though expressed in the design, would not have represented sufficient of the author's skill and labour as to attract copyright protection.[4]

---

[1] Such as the Berne Convention for the Protection of Literary and Artistic Works 1886 and the Rome Convention for the Protection of Performers, Producers of Phonograms and Broadcasting Organisations 1961.

[2] The familiar copyright notice—that is, '© name of the copyright owner and year of first publication'—is a formality required not by the Berne Convention, but by the Universal Copyright Convention (UCC); it is required if a published work is to attract copyright in a country that adheres only to the UCC.

[3] [2000] 1 WLR 2416.

[4] Ibid. at 2423.

As is clear from this quote, the author needs to invest a minimum amount of skill and labour in his or her work. That makes it an expression of an idea and it can therefore be protected by copyright.

In those cases, the expression will be original. Originality is therefore linked to the idea–expression dichotomy. Copyright uses the concepts of idea–expression and originality to determine what can be appropriated through the grant of copyright; anything else will be in the public domain and will not be subject to an exclusive right. Through these concepts, copyright really regulates the balance and tension that was set out in Chapter 1. Striking a correct balance is essential to justify copyright as an exclusive right.[5]

Fixation

It follows from the need for there to be the expression of an idea that all subject matter—all works—needs to exist in some permanent form before attracting copyright. In practice, this issue gives rise to interesting interpretation problems in the sphere of artistic activity: for example, is a face make-up that is used repeatedly permanent enough in nature,[6] and what about a device used to make sand pictures that contained sand and glycerine?[7] In both of cases, the answer was negative.

For many works, however, this does not create a problem, because the creation and fixation of the work take place at the same time. For example, the idea in a painting is only expressed—and can, as a consequence, only attract protection—when the work is executed and fixation takes place automatically. But we will have to come back to this issue, because its application to certain other works is more problematical.

An overview

Copyright has come a long way from its roots as a right to copy in the sphere of literary and artistic works. It has proven itself to be a very flexible tool that can also cope with various new technological developments and very different types of work.

Copyright is based on a couple of key concepts. Firstly, it protects works and, if these meet the requirements, they become copyright works. But ideas are not protected by copyright, only expressions of ideas are covered—and, in making that distinction, the originality requirement as a precondition to copyright protection plays a vital role. Additionally, works have to be fixated if they are to attract copyright protection.

Further reading

DREIER, T. (2001) 'Balancing proprietary and public domain interests: inside or outside of proprietary rights', in R. Dreyfuss, D. Zimmerman and H. First, *Expanding the Boundaries of Intellectual Property: Innovation Policy for the Knowledge Society*, Oxford: Oxford University Press, pp. 295–316.

---

[5] See T. Dreier (2001) 'Balancing proprietary and public domain interests: inside or outside of proprietary rights', in R. Dreyfuss, D. Zimmerman and H. First, *Expanding the Boundaries of Intellectual Property: Innovation Policy for the Knowledge Society*, Oxford: Oxford University Press, p. 303.

[6] *Merchandising Corp. of America Inc. v. Harpbond Inc.* [1983] FSR 32 (the *Adam Ant* case).

[7] *Komesaroff v. Mickle* [1988] RPC 204.

10

The various types of copyright and the quality issue

Section 1(1) of the Copyright, Designs and Patents Act 1988 lists the various types of copyright, which are further defined in the following sections. The case law is also a helpful source of information in this respect. In reality, various types of work are defined. Every work that can be classified as one of these types of work will attract copyright, if all of the other requirements are met.

This classification of works is an important aspect of our copyright system: a work that does not come within the definition of any of the types of work will not be protected by copyright. It might also be argued that each work must be classified in one category: a work would not be able to get copyright protection under two different classifications at the same time. Indeed, slight differences may exist between the various regimes of copyright protection for each of the types of work and this could give rise to problems. A product may include more than one work for copyright purposes, but each of these works will be classified and protected as a single type of work. This point was summarized as follows by Laddie J:[1]

> although different copyrights can protect simultaneously a particular product and an author can produce more than one copyright work during the course of a single episode of creative effort, for example a competent musician may write the words and the music for a song at the same time, it is quite another thing to say that a single piece of work by an author gives rise to two or more copyrights in respect of the same creative effort.[2]

This point has now been addressed further by the Court of Appeal, however, and it is submitted that the view of Laddie J now needs to be confined to those copyrights that are listed in s. 1(1)(a) of the 1988 Act.

This seems to flow logically from the decision of the Court of Appeal in *Norowzian v. Arks*,[3] in which the Court held that a film could also constitute a dramatic work, as long as the criteria for both categories were met. This means that a work can, at the same time, be protected as an original work in one of the categories listed in s. 1(1)(a) of the 1988 Act and as sound recording, film, or broadcast under s. 1(1)(b) of that Act.

---

[1] *Electronic Techniques (Anglia) Ltd v. Critchley Components Ltd* [1997] FSR 401, *per* Laddie J; see also *Anacon Corp. Ltd v. Environmental Research Technology Ltd* [1994] FSR 659.

[2] *Electronic Techniques (Anglia) Ltd v. Critchley Components Ltd* [1997] FSR 401, *per* Laddie J at 412.

[3] *Norowzian v. Arks Ltd (No. 2)* [2000] FSR 363.

Original literary, dramatic, musical, and artistic works

The originality requirement

All works in this first category have in common the originality requirement. Originality should not, however, be taken in the normal sense: neither novelty, nor innovation is required; the starting point is that the work is not copied and originates from the author.[4] The author must produce his or her own expression of the idea, but the test to establish whether the work originates from the author is only a minimum effort standard. It is not required that the idea is new, because the *idea* is not covered by copyright at all. A radically new and different expression of the idea of the passionate love story between two people with irreconcilable cultural backgrounds set in outer space is equally not required; the author's own expression of the classic *Romeo and Juliet* tale will suffice. The author must only have expended 'skill, judgment and labour', or 'selection, judgment and experience', or 'labour, skill and capital' in creating the work.[5]

In reality, two cumulative requirements are involved: firstly, the work must originate from the author; secondly, there must have been a minimum investment by the author of skill, judgment, and labour. Both requirements have to be met. The investment of skill, judgment, and labour merely in the process of copying someone else's work cannot confer originality.[6] But even if that threshold is low, works that do not meet this minimum standard will not attract copyright protection: a copy that incorporates some minor alterations of a work which is no longer protected under copyright, for example, will not attract copyright.[7] Even if the content of a work may be nothing more than a compilation of existing elements, some skill and labour must have been invested in the way in which those elements are organized and expressed.[8] On the one hand, that skill and labour must not be so trivial that it could be characterized as a purely mechanical exercise; on the other, creativity, as such, is not required either.[9] Football pool coupon lists, for example, can be protected, but only if it can be shown that the presentation of the material is special: it must be shown that the author has invested skill and labour in the way in which the table is organized. There must be '*a relation of creation between the work and the author whatever this act of creation (sometimes only presentation) means*'.[10] But what amounts to a sufficient amount of independent skill, labour, and judgment is not capable of definition in advance; it has to be determined on the facts of each case.[11]

Most other European countries have a slightly higher originality threshold. They define an original work as a work that constitutes the expression of the personality of its author and a work should be the author's own intellectual creation. This version of originality

---

[4] *Ladbroke (Football) Ltd v. William Hill (Football) Ltd* [1964] 1 All ER 465, [1964] 1 WLR 273, *per* Lord Pearce at 479 and 291; *University of London Press Ltd v. University Tutorial Press Ltd* [1916] 2 Ch 601, *per* Peterson J at 609.

[5] Ibid.

[6] This was reconfirmed by the Court of Appeal in *Biotrading & Financing OY v. Biohit Ltd* [1998] FSR 109 at 116; see also Lord Oliver's opinion in *Interlego AG v. Tyco Industries Inc.* [1989] AC 217 at 258.

[7] See *Interlego AG v. Tyco Industries Inc.* [1989] AC 217, [1988] 3 All ER 949.

[8] See *Cramp (GA) & Sons Ltd v. Smythson* [1944] AC 329, [1944] 2 All ER 92.

[9] See the decision of the Supreme Court of Canada in *The Law Society of Upper Canada v. CCH Canadian Ltd, Thomson Canada Ltd & Canada Law Book Inc.* [2004] SCC 13.

[10] A. Dietz, 'The artist's right of integrity under copyright law: a comparative approach' (1994) 25 IIC 177 at 182.

[11] *Biotrading & Financing OY v. Biohit Ltd* [1998] FSR 109 at 116.

is found in the European Community Copyright Directives,[12] which introduced a very partial harmonization of copyright in the Community.[13]

We will have to come back to this issue when we discuss the relevant types of work in detail. Suffice it to say here that this higher originality requirement has now been included in the Copyright, Designs and Patents Act 1988,[14] in relation to copyright in databases, as a result of the implementation of the Database Directive.[15] The UK may have to redefine its own originality requirement should a further European harmonization of copyright take place.

An attempt at clarification in Hyperion

The exact meaning of the concept of originality has never been absolutely clear, but a recent case allowed the Court of Appeal to shed some more light on it. In *Hyperion Records v. Lionel Sawkins*,[16] the question arose of whether originality could be found in a restored musical work. The original musical work by Lalande was out of copyright, but Dr Lionel Sawkins had restored the work by making performing editions that allowed the work to be played again. In doing so, Sawkins had made additions and corrections, but he had done so with the aim of restoring the work in its original format—that is, as Lalande would have composed it.

A lot has been made in relation to this case of the public policy issue that granting copyright in a restored, out-of-copyright work would hinder access to the work itself. The underlying argument seems to be that the real originality and the real work is that which is out of copyright, and, in that line of thought, granting a new copyright would clash with public policy. The *Hyperion* case offered a unique opportunity to dispel that myth. Copyright only protects a particular expression of a certain idea and not the idea itself. Copyright in a restored or reconstituted version of an out-of-copyright work will protect only the expression of the restored or reconstituted version; everyone remains free to use the out-of-copyright material itself. To use the specific facts of *Hyperion*: granting Lionel Sawkins copyright in his performing editions will not protect anyone from copying Lalande's music or from making their own performing editions. All they cannot do is use the short cut offered by the existence of the Sawkins' performing editions by copying these without his consent.

This last point is the most basic expression of the public policy of copyright—namely, to prevent the unauthorized copying of certain material forms of expression. One should therefore be very careful in using the public policy argument in this type of case.

The broad perspective restated

The key point is, however, found in the fact that only certain material forms of expression are, from a public policy point of view, worth protecting by copyright. Only original forms of expression are to be protected.

Let us look at this from a broad perspective. Remember that originality should not be taken in the normal (dictionary) sense here: neither novelty, nor innovation is required; the starting point is that the work is not copied and originates from the author, as the

---

[12]   See, e.g., Art. 1(3) of the Council Directive of 14 May 1991 on the legal protection of computer programs (1991) OJ L 122/42.

[13]   See also the amended draft Directive (1998) OJ L 289/28 and Regulation (2001) OJ C 120/12 on industrial design.

[14]   As s. 3A.

[15]   European Parliament and Council Directive 96/9/EC (1996) OJ L 77/20 and the Copyright and Rights in Databases Regulations 1997.

[16]   [2005] 3 All ER 636, [2005] 1 WLR 3281 (CA).

House of Lords made clear in *Ladbroke v. William Hill*.[17] The author must produce his or
her own expression of the idea, but the test to establish whether the work indeed originates from the author is only a minimum effort standard. It is not required that the idea
is new, because the idea is not covered by copyright at all. The author must only have
expended 'skill, judgment and labour', or 'selection, judgment and experience', or 'labour,
skill and capital' in creating the work, in relation to which, two cumulative requirements
are involved: that the work must originate from the author and that there must have been
a minimum investment by the author of skill, judgment and labour. The investment of
'skill, judgment and labour' merely in the process of copying someone else's work cannot
confer originality, as was confirmed by the Court of Appeal in *Biotrading v. Biohit*,[18] with
reference to Lord Oliver's famous dictum in *Interlego v. Tyco*.[19]

But even if the threshold is low, works that do not meet this minimum standard will not
attract copyright protection. The question of whether an item that is similar to a copyright
work is, in its own right, an original copyright work is a difficult question, in relation to
which the Court of Appeal provided some guidance in *Guild v. Eskander Ltd*.[20] A piecemeal approach should be guarded against; the question was, instead, whether all—and
not just any one or more—of the additional features gave rise to the requisite quality of
originality. The need to look at the work as a whole is crucial and the Court of Appeal
also emphasizes this in *Hyperion*. Despite that, some consideration of individual features
would be unavoidable in answering that question.

A copy that incorporates some minor alterations of a work that is no longer protected
under copyright will not attract copyright.[21] The principle is clearly stated in the *Interlego*
case and is widely accepted. Its exact coverage, however, and the answer to the question
of whether it can be reconciled with the judgment of the House of Lords in *Walter v.
Lane*,[22] are less clear. The *Hyperion* case obliged the Court of Appeal to rule on these
points and we will return to that ruling shortly, but here we will mention only that copyright infringement in a performing edition of a fourth work was ruled out, because there
had been only a very limited editiorial input by Dr Sawkins.

Even if the content of a work may be nothing other than a compilation of existing
elements, some skill and labour must have been invested in the way in which they are
organized and expressed.[23] That skill and labour must not be so trivial that it could be
characterized as a purely mechanical exercise, but creativity as such is not required either,
as can be seen from the decision of the Supreme Court of Canada in *The Law Society of
Upper Canada v. CCH Canadian Ltd, Thomson Canada Ltd & Canada Law Book Inc*.[24]

There is no better way to conclude this overview of the general approach to originality in English law than to quote Dr Dietz, who wrote that there must be '*a relation of
creation between the work and the author whatever this act of creation (sometimes only
presentation) means*'.[25] With hindsight, these wise words almost sound prophetic in a
Hyperion context. What amounts to a sufficient amount of independent 'skill, labour and

[17] *Ladbroke (Football) Ltd v. William Hill (Football) Ltd* [1964] 1 All ER 465, [1964] 1 WLR 273, *per* Lord
Pearce at 479 and 291; *University of London Press Ltd v. University Tutorial Press Ltd* [1916] 2 Ch 601, *per*
Peterson J at 609.
[18] *Biotrading & Financing OY v. Biohit Ltd* [1998] FSR 109 at 116.
[19] *Interlego AG v. Tyco Industries Inc.* [1989] AC 217 at 258.
[20] *Guild v. Eskander Ltd* [2003] FSR 23.
[21] See *Interlego AG v. Tyco Industries Inc.* [1989] AC 217, [1988] 3 All ER 949.
[22] *Walter v. Lane* [1900] AC 539 (HL).
[23] See *Cramp (GA) & Sons Ltd v. Smythson* [1944] AC 329, [1944] 2 All ER 92.
[24] *The Law Society of Upper Canada v. CCH Canadian Ltd, Thomson Canada Ltd & Canada Law Book
Inc.* [2004] SCC 13.
[25] Dietz (1994) at 182.

judgment' is not capable of definition in advance; it has to be determined on the facts of each case.[26]

How does Hyperion apply in practice?

It is now time to return to the somewhat narrower perspective of the *Hyperion* case and to apply these principles in detail. Lord Justice Mummery looks at this from the following angle:

> The first question is whether the performing editions are incapable of being regarded as 'original' works because Lalande composed the music and Dr Sawkins made his editions of that music with the intention that they should be as close as possible to the Lalande originals.[27]

The Court of Appeal answers that question by relying very strongly on the dictum of the House of Lords of over century ago in *Walter v. Lane*.[28] The Court of Appeal suggests that that decision is still good law as a result of the confirmation it received in *Express Newspapers plc v. News (UK) Ltd*.[29]

In *Walter v. Lane*, the House of Lords held that copyright subsisted in shorthand writers' reports of public speeches as 'original literary' works. The Earl of Rosebery had made the speeches in public, with the reporters present. The reporters had made notes in shorthand; they had later transcribed them, corrected, revised, and punctuated them, and they had published them in newspapers as verbatim reports of the speeches. From the copyright point of view adopted by the House of Lords, a speech and a *report* of a speech are two different things. Lord Rosebery was the author of his speeches; the shorthand writers were the authors of their reports of his speeches. They spent effort, skill, and time in writing up their reports of speeches that they themselves had not written. For our current purposes, it is very important to note that the reports were held to be 'original' literary works, even though the intention of the reporters was to produce as accurate a report as possible of a work of which they were not the authors.

This analysis led Lord Justice Mummery to the following conclusion in the *Hyperion* case:[30]

> In my judgment, on the application of Walter v. Lane to this case, the effort, skill and time which the judge found Dr Sawkins spent in making the 3 performing editions were sufficient to satisfy the requirement that they should be 'original' works in the copyright sense. This is so even though (a) Dr Sawkins worked on the scores of existing musical works composed by another person (Lalande); (b) Lalande's works are out of copyright; and (c) Dr Sawkins had no intention of adding any new notes of music of his own.

This reliance on *Walter v. Lane* cannot be accepted, however, without considering the dictum in the *Interlego* case with which it seems at odds. One has, indeed, in the past derived a *de minimis* rule from the words of Lord Oliver in that case[31]—that is, that a copy incorporating some minor alterations of a work that is no longer protected under

---

[26] *Biotrading & Financing OY v. Biohit Ltd* [1998] FSR 109 at 116.

[27] *Hyperion Records v. Lionel Sawkins* [2005] 3 All ER 636, [2005] 1 WLR 3281 (CA), at [32] of the judgment.

[28] *Walter v. Lane* [1900] AC 539 (HL), a decision on the Copyright Act 1842 that used a different kind of wording when compared to the CDPA 1988.

[29] *Express Newspapers plc v. News (UK) Ltd* [1990] FSR 359 at 365–6.

[30] *Hyperion Records v. Lionel Sawkins* [2005] 3 All ER 636, [2005] 1 WLR 3281 (CA), at [36] of the judgment.

[31] See, e.g., the fourth edition of this book, p. 175.

copyright will not attract copyright. But the question must be asked whether the impact of the following words does not go further:

> Take the simplest case of artistic copyright, a painting or photograph. It takes great skill, judgment and labour to produce a good copy by painting or to produce an enlarged photograph from a positive print, but no one would reasonably contend that the copy painting or enlargement was an 'original' artistic work in which the copier is entitled to claim copyright. Skill, labour or judgment merely in the process of copying cannot confer originality.[32]

In other words, does this dictum in any way reverse what was said in *Walter v. Lane* in the context of a somewhat differently worded statutory provision?

It is submitted that the two provisions are not incompatible and that the dictum in *Interlego* needs to be interpreted restrictively. The Court was, after all, dealing with drawings for plastic toy blocks that had barely been touched and the attempt of the producer of the blocks effectively to prolong the term of their protection was all too obvious. Lord Justice Jacob makes this point very clearly in the second (concurring) judgment in *Hyperion*.[33] Like him, I would like to refer to the authors of the *Modern Law of Copyright*,[34] who interpret the dictum in *Interlego* as follows:

> However, whilst the remarks made in *Interlego* may be valid if confined to the subject matter then before the Privy Council, they are stated too widely. The Privy Council was there considering fairly simple technical drawings. This is a rather special subject-matter. While the drawing of such a work is more laborious than it looks, it is a fact that any competent draftsman (perhaps, any conscientious amateur) who sets out to reproduce it exactly will almost certainly succeed in the end, because of the mathematical precision of the lines and measurements. This should be contrasted with, eg a painting by Vermeer, where it will be obvious that very few persons, if any, are capable of making an exact replica. Now, assume a number of persons do set out to copy such a painting, each according to his own personal skill. Most will only succeed in making something which all too obviously differs from the original—some of them embarrassingly so. They will get a copyright seeing that in each instance the end result does not differ from the original yet it took a measure of skill and labour to produce. If, however, one of these renders the original with all the skill and precision of a Salvador Dali, is he to be denied a copyright where a mere dauber is not? The difference between the two cases (technical drawing and old master painting) is that in the latter there is room for individual interpretation even where faithful replication is sought to be attempted while in the former there is not. Further, a photographer who carefully took a photograph of an original painting might get a copyright and, if this is so, it is rather hard to see why a copy of the same degree of fidelity, if rendered by an artist of the calibre aforementioned, would not be copyright. These considerations suggest that the proposition under discussion is suspect. It is therefore submitted that, for example, a picture restorer may get a copyright for the result of his efforts. Be that as it may, it is submitted that the *Interlego* proposition is anyway distinguishable where the replicator succeeds in preserving for posterity an original to which access is difficult.[35]

To quote Jane Ginsburg:[36]

> Reproductions requiring great talent and technical skill may qualify as protectable works of authorship, even if they are *copies* of pre-existing works. This would be the case for photographic and other high quality replicas of works of art.

---

[32] *Interlego v. Tyco* [1988] RPC 343, *per* Lord Oliver at 371.

[33] At [79]–[82] of the judgment.

[34] H. Laddie, P. Prescott and M. Vitoria (1995) *The Modern Law of Copyright and Designs*, 2nd edn, London: Butterworths.

[35] At para. 4.39.

[36] J. Ginsberg, 'The concept of authorship in comparative copyright law' (2003) 52 DePaul L Rev1063.

In conclusion, the two dicta are not incompatible: *Walter v. Lane* sets out the rule, but presupposes some creative input; *Interlego* deals with the other end of the spectrum, at which there is only mere copying.

In the words of Lord Justice Jacob:[37]

> I think the true position is that one has to consider the extent to which the 'copyist' is a mere copyist—merely performing an easy mechanical function. The more that is so the less is his contribution likely to be taken as 'original'.

One should not underestimate the importance for English copyright law of the fact that the Court of Appeal has now, in *Hyperion*, clarified the approach that is to be taken to originality by reconfirming the dictum in *Walter v. Lane* and by ruling out any conflict with *Interlego*, which is confined to its particular mere copying scenario.

Recorded expression

Another essential rule is that copyright does not protect ideas; only a particular expression of an idea is protected. This does not create a specific problem for artistic works, but, if one is not to protect the idea in a literary, dramatic, or musical work, the expression should be recorded in a permanent form. This can be in writing or in any other form and all new technological recording or fixation methods are automatically included.

One could see an impromptu speech and a tune devised while playing the guitar, which are not recorded, as the perfect illustration of this problem. The author can record the work him or herself, but this is not required; the requirement only mentions recording—in relation to which, not even the permission of the author is required.[38] This means that the recording requirement will be met as soon as *someone* records the work.

Apart from the permanent fixation aspect, the rule that copyright protects expression, but not ideas, has an even more fundamental aspect to it. Two situations arise in this context. In the first, a copyright work may express ideas that are not protected, because they lack any connection with the literary, dramatic, musical, or artistic nature of the work.[39] This could be the case, for example, if a literary work expresses the idea of a technical innovation.[40] In the second situation, certain ideas protected by a copyright work may themselves be denied protection, because they are not original or because they are commonplace,[41] despite the fact that they are ideas of a literary, dramatic, musical, or artistic nature.[42]

Literary works

A definition and some examples

The Act characterizes literary works as '*any work, other than a dramatic or musical work, which is written, spoken or sung*'.[43] This category should not be restricted to works of literature. As Peterson J put it, this category contains every '*work which is expressed in print or writing, irrespective of the question whether the quality or style is high*'.[44]

---

[37] *Hyperion Records v. Lionel Sawkins* [2005] 3 All ER 636, [2005] 1 WLR 3281 (CA), at [82] of the judgment.
[38] Copyright, Designs and Patents Act 1988, s. 3(3).
[39] See, e.g., *Kleeneze Ltd v. DRG (UK) Ltd* [1984] FSR 399.
[40] *Designer Guild Ltd v. Russell Williams Textiles Ltd* [2000] 1 WLR 2416, *per* Lord Hoffmann at 2423; *Ultra Marketing (UK) Ltd & Thomas Alexander Scott v. Universal Components Ltd*, judgment of 12 March 2004, Ch D, unreported.
[41] See, e.g., *Kenrick & Co. v. Lawrence & Co.* (1890) 25 QBD 99.
[42] *Designer Guild Ltd v. Russell Williams (Textiles) Ltd* [2001] 1 All ER 700, [2000] 1 WLR 2416, *per* Lord Hoffmann.
[43] CDPA 1988, s. 3(1).
[44] *University of London Press Ltd v. University Tutorial Press* [1916] 2 Ch 601 at 608.

The case law supplements high-quality works with all kinds of compilations and tables.[45] Trade catalogues,[46] street directories,[47] timetable indexes,[48] examination papers,[49] football fixtures lists,[50] a listing of programmes to be broadcast,[51] a racing information service,[52] business letters,[53] and consignment notes[54] have all been held to be literary works protected by copyright. Lyrics for songs and computer programs are also protected.

An exception is presented by compilations of (only) artistic works. Compilations are protected as literary works, but only if they are written. Most artistic works are not written and such compilations of artistic works will therefore not attract copyright protection.[55] The addition of a substantial quantity of written work will solve this problem, because the originality requirement will be met in these cases.

Originality as a de minimis rule

In practice, the originality requirement requires such a low amount of skill, labour, and judgment to be invested in a literary work that it operates as a *de minimis* rule. Only works that are not substantial enough do not attract copyright protection. A first group of works falls in this category because the amount of skill and labour invested in them is almost non-existent: case law examples include a card containing spaces and directions for eliciting statutory information,[56] and an advertisement consisting of four commonplace sentences.[57] Recently, it was held that a formula for calculating racing forecasts was not an original literary work; nor were the forecasts produced by using the formula. The calculation was held to be a routine repetitive task that involved feeding the relevant information into a computer and that task did not involve sufficient skill, labour, or judgment to produce an original literary work each time the formula was used.[58]

A second group of works falls into this category because the volume of these works is not substantial enough. There is not enough space to distinguish between ideas and expression, if there is an underlying idea at all, and copyright should not be used to monopolize words. Obvious examples in this category are trade marks[59] and most titles of books, plays, films, etc.[60]

---

[45] See also CDPA 1988, s. 3(1)(a).

[46] *Collis v. Cater* (1898) 78 LT 613; *Purefoy Engineering Co. Ltd v. Sykes Boxall* (1955) 72 RPC 89.

[47] *Kelly v. Morris* (1866) LR 1 Eq 697.

[48] *Blacklock (H) & Co. Ltd v. Pearson* [1915] 2 Ch 376.

[49] *University of London Press v. University Tutorial Press* [1916] 2 Ch 601.

[50] *Football League v. Littlewoods* [1959] Ch 637, [1959] 2 All ER 546; L*adbroke (Football) Ltd v. William Hill (Football) Ltd* [1964] 1 All ER 465, [1964] 1 WLR 273.

[51] *Independent Television Publications v. Time Out Ltd* [1984] FSR 64; a subsequent competition law initiative made the copyright owners grant licences and made the listings available to other publishers.

[52] *Portway Press v. Hague* [1957] RPC 426.

[53] *British Oxygen Co. Ltd v. Liquid Air Ltd* [1925] Ch 383.

[54] *Van Oppen & Co. Ltd v. Van Oppen* (1903) 20 RPC 617.

[55] A. Monotti, 'The extent of copyright protection for compilations of artistic works' [1993] 5 EIPR 156 at 160–1.

[56] *Libraco v. Shaw* (1913) 30 TLR 22.

[57] *Kirk v. Fleming Macg Cap Cas* (1928) 44.

[58] *Bookmakers' Afternoon Greyhound Services Ltd v. Wilf Gilbert (Staffordshire) Ltd* [1994] FSR 723.

[59] *Exxon Corp. v. Exxon Insurance Consultants International Ltd* [1982] Ch 119; aff'd [1981] 3 All ER 241; copyright should not be used to expand the protection granted by a trade mark to a well-known brand name to an entirely different category of products or services.

[60] See *Ladbroke (Football) Ltd v. William Hill (Football) Ltd* [1964] 1 All ER 465, [1964] 1 WLR 273, *per* Lord Hodson at 476 and 286; *Francis Day & Hunter Ltd v. Twentieth Century Fox Corp. Ltd* [1940] AC 112, *per* Lord Wright at 123.

A literary work based on existing sources can be seen as a different expression of the same idea if no substantial amount of copying is involved, and if skill and labour has been invested in the new work. Because the idea is not protected, no infringement problem arises and the new work can attract copyright protection as a literary work. Translations,[61] compilations,[62] selection and abridgment,[63] critical annotation and explanation,[64] and editorial work that involves amendments[65] all come under the head of literary works and qualify for protection irrespective whether the material taken from existing sources is in, or out, of copyright. As for all literary works, the *de minimis* principle applies. On this basis, copyright protection for the times of local trains, extracted from a general timetable,[66] and for a collection of existing tables made for the front of a pocket diary[67] was refused.

It may, at first, seem contradictory, but certain similar works do not fall foul of the *de minimis* rule. These works involve a sufficient amount of skill and labour in the selection and use of the existing elements on the basis of a commercial judgment. Skill and labour are not restricted to literary selection, expression, and presentation, as became clear in *Ladbroke v. William Hill.*[68] Copyright protection was granted to a fixed-odds football pool that consisted of a compilation of 16 known forms of bet, when the commercial judgment and skill used in the selection of these forms of bet was taken into account and reference was not solely made to the presentation on the pool form.[69]

Works that derive, in some way, from an earlier source—such as a selection of poetry or a selection of letters written by a celebrity—attract copyright if more than a minimal amount of skill and labour is invested in the choice and presentation of the material.[70] The poems or letters that are reproduced by a substantial amount may still attract copyright, which will coexist with the copyright in the new work. It is obvious that the permission of all owners of a copyright is required to reproduce their work or to deal with the copyright in any other way; each copyright creates an independent exclusive right in this respect. All of this follows logically from the restrictive definition that is given to the originality requirement.

Works can also derive from an earlier source in another way. Many literary works go through many drafts before they are eventually published: each one of these (unpublished) drafts will attract its own copyright as a literary work, as long as a minimum amount of skill and labour has been invested in adapting the previous draft. Correcting obvious incorrect typing errors will not suffice for that purpose, but any alterations to the work itself almost inevitably will.[71]

---

[61] *Byrne v. Statist Co.* [1914] 1 KB 622; *Cummins v. Bond* [1927] 1 Ch 167.

[62] *Portway Press v. Hague* [1957] RPC 426; *Football League v. Littlewoods* [1959] Ch 637, [1959] 2 All ER 546; *Ladbroke (Football) Ltd v. William Hill (Football) Ltd* [1964] 1 All ER 465, [1964] 1 WLR 273.

[63] *Macmillan v. Cooper* (1923) 93 LJPC 113; condensation of a single text may not be sufficient, but collecting an anthology of verse is likely to be sufficient: *Sweet v. Benning* (1855) 16 CB 459.

[64] The notes appended to a condensed text showed sufficient literary skill, taste, and judgment in *Macmillan v. Cooper* (1923) 93 LJPC 113.

[65] *Warwick Film Productions Ltd v. Eisinger* [1969] 1 Ch 508, [1967] 3 All ER 367 was concerned with an edited version of a trial transcript.

[66] *Leslie v. Young* [1894] AC 335; see also *Blacklock v. Pearson* [1915] 2 Ch 376.

[67] *Cramp v. Smythson* [1944] AC 329; see also *Rose v. Information Services* [1987] FSR 254.

[68] [1964] 1 All ER 465, [1964] 1 WLR 273.

[69] For another example that attracted copyright (a random choice game in a newspaper with grids of letters printed on cards as the only literary material), see *Express Newspapers v. Liverpool Daily Post* [1985] 3 All ER 680, [1985] 1 WLR 1089; see also *Mirror Newspapers Ltd v. Queensland Newspapers Pty* [1982] Qd R 305; *Kalamazoo (Aust) Pty Ltd v. Compact Business Systems Pty Ltd* (1985) 5 IPR 213.

[70] See the comparison in *Ladbroke (Football) Ltd v. William Hill (Football) Ltd* [1964] 1 All ER 465, [1964] 1 WLR 273.

[71] *Sweeney v. Macmillan Publishers Ltd* [2002] RPC 35 at 651. See also *LA Gear Inc. v. Hi-Tec Sports* [1992] FSR 121, *per* Nourse LJ at 136; *Robin Ray v. Classic FM Ltd* [1998] FSR 622.

At a more fundamental level, one needs to identify what exactly one is looking for as a work. In a book, each chapter, page, or maybe even each sentence can be said to amount to a (separate) literary work, but when each of them is incorporated into a larger work—that is, the book—one looks at the larger work or book in which it existed.[72] For copyright purposes, one looks primarily at the format in which the work is released onto the market.

When compared to the wider European originality concept, which would probably deny copyright protection to certain works that are purely functional and do not require creative activity by the author, the UK originality concept makes copyright protection available for works that are used only in a business context. Copyright therefore makes it impossible for the direct business competitor to express his or her business message in an identical way. In these cases, copyright is used to remedy the lack of an unfair competition concept. It is arguable, however, that the use of copyright to protect items that are fundamentally different in nature is not desirable and that the Continental combination of a tighter originality requirement and an unfair competition concept is a more adequate solution, because it creates a suitable and well-defined solution for each of the different problems.

The exclusion of dramatic and musical works

Let us return briefly to the definition that the 1988 Act gives of a 'literary work'.[73] A literary work is defined widely as any work that is written, spoken, or sung, and that is not a dramatic or musical work. The exclusion of any work that comes within the definition of a musical or a dramatic work from the category of literary works implements the basic principle that every original work can only fall within a single category of original types of work. This exclusion slightly narrows the category of literary works, but it remains rather wide.

The last point is demonstrated by the fact that a literary work need not be expressed in words or any particular notation: any kind of notation can turn a work into a work that is written.[74] As a result of this, a software program that is written in any kind of computer programming language will fall within the category of literary works.

Computer programs, tables, and compilations as literary works

That brings us to the types of work that are explicitly included in the definition of a 'literary work'. Section 3(1) of the 1988 Act mentions specifically that a computer program and the preparatory design material for a computer program are literary works. The same goes for tables and compilations. A table consists of a series of facts or numbers that have been arranged in a systematic way; a compilation is mainly a body of materials that have been brought together. There is no need to distinguish whether a particular work is a table or a compilation, because the Act treats them in exactly the same way.

It is important to note that the Act does not require that the author of the table or compilation is also the person from whom the materials, numbers, or facts that are included in these works originate. Copyright in a table or compilation consists in protecting the skill and labour employed in selecting, collecting, or arranging the materials, numbers, or facts. The materials, numbers, or facts, as such and on their own, are not protected by the copyright in the table or compilation, but they may, or may not be protected by copyright in their own right: for example, five short stories in a compilation may be protected by copyright as five separate literary works. Any copyright in the compilation comes on

---

[72] *Sweeney v. Macmillan Publishers Ltd* [2002] RPC 35 at 651.
[73] CDPA 1988, s. 3(1).
[74] See Laddie et al. (2000) p. 64.

top of existing separate copyrights in the contents of the compilation and leaves the latter unchanged.

Finally, databases are also defined as literary works for copyright purposes.

Databases

Databases have a lot in common with compilations. Most databases could be described as a kind of compilation. The Act makes it clear, however, that no overlap between the two types of literary work can exist for copyright purposes, by defining compilations as *'compilations, other than a database'*.[75] A database such as the LEXIS legal information system would be a good example: legal materials from a range of sources are collated by the publisher into a database, which is used skilfully by the subscriber.

Section 3A of the 1988 Act defines a database. The starting point is that a database is a collection of works, data, or other materials. Firstly, these works, data, or other materials that form the components of, or items of content comprised in, the collection need to be independent from one another. A collection of titles and names of authors of all books published in English in the nineteenth century might be a good example. Each title or name of an author would be able to stand on its own; this independence would not be destroyed were a search facility to allow the user of the database to retrieve several of these data from the database at the same time. Each title or name of an author would remain independent when jointly listed on the screen as the search result, for example, of a search for all titles of books that were published in 1830. But such independence does not exist, for example, in relation to a film. A cinematographic film is composed of a succession of still frames. Each frame can stand on its own as a photograph, but, in the context of the film, the frames are dependent on other frames. The essence of the film is the moving image and that moving image can only be produced by a combination of frames. That means that the individual frames cannot be considered to be independent from one another.

Secondly, a collection will only be a database if the independent works, data, or other materials that form the collection are arranged in a systematic or methodical way.[76] In relation to our earlier example of titles and names of authors of books published in English during the nineteenth century, this means that the data must, for example, be organized by year of publication, or alphabetically by name of author, or on the basis of all books published by a certain author in that period. A random collection of names of authors and titles from the nineteenth century will not do. It is, however, sufficient that the data has been given a systematic code in the database and can be retrieved—for example, on the screen of the terminal in relation to an electronic database—in a systematic way. The precise way or order in which they are technically stored in any electronic storage medium is irrelevant for this purpose.

Thirdly, the works, data, or other materials need to be individually accessible.[77] Access to each individual and independent work needs to be possible. In our example, this means that it must be possible to retrieve the data about a specific name of an author or a specific title of a book from the database. Such access can be by electronic or other means, which provision makes it clear that electronic databases are not the only ones that are protected. Hard-copy databases—for example, in card or book format—also come under the definition.

An additional hurdle remains, even if a collection meets these three requirements: such a collection will only be a database if it is original. Originality is defined in a specific

---

[75] One could wonder, however, whether, in the light of the wide definition that is given to the concept of a database, there are de facto any compilations left.

[76] CDPA 1988, s. 3A(1)(a).

[77] Ibid., (b).

way for the purposes of a database.[78] A slightly higher criterion than the normal UK originality criterion is used. The database must constitute the author's own intellectual creation, by reason of the selection or arrangement of the contents of the database, with the emphasis firmly placed on the selection or the arrangement of the contents of the database. Copyright in a database is not concerned with the contents of the database as such. The selection and arrangement criterion, and the way in which they take place, must be the author's own intellectual creation: he or she must have devised them and they cannot, therefore, be commonplace. For example, a standard alphabetical arrangement by name in a telephone directory, comprising all people with a telephone connection in a certain area, must be commonplace and that arrangement cannot be seen as the author's own intellectual creation.

Any collection that does not meet the three requirements above and the special originality requirement will not be a database for the purposes of the Act. It may nevertheless attract copyright protection as a compilation, for example, if it only meets the lower standard originality criterion. Those collections that meet the three requirements and the originality criterion will attract copyright protection as a database—but that protection does not cover the contents of the database though. What is protected is the structure of the database, because that is the expression of the author's original selection and arrangement of the contents of the database. Other aspects of a database may be protected by a *sui generis* right.[79]

The introduction of a new originality criterion for databases in s. 3A(2) of the 1988 Act creates problems in relation to computer programs. Both databases and computer programs are the subject matter of EC Directives.[80] Both Directives contain the same originality criterion of *'author's own intellectual creation'*,[81] but this criterion has only been transposed into the 1988 Act in relation to databases. After the Software Directive, it could be argued that the Act did not define originality and that we, therefore, did not have to copy the Directive's originality criterion. In the absence of a definition in the Act, we could simply interpret the level of originality required for computer programs in the light of the Directive and apply our old originality criterion to all other works. Alternatively, one might unconvincingly argue that, in practice, there was no difference between the Directive's originality criterion, and the skill and labour approach in the first place. If either of these explanations were true, there was no need to include the 'author's own intellectual creation' originality criterion in the 1988 Act in relation to databases.

The only logical conclusion must be that the new originality criterion that is specifically defined for databases departs from the originality criterion that applies to other works. That means that we have failed to implement the Software Directive correctly.[82] The 'author's own intellectual creation' originality criterion should at least apply to databases and computer programs.

Dramatic works

The category of 'dramatic works' shares the same set of general rules with the literary works category from which it is excluded by s. 3(1) of the Act. The obvious example is a

[78] Ibid., s. 3A(2).

[79] See Chapter 30.

[80] European Parliament and Council Directive 96/9/EC on the legal protection of databases (1996) OJ L 77/20 and Council Directive 91/250/EEC on the legal protection of computer programs (1991) OJ L 122/42 (the Software Directive).

[81] Articles 3(1) and 1(3) respectively.

[82] See, in this context, the broader discussion in Laddie et al (2000) preface and ch. 3.

synopsis or script for a play or for a film,[83] but dance and mime are also included in this category.[84] An interesting issue is raised by certain contributions to scripts made by other writers. It is clear that someone who suggests a series of ideas and key story lines for a work written by others will not share in the copyright protection in the work.[85] All that he or she contributes are ideas, which are expressed by the writer, and only the expression is protected by copyright. This would seem to require a contribution to the precise expression of the ideas, such as the full text of a scene or a number of lines for a synopsis, script, or play. Another relevant rule is the recording requirement: no copyright can be granted if those lines are not recorded and this same conclusion was reached in a case that was concerned with an elaborated visual skit for a music hall sketch involving the use of fireworks.[86]

Titles are excluded from protection on the basis of the restrictive UK originality requirement, which applies to this category as well and results in a *de minimis* rule. This rule also covers the names of characters and the typical way in which they behave,[87] unless the link and the characteristics are so strong that they become an independent and recognizable entity.[88] But the protection granted to scripts for plays and movies does not extend to costumes and scenic effects, which will only attract copyright if they are artistic works. Characters and the merchandising rights involved can be protected under passing off, but only in the cases in which they benefit from an established trading reputation.[89]

What has become clear from the examples is that dramatic works involve action and movement. This is also reflected in the comment by Lord Bridge that a dramatic work must be capable of performance.[90] It is submitted that a dramatic work can be best defined as '*a work created in order to be communicated in motion, that is, through a sequence of actions, movements, irrespective of the technique by which this movement is retrieved or expressed*'.[91]

The communication in motion must be required for the proper representation of the work if the work is to be classified as a dramatic work. Any work can be performed before an audience—for example, a literary work can be read—but communication in motion is not required for the proper representation of a literary work. The Court of Appeal has now gone down the same path in holding that a dramatic work is any work of action, with or without words or music, that is capable of being performed before an audience.[92]

This definition implies that a cinematographic or audio-visual work will be a dramatic work, because it clearly meets the requirement of a work created to be communicated in motion. This dramatic work is distinct from the script: various other aspects—such as music, dance, etc.—have been added, making the cinematographic or audio-visual work more than a performance of the script. Although based on the script, it will constitute

---

[83] The film itself attracts a separate copyright.

[84] CDPA 1988, s. 3(1)

[85] *Tate v. Thomas* [1921] 1 Ch 503; see also *Wiseman v. Weidenfeld & Nicolson Ltd* [1985] FSR 525; *Ashmore v. Douglas-Home* [1987] FSR 553.

[86] *Tate v. Fullbrook* [1908] 1 KB 821.

[87] See *Kelly v. Cinema Houses Macg Cap Cas* (1932) 362, *per* Maugham J at 368.

[88] *Exxon Corp. v. Exxon Insurance Consultants International Ltd* [1982] Ch 119, [1981] 2 All ER 495, which refers to Lewis Carroll's *Jabberwocky* as an example.

[89] See Chapter 31 on 'Character merchandising'.

[90] *Green v. Broadcasting Corp. of New Zealand* [1989] 2 All ER 1056, [1989] RPC 700.

[91] P. Kamina, 'Authorship of films and implementation of the Term Directive: the dramatic tale of two copyrights' [1994] 8 EIPR 319 at 320; compare J. Phillips, R. Durie and I. Karet (1993) *Whale on Copyright*, 4th edn, London: Sweet and Maxwell, p. 27.

[92] *Norowzian v. Arks Ltd (No. 2)* [2000] FSR 363.

a new (derivative) dramatic work.[93] The Court of Appeal formally adopted this line of argument in the *Norowzian* case,[94] in which it was held that a film could also be a dramatic work, apart from being eventually the recording of another dramatic work. The Court argued that a film would often, athough not always, be a work of action that was capable of being performed before an audience.

A proper distinction does, however, need to be drawn between a dramatic work and a performance. Copyright in a dramatic work will only cover the work as such—that is, what can be printed and published[95]—and not the interpretation that is given to it by the person who performs it in motion.

Musical works

A first definition

Lyrics are protected as literary works, so what remains of a song is the music. Every overlap is excluded, because a musical work is defined as a work consisting of music, exclusive of any words or action intended to be sung, spoken, or performed with it.[96] For copyright purposes, music and lyrics are distinct works. They can be owned by different persons and can expire at different times, etc. A musical work is, then, '*intended to be performed by the production of a combination of sounds to be appreciated by the ear*'.[97]

Originality

The general rules governing the two previous categories apply to musical works as well. There is no subjective quality requirement: what is a beautiful piece of music to one person is nothing more than an awful cacophony and noise to another person, and a couple of notes and chords will be sufficient to attract copyright.[98] Secondary musical works based on an existing musical work may attract their own copyright. In this category, we find, for example, arrangements or transcriptions for another type of orchestra.[99] These will attract their own copyright if the minimum amount of skill and labour requested by the originality requirement is invested in them, but this does not rule out the possibility of infringement of the copyright in the earlier musical work if, for example, the arrangement is made without the permission of the owner of the copyright in the earlier work.

The situation in relation to arrangements must be distinguished from that in relation to the mere interpretation in a performance of a work. In the latter case, there will be no separate copyright in a (new) musical work, but a right in the performance may arise.

Exploring the boundaries

The 1988 Act does not offer a definition of a musical work. In many cases, one recognizes a musical work if one sees (or hears) one, but, on the borderlines, problems were bound to arise, as happened in the *Hyperion* case,[100] which gave the Court of Appeal the opportunity to clarify the concept of a musical work. It will be recalled that Dr Lionel Sawkins

---

[93] Kamina [1994] at 320–1.

[94] *Norowzian v. Arks Ltd (No. 2)* [2000] FSR 363.

[95] See *Tate v. Fullbrook* [1908] 1 KB 821.

[96] CDPA 1988, ss. 1(1)(a) and 3(1).

[97] Laddie et al. (2000) p. 79.

[98] See *Lawson v. Dundas* (1985) The Times, 13 June, copyright in the then Channel 4 television logo music.

[99] *Metzler & Co. (1920) Ltd v. Curwen* (1928–1935) MacG Cap Cas 127; *Wood v. Boosey* (1868) LR 3 QB 223; *Redwood Music v. Chappell* [1982] RPC 109.

[100] *Hyperion Records v. Lionel Sawkins* [2005] 3 All ER 636, [2005] 1 WLR 3281 (CA).

had restored out-of-copyright musical works by Lalande, with the aim of recreating the works as Lalande would originally have created them. The question arose whether such a restoration effort that led to new performing editions of the works involved the creation of musical works. Hyperion did not want to pay royalties to Sawkins for the use of the performing editions when it recorded its CD and had argued that no new musical work had been created. In its view, the performing edition has no impact on the sound that is produced and perceived by the audience. That sound is essentially the result of Lalande's musical work and has nothing to do with Sawkins' work. The fact that Sawkins wanted to stay as close as possible to Lalande's original work provides a further argument for denying the existence of a new copyright work.

The Court summarized that argument as follows:[101]

> The effect of the editorial interventions of Dr Sawkins was, as he asserted was his intention, only to produce more faithful and better copies of Lalande's original music and to make it playable, rather than to create new music of his own. The kind of effort and skill expended by Dr Sawkins was not appropriate or relevant to the creation of a fresh musical copyright, such as might be achieved by changes to the melody and harmony of the underlying work.

At first instance, Patten J had summarized Hyperion's position on subsistence as follows:[102]

> [U]nless the edition includes the composition of new music in the form of the notes on the score (and not merely the correction of wrong or unsatisfactory notes in the scores used) then no copyright would exist in the edition as a musical work.

Both Patten J and the Court of Appeal refused to follow this unduly narrow approach. It seems, indeed, that there is more to music than notes on a score. Any plain language definition will, for example, also refer to sound and rhythm, and the impact on the ear in general. By focusing narrowly on notes only, Hyperion's argument is also inconsistent with the approach of assessing the work as a whole that the House of Lords laid down in *Ladbroke v. William Hill*.[103]

The Court of Appeal summarized these two points as follows, on the basis of which it rejected Hyperion's argument and held the performing editions to amount to a musical work:[104]

> In my judgment, the fallacies in Hyperion's arguments are that (a) they only treat the actual notes in the score as music and (b) they approach the issue of subsistence from the wrong direction by dividing the whole of the performing edition into separate segments and by then discarding particular segments on the basis that they are not music and not therefore covered by copyright. That is contrary to the correct approach to subsistence of copyright laid down by the House of Lords in Ladbroke (Football) Ltd v. William Hill (Football) Ltd... The subsistence of copyright involves an assessment of the whole work in which copyright is claimed. It is wrong to make that assessment by dissecting the whole into separate parts and then submitting that there is no copyright in the parts. Hyperion's arguments ignore the fact that the totality of the sounds produced by the musicians are affected, or potentially

---

[101] Ibid., at [41] of the judgment.

[102] At [50] of his judgment, which the Court of Appeal praised unanimously and which is reported at [2004] 4 All ER 418. See also V. Jones, 'Musical works: out with the old and in with the new' [2005] Ent LR 89; Groves, 'Better than it sounds: originality of musical works' [2005] Ent LR 20; V. Jones, 'What constitutes a copyright work: does it really matter?' [2005] Ent LR 129.

[103] *Ladbroke (Football) Ltd v. William Hill (Football) Ltd* [1964] 1 WLR 273, at 277–91 (HL).

[104] *Hyperion Records v. Lionel Sawkins* [2005] 3 All ER 636, [2005] 1 WLR 3281 (CA), at [49] of the judgment.

affected, by the information inserted in the performing editions produced by Dr Sawkins. The sound on the CD is not just that of the musicians playing music composed by Lalande. In order to produce the sounds the musicians played from Dr Sawkins' scores of his edition. Without them Ex Cathedra would not have produced the combination of sounds of *Te Deum*, *La Grande Piece Royale* or *Venite Exultemus* for recording on the CD.

There is indeed no reason for restricting the coverage of musical copyright to the actual notes of the music only; after all, a dramatic work is not limited to the words that are to be spoken by the actors either. It is thus common sense that a recording of a person's spontaneous singing or any form of improvization also amounts to music for copyright purposes.

Sawkins' work was required for the musician to play Lalande's work in the way that they did and, more importantly, it produced aural effects—that is, it changed what people heard. From a subsistence point of view, a separate musical work had therefore been created. Music is therefore more than notes on a score: what the audience hears also counts. The Court did not arrive at a definition in statutory language, but the concept of a musical work has at least been clarified somewhat.

Artistic works

This category of original works is wide in scope and can be subdivided into three parts.[105] There are works that are protected irrespective of artistic quality, which are followed by the intermediate group of works of architecture; after this, there are works of artistic craftsmanship. In relation to the last of these works, artistic quality might play a role. This represents a clear departure from the previous categories of work, for which the possession of artistic quality was irrelevant.

Artistic works irrespective of their artistic quality

Graphic works, photographs, sculptures, or collages are protected as artistic works irrespective of their artistic quality.[106] 'Graphic works' include any painting, drawing, diagram, map, chart, plan, engraving, etching, lithograph, woodcut, or similar work.[107] This means that works ranging from a painting by Salvador Dali, to an engineer's plans and drawings for an electromagnetic train, are protected in the same way: no distinction is made between aesthetic, functional and utilitarian works.

Casts, moulds, or models made for a sculpture are treated as a sculpture.[108] The word 'sculpture' should, however, be given its normal plain English meaning. In that sense, for a work to be a sculpture in the first place, it must be a three-dimensional work made by an artist's hand. It follows therefore that not every mould is an artistic work. A mould will not be an artistic work if nothing:

suggests that the manufacturers of [this] mould considered themselves, or were considered by anybody else, to be artists when they designed the [mould] or that they were concerned in any way with the shape or appearance of what they were making, save for the purpose of achieving a precise functional effect.[109]

An attempt was also made to keep pace with future technological developments: a photograph was defined as '*a recording of light or other radiation on any medium on which an*

105 CDPA 1988, ss. 1(1)(a) and 4(1)(a), (b), and (c).
106 Ibid., s. 4(1)(a).
107 Ibid., s. 4(2).
108 Ibid.
109 *Metix (UK) Ltd v. GH Maughlan (Plastics) Ltd* [1997] FSR 718, *per* Laddie J.

image is produced or from which an image may by any means be produced, and which is not part of a film'.[110] Any conflict with films, which may be seen as a succession of a huge number of photographs, is thus ruled out.

Technological developments are nonetheless bound to raise questions. Computer and video games involves a succession of frames, and the question has arisen of whether they are to be considered artistic works. The individual frames might be seen as graphic works—but the question was also asked whether the series for frames as an entity could also be considered to be a graphic work, as part of the wider category of artistic works. In *Nova Productions*,[111] the Court of Appeal held that an artistic work was defined in the Act as including the types of things listed in s. 4, all of which shared the characteristic of being static—that is, non-moving. A series of drawings or frames is therefore a series of graphic works and not a single graphic work or artistic work in itself. Individual frames are graphic works, however, and, as such, they come within the category of artistic works. Section 4 therefore also covers images that are generated on a screen and bitmap files.

The originality requirement for this first group of artistic works is the same as that for all previous types of work. The work should not be copied, should originate from the author, and its creation should involve the minimal amount of skill and labour. That originality relates to artistic matters, rather than, for example, to technical matters in relation to the content of the drawing. The term 'artistic' should be defined here as anything that is visually significant.[112] That minimal amount of skill and labour is clearly present when a photographer makes a photograph from a picture[113] or any other single static object.[114] This is shown by the choice of the angle under which the picture is taken, the exposure time, the degree of focus, the positioning of the object, etc.[115] Often the skill, and therefore the originality, of the photographer is found in reproducing faithfully what is in front of the lens. And the visually significant aspect of the work is found not in the scene or object before the lens, but in the image of it, which is produced on the photograph. Other good examples are a woodcut made from a drawing[116] and the label design for a sweet tin.[117]

But the skill and labour does not necessarily need to be artistic: a plan for a technical device containing three concentric circles was protected, because technical judgment was involved in drawing them to precise measurements, which allowed the technical device to work.[118] Meanwhile, a plan containing a design for toy bricks that was only different from

---

[110] CDPA 1988, s. 4(2).

[111] *Nova Productions Ltd v. Mazooma Games Ltd & ors; Nova Productions Ltd v. Bell Fruit Games Ltd* [2007] RPC 25 (CA).

[112] *Interlego AG v. Tyco Industries Inc.* [1989] AC 217, *per* Lord Oliver at 266; *Ultra Marketing (UK) Ltd & Thomas Alexander Scott v. Universal Components Ltd*, judgment of 12 March 2004, Ch D, unreported.

[113] *Graves' Case* (1869) LR 4 QB 715. For a detailed analysis of copyright in relation to photographs, see Y. Gendreau, A. Nordemann and R. Oesch (1999) *Copyright and Photographs*, London: Kluwer Law International.

[114] *Antiquesportfolio.com plc v. Rodney Fitch & Co. Ltd* [2001] FSR 23. There may also be cases in which the person who arranges the scene that is to be photographed specifically for a picture to be taken is the joint author of the photograph. That will, however, not be the case of any later pictures taken of the same scene without authorization: see *Creation Records v. News Group* [1997] EMLR 444.

[115] *Antiquesportfolio.com plc v. Rodney Fitch & Co. Ltd* [2001] FSR 23; see K. Garnett, G. Davies and G. Harbottle (2005) *Copinger and Skone James on Copyright*, 15th edn, London: Sweet and Maxwell, pp. 128–9; K. Garnett, 'Copyright in photographs' [2000] EIPR 229.

[116] Or a coin engraved in three dimensions from a drawing: *Martin v. Polyplas Manufacturers Ltd* [1969] NZLR 1046; see also *Wham-O Manufacturing Co. v. Lincoln Industries Ltd* [1985] RPC 127, the New Zealand frisbee case in which wooden models from which moulds for the plastic frisbees were made were protected as sculptures, while the moulds themselves were protected as engravings.

[117] *Tavener Rutledge v. Specters* [1959] RPC 355.

[118] *Solar Thomson Engineering Co. Ltd v. Barton* [1977] RPC 537 at 558.

an earlier plan because minor variations were mentioned in words and figures, which are not themselves artistic works, fell foul of the originality requirement and was not awarded distinct copyright.[119]

Works of architecture

A second group of artistic works comprises works of architecture.[120] Buildings or models for a building, which are commonly used to attract potential investors, fall into this group, but the architect's plans are protected as a graphic work and fall into the previous group. A model made of a building also falls outside of this group.

Section 4(1)(b) does not contain the rule that works in this group are protected irrespective of their artistic quality. This omission means that we have to consider the originality requirement carefully. It is submitted that artistic quality is not required: the addition of the additional line in s. 4(1)(a) was necessary to avoid all arguments about the artistic quality of such items as a sculpture that consists only of a rectangular piece of metal. Such arguments do not normally arise concerning buildings and it was not necessary to specify once more that the originality requirement is not an artistic quality test.[121]

Works of artistic craftsmanship[122]

Works of artistic craftsmanship comprise the last—but, admittedly, the most difficult—part of the category of artistic works. Many items or artefacts might be called works of craftsmanship. Jewellery made to a special design, furniture, clothing, or cutlery can all be called works of craftsmanship. The Act offers no definition of this term, but, through the inclusion of the word 'artistic', makes it clear that some artistic quality is required if a work of craftsmanship is to attract copyright protection.

Hensher v. Restawhile

The House of Lords was given the opportunity to consider the issues raised by works of artistic craftsmanship in *George Hensher Ltd v. Restawhile Upholstery (Lancs) Ltd*.[123] This case was concerned with a prototype for a suite of furniture, the boat shape of which was said, by the House, to have given it a particular low-brow appeal. The first important issue is whether artistic quality is required and what level must be attempted or reached. The House of Lords disagreed with the lower court, which had held that the work qualified for copyright, and the judgment makes it clear that some artistic quality is required. The fact that the work is a work of craftsmanship that is not purely utilitarian is not sufficient; artistry and craftsmanship are both required. This is the real significance of the judgment, because this is the only point on which their Lordships agreed. Lord Reid and Lord Morris seem to think that a prototype can never satisfy the artistry requirement, because it is, by definition, not intended to have any value or permanence.[124] It is submitted that the intention of the craftsman is more relevant to a second and separate issue.

Should one look at the craftsman's intention to create something artistic or should one focus on the public's perception of artistic quality? The Court of Appeal had suggested that one should ask whether the public would purchase the thing for its aesthetic appeal,

---

[119] *Interlego AG v. Tyco Industries Inc.* [1989] AC 217, [1988] 3 All ER 949.

[120] CDPA 1988, s. 4(1)(b).

[121] Along the same lines. Laddie et al. (2000) pp. 194–5; cf W. Cornish (1999) *Intellectual Property: Patents, Copyright, Trade Marks and Allied Rights*, 4th edn, London: Sweet and Maxwell, p. 390.

[122] CDPA 1988, s. 4(1)(c).

[123] [1976] AC 64; aff'd [1974] 2 All ER 420.

[124] Ibid. at 77, 80, 423, and 425.

rather than for its functional utility,[125] but this approach was rejected by the House of Lords. Lord Simon of Glaisdale suggested that the Court of Appeal's approach was wrong, because aesthetic appeal was derived from functional utility and vice versa in the English aesthetical tradition.[126] But the speeches do not offer a clear-cut alternative approach. Lord Morris and Viscount Dilhorne suggest that an objective approach on the basis of a detached judgment of the work, without giving priority to the craftsman's intention or the perception by the public, is the better approach.[127] Lord Kilbrandon[128] and Lord Simon[129] attach more importance to the intention of the craftsman, although Lord Simon would also look at the work. And Lord Reid suggested that a work of craftsmanship could only be artistic if a substantial part of the public valued it positively for its appearance.[130]

Some further guidance is provided by *Merlet v. Mothercare*.[131] The criterion suggested by Walton J is whether the craftsman had the conscious purpose of creating a work of art.[132] In his view, the work must be a work of art and he considered this to be the common ground in the speeches in the House of Lords in the *Hensher* case. This leads to the conclusion that the intention of the creator prevails. This case was concerned with a prototype of a cape for babies, called 'Raincosy', and provides helpful guidance by making it clear that only the work itself should be submitted to the test; the use of the work should not be taken into account. In this case, this meant that the cape should be considered without a baby in it and one should clearly not look at the combination of a mother wearing the baby in a baby sling, with the baby protected by the 'Raincosy'.

A last interesting point is that the judge can rely on expert witnesses to determine whether the work meets the relevant standards. Their Lordships did not adopt a common position in this respect in the *Hensher* case, but it is clear that they all refer to expert evidence as a determining factor.

Uncertainty remains

All of this leaves us with a considerable amount of uncertainty. It is not clear what level of artistic quality is required, and no proper and comprehensive test is available. In practice, no problems arise for handcrafted jewellery and similar items, but the position for machine-made objects is problematic. In *Hensher*, Lord Simon seems to suggest that this should not disqualify an object and that copyright protection would still be possible,[133] but Lord Reid seems to disagree.[134] The problem is potentially aggravated if the object is utilitarian in nature and is produced in mass. This is especially the case, because a lot of money is invested in the development of these objects. This situation is particularly regrettable, because this category of works is becoming more and more important now that a proper industrial design right has been created. This will create more intellectual property activity in this area, and requires a clear delimitation of the copyright and design areas respectively—all of which is hampered by the absence of a clear definition of what constitutes a work of artistic craftsmanship.

---

[125] [1976] AC 64 at 71, [1973] 3 All ER 414 at 419.

[126] [1976] AC 64 at 90–2; aff'd [1974] 2 All ER 420 at 433–5.

[127] Ibid. at 81, 86, 426, and 430.

[128] Ibid. at 97 and 439.

[129] Ibid. at 95 and 437.

[130] Ibid. at 78 and 424; see also *Cuisenaire v. Reed* [1963] VR 719 for a similar approach.

[131] *Merlet v. Mothercare plc* [1986] RPC 115. The case went up to the Court of Appeal, but only the point of infringement of the drawing was considered: see [1986] RPC 115.

[132] [1984] FSR 358.

[133] [1976] AC 64 at 90–2; aff'd [1974] 2 All ER 420 at 433–5.

[134] Ibid. at 77 and 423.

No clear solution is available either for the situation in which one person supplies the craftsmanship, but another supplies the idea for the work of artistic craftsmanship. An old precedent[135] suggests that no copyright is available in such a case, but it is submitted that this approach is wrong as long as the craftsman's contribution gives the required level of artistic quality to the work.[136] A recent case goes even further, and allows the craftsman and the artist to be two separate persons.[137]

This situation of twenty years' legal uncertainty is undesirable and unacceptable. The scope of copyright protection is, in general, extremely wide, which allows it to be used to prevent unfair competition. The stricter requirements for works of artistic craftsmanship are an exception to this rule. But even if, as submitted above, one would prefer a narrower scope of copyright protection coupled with a proper unfair competition tort, it is hard to justify why works of artistic craftsmanship should be treated differently. This is clearly an area in which statutory clarification would be desirable.

Towards a way forward

What we have described above is the generally accepted position. We think, however, that the case law allows for an alternative interpretation that may clarify things on a number of points.

This interpretation starts from Lord Simon's speech in the *Hensher* case: what is protected is a work of artistic craftsmanship, not an artistic work of craftsmanship.[138] A glazier, a plumber, and others are all craftsmen,[139] although it is clear that the legislator did not seek to protect all of their professional activities, because craftsmanship requires only that one is able to make something in a skilful way—that is, that one knows one's trade properly.[140] The purpose was to protect a certain type of craftsmanship and the legislator attempted to distinguish that activity by calling it 'artistic craftsmanship'.[141] The glazier who makes stained-glass windows, for example, engages in artistic craftsmanship.[142] In making the distinction, the judge can rely on the evidence provided by expert witnesses.[143]

It follows from this starting point that it is not required that each individual work produced is a work of art, as long as it is the result of an activity that is considered, by the relevant circles, to be an activity of artistic craftsmanship as opposed to ordinary craftsmanship. This brings this type of work in line with the rest of the copyright works, for which no artistic value of the individual work is required, and leads to the application of the normal originality requirement to the individual work.

Or does it?

In deciding whether artistic craftsmanship is involved, the expert evidence will be directed towards the fact that '*artists have vocationally an aim and impact which differ*

---

[135] *Burke & Margot Burke v. Spicers Dress Designs* [1936] Ch 400.

[136] Some more recent decisions expressed disagreement with the case: see *Radley Gowns Ltd v. C Spyrou* [1975] FSR 455, *per* Oliver J; *Bernstein v. Sydney Murray* [1981] RPC 303, *per* Fox J; *Merlet v. Mothercare plc* [1986] RPC 115, *per* Walton J at 123–4.

[137] *Vermaat & Powell v. Boncrest Ltd* [2001] FSR 43.

[138] *George Hensher Ltd v. Restawhile Upholstery (Lancs) Ltd* [1976] AC 64 at 94; aff'd [1974] 2 All ER 420, *per* Lord Simon at 437.

[139] Ibid., *per* Lord Simon at 91 and 434.

[140] See *Vermaat & Powell v. Boncrest Ltd* [2001] FSR 143.

[141] *George Hensher Ltd v. Restawhile Upholstery (Lancs) Ltd* [1976] AC 64; aff'd [1974] 2 All ER 420, *per* Lord Simon at 89–91 and 432–4.

[142] Ibid., *per* Lord Simon at 91 and 434.

[143] Ibid., *per* Lord Simon at 94 and 437.

from those of the ordinary run of humankind'.[144] This covers both the intention of the creator and the result of his or her activity.[145] So the work that is produced is taken into account in deciding whether the activity is artistic in nature.[146] But this refers to the work of the author and the relevant kind of activity in general in requiring some artistic level, and has the advantage of not referring to the individual piece of work under consideration for the purpose of copyright. Artistic craftsmanship thus involves a type of work with material that requires manual dexterity, which leads to the creation of an object that certain members of the public wish to acquire and retain for its visual appearance, rather than for its functional purpose. In this test, the artistic element applies to the type of work carried out by the craftsman and not to the issue of whether each individual work is a piece of art. It is submitted that this approach could remove some of the doubts present in the speeches in the House of Lords and that it would provide us with a workable solution. It would not affect the outcome of the *Hensher* and *Merlet* cases, because both types of activity would be held not to be artistic craftsmanship.

This approach is also reflected in a recent Australian decision. In *Burge v. Swarbrick*,[147] the High Court of Australia held that, while an exhaustive definition should not be attempted, it could be said that the determination of whether a work was a work of artistic craftsmanship '*does no turn on assessing the beauty or aesthetic appeal of the work or on assessing any harmony between its visual appeal and its utility*'.[148] What is vital is the extent to which the particular work's artistic expression, in its form, is unconstrained by functional considerations: if the expression is fully constrained by functional considerations, there may well be a work of craftsmanship, but it will not amount to a work of artistic craftsmanship. The latter requires creative expression outside the constraints of functional considerations and, as such, it is not incompatible with machine and mass production. There is no antithesis between utility and beauty, or between function and creativity. A work of artistic craftsmanship requires both.

Entrepreneurial rights

Section 1 of the 1988 Act also grants copyright protection to sound recordings, films, broadcasts, and typographical arrangements of published editions. These are, in most cases, derivative rights that protect the entrepreneur and the commercial exploitation of copyright. A sound recording of a pop song is a typical example. Original copyrights exist in the lyrics and the music of the song, and are, at least in the first stage, owned by their respective authors. An additional copyright is granted to the sound recording and this copyright is derivative. These rights were introduced to give the entrepreneur his or her own protection. This protection is particularly important, because, often, the financial cost of copyright exploitation is high. Many of the derivative works incorporate a series of original works protected by copyright. A film may incorporate lyrics, music, and a script, which is a dramatic work. In case of infringement, it is extremely helpful that the owner of the copyright in the film can sue. This avoids a series of parallel lawsuits by the owners of the original rights, which may each face the problem of demonstrating that his or her copyright was infringed. The absence of a derivative right would, in practice, greatly facilitate film piracy.

---

[144] Ibid.
[145] Ibid.
[146] Cf *Vermaat & Powell v. Boncrest Ltd* [2001] FSR 143.
[147] *Burge v. Swarbrick* [2007] FSR 27 (High Court of Australia).
[148] Ibid. at 708.

In fact, all of these derivative copyrights are neighbouring rights when compared to the original copyrights. They need, in general, an original copyright work as their basis. A sound recording of a musical work is a good example and so is the script as the dramatic work that is a basis for a film. In a sense, they involve a first exploitation of the original work. This distinction is reflected in many provisions of the Act[149] and is not just of theoretical importance. Unfortunately, the Act does not adopt this terminology and calls all of these rights 'copyrights', although it is clear that they are, in many respects, different from the original copyrights.

These works need not be based on works protected by copyright. If we go back to the example of the sound recording and replace the pop song by the noise of the sea unleashing its forces on the Cornish coast, the conclusion is that the recording is still a sound recording for the purposes of the Act and will attract copyright. Whether the derivative work is based on works protected by copyright or not, the originality requirement for original works will not apply to it.

Sound recordings

The Act defines the term 'sound recording' in s. 5A(1) as:

> a recording of sounds, from which the sounds may be reproduced, or ... a recording of the whole or any part of a literary, dramatic or musical work, from which sounds reproducing the work or part may be produced, regardless of the medium on which the recording is made or the method by which the sounds are reproduced or produced.

It is important to stress that the Act deliberately uses the word 'sound' and not the word 'music'. Not only does this eliminate the discussion on the quality issue, but it also means that speech and other noises are included. In brief, all non-musical works are also included.

The 'recording' part of the definition is equally wide in scope. All that is required is the recording of the sound and the possibility of reproducing it; the medium on which the recording is made and the method by which the sound is produced or reproduced is irrelevant.[150] This means that all existing formats—such as CD, magnetic tape, and digital audio tape (DAT)—are included and that all new formats that may be developed in the years to come will automatically be included. It is obvious that the sound that is recorded may include the whole, or part of, a literary, musical, or dramatic work, but copyright will not exist in a sound recording that is, or to the extent that it is, taken from a previous sound recording.[151] In the music industry—or, perhaps more appropriately, the sound industry—this means that copyright will subsist in the master copy of the recording. This master copy is used to produce the copies on sale to the public. The CDs and cassettes do not attract their own copyright, but are protected indirectly through the copyright in the master copy.[152] This technique does not reduce the level of copyright protection, but eliminates the possibility that, in the absence of an originality requirement, each new and identical copy would attract copyright and extend the duration of copyright protection.

Each recording made independently will, however, attract copyright. If we take the Cornish example, and many persons make their own recording of the noise of the sea at the same time and place, each of these recordings will attract its own copyright and the

---

[149] See, e.g., CDPA 1988, s. 9(2).

[150] CDPA 1988, s. 5A(1).

[151] Ibid., (2).

[152] For more details on the indirect infringement issue, see Chapter 15 on infringement.

person making his or her recording will be able to sue for infringement if someone makes, without permission, a copy of his or her recording. Such a copy will not only infringe, but it will also not attract copyright in its own right.[153]

Films

The Act defines a film in s. 5B(1) as '*a recording on any medium from which a moving image may by any means be reproduced*'. The essential element here is the recording from which a moving image may be reproduced; the technique used to make the recording, the medium on which it is made, and the means of reproduction are irrelevant.[154] All existing formats—such as celluloid film, video, and laser disc—are included and all new formats will also be included, the provision being drafted in such a way that it will not be outdated by technological developments.

Another important point is that only images are referred to: the soundtrack will attract its own separate copyright as a sound recording. Nevertheless, the term 'film' should be taken to include the soundtrack accompanying the moving images, because s. 5B(2) makes it clear that the soundtrack shall be treated as part of the film. This solution is unfortunate in so far as it represents a departure from the basic rule that one work should only be classified and protected as a single type of work, but the solution does reflect the way in which soundtracks are exploited. They are nowadays, on the one hand, an integral part of a film and it might be argued that they deserve protection as such; on the other hand, they are also exploited as separate sound recordings and people buy them separately on CDs or cassettes. Neither is there therefore any reason to take away the protection of a soundtrack as a sound recording simply because it is also used in a film.

Only the master copy of a film will attract copyright protection; this rule applies to films in exactly the same way as it applies to sound recordings. Copyright will not subsist in a film that is, or to the extent that it is, a copy of a previous film.[155] On the one hand, indirect protection for authorized copies is eventually available, because copying them means indirectly copying the original master version; on the other, an unauthorized copy will not only not attract copyright, but will also infringe the copyright in the master copy.

It has to be emphasized that this form of copyright in a film is independent from, and does not influence, the copyright as a dramatic work in the cinematographic or audiovisual work that will, in many cases, be recorded in the film. That copyright as a dramatic work may arise if the director adds significantly to the scenario or script of an acted film, or even in the absence of a pre-existing dramatic work if the film or cinematographic work is a work of action that is capable of being performed before an audience.[156]

The breadth of the references to a recording on any medium and to the reproduction of moving images in the definition of a film do not only allow the wording of the Act to cope with further technological developments in terms of recording medium; it also allows for the classification as films of certain works that would not necessarily be described as films in the plain English sense of the word. For example, many multimedia products that are produced in a digital format seem to fall within the Act's definition of a film. Digital

---

[153] *Metix (UK) Ltd v. GH Maughlan (Plastics) Ltd* [1997] FSR 718, *per* Laddie J.

[154] CDPA 1988, s. 5B(1).

[155] Ibid., (4).

[156] *Norowzian v. Arks Ltd (No. 2)* [2000] FSR 363. In this sense, this recreates the distinction between the work and the recording, and the protection as a dramatic work may be necessary to meet our obligations under the Berne Convention to protect cinematographic works: ibid., *per* Buxton LJ. It is also interesting to see the parallelism with the dual-track approach to musical works and sound recordings. This case does away with the idea that the Act proposed a one-track approach in relation to films.

recording media do not create a problem and the requirement that a moving image can be reproduced from the recording is also met. Most of these products do, indeed, include moving images, in addition to texts, photographs, sound recordings, and computer programs. These additional elements, as well as the potential for interactivity, cannot reverse the reality that all elements of the definition of a film are met. Once again, the copyright as a film in the multimedia work comes on top of, and is independent from, the copyright that may exist in any of the works that are included in it. For example, if a photograph is included in a multimedia work, the film copyright in the multimedia work does not affect the copyright in the photograph as an artistic work. The maker of the multimedia work will require a licence to use the photograph if he or she does not own the copyright in it.

Broadcasts

Terrestrial broadcasts

The Copyright, Designs and Patents Act 1988 grants copyright protection to broadcasts.[157] Originally, a distinction was made between wireless transmissions, which were protected as broadcasts, and transmissions by wire, which were protected as cable programmes. That distinction has now been swept away and the category of broadcasts has been widened.[158]

The Act, as amended, defines a broadcast as:

an electronic transmission of visual images, sounds or other information which—

(a) is transmitted for simultaneous reception by members of the public and is capable of being lawfully received by them, or

(b) is transmitted at a time determined solely by the person making the transmission for presentation to members of the public.[159]

The concept of transmission includes both cable transmissions and wireless broadcasts; all that is required is that the transmission is electronic.

This is a clear attempt to make the definition technology-neutral in order to cover any future developments. The definition is even wider, because it includes the transmission of information, any kind of information, on top of sounds and visual images. It is also important to keep in mind that the law attempts here to protect the investment in transmitting the signal and the provision of the service, and not anything fixed on a certain support of the works included in the transmission. The transmission can either be made for simultaneous reception by members of the public—that is, the traditional radio and television broadcasts—or at a time that is determined solely by the person making the transmission—that is, by the radio or television station. If we analyse the definition even further, we see that broadcasts that cannot be lawfully received by members of the public—such as certain military broadcasts—do not attract copyright. An interesting problem arises when broadcasts are encrypted. This means that the sound and image are emitted in a way that will result in a distorted image and sound being produced on a normal television set. Commercial satellite broadcasters, who charge fees to viewers, often do this. One needs to subscribe to the service, and one then receives a decoder to recreate the normal sound and image. These broadcasts are regarded as capable of being lawfully received if—and only if—decoding equipment has been made available to members of

---

[157] CDPA 1988, s. 6.

[158] The Copyright and Related Rights Regulations 2003, regs 4 and 5. Among other things, CDPA 1988, s. 7, which dealt with cable programmes, has been abolished.

[159] CDPA 1988, s. 6(1).

the public by, or with the authority of, the person making the transmission. The person providing the contents of the transmission can replace the latter.[160]

What is meant by transmission for presentation to members of the public? This becomes clear if we contemplate the example of a giant rock concert, in Hyde Park, for example. Not all fans can attend, and giant screens may be placed in halls in Edinburgh and Manchester where fans who pay an entrance fee can attend to watch the concert on a large screen. The transmission from Hyde Park to Manchester and Edinburgh is a transmission of sound and images for presentation to members of the public, and will attract copyright as a broadcast. Reception of a broadcast may be by means of a telecommunications system[161] and copyright does not subsist in a broadcast that infringes, or to the extent that it infringes, the copyright in another broadcast.[162] Broadcasts are also often relayed. Section 5(A) of the Act now stipulates that the relaying of a broadcast by reception and immediate retransmission is to be regarded as a separate act of broadcasting from that which is being retransmitted.[163]

In principle, there is one major exception from the wide definition of a broadcast: any Internet transmission is not a broadcast, unless the transmission takes place simultaneously on the Internet and by other means, unless it is a concurrent transmission of a live event, or unless it is a transmission of recorded moving images or sounds that form part of a programme service that is offered by the person making the transmission.[164] In the later circumstances, the service concerned must be a service in which programmes are transmitted at scheduled times that are determined by the person making the transmission. These three exceptions, which will bring Internet transmissions within the scope of the definition of a broadcast, are explained easily: in each of the circumstances, the Internet is used as a medium for what amount effectively to a traditional broadcast. The medium used may be different, but the transmission, as such, is not. It is therefore logical to treat these kinds of transmissions as broadcasts for copyright purposes. This means that an Internet transmission has, as a key element, the fact that it is the recipient—that is, the user—who chooses to receive the transmission at a place and time chosen by him or her and, on top of that, these transmissions tend to be interactive. Near on-demand services will, however, still be broadcasts, because they come within the third exception.

Satellite broadcasts

Satellite broadcasting is a form of broadcasting that raises additional problems.[165] The signal is transmitted to the satellite (the 'up-leg') from where it is retransmitted towards the earth (the 'down-leg'). Many countries are covered by the foot of the satellite and the question can be raised which copyright law will be applicable to the broadcasts. The choice is restricted by the fact that the Berne Convention for the Protection of Literary and Artistic Works 1886 speaks about broadcasting in terms of communication to the public.[166] This could lead to the conclusion that both emission and reception are essential elements, and that the copyright law of the emission country and the copyright laws of the countries inside the foot of the satellite should be applied cumulatively.[167]

---

[160] Ibid., (2).

[161] Ibid., (5).

[162] Ibid., (6).

[163] CDPA 1988, s. 5(A), inserted by Copyright and Related Rights Regulations 2003, reg. 4(d).

[164] CDPA 1988, s. 6(1A), inserted by Copyright and Related Rights Regulations 2003, reg. 4(a).

[165] See A. Dietz, 'Copyright and satellite broadcasts' (1989) 20 IIC 135–50.

[166] Berne Convention, Art. 11bis.

[167] This theory is called the 'Bogsch theory': see M. Ficsor, 'Direct broadcasting by satellite and the "Bogsch Theory"' [1990] IBL 258. Dr Arpad Bogsch is the former Director General of the World Intellectual Property Organization (WIPO).

.The Copyright, Designs and Patents Act 1988[168] and the EC Council Directive on Satellite Broadcasting[169] reject this approach, focusing instead on the 'up-leg' and applying only the copyright law of the country of emission.[170] Communication to the public occurs, from the perspective of those instruments, solely in the country from which the signal is emitted (to the satellite). This approach carries with it the risk that satellite broadcasters will locate their uplink stations in countries with weak copyright laws to evade paying royalties to the largest possible extent. The Directive provides, therefore, for an exception in case the emission takes place in a non-.ember State that does not provide a sufficient level of copyright protection.[171] That exception has now been implemented by the UK as s/ 6A of the 1988 Act and its scope has been extended to include the states adhering to the European Economic Area (EEA) as well as the EU member States.

Regulation 5 of the Copyright and Related Rights Regulations 2003[172] makes it clear, in line with the widening of the definition of a broadcast, that we are here concerned uniquely with wireless transmission and wireless broadcasting, because no wires or cables are used to carry the signal. If the signal is emitted to the satellite from the territory of a member State of the EEA, the copyright laws of that member State will apply[173] and the person operating the uplink station will be treated as the person making the broadcast.[174] In all member States, the level of copyright protection will be at a harmonized level. If the signal is emitted from the territory of a non-member State and that country does not provide a minimum level of protection, the exceptional rule comes into operation. The minimum level of protection is defined as equivalent rights for authors of literary, dramatic, musical and artistic works, films, and broadcasts to those given to them by s. 20 of the 1988 Act in relation to the broadcasting of their works, plus the requirement that the consent of the performer be obtained before a performance is broadcast live, and a right for authors of sound recordings and performers to share in a single equitable remuneration in respect of the broadcasting of sound recordings.[175] The exceptional rule states that, if the emission has been commissioned by a person or a broadcasting organization established in a member State, then the laws of the member State in which that person or the broadcasting organization has its principal establishment will apply.[176]

The copyright protection for satellite broadcasts is not dependent on the type of satellite used, as long as the signals can be lawfully received by members of the public. As a result, only point-to-point communication is excluded if it is exclusively meant for reception and retransmission by a local broadcaster.[177]

Typographical arrangements

This category of works is concerned with the typographical arrangements of published editions. The type and size of the letters used, the number of words on a page, and the

---

[168] CDPA 1988, s. 6(4).

[169] EC Council Directive 93/83/EEC of 27 September 1993 on the coordination of certain rules concerning copyright and rights related to copyright applicable to satellite broadcasting and cable retransmission (1993) OJ L 248/15 at Art .1(2)(b); see also P. Kern, 'The EC "common position" on copyright applicable to satellite broadcasting and cable retransmission' [1993] 8 EIPR 276.

[170] On the emission theory, see G. Karnell, 'A refutation of the Bogsch Theory on DIRECT SATELLITE BROADCASTING RIGHTS' [1990] IBL 263; this theory provides, in practice, a more workable solution.

[171] CDPA 1988, s. 5A(2).

[172] SI 2003/2498

[173] See Art. 1(2)(d) of the Directive.

[174] See CDPA 1988, s. 6A(2).

[175] Ibid.   [176] Ibid., (1).

[177] See Art. 1(1) of the Directive.

place of illustrations in relation to the text are all examples of typographical arrangements. Typographical arrangements have been described as *'graphical images pertaining or relating to printing by which literary, dramatic or musical works may be conveyed to the reader'*.[178]

The typographical arrangement copyright arises in relation to published editions of the whole, or any part, of one or more literary, dramatic, or musical works.[179] The copyright exists, however, only in relation to the published edition as a whole as it is published by the publisher, irrespective of how its content is composed.[180] For example, in relation to a newspaper, the copyright existed in relation to the newspaper, as published, rather than in relation to the arrangement of individual articles within the newspaper.[181]

The typographical arrangement copyright does not arise in relation to artistic works and does not subsist in the typographical arrangement of a published edition if, or to the extent that, it simply reproduces the typographical arrangement of a previous edition.[182]

An overview

Copyright will only exist if a work comes within the scope of a category of works that has been defined in the Copyright, Designs and Patents Act 1988. A first set of categories requires some level of originality. It comprises literary, dramatic, musical, and artistic works. The precise definition of each of these types of work has given rise to a considerable amount of case law, because the Act does not always offer a definition. Sometimes, a list of works is given instead of a definition, but even then problems remain.

Original works do not, however, require artistic quality, even if the concept of originality is not always very specific and seems to be influenced by the type of work under consideration. All of these definitional problems unite to make the case of works of artistic craftsmanship into a very colourful example in point.

A second set could be said to involve mainly entrepreneurial rights. Originality as such is not required; often, these are derivative rights. In this category, we find films, sound recordings, broadcasts, and typographical arrangements of published editions.

Further reading

GENDREAU, Y., NORDEMANN, A. and OESCH, R. (eds) (1999) *Copyright and Photographs: An International Survey*, London: Kluwer Law International.

HINTON, C., 'Can I protect my TV format?' (2006) 17 Ent LR 3, 91.

JONES, V., 'What constitutes a copyright work: does it really matter?' (2005) 16 Ent LR 5, 129.

RAHMATIAN, A., 'Music and creativity as perceived by copyright law' [2005] IPQ 267.

TORREMANS, P. (2007) 'Legal issues pertaining to the restoration and reconstitution of manuscripts, sheet music, paintings and films for marketing purposes', in P. Torremans, *Copyright Law: A Handbook of Contemporary Research*, Cheltenham/Northampton, MA: Edward Elgar, pp. 28–48.

[178] Laddie et al. (2000) p. 435.
[179] CDPA 1988, s. 8(1).
[180] *Newspaper Licensing Agency Ltd v. Marks & Spencer plc* [2001] Ch 257, [2000] All ER 239, [2001] Ch 281, *per* Mance LJ.
[181] Ibid.
[182] CDPA 1988, s. 8(2).

11
Qualification

Works that come under one of the categories described in the previous chapter have to pass one more hurdle to secure copyright protection—namely, the qualification requirement. This requirement is linked to the principle of national treatment contained in the Berne Convention for the Protection of Literary and Artistic Works 1886, in the Universal Copyright Convention, and now also in the TRIPS Agreement.[1] Authors connected with another member State are to be treated in the same way as a member State's own authors and should receive the same copyright. That connection with a member State might be provided in two ways: the author may have a personal relationship with the member State or the work may be first published in that member State.[2] The latter option is not available as long as a work remains unpublished.

This principle is implemented in the UK through a two-stage process.

1. The criteria used to establish a connection with the UK[3]—whether through the author or through publication—are laid down.

2. The system is applied to works connected with other member States of both Conventions. Such application is effected by an Order in Council.[4]

Things become further complicated because countries adhere to one, or both, Conventions at different dates. This creates problems for works published before the date on which the country adheres to the Conventions. Unfortunately, the provisions dealing with this issue are not identical in both Conventions. On the one hand, the Berne Convention works, in part, retroactively. If a work is still in copyright under its own national copyright legislation when a country adheres to the Convention, the work will attract copyright protection in the UK for the remaining part of the term of copyright. On the other hand, the Universal Copyright Convention does not work retroactively and a work published before a country, which is not a member of the Berne Convention, adheres to the Universal Copyright Convention will not be granted copyright in the UK.

---

[1] Berne Convention, Art. 3; Universal Copyright Convention, Art. 2; TRIPS Agreement, Art. 3.

[2] See also, for the implementation of this Convention rule, CDPA 1988, s. 153.

[3] And with dependent territories to which the CDPA 1988 is extended—the Isle of Man, the Channel Islands, etc.—see CDPA 1988, s. 157 and the relevant Orders in Council taken on the basis of that section.

[4] Ibid., s. 159.

Qualification by means of the personal status of the author

The issue here is whether the author of the work, being the creator of the work,[5] is a qualifying person. This will be the case if the author is a British national,[6] is domiciled or resident in the UK, or is a body incorporated under the laws of the UK. Application to a foreign work depends on the question of whether the author is a citizen, subject, domiciliary, or resident of a Convention country listed in an Order in Council, or a company incorporated in such country.[7]

Because all of these connecting factors can change over time, the connection has to exist at the material time—that is, at the date on which the work is made for unpublished literary, dramatic, musical, and artistic works. If the work is published, reference is made to the date of first publication and the author's status at that date, or on the date on which the author died if that occurs before the work is published.[8] There is only one rule for works that do not come within the scope of the 'original' category: the date on which a sound recording or film is made is the material time for these works. For broadcasts, the date of transmission is the material time, and for typographical arrangements, this is the time of first publication.[9]

Once qualification has been achieved, subsequent events cannot take it away.[10]

Qualification by means of first publication

The country of first publication is also a separate connecting factor. A work that is first published in the UK will qualify for copyright protection and so will a work first published in another Convention country.[11] The country of transmission is the connecting factor for broadcasts.[12]

Really simultaneous publication does not create a problem if one of the countries in which the work is published is the UK or another contracting state, but a problem may be created if the country in which publication takes place a couple of days before publication in other countries is not a contracting state to one of the copyright conventions. This would normally jeopardize the option of qualification for copyright protection through first publication in a contracting state, but a period of grace of 30 days has been built in. Publication in that period in the UK or another contracting state will be treated as really simultaneous publication and will secure qualification for copyright protection.[13]

But what amounts to publication? The definition of the term 'publication' is, first of all, relevant for the qualification issue, but, in many cases, it is also of importance for the term

---

[5] Defined more precisely in Chapter 13.

[6] British dependent territories citizens, british nationals (overseas), british overseas citizens, british subjects and british protected persons within the meaning of the British Nationality Act 1981 are added to this category: CDPA 1988, see s. 154(1)(a).

[7] Ibid., s. 154.

[8] Ibid., (4).

[9] Ibid., (5).

[10] Ibid., s. 153(3).

[11] Ibid., s. 155(1) and (2).

[12] Ibid., s. 156.

[13] Ibid., s. 155(3).

of copyright protection, as we will discuss in the next chapter. For copyright purposes, 'publication' means issuing copies of the work to the public in sufficient quantities with the intention of satisfying public demand.[14] Copies are issued to the public if they are put into circulation by sale, gift, or hire[15] and this takes place if the publisher invites the public to acquire the copies.[16] The intention of the publisher is an important element, because he or she must be prepared to meet public demand.[17]

For literary, dramatic, musical, and artistic works, copies can also be issued to the public through the inclusion of the work in an electronic retrieval system that makes the work available to the public.[18] The number of copies issued is of secondary importance,[19] as shown by the Court of Appeal's decision to accept that the release for sale of six copies of a song that was not (yet) known amounted to publication.[20]

Copies are <u>not issued</u> to the public by the performance of a literary, dramatic, or musical work. The same goes for broadcasting, exhibiting an artistic work, and issuing graphic works or photographs of sculptures, works of architecture, or works of artistic craftsmanship.[21]

The concept of copies is to be construed along the lines of s. 17 of the Copyright, Designs and Patents Act 1988. The main outstanding question is how exact the copies should be in order to constitute publication of the original work. The infringement criterion of a substantial part of the work is not suitable in this context; the whole work should be contained in the copies. There should be no difference in material respects between the copies and the original work, even if minor variations can be accepted.[22]

Unauthorized acts are not taken into account when it is established whether a work has been published or not.[23] A related, but fairly specific and exceptional, problem is raised by an adaptation—by the author, or with his or her consent—of an unpublished work. Does the translation into English of an unpublished African Swahili literary tale, or the conversion of an unpublished novel into a play, have the effect of publishing the original if copies of the adaptation are issued to the public? The Act provides no clear guidance, but it seems reasonable to assume that, if the adaptation is 'original' enough to attract its own copyright, it is distinct enough from the original to conclude that it does not constitute publication of the original work, which is clearly distinct from the adaptation. If, however, the adaptation merely reproduces the older unpublished work, publication of the adaptation will probably have the effect of publication of the older work. An example of the latter case would be a three-dimensional embodiment of a two-dimensional drawing.[24] As we will see later in Chapter 15 on infringement, this latter example is very similar to cases of copyright infringement.

---

[14] Ibid., s. 175(1)(a).

[15] See *British Northrop v. Texteam Blackburn Ltd* [1974] RPC 57, *per* Megarry J at 67.

[16] Ibid. It would not be workable to take into account the place where the public receives the copies, because this would make the country of first publication dependent on where shipments of the work were received first.

[17] Cf *Copex v. Flegon* (1967) The Times, 18 August.

[18] CDPA 1988, s. 175(1)(b).

[19] Mere colourable publication, which is not intended to satisfy public demand, is not taken into account: CDPA 1988, s. 175(5).

[20] *Francis Day & Hunter v. Feldman* [1914] 2 Ch 728; see also *Bodley Head Ltd v. Flegon* [1972] 1 WLR 680, [1972] RPC 587.

[21] CDPA 1988, s. 175(4).

[22] See *Sweeney v. Macmillan Publishers Ltd* [2002] RPC 35 at 651.

[23] CDPA 1988, s. 175(6).

[24] *Merchant Adventurers v. Grew* [1973] RPC 1 at 10.

The Berne Convention has a built-in preference for qualification by means of the country of first publication over qualification by means of the personal status of the owner.[25] The latter option will only be taken into account once it has been established that first publication did not take place in a contracting state. This preference is not found in the 1988 Act: the Act treats both methods of qualification as equal.

An overview

The UK copyright system is based on a series of international conventions, which have been implemented into national law. The main principle of the international copyright system is that foreign authors and their works will, in each member State be given national treatment. In practice, this requires a tool with which to determine whether an author or a work qualifies for this national treatment and therefore for copyright protection in the UK. The qualification rules deal with this matter. Authors and works that pass the test will have access to the copyright system in the UK; authors and works that do not qualify will not benefit from copyright protection. Qualification can be achieved by means of the personal status of the author or by means of first publication of the work.

Further reading

GARNETT, K., DAVIES, G. and HARBOTTLE, G. (2005) *Copinger and Skone James on Copyright*, 15th edn, London: Sweet and Maxwell, pp. 135–52.

RICKETSON, S. and GINSBURG, J. (2006) *International Copyright and Neighbouring Rights: The Berne Convention and Beyond*, Oxford: Oxford University Press, pp. 239–78.

STERLING, J. A. L. (2003) *World Copyright Law*, 2nd edn, London: Sweet and Maxwell, pp. 604–7.

---

[25] Berne Convention, Art. 5(4). Under the Convention, this is the normal way to determine the country of origin of a work. First publication is, relatively speaking, easier to determine for any third party and is relatively easily proved in comparison with any aspect of the personal status of the author.

12
The term of copyright

General principles

A harmonized term of protection

We have now established which works attract copyright, but what is the duration of copyright? We will mainly have to distinguish between 'original' works and films, on the one hand,[1] and all other works, on the other.

The term of copyright in 'original' works used to be 50 years in the UK.[2] In other member States of the European Union (EU), longer terms of protection were in force—such as 70 years in Germany and 60–80 years in Spain. This was possible because the Berne Convention for the Protection of Literary and Artistic Works 1886 only imposes a minimum term of protection upon its members,[3] but it could impede the free movement of goods within the EU and was therefore held to be undesirable.

A Directive was adopted with the aim of harmonizing the term of copyright protection in the EU, broadly speaking, at the 70-year level.[4] This Directive brought radical change to the relevant sections of the Copyright, Designs and Patents Act 1988 when it was eventually implemented by the Duration of Copyright and Rights in Performances Regulations 1995.[5] In the UK, the changes took effect on 1 January 1996.

Comparison of term

A preliminary point that affects the transition from a 50-year term to a 70-year term is the issue of the comparison of term. This technique is introduced—or perhaps one should say 'tolerated'—by Art. 7(8) of the Berne Convention. It means that works in relation to which the country of origin has a shorter term of copyright protection will not attract copyright protection in a country with a longer term of protection once the term of protection in the country of origin has expired. In practical terms, this means, for example, that a Canadian work with a Canadian term of protection would not attract 20 extra years of copyright protection in Germany; the Germans are allowed to discriminate and apply the 70-year term only to works in relation to which the country of origin is Germany or any

---

[1] Article 1 of the Directive refers to works in the meaning of Art. 2 of the Berne Convention.

[2] CDPA 1988, s. 12, as it stood before the amended version that was contained in the Duration of Copyright and Rights in Performances Regulations 1995, SI 1995/3297, regs 4 and 5(1), took effect on 1 January 1996.

[3] Berne Convention, Art. 7(6). The minimum term is 50 years.

[4] EC Council Directive 93/98/EEC of 29 October 1993 on the harmonizing of the term of copyright and certain related rights (1993) OJ L 290.

[5] SI 1995/3297.

other country that allows a minimum term of protection of 70 years for German works. Article 7 of the Directive makes the application of the comparison of term rule mandatory for all member States. Works originating in third countries that do not offer at least a 70-year copyright term will not benefit from the longer protection in the EU, the obvious aim of which is to convince third countries also to adopt a 70-year term of copyright.

The UK has implemented Art. 7 by inserting into the 1988 Act a provision that stipulates that a work that has a state that is not part of the European Economic Area (EEA) as its country of origin and the author of which is not a national of a EEA state will only be protected in the UK for the term for which it is granted protection in its country of origin.[6] On top of that, the provision stipulates that, under no circumstances, will a term that is longer than the new UK term of protection will be granted. This means, for example, that the UK will only grant a 50-year term of protection to a novel published in Toronto by a Canadian national. Should Canada put in place a copyright system that grants protection for an 80-year term, the UK will still only protect the work for its own 70-year term.

The new UK provision applies to all types of copyright work.[7] The country of origin is defined as follows for the purposes of the 1988 Act: if the work is first published in a contracting state to the Berne Convention, that country of first publication will be the country of origin of the work;[8] for unpublished works and works that are first published in a country that is not a Berne Convention country, the country of which the author of the work is a national will normally be the country of origin of the work.[9] Special rules that depart from this latter rule exist for films, works of architecture, and artistic works that are incorporated in a building. The country in which the maker of the film has either its headquarters, its domicile, or its residence will be the country of origin of the film if that country is a contracting state to the Berne Convention.[10] The Berne Convention country in which the work of architecture is constructed, or in which the building or structure in which the artistic work is incorporated is situated, will be the country of origin of the work of architecture or the artistic work, respectively.[11]

Non-discrimination in the EU

The provision in Art. 7(8) of the Berne Convention has strange implications in relation to the Term Directive, due to the transition from a 50-year term to a 70-year term in the majority of member States. Indeed, Art. 12 (formerly 6) of the EC Treaty rules out any discrimination on the basis of nationality and this rule applies also to copyright issues. Thus Germany was not entitled to use its comparison of term rule in relation to works of nationals of another member State:[12] these works should have enjoyed a 70-year term of protection in Germany all along.

When the Directive came into force, the area in which these works enjoy protection became the whole territory of the EU. As a strange consequence, all works that were still

---

[6] CDPA 1988, ss. 12(6), 13A(4), 13B(7), and 14(3).

[7] Ibid. The comparison of term rule is dropped in relation to sound recordings and broadcasts in those cases in which its application would be at variance with the UK's international obligations as they stood on 29 October 1993: CDPA 1988, ss. 13A(5) and 14(4).

[8] CDPA 1988, s. 15A(2). Special provisions for cases of simultaneous publication are found in s. 15A(3) and (4).

[9] Ibid., s. 15A(5)(c).

[10] Ibid., s. 15A(5)(a).

[11] Ibid., (b).

[12] Cases C-92 and 326/92 *Phil Collins v. Imtrat Handelsgesellschaft GmbH* [1993] ECR I-5145, [1993] 3 CMLR 773.

protected in Germany did benefit from the 70-year term in the whole of the EU, even if some of these works were out of copyright and in the public domain in a number of member States, eventually including the member State of origin, which used to have a 50-year term. An English literary work, written by an English author who died in 1943 and first published in the UK, no longer attracted copyright protection in the UK under the old provisions of the 1988 Act when the Directive came into force, its term of protection having expired at the end of 1993—but it did still attract copyright in Germany until the end of 2013. The work came back into copyright through the implementation of the Directive and its term of copyright protection will expire at the end of the year 2013 in the whole of the EU, including the UK.

All of this is the inevitable result of the combined application of Art. 12 (formerly 6) of the EC Treaty, as applied in the *Phil Collins*[13] case, and Art. 7 of the Term Directive.[14]

Transition issues

In practical terms, all of those works to which a new longer term would now apply if they were created after the date on which the Directive was implemented saw their term of protection increased to the new longer period. For example, the first edition of this book was written in 1995; the old 50-year term applied to it at first, but, from 1 January 1996 onwards, its term of protection in the UK was increased under the new 70-year rule. If the copyright had already lapsed under the old rules, but the new longer period had not yet expired, the copyright would have been revived for the remaining period of the new longer term.

For example, the works of an author such as D. H. Lawrence, who died in 1930, went out of copyright at the end of 1980, but their copyright was revived under the new rules for the period between 1 January 1996 and the end of the year 2000. While this may have been good news for right holders and those who held copyrights before they lapsed under the old rules, it created an odd situation for those who had exploited the works, for example, by publishing a complete collection of the works of D. H. Lawrence in 1990, on the understanding that they were out of copyright.

This situation has been addressed by the implementing statutory instrument[15] and transition measures have been put in place.[16] Anything done before the UK's implementation date of 1 January 1996 cannot amount to infringement and copies that were made before the Directive's implementation date of 1 July 1995 can be issued to the public without giving rise to copyright infringement, even if that effectively takes place once the new system is in force. This means that no royalties will be payable for the collection of the works of D. H. Lawrence that was published in 1990 in our example and that its publishers can continue to sell existing copies of the collection. On top of that, any allegedly infringing acts for which arrangements were made before 1 January 1995 and which are subsequently implemented in relation to works that were out of copyright at that time will not amount to copyright infringement.

---

[13] Ibid.

[14] G. Dworkin and J. A. L. Sterling, '*Phil Collins* and the Term Directive' [1994] 5 EIPR 187.

[15] See reg. 23.

[16] Bizarre situations remain, however, especially because the 1988 Act also contained transitional measures in relation to works created under previous UK Copyright Acts. The combination of the various transition measures can give rise to odd results: see J. N. Adams and M. Edenborough, 'The duration of copyright in the UK after the 1995 Regulations' [1996] 11 EIPR 590.

Original works

The term of copyright protection is calculated from the end of the year in which the author dies and runs for 70 years.[17] As a result, copyright in original literary, dramatic, musical, and artistic works expires 70 years after the end of the year in which the author of the work died. The term of protection for computer-generated works, which have no human author who can die, continues to run for 50 years and the death of the author is replaced by the date on which the work was made.[18]

Computer-generated works are virtually unknown outside the UK. Their introduction in the 1988 Act was not followed by similar moves in other European countries. The Term Directive does not affect these works and the UK opted to keep its term of protection at 50 years. All terms are, for reasons of simplicity, calculated from 1 January of the year following the event that gives rise to them.[19] In the case of joint authorship, the 70-year term of protection for the work is calculated from the end of the year in which the last surviving author dies.[20]

Anonymous or pseudonymous works create a problem for the application of these rules. For these works, the term of protection runs for 70 years from the lawful publication[21] of the work. That lawful publication needs to occur within a period of 70 years from the end of the calendar year in which the work was made. If no lawful publication takes place within that period, the copyright expires at the end of the 70 years after the work was made.[22] These rules apply unless the author discloses his or her identity during the 70-year period, or if his or her identity becomes known during that period. In this situation, the normal rule for non-anonymous and non-pseudonymous works will apply.[23]

Films

Cinematographic and audio-visual works present a different case. The Directive does not simply lay down a term of protection, but also stipulates that the principal director of such a work shall be considered as its author or as one of its authors. Member States are, in addition, given the freedom to designate other co-authors for these works. The latter provision can be seen as a compromise between the Continental tendency to give directors rights in a film and the UK's tradition to give the same rights to producers.

It also becomes clear from these provisions that films, to use the UK term, are increasingly associated with, or considered as, original works, rather than entrepreneurial recording rights. Historically, films were very much part of the latter category, which was illustrated by the fact that the original version of the 1988 Act dealt with the duration of sound recordings and films in a single section. Originality is still not required for films, but the fact that the 'artistic' creators of a film are now seen as its authors—with the emphasis shifting somewhat away from the 'entrepreneurial' producers—explains why

---

[17] CDPA 1988, s. 12(2).
[18] Ibid., (7).
[19] Article 8 of the Directive confirms this existing principle in UK copyright law.
[20] CDPA 1988, s. 12(8).
[21] As defined in CDPA 1988, s. 12(5).
[22] Ibid., s. 12(3).
[23] Ibid., (4).

films are now given a duration regime that resembles, above all, the regime for original works.

From 1 January 1996 onwards, the following regime applies. The term of copyright protection for a film will expire 70 years after the end of the year in which the last of the following persons dies:

- the principal director;
- the author of the screenplay;
- the author of the dialogue;
- the composer of the music specifically created for use in the film.[24]

If the identity of one or more of the persons concerned is not known, these persons can be deleted from the list and the death of the last known person will trigger the start of the 70-year term.[25] If the identity of all of the persons concerned is unknown, the film will be protected for 70 years from the end of the calendar year in which it was made. This period is extended to 70 years from the end of the calendar year in which the film was made available to the public if the film is made available before the 70-year period after making expires.[26] A film is made available to the public when it is first shown in public or broadcast, unless it is the consequence of an unauthorized act.[27] If the identity of at least one of the persons concerned becomes known before the 70-year period for anonymous films expires, the normal rules that rely on the death of the author or of the last of the co-authors as the triggering event replace the rules for anonymous films in determining the term of protection for the film.[28] An author's identity shall not be assumed to be unknown simply because the person who wants to find out whether a film is still in copyright does not know it; the criterion is rather that it is not possible to ascertain the identity by reasonable inquiry.[29]

Regrettably, the UK took a minimalist approach when implementing the Directive. This means that the list of people that are referred to in relation to the term of copyright in a film does not correspond with that used in relation to the authorship of a film. On the latter point, the UK was obliged to include the director in addition to the producer, who was traditionally included under UK law, but it declined to use the option to add other people. There seemed to be an unwritten rule that the rules on the term of copyright referred to the authors of the work; this rule has now been set aside in relation to films, and the 1988 Act no longer displays a clear and systematic approach to this matter. Such a political compromise, or a bending of the rules in favour of one group of lobbyists, does not enhance the transparency and the inherent logic of the copyright system in the UK, and is therefore to be regretted. This also represents a missed chance to achieve harmonized rules for films that are, after all, exploited across Europe and not only in the UK.

It is submitted that the better solution would have been the creation of a new heading in the 1988 Act, which would cover cinematographic and audio-visual works. These would then be expressly excluded from the scope of the dramatic works provision.[30] This approach would lead to two separate rights: one for, eventually among others, the director

---

[24] Ibid., s. 13B(2).
[25] Ibid., (3).
[26] Ibid., (4).
[27] Ibid., (6).
[28] Ibid., (5).
[29] Ibid., (10).
[30] Cf P. Kamina, 'Authorship of films and implementation of the Term Directive: the dramatic tale of two copyrights' [1994] 8 EIPR 319.

in the cinematographical or audio-visual work, and a second right for the producer in the film as the recording of the cinematographical or audio-visual work.[31] This is also the approach taken in the Belgian Copyright Act of 1994, which was adopted after the Directive had been adopted.[32] Such an approach would underscore the fact that films are increasingly seen as original works. A separate recording right, or right in the first fixation, would then exist on top of the original right. But maybe such a coherent and systematic approach has too much of a Continental flavour to it for the pragmatic UK copyright lawyer.

The current state of confusion is shown by two contrasting developments. On the one hand, there is the implementation in the UK of the Term Directive, which clearly treats films as a single category, including both the fixation and the cinematographic work. Arguably, this is a breach of the provisions of the Directive, because, in taking the fixation on board, the UK also extended the term for moral rights protection in films, which is something for which the Directive did not provide a mandate.[33] On the other hand, there is the Court of Appeal's decision in *Norowzian*.[34] While it was not open to the Court to create a separate copyright category of cinematographic works, the Court did offer a form of dual protection, by arguing that some works can be protected as films and as dramatic works at the same time.

Other entrepreneurial works

Sound recordings are the first 'other' type of work. Sound recordings are protected for 50 years from the end of the calendar year in which the sound recording was made. This period is extended to 50 years from publication[35] if the recording is published before the 50-year period after making expires.[36] In the absence of publication, a recording can still be made available to the public during the 50 year period after the recording was made. Publication can take the form of the recording being played in public or communicated to the public and the term of protection will then expire at the end of a 50 years term that starts running from the end of the calendar year in which the recording is made available. In determining whether a sound recording has been published, played in public, or communicated to the public, no account is to be taken of an unauthorized act.[37]

The term of protection for broadcasts is 50 years from first transmission.[38] A broadcast that is a repeat of a broadcast previously made is not able to prolong the term of copyright in the broadcast or to attract a new copyright after the original term has expired. The copyright in the repeat broadcast will expire at the same time as the copyright in the

---

[31] The provisions on employer ownership of the copyright in the work and assignment of copyright could still grant the producer most of the rights. Contractual provisions will continue to play an important role in this area.

[32] Wet betreffende het auteursrecht en de naburige rechten—Loi relative au droit d'auteur et aux droits voisins of 30 June 1994 [1994] Belgisch Staatsblad—Moniteur Belge, 27 July, p. 19297 *et seq.*; see Arts 2, 14, and 39.

[33] See H. Laddie, P. Prescott and M. Vitoria (2000) *The Modern Law of Copyright and Designs*, 3rd edn, London: Butterworths, p. 19.

[34] *Norowzian v. Arks Ltd (No. 2)* [2000] FSR 363.

[35] Starting at the end of the calendar year during which publication took place.

[36] CDPA 1988, s. 13A(2), as amended by Copyright and Related Rights Regulations 2003, reg. 29.

[37] Ibid.

[38] CDPA 1988, s. 14(2).

original broadcast.[39] For typographical arrangements, the term of copyright protection is only 25 years from first publication.[40]

All of these terms start to run from the end of the year in which the triggering event takes place.

An overview

The basic rule is simple: the term of copyright has been harmonized at life of the author plus 70 years in the EU. One can ask plenty of questions about the justification for this move, but, because the USA followed suit, it is unlikely to be reversed in the near future. The basic rule applies to the original category of works—that is, literary, dramatic, musical, and artistic works—and to films.

Entrepreneurial works, such as sound recordings and broadcasts, benefit from 50 years of copyright protection. There have recently been attempts to lengthen the term for sound recordings, but these have, for the time being, come to nothing.

The term of protection for typographical arrangements is 25 years.

Further reading

ADAMS, J. N. and EDENBOROUGH, M., 'The duration of copyright in the UK after the 1995 Regulations' [1996] 11 EIPR 590.

EMILIANIDES, A. C., 'The author revived: harmonisation without justification' (2004) 26 EIPR 12, 538.

GARNETT, K., DAVIES, G. and HARBOTTLE, G. (2005) *Copinger and Skone James on Copyright*, 15th edn, London: Sweet and Maxwell, ch. 6.

LADDIE, H., PRESCOTT, P. and VITORIA, M. (2000) *The Modern Law of Copyright and Designs*, 3rd edn, London: Butterworths, ch. 10.

PARKER, N., 'A raw deal for performers: Part 1—term of copyright' (2006) 17 Ent LR 6, 161.

[39] Ibid., (5) and (6).
[40] Ibid., s. 15.

13

Authorship and ownership of copyright

Authorship

The creator as author

The person who creates the work is the author of the work.[1] This hardly creates problems for the original literary, dramatic, musical, and artistic works. Thus the writer of a literary work, such as a novel, will be its author; the composer will be the author of a musical work;[2] the sculptor will be the author of a sculpture; the photographer will be the author of a photograph. For derivative works, however, the application of this principle is not as easy: who creates a sound recording? *not disk only*

The Copyright, Designs and Patents Act 1988 provides further guidance on this point in s. 9(2). The original rule in the UK in 1988 was that the person who creates a sound recording and becomes its author is the person who makes the necessary arrangements for the making of the recording. The same solution was adopted for films. In practice, this meant that the producer becomes the author of a film, because he or she makes the arrangements for making the film. But most other European countries adopted a different approach: from their point of view, the director of a film was the creator of the work, even if he or she was not always the sole creator of the work. In an attempt to harmonize these provisions, the Community *EU* introduced the obligation to consider the principal director of a film as its author and left it to the member States to designate other co-authors if they so wished.[3] In the UK, the 1988 Act was amended in the light of the Directive by the Copyright and Related Rights Regulations 1996.[4] The original rule in relation to sound recordings and films disappeared entirely. For films, it was replaced by a rule that designates the director and the producer as the co-authors of a film,[5] and the Act now expressly states that the producer is the author of a sound recording.[6]

But who creates a computer-generated literary, dramatic, musical, or artistic work? The obvious answer would be the computer—but then the computer becomes the author of the work and it would be absurd to have a machine as a player in a system that grants property rights. The 1988 Act solves this problem by adopting an approach that is identical to

---

[1] CDPA 1988, s. 9(1).

[2] For an interesting example, see *Hyperion Records Ltd v. Lionel Sawkins* [2005] 3 All ER 636, [2005] 1 WLR 3281 (CA).

[3] EC Council Directive 93/98/EEC of 29 October 1993 harmonizing the term of protection of copyright and certain related rights (1993) OJ L 290/9, Art. 2(1).

[4] SI 1996/2967, regs 4 and 18(1).

[5] CDPA 1988, s. 9(2)(ab).

[6] Ibid., (aa).

that originally taken in relation to sound recordings and films: the person who makes the necessary arrangements for the creation of the work becomes the author of the work.[7]

In relation to broadcasts, the person making the broadcast is its creator, unless it relays another broadcast by reception and immediate retransmission. In the latter case, the person making that other broadcast will be the creator and author.[8] This avoids the unhealthy situation of two equal authors for one work, which one of them created and transmitted, and which the other one only retransmits. In relation to a typographical arrangement, meanwhile, the publisher of the edition is its author.[9]

It is recognized that the identity of the author is not always known: obvious examples of such a situation are presented by anonymous works. A work is of unknown authorship[10] if a person cannot identify the identity of the author by reasonable enquiry.[11] It is not clear, however, which person undertakes this reasonable inquiry. A logical solution would be to make this a subjective test, to be performed by the person who wishes to deal with the work and therefore needs to trace the origin of the work, starting with its author, if he or she wants to obtain the permission to deal with the work.[12]

Multiple authors—joint authorship

An increasing number of works are produced as a result of collaboration between two or more authors. In this case, the rules outlined above apply to each of the authors, as long as it is possible to distinguish and identify the individual contribution of each to the work. Each will be treated as the creator and author of his or her own individual contribution to the work.

This approach does not work, however, when a group of jazz musicians records its own impromptu jazz session. It is impossible to distinguish afterwards between the contribution of one musician and that of another musician. The Act calls this a work of 'joint authorship'[13]—but in order to be a joint author, a person must establish a significant and original contribution to the creation of the work, albeit not necessarily equal to that of the other joint authors. This will apply even if the performance of an existing work involves an improvization.[14]

The contribution must be to the work, rather than to its performance. For example, a director of a play who made a contribution to the script in the course of the rehearsals, even before the first performance, did not become the joint author of the play. She was only carrying out her task as a director in relation to the performance of the work.[15] Similarly, a university that cooperated with a company to design new software was not a joint author either, because its contribution was limited to providing background information about the existing software, assistance in the compilation of the technical specifications, and

---

7 Ibid., s. 9(3).

8 Ibid., (2)(b).

9 Ibid., (d).

10 If the identity of the author is, or becomes, known at one stage, the work can no longer fall in this category: CDPA 1988, s. 9(5).

11 Ibid., (4) and (5).

12 See R. Merkin (1989) *Copyright, Designs and Patents: The New Law*, Harlow: Longman, p. 50; the alternative option of relying on the concept of the ubiquitous reasonable man is less attractive.

13 CDPA 1988, s. 10(1).

14 *Hadley v. Kemp* [1999] EMLR 589 (the *Spandau Ballet* case). A common intention to produce a joint work is not required; collaboration in the execution, the creation of the work is the essence: see *Beckingham v. Hodgens* [2003] EMLR 18 (CA).

15 *Pamela Dallas Brighton & Dubbeljoint Co. Ltd v. Marie Jones* [2005] FSR 16, 288.

vetting of the suggestions of third parties.[16] In this case, there was no contribution to the creation of the new work itself. This can be contrasted with the case of the lyrics for a rap song, in relation to which one person had been responsible for a draft that was then amended by a second person. Some of the language had been changed, Jamaican English had been introduced to match word rhythm to music, and exclamations had been added. In this case, both persons were joint authors, because they had collaborated on the final work and it was no longer possible to separate their contributions in the final work.[17]

In the case of a work of joint authorship, all authors are referred to as the author of the work for the purposes of the 1988 Act.[18] Rather than become the author of a part of the work, each of them becomes (joint) author of the whole work. This has important consequences for the ownership of the copyright in the work that we will discuss in the next section of this chapter.

Section 10(1A) of the 1988 Act clarifies the relationship between the director and the producer as co-authors of a film. They are to be treated as joint authors and the film is to be treated as a work of joint authorship, unless the producer and the principal director are the same person. Section 10(2) deals with joint authorship in broadcasts. The person making the broadcast is the person transmitting the programme, if he or she has responsibility to any extent for its content, and any person providing the programme who makes, along with the person transmitting it, the arrangements necessary for its transmission.[19] In many cases, this results in more than one person making the broadcast and joint authorship for these persons.

Creators and fixators

The rule that the creator of the work is the author of it has to be combined with the necessity of recording, or fixating, original literary, musical, and dramatic works. Remember that ideas are not protected,[20] while their expression is protected only when it is recorded or fixated. This creates problems in a situation such as that which arose in *Walter v. Lane*.[21] Reporters from *The Times* recorded speeches by Lord Rosebery in writing. As we have seen above, the speeches attract copyright as a literary work once they are recorded and it is not necessary that the speaker records them himself—so who is the author of the literary work so created? In this case, it was held that the reporters were the creators of the work and, as such, the authors.

This case was decided before the introduction of the originality requirement.[22] It is submitted that a verbatim report[23] of the complete speech would not now pass this originality requirement. The report would not be an original literary work and would not attract copyright, but, because they are now recorded, the speeches themselves would

---

[16] *Cyprotex Discovery Ltd v. University of Sheffield* [2004] RPC 4, aff'd in other grounds [2004] RPC 44 (CA).

[17] *Brown v. Mcasso Music* [2005] FSR 40.

[18] CDPA 1988, s. 10(3).

[19] Ibid., s. 6(3).

[20] As shown by the case in which a journalist supplied the idea for an article written by his editor. His idea did not attract copyright—he was not the creator of the literary work—but his editor's expression of the idea attracted copyright. The editor was the creator of the expression of the idea and thus as creator of a literary work its author: *Springfield v. Thame* (1903) 19 TLR 650.

[21] [1900] AC 539.

[22] The originality requirement was introduced by the Copyright Act 1911.

[23] The case refers to the corrections and revisions made by the reporters. This should be seen as correcting the spelling and other small mistakes, while taking down in a hurry the words of the speaker and checking that the report is, indeed, a full and correct account or written version of the speech.

attract copyright and the speaker would be the author. This situation corresponds to that of a secretary writing down dictation. For the purposes of copyright, the person dictating will be the author of the work. The secretary who does the writing can, at best, be said to be acting as an agent. If the reporters had edited the work by selecting parts of the speech and had added their own comments—for example, on the venue at which the speech was delivered—the situation would have been different. The report would have been an original literary work and would have attracted its own copyright, because the reporters would have applied skill, labour, and judgment in drafting the report.

Corporate bodies

A final issue in relation to authorship of copyright is the question of whether a corporate body can be the author of a work. This is particularly relevant in the film and music industries, within which many arrangements for the making of a sound recording or movie[24] are made by large production companies that may de facto become the producers of the works.

It is submitted that this question receives a positive answer under copyright law. Works of a body incorporated under the laws of the UK qualify for copyright protection according to s. 154(1)(c) of the 1988 Act. There would be no reason to deal with this qualification issue if corporate bodies could not create works that attract copyright.[25] In theory, there could be a problem in relation to sound recordings and film, because an author (company) that never dies could give rise to a never-ending copyright. This problem is avoided, in practice, because the duration of copyright in a sound recording is not dependent on the concept of the author and because the duration of copyright in a film is now calculated according to s. 13B(2) of the 1988 Act, on the basis of a list of persons that does not include the producer (which can be a company).

Ownership

The starting point—the author as first owner

The general principle of ownership is that the author is the first owner of the copyright.[26] A sculptor will be the first owner of his or her sculpture and I will be the first owner of the copyright in the poems I write for my own enjoyment. But contracts of employment undermine this general principle. The first owner of the copyright in a literary, dramatic, musical, or artistic work, or in a film,[27] created by an employee in the course of his or her employment, will be the employer. Agreements to the contrary are, however, possible.[28]

---

[24] Even in the new regime for films, the question of whether or not they will be co-authors remains.

[25] The position that companies can be authors receives support in *Mad Hat Music Ltd v. Pulse 8 Records Ltd* [1993] EMLR 172; *Adventure Film Productions SA v. Tully* [1993] EMLR 376; *Century Communications Ltd v. Mayfair Entertainment UK Ltd* [1993] EMLR 335. See also H. Laddie, P. Prescott and M. Vitoria (2000) *The Modern Law of Copyright and Designs*, 3rd edn, London: Butterworths, p. 355.

[26] CDPA 1988, s. 11(1).

[27] This addition to CDPA 1988, s. 11(2), was made by the Copyright and Related Rights Regulations 1996, SI 1996/2967, regs 4 and 18(3). Once more, copyright in a film was treated as copyright in an original work, rather than in an entrepreneurial work, although the roots of copyright in a film are found in the latter category.

[28] CDPA 1988, s. 11(2).

This provision creates some difficulties:[29] who is an employee? What are the characteristics of the employer–employee relationship? And what is the meaning of this in the course of his or her employment?

Let us start with some obvious examples. On the one hand, a cleaner who writes poetry in her own time will be the first owner of the copyright in his or her poems.[30] The poems are clearly not written in the course of that employment and that individual is not in employment as a poet. If, on the other hand, a purchasing manager of an engineering company writes, for the board of directors of the company and during normal working hours, a report on the options open for his or her company to find an alternative supplier of cylinder valves, this work will obviously have been made in the course of that employment and the employer will be the first owner of the work. The contract of employment and the job description contained in it are important elements in this respect. They can facilitate the application of the test of whether the skill, labour, and judgment invested by the employee in the creation of the work are part of the employee's normal duties—which can be either express or implied in the contract—or come within the special duties that the employer has assigned to the employee, because they reveal the intentions of the parties. If the answer is affirmative, the work will have been created in the course of employment and the employer will be the first owner of the copyright in it.

This approach is supported by *Stephenson Jordan & Harrison Ltd v. MacDonald*.[31] An accountant was employed to advise clients. He started giving lectures and, eventually, he published them. He owned the copyright in the book, because giving lectures was not part of his normal duties and he had not been instructed by his employers to give the lectures or produce the book—but two elements complicate this case. Firstly, his employer had provided secretarial help, which he had used for his project: the Court held that the use of the employer's facilities or assistance is not relevant to this copyright test.[32] Secondly, the accountant had used a report that he had written for a client of his employer in the book: the copyright in this part of the book was owned by his employer.

It is in the interest of both employer and employee that there is no doubt about the ownership of copyright. A clear and detailed job description is required and, if the content of a job changes, a new description of the employee's duties should be drafted. This does not rule out that a job description can be wide in scope. When someone is employed as a research and development (R&D) engineer, this description makes it clear that the copyright in every work that is useful to his or her employer will be owned by the employer. But this system depends on the classification of the author of the work as employee, which itself depends on the existence of a contract of service or apprenticeship between the author and the alleged employer claiming the ownership of the copyright in the work.[33] The establishment of such a relationship is not obvious if the author is a freelance worker or a consultant.

It is submitted that these consultants and freelancers have a contract to do a certain job or a certain amount of work, but are not directly subject to the instructions of the

---

[29] For a good, but somewhat complex, example, see *Cyprotex Discovery Ltd v. University of Sheffield* [2004] RPC 44, (2004) 148 SJLB 421 (CA).

[30] For a somewhat more complex example, see *Ultra Marketing (UK) Ltd & Thomas Scott v. Universal Components Ltd* [2002] EWHC 2285.

[31] (1952) 69 RPC 10.

[32] But it may well have its relevance for other aspects of the employer–employee relationship—e.g. breach of the contract of employment.

[33] CDPA 1988, s. 178.

employer. For example, a management consultant will be asked to produce a report on the management of a company, but he or she will decide how to produce that report. The consultant's only obligation is to submit a report that meets the standards laid down in the contract by the date agreed in the contract. Employees, on the contrary, are subject to the instructions of their employer. For them, there is a mutuality of agreement, in the sense that they are subject to an obligation to accept and perform some minimum—or at least reasonable—amount of work for their alleged employer.[34] The freelance worker and the consultant will own the copyright in their work, because they do not come within the definition of an employee.

The employer may allow the employee to become the first owner of the copyright in the work created in the course of employment. This option is left open by s. 11(2) of the 1988 Act. For normal transfers of ownership of copyright, the Act requires the transfer to be in writing and signed by, or on behalf of, the copyright owner,[35] but this requirement does not apply here. In this situation, there is no transfer of copyright ownership—that is, no one owning the copyright before the first owner of the copyright in the work. This case should be contrasted with the case of a work produced by a consultant or a freelancer. Because they are not employees, s. 11(1) will apply and the freelancer or consultant will be the first owner of the copyright. Any subsequent transfer of the copyright will have to be in writing and will have to be signed by the owner or on his behalf.[36]

A clause in the contract concluded with the freelancer or consultant stipulating that the ownership of the work produced will be transferred is more than advisable. Otherwise, one has to rely on the concept of the implied licence. Someone ordering a report from a consultant will have necessarily included in the contract a right to use the result of the consultant's activity. Someone who requests a plan for a house to be built on a certain plot of land from an architect implies, in the contract with the architect, a clause giving him or her the right to build the house on that plot, because the contract is necessarily for a plan that is to be used to build a house. The architect keeps the ownership of the copyright in the plans, but grants an (implied) licence to use them to build the house.[37]

Joint owners

It is possible that there are two or more joint owners of the copyright in a work if it is a work of joint authorship. The latter possibility was raised above and we will now discuss its implications on the issue of ownership.

These owners will own the copyright in the work as tenants in common[38] and will each have their own individual rights in the work that they can assign individually. They can also act individually against infringement. But, because they will never own the whole copyright individually, they will not be able to license someone to exploit the

[34] See *Nethermere (St Neots) Ltd v. Taverna* [1984] IRLR 240, *per* Kerr LJ.
[35] CDPA 1988, s. 90(3).
[36] The use of the concept of beneficial ownership was suggested in *Warner v. Gestetner Ltd* [1988] EIPR D-89. It is submitted that this approach cannot be accepted, because it includes a partial assignment of the ownership of copyright that does not satisfy the requirements laid down in CDPA 1988, s. 90(3). See *R Griggs Group Ltd v. Evans (No. 1)* [2005] FSR 31, [2005] ECDR 30 (CA).
[37] See *Blair v. Osborne & Tomkins* [1971] 2 QB 78, [1971] 1 All ER 468, *per* Lord Denning MR at 470 and 507.
[38] Not as joint tenants—see *Lauri v. Renad* [1892] 3 Ch 402—because this would deny them individual rights and oblige them to act together on each occasion.

work without the consent of their co-owners;[39] otherwise, they would be able to transfer rights that they do not fully own. The co-owner of the copyright in a book will be able to assign his or her right to one of his or her creditors, which will allow that creditor to recuperate—through the royalties—the debt owed, but the creditor does not deal with the copyright.

The same co-owner will not be able to allow a film director to make a movie based on the book without the consent of the co-owners.

Anonymous works

Until now, we have examined the ownership issue, assuming that the author with whom the ownership chain starts is known. An anonymous work would, in this system, lead to an unknown owner of the copyright. This system would endanger the commercial exploitation of the work and would be undesirable. Therefore, the 1988 Act contains a presumption that the publisher of an anonymous work is the owner of the copyright in it at the time of publication.[40] This presumption can, however, be rebutted.[41]

A caveat—moral rights

The issue of ownership touches upon the commercial exploitation of copyright. We will come back to this issue later, but it is worth noting here that not all aspects of copyright are directed to commercial exploitation. Copyright is, to a certain extent, also an author's right. This will become clear in the next chapter, through the analysis of the new, separate, but closely related, moral rights that the 1988 Act grants to authors, and which protect them and their works against certain aspects of abusive commercial exploitation.

An overview

The concept of authorship is approached in a very pragmatic way. The creator of a work will, in principle, be its author. There can be more than one creator for a work and therefore also more than one author. Joint authorship, and the specific rules that go with it, arises when more than one creator is involved in the creation of the work and the contribution of each creator can no longer be separated out in the final result.

From authorship, the law moves on to ownership. Copyright is a property right and, as such, it needs an owner. The general principle is that the author will be the first owner of the copyright in his or her work. Works created by employees complicate life somewhat in this area. There is a legal presumption that the employer, rather than the employee-creator, will be the first owner of the copyright in the work that is created in the course of employment, but agreements to the contrary are possible. This rule has nothing to do with high principle. In a business context, it simply makes sense to have the employer own the rights and a systematic need for a contractual transfer of rights would be somewhat cumbersome.

---

[39] *Cescinsky v. George Routledge & Sons Ltd* [1916] 2 KB 325. The opposite is true in patent law: see Patents Act 1977, s. 36.

[40] CDPA 1988, s. 104(4).

[41] For an example of an unsuccessful attempt to rebut the presumption, see *Warwick Film Productions Ltd v. Eisinger* [1969] 1 Ch 508, [1967] 3 All ER 367.

Further reading

BAINES, R., 'Copyright in commissioned works: a cause for uncertainty' (2005) 27 EIPR 3, 122.

CHRISTY, L., 'Joint authorship and infringement by "altered copying": some lessons from the *Stones in his Pockets* case' (2004) 26 EIPR 10, 472.

GRIFFIN, J., 'The changing nature of authorship: why copyright law must focus on the increased role of technology' (2005) 2 IPQ135.

LAUTERBACH, T., 'Joint authorship in a copyright work revisited' (2005) 27 EIPR 3, 119.

ZEMER, L., 'Contributions and collaboration in joint authorship: too many misconceptions' (2006) 1 JIPLP 4, 283.

14
Moral rights

Moral Rights - formally included in CDPA 1988

General principles

Copyright in Continental Europe is, in the first place, an author's right. Much attention is paid to the rights of the creator.[1] Because copyright law is based on international conventions, a compromise with the UK's more entrepreneurial approach was reached in the Berne Convention for the Protection of Literary and Artistic Works 1886. This led eventually to the formal inclusion of moral rights in UK in the Copyright, Designs and Patents Act 1988.[2] Previous Acts did not explicitly acknowledge these moral rights, although some protection was offered through, for example, the torts of defamation[3] or passing off.[4]

We submit that the compromise should go much further. The focal points of both approaches work in a complementary manner: everything starts with the author, who has to create works; if there are no works, there is nothing for the entrepreneur to exploit. But if one offers an extremely strong protection to the author-creator, this may make the work of the entrepreneur impossible. If the author has all of the rights and the entrepreneur is left with no flexibility or bargaining power based on legal rights, the exploitation of the work becomes impossible, or at least economically unsound. This could seriously affect the incentive of the author to create works, because it would reduce the chances of making a living as an author. It is clear that the volume of the works created would be seriously affected: what is needed in a perfect copyright system is a sound balance between the rights of the author-creator and those of the entrepreneur who exploits the work. We submit that the Continental approach has much to contribute to such a perfect system in relation to the rights of the author, while the UK's traditional approach would be the dominant contributor in relation to the rights given to the entrepreneur.

Such a perfect copyright system is not just an ideal. European integration and harmonization of the provisions dealing with copyright means that, inevitably, a compromise has to be reached each time, between both approaches, in an attempt to make copyright

---

[1] See N. Walravens, 'La protection de l'oeuvre d'art et le droit moral de l'artiste' (2003) 197 RIDA 2; A. Lucas and H.-J. Lucas (2000) *Traité de la Propriété Littéraire et Artistique*, 2nd edn, Paris: Litec, p. 45. See also E. Adeney (2006) *The Moral Rights of Authors and Performers: An International and Comparative Analysis*, Oxford: Oxford University Press.

[2] See, in general, I. Stamatoudi, 'Moral rights of authors in England: the missing emphasis on the role of creators' [1997] IPQ 478.

[3] See *Humphreys v. Thomson* (1908) Mac CC 148.

[4] See *Samuelson v. Producers Distributing* [1932] 1 Ch 201.

in the European Union (EU) resemble the perfect model.[5] But how does this relate to the issue of moral rights?

It is submitted that the author-creator should not only become the first owner of the work and, by implication, lose control over the work almost immediately afterwards. On the one hand, the possibility of unfair use of the work can deter the author from creating works and so he or she should be protected against that possibility; on the other, a good exploitation of the work requires as much freedom for the entrepreneur as possible. Moral rights reconcile these two aims. They give minimum long-lasting rights against manifestly unfair use of the work to the author-creator, while allowing maximum flexibility for the entrepreneur, because only manifestly unfair forms of exploitation will be affected. In this approach, moral rights are an essential component of the bundle of rights that is given by copyright—and it is for this reason that we discuss them here, rather than at the end of chapters on copyright. All the authors of original works and directors of films[6] are given moral rights, while the owners of the entrepreneurial neighbouring rights are not granted any moral rights.[7] This clearly vindicates our approach. The real copyrights are the original ones and moral rights are an essential component of the rights granted by copyright. Neighbouring rights often rely on copyright works and are secondary rights, such as the recording of an original musical work. They are linked to the entrepreneurial exploitation of copyright and therefore moral rights are not needed in relation to such secondary rights. And there is another argument that we may wish to consider: the Berne Convention—which is the international basis of the UK's copyright regime—deals with moral rights in Art. 6bis. It is situated right in the middle of the Articles that deal with the substance of copyright, suggesting that moral rights are an essential element of copyright, rather than an addendum to it.

Four moral rights are included in the UK's 1988 Act:

- the right to be identified as the author or director of a work—that is, the 'paternity right';[8]
- the right of the author or a director of a work to object to derogatory treatment of that work—that is, the 'integrity right';[9]
- the right for everyone not to have a work falsely attributed to him;[10]
- the commissioner's right of privacy in respect of a photograph or film made for private and domestic purposes.[11]

Only the first two rights are full moral rights, while the latter two are hybrid in nature, because they do not confer special rights on the creator of the work.

All of these rights aim to restore the balance between the interests of the commercial exploitation of the work and the interests of the creator of the work. This cannot be done through contractual negotiations, in which the author or director quite often occupies a weak bargaining position. To protect the author or director as the weaker party, moral rights are inalienable to others—but they are transmissible on death.[12] Because they are coupled to the commercial rights granted by copyright, the term of moral rights is coupled

---

[5] See J. F. Verstrynghe, 'The spring 1993 Horace S Manges Lecture: the European Commission's direction on copyright and neighbouring rights—toward the regime of the twenty-first century' (1993) 17 Colum-VLA JL & Arts 187 at 206–9.

[6] Note that films are treated, once more, in the same way as original works.

[7] CDPA 1988, ss. 77, 80, and 84.

[8] CDPA 1988, ss. 77–79.

[9] Ibid., ss. 80–83.

[10] Ibid., s. 84.

[11] Ibid., s. 85.

[12] Ibid., ss. 94 and 95.

to that of copyright in the work to which they relate.[13] The one exception to the latter rule is the right to object to false attribution, which expires 20 years after a person's death.[14]

The paternity right

The right to be identified

The creator of a work has the right to be identified as its author; this is the basic concept behind the paternity right. Because this right has to restore the balance with the commercial exploitation of the work that attracts copyright protection, it is also restricted to those works that attract copyright. The scope of the right is further restricted to literary, dramatic, musical, or artistic works, and films, and identification should only take place in certain cases.[15] These cases are different for the various categories of work and the categories themselves are different from those used in relation to the existence of copyright. In particular, lyrics for songs are not treated as literary works, but as musical works, and films are the only category of non-'original' works to be included.

The author of a literary work that is not intended to be spoken or sung with music and the author of a dramatic work both have the right to be identified whenever the work is published commercially, performed in public, or broadcast, or whenever copies of a film or sound recording of the work are issued to the public.[16] Non-commercial exploitation—such as the private performance of a play—does not give rise to the obligation to identify the author. This fits in with the logic that this moral right only restores the balance with the commercial exploitation of the work. Another interesting point is the meaning given to 'issuing copies of the work'. It cannot be restricted to the narrow meaning it has in s. 18(2) of the Act: every commercial publication and every public performance requires the identification of the author, and not only the first publication or first performance. Issuing copies is mentioned together with publication and performance, and should mean making copies available, not only making them available in the UK for the first time. Only this interpretation conforms to the logical sense of the system.

Musical works and lyrics are subjected to the same regime.[17] Their commercial publication and the issuing of copies of a sound recording of the work to the public give rise to the obligation to identify the author.[18] Performance of the work—which was included in relation to literary and dramatic works—is not included here, because it would not be practicable to require that, for example, a disc jockey identify the author of every song before or after playing it. If a film, the soundtrack of which includes the work, is shown in public or copies of the film are issued to the public, however, the author of the musical works and their lyrics should be identified. This provision fits in with the rules for films. Indeed, the director of a film has the right to be identified each time that the film is shown in public or broadcast, and when copies of the film are issued to the public.[19] The director of the film gets preference over the producer in relation to moral rights. The creative activity is the director's contribution, which deserves the special moral rights protection, while the entrepreneurial contribution of the producer does not deserve that. The provisions for artistic works are similar, but include also public exhibition of the work.[20]

---

[13] Ibid., s. 86(1).   [14] Ibid., (2).
[15] Ibid., s. 77(1).   [16] Ibid., (2).
[17] See *Hyperion Records Ltd v. Leonard Sawkins* [2005] 3 All ER 636, [2005] 1 WLR 3281 (CA).
[18] CDPA 1988, s. 77(3).
[19] Ibid., (6).
[20] Ibid., (4); see also s. 77(5) on works of architecture.

Identification should take place in a clear and prominent way—for example, in or on each copy of the work[21]—or in any other way that brings the identity of the author or director to the attention of the person who acquires a copy of the work.[22] The author or director also has the right to be identified in relation to an adaptation of the work. When a textbook on public international law written by an English professor is translated into Russian, the English author has the right to be identified in the Russian translation. If we assume that it is not the whole work that is translated, but only a couple of chapters, the right to be identified will still apply, because it applies in relation to the whole work or to a substantial part of it.[23] The test to determine whether or not a part is substantial is probably the same as that used in relation to copyright infringement.[24]

Preconditions and exceptions

This leaves us with one major precondition and some exceptions to the right to be identi-fied. The paternity right is not granted automatically: the author or director who seeks its benefit has to assert it.[25] Such an assertion can be general in nature or can be in relation only to specified acts. This can be done in the form of a statement that is included in an instrument assigning copyright in the work. Such a document has to be in writing and has to be signed by, or on behalf of, the author.[26] This method of asserting the paternity right has to be recommended, because it will not only bind the assignee, but also anyone claiming through him—such as the person to whom the assignee assigns part of his or her rights—even if those other persons did not receive notice of the assertion.[27] The assertion can also be made by another written instrument signed by the author or director, but this assertion will only bind those with notice of it.[28] The paternity right can be asserted at any time during the life of the author, but it is not retrospective in nature—that is, the right only arises once it has been asserted.[29] The assertion does not cover past use of the work. Any delay in asserting the right can only work to the detriment of the author or director, because it should be taken into account in determining whether an injunction should be granted, and in the determination of damages and other relief.[30]

There is also a long list of exceptions to the paternity right contained in s. 79 of the 1988 Act. Some of them are particularly important. No paternity right exists in relation to com-puter programs, computer-generated works, and typefaces,[31] and publications in news-papers, periodicals, encyclopaedias, and dictionaries are excluded.[32] The first category is clearly too much linked to technical and technological elements, and too far away from the moral rights idea of the artist-creator who should be identified; in the second category, identification of the author of each article or contribution would overload the works and would be impractical, because editors edit and each edition of a newspaper may change

---

[21] The obvious technique for, e.g., books.

[22] For example, when a play is performed, the programme can contain the name of the author of the play.

[23] CPDA 1988, s. 89(1).

[24] See Chapter 15 on Copyright infringement.

[25] Ibid., s. 78(1).

[26] Ibid., (2).

[27] Ibid., (4).

[28] Ibid., (2) and (4).

[29] Ibid., (1).

[30] Ibid., (5).

[31] Ibid., s. 79(2).

[32] Ibid., (6).

dramatically. All of these identifications could effectively take up a substantial percentage of the whole work.

Additionally, the employer or first owner of the copyright in a work created in the course of employment, or anyone acting with his or her authority, is not obliged to identify the creator-employee.[33] This avoids the considerable problem that would have been created had an employee-engineer—or later, eventually, an ex-employee-engineer—been allowed to interfere with the exploitation of the drawings he made for a series of products through the exercise of his moral rights. The paternity right will, under certain circumstances, not be infringed by acts done in relation to the reporting of current events or by incidental inclusion of the work.[34]

Performers

The paternity right, as it existed at the time that the 1988 Act was passed, applied only to literary, dramatic, musical, or artistic works and to films, but Art. 5 of the World Intellectual Property Organization (WIPO) Performances and Phonograms Treaty 1996 introduced a right of paternity for performers. The UK has implemented this Treaty obligation by means of the Performances (Moral Rights, etc.) Regulations 2006.[35] This has resulted in the performer being given a right of paternity in his or her live aural performances and his or her performances fixed in phonograms. The performer has the right to be identified as such when he or she perfoms live, when the performance is broadcast, or when a recording of the performance is communicated to the public, or when copies of it are issued to the public.[36] That identification needs to take place in such a way that it is likely to be noticed by the audience.[37] No identification is required when it is not reasonably practical or when the performance is given for reasons relating to advertising or news reporting.[38]

Unfortunately, the provisions do not offer guidance on what is meant by 'not reasonably practical'. Does this, for example, include a failure to name all musicians performing on a recording when it is played as part of a radio show?

The moral right to be identified is not infringed unless the performer has first asserted his or her moral right in writing.[39] The approach that has been taken is therefore similar to that taken in relation to the moral rights of authors. It therefore comes as no surprise that the duration of the moral rights of performers are also linked to the duration of the (economic) rights in the performance.[40]

The integrity right

The nature of the right to object to derogatory treatment

The beneficiaries of this moral right—the integrity right—are the same as those of the paternity right: authors of literary, dramatic, musical, and artistic works and directors of films. The integrity right applies only to the extent that works are, and remain, in

---

[33] Ibid., (3)(a).

[34] The fair dealing and incidental inclusion concepts will be analysed fully in Chapter 15 on copyright infringement, in which they find their roots; see CDPA 1988, s. 79(4).

[35] SI 2006/18, in force since 1 February 2006.

[36] CDPA 1988, s. 205C.

[37] Ibid.

[38] Ibid., s. 205E.

[39] Ibid., s. 205D.   [40] Ibid., s. 205I.

copyright.[41] Derogatory treatment of the work involves addition,[42] deletion, alteration, or adaptation that amounts to distortion or mutilation of the work, or which is otherwise prejudicial to the honour or reputation of the author or the director.[43] This would be the case, for example, if a tale for young children written by a reputed children's author were to be turned into a pornographic story through addition and alteration.

Criticism of a work, however, is in no way complicated by this integrity right. Criticism does not involve distortion or mutilation and does not affect the honour or reputation of the author. It takes place at a different level and derogatory criticism should not be called criticism, but should be called instead by its true name: derogatory treatment. The focus on the treatment should not hide the fact that there is a second cumulative requirement that involves proof of honour or reputation, as well as evidence of prejudice to that honour or reputation.[44]

The essential issue is when does an act amount to distortion or mutilation of the work, or when is it otherwise prejudicial to the honour or reputation of the author or the director? The integrity right can clearly not be exercised at the discretion of the author or the director.[45] It has to be proven *'that the distortion or other mutilation of* [the] *work really prejudices* [the author's] *lawful intellectual or personal interests in the work'*.[46] This involves the balancing of all of the relevant interests involved.

In this process, the nature and the purpose of the work to which the allegedly infringing act is done is an important factor. It is submitted that, for example, an act done to a drawing containing technical details and a draft plan for an industrial product will less easily infringe the integrity right of the author than will a similar act done to a work of fine art, such as a painting. The author of the drawing knows that his or her work is just the starting point for a long process of development and change involving many other people. The painter who delivers the painting to an art dealer, however, readily assumes that the painting will not be changed at all. A first criterion in the balancing test is thus whether the work is, relatively speaking, more utilitarian or more artistic in nature.[47]

In a recent case, it was, indeed, held that the integrity right of the author of a cut-away drawing for a tourist brochure had not been infringed by little changes that were so trivial that they could only be detected upon close inspection.[48]

> Additional criteria could be, for example, the nature and the extent of the alteration of the work and also how far the latter is reversible or irreversible; the number of people or the size of the public addressed by the user of the work in altered form; the fact whether the author created the work in an employment relationship or as a self-employed author, or else whether a commissioning party did not have a decisive influence on the final result of the creation.... [A]lso the possible consequences for the professional life of the author and, of course, for his or her reputation have to be taken into consideration.[49]

---

[41] Ibid., s. 80(1).

[42] For example, the addition of a rap line to the recording of a piece of music: see *Confetti Records, Fundamental Records & Andrew Alcee v. Warner Music UK Ltd (t/a East West Records)* [2003] ECDR 336.

[43] CDPA 1988, s. 80(1) and (2).

[44] See *Confetti Records, Fundamental Records & Andrew Alcee v. Warner Music UK Ltd (t/a East West Records)* [2003] ECDR 336.

[45] See the decision of the Supreme Court of Canada in *Galérie d'Art du Petit Champlain Inc, Galérie d'Art Yves Laroche Inc, Editions Multi-Graph Itée, Galérie d'Art Laroche, Denis Inc. & Serge Rosa v. Claude Théberge* [2002] SCC 34.

[46] A. Dietz, 'The artist's right of integrity under copyright law: a comparative approach' (1994) 25 IIC 177 at 183.

[47] Dietz (1994) at 184–5.

[48] *Pasterfield v. Denham* [1999] FSR 168 (a decision of the Plymouth County Court).

[49] Ibid., at 185.

Because the integrity right and other moral rights very strongly involve the issue of fundamental fairness between the author and the user of the work, one might add the purpose and the character of the use of the work as another relevant criterion. Finally, certain well-established customs and traditions in certain parts of industry may also be taken into account.[50]

All of these elements point towards a rather objective test. It is submitted that the determination of whether the author's, or the director's, honour or reputation has been prejudiced by the treatment of the work by a third party is to be effected by answering the question of whether right-thinking members of the public would think less of him or her as a result of the treatment.[51] This test bears similarities to that which is applied in cases of defamation and the view that a *certain subjective element or judgment on the part of the author so long as it is reasonably arrived at*[52] is involved needs to be rejected. The latter view would push the integrity right beyond its role as a fundamental right that preserves the balance of rights between the author or director and those exploiting the work. It is encouraging to note, in this respect, that, in a recent case,[53] it has indeed been held that the fact that the author was aggrieved by what had occurred was not sufficient to hold that the author's honour and reputation had been affected.

The courts in the UK have not yet decided any major case on moral rights since the introduction of the 1988 Act.[54] German and Swiss courts, however, have used the balancing test on the basis of similar provisions.[55] The Swiss Federal Supreme Court used it to rule that the proposed alterations to a school building—which involved, among other things, the replacement of the original flat roof by a saddleback roof—did not amount to a mutilation of the architectural work and did not infringe the integrity right of the architect.[56]

Authors and directors can invoke this right to object to derogatory treatment of their work if it occurs when copies of the work are published commercially, when copies of a sound recording or film are made available to the public, when the work is performed, played, or shown in public,[57] and when it is broadcast.[58] The right also applies to parts of works that were previously adapted or translated by someone else. When a French translation of a novel by Dame Barbara Cartland is subjected to derogatory treatment, she will still be able to object to the infringement of her integrity right.[59]

Exceptions

The wide scope of the right is, however, subject to a series of exceptions. The integrity right is not infringed if the treatment of the work does not go further than the translation of a literary or dramatic work, or the arrangement or transcription of a musical work

---

[50] Ibid., at 185–7.

[51] See *Tidy v. Trustees of the Natural History Museum* [1996] 3 EIPR D-81.

[52] *Snow v. Eaton Centre* (1982) 70 CPR 105 (2d) (a decision of the Canadian High Court).

[53] *Pasterfield v. Denham* [1999] FSR 168.

[54] For a first timid attempt, see ibid. and *Tidy v. Trustees of the Natural History Museum* [1996] 3 EIPR D-81. See also *Confetti Records, Fundamental Records & Andrew Alcee v. Warner Music UK Ltd (t/a East West Records)* [2003] ECDR 336.

[55] German Supreme Court Decision of 31 May 1974 [1974] GRUR 675; see also German Supreme Court Decision of 2 October 1981 [1982] GRUR 107; both cases cited by Dietz (1994) at 188.

[56] Swiss Federal Supreme Court Decision of 24 September 1991 [1992] GRUR 473, cited by Dietz (1994) at 188.

[57] For a French example, see *Lindon v. Boussagol*, judgment of the Tribunal de Grande Instance de Paris, 3rd Chamber, 15 October 1992, 155 (1993) RIDA Chronique de Jurisprudence.

[58] CDPA 1988, s. 80(3)–(6).

[59] Ibid., (7).

involving no more than a change of key or register.[60] Furthermore, the integrity right does not apply to computer programs and computer-generated works; nor does it apply in relation to publication in a newspaper, periodical, encyclopaedia, or yearbook and any subsequent unmodified republication thereof. Should the author or director of a work made in the course of employment that is altered be identified, the right is restricted to a sufficient disclaimer of association with the altered work.[61] The impact of the right is further compromised by the introduction of a special remedy for this moral right. By means of an injunction, the court may allow the act complained of to continue once a disclaimer dissociating the author or director from the altered work is made.[62] A clear example of this is that an architect's integrity right is restricted to him being allowed to request the removal of his identification from the building.[63]

A broadcasting authority may, in certain circumstances, wish to censor certain works, and to make excisions and alterations, because its broadcasts should not incite crime, offend good taste and decency, lead to disorder, or be offensive to public feeling. Because this could eventually amount to derogatory treatment of the works concerned, the Act explicitly allows the BBC—but, oddly, not the commercial channels—to censor the works by stipulating that this will not infringe the integrity right in the work.[64]

The scope of the right and its effectiveness are, however, widened by the fact that the right is also infringed by possessing, in the course of a business, or dealing with an infringing item if such a person knows, or has reason to believe, that there is a false attribution.[65] It may be easier to find someone in possession of, or dealing with, the infringing item than to find the person responsible for the alterations. An action for infringement is now more readily available, which makes it easier to enforce the integrity right.

Performers

The integrity right as it existed at the time that the 1988 Act was passed applied only to literary, dramatic, musical, or artistic works and to films, but Art. 5 of the WIPO Performances and Phonograms Treaty 1996 introduced a right of integrity for performers. The UK has implemented this Treaty obligation by means of the Performances (Moral Rights, etc.) Regulations 2006.[66] The integrity right will be infringed if the performance is broadcast live, or if it is played in public or communicated to the public by means of a sound recording, with any distortion, mutilation, or other modification that is prejudicial to the reputation of the performer.[67]

Further exceptions to the right of integrity include modifications that are consistent with normal editorial practice and performances that are given for reasons related to advertising or news reporting.[68] No guidance is provided as to the interpretation of the concept of normal editorial practice. Possessing infringing copies of the work in the course of business or dealing in them is also an infringement of the integrity right.[69] The

---

[60] Ibid., (2)(a).

[61] Ibid., ss. 81 and 82.

[62] Ibid., s. 103(2).

[63] Ibid., s. 80(5).

[64] Ibid., s. 81(5)(c).

[65] See Chapter 15 on copyright infringement for a proper definition of the concepts of possessing or dealing with an infringing copy; CDPA 1988, s. 81.

[66] SI 2006/18, in force since 1 February 2006.

[67] CDPA 1988, s. 205F.

[68] CDPA 1988, s. 205G.

[69] Ibid., s. 205H.

approach that has been taken is therefore similar to that taken in relation of the moral rights of authors. It therefore comes as no surprise that the duration of the moral rights of performers are also linked to the duration of the (economic) rights in the performance.[70]

The right against false attribution of the work

The author or director of the work has the right to be identified as such; he or she should also have a right only to be identified if he or she really is the creator of the work. This right is laid down by the 1988 Act as the right to oppose '*false attribution of the work*'.[71] It applies to literary, dramatic, musical, and artistic works and to films. Any person to whom such a work is attributed falsely and who is not its creator may object to it.[72] This right would be useful, for example, if someone were to plagiarize the style of a famous novelist, such as Stephen King, in producing a mediocre work in which he or she advocates the imposition of Mafia-style taxes—that is, extortion—to generate funds for a political party and prints Stephen King's name on the cover page. We may assume that the famous novelist would like to object to the attribution of this work to him.

The opportunity to object arises when copies of the work containing the false attribution are issued to the public, when an artistic work or a copy of it in or on which there is a false attribution is exhibited in public, when a literary, dramatic, or musical work is performed in public, or broadcast as being the work of the plaintiff, and when a film is shown in public, or broadcast as being directed by the plaintiff.[73] The plaintiff is also given a right of action against anyone possessing a copy of the work in the course of business or dealing with a copy of the work if such a person knows, or has reason to believe, that there is a false attribution.[74] A special problem arises in relation to an artistic work that is left in the possession of a dealer before it is altered. When such a work is dealt with afterwards as the unaltered work of the author, he or she will have the right to object to this as being a false attribution.[75]

The right also applies to adaptations that are falsely being presented as adaptations of the work of a person. In the case of an artistic work, this means a copy of a work that is falsely presented as being a copy made by the author of the artistic work.[76]

The right expires 20 years after the death of the person to whom the work is attributed falsely.[77] In this sense, it comprises an exception to the rule that the term of moral rights and commercial copyright are the same. This rule cannot be applied in this case, because there is no equivalent copyright for the person to whom a work is attributed falsely.

The right to object to false attribution is particularly relevant in relation to certain forms of parody. By definition, a parody has to resemble the original work closely enough that people can make the link between the two works. It is easy to see how the impression can be created that the parody is the work of the author of the original work in this context. A good example of such a situation is found in *Clark v. Associated Newspapers Ltd.*[78] Alan Clark famously published his diaries some years ago; the defendants published a parody of the diaries as a column in *The Evening Standard*. A Mr Peter Bradshaw wrote the newspaper columns, and they carried the headings 'Alan Clark's secret Election' and 'Alan Clark's political diary'. A photograph of Mr Clark accompanied the headings and Mr Bradshaw's name, albeit in capital letters, appeared only in the introductory

---

[70] Ibid., s. 205I.   [71] Ibid., s. 84.
[72] Ibid., s. 84(1).   [73] Ibid., s. 84(2)–(4).
[74] Ibid., (5).   [75] Ibid., (6).
[76] Ibid., (8).   [77] Ibid., s. 86(2).
[78] [1998] 1 All ER 959, [1998] 1 WLR 1558.

paragraph. That paragraph mentioned the fact that the column was, in fact, all about how Mr Bradshaw imagined Mr Clark might record certain events. Mr Clark brought a case in passing off and he relied also on s. 84 of the 1988 Act. In relation to the latter point, he argued that the readers of *The Evening Standard*—or, at least, a large number of them—would assume that he was the author of the column. In his view, confusion as to who is the author was sufficient for the purposes of s. 84.

The court started its analysis of s. 84 by stating that:

> Two distinctive features of the statutory tort are: (a) that it is unnecessary that the plaintiff be a professional author and accordingly that he has any goodwill or reputation as an author to protect or which may be damaged by false attribution; and (b) consequently the tort is actionable per se without proof of damage. In short s 84 confers a personal or civic right on everyone not to have authorship of any literary work falsely attributed to him.[79]

It is, however, up to the plaintiff to establish that the work contains what is a false attribution of authorship. It is not sufficient that a few, or more, people may understand it to be a false attribution.[80] On this basis, the court ruled that '[t]*he proper approach…is to determine what is the single meaning which the literary work conveys to the notional reasonable reader*'.[81] On the basis of the facts of this case, the court concluded that the articles contained, in their title and through the addition of a photograph, a clear and unequivocal false statement attributing their authorship to Mr Clark. The court accepted that such a statement could, in certain cases, be neutralized by an express contradiction—but such a contradiction had to be as bold, precise, and compelling as the false statement, and this requirement had not been met in this case.

Similarly, s. 84 could also be used to object to the attribution to an interviewee of the comments made in an interview in circumstances in which the interviewer added or made up 90 per cent of the comments.[82]

The right to privacy in relation to commissioned photographs

When someone commissions a photograph, the photographer gets the ownership of the copyright as creator of the work. He or she can use the negatives for all kinds of purposes and does not need the consent of the commissioner.[83] This can be undesirable if the photograph is commissioned for private and domestic purposes: for example, one would not want to see one's own wedding pictures as part of a billboard advertising campaign for life insurance policies or on the front page of the tabloids next to a story headed 'How many husbands are unfaithful right from the start?'.

The right to privacy grants the commissioner some protection in this respect. The commissioner has the right not to have copies of the photograph issued to the public, not to have them exhibited in public, and not to have the photograph included in a broadcast. Anyone who does, or who authorizes, these acts infringes the right to privacy—but two further

---

[79] [1998] 1 WLR 1558 at 1564.

[80] Support for the single meaning view can be found in *Moore v. News of the World Ltd* [1972] 1 QB 441, [1972] 1 All ER 915, at 451–2 and 921–2.

[81] [1998] 1 WLR 1558 at 1568.

[82] See *Moore v. News of the World Ltd* [1972] 1 QB 441 and [1972] 1 All ER 915; see also *Noah v. Shuba* [1991] FSR 14.

[83] See Y. Gendreau, 'Copyright ownership of photographs in Anglo-American law' [1993] 6 EIPR 207 at 211–13. See also Chapter 31 on character merchandising.

requirements have to be met: the photograph has to have been commissioned for private and domestic purposes, and needs to attract copyright. An identical right exists in relation to films commissioned for private and domestic purposes.[84] There are no other requirements for the existence of the right: it is, for example, immaterial whether the commissioner hired a professional photographer at an enormous price or an unpaid friend or relative.

The term of the right is equal to that of the copyright in the photograph or film[85] and the right is given independently to each joint co-commissioner.[86] It applies to the whole work or to a substantial part of it.[87]

There are some minor exceptions to the right.[88] The most important is that the right to privacy is not infringed in case of the incidental inclusion in an artistic work, film, or broadcast.[89] This right compensates, in this particular area, the lack of a general right to privacy, even if the adoption of the Human Rights Act 1998 alleviated the problem somewhat. This became necessary because the 1988 Act no longer gives the commissioner any ownership of the copyright in the commissioned work.

An interesting case, in this respect, was decided before the 1988 Act came into force. In *Mail Newspapers plc v. Express Newspapers plc*,[90] wedding pictures were at the centre of the debate. The wife had suffered a brain haemorrhage and was kept alive artificially to give birth. The husband had sold the exclusive right in the pictures to one newspaper and the other newspaper tried to obtain copies from the photographer. Under the new provision, the husband could have stopped the photographer from giving copies of the picture to the newspaper. This case is also interesting, because it illustrates that the right is not only a negative right: in practice, it will often be used to secure exclusivity and gain a higher price for the use of the photographs or films. In the example, it is clear that the husband could stop the photographer without having to rely on the consent of his wife. The interesting point is whether the photographer-owner of the copyright can interfere with the exclusivity contract. It is submitted that the commissioner has an implied licence to use the photographs and the privacy right does not play any special role.

Interestingly, the right is given to the commissioner rather than to the person in the photograph or film, while, in most cases, it is the latter's privacy that is at issue. The problem obviously only arises when the commissioner is not the person in the photograph or film. But the rule can be justified on the basis that it is much easier to identify and contact the commissioner, whose name and address will be known to the photographer or the maker of the film. There may also be a single commissioner, but many people may figure in the photograph or film. The owners of the copyright in the work may also not necessarily have known names and addresses of the latter parties.

Consent and waiver

It could be accepted that the moral rights of a person who consented to an act being done are not infringed.[91] When the author consents to the publication of his or her novel

---

[84] CDPA 1988, s. 85(1).

[85] Ibid., s. 86(1).

[86] Ibid., s. 88(6). This must mean that the right does not disappear when the commissioner dies, but is transmissible on death.

[87] Ibid., s. 89(1).

[88] Ibid., s. 85(2).

[89] Ibid., (2)(a).

[90] [1987] FSR 90.

[91] CDPA 1988, s. 87(1).

without being identified, he or she cannot complain about the infringement of his or her identity immediately afterwards. But the Act goes further and allows moral rights to be waived. The person entitled to any of the four moral rights can surrender them in a written and signed instrument.[92] Contractual consideration is not required.

This can be done even before an issue arises. Such a waiver may relate to one or more specific rights, or to all moral rights; it may relate to one specific work, to a class of works, to all works, and even to future works. The waiver can be conditional or unconditional, and can also be expressed to be subject to revocation.[93] This possibility for the author to waive his or her moral rights substantially weakens the impact and value of the moral rights. An author or director quite often occupies a weak bargaining position in negotiating the conditions for the creation and the commercial exploitation of the work, and can be leaned upon to waive all moral rights. It is submitted that the possibility of waiving moral rights contradicts the essence of the concept of moral rights as essential safeguards for the author or director as the weaker party. Nevertheless, a similar waiver provision has also been introduced in relation to the moral rights of performers.[94]

Even worse in its weakening impact is the possibility of an informal waiver under the general principles of contract or estoppel.[95] The enforcement of the identity right may become impossible if conduct of the author or director leads another person to believe that he or she will not insist upon identification.

The introduction of moral rights in the Act was clearly a step in the right direction: the protection of the weaker party cannot be left entirely to the contractual freedom of the parties. But the flexible waiver facility undermines the whole system. It is clear, then, that the concept of moral rights is not yet fully integrated in the UK's entrepreneurial style copyright system.[96]

An overview

Moral rights emphasize the strong link between the work and its author. Whatever form the commercial exploitation of the work takes, that link survives. Moral rights are therefore inalienable and stay with the author.

There are two core moral rights. Firstly, there is the right to be identified, or the paternity right. This applies traditionally to literary, dramatic, musical, or artistic works, but it has been expanded to include films and performances. While important for the author, the paternity right also has its importance of the user of copyright works. Many copyright works are bought or consumed because of the fame of the author and because the buyer or consumer sees, in the name of the author, a guarantee of quality.

Secondly, there is the right of integrity, or the right to object to derogatory treatment of the work. This protects the reputation of the author, which again also has its value for users of the work.

Both of these rights are minimal rights that protect fundamental aspects of the link between the author, the work, and the public. It is clearly not envisaged that moral rights will constantly interfere with the normal exploitation of the work; they are essentially

---

[92] Ibid., (2). But the passing of equitable title in the copyright or the grant of an implied licence to use the copyright work are not sufficient: see *Pasterfield v. Denham* [1999] FSR 168.

[93] CDPA 1988, s. 87(3).

[94] Ibid., s. 205J.

[95] Ibid., s. 87(4).

[96] See Stamatoudi [1997] at 478.

there to stop abuses. From that perspective, the relative important scope of certain exceptions to these rights, and, specifically, the fact that they can be waived or need to be asserted before they come into force, is to be regretted. They do not correspond with the goal of moral rights and hinder their proper functioning within our copyright system.

The legislature has also used the chapter on moral rights to deal with the right to object to false attribution, which can be seen as the other side of the paternity right coin, and the right to privacy in relation to commissioned photographs.

Further reading

ADENEY, E. (2006) *The Moral Rights of Authors and Performers: An International and Comparative Analysis*, Oxford: Oxford University Press.

GARNETT, K., DAVIES, G. and HARBOTTLE, G. (2005) *Copinger and Skone James on Copyright*, 15th edn, London: Sweet and Maxwell, ch. 11.

MASIYAKURIMA, P., 'The trouble with moral rights' (2005) 68 MLR 3, 411.

RIGAMONTI, C., 'Deconstructing moral rights' (2006) 47 Harv Int LJ 2, 353.

SIMON, I., 'The introduction of performers' moral rights: Part I' (2006) 28 EIPR 11, 552.

SIMON, I., 'The introduction of performers' moral rights: Part II' (2006) 28 EIPR 12, 600.

15
Copyright infringement

The owner of the copyright in a work is given a property right according to s. 1 of the Copyright, Designs and Patents Act 1988—but what is the content of this property right? The owner is given the exclusive right to perform certain acts in relation to the work, but in relation to an intangible right, it is easier to approach things from an infringement perspective. Anyone who performs an act that has been reserved exclusively for the copyright-owner will infringe the copyright in the work if he or she has not, in advance, obtained the permission of the copyright owner to perform that act. This chapter will therefore be concerned with the various acts that can infringe copyright and the content of the property right of the copyright owner will be defined in this indirect way.

Essentially, copyright is a right to make copies; copyright infringement can therefore be seen as making unauthorized copies of a work. At least, this was the historical starting point: now, much refinement has taken place, and a distinction is made between primary and secondary infringement.

Primary infringement

In one way or another, all forms of primary infringement involve copying, whether through reproduction or through performance of the work. According to s. 16(1) of the 1988 Act, the rights of the copyright owner are infringed if:

- the work is copied;
- copies of the work are issued to the public;
- the work is lent or rented to the public;
- the work is performed, shown, or played in public;
- the work is communicated to the public;
- an adaptation is made of the work or any of the above is done in relation to an adaptation.[1]

It is an infringement to do these acts, but also to authorize someone else to do them.[2] These acts are called 'restricted acts' and only the owner of the copyright, or someone with his or her consent, can do them.

Normally, infringing acts are carried out by one party, or by several parties, each of which carries out separate infringing acts. There are, however, cases in which

---

[1] Inserted by Copyright and Related Rights Regulations 2003, reg. 6(2).
[2] CDPA 1988, s. 16(2).

the alleged infringers really act together in carrying out a single infringing act. Such copyright infringement cases in which the alleged infringers are sued jointly as joint tortfeasors require proof of an intended, procured, and shared common design for such infringement.[3]

Copyright infringement is the infringement of an intangible right in the expression of an idea. The idea is not protected and copying the idea is not an infringement of copyright.[4] The work should also be dissociated from its physical, tangible carrier: when you buy a wooden sculpture, you buy the piece of wood; the ownership of the copyright is not transferred.[5]

Infringement requires misappropriation

The causal link

Appropriation of the expression of the copyright work is an essential element of copyright infringement. Because only the particular expression of an idea is protected by copyright, a work expressing the same idea is not necessarily an infringement. This will be the case and no infringement will arise if the result is reached independently[6] or if a common source is relied upon.[7] This will, for example, be the case if two authors describe the Venice Marathon race in a very similar way, while sitting at opposite sides of the Rialto Bridge over the Canal Grande: they will reach the similar result independently. A common source may be found in two very different tables of matches on football pools coupons, each of which has to rely on the list of matches provided by the Football Association. It is necessary to demonstrate that the alleged infringement is linked to the original work and that part of its expression has been taken.

Recent case law provides a straightforward example in relation to a film.[8] The plaintiff had shown the defendant an advertising film. The defendant had declined the offer to utilize the film, but he had afterwards taken the idea that was contained in it to make his own film. It was held that copyright in the original film is not infringed when the defendant does not make an exact copy of the film itself, but makes another film in a way that is designed to, and which does, closely resemble and imitate the film in which copyright subsists.[9]

The burden of proof

The owner who alleges infringement of his or her copyright bears the burden of proving that the similarity between his or her work and the alleged infringement is explained by this causal connection. Part of the evidence required is that the plaintiff's work was created *before* the alleged infringement, which rules out the possibility that it borrowed subject matter from the alleged infringement.

In practice, it is extremely difficult to demonstrate the causal link fully. In most cases, all that the claimant can do is demonstrate strong similarities between the earlier work and the allegedly infringing work, which are of evidential value, but not conclusive; these are then coupled with evidence that the defendant had the opportunity to know the

---

[3] *MCA Records Inc. v. Charly Records Ltd* [2002] FSR 401, [2002] EMLR 1 (CA).

[4] *IPC Media Ltd v. Highbury-Leisure Publishing Ltd (No. 2)* [2005] FSR 20.

[5] This does not exclude a separate transfer of copyright.

[6] See *Francis Day & Hunter Ltd v. Bron* [1963] Ch 587, [1963] 2 All ER 16.

[7] For example, factual, scientific, and historical data, which is readily available and forms the basis of a number of works: see *Harman Pictures NV v. Osborne* [1967] 2 All ER 324, [1967] 1 WLR 723, at 328 and 728.

[8] *Norowzian v. Arks Ltd* [1998] FSR 394.

[9] The fact that the work was a film explains certain peculiarities of the case.

plaintiff's work. If the defendant does not provide another convincing explanation for the similarities, most judges will accept that the plaintiff has discharged the burden of proof and will find copying proved.

Lord Millett summarized it as follows in *Designers Guild Ltd v. Russell Williams Textiles Ltd:*[10]

> The first step in an action for infringement of artistic copyright is to identify those features of the defendant's design which the plaintiff alleges have been copied from the copyright work. The court undertakes a visual comparison of the two designs, noting the similarities and the differences. The purpose of the examination is not to see whether the overall appearance of the two designs is similar, but to judge whether the particular similarities relied on are sufficiently close, numerous or extensive to be more likely to be the result of copying than of coincidence. It is at this stage that similarities may be disregarded because they are commonplace, unoriginal, or consist of general ideas. If the plaintiff demonstrates sufficient similarity, not in the works as a whole but in the features which he alleges have been copied, and establishes that the defendant had prior access to the copyright work, the burden passes to the defendant to satisfy the judge that, despite the similarities, they did not result from copying. Even at this stage, therefore, the inquiry is directed to the similarities rather than the differences. This is not to say that the differences are unimportant. They may indicate an independent source and so rebut any inference of copying, but differences in the overall appearance of the two works due to the presence of features of the defendant's work about which no complaint is made are not material.[11]

The nexus that needs to be shown between the original work and the alleged copy should be one in terms of expression. A nexus at a high level of abstraction at which only the ideas are linked is not sufficient, because copyright protection does not operate at that level.[12]

It should be kept in mind, however, that the underlying rule requires proof of borrowing and a causal connection. In the absence of proof of actual knowledge of the original work, it was therefore held that infringement was not established in a case in which a designer created a pattern for a carpet on the basis of instructions that led to strong similarities with the original design.[13] The alleged infringer did not have to be able to explain in full detail how he came up independently with the similar aspects of the design. In these circumstances, the claimant-copyright owner can only succeed on the issue of copying by demonstrating similarities between the works that could not be coincidental.[14] The presence in both the original work and the alleged copy of a host of small, unimportant details is often an indication of copying.[15] Similarly, a particular feature—especially in a technical drawing, for example, of a design feature that solves a technical problem—may also be so ingenious and unique that any subsequent appearance of it must be the result of borrowing, because it is unrealistic to assume that someone could independently have arrived at exactly the same solution.[16] In the latter case, a lot will obviously depend upon the extreme nature of the facts of the case.

---

[10] [2000] 1 WLR 2413, [2001] FSR 113, at 2425 and 124.

[11] See also *Ultra Marketing (UK) Ltd & Thomas Alexander Scott v. Universal Components Ltd* [2004] EWHC 468; *Nouveau Fabrics Ltd v. Voyage Decoration Ltd & Dunelm Soft Furnishings Ltd* [2004] EWHC 895.

[12] *IPC Media Ltd v. Highbury-Leisure Publishing Ltd (No. 2)* [2005] FSR 20.

[13] *Stoddard International plc v. William Lomas Carpets Ltd* [2001] FSR 848.

[14] *Stephan Malmstedt v. EMI Records Ltd & Per Gessle* [2003] ECDR 162.

[15] *Nova Productons Ltd v. Mazooma Games Ltd & ors; Nova Productions Ltd v. Bell Fruit Games Ltd* [2007] RPC 25, [2007] EMLR 14 (CA).

[16] *George Jones v. Tower Hamlets London Borough Council & Samuel Lewis Housing Association* [2001] RPC 407.

The intention of the infringer and subconscious copying

The intention of the defendant is not relevant. The fact that he or she believed that, for whatever reason, he or she was allowed to reproduce or perform the work does not influence the finding of infringement. The defendant may not realize that he or she is infringing copyright; one also finds situations in which the defendant does not realize that he or she is copying. We all frequently come into contact with copyright works. Some of them leave untraceable impressions in our memory. Unconsciously, we may copy these works or parts of them when creating our own work. This will also constitute infringement, because copying does not need to happen consciously.[17] The obvious example is that of a composer who listens to hundreds of melodies and, when composing his own music, unconsciously copies fragments of the melodies that he heard.[18]

Full proof of a causal link will be even more difficult in cases of unconscious copying. Judges will consider:

> the degree of familiarity (if proved at all, or properly inferred) with the plaintiff's work, the character of the work, particularly its qualities of impressing the mind and memory, the objective similarity of the defendant's work, the inherent probability that such similarities as found could be due to coincidence, the existence of other influences on the defendant...the quality of the defendant's...own evidence on the presence in his mind of the plaintiff's work.[19]

Indirect copying

The causal relationship can be turned into a causal chain: a copy of a copy indirectly copies the original work and constitutes an infringement.[20] Drawings are often made before a three-dimensional object is made; if someone makes his or her own drawing after having seen the object, but without having seen the original drawing, the copyright in that drawing will nevertheless be infringed.[21]

This chain can be long, but it must be uninterrupted and run in the same direction. The final infringing copy must be linked to the original work, the copyright in which it is infringing—but it is not required that all intermediate acts produce works that can attract copyright.[22] To go back to our example, it is not required that the three-dimensional object attracts copyright. A recent case law example concerned parts of cartridges for laser printers and photocopiers.[23] The copying by the defendant of parts of the plaintiff's cartridges constituted an indirect reproduction of the plaintiff's drawings, in which artistic copyright existed. The fact that the cartridges were functional three-dimensional objects was irrelevant.

The provision cannot be used, however, if two similar objects are created and drawings of each of these objects are made. In that situation, there is no indirect infringement of

---

[17] See *Rees v. Melville* (1911–16) Macq Cop Cas 168; *Ricordi v. Clayton & Waller* (1928–30) Macq Cop Cas 154; *Francis Day & Hunter Ltd v. Bron* [1963] Ch 587, [1963] 2 All ER 16; *Industrial Furnaces v. Reaves* [1970] RPC 605 at 623.

[18] See *Stephan Malmstedt v. EMI Records Ltd & Per Gessle* [2003] ECDR 162.

[19] *Francis Day & Hunter Ltd v. Bron* [1963] Ch 587, [1963] 2 All ER 16, *per* Willmer LJ at 614, adopting the words of Wilberforce J at first instance.

[20] CDPA 1988, s. 16(3); this provision is based on the case law of, e.g., *King Features Syndicate v. Kleeman* [1941] AC 417, [1941] 2 All ER 403 and *British Leyland Motor Corp. v. Armstrong Patents Co. Ltd* [1986] RPC 279.

[21] See *LB (Plastics) v. Swish Products Ltd* [1979] RPC 551.

[22] CDPA 1988, s. 16(3).

[23] *Canon Kabushiki Kaisha v. Green Cartridge Co. (Hong Kong) Ltd* [1997] 3 WLR 13, [1997] FSR 817 (PC).

the drawing of the first object, because the objects are the starting point in the chain, not the drawing.[24]

Substantial copying

Two separate requirements

Copying is all about reproducing. This means, traditionally, that new copies of the work are produced in material form. This new copy, or these new copies, can now also be produced in digital form, but there still needs to be at least one 'new' copy. This was held not to be the case, for example, when an art gallery used a special technique to transfer the ink by which an authorized reproduction of a painter's work had been made on a poster to a canvas. No ink was left on the original poster and hence no 'new' copy of the work had been made.[25]

It remains equally true that not every act of copying is actionable: the defendant must have copied either the whole work or a substantial part of it.[26] This is the issue of 'substantiality', which comes on top of that of copying as such. It should be stressed that copying and taking a substantial part are two separate things: both are required and it is not correct to say that, when copying is found, it will follow that a substantial part has been taken.[27]

A qualitative approach

Cases in which the whole work has been copied are not problematic, but what is a 'substantial part' of a work? It is not determined on a quantitative basis: it is not possible to derive, from the 1988 Act and the case law, a rule that the copying of X per cent of a work will not be substantial copying, while the copying of Y per cent of the work will be such. Although, obviously, the quantity taken from the original work plays a certain role, it is much more a qualitative approach that is taken to determine whether the copying was substantial.[28]

Substantial taking also needs to be demonstrated in relation to each copyright work individually. If elements of more than one copyright work have been taken, the taking of a substantial part has to be demonstrated for each work.[29] This is linked to the fact that copyright is used in the UK as a tool against unfair competition. Copying will be allowed only in so far as it does not lead to unfair competition. A qualitative approach fits this purpose much more easily. Another relevant factor is the principle that ideas are not protected. A substantial part of the expression of the idea can be copied, but it is not possible to translate that into a percentage of the work, because one does not know the balance between idea and expression in the work.

Whether or not a substantial part of the work has been copied will have to be determined on a case-by-case basis. It is a matter of fact and degree, and will depend on the

---

[24] *Purefoy Engineering Co. Ltd v. Sykes Boxall* (1954) 71 RPC 227 at 232. Cf the Court of Appeal's approach in the same case, which is differently worded: (1955) 72 RPC 89 at 99.

[25] See the decision of the Supreme Court of Canada in *Galérie d'Art du Petit Champlain Inc., Galérie d'Art Yves Laroche Inc., Editions Multi-Graph Itée, Galérie d'Art Laroche, Denis Inc. & Serge Rosa v. Claude Théberge* [2002] SCC 34.

[26] CDPA 1988, s. 16(3)(a).

[27] *Nova Productons Ltd v. Mazooma Games Ltd & ors; Nova Productions Ltd v. Bell Fruit Games Ltd* [2007] RPC 25, [2007] EMLR 14 (CA).

[28] *Ladbroke (Football) Ltd v. William Hill (Football) Ltd* [1964] 1 All ER 465, [1964] 1 WLR 273, *per* Lord Reid at 469 and 276; see also Lord Pearce's speech at 481 and 293.

[29] *IPC Media Ltd v. Highbury-Leisure Publishing Ltd (No. 2)* [2005] FSR 20.

circumstances of the case.[30] Lord Hoffmann recently summarized the basic position as follows:

> The House of Lords decided in *Ladbroke (Football) Ltd v. William Hill (Football) Ltd* [1964] 1 All ER 465, [1964] 1 WLR 273 that the question of substantiality is a matter of quality rather than quantity. The relevant passages are too well known to require citation...But what quality is one looking for? That question, as it seems to me, must be answered by reference to the reason why the work is given copyright protection. In literary copyright, for example, copyright is conferred (irrespective of literary merit) upon an original literary work. It follows that the quality relevant for the purposes of substantiality is the literary originality of that which has been copied. In the case of an artistic work, it is the artistic originality of that which has been copied. So, in the recent case of *Designer Guild Ltd v. Russell Williams (Textiles) Ltd* [2001] 1 All ER 700, [2000] 1 WLR 2416, the House decided that although not the smallest part of a fabric had been reproduced with anything approaching photographic fidelity, the copying of certain of the ideas expressed in that design which, in their conjoined expression, had involved original artistic skill and labour, constituted the copying of a substantial part of the artistic work.[31]

Further guidance

Some further general guidance can, however, be given. The court will have to concentrate on the similarities between the part of the work that has allegedly been copied and the equivalent part in the alleged copy. Differences between the two can only be used to ascertain the similarities.[32] The qualitative approach to determining whether a substantial part of the work has been copied means that particular weight will be given to the copying of the most important and interesting parts of the original work.[33] In a case that was concerned with cacao crop reports, the copying of the pod count summary from the much longer report was held to constitute the copying of a substantial part of the work for this very reason.[34] In another case, a few lines had been taken from a manuscript authored by James Joyce.[35] The earlier edition of the work did not contain these lines, because they had been omitted at the typescript stage; they had been reinstated in the allegedly infringing edition. Even though only a few lines of text were at issue, they were held to amount to a substantial part of the work, because they were particularly important. Their reinstatement gave the public access to the complete original manuscript. If parts of more than one work—for example, a series of articles—are copied in the allegedly infringing work, each of the original works must be considered separately for the purposes of determining whether a substantial part of it has been copied.[36]

---

[30] For example, in *Hawkes & Sons (London) Ltd v. Paramount Film Service Ltd* [1934] Ch 593, it was held that the inclusion of a 20-second portion of the main melody of the march 'Colonel Bogey', which lasts for four minutes, in a newsreel amounted to substantial copying.

[31] *Newspaper Licensing Agency Ltd v. Marks & Spencer plc* [2001] UKHL 38, [2001] 3 WLR 290 at [19].

[32] *Biotrading & Financing OY v. Biohit Ltd* [1998] FSR 109 at 121.

[33] Care needs to be taken, though, that these do not include underlying ideas and concepts, because these are not protected by copyright. See *Baigent & anor v. Random House Group Ltd* [2007] FSR 24 (CA) (the *Da Vinci Code* case).

[34] *PCR Ltd v. Dow Jones Telerate Ltd* [1998] FSR 170.

[35] *Sweeney v. Macmillan Publishers Ltd* [2002] RPC 35 at 651. The judgment gives the impression that the lines also amount to a substantial part of the work, because they make the allegedly infringing edition special and distinct. It is respectfully submitted that this argument is not acceptable, because it refers to the allegedly infringing work, whereas the real issue is whether a substantial part—in a qualitative sense—of the copyright work has been copied.

[36] *PCR Ltd v. Dow Jones Telerate Ltd* [1998] FSR 170.

Once the court is convinced that unfair competition is taking place,[37] it will be hard to convince it that the alterations made are so substantial that the part of the original work that is copied is no longer substantial.[38] Indeed, the mere presence of additional new material is, as such, not diminishing the substantial copying.[39] This should also be seen against the background of the vague dividing line between idea and expression. Judges in the type of case described often take the view that the idea is restricted to the thought underlying the work, such as a joke underlying a cartoon.[40] The only way in which the defendant can avoid copying the expression is by drawing a different cartoon starting from the same joke, but not based on the completed original cartoon.[41] This extremely wide interpretation of what is expression facilitates, of course, the finding that a substantial part of it has been copied. The case law contains various examples of this approach in relation to scripts for plays or films based on plots found in a play or a novel.[42] The actual words were often not copied; only the plot, as such, was taken and eventually slightly adapted.[43] The courts decided that substantial copying had, nevertheless, taken place. In their view, the idea was confined to the thought that was the starting point for the development of the plot, such as making a play about the homecoming of a husband who was presumed dead.[44]

It is submitted that this approach should be confined to cases in which there is a very strong sense of unfair competition or in which the starting point is the essential element of the work that determines its economic value. The economic value of a plot, and that of the play or film based on it, is often determined on the basis of the value of the initial starting point. This is less so for a novel, in relation to which literary style is also extremely important, or for an artistic work, in relation to which visual appeal is the other extremely important factor.[45]

Alterations while copying

In all other circumstances, the idea is wider in scope. Under these circumstances, other elements become prominent in determining whether substantial copying has taken place. One obvious element is the unaltered copying of a key element of the original work, such as the refrain of a song.[46] This amounts, qualitatively speaking, to substantial copying, even if the amount taken is not large in comparison to the whole work.[47]

---

[37] Especially if the judges adhere to the hard-line approach suggested by Peterson J that 'what is worth copying is prima facie worth protecting': *University of London Press v. Universal Tutorial Press* [1916] 2 Ch 601 at 610 (quoted in *Ladbroke (Football) Ltd v. William Hill (Football) Ltd* [1964] 1 All ER 465, [1964] 1 WLR 273 at 279).

[38] An excellent example is found in *Elanco Products v. Mandops (Agrochemical Specialists) Ltd* [1980] RPC 213.

[39] *Hyperion Records Ltd v. Lionel Sawkins* [2005] 1 WLR 3281 (CA).

[40] *McCrum v. Eisner* (1917) 87 LJ Ch 99, 117 LT 536.

[41] Ibid.; see also *Krisarts SA v. Briarfine Ltd* [1977] FSR 557 (defendant painting independently a scene that the plaintiff painted at an earlier time, resulting in a similar process of creation, while only the idea was borrowed).

[42] *Corelli v. Gray* (1913) 30 TLR 116; *Vane v. Famous Players* (1928–35) Macq Cop Cas 394, are good examples of this approach.

[43] *Kelly v. Cinema Houses Ltd* (1928–35) Macq Cop Cas 362; *Dagnall v. British & Dominion Film Corp.* (1928–1935) Macq Cop Cas 391; *Fernald v. Jay Lewis* [1975] FSR 499 (case decided in 1953).

[44] An example given in *Vane v. Famous Players* (1928–35) Macq Cop Cas 394, *per* Scrutton LJ.

[45] See *Bauman v. Fussell* [1978] RPC 485, *per* Somervell LJ at 487.

[46] Cf *Hawkes & Sons (London) Ltd v. Paramount Film Service Ltd* [1934] Ch 593.

[47] But one line taken from the refrain of a popular song did not amount to substantial copying in *Joy Music Ltd v. Sunday Pictorial Newspapers (1920) Ltd* [1960] 2 QB 60; see below.

A smart copier alters and reworks the part that he or she has copied: does this still amount to substantial copying? The test is whether a substantial part of the original work survives in the new work.[48] It has been suggested that this means that no substantial and actionable copying will occur if the copier has invested enough skill and labour in the alteration of the copied parts[49] for the result to attract its own copyright.[50] This is, however, not the real test, and it should be emphasized that the skill and labour approach should, in any case, be restricted to the parts based on the copying. Other parts of the allegedly infringing work, and the skill and labour invested in them, should not be taken into account when discussing the infringement issue. It is therefore possible to determine whether the production of an altered copy constitutes a copyright infringement by asking whether the infringer has incorporated a substantial part of the independent skill and labour contributed by the original author in creating the copyright work.[51]

Two excellent examples of circumstances in which alterations lead to difficulties in this respect are satirical versions of works and summaries of works. The satirical version has to stay close enough to the original for people to recognize the link and, for reasons of accuracy, a summary has to contain the essential elements of the original work. A song, the lyrics of which had been altered and parodied in pursuit of Prince Philip, was held not to be an infringing copy, because only one repeated phrase had been taken from the original lyrics.[52] Selection of the essential elements of the work,[53] condensation, and revision must amount to enough skill and labour to attract copyright for a summary to escape the infringement sanction.[54]

The originality of what is copied

The work that has been copied may also contain unoriginal parts. This leads to special problems if the part that was copied included the unoriginal parts. It was held that, if an unoriginal part was taken, and that part was used in a similar context and way as in the original copyright work, the latter aspect meant that also part of the work of the author that provided originality was taken.[55] It is likely that, in these circumstances, the amount taken would be likely to amount to a substantial part of the work.[56]

Industrial drawings are a good example in this context. They often consist of unoriginal shapes, which are copied from earlier drawings, in combination with new original

---

[48] *Schweppes Ltd v. Wellington Ltd* [1984] FSR 210; *Redwood Music v. Chappell & Co. Ltd* [1982] RPC 109.

[49] It is essential that the copied work does not rely exclusively on information gathered by the plaintiff, using his or her skill and judgment: see *Elanco Products v. Mandops (Agrochemical Specialists) Ltd* [1980] RPC 213. It must be remembered, however, that this was a case in which there were strong indications of unfair competition, because the first version of the instruction leaflet for a weed killer was an exact copy of the plaintiff's leaflet and the second version was only revised to such extent as to give the same information in other words; the judgment can be criticized, because it gives the plaintiffs—authors of a trivial work—an almost absolute monopoly in the only possible way to express these instructions efficiently, concisely, and accurately.

[50] *Joy Music Ltd v. Sunday Pictorial Newspapers (1920) Ltd* [1960] 2 QB 60, [1960] 1 All ER 703; *Glyn v. Weston Feature Film Co.* [1916] 1 Ch 261.

[51] *Designers Guild Ltd v. Russell Williams Textiles Ltd* [2001] FSR 113, *per* Lord Scott at 131, with reference to H. Laddie, P. Prescott and M. Vitoria (2000) *The Modern Law of Copyright*, 3rd edn, London: Butterworths, pp. 92–3. See also *Nouveau Fabrics Ltd v. Voyage Decoration Ltd & Dunelm Soft Furnishings Ltd* [2004] EWHC 895.

[52] *Joy Music Ltd v. Sunday Pictorial Newspapers (1920) Ltd* [1960] 2 QB 60, [1960] 1 All ER 703.

[53] This aspect is essential, because the Court of Appeal held, in *Elanco Products v. Mandops (Agrochemical Specialists) Ltd* [1980] RPC 213, that the defendant could not rely exclusively on the plaintiff's effort and judgment in selecting the information.

[54] See *Sweet v. Benning* (1855) 16 CB 459, *per* Jervis CJ at 483.

[55] *Biotrading & Financing OY v. Biohit Ltd* [1998] FSR 109 at 121.

[56] Ibid.

shapes. When such an industrial drawing is copied, the copying of the unoriginal shape may not amount to the copying of a substantial part, but substantial copying may be involved when the amount copied includes the context in which the shape was portrayed. The latter conclusion is reached because the copier has also taken much of the work of the author in deciding how, and in what way, the unoriginal shape should be combined with the original shape. The inclusion of the unoriginal shape in what is copied has little relevance in deciding whether or not a substantial part has been copied.[57]

It cannot be the aim of copyright to give the plaintiff a wide-ranging monopoly. This could happen if works involving substantial copying of a part of a work that itself involves only the minimum amount of skill and labour to attract copyright are held to be infringements. This would be an undesirable consequence of the low requirements for a work to attract copyright and judges have fortunately responded to it by taking the extent of the effort invested by the plaintiff into account when deciding whether substantial copying has occurred. The answer will only be affirmative if an exact copy of the work, which itself involved an extremely low level of creativity, is produced.[58]

A particular problem arises when a work that is itself an edited version, or which consists of selected and compiled material, is allegedly copied to a substantial extent. This might occur in relation to a collection of selected poems, of which some poems are copied, together with some of the annotation. It occurs also in cases concerning tables, in relation to which the commercial judgment in selecting the material secures copyright and in which that selection is copied. Copyright arises in the whole work, but it is obvious that the real skill and labour expended by the plaintiff are located in the areas of selection, editing, and annotation. This is taken into account when determining whether the material copied amounts to a substantial part of the work.[59] The infringement of the plaintiff's contribution must be substantial as well.

Copying the various types of work

As a general rule, the idea of copying can be said to involve two elements:

> first, there must be sufficient objective similarity between the infringing work and the copyright work, or a substantial part thereof, for the former to be properly described, not necessarily as identical with, but as a reproduction or adaptation of the latter; secondly, the copyright work must be the source from which the infringing work is derived.[60]

The technical definition of copying depends on the type of work. But once such a case arises, the principles laid down above apply to it.

Original literary, artistic, dramatic, and musical works
An original work is copied through reproduction in any material form.[61] This includes storing the work in any medium by electronic means, such as storing the content of a book on a CD-ROM; it also includes materialization on a television monitor.[62] A special option

---

[57] Ibid., at 122.

[58] *Kenrick v. Lawrence & Co.* (1890) 25 QBD 99 (a drawing of a hand, showing voters where to cast their vote).

[59] *Warwick Film Productions Ltd v. Eisinger* [1969] 1 Ch 508, [1967] 3 All ER 367.

[60] *Francis Day & Hunter Ltd v. Bron* [1963] Ch 587, *per* Diplock LJ at 583.

[61] CDPA 1988, s. 17(2). See *HRH Prince of Wales v. Associated Newspapers Ltd* [2006] ECDR, confirmed on appeal [2007] 3 WLR 222.

[62] *Bookmakers' Afternoon Greyhound Services Ltd v. Wilf Gilbert (Staffordshire) Ltd* [1994] FSR 723.

arises for artistic works.[63] A two-dimensional copy can be made of a three-dimensional work, or a three-dimensional copy can be made of a two-dimensional work. The work is also reproduced in a material way in these cases. Such a case arises, for example, when a cartoon is enacted.[64]

Films and television broadcasts

Films and television broadcasts are copied when they are reproduced.[65] This can take place when a film is made of a film or a broadcast; it also takes place when a photograph of the whole, or of any substantial part, of an image that forms part of the film or broadcast is made.[66] The courts held that making a photograph of a single frame of a *Starsky and Hutch* film was an infringement.[67] This situation also covers the case in which a photograph of a television screen, on which the work is momentarily displayed, is made.

Typographical arrangements of published editions

Copying a typographical arrangement involves making a facsimile copy of that arrangement.[68] That copy can be enlarged or reduced in scale,[69] which means that infringement often takes place by means of a photocopy or a fax.

All works

Copying of any kind of work also includes making copies that are transient or incidental to some other use of the work.[70] The prime example in this case would be making a series of photographs while copying a film.

Issuing copies to the public

Copying is not the only restricted act: copyright is also infringed when copies of a work are issued to the public. This applies to all works; no distinction is made between the various categories. Copies are issued to the public when they are put into circulation for the first time. It is essential that copies of the work were not previously available and that they are now put into circulation.[71]

A distinction is made between putting copies into circulation in the UK or in any other member State of the European Economic Area (EEA), on the one hand, and putting copies into circulation outside the EEA member States, on the other. Copies are issued to the public by putting them into circulation in the territory of the EEA if these copies have not previously been put into circulation in that territory by, or with the consent of, the copyright owner. Copies are also issued to the public when they are put into circulation outside the territory of the EEA if they have not previously been put into circulation in that territory or elsewhere. All of this reflects also in the fact that subsequent dealings

---

[63] CDPA 1988, s. 17(3).

[64] *Bradbury, Agnew & Co. v. Day* [1916] WN 114. The dimensional shift rule only applies to artistic works; it does not apply when, e.g., a literary work is involved: see *Brigid Foley Ltd v. Eliott* [1982] RPC 433.

[65] CDPA 1988, s. 17(4).

[66] On a conceptual basis, copying needs to be distinguished from making another film in a way that is designed to, and which does, closely resemble and imitate the film in which copyright subsists, if no exact copy is made in the latter case: see *Norowzian v. Arks Ltd* [1998] FSR 394.

[67] *Spelling Goldberg Productions Inc. v. BPC Publishing Ltd* [1981] RPC 283.

[68] CDPA 1988, s. 17(5).

[69] Ibid., (8).

[70] Ibid., (6).

[71] See *HRH Prince of Wales v. Associated Newspapers Ltd* [2006] ECDR, confirmed on appeal [2007] 3 WLR 222.

with a copy that is put into circulation do not constitute the restricted act of issuing copies to the public. When a book that has not been published is put into circulation, this will be an infringement of the copyright in the book, but subsequent importation of copies of the book and the loan of these copies will not constitute issuing copies to the public.[72] Rental and lending are, however, subject to special provisions, and it is to these provisions that we now turn.

Rental and lending of the work to the public

Rental and lending of a work[73] mean that a copy of the work is made available for use, on terms that it will, or may, be returned. Hire purchase-type deals are therefore also included. In the case of rental, the work is made available for direct or indirect commercial or economic advantage. The activities of video shops come to mind as an obvious example. Lending covers all cases in which no direct or indirect commercial or economic advantage is involved[74] and the copy of the work is made available through an establishment that is accessible to the public, such as a library.[75] Unauthorized rental or lending of copies of certain types of work to the public will constitute an infringement of the copyright in the work. The types of work involved are literary, dramatic, and musical works, films, and sound recordings. Artistic works are only involved in so far as they are not a work of architecture in the form of a building or a model for a building, or a work of applied art.[76]

The right to object to unauthorized rental and lending does not apply to a limited number of cases, because they have been excluded from the scope of the definition of rental and lending. These exclusions cover making a copy of the work available for the purpose of public performance, playing, or showing in public, broadcasting, and making a copy available for the purpose of exhibition in public, as well as making the copy available for on-the-spot reference use.[77] The latter excludes for example, all use of a work inside a library without taking it out.

Rental and lending are based on the European Copyright (Rental and Lending) Directive,[78] which contains a minimum principle of equitable remuneration to which the right holder is entitled despite any potential contractual provisions by means of which he or she may have renounced his or her rights. The European Court of Justice has now expressed its views on the interpretation of that concept of equitable remuneration. The equitable remuneration for performing artists and phonogram producers was the point of discussion in *SENA v. NOS*.[79] The Court held that the member States are free to establish their own criteria within the boundaries set by the Directive and by Community law. It then applied that test to the Dutch criteria and found that the Dutch model passes the test, in so far as it relies on a combination of fixed and variable factors:

- the number of hours of phonograms broadcast;
- the viewing and listening densities achieved by the radio and television broadcasters represented by the broadcast organization;

[72] CDPA 1988, s. 18.
[73] Ibid., 18A(2).
[74] This does not exclude the payment of an amount to cover the operating costs of the establishment: ibid., (5).
[75] Interlibrary transactions are excluded from the scope of lending: ibid., (4).
[76] Ibid., (1).
[77] Ibid., (3).
[78] Council Directive 92/100/EEC on rental and lending right and on certain rights related to copyright in the field of intellectual property (1992) OJ L 346/61.
[79] [2003] ECR I-1251.

- the tariffs fixed by agreement in the field of performance rights and broadcast rights in respect of musical works protected by copyright;
- the tariffs set by the public broadcast organizations in the member States bordering on the Netherlands;
- the amounts paid by commercial stations.

This conclusion was reached in the understanding that the model is such that it will enable a proper balance to be achieved between the interests of performing artists and producers in obtaining remuneration for the broadcast of a particular phonogram, and the interests of third parties in being able to broadcast the phonogram on terms that are reasonable. While this is perhaps not a turnkey solution offered by the Court, it is nevertheless some kind of a workable tool for those concerned.

Public performance of the work and showing or playing the work in public

In this category of restricted acts, public performances apply to literary, dramatic, and musical works only. The copyright in these works is infringed by the public performance of the work. This includes any visual or acoustic presentation of the work, even if the presentation is done by means of sound recordings, films, or broadcasts. Lectures, speeches, and addresses obviously come within this category.[80]

It is also an infringement of copyright to play or show a sound recording, film, or broadcast in public.[81] This kind of infringement arises, for example, when background music is played in a shop or restaurant.[82] The application of this provision is not, however, without problems: how do we define 'in public'? It is clear that this is not a reference to the public at large: showing the work to a group of ten members of the public can be an infringement,[83] but private showings, even if to a larger number of people than ten, are not caught. To avoid infringement, then, the audience has to be of a domestic nature: copyright will not be infringed when a father plays a record and the rest of the family is listening in the lounge of the family home. This distinction is not, however, always clear: is the showing of a film in a hotel equipped with a central video recorder and a television set in every room private or public?[84] People will watch the film in the private atmosphere of their room, but the work will be available to a large group of people. Judges seem to attach a lot of importance to the question of whether the economic interests of the copyright owner are harmed.[85] If the answer is positive, the showing or playing will be public and will infringe. This will often be the case if everyone can gain access to the place at which the showing or playing takes place, with or without payment.

When a work is performed, played, or shown by means of apparatus receiving visual images or sounds that are conveyed by electronic means, the infringer will not be the

---

[80] CDPA 1988, s. 19(1) and (2).

[81] Ibid., (3).

[82] Blanket licences are available from collecting societies: see Chapter 18.

[83] Cf Art. 3(1) of the Directive 2001/29/EC of the European Parliament and the Council on the harmonization of certain aspects of copyright and related rights in the information society [2001] OJ L 167/10.

[84] The European Court of Justice has held that Art. 1 of the Cable and Satellite Directive (Directive 93/83 on the coordination of certain rules concerning copyright and rights related to copyright applicable to satellite broadcasting and cable retransmission [1993] OJ L 248/15) did not define whether this amounted to communication to the public and that this was a matter for national law: Case C-293/98 *EGEDA v. Hosteleria Asturiana SA* [2000] ECR 231.

[85] See *Duck v. Bates* (1884) 13 QBD 843; *Ernest Turner Electrical Instruments Ltd v. Performing Right Society Ltd* [1943] Ch 167, [1943] 1 All ER 413; see also *Performing Right Society Ltd v. Harlequin Record Shops* [1979] FSR 233.

person who sends the sounds or images (and the performer, in case of a performance),[86] but the person who makes the arrangements for the infringing act to take place.

Communication to the public

In implementing the Information Society Directive,[87] the new, broader concept of broadcast has now also been reflected in the new s. 20 of the 1988 Act.[88] Infringement by broadcasting or inclusion in a cable programme service has been replaced by infringement by communication to the public. That communication to the public of the work is now an act restricted by the copyright in a literary, dramatic, musical or artistic work, a sound recording or film, or a broadcast, and any reference to 'communication to the public' is to communication to the public by electronic transmission. In relation to a work, this includes the broadcasting of the work and the making available to the public of the work by electronic transmission in such a way that members of the public may access it from a place, and at a time, individually chosen by them.

Whereas s. 19 is concerned with public performance in cases in which the public is present, s. 20 is solely concerned with communication to the public in cases in which the public is not present at the place of communication:[89] for example, in relation to the place at which the act of broadcasting takes place.[90] Communication is, by definition, also concerned only with the electronic transmission of the work[91]—but all forms of electronic transmission are covered, which includes on-demand services. Internet transmissions are also included, because they are electronic transmissions through which members of the public may access the work from a place, and at a time, that they individually choose. They come therefore within the definition of communication to the public.[92]

Making an adaptation

Making an adaptation of a literary, dramatic, or musical work is also a restricted act.[93] Adaptations of artistic works are excluded. The adaptation is made when it is recorded, in writing or otherwise. Examples are the translation of a literary work into a foreign language, adapting a novel into a play, or making an arrangement of a musical work. The making of an adaptation of an adaptation or doing any other restricted act to an adaptation—for example, including it in a broadcast—is also an act restricted by the copyright in the work and will constitute an infringement.[94]

---

[86] CDPA 1988, s. 19(4).

[87] Directive 2001/29/EC of the European Parliament and the Council on the harmonization of certain aspects of copyright and related rights in the information society [2001] OJ L 167/10.

[88] Inserted by Copyright and Related Rights Regulations 2003, reg. 6.

[89] See Recital 23 to the Directive.

[90] Broadcasting, and therefore communication to the public, will take place in both the country in which the principal audience and the seat of the organization is located, and in the country in which the transmitter is located in a scenario within which the latter is, for technical reasons, located on the other side of the border: Case C-192/04 *Lagardère Active Broadcast v. SPRE & GVL* [2005] ECR I-07199 (ECJ).

[91] A hotel that makes available television sets in individual bedrooms is communicating television programmes as copyright works to the public. Liability under copyright arises despite the fact that each guests watches in the privacy of his or her room; that does not mean that no communication to the public is involved. Case C-306/05 *SGAE v. Rafael Hoteles SA* [2006] ECR I-11519 (ECJ).

[92] See, under the original text of the CDPA 1988, *Shetland Times v. Wills* [1997] FSR 604.

[93] CDPA 1988, s. 21(1).

[94] Ibid., (2).

Secondary infringement

Copyright can also be infringed by dealing commercially with copies of works that attract copyright.[95] This is known as 'secondary infringement', because, in all forms of primary infringement, an infringing copy of the work is made, while in this type of infringement case, these copies are only exploited commercially. The other main difference between primary and secondary infringement is found in the psychological element relating to the infringer: the intention to infringe, or the fact that one is infringing copyright knowingly, is irrelevant for primary infringement—but it is also possible to infringe copyright unconsciously. In cases of secondary infringement, however, the alleged infringer must have had knowledge or reason to believe that his or her activity would be a secondary infringement of copyright.[96] This requirement is approached objectively. It should have been obvious to the defendant that his or her activity would infringe copyright.[97] Obviousness may be tested by taking the 'reasonable man' approach:[98] would it have been obvious to a reasonable man that the activity would infringe?

Knowledge of infringement proceedings is not sufficient to establish that the alleged infringer must have had knowledge or a reasonable belief that the activities would be an infringement. Setting aside money for a fighting fund does not change that. On the one hand, this is a logical conclusion, because, in certain cases, the reasonable man might expect the alleged infringer to win the case;[99] on the other, the alleged infringer must make the reasonable man assessment in all of the circumstances and cannot escape liability for secondary infringement simply by relying on a representation, to the extent that no infringement is involved, made by a business partner who has a self-interest in the case. In a recent case, it was indeed held that a distributor of records could not rely on a representation that everything was in order, made by the recording company involved, to escape secondary infringement liability.[100] Newspaper stories and an interlocutory injunction in a foreign court should have led any reasonable man to the obvious belief that the activity would infringe.

Despite all of this, it is fair to say that the precise meaning of having 'reason to believe' is not entirely clear. What seems clear, however, is that there has to be more than mere knowledge of certain facts, because the facts need to lead to a belief. In the words of Morritt J:[101]

> Nevertheless, it seems to me that 'reason to believe' must involve the concept of knowledge of facts from which a reasonable man would arrive at the relevant belief. Facts from which a reasonable man might suspect the relevant conclusion cannot be enough. Moreover, as it seems to me, the phrase does connote the allowance of a period of time to enable the reasonable man to evaluate those facts so as to convert the facts into a reasonable belief.

---

[95] Ibid., ss. 22–26.

[96] Ibid., each section *in fine*.

[97] It has been held that a failure of the claimant to provide details of the alleged infringement may mean that the defendant has no reason to believe that his or her activities infringe the claimant's copyright: see *Vermaat (t/a Cotton Productions) v. Boncrest Ltd (No. 2)* [2002] FSR 21.

[98] See *Infabrics Ltd v. Jaytex Shirt Co.* [1978] FSR 451, *per* Whitford J at 464–5 (a case interpreting the similar provisions of the previous Copyright Act). This approach, adopted by the courts before the introduction of the new criteria in the 1988 Act, will be continued: see also *LA Gear Inc. v. Hi-Tech Sports plc* [1992] FSR 121.

[99] *Metix (UK) Ltd v. GH Maughan (Plastics) Ltd* [1997] FSR 718; see also *Hutchison Personal Communications Ltd v. Hook Advertising Ltd* [1995] FSR 365.

[100] *ZYX Music GmbH v. King* [1997] 2 All ER 129, [1997] EMLR 319.

[101] *LA Gear Inc. v. Hi-Tec Sports plc* [1992] FSR 121 at 129.

Facts giving rise to a 'reason to suspect' are therefore not enough. The defendant must also evaluate all factors known to him or her, without accepting the claimant's assertions at face value, but also without ignoring them. The grounds for suspicion have to harden into grounds for belief, which has to be assessed on an objective basis—that is, by taking the reasonable man's beliefs into account, rather than the actual beliefs of the defendant. The defendant's evaluation will often involve him or her in making enquiries and the answers received will help to determine whether the defendant acquired 'reason to believe'. A defendant who fails to carry out sensible enquiries, having received assertions of infringement and who had 'reason to suspect', is, however, capable of becoming a person with 'reason to believe'.[102]

Various types of secondary infringement in the exploitation of copies of a work are listed in the 1988 Act. All apply in relation to any kind of work that attracts copyright and the list includes the following:

• importing into the UK an infringing copy of the work, if this copy is not imported for the importer's private and domestic use.[103] If we assume that a novel is translated without the consent of the copyright owner, you can import an infringing copy to read it at home, but you cannot import ten copies to sell them as exclusive pieces in your book shop without infringing copyright;

• possessing an infringing copy in the course of a business, selling it, letting it for hire, offering or exposing it for sale or hire, exhibiting it in public in the course of a business or otherwise, to such an extent that it affects the copyright owner prejudicially;[104]

• providing the medium with which to make infringing copies of the work, which medium—such as machines—must be designed specifically for this purpose.[105] The double cassette or video recorder, for example, is not specifically designed for the purpose of copying films from one cassette to the other, because it can also be used to record legally something that is not protected by copyright, the length of which exceeds the maximum recording time of one cassette;[106]

• transmission of the work by means of a telecommunications system when it is likely that infringing copies of the work will be made due to the reception of the transmission. Broadcasting the work will not constitute transmission of the work for the purposes of this provision;[107]

• permitting the use of a place of public entertainment for an infringing performance of the work. The person permitting the use of such a place will escape liability if he or she believed, on reasonable grounds, that the performance would not infringe copyright;[108]

• the provision of material or equipment required for the infringing performance, if the person providing the material or equipment knows, or has reason to believe, that it will be used for an infringing performance.[109]

These provisions all refer to the concept of an infringing copy of the work. This concept is defined in s. 27 of the Act. An item, the making of which constituted an infringement

---

[102] *Nouveau Fabrics Ltd v. Voyage Decoration Ltd & Dunelm Soft Furnishings Ltd* [2004] EWHC 895.
[103] CDPA 1988, s. 22.
[104] Ibid., s. 23.
[105] Ibid., s. 24(1).
[106] *CBS Songs Ltd v. Amstrad Consumer Electronics plc* [1988] AC 1013, [1988] 2 All ER 484.
[107] CDPA 1988, s. 24(2).
[108] Ibid., s. 25.
[109] Ibid., s. 26.

of copyright, is an infringing copy; items, the making of which would have constituted an infringement of copyright had they been made in the UK, or a breach of an exclusive licence agreement, and which have been, or will be, imported into the UK are also infringing copies, as are copies that are infringing copies by virtue of several provisions relating to the acts permitted in relation to copyright.[110] The latter are defences to copyright infringement and will be analysed in the next chapter.

Technical measures

Increasingly, copyright holders use technical devices to prevent the unauthorized copying of their works. This development will now get legal support to protect it, primarily against the persistent attempt by hackers and others to circumvent any such device or measure. The Information Society Directive describes a technological measure as '*any technology, device, or component that, in the normal course of its operation, is designed to prevent or restrict acts, which are not authorized by the rightholder of any copyright*'.[111] Member States are required to provide:

> adequate legal protection against the circumvention of any effective technological measure, which the person concerned carries out in the knowledge, or with reasonable grounds to believe that he or she is pursuing that objective.[112]

The additional requirement that the measure must be effective is defined as the situation in which

> the use of the protected work or other subject-matter is controlled by the rightholders through application of an access control or protection process, such as encryption, scrambling or other transformation of the work or other subject-matter or a copy control mechanism, which achieves the protection objective.[113]

The implementation in the UK of the Directive, by means of the Copyright and Related Rights Regulations 2003, is a classical example of highly complex and detailed legislation. In essence, a distinction is made between the circumvention of technical devices applied to computer programs and technical devices applied to other copyright works. Technical devices applied to a computer program are defined as '*any device intended to prevent or restrict acts that are not authorized by the copyright owner of that program and are restricted by copyright*'.[114] When such a device has been applied to a computer program, the copyright owner and certain other persons are given the same rights that the copyright owner has in relation to copyright infringement. These rights are given if a person knowing, or having reason to believe, that it will be used to make infringing copies either manufactures for sale or hire, imports, distributes, sells, or lets for hire, offers or exposes for sale or hire, advertises for sale or hire, or has in his or her possession for commercial purposes any medium, the sole intended purpose of which is to facilitate the unauthorized removal or circumvention of the technical device, or if such a person publishes information that is intended to enable or assist persons to remove or circumvent the technical device.[115] A similar right of action and entitlement to a remedy is provided when effective technological measures have been applied to copyright work that is not a computer

---

[110] Ibid., s. 27.
[111] Article 6(3).
[112] Article 6(1).
[113] Article 6(3).
[114] CDPA 1988, s. 296(6), inserted by Copyright and Related Rights Regulations 2003, reg. 24.
[115] CDPA 1988, s. 296(1) and (2), inserted by Copyright and Related Rights Regulations 2003, reg. 24.

program and a person does anything that circumvents those measures, while knowing, or having reasonable grounds to know, that he or she is pursuing that objective.[116]

This affects the act of circumvention itself, but there is an additional provision that deals directly with the devices, components, or services that are used to achieve circumvention. Member States are required to provide adequate legal protection against the manufacture, import, distribution, sale, rental, advertisement for sale or rental, or possession for commercial purposes of devices, products, or components, or the provision of services that are promoted, advertised, or marketed for the purpose of circumvention of any effective technological measure, or which have only a limited commercially significant purpose or use other than circumvention, or which are primarily designed, produced, adapted, or performed for the purpose of enabling or facilitating the circumvention of effective technological measures.[117] As the new s. 296ZB of the 1988 Act puts it:

(1) A person commits an offence if he—

  (a) manufactures for sale or hire, or

  (b) imports otherwise than for his private and domestic use, or

  (c) in the course of a business—

    (i)   sells or lets for hire, or

    (ii) offers or exposes for sale or hire, or

    (iii) advertises for sale or hire, or

    (iv) possesses, or

    (v)   distributes, or

  (d) distributes otherwise than in the course of a business to such an extent as to affect prejudicially the copyright owner,

any device, product or component which is primarily designed, produced, or adapted for the purpose of enabling or facilitating the circumvention of effective technological measures.

(2) A person commits an offence if he provides, promotes, advertises or markets—

  (a) in the course of a business, or

  (b) otherwise than in the course of a business to such an extent as to affect prejudicially the copyright owner,

a service the purpose of which is to enable or facilitate the circumvention of effective technological measures.[118]

Apart from technological measures, rights holders often add electronic rights management information to copies of the work, in order to be able to trace copies of the work, for example. The Directive defines such information as any information provided by rights holders that identifies the work, the author, or any other right holder, or information about the terms and conditions of use of the work, and any numbers or codes that represent such information.[119] Member States are required to provide adequate legal protection against any person who knowingly and without authorization removes or alters any electronic rights management information, or who distributes, imports for distribution, broadcasts, communicates, or makes available to the public works from which electronic rights management information has been removed or altered without authority, if such a

---

[116] CDPA 1988, s. 296ZA(1), inserted by Copyright and Related Rights Regulations 2003, reg. 24.
[117] Article 6(2) of the Directive.
[118] Inserted by Copyright and Related Rights Regulations 2003, reg. 24.
[119] See CDPA 1988, s, 296ZG(7)(b), inserted by Copyright and Related Rights Regulations 2003, reg. 25.

person knows, or had reasonable grounds to know, that, by so doing, he or she is inducing, enabling, facilitating, or concealing an infringement of any copyright.[120] In terms of UK copyright infringement in the new s. 296ZG of the 1988 Act:

(1) This section applies where a person (D), knowingly and without authority, removes or alters electronic rights management information which—

  (a) is associated with a copy of a copyright work, or

  (b) appears in connection with the communication to the public of a copyright work, and

  where D knows, or has reason to believe, that by so doing he is inducing, enabling, facilitating or concealing an infringement of copyright.

(2) This section also applies where a person (E), knowingly and without authority, distributes, imports for distribution or communicates to the public copies of a copyright work from which electronic rights management information—

  (a) associated with the copies, or

  (b) appearing in connection with the communication to the public of the work,

  has been removed or altered without authority and where E knows, or has reason to believe, that by so doing he is inducing, enabling, facilitating or concealing an infringement of copyright.[121]

The artists' resale right

A Directive has been adopted that puts in place a resale right for authors of an original work of art.[122] These works are mainly exploited through the sale of the original, or of a few copies of the work, and this is to be contrasted with the exploitation by means of multiple copies or uses of other copyright works. Some member States felt that this disadvantaged authors of original rights, whose works are often resold at a later stage for a much higher price. These member States had, therefore, introduced a resale right—or *droit de suite*—and the Artists' Resale Right Directive 2001 is an attempt to harmonize the existing rules on this point. The Directive was highly controversial, and the Council and the Parliament adopted very different positions.[123] Finally, a reconciliation procedure produced a compromise to which all parties could agree. The member States had to implement the Directive by 1 January 2006.[124]

Despite being strongly opposed to the introduction of an artists' resale right during the negotiations, the UK transposed the Directive into national law on 14 February 2006 by means of the Artist's Resale Right Regulations 2006.[125] The author of an original work of art shall be given an additional exclusive right as part of his or her copyright. This right is inalienable[126] and cannot be waived,[127] even in advance, but it can transmitted on death[128]

120   Article 7 of the Directive.

121   Inserted by Copyright and Related Rights Regulations 2003, reg. 25.

122   European Parliament and Council Directive 2001/84/EC on the resale right for the benefit of the author of an original work of art (2001) OJ L 272/32.

123   See, in general, P. Torremans (2000) 'The proposed *droit de suite*: a critique and a Euro–Polish comparison', in P. Torremans (ed.) *Legal Convergence in the Enlarged Europe of the New Millennium*, London: Kluwer Law International, p. 71.

124   Article 12 of the Directive.

125   SI 2006/346.

126   No assignments are possible: reg. 7(1).

127   Regulation 8(1).

128   Regulation 9.

or transferred to a charity.[129] While the aim behind the creation of the resale right is clearly economic, these latter aspects emerge from its strong link with the person of the author and are reminiscent of certain key aspects of moral rights.

The right will entitle the author to a royalty, based on the price at which the work of art is sold on any occasion after the initial sale,[130] until the end of the copyright term,[131] as long as a professional market professional is involved in one way or another.[132] Sales between private individuals are exempted, because such a right could not be enforced for such transactions. The works that are covered by the right are any work of graphic or plastic art, such as a picture, a collage, a painting, a drawing, an engraving, a print, a lithograph, a sculpture, a tapestry, a ceramic, an item of glassware, or a photograph, according to reg. 4. In essence, originals are covered, but copies that are made by the artist or under his or her authority will also be considered to be original works of art if they have been made in limited numbers.[133] This will, for example, be the case for a limited series of numbered prints, or for any other copies that have (normally) been numbered, signed, or otherwise been duly authorized by the artist.

The royalty is calculated according to a decreasing scale in relation to the resale price:[134]

From €0–50,000	4%
From €50,000.01–200,000	3%
From €200,000.01–350,000	1%
From €350,000.01–500.000	0.5%
Exceeding €500,000	0.25%

In any case, however, the total amount of royalty payable on the sale shall not exceed €12,500.[135] Sales of less than €1,000 are not subject to the resale right as sales of up to €10,000, on condition that the seller previously acquired the work directly from the author less than three years before the sale.[136]

The exercise of the resale right and the collection of the royalty can only take place through a collecting society. The artist is free to choose a collecting society, but, in the absence of choice, the task shall be carried out by the collecting society that manages copyright on behalf of artists: for example, the Design and Artists Copyright Society (DACS).[137] Those liable to pay the resale right are the seller and, if acting in the course of a business of dealing in works of art, the seller's agent, the buyer's agent (if there is no seller's agent), and the buyer (if there are no such agents). Liability is joint and several, and arises upon completion of the sale.[138]

Third-country nationals will only be able to benefit from the right if their own national legislation offers a similar right to those of EU authors.[139] This should be seen as a way of encouraging other countries to adopt a resale right, which Art. 14ter of the Berne

---

[129] Regulation 7(3)–(5).

[130] A resale after the first transfer of ownership of the work of art by the author is required: reg. 12.

[131] Regulation 3.

[132] Regulation 12(2)–(3).

[133] Regulation 4(2).

[134] Which, according to reg. 3(4), is defined as '*the price obtained for the sale, net of the tax payable on the sale, and converted into euro at the European Central Bank reference rate prevailing at the contract date*'.

[135] Schedule 1 to the Regulations.

[136] Regulation 12.

[137] Regulation 14.

[138] Regulation 13.

[139] Regulation 10 and Sch. 2 to the Regulations.

Convention for the Protection of Literary and Artistic Works 1886 still describes as an optional right that contracting states are not bound to implement.

Finally, the right holder will have a three-year period, following every sale, during which any information necessary to secure the payment of the royalty can be requested from any art market professional involved with such a sale.[140]

An overview

In the aftermath of the implementation of the Information Society Directive, copyright provides essentially for three main rights, which are also available in a digital online environment: the reproduction right; the right of communication to the public and of making available to the public; the distribution right.

In relation to the reproduction right, authors have the exclusive right to authorize or to prohibit direct or indirect, temporary or permanent reproduction of their work by any means, and in any form, in whole or in part. Copying and borrowing remain infringements, irrespective of the analogue or digital environment in which they may take place. Similarly, a reproduction right is given to producers of films in respect of the original and copies of their films, and to broadcasting organizations in respect of their broadcasts, irrespective of whether these broadcasts are transmitted by wire or over the air (including cable and satellite broadcasting). The crucial element in this case is that it is accepted as a starting point that temporary reproduction, as well as permanent reproduction, amounts to an infringement of copyright if it is done without the prior authorization of the right holder. Such temporary reproductions are made on numerous occasions in a digital online environment.[141]

In a digital online environment, many works are no longer dealt with in hard copy, but they are instead delivered online. Right holders are therefore given a right to authorize or to prohibit the communication of their works to the public by wire or by wireless means. The most important aspect of this right is that it also applies to on-demand services, in relation to which the work is made available to the public in such a way that members of the public may access the work from a place and time that they have chosen. This removes the doubt that still existed on this point under the old existing legislation.

Producers of the first fixations of films receive an exclusive right to authorize or to prohibit the making available to the public, by wire or by wireless means, of the original or of copies of their films. Again, this right is explicitly held to apply also to on-demand systems and a similar right is given to broadcasting organizations in relation to fixations of their broadcasts. This right is independent of the way in which the broadcast was transmitted: transmission by wire or over the air, or by cable or satellite are all included.[142]

The third right is the distribution right, which mainly affects hard copies of the work. The right applies to originals or copies of works that are distributed to the public through sale or otherwise.[143]

In addition copyright owners are also protected through the provisions on indirect infringement, but in relation to this type of infringement, they will have to prove knowledge or reason to believe on the part of the alleged infringer.

---

[140] Regulation 15.
[141] Article 2 of the Directive.
[142] Article 3.
[143] Article 4.

Further reading

CONNOR, I., '*IPC Media Ltd v. Highbury-SPL Publishing Ltd*' (2005) 27 EIPR 9, 338.

GARNETT, K., DAVIES, G. and HARBOTTLE, G. (2005) *Copinger and Skone James on Copyright*, 15th edn, London: Sweet and Maxwell, chs 7 and 8.

HAYS, T., 'The evolution and decentralisation of secondary liability for infringements of copyright-protected works' (2006) 28 EIPR 12, 617.

HAYS, T., 'Secondary liability for infringements of copyright-protected works' (2007) 29 EIPR 1, 15.

KLEMENT, U., 'Copyright protection of unauthorised sequels under the Copyright, Designs and Patents Act 1988' (2007) 18 Ent LR 1, 13.

16

Defences to copyright infringement

Certain acts that constitute infringements of copyright on the basis of the provisions analysed in the previous chapter are permitted acts. In particular, circumstances copyright will not be infringed, because a defence is available, making the allegedly infringing act a permitted act. These defences exist in order to restore the balance between the rights of the owner of copyright and the rights of society at large. They restrict the exclusive rights granted by copyright in cases in which it is felt that they go too far. This is particularly useful, because copyright is extremely wide in scope and its term of protection is long.

But before we start our analysis of the permitted acts or the exceptions to copyright infringement, it has to be emphasized that these exceptions are exceptions to copyright infringement only.[1] If a case also involves a breach of confidence, the exception will not apply to the breach of confidence.

The first two defences are of a general nature and are not listed in Ch. III of the Copyright, Designs and Patents Act 1988 as permitted acts.

Authorization or consent of the owner

Copyright in a work is not infringed if the owner of the copyright in the work authorized or consented to the allegedly infringing act.[2] No formal contractual licence to do these acts is required: informal, or even implied,[3] licences are acceptable. An amateur musician does not infringe the copyright in a musical work when he or she makes a copy of it with the authorization of the composer of the musical work who owns the copyright in it. In cases of joint ownership of copyright, a licence from all of the joint owners is required.[4]

Public interest

The concept

If the allegedly infringing act is in the public interest, this will provide a valid defence against the alleged infringement, despite the fact that the 1988 Act did not give the court

---

[1] CDPA 1988, s. 28(1).

[2] Ibid., s. 16(2). See *Confetti Records, Fundamental Records & Andrew Alcee v. Warner Music UK Ltd (t/a East West Records)* [2003] ECDR 336.

[3] Although the use of an implied licence may lead to problems: see *Warner v. Gestetner Ltd* [1988] EIPR D-89; *Blair v. Osborne & Tomkins* [1971] 2 QB 78, [1971] 1 All ER 468.

[4] CDPA 1988, s. 173.

any general power to enable an infringer to use another's copyright in the public interest. Instead, the public interest defence is based on the court's inherent jurisdiction to refuse an action for infringement of copyright in cases in which the enforcement of copyright would offend against the policy of the law. This inherent power has been preserved by s. 171(3) of the 1988 Act.[5] This defence also applies to the law of confidence, but in that respect, it is based on different grounds.[6]

It remains difficult to determine precisely what is in the public interest in a theoretical way. What *is* clear is that the circumstances in which the court could invoke its inherent jurisdiction depend on the work at issue, rather than on the issue of the ownership of the work.[7] These circumstances include those in which the work was immoral, scandalous, or contrary to family life,[8] or in which the work is injurious to public life, public health and safety, or the administration of justice. Also included are circumstances in which the work would encourage others to act in a way that would cause such injury.[9]

The Court of Appeal's judgment in *Ashdown v. Telegraph Group Ltd*[10] makes it clear, however, that the public interest defence cannot be restricted solely to these circumstances—that is, to circumstances in which where there had been serious wrong-doing on the part of the claimant. The Court held that the circumstances in which the public interest could override copyright were not capable of precise categorization or definition. This is in line with the public policy role of the public interest defence, which is to refuse an action for infringement of copyright if the enforcement of copyright would offend against the policy of the law. Like all such broad emergency brakes, it is not capable of precise definition.

Let us turn to the practical implications of all of this by way of the facts of the *Hyde Park Residence* case.[11] Photographs that had been taken from a security video recording of a brief visit paid by the late Diana, Princess of Wales, and Dodi Fayed to a villa in France were an infringement of copyright, and the publication of these pictures in *The Sun* more than one year after their tragic deaths could not be justified by means of the public interest defence—even if they showed that statements made by Mr Fayed's father were anything but accurate. The latter point could be made without there being a need for copyright infringement and therefore no circumstances remained that made it necessary to breach copyright in the public interest. All that could be said was that these pictures remained of interest to the public, but that is something rather different altogether.[12]

In general, in the copyright context, the defence is often used to justify publication of information in breach of copyright and confidence in the information,[13] because—especially when that information is embarrassing for someone—an attempt to use copyright to stop the publication of the information will be launched.

Freedom of expression

The interaction between copyright and human rights has been at the centre of attention in recent times. The Human Rights Act 1998 incorporated into UK law the European

[5] *Hyde Park Residence Ltd v. Yelland* [2000] 3 WLR 215, *per* Aldous LJ at 160.

[6] Ibid., at 167.

[7] Ibid., at 168.

[8] See also *A v. B* [2000] EMLR 1007.

[9] *Hyde Park Residence Ltd v. Yelland* [2000] 3 WLR 215, *per* Aldous LJ at 168.

[10] *Ashdown v. Telegraph Group Ltd* [2001] 4 All ER 666, [2002] RPC 235.

[11] *Hyde Park Residence Ltd v. Yelland* [2000] 3 WLR 215.

[12] Ibid., at 168.

[13] See *Beloff v. Pressdram Ltd* [1973] 1 All ER 241 at 259.

Convention on Human Rights and, with it, the Art. 10 right to freedom of expression. It is easy to see how a right to freedom of expression may clash with copyright, which creates an exclusive right in certain expressions—but that exclusive right takes the form of a property right and the latter is also protected by Art. 1 of the Convention.[14] These conflicting interest have been reconciled in the 1988 Act and that reconciliation has mainly been achieved by the following tools:

- the idea–expression dichotomy—that is, the fact that ideas are not protected and that freedom of expression is guaranteed by the option to express the same idea differently;

- the fair dealing defence, as will be seen below;

- the public interest defence—that is, the denial of copyright enforcement in cases in which the inappropriate use of copyright would crush freedom of expression.

This is the argument that there are internal safeguards in copyright to deal with the issue. In most cases, these internal safeguards will indeed suffice, but there are cases in which that will not be the case and in which the application of copyright law will not suffice to solve the external conflict between copyright and human rights.[15]

The Court of Appeal recognized this in *Ashdown v. Telegraph Group Ltd.*[16] The newspaper had used substantial quotes from a (confidential) memo of a meeting between Paddy Ashdown and the Prime Minister. Mr Ashdown had dictated the memo and claimed copyright infringement. The newspaper defended itself by relying on the fair dealing exception, the public interest defence, and freedom of expression.[17] The newspaper mainly criticized the actions of those involved in the meeting, which made it harder to rely on fair dealing. The Court therefore turned to the question of whether the right of freedom of expression could justice the verbatim publication of the copyright work at issue. It ruled that, in principle, the use of the exact words used by the author is not justifiable by the right to freedom of expression and the public interest defence, and that the alleged infringer could express the matter in a different way.

The Court also recognized, however, that there may be exceptional circumstances in which the exact words and format were of interest to the public—that is, circumstances in which the point cannot be made without copying the exact words and or format used by the author. In this case, there was a need to use the exact words of the memo to convince the public that the newspaper had a copy of the memo and was able to give an authentic account of events—but such a reason justified only a short quotation and the real motivation for the large quotes had been commercially motivated in order to appeal to reader, rather than being necessary for journalistic reasons. Only those necessary quotes could be defended by invoking freedom of expression and, even then, the use of the work is not free. In other words, the freedom of expression argument may serve to avoid an injunction against use, but not to avoid a claim for indemnification.[18] Allowing an injunction to enforce copyright would be against the public interest in such a case.

---

[14] The right of every person to peaceful enjoyment of his possessions in this Article has been understood in such a way that possession can include copyright.

[15] See M. Birnhack, 'Acknowledging the conflict between copyright law and freedom of expression under the Human Rights Act' [2003] Ent LR 24.

[16] [2001] 4 All ER 666, [2002] RPC 235.

[17] See P. Masuyakurima (2004) 'Fair dealing and freedom of expression', in P. Torremans (ed.) *Copyright and Human Rights*, London: Kluwer Law International.

[18] *Ashdown v. Telegraph Group Ltd* [2001] 4 All ER 666, [2002] RPC 235.

Copyright not enforced in the public interest

The public interest defence can be used to punish anyone who acts against the public interest and who has a copyright interest that results from that act. The public interest concept will allow the courts in such a case not to enforce that copyright and infringers will no longer be liable for copyright infringement.

The concept was applied in this way in the *Spycatcher* case.[19] The House of Lords held that the book's author, Peter Wright, had acted against the public interest in revealing details about the operations of the secret service, because it is in the public interest that the operations of the nation's secret service are kept secret. His conduct could harm national security. The courts in this country would, as a result—or perhaps as a punishment—not enforce the copyright in his book *Spycatcher*.[20] In terms of the facts of the case, everyone was free to publish substantial extracts from the book without being liable for copyright infringement.

The rule can be phrased in a slightly wider way. The public interest can also be used to back positive action, rather than purely negative non-enforcement. It can be said that it is against the public interest that a convicted criminal should benefit from his or her crime and that he or she should therefore not be allowed to receive, or retain, profit directly derived from the commission of the crime. Copyright royalties for the publication of a book in which the crime is described should therefore not be paid to the offender and the courts are authorized to use the public interest principle to grant an injunction to that extent (upon the application of the Attorney-General).[21]

Alleged infringement is not relevant

Alleged infringement of copyright by the plaintiff does not, however, warrant the operation of the public interest principle. In this case, the private interest of a copyright holder is at stake, rather than the public interest. The (alleged) infringement of the copyright of a third party by the plaintiff, when he or she made the adaptation of the original work, is therefore not a public interest defence to the infringement of the plaintiff's copyright by the defendant's arrangement of a further adaptation of that first adaptation.[22] If the concept of originality is satisfied, the author of the first adaptation will receive copyright in it, notwithstanding the fact that he or she may, at the same time, have infringed the copyright in the original work.[23] Any damages for copyright infringement that the plaintiff recovers from the author of the second adaptation will have to be shared with the author of the original work.[24]

The concept of public interest needs, therefore, to be described narrowly.

The Copyright (Visually Impaired Persons) Act 2002

New legislation has been put in place in the form of the Copyright (Visually Impaired Persons) Act 2002 to address the specific problems that are faced by visually impaired persons. This instrument allows the copying in large fonts—or in any other way that is

[19] *A-G v. Guardian Newspapers Ltd (No. 2)* [1990] 1 AC 109, [1988] 3 All ER 545; see also *A-G v. Times Newspapers Ltd* [1992] 1 AC 191, [1991] 2 All ER 398.
[20] *A-G v. Guardian Newspapers Ltd (No. 2)* [1990] 1 AC 109, [1988] 3 All ER 545.
[21] See *A-G v. Chaudry* [1971] 3 All ER 938, [1971] 1 WLR 1614; *A-G v. Blake (Jonathan Cape Ltd, third party)* [1998] Ch 439, [1998] 1 All ER 833.
[22] *ZYX Music GmbH v. King* [1995] 3 All ER 1.
[23] See also *Redwood Music Ltd v. Chappell & Co. Ltd* [1982] RPC 109 at 120.
[24] *ZYX Music GmbH v. King* [1995] 3 All ER 1.

necessary to make the work accessible—of copyright material to assist visually impaired people on the basis of a lawfully obtained copy of the work. This will no longer infringe copyright. The exception applies to literary, dramatic, musical, or artistic works, or to a published edition, in so far as the copyright owner has not made accessible formats of the work available on a commercial basis. On each occasion, a statement that the exception is used is a sufficient acknowledgment. Third persons can only make such copies for a visually impaired person if the amount that they charge for that service does not exceed the cost of making and supplying the copy.

The Act allows for the making of single copies for personal use,[25] as well as for the making of multiple copies by approved bodies.[26] In the latter case, commercial publication of the work copied is a precondition and the exception can also be replaced by a licensing scheme.[27]

The making of temporary copies

The implementation of the Information Society Directive[28] by the Copyright and Related Rights Regulations 2003, and the changes to the 1988 Act that resulted from it, have removed any remaining doubts about the fact that even temporary copies infringe copyright. Modern digital technology, such as computers accessing the Internet, makes frequent use of such temporary copies to access works and declaring any such use an infringement was therefore an unduly blunt tool. The solution was the creation of a new s. 28A[29] of the 1988 Act, in which an exemption for temporary reproduction is contained. According to its wording, copyright in a literary work—other than a computer program or a database—or in a dramatic, musical, or artistic work, the typographical arrangement of a published edition, a sound recording, or a film, is not infringed by the making of a temporary copy that is transient or incidental, that is an integral and essential part of a technological process, and the sole purpose of which is to enable a transmission of the work in a network between third parties by an intermediary; or a lawful use of the work, and which has no independent economic significance. Only those temporary copies that meet all of these requirements will benefit from the exemption.

This exception is of particular benefit to Internet service providers, which will escape liability for activities such as caching.

Fair dealing

The Act allows 'fair dealing' with the work that attracts copyright. This means, roughly, that there will be no copyright infringement if the use made of the work is fair. The defence only becomes relevant when the part taken from the work is substantial; otherwise no copying arises in the first place and any defence is without purpose.[30]

---

[25] CDPA 1988, s. 31A, inserted by Copyright (Visually Impaired Persons) Act 2002, s. 1.
[26] CDPA 1988, s. 31B, inserted by Copyright (Visually Impaired Persons) Act 2002, s. 2.
[27] CDPA 1988, s. 31D, inserted by Copyright (Visually Impaired Persons) Act 2002, s. 4.
[28] European Parliament and Council Directive 2001/29/EC on the harmonization of certain aspects of copyright and related rights in the information society [2001] OJ L 167/10.
[29] Inserted by Copyright and Related Rights Regulations 2003, reg. 8.
[30] Contra, but with respect, arguably wrong. *'Indeed once the conclusion is reached that the whole or a substantial part of the copyright work has been taken, a defence under (the fair dealing provisions) is unlikely to*

The fairness issue will have to be determined by the judge, taking into account all circumstances of the case. The Act provides no definition, but restricts the defence to fair use for a number of purposes. In *Hubbard v. Vosper*,[31] a case on fair dealing for the purposes of review and criticism, Lord Denning described the scope of the fair dealing defence and how a judge should assess it when he said:

> You must first consider the number and the extent of the quotations...Then you must consider the use made of them. If they are used as a basis of comment, criticism or review, that may be fair dealing. If they are used to convey the same information as the author, for a rival purpose, they may be unfair. Next you must consider the proportions. To take long extracts and attach short comments may be unfair. But short extracts and long comments may be fair. Other considerations may come to mind also. But...it must be a matter of impression.[32]

There is no reason to restrict the scope of this quote to one particular type of fair dealing; it applies to fair dealing in general.

A number of factors are extremely important in the assessment.

- For which purpose was a substantial part of the work copied? The degree to which the challenged use competes with the exploitation of the copyright by its owner will be an important consideration.[33]

- What is the proportion of the copied part in relation to the whole work? The relevance of this extent of use will, however, depend very much on the particular circumstances of the case.[34]

- What motive led to the copying? If the motive was to compete with the original work, this is likely to make the dealing with the work unfair and the defence unavailable.[35]

- And finally, what is the status of the work from which a substantial part is copied? If that work is not published or confidential, the defence is unlikely to succeed;[36] the same conclusion is reached in case of a 'leak'.[37]

Although a number of quantitative elements are taken into account, the final assessment will be qualitative in nature. In practice, this means that, depending upon the circumstances of the case, the fair dealing defence may be unavailable for someone who copies only marginally more than the minimal substantial part of a work, or may be available, in the other extreme case, to someone who copies almost the whole work.

In the end, then, '*the court must judge the fairness by the objective standard of whether a fair-minded and honest person would have dealt with the copyright, in the manner that* [the alleged infringer] *did*'.[38]

---

succeed': *Independent Television Publications Ltd v. Time Out Ltd* [1984] FSR 64, *per* Whitford J at 75. In this view, the defence would justify only insubstantial copying, but insubstantial copying is no infringement. It cannot be accepted that Parliament included a useless and unneeded defence in the 1988 Act.

[31] [1972] 2 QB 84, [1972] 1 All ER 1023.

[32] Ibid., *per* Lord Denning MR at 94.

[33] *Pro Sieben Media AG v. Carlton UK Television Ltd* [1999] 1 WLR 605, [1999] FSR 610, *per* Robert Walker LJ at 619.

[34] Ibid.

[35] *Wheatherby & Sons Ltd v. International Horse Agency & Exchange Ltd* [1910] 2 Ch 297.

[36] *Hyde Park Residence Ltd v. Yelland* [2000] 3 WLR 215, *per* Aldous LJ at 158. Article 5(3)(d) of the Information Society Directive even makes the fact that the work must already have been made available lawfully to the public a prerequisite for the existence of the defence.

[37] *British Oxygen Co. Ltd v. Liquid Air Ltd* [1925] Ch 383; *Beloff v. Pressdram Ltd* [1973] 1 All ER 241, [1973] FSR 33.

[38] *Hyde Park Residence Ltd v. Yelland* [2000] 3 WLR 215, *per* Aldous LJ at 158.

Research and private study

Fair dealing with a work may be for the purposes of research and private study.[39] This defence applies, first of all, to substantial copying in relation to literary, dramatic, musical, and artistic works.[40] It will allow me to copy a passage of a book on the history of Crete by hand, but a problem may arise if I use a photocopier to make the copy, because the typographical arrangement will be copied as well. Therefore, the defence applies also to typographical arrangements. This becomes particularly relevant in cases in which the work as such is out of copyright, but the typographical arrangement is not. There will be no infringement through the fair dealing with the published edition, indirectly affecting the copyright in the typographical arrangement, nor will there be infringement through fair dealing with the typographical arrangement itself.[41]

Research

The 1988 Act distinguishes between fair use for the purposes of research, on the one hand, and fair dealing for the purposes of private study, on the other. Fair dealing with a literary, dramatic, musical, or artistic work for the purposes of research for a non-commercial purpose does not infringe any copyright in the work, provided that it is accompanied by a sufficient acknowledgment.[42] The key points to note are the exclusion of research for a commercial purpose and the need for an acknowledgment—but no acknowledgment is required in connection with fair dealing for the purposes of research if this would be impossible for reasons of practicality or otherwise.

The exclusion of research for commercial purposes is not entirely straightforward either. There is, of course, the obvious problem of defining research. Research may be said to be scientific by definition, and to involve a diligent and systematic enquiry or investigation of a particular subject, but the Act does not contain a precise definition. In addition, there is the problem that non-commercial academic research may, sooner or later, feed directly or indirectly into a commercial (scientific) publication. Would that make the original research commercial in nature? Or does the commercial nature of the research depend, to a large extent, on the environment in which it is carried out? Research by commercial entities such as companies would then, by definition, be commercial in nature, while academic research would be non-commercial (except, perhaps, for contract research). Sooner or later, the courts will have to provide clarification on this point.

In summary, the fair dealing exception for the purposes of research is subject to four conditions:

- there must be fair use;
- the use must be for the purposes of research;
- the research must be non-commercial;
- there must be a sufficient acknowledgment of the source of the material that has been used.

Private study

Fair dealing with a literary, dramatic, musical, or artistic work for the purposes of private study does not infringe any copyright in the work either.[43] In relation to private study,

---

[39] CDPA 1988, s. 29.
[40] Ibid., (1) and (1C), inserted by Copyright and Related Rights Regulations 2003, reg. 9.
[41] CDPA 1988, s. 29(2).
[42] Ibid., (1), inserted by Copyright and Related Rights Regulations 2003, reg. 9.
[43] Ibid., (1C), inserted by Copyright and Related Rights Regulations 2003, reg. 9.

there appear to be only two conditions—that is, fair use and use for the purposes of private study—but, in fact, there are three. Private study was always deemed to be non-commercial and this has now been made explicit in s. 178 of the 1988 Act, where the definition of private study excludes any form of study that is either directly or indirectly undertaken for a commercial purpose. There is, however, no need for an acknowledgment.

The publication in breach of copyright of a student textbook was held not to be fair dealing for the purposes of research and private study.[44] This book involved substantial copying to facilitate someone else's research and private study, the defendant itself not being involved in research or private study. This does not mean that the researcher or student has to make his or her own copies, but the person who makes the copies should not know, or have reason to believe, that the copying will result in copies of substantially the same material being provided to more than one person at substantially the same time and for substantially the same purpose.[45]

How much can be taken?

It is submitted that even the copying of a fairly large part of a work can amount to fair dealing with the work for the purposes of research and private study. Very large parts of books and, eventually, whole articles may be copied if the number of them needed for one's research and private study, in combination with the limited direct use of the information contained in them for the purposes of that research and private study, makes it impracticable to buy all of the books and to subscribe to all of the periodicals containing these articles. The situation will be entirely different when one book is used and a photocopy is made even though it would still be possible to buy a copy of the book (at a slightly higher price). In the latter case, the dealing with the book would be unfair.

The defence clearly aims to facilitate research and private study. Copyright should not become a financial and practical factor obstructing research and private study. There needs to be a balance between the interests of copyright owners and society in the good functioning of the copyright system, and the interest of society in the development, by means of the research and private study, of its members.

Computer programs

The observation, study, or testing of the functioning of a computer in order to determine the ideas and principles underlying the program will not amount to fair dealing. This exclusion is a logical one, because s. 50BA of the 1988 Act deals with this specific issue.[46]

Review and criticism

The starting point

Fair dealing, for the purpose of review and criticism, applies to any form of work or to a performance of a work.[47] Copyright will not be infringed if a sufficient acknowledgment[48]—comprising the title, or another description, of the work and the

---

[44] *Sillitoe v. McGraw-Hill Book Co. (UK) Ltd* [1983] FSR 545.

[45] CDPA 1988, s. 29(3).

[46] Ibid., (4A), inserted by Copyright and Related Rights Regulations 2003, reg. 9.

[47] Ibid., s. 30(1). The issue of ownership of the work is entirely irrelevant: see *Hyde Park Residence Ltd v. Yelland* [2001] Ch 143, *per* Aldous LJ at 158.

[48] See *Sillitoe v. McGraw-Hill Book Co. (UK) Ltd* [1983] FSR 545.

identification of the author—is given.[49] The identification has to be to the audience and any wording or other indication that would make the reasonably alert member of the audience realize that the person that is identified is the author of the work will be sufficient.[50] The presence of the logo of the television company on the screen when borrowed images were shown was sufficient in this respect, because the majority of viewers would be able to identify the author in this way.[51]

The bottom line seems therefore to be that there needs to be sufficient acknowledgment, even if it does not amount to express identification.[52] It is fair to deal with one work in order to criticize another work or a performance of the work. There is no requirement that parts of only the work that is reviewed or criticized should be used; this book can be reviewed or criticized using parts and quotes from other textbooks on intellectual property. There is, however, a requirement that the dealing with a work should be for the purposes of review and criticism, whether of the subject matter of the work or of its style. Criticism of the work may extend to the ideas found in the work, but the defence does not cover those cases in which only ideas, doctrine, philosophy, and events are criticized.

Pro Sieben

Laddie J repeated this in the *Pro Sieben* case[53] when he ruled that:

> The Act does not provide a general defence to the effect that it is permissible to fairly deal in any copyright work for the purpose of criticizing or reviewing that work or anything else[;] the defence is limited to criticizing or reviewing that or another work or a performance of a work.[54]

In *Pro Sieben*, the plaintiffs, Pro Sieben, had conducted an interview with Mandy Allwood and her boyfriend about Ms Allwood's decision to carry on with her pregnancy after it had been revealed that she was carrying eight live embryos, and a television programme had resulted from this. The defendants copied parts of the German programme and included it in one of their own programmes. It was held, in the High Court, that the defendants could not rely on the fair dealing defence to justify their copying, because their programme did not criticize or review the Pro Sieben programme, but rather Pro Sieben's decision to pay for an interview.

The Court of Appeal later overturned that decision and held that the Carlton programme was criticizing various works representing the fruits of chequebook journalism, of which the allegedly copied work was only one example. In that context, there was reason to allow the application of the fair dealing defence. Indeed, fair dealing refers to the true purpose of the allegedly infringing activity in the sense of its good faith, intention, and genuineness. The Court held that, in this case, the programme incorporating the infringing material was a genuine piece of criticism or review, rather than an attempt to dress ordinary copyright infringement up as criticism; in the latter case, the defence should not apply. One should be careful, however, not to rely solely on the intentions and motives of the alleged infringer. The notion that all that is required is for the alleged

---

[49] Ibid.; see also CDPA 1988, s. 178. There is no need to include the name of the author if the work is published anonymously (see *PCR Ltd v. Dow Jones Telerate Ltd* [1998] FSR 170) or if the name of the author cannot be ascertained by reasonable enquiry.

[50] *Pro Sieben Media AG v. Carlton UK Television Ltd* [1998] FSR 43.

[51] *Pro Sieben Media AG v. Carlton UK Television Ltd* [1999] 1 WLR 605, [1999] FSR 610, *per* Robert Walker LJ at 625.

[52] It all comes down to a matter of fact: *Fraser-Woodward v. BBC* [2005] EMLR 22, [2005] FSR 35

[53] *Pro Sieben Media AG v. Carlton UK Television Ltd* [1999] 1 WLR 605, [1999] FSR 610.

[54] Ibid., *per* Robert Walker LJ at 625.

infringer to have the sincere belief, however misguided, that he or she is criticizing a work should not be encouraged. It is therefore better to construe the phrase for the purposes of review and criticism as a whole, and to treat it as the equivalent of making use of the work in the context of review and criticism.[55]

Once it has been established that proper criticism is at stake, that criticism should not be limited to criticism of style. The ideas that are found in the work and its social or moral implications can also be criticized. Carlton could therefore use the extracts of the Pro Sieben programme to criticize chequebook journalism and its consequences.[56] In finding that Carlton's action were covered by the fair dealing doctrine, the Court of Appeal also attached importance to the fact there was no unfair competition with the copied work.[57]

Fraser-Woodward

The unauthorized use of photographs of David and Victoria Beckham, and their family, in a British Broadcasting Corporation (BBC) programme about celebrity journalism, and the links between the press and celebrities, provided an interesting factual background for a further analysis of the exemption for fair dealing for the purposes of review and criticism in *Fraser-Woodward Ltd v. BBC*.[58]

The court dealt, first of all, with the concepts of review and criticism. 'Criticism or review' was held to be n expression of wide and indefinite scope that was to be interpreted liberally. It is therefore not possible to define the boundaries of the expression precisely, and it is therefore not helpful to attempt to draw a distinction between bare comment and something that went further into criticism.[59] More importantly, criticism or review of the photographs could also extend to the philosophy or ideas underlying them, including the ideas or philosophy underlying a certain style of journalism, as manifested in the works themselves. But one should not confine the notion of ideas and philosophy narrowly, or see it in a strictly scientific sense: ideas and philosophy are merely a formulation of the extent to which criticism might extend. That review or criticism can be concerned with another work: in this case, the works of celebrity journalism.

In relation to the facts in *Fraser-Woodward*, this meant that the programme contained frequent shots of newspapers, their mastheads and stories, as well as pictures showing the public presentation of the Beckhams. All of the material was there to demonstrate a certain style of journalism—namely, the coverage of celebrity—and to comment on that style as manifested in the relevant publications. Various points were made about the fact that certain celebrity items were covered at all on the grounds of newsworthiness, the manipulation by the Beckhams of media interest in their lives, the extent of coverage, and the extent to which rival publications covered or disdained celebrity stories. Most photographs were used in that critical context and in order to illustrate the themes of the programme. Accordingly, these photographs were deployed in the context, and for the purpose, of criticism or review of other works—namely, the tabloid press and magazines. As such, the defence was deployed successfully.

Banier

Many of these factors were missing in another case[60] and therefore, when *The Sun* newspaper copied and published a photograph of Princess Caroline of Monaco without having

[55] Ibid., at 620.
[56] Ibid.
[57] Ibid., at 624.
[58] *Fraser-Woodward v. BBC* [2005] EMLR 22, [2005] FSR 35.
[59] Ibid.; see also *IPC Media Ltd v. News Group Newspapers Ltd* [2005] EMLR 23.
[60] *Banier v. News Group Newspapers Ltd* [1997] FSR 812.

obtained the prior authorization of the photographer, Mr Banier, it could not successfully invoke the defence. The photograph was not used to illustrate any review or criticism of the copyright work—that is, the photograph itself; it was plain copying and competing use, with an attempt to disguise it as review and criticism.

Factors to be taken into account

The aim of the defence is to give a critic or a reviewer a reasonable freedom of quotation or copying for the purpose of criticism or review. This means, as indicated above, that one has to take into account the state of the reviewer or critic's mind at the time of the alleged infringement, but that one should also consider the likely impact on the audience.[61] The dealing with the work must also be fair, even in those cases in which the reviewer or critic had the right state of mind, in that he or she intended to deal with the work for the purposes of review or criticism. This does not mean that the judge should decide whether the criticism or the review is fair, but it does mean that the extent of the copying must be fair, in all of the circumstances, to support or illustrate the criticisms or the review.

The dealing or copying must be directed at supporting or illustrating the review or criticism; the defence cannot justify any other dealing with the work or any dealing with the work that goes further. Copying with the main aim of advancing one's own competing purposes therefore falls outside the scope of the defence, even if it is accompanied by some review or criticism.[62] The examination of this point should not, however, involve a requirement for the defendant to demonstrate that no alternative way of reviewing or criticizing the work was available.[63] There is no requirement of necessity and it is irrelevant that the criticism or review might have been achieved without use of the copyright work as long as the requirement of fair dealing is met.[64]

Thus this defence will not apply in cases of copying in which there is neither review nor criticism, or in which there is only review and criticism to a minimal extent. It is not fair dealing with the correspondence between the Duke and Duchess of Windsor when extracts are published without review or criticism.[65] The defence covers any type of review or criticism, from the most polite and laudatory forms, to the most scathing—or, in the words of Robert Walker LJ:[66]

> If the fair dealing is for the purpose of criticism that criticism may be strongly expressed and unbalanced without forfeiting the fair dealing defence; an author's remedy for malicious and unjustified criticism lies (if it lies anywhere) in the law of defamation, not copyright.

How much can be taken?

If the defence is to have any proper value, it has to apply to cases in which the review and criticism involve a substantial part of a work. In *Hubbard v. Vosper*,[67] substantial parts of confidential, as well as non-confidential, works—such as books and letters—written by the plaintiff were used in a book written by the defendant who was an ex-member of the Church of Scientology. The book was highly critical of the movement, and reviewed and criticized its views. The defence of fair use for the purpose of review and criticism was raised successfully against the alleged copyright infringement. The proportion of the work

---

[61] *Pro Sieben Media AG v. Carlton UK Television Ltd* [1999] 1 WLR 605, [1999] FSR 610, *per* Robert Walker LJ at 622.

[62] *IPC Media Ltd v. News Group Newspapers Ltd* [2005] FSR 35; [2005] EMLR 23.

[63] *Pro Sieben Media AG v. Carlton UK Television Ltd* [1998] FSR 43.

[64] *Fraser-Woodward v. BBC* [2005] EMLR 22, [2005] FSR 35.

[65] *Associated Newspapers Group plc v. News Group Newspapers Ltd* [1986] RPC 515.

[66] *Pro Sieben Media AG v. Carlton UK Television Ltd* [1999] FSR 610, at 619.

[67] [1972] 2 QB 84, [1972] 1 All ER 1023.

that can be taken may be large, but review and criticism do not require such large amounts of the work to be taken as what is possible for the purpose of research and private study.[68]

Recently, further clarification on this point was provided by *Time Warner v. Channel 4.*[69] Channel 4 wished to use fragments from Stanley Kubrick's notorious film *A Clockwork Orange* in an arts documentary. Time Warner had withdrawn the film from British cinemas twenty years ago at the request of the director himself and was not prepared to give Channel 4 a licence to show the fragments. When Channel 4 proceeded without a licence, Time Warner obtained an injunction, which was lifted by the Court of Appeal, which accepted that Channel 4 was engaging in fair dealing for the purpose of the review and criticism defence.

In this case, the fragments shown by Channel 4 amounted to almost 10 per cent of the film. It is submitted that this high percentage of allowed copying under the defence was reached because of the very large amount, and high quality, of review and criticism equally included in the programme, and the fact that a documentary is particularly suited for review and criticism. But it gives an impression of how far-reaching the defence can potentially be.

A work that is available to the public

Fair dealing for the purposes of review and criticism is, however, limited in one important way:[70] the work that is used must previously have been made available to the public. Any infringement for criticism, review, and news reporting will therefore only be exempted if the work used has previously been made available to the public.[71]

A work has been made available to the public if it has been made available by any means, including the issue of copies to the public, an electronic retrieval system, the rental or lending of copies of the work to the public, the performance, exhibition, playing, or showing of the work in public, and the communication to the public of the work; in determining generally whether a work has been made available to the public, no account shall be taken of any unauthorized act.[72]

A summary of conditions

In summary, four conditions need to be met for the exception of fair dealing for the purpose of review and criticism to apply.

1. The use has to be fair.
2. The use must be for the purposes of review and criticism.
3. There must be a sufficient acknowledgment.
4. The work must have been made available to the public.

The concept of fairness is itself linked to certain requirements that were set out by Mann J in *Fraser-Woodward*.

1. Regard should be had to the motives of the user.
2. Fair dealing is a matter of impression.

---

[68] See *Hubbard v. Vosper* [1972] 2 QB 84, [1972] 1 All ER 1023; *Walter v. Steinkopff* [1892] 3 Ch 489.

[69] *Time Warner Entertainments Co. v. Channel 4 Television plc* (1993) The Independent, 23 October, [1994] EMLR 1 (CA).

[70] CDPA 1988, s. 30, as amended by Copyright and Related Rights Regulations 2003, reg. 10.

[71] Because the diaries of the Prince of Wales had not previously been made available to the public, the defence failed in *HRH Prince of Wales v. Associated Newspapers Ltd* [2006] ECDR 20, upheld on appeal [2007] 3 WLR 222.

[72] CDPA 1988, s. 30(1A).

3. The amount of the work used is relevant and excessive use could render the use of the work unfair.

4. The court can have regard to the purpose of the use to determine whether it is a genuine piece of review or criticism or something else.[73]

Finally, the three-step test found in the international treaties and the Information Society Directive comes into play. Indeed, irrespective of the factors mentioned above, the use should not unreasonably prejudice the legitimate interests of the author or conflict with the author's normal exploitation of the work. It follows that risk to the commercial value of the copyright of the work involved might go towards demonstrating unfairness, even if no damage or risk makes any use of the material unfair.[74] The three-step test is not a separate requirement, but it is clearly part of any determination of fairness.

Reporting current events

The defence includes fair dealing with a work in order to report current events. Copyright will not be infringed unless the work is a photograph. Newspapers quite often copy stories that were published 24 hours earlier by another newspaper. The defence covers this, but, without copyright permission, they will not be able to copy the photograph accompanying the story. A sufficient acknowledgment is required.[75] Due to practical problems and the speed at which these media work, an acknowledgment is not required in connection with the reporting of current events by means of a sound recording, film, or broadcast, of this would be impossible for reasons of practicality or otherwise.[76]

It is hard to understand why the special treatment accorded to photographs should not be applied to broadcasts and films. The definition of the concept of 'current events' is an important issue in this respect. That concept must include all matters of current interest or concern,[77] as opposed to matters of historical interest or concern. On top of that, the concept should be construed liberally and the fair use of copyright material cannot be restricted, for example, to the reporting of news events that are less than 24 hours old.[78]

In a case in which the defendant copied substantial parts of the plaintiff's reports of the current status of cacao crops around the world,[79] the defendant could argue that the following points came within the concept of current events:

- the fact that the reports had been published;
- the broad substance of the reports;
- the impact of the reports on the market.

The defendant could copy parts of the reports to report these issues, but, once more, the nature and the extent of the copying should not go beyond what is reasonable and appropriate to report these current events.[80]

---

[73] *Fraser-Woodward v. BBC* [2005] EMLR 22, [2005] FSR 35.

[74] Ibid.; see also *IPC Media Ltd v. News Group Newspapers Ltd* [2005] EMLR 23, in which it was held that the issue of whether the work was commercially competing with the exploitation of the copyright work was the most important factor in assessing fair dealing.

[75] CDPA 1988, s. 30(2).

[76] Ibid., (3), as amended by Copyright and Related Rights Regulations 2003, reg. 10; see also *BBC v. British Satellite Broadcasting Ltd* [1992] Ch 141, [1991] 3 All ER 833.

[77] See *Pro Sieben Media AG v. Carlton UK Television Ltd* [1999] 1 WLR 605, [1999] FSR 610, *per* Robert Walker LJ at 625.

[78] *Pro Sieben Media AG v. Carlton UK Television Ltd* [1998] FSR 43.

[79] *PCR Ltd v. Dow Jones Telerate Ltd* [1998] FSR 170.

[80] See *Hyde Park Residence Ltd v. Yelland* [2001] Ch 143.

This last decision is ultimately one of impression. In the *Cacoa Reports* case, it was held that the copying of the full pod-count report went beyond what is fair dealing to report the current events as described above. In this case, the concept of fair dealing involved a balancing of the interests of the owner of the copyright and those of the news reporter.[81]

Incidental inclusion

When a foreign tourist visits London and takes some photographs, it is almost inevitable that at least one of the photographs will include a work protected by copyright, such as a building, an artistic work, or simply the front page of a newspaper. The same applies when a television news crew films a demonstration in the City and the report is broadcast. It is not feasible to require that, on each of these occasions, copyright permission is obtained in advance or it would be impossible to make these photographs, films, and broadcasts. The 1988 Act gets around this problem by introducing a rule that copyright in a work that is accidentally included in an artistic work, a sound recording, a film, or a broadcast will not be infringed.[82]

Subsequent dealings with the work in which another work was accidentally included are also exempted.[83] Copies can be issued to the public, the work can be shown or played, or it can be broadcast. The film made in the City can be broadcast without infringing indirectly the copyright in the works accidentally included in it. But the inclusion must be accidental: this defence will not be available if a work is included deliberately. If we go back to our news crew, they may decide to add some background music to the soundtrack of the film. The background music will not be included accidentally and, if the copying through the inclusion is substantial, copyright in the musical work will be infringed if no advance copyright permission was obtained.

This rule applies to all musical works, lyrics, and all works embodying them.[84] In *Hawkes & Sons (London) Ltd v. Paramount Film Service Ltd*,[85] copyright infringement took place and the accidental inclusion defence did not apply, because the 28 bars of the march 'Colonel Bogey' were included deliberately in the newsreel as background music. The outcome of the case would have been different if the newsreel's topic had been a parade by a band playing the march. Then, the inclusion of part of the march—recorded live during the parade together with the images—would have been accidental.

The Court of Appeal handed down a major judgment interpreting the scope of this defence to copyright infringement in *Football Association Premier League Ltd v. Panini UK Ltd*.[86] Panini had reproduced, without the permission of the claimant, photographs of football players. These included the logos of the football clubs and of the Premier League, in which the claimants claimed copyright. Panini argued that the logos had been included incidentally. A first important point mentioned by the Court of Appeal is that incidental inclusion does not rule out that the work is included in its entirety and is therefore not limited to partial inclusion. More importantly, though, the Court of Appeal ruled that one must look at all of the circumstances in which the derivative work has been created and the reasons why, in that context, the copyright work has been included. This evaluation

[81] CDPA 1988, s. 36A.
[82] Ibid., s. 31(1).
[83] Ibid., (2).
[84] Ibid., (3).
[85] [1934] Ch 593.
[86] [2003] 4 All ER 1290, [2004] FSR 1.

can include aesthetic, as well as commercial, motives, but the incidental inclusion can hardly be defended on aesthetic grounds if the decision to include the work was based on commercial motives. In the case at issue, commercial motives had prevailed, because players pictured in their club outfits would probably enhance sales. The conclusion was, therefore, that the inclusion was, from this point of view, essential to success from an economic point of view and could therefore not be characterized as incidental.[87]

Educational use[88]

Instruction and examination

Copyright will not be infringed if a literary, dramatic, artistic, or musical work, or a substantial part of any of them, is copied in the course of instruction or while preparing instruction if four preconditions are met. The first two preconditions are that the person giving instruction or the person receiving instruction must do the copying and that it may not be done by means of a reprographic process.[89] When a student writes down a substantial part of a legal article in his or her essay in support of his or her own point of view, for example, copyright in the article as a literary work will not be infringed. Neither will it be infringed when a lecturer writes down the same quote on his or her whiteboard, for discussion with the students during a tutorial.

The two further preconditions are that the instruction must be carried out for a non-commercial purpose and that, where practicable, an acknowledgment of the source is required. On top of that, the copying of any literary, dramatic, artistic, or musical work that has previously been made available to the public must also meet the fair dealing requirements.[90]

In the same circumstances, copies of a sound recording, a film, or a broadcast can be made in making a film or soundtrack for the purpose of instruction, without infringing copyright.[91]

In an exam situation, copyright will not be infringed by anything done in setting the questions, communicating them to the students, or answering them. But, even in an examination context, an acknowledgment is required.[92] The question can thus contain a large quote taken from a literary work before asking students to analyse it and comment on it. The only exception to this rule is the making of reprographical copies of a musical work that is to be performed by the students during the examination.[93] In this case, copyright permission is required.

This educational exception does not cover any subsequent dealings in the copies made for educational use. Copyright will be infringed when they are sold, let for hire, or offered or exposed for sale or hire.[94] A poem may be copied for the purpose of setting an exam question, but the subsequent sale of the exam paper containing the poem will infringe the copyright in the poem.

---

[87] See also *Fraser-Woodward v. BBC* [2005] EMLR 22, [2005] FSR 35.

[88] See Copyright (Educational Establishments) (No. 2) Order 1989.

[89] CDPA 1988, s. 32(1).

[90] Ibid. These extra requirements have been inserted by Copyright and Related Rights Regulations 2003, reg. 11.

[91] CDPA 1988, s. 32(2), as amended by Copyright and Related Rights Regulations 2003, reg. 11. Obviously, the conditions that no reprographic means can be used does not apply here.

[92] Ibid., (3).

[93] Ibid., (4).

[94] Ibid., (5).

Anthologies

Short passages of published literary and dramatic works may be included in a book that consists of a collection of passages, mainly taken from works that are not, or no longer, protected by copyright. The book—known as an anthology—has to be clearly intended for educational use.[95]

Performing, playing, or showing a work

Literary, dramatic, and musical works can be shown, played, or performed at an educational establishment without infringing copyright. This can either be done by the students and teachers, in the course of the activities of the educational establishment, or by a third person, in the course of instruction. Students, teachers, and other persons directly connected with the activities of the establishment may form part of the audience,[96] but parents and any other persons that are only connected indirectly to the activities of the educational establishment may not.[97] School plays to which parents are invited will require copyright permission to perform the work.

Neither will copyright will not be infringed if a sound recording, film, or broadcast is played or shown before a similar audience, as long as the event takes place at the educational institution for the purposes of instruction.[98]

Recording, reprographic copying,[99] and lending

An educational establishment[100] may record, for educational purposes and for its own use, broadcasts.[101] Under the same preconditions, it can copy reprographically—in practice, with a photocopier—passages of published works. The latter copying is restricted to 1 per cent of each work per term.[102]

If the educational institution stays within the framework of these two exceptions, copyright in the recorded or copied works will not be infringed. But these two exceptions have two further aspects in common. Copyright will be infringed if the authorized recordings and copies are subsequently dealt with, and both exceptions can, in practice, be superseded by a licensing scheme allowing the educational institutions to make recordings and reprographic copies subject to certain conditions.[103]

There is also a special exception to the lending right of copyright owners. Lending of copies of the work by an educational establishment[104] will not infringe the copyright in

---

[95] Ibid., s. 33(1).
[96] Ibid., s. 34(1).
[97] Ibid., (3).
[98] Ibid., (2).
[99] See Copyright (Certification of Licensing Scheme for Educational Recording of Broadcast and Cable Programmes) (Educational Recording Agency Limited) Order 1990, SI 1990/879; Copyright (Certification of Licensing Scheme for Educational Recording of Broadcast and Cable Programmes) (Educational Recording Agency Limited) (Amendment) Order 1993, SI 1993/193; Copyright (Certification of Licensing Scheme for Educational Recording of Broadcasts) (Open University Educational Enterprises Limited) Order 1993, SI 1993/2755; Copyright (Certification of Licensing Scheme for Educational Recording of Broadcast and Cable Programmes) (Educational Recording Agency Limited) (Amendment) Order 1994, SI 1994/247.
[100] As defined in CDPA 1988, s. 174.
[101] Ibid., s. 35(1).
[102] Ibid., s. 36(1) and (2).
[103] Ibid., ss. 35 and 36.
[104] Ibid.

the work. As a result of the implementation of the Information Society Directive, ss. 35 and 36[105] of the 1988 Act—that is, the sections with which we are concerned in relation to this area—have seen the introduction of the requirements that instruction and education for commercial purposes falls outside the scope of the exemptions, and that, wherever practicable, an acknowledgment is required. The broadcast that has been recorded can now also explicitly be communicated to the public, albeit strictly within the borders of the educational establishment concerned.

Libraries, archives, and public administration

Further exceptions to copyright infringement are provided for the benefit of libraries, archives, and public administration.[106] We will only refer generally to a couple of these detailed exceptions; none of the acts specified in the following will give rise to copyright infringement.

The exceptions for libraries and archives only apply to those libraries and archives that are prescribed by statutory instrument.[107] A librarian can make one copy of an article in a periodical for a person who requires it for the purposes of non-commercial research and private study. It is essential that no person is supplied with more than one copy of the article at the same time[108] and that not more than one article from the same issue of the periodical is supplied.[109] Under the same conditions, librarians can copy part of a published edition of a literary, dramatic, or musical work.[110] The person supplied with the copies must pay the costs. The readers of this book will all be familiar with the system of interlibrary loans, and will recognize the legal basis for this system and the particular format of the copyright declaration accompanying them. The librarian or archivist may rely on the contents of that declaration: if the declaration is false, the person making the declaration will have infringed the copyright in the work of which he or she obtained copies, as if he or she made them him or herself, and the copies will be infringing copies.

The lending of copies of a work by libraries or archives is also subject to a special regime.[111] The copyright in any work is not infringed by the lending of a book that is within the public lending right scheme if the lending takes place through a public library; neither is copyright in a work infringed through the lending of copies of the work by a prescribed library or archive[112] if that lending is not conducted for profit.

Librarians can also supply each other with copies of articles in periodicals or, if the identity of the person who can authorize the copying is unknown and cannot be ascertained by reasonable enquiry, the whole or part of a published edition of a literary, dramatic, or musical work.[113] Copies can also be made to replace copies of works that have been lost, destroyed, or damaged, or to preserve the original.[114] The latter will only be possible if it is not reasonably practicable to buy another copy of the work.[115]

---

[105] As amended by Copyright and Related Rights Regulations 2003, regs 12 and 13.
[106] CDPA 1988, ss. 37–50.
[107] See Copyright (Librarian Archivists) (Copying of Copyright Material) Regulations 1989, SI 1989/1212.
[108] Multiple copies are banned by the Act.
[109] CDPA 1988, s. 38.
[110] Ibid., s. 39.
[111] Ibid., s. 40A.
[112] Other than a public library.
[113] CDPA 1988, s. 41.
[114] Which may be particularly valuable or fragile.
[115] CDPA 1988, s. 42.

Acts done for the purposes of public administration will not infringe copyright. In copyright infringement cases, copies of the respective works can be made in the course of the proceedings, judicial proceedings can be reported,[116] entries in the Register of Trade Marks can be copied, and copies of works can be made for the purposes of judicial proceedings,[117] etc.

Miscellaneous

Copyright infringement does not occur if buildings, sculptures, works of artistic craftsmanship, or models for buildings that are permanently situated in a public place or premises open to the public are photographed. One may also make a graphic work of them—that is, a drawing or painting—film them, and include a visual image of them in a broadcast.[118] The reconstruction of a building will not involve an infringement of the copyright that exists in the building or in the plans for the building.[119]

When artistic works are put up for sale, copies made for advertising purposes will not infringe the copyright in the artistic work. This will occur only if the copies are subsequently dealt with for other purposes[120]—that is, if they are sold themselves.

Video recorders, DVD recorders, and other recording devices are quite useful if you want to watch a broadcast that is emitted when you have something else to do or when you are not at home. You let the recording device do its work and you can watch it any time you want. There is only one small problem: you have recorded the broadcast and your activity may infringe copyright. The Act solves this problem by allowing anyone to record a broadcast for private and domestic use if this recording is made for the purpose of time shifting[121]—that is, the recording may only be made if it is made in order to view the broadcast at a (more) convenient time. Only in these particular circumstances is the recording exempted.

Sony Music Entertainment (UK) & ors v. Easyinternetcafé Ltd[122] was concerned with the scope of the time-shifting defence to copyright infringement. The defendant allowed clients to download material from the Internet and to store the files on a private part of the server used by it. Its employees did not have access to that part of the server, but offered a CD-burning service. Confronted with a claim of illegal copying of music files, the defendant ran the defence of time shifting. The Court held that it had not been proven that the copies were made for time-shifting purposes and that, in any case, such copies were supposed to be made privately by the person concerned and not by a third party, such as the internet cafe that was involved in the business for commercial purposes.

The Copyright and Related Rights Regulations 2003[123] have now further tightened up the conditions for the application of the time-shifting exemption. The exemption will now apply only if the act of copying takes place '*in domestic premises*' and if a copy that would otherwise be an infringing copy is made in accordance with the regulation, but is subsequently dealt with, it shall be treated as an infringing copy for the purposes of that

---

[116] Obviously, this does not cover the copying of published reports of judicial proceedings.

[117] *A v. B* [2000] EMLR 1007, in which copies of confidential diaries had been made for use by the other partner in divorce proceedings.

[118] CDPA 1988, s. 62; copies may also be issued to the public.

[119] Ibid., s. 65.

[120] Ibid., s. 63.

[121] Ibid., s. 70.

[122] *Sony Music Entertainment (UK) & ors v. Easyinternetcafé Ltd* [2003] FSR 48.

[123] SI 2003/2498, reg. 19.

dealing; if that dealing infringes copyright, it shall be treated as an infringing copy for all subsequent purposes. The exemption in s. 71 of the 1988 Act for photographs taken of television broadcasts has been the object of similar changes.[124]

A club or society that was not established for profit and the main objectives of which are charitable can play sound recordings in the course of its activities without infringing copyright, if the proceeds of such activity are applied solely for the purposes of the organization concerned.[125] The Copyright and Related Rights Regulations have also tightened the requirements for this exception. Additional requirements have been added,[126] according to which it is required that the sound recording is played by a person who is acting primarily and directly for the benefit of the organization, and who is not acting with a view to gain, that the proceeds of any charge for admission to the place at which the recording is to be heard are applied solely for the purposes of the organization, and that the proceeds from any goods or services sold by, or on behalf of, the organization in the place at which the sound recording is heard and on the occasion when the sound recording is played are applied solely for the purposes of the organization. A local council that organized aerobics classes was held not to qualify for this exemption.[127] The status of the organization, rather than the activity, is of primary importance in this respect.

If anything done to an adaptation is exempted on the basis of the provisions analysed above, the copyright in the original work will not be infringed.[128]

Having been excluded from the scope of fair dealing, a new exception covering the acts of observing, studying, and testing of computer programs was in order. According to the new s. 50BA[129] of the 1988 Act, it is not an infringement of copyright for a lawful user of a copy of a computer program to observe, study, or test the functioning of the program in order to determine the ideas and principles that underlie any element if he or she does so while performing any of the acts of loading, displaying, running, transmitting, or storing the program that he or she is entitled to do. And if an act is permitted under this section, it is irrelevant whether or not there exists any term or condition in an agreement that purports to prohibit or restrict the act.

Once more, the Information Society Directive

In the subject matter covered in this chapter, the implementation of the Information Society Directive has been the source of quite a few changes; one additional important point is to be retained. Article 5(5) of the Directive formally adopts the three-step test of the Berne Convention for the Protection of Literary and Artistic Works 1886 to any exception. Exceptions can therefore only be introduced and applied if they refer to certain special cases, if these cases do not conflict with the normal exploitation of the work, and if the exception does not unreasonably prejudice the legitimate interests of the right holder.

---

[124] See reg. 20.
[125] *Phonographic Performance Ltd v. South Tyneside Metropolitan Borough Council* [2001] 1 WLR 400; see also CDPA 1988, s. 67.
[126] Regulation 18.
[127] CDPA 1988, s. 76.
[128] European Parliament and Council Directive 2001/29/EC on the harmonization of certain aspects of copyright and related rights in the information society [2001] OJ L 167/10.
[129] Inserted by Copyright and Related Rights Regulations 2003, SI 2003/2498, reg. 15.

The inclusion of this overarching principle into EU law represents an important step, also enabling the use of the three-step test in interpreting the exact scope that is to be given to each of the exceptions under EU and national law.[130]

An overview

Once we have ascertained that copyright does subsist in the work, we examine the allegedly infringing act.

- Is it a restricted act, such as copying?
- Has the act been done to a substantial part of the work?

Only if these two questions are answered affirmatively, can there potentially be infringement.

There will nevertheless be no infringement if any of the next stages of our examination receives a positive answer.

- Did the owner of the copyright in the work authorize the act or consent to it, whether expressly or impliedly?
- Is the copyright infringement in the public interest?
- Is the act covered by any of the permitted acts?

Only a negative answer to these three further questions will allow us to conclude that the copyright in the work has been infringed.

Further reading

DE ZWART, M., 'A historical analysis of the birth of fair dealing and fair use: lessons for the digital age' (2007) 1 IPQ 60.

GARNETT, K., DAVIES, G. and HARBOTTLE, G. (2005) *Copinger and Skone James on Copyright*, 15th edn, London: Sweet and Maxwell, ch. 9.

MASUYAKURIMA, P. (2004) 'Fair dealing and freedom of expression', in P. Torremans (ed.) *Copyright and Human Rights*, London: Kluwer Law International.

MITCHELL, P. and BOURN, S., '*HRH The Prince of Wales v. Associated Newspapers Ltd*: copyright versus the public interest' (2006) 17 Ent LR 7, 210.

SENFTLEBEN, M. (2004) *Copyright, Limitations and the Three-Step Test: An Analysis of the Three-Step Test in International and EC Copyright Law*, London: Kluwer Law International.

SIMS, A., 'The public interest defence in copyright law: myth or reality?' (2006) 28 EIPR 6, 335.

THEOBALD, T., 'Copyright infringement or is it just fair dealing?' (2005) 16 Ent LR 6, 153.

---

[130] See M. Senftleben (2004) *Copyright, Limitations and the Three-Step Test: An Analysis of the Three-Step Test in International and EC Copyright Law*, London: Kluwer Law International.

17

Rights in performances

The problem

Luciano Pavarotti adored live performances in front of mass audiences.[1] Imagine him performing, live at Wembley, a series of songs taken from Gaetano Donizetti's famous opera *Lucia di Lammermoor*. Someone in the audience makes a bootleg recording of Pavarotti's performance and sells it to a record company other than Decca, with whom Pavarotti had a recording contract. There is very little that can be done on the basis of the copyright rules that we have described in earlier chapters: Donizetti died in 1848, the copyright in the music and the libretto have long expired. The Decca recording is not copied or dealt with; the bootleg recording is an entirely separate and independent recording. No copyright infringement can be found, and both Pavarotti as the performer and Decca as the recording company are left unprotected.

This was felt to be undesirable, because both performers and recording companies[2] make a substantial contribution, and would be less inclined to do so if they were unable to secure a proper return for their contribution. Apart from the financial implications, the performer contributes to the artistic value of the work in bringing it to life and the recording company's entrepreneurial investment is considerable. To remedy the absence of protection for these groups under traditional copyright rules, the Convention for the Protection of Performers, Producers of Phonograms and Broadcasting Organizations was concluded in Rome in 1961.

Before the Copyright, Designs and Patents Act 1988 entered into force, the old rules[3] in the UK tried to offer some protection. The performers were given a right to civil remedies on top of the statutory criminal penalties in *Rickless v. United Artists Corp.*[4] The defendant took clips and discarded excerpts from old *Pink Panther* films starring the late Peter Sellers to make a new film without obtaining the permission of the actor's executors. The Court of Appeal argued that the statutory provision of criminal penalties created an obligation or prohibition for the benefit of the performers. Any aggrieved performer thus had a cause of action. The same Court of Appeal felt obliged, however, to deny similar civil remedies to a recording company that wished to act against the making of a bootleg recording.[5]

---

[1] Luciano Pavarotti passed away recently, but that does not affect the example. As we will see, rights remain in place for 50 years and rights given to the performer are transmissible *ex mortem*, by testamentary disposition or otherwise.

[2] See G. Boytha, 'The intellectual property status of sound recordings' (1993) 24 IIC 295–306.

[3] See the Dramatic and Musical Performer's Protection Act 1925, the Dramatic and Musical Performer's Protection Act 1958, the Performer's Protection Act 1963 and the Performer's Protection Act 1972; criminal penalties were made available.

[4] *Rickless v. United Artists Corp.* [1988] QB 40, [1987] 1 All ER 679.

[5] *RCA Corp. v. Pollard* [1983] Ch 135, [1982] 3 All ER 771.

Effective protection is only achievable when the interested parties can enforce their rights themselves and have access to civil remedies. The old system could not provide that in all cases and was replaced by Pt II of the 1988 Act.[6]

Subsistence of rights

Rights in performances are given to the performers and to the person who has recording rights in relation to the performance. A performance, in this context, means a live performance by one person or a group of persons. It can be a musical performance, such as Pavarotti's performance in our example, a dramatic performance, a dance, or a mime. It can also be the reading or recitation of a literary work, a performance of a variety act, or a similar presentation.[7] This definition is extremely wide in scope. The consent of the performer(s) is required for any exploitation of such a performance.[8]

No film or sound recording can be made of a performance without the consent of the performer or the person having recording rights in relation to the performance. The latter will have an exclusive recording contract, such as that which Pavarotti had with Decca, under which he alone has the right to make the recording. The Act covers recordings made directly from the live performance, recordings made from a broadcast of, or a cable programme including, the performance, as well as any recording made, directly or indirectly, from another recording of the performance.[9] Once again, this is a definition that is very wide in scope.

Term of protection

These rights in performances come on top of the rights conferred by copyright and they are independent rights[10] that expire after a 50-year term. The rights in the performance normally expire 50 years after the end of the calendar year in which the performance to which they relate took place. But if a recording of the performance is lawfully released during this normal 50-year period, the rule changes and the rights shall only expire 50 years after the end of the calendar year in which the first release of the recording of the performance took place.[11] The concept of 'release' includes the first publication, showing, or playing in public, broadcasting, or inclusion in a cable programme service of a recording.[12] Unauthorized acts cannot be taken into account to determine whether or not a recording has been released or to determine the date of release.[13]

---

[6] For a detailed analysis, see R. Arnold (2004) *Performer's Rights*, 3rd edn, London: Sweet and Maxwell.

[7] CDPA 1988, s. 180(2).

[8] Ibid., (1).   [9] Ibid., ss. 180(1), (2), and 185(1).

[10] Ibid., s. 180(4).   [11] Ibid., s. 191(2).

[12] The Term Directive did not distinguish between publication and communication to the public, and such a distinction is therefore also not found in the current provisions of the 1988 Act. In order to avoid uncertainty over the term of a right if publication and communication to the public both took place, but on different dates, the Term Directive gave preference to the earlier date. The combination of two dates could, however, give rise to problems—especially because the date of communication to the public is not always easy to ascertain. The new Information Society Directive (European Parliament and Council Directive 2001/29/EC on the harmonization of certain aspects of copyright and related rights in the information society [2001] OJ L 167/10) has, therefore, changed the system and gives preference to the publication of the phonogram to determine the duration of the right of its producer. Only in cases in which no publication occurs in the relevant period will the lawful communication to the public be taken into account as a starting point for the calculation of the term of the right: Art. 11(2).

[13] CDPA 1988, s. 191(3).

These rules are different from those that are normal in copyright, which refer to the life of the author: in this case, no reference is made to the life of the performer. The restriction of the term of protection to that offered in the country of which the performer is a national for performers who are not nationals of a European Economic Area (EEA) state, meanwhile, shows strong similarities with the copyright comparison of term regime.[14]

If we go back to Pavarotti's Wembley performance, his performer's right will expire 50 years after the end of the year in which the concert takes place. The situation changes when Decca makes a lawful recording of the concert. This constitutes a fixation of the performance and, assuming that no other communication to the public takes place, Pavarotti's performer's right will expire 50 years after the end of the year in which the recording was released. Decca's recording right expires 50 years after the end of the year in which the recording of the performance is released, assuming that the recording will be released before the expiry of the period of 50 years from the end of the year in which the recorded performance took place.

The qualification requirement

The qualification requirement also exists for rights in performances.[15] The performance must be a qualifying performance—that is, a performance given in a qualifying country, or by a person who is a citizen or a subject of such a qualifying country. A country qualifies if it offers reciprocal protection.[16] The UK, the other member States of the European Union (EU), and some other countries designated by Order in Council are qualifying countries, but the complete list is much shorter because the Rome Convention has only been adhered to by approximately one-third of the states that adhere to the Berne Convention for the Protection of Literary and Artistic Works 1886. This weakens the international protection for rights in relation to performances, performers, and recorders.

Content and infringement

The content of the intangible right in a performance is best examined by means of the list of those acts that will constitute an infringement of the right. In general, the rights in performances are infringed whenever a performance is exploited without the consent of the performer, or whenever the performance is recorded without the consent of the person who owns the exclusive recording right. The consent of the owners of the rights in the performance is essential.[17] Helpfully, consent given in respect of one particular use does not mean that no consent is given for any other use unless there are special indications that further consent was required.[18]

The performer's right is infringed when certain acts are done to the whole, or a substantial part, of the performance. Within the scope of these acts fall:

- making a recording of the live performance,[19] which is not exclusively for private and domestic use;[20]

---

[14] The new term can only be shorter than that put in place by s. 191(2) of the 1988 Act; see CDPA 1988, s. 191(4).

[15] Ibid., s. 181. [16] Ibid., ss. 206–208. [17] Ibid., see s. 197.

[18] See *Grower v. British Broadcasting Corp.* [1990] FSR 595: consent given for the broadcasting of a recording of a performance in a radio programme does not exclude consent for other use of the recording in the absence of special indications to the contrary.

[19] CDPA 1988, s. 182(1)(a). [20] Ibid., (2).

- broadcasting the performance live or including it live in a cable programme service;[21]

- making, otherwise than for private and domestic use, either directly or indirectly,[22] a copy of a recording of the performance[23]—that is, the reproduction right.[24] The making of a copy of a recording includes the making of a copy that is transient or incidental to another use of the original recording;[25]

- issuing copies or the original[26] of a recording of the performance to the public[27]— that is, the distribution right;[28]

- renting or lending copies of a recording of the performance[29] to the public;[30]

- making a recording of the performance directly from a broadcast of, or a cable programme including, the live performance;[31]

- showing a recording of the performance in public, broadcasting it, or including it in a cable programme service;[32]

- importing into the UK an illicit recording of the performance if the person importing it knows, or has reason to believe, that it is an infringing copy;[33]

- possessing, in the course of business, selling or letting for sale, offering or exposing for sale or hire, or distributing an illicit recording of the performance if the person importing it knows, or has reason to believe, that it is an infringing copy.[34]

Broadly speaking, these rights might be described as the reproduction and the distribution right. The Information Society Directive[35] and the Copyright and Related Rights Regulations 2003[36] that implemented it under UK law have added a third major right: that of making available a recording. Section 182 CA of the 1988 Act now stipulates that a performer's rights are infringed by a person who, without that performer's consent, makes available to the public a recording of the whole, or any substantial part, of a qualifying performance by electronic transmission in such a way that members of the public may access the recording from a place and at a time individually chosen by them. The inclusion in this definition of a 'making available' right for performers, which can be seen as the equivalent of the right of communication to the public for copyright owners of on-demand services, is of vital importance in the digital age.

---

[21] Ibid., (1)(b).

[22] Ibid., s. 182A(2).

[23] Ibid., (1).

[24] Ibid., (3).

[25] Ibid., s. 182A(1A), inserted by Copyright and Related Rights Regulations 2003, reg. 8(3).

[26] Ibid., s. 182B(4).

[27] Ibid., (1). Issuing to the public is defined in s. 182B(2) and (3) as including exclusively '*the act of putting into circulation in the EEA copies not previously put into circulation in the EEA by or with the consent of the performer*' or '*the act of putting into circulation outside the EEA copies not previously put into circulation in the EEA or elsewhere*'.

[28] Ibid., (5).

[29] See T. Dreier and B. Hugenholtz (eds) (2006) *Concise European Copyright Law*, London: Kluwer Law International, pp. 245–58.

[30] CDPA 1988, s. 182C, in which 'rental' and 'lending' are defined.

[31] Ibid., s. 182(1)(c).

[32] Ibid., s. 183.

[33] Ibid., s. 184(1)(a).

[34] Ibid., (b).

[35] European Parliament and Council Directive 2001/29/EC on the harmonization of certain aspects of copyright and related rights in the information society [2001] OJ L 167/10.

[36] Regulation 7.

The performer is also given a right to equitable remuneration for the exploitation of a sound recording of the whole, or a substantial part, of the performance, but the right only applies to cases in which the sound recording is communicated to the public otherwise than by being made available to the public.[37] This remuneration is to be paid by the owner of the copyright in the commercially published sound recording when it is played in public or when it is included in a broadcast. The determination of the exact amount payable is to be determined in negotiations between the parties and, in default of agreement, the amount will be determined by the Copyright Tribunal. The right to equitable remuneration cannot be assigned, except to a collecting society that will enforce the right on behalf of the right holder.[38]

The rights of a person who has the exclusive recording right of a performance are infringed when the same acts are done to the whole, or a substantial part, of the performance, but the person having recording rights is not given the rights of reproduction, distribution, rental, and lending.[39] There is one further exception to this rule that the rights of such a person are similar to those of the performer: the recording rights are not infringed by a live broadcast of the performance or by the live inclusion of the performance in a cable programme service.[40] One might argue that this does not involve the recording of the performance, nor any dealings with illicit copies.

These lists contain forms of primary and secondary infringement, and bear similarities to the regime for normal copyright infringement.

Defences against alleged infringements

The defences available are very similar to those available in cases of alleged copyright infringement. They are contained in Sch. 2 to the 1988 Act: review and criticism; reporting current events;[41] educational use (although it is slightly less extensive in this context); incidental inclusion; public administration, etc. It has to be noted that there is no exception for research and private study.

The nature of the performer's rights and their transfer

Two types of right are given to the performer: some rights are property rights and others are non-property rights. The reproduction right, the distribution right, and the rental and lending right fall into the first category. They are the performer's property rights.[42] These property rights can be assigned and they are transmissible, just as any other item of personal or moveable property. Just as can any other assignment, this type of assignment can be partial, and needs to be in writing and signed by, or on behalf of, the assignor.[43] Normally, such an assignment cannot be presumed—but the Act contains an exception to

---

[37] CDPA 1988, s. 182D, as modified by Copyright and Related Rights Regulations 2003, reg. 7(2).

[38] Ibid.

[39] These will nevertheless exist in relation to the copyright in the sound recording (or film) that results from the exercise of the recording right. In practice, the owners of these various rights will often be the same persons.

[40] CDPA 1988, ss. 185–188.

[41] These three defences do not seem to require a sufficient acknowledgment, at least in cases in which it is not required by copyright itself.

[42] CDPA 1988, s. 191A.   [43] Ibid., s. 191B.

this rule. This exception operates in cases in which an agreement relating to film production is concluded between a performer and a film producer. To avoid a situation in which too many persons—each of whom has made a small contribution to the film—need to give their approval for the exploitation of the film, the performer shall be presumed to have transferred to the producer any rental right in relation to the film. That rental right would arise due to the inclusion of the recording of the performer's performance in the film. The presumption is overturned in case the agreement provides to the contrary.[44] In any event, the performer retains always a right to equitable remuneration when he or she has transferred his or her rental rights concerning a sound recording or a film to the producer of the latter works.[45]

The performer is also given certain non-property rights,[46] which include the rights granted by ss. 182–184 of the 1988 Act. This list comprises all rights that are not specifically listed as property rights. The non-property rights in performances are normally not assignable or transmissible[47]—but the right given to the performer is transmissible *ex mortem*, by testamentary disposition or otherwise, and the exclusive recording licence, as the benefit of the rights in the performance, can be assigned, for example, from one recording company to another.[48]

Moral rights

At the international level, the Rome Convention, on which the rights in performances are based, never attracted the level of support that is enjoyed by the Berne Convention in the copyright area. The TRIPS Agreement only managed to provide a basic framework in 1994. The World Intellectual Property Organization (WIPO) tried to remedy this lack of international recognition for rights in performances and build on the minimum framework that had been achieved. That attempt resulted, on 20 December 1996, in the signing of the WIPO Performances and Phonograms Treaty (WPPT). This treaty offers enhanced levels of international protection, and it is hoped that its link with the Berne Convention will convince the vast majority of countries to sign up to it and ratify it. It entered into force on 20 May 2002 and has rapidly been attracting ratifications ever since. One of its main achievements is that it gives the performer inalienable moral rights[49] and this is a significant step forward.

The UK has implemented its Treaty obligation by means of the Performances (Moral Rights, etc.) Regulations 2006.[50] Performers have been given a paternity right and an integrity right. The performer has the right to be identified as such when he or she performs live, when the performance is broadcast, when a recording of the performance is communicated to the public, or when copies of it are issued to the public.[51] That identification needs to take place in such a way that it is likely to be noticed by the audience.[52] No identification is required when it is not reasonably practical or when the performance is given for reasons relating to advertising or news reporting.[53] Unfortunately, the

---

[44] Ibid., s. 191F.
[45] Ibid., s. 191G.
[46] Ibid., s. 192A.
[47] Ibid., ss. 192A and 192B.
[48] Ibid., ss. 192A(2), 192B(2), and 185(2)(b) and (3)(b).
[49] WIPO Performances and Phonograms Treaty, Art. 5.
[50] SI 2006/18, in force since 1 February 2006.
[51] CDPA 1988, s. 205C.
[52] Ibid.
[53] Ibid., s. 205E.

provisions do not offer guidance on what is meant by 'not reasonably practical': does this, for example, include a failure to name all musicians performing on a recording when it is played as part of a radio show? The moral right to be identified is not infringed unless the performer has first asserted his or her moral right in writing.[54]

The integrity right will be infringed if the performance is broadcast live, or if it is played in public or communicated to the public by means of a sound recording, with any distortion, mutilation, or other modification that is prejudicial to the reputation of the performer.[55] The performer therefore faces a high burden of proof. There are also a series of exceptions to the right of integrity. These include modifications that are consistent with normal editorial practice and performances that are given for reasons related to advertising or news reporting.[56] No guidance is provided as to the interpretation of the concept of 'normal editorial practice'. Possessing infringing copies of the work in the course of business or dealing in them is also an infringement of the integrity right.[57]

The overall approach that has been taken is therefore similar to that in relation of the moral rights of authors. It therefore comes as no surprise that the duration of the moral rights of performers are also linked to the duration of the (economic) rights in the performance.[58] The grant of moral rights to performers is clearly a positive development, and their similarity to the moral rights for authors underlines the increasing recognition for the creative efforts of performers and the role that they play.

An overview

Performers play an important role in bringing copyright works to a wider audience; recordings of their performances also make a vast contribution. The interests of those that are involved with performances are, nevertheless, not necessarily the same as those of copyright owners. Copyright on its own was therefore not sufficient to protect the contribution of those involved with performances.

A separate set of rights in performances has consequently been created, which covers all aspects of the making of a recording of a performance and its subsequent exploitation. The rights follow the commercial needs on this point. They involve a reproduction right, a distribution right, and a rental and lending right, but, recently, moral rights have been added, in the form of a paternity and an integrity right.

Further reading

ARNOLD, R. (2004) *Performer's Rights,* 3rd edn, London: Sweet and Maxwell.

BOYTHA, G., 'The intellectual property status of sound recordings' (1993) 24 IIC 295.

DREIER, T. and HUGENHOLTZ, B. (eds) (2006) *Concise European Copyright Law,* London: Kluwer Law International, pp. 245–58.

GARNETT, K., DAVIES, G. and HARBOTTLE, G. (2005) *Copinger and Skone James on Copyright,* 15th edn, London: Sweet and Maxwell, ch. 12.

LADDIE, H., PRESCOTT, P. and VITORIA, M. (2000) *The Modern Law of Copyright and Designs,* 3rd edn, London: Butterworths, ch. 12.

---

[54] Ibid., s. 205D. [55] Ibid., s. 205F.
[56] Ibid., s. 205G. [57] Ibid., s. 205H.
[58] Ibid., s. 205I.

18
Dealing in copyright

Crown copyright

It is clear, in principle, that works made by Her Majesty or by officers or servants of the Crown will attract copyright if they come within the normal copyright rules described above. But the Copyright, Designs and Patents Act 1988 contains a few special provisions in relation to Crown copyright. These rules apply to works made by Her Majesty and, if the works are made in the course of his or her duties, works made by an officer or servant of the Crown.[1]

It is clear that the Crown will own the copyright in these works.[2] If no special rules exist, the normal copyright rules apply. A first rule affects literary, dramatic, musical, and artistic works. The term of copyright protection for such a work is 125 years from the end of the calendar year in which they were made if the work is not published commercially.[3] The term of copyright protection is, however, reduced to the more standard 50-year term if the work is published commercially during the first 75 years of the 125-year term. This reduced 50-year term—which the UK may, in due course, decide to harmonize with the new standard term of 70 years—starts running from the end of the calendar year in which first commercial publication took place.[4] As we know, 'commercial publication' is defined by the 1988 Act as:

> issuing copies to the public at a time when copies made in advance of the receipt of orders are generally available to the public [or] making the work available by means of an electronic retrieval system.[5]

Most works that are protected by Crown copyright will be published as soon as they are created. In practice, the 50-year term therefore seems to be the rule rather than that of 125 years.

Acts of Parliament and Measures of the General Synod of the Church of England present us with another copyright particularity. They will attract copyright protection, owned by Her Majesty, for a 50-year term, which will start running from the end of the calendar year in which they received royal assent.[6] Parliamentary copyright is copyright in works that are made by, or under the direction or control of, the House of Commons or the House of Lords. The House will own the copyright in the works so produced. In

---

[1] CDPA 1988, s. 163.
[2] Ibid., (1)(b).
[3] Ibid., (3)(a).
[4] Ibid., (3)(b).
[5] Ibid., s. 175(2).
[6] Ibid., s. 164.

general, these works are subject to the normal copyright rules, but the term of protection for literary, dramatic, musical, or artistic works is 50 years from the end of the calendar year in which the work was made.[7] In these categories, we find works such as reports of select committees; only Parliamentary Bills are catered for separately. Copyright in Bills will expire when they receive royal assent,[8] or when they are rejected or withdrawn at the end of the session.[9]

While retaining the principle of Crown copyright,[10] the 1999 White Paper on the *Future Management of Crown Copyright*[11] introduced the idea of a waiver of crown copyright in respect of, among other works, primary and secondary legislation, such as Acts of Parliament and statutory instruments, and their typographical arrangements.[12] The retention of the right guarantees the possibility of controlling the integrity of the works, while the waiver in respect of any enforcement enables their unrestricted use and wide dissemination.

Commercial exploitation of copyright in the UK

Copyright, as a form of intellectual property, has the same kind of commercial value as any other property right. Its contractual exploitation can take various forms, such as a sale or a more restricted right to do something in relation to the subject matter of the right. Authors can exploit their works themselves, but they may not be interested in doing so. Often they do not have the financial, material, and organizational means to exploit their works, or at least to do so efficiently. They can then leave the exploitation to a third party. This normally involves the transfer of some, or all, of the rights in the work to that third party.[13]

Some aspects of copyright are, however, slightly peculiar: firstly, exploitation of copyright takes place through a material item in which the work is recorded. This implies that, if one acquires that material item, one does not normally acquire the intellectual property right as well. If I buy a book, as a recording of a literary work, for example, I buy the paper and the ink, but not the copyright in the book or any right in relation to the copyright, such as the right to reproduce the work. This separation between the copyright and the right in the carrier is a special characteristic of intellectual property rights.

Secondly, copyright works are normally still created by an individual author or by a couple of individuals. These individuals will normally rely on a third party to exploit their work and that third party is often a corporate body. This results in the fact that the balance of bargaining and negotiating powers tilts almost necessarily in favour of the party exploiting the work, while the author is left behind as the weaker party.

Thirdly, copyright offers only a weak form of protection, because only the reproduction of expression is protected. This leaves the idea of the work unprotected and leaves the author powerless to act against various things that can be done to his or her work, such as

---

[7] Ibid., s. 165.

[8] The copyright in the Act commences at this point.

[9] CDPA 1988, s. 166.

[10] See S. Saxby, 'Crown copyright regulation in the UK: is the debate still alive?' (2005) 13 Int JL & IT 3, 299.

[11] Cm 4300, March 1999, available online at www.opsi.gov.uk/advice/crown-copyright/future-management-of-crown-copyright.pdf.

[12] Ibid., ch. 5.

[13] On the economic importance of the exploitation of copyright, see H. Cohen-Jehoram, 'Critical reflections on the economic importance of copyright' (1989) 20 IIC 485–97.

the production of a satirical work that clearly, through the borrowing of the idea, refers to the author's work. This reinforces the view that the author is in a weak position.

In the UK, we have historically not been too bothered about this: we have seen copyright as an entrepreneurial right that primarily protects the interests of the person who exploits the work. In contrast, Continental copyright emphasized the role of the artist— that is, the creator of the copyright work. The focus on moral rights is a good example of this emphasis on the artist. Now, we have seen the introduction of moral rights in the 1988 Act in the UK and we see the European Union (EU) developing initiatives in the copyright area: have we therefore arrived at a compromise? It is submitted that the use of the word 'compromise' would be misleading in this context, because it implies that concessions have been made on both sides; instead, what has happened is that the UK has moved towards a better and more complete set of copyright rules.

It is logical to start with the author. If the author does not create copyright works, there will be nothing to exploit and performing artists will have no works to perform. We may encounter the odd artist who keeps all of his or her works to themselves, but the vast majority of creators of copyright works want to see their works exploited. This can be explained by the desire to disseminate their work and the ideas behind it, or simply through the need for remuneration to allow them to keep creating works. The role of the person who exploits the copyright work is therefore in no way secondary in importance to the role of the author.

If we go back to the author who comes first, he or she becomes the first owner of the copyright in the work. The author is also given certain moral rights to compensate for the weak position in which he or she finds him or herself and which we described above. These moral rights are minimal rights and, as such, they do not in any way obstruct the normal exploitation of the work, because they only allow the author to act against forms of abusive exploitation of the work. It is therefore extremely important—also taking the weak position of the author into account—that these moral rights are inalienable. It is submitted that the possibility for the author to waive the moral rights has no place in this system.[14]

The person who exploits the rights should also have an exclusive right. There should be a transfer of all economic rights if each of these rights has been contracted against an equitable remuneration. A producer who has acquired exploitation rights from authors or performers has to possess all of the exclusive rights that are required for an efficient exploitation in the interest of all right holders. Clearly, a right to act independently against infringers should form part of these exclusive rights. This should be the starting point of the legislation and it should be left to the contractual freedom of the parties to add to this set of rules or to derogate from it.[15]

The essential feature of this system is that neither party gains total control over each other: both are given parallel exclusive rights and this should incite them to cooperate, which is in the best interests of both parties and in the best interest of copyright.[16] It is probably also the only system that will be able to cope with the challenge of the digital exploitation of copyright, which will make worldwide, high-speed exploitation of copyright in various formats possible, and which offers the opportunity to play around with an original work and to amend it efficiently, speedily, and, in practice, on a worrying number of occasions.[17]

---

[14] See J.-F. Verstrynghe, 'The Spring 1993 Horace S Manges Lecture: the European Commission's direction on copyright and neighbouring rights—toward the regime of the twenty-first century' (1993) 17 Colum-VLA JL & Arts 187 at 206–8.

[15] Ibid., at 206–7.

[16] Ibid.

[17] Dreier (1993).

Assignment of copyright and copyright licences

Assignment of copyright and copyright licences are the two forms of contract involved in the exploitation of a copyright work by a third party.[18] Each has its own distinct characteristics.

Assignment

An assignment involves the disposal of the copyright: the author (the assignor) assigns the copyright to another person (the assignee). The 1988 Act requires that an assignment is in writing[19] and is signed by, or on behalf of, the assignor.[20] The standard type of assignment involves the transfer of the complete copyright, but this need not be the case.[21] Two forms of partial assignment are possible: it is possible to assign only certain aspects of the copyright or certain rights, and not the whole copyright, and it is also possible to restrict the assignment to a certain period.[22] This makes it possible to assign, for example, the copyright in the novel, to assign only the public performance right or the translation right, or to assign all or any of these rights only for a period of ten years. The assignor will normally receive a lump sum in return for the assignment of the copyright in the work.

An assignment can also take place in relation to a work that has yet to be created. The Act calls this the assignment of 'future copyright'—that is, of copyright that will come into existence once the potential author decides to create the work and the work is effectively created. The author will then become the first owner of the copyright and the assignment will take effect immediately.[23]

A difficult point is presented by the assignment of copyright in equity. The courts have, on a couple of occasions, accepted that an assignment can take place even if the formal requirements of s. 90 of the 1988 Act are not met. In *Warner v. Gestetner*,[24] the court held that there had been an assignment of copyright in equity only.[25] Warner had produced drawings of cats for Gestetner. These drawings were to be used to produce a new product at a fair and Warner would remain the owner of the copyright in the drawings. Gestetner later used them in promotional literature. The court decided that Gestetner was entitled to use the drawings and implied a clause assigning beneficial ownership of the copyright to Gestetner. In this construction, there is a legal owner of the copyright and an owner at equity who is free to use the work. It seems to be the case, however, that an equitable owner of copyright cannot bring an infringement case without the assistance of the legal owner of the copyright in the work.[26]

Licences

A licence does not involve a transfer of the copyright in the work: the owner of the copyright (the licensor) simply grants permission to a third party (the licensee) to do certain

---

[18] CDPA 1988, s. 90(1).

[19] But secondary evidence can be admitted in later proceedings if the written original can no longer be traced: see the decision of the Court of Appeal in *Masquerade Music Ltd v. Bruce Springsteen* [2001] EMLR 25.

[20] CDPA 1988, s. 90(3).

[21] See *Peer International Corp., Southern Music Publishing Co. Inc. & Peermusic (UK) Ltd v. Termidor Music Publishers Ltd, Termidor Musikverlag GmbH & Co. KG & Editora Musical de Cuba* [2004] RPC 455, which also raises interesting points of private international law.

[22] CDPA 1988, s. 90(2).

[23] Ibid., s. 91(1) and (2).

[24] [1988] EIPR D-89.

[25] See also the unreported decision of the Court of Appeal of 26 November 1999 in *Lakeview Computers plc v. Steadman*.

[26] *Performing Right Society Ltd v. London Theatre of Varieties Ltd* [1924] AC 1.

acts in relation to the copyright work that would otherwise constitute an infringement. An obvious example is a licence to perform a play: without the licence being granted, the performance would have constituted an infringement of the copyright in the play. A licence can be granted in return for the payment of a lump sum or royalties, which involve the payment of a fixed sum or a percentage of the return each time that the act allowed by the licence takes place.

In the same way as an assignment, the licence can be restricted in relation to its scope— that is, in relation to the acts that are allowed or in relation to its term.[27] It is indeed quite common to grant various licences—eventually in combination with a partial assignment—to various persons in relation to the exploitation of a work. Let us consider a novel as an example: the owner of the copyright in the novel can assign the publication rights in the UK to a publisher, can license the performing rights, can license another publisher to produce a translation in French, can license a German producer to make a sound recording, and can assign the film rights to MGM in the USA, etc.

A licence can be exclusive or non-exclusive. An exclusive licence is subject to certain additional provisions. It is the only type of licence for which the 1988 Act requires a written format, which has to be signed by, or on behalf of, the copyright owner-licensor.[28] It allows the exclusive licensee to exercise certain rights in relation to the copyright work on an exclusive basis. This means that all other persons, including the licensor, will be excluded from exercising that right. The exclusive licensee can also bring an independent infringement action after joining the owner or by leave of the court; a non-exclusive licensee needs the assistance of the licensor to do so, because, in that case only the owner can sue. The exclusive licensee also has the same rights against a successor in title who is bound by the licence as he or she has against the original licensor.[29]

This brings us to the question of who is bound by a licence. In principle, the licence binds every successor in title to the licensor and there is only one exception to this rule. A purchaser in good faith and for valuable consideration, or someone deriving his or her title from such a purchaser, is not bound by the terms of the licence if he or she had no actual or constructive notice of the licence.[30] These requirements are extremely difficult to meet in practice, because, once exploitation has taken place, it is almost impossible for a purchaser to prove that he or she did not even have constructive notice of the licence. Nevertheless, this rule is one of the reasons why publishers prefer an assignment of copyright to an exclusive licence.

A prospective owner can license future copyright, in the same way as it can be assigned.[31] In this case again, however, the purchaser in good faith is granted protection.[32]

It is clear that it is extremely difficult to distinguish certain copyright licences from certain assignments of copyright: it is a matter of construction and the actual words used by the parties are not conclusive.[33] The payment of royalties points towards a licence and the difference regarding the right to sue independently is also an important factor in this respect.

Collecting societies

The normal way of exploiting copyright by way of licences involves the grant of a licence for every use that is made of the copyright work. In cases in which the work is a recording,

---

[27] CDPA 1988, s. 90(2).
[28] Ibid., s. 92(1).
[29] Ibid., (2).
[30] Ibid., s. 90(4).
[31] Ibid., s. 91(3).
[32] Ibid., (3).
[33] *Jonathan Cape Ltd v. Consolidated Press Ltd* [1954] 3 All ER 253, [1954] 1 WLR 1313.

to do so would involve the creation of a licence every time that the recording is played. It is probably not very convenient for the copyright owner to collect a minimum fee on every occasion. The overhead costs would be tremendous; it would take up all of his or her time and he or she would, in practice, only be able to collect a fraction of royalties owed to him or her. The user of these records is in a similar position. If a restaurant owner wants to play background music in the restaurant, to so do requires a separate licence for every work that is played: how is the restaurant owner going to find all of the right owners in the first place?

This problem is addressed by the creation of collecting societies, such as the Performing Right Society (PRS) or Phonographic Performance Ltd (PPL).[34] There is normally one collecting society per type of work and per country. Owners of the copyright become members of this body, which will license the use of their works and collect the royalties for them. The PRS takes an assignment of the copyright in the performance and broadcasting of musical works, grants licences, collects royalties, and distributes these among its members after the deduction of administration costs. This presents a tremendous advantage to copyright owners, but it is also advantageous for the users of the works. They now have to deal only with one body and they will be able to get a blanket licence that will allow them to use any work that is among the repertoire of the society.[35]

Certain members of the collecting society may also bring infringement proceedings against those who do not have a licence or who are in breach of its terms if they are, for example, exclusive licensees of the copyright in various sound recordings. Despite not having actual authority from the members of the collective society, it is accepted that they can sue as a representative claimant in a representative capacity if they, and the other members, have a common interest and a common grievance, and if the relief sought would, in its nature, be beneficial to the relevant members of the collecting society.[36]

But the fact that a society has a double monopoly creates some problems. Copyright owners are obliged to deal with the one existing society if they want to exploit their works effectively. This situation can give rise to discrimination by the society against certain of its members by imposing different membership rules, for example, for foreign owners of copyright, or by the adoption of discriminatory royalty distribution rules for certain types of work or certain classes of member. The society is also an unavoidable partner for the users of copyright works and abuse could consist in this area, for example, in charging exorbitant royalties. The 1988 Act took this into account and gave the Copyright Tribunal jurisdiction to deal with such cases.[37]

Licensing schemes

The owner of the copyright in a work may be willing to set standard conditions on which licences to do certain acts are available. This is, for example, the case in relation to the photocopying of literary works. Every owner knows that this is happening and that it is unrealistic to expect every person who engages in the photocopying of the work to apply for a separate licence for each work of which he or she wishes to copy a part. It is also unrealistic to assume that the copyright owner could act effectively against this form of infringement

---

[34] See P. Torremans (2006) 'Collective management in the United Kingdom (and Ireland)', in D. Gervais (ed.) *Collective Management of Copyright and Related Rights*, London: Kluwer Law International, pp. 227–55.

[35] See D. Gervais (2006) 'The changing role of copyright collectives', in D. Gervais (ed.) *Collective Management of Copyright and Related Rights*, London: Kluwer Law International, pp. 3–36.

[36] *Independiente Ltd & ors v. Music Trading OnLine (HK) Ltd & ors* [2003] EWHC 470 (Ch).

[37] See also *Association of Independent Radio Companies Ltd v. Phonographic Performance Ltd* [1994] RPC 143.

in cases in which no licence is applied for. The solution is to pool resources and to arrive at standard conditions on which licences are available, and to do so with a large group of copyright owners. More copiers will be prepared to take a licence and the body administering the licence will be more effective in acting against infringement. The Act also sees this from another perspective: by giving the Copyright Tribunal jurisdiction over these schemes, it can prevent the abuse of monopoly powers by the copyright owners.

A licensing scheme is defined as:

> a scheme setting out the classes of case in which the operator of the scheme, or the person on whose behalf he acts, is willing to grant copyright licences, and the terms on which licences would be granted in those classes of case.[38]

A licensing body, meanwhile, means:

> a society or other organisation which has as its main object, or one of its main objects, the negotiation or granting, either as owner or prospective owner of copyright or as agent for him, of copyright licences, and whose objects include the granting of licences covering works of more than one author.[39]

The Copyright Tribunal

The Copyright Tribunal has a wide jurisdiction. The following types of case can be referred to it:

• the determination of the royalty or other remuneration to be paid with respect to the retransmission of a broadcast that includes the work;

• an application to determine the amount of the equitable remuneration that remains payable in those cases in which the author has transferred his or her rental rights, relating to a sound recording or film, to the producer;

• disputes about the terms or the operation of a proposed or existing licensing scheme,[40] which is operated by a licensing body and which covers works of more than one author. (Such an action can, for example, be brought by an organization that represents persons who require licences that are covered by the scheme.) The licences must cover[41] the copying of the work, the rental or lending of copies of the work, the performing, showing, or playing of the work in public, or the broadcasting of the work;

• an application in relation to entitlement under such a licensing scheme—that is, if someone is refused a licence;

• a reference in relation to licensing by a licensing body—for example, a case relating to the terms of a licence. The licences must cover the same acts as those listed in relation to licensing schemes;[42]

• an application or reference in relation to the use as of right of sound recordings in broadcasts;[43]

• an appeal against the coverage of a licensing scheme or a licence;

[38] CDPA 1988, s. 116(1); see *Universities UK Ltd v. Copyright Licensing Agency Ltd* [2002] RPC 693.
[39] CDPA 1988, s. 116(2); see *Universities UK Ltd v. Copyright Licensing Agency Ltd* [2002] RPC 693.
[40] CDPA 1988, ss. 118 and 119; see *Universities UK Ltd v. Copyright Licensing Agency Ltd* [2002] RPC 693.
[41] CDPA 1988, s. 117.
[42] Ibid., s. 124.
[43] Ibid., ss. 135D and 135E; see *Phonographic Performance Ltd v. Virgin Retail Ltd* [2001] EMLR 139.

- an application to settle the royalties for the rental of sound recordings, films, or computer programs in cases in which the Secretary of State uses the exceptional powers contained in s. 66 of the 1988 Act;

- an application to settle the terms of a copyright licence that has become available as of right.[44]

Appeals on a point of law from the decisions of the Copyright Tribunal can be made to the High Court, or, in Scotland, to the Court of Session.[45]

The rental and the lending right

If we consider video cassettes or DVDs containing a copy of a film as an example, it is easy to understand that exploitation through rental of a film has become one of the leading ways of exploiting a film. Rental and lending of copyright works have, indeed, acquired an important status in the field of copyright exploitation and, because they have replaced, in a number of cases, the acquisition of a copy of the work and the royalty payment that goes with it, it was felt that the authors of the works that are exploited in this way were entitled to some form of remuneration. Section 66 of the 1988 Act provides for the payment of a reasonable royalty in rental cases—but this provision is, in fact, a last remedy against abuse by the owners of copyright in sound recordings, films, and computer programs of their copyright, and it is unlikely that the Secretary of State will ever use his power under this section to grant licences and ask the Copyright Tribunal to determine the reasonable royalty in default of agreement. In the absence of any substantial rental or lending provisions in many of its member States, the EU took the initiative to introduce these rights in a harmonized way and this resulted in a Council Directive.[46]

The implementation of the Directive[47] in the UK added the rental and lending of the work or of copies of it to the list of restricted acts.[48] The fact that these acts are now restricted to the owner of the copyright in the work enables the copyright owner to charge royalties for the rental and lending of the work, and to receive payment for this new way of exploiting his or her work. The general structure of the relevant provisions has been discussed above and need not be repeated here.[49] We also discussed the introduction of rental and lending rights as part of the rights in performances. We therefore turn our attention to a few special aspects of the rental and lending rights regime.

As the credits that appear on the screen at the end of the showing of a film demonstrate, a long list of people are generally involved in the making of a film. The list of those people that will possess rental rights is significantly shorter, but can nevertheless still be rather long. Once the film is made, each of them will normally go his or her own way; it might therefore be rather impractical to impose a system whereby the film can only be exploited through rental if the authorization of each contributor has been obtained. Some of the contributors may be hard to trace, or even a single one might hold the whole project to ransom.

---

[44] CDPA 1988, s. 149.

[45] Ibid., s. 152.

[46] Council Directive 92/100 on rental right and lending right and on certain rights related to copyright in the field of intellectual property (1992) OJ L 346/61.

[47] A challenge against the Directive, in which its validity was questioned, was rejected by the European Court of Justice on 28 April 1998 in Case C-200/96 *Metronome Musik GmbH v. Music Point Hokamp GmbH* [1998] ECR I-1953; [1998] 3 CMLR 919.

[48] CDPA 1988, s. 16(1)(ba).

[49] See Chapter 15; see also Case C-245/00 *SENA v. NOS* [2003] ECR I-1251 on the point of equitable remuneration.

The Directive and the 1988 Act therefore provide the possibility of concentrating the rental rights in a single pair of hands. The Act contains a presumption[50] that, unless the agreement provides to the contrary, the conclusion of an agreement concerning the production of a film between the producer and an author of a literary, musical, dramatic, or artistic work[51] is presumed to include a transfer to the producer of any rental right in relation to the film arising by virtue of the inclusion of a copy of the author's work in the film. As we saw in the last chapter, an identical provision exists in relation to performers.[52] Due to the higher level of bargaining power of the producer, such a presumption might be to the detriment of authors or performers, who would hardly be able to secure a proper remuneration for the transfer of their rental rights in the production agreement. The Act tries to overcome this problem by introducing a rule that the authors or performers remain entitled to an equitable remuneration for the rental, even after the transfer of their right.[53]

The producer may be the only person that can authorize the rental of the work, but he or she has to provide an equitable remuneration for those whose rights have been transferred. That right of equitable remuneration cannot be assigned, except to a collecting society that will enforce the right on behalf of the right holder.[54] For the purposes of this rule, the category of authors also includes the principal director of the film, in addition to the author of a literary, dramatic, musical, or artistic work.[55]

The amount payable by way of equitable remuneration is to be agreed between the author and performers, on the one hand, and the producers or his or her successor in title as assignee of the rental rights in the film, on the other.[56] In default of an agreement, the Copyright Tribunal will determine the amount upon application.[57]

These provisions successfully overcome the problems that arise when too many persons potentially get rental rights in relation to a single work. The general conclusion must therefore be that the system of rental rights enhances the copyright position of the people involved, and constitutes an appropriate and necessary response to the change in the way in which certain copyright works are exploited commercially. The position of the performers is especially enhanced by this change, because their protection was, until now, rather weak.

The exploitation of copyright works through hard copy has further been eroded through the rise of the Internet. Many works are now available online and their use online reduces the use of hard copies. The existing provisions of copyright—including those concerning rental and lending—are, perhaps, not entirely capable of successfully tackling the problems that arise. The World Intellectual Property Organization (WIPO) Copyright Treaty 1996 and the WIPO Performances and Phonograms Treaty 1996 are attempts, at an international level, to update copyright in this respect. The EU has translated these international commitments into the Information Society Directive,[58] which is now in the process of being implemented by its member States. The UK has already implemented the Directive through the Copyright and Related Rights Regulations 2003.[59] This process will,

---

[50] CDPA 1988, s. 93A.

[51] Screenplays, dialogues, or music that are specifically created for, and used in, a film are excluded according to CDPA 1988, s. 93A(3).

[52] Ibid., s. 191F.

[53] Ibid., s. 93B(1).

[54] Ibid., s. 93B(2).

[55] Ibid., (1).

[56] Ibid., (4); see Chapter 15; see also Case C-245/00 *SENA v. NOS* [2003] ECR I-1251.

[57] CDPA 1988, ss. 93C and 191G.

[58] Directive 2001/29/EC on the harmonization of certain aspects of copyright and related rights in the information society [2001] OJ L 167/10.

[59] SI 2003/2498.

in the near future, lead to the ratification by the whole of the EU of both WIPO Treaties. The provisions of the Directive—especially the enhanced bundle of rights consisting of the reproduction right, the distribution right, and the right to communicate the work to the public and to make it available to the public—have been discussed above. Suffice it to mention here that the Directive fully preserves the existing rental and lending rights.[60]

Apart from the Internet, there are other forms of exploitation of copyright works in this area in addition to online services, which include pay-per-view television, video or music on demand, and electronic publishing. These can be called 'conditional access' services. Authors can only be paid properly in this context if unauthorized (pirate) access without payment to these services is prohibited and prevented. The EU harmonized the law on conditional access services and their protection through the adoption of a Directive.[61] The purpose of the Directive was to create a uniform legal environment for the protection of these conditional access services—that is, services offered to the public in relation to which access is subject to payment of subscriptions, such as pay-per-view television and interactive online services. The Directive required member States to prohibit, and provide suitable sanctions against, the manufacture and commercial dealing in illegal decoders, smart cards, and software, etc.. In the UK, this resulted in the insertion of s. 297A into the 1988 Act, which does exactly that.[62]

Copyright exploitation and free competition

The position in the UK under domestic law in relation to the conflict between copyright exploitation and free competition is clear, in that it gives priority to copyright exploitation. Section 66 of the 1988 Act could lead to compulsory licences in a restricted area, but, as discussed above, the provision will probably never be used. This leaves us with the licences of right as the only effective tool with which to act against an abuse during the exploitation of the rights granted by copyright law. A report of the Competition Commission[63] may lead to the creation of licences of right, which means essentially that licences become available to anyone who applies for them. What is required for the creation of such licences is that the public interest is, or has been, or may be, prejudiced. This can be on the basis of conditions in licences restricting the use of the work or the right of the owner to grant other licences, or on the basis of a refusal of the copyright owner to grant licences on reasonable terms.[64] The UK's improved general competition provisions, contained in the Competition Act 1998, are based on the example found in the Treaty of Rome. The latter provisions have shown to be of real practical importance and it is to these that we now turn.

Exploitation under European law—copyright and the free movement of goods

Article 30 of the Treaty of Rome refers to '*industrial and commercial property*', and this clearly includes patents and trade marks—but does it also include copyright? Does it really mean the same as 'intellectual property'? The European Court of Justice has now given a

---

[60] Article 1(2)(b) of the Directive.
[61] European Parliament and Council Directive 98/84/EC on the legal protection of services based on, or consisting of, conditional access (1998) OJ L 320/54.
[62] Inserted by Conditional Access (Unauthorized Decoders) Regulations 2000, SI 2000/1175, reg. 2.
[63] CDPA 1988, s. 144.
[64] Ibid.

positive answer to these questions[65] and all of the general principles that we outlined in Chapter 5 on patents can now be applied to copyright, subject to what follows.

Copyright is a difficult area, because its scope is so extremely wide and because it protects, as a result, very different types of work. This makes it extremely difficult to define the specific subject matter of copyright and the European Court of Justice has not yet made an attempt to do so. It is submitted that, for these purposes, there are two types of copyright, which probably have a different specific subject matter: the first category comprises all non-performance copyrights, such as those in books, paintings, and sound-recordings; the second comprises all performance copyrights. The latter category includes live performances, but also all performances of films. We will discuss both categories separately.

The Treaty obviously deals with matters at EU level, but questions can remain as to what member States can do at a purely international level. The Court was asked, in *Laserdisken ApS v. Kulturministeriet*,[66] whether the rule on exhaustion was, in relation to copyright, limited to exhaustion within the European Economic Area (EEA) or whether the member states remained free to apply the principle of international exhaustion. This case concerned the right of distribution. The Court declined to open the door for international exhaustion and clarified that, in the area of copyright, exhaustion is also limited to the EEA level.[67]

Non-performance copyrights

Deutsche Grammophon

Non-performance copyrights are treated very similarly to patents. In fact, the oldest case in which the exhaustion doctrine was applied was a case relating to records. In *Deutsche Grammophon v. Metro*,[68] the Court was faced with the following issue. Deutsche Grammophon sold the same records in Germany and in France, but its French subsidiary, Polydor, could only charge a lower price due to market conditions. Metro bought the records in France for resale in Germany at a price below the price that Deutsche Grammophon charged. Deutsche Grammophon invoked its copyright[69] in the records to stop this practice. The Court ruled that Deutsche Grammophon had exhausted its copyright in the records by putting them on the market in France with its consent and could not oppose the importation of the records by Metro.[70]

This approach was confirmed in *Musik-Vertrieb Membran v. GEMA*.[71] Once more, records and cassettes were being imported into Germany after they had been put on the market in another member State with the consent of the copyright owner. The German collecting society, GEMA (*die Gesellschaft für musikalische Aufführungs*) tried to rely on the German copyright in the works to levy the difference between the low royalty that had

---

[65] Cases 55 and 57/80 *Musik-Vertrieb Membran GmbH & K-tel International v. GEMA* [1981] ECR 147, [1981] 2 CMLR 44.

[66] Case C-479/04 *Laserdisken ApS v. Kulturministeriet* [2006] ECDR 30.

[67] See Chapter 27 for a broader discussion in the context of trade marks.

[68] Case 78/70 *Deutsche Grammophon GmbH v. Metro-SB-Grossmarkte GmbH & Co. KG* [1971] ECR 487, [1971] CMLR 631.

[69] For the purposes of our discussion of the case, we can assume that the German exclusive distribution right is akin to copyright.

[70] Case 78/70 *Deutsche Grammophon GmbH v. Metro-SB-Grossmarkte GmbH & Co. KG* [1971] ECR 487 at 500.

[71] Joined cases 55 and 57/80 *Musik-Vertrieb Membran v. GEMA* [1981] ECR 147, [1981] 2 CMLR 44; see also Case 58/80 *Dansk Supermarked A/S v. Imerco A/S* [1981] ECR 181, [1981] 3 CMLR 590.

been paid abroad and the higher German royalty. The Court reiterated that, by putting the records and cassettes on the market with its consent, the owner of the copyright had exhausted all copyright in them. It could, as a result, not rely on any copyright to prevent the importation, nor could it rely on that copyright to charge an additional royalty. In the Court's view, the copyright owner who markets its works in member States in which the royalties are low has to abide by that decision and accept its consequences.

The approach sounds identical to that taken in the patent case of *Merck v. Stephar*[72] and the case law of the Court has now also been reflected in the Information Society Directive, Art. 4(2) of which stipulates that:

> the distribution right shall not be exhausted within the Community in respect of the original or copies of the work, except where the first sale or other transfer of ownership in the Community of that object is made by the rightholder or with his consent.

Warner Bros

In *Warner Bros v. Christiansen*,[73] a difficult problem arose. Video cassettes, which were put on the market in both the UK and Denmark, were being imported from the UK into Denmark. It is clear that the plaintiff could not rely on its Danish copyright to stop the importation of the video cassettes, because this only requires a normal application of the dictum in the two previous cases. The problem arose because Danish law granted a rental right to the author or the producer, while such a right did not exist in the UK and Christiansen had imported the cassettes to hire them out afterwards. Christiansen argued that the rights in the cassettes had been exhausted, because they had been marketed in the UK with the consent of the owner, but the Court rejected this argument. Indeed, the rental right has to be treated as a separate right and, because it did not exist in the UK, it could not have been exhausted.[74] Warner Bros could invoke the Danish rental right to stop Christiansen hiring out the video cassettes.[75]

It is easier to understand why the rental right should be treated as a separate right by looking at the consequences of not doing so: that would effectively have rendered the rental right worthless, because it would have been exhausted by sale in a member State in which the right is not known. As we discussed in relation to patents in Chapter 5, Arts 28 and 30 are construed in such a way that they must leave the existence of the right and a certain exercise untouched, because any other interpretation would render them senseless. The approach taken by the Court must therefore be correct.

It may be tempting to argue that this case presented similar features to those of the *Merck v. Stephar*[76] in relation to patents and that, as a result, the Court should have ruled that Warner Bros could not rely on the Danish rental right, because it should accept the consequences of its decision to market the video cassettes in a country where no rental right is available. It is submitted that this approach is wrong. In *Merck*, Italy had a patent law, but excluded pharmaceuticals from its scope. The Court argued that Merck should accept the consequences of a weaker or absent patent protection in Italy and could not invoke its Dutch patent. Only one right was involved. In the *Warner* case, however, two rights were involved. The copyright had been exhausted, but was not relied upon, because only the Danish rental right was used—and it is this that allows us to distinguish the cases.

---

[72] Case 187/80 *Merck & Co. Inc. v. Stephar BV* [1981] ECR 2063, discussed in Chapter 5.

[73] Case 158/86 *Warner Bros Inc. v. Christiansen* [1988] ECR 2605.

[74] See M. Henry, 'Rental and duration directives: issues arising from current EC reforms' [1993] 12 EIPR 437 at 439.

[75] Ibid.

[76] Case 187/80 *Merck & Co. Inc. v. Stephar BV* [1981] ECR 2063, discussed above in Chapter 5.

EMI Electrola

A problem relating to the term of copyright arose in *EMI Electrola GmbH v. Patricia*,[77] because the term of copyright protection for records in Denmark was shorter than that available in Germany. Patricia bought Cliff Richard sound recordings in Denmark once they were out of copyright and imported them into Germany, where EMI Electrola tried to stop it by relying on the German copyright in the recordings that had not yet expired. The European Court of Justice held that the German copyright had not been exhausted, because the marketing in Denmark had not occurred with the consent of the copyright owner, but was due to the fact that the term of copyright had expired.

This case can now be described as legal history, because the term of copyright has now been harmonized in the Community and because the *Phil Collins* judgment[78] would now result in the work in a similar case remaining in copyright in the whole of the EU, as discussed in relation to the term of copyright. The problem will therefore not reoccur.

The difficulty of defining the essential function of copyright

The essential function of copyright was first described by the Court of First Instance in the *Magill* cases,[79] which are concerned with competition law, as being '*to protect the moral rights in the work and to ensure a reward for the creative effort, while respecting the aims of, in particular, Article* [82]'. This definition is not precise enough, although it rightly indicates the two essential elements of copyright—moral rights and economic rights—that are granted to the author. The reference to creativity must be understood against the background of the low originality requirement in copyright. This definition should, therefore, be treated with caution.

The *Warner Bros* case[80] shows clearly that there are many facets to the essential function of copyright and, especially, to the specific subject matter of copyright. The rental right point was clearly a separate aspect within the latter. This should not come as a surprise: copyright is a broad right that protects a wide variety of products. It may, in each case and broadly speaking, be the aim to protect the author and the subsequent right holders, because it is felt that their creative efforts deserve encouragement and protection, but the exact way in which this is put into practice by including different aspects within the specific subject matter of copyright is not always as easy to determine as it is with the narrower patent right.

While it can be understood that rental, as a separate way in which the work is exploited, may have been entitled to be promoted to a separate aspect of the specific subject matter, one should not construe the latter too broadly either. The *Dior* case[81] illustrates this point. Dior had exhausted all copyrights in the box in which it sold its perfume bottles by putting the perfumes, in the box, on the market for the first time. This is normal copyright exhaustion and the reward for the copyright in the design of the boxes is seen as being included in the sales price of the perfume. Any further use of the copyright in the design of the boxes would therefore go beyond the specific subject matter of copyright in this case. A problem arose because the parallel importer wanted to reproduce the design of the boxes in its publicity. Printing a photograph of the boxes to advertise the fact that the

---

[77] Case 341/87 *EMI Electrola GmbH v. Patricia Im- und Export* [1989] ECR 79, [1989] 2 CMLR 413.

[78] Case C-92/92 *Phil Collins v. Imtrat Handelsgesellschaft MbH* [1993] 3 CMLR 773, in which the parallel case Case 362/92 *Patricia v. EMI Electrola*, concerning Cliff Richard's work, is also reported; see also G. Dworkin and J. A. L. Sterling '*Phil Collins* and the Term Directive' [1994] 5 EIPR 187.

[79] Cases T-69/89 *Radio Telefis Éireann v. Commission* [1991] ECR II-485, [1991] 4 CMLR 586; T-70/89 *BBC v. EC Commission* [1991] ECR II-535, [1991] 4 CMLR 669; T-76/89 *Independent Television Productions v. EC Commission* [1991] ECR II-575, [1991] 4 CMLR 745.

[80] Case 158/86 *Warner Bros v. Christiansen* [1988] ECR 2605, [1990] 3 CMLR 684.

[81] Case C-337/95 *Parfums Christian Dior SA v. Evora BV* [1998] RPC 166.

perfume is now available at a lower price from certain outlets certainly involves copying: could Dior stop this on the basis of its copyright?

The European Court of Justice ruled that it could not. The exhaustion of the copyright by putting the product on the market exhausted all rights. Reprinting for publicity purposes is clearly not a separate aspect of the specific subject matter of the right; it is part of the main aspect of copyright. It could rather be argued that the parallel importer, who has the right to import the perfume bottles that Dior put on the market in another member State, must also have the right to advertise these products. Otherwise, the consumer will not be informed and, in the absence of real sales, the whole system of parallel import will de facto collapse. Any use of copyright to stop the advertising of the products would therefore be a use to block parallel imports of legitimately acquired products. This cannot be part of the essential function of copyright; it must be an abusive use of the right. It must therefore be treated as falling outside the specific subject matter of the right and the right must be treated as having been exhausted for this purpose.[82]

Performance copyrights

The category of performance copyrights is concerned with plays and films, and their performance. The exploitation of these works takes place through public exhibitions, which can be repeated an indefinite number of times. It is like rendering a service and the whole area has more links with the free movement of services provided for in Art. 49 of the Treaty of Rome than with the free movement of goods. This implies that this category of rights should be treated differently.

The European Court of Justice was confronted with this problem in the *Coditel* case.[83] This case made the French film *Le Boucher*—the copyright in which was owned by the French company Les Films la Boétie—famous. A seven-year exclusive licence to exhibit the film in Belgium had been given to Ciné Vog. One of the clauses of the licence stipulated that Ciné Vog could only allow the film to be broadcast on Belgian television 40 months after its first cinema showing. A different exclusive licensee was appointed for Germany and that licence contract did not restrict the showing of the film on television. The film was shown on German television before it could have been shown on Belgian, and the Belgian cable company Coditel picked up the German signal and retransmitted it on its cable network. This required the authorization of the Belgian licensee under Belgian copyright law, because it was held to be a communication to the public. Because no authorization had been applied for and because it feared loss of revenue, because the Belgian television stations would be less interested in acquiring the right to broadcast a film that many of their viewers had already seen in the German version, Ciné Vog sued Coditel for infringement of copyright. Coditel based its defence, inter alia, on the freedom to provide services and argued that, because the film had been shown with the consent of the owner of the copyright, all copyright in it had been exhausted.

The problem with the free movement of services provision of the Treaty, however, is that it does not provide for an exception for intellectual property. This did not prevent Advocate-General Warner suggesting that Art. 30 applied by analogy in this context. The Court must have agreed with this suggestion because it ruled that:

> Whilst Article 49 of the Treaty prohibits restrictions upon the freedom to provide services, it does not hereby encompass limits upon the exercise of certain economic activities which

[82] See also I. Stamatoudi, 'From drugs to spirits and from boxes to publicity: decided and undecided issues in relation to trade mark and copyright exhaustion' [1999] IPQ 95.

[83] Case 62/79 *Coditel SA v. Ciné Vog Films SA* [1980] ECR 881, [1981] 2 CMLR 362.

have their origin in the application of national legislation for the protection of intellectual property, save where such application constitutes a means of arbitrary discrimination or a disguised restriction on trade between member states. Such would be the case if that application enabled parties to create artificial barriers to trade between member states.[84]

In a next step, the specific subject matter of the performing right in a film was defined as the right of authorities to forbid each and every performance of the film, including the right of it being televised. Because the retransmission of the film by Coditel amounted to a new performance, the performing right in the film had not been exhausted and Ciné Vog could rely on it. The restriction on the showing of the film that Ciné Vog claimed was necessary in order to guarantee it the benefit of the essence of the exclusive performing right. The remaining issue was whether the practice of having one exclusive licensee per member State was an example of the artificial barriers to trade to which the Court objected. But the Court did not see it as such and accepted that such an approach was objectively justifiable, because, at that time, all television services were organized on the national basis of a legal broadcasting monopoly.[85] Its conclusion was that:

> the provisions of the Treaty relating to the freedom to provide services did not preclude an assignee of the performing right in a cinematographic film in a member state from relying upon his right to prohibit the exhibition of that film in that State, without its authority, by means of cable diffusion if the film so exhibited is picked up and transmitted after being broadcast in another member state by a third party with the consent of the original owner of the right.[86]

In a digital online environment, similar situations arise. Works are, for example, delivered online whenever the user needs them: for example, through access to a database. Concepts such as communication to the public and making the work available to the public carry with them an element of services, rather than a material copy of the work, being provided to the user. The Information Society Directive takes this into account and stipulates, in its Art. 3(3), that the communication to the public right and the making available to the public right will '*not be exhausted by any act of communication to the public or making available to the public as set out in this Article*'.

Exploitation under European law—copyright and competition law

Article 81

Agreements related to copyright may restrict competition and thus may fall within the scope of Article 81 of the EC Treaty. Such infringing agreements will involve an improper or abusive exercise of copyright, as confirmed by the European Court of Justice in the *Coditel (No. 2)* case.[87] It cannot be said that many cases arose in this area, but the practice of the Commission shows that its approach is similar to its approach in patent licence cases.

---

[84] Case 62/79 *Coditel SA v. Ciné Vog Films SA* [1980] ECR 881 at 903.

[85] Arguably, this is no longer the case now that Directive 93/83 on copyright and neighbouring rights relating to satellite broadcasting and cable retransmission (1993) OJ L 248/15 has been adopted. For example, Art. 7(3) of that Directive, on co-production agreements, shows that licences may have to be granted on a Community scale, thereby excluding territorial licensing. See P. Kern, 'The EC "common position" on copyright applicable to satellite broadcasting and cable retransmission' [1993] 8 EIPR 276 at 280.

[86] Case 62/79 *Coditel SA v. Ciné Vog Films SA* [1980] ECR 881 at 904.

[87] Case 262/81 *Coditel SA v. Ciné Vog Films SA* [1982] ECR 3381, [1983] 1 CMLR 49.

For example, 'no challenge' clauses, royalty clauses that were extended to non-protected goods or works, non-competition clauses that were to continue after the expiry date of the agreement, an exclusive grant-back clause,[88] export bans,[89] and attempts to guarantee absolute exclusivity[90] were disputed by the Commission and the relevant agreements were modified at the Commission's request so that no formal decisions were issued.

Article 82—collecting societies

The largest number of cases in which Art. 82 of the EC Treaty has been applied to copyright relates to those involving collecting societies. The European Court of Justice has indicated that there is nothing intrinsically objectionable about the establishment of collecting societies, which may be necessary in order that individual artists can obtain a reasonable return for their endeavour[91]—but, usually, these collecting societies occupy a dominant position, because they operate as a de facto monopoly in the member States—that is, in relation to a substantial part of the Common Market. Trade between member States is affected by the fact that the creation of a single market for copyright services is prevented. So the way in which these collecting societies exploit their dominant position will be closely examined and improper exploitation will be an infringement of Art. 82.[92]

The early cases

The internal rules of the collecting societies have to take account of all of the the relevant interests and the result must be a balance between '*the requirement of maximum freedom for authors, composers, and publishers to dispose of their works and that of the effective management of their rights*'.[93] Every exaggeration towards one side can imply an abuse of dominant position. This abuse takes the form of discrimination against nationals of other member States and among members, or the binding of members with excessive obligations.[94]

There is no doubt that any discrimination on grounds of nationality is an abuse of dominant position. The Commission made that clear in its *GEMA* decision.[95] Membership cannot be made dependent on the establishment of a tax domicile in the member State in which the collecting society operates and special forms of membership, or membership of the organs of the society, cannot be denied to persons or companies that have the nationality of a different member State from that of the collecting society. Account should also be taken of income received from other collecting societies in order to determine if a member qualifies for a special form of membership.[96] GEMA did not appeal to the European Court of Justice, but the Court approved of the Commission's point of view

---

[88] *Neilsen-Hordell/Reichmark*, reported in EC Commission (1982) *Twelfth Annual Report on Competition Policy*, points 88–9.

[89] *Re Ernest Benn Ltd*, reported in EC Commission (1979) Ninth Annual Report on Competition Policy.

[90] *Knoll/Hille-Form*, reported in EC Commission (1983) Thirteenth Annual Report on Competition Policy, points 142–6.

[91] Case 127/73 *Belgische Radio en Televisie & Société Belge des Auteurs, Compositeurs et Editeurs v. SV SABAM & NV Fonior* [1974] ECR 313, [1974] 2 CMLR 238.

[92] See J.-F. Bellis (1989) 'Collecting societies and EEC law', in D. Peeperhorn and C. van Rij (eds) *Collecting Societies in the Music Business*, Reports presented at the meeting of the International Association of Entertainment Lawyers, MIDEM, Cannes, Apeldoorn: Maklu, p. 78; B. Cawthra (1973) *Industrial Property Rights in the EEC*, Farnborough: Gower Press, pp. 70–1.

[93] Case 127/73 *Belgische Radio en Televisie & Société Belge des Auteurs, Compositeurs et Editeurs v. SV SABAM & NV Fonior* [1974] ECR 313, [1974] 2 CMLR 238.

[94] Bellis (1989) p. 78.

[95] (1971) OJ L 134/15.

[96] Ibid.

by giving judgment against GVL when it refused to represent anyone not resident in Germany, because secondary exploitation rights in other member States were generally less comprehensive and more difficult to assert.[97]

Discrimination among members in relation to the distribution of income is also an abuse. Every classification procedure has to be cost-justified and, without cost-justification, an undertaking in a dominant position cannot pay loyalty bonuses[98]—especially not to certain members with funds coming from all members. The Commission found that GEMA was infringing these principles.[99] But if royalty income from all sources is taken into account, a collecting society is still permitted to set a reasonable level of royalty income as a condition of membership.[100] It was stated:[101]

> The abuse also lies in the fact that GEMA binds its members by obligations which are not objectively justified and which, in particular, unfairly complicate the movement of its members to another society.

It cannot be accepted that members are required to assign their rights for all categories of works and for the entire world to the collecting society, especially not if the assignment period and the waiting period for the acquisition of certain benefits are excessive and if future works also have to be assigned. The two latter points are already abuses when considered on their own.[102] The Commission held that members should be free to assign all, or part, of their rights for the countries in which the collecting society does not operate directly to other societies, and that they should be equally free to assign only certain categories of rights to the collecting society and to withdraw from it the administration of certain categories at the end of a three-year period.[103]

Members must have the opportunity to choose another collecting society to represent them outside the Community. An abuse that relates only to performance outside the Community stays an infringement of Art. 82 if parties within the jurisdiction of one of the member States concluded the contract in the Community.[104]

A couple of final details can be added, such as the rule that the right of judicial recourse may not be excluded by an undertaking occupying a dominant position[105] and that, if they are essential to strengthen the position of the collecting society in negotiations with powerful large customers such as national radio and television stations, restrictions imposed on members can be accepted.[106]

---

[97] Case 7/82 *Gesellschaft zur Verwertung von Leistungsschutzrechten mbH (GVL) v. EC Commission* [1983] ECR 483, [1983] 3 CMLR 645.

[98] See Case 85/76 *Hoffmann-La Roche & Co. AG v. EC Commission* [1979] ECR 461, [1979] 3 CMLR 211.

[99] *GEMA decision* (1971) OJ L 134/15.

[100] Bellis (1989) p. 79.

[101] *GEMA decision* (1971) OJ L 134/15.

[102] Ibid.

[103] The original period was one year and seven categories were defined. This option is still open: *GEMA decision* (1971) OJ L 134/15. The Commission's decision of 6 July 1972—(1972) OJ L 166 22—offered the alternative of a three-year period compensated by these narrower categories: the general performance right; the radio broadcasting right; the public performing right of broadcast works; the right to transmit by television; the public performing right of televised works; the motion picture performance right; the right of mechanical reproduction and distribution; the public performing right of mechanically reproduced works; the motion picture production right; the right to produce, reproduce, and distribute on videotape; the public performing right of works reproduced on videotape; the utilization rights arising in the future as a result of technical development or a change in legislation.

[104] Case 22/79 *Greenwich Film Production, Paris v. SACEM* [1979] ECR 3275, [1980] 1 CMLR 629.

[105] *GEMA decision* (1971) OJ L 134/15.

[106] Case 127/73 *Belgische Radio en Televisie & Société Belge des Auteurs, Compositeurs et Editeurs v. SV SABAM & NV Fonior* [1974] ECR 313, [1974] 2 CMLR 238.

The relationship between collecting societies and third parties can also be problematic, and raises certain issues in relation to Art. 82. The first abuses to be found in this area were the imposition of a higher royalty on imported tape and video recorders than that levied on equipment produced in the member State in which the collecting society is established and the contractual extension of royalty payments to works that are no longer protected.[107]

The more recent cases provide more details

A series of recent cases allowed the European Court of Justice to work out a more detailed point of view. In the *Basset v. SACEM* case,[108] the Court ruled that it is no abuse, in the sense of Art. 82, if a collecting society charges a royalty called a 'supplementary mechanical reproduction fee', in addition to a performance royalty, on the public performance of sound recordings. This only amounted to a normal copyright exploitation and no act of arbitrary discrimination, nor a disguised restriction on trade between member States, could be seen in it, because the fee was charged for all sound recordings, regardless of their origin. The fact that such a fee did not exist in the member State in which the sounds recorded were lawfully placed on the market did not influence this conclusion.

Even more important in that case was the following *obiter dictum*: 'It is not impossible, however, that the amount of the royalty, or of the combined royalties, charged by the copyright-management society may be such that Article [82] applies.'[109] The Court elaborated this *obiter dictum* further by laying the burden of proving that an appreciably higher scale of royalty fees is justified by a better copyright protection on the collecting society. If such proof is not brought, the imposition of the higher fees forms an abuse of dominant position.

In the subsequent *Lucazeau* cases,[110] the Court ruled:

> When an undertaking holding a dominant position imposes scales of fees for its services which are appreciably higher than those charged in other member states and where a comparison of the fee levels has been made on a consistent basis, that difference must be regarded as indicative of an abuse of a dominant position. In such a case it is for the undertaking in question to justify the difference with reference to objective dissimilarities between the situation in the member state concerned and the situation prevailing in all the other member states.[111]

The Court had reached the same conclusion some weeks earlier in the *Tournier* case.[112] But in *Tournier*, the Court ruled also that a collecting society that refuses to grant the users of recorded music access only to its foreign repertoire does not abuse its dominant position, in the sense of Art. 82:

> unless access to a part of the protected repertoire could entirely safeguard the interests of the authors, composers and publishers of music without thereby increasing the costs of managing contracts and monitoring the use of protected musical works.[113]

---

[107] *GEMA decision* (1971) OJ L 134/15, but collecting societies have the right to round off the playing time to the nearest minute.

[108] Case 402/85 *G Basset v. Société des Auteurs, Compositeurs et Editeurs de Musique (SACEM)* [1987] ECR 1747, [1987] 3 CMLR 173.

[109] Ibid., at 1769. This dictum fell outside the scope of the prejudicial question referred to the Court by the French judge.

[110] Cases 110/88, 241/88 and 242/88 *François Lucazeau v. Société des Auteurs, Compositeurs et Editeurs de Musique (SACEM)* [1989] ECR 2811.

[111] Ibid., at 2831.

[112] Case 395/87 *Ministère Public v. Jean-Louis Tournier* [1989] ECR 2521, [1991] 4 CMLR 248.

[113] Ibid., at 2580.

The main issues with a Community interest in relation to collecting societies have now been addressed. *BEMIM*[114] and *Tremblay*[115] showed that the outstanding issues lack a Community interest and therefore fall under the jurisdiction of the national courts. This may suit the EU well, because it becomes clear that it will need the cooperation of the collecting societies if these are to be increasingly involved in collecting royalties for the exploitation of copyright works in the information society.[116] These developments do not, however, involve a change in policy as far as the points of substantive law are involved.

Article 82—does dominance force an undertaking to grant a licence?

The central issue involved in relation to the question of whether dominance forces an undertaking to grant a licence is whether an undertaking in a dominant position can itself be forced to grant a 'licence' of an intellectual property right that it holds and if a refusal to do so implies an abuse of its dominant position. In recent years, this issue arose on several occasions in the areas of design and copyright. We discuss these design and copyright cases here together, because they strongly draw upon each other.

Volvo *and* Renault

The issue arose for the first time in two cases that were concerned with designs for spare parts for cars: *Maxicar v. Renault*[117] and *Volvo v. Veng*.[118] Maxicar and Veng were involved in car repairs and maintenance, and wanted to obtain a licence to produce spare parts themselves. When unsuccessful in obtaining these licences, they argued that Volvo and Renault occupied a dominant position in the relevant market and that, by refusing to grant licences, they abused their dominant position. They wanted to see Volvo and Renault obliged to grant the licences, and submitted that the European Court of Justice should interpret Art. 82 accordingly.

The Court started its analysis by ruling out the possibility that the existence of the fact that an intellectual property right was obtained could be an abuse of a dominant position. The Court held that the existence and the issue of obtaining an intellectual property right is a matter for the national rules of the member States, which rules determine the nature and extent of the protection.[119] In the *Maxicar* case, the Court stated that '*the mere fact of obtaining protective rights ... does not constitute an abuse of a dominant position within the meaning of Article* [82]'.[120]

---

[114] Case T-114/92 *Bureau Européen des Médias de l'industrie Musicale (BEMIM) v. EC Commission* [1995] ECR II-147, [1996] 4 CMLR 305.

[115] Case T-5/93 *Roger Tremblay v. EC Commission (Syndicat des Exploitants de Lieux de Loisirs (SELL), intervening)* [1995] ECR II-185, [1996] 4 CMLR 305; Case C-91/95P *Roger Tremblay v. EC Commission* [1996] ECR I-5547, [1997] 4 CMLR 211.

[116] See P. Torremans and I. Stamatoudi, 'Collecting societies: sorry, the Community is no longer interested!' (1997) 22 EL Rev 352; see also I. Stamatoudi, 'The European Court's share–state relationship with collecting societies' [1997] 6 EIPR 289–97.

[117] Case 53/87 *Consorzio Italiano della Componentistica di Ricambio per Autoveicoli & Maxicar v. Régie nationale des usines Renault* [1988] ECR 6039, [1990] 4 CMLR 265.

[118] Case 238/87 *AB Volvo v. Erik Veng (UK) Ltd* [1988] ECR 6211, [1989] 4 CMLR 122.

[119] Ibid., with reference to Case 144/81 *Keurkoop BV v. Nancy Kean Gifts BV* [1982] ECR 2853, [1983] 2 CMLR 47.

[120] Case 53/87 *Consorzio Italiano della Componentistica di Ricambio per Autoveicoli & Maxicar v. Régie nationale des usines Renault* [1988] ECR 6039, [1990] 4 CMLR 265 at 6073.

The obligation for a dominant undertaking to grant a licence[121] was ruled out in the *Veng* case:

> the right of the proprietor of a protected design to prevent third parties from manufacturing and selling or importing, without its consent, products incorporating the design constitutes the very subject-matter of his exclusive right. It follows that an obligation imposed upon the proprietor of a protected design to grant to third parties, even in return for a reasonable royalty, a licence for the supply of products incorporating the design would lead to the proprietor thereof being deprived of the substance of his exclusive right, and that a refusal to grant such a licence cannot in itself constitute an abuse of a dominant position.[122]

The situation may, however, be different if the owner of the right refuses to supply spare parts, fixes prices at an unfair level,[123] or discontinues production. Provided that such conduct is liable to affect trade between member States, such exercise of the intellectual property right is prohibited by Art. 82 and, in this situation, the grant of a 'compulsory' licence becomes possible.[124] But it is clear from the cases that more than the existence of the right creating a dominant position and the simple refusal to grant a licence is required if an abuse is to be proved. The starting point must be that the power to decide whether or not to grant licences is an essential component of the right with which Art. 82 does not interfere. *Volvo v. Veng* dealt with designs, but the Court's ruling in *Maxicar v. Renault* does not permit any different conclusion when patents are concerned.[125]

Magill

Facts and early stages of the Magill *litigation*

In the *Magill* cases,[126] the problem arose when Magill wished to publish the listings of programmes of the British Broadcasting Corporation (BBC), Independent Television (ITV), and Radio Telefís Éireann (RTE) in a single weekly publication. The three companies refused to supply those listings and invoked their copyright in the listings to do so. It should be noted that they published their own guides, which thus enjoyed a form of monopoly, and supplied, free of charge, the weekly listings to foreign publications; they also supplied daily listings to the press. The Commission[127] ruled that the three companies abused their dominant position in exercising their copyright in such a way and required that advance information be supplied to Magill.

---

[121] See V. Korah, 'No duty to license independent repairers to make spare parts: the *Renault, Volvo* and *Bayer* cases' [1988] 12 EIPR 381.

[122] Case 238/87 *AB Volvo v. Erik Veng (UK) Ltd* [1988] ECR 6211, [1989] 4 CMLR 122 at 6235.

[123] Products protected by an intellectual property right may be sold at a higher price than similar unprotected products if the price difference forms a reasonable return of the investments made: see Case 24/67 *Parke, Davis & Co. v. Probel, Reese, Beintema-Interfarm & Centrafarm* [1968] ECR 55, [1968] CMLR 47, confirmed in Case 53/87 *Maxicar v. Régie nationale des usines Renault* [1988] ECR 6039, [1990] 4 CMLR 265.

[124] Case 238/87 *AB Volvo v. Erik Veng (UK) Ltd* [1988] ECR 6211, [1989] 4 CMLR 122; Case 53/87 *Maxicar v. Régie nationale des usines Renault* [1988] ECR 6039, [1990] 4 CMLR 265.

[125] Ibid.; see C. Bellamy and G. Child (1991) *Common Market Law of Competition*, 1st Supp. to 3rd edn, London: Sweet and Maxwell, p. 86. The Patents Court in London dealt with an application to patents in *Philips Electronics NV v. Ingman Ltd & the Video Duplicating Co. Ltd* [1999] FSR 112.

[126] Case T-69/89 *Radio Telefís Éireann v. EC Commission (Magill TV Guide Ltd intervening)* [1991] ECR II-485, [1991] 4 CMLR 586; Case T-70/89 *British Broadcasting Corp. & BBC Enterprises Ltd v. EC Commission (Magill TV Guide Ltd intervening)* [1991] ECR II-535, [1991] 4 CMLR 669; Case T-76/89 *Independent Television Publications Ltd v. EC Commission (Magill TV Guide Ltd intervening)* [1991] ECR II-575, [1991] 4 CMLR 745.

[127] *Magill TV Guide/ITP, BBC & RTE decision* (1989) OJ L 78/43, [1989] 4 CMLR 757.

The Court of First Instance upheld the decision on this point.[128] The judgment of the Court of First Instance reads:

> conduct of that type (the exercise of the copyright in the way described above)…clearly goes beyond what is necessary to fulfil the essential function of the copyright as permitted in Community law.[129]

After failing to find an objective and specific justification for this conduct, the Court of First Instance continued:

> the aim and effect of the applicant's exclusive reproduction of its programme listings was to exclude any potential competition…in order to maintain the monopoly enjoyed…by the applicant on that market. From the point of view of outside undertakings interested in publishing a television magazine, the applicant's refusal to authorise, on request and on a non-discriminatory basis, any third party to publish its programme listings is therefore comparable…to an arbitrary refusal by a car manufacturer to supply spare parts…to an independent repairer…[130]

The Court of First Instance applied the *Volvo v. Veng* doctrine to copyright. This situation falls under the exception in the doctrine in relation to which the grant of a 'compulsory' licence is possible, because the intellectual property right is exercised in a way that is prohibited by Art. 82.[131]

The Court of First Instance also stressed that it is enough, in order for Art. 82 to be applicable, that the abusive conduct is capable of affecting trade between member States; no present and real effect on such trade is requested.[132]

Magill *before the Court of Justice—a turning point*

The *Magill* cases went on to be appealed before the European Court of Justice.[133] The main problem with the approach taken by the Commission and the Court of First Instance is that it could suggest that, once an undertaking occupies a dominant position, the simple refusal to grant a licence could constitute an abuse of that dominant position.[134] This cannot be a correct interpretation of Art. 82. As suggested in *Volvo* and *Renault*, the interpretation of Art. 82 develops along the lines of the interpretation of Arts 28 and 30. This is the approach that we advocated above in relation to the free movement of goods and it was also the approach taken by Advocate-General Gulmann in his conclusion, which was delivered in June 1994.[135]

---

[128] Case T-69/89 *Radio Telefis Éireann v. EC Commission (Magill TV Guide Ltd intervening)* [1991] ECR II-485, [1991] 4 CMLR 586; Case T-70/89 *BBC & BBC Enterprises Ltd v. EC Commission (Magill TV Guide Ltd intervening)* [1991] ECR II-535, [1991] 4 CMLR 669; Case T-76/89 *Independent Television Publications Ltd v. EC Commission (Magill TV Guide Ltd intervening)* [1991] ECR II-575, [1991] 4 CMLR 745.

[129] Case T-69/89 *Radio Telefis Éireann v. EC Commission (Magill TV Guide Ltd intervening)* [1991] 4 CMLR 586 at 618.

[130] Ibid.; similar rulings are found in the other *Magill* cases.

[131] Compare R. Whish (1993) *Competition Law*, 3rd edn, London: Butterworths, p. 648; Bellamy and Child (1991) p. 87 could not reconcile the Commission's decision with the *Volvo v. Veng* doctrine.

[132] Case T-69/89 *Radio Telefis Éireann v. EC Commission (Magill TV Guide Ltd intervening)* [1991] ECR II-485, [1991] 4 CMLR 586; Case T-70/89 *BBC & BBC Enterprises Ltd v. EC Commission (Magill TV Guide Ltd intervening)* [1991] ECR II-535, [1991] 4 CMLR 669; Case T-76/89 *Independent Television Publications Ltd v. EC Commission (Magill TV Guide Ltd intervening)* [1991] ECR II-575, [1991] 4 CMLR 745.

[133] Joined cases C-241/91 P and C-242/91 P *Radio Telefis Éireann & Independent Television Publications Ltd v. EC Commission* [1995] ECR I-743, [1995] 4 CMLR 718.

[134] See S. Haines, 'Copyright takes the dominant position: the Advocate-General's Opinion in *Magill*' [1994] 9 EIPR 401 at 401.

[135] See ibid.

In a controversial judgment, the wording of which strongly resembles the *Commercial Solvents*[136] line of thought, the Court declined to overrule the Court of First Instance. The reasons given and the implications of the judgment do, however, require some careful examination.[137] The main principle is that a refusal to license intellectual property rights can contravene Art. 82 in 'exceptional circumstances'. In those cases, compulsory licensing is an available remedy.[138]

When it established that the broadcasters occupied a dominant position, the Court indicated, first of all, that it accepted that the relevant product and geographical market should be defined as the market in comprehensive television listings guides in Ireland and Northern Ireland. The Court went on to confirm that the mere ownership of an intellectual property right—in this case, the copyright in the programme listings—does not confer a dominant position.[139] That dominant position did, however, exist in the particular circumstances of the case. This was derived from the fact that the broadcasters were the only source of the basic programming information, that they had a de facto monopoly over the raw material that the programming information constituted,[140] and that they could therefore prevent effective competition in the secondary market of weekly television magazines.[141]

Even so, the question remained whether the refusal to license amounted to an abuse of that dominant position. The existing case law pointed towards the fact that the mere existence of the intellectual property right and a use that stays within the specific subject matter of the right cannot amount to an abuse. If the possession of the immaterial right is to have any value, its owner must be free to decide under which circumstances and under which financial conditions he or she is prepared to grant a licence. A right to refuse to grant a licence must be part of such a system and must therefore come within the specific subject matter of the right. In normal circumstances, such a refusal can therefore not be in breach of Art. 82. There may, however, be circumstances in which the intellectual property right is used improperly, to serve purposes that have nothing to do with the real purpose and essential function of the right. If the right is abused, the refusal to grant a licence is no longer used to implement the essential function of the right and, just as anything else in relation to an exclusive or monopoly intellectual property right, exposes itself to the sanction of Art. 82.

This approach is endorsed by the Court's judgment. The Court argued that a refusal might, in exceptional circumstances, constitute an abuse.[142] These exceptional circumstances involved the following in this case: the broadcaster's main activity is broadcasting; the television guides market is only a secondary market for the broadcaster. By refusing to provide the basic programme listing information, of which they were the only source, the broadcasters prevented the appearance of new products that they did not offer and for which there was a consumer demand. The refusal could not be justified by virtue of their normal activities and, by denying access to the basic information that was required to make the new product, the broadcasters were effectively reserving the secondary market for weekly television guides to themselves. The use of copyright to block the appearance of a new product for which the copyright information is essential, and to reserve a

---

[136] See Case 6, 7/73 *ICI & Commercial Solvents v. EC Commission* [1974] ECR 223, [1974] 1 CMLR 309.

[137] See I. Stamatoudi, 'The hidden agenda in *Magill* and its impact on new technologies' (1998) 1 JWIP 153.

[138] Joined cases C-241/91 P and C-242/91 P *Radio Telefis Eireann & Independent Television Publications Ltd v. EC Commission* [1995] ECR I-743, [1995] All ER (EC) 4161.

[139] Ibid., at [46].

[140] Ibid., at [53].

[141] Ibid., at [47].

[142] Ibid., at [54] and [57].

secondary market to oneself, is an abuse and cannot be said to be necessary to fulfil the essential function—that is, the reward and encouragement of the author—of copyright. This is especially so if one is the only source of the copyright information or material, and especially the latter element is of vital importance. It may not be part of the abuse, but the availability of other sources for the material would take away the element of dominance. Without dominance, there can simply be no abuse of a dominant position.

Looking at it this way, the Court has allayed the fears that had arisen on the basis of the problematically worded judgment of the Court of First Instance. It is also clear that the judgment of the European Court of Justice in *Magill* is by no means a departure from its existing case law; it is rather an application of that case law in an extreme set of circumstances. All intellectual property rights still have their role in a free market economy, but, as we explained earlier, that role is restricted to their capacity to enhance overall levels of competition. This means that intellectual property rights can only be used to fulfil their essential function. This point has been overlooked on too many occasions and the specific subject matter of a right has too often been seen as a list, set in stone, of things that the right holder is allowed to do. Refusing a licence had to be on that list. But *Magill* has shown that the list is by no means so set and that the listed items are only included in so far as they fulfil the essential pro-competitive function of the intellectual property right involved. They will be caught by the operation of competition law if they are (ab)used for other purposes. This will be the case in what the Court described as 'exceptional circumstances' and the essential facilities doctrine, which is so prominently present in the judgment, provides just one—albeit a poignant—example of exceptional circumstances in which the use of an intellectual property right falls outside of what is required for the fulfilment of the essential function of the intellectual property right concerned.

One can find, between the lines of the *Magill* case, criticism of the fact that the UK and Ireland grant copyright to basic programme information listings that have such a low level of originality. But this point will have to be addressed by the member States concerned or by means of a Parliament and Council Directive. The Court has no power to interfere with issues such as what is original enough to attract copyright or, in trade marks terms, with the determination of whether there is de facto confusion between two trade marks. The Court made this clear in *Deutsche Renault v. Audi*.[143] These issues of substantive law are part of the sovereign powers of the member States in the absence of Community harmonization measures on the points concerned.

It must be obvious that these exceptional circumstances will rarely be found and that the operation of the rule in *Magill* will be restricted to unusual and special cases, but the essential function is by no means a narrow concept. *Magill* must also be seen against the background of the fact that a weak copyright was involved. Most other member States would not even have given copyright in the basic programme information concerned. Basic information is more easily an indispensable raw material for new products than the more traditional highly creative personal expressions of certain ideas by authors. This means that the *Magill* rule will more easily bite in the former cases. The more original the work is, the more creative the expression that has gone in a particular expression of an idea, the more unlikely it is that a refusal to licence will be an abuse. The refusal to grant a licence for the television listings became abusive, among other things, because, without the licence, Magill could not publish any guide: the whole market and the emergence of a new product were blocked. A refusal to grant a licence to turn a novel into a movie is clearly not in the same league: plenty of other films can be made and the monopolization of any secondary market is simply not present.

---

[143] Case C-317/91 *Deutsche Renault v. Audi* [1993] ECR I-6227, [1995] 1 CMLR 461.

Ladbroke

The conclusion that *Magill* needs to be confined to a small number of extreme cases is also supported by the judgment of the Court of First Instance in one of the many *Ladbroke* cases.[144] This case was concerned with the question of whether a refusal by the French copyright owners to license sound and pictures of French horse races to a Belgian betting agency amounted to a *Magill*-style abuse of a dominant position.[145]

The emphasis in this case lies squarely on the issue of abuse. That abuse must be found on the relevant geographical market and any activity or decision outside that market is irrelevant. The Court of First Instance ruled that no *Magill*-style abuse could be found. It reached this conclusion for a couple of reasons.[146] Firstly, Ladbroke was not prevented from entering another market by the refusal to license. It was already an important player in the market concerned and it could not be argued that the French horse racing organizations reserved that betting market for themselves, especially because they were not even present in it. The pictures were not essential for the exercise of the activity in question.

Secondly, the emergence of a new product was not blocked and, in any case, the sound and pictures were not the essential ingredient of such a product; Ladbroke rather wanted to offer an additional service to its clients for its main betting activity. Only a refusal to license that concerned either a new product, the introduction of which might be prevented, despite specific, constant, and regular potential consumer demand, or a product of service that was essential, due to the absence of a real or potential substitute for the activity concerned would fall foul of Art. 82.

Ladbroke was also not excluded from a market in which the French horse racing organizations were operating by the refusal to license and neither was it discriminated against on the Belgian market.[147]

IMS Health

Facts and issues

It has become clear from the discussion above that it is at least arguable that *Magill* had left open several issues.[148] These issues were primarily open to argument, because it was not clear whether the decision on that point in *Magill* depended entirely on the facts of the case—that is, on whether other facts could receive a different treatment—or whether they were a necessary element from a legal point of view. One of the issues left open is the question of whether a finding of exceptional circumstances required, cumulatively, the facts that the intellectual property right was linked to essential inputs for secondary markets, on the one hand, and that a new product had to be introduced in that market for which there was significant and unmet demand, on the other. Do the conditions in *Magill* apply cumulatively—as was the case in *Magill* on its facts—or are they alternative

---

[144] Case T-504/93 *Tiercé Ladbroke SA v. EC Commission (Société d'Encouragement et des Steeple-Chases de France intervening)* [1997] ECR II-923, [1997] 5 CMLR 309. The same conclusion was also strongly emphasized in the UK courts in *Philips Electronics NV v. Ingman Ltd & the Video Duplicating Co. Ltd* [1999] FSR 112. See also Case C-7/97 *Oscar Bronner GmbH & Co. KG v. Mediaprint Zeitungs- und Zeitschriftenverlag GmbH & Co. KG* [1998] ECR I-7791, [1999] 4 CMLR 112.

[145] See D. Fitzgerald, 'Magill revisited: Tiecé Ladbroke SA v. The Commission' [1998] EIPR 154.

[146] See Case T-504/93 *Tiercé Ladbroke SA v. EC Commission (Société d'Encouragement et des Steeple-Chases de France intervening)* [1997] ECR II-923, [1997] 5 CMLR 309 at [129]–[131].

[147] Ibid., at [124]–[128] and [133].

[148] See the discussion in [88]–[105] and the conclusion in [106] that there is 'a very serious dispute' concerning these in the Order of the President of the Court of First Instance of 26 October 2001 in Case T-184/01 R [2001] ECR II-3193. This Order was upheld by the Order of the President of the Court of Justice of 11 April 2002 in Case C-481/01 P(R) [2002] 5 CMLR 44. See also *Intel Corp. v. Via Technologies Inc.* [2003] FSR 574 (CA).

conditions? The latter option would see the essential facilities doctrine apply to many more cases, because there would be more exceptional circumstances. *Magill* also stresses the need for monopolization of a secondary market—but how secondary should that market be? Is it simply a separate or derivative market? And could the essential facilities doctrine apply if the competitor that was refused a licence wanted to compete on the right holder's main market? In other words, how close to the core business of the right holder can one come?

The *IMS Health* saga provided an opportunity to answer some of these questions. *IMS Health* is developing along two parallel tracks on the basis of the following facts. IMS Health is a major supplier of marketing data to pharmaceutical and other health-care companies. In the German market, it has established a structure of local geographic segments—1,860 in total—called 'bricks', each containing a comparable number of pharmacies, in order to collect standardized data without violating data protection laws, which do not allow for the identification of individual pharmacies' data. That structure is protected by copyright under German copyright law. That point as such is not in dispute, but there is more to it than pure copyright.

From the user or consumer perspective, there is a high demand for the data collected through use of the brick structure, which has become an impressive success on the market. The brick structure has de facto become the industry standard and its competitors asked for it to be licensed to them in order for them to be able to compete. The user is, indeed, only interested in data that is presented in a comparable fashion. When IMS Health's competitors, NDC Health and AzyX Deutschland GmbH Geopharma Information Services, applied for a licence covering the brick structure at various stages during the complex timeline and developments of the case, the details of which are not necessary for our present purposes, the grant of such a licence was refused by IMS Health and that resulted, in the end, in a complaint by NDC and AzyX to the European Commission for abuse of dominant position. In due course, the Commission issued its decision, in which it went against IMS in a first stage, but without reaching a final conclusion. Interim measures were imposed. That Commission decision was appealed and, as a result, two Orders of the President of the Court of First Instance[149] and one Order from the President of the European Court of Justice,[150] which suspended those interim measures, followed. In the light of that suspension and of the sceptical attitude that the Presidents of the two courts took towards the Commission's approach, the Commission withdrew its interim measures decision.[151]

At the same time, however, IMS Health's competitors had decided to make use of the brick structure anyway, without waiting for the grant of the licence. IMS Health therefore brought copyright proceedings against them in the German courts. In the course of these copyright proceedings, the German court referred the case to the European Court of Justice for a preliminary ruling.[152] The Court has now given its judgment in that case. That means that the two elements that remain outstanding in this case are the final decision of the Commission on the competition issue and the judgment of the German court, which will have to apply the guidance from the European Court of Justice.

---

[149] Order of the President of the Court of First Instance of 10 August 2001 in Case T-184/01 R [2001] ECR II-2349; Order of the President of the Court of First Instance of 26 October 2001 in Case T-184/01 R [2001] ECR II-3193.

[150] Order of the President of the Court of Justice of 11 April 2002 in Case C-481/01 P(R) [2002] 5 CMLR 44.

[151] Commission Decision of 13 August 2003 (2003) OJ L 268/59, based on the fact that urgent measures were no longer needed.

[152] Case C-418/01 *IMS Health v. NDC Health* [2004] 4 CMLR 1543.

The Commission's approach

We will start by analysing the Commission's decision first. In this way, the approach the Commission takes to the wider issue of the essential facilities doctrine in relation to intellectual property rights will become clear. Afterwards, we will move on to consider the decision of the European Court of Justice. Let us therefore now, first of all, have a look at the process followed by the Commission in giving its decision,[153] in order to find out how it interpreted and applied the essential facilities doctrine in this case.

Following the standard provisions for any case in which the abuse of a dominant position is alleged, the Commission first of all identified the relevant geographical market. In its view, that relevant geographical market is Germany,[154] whereas the relevant product market is the regional sales data services.[155]

In relation to the position of dominance, IMS Health is found to be dominant after examining several factors, but the Commission primarily refers to the fact that IMS Health holds a high market share not only in Germany, but also in Europe.[156] Because Germany is the country that has '*the largest market for regional sales data services in Europe*',[157] it may therefore be regarded as a '*substantial part of the common market*' in this respect.[158]

Let us now return to the relevant market for German regional sales data services. In order to understand the background to the case, we need to know what these services are in this case and why they are needed. Pharmaceutical companies need the brick system and, in particular, the system put in place by IMS, because this system enables them to gather data in which they can record sales of a particular drug, comparing the sales figures for each of their products with those for the products of their competitors; it also offers them a tool to measure the performance of their sales representatives.[159] In the brick structure, this data is collected in each brick for a small number of pharmacies in a local area. This allows the pharmaceutical companies to obtain a detailed picture showing possible local differences, without, at the same time, infringing German data protection laws, under which the use of data relating to individual doctors or pharmacies would cause problems.

The Commission adopts the conclusion that IMS Health occupies a position of quasi-monopoly,[160] and this is, according to the Commission, due to the fact that IMS Health owns the copyright in a unique structure for recording sales data for pharmaceutical products and services and that, in the relevant market, there was simply no competition before the arrival on the market of NDC and AzyX. The Commission argues that IMS obtained this quasi-monopoly position through a close collaboration with the German pharmaceutical industry, which lead it to the creation of a 1,860-brick structure[161] that is segmenting the German market in several sectors in which many data is collected, including those of names of sales representatives, customers, doctors, etc. The exact shape of the brick structure is therefore, to a large part, the outcome of that collaborative effort. That involvement of the primary customer in the establishment of the structure also helps to explain why this structure seems to be indispensable for other competitors, which made

---

[153] Commission Decision 2001/165/EC of 3 July 2001 in Case COMP D3/38.044—*NDC Health/IMS Health*: Interim Measures [2002] OJ L 59/18.

[154] Commission Decision 2001/165/EC, at [55].

[155] Ibid., at [51].

[156] Ibid., at [59], where the Commission refers on this point to the Court of Justice's judgment in Case C-62/86 *AKZO Chemie BV v. Commission* [1991] ECR I-3359.

[157] Commission Decision 2001/165/EC, at [60].

[158] Ibid.   [159] Ibid., at [93].

[160] Ibid., at [58].

[161] See the first sentence of [83] and the first sentence of [86] of Commission Decision 2001/165/EC; see also [87] of the Decision and the opinion expressed by some pharmaceutical companies; see also [185] of the Decision.

enormous investments to enter into that market and yet found it impossible to build a new structure due primarily to the unwillingness[162] of the pharmaceutical industry to switch to another—a process in which the industry would incur important additional costs.[163]

The Commission is further sustaining that the IMS brick structure is becoming a de facto industry standard or a 'common language', as defined by the Commission,[164] in the sense that the common language of that structure is well known and commonly used. For the Commission, the '*1860 brick structure is becoming a common language for communicating the information*'[165] and all of the pharmaceutical companies that assisted with its creation are, in the end, effectively 'locked in' in relation to that structure—even if one needs to add that they are locked in on a voluntarily basis. Everything turns around that structure[166] and the situation in Germany does not offer so much space for a substitution. The 1,860-brick structure is especially a large and unique source of information[167]—and it is in this respect that the Commission sees parallels with the *Magill* case, in which the information concerned was contained in the television listings on the basis of which the broadcasters had, indeed, a unique source of information.[168]

The possibility of changing the system for the collection of data exists, but, despite the fact that competing companies tried it,[169] this did not lead to a structure very different from that put in place by IMS Health. Changing that structure will also mean changing other data[170] linked to that structure, and this will therefore increase the costs and work as a deterrent for any such change. Also, the relationship of the companies using the (new) structure with their sales representatives will be harmed, because this relationship has also been shaped around the 1,860-brick structure.[171] The Commission's analysis—despite the fact that, in its defence, IMS Health accuses the Commission on more than one occasion of not being precise enough[172]—has shown that IMS Health's brick structure became indispensable and the overall standard.

Moreover, there are '*technical and legal constraints*'[173] that make it even more difficult and, in the Commission's view, even impossible for other companies to create a new

---

[162] See final sentence of [86] of Commission Decision 2001/165/EC.

[163] Especially, it has been argued by the competitors of IMS that a change to the brick structure involves a change in working conditions under German labour law, and that the additional costs therefore include the fact that the contract of service of the sales representatives has to be renegotiated using the German system of codetermination, and that any such change to the brick structure used will therefore mean a long and costly procedure due to the involving the workers' council in the renegotiation procedure: see [115] of Commission Decision 2001/165/EC.

[164] In [123] of Commission Decision 2001/165/EC and in [86] and [89] in response to the defence of IMS Health (in [88]) regarding the legal requirements for something to be considered an industry standard.

[165] Commission Decision 2001/165/EC, at [89].

[166] Also marketing campaigns and market research are organized according to the data in this structure.

[167] Commission Decision 2001/165/EC, at [102]–[104]. Also data companies, as well as software companies, make use of the brick structure and deliver their products in it. All of the other data effectively follows the 1,860-brick structure.

[168] The crucial fact in *Magill* is that the monopoly was a monopoly over information and that information happened to be the raw material required by a third party. Therefore *Magill* is now no longer the only case to be remembered for its unusual facts: the unusual protection of copyright of factual information.

[169] See the comments in [124] and [128] of Commission Decision 2001/165/EC.

[170] Commission Decision 2001/165/EC, at [100].

[171] Ibid., at [107] and [108]. Pharmacia also stated that '*each restructuring of sales force destroys customers' relationships with our reps, which means that we would lose significant numbers of sales at the end of the day*': Commission Decision 2001/165/EC, at [107]. See also Commission Decision 2001/165/EC, at [114], where the loss of the special relationship between doctors and sales representatives in case of a change of the brick structure is highlighted.

[172] Commission Decision 2001/165/EC, at [122].

[173] Ibid., at [124].

structure for regional sales data in Germany that is able to compete with the 1,860-brick structure. The Commission concluded, therefore, that IMS Health should grant all of its competitors a licence upon payment of a reasonable royalty for the use of its copyright work. The Commission justifies its conclusion as follows: there is an abuse that is due to the dominant position occupied by IMS Health and, moreover, IMS Health owns an essential facility that is impossible to substitute.

In its decision, the Commission refers repeatedly to the essential facility doctrine—especially in the sense in which it was set out by the European Court of Justice in the *Oscar Bronner* case.[174] *Bronner* was not a case concerned with intellectual property rights, but it may nonetheless be important, because it is clearly a case about essential facilities. *Bronner* could therefore shed light on the correct interpretation of the essential facilities doctrine in European competition law.

Bronner dealt with a system for the house-to-house distribution of newspapers in Austria, set up by the major national newspaper. A smaller competitor argued that it should be allowed to make use of the system in order to be able to compete. In its view, the system had become an essential facility. The Court followed the suggestion of its Advocate General Francis Jacobs in interpreting the essential facilities doctrine restrictively and then ruled that it did not apply here. Important for our current purposes is the establishment of a test that a firm violates Art. 82 if:

- the refusal of access to the facility is likely to eliminate all competition in the relevant market;
- such refusal is not capable of being objectively justified; and
- the facility itself is indispensable to carry on business, inasmuch as there is no actual or potential substitute in existence for that facility.[175]

The Commission forgets to mention, however, that *Bronner* is a case that can only show how the essential facilities doctrine can be applied in a European competition law context in general, being a case of pure competition rules application. It is indeed vital to recall that, in a normal situation, competition rules are the only set of rules used to regulate market behaviour; this is the case in *Bronner*.

The presence of copyright does, however, complicate things. Because copyright confers an exclusive right, there is, almost by definition, also a possibility that such an exclusive right will be used in one way or another to restrict competition. There may therefore be a conflict between competition law, on the one hand, and copyright law, on the other, in a given situation.[176] But in order to understand the nature of such a potential conflict better, one needs to see how both regulatory systems—that is, copyright and competition law—operate.

Copyright operates at a structural level. It puts in place a rewards and incentives structure that applies to all relevant cases, and which aims to enhance competition at creation and innovation level by granting an exclusive right in the copyright work that restricts, to some extent, competition at the production level. In so doing, copyright defines (intellectual) property rights. Competition law, meanwhile, operates in an entirely different way. It operates at the behavioural level and it does so almost on a case-by-case basis. It is therefore not the case that there is a conflict between two sets of rules that operate in the same

---

[174] Case C-7/97 *Oscar Bronner GmbH andCo KG v. Mediaprint Zeitungs- und Zeitschriftenverlag GmbH & Co. KG* [1998] ECR I-7791, [1999] 4 CMLR 112.

[175] Ibid.

[176] See M. Furse (2002) *Competition Law of the UK and the EC*, 3rd edn, Oxford: Oxford University Press, pp. 205 and 214.

way and at the same level.[177] Copyright and competition law share the same objective, but they have different ways of achieving it and they operate at a different level.[178]

Competition law does not operate at the structural level and, as such, it does not interfere with the structure created by copyright to enhance creation and innovation at competition at that stage. What is true, however, is that it may interfere, at a later stage, with some of the behaviour that flows from the grant of copyright. In more down-to-earth terms, copyright may be used or exercised in an improper way, and such behaviour is then regulated and addressed by means of competition law. The factor that complicates matters is that it is, to a fair extent, the incentives and exclusive rights created at the structural level by copyright that facilitate, or at least make possible, the emergence of inefficient behaviour that might infringe competition law rules. What can be derived at this early stage is that a system that is designed to regulate behaviour should not operate in a way that undoes the structure put in place by a system such as copyright. The legislator has made a policy decision to put a structure such as copyright in place to enhance, and reward, creativity and innovation, and that decision should be respected. In other words, competition law should restrict itself to its proper role, which is to address anticompetitive behaviour—such as any use of copyright that is not pro-competitive—as was envisaged when the structural system was set up.[179] This conclusion should not surprise anyone, because it should be kept in mind that it is competition law itself that allows for the grant of exclusive rights if, on the one hand, they are necessary and unavoidable to obtain the benefits that the right holder brings about for the consumer, and if, on the other hand, they do not lead to a complete elimination of competition.[180]

As we have demonstrated above, in intellectual property cases in general—and particularly in copyright cases—there is not only one set of rules that affects the market behaviour regulation point: both intellectual property and copyright rules, on the one hand, and competition rules, on the other, set out to regulate competition conditions, and to steer certain forms of behaviour, on the market. The presence of such a second set of rules must have an impact on the test that is used, otherwise its vital role is completely ignored. It is therefore submitted that it is not possible to transfer the test set out in the *Bronner* case to intellectual property and copyright related cases without modifying it.[181] This must mean that any strict reliance by the Commission on the *Bronner* case in its *IMS Health* decision must be misguided. The decision cannot be based solely and straightforwardly on the Court's judgment in *Bronner*.

To be fair to the Commission, it also argues that its decision follows from the judgments in *Magill*[182] and *Ladbroke*[183]. The exceptional circumstances referred to by the Court in

---

[177] G. Ramello (2002) 'Copyright and antitrust issues', SERCI research paper, available online at www.serci.org/2002/ramello.pdf, p. 28.

[178] S. Lemarchand, O. Fréget, and F. Sardain, 'Biens informationnels: entre droits intellectuels et droit de la concurrence' [2003] Propriétés Intellectuelles 11 at 17–19.

[179] See the introductory comments in R. Whish (2001) *Competition Law*, 4th edn, London: Butterworths, p. 676.

[180] Lemarchand, Fréget and Sardain [2003] at 19.

[181] For a complete analysis of the case, see P. Treacy, 'Essential facilities: is the tide turning?' [1999] IPQ 501; C. Stothers, 'Refusal to supply as abuse of a dominant position: essential facilities in the European Union' [2001] Eur Competition LR 256.

[182] Case T-69/89 *Radio Telefis Éireann v. Commission (Magill TV Guide Ltd intervening)* [1991] 4 CMLR 586; Case T-70/89 *British Broadcasting Corp. & BBC Enterprises Ltd v. Commission (Magill TV Guide Ltd intervening)* [1991] 4 CMLR 669; Case T-76/89 *Independent Television Publications Ltd v. Commission (Magill TV Guide Ltd intervening)* [1991] ECR II-575, [1991] 4 CMLR 745.

[183] Case T-504/93 *Tiercé Ladbroke SA v. Commission (Société d'Encouragement et des Steeple-Chases de France intervening)* [1997] ECR II-923, [1997] 5 CMLR 309.

relation to the broadcasters' refusal to license the programme listings in *Magill* come down to two elements. By refusing to make programme listings available to Magill under licence, the broadcasters prevented the appearance of a new product that they did not offer, but for which there was a clear demand from the side of the consumer. It is important to add, in relation to this first element, that, as a result of their exclusive copyright in the listings, the broadcasters were the only source for any such information, which is vital for anyone wishing to publish a weekly television guide.

The second element is that, by denying access to that vital material without which the new product could not see the light of day, the broadcasters were effectively reserving the secondary market for weekly television guides to themselves. The Court clearly emphasizes the secondary market point by indicating that the broadcasters' main activity is broadcasting and that the prohibited activity therefore did not affect that primary activity, but only the guides market that is only a secondary market for the broadcasters. The refusal therefore could not be justified by virtue of the broadcasters' normal activities.

At this stage, one clearly sees the appearance of the essential facilities doctrine. Because the broadcasters are the only source of the necessary copyright material and because that material is essential—that is, the television guide cannot be produced without it—the copyright-protected information concerning programme listings has become an essential facility for any company that wishes to operate on the relevant market. *Magill* can therefore be seen as an application of the essential facilities doctrine in a copyright case, whereas *Bronner* applies the same doctrine to a 'normal', non-intellectual property-related case, as discussed above.[184] It is also important to highlight the fact that the Court emphasized that there was a clear and unmet demand on the consumers' side. Like all essential facilities cases in the USA, *Magill* also links the essential facilities doctrine to the benefit that arises for the consumer from its application.[185]

When the Commission refers to the Court's judgment in *Magill*, it summarizes the position adopted by the Court as follows:

> The Court therefore recognised that in exceptional circumstances the exercise of an exclusive right deriving from an intellectual copyright may be abusive even in the absence of additional abusive conduct when, *inter alia*, it prevents the appearance of a new product.[186]

This summary is causing problems in so far as the use of the term 'inter alia' is possibly a misrepresentation of the Court's judgment in *Magill*. Indeed, the Commission seems to suggest that the appearance of a new product is not a necessary element and that other elements might replace it. In the Commission's view, the appearance of a new product is only one of the exceptional circumstances to which the Court refers. It is submitted that it is wrong to use the term 'inter alia' in this way and to give this interpretation to the judgment of the Court. Instead, it is submitted that the 'inter alia' type of exceptional circumstances that the Court saw in *Magill* amounts to the fact that the information concerned had become an essential facility for the publishers of television guides. The judgment in *Magill* supports the point of view that the application of the essential facilities doctrine in relation to intellectual property—that is, for there to be an abuse of the dominant position, the possession of which is not an abuse per se—requires the presence of all elements set out above. The prevention of the emergence of a new product is therefore a necessary component and not only an optional element, as suggested by the Commission.

---

[184] See F. Woolridge, 'The essential facilities doctrine and *Magill II*: the fecision of the ECJ in *Oscar Bronner*' [1999] IPQ 256; Treacy [1999]; Stothers [2001].

[185] See P. Areeda, 'Essential facilities: an epithet in need of limiting principles' [1989] 58 ATLJ 84.

[186] Commission Decision 2001/165/EC, at [67].

The Commission also argues that its point of view is supported by the judgment of the Court of First Instance in *Ladbroke*.[187] That Court came to the conclusion that the facts of the *Ladbroke* case did not warrant the application of the rules set out in *Magill*. One could argue that the main reason behind the Court not examining the point of the emergence of a new product is the fact that, if one condition had not been met, the case was bound to fail, because the conditions apply cumulatively. But one might go further, as the Commission seems to be doing in its *IMS Health* decision, and highlight the statement of the Court of First Instance that:

> [the] refusal to supply the applicant could not fall within the prohibition laid down by Article [82] unless it concerned a product or service which was either essential for the exercise of the activity in question, in that there was no real or potential substitute, OR was a new product whose introduction might be prevented, despite specific, constant and regular potential demand on the part of the consumer.[188]

Taken on its own, this quote might suggest that there is no need to establish that the abuse takes place on a downstream market before *Magill* can be applied and, even more importantly, that the conditions found in *Magill* might be alternatives, which excludes the need for their cumulative application.

It is submitted that this is not a correct approach. The whole approach hinges on the literal interpretation, out of context of the single word 'or'; if one adds that context, that interpretation becomes difficult. The Court of First Instance felt hardly any need to investigate the second point.[189] It dismissed the case on the first ground. Anything that it said about the second point is therefore obiter. If it had seen the requirements as real alternatives, as the Commission suggests, it would have needed to deal with the second point in much more depth, even if the truth is probably that the emergence of a new product was not blocked and that, in any case, the sound and pictures were not the essential ingredient of any such product.

The Commission's interpretation, which dismisses the new product requirement that seemed so prominent in *Magill*, is therefore based on flimsy grounds and reliance on the passage from the judgment of the lower European court in *Ladbroke* to achieve this is precarious.[190] This is even more so because it disregards the economic analysis set out above. The approach may well work in a non-intellectual property context. The *Bronner* case showed how the essential facilities doctrine could work in this context; similarly, the *Commercial Solvents*[191] judgment leads one to the conclusion that there is an abuse of a dominant position on the sole ground of the monopolization of a secondary market. In non-intellectual property cases, that is an abuse as such even if a new product is not prevented from appearing on the market; in this case, the requirements do not need to be applied cumulatively. But we have already explained that the presence of intellectual property rights and their competition-regulating function change the picture dramatically. It is therefore submitted that the Commission is misguided in its reliance on *Ladbroke* for its views in the *IMS Health* decision.[192]

---

[187] Case T-504/93 *Tiercé Ladbroke SA v. European Commission (Société d'Encouragement et des Steeple-Chases de France intervening)* [1997] 5 CMLR 309. For a complete overview of the case, see Fitzgerald [1998].
[188] Commission Decision 2001/165/EC, at [68].
[189] D. Hull, J. Atwood and J. Perrine, 'Intellectual property: compulsory licensing' [2002] European Antitrust Review 36, at 37 (a global competition review special report).
[190] Ibid.
[191] See *ICI & Commercial Solvents v. Commission* [1974] ECR 223.
[192] Hull et al. [2002] at 37.

IMS *in the European Court of Justice*

The scepticism towards the broad interpretation of the essential facilities doctrine proposed by the Commission that has been expressed in the foregoing analysis was also reflected in the Orders of the President of the Court of First Instance and the President of the Court of Justice. It is therefore welcome to see that the European Court of Justice adopted a much more careful and sensible approach in its judgment in *IMS Health v. NDC Health*.[193]

The Court, first of all, turned its attention to the vital question of when, in a copyright context, a facility has become an essential facility. The Court held that, in order to determine whether a product or service is indispensable for the purposes of enabling an undertaking to carry on business in a particular market, it must be determined whether there are products or services that constitute alternative solutions. It does not matter in that respect that these alternative solutions are less advantageous, or whether there are technical, legal, or economic obstacles capable of making it impossible—or at least unreasonably difficult—for any undertaking seeking to operate in the market to create—possibly in cooperation with other operators—the alternative products or services. The existence of economic obstacles will only be able to rule out an alternative solution if it is established, at the very least, that the creation of those products or services is not economically viable for production on a scale that is comparable to that of the undertaking in control of the existing product or service. This is a very strict interpretation of the essential facility point and, because the existence of an essential facility is a prerequisite that must be met before even the issue of abuse can be addressed, this will severely limit the number of cases in which the exercise of copyright will be interfered with.

In the *IMS* case, the Court advised the German court that, in applying the test, account must be taken of the fact that a high level of participation by the pharmaceutical laboratories in the improvement of the 1,860-brick structure protected by copyright has created a dependency by users in relation to that structure, particularly at a technical level. The Court went on to say that:

> In such circumstances, it is likely that those laboratories would have to make exceptional organisational and financial efforts in order to acquire the studies on regional sales of pharmaceutical products presented on the basis of a structure other than that protected by copyright. The supplier of that alternative structure might therefore be obliged to offer terms which are such as to rule out any economic viability of business on a scale comparable to that of the undertaking which controls the protected structure.[194]

The strong suggestion to the German court is therefore no doubt that these additional circumstances have turned the block structure into an essential facility.

Once it has been established that the facility—in this case, the block structure, as protected by copyright—is an essential facility, the second step—that is, the issue of whether there has been an abuse of a dominant position, in this case, by refusing to license the block structure—can be addressed. The Court ruled on this point that three conditions have to be met cumulatively for there to be an abuse:

- the refusal is preventing the emergence of a new product for which there is a potential consumer demand;
- there is no objective justification for this refusal;
- the refusal is such as to exclude any competition on a secondary market.[195]

---

[193] Case C-418/01 [2004] 4 CMLR 1543.
[194] Ibid., at 1577.
[195] Ibid., at 1579.

In this way, the Court clearly adopts a very restrictive interpretation of its earlier dicta in *Magill* and *Bronner*. The Commission's suggestions that the criteria could be applied alternatively, rather than cumulatively, and, in particular, that the existence of separate markets was not required has been straightforwardly rejected. The point is now clear: all three requirements apply cumulatively if there is to be a finding of abuse.

The Court then went on to clarify each of the three requirements and their application to the *IMS Health* case. The third condition—relating to the likelihood of excluding all competition on a secondary market—requires that it is possible to distinguish an upstream market, constituted by the product or service that forms the essential facility (for example, in *Bronner*, the market for home delivery of daily newspapers, and in *IMS Health*, the market for brick structures) and a (secondary) downstream market, on which the product or service in question—that is, the essential facility—is used for the production of another product or the supply of another service (for example, in *Bronner*, the market for daily newspapers themselves, and in *IMS Health*, the market for the supply of sales data).[196] The fact that the essential facility is not marketed separately is not regarded as precluding, from the outset, the possibility of identifying a separate market. It is indeed sufficient that a potential market, or even a hypothetical market, can be identified.[197] One of the positive aspects of this approach is that an abuse can also be found in those circumstances in which the right holder's behaviour does not simply hinder competition, but acts to exclude competition completely to such an extent that, in reality, no downstream market exists.

Secondly, it is now clear that a secondary market does not have to be of secondary importance to the right holder, as was the case on the facts in *Magill*. All that is required is the existence of two markets—or in the words of the Court:

> Accordingly, it is determinative that two different stages of production may be identified and that they are interconnected, the upstream product is indispensable inasmuch as for supply of the downstream product.[198]

It is therefore possible that the applicant for the licence that is refused wanted to compete head on with the right holder on the same market.

In practical business terms, it will be relatively easy to determine the markets involved in those cases in which there is a real existing market for the goods or services that allegedly amount to an essential facility, but things get more difficult when one is looking at the potential or hypothetical markets that the Court mentions and which are likely to represent the majority of cases. Indeed, the abuse complained of prevents the existence of a real market in business terms. The Court's approach is to argue that there is a potential or a hypothetical market if two conditions are met:

- the products or services must indispensable in order to carry on a particular business;
- there is an actual demand for them on the part of undertakings, which seek to carry on the business for which they are indispensable.

In terms of the *IMS Health* case, this means asking whether the 1,860-brick structure constitutes, upstream, an indispensable factor in the downstream supply of German regional sales data for pharmaceutical products, coupled with the demand on the part of the competitors of IMS.[199]

---

[196] Ibid., at 1580.
[197] See V.-L. Bénabou, 'Chroniques: transversales' [2004] Propriétés Intellectuelles 807 at 825.
[198] Case C-418/01 *IMS Health v. NDC Health* [2004] 4 CMLR 1543 at 1580.
[199] Ibid.

The approach adopted by the Court refers back to the criteria used to determine whether or not a facility is indeed an essential facility. One could allege that it is therefore a circular reasoning. More importantly, however, this may well be a workable solution. Admittedly, copyright itself is narrowly associated with its exploitation: for example, IMS only created the brick structure in order to be able to supply the sales data, and the brick structure and the copyright in it have little, or no, value outside the sales data business. The distinction between two markets for the creation of the copyright work, and the right and the work, on the one hand, and for the exploitation of the work on the sales data market, on the other, may therefore seem artificial. But this is a peculiarity of copyright and one should resist the temptation to argue that the creation of two, somewhat artificial, markets in this way opens the door for the application of the essential facilities doctrine in a vast number of cases to the detriment of copyright.[200] It should indeed be remembered that two additional requirements must to be met before the essential facilities doctrine can be applied.

It is to these two other requirements that we now turn. The first condition relates to the emergence of a new product. The Court clarified, in this respect, that, in the balancing of the interest in protection of copyright and the economic freedom of its owner against the interest in protection of free competition, the latter interest can only prevail over the copyright interest if refusal to grant a licence prevents the development of the second-ary market to the detriment of consumers. There is therefore a need for the applicant for a licence to offer a new and different product, and to show consumer demand for such a product. The consumer interest point is therefore of vital importance. Copyright is indeed not granted to stop the emergence of new and different products for which there is a demand; any use of copyright to that end must amount to an abuse of right.

The final requirement is that the refusal to license must be unjustified. This means simply that the court is to examine whether the refusal of the request for a licence is justified by objective considerations.

In conclusion, despite the fact that we are not yet at the end of the *IMS* saga, a lot of points have been clarified in relation to the essential facilities doctrine and its application in relation to copyright (and intellectual property rights in general).[201] It is submitted that the Court's restrictive approach is to be applauded, because it does justice to the pro-competitive role of copyright (and other intellectual property rights), on the one hand, and because it allows, on the other, competition law to stop any abuse for undue purposes of copyright (or other intellectual property rights). Those cases in which copyright (or intellectual property rights in general) will be interfered with will be limited to a small number and this may well be rightly so. The Court may not have ruled out all difficulties in applying the test in practice and further difficult cases will no doubt arise, but it did at least did get the balance right in theory.

An overview

The exclusive rights granted by copyright come to life through their commercial exploitation. Assignment and licence contracts take centre stage in this context. There are, of course, plenty of contractual dealings between right holders and individual users, and these may concern one or more works, and single or multiple uses of works. All of this is

---

[200] See Bénabou [2004] at 825.

[201] For a UK application of the *Magill–IMS* case law, see *Attheraces Ltd v. British Horse Racing Board Ltd* [2006] FSR 20, rev'd on appeal [2007] ECC 7.

left to the contractual freedom of the parties. To facilitate the exploitation of rights—both from the point of view of the right holders and from the point of view from the users—multiple contracts for use of many works and contracts with a low monetary value are often replaced by a system of collective licensing.

As an exclusive right, copyright can contribute to the creation of a dominant position. Due to the fact that there is often one collecting society per country, collecting societies find themselves, almost by nature, in a dominant position in relation both to their members (the right holders) and in relation to their users. Certain items that are protected by copyright may also become an essential facility. These aspects of the commercial exploitation have come under intense scrutiny of the competition authorities. The bottom line is, however, that copyright establishes a structure that has a pro-competitive orientation. Copyright and its use are, as such, therefore not leading to a breach of competition law. But like many instruments, copyright can also be used for the wrong purposes: one can speak of a possible abuse of right. Such abuse takes place at behavioural level and it is at this level that competition law intervenes to stop the abuse. Rather than a straight fight for dominance, then, the interaction between copyright and competition law turned out to be all about complementary actors.

Exhaustion and the rules on free movement also intervene with the exploitation of copyright in the EU. In this respect, an important distinction appears between non-performance copyrights, on the one hand, in relation to which one is typically concerned with the physical distribution of copyright goods, and performance copyright, on the other, in relation to which one is typically concerned with broadcasting and communication to the public of copyright works.

Further reading

DREXL, J. (2007) 'Competition in the field of collective management: preferring "creative competition" to allocative efficiency in European copyright law', in P. Torremans (ed.) *Copyright Law: A Handbook of Contemporary Research*, Cheltenham/Northampton, MA: Edward Elgar, pp. 255–82.

GERVAIS, D. (2006) 'The changing role of copyright collectives', in D. Gervais (ed.) *Collective Management of Copyright and Related Rights*, London: Kluwer Law International, pp. 3–36.

RICOLFI, M. (2007) 'Individual and collective management of copyright in a digital environment', in P. Torremans (ed.) *Copyright Law: A Handbook of Contemporary Research*, Cheltenham/Northampton, MA: Edward Elgar, pp. 283–314.

TORREMANS, P. (2006) 'Collective management in the United Kingdom (and Ireland)', in D. Gervais (ed.) *Collective Management of Copyright and Related Rights*, London: Kluwer Law International, pp. 227–55.

TORREMANS, P. (2007) 'The ongoing copyright as an essential facility saga', in G. Ramello and D. Porrini (eds) *Property Rights Dynamics: A Law and Economics Perspective*, London: Routledge-Taylor and Francis, pp. 157–76.

19
Copyright—an overview

Copyright is a right of diversity. We started our analysis by referring to the dual roots of the right and this element proved to be omnipresent in the rest of our analysis. Copyright is a constant balancing act between the author and his or her rights, and the entrepreneur (who exploits copyright works) and his or her rights. This is inevitable, because the two parties are heavily interdependent.

We discussed the wide variety of, sometimes very different, types of work that attract copyright protection. The one point that they have in common is that they form the original expression of an idea, or that, if they are derivative works, they are a technical format that allows the exploitation of that expression.

The essence of the copyright in a work is the exclusive right to make copies of the work. This right is often transferred to the entrepreneur who undertakes the commercial exploitation of the work. The author then maintains his or her moral rights to prohibit any abusive form of exploitation of the work and the transfer of rights normally also involves a form of remuneration for the author.

The constant evolution in the way in which copyright works are exploited resulted in rights for performers and producers of phonograms, on the one hand—now even including moral rights—and in things such as rental and lending rights, on the other hand. The exploitation of copyright is also linked very strongly to the evolution of the reproduction technology.

Because copyright is a rather weak right that only protects the expression and not the idea, it offers, as a form of compensation, a rather long term of protection. In general, this term is now 70 years from the death of the author, although some 50-year terms still exist.

Copyright has, over the years, proved to be a flexible and extremely useful tool; it also plays an important economic role. New technical developments in the area of computing are, however, stretching it to the limit. We will discuss some of these developments in Chapter 30 on computers and intellectual property rights—but suffice it to say here that it is essential that copyright sticks to the core elements of the right that we have described, because bending these too strongly would turn a flexible right into a hollow right. We have to preserve the common core that is formed by the essential copyright requirements.

Further reading

TORREMANS, P. (2007) *Copyright Law: A Handbook of Contemporary Research*, Cheltenham/ Northampton, MA: Edward Elgar.

SECTION D

DESIGNS

20
Design and copyright

Introduction

Various definitions of what is a design might be given. Design law sees design as features of shape or configuration, which can be either of an aesthetic or a functional nature. For each of these, there is now a separate design right: aesthetic designs are protected under the provisions of the Registered Designs Act 1949, while functional designs are governed by the provisions of the Copyright, Designs, and Patents Act 1988. This has always been an area of substantial complexity, due in part to the influence of copyright.

The wall between design and copyright

There seems to be a natural overlap between design law and copyright, because, in the majority of cases, designs are laid down in drawings, plans, or blueprints that attract copyright protection. A copy of an item incorporating the design involves making a three-dimensional copy of the drawing, plan, or blueprint and infringes its copyright.

The overlap problem

The problems involved became very clear in the famous case of *British Leyland Motor Corp. Ltd v. Armstrong Patents Co. Ltd*,[1] which deals with functional designs. British Leyland owned the copyright in the drawings for exhaust pipes for its vehicles, which were built to a functional design. Armstrong reverse engineered the exhaust pipes—that is, it made its own exhaust pipes by taking the original apart and using the information acquired to make identical copies. Armstrong wanted to sell these pipes as spare parts for British Leyland cars.

On the basis of our above analysis, British Leyland could successfully bring a case for copyright infringement—but this would lead to the undesirable situation that a manufacturer has a de facto monopoly in the supply of spare parts for the life of the author plus (then) 50 years and could eventually abuse that monopoly. The House of Lords attempted to get around the problem by applying the land law principle of non-derogation from grant to soften the exaggerated strength of copyright protection for functional designs. By selling cars, British Leyland had impliedly promised to make spare parts available during the life of the car to facilitate its maintenance. It was clear that law reform was needed.

---

[1] [1986] AC 577, [1986] 1 All ER 850.

The solution in the Copyright, Designs and Patents Act 1988

The 1988 Act tried to remove the overlap between copyright and designs once and for always. Section 51 is the provision that is supposed to take care of that. Section 51(1) reads:

> it is not an infringement of any copyright in a design document or model recording or embodying a design for anything other than an artistic work or a typeface to make an article to the design or to copy an article made to the design.

The section goes back to the old method of protecting a design through the copyright in the design drawings. It does not abolish copyright in these drawings, or in any other design document, but it provides an exception in relation to copyright infringement. It is no longer an (indirect) infringement of the copyright in the design document, or in a model recording or embodying the design, to make an item to that design or to copy an item made to that design. This means that a photocopy of the design document will still infringe the copyright in the design document, but that an item made on the basis of that design document will no longer infringe the copyright in the design document as a three-dimensional copy of a two-dimensional work. Instead, the infringement action will now have to be brought under the new design right provisions.

In a case such as *British Leyland*, the copyright in the two-dimensional drawing of the three-dimensional product would not be infringed. An action for infringement of the design right in the copied design is the only available option.

Section 51 explained

A couple of points in this system need clarification and a number of details need to be added.

A 'design document' includes any record of a design. This can, for example, take the format of a literary work, a set of computer data, a model, or a photograph, apart from the obvious drawing.[2] It has to be a design document or model that records or embodies the design; this clearly refers to a document or model made for that purpose. Taken on its own, a drawing of Mickey Mouse made for a comic strip is not made for the production of items, such as toy figures, to that design. It is submitted that such drawings are therefore not design documents for the purposes of s. 51. Otherwise, all kinds of drawings and photographs would lose a substantial part of their copyright protection, especially the possibility of infringement by making a three-dimensional copy of the two-dimensional original, just because someone may, at one stage, want to use them for design purposes.

More importantly, s. 51 excludes design documents or models for artistic works or typefaces from its scope. Copyright in these will still be infringed if an item is made to their design or if an item made to that design is copied. The exclusion of artistic works evidently applied in a case in which an attempt was made to apply s. 51 to drawings made by a freelance graphic designer and that were to be applied to the surface of a set of badges.[3] As designs for artistic works, these clearly fell outside the scope of s. 51.

Another good example may be found in the production of furniture.[4] It will not be an infringement to make furniture to someone else's design without having obtained permission to do so unless the furniture, as such, is an artistic work. Furniture can indeed

---

[2] CDPA 1988, s. 51(1) and (3).

[3] *Flashing Badge Co. Ltd v. Brian David Groves (t/a Flashing Badges by Virgo & Virgo Distribution)* [2007] ECDR 17.

[4] CDPA 1988, s. 51 (1).

qualify for copyright protection as an artistic work, whether as a sculpture or a work of artistic craftsmanship, and, if this is the case, the exclusion clause in s. 51 will apply and copyright will still be infringed.[5] In everyday life, most cases of furniture production rely on mass industrial production and artistic copyright protection is unlikely to exist in these cases. Nonetheless, one should not underestimate the impact of the exclusion of artistic works from the scope of s. 51. It has been held that the design of rubber mats for cars that were made by using a metal plate as a mould involved artistic works, both in the shape of the drawing and the shape of the metal plate.[6] Both the metal plates and the impression made on the mats in the mould amounted to engraving, and were therefore artistic works.

One should, however, keep in mind that the exception covers a design 'for' an artistic work or typeface. This means, as we have seen, that s. 51 will not exclude copyright infringement if the (design) document is made for the purpose of making an engraving, sculpture, or etching as an artistic work. But if the design is for something that, in itself, is not an artistic work, such as a design for dolls—even the fact that a three-dimensional model is made as an intermediate stage towards final production—will not exclude the application of s. 51 and the exception for artistic works will not apply.[7]

The definition of a design

The definition of a 'design' in s. 51(3) is also important. Apart from any aspect of shape, the design can also consist of any aspect of the configuration of the whole, or part, of an item. The concept of configuration is a broad one and includes the relative arrangement of the parts or elements of an item. It cannot be limited to the physical geometry of the item concerned.[8]

But the definition excludes surface decoration. An example of this was found when a graphic design was applied to badges with a shape that followed the contours of the graphic design: that graphic design provided the surface decoration of the badges and was therefore excluded from the scope of the definition of a design under s. 51(3).[9] The existence, in s. 51(3), of a separate definition of a design has important consequences. Section 51 does not require the existence of a design right to operate; as long as the design meets the requirements of the definition of a design (and a design document) contained in s. 51(3), the exclusion rule in s. 51 will operate and copyright infringement cannot be relied upon. For example, if the design of a tracksuit top involving a colour pattern applied to the shape of the garment did not meet the requirements for design right protection, this did not mean that s. 51 did not apply and that copyright could be relied upon.[10] The only thing that mattered was the question of whether the design met the criteria contained in the definition in s. 51(3). Because the answer to that question was positive, the exclusion of copyright infringement applied, irrespective of the issue of design right protection. The majority in the Court of Appeal disregarded this, but it should be kept in mind that s. 51(3) refers *expressis verbis* to the design of any aspect of the shape or configuration of an item.

---

[5] See H. MacQueen, 'A Scottish case on unregistered designs' [1994] 2 EIPR 86, on *Squirewood Ltd v. Morris & Co. Ltd* at 87. The case was not reported, but is available on Lexis.

[6] *Hi Tech Autoparts Ltd v. Towergate Two Ltd (No. 2)* [2002] FSR 270.

[7] *BBC Worldwide Ltd v. Pally Screen Printing Ltd* [1998] FSR 665.

[8] *Mackie Designs Inc. v. Behringer Specialised Studio Equipment (UK) Ltd* [1999] RPC 717. The correctness of this view has been disputed, because it could lead to an unduly broad right: see H. Laddie, P. Prescott and M. Vitoria (2000) *The Modern Law of Copyright and Designs*, 3rd edn, London: Butterworths, pp. 2171–3.

[9] *Flashing Badge Co. Ltd v. Brian David Groves (t/a Flashing Badges by Virgo & Virgo Distribution)* [2007] ECDR 17.

[10] *Lambretta Clothing Co. Ltd v. Teddy Smith (UK) & anor* [2005] RPC 6 (CA).

One might therefore argue that, as long as one only copies surface decoration and colour patterns, that does not involve the shape and configuration of the item, and s. 51 should therefore not apply.[11] The majority clearly felt this to be an unduly fine distinction.

Items made to the design

Section 51 covers items made to the design and copies of such items made to the design. Here, too, a wide definition is in order and no additional requirements relating to the result of the copying can be imposed. Lists of components, circuit diagrams, and boards that resulted from the analysis of an existing mixing desk for use in recording studios carried out by a competitor with the aim of gathering knowledge for the construction of its own mixing desk were therefore covered by the definition and by implication by s. 51.[12] Items that are not infringing copyright can also be issued to the public or included in films, broadcasts, or cable programme services without infringing copyright.[13] This completes the copyright exception, which would otherwise have little practical economical importance.

The scope of s. 51

If s. 51 is to be really effective in reducing the overlap and the confusion, it should cover both the overlap between copyright and unregistered-functional design, and the overlap between registered aesthetic design and copyright. There is no doubt that it covers the overlap with unregistered designs, because cases such as *British Leyland* arose in relation to functional designs, and we will see that the definition of an unregistered design is identical to that found in s. 51.

Although it is submitted that that definition is, at first glance, wide enough in scope to encompass the definition of registered designs,[14] there are a number of elements that complicate things. Firstly, most design documents that are copied in aesthetic designs will be artistic works and this category of copyright works is excluded from the scope of s. 51. Secondly, surface decoration is also excluded from the scope of s. 51, while it may come inside the scope of the definition of a registered design, in relation to which no similar exclusion is found.

It is not necessary to go into the detail of the various definitions right now before we discuss the two design rights in substance. It is indeed clear that, in practice, s. 51 is almost exclusively restricted to cases of unregistered design. This creates the impression that the overlap between copyright and registered design is left untouched, and may still create problems, but this impression is not correct.

Section 52

Indeed, for purposes of completeness, a brief reference should be made to s. 52 of the 1988 Act. This section refers to authorized use of an artistic work and restricts the term of copyright protection in these works to 25 years if copies of the work are made by an industrial process or if such copies are marketed.[15] Items can be made to the description of the artistic work without infringing copyright, starting 25 years after the end of the calendar year in which the first marketing of the items authorized by the owner of the artistic copyright were first marketed.[16] This effectively reduces the duration of copyright to that of the registered design right, as we will see. The two rights coexist, but no substantial

---

[11] See the dissenting opinion of Mance LJ, ibid., at [80].

[12] Ibid.; *BBC Worldwide Ltd v. Pally Screen Printing Ltd* [1998] FSR 665.

[13] CDPA 1988, s. 51(2).

[14] Registered Designs Act 1949, s. 1; see Chapter 21.

[15] In the UK or elsewhere: CDPA 1988, s. 52(1)(b).

[16] Ibid., s. 52.

problems arise, because the two forms of protection have the same coverage and will disappear together.

Does the British Leyland defence survive?

But what was the influence of the law reform on the defence created in the *British Leyland* case? The provisions of the 1988 Act—and especially ss. 51 and 52—effectively replaced the existing law in this area. One of the reasons why Parliament introduced new legislation in this area was that the old law was not satisfactory. It is submitted that, in practice, the *British Leyland* defence no longer exists under the regime of the 1988 Act. Section 171(3) keeps the defence alive only in theory, because it stipulates that the provisions of the 1988 Act do not affect any rule of law that prevents or restricts the enforcement of copyright. The *British Leyland* defence clearly had that effect. But for the defence to operate, there must, first of all, be a case of copyright infringement and the effect of s. 51 is exactly that this will no longer be possible in design-related cases. The copyright in the design document will not be infringed, so, in practice, there is no use for a rule restricting the enforcement of copyright. Making items, such as the infamous exhaust pipes, to the design contained in the design document, such as the drawing of the exhaust pipe, will not infringe the copyright in the design document.[17] The alleged copyright infringer does not infringe and the production can go ahead. There is no need for the *British Leyland* defence against copyright infringement to arrive at this conclusion.

Nevertheless, the Act has not abolished the *British Leyland* defence. Maybe the defence can still play a role, when defined properly—which proper definition was provided by the Privy Council in the *Canon* case.[18] The Privy Council ruled that the *British Leyland* spare parts exception must be seen as a proper exception from copyright infringement. It is the expression of the public policy rule that will prevent manufacturers using their copyright to control the aftermarket in spare parts. That public policy rule will operate if two requirements are met: firstly, there must be a manifest unfairness to the consumer, who is using the original product for which the spare part is intended; secondly, the monopoly must plainly be anti-competitive in nature. The Privy Council added that the jurisprudential and economic basis for the doctrine of the exception becomes very fragile if these requirements are not met.

The *Canon* case applied this to a situation in which replacement ink cartridges for photocopiers and laser printers infringed the copyright in the drawings of the original Canon cartridges. It was held that the defence did not apply, because the replacement of a cartridge was not a repair that an ordinary purchaser would assume he or she could carry out him or herself in order to have the continuing enjoyment of the product purchased. The manufacture of the cartridges was an infringement of the copyright in the drawings and the defence could not change that position (the provisions of the 1988 Act did not apply in this case), because the purchaser accepted that he or she would, every so often, need to buy a replacement cartridge. The interests of the consumer were not affected unfairly and the practices of Canon were not anti-competitive.[19]

---

[17] Contra, *Flogates Ltd, USX Corp. & USX Engineers & Consultants Inc. v. Refco Ltd & Graham Peter Briggs* [1996] FSR 935. The comments by Jacob J were obiter, because the case was concerned with the transitional provisions of the 1988 Act. (CDPA 1988, Sch. 1, para. 19(9) keeps the defence alive for cases that come under the transitional provisions.)

[18] *Canon Kabushiki Kaisha v. Green Cartridge Co. (Hong Kong) Ltd* [1997] AC 728, [1997] 3 WLR 13.

[19] Ibid.

It is submitted that the decision to found the *British Leyland* spare parts exception—also called the common law spare parts exception—on grounds of public policy needs to be applauded.[20] It must, indeed, be the case that, even in a purely domestic context, intellectual property rights need to be fitted in with the overall principle of the enhancement of free competition. Public policy rules should be able to stop the operation of intellectual property whenever these rights are put to improper use, whenever they are abused, and whenever they are used for an anti-competitive goal for which they were not intended. Although narrowly focused on the spare parts issue, the decision of the Privy Council could open the door for a wider application of this exceptional public policy safeguard in other cases of abuse. It could eventually be developed into a rule that fulfils the same role in domestic competition law as that fulfilled by the essential function–specific subject matter doctrine in the *Magill* case at European level in relation to intellectual property rights.

The next chapter will, however, look at the substantive provisions on registered designs.

An overview

Overlaps in protection between intellectual property rights with different aims and rationales are never desirable. Attempts have therefore been made to avoid an overlap between copyright and design rights. The courts struggled on this point, but, in *British Leyland*, a solution was found, albeit on the basis of principles that are alien to intellectual property.

The legislature then intervened and s. 51 of the 1988 Act was an attempt at a comprehensive solution. According to its terms:

> it is not an infringement of any copyright in a design document or model recording or embodying a design for anything other than an artistic work or a typeface to make an article to the design or to copy an article made to the design.

As it turned out, the solution was more problematic, and less clear and comprehensive than envisaged. Section 51(1) excludes designs for artistic works or typefaces; the definition of a design in s. 51(3) excludes surface decoration. The exact circumscription of these exclusions and their impact on the overall solution to the problem has been causing problems. Gradually, a picture of a workable, but not watertight, separation between copyright and designs is emerging—but it is clear that there is also still a place for the *British Leyland* defence.

Further reading

MacQueen, H., 'A Scottish case on unregistered designs' [1994] 2 EIPR 86.

Scanlan, G., 'The future of the design right: putting s. 51 Copyright, Designs and Patents Act 1988 in its place' (2005) 26 Stat LR 3, 146.

---

[20] See *Mars UK Ltd v. Teknowledge Ltd (No. 1)* [2000] FSR 138; cf *Hyde Park Residence Ltd v. Yelland* [2000] RPC 604.

21

Registered designs

Starting points

One could be forgiven for thinking that a design is a plan or blueprint that shows how an item is to be constructed or how the elements of the item are arranged. Intellectual property law, however, has never accepted that simple definition. For our purposes, a design is concerned with aspects of an item or with features applied to it, and is never concerned with the item itself. To complicate things further, two types of designs exist in the UK: registered designs—based on the Registered Designs Act 1949, as amended—and (unregistered) designs—based on the Copyright, Designs and Patents Act 1988.

Design law has now been harmonized in Europe, by means of the Design Directive.[1] For the UK, this has resulted in the original Registered Designs Act 1949 virtually being emptied of its original content. The new provisions that have been inserted by the Registered Design Regulations 2001[2] and the Registered Design Regulations 2003[3] are entirely based on the provisions of the Directive.[4] In this book, we will deal exclusively with these new provisions.[5]

On top of these (harmonized) national design laws, a Community registered design has been put in place by the Community Designs Regulation.[6] Under this additional system, a single registered design right is granted for the whole of the European Union (EU). That system is administered by the Office for the Harmonization of the Internal Market (OHIM), which is based in Alicante, Spain, and which also administers the Community trade mark.[7] In this chapter, we will examine the registered designs system and look at the Regulation. The UK system of unregistered designs—also referred to as 'design rights'— will be analysed in Chapter 22.

Registered designs were, in origin under English law, aesthetic designs that were intended to appeal to the eye. Decorative features or items such as a beautifully decorated crystal vase, or patterns applied to household porcelain, would attract registered design protection. But registered designs may also be functional in nature. Exhaust pipes for cars are the prime example,[8] but there are plenty of other examples, such as kitchen utensils

---

[1] European Parliament and Council Directive 98/71/EC on the legal protection of designs [1998] OJ L 289/28.

[2] SI 2001/3949.

[3] SI 2003/550.

[4] See also M. Howe (ed.) (2005) *Russell Clarke and Howe on Industrial Design*, 7th edn, London: Sweet and Maxwell.

[5] The old provisions were discussed at length in Chapter 20 of the third edition of this book (2001).

[6] Council Regulation (EC) 6/2002 of 12 December 2001 on community designs [2002] OJ L 3/1.

[7] Article 2 of the Regulation.

[8] Spare parts occupy a special position in design law: see *British Leyland Motor Corp. Ltd v. Armstrong Patents Co. Ltd* [1986] AC 577, [1986] 1 All ER 850.

that fall within the scope of the (unregistered) design right. Oversimplification led to the rule that aesthetic designs were covered by the registered design, while the (unregistered) design right covered functional designs. In reality, there was—and still is—a considerable overlap. Many aesthetic designs are also functional and may meet the requirements of the (unregistered) design right, such as food containers of a particular shape made to distinguish the product of one manufacturer from the identical product of a competitor, while some primarily functional designs may also have eye appeal and may also be covered by the new system of registered designs.

In analysing registered designs, then, we will refer to the Registered Designs Act 1949, as amended by the Copyright, Designs and Patents Act 1988.

Requirements for the grant of a registered design before the implementation of the Design Directive

The system put in place by the Design Directive is still relatively new and very little exists in the form of case law to clarify its provisions. It should also be kept in mind that, as with any European Directive, it will eventually be up to the European Court of Justice to rule on its interpretation.

Whereas the old system required the registration of a design for each product separately, the essence of the new system is that it protects a design for a product. The emphasis is on the design, even if it has to be a design for a product. This gives the protection potentially a very wide scope indeed and it is therefore of capital importance to consider carefully how the concepts involved are defined.

A design

The concept of a 'design' is now defined as '*the appearance of the whole or a part of a product resulting from the features of, in particular, the lines, contours, colours, shape, texture of materials of the product or its ornamentation*'.[9] A design is therefore an element of appearance in products.

This definition is much wider than that under the old law and the requirement of 'eye appeal' that characterized the old system no longer exists. The Directive emphasizes this by indicating, in its Recital 14, that no aesthetic quality is required, meaning that arbitrary, but non-appealing, features can now be covered by the definition. What comes in its place, however, is a reference in Recital 11 to '*features which are shown visibly*'. This has to be combined with the use of the word 'appearance' in the definition of a design and, as such, the definition clearly points primarily to aesthetic elements and to an aesthetic impression being created in the mind of the consumer on seeing the design. We are primarily concerned, in this respect, with the 'look and feel'[10] of the product. The design should primarily have been adopted for aesthetic or associative reasons, rather than for technical reasons. We will return to this point in more detail at a later stage. It is, however, worth pointing out that this wide design definition clearly covers the appearance of some trade marks. This will therefore create an overlap in protection, also referred to as the 'convergence' of intellectual property rights.

---

[9] RDA 1949, s. 1(2).
[10] See *Apple Computer Inc. v. Design Registry* [2002] ECDR 191, *per* Jacob J.

A design for a product

What is protected is a 'design for a product'. That concept of a 'product' is defined, in turn, and is said to mean '*any industrial or handicraft item other than a computer program; and, in particular, includes packaging, get-up, graphic symbols and typographical typefaces and parts intended to be assembled into a complex product*', while a complex product is, in turn, defined as '*a product which is composed of at least two replaceable components permitting disassembly and re-assembly of the product*'.[11] In reality, in relation to the latter, the legislator had primarily costly, complex, and long-lasting products—such as cars or computers—in mind.

The only restrictive element in this definition is the exclusion of computer programs[12]—but this is a logical exclusion, because a special regime of protection has already been established for computer programs. Apart from that, the definition is very wide and does away with the restrictions that had surfaced in the UK in relation to what amounts to an item. There is no longer a need for the design to be applied to a product by an industrial process, as is evidenced by the inclusion of handicrafts in the definition. Another consequence of this wide definition will be a substantial weakening of the link between the design and the item or product to which it is applied. The inclusion of 'get-up' in the definition will increasingly make it possible to register the design almost as such, or at least to see its scope of protection against infringement widened in practice. In general, there is no longer a need to register the design in respect of every specific item or group of items. The use of the word 'item' in the definition leads to a degree of uncertainty. The word 'item' seems to suggest some physical form, which is easy to understand in relation to packaging and get-up, because bottle shapes and distinctive labels come to mind, but what is meant by items that consist of graphic symbols or typefaces?

It is likely that the legislator wanted to indicate that the design could be on any kind of surface. Things printed on paper, stamps and posters are therefore, for example, also covered, as are the more traditional designs for curtains and wallpapers. This clearly expands the traditional scope of design law and some even argue that the carrying medium or product does not need to be permanent.[13] It could therefore even include things such as computer screen icons.[14] Designs can also be for a part of an item; there is no longer a need for the product to which the design refers to be sold separately.

Novelty

In order to be registrable, a design must also be new.[15] Novelty is defined in a far less strict way than in patent law: '*a design is new if no identical design or no design whose features differ only in immaterial details has been made available to the public before the relevant date.*'[16]

The first point in this definition of novelty that needs to be clarified is the concept of the 'relevant date'. Normally, this will be the date on which the application for protection is filed. In international cases, however, the applicant may be able to take advantage of the rule in the Paris Convention for the Protection of Industrial Property 1883 that allows an applicant to rely on the date of his or her first application in a contracting state during

---

[11] RDA 1949, s. 1(3).

[12] Ibid.

[13] See A. Kur, 'Protection of graphical user interfaces under European design legislation' (2003) 34 IIC 50.

[14] *Apple Computer Inc. v. Design Registry* [2002] ECDR 191, *per* Jacob J.

[15] RDA 1949, s. 1B(1).

[16] Ibid., (2).

a six-month period whenever an application in another contracting state is filed within that period.[17]

On that relevant date, the test that should be applied is whether the same design—or one with a similar character—is already available to the public through publication, whether following registration or otherwise, through exhibition, through use in trade or through any other form of disclosure. Any design that is already available to the public in this way will no longer be new and cannot be registered, because it is part of the prior art. That prior art is composed of designs. In other words, only designs, as defined in the s. 1(2) of the 1949 Act, are to be taken into account. Even if that is now a wide definition, which will include many artistic works of copyright and general designs for any kind of item, there are still limitations: for example, human beings are excluded even if they have become icons and are used as such in publicity campaigns.[18]

Certain disclosures will, however, be disregarded when novelty is examined.[19] Firstly, any disclosure that is made in confidence to outsiders is not taken into account. Secondly, in a certain sense, novelty—unlike in patent law—is limited to novelty within Europe, by disregarding any disclosures that could not reasonably have become known in the normal course of business to persons carrying out business in the European Economic Area (EEA) and who specialize in the relevant design area. Thirdly, there is a set of exclusions that are based on the same 12-month grace period principle. On the basis of this principle, disclosures made in that period by the designer or a successor in title, disclosures made by the recipient of information from the designer or such a successor, or disclosures made by anyone in abuse of a relation with the designer or such a successor are to be disregarded. This latter limitation may be an advantage, as well as a disadvantage. On the positive side, it allows a designer to show—that is, disclose—the design at a trade exhibition to assess its success before filing an application for protection. This will only trigger the start of the grace period and the designer will still be able to claim novelty during that grace period. The negative consequences—that is, the destruction of the novelty of the design—will surface if another designer picks up the design at the exhibition, copies it, and brings the product on the market within the EEA before the designer files its application. Such behaviour is, on top of anything else, not at all uncommon in the relevant trade circles.

Not only an identical design, but also a design that differs only in immaterial details can destroy novelty. A good example is an application for a design for a bottle carrier. An existing design for a bottle carrier had many features in common with the new design, but the two differed in that:

- they had a different ratio between width and height;
- the handle part in the design applied for encompassed its top half, while that in the existing design comprised only its top third;
- the hole in the handle was circular in shape in the design applied for, while it was oval in the existing design;
- the body part in the design applied for encompassed its bottom half, while in the existing design it encompassed its bottom two-thirds.[20]

These were held to be more than immaterial differences and the design that was applied for satisfied the novelty requirement.

---

[17] Ibid., ss. 1B(7) and 14(2).

[18] See *Spice Girls' Application* [2000] ECDR 148.

[19] RDA 1949, s. 1B(6).

[20] *Built NY Inc. v. I-Feng Kao*, decision of 8 May 2006, OHIM Invalidity Division.

A design for a heater radiator that shared the same pattern of arrangement of features, shapes, and contours with an existing design for radiators was, however, held not to be new, despite the fact that the ratio between width and height had been changed from 1:2.5 to 1:2. In this case, these differences were held to be immaterial details.[21]

Individual character

In addition to being new, the new registered design system requires the design to have 'individual character', which is defined as follows:

> A design has individual character if the overall impression it produces on the informed user differs from the overall impression produced on such a user by any design which has been made available to the public before the relevant date.[22]

Whereas novelty essentially looks at whether the design is, save for immaterial details, identical to a pre-existing design, the requirement of individual character is much more in the eye of the particular beholder. The question that is asked is whether the overall impression that the design produces on the informed user differs from the overall impression that a prior design produced on that person. The emphasis is on the overall impression, so bringing together existing features that exist in different products may suffice.[23]

This should not obscure the fact, however, that this is a tough test. In many cases, a design will show differences when compared with prior designs, but that by no means guarantees that the informed user will judge that a different overall impression is created. The new law offers no definition of the concept of the 'informed user'. But the fact that the words 'user' and 'informed' are combined suggest that we are dealing with someone who has a certain level of knowledge of the design area concerned, either as a professional working in that field, or as a consumer. That, yet again, makes the test harder, because such users will be particularly well aware of the design features that already exist in the field.

The only flexibility that has been built into the system is the sensible approach by which the degree of freedom that was available to the author of the design in creating it should be taken into account when assessing individual character.[24] Indeed, if there is little room for manoeuvre—maybe for technical reasons—small differences between a new design and existing designs may be particularly telling, and may therefore confer individual character.

A first good example concerned designs for bicycle wheels.[25] The individual character of an application was challenged on the basis of a 2002 international patent application that contained a bicycle wheel. The informed user was obviously aware of the functional requirements of such wheels and of the prior art known to those who specialize in this area. The informed user would also be aware of the fact that design freedom was limited by the need to lace the wheel with spokes between the hub and the rim. That would focus attention on areas in relation to which design freedom remained, such as the pattern of distribution of spokes around the hub. In this case, the number of spokes was the same, and the same symmetrical, orderly arrangement and pattern had been used.

---

[21] *Pitacs Ltd v. Kamil Korhan Karagülle*, decision of 26 April 2006, OHIM Invalidity Division.

[22] RDA 1949, s. 1B(3).

[23] Cf *Household Article's Registered Design* [1998] FSR 676.

[24] RDA 1949, s. 1B(4).

[25] *Rodi Comercial SA v. Vuelta International SpA*, decision of 20 December 2005, OHIM Invalidity Division.

This consequently produced the same overall impression on the user and the design failed the individual character test.

Another example concerned dolls.[26] The dolls in question were very similar, but the addition of features such as the shape of the nose or belly button, which made the dolls appear more human, made the design pass the novelty test. Despite that finding, however, the dolls still produced the same overall impression on the informed user and they therefore failed the individual character test.

Component parts of complex products

Additionally, novelty and individual character are said to require that a design that is applied to a component part of a complex product remains visible during the normal use of the complex product, and the novelty and individual character requirements obviously have to be met by the visual features of the component part.[27] This additional rule applies to separate removable parts of a product, rather than to the inside surface of the product. Consumables, such as staples in a staple gun, are also not component parts of the product—that is, the staple gun.

Normal use is defined as use by the end user,[28] with the exclusion of maintenance, servicing, or repair work in relation to the product. The requirement that the design must remain visible in normal use applies therefore in relation to use by the user, rather than by a maintenance technician. Components of an engine that are only visible when the latter is carrying out maintenance work on the engine of a car, for example, are therefore excluded.

Grounds for refusal of registration

Technical function

As we have already indicated, registered designs are not available to grant rights in technical effects; they are rather oriented towards aesthetic designs. While this works well as a starting point, its implementation, in practice, is not entirely straightforward. The legislator has decided that no registered design right shall subsist in features of the appearance of a product that are solely dictated by the product's technical function.[29] Much will depend on the interpretation of this provision. A narrow interpretation will exclude virtually nothing and might allow a designer to monopolize the product by registering a few designs for all of the practical ways of giving effect to a clever technical idea, while a wide interpretation may limit design registrations unduly.

What seems relatively clear from the wording of the provision is that the exclusion will only operate if the features concerned are solely dictated by the product's technical function. This must mean that the main idea is to cover those cases in which the designer had no choice, due to technical constraints linked to the technical function of the product. The exclusion will not apply if the designer can show that there is sufficient design freedom for the product at issue to enable others to create a product that performs the

---

[26] *Aktiebolaget Design Rubens Sweden v. Marie Ekman Bäcklund*, decision of 20 December 2005, OHIM Invalidity Division.

[27] RDA 1949, s. 1B(8).

[28] Ibid., (9).

[29] Ibid., s. 1C(1).

same technical function, while being designed differently. It may be that the exact line separating both options might be drawn up to which the features are essential to obtain a technical result—that is, to allow the product to fulfil its technical function up to the same standard; those features that are not essential in this sense can be the subject of design registration, while essential features, in the sense that they are dictated by technical necessity, cannot.[30]

It is important, however, to add that the exception does not directly exclude designs. All that it excludes are features of appearance that are solely dictated by the product's technical function; all features that are not solely dictated by the product's technical function remain open for design protection. A design for the appearance of a product is therefore still possible if there are enough non-technical features left to meet the criteria for design registration. It is not the case that the presence of one or more technical features excludes the whole appearance of the product from design registration. This makes a lot of business sense, because competitors need those technical features in order to compete, but there is no need for them to copy the non-technical features.

Overall, this interpretation of the provision does, it is submitted, strike a correct competition-friendly balance between adequate design protection and the risk of competition excluding technical designs.[31]

The 'must fit' exception

The other important exception for non-aesthetical features from the scope of registered designs is the 'must fit' exception, which deals with a type of functional design features. Section 1C(2) defines the scope of the exception in the following way:

> A right in a registered design shall not subsist in features of appearance of a product which must necessarily be reproduced in their exact form and dimensions so as to permit the product in which the design is incorporated or to which it is applied to be mechanically connected to, or placed in, around or against, another product so that either product may perform its function...[32]

Clear examples in practice are electrical plugs and sockets, connectors for lamps to fit into sockets, and batteries to fit into watches. In all of these cases, there is a need for the features of appearance to be reproduced in their exact form and dimensions, and this necessity for exact reproduction is therefore the key element in the exception.

This exception is clearly very similar to the technical function exception and there could arguably be an overlap. In fairness to the drafters of the legislation, it can be said that the technical function exception primarily deals with a product that works on its own and in relation to which the design features are dictated by the technical function of that product, whereas the 'must fit' exception deals with two products that need to be connected, etc., in order for them to work. Rather than a technical, this is more a functional exception. But it is clear that the exception is vital to make sure that no single designer or trader monopolizes a connector system due to the fact that interoperability of products is a vital element to enhance competition. The technical function exception on its own may not have been able to achieve this result, because the shape of the connector is not dictated

---

[30] Cf the decision of the European Court of Justice on trade marks for shapes that are necessary to obtain a technical result in Case C-299/99 *Koninklijke Philips v. Remington* [2002] ECR I-5475, [2003] RPC 14.

[31] Cf, under the old law, *Cow (PB) & Co. Ltd v. Cannon Rubber Manufacturers Ltd* [1959] RPC 240; the slightly different approach adopted by the House of Lords in *Amp Inc. v. Utilux Pty Ltd* [1972] RPC 103.

[32] RDA 1949, s. 1C(2).

solely by the product's technical function. Indeed, as the electrical plug and socket example shows, for example, different plugs and sockets can be devised, and are in use in the UK and in Continental Europe. A narrowly defined technical function exception would therefore not cover this example, because the design features of one system are not essential for any product to carry out its technical function.

There is one exception to the 'must fit' exception: designs that serve *'the purpose of allowing multiple assembly or connection of mutually interchangeable products within a modular system'*[33] will still be registrable. Lego toy bricks or stackable chairs come to mind by way of examples. This exception is not based on any particular logic or argument, but is the result of effective lobbying by the toy industry.

Public policy and morality

Designs that are contrary to public policy or to accepted principles of morality will not be registered.[34] Morality can only be invoked, however, if the design would offend against the moral principles of right-thinking members of society; the fact that some people might find the design distasteful is not sufficient.[35]

This is a standard prohibition. The theoretical reason for its existence is clear, but its application, in practice, is often problematic, because public policy and public morality are hard to define.

General exception

There is, of course, also a provision that excludes from registrability anything that does not come within the definition of a design in s. 1(2) of the 1949 Act—and neither will a design that does not meet the requirements of novelty and individual character be registered.[36]

Ownership of a registered design

The author of a design—as the person who creates the design[37]—will be the first owner of the registered design.[38] There are only two exceptions to this rule: the employer of the employee who creates a design will be the first owner of the registered design if the design is created in the course of employment;[39] the person who commissions a design will be the first owner of the registered design if the design was commissioned for money, or for money's worth.[40] A specific problem arises when a design is computer-generated. The computer is not a person and cannot become the first owner of the registered design, but there is no human author. In such a case, the ownership of the registered design is then

---

[33] Ibid., (3).

[34] Ibid., s. 1D.

[35] *Re Masterman's Design* [1991] RPC 89 (a design for a Scottish doll with a kilt, which exposed male genitalia when lifted), but note that a design that shows directly representations of genitalia may still infringe morality.

[36] RDA 1949, s. 1A(1).

[37] Ibid., s. 2(3).

[38] Ibid., (1).

[39] Ibid., (1B).

[40] Ibid., (1A).

attributed to the nearest person involved in its creation—that is, to the person who made the arrangements necessary for the creation of the design.[41]

Ownership, of course, presupposes the registration of the design. The provisions governing such registration can be found in ss. 3 and 3A–3D of the Act. It should be kept in mind that a registration is effective against the use of the design on any item in so far as no different overall impression is created. The design will nevertheless have to be registered for a specific product on which it is to be used. This will be done on the basis of an international classification,[42] which facilitates searches of the register by interested parties. Registration in multiple categories is possible.

The ownership of a registered design right or the right to apply the design to any item can be transferred. This can be done by an assignment or any other form of transmission.[43] The transferee can either become the full owner of the right, or he or she can become joint owner of the right together with the assignor.[44] Licences can also be granted.[45] Partial transfers, such as of the right to apply the design to one specific item, and transfers to more than one party, resulting in joint ownership, are possible. But all assignments of a registered design right must be registered. This means that, in practice, it is advisable that assignments and licences are in writing, although this is, in theory, not an express requirement.[46]

Rights of the owner and infringement

The Design Directive led to changes in UK law in the areas of the rights of the owner and infringement. In terms of the rights that are granted by a registered design, the basic principles are found in Art. 12 of the Directive, which provides that:

> The registration of a design shall confer on its holder the exclusive right to use it and to prevent any third party not having its consent from using it. The aforementioned use shall cover, in particular, the making, offering, putting on the market, importing, exporting or using of a product in which the design is incorporated or to which it is applied, or stocking such a product for those purposes.

These basic principles must be interpreted in the light of the two provisos found in Art. 9:

(1) The scope of the protection conferred by a design right shall include any design which does not produce on the informed user a different overall impression.

(2) In assessing the scope of the protection, the degree of freedom of the designer in developing his design shall be taken into consideration.

Section 7 of the 1949 Act puts this into practice under UK law by granting the owner of the design the exclusive right to use the design, as well as any design that does not produce a different overall impression on the informed user.[47] The concept of 'use' is wider than that used previously and includes making, offering, putting on the market, exporting, or

---

[41] Ibid., (4).
[42] See the Locarno Agreement 1968.
[43] RDA 1949, s. 2(2).
[44] Ibid.
[45] Ibid., s. 19(4).
[46] Ibid., s. 19.
[47] Ibid., s. 7(1).

using a product in which the design is incorporated, or to which it has been applied, or stocking such a product for any of these purposes.[48]

Infringement, then, logically occurs if, without the consent of the owner of the design right, a person does anything that, by virtue of s. 7, is the exclusive right of the owner of the registered design right.[49] The key test on this point is whether a different overall impression is created on the informed user by the allegedly infringing design; there will only be an infringement if no different overall impression is created. In assessing this issue of different overall impression, the degree of freedom of the author in creating the design is to be taken into account.[50] Article 9(2) is, in this respect, a limiting provision.

But this does not solve our main problem: how does one deal with the relationship between the design, on the one hand, and the item, on the other? The design will still be registered for a product, or a class of products, and any infringement case is almost bound to compare design, as applied to products, rather than design in isolation, but infringement is, in the new law, no longer confined to use on the product for which the design is registered. The design may be infringed if no different overall impression is created, irrespective of the type of product to which it is applied. The design may also only affect a part of a product. This may make it rather difficult to apply the negative test of not creating a different impression to the design. How, in practice, is one going to make abstraction of the product to assess the overall impression created by the allegedly infringing design? On top of that, the negative formulation of the test does nothing to alleviate the problem (which is fairly inevitable in relation to designs). Does 'different' mean that the design must not create the same identical impression or will some (strong) form of similarity infringe in practice? It will be up to the courts—and, eventually, the European Court of Justice—to determine the exact boundaries in this respect.

The Court of Appeal made a start in *Procter & Gamble v. Reckitt Benckiser.*[51] This case was concerned with a design applied to sprayers for air freshener products. The canister for the defendant's 'Air-Wick' product was inspired by the claimant's design for its 'Febreze' canister. The question arose whether there was more than inspiration and whether an infringement had occurred.

The Court of Appeal, first of all, turned its attention to the concept of the 'informed user'. Similar characters in both patent and trade mark law were held not to be of assistance. What we are dealing with here is a user who is aware of the existing design corpus in the area. Such a user has experience of other similar items and designs, and will therefore be reasonably discriminatory. He or she will be able to appreciate enough detail to decide whether a design creates an allegedly infringing design or produces a different overall impression. In doing so, there is no decisive role for the idea that the user must have an imperfect recollection. He or she would view things carefully and, as such, remember more details. What matters in making the decision is what strikes the mind of the informed user when the designs are viewed carefully. The informed user therefore has more extensive knowledge than an average consumer in possession of average information, awareness, and understanding. In particular, the informed user is open to design issues and is fairly familiar with them.[52] This includes the knowledge of the fact that, by

---

[48] Ibid., (2).

[49] Ibid., s. 7A(1).

[50] Ibid., (3).

[51] *Procter & Gamble Co. v. Reckitt Benckiser (UK) Ltd* [2007] EWCA Civ 936.

[52] The Court of Appeal cited, with approval, the conclusion reached in a case between the same parties by the Higher Provisional Court in Vienna 4Ob 239/04g: *Procter & Gamble Co. v. Reckitt Benckiser (UK) Ltd* [2007] EWCA Civ 936, at [26]; see also *Woodhouse v. Architectural Lighting* [2006] RPC 1.

reason of function, shapes can be, to a certain extent, required to conform to a certain standard.

The Court then turned its attention to the concept of 'a different overall impression'. A difference that allows the informed user to discriminate between the two designs is required, but it is not required that the allegedly infringing design 'clearly differs' from the registered design. What one has in mind is the question of whether or not the designs are substantially different. The Court offered the following guidelines for the application of the test:

i) ...the test is 'different' not 'clearly different.'

ii) The notional informed user is 'fairly familiar' with design issues....

iii) Next [it] is not a proposition of law but a statement about the way people (and thus the notional informed user) perceive things. It is simply that if a new design is markedly different from anything that has gone before, it is likely to have a greater overall visual impact than if it is 'surrounded by kindred prior art.' ...It follows that the 'overall impression' created by such a design will be more significant and the room for differences which do not create a substantially different overall impression is greater. So protection for a striking novel product will be correspondingly greater than for a product which is incrementally different from the prior art, though different enough to have its own individual character and thus be validly registered.

iv) On the other hand it does not follow, in a case of markedly new design (or indeed any design) that it is sufficient to ask 'is the alleged infringement closer to the registered design or to the prior art', if the former infringement, if the latter not. The test remains 'is the overall impression different?'

v) It is legitimate to compare the registered design and the alleged infringement with a reasonable degree of care. The court must 'don the spectacles of the informed user' to adapt the hackneyed but convenient metaphor of patent law. The possibility of imperfect recollection has a limited part to play in this exercise.

vi) The court must identify the 'overall impression' of the registered design with care. True it is that it is difficult to put into language, and it is helpful to use pictures as part of the identification, but the exercise must be done.

vii) In this exercise the level of generality to which the court must descend is important. Here, for instance, it would be too general to say that the overall impression of the registered design is 'a canister fitted with a trigger spray device on the top.' The appropriate level of generality is that which would be taken by the notional informed user.

viii) The court should then do the same exercise for the alleged infringement.

ix) Finally the court should ask whether the overall impression of each is different. This is almost the equivalent to asking whether they are the same—the difference is nuanced, probably, involving a question of onus and no more.[53]

When the Court applied these guidelines to the case at issue, it again agreed with the Austrian court's decision that:

In reality, even though the same features are found in both, there are clear differences between the two sprayers resulting from the different mode of their execution: the Febreze sprayer is smaller, has a slightly larger diameter and so looks more compact. The head of this sprayer is shallower but also broader, so that the Febreze sprayer fits the hand differently than the Airwick sprayer (with the Airwick sprayer, which has the considerably narrower head, there is a feeling that it could slip out of the user's hand). In contrast to the Airwick sprayer, the metal

53 *Procter & Gamble Co v. Reckitt Benckiser (UK) Ltd* [2007] EWCA Civ 936, at [35].

can of the Febreze sprayer tapers upwards, so that the waist begins lower down than in the Airwick sprayer. The 'train' goes down much further in the Febreze sprayer, so that the lower boundary of the plastic part echoes the angle of the head part far more markedly than in the Airwick sprayer. The shape of head too is different: while the head of the Febreze sprayer—to draw a comparison from the animal kingdom—is reminiscent of a snake's head, the shape of the Airwick sprayer head is like a lizard's head.[54]

The similarities are clearly only found at a general level and it was therefore held that a different overall impression was produced on the informed user. On that basis, the infringement case failed.[55]

Exclusion from protection—defences to infringement

The exclusive rights of the right holder are subject to certain limitations and exclusions. For an alleged infringer, these turn into a series of defences.

1. Acts done privately and for non-commercial purposes will not constitute an infringement.[56]

2. Acts done for experimental purposes are exempted.[57]

3. Acts of reproduction for the purposes of making citations or of teaching are also exempted provided that the act of reproduction is compatible with fair trade practices and does not unduly prejudice the normal exploitation of the design, on the one hand, and that the source is mentioned, on the other.[58]

4. There are specific exceptions in relation to foreign registered ships and aircraft, which are temporarily in the UK, the repairing of these, and the importation of spare parts for that purpose.[59]

These limitations and defence are subject to the condition that such acts are compatible with fair trade practice, do not unduly prejudice the normal exploitation of the design, and that mention is made of the source.[60]

The exhaustion rule will also apply at EEA level. The usual rule applies in this respect. Accordingly, s. 7A(4) of the 1949 Act stipulates that:

The right in a registered design is not infringed by an act which relates to a product in which any design protected by the registration is incorporated or to which it is applied if the product has been put on the market in the European Economic Area by the registered proprietor or with his consent.

The Crown has the right to use a registered design for the services of the Crown or to authorize such use, normally against compensation.[61] This is not an exclusion from protection in the purest sense, but it does limit the exclusive right of the right holder to some extent.

Invalidity

A design may be declared invalid on the basis of four grounds of invalidity. The first ground of invalidity is that the design does not meet the requirements set out in s. 1A of

---

[54] Ibid., at [61].
[56] RDA 1949, s. 7A(2)a.
[58] Ibid., s. 7A(2)c.
[60] Ibid., (3).

[55] Ibid., at [62]–[63].
[57] Ibid., (2)b.
[59] Ibid., (2)d–f.
[61] Ibid., s. 12.

the Act.[62] The second ground is that the registered proprietor is not the real proprietor of the design and that the real proprietor objects to the existing registration.[63] These two grounds refer to deficiencies in the registration.

The other two grounds focus on clashes with other rights. A design registration can also be declared invalid if it incorporates a registered or unregistered trade mark;[64] the final ground of invalidity is that the registered design constitutes the unauthorized use of a copyright work.[65] In both of these cases, the right holder in the mark or copyright needs to object to the design registration.

Duration of the registered design right

If the design is registered and published[66] after the examination of the application by the Designs Registry, a branch of the Patent Office, that registration will initially be valid for a period of five years[67] from the date of registration.[68] The registration of the design can be renewed four times, bringing the maximum term of protection to 25 years.[69]

The Directive contains a similar 25-year maximum term of protection, but, according to Art. 10, the term is to be calculated from the date of filing of the application. Section 3C(1) of the 1949 Act now overcomes this difference by stipulating that a design shall be registered as of the date of application, which means that the two approaches will now overlap. In practice, the commercial life of an aesthetic design will often be shorter than 25 years and it can be expected that many registered designs will be allowed to lapse, because their owners request no further renewal. Fashions do indeed exist in eye-appealing designs. Many features of appearance that were very popular around 1990 are no longer popular, so there is no need to renew the design registration. In doing so, one would incur a cost that could no longer be recuperated by profits through sales of items made to the design.

The application for renewal of the registered design right must be addressed to the Registrar during the last six months of the previous five-year period; in the absence of such an application, the right will cease to exist upon expiry of the previous five-year period.[70] The owner of the right is, however, given an additional six-month period during which he or she can renew the right,[71] although a restoration fee will be payable on top of the normal renewal fee. If the right is restored, it shall be treated as if it had never expired.[72]

Spare parts

Spare parts have been a stumbling block in relation to design law for several years. The idea that manufacturers of consumer products would be able to monopolize the spare

---

[62] Ibid., s. 11ZA(1).
[63] Ibid., (2).
[64] Ibid., (3).
[65] Ibid., (4).
[66] But see ibid., s. 5, which contains exceptional rules.
[67] Ibid., s. 8(1).
[68] Earlier applications will have a priority right that can be claimed for up to six months.
[69] RDA 1949, s. 8(2).
[70] Ibid., (3).
[71] This is not an automatic right; the Registrar has a discretion: see ibid., s. 8A.
[72] Ibid., s. 8(4).

part market by means of design registrations has proved to be at least controversial, if not straightforwardly unacceptable. It is indeed true that many parts take distinctive shapes; some of these shapes reflect the design features of the larger part in which they are inserted. One might think, for example, of doors for a certain make of car. Others may have a functional shape and, in this respect, one might think, for example, of exhaust pipes for a certain make of car. All of these, when bought as spare parts, will, in most cases, need to take the same shape if they are to be suitable for repair or replacement purposes. The consumer will therefore have no choice of supplier if a design registration allows the manufacturer of the original product to be the only parts supplier. The risk of monopoly pricing and other abuses, such as failure to supply parts for older products, is then not simply remote prospect.

As a result, many legislators and courts have acted by providing a special regime for design rights in spare parts. When the EU agreed the Directive (and the Regulation), no agreement could be reached on this point. In relation to spare parts and registered designs, the member States have therefore, in the end, retained the right to maintain their existing national provisions. They can, however, only introduce changes to these provisions if the changes have the effect of liberalizing the market for spare parts.[73] The Commission was to draft a report by the end of 2004, on the basis of which a new attempt to solve the outstanding spare parts issue is being undertaken.[74] Looking back at the controversy surrounding this area, it is hard to see how this will be achieved in the short term.

In the UK Act, the spare parts issue is now addressed in s. 7A(5). A registered design right in a component part that may be used for the purpose of the repair of a complex product so as to restore its original appearance is not infringed by the use for that purpose of any design protected by the registration.[75] Spare parts can therefore be manufactured without infringing the registered design, but it is important to note that the provision does not take the design right away altogether; it will simply not be infringed if the part involving the design is used to restore the original appearance of a complex product. The latter is also an important limitation that is placed on the exception. Any use that goes beyond restoring the original appearance of the complex product will still amount to an infringement of the registered design.

It is also important to note that the current solution is rather more consumer-friendly than it looks at first sight. Indeed, complex products are those in relation to which the spare parts issue arises most frequently. The existence of design requires that a design that is applied to a component part of a complex product remains visible during the normal use of the complex product, and also that the component itself is new and has individual character. Because complex products have been defined in a loose way, this will reduce the number of possible design registrations for spare parts.

International commercial exploitation

International exploitation of registered designs is facilitated by the fact that the Paris Convention, to which the UK is a party, covers this area. A design application in one

---

[73] Design Directive, Art. 14.

[74] Ibid., Art. 18. The Commission accordingly produced its Proposal for a Directive of the European Parliament and of the Council amending Directive 98/71/EC on the legal protection of designs, SEC (2004) 1097, COM/2004/0582 final, available online at eur-lex.europa.eu/smartapi/cgi/sga_doc?smartapi!celexapi! prod!CELEXnumdoc&lg=en&model=guicheti&numdoc=52004PC0582.

[75] RDA 1949, s. 7A(5).

of the contracting states will result in a priority right, the term of which is six months, in relation to applications made in other contracting states.[76] But substantial problems relating to the international exploitation of a registered design are created by the tremendous international disparity in design protection systems. So, contrary to the UK system, many foreign systems do not provide for a search, but operate a deposit system, which means that designs are entered into the register upon application, with a possibility for all interested parties to object to the validity of the design and to request its removal from the register. The latter option was also taken by the contracting parties to the Hague Agreement 1925,[77] which aimed at creating a unified registration system for designs, but this system never managed to attract much international support (and, obviously, the UK never adhered to it).

Many Commonwealth countries copied the principles of the UK's registered design system. A large group among them extends protection to UK registered designs without requiring local registration.[78] These countries even request that local applicants register their designs in the UK. Some other countries and territories[79] require local re-registration before they extend protection to the design.

The Community design

We indicated above that the EU approach to registered designs has been based on two tracks. The first track consisted of the Directive, aimed at harmonizing national registered design laws. In the UK, this resulted in the substantial revision of the Registered Designs Act 1949, the provisions of which we have analysed in depth.

The second track consists of the Regulation,[80] which puts in place a system under which a single Community (registered) design will be granted as a result of a central single application with the Community Design Office, which will be located in Alicante as part of the existing OHIM structure. Once granted, the Community design will apply in the whole of the community.

The Community design is separate from any national design rights.

Procedural issues

In procedural terms, OHIM will deal with the registration of Community designs.[81] It will examine whether the formal requirements and the definition of a design have been met. Novelty and individual character will not be examined, but third parties can bring invalidity proceedings before the Office if they consider that the design should not be registered validly, because of lack of such.[82]

---

[76] Ibid., s. 14. A resident of the UK can only make a second application six weeks after the application in the UK was made: ibid., s. 5.

[77] Which had attracted 47 contracting states as of November 2007. The 1999 Act of the Agreement entered into force on 23 December 2003 (at present between 51 of the contracting states, if EU states are counted individually).

[78] Antigua, Bermuda, Botswana, Cyprus, Fiji, Ghana, Gibraltar, Hong Kong, Kenya, Malaysia, Sierra Leone, Singapore, and Uganda are all included in this group.

[79] For example, the Channel Islands, Malta, and Tanzania.

[80] Council Regulation (EC) 6/2002 on community designs [2002] OJ L 3/1.

[81] Title IV of the Regulation.

[82] Articles 24 and 25 of the Regulation.

Appeals against a decision made by OHIM—such as a decision to refuse registration—can be brought before the OHIM Boards of Appeal. A further appeal can then be brought before the European Court of Justice, via the Court of First Instance and, ultimately, before the Court of Justice itself.[83] Invalidity can also be raised as a counterclaim before the national courts, which will also deal with infringement cases. Each member State has selected, for this purpose, a limited number of community design courts among its national courts, both at first instance and on appeal.[84]

Substantive provisions

The substantive provisions of the Regulation are supposed to mirror those of the Directive. We will therefore not repeat here what has been said above, but one important point of difference can be found in the provisions on initial ownership of the Community design. The Directive had left that matter to the national laws of the member States and no harmonization had taken place; this solution was unworkable in relation to a single Community design. The Regulation therefore provides that *'the design shall vest in the designer or his successor in title'* and that the employer is presumptively the person who becomes the first owner of a design made by the employee in the course of employment.[85] There is, however, no presumptive transfer of ownership to the commissioner of the design. This is an important departure from the traditional UK approach. It may nevertheless be possible for the courts to read an implied licence transferring ownership to the commissioner into the contract between the designer and the commissioner in cases in which all of the circumstances suggest it.[86] This will, of course, not apply to all cases and it does therefore not solve the problem as such.

A few points were not covered at Community level. This lacuna has been filled at national level by the Community Design Regulations 2005.[87] Regulation 2 provides for an action against groundless threats.

A somewhat peculiar situation in this respect arose in *Quads 4 Kids v. Campbell.*[88] The defendant had applied to register a number of Community design rights, but had requested the deferment of the publication of that registration. When the claimant sold children's bikes made to an allegedly similar design on eBay, the defendant used eBay's own verified rights owner (VERO) programme, but made it clear that no further action would be taken. eBay uses the VERO system to allow intellectual property right holders to report infringements of their rights. eBay then removes the allegedly infringing listings, without any investigation. The seller whose listings are removed is simply informed of their removal. The sole purpose of the system is to make sure that eBay cannot be liable for infringement.

The normal test in groundless threat cases is whether the reasonable person in the position of the threatened would have understood that he or she might have been subject to infringement proceedings at some point in the future. This was not the case in *Quads*, because the defendant had made it clear that no further action would be taken. Nevertheless, the claimant was no longer able to trade on the basis of allegations that had not been proven. This was exactly the situation that the groundless threats provision was

---

[83] Title VII of the Regulation.
[84] Articles 80 and 81 of the Regulation.
[85] Article 14 of the Regulation.
[86] See *Blair v. Osborne & Tomkins* [1971] 2 QB 78 (CA).
[87] SI 2005/2339.
[88] *Quads 4 Kids v. Campbell* [2006] EWHC 2482, [2006] All ER (D) 162.

supposed to address. Mr Justice Pumfrey proposed, therefore, a new test for this type of cases.[89] This involved determining whether eBay would have understood that it could be subject to future infringement proceedings, had it not adopted the policy, via the VERO system, of removing any items alleged to infringe. In this case, the answer was affirmative and the claimant was therefore successful in securing the injunction for which it had applied.

The Community unregistered design right

The Regulation also created a Community *unregistered* design right, which complements the registered right. We will discuss it here because of that link and because, as such, it provides a link with the next chapter.

The need for an unregistered right had become apparent in those industries in which fashion changes every couple of months and for which the registration process will simply last too long. There are also many cases in which registration will be costly and in relation to which the applicant would rather test the market for the design first before deciding on registration.[90]

The Community unregistered design right addresses these concerns by providing for a three-year term of protection without registration or other formalities. In order to be protected, the design will need to meet the same requirements as its registered counterpart. The three-year term starts to run on the date on which the design was first made available to the public by publication, exhibition, use in trade, or any other way of disclosing the design if it could be reasonably known in specialized Community circles.[91] In this respect, again, there are important similarities with its registered counterpart.

Infringement of the Community unregistered design right occurs in the same way as infringement of the registered right, apart from the fact that, in the absence of registration, the claimant must also prove that the defendant copied the protected design.[92]

The seamless connection with the registered right is assured by the provision that allows a one-year grace period between the publication and the application for the registered right.[93] Novelty will, in other words, not be lost by publication giving right to a Community unregistered design right. This allows the designer to test the market before deciding on an application.

An overview

This is an area of the law of intellectual property that is undergoing important and radical changes at present. Much of the 1949 Act had become outdated and the courts had struggled to maintain a workable system. The Design Directive and its implementation, in the form of the recent radical shake-up of the 1949 Act, puts in place a harmonized and more modern approach to registered designs. That approach is rather radically different on a number of key points and this will inevitably bring with it some uncertainty in its initial implementation. It will eventually be up to the courts, both at national and at EU levels, to provide the necessary clarifications.

89 Ibid. at [30].
90 See V. Saez, 'The unregistered Community design' [2002] EIPR 585.
91 Article 11 of the Regulation.
92 Article 19(2) of the Regulation.
93 Article 7(2) of the Regulation.

What remains true, however, and what drives this whole overhaul of the system is the fact that designs can be of a tremendous commercial value. They do not amount to an invention and are not necessarily a trade mark; neither does copyright protect the idea behind the design. So there is a very real need to register the design as a registered design. It is the only way in which to prevent competitors from cashing in on a good and valuable design by using one that is substantially identical.

The new system should be far better equipped to allow designers to secure adequate protection for their valuable designs.

Further reading

DREXL, J., HILTY, R. and KUR, A. 'Design protection for spare parts and the Commission's proposal for a repairs clause' (2005) 36 IIC 448.

HOWE, M. (ed.) (2005) *Russell Clarke and Howe on Industrial Design*, 7th edn, London: Sweet and Maxwell.

IZQUIERDO PERIS, J.J. 'Registered Community design: first two-year balance from an insider's perspective' [2006] EIPR 146.

SAEZ, V. 'The unregistered Community design' [2002] EIPR 585.

SCANLAN, G. and GALE, S. 'Industrial design and the Design Directive: continuing and future problems in design rights' [2005] JBL 91.

SYKES, J. (2005) *Intellectual Property in Designs*, London: Butterworths Lexis-Nexis.

22
Unregistered designs

Introduction

The unregistered design right was introduced by the Copyright, Designs and Patents Act 1988 in an attempt to overcome various problems. Before that time, functional, non-aesthetic designs—such as those for exhaust pipes for cars—did not qualify for registered design protection and neither were they covered by a special intellectual property right. But there was an overlap with copyright, because, in the majority of cases, functional designs are laid down in drawings, plans, or blueprints that attract copyright protection. A copy of an item incorporating the design involves making a three-dimensional copy of the drawing, plan, or blueprint and infringes their copyright. This system provided indirect protection for the majority of functional designs, but it is hard to see why a certain category of designs—those that are aesthetic—deserve the creation of a special intellectual property right, while the other designs—that are purely functional in nature—should only be protected indirectly through copyright.

This argument becomes even more forceful if one considers that, in theory, all design rights—both aesthetical and functional—benefit potentially from the overlap with copyright. In practice, designs that met all of the requirements for registration were often not registered, because the non-bureaucratic and fee-free copyright system offered long-term protection. Parliament tried to remedy this by means of a series of arbitrary measures: in the Copyright Act 1956, copyright protection was denied to designs that could have been registered; in the Design Copyright Act 1968, copyright was once again permitted, but the term of copyright protection in such cases was restricted to the term of the registered design right.[1]

This created absurd situations such as that in *Dorling v. Honnor Marine*.[2] This case was concerned with a sailing dinghy. The design for the dinghy met the requirements for registration, but had not been registered. Before their relationship turned sour, the defendant built the dinghies—both in complete and in kit forms—under a licence granted by the plaintiff. The case arose when the defendant went on to assign his licence to a limited company that he had formed; the company became the co-defendant in the case. Drawings of the dinghy and of all its parts existed, and, theoretically speaking, the copyright in them was infringed by making three-dimensional copies. In practice, the Copyright Act 1956 had removed copyright protection for designs that could have been registered, so no intellectual property right had been infringed in building the dinghies. But kits of parts were also made: the design of each of the included parts was purely functional and could not be registered. As a result, the provisions of the Copyright Act 1956 did not exclude copyright

---

[1] At that stage, 15 years; now extended to 25 years, as discussed in the previous chapter.
[2] *Dorling v. Honnor Marine Ltd* [1965] Ch 1, [1964] 1 All ER 241.

protection in the drawings for the kit parts and the production of the parts formed an indirect infringement of the copyright in the drawings by making three-dimensional copies of these two-dimensional drawings. The functional design of the parts enjoyed protection for the life of the author plus 50 years, while no protection was available for the aesthetical design of the complete dinghy.[3] This discrepancy in protection for the two types of design could not be justified.

But it is not only the discrepancy that caused problems: copyright protection for functional designs also proved to be an inadequate solution. This became clear in the famous *British Leyland Motor Corp. Ltd v. Armstrong Patents Co. Ltd*,[4] which we discussed in Chapter 20. The case most strongly indicated the need for design law reform and action needed to be undertaken on two points. A specific intellectual property right needed to be created for functional designs, meaning that the whole design area would be covered by two specific design rights: aesthetical designs would still be protected by the registered design right and the non-aesthetical functional designs would be covered by the new design right.

The second point that needed to be addressed is the overlap with copyright: a clear delimitation of both the copyright and the design area was required. The reform of the 1988 Act attempted to reach that conclusion and created the (unregistered) design right, which is officially called the design right—but, in order to distinguish it from the registered design and because there is no registration requirement, we will describe it as the (unregistered) design.

Subsistence of the (unregistered) design right

A design

The technical definition of a 'design' given is that it is *'the design of any aspect of the shape or configuration (whether internal or external) of the whole or part of an article'*.[5] The concept of 'shape' is understood relatively easily, but that of 'configuration' is somewhat more vague. In relation to the former, suffice it to say that there is no reason why a simple geometric shape could not be a protectable design for an item.[6] In relation to the latter, however, the Court of Appeal has indicated that 'configuration' refers to the relative arrangement of three-dimensional elements.[7] These elements need to be configured and the mere choice of colourways of a standard track top was therefore not an aspect of the shape or configuration of an item or of a part of an item.[8] The addition of the term 'aspect' to the notions of shape and configuration refers to something discernible or recognizable.[9]

This definition and approach means that various aspects of the shape or configuration of an item can be the subjects of different design rights, and that a design does not necessarily relate to the whole item. It is, however, quite possible that both the individual parts and the machine as a whole come within the definition of a design.[10] This was, for example, the case for a slurry machine as a whole, on the one hand, and its various components, on the other.[11]

---

[3] Even if the design had been registered, the term of protection would have been much shorter.
[4] [1986] AC 577, [1986] 1 All ER 850.
[5] CDPA 1988, s. 213 (2).
[6] *Sales v. Stromberg* [2006] FSR 7.
[7] *Lambretta Clothing Co. Ltd v. Teddy Smith (UK) Ltd & anor* [2005] RPC 6 (CA).
[8] Ibid.
[9] *A Fulton Co. Ltd v. Totes Isotoner (UK) Ltd* [2004] RPC 301 (CA), at 311.
[10] Ibid. at 307–11.
[11] *Farmers Build Ltd (in liq.) v. Carier Bulk Materials Handling Ltd* [1999] RPC 461.

The case law also offers another example in a case concerning pig fenders for use in pig arks, which provide shelter for a single sow and her piglets. A two-inch tube protected the teats of the sow; this two-inch tube was held to be an aspect of the shape or configuration of a part of the fender—that is, the tube element constituted a design.[12] A clear distinction must, however, be made between the design and the item to which it is applied: the design is protected, while the item is not; the right protects the design itself and not the item on which it has been recorded or to which it has been applied.[13] The right in the design is not a right in the item itself.[14]

Aspects of the internal shape or configuration of the whole, or part, of an item can also be taken into account. This marks a clear difference from the 'eye appeal' requirement for registered designs. (Unregistered) designs are intended to offer protection for functional designs; eye appeal is not required. The worth and ingenuity of such a design might be found in its detailed relative dimensions. A design might even exist (and be different and new) if the eye is not able to distinguish the shape (in relation to other designs).[15] Larger, and more clearly visible, shapes are obviously also possible and remain eligible for protection.

An original design

The design right will only subsist in designs that are original. This clearly means that the design should not be copied and that it should be the result of its creator's own work. The design should be the independent work of the designer and should not be copied from previous designs. Time, labour, and skill should have been invested to such an extent that copyright protection could have been attracted.[16] When examining originality, one should ask whether all of the additional features added by the designer give rise to the requisite quality of originality. One should not focus exclusively on one or more features or adopt a piecemeal approach, even if individual features will unavoidably require some attention and consideration.[17] But that is not all: s. 213(4) of the 1988 Act specifies that '*a design is not "original" if it is commonplace in the design field in question at the time of its creation*'.

The concept of 'commonplace'

Laddie J has defined as 'commonplace' any design that is '*trite, trivial, common or garden, hackneyed or of the type which would excite no particular attention in those in the relevant art*'.[18] For example, in a case that was concerned with designs for leather cases for individual models of mobile phones, it was held that those aspects of the design that were found in industry standard cases were commonplace;[19] they were therefore excluded from the

---

[12] *C & H Engineering v. Klucznik & Sons Ltd* [1992] FSR 421, *per* Aldous J at 428; see J. Turner, 'A true design right: *C & H Engineering v. Klucznik and Sons*' [1993] 1 EIPR 24 at 24.

[13] *Electronic Techniques (Anglia) Ltd v. Critchley Components Ltd* [1997] FSR 401; *Scholes Windows Ltd v. Magnet Ltd (No. 1)* [2002] FSR 172 (CA), at 180.

[14] *Scholes Windows Ltd v. Magnet Ltd (No. 1)* [2002] FSR 172 (CA), at 180.

[15] *Ocular Sciences Ltd & ANR v. Aspect Vision Care Ltd; Geoffrey Harrison Galley v. Ocular Sciences Ltd* [1997] RPC 289 at 423.

[16] *Farmers Build Ltd (in liq.) v. Carier Bulk Materials Handling Ltd* [1999] RPC 461, *per* Mummery LJ at 475; *C & H Engineering v. F Klucznik & Sons Ltd* [1992] FSR 421.

[17] *Guild v. Eskander Ltd* [2003] FSR 23 (CA), at 39.

[18] *Ocular Sciences Ltd & ANR v. Aspect Vision Care Ltd; Geoffrey Harrison Galley v. Ocular Sciences Ltd* [1997] RPC 289 at 429, in which there was a reference to semiconductor products and the design right in them. The definition was repeated in *Mayfair Brassware v. Aqualine International Ltd* [1998] FSR 135, in a context that refers to design rights.

[19] *Philip Parker v. Stephen Tidball* [1997] FSR 680.

design right. It is possible, however, to arrive at a design that is not commonplace through the combination of commonplace and trite ingredients. The test applies to the design: if the design is a combination of ingredients, that combination itself must not be commonplace.[20] It should be kept in mind, however, that no design right is conferred on the item; the right is conferred on aspects of shape of configuration of the item. One should therefore not derive any conclusion from the fact that the item itself is commonplace: its shape and configuration may still not be commonplace.[21]

The provision that is contained in s. 213(4) of the 1988 Act makes the originality requirement for designs clearly more stringent than that for copyright. Indeed, it introduces an objective component akin to the novelty consideration in patents.[22] Some form of objective assessment is required.[23] A design that is already known and is, in reality, nothing more than a copy of an existing design will not be original;[24] neither will mere changes in scale produce a different or new design.[25] It is submitted that the design must be innovative, although the fact that it is new does not carry with it any qualitative judgment. The design must not be good or better than all existing designs, nor should it present a technical advantage. But this does not imply that one should simply use the novelty requirement as applied in patent law,[26] nor is it possible to import concepts such as 'novelty' and 'variants commonly used in trade' from the law on registered designs.[27] The 1988 Act itself restricts the scope of the provision to the design field in question and nothing outside that specific design field will influence the decision regarding the originality of the design. A design that is known in another unrelated design field will still be original. (Patent anticipation is clearly much wider in scope.)

In a case that was concerned with design rights in a slurry separator for use in the agricultural industries, it was held that the relevant design field was that of slurry separators, rather than any wider agricultural field. Evidence relating to agricultural machines or engineering outside this narrow field was irrelevant for the determination whether the designs for the slurry separators were commonplace.[28]

The design field

Such a determination of the relevant design field remains, however, one of fact and degree.[29] The court is quite entitled to take the views of the customer, rather than the view of a design expert, into account when determining how broad the relevant field should be. For example, the customer would compare all types of window, whether made of aluminium, uPVC, or wood, rather than restrict him or herself to uPVC windows, as might an expert.[30] In addition, by pointing out that the design should not be commonplace, the Act clearly does not deprive of the required level of originality any design that has been circulated to a limited extent. Showing a limited number of items incorporating the new design at a trade fair, or consulting colleagues or potential customers on the qualities of

---

[20] *Farmers Build Ltd (in liq.) v. Carier Bulk Materials Handling Ltd* [1999] RPC 461, *per* Mummery LJ at 476.
[21] Ibid., *per* Mummery LJ at 483.
[22] *Philip Parker v. Stephen Tidball* [1997] FSR 680.
[23] *Farmers Build Ltd (in liq.) v. Carier Bulk Materials Handling Ltd* [1999] RPC 461, *per* Mummery LJ at 476.
[24] The fact that a design becomes well known does not mean it looses its design right, but further variations may become commonplace: see *Dyson Ltd v. Qualtex (UK) Ltd* [2006] RPC 31 (CA).
[25] *Ocular Sciences Ltd v. Aspect Vision Care Ltd; Geoffrey Harrison Galley v. Ocular Sciences Ltd* [1997] RPC 289 at 423.
[26] See *Dyson Ltd v. Qualtex (UK) Ltd* [2005] RPC 19.
[27] *Farmers Build Ltd (in liq.) v. Carier Bulk Materials Handling Ltd* [1999] RPC 461, *per* Mummery LJ at 481.
[28] Ibid., *per* Mummery LJ at 476.
[29] See *Ultraframe (UK) Ltd v. Eurocell Building Plastics Ltd* [2005] RPC 36 (CA).
[30] See *Scholes Windows Ltd v. Magnet Ltd (No. 1)* [2002] FSR 172 (CA), at 182.

the new design by showing them a drawing of it, will not necessarily make the design commonplace.

Further, the relevant moment in time is the creation of the design rather than the filing date of the application used in patent law. This is, of course, a consequence of the fact that there is no registration requirement for this design right. Arguably, this originality requirement comes close to the novelty requirement for registered designs, although there is a clear difference in relation to anticipation by publication for certain purposes in restricted circles.

When looking at the design field in question, no attention should be paid to when other designs in a certain field with which comparison was made were first produced, or to whether they were still in use or had fallen in disuse at the time at which the new design appeared. Old designs could not be excluded from the design field, because they could still form part of the design field in question, because, for example, designers and members of the public can still see them.[31]

A narrow approach

All of these elements are mere signposts in the direction of a commonplace test. What is clear is that the concept of 'commonplace' is to be given a narrow interpretation, because the design right itself should cover designs of functional items. A broad definition would—in combination with the shorter life of the right and the narrower protection against copying—effectively remove protection for the majority of such designs for functional items.[32]

A test was outlined by Mummery LJ in *Farmers Build Ltd (in liq.) v. Carier Bulk Materials Handling Ltd.*[33] It can be summarized in the following four steps.

1. In a first stage, the court needs to ascertain how similar the design under consideration is to the design of similar items in the same design field that are made by third parties.

2. That comparative exercise needs to be carried out objectively in the light of expert evidence that highlights the similarities and differences between the various designs, and which explains their respective significance. The final decision whether a design is commonplace rests with the court, and it involves a judgment of fact and degree that reflects the evidence of the particular case.

3. Designs are more likely to be commonplace if, in the absence of copying, they are close to one another. The closer the designs are, the more likely it becomes that they are commonplace, because this may be evidence of the fact that only one—commonplace— way of designing the item exists.

4. A design is not commonplace if it contains various aspects that are not found in any other design in the relevant design field, even if these aspects are found in the alleged infringer's design.[34]

The tangible form requirement

No registration is required before a design can attract design protection, but one cannot protect something if the content—and thus the precise subject of protection—is not

---

[31] Ibid., at 181–182.
[32] *Farmers Build Ltd (in liq.) v. Carier Bulk Materials Handling Ltd* [1999] RPC 461, *per* Mummery LJ at 481.
[33] Ibid.
[34] Ibid., *per* Mummery LJ at 482. See also *A Fulton Co. Ltd v. Grant Barnett & Co. Ltd* [2001] RPC 257.

known. A design therefore has to have a tangible form if it is to attract design protection.[35] This requirement can be met in two ways: the design can be recorded in a design document, as defined above, or an item can be made to the design. The design right will subsist from the moment of recording or from the moment of incorporation onwards.[36] And it is clear that the recording does not need to be made by the designer for this requirement to be met.[37]

In the case of registered designs, the tangible form is evidently required for the purposes of registration. One cannot, materially speaking, put together an application if the design does not exist, in the application, in a tangible form. In the registration system, the date of registration is the starting point for the term of protection. Because that element is not available in a system without registration, the date of recording is substituted for the date of registration.

The commencement date for the new design regime was 1 August 1989. Designs that were recorded in a design document or which were applied to an item before that date will not attract design right protection.[38]

Exceptions to the design right

Design rights will not subsist in a number of items. These are listed in s. 213(3) of the 1988 Act, as follows.

Methods or principles of construction

The first items on the list are 'methods or principles of construction'.[39] This is an obvious exception, which also exists in relation to registered designs.[40] Particular features of shape or configuration—as applied to an item or a part of it—are protected, but not general, theoretical, and eventually underlying principles. This exception is similar in nature to the scientific theories and mathematical methods exceptions that relate to patentable subject matter.[41]

An interesting example of the operation of s. 213(3)(a) is provided by a case that was concerned with a design of a polyvinyl alcohol (PVA), warp-knitted, ladder-resistant, micromesh bait bag for anglers. The Court held that the basic appearance of the design was generated by the Atlas warp-stitch method that had been used and that it therefore was nothing more than a method or principle of construction. As such, the design was excluded from protection as an unregistered design.[42]

The arrangement of zippers and piping for the expansion section of a suitcase design, meanwhile, was held not to be a principle or method of construction.[43] Indeed, the exception does not aim to preclude a design from protection merely because it has a functional purpose and other designers can still use the construction features in quite distinct designs. The exception aims rather to avoid monopolization of the entire principle of method of construction and such monopolization did not occur in this case.

---

[35] CDPA 1988, s. 213(6).
[36] Ibid.
[37] *C & H Engineering v. Klucznik & Sons Ltd* [1992] FSR 421, *per* Aldous J at 428.
[38] CDPA 1988, s. 213(7).
[39] Ibid., (3)(a).
[40] See Registered Designs Act 1949, s. 1(1)(a).
[41] Patents Act 1977, s. 1(2)(a).
[42] *Bailey (t/a Elite Angling Products) v. Haynes (t/a Rags)* [2007] FSR 10.
[43] *Landor & Hawa International Ltd v. Azure Designs Ltd* [2006] ECDR 31 (CA).

Surface decoration

Also on the list is *'surface decoration'*,[44] which does not come within the category of functional, rather than aesthetic, design that the 1988 Act set out to protect. Surface decoration
includes two things: firstly, it includes decoration lying on the surface of the item; secondly,
it includes decorative features of the surface itself. Surface decoration cannot be confined
to features that are essentially two-dimensional and it also includes, potentially, those features that serve a functional purpose.[45] Accordingly, the painted finish, cockbeading, and
V-grooves that were all aspects of the external appearance of a single wall unit in a range
of kitchens were excluded from the scope of the design protection that was held to exist in
the unit.[46] And as a case involving dying the fabric used for a standard track top and the
colourways used for that purpose demonstrates, the concept of surface decoration not only
involves cases in which the surface was covered with a thin layer, but also cases in which
the decoration ran right through the item.[47] The exclusion of certain aspects of the design
as surface decoration does not mean, for example, that the rest of the aspects of the shape
of the kitchen unit could not attract an (unregistered) design right.[48]

'Must fit'

One of the most important exceptions on the list is the *'must fit'*[49] exception, which
excludes *'features of shape or configuration which enable the article to be connected to,
placed in, around or against another article so that either article may perform its function'*[50] from the scope of the design right. The exception—which is also referred to as the
'interface provision'—is confined to those situations in which two items, produced by
one or two producers, are linked and certain features of shape or configuration enable
either item to perform its function. It also applies to the interface features of two interfit-
ting items that are later assembled together to form the whole, or part, of another, larger,
item.[51] The exception is confined strictly to those features that play this enabling role
and which must be of a certain precise shape or configuration to be able to play it; other
features of shape or configuration of the same item may well attract design protection.

No feature of shape of configuration will escape from the scope of the exception because
it also performed some other purpose: for example, because it was also attractive.[52] In certain cases, two or more different designs would enable the items to be fitted together in a
way that allowed one or all of them to perform their function. In such cases, all of these
designs fall within the exclusion and no (unregistered) design right will exist in them.
This indicates the wide scope of the exception, which has, as its purpose, the prevention of
*'the designer of a piece of equipment from using design right to prevent others from making
parts which fitted his equipment'*.[53] That purpose will only be met if the drafting, in wide
terms of the exception, is given its proper wide and extensive interpretation. The word
'article'—that is, item—can therefore be applied to living and formerly living things, as

---

[44] CDPA 1988, s. 213(3)(c).
[45] A visor-stiffening effect of the double-scalloping feature of a firefighter's helmet does not bring it outside the scope of the exception for surface decoration: see *Helmut Integrated Systems Ltd v. Tunnard* [2006]
FSR 41.
[46] *Mark Wilkinson Furniture Ltd v. Woodcraft Designs (Radcliffe) Ltd* [1998] FSR 63.
[47] *Lambretta Clothing Co. Ltd v. Teddy Smith (UK) Ltd & anor* [2005] RPC 6 (CA).
[48] *Mark Wilkinson Furniture Ltd v. Woodcraft Designs (Radcliffe) Ltd* [1998] FSR 63.
[49] CDPA 1988, s. 213(3)(b)(i).
[50] Ibid.
[51] *Electronic Techniques (Anglia) Ltd v. Critchley Components Ltd* [1997] FSR 401.
[52] *Ocular Sciences Ltd v. Aspect Vision Care Ltd; Geoffrey Harrison Galley v. Ocular Sciences Ltd* [1997]
RPC 289 at 424.
[53] Ibid., *per* Laddie J.

well as to inanimate things. This means that, in a case, concerning contact lenses, the back radius, the diameter, and the parallel peripheral carrier of the contact lens were all excluded from the design right, because they were features that enabled the lens to fit against the eyeball so as to allow the lens to perform its function of correcting the focusing ability of the eye and to remain in a stable position in the eye.[54] Another example is found in an electrical currency adaptor that allows the use of equipment built for 110V on the UK's 220V system and which has many peculiar functional features of shape, but also rods that fit into a wall socket. This example may well result in design rights for the various features of shape, but no design right will subsist in the shape of the rods, because this shape will be dependent upon the shape of the socket, enabling the adaptor to be connected to the socket and the electricity network, and allowing the socket and the adaptor to perform their functions. Those features of the shape of leather cases for individual mobile phones that enable the cases to be placed around the phones, so that either the phones or the cases may perform their function, are yet another example of design features that fall foul of the exception.[55]

Many of these aspects of the 'must fit' exception have now been reviewed by the Court of Appeal in *Dyson v. Qualtex.*[56] This case concerned spare parts for Dyson vacuum cleaners. Dyson claimed design protection, while Qualtex relied on the exception. The Court determined that once a handle is shaped in a certain way, for example, the catch must necessarily adopt a certain shape to fit with the handle. That latter shape is therefore covered by the exception. The words of the exception should not be interpreted particularly narrowly or widely. It does not matter that there are two ways of achieving the necessary fit or connection between the item and the item to which it fits. If the design chosen by the design right holder is a way of achieving that fit or interface, then it does not attract design right, no matter how many alternative ways of achieving the same fit or interface might be available. It is also not necessary for the items to touch each other for the exception to apply.[57]

This exception has an equivalent in section 1(1)(b)(i) of the Registered Designs Act 1949, but the latter refers to the 'purpose solely dictated by function' and is therefore wider in scope.

'Must match'

The second of the most important exceptions is the '*must match*'[58] exception, which covers all features of shape or configuration that '*are dependent upon the appearance of another article of which the article is intended by the designer to form an integral part*',[59] the classic example of which would be the doors of a car. The design of the doors is determined by the appearance of the bodywork of the car. If I were to buy a door as a spare part for my car, it would be rather essential that it fit in the gap left in the body. When considering the 'must match' exception, the court will have to consider whether there is a dependency of the kind, or to the extent, that it would make the overall item in question radically different in appearance if the first item were not shaped as at present. Ultimately, this is a matter of fact, degree, and impression.[60]

---

[54] Ibid., at 425–8.
[55] *Philip Parker v. Stephen Tidball* [1997] FSR 680.
[56] *Dyson Ltd v. Qualtex (UK) Ltd* [2005] RPC 19, affirmed [2006] RPC 31 (CA).
[57] Ibid.
[58] CDPA 1988, s. 213(3)(b)(ii).
[59] Ibid.
[60] *Dyson Ltd v. Qualtex (UK) Ltd* [2005] RPC 19, affirmed [2006] RPC 31 (CA).

Of course, the exception—like the 'must fit' exception—does not extend to other features of the same item; it does not apply if one item was not intended to form an integral part of another. For example, the features of a kitchen unit were not caught by the exclusion, because the complete kitchen unit was a series of matching items, none of which formed an integral part of another.[61] The fact that one item could incidentally be made to form an integral part of another is not relevant. This makes it also clear that things made in sets—such as plates and glasses—are not covered by the exception. In these cases, one design will be applied to the whole set.

The example concerning the design of the doors of a car that already indicates that spare parts occupy a special position in relation to the design right—but not only do they cover a very substantial part of the whole design activity, the exceptions also seem to exclude them almost entirely from design protection. This meets the need for competition in this area. The legislature found it unacceptable that the producer of an item could, through copyright (at one time) and design protection regimes, monopolize the spare parts market. This market is opened up for competition by means of the 'must fit' and 'must match' exceptions to the design right. But the fact that other features are not covered by the exception can create some difficulty: on the one hand, the alternative producer of spare parts should be careful not to infringe the design right in these features, should it exist; on the other, the fact can be seen as a tool through which the original producer to distinguish its spare parts from those of alternative producers.

Qualification

Designs that meet all previous requirements will only be protected if they meet one additional requirement: the design should also qualify for protection. This requirement is very similar to the qualification requirement in copyright, and forms an inherent part of any intellectual property right that is not subject to a registration requirement and which is, after all, granted on a national basis. The qualification requirement is met if the designer,[62] the commissioner of the design[63] (if the design is commissioned for money or money's worth),[64] or the employer of the designer[65] (for designs created in the course of employment) is a qualifying person. The position of the designer is only relevant if the design is neither created in the course of employment, nor in pursuance of a commission.[66]

The system starts with the definition of what is a 'qualifying country'.[67] This is defined as the UK and the other member States of the European Union (EU), eventually supplemented by other countries by an Order in Council.[68] A qualifying individual is a citizen of, or an individual habitually resident in, such a qualifying country. Together with any corporate body or any body having legal personality that is formed under the law of a qualifying country or which has at least a place of business at which substantial business activity[69] is carried out in a qualifying country, these qualifying individuals comprise the category of the qualifying persons.[70]

The qualification requirement can also be met by reference to the country and person of first marketing of items made to the design if the designer, and, eventually, the

[61] *Mark Wilkinson Furniture Ltd v. Woodcraft Designs (Radcliffe) Ltd* [1998] FSR 63.
[62] CDPA 1988, s. 218(2).   [63] Ibid., s. 219(1).
[64] Ibid., s. 263(1).   [65] Ibid., s. 219(1).
[66] Ibid., s. 218(1).   [67] Ibid., s. 217(3).
[68] See Design Right (Reciprocal Protection) (No. 2) Order 1989, SI 1989/1294.
[69] *'Dealings in goods which are at all material times outside the country'* shall not be taken into account: CDPA 1988, s. 217(5).
[70] Ibid., (1).

commissioner or employer do not qualify.[71] This is the case if the first marketing takes place by a qualifying person in a qualifying country. On top of that, the qualifying person must be exclusively authorized by the person who would have been the first owner of the design right, if it came into existence, to put the items made to the design on the market in the UK and that exclusivity must be enforceable by legal proceedings in the UK. For qualification purposes, the place at which the design was created is utterly irrelevant.

The substance of the design right

The design right is a property right[72] that grants to its owner the exclusive right to reproduce the design for commercial purposes. The obvious way to do so is by making items to the design, but the owner can also make a design document in which the design is recorded and which enables such items to be made by a third party.[73] An item is reproduced for 'commercial purposes' if the reproduction is undertaken with a view to its being sold or hired in the course of business.[74]

The person behind the design

The preceding analysis refers often to the 'person behind the design'; it is now time to fill in that notion. The designer is the person who creates the design.[75] Should this rule lead us to a computer, the person that undertakes the necessary arrangements for the creation of the design by the computer will be regarded as the designer.[76] Creation should be interpreted as having the idea for the design; it does not necessarily include the recording of the design.[77]

This leads us to the issue of who will be the first owner of the design. If the design is neither commissioned, nor created in the course of employment, the designer will be the first owner of the design right.[78] The commissioner and the employer are the first owners of the design right in a design created in pursuance of a commission or in the course of employment, respectively.[79] A particular problem arises, in practice, when a design is created by a 100 per cent shareholder of a company through which he or she carries on business: is such a person employed by the company or did the company commission the design?

The Court of Appeal has shed some light on the matter by holding that a contract of employment—even if it can be concluded entirely orally—requires the presence of three elements, as follows.[80]

1. The alleged employee must have agreed that, in consideration for a wage or any other form of consideration, he or she would provide skill and labour in the performance of some service for his or her employer.

---

[71]   Ibid., s. 220.
[72]   Ibid., s. 213(1).
[73]   Ibid., s. 226(1).
[74]   Ibid., s. 263(3).
[75]   Ibid., s. 214(1).
[76]   Ibid., (2).
[77]   *C & H Engineering v. Klucznik & Sons Ltd* [1992] FSR 421, *per* Aldous J at 428.
[78]   CDPA 1988, s. 215(1).
[79]   Ibid., (2) and (3).
[80]   *Ultraframe UK Ltd v. Fielding* [2004] RPC 479 (CA).

2. Expressly or impliedly, the alleged employee must have accepted that, in the performance of that service, he or she would be subject to the control of the employer to such an extent that the employer can be described as his or her 'master'.

3. The other provisions of the contract must be consistent with it being a contract of employment.[81]

The idea of commissioning a work involved, in the eyes of the Court of Appeal, a contract involving mutual obligations prior to the production of the relevant design.[82] If neither of these situations occur, but if the 100 per cent shareholder acts for the company and created the design through the company, the shareholder will hold the design and any rights in it in trust for the company.[83]

These rules apply in all circumstances except in those of s. 220 of the 1988 Act: if the design qualifies through first marketing only, the first owner of the design right will be the person that markets the items made to the design.[84]

Joint creation—which will arise when the contribution of two or more designers is not distinct and cannot be distinguished—and joint ownership are also possible, and do not create specific problems. It is worth pointing out, however, that in cases in which not all of the persons involved are qualifying persons, only those that are will be entitled to the design right;[85] the design, meanwhile, will meet the qualifying requirement as soon as any of the persons involved is a qualifying person.[86] A design jointly created by eight designers, for example, will qualify for design protection as long as one of the designers is a qualifying person. In that case, that one (qualifying) person alone will be entitled to the design right. Should four of the designers qualify, the four of them will be jointly entitled to the design right. In any case, designers that are not qualifying persons will not be entitled to the design right.

The term of (unregistered) design protection

We have already discussed the fact that the design right comes into existence at the moment at which it is either recorded in a design document or when an item is made to the design. As with most terms in copyright, the duration of the design right is then linked to the end of the calendar year in which such recording or production takes place. We will call this important point the 'end of the creation year'.

Most designs will be exploited before the end of a five-year period, which starts running from the end of the creation year. If such exploitation takes the form of items made to the design being made available for sale or hire, the term of (unregistered) design protection is ten years. This term starts running at the end of the calendar year during which the exploitation first occurred.[87] The exploitation can take place anywhere in the world, as long as it is done by the owner of the design right or with its licence.[88]

---

[81] Ibid.; *Ready Mixed Concrete (South East) Ltd v. Minister of Pensions & National Insurance* [1968] 2 QB 497.

[82] Ibid.; *Apple Corps Ltd v. Cooper* [1993] FSR 286.

[83] *Ultraframe UK Ltd v. Fielding* [2004] RPC 479 (CA).

[84] CDPA 1988, s. 215(4).

[85] Ibid., ss. 218(4) and 219(3).

[86] Ibid., (3) and 219(2).

[87] Ibid., s. 216(1)(b).

[88] Ibid., (2).

The absence of exploitation, as defined above, within the first five years does not, however, lead to an unlimited design right protection. In that case, the term of (unregistered) design protection expires 15 years after the end of the creation year.[89]

These terms of protection are substantially shorter than those used in copyright and are much more in line with those used in patent law. This is probably a recognition of the fact that functional designs are, in general, an industrial property right and that a fair return on the investment they require can be obtained in a relatively short period. As we have seen in Chapter 1 of this book, the term of protection should indeed be linked to the determination of the correct balance between the innovation (creation of new designs) and production levels (items produced to the design). Approximately ten years of design exclusivity will allow for the ongoing creation of new designs and will not unduly restrict the free use of the design.

Infringement and remedies

Primary infringement

Because the owner of the design right has the exclusive right to reproduce the design for commercial purposes, the design right will, first of all, be infringed by anyone making an item to the design without the licence of the owner of the design right and by anyone making a design document that records the design for the purpose of enabling someone to make items to it, once again, if this is done without the licence of the design right owner. One can immediately add to this the case in which someone authorizes someone else to do one of these two things.

Design right infringement is subject to the same principles as copyright infringement.[90] This means, firstly, that an objective similarity between the allegedly infringing item and the design must exist. All features that are covered by an exclusion—such as the interface exclusion—should be disregarded for this purpose. Secondly, a causal connection between the design and the allegedly infringing item needs to be established.[91]

Making items to the design

The act of making items to the design is circumscribed more precisely: the design has to be copied in such a way that items exactly or substantially similar to the design are produced. This latter element involves an objective test that should be decided through the eyes of the person to whom the design is directed[92]—that is, the person who will use the items made to the design. In a case that was concerned with design rights in the features of shape of a kitchen unit, the design was held to be directed to the person interested in buying a fitted kitchen.[93]

That person should look at the similarities and differences between the two designs. Infringement will arise if the allegedly infringing item is simply made to the plaintiff's design or if it is made substantially to that design. The latter situation will definitely cover

[89] Ibid., (1)(a).
[90] *Mark Wilkinson Furniture Ltd v. Woodcraft Designs (Radcliffe) Ltd* [1998] FSR 63.
[91] As in the equivalent copyright cases, it is not required that the infringer has the protected design in front of him or her when the allegedly infringing item is made: see *Philip Parker v. Stephen Tidball* [1997] FSR 680.
[92] *C & H Engineering v. Klucznik & Sons Ltd* [1992] FSR 421, *per* Aldous J at 428.
[93] *Mark Wilkinson Furniture Ltd v. Woodcraft Designs (Radcliffe) Ltd* [1998] FSR 63.

all occasions on which all of the elements linked to the functional role of the design have been copied and the differences are not relevant for that role. It is submitted that the approach should bear important similarities to that adopted in relation to patent law in the *Catnic* case,[94] but only the case law can shed some more light on this issue in a decisive way over the next few years. In addition, it should be emphasized that the objective test through the eyes of the person to whom the design is directed may involve the item being dismantled to allow that person to compare the designs if they apply to a internal part of the item, because design rights can exist in features of shape or configuration of an internal part of the item. Despite the fact that design right infringement shares some of its principles with copyright infringement, it is important to stress that, on this point, there clearly are differences and that similarities with patent law also creep in. As the Court of Appeal put it, there is a difference between an enquiry into whether the item copied forms a substantial part of a copyright work and an enquiry into whether the whole design containing the element that had been copied was substantially the same design as that which enjoyed design right protection.[95]

An objective test

It is extremely important, however, to see what is being compared in the objective test and it is respectfully submitted that the approach taken obiter[96] in the *Klucznik* case[97] is not detailed enough.[98] Infringement is situated in the fact of making items to the design without having obtained a licence to do so—but the design right covers features of shape or configuration of the whole, or part, of the item and the test is directed to see whether the design right has been infringed. It is submitted that s. 226(2) of the 1988 Act directs us to look at the similarities and differences between the designs, rather than between the items. If the design right covers features of shape or configuration of the whole item, the result will not necessarily vary, but the importance of the nuance is found in the fact that the design right can also cover features of shape or configuration of a part of the item. Making reference to the whole item would, in such a case, reduce the number of cases in which infringements would be found substantially and weaken the design right as such. It would also be absurd to take into account additional non-protected features and, eventually, features that form the subject of another design right, and which are applied to another part of the same item in deciding whether a design right has been infringed. The test should only take into consideration those parts of the item to which the design refers, although this can eventually be the whole item;[99] otherwise, there could almost never be an infringement when only the design for part of an item is reproduced. But the emphasis on the design does not change the fact that the observer is forced to compare the original design to the item in which allegedly a substantial part of the design has been copied. One should '*ask oneself what by way of comparative design would be suggested to the interested observer*'[100] and this should be done in the light of the entirety of the allegedly infringing item.

---

94   *Catnic Components Ltd & anor v. Hill & Smith Ltd* [1982] RPC 183.

95   *L Woolley Jewellers Ltd v. A and A Jewellery Ltd* [2003] FSR 255 (CA).

96   Klucznik's claim to the design right failed, because Aldous J was unable to reach the conclusion that it was the owner of the design (had Klucznik thought of it or had C & H Engineering thought of it?), thus the infringement action accordingly also failed. Aldous J nevertheless considered the infringement issue, but that part of the judgment is thus obiter.

97   *C & H Engineering v. Klucznik & Sons Ltd* [1992] FSR 421.

98   Ibid., *per* Aldous J at 428, but the approach received nevertheless support from a differently constituted Court of Appeal in *L Woolley Jewellers Ltd v. A and A Jewellery Ltd* [2003] FSR 255 (CA).

99   Cf Turner [1993] at 25.

100   *Philip Parker v. Stephen Tidball* [1997] FSR 680.

In the *Klucznik* case, the test was indeed described as an objective one, having the pig farmer—as the person to whom the design is directed—look at the similarities and differences between the two pig fenders. The conclusion reached was that the designs were not substantially the same, but it is submitted that this conclusion could be wrong, because it relies on an additional feature of the allegedly infringing fender. This feature was not part of the design right that was allegedly infringed and the features of shape covered by the design right—that is, the two-inch tube—were only features of the shape of a part of the fender. Attention should, in this case, primarily be directed to that part of the fender and other additional features should be left aside. One should only turn to the whole of the allegedly infringing item in a second stage to determine whether its overall features allow for a conclusion that the overall impression of the observer is not that the allegedly infringing item has been made to the original design; this should only be the case if the other features have become its essential features. In that case, the item is no longer produced to the original design, even if the two have certain aspects in common. This slightly more complicated test follows from the fact that design infringement is not completely similar to copyright infringement and that additional emphasis is put on the point that the copying must lead to the production of an item exactly, or substantially, to the design. That judgment, in relation to the allegedly infringing item, comes on top of the copyright-style substantial copying test (from one design to another, or to the relevant part of the allegedly infringing item).

An enabling recording

The enabling recording of a design document as an infringing activity bears strong similarities to its equivalent in copyright, but it is slightly harder to prove the design version. The recording should be made for the purpose of enabling someone to make items to the design. The only purpose one needs to establish for its copyright infringement alternative is the purpose to copy;[101] the design intention should be present at the time at which the recording was made, otherwise the recording was not made for that purpose. It is, indeed, not sufficient that the recording can eventually later be used to enable someone to make items to the design.

Direct or indirect reproduction

The reproduction of the design may be direct or indirect. Indirect reproduction will still infringe, even if the intervening acts do not infringe the design right themselves.[102] This has important consequences in relation to the reverse engineering of designs. One can easily take apart an item made to the design, analyse the design, and copy the non-protected elements; eventually, this can lead to the creation of a new original design. But if reverse engineering simply precedes reproduction, making an item to the design will still infringe.

Innocent infringement

Innocent infringement is possible. This clarification is made indirectly in s. 233 of the 1988 Act. If, at the time of the infringement, the defendant was unaware and had no reason to believe that design right subsisted in the design, the plaintiff will not be entitled to damages against the defendant. Other remedies do, however, remain available.[103] This provision offers a limited amount of protection to the reasonable bona fide user of the design who thought that there was no design right he or she could be infringing. This

---

[101] H. MacQueen, 'A Scottish case on unregistered designs' [1994] 2 EIPR 86 at 87.
[102] CDPA 1988, s. 226(4).
[103] Ibid., s. 233(1).

is bound to happen on a number of occasions, such as when a user cannot check in any register of designs in order to pre-empt this situation.

Secondary infringement

The design right will also be infringed if a person does any of the following acts in relation to an infringing item without the licence of the owner of the design right:

- imports the item into the UK for commercial purposes;[104]
- has the item in his or her possession for commercial purposes;[105]
- sells, hires, or offers or exposes for sale or hire, the item in the course of a business.[106]

Apart from the possession for commercial purposes, similar provisions are found in s. 7 of the Registered Designs Act 1949.

First of all, what is an infringing item? An item is an infringing item if the making of the item to the design constituted an infringement of the design right in the design.[107] Items that have been imported into the UK, or which are proposed to be imported into it, and the making of which would have constituted an infringement of the design right (or a breach of an exclusive licence agreement) had the items been made in the UK are also infringing items.[108] In addition, an action for secondary design infringement can only be successful if it is proven that the defendant knew, or had reason to believe, that the item was infringing.[109] This additional knowledge requirement is identical to that found in copyright and does not exist for registered designs.[110]

This knowledge requirement, taken in combination with the fact that only designs created after the commencement date of the design provisions of the 1988 Act attract design protection, could create a problem for the plaintiff in proving that the item was made at a time when the right subsisted and is thus an infringing item. The Act therefore introduced a presumption in favour of the plaintiff. The item made to the design is presumed to have been made at a time when the design right in the design subsisted, unless the contrary can be proven.[111] This is even more favourable for the plaintiff, because he or she will quite often be the only person able to prove when the design right first arose.

If the defendant in an action for secondary infringement is able to show that he or she, or a predecessor in title, acquired the infringing item innocently, this will not imply that the action is bound to fail; rather, it only restricts the remedies available to damages of up to what would be a reasonable amount of royalties in respect of the complained-of act.[112]

Defences

A defendant in a design right infringement action can try to argue that the design right has expired, or that it was not valid in the first place, because one of the requirements was

---

104 Ibid., s. 227(1)(a).
105 Ibid., (1)(b).
106 Ibid., (c).
107 Ibid., s. 228(2).
108 Ibid., (3).
109 Ibid., s. 227(1).
110 See Chapters 15 and 21.
111 CDPA 1988, s. 228(4).
112 Ibid., s. 233(2). See *Badge Sales v. PSM International* [2006] FSR 1.

not met and that the design right thus never came into existence. Apart from these arguments, it is obvious that the defendant will try to argue that the requirements for primary and secondary infringement to take place are not met. A last defence could, in relevant cases, be based on s. 236 of the 1988 Act.

These relevant cases are those in which copyright exists in a work that consists of, or includes, a design in which a design right subsists. Anything that is an infringement of the copyright in the work will not be an infringement of the design right.[113] This provision clearly aims to complete the separation between copyright and design right. It applies to design right infringement cases, whereas s. 51 applies to the copyright infringement cases.

Commercial exploitation

Assignment and licences

As is the case with most other intellectual property rights, an (unregistered) design right can be exploited commercially in various ways. Owners of the design right can exploit the right themselves by making an item to the design, but can also leave the exploitation or part of it to a third party. In such cases, the design right can be assigned or a licence can be granted. An assignment can be compared to a sale and is particularly appropriate if the owners of the design right do not want to exploit the design themselves. Granting a licence is more like hiring out the right to use the design. If the licence is not exclusive, it allows the owners to exploit the design themselves too and the exclusive licence may ultimately even expire, at which point the exploitation right will return to the owners.

This is, of course, only a rough description of assignments and licences. They can be moulded to perform special functions through the insertion of special clauses in the contract. A future design right—that is, one that will, or may, come into being—can be the subject of an assignment or of a licence. The same rules apply to the exploitation of both the existing design right and the future design right.[114]

Assignments
When the design right is assigned, this must be done in writing and the assignment must be signed by, or on behalf of, the owner-assignor.[115] An assignment effectively transfers the design right to the assignee, but it can be partial in two ways.[116]

- The assignment can be limited in terms of its duration. This implies that the design right returns to the assignor after the expiry of the term agreed in the assignment contract.
- It can also be limited in scope, in the sense that not all of the exclusive rights of the owner are assigned to the assignee.

In relation to the rights assigned to him or her, the assignee has exactly the same rights as those that the owner-assignor had before the assignment and would have had if the assignment had not taken place.

---

[113] CDPA 1988, s. 236.
[114] Ibid., s. 223.
[115] Ibid., s. 222(3).
[116] Ibid., (2).

Apart from by assignment, the design right can also be transferred by testamentary disposition or by the operation of law,[117] such as in the case of a liquidation of a company that owned a design right.

Licences

The alternative to an assignment is a licence, which authorizes the licensee to do certain things in relation to the design right. The owner can grant an exclusive licence or a non-exclusive licence: an exclusive licence gives the licensee the exclusive right to exploit the design right in a certain area and/or the exclusive right to exploit the design right in a certain way. All other persons—including the owner-licensor—are excluded from exploiting the design right in the area and/or form of exploitation covered by the exclusive licence. Such a licence has to be in writing and signed by, or on behalf of, the owner-licensor of the design right,[118] and it gives the exclusive licensee the same rights and remedies as an assignment. But there is one exception to the latter point: the rights and remedies are not the same in relation to the owner-licensor. The exclusive licensee can, as can the assignee, act independently against infringers[119]—but because the licensor retains certain rights in relation to the design right, there will be cases in which the two parties have a right of action. The Act calls this a 'concurrent right of action' and requires that the other party is either joined as a plaintiff or added as a defendant before the action proceeds.[120]

One or more non-exclusive licences can also be granted and these may give the licensee the non-exclusive right to exploit the design right in a certain area and/or the non-exclusive right to exploit the design right in a certain way. The licensor will remain free to exploit the design right him or herself and may also appoint other licensees. There are no requirements regarding the format of a non-exclusive licence and the licensor will have to rely on the contract in infringement cases. No rights to act independently are transferred; the licensee will have to request the licensor to take action against the infringer. A licence granted by the owner of the design right shall normally bind him or her and every successor in title. It will not bind a purchaser of the design right who purchases in good faith, for valuable consideration, and who has no actual or constructive notice of the licence.[121] An assignor who meets the additional requirements could be such a purchaser. This clearly puts the licensee in a weaker position than the licensor and makes an assignment theoretically more attractive than a licence. It remains to be seen, however, whether an assignment is available in practice and, even if that is the case, the higher price linked to it may well outweigh the advantage.

Licences of right

Licences of right are available during the last five years of the term of protection offered by the design right. This weakens the value of the design right, but opens another opportunity for the exploitation of the design right. The Comptroller-General of Patents, Designs and Trade Marks will settle the terms of the licence if the parties fail to agree upon it.[122] It will not always be easy for the potential licensee to find out when these licences of right become available, because, in cases in which the design is recorded some time before it is exploited, the owner of the design right is often the only person to know the real date on which the design right came into existence.

---

[117] Ibid., (1).
[118] Ibid., s. 225(1).
[119] Ibid., s. 234.
[120] Ibid., s. 235(1).
[121] Ibid., s. 222(4).
[122] Ibid., s. 237.

One design, two design rights

Some designs meet the requirements of the Registered Designs Act 1949 as well as those for the (unregistered) design right. If they are registered, they will attract double design protection. An example may be a teapot, the spout or handle of which is both aesthetically pleasing and also fulfils a functional role. This could create problems when only one right is assigned or licensed and commercial exploitation of the design takes place. This could constitute an infringement of the other design. The Act therefore provides that, if the owners of both design rights are the same persons, an assignment of the registered design will include an assignment of the (unregistered) design right unless an intention to the contrary appears from the transaction or its circumstances.[123] The opposite situation is covered by s. 19(3B) of the Registered Designs Act 1949, which provides that, if the owners of both design rights are the same persons, an assignment of the (unregistered) design right will include an assignment of the registered design unless an intention to the contrary appears.

This is, of course, only a partial solution. The presumption may be rebutted and the rights may become separated, should different persons own them. The latter risk is reduced by the fact that the Registrar is not supposed to register a registered design if the person who claims to be the owner of the design right does not make the application.[124] The legislature clearly attempts to keep the ownership of both design rights in the same hands, while leaving it up to the parties to negotiate the terms of the licences, which are just a temporary right to use. It can indeed be accepted that no one would agree to a licence for one of the rights if the use of that right would infringe the second design right and that, even if that were the case, the courts might imply a licence for the second design right.

Crown use

The 1988 Act also contains provisions on Crown use of design rights. It refers to the use by the Crown without a licence, but with a form of remuneration of designs protected by design rights, for purposes such as health and other needs of the services of the Crown. There are also provisions on the supply of items made to the design for foreign defence purposes.[125]

Competition law

Agreements on the exploitation of design rights may infringe competition law. In relation to UK competition law, the 1988 Act allows action to be taken in such cases,[126] but the most relevant provisions are to be found in the EC Treaty. Licence agreements in relation to design rights may infringe Art. 81. We may refer here to our discussion of this Treaty provision in the previous chapter, because it applies in the same way to all intellectual property rights. Suffice it to say that no block exemption covers design rights. In theory, there is also no reason why Art. 82 on the abuse of a dominant position could not apply in relation to a design right, although it is not too likely that such a case will often arise in practice.

The European Court of Justice was invited to rule on the relationship between design rights and the free movement provisions of the EC Treaty in *Keurkoop v. Nancy Kean Gifts*.[127] The judgment makes it clear that designs form an intellectual property right for

---

[123] Ibid., s. 224.
[124] Registered Designs Act 1949, s. 3.
[125] CDPA 1988, see ss. 240–244.
[126] Ibid., s. 238.
[127] Case 144/81 *Keurkoop BV v. Nancy Kean Gifts BV* [1982] ECR 2853, [1983] 2 CMLR 47.

the purposes of these provisions and that the exhaustion doctrine applies to them. The Court did not find it necessary, however, to define the specific subject matter of designs, because it could reach its conclusion without doing so. It said that, in the absence of Community harmonization, it is left to the member States to decide which system of design rights they have, and to decide accordingly on the terms and conditions under which protection is granted. The existing disparity did not influence the applicability of the free movement provisions to design rights. This means that there is nothing special about design rights in this context and that the principles that we have discussed in relation to other intellectual property rights apply equally to them.

An overview

Unregistered designs are essentially functional, non-aesthetic designs. The 1988 Act defines them as the design of any aspect of the shape or configuration (whether internal or external) of the whole, or part, of an item. In order to attract protection, such a design must be original, in the sense that it should not be commonplace in the design field in question at the time of its creation.

Certain items are excluded from design protection, essentially because a design right in them would confer upon the right holder an unduly broad exclusive right. There is clearly an underlying logic that other designers should be able to come up with another design that has the same functional effectiveness. Granting designs rights for methods or principles of construction, or for designs that must fit or must match, would undermine that logic. Surface decoration is also excluded, because its functional credentials are weaker.

Unregistered design rights roughly offer 15 years of protection during which the right holder has the exclusive right to reproduce the design for commercial purposes. Infringement will therefore consist in anyone making an item to the design without authorization and in the making of a design document that records the design for the purposes of enabling someone else to make items to it, again without authorization. Authorizing someone else to do either of these two things will also constitute an infringement. Just as in copyright, there are also provisions on secondary infringement that cover dealing with infringing items.

Further reading

GARNETT, K., DAVIES, G. and HARBOTTLE, G. (2005) *Copinger and Skone James on Copyright*, 15th edn, London: Sweet and Maxwell, ch. 13.

MALLINSON, R. and YOUNG, C., 'Industrial plagiarism and the "gap" in design protection' (2005) 27 EIPR 2, 68.

MICHAELS, A., 'The end of the road for "pattern spare" parts? *Dyson Ltd v. Qualtex (UK) Ltd*' (2006) 28 EIPR 7, 396.

SYKES, J., 'The unregistered design right: interpretation and practical application of the must-match exemption' (2006) 1 JIPL P 442.

WILKINSON, D., 'Case closed: functional designs protected by design right' (2007) 29 EIPR 3, 118.

23
Designs—an overview

Registered design is like the 'little brother' of patents and trade marks, but that does not mean that design rights are not valuable for industry; in the contrary, enormous amounts of money are spent on designs. Registration alone is simply not the best way of protecting designs and it would be wrong to disregard anything smaller than patents and trade marks as not important.

The old UK system was based on a strict separation between registered and unregistered design, and between aesthetical and functional designs. Aesthetical designs were protected as registered designs and functional designs were protected by means of an unregistered right. The problems that aesthetical designs often change rapidly, and that the delays and costs involved in a registered designs system represent major hurdles in substantial number of cases, were not addressed under this two-part system. The two types of design had been separated on, allegedly, the wrong basis. We had therefore already concluded, in the third edition of this book, that having one design right that could serve both aesthetic and functional designs would eliminate much confusion—this suggestion was made before the EU reforms were implemented.

It is submitted that the situation now is worse. The Design Directive, as implemented in the revised version of the Registered Designs Act 1949, has put in place a modern system of registered design protection. That system does away with the aesthetical requirements of the old 1949 Act and the new concept of a design only attempts to exclude technical matters that should, in principle, be dealt with by patent, rather than design, law. Design law should not become a second-best option for failed patent applications. Such a system can cover the whole design spectrum at national level and the Community design, as introduced by the Community Designs Regulation, duplicates that at Community level. The Regulation also complements the registered rights system with an unregistered design right that is strictly limited in time, so as not to compete with the registered right, while at the same time offering an effective and fast protection at no cost for designs for which the registered system is too slow and costly.

It is submitted that maintaining in force, on top of all of this, a domestic unregistered design right that was supposed to fit in seamlessly with a system of registered rights that no longer exists is itself no longer necessary. The overlap of protection creates confusion and an undue duplication of rights. The fact that some designs will get protection under a UK unregistered right while failing to be protected—or worse, while expressly being excluded from protection—under its European counterpart or by the European registered design is clearly an absurd and unjustifiable consequence of a historical legal maze. Especially hard to justify is the fact that the UK keeps in force an unregistered right that has a much longer term than that of its Community counterpart.

The only reason why the UK unregistered right may justifiably survive is the fact that, unlike the Community right, it does not exclude purely technical designs, apart from those covered by its 'must fit' exemption. This justification disappears, however, if the EU technical exemption is defined sensibly and not too widely, as suggested in Chapter 21. As demonstrated earlier, the technical exemption would then only eliminate a limited number of cases and all of these would be cases in which there are good competition-related reasons to deny any form of protection whatsoever.

Maybe the time has therefore come to reconsider the existence of a UK unregistered design right on the basis of the Copyright, Designs and Patents Act 1988.[1] Especially at a time of increasing duplication of protection and overprotection, any opportunity to reduce these problems should be looked at seriously. After all, there will still be a wide design right, as well as a potential overlap at the fringes with copyright, trade marks, and—to a lesser extent—patents.[2]

Further reading

DERCLAYE, E., 'The British unregistered design right: will it survive its new Community counterpart to influence future European case law?' (2004) 10 Colum J Eur L 265.

---

[1] See also the obiter comment by Jacob LJ in *Lambretta Clothing Co. Ltd v Teddy Smith (UK) Ltd & anor* [2005] RPC 6 at [41].

[2] See Recital 31 of Council Regulation (EC) 6/2002 on Community Design [2002] OJ L 3/1.

SECTION E

IMAGE RIGHTS

24
Trade marks— an introduction

Today, the trade mark industry is such a vital component of the whole structure of the advertising and marketing that is a key feature of the commercial scene. Logos, catch-phrases, and images all fall within the ambit of the trade mark and form a valuable part of the goodwill of the business with which they are associated. In law, however, trade marks have in recent years been the subject of increasing controversy; this has culminated in an entirely new legislative framework, in the form of the Trade Marks Act 1994.[1]

Trade marks—development

The earliest form of trade mark is both the most obvious and the type that is still at the heart of the law of trade marks today. Even in Roman times, pottery was made (and has survived) bearing the name of the potter responsible for it. Then, as now, the trade mark was an important badge of origin for the product; the origin, of course, also being indicative of the quality of the product associated. Many major brand names are the names of the founder of the brand: Ford for cars or Kelloggs for breakfast cereals are obvious examples. Exceptionally, the name may even become synonymous with the product itself: people will often refer to any brand of vacuum cleaner as a 'Hoover', for example.

But throughout history, with only a couple of minor exceptions, trade marks were essentially a part of the private sector, attracting legal protection by use, rather than by formal grant by the state. This was unacceptable in a society that was rapidly changing and industrializing, and it became clear both that a more formal system was required and that the central authority of the state should form a central feature of that system. In 1862, a Trade Marks Bill was considered, but did not go ahead for various reasons. There were doubts about whether a formal and transferable legal right was appropriate to reflect the personal nature of the typical trade mark, and the common law of passing off was, as will be seen later, already in the process of development. Deliberate counterfeiting was seen to be more of a problem abroad than at home and this called into question the effectiveness of the proposed new law. Nonetheless, pressure continued to mount in favour of a statutory system of trade marks and that demand was ultimately fulfilled, in the first instance, by the Trade Marks Act 1875.

---

[1] See, in general, C. Morcom, A. Roughton, J. Graham and S. Malynicz (2005) *The Modern Law of Trade Marks*, 2nd edn, London: Butterworths Lexis-Nexis; D. Kitchin, D. Llewelyn, J. Mellor, R.Meade, T. Moody-Stuart and D. Keeling (2005) *Kerly's Law of Trade Marks and Trade Names*, 14th edn, London: Sweet and Maxwell.

The 1875 Act created a central Trade Marks Registry (now subsumed within the Patent Office), which could award a proprietary right in the form of a trade mark, and also register its existence and ownership for the benefit and guidance of future prospective applicants. Then, as now, at the heart of the notion of the trade mark lay the idea that it should be distinctive, thus going far beyond the notion of the mark as being a badge of origin. From 1875, then, the essence of the modern system of trade mark law and practice was in place, but the law was never likely to stay in a settled form for too long. New Acts extended the law in 1883, 1905, and 1919, the last of which split the Register into two sections; the keynote Act was, until recently, the further Act of 1938. But the 1938 Act did not survive unadorned, with some of the recommendations of the Mathys Committee of 1974[2] being enacted by the Trade Marks (Amendment) Act 1984, which created, among other things, a mark for services as well as for goods.

But even more change was considered necessary.

The need for reform

Reform was canvassed in a government White Paper titled *Reform of Trade Marks Law*[3] in 1990. The Paper recognized that many of the recommendations of the Mathys Committee had never been taken up, but that there were other factors that tended to suggest that more fundamental reform was needed. First and foremost among these factors was the 'Europeanization' of yet another area of intellectual property.

The influence of the European Union (EU) on trade mark law takes two separate, but related, forms. Firstly, a Directive was passed as far back as 1988[4] that sought to harmonize the national laws relating to trade marks so as to remove potential barriers to freer trade. The terms of the Directive required compliance with its terms by the end of 1991 (later extended by a year)—a deadline that was well missed by the UK, although the 1994 Act appears now to fulfil this requirement in almost all respects.

The second aspect of EU activity that has had a significant impact on the reform process is the establishment of a Community-wide trade mark, distinct from the individual national marks. After interminable discussion and the traditional haggling, the Regulation approving the creation of such a mark was finalized in 1994.[5] The Community Trade Marks Office is sited in Alicante in Spain and it has been confronted with an (unexpected) flood of applications ever since it opened its doors to the public. This new mark is, of course, not subject to amendment by domestic legislation, but, conversely, has represented a sensible opportunity to try to match the domestic and European procedures so as to minimize any conflict or duplication between the two systems.

A third international factor also at play in the formulation of the 1994 legislation was that trade—and thus trade marks—takes on an increasingly international dimension all the time and that, thus, the international protectability of trade mark rights takes on an even greater importance. For over a century, an international register of trade marks has been maintained under the provisions of the Madrid Agreement[6] with an International Register maintained by the World Intellectual Property Organization (WIPO) in Geneva.

---

[2] Cmnd 5601.

[3] Cm 1203.

[4] Council Directive 89/104 EEC to approximate the laws of the member States relating to trade marks (1989) OJ L 40/1.

[5] Council Regulation (EC) 40/94 on the Community trade mark (1994) OJ L 11/1.

[6] Madrid Agreement Concerning the International Registration of Marks of 14 April 1891.

This system was not entirely successful, because it reflected Continental rather than common law approaches to the topic, but the era of harmonization meant that change was not only appropriate, but also necessary. In consequence, a Protocol[7] was added to the Madrid Agreement enabling the UK and many other countries to fall within its scope, and the 1994 Act had the further task of adapting domestic law to this new international agreement.[8] Finally, further implementation of the Paris Convention for the Protection of Intellectual Property of 1883 is facilitated by the new legislation.

Other, domestic, factors also shaped the new law of trade marks. There is no doubt that the old law was in a messy state. The 1938 Act—which was far from clear in certain aspects even from day one—had been changed by successive amendments in 1984, 1986, and 1988, and divining the precise text of the legislation on service marks, in particular, was not an easy task. This alone suggested that an urgent clarification of the law was required, but broader political forces were also at play. The government was consistently in favour of the promotion of the interests of business groups and this, in its own right—coupled with the related drive towards deregulation—meant that a simpler, clearer, and more market-focused system of trade marks law was deemed to be a necessity.[9] An efficient and less costly system has consequently emerged from the 1994 reforms.

As part of this process of simplification, there were mysteries created by the law that it was opportune to resolve. The fact, for example, that the shape of a container such as a Coca-Cola bottle could not be registered[10] may or may not be objectionable, but it is difficult to justify such a view when the entire surface of a two-coloured pill could be registered.[11] Such narrow distinctions may have been the stuff of life to medieval philosophers, but were less familiar to provincial solicitors.

Equally arcane distinctions between the different types of trade mark—the Part A and the Part B marks—were also found to pose problems. The need in a Part A mark was to establish its distinctiveness by considering whether it was 'adapted to distinguish' the goods of its proprietors from those of others.[12] This was to be done with reference to its inherent adaptability to distinguish and the extent to which its use, in fact, adapted it to distinguish. For a Part B trade mark, the test of distinctiveness was whether the mark was capable of distinguishing the goods from others,[13] but this was done with reference to inherent capability and factual capability. The difference between 'adapted' and 'capable' was at once vital and obscure. Any thoughts that a Part B mark could be identified by the presence of 100 per cent factual distinctiveness was scotched by the House of Lords in *York Trailers Holdings v. Registrar of Trade Marks*,[14] in which the fact that the applicant was the only manufacturer of trailers in York, Canada (or indeed, it seems, any other York), did not justify the grant of a trade mark on the grounds that it would create too great a monopoly were the claim by one manufacturer to use as a trade mark the name of a substantial chunk of territory to be allowed. Thus additional rules of law were created to complicate further an already tangled web.

---

[7] Protocol Relating to the Madrid Agreement Concerning the International Registration of Marks of 28 June 1989.

[8] The UK became a party to the Protocol to the Madrid Agreement on 1 December 1995: see the Trade Marks (International Registration) Order 1996, SI 1996/714. The Protocol itself became operational on 1 April 1996. The UK is still not a party to the Madrid Agreement. The EU (the Community Trade Mark) adhered to the Madrid Protocol on 1 October 2004.

[9] Cm 1203, at 2.

[10] *Re Coca-Cola Co's Applications* [1986] 2 All ER 274, *sub nom. In re Coca-Cola Co.* [1986] 1 WLR 695.

[11] *Smith, Kline & French Laboratories v. Sterling-Winthrop Group* [1975] 2 All ER 578, [1975] 1 WLR 914.

[12] TMA 1938, s. 9(3)(b).

[13] Ibid., s. 10(2).

[14] [1982] 1 All ER 257, *sub nom. In re Coca-Cola Co.* [1982] 1 WLR 195.

A third example can be given from the world of infringement. It is obvious that it is wrong to claim the trade mark of another for your own use on rival goods or services—but the old law also treated as an infringement the situation in which the use of another's mark in some way connoted that the use of the mark was with the proprietor's permission or otherwise—in the words of s. 4(1)(b) of the 1938 Act—that the use *imported a reference to some person having the right as proprietor to use the trade mark*.

A good example of the perhaps surprising consequences of this is offered in the comparative advertising case of *News Group Ltd v. Mirror Group Ltd*.[15] In this case, the publishers of the *Daily Mirror* decided to exploit the unpopularity of the Conservative government and its then leader, and the slavish support that was nevertheless afforded to it by most other newspapers, by launching an advertising campaign. One poster featured, under the words 'Yes, Prime Minister', the masthead logos of all of the pro-Conservative papers, including the claimant's organ, *The Sun*. Another poster, under the words 'No, Prime Minister', featured, in solitary splendour, the masthead logo of the *Daily Mirror*. In spite of the context in which *The Sun* was appearing to be criticized for its editorial stance, it was still found that its trade-marked logo had been infringed as a result of the route of 'importing a reference'.

But all of this is now part of history, as cases arising from the old law and the various transitional provisions have worked their weary way through the system. The Trade Marks Act 1994 summarily repeals the 1938 legislation in its entirety and replaces it with a new code. It is also clearly the case that the myriad complexities of the case law arising from earlier legislation are now of little value, because the new law is based on different principles. Therefore reliance will not, for the most part, be placed on the old law as such, although, of course, there will be ample occasions to cite past cases as examples of areas of difficulty that may—or may not—have been resolved by the new law.

Why trade marks?

Before examining the detail of the new law, it is appropriate to investigate the rationale of a system of trade marks. It is clear that trade mark law has to achieve a balance between various potentially competing interests: the trader seeks to protect the image and reputation of his or her goods, but the rival trader—in a society based on free competition—has every reason to wish to compete on level terms within the same market and will, at the very least, hope that the monopoly conferred by the grant of a trade mark is confined to reasonable limits so as not to inhibit legitimate competition. The consumer also has an interest: he or she associates the product or service and its quality with its associated brand name or logo, and will not wish to be confused by similar names or logos placed on different—particularly inferior—products.

As has been seen, the trade mark originally evolved in the private sector at the behest of the traders themselves and this has generally been the principal interest given protection by the trade marks system. The protection afforded has centred on the origin of the goods and, while this has also been of benefit to consumer interests, this has been, first and foremost, in the interests of the proprietor of the trade mark. In indicating origin, the mark, being distinctive, differentiates that product from another and by doing so, in turn, guides the consumer in the exercise of choice. This, it is suggested, may now be seen as the 'core' function of trade marks and it will be pertinent to bear this view in mind, particularly when considering the direction taken by the new law of trade marks.

---

[15] [1989] FSR 126.

There can be no doubt as to the commercial significance of trade marks in modern society. Brand names or product identities, such as that of Guinness or Coca-Cola, are hugely valuable assets to their owners and are vigorously protected by them. It may be confidently predicted that the advent of a new and more flexible law of trade marks will continue to give rise to a flood of new registrations of previously unregistrable marks, thus adding further to the value of this sector.

An overview

The historical roots of trade marks go back a very long time. There is also something fashionable about trade marks: they are very commercial in nature. Over the last decades, trade mark law has been harmonized in Europe and, in the UK, the 1994 Act saw a sea change in the law of trade marks. An abundant flow of cases followed and they have gone a long way in clarifying the new system, as we will see in the next chapters.

Trade marks are essentially pro-competitive, because they allow the origin of goods to be distinguished. A producer of goods can therefore distinguish his or her goods from those of other producers of the same goods. That allows each to set itself apart and to compete with one another. At least in theory, each can always pick another trade mark. Exclusive rights in one or other mark therefore do not restrict the opportunity for competitors to pick their own mark and compete.

A mark therefore allows one to create goodwill in a brand; that goodwill necessarily exists in the relationship with the consumer. The mark allows the consumer to get information about the goods or services and the consumer should be able to rely on that information. Trade marks operate in the relationship between right holder and consumers, and the interests of both sides to the relationship are necessarily reflected in trade mark law.

Further reading

KITCHIN, D., LLEWELYN, D., MELLOR, J., MEADE, R., MOODY-STUART, T. and KEELING, D. (2005) *Kerly's Law of Trade Marks and Trade Names*, 14th edn, London: Sweet and Maxwell.

MORCOM, C., ROUGHTON, A., GRAHAM, J. and MALYNICZ, S. (2005) *The Modern Law of Trade Marks*, 2nd edn, London: Butterworths Lexis-Nexis.

25

Trade marks— registrability and use

Trade mark recognition—the UK framework

The Register of Trade Marks is a public document that can be consulted by interested parties. Joining it—and thus gaining access to the alleged prosperity that will then ensue—is a matter of formal application and examination before a registration is awarded. The applicant must provide, by virtue of s. 32 of the Trade Marks Act 1994:

- a request for registration of the mark;
- a statement of the goods or services in relation to which the mark is sought;
- a representation of the mark;
- a statement that the mark is used or is intended to be used, whether by the applicant him or herself or with his or her consent, in connection with those goods or services.

Non-use of a mark will prevent its registration. On receipt of all bar the last of these items, the application receives an official filing date, which may be of importance in deciding which of two rival marks has priority—a problem that we have already encountered in the system for the registration of patents.

The Registrar of Trade Marks then examines the application to see that the proposed mark fulfils the legal requirements necessary for a trade mark and, in so doing, is likely to search pre-existing trade marks to ensure that there is no duplication.[1] The Registrar must ask for further details from the applicant if not satisfied[2] and must publish the application[3] so that other interested parties can oppose or make comments on the proposed mark. If the necessary criteria have been met, the Registrar '*shall accept the application*',[4] but only '*if it appears to the Registrar*' that the criteria have been fulfilled. This suggests that some discretionary powers remain with the Registrar and it would seem that registration is not automatic, because it is for the Registrar to determine, in his own opinion, whether the, at times vague, requirements for registration have been met before permitting it to take place. If and when it occurs, the registered trade mark is deemed (by s. 2 of the Act) to be a property right.

A trade mark is granted not for all purposes, but only for those classes of goods and services for which an application has been made,[5] although one of the advantages of the

---

[1] TMA 1994, s. 37(2).   [2] Ibid., (3).
[3] Ibid., s. 38.   [4] Ibid., s. 37(5).
[5] The final decision on classification is a matter of administrative convenience and rests with the Registrar, rather than with the applicant: *Altecnic Ltd v. Reliance Water Controls Ltd*, judgment of 12 December 2000, unreported.

1994 Act is to make multiple applications easier by allowing one application to be made for more than one class, unlike in the old law. The classification of goods and services is carried out in accordance with the Nice Classification[6] (sixth edition), an international agreement that splits goods and services into, respectively, 34 and eight classes. These are incorporated into domestic law by reference to the *'prescribed system of classification'* in s. 34 of the 1994 Act, but new Rules have had to be promulgated to incorporate the classification into the law, there formerly having been a Schedule to the old Trade Marks Act.[7] Internationally, there is also the 1985 Vienna Agreement Establishing an International Classification of the Figurative Elements of Marks; this, however, does not form part of the domestic law.

The Nice Classification is designed to be comprehensive and, by definition, covers the whole range of manufacturing and service industry. Thus, as a random example, Class 12 of the classification comprises all vehicles, while firearms, ammunition, explosives, and fireworks comprise Class 13. Inevitably, there are anomalies: beers and soft drinks form one Class 32, while all alcoholic drinks other than beers form Class 33.

Clearly, the requirements for registration lie at the heart of this process and it is to these and, first and foremost, to the key question of what is a trade mark that we now turn.

Trade marks defined

The basic definition of a 'trade mark' is given by s. 1(1) of the 1994 Act and appears alarmingly straightforward. The Act states that a 'trade mark' is *'any sign capable of being represented graphically which is capable of distinguishing goods or services of one undertaking from those of another'*. (It should immediately be stated that certain marks that fall within this broad definition are nevertheless refused registration in accordance with ss. 3, 4, and 5 of the 1994 Act, considered subsequently.)

On its own, s. 1(1) contains three elements. The graphical representation point and the distinctiveness point will be discussed in more detail later on, but it is important to mention the third element at this stage: a trade mark is described as 'any sign'. This term is very wide in scope and should be taken to mean 'anything which can convey information'.[8] There are nevertheless limits to what can be a sign. Dyson attempted to register two trade marks consisting of a transparent bin or collection chamber forming part of the external surface of a vacuum cleaner. It tried to register the marks as a concept, which could then be applied in a specific way to each of its vacuum cleaners. The European Court of Justice refused to allow the registration, because, in the Court's view, the requirement that there needs firstly to be a sign was not fulfilled. Abstract concepts are not signs; the latter need to take a specific format.[9]

Once it is decided that a mark may fall within s. 1(1), it is necessary to consider whether it will fall foul of the inherent bars to registration, in ss. 3 and 4 of the 1994 Act, and then to see whether there are problems relating to the existence of other marks that may also present a difficulty in the way of registration, as per s. 5 of the Act. Meanwhile, the initial section of the Act continues: *'A trade mark may, in particular, consist of words (including*

---

[6] Under the World Intellectual Property Organization (WIPO) Nice Agreement concerning the International Classification of Goods and Services for the Purposes of the Registration of Marks of 1957, available online at www.wipo.int/treaties/en/classification/nice/index.html.

[7] By Sch. 4 of the Trade Marks Rules 1994, SI 1994/2583.

[8] *Philips Electronics BV v. Remington Consumer Products* [1998] RPC 283, *per* Jacob J.

[9] Case C-321/03 *Dyson Ltd v. Registrar of Trade Marks* [2007] 2 CMLR 14, [2007] RPC 27.

personal names), designs, letters, numerals or the shape of goods or their packaging.' These provisions closely follow—and clearly equate to—the words of Art. 2 of the Harmonization Directive.[10]

These definitions need to be examined closely, but their import is clear. To be registrable, a mark can consist of anything, with the items in the second paragraph of s. 1(1) clearly being no more than illustrations. It is clear, however, that no mark can be registered unless it satisfies the two vital, but related, factors of being capable of being represented graphically and also capable of distinguishing one trader's products from those of others.

Capable of being represented graphically

The concept of distinctiveness will, in due course, warrant further examination, but the requirement of capability of graphical representation may, in certain cases, create more of a problem than was first thought. Swizzels Matlow's trade mark application for a chewy sweet on a stick[11] illustrates that point clearly. The application was rejected, because it was not possible to understand the mark precisely without reference to samples of the goods. This meant that the mark, in all of its aspects, was not capable of being represented graphically.

In recent years, the issue of graphical representation has become the focus of attention in relation to olfactory (smell), sound, and colour marks.

Olfactory marks

A first question mark arises from the fact that all of the examples of registrable signs that are listed in s. 1(1) of the 1994 Act are, in themselves, capable of being perceived visually, whereas an olfactory sign is not and relies on an indirect route in this respect. But when confronted with this question for the first time in *Ralf Sieckmann v. Deutsches Patent- und Markenamt,*[12] the European Court of Justice brushed the suggestion aside, confirming that there is no fourth requirement in this respect and that the list should be considered as containing nothing more than random examples. In the words of the Court:

> The Directive must be interpreted as meaning that a trade mark may consist of a sign which is not in itself capable of being perceived visually, provided that it can be represented graphically.[13]

This quotation draws attention to what has become the major issue—that is, is the olfactory mark capable of being represented graphically? Looking back at olfactory marks that were granted at an early stage, it cannot be denied, on the one hand, that the Sumitomo mark (the smell of roses for tyres and wheels) and marks such as 'the smell of freshly cut grass' are not defined very precisely. Both roses and freshly cut grass can mean many different things in different circumstances and to different persons. On the other hand, any third party should be able to find out exactly what the trade mark is from consulting the register, not only to avoid infringement, but also to find out whether another mark can still be registered. The Register of Trade Marks must also know exactly what the mark is in order to carry out its examination and publication role. And all of this must be done on the basis of the register—that is, the graphic representation only—because that is

---

[10]   Council Directive 89/104 EEC to approximate the laws of the member States relating to trade marks (1989) OJ L 40/1.

[11]   [1998] RPC 244.

[12]   Case 273/00 [2002] ECR I-11737, [2003] Ch 487, [2003] RPC 685.

[13]   Ibid. [2003] Ch 487 at 509.

the material that is in the public domain and therefore accessible to third parties. In the *Sieckmann* case, the Court drew from this the conclusion that:

> If the users of that register are to be able to determine the precise nature of a mark on the basis of its registration, its graphic representation in the register must be self-contained, easily accessible and intelligible.
>
> Furthermore, in order to fulfil its role as a registered trade mark a sign must always be perceived unambiguously and in the same way so that the mark is guaranteed as an indication of origin. In the light of the duration of a mark's registration and the fact that, as the Directive provides, it can be renewed for varying periods, the representation must be durable.
>
> Finally, the object of the representation is specifically to avoid any element of subjectivity in the process of identifying and perceiving the sign. Consequently, the means of graphic representation must be unequivocal and objective.
>
> In the light of the foregoing observations, the answer to the first question must be that [...] the Directive must be interpreted as meaning that a trade mark may consist of a sign which is not in itself capable of being perceived visually, provided that it can be represented graphically, particularly by means of images, lines or characters, and that the representation is clear, precise, self-contained, easily accessible, intelligible, durable and objective.[14]

But what did that mean in practice? Mr Sieckmann had described, and represented graphically, the olfactory trade mark he applied for as follows:

> Trade mark protection is sought for the olfactory mark deposited with the Deutsches Patent- und Markenamt of the pure chemical substance methyl cinnamate (= cinnamic acid methyl ester), whose structural formula is set out below. Samples of this olfactory mark can also be obtained via local laboratories listed in the Gelbe Seiten (Yellow Pages) of Deutsche Telekom AG or, for example, via the firm E. Merck in Darmstadt.
>
> C_6H_5-CH = CHCOOCH3.

Mr Sieckmann also submitted, with his application, an odour sample of the sign in a container and stated that the scent was usually described as '*balsamically fruity with a slight hint of cinnamon*'.

The question was therefore whether, in relation to an olfactory mark, a chemical formula, a description in words, the deposit of an odour sample, or any combination of these elements could satisfy the requirements concerning the mark's capability of being represented graphically, as set out by the Court. The Court came to the conclusion that it could not and gave the following reasons for reaching that conclusion:

> As regards a chemical formula...few people would recognise in such a formula the odour in question. Such a formula is not sufficiently intelligible. In addition...a chemical formula does not represent the odour of a substance, but the substance as such, and nor is it sufficiently clear and precise. It is therefore not a representation for the purposes of...the Directive.
>
> In respect of the description of an odour, although it is graphic, it is not sufficiently clear, precise and objective.
>
> As to the deposit of an odour sample, it does not constitute a graphic representation for the purposes of...the Directive. Moreover, an odour sample is not sufficiently stable or durable...
>
> In the light of the foregoing considerations, the answer to the second question must be that, in respect of an olfactory sign, the requirements of graphic representability are not satisfied by a chemical formula, by a description in written words, by the deposit of an odour sample or by a combination of those elements.[15]

---

14 Ibid.   15 Ibid. at 511.

This seems to leave very little room indeed for olfactory marks and most of the marks already granted do not meet these stringent requirements.

Sound marks

Let us now move on to sound marks, as did the European Court of Justice 11 months after the *Sieckmann* case, when it delivered its judgment in *Shield Mark BV v. Joost Kist hodn Memex*.[16] Shield Mark had registered various signature tunes or jungles as sound trade marks with the Benelux Trade Marks Office. Let us consider the following Shield Mark marks as an example:

> Four of those trade marks consist of a musical stave with the first nine notes of the musical composition *Für Elise*, by Ludwig von Beethoven. Two of them also state: Sound mark. The trade mark consists of the representation of the melody formed by the notes (graphically) transcribed on the stave, plus, in one case, played on a piano...
>
> Three further marks consist of the sequence of musical notes E, D#, E, D#, E, B, D, C, A. Two of them also state: Sound mark. The trade mark consists of the reproduction of the melody formed by the sequence of notes as described, plus, in one case, played on a piano.
>
> Two of the trade marks registered by Shield Mark consist of the denomination Kukelekuuuuu (an onomatopoeia suggesting, in Dutch, a cockcrow). One of them states: Sound mark, the trade mark consists of an onomatopoeia imitating a cockcrow.

As a preliminary matter, the issue was raised whether sound marks could, by their nature, be distinctive. Having disposed of that issue by ruling that sound signs are not, by nature, incapable of distinguishing the goods or services of one undertaking from those of other undertakings, the Court returned to the key issue of graphical representation and applied its *Sieckmann* approach to sound marks. The written description of a sound, the onomatopoeia, and the musical notes all failed to pass the *Sieckmann* test: they were neither clear, nor precise, nor objective enough.

But whereas the Court did not have a suggestion as to how olfactory marks could pass the test, it did come up with a solution for sound marks:

> ...a stave divided into bars and showing, in particular, a clef (a treble clef, bass clef or alto or tenor clef), musical notes and rests whose form (for the notes: semibreve, minim, crotchet, quaver, semiquaver, etc.; for the rests: semibreve rest, minim rest, crotchet rest, quaver rest, etc.) indicates the relative value and, where appropriate, accidentals (sharp, flat, natural)—all of this notation determining the pitch and duration of the sounds—may constitute a faithful representation of the sequence of sounds forming the melody in respect of which registration is sought. This mode of graphical representation of the sounds meets the requirements of the case-law of the Court that such representation must be clear, precise, self-contained, easily accessible, intelligible, durable and objective.
>
> Even if such a representation is not immediately intelligible, the fact remains that it may be easily intelligible, thus allowing the competent authorities and the public, in particular traders, to know precisely the sign whose registration as a trade mark is sought.[17]

Colour marks

That leaves us with the question of whether the door also remains open—even if not wide open—for the registration of a single colour as a trade mark. This extreme scenario was put before the European Court of Justice in May 2003 in *Libertel Groep*

---

[16] Case C-283/01 [2003] ECR I-14313, [2004] Ch 97, [2004] RPC 315.
[17] Ibid. [2004] Ch 97 at 118.

BV v. Benelux-Merkenbureau.[18] Libertel had applied for the registration of the colour orange, per se, and, in the box for reproducing the trade mark, the application form contained an orange rectangle and in the space for describing the mark it contained the word 'orange' without reference to any colour code. The Court once more put the focus on graphical representation and the need for it to be clear, precise, self-contained, easily accessible, intelligible, durable, and objective, along the lines of the approach set out in the *Sieckmann* case.

The Court held that a mere sample of a colour is not durable enough, because it may fade; it may also change slightly depending on the background on which it is printed or against which it is put. The mere sample therefore fails the *Sieckmann* test, but, in the view of the Court, a verbal description of a colour could pass the test, depending on the circumstances of the case, as may the combination of a sample and a verbal description. The Court also deemed an internationally recognized colour identification code to be precise and stable enough to pass the test. *Libertel* therefore failed—but the addition of a colour code to the sample and the (maybe somewhat fuller) verbal description might have seen the colour orange being registered successfully.

But even in those cases, the mark will still have to pass the distinctiveness test.[19]

Distinctiveness in trade

Several issues need to be addressed further in the context of what a mark can be, but it is first appropriate to consider the significance of the use of the word 'mark', especially if such a mark has to be capable of distinguishing.

Names and signatures as marks

People's signatures may quite appropriately be regarded as their 'mark', but although a person's signature is both graphic and distinctive,[20] it is not a trade mark, because no trade is normally likely to be involved. That is not, however, to say that it could never be: the Trade Marks Act 1938 expressly permitted registration of a signature of the proprietor of a mark or his or her predecessor in business[21]—but it is this last word that is the clue: personal marks are not registrable and only those that are used in business—that is, trade—are. Under s. 103(1) of the 1994 Act, 'trade' is unhelpfully stated to '*include any profession or business*', but this nevertheless gives some indication that this whole area is once again concerned solely with the commercial exploitation of the relevant intellectual property rights.

Ex-footballer Paul Gascoigne, like many others with a similar name, has the nickname 'Gazza'—this, as such, is not registrable; once this particular 'Gazza' attains fame or notoriety and can enter trade—for example, in the character merchandising industry—then the name or signature can be registered as a *trade* mark (as long as all other criteria are satisfied). Thus there has to be trade, but—unlike in the old law[22]—there does not appear to be any need for the trade in question to be for valuable consideration. This is not to say, however, that the registration of a name or a signature as a trade mark is now a straightforward

[18] Case C-104/01 [2003] ECR I-3793, [2004] FSR 65.

[19] See Case T-173/00 *KWS Saat v. OHIM* [2002] ECR II-3843.

[20] Laddie J's judgment in *Re Elvis Presley Trade Marks* [1997] RPC 543 correctly qualifies this basic starting point and argues that signatures, although prima facie distinctive, are not inevitably distinctive. Only those signatures that are stylistically unique are really distinctive. In practice, the latter are often a highly distorted way of writing a name and can be seen as a private graphic tied to one person.

[21] TMA 1938, s. 9(1)(b).

[22] See *Re Dee Corp. plc's Application* [1990] RPC 159.

issue. The distinctiveness requirement can still create major problems if the mark is not adapted to distinguish the goods of the applicant from those of other traders.

The *Elvis Presley* case[23] graphically illustrates these problems. In that case, a cursive rendition of the singer's name was held not to be distinctive. Laddie J ruled that the public bought memorabilia carrying the Elvis name, because it referred to the singer; the public did not assume that these goods came from one source that was linked to the singer. The proposed mark was therefore not capable of distinguishing memorabilia marketed by the applicant from those marketed by other traders. A famous name refers to the person and, as such, it does not necessarily possess the distinctiveness required to distinguish goods from one source from those of another.[24]

Overall, the distinctiveness requirement means that the main purpose of a trade mark is to convey a message about the source of, and responsibility for, quality of the goods or services that are labelled with the mark.[25] This does not exclude the option that the goods are made for the trade mark owner by a third party using the trade mark owner's specification or that the services are provided by a third party according to the trade mark owner's specification, but the trade mark owner must adopt the goods or services as his or her own in those cases after having checked that they match his or her specification.[26]

This approach has now been confirmed by the European Court of Justice. The question of whether a common surname could be a trade mark arose in *Nichols plc v. Registrar of Trade Marks.*[27] The Court held that the distinctive character of such a mark needed to be assessed in the same way as that of any other mark. No special criteria applied and such an assessment should therefore focus, firstly, on the products or services in respect of which registration is applied for and, secondly, on the perception of the relevant consumers. In other words, one needs to determine whether, in relation to the relevant product or service, the relevant consumers would see the name as a mark distinguishing the goods or services of one source from the goods or services of another, or whether they would see it as nothing more than a surname.

Kinds of mark

From this, then, we can return to the issue of the kinds of marks that will attract registration. The 1938 Act, by virtue of s. 68(1), gave a list of things that could count as marks and most of these have been retained within the similarly non-inclusive list in s. 1(1) of the new law. (Those that have not, such as devices or headings are not incapable of trade mark registration, but must simply satisfy the general requirements of the first paragraph of s. 1(1).) It must be emphasized, however, that even the types of mark listed must also satisfy these requirements. It is not every word or numeral that can now be registered as a trade mark; only those that can be both graphically represented and are product-distinctive, the latter point often giving difficulty.

It is important to point out, at this stage, that the list of potential marks does expressly include an important new area. By clarifying that 'the shape of goods or their packaging' can be registrable in appropriate circumstances, the 1994 Act at once removes not only

---

[23] *Re Elvis Presley Trade Marks* [1997] RPC 543.

[24] Ibid. The test for name trade marks is not different from that for any other trade, however, and s. 11 (2) has no influence: see Case C-404/02 *Nichols plc v. Registrar of Trade Marks* [2004] ECR I-8499, [2005] 1 WLR 1418.

[25] *Glaxo Group v. Dowelhurst Ltd* [2000] FSR 529. For an example of a mark that failed to clear this hurdle at the time of the application for registration, see *'800-Flowers' Trade Mark* [2001] FSR 191 (CA).

[26] *Primark Stores Ltd & Primark Holdings v. Lollypop Clothing Ltd* [2001] ETMR 30.

[27] Case C-404/02 *Nichols plc v. Registrar of Trade Marks* [2004] ECR I-8499, [2005] 1 WLR 1418.

such awkward cases as *Re Coca-Cola*,[28] thus allowing registration of a suitably distinct bottle and other containers (a picture of the container will count as a graphic representation), but also appears to go even further back to overrule cases such as *James v. Soulby*,[29] which prevented the registration of the distinctive shape of the thing itself. Registration of the shape, if distinctive, is now permissible under the 1994 Act.

It is appropriate to consider some of the problems that dogged the old law here and to use some examples from the previous case law to illustrate those problems. The use of a name, per se, may well not be distinctive, if the name is relatively common. The old law, by s. 9(1)(a) of the 1938 Act, insisted that a name could only be registered if in a special or particular manner, as demonstrated by *Re Standard Cameras Ltd's Application*.[30] In this case, the name 'Robin Hood' was used for a camera and registration was allowed, because the first letter was shaped as an archer similar to the well-known historical figure and the last letter in the name portrayed as a target. Under the new regime, the answer would appear to be the same—but by the simpler route of the clear factual distinctiveness that such a mark would appear to enjoy.

The category of words has given rise to various problems, because the courts were constrained by the 1938 Act[31] to allow only invented words or words that conveyed no connection with the object itself and which were neither a geographical name nor a surname. The goal for trade mark proprietors was to sail as close to the wind as possible, so as to try to associate the goods as directly as possible with the name chosen. Thus in *De Cordova v. Vick Chemical Co.*,[32] a chest rub was named 'Vaporub'. The claim that was made was that this was an invented word and thus registrable. In a narrow sense, the word was not to be found in any dictionary, but it was too obvious in its origins to be regarded as invented and thus registrable. In *Re Hallgarten*,[33] however, a whisky-based liqueur marketed as 'Whisquer' was seen as sufficient of a variant from the new word's origins that it was to be regarded as invented and thus could be registered. Now, under s. 1(1) of the 1994 Act, the test is whether the names distinguish their product from others and it would seem likely that the presence of other products of that type on the market would mean that 'Vaporub' would remain unregistrable, while 'Whisquer' might survive in the absence—as far as is known—of any similar product name or description in the marketplace.

The law has taken and, it seems likely, will continue to take cognisance of the problem of phonetic equivalence. This is shown by the case of *Re Exxate Trade Mark*,[34] in which the use of Exxate on petrochemical products was allowed not as an invented word, the origin being too obvious, but as a mark that was nevertheless distinctive, bearing no obvious relation to the goods. This would seem still to represent the conclusion that the law is likely to reach even after its rewriting.

This argument is reinforced by the decision of the appointed person in the *Froot Loops Trade Mark* case.[35] Trade mark registration for 'Froot Loops' in relation to cereals and cereal preparations was refused, because it was the phonetic equivalent of 'fruit loops'. As such, the mark lost its distinctiveness and became a description of the goods involved.

---

[28] *Re Coca-Cola Co's Applications* [1986] 2 All ER 274, *sub nom. In re Coca-Cola Co.* [1986] 1 WLR 695, discussed in the previous chapter.

[29] (1886) 33 Ch D 392.

[30] (1952) 69 RPC 125.

[31] Section 9(1)(c) and (d).

[32] (1951) 68 RPC 103.

[33] (1948) 66 RPC 105.

[34] [1986] RPC 567.

[35] [1998] RPC 240.

The law's concern to restrict the use of laudatory epithets, lest an over-extensive monop-oly be created, is perhaps harder to retain under the new law. In *Re Joseph Crosfield & Sons Ltd*,[36] the name 'Perfection' was denied trade mark registration for a soap as being too broad a monopoly and as being, in the future, potentially misleading. It seems diffi-cult to argue today that such a general word could be distinctive even within a particular category of goods, although, of course, distinctiveness will ultimately be a question of fact. In the first case to raise this issue under the 1994 Act, Jacob J denied trade mark protection to the laudatory epithet 'Treat', which was used in relation to dessert sauces and syrups.[37]

The law may, however, be more helpful to a laudatory epithet that is less likely to be in common use. The case of *My Mum's Cola Trade Mark*[38] was decided in relation to a Part B mark and thus should be relevant in the new era, in which factual distinctiveness is at the heart of all marks. The mark was held to be registrable, notwithstanding its laudatory character, because its use of the words 'My Mum's' was not a use that other traders would have any reason to employ. Now, we would simply look to see whether any trader had, in fact, used such an epithet and would consider the compound trade mark as a whole.

Disclaimers

Some trade marks may be created from more than one image: for example, a distinctive name written in a distinctive manner, such as the way in which 'Coca-Cola' is written on its tins. The question that arises is whether a problem is created if one of the elements is not distinctive and thus, in itself, not able to gain trade mark protection. This problem is dealt with, at least in part, by the system of disclaimers under which an applicant can disclaim parts of his or her trade mark by denying any claim to the exclusive use of that element.[39] The classic illustration of this is the old case of *Re Diamond T Trade Mark*,[40] in which a mark had three distinct elements—namely, the word 'diamond', the shape of a diamond, and the letter 'T'. None of these were, in themselves, distinctive and each of the individual items was thus the subject of a disclaimer, but a trade mark was held to subsist in what was left—namely, the (distinctive) combination of the three items.

The 1994 Act varies from its predecessor in one vital way in relation to cases in which the use of disclaimers is concerned. Formerly, the Registrar could impose disclaimers, but this is now a voluntary matter for the applicant. There is a clear incentive for the applicant to avail him or herself of this facility: there is always a risk that the failure so to do will often be counterproductive, because, as will be seen, a mark may be refused or may sub-sequently be struck down at the instigation of a rival trader if, for example, it is thought to be likely to cause confusion with other similar marks or other similar goods. Clearly, the incorporation of non-distinctive matter will readily raise such potential confusion.

That said, the use of the disclaimer enables trade marks to incorporate, albeit under the disclaimer, much valuable descriptive matter. The proprietor of 'Torremans' Fresh Orange Juice' cannot monopolize the description of the product—but if the name is printed in distinctive purple spiky lettering, a trade mark can be obtained in the overall mark and it may then be that, as a matter of fact, the public associates the general product description with the particular trade marked product.

---

[36] [1910] 1 Ch 118, HC; on appeal [1910] 1 Ch 130 at 142–3, CA.

[37] *British Sugar plc v. James Robertson & Sons Ltd* [1996] RPC 281.

[38] [1988] RPC 130; Case C-329/02 *Satellitenfernsehen GmbH v Office for Harmonisation of the Internal Market* [2004] ECR I-8317.

[39] TMA 1994, s. 13.

[40] (1921) 38 RPC 373.

It is important to note, however, that the effect of a disclaimer is not limited to the grant of a trade mark: it also has an effect when it comes to infringement and opposition. So if the only point of similarity with a registered trade mark is the disclaimed element, that disclaimed element can also no longer be relied on in opposition or infringement proceedings.[41]

Unregistrable marks

Fulfilling the basic requirements of trade mark registration does not guarantee that a trade mark will be obtained. The 1994 Act makes clear that certain marks are either never registrable or are unregistrable in the light of market conditions. It is the first category that we now examine.

Absolute grounds for refusal of registration

Section 3 of the 1994 Act establishes the principal rules relating to absolute unregistrability. It lists a range of different grounds and, by subs. (1), states that the following marks shall not be registered:

(a) signs which do not satisfy the requirements of section 1(1),

(b) trade marks which are devoid of any distinctive character,

(c) trade marks which consist exclusively of signs or indications which may serve, in trade, to designate the kind, quality, quantity, intended purpose, value, geographical origin, the time of production of goods or of rendering of services, or other characteristics of goods or services,

(d) trade marks which consist exclusively of signs or indications which have become customary in the current language or in the bona fide and established practices of the trade;

provided that a trade mark shall not be refused registration by virtue of paragraph (b), (c) or (d) above if, before the date of application for registration, it has in fact acquired a distinctive character as a result of the use made of it.

These complex provisions go to the heart of the issue of distinctiveness already flagged up as crucial by s. 1 of the Act. The four paragraphs of s. 3(1) are by no means mutually exclusive and may apply in combination in any given case.[42] The first paragraph of s. 3 is self-evident—but the Court of Appeal's judgment in *Bach & Bach Flower Remedies Trade Marks*,[43] which dealt with this point, had the potential to create confusion and could be seen as irreconcilable with the decision of the European Court of Justice in *Philips Electronics NV v. Remington Consumer Products Ltd.*[44] The Court of Appeal sought to clarify the matter in *West (t/a Eastenders) v. Fuller Smith & Turner plc*[45] and held that the rule was that the second half of the definition of a trade mark in s. 1(1) of the 1994 Act does not impose any requirement of distinctiveness separate from that imposed by s. 3(1)(b), (c), and (d), and that there was no requirement that a mark be both 'capable of distinguishing' and 'not devoid of distinctive character'.

---

[41] *General Cigar Co. Ltd v. Partagas y Cia SA* [2005] FSR 45.
[42] *Bach & Bach Flower Remedies Trade Marks* [2000] RPC 512, CA.
[43] [2000] RPC 513.
[44] Case C-299/99 [2002] ECR I-5475, [2003] Ch 159, [2003] RPC 14.
[45] [2003] FSR 816.

Marks that consist of several components must be considered as a whole for the purposes of s. 3(1).[46] Section 3(1)(b) denies trade mark registration to trade marks that are devoid of any distinctive character. It basically repeats the requirement in s. 1 that the trade mark must be capable of distinguishing. A trade mark must, at the very least, be able to serve as a guarantee of trade origin—that is, it must be capable of distinguishing the goods that originate with one trader from similar goods that originate with another.[47]

Section 3(1)(b)

A mark that is devoid of any distinctive character can never convey the message 'these are the goods of a particular trader'; that conclusion is reached by considering the mark on its own, taking into account no use. It was, for example, held that the word 'treat' was devoid of any distinctive character, when looked at on its own.[48] The same applied to the PREPARE mark, which, as such, was unable to distinguish the teaching aids of one trader from those of another trader and only referred to the word 'prepare'.[49] 'Eurolamb',[50] as an abbreviation of European lamb,[51] and 'Froot Loops',[52] as the phonetic equivalent of fruit loops (cereals), were also held not to be distinctive and therefore excluded from registration through the operation of s. 3(1)(b). And when Philips tried to register its three-headed rotary shaver as a trade mark, it was held that the shaver as a *'sign can never only denote shavers made by Philips and no one else because it primarily says "here is a three-headed rotary shaver"'* and that the sign *'is not "capable" of denoting only Philips goods'.*[53] The mark was therefore invalid. It is important to note that the Philips sign did not include the name 'Philips' and that any other three-headed rotary shaver design would have infringed the mark if it had been granted. It was also irrelevant that no other manufacturer had hitherto made such shavers.

The European Court of Justice has also rendered its judgment in the *Philips* case.[54] The Court agreed that the shape of a three-headed rotary shaver as such could not be a trade mark, because it only conveyed the message that the item was a three-headed rotary shaver and could therefore not distinguish one such shaver from one manufacturer from another such shaver from another manufacturer.

---

[46] Case C-329/02 *Satellitenfernsehen GmbH v Office for Harmonisation of the Internal Market* [2004] ECR I-8317.

[47] *Philips Electronics BV v. Remington Consumer Products Ltd* [1998] RPC 283. The case went on to the Court of Appeal, which made a reference for a preliminary ruling to the European Court of Justice: [1999] RPC 809; see Case C-299/99 *Philips Electronics NV v. Remington Consumer Products Ltd* [2002] ECR I-5475, [2003] CH 159, [2003] RPC 14.

[48] *British Sugar plc v. James Robertson & Sons Ltd* [1996] RPC 281.

[49] [1997] RPC 884.

[50] *Eurolamb Trade Mark* [1997] RPC 279.

[51] The Court of First Instance also held that two generic words that describe the range of products of a manufacturer cannot be registered as a trade mark, because they lack distinctive character, even if the two words are stuck together: see Case T-19/99 *DKV v. OHIM (Companyline)* [2000] ECR II-1.

[52] *Froot Loops Trade Mark* [1998] RPC 240.

[53] *Philips Electronics NV v. Remington Consumer Products Ltd* [1998] RPC 283, *per* Jacob J. Similarly, the Court of First Instance held that the rectangular shape of washing powder tablets in two colours could not be registered as a trade mark, because it indicated the product, and did not allow the consumer to distinguish between the product and another tablet from another manufacturer, because the shape was used commonly: see Case T-335/99 *Henkel v. OHIM* [2001] ECR II-2581. The cylindrical shape of a torch was not registrable, because it referred to the product rather than to a specific manufacturer; again, the distinctive character of the mark was lacking: see Case T-88/00 *Mag Instrument v. OHIM* [2002] ECR II-467.

[54] Case C-299/99 *Philips Electronics NV v. Remington Consumer Products Ltd* [2002] ECR I-5475, [2003] Ch 159, [2003] RPC 14.

Similarly, Lego was denied trade mark registration for its toy plastic bricks when it tried to register them without the name 'Lego' stamped on them.[55] This does not mean that trade mark protection for shapes of goods is to be ruled out altogether: the distinctive Coca-Cola bottle is probably a good example of a successful case. In relation to word marks, the meaning of a word can depend on its usage, and it is permissible and necessary to determine the meaning of a word as used at the time of the application for registration. 'Usage' means usage by those engaged in the relevant trade and includes the average consumer, as well as manufacturers, wholesalers, and retailers. Through usage, a word could acquire—but also lose—a distinctive character. It was therefore necessary to determine the meaning of the word on the basis of the usage before deciding whether, under s. 3(1)(b), the mark was, or had become, devoid of distinctive character, or whether instead distinctive character had been acquired.[56]

West (t/a Eastenders) v. Fuller Smith & Turner plc[57] raised interesting questions concerning s. 3(1) of the 1994 Act. The trade mark concerned was 'E.S.B.', an acronym of Extra Strong Bitter, and its revocation was sought on the basis that it was devoid of distinctive character and that is was merely descriptive. In the Court of Appeal, it was held that if, at the date of registration, the mark served as a trade mark to the interested public (as the judge had held it did in fact), it could not be regarded as being devoid of distinctive character. The mark would offend against s. 3(1)(b) only if the average consumer knew that the sign 'E.S.B.' was used exclusively as an indication or the kind or quality of the goods or was in common use. The word 'devoid' had to be construed strictly and the concession that the mark possessed distinctiveness *in vacuo* was fatal to the objection under this subsection. The Court followed the guidance of the European Court of Justice in *Procter & Gamble v. OHIM*[58] on this point.

Section 3(1)(b) is therefore particularly concerned with those marks that, from the point of view of the relevant public, are commonly used, in trade, for the presentation of the goods or services concerned, or in connection with which there exists, at the very least, concrete evidence justifying the conclusion that they are capable of being used in that manner.[59] Moreover, these marks are incapable of performing the essential function of a trade mark—namely, that of identifying the origin of the goods or services— thus enabling the consumer who acquired them to repeat or avoid the experience on a subsequent occasion.[60]

It is important to note that, for the purposes of s. 3(1)(b), no distinction should be made between different categories of mark. It is therefore not appropriate to apply more stringent criteria when assessing the distinctiveness of three-dimensional marks comprising the shape of the goods themselves or the shape of the packaging of those goods than in the case of other categories of mark, even if, in practice, fewer three-dimensional marks will pass the test.[61] But nonetheless one needs to keep in mind, when applying those criteria, that the relevant public perception is not necessarily the same in the case

---

[55] *Interlego AG's Trade Mark Application* [1998] RPC 69 (a case under the 1938 Act).

[56] *Bach & Bach Flower Remedies Trade Marks* [2000] RPC 513, CA.

[57] [2003] FSR 816.

[58] Case C-383/99 P [2001] ECR I-6251.

[59] Case T-305/02 *Nestlé Waters France v. OHIM* [2004] ETMR 566 at [28]; Joined Cases T-79/01 and T-86/01 *Bosch v. OHIM (Kit Pro & Kit Super Pro)* [2002] ECR I1-4881 at [19].

[60] Case T-79/00 *Rewe Zentral v. OHIM (LITE)* [2002] ECR I1-705 at [26]; Case T-305/02 *Nestlé Waters France v. OHIM* [2004] ETMR 566 at [28].

[61] Joined Cases C-53/01 and C-55/01 *Linde AG & ors v. Deutsches Patent- und Markenamt* [2003] ECR I-3161 at [49]. See also Case T-88/00 *Mag Instrument v. OHIM* [2002] ECR II-467 at [32]; Case T-305/02 *Nestlé Waters France v. OHIM* [2004] ETMR 566 at [35].

of a three-dimensional mark that consists of the appearance of a product itself as it is in case of word or figurative marks that consist of signs that are unrelated to the appearance of the product. Consumers are simply not used to make assumptions about the origin of products on the basis of their shape, or of the shape of their packaging, without reference to any word or graphic element. It must therefore be more difficult to establish distinctiveness for three-dimensional marks. The practical outcome is therefore that only a mark that departs significantly from the norm of the sector can fulfil its essential function of indicating origin and can therefore potentially escape being devoid of distinctive character.[62] But even in those cases, the fact that they now fulfil the essential function of indicating origin on their own is not a foregone conclusion and needs to be demonstrated.[63]

A minimum degree of distinctive character is, on the other hand, sufficient to render inapplicable the ground for refusal set out in s. 3(1)(b). In a case involving bottles for mineral water,[64] the sign claimed consisted of the shape of the packaging of the product, rather than the product itself, because beverages, such as mineral waters, cannot be sold without packaging. That three-dimensional mark was composed of commonly used elements, but they were combined in a particular way that made the combination stand out. The mark therefore had the minimum degree of distinctiveness required.

Language issues can also arise: is a descriptive word in one language necessarily devoid of distinctiveness when it is used as a trade mark in another language area? In *Matratzen Concord AG v. Hulka SA*,[65] the mark concerned was 'Matratzen'—'mattresses' in German. The mark was, however, registered and used in Spain. In Spanish, the word has no meaning and the European Court of Justice ruled therefore that it could be distinctive for mattresses, unless the relevant parties in the member State in relation to which registration was sought were capable of identifying the meaning of the term. Unless the latter situation arises, the mark is not caught by s. 3(1).

Finally, it should be noted that the European Court of Justice has held that the distinctiveness of a trade mark must be assessed by reference to, firstly, the goods or services in respect of which registration is sought and, secondly, the perception of the relevant persons—namely, the consumers of the goods or services. According to the Court, that means the presumed expectations of an average consumer of the category of goods or services in question, who is reasonably well informed, and reasonably observant and circumspect.[66]

Section 3(1)(d)

A similar approach applies to s. 3(1)(d) of the 1994 Act.[67] The starting point for paragraph (d) is that, for it to apply, the mark must consist exclusively of signs or indications that have become customary in the current language or in the established practices of the trade in the products or services in respect of which the mark is to be registered. This should not be taken to mean, however, that the signs or indications must have become a direct description of the goods or services concerned and that they describe their essential

---

[62] Case C-24/05 *Storck KG v. OHIM* [2006] ECR I-5677; Case C-173/04 *Deutsche SiSi-Werke GmbH & Co. Betriebs KG v. OHIM* [2006] ECR I-551, [2006] ETMR 41.

[63] *Bongrain SA's Trade Mark Application* [2005] RPC 14 (CA). A six-lobed shape for cheese, unusual as it may be, was held not to be distinctive.

[64] Case T-305/02 *Nestlé Waters France v. OHIM* [2004] ETMR 566.

[65] Case C-421/04 *Matratzen Concord AG v. Hulka SA* [2006] ECR I-2303, [2006] ETMR 48.

[66] Case C-210/96 *Gut Springenheide & Tusky* [1998] ECR I-4657 at [31]; Joined Cases C-53/01 and C-55/01 *Linde AG & ors v. Deutsches Patent- und Markenamt* [2003] ECR I-3161 at [41].

[67] Ibid.

elements or characteristics; it is sufficient that the signs or indications bring the goods or services to mind to the average consumer.[68]

Section 3(1)(c)

Section 3(1)(c) is designed to deny trade mark registration to descriptive marks that, as such, are likely not to be distinctive. Once more, the *Treat* case[69] can serve as an example: 'Treat' was held to be a sign that designated exclusively the kind, quality, and intended purpose of the product. Similarly, Philips' shaver head fell foul of this provision in so far as the public took it as a picture of the goods[70] and not as a trade mark.[71] It is important to note that the bar on registration applies only if the mark is exclusively composed of these types of descriptive matter and marks can be registered that, among other elements, include matters of this sort, whether the subject of a disclaimer or not. A trade mark can therefore include descriptive matter, as long as it does so in combination with other matter that adds a distinctive character to the combination.

West (t/a Eastenders) v. Fuller Smith & Turner plc[72] raised interesting questions concerning s. 3(1) of the 1994 Act. The trade mark concerned was 'E.S.B.' (an acronym of Extra Strong Bitter) and its revocation was sought on the basis that it was devoid of distinctive character and that is was merely descriptive. In relation to the descriptiveness argument, the Court of Appeal held that s. 3(1)(c) of the Act did not present a high hurdle to an applicant. The principles summarized by the judge in the following four propositions were held to be correct:

(i) s. 3(1)(b), (c), and (d) were not designed to exclude from registration marks that merely possessed an indirect descriptive connotation—the words 'devoid of any' in subsection (b) and 'exclusively' in (c) were to be given effect to;

(ii) the fact that some mental activity was necessary to discern a reference to the quality, or characteristic, of the goods could assist in its registrability;

(iii) uncertainty as to the precise nature of the reference to the quality or character of the goods would also be of assistance;

(iv) marks that could only refer to the quality or character of the goods had to be refused registration, because such a mark did not *differ from the usual way of designating the goods or their characteristics*' and because it might serve in normal usage, from a customer's point of view, to designate the relevant goods either directly or indirectly, or by reference to one of their essential characteristics.[73]

Common words

The distinctive character of trade marks that consist of common words has also taken up a lot the time in the courts. The European Court of Justice held, in *Procter v. Gamble Co. v. OHIM* (the *Baby-Dry* case),[74] that the combination of the words 'baby' and 'dry' was not simply descriptive, and that the distinctive character of the mark could be established. In

[68] Conclusion of Advocate-General Damaso Ruiz-Jarabo Colomer in Case C-517/99 *Merz & Krell & Co.*, delivered on 18 January 2001, [2001] ETMR 48.
[69] *British Sugar plc v. James Robertson & Sons Ltd* [1996] RPC 281.
[70] See also *Froot Loops Trade Mark* [1998] RPC 240 (the trade mark is understood as fruit loops and, as such, describes the cereals involved); *Eurolamb Trade Mark* [1997] RPC 279 (the trade mark means European lamb and that is a description of the product).
[71] *Philips Electronics NV v. Remington Consumer Products Ltd* [1998] RPC 283.
[72] [2003] FSR 816.
[73] Ibid. at 829.
[74] Case C-383/99 P [2001] ECR I-6251, [2002] Ch 82.

order to do so, the Court held that the descriptive character does not solely relate to the individual words, but also to the sign of which they form part. The distinctive character can, in other words, be shown by any difference in use and expression between the combination of words and the normal terminology, and the normal use of the words in everyday language. In the *Baby-Dry* case, the distinctive character was derived from the fact that the words 'baby' and 'dry' are not normally used in that particular combination in relation to nappies. Such a difference should be in relation to important aspects of form or meaning of the sign. It is submitted that the key element in the *Baby-Dry* case was, indeed, the fact that, while common words were used, they were used in a weird combination that, on its own, is not a common word and that is not part of normal everyday language.

The debate surrounding trade marks that consist of common words continued though and came to a climax in the *Doublemint* case.[75] Wrigley wanted to register 'Doublemint' as a trade mark for mint-flavoured chewing gum. The European Court of Justice was eventually called upon to sort out the *Doublemint* saga. The key question was whether the absolute ground for refusal of marks that are descriptive under s. 3(1)(c) of the 1994 Act applies only if the mark is exclusively descriptive. The Court of First Instance had held that the word 'Doublemint' was not exclusively descriptive in this case.[76] It found that the adjective 'double' was unusual when compared with other English words, such as 'much', 'strong', 'extra', 'best', or 'finest', and that, when combined with the word 'mint', it had two distinct meanings for the potential consumer: twice the usual amount of mint or flavoured with two varieties of mint. Furthermore, it found that mint is a generic term that includes spearmint, peppermint, and other culinary herbs, and that there are several possible ways of combining two sorts of mint and, in addition, various strengths of flavour are possible in the case of each combination. The registration had therefore been allowed.

On appeal, the Court of Justice overturned that decision. According to the Court, se. 3(1)(c) pursues an aim that is in the public interest—namely, that descriptive signs or indications relating to the characteristics of goods or services in respect of which registration is sought may be freely used by all. That provision accordingly prevents such signs and indications from being reserved to one undertaking alone, because they have been registered as trade marks. In order for the registration to be refused, it is therefore not necessary that the signs and indications composing the mark that are referred to in that section actually be in use at the time of the application for registration in a way that is descriptive of goods or services such as those in relation to which the application is filed, or of characteristics of those goods or services. It is sufficient, as the wording of that provisions itself indicates, that such signs and indications could be used for such purposes. The rule that has been established is therefore clearly that a sign must be refused registration under that provision if at least one of its possible meanings designates a characteristic of the goods or services concerned. Because, at least in one sense, 'Doublemint' was descriptive, its registration as a trade mark therefore had to be refused.[77]

Slightly different issues arise, as we saw earlier in relation to distinctiveness, when a descriptive word from another language is used as a mark. In *Matratzen Concord AG v. Hulka SA*,[78] the mark concerned was 'Matratzen', which means 'mattresses' in German. The mark was, however, registered and used in Spain. In Spanish, the word has no meaning and the European Court of Justice ruled therefore that it could be distinctive for

---

[75] Case C-191/01 P *OHIM v. Wm Wrigley Jr Co.* [2004] RPC 327, [2004] ETMR 121.

[76] Case T-193/99 *Wm Wrigley Jr Co. y v. OHIM* [2001] ECR II-417.

[77] Case C-191/01 P *OHIM v. Wm Wrigley Jr Co.* [2004] RPC 327, [2004] ETMR 121.

[78] Case C-421/04 *Matratzen Concord AG v. Hulka SA* [2006] ECR I-2303, [2006] ETMR 48.

mattresses, unless the relevant parties in the member State in relation to which registration was sought were capable of identifying the meaning of the term. Unless the latter situation arises, the mark is not caught by s. 3(1); if, however, the word is descriptive and understood as such by the public, any particular representation of the word will remain caught by the exclusion.[79]

A need to look at all of the circumstances

The same approach was used by Advocate General Ruiz-Jarabo Colomer in his conclusions in *Campina Melkunie BV v. Benelux-Merkenbureau* (the *Biomild* case)[80] and in *Koninklijke KPN Nederland NV v. Benelux-Merkenbureau* (the *Postkantoor* case).[81] He added that, in examining whether a sign is suitable for registration as a trade mark, the trade mark office should not limit its analysis to the sign as it appears in the application; attention should also be paid to all other relevant circumstances and these include the acquisition of distinctive character through use that has been made of the sign, as well as the danger that the average consumer will be confused or misled by the use of the mark for the goods or services in relation of which registration is sought.

The European Court of Justice confirmed the approach in the *KPN Postkantoor* case in the following terms:

> Article 3(1)(c) of Directive 89/104 must be interpreted as meaning that a mark consisting of a word composed of elements, each of which is descriptive of characteristics of the goods or services in respect of which registration is sought, is itself descriptive of the characteristics of those goods or services for the purposes of that provision, unless there is a perceptible difference between the word and the mere sum of its parts: that assumes either that because of the unusual nature of the combination in relation to the goods or services the word creates an impression which is sufficiently far removed from that produced by the mere combination of meanings lent by the elements of which it is composed, with the result that the word is more than the sum of its parts, or that the word has become part of everyday language and has acquired its own meaning, with the result that it is now independent of its components. In the latter case, it is necessary to ascertain whether a word which has acquired its own meaning is not itself descriptive for the purposes of the same provision.
>
> For the purposes of determining whether Art.3(1)(c) of Directive 89/104 applies to such a mark, it is irrelevant whether or not there are synonyms capable of designating the same characteristics of the goods or services mentioned in the application for registration or that the characteristics of the goods or services which may be the subject of the description are commercially essential or merely ancillary.[82]

Three-dimensional marks

It has also been argued that s. 3(1)(c) of the 1994 Act has no relevance for three-dimensional shape of product trade marks. The European Court of Justice has rejected that argument and has added that:

> When examining the ground for refusing registration in Article 3(1)(c) of the Directive in a concrete case, regard must be had to the public interest underlying that provision, which is that all three-dimensional shape of product trade marks which consist exclusively of signs or indications which may serve to designate the characteristics of the goods or service within

---

[79] *Hormel Foods Corp. v. Antilles Landscape Investments NV* [2005] RPC 28.
[80] Case C-265/00 *Campina Melkunie BV v. Benelux-Merkenbureau* [2004] ETMR 821.
[81] Case C-363/99 *Koninklijke KPN Nederland NV v. Benelux-Merkenbureau* [2004] ETMR 771.
[82] Case C-363/99 *Koninklijke KPN Nederland NV v. Benelux-Merkenbureau* [2004] ETMR 771. See also Case C-265/00 *Campina Melkunie BV v. Benelux-Merkenbureau* [2004] ETMR 821.

the meaning of that provision should be freely available to all and, subject always to Article 3(3) of the Directive, cannot be registered.[83]

This policy consideration is of crucial importance in relation to the application of s. 3(1)(c) in practice and applies across the board.

The proviso

Obviously, certain—but not all—marks can become distinctive and capable of distinguishing through use,[84] and through educating the public that the sign is a trade mark.[85] If there is evidence that this has happened before an application is made to register the marks, then there is no problem. Indeed, in such a case, the position of the applicant is further enhanced by the proviso to s. 3(1)(b), (c), and (d), which provides that, in such a case, registration of the trade mark shall not be refused.[86]

The European Court of Justice has held that this proviso constitutes a major exception to the rules laid down in s. 3(1)(b), (c), and (d).[87] The distinctive character that can be obtained through use must therefore 'serve to identify the product... as originating from a particular undertaking and thus to distinguish that product from goods of another undertaking'.[88] Only then will the geographical indication—or any of the other items listed in s. 3(1)(c)—have gained a new significance and will its connotation, which is no longer purely descriptive, justify its registration as a trade mark. In making the assessment of whether the mark has acquired such a distinctive character, the court may take account of points such as the market share held by the mark, how intensive, geographically widespread and long-standing the use of the mark has been, the amount that the applicant has invested in promoting the mark, the proportion of the relevant class of persons who identify the goods as originating from a particular undertaking as a result of the use of the mark, and statements from trade and professional associations. The final test in this respect is that at least a significant part of the relevant class of persons must identify goods as originating from a particular undertaking because they are labelled with the mark. If this is the case, the distinctive character will have been acquired. It is therefore not required that the goods are also manufactured in the desired location. In cases in which a real link between the location and the goods or services is absent, nothing stands, in principle, in the way of registering a geographical location as a trade mark for those goods or services, as long as that location does not evoke any connotation in the mind of the consumer.[89]

A somewhat complex set of facts arose in *Bovemij v. Benelux-Merkenbureau*,[90] in which the mark involved was 'Europolis'. In Dutch (one of the languages spoken in the Benelux), this is a contraction of 'euro' and 'polis', the latter word meaning policy, as in insurance policy. The mark was indeed to be used in relation to insurance. At first glance, the mark

---

[83] Joined Cases C-53/01 and C-55/01 *Linde AG & ors v. Deutsches Patent- und Markenamt* [2003] ECR I-3161 at [76]–[77].

[84] The Coca-Cola bottle may be seen as an example. The shape of the bottle clearly became a sign that refers uniquely to the Coca-Cola Company.

[85] See Jacob J's comments concerning the 'Treat' mark in *British Sugar plc v. James Robertson & Sons Ltd* [1996] RPC 281.

[86] For an application, see *Waterford Wedgwood plc v. David Nagli Ltd* [1998] FSR 92.

[87] Cases C-108/97 *Windsurfing Chiemsee Produktions und Vertriebs GmbH v. Boots- und Segelzubehör Walter Huber*; C-109/97 *Windsurfing Chiemsee Produktions und Vertriebs GmbH v. Attenberger* [1999] ECR I-2779.

[88] Ibid.

[89] Ibid. Further questions on the interpretation of the proviso have been referred to the European Court of Justice: see *Société des Produits Nestlé SA v. Mars UK Ltd* [2004] FSR 16, [2003] ETMR 1235 (CA); *Dyson Ltd v. Registrar of Trademarks* [2003] RPC 821.

[90] Case C-108/05 *Bovemij v. Benelux-Merkenbureau* [2006] ECR I-7605.

therefore failed the test in s. 3(1). The Court ruled that the proviso could only save the application if the sign has acquired distinctive character throughout the member State concerned. For the Benelux, this means the part of the territory for which the ground of refusal exists. When the ground for refusal is based on the use of a language in a part of a member State or on the Benelux, evidence of acquired distinctiveness in that part of the member State or the Benelux will suffice.

As such, there is nothing special about the judgment: it is a logical application of the provision concerned. It is, however, interesting to contrast the decision with another decision of the European Court of Justice on s. 3(1) in *Matratzen Concord AG v. Hulka SA*.[91] It is important to see, though, that the second decision is not concerned with the proviso, but with s. 3(1)(b) and (c) itself. The mark concerned was 'Matratzen', which means 'mattresses' in German. The mark was however registered and used in Spain. In Spanish, the word has no meaning and the Court ruled therefore that it could be distinctive for mattresses, unless the relevant parties in the member State in relation to which registration was sought were capable of identifying the meaning of the term. Unless the latter situation arises, the mark is not caught by s. 3(1) in the first place and there is therefore no need to turn to the proviso.

The use that is required to acquire distinctiveness through use may be the result of the use of the mark in conjunction with, or as part of, another registered trade mark. The Court of Justice held so in *Nestlé v. Mars UK*.[92] The case turned around Nestlé's attempt to register 'Have a Break' as a trade mark, while they already had trade marks in the name KIT KAT and in the slogan 'Have a break…have a KIT KAT'.

The proviso to s. 3(1)(b), (c), and (d) of the 1994 Act fits in with its emphasis on factual distinctiveness as being the test for trade mark protection and irrevocably overturns the *York Trailers*[93] decision that had occasioned so much controversy. Thus, whether the mark in question is not distinctive, is exclusively descriptive, or has become a common or generic name will not be a bar to registration if it can be proven that, at that time, the mark was already 100 per cent factually distinctive. This meets head-on one of the strongest objections to the old law of trade marks. But if the mark is registered while still not being distinctive, the registration can normally be declared invalid. The proviso to s. 47(1), however, allows for the mark to stay on the register and for it not to be declared invalid in those cases in which the mark has, after registration, acquired a distinctive character in relation to the goods or services for which it is registered. But it must be added that, in the case of descriptive or laudatory words, the burden of proof will be very high. Evidence of the fact that 60 per cent of the public would recognize the word 'Treat' as a British Sugar Silver Spoon trade mark was held to be insufficient in this respect.[94]

Section 3(2)

Section 3(2) creates further instances of unregistrability arising directly from the extension of trade mark protection to shapes of items.

Shapes resulting from the nature of the goods and shapes necessary to achieve a technical result

Clearly, there is a risk of overlap between trade marks and other intellectual property rights, and this is addressed by the provision that shapes (in each case exclusively)

[91] Case C-421/04 *Matratzen Concord AG v. Hulka SA* [2006] ECR I-2303, [2006] ETMR 48.
[92] Case C-353/03 *Societe des Produits Nestlé SA v. Mars UK Ltd* [2005] ECR I-6135, [2005] 3 CMLR 12.
[93] [1982] 1 All ER 257.
[94] *British Sugar plc v. James Robertson & Sons Ltd* [1996] RPC 281, but Jacob J was happy to accept that 90 per cent would clearly do.

resulting from the nature of the goods themselves[95] and shapes necessary to achieve a technical result[96] shall not be registered. But how does one determine whether a sign consists exclusively of a shape that results from the nature of the goods themselves? The definition that is given to the concept of the goods themselves is vital in this respect. If the goods are defined narrowly—for example, as three-headed rotary shavers in the *Philips* case—any shape mark would be rendered invalid. It could, of course, be argued that the goods should be taken to mean the specification of goods for which the mark is intended to be registered.

Jacob J rejected that argument in the *Philips* case and called the whole issue 'a practical business matter'.[97] He arrived at his ruling that the goods in the case at issue were electric shavers on the basis of the criterion that this was how things were in practice, as articles of commerce. Alternatively, the problem under s. 3(2) may lie in the fact that the shape of the goods is necessary to achieve a technical result. This was held not to mean that there was no other route to that result;[98] rather it means that, in substance, the shape is motivated by function. The test was established as whether, in substance, the shape solely achieves a technical result.[99] The Philips three-headed rotary shaver shape was held to have been chosen to achieve a technical result and it therefore fell foul of s. 3(2)(b),[100] which approach has now been confirmed by the European Court of Justice. The Court additionally explained in the *Philips* case, that the exclusion from trade mark registrability of a shape that is necessary to achieve a technical result still applies if other shapes could allow the same or a similar result to be reached, as long as the essential features of the shape were chosen to achieve the result.[101]

Patent and design law may offer alternative routes to intellectual property protection in appropriate cases that are excluded from trade mark law through the operation of s. 3(2).

Shapes that give substantial value to the goods

More difficulty is provided by the third exclusion in this group—namely, the exclusion under s. 3(2)(c) of a shape 'which (exclusively) gives substantial value to the goods'. This is an entirely new provision in the law and has its origins in the trade marks law of the Benelux countries. Taken at face value, it appears to exclude a significant range of products from trade mark protection, because those involved in marketing will obviously seek to attract customers to a product by, among other things, its distinctive shape and, if this ploy succeeds, they will have enhanced the value of the product.

Examples are manifold. The success of the film *Jurassic Park* caused many manufacturers of such foodstuffs as fish fingers and burgers to shape their products so as to resemble dinosaurs. It would be reasonable to assume that this helped the sales of the products and thus the shape gave added value (although there is a query as to whether it gave substantial added value) to the product. Many items of designer clothing or jewellery also seem to fall within this exception, and significant litigation has occurred in the Benelux countries from which this new provision is derived. The guidance provided by Benelux decisions may not be followed in the UK; the 1994 Act does not require reference to be made to it.

---

[95] TMA 1994, s. 3(2)(a).

[96] Ibid., (b).

[97] *Philips Electronics BV v. Remington Consumer Products Ltd* [1998] RPC 283 at 305.

[98] Conclusion of Advocate-General Damaso Ruiz-Jarabo Colomer in Case C-299/99 *Philips Electronics BV v. Remington Consumer Products Ltd*, delivered on 23 January 2001, [2001] ETMR 48.

[99] Ibid.; *Philips Electronics BV v. Remington Consumer Products Ltd* [1998] RPC 283.

[100] *Philips Electronics BV v. Remington Consumer Products Ltd* [1998] RPC 283.

[101] Case C-299/99 *Philips Electronics NV v. Remington Consumer Products Ltd* [2002] ECR I-5475, [2003] Ch 159, [2003] RPC 14.

Nevertheless, it would seem sensible to see what issues this provision can raise. The need for the value conferred by the shape to be substantial has been emphasized,[102] and it must be the shape itself, rather than the overall image of the product, that must be responsible for the extra value.[103]

The section was invoked in the *Philips* case and this gave an English court the opportunity to express itself on the matter for the first time. It was held that the provision excluded '*shapes which exclusively add some sort of value (design or functional appearance or perhaps something else …) to the goods* disregarding *any value attributable to the trade mark* [that is, source identification] *function*'.[104] In the case at issue, the shaving head had an engineering function that rendered it very effective and this was seen as adding substantial value to the product, especially because it had already been held that the shape was not distinctive and could therefore not have a source identification function. The exception is only logical in so far as it targets the trade mark protection of the sign when it does not fulfil the traditional trade mark function of source identification. The *Philips* case is an extreme example of such a case, because the sign was held not to be distinctive and capable of identifying a source at all.

A case in which the shape does allow source identification, but nevertheless gives substantive value to the goods presents more of a dilemma. Trade mark protection will necessarily apply to both aspects, comprised in a single shape, and not just to the trade mark function. Jacob J's ruling in the *Philips* case seems to suggest that this case will not be covered by the exception, because the shape does not 'exclusively' add some other value to the goods. This approach is to be supported. Only those extreme cases in which trade mark protection would be granted to a shape that would have no—or almost no—value as a source identification function should be targeted by the exception. Those extreme cases do not belong in trade mark law, because the basic function of a trade mark is not fulfilled by such a mark and perhaps such shapes should seek protection in the various design rights, reflecting their success in coming up with an aesthetically pleasing design for their product.

Even heavy advertising cannot overcome the hurdle. An advertising campaign before an attempt at registration can make the public familiar with the mark and get the mark recognized as a distinctive sign, but it remains a shape that adds substantial value and, because there is no proviso for this provision, such a shape simply cannot constitute a trade mark. There seems to be underlying policy reason that such a shape must be available to all traders.

The European Court of Justice confirmed this in a case that dealt with an application for the registration of sloping stitching, contrasting colour bands, seams, and further stitching for trousers (G-Star trousers).[105] The national court had accepted that such a sign added substantial value to the goods: the shape of the trousers that resulted from it had indeed become the example par excellence of a style or fashion. That added substantial value, but also made it necessary, from a policy point of view, that other traders could compete with goods of the same style or fashion. From a UK point of view, however, the conclusion that stitching, etc., can amount to a shape and that substantial value was added even if the mark had also a certain level of distinctiveness is not so obvious.

---

[102] *Adidas v. De Laet*, Benelux Court, 23 December 1985, [1985] Jun 38.

[103] *Superconfex v. Burberrys*, Benelux Court, 14 April 1989, [1989] Jun 19.

[104] *Philips Electronics BV v. Remington Consumer Products Ltd* [1998] RPC 283, *per* Jacob J.

[105] Case C-371/06 *Benetton Group SpA v. G-Star International BV*, judgment of 20 September 2007, not yet reported, available online at curia.europa.eu.

Section 3(3)

The next part of the Act, s. 3(3), adds further restrictions. No mark may be registered if, first, it is contrary to public policy or accepted principles of morality or, secondly, if it would have the effect of deceiving the public.

Morality

The first category will, of course, be one that will be hard to predict given the inherent changeability of such issues as public policy and morality. On the one hand, the Registrar has taken the view that the religious connotations of the word 'Hallelujah' meant that it was inappropriate to allow it as a trade mark for women's clothing,[106] and presumably there would be similar protection granted to, for example, symbols of significance to Muslims or Buddhists. On the other hand, claims that the use of the mark 'Oomphies' for footwear should be refused, because of its connotations of sex appeal and even its potential encouragement for foot fetishists, were ignored and registration allowed in *Re La Marquise Footwear's Application*.[107]

The logic behind these cases seems to be that one needs to look at the intrinsic qualities of the mark. These intrinsic qualities need to contravene generally accepted moral principles for the prohibition to apply.[108] Marks that needed to be used in a certain context to become objectionable are not covered by the prohibition. An example of the latter scenario was the mark 'FCUK', which was capable of being seen as a swear word, but to whether and to which extent this would be the case depended on the circumstances of its use.[109] It escaped the prohibition. An example of the former scenario was the mark 'Jesus' for clothing. Any commercial use or appropriation of that name would be anathema to Christians.[110]

Deceiving the public

The second category of prohibited marks in s. 3(3) of the 1994 Act has given rise—in its earlier, but similar, formulations—to more extensive discussion. The subsection itself points out, inter alia, that the deception may arise in connection with the nature of the goods or services, their quality, or their geographical origin. In *Re Royal Worcester Corset Co's Application*,[111] trade mark registration was refused for the use of the company's name as a trade mark on corsets, because the application did not distinguish between corsets made by the company in Worcester, Massachusetts, and other corsets, and, in any event, no royal patronage had been conferred on the goods.[112] Thus the proposed mark was doubly deceptive. Likewise, the word 'Orlwoola' could not be registered for use on goods that were not all wool;[113] here the phonetic equivalence gave rise to the deception. More fortunate was the proprietor of the *Queen Diana Trade Mark*[114] used on Scotch whisky. The typical consumer may have assumed that there had been royal patronage of a drink named after the then likely future designation of Diana Princess of Wales, but it was held that there was no deception because—by what, at the time, must have seemed to the

---

[106] *Re Hallelujah Trade Mark* [1976] RPC 605.
[107] (1946) 64 RPC 27.
[108] Case T-140/02 *Sportwetten GmbH Gera v. OHIM* [2005] ECR II-3247.
[109] *Woodman v. French Connection Ltd* [2007] RPC 1.
[110] *Basic Trademark SA's Trade Mark Application* [2005] RPC 25, but religous significance on its own is not sufficient.
[111] (1909) 26 RPC 185.
[112] See also *Waterford Wedgwood plc v. David Nagli Ltd* [1998] FSR 92 (a case decided under the 1994 Act).
[113] (1909) 26 RPC 185.
[114] [1991] RPC 395.

proprietor a remarkable stroke of good fortune—the name had been in use since 1971 and this honest use, during which time a reputation had been gained, was sufficient to deny any allegation of deception.

Elizabeth Florence Emanuel v. Continental Shelf 128 Ltd[115] provided the European Court of Justice with an opportunity to explain the underlying provision in the Directive on which s. 3(3)(b) is based. Ms Emanuel is a well-known designer of wedding wear. She registered the trade mark 'Elizabeth Emanuel' for her company. Later, the business, good-will, and the registered trade mark were assigned to Frostprint Ltd, which immediately changed its name to Elizabeth Emanuel International. Soon afterwards, Ms Emanuel left the business. After another assignment, the new company, with which Ms Emanuel has no links, applied to register another trade mark, 'ELIZABETH EMANUEL'. Ms Emanuel filed a notice of opposition to that application and, in September 1999, she lodged an application to revoke the registered trade mark 'ELIZABETH EMANUEL'. In her view, the registration of her name by a company with which she has no links is likely to deceive the public that still associates her name with wedding gear, but she has no involvement whatsoever in that company's wedding gear.

The Court refused to establish the narrow link between the use of a name and decep-tion, simply because the person whose name is used is no longer involved. In the view of the Court:

(i) A trade mark corresponding to the name of the designer and first manufacturer of the goods bearing that mark may not, by reason of that particular feature alone, be refused registration on the ground that it would deceive the public, ... in particular where the goodwill associated with that trade mark, previously registered in a different graphic form, has been assigned together with the business making the goods to which the mark relates.

(ii) A trade mark corresponding to the name of the designer and first manufacturer of the goods bearing that mark is not, by reason of that particular feature alone, liable to revocation on the ground that that mark would mislead the public, ... in particular where the goodwill associated with that mark has been assigned together with the business making the goods to which the mark relates.[116]

The applicant is therefore required to prove actual deception. In the absence of that proof, the right holder that has acquired the trade mark in a bona fide way as a tradable com-modity in its own right can continue to use it. Or, having obtained the business, nothing will stand in the way of additional trade mark registrations.

Clearly, s. 3(3) represents a sensible and necessary set of controls.

Section 3(4)

It is not possible to register any mark use of which is forbidden by other laws, according to s. 3(4). The best example of this is the provision preventing the use of red crosses or red crescents for any purpose apart from the humanitarian activities of the Red Cross and related organizations.[117] Section 3(5) prevents registration of specially protected emblems. This is a reference to s. 4, which establishes that the use of a wide range of royal arms and insignia is only allowed with the permission of royalty, and also makes clear[118] that a representation of either the Union Jack or of the national flags of the component

---

[115] Case C-259/04 *Elizabeth Florence Emanuel v. Continental Shelf 128 Ltd* [2006] ECR I-3089, [2006] ETMR 56.

[116] Ibid., at [51] and [53].

[117] Geneva Conventions Act 1957, s. 6; *Harrison v. Teton Valley Trading Co. Ltd* [2004] 1 WLR 2577 (CA).

[118] TMA 1994, s. 4(2).

countries of the UK shall not be registered if that use would be either misleading or grossly offensive.

There is analogous protection, conferred by s. 4(3), for national emblems and other such insignia of all signatory states to the Paris Convention,[119] and of international agencies of which any Paris Convention state is a member.[120] Thus the unauthorized use of a wide range of insignia is controlled as a matter of law, rather than as one of discretion. In this and other ways, the 1994 Act has fulfilled the government's aim of reducing the (inherently unpredictable) discretionary powers of the Registrar.

Section 3(6)

Having said that, however, the final part of s. 3 appears to lead in an entirely opposite direction. Under s. 3(6), a trade mark shall not be registered if the application is made in bad faith. The Court of Appeal dealt with the concept of registration in bad faith in *Harrison v. Teton Valley Trading Co. Ltd*.[121] The Court held that, when determining whether an application to register was made in bad faith within s. 3(6) of the 1994 Act, the court was required to consider the applicant's mental state and all of the relevant circumstances of the particular case. And, because registration of a trade mark was designed to enable bona fide proprietors to protect their proprietary rights without having to prove unfair trading, the dishonest person or the person with low standards could not be permitted to obtain such a registration in circumstances under which a person abiding by a reasonable standard would not proceed with the registration. The test, in this respect, is a combined objective and subjective test, and the proper standard is that of acceptable commercial behaviour as observed by reasonable and experienced persons in the particular commercial area being examined—which excludes behaviour that might have become prevalent, but which, on examination, would not be deemed acceptable.

In the case at issue, the applicant had applied to trade mark the name of a drink ('Chinawhite'), the recipe of which he had received from the bar manager of the bar with the same name, which had developed the recipe and made its staff sign an agreement of confidentiality. In the circumstances, a person in the applicant's position, adopting proper standards and despite believing what the bar manager had told him—that is, that he was not bound by such an agreement—would not have applied for a monopoly that would enable him to prevent opponents carrying on their business of selling Chinawhite cocktails and drinks under that name as they presently were. Accordingly, the application to register was made in bad faith.

Section 3(6) of the 1994 Act was also raised in *Mickey Dees (Nightclub) Trade Mark*,[122] a case that came before the Register of Trade Marks and which, to a certain degree, involved both examples. MD—known as 'Mickey Dee'—had applied for a trade mark in the name 'Mickey Dees' in respect of '*provision of nightclub services; presentation of live music performances*'. He only provided the latter of the range of services listed in the application, however, and, at the same time, he was employed as manager of a nightclub that his employer had baptized Mickey Dees. It was held that he acted in bad faith when he applied for the mark in respect of the provision of nightclub services;[123] his application resulted in his employer being unable to register the trade mark.

---

[119] Ibid., s. 57.
[120] Ibid., s. 58.
[121] *Harrison v. Teton Valley Trading Co. Ltd* [2004] 1 WLR 2577, [2005] FSR 10 (CA).
[122] [1998] RPC 359.
[123] Ibid.

A similar result was reached when a sole distributor for the UK registered the 'Travelpro' trade mark in the UK for goods that were very similar to those that he distributed under the contract and in respect of which his US partner had obtained a trade mark registration in the USA. The distributor's application was held to have been made in bad faith.[124]

Section 3(6) presents a clear overlap with the earlier provisions of the section: an application that is clearly deceptive, or which implies, without permission, some royal connection, will also be an application not made in good faith. It also overlaps with the protection conferred by s. 5 on owners of previous marks, because clearly a later attempt to register an already registered name is likely to be one made in bad faith. Thus the 'bad faith' exception has potential for considerable use; it may best be regarded as a general catch-all provision.

Relative grounds for refusal of registration

It is now necessary to turn to the second group of unregistrable marks—namely, those that cannot be registered not because of their own inherent problems, but because of the pre-existing presence in the market of other similar or identical marks on other similar or identical goods or services. Section 5 of the 1994 Act and its related provisions provide the relevant rules.[125]

An earlier mark

The first thing to establish is that, in looking at the pre-existing marks that may affect the registrability of a new mark, it is necessary to cast the net widely and look beyond merely what trade marks have been registered in the UK. Section 5 refers to an 'earlier trade mark' and this key phrase is explained by the following section as including all UK marks, the Community trade mark and trade marks registered through the provisions of the Madrid Protocol, and also applications for trade marks[126] in each case in which that mark has, in effect, an earlier priority date. Even marks that have lapsed are protected for a year after their expiry unless they have not been used in the two years prior to their expiry, according to s. 6(3) of the Act.

That phrase, by virtue of s. 6(1)(c) of the 1994 Act, also covers well-known trade marks— that is, those marks explained by s. 56 of the Act as being well-known for the purposes of the Paris Convention—namely, a mark of a person or business from any signatory country who, although not in business or even in possession of business goodwill in the UK, nevertheless has a mark that is well known. It is not clear from the wording of the legislation whether the mark in question has to be well known in the UK or merely in one or more other signatory state. If the latter is the case, then an example of such a mark may be the logo of a major airline, but one that does not fly into the UK; if the former is the case,[127] the airline, in order to benefit from this protection, would have to show that its mark was well known in the UK, which is difficult to disassociate from the presence of goodwill. If the airline is, in fact, used by many UK travellers, this will suggest that it has goodwill in the UK and is also well known, but if it confines itself primarily to flying citizens of its own state, it seems that it will neither be well known in the UK, nor have goodwill here, and thus will not be protected by these provisions.

---

[124] *Travelpro Trade Mark* [1997] RPC 867.
[125] See *Wild Child Trade Mark* [1998] RPC 455.
[126] TMA 1994, s. 6(2).
[127] As suggested by R. Annand and H. Norman (1994) *Blackstone's Guide to the Trade Marks Act 1994*, Oxford: Blackstone Press, p. 31. See also M. Blakeney '"Well-known" marks' (1994) 11 EIPR 481.

If there is goodwill in the UK, which will therefore be protected separately by the tort of passing off, a further route exists to protect that goodwill against the possibility of the subsequent registration of an overlapping trade mark. Section 5(4) of the 1994 Act makes clear that registration of a later trade mark will be denied if its use will be prevented by any prior legal right, including by a specific reference the tort of passing off (and also copyright and design law).[128] Thus the holder of a non-proprietary right in goodwill is also regarded as the holder of a relevant 'earlier right', although not an 'earlier trade mark', and this will give rights not under the rest of s. 5, but, for example, in s. 7.

The relative grounds

Having ascertained what is an 'earlier trade mark', it is now necessary to consider the ways in which such a mark will intervene so as to prevent a subsequent registration. The Act offers a three-tier system of protection. This system is, in essence, the same as that used for infringement cases. We therefore refer the reader to the next chapter for a more in-depth analysis.

Section 5(1)

Firstly, and most simply, no trade mark can ever be registered if it is identical to an earlier mark and is used on identical goods or services,[129] this being perhaps a relatively unlikely scenario. The more likely situation is that in which either, or both, the mark, or the goods or services are not identical, but merely similar.

Section 5(2)

So, secondly, a mark must also not be registered if it is *either* identical to an earlier mark and to be used on similar goods and services, *or* similar to an earlier mark and to be used on identical *or* similar goods and services.[130] This is, however, subject to a proviso—namely, that the overlap must cause confusion on the part of the public. So the essential question to ask is whether the similarities in question are likely to confuse. Obviously there is a likelihood that any such proposed mark may already have hit trouble under s. 3 as being either a deceptive mark or one sought in bad faith.

What will be regarded as 'similar' for the purpose of s. 5(2) is unclear, but the courts have experience of considering this type of issue under s. 12 of the 1938 Act. It is clear from the old case law, which still appears to be relevant here, that the question of similarity cannot really be untangled from the necessary presence of confusion. So, in *Re Revue Trade Mark*,[131] 'Revue' had been registered for a range of photographic equipment—including cameras, light meters, exposure meters, binoculars, and other apparatus—and the applicants for a mark in 'Revuetronic' sought to remove it from the register on the grounds of non-use. There was, however, clear use—at the least in relation to binoculars and exposure meters—and this was regarded as evidence of use in the photographic trade. The Registrar pointed out that exposure meters were the same type of goods as cameras, flashguns, and other items used in the actual process of photography, but that goods such as projectors and enlargers used in the process of developing the film were in a separate category. Clearly, there may be some confusion between the various items used to take a photograph, but not between those items and the physically quite separate items used to develop the film, elsewhere, later, and often by someone else.

---

[128] See *Wild Child Trade Mark* [1998] RPC 455.
[129] TMA 1994, s. 5(1).
[130] Ibid., (2).
[131] [1979] RPC 27.

Another illustration of this is the splendid case of *Re Seahorse Trade Mark*.[132] 'Seahorse' was already registered for marine engines, but its proprietor was in the business of making outboard motors for dinghies and suchlike with a horsepower ranging from 1 to 115. A new application was made to register 'Seahorse', again for marine engines, but this time the engines were huge engines designed to power large seagoing ships of over 5,000 horsepower. The registration was allowed, because the different character of the products ensured that there would be no confusion.

Re Hack's Application[133] provides a final instance in which the similarity of the goods was the subject of discussion. The mark 'Black Magic' had already been registered for what remains a widely recognized box of chocolates and the proprietors of that mark objected to the proposed use of the same words on a new brand of laxatives. Evidence that some laxatives were sold with a chocolate flavouring, and further evidence that many shops sold both chocolates and laxatives, combined to enable Morton J to find that there was a clear risk of confusion and thus that the application in respect of laxatives should not be registered.

From cases concerned with the similarity of goods, we can now turn to cases that consider similarities between marks. Again, this will be a question of fact and relevant factors may include not only the mark itself, but also the surrounding circumstances of its use. Clearly, the marks 'Lancia' and 'Lancer' are, in themselves, very similar and, if the products in question were sold in a crowded market or a busy pub, registration of one would not be appropriate if there was a prior registration of the other. In *Re Lancer Trade Mark*,[134] however, the products in question were two types of car. Cars are bought with care, and with the likelihood of inspections, detailed brochures, and guidance (or persuasion) by attentive sales staff. In those circumstances, both could be registered, because all of the circumstances indicated that confusion would not be caused.

Section 5(3)

There is a third level of protection. In certain circumstances, prior use of a mark, whether similar or identical, will prevent a subsequent registration even for totally dissimilar goods or services. This arises in cases in which the earlier mark has gained a reputation and the subsequent use of the same mark in a different context would either take unfair advantage of, or be detrimental to, the distinctive character or repute of the earlier trade mark.[135] This is an entirely new provision in the UK trade mark law[136] and its effect is therefore not entirely clear. It seems to revolve around the mark having developed a reputation such that people associate the mark with that proprietor. It is less clear what form the subsequent use might take. Clearly, if a subsequent trade mark applicant were to seek to use a renowned mark such as, for example, the masthead logo of *The Independent* newspaper as a trade mark on a range of violent videos, clear detriment would be caused to the newspaper proprietors—but the phrase 'unfair advantage' appears to go much further.[137] Arguably, any use of a renowned trade mark by another is making an unwarranted and unfair use of the mark to the repute of which the later applicant has done nothing to contribute. It has nevertheless been held that dilution and detriment need to be demonstrated, and cannot simply be assumed to exist.[138]

Thus identical marks used on identical goods lead to immediate unregistrability. In cases in which similarities are involved, it is the presence of confusion that leads to

---

[132] [1980] RPC 250.   [133] (1940) 58 RPC 91.

[134] [1987] RPC 303.   [135] TMA 1994, s. 5(3).

[136] Although cf the passing-off case of *Lego System A/S v. Lego M Lemelstrich* [1983] FSR 155, discussed in Chapter 28.

[137] See H. Carty, 'Do marks with a reputation merit special protection?' [1997] 12 EIPR 684.

[138] *Intel Corp. Inc. v. CPM United Kingdom Ltd* [2007] RPC 35.

unregistrability. And in those in which identical or similar marks are used on dissimilar goods and services, it is the presence of harm to the reputation of the earlier mark that will prevent registration of the later mark.

In all cases, the consent of the proprietor of the earlier mark negates the operation of the section.[139]

Section 7

This clear framework, designed to ensure that there is no damaging duplication of trade marks, has, however, one clear and surprising exception. This is created by s. 7 of the 1994 Act. This provides that the Registrar can still register a trade mark even when there is already an earlier trade mark as designated by s. 5(1), (2), or (3), or an earlier right, as defined by subsection (4). This possibility arises in cases in which there has been 'honest concurrent use'[140] of the two marks and this phrase is stated to have the same meaning as in s. 12(2) of the 1938 Act.[141]

In deciding whether the honest concurrent use should be allowed, the principles laid down by Lord Tomlin in *Re Alex Pirie & Sons Ltd's Application*[142] remain relevant. The extent of confusion, the honesty of the parties, the length of the use, and the size of the applicant's trade are all factors to be brought into the equation. Longer use and larger trade will both help the honest applicant.

Problems are caused by this provision. Firstly, the very fact that honest concurrent use may be permitted means that the risk of confusion to the consumer remains a clear possibility, and this clearly undermines and devalues the entire concept of the trade mark as a clear badge of origin, and as a valuable trading asset. Secondly, the effect of the section is limited in that the presence of earlier rights of all kinds in respect of which there has been honest concurrent use, although no bar to a registration as such, is stated[143] to confer on the proprietor of those earlier rights a right to object to the later registration. The Registrar, in the first place, will then have to decide whether confusion or harm to reputation will ensue from the prospective dual registration. So considerable additional uncertainty will arise from the operation of the section.

The third problem is, however, more fundamental: there is no provision whatsoever in the Harmonization Directive for an exception of this type. Indeed, the position is quite the opposite under Art. 4, which is the basis of s. 5 of the 1994 Act. Article 4 states clearly that a mark shall not be registered in the cases to which s. 5 of the 1994 Act applies, while s. 7 of the 1994 Act specifically applies as an exception to cases in relation to which s. 5 of the Act would otherwise apply. It is hard to see any reason why the proprietor of an earlier mark whose interests are harmed by a subsequent registration based on the honest concurrent use exception should not jump on the first plane to Luxembourg and require that the European Court of Justice (assuming that no domestic tribunal is so willing) strike out s. 7 of the 1994 Act as being wholly incompatible with both the Directive that it ostensibly seeks to implement and, for good measure, with the Community trade marks system as well.

The examination system

When the 1994 Act was first passed, the Registrar would examine the application on the point of relative grounds and eventually decide whether or not to grant the trade mark. Many other European countries already at that stage had an opposition system instead. An

---

[139] TMA 1994, s. 5(5).   [140] Ibid., s. 7(1).
[141] Ibid., (3).   [142] (1933) 50 RPC 147 at 159–60.
[143] TMA 1994, s. 7(2).

opposition system leaves it to the existing right holders to defend their rights by raising an opposition against a new application that could fall foul of s. 5 of the UK's 1994 Act.

The Act allowed for the eventual introduction of such a system in the UK and this has now happened as of 1 October 2007. The Registrar will still search the relevant registers and send the results to the applicant; if, in the view of the examiner, there are existing marks that conflict with the mark applied for, the applicant is given a choice of whether to continue with the application, to amend it by reducing the list of goods or services, or to withdraw it. If the application is not withdrawn, the Registrar will notify all existing rights holders: holders of UK trade marks are notified automatically; EU trade mark owners need to opt in and pay a fee. It is then up to the existing rights holders to oppose the registration and launch the opposition procedure.[144]

The final word

Much of the new law on unregistrable marks is nothing but sensible, for the most part building on previous good practice—but the new law provides, in places, for great potential uncertainty, for example in denying registration for shapes that add value to a product and in creating the bad faith exception.

Special marks

So far, we have been concerned entirely with registration by a proprietor of the trade mark that he or she uses him or herself on his or her own goods. There are now, however, two quite distinct ways in which groups of traders, rather than individuals, can seek a form of joint trade mark that protects their joint, rather than individual, reputation. The 1994 Act retains the pre-existing category of certification marks, but adds the new concept of the collective mark.

Certification marks

Certification marks are unique in that, until 1994, they were the only way in which a group of traders could obtain trade mark protection as a group and also unique in that, then and now, they are the only form of trade mark under which the quality of the product is testified to by the existence of the trade marks. Of course, many trade marks, in reality, make a link in the consumer's mind between the mark and the quality of the goods or services provided, but a mark can equally be created in respect of poor quality goods or services, other than in this field.

The principal provision of the 1994 Act in respect of these marks is s. 50. This defines a certification mark as an indication that the goods or services in question are, by the mark, '*certified by the proprietor of the mark in respect of origin, material, mode of manufacture of goods or performance of services, quality, accuracy or other characteristics*'. Note that this is a mark rather than a trade mark; there appears to be no requirement that the mark is used in the course of trading activity under the 1994 Act.[145] Indeed no such mark can be granted if the proprietors of the certification mark are in the business of supplying goods

---

[144] The Trade Marks (Relative Grounds) Order 2007, SI 2007/1976 and The Trade Marks (Amendment) Rules 2007, SI 2007/2076. The power to make these changes was conferred on the Secretary of State by TMA 1994, s. 8.

[145] Cf '*Sea Island Cotton*' *Certification Trade Mark* [1989] RPC 87.

or services of the kind certified.[146] It will thus normally be a trade association who will seek this type of mark.

Detailed regulations adapting the general trade mark regime to the needs of this different type of mark are found in Sch. 2 to the 1994 Act, but the general principles remain applicable. The main change of any significance is that the geographical origin of goods or services—normally unregistrable unless prior factual distinctiveness can be shown[147]—can be appropriately—indeed, typically—registered as a certification mark, because the origin of goods or services is often the hallmark of their quality. Champagne, from that region of France, would be an excellent example.

Problems of geographical origin arose in one of the few reported cases on these marks. In *Re Stilton Trade Mark*,[148] a certification trade mark was sought by an association of manufacturers of Stilton cheese, a business long associated with the area around the Leicestershire town of Melton Mowbray. The problem arose, however, that Stilton is itself a village some 50 miles away. The court was, however, satisfied that no cheese of any kind had been made in the village for many years, and that there was ample evidence of the connection between the cheese and the Melton Mowbray area so as to justify the award of a certification trade mark.

Unfortunately, the other grounds for refusal of registration in s. 3(1)(c) of the 1994 Act have not been waived and apply equally to certification marks. Thus a certification mark certifying the quality of the goods—as did the mark in the *Stilton* case, for example—which is a criterion in s. 50 of the Act for the grant of such a mark will fall foul of s. 3(1)(c), which excludes quality if a trade mark exclusively consists of a mark indicating the quality of the goods unless prior factual distinctiveness can be shown. Thus the need to show either such distinctiveness or to include other material in the mark, which may not fall within the rules on certification marks, will pose further problems that will, in all likelihood, further restrict the already limited use made of certification marks.

Collective marks

This is, then, an appropriate moment to introduce the new collective mark. This is introduced into UK law (the concept having long been familiar in Europe and the USA) by s. 49 of the 1994 Act. This states that a collective mark is one that '*distinguishes the goods or services of members of the association which is the proprietor of the mark from those of other undertakings*'. Thus the only lawful proprietor of this type of mark will be a trade association.

Again there are detailed rules applying to such marks, found in Sch. 1 to the 1994 Act, but, again, these adapt the mainstream rules to this type of mark. As with certification marks, an indication of geographical origin—but no other matter excluded by s. 3(1)(c)—can be registered as a collective mark, but this does not entitle the proprietor to prohibit others from using such indications themselves, as long as that use is '*in accordance with honest practices in industrial or commercial matters*'.[149] No definition of this phrase is provided.

Such marks, being easier to obtain, may well replace the certification mark over a period of time. In any event, it is easy to envisage situations in which a group of small traders decides to pool their energies and resources, and seek to obtain a collective mark

---

146   TMA 1994, Sch. 2, para. 4.
147   TMA 1994, s. 3(1)(c).
148   [1967] RPC 173.
149   TMA 1994, Sch. 1, para. 3.

in relation to which it would be beyond them to gain individual trade mark registration, either through lack of resources or, if all in a common trade, because of potential problems with lack of distinctiveness. The 1994 Act has sought to ease the burden placed on the applicant for a trade mark. To a great extent, the criteria for registration have been eased in favour of the applicant and against the exercise of discretion by the Registrar. It is, however, clear from this area of the law in particular that fuller thought could, and should, have been given to the precise drafting of the 1994 Act.

Uses of trade marks

If a trade mark is registered in accordance with the foregoing rules, it confers on the proprietor of the mark exclusive rights in the mark and the right to bring actions for infringement of the mark;[150] the mark becomes an item of personal property.[151] The effect of the registration is to confer these exclusive rights for a period of ten years, which is renewable for further periods of ten years[152]—an extension of the seven-year period provided by the law prior to 1994 and bringing UK law into harmony with that of most other countries.

Given that a trade mark is an item of property, naturally, proprietors of trade marks will wish to trade with them and the 1994 Act understands that this is the case. Clear provisions exist permitting (relatively) unrestricted dealing with trade marks.

Assignment

The first major provision is found in s. 24 of the 1994 Act, which permits assignment or other disposition of a trade mark in just the same way as is the case with any other items of personal property. This right to assign is expressly stated to exist irrespective of whether business goodwill is assigned at the same time or not, and is also capable of being exercised in part, rather than wholly: for example, in respect of particular uses of the mark or its application to particular goods. Assignments must be made in writing or, in case of an English company, by the affixing of the company's seal.

Although clearly a sensible provision and one that reflects commercial reality, the ease by which assignment is permitted clearly goes far towards breaking down the traditional link between the mark and its proprietor. This is echoed by s. 32(3) of the 1994 Act, which, as has been seen, insists that the proposed use of the mark has to be declared as part of the registration procedure, but that use does not have to be by the applicant him or herself and may merely be with his or her consent. Thus use by an assignee will count as use for these purposes, as will use by a licensee.

Licensing

Licensing of trade marks is permitted by s. 28 of the 1994 Act and the sections that follow it. The restriction under the old s. 28 of the 1938 Act on the registration of a mark if the purpose of that registration was to facilitate trafficking or dealing in the mark has been completely swept away,[153] again reflecting the commercial need to use a trade mark as a

---

[150] Ibid., s. 9.

[151] Ibid., s. 72.

[152] Ibid., s. 42.

[153] For criticism of this provision, see *Re American Greeting Corp's Application* [1984] 1 All ER 426, [1984] 1 WLR 189.

tradable asset. A licence may be granted in whole, or in part, but, in any event, there is a requirement that, to be valid, the licence must be put in writing by its grantor.[154] A licensee of a trade mark is entitled, subject to any agreement to the contrary, to require the proprietor of the mark to take infringement proceedings if his or her interests are threatened and, in the case of inaction by the proprietor, after two months, the licensee is granted the right to take proceedings in his or her own name.[155] This approach fits in with the fact that a trade mark licence is traditionally seen as a right to use the trade mark, which remains owned by the licensor. Any goodwill created through the use of the trade mark accrues in the mark and is owned by the right holder-licensor.[156]

In many cases, the parties will wish to restrict the number of licences so that the licensee gains the monopoly benefits normally enjoyed by the proprietor of a mark. This can be done in the form of an exclusive licence, under which the licensee has the sole right to use a trade mark, excluding even exploitation by the proprietor of the mark him or herself.[157] An exclusive licensee has his or her own right to bring infringement proceedings that is not contingent on any action by the proprietor and is, in effect, in the same position as an assignee of the trade mark,[158] subject again to the terms of the agreement.

There is, of course, a problem that arises in relation to exclusive licences. Any such licence has the effect of moving the monopoly right from the originator of the trade mark, who may, in broad terms, be regarded as having deserved such a privilege, to another. Such extensions of monopoly rights have naturally attracted the interest of the EU, but in this area, there are no block exemptions, making the likely interest of EU competition law all the stronger at first glance.

Registering the transaction

The fact that both assignees and licensees may enjoy rights of action means that care needs to be taken to alert others to the existence of their interests. This is achieved by s. 25 of the 1994 Act, which insists that various transactions relating to trade marks can be registered alongside the mark itself. The process is voluntary in that it is up to, for example, an assignee or licensee to seek registration of the transaction in question, but there is, to put it mildly, an incentive to register the transaction, because, by virtue of s. 25(3), rights against persons claiming a conflicting interest in the mark in ignorance of any such transaction and all the rights of licensees are ineffective in the absence of an application to register the relevant transaction. So, in reality, all affected transactions are likely to be formally registered.

An overview

That the old law needed reform was undoubted: its convolutions and complexities were considerable, and became worse as amendment after amendment was made. Its failure to

---

[154]   TMA 1994, s. 28(2).

[155]   Ibid., s. 30(2) and (3).

[156]   The latter point seems to have been doubted in the recent *Scandecor Development AB v. Scandecor Marketing AB* [1998] FSR 500, HC and [1999] FSR 26, CA (23 July 1998, unreported). It is submitted, however, that this case must be seen as a special case, due to the fact that the rights in the mark were at first owned by one company and that the licence deal formed part of the splitting-up process of that original company. In general, there is an absolute lack of cases in this area relating to licence contracts.

[157]   TMA 1994, s. 29(1).

[158]   Ibid., s. 31(1).

slot in with internationally recognized approaches was equally regrettable—but does the Trade Marks Act 1994 meet the objective of redressing these difficulties?

The answer must be that, in broad measure, it does. The new law creates a simpler, clearer, and better internationally coordinated approach and this is obviously to be welcomed. There is a pleasing symmetry, too, to the interrelationship and overlap between the principal provisions on registrability, infringement, and revocation, and it reflects an understanding of reality in terms of the need to assign or licence trade marks.

That there turned out to be gremlins in the drafting of the new law was inevitable and that there has been, and will have to be, considerable litigation to mark the boundaries of the new law in relation to new types of mark, such as shape and, in particular, tastes and smells, is unavoidable. Less justifiable perhaps are some of the inherently vague items of terminology that, for the most part, are, unsurprisingly, inherited from the Directive. Clearly, it takes time before a clear picture emerges as to what, for example, is a shape that gives value to a product or in what circumstances registration will be refused on the grounds of bad faith. Some clarifications have already been provided, but we are not yet there entirely. The retention of honest concurrent use as a defence seems particularly unfortunate, because it is flying in the face of the words of the Directive itself.

In terms of requirements for registration, the 1994 Act represents a move away from the role of trade mark law as a method of consumer protection and does not have the traditional assurance provided by the mark as a badge of quality. It offers registration to those trade marks that function (as a minimum) as a badge of origin, protecting a business against predatory rivals often engaged in cynical counterfeiting activity. Indeed, in this respect, the best litmus test of the new law—both in its pure domestic context and in its promotion of international accord—is whether it is successful in going at least some way to stemming the tidal wave of blatantly counterfeit goods that form a major blot on our trading landscape.

Further reading

CLARK, J., 'Adorning shavers with clover leaves: *Koninklijke Philips Electronics NV v. Remington Consumer Products Ltd*' (2006) 28 EIPR 6, 352.

GIOLA, F., 'Alicante and the harmonisation of intellectual property law in Europe: trade marks and beyond' (2004) 41 CML Rev 4, 975.

HANDLER, M., 'The distinctive problem of European trade mark law' (2005) 27 EIPR 9, 306.

KITCHIN, D., LLEWELYN, D., MELLOR, J., MEADE, R., MOODY-STUART, T. and KEELING, D. (2005) *Kerly's Law of Trade Marks and Trade Names*, 14th edn, London: Sweet and Maxwell, chs 8 and 9.

THOMPSON, C. and LADAS, B., 'How green is my trade mark? *Woolworths v. BP*' (2007) 29 EIPR 1, 29.

26
Trade marks—infringement and revocation

In trade mark law, just as in patent law, the issues of infringement and revocation, although separate, are inevitably interlocked in many examples of litigation. It is typical for a claim that a trade mark has been infringed to be countered by the argument that the trade mark has been wrongly registered in the first place; similarly, a revocation claim may be met by the counter-threat of an infringement allegation. The Trade Marks Act 1994 recognizes this symbiosis and the two separate concepts are the subject of well-coordinated legislation. It can be added that, in defining what will amount to an infringement, the Act also indirectly defines the scope of the rights that are given to the trade mark owner.

Infringement

Section 10 of the 1994 Act establishes the basic criteria for an infringement action. It is written to accord with the provisions of s. 5 of the Act, which, as has been seen, is designed to prevent the concurrent use of duplicate or similar marks. If a mark is already on the Trade Marks Register, it is an infringement to use the same mark for the same goods or services.[1] If either, or both, of the two marks and the product in question are similar rather than identical, there will be an infringement if the later use of the earlier mark will be likely to cause confusion to the public.[2] Finally, unauthorized use of an identical or a similar mark on totally different goods will also be an infringement if the repute of the original mark would be harmed by such a use.[3]

This crucial section is worded as follows:

10 Infringement of registered trade mark

(1) A person infringes a registered trade mark if he uses in the course of trade a sign which is identical with the trade mark in relation to goods or services which are identical with those for which it is registered.

(2) A person infringes a registered trade mark if he uses in the course of trade a sign where because—

    (a) the sign is identical with the trade mark and is used in relation to goods or services similar to those for which the trade mark is registered, or

    (b) the sign is similar to the trade mark and is used in relation to goods or services identical with or similar to those for which the trade mark is registered,

---

[1] TMA 1994, s. 10(1).

[2] Ibid., (2).

[3] Ibid., (3).

there exists a likelihood of confusion on the part of the public which includes the likelihood of association with the trade mark.

(3) A person infringes a registered trade mark if he uses in the course of trade a sign which—

(a) is identical with or similar to the trade mark, and

(b) is used in relation to goods or services which are not similar to those for which the trade mark is registered,[4]

where the trade mark has a reputation in the United Kingdom and the use of the sign, being without due cause, takes unfair advantage of, or is detrimental to, the distinctive character or the repute of the trade mark.

...

The application of each of these three subsections gives rise to a number of issues. Before turning to these issues, however, one preliminary matter is worth highlighting: a trade mark is often used as a shorthand term to describe the goods—but might this be an infringement of the mark? In other words, exactly how far do the rights of the trade mark owner under s. 10(1) and (2) of the 1994 Act go to stop use in the course of trade?

The judgment of the European Court of Justice in *Holterhoff v. Freiesleben*[5] sheds some light on this. Mr Freiesleben had registered the marks 'Spirit Sun' and 'Context Cut' in relation to diamonds and precious stones. Both marks correspond to a particular cut of precious stone and Mr Holterhoff had used the names to describe the kind of cut to his clients. Did this amount to trade mark infringement? The Court held that it did not, on the basis that the proprietor of a trade mark cannot rely on his or her exclusive right if a third party, in the course of commercial negotiations, reveals the origin of goods that he or she has produced him or herself and uses the sign in question solely to denote the particular characteristics of the goods on offer for sale, in such a way that there can be no question of the trade mark used being perceived as a sign indicative of the undertaking of origin.

Trade mark infringement requires the 'use in the course of trade' of the goods labelled with the trade mark. It is generally accepted that 'use' includes importation, even if the territorial scope of the 1994 Act is limited to the UK. So what exactly is the meaning of the concepts of 'use' and 'importation'? This is what the judgment of the European Court of Justice in *Class International BV v. Colgate-Palmolive Co. & ors*[6] addressed.

In this case, the goods—branded toothpaste—were lawfully under the external transit procedure or the customs warehousing procedure. There was no evidence that a purchaser had already been found. The Court had to define what was meant by the concept of 'importation' and whether it also covered the external transit procedure or the customs warehousing procedure. The Court held that interference with the exclusive right of the right holder needed to be shown. That exclusive right is necessarily limited to the member State concerned, or to the Community, in case of a Community trade mark. The interference that may be pleaded consists, in the Court's view, either in the release for free circulation of the goods or an offering or sale of those goods that necessarily entails putting them on the market in the Community. In the absence of such interference, the goods have not been imported and the right holder cannot invoke infringement of its trade mark. In this case ,such interference had not been shown, because only warehousing under the

---

4 Ibid., s. 10(3)(b) has now been deleted in the aftermath of the *Adidas* case (see later in this chapter), by means of the Trade Marks (Proof of Use, etc.) Regulations 2004, SI 2004/946.

5 Case C-2/00 *Holterhoff v. Freiesleben* [2002] ECR I-4187.

6 Case C-405/03 *Class International BV v. Colgate-Palmolive Co. & ors* [2006] 1 CMLR 14, [2006] 2 WLR 507.

customs procedure and the use of the external transit procedure had been demonstrated. The infringement claim was therefore bound to fail.[7]

Section 10(1)

A sign used in the course of trade

Section 10(1) of the 1994 Act refers to a 'sign' that is allegedly infringing and that is used by the alleged infringer. It is, first of all, necessary to define what is a 'sign' in any particular case.

In the *British Sugar* case,[8] Jacob J took the sign to be the word 'Treat'. The defendant, Robertson, had also used the phrase 'Robertson's Toffee Treat', but the two first words were regarded as added matter that described the goods. 'Treat' was the sign, or label, that was used to distinguish the goods. Additionally, s. 10(1) requires that the sign is used in the course of trade. That does not mean, however, that the sign should be used in a trade mark sense—that is, as a distinctive sign. In the *British Sugar* case, Jacob J gave the example of the phrase *'give your child a treat, give it Robertson's marmalade'*.[9] He argued that the use of the word 'treat' in that sentence, while clearly not used in a trade mark sense, could still come within the provisions of s. 10.[10] On the other hand, the use of the sign 'Crate & barrel', which was identical to the 'Crate & Barrel' mark registered in the UK, on the website of a shop in the Irish capital Dublin was not used in the course of trade in the UK, because the advertisement was merely intended to address a local Irish clientele to the shop premises and because no trade was taking place on the Internet through the website.[11]

One should not be carried away too easily by this 'use in the course of trade' argument, however, and one should, in any case, not rush too easily to the conclusion that there was no use in the course of trade—as the *Arsenal v. Reed* saga demonstrates clearly. Arsenal had registered a series of trade marks in relation to memorabilia. Reed sold Arsenal memorabilia bearing these or similar marks without having obtained a licence from Arsenal Football Club. When sued for trade mark infringement, Reed ran as a defence the argument that there was no use in the course of trade, because he was only using the marks to express loyalty towards the club. In the High Court,[12] Laddie J had accepted Reed's defence, and ruled that such use to express loyalty was not use in the course of trade and did therefore not amount to infringement. Nevertheless, he referred the matter to the European Court of Justice for a preliminary opinion.

That Court[13] disagreed with Laddie J's view and ruled that, in cases such as this, there would be infringement and that it is immaterial that, in the context of the use of the mark, the sign is perceived as a badge of support for, or loyalty or affiliation to, the trade mark proprietor. Laddie J, in his second judgment,[14] argued that, in coming to this conclusion, the European Court of Justice had reached a different conclusion on the fact and had therefore gone beyond its powers. He felt not bound by the judgment and ruled again in favour of Matthew Reed.

---

[7] See also *Mastercigars Direct Ltd v. Hunters & Frankau Ltd* [2006] RPC 32.

[8] *British Sugar plc v. James Robertson & Sons Ltd* [1996] RPC 281.

[9] Ibid.

[10] It had been accepted in the Scottish case *Bravado Merchandising Services Ltd v. Mainstream Publishing (Edinburgh) Ltd* [1996] FSR 205—the *Wet Wet Wet* case—that s. 10(1) required use in a trade mark sense. While applauding the outcome of the case, Jacob J disagreed with that view.

[11] *Euromarket Designs Inc. v. Peters* [2001] FSR 20.

[12] *Arsenal v. Reed* [2001] 2 CMLR 481, [2001] RPC 922.

[13] Case C-206/01 *Arsenal v. Reed* [2002] ECR I-7945, [2003] Ch 454.

[14] *Arsenal v. Reed* [2003] 1 All ER 137, [2003] 1 CMLR 382.

On appeal, the Court of Appeal[15] rejected Laddie J's approach to the interpretation and application of the European Court of Justice's opinion. The Court of Appeal's judgment highlights a couple of important points. Firstly, the reference to the European Court of Justice started from the point of view that any decision on infringement hinged on whether or not the use of the mark was use in the course of trade—that is, on trade mark use and an indication of origin. That issue was a separate point and a prerequisite for s. 10(1); if the prerequisite was not met, there was no need to continue the infringement examination under s. 10(1). The Court of Appeal, as well as the European Court of Justice, disagreed. In its view, one has to consider the mark as a property right and the question that needs to be asked is whether the use of the sign causes damage to the trade mark as a property right. In other words, would there be damage to the essential function of the trade mark as a badge of origin? There is therefore no prerequisite, but rather one substantial test that includes the trade issue. There is an inextricable link between the property-essential function issues and the use in the course of trade issue.

In this case, once Mr Reed's memorabilia left his stand, no one was able to determine any more whether they originated from him or from Arsenal. The origin function of the mark was therefore affected. That confusion element is vital in this context. This case is also remarkable because, in this way, it represents the first application of the after-sale confusion doctrine in English trade mark law: the confusion only arose when the consumers and the goods had left Mr Reed's stand.

The comparison

The main point in s. 10(1), and the test for infringement, is the comparison that needs to be made between the use of the claimant's trade mark in a normal and fair manner in relation to the goods for which it has been registered, and the way in which the defendant actually used its allegedly infringing sign, discounting added or surrounding[16] matter or circumstances.[17] For example, the use by the defendant of the surrounding words 'independent' and 'specialist' in combination with the claimant's 'Volvo' trade mark in a style that was similar to that of the registered trade mark had to be discounted.[18] The defendant still used an identical word in the course of trade and that constituted prima facie infringement under s. 10(1).

This brings us back to the test in relation to s. 10(1).

Identical signs

Firstly, this test will have to determine whether the sign and the trade mark can be considered to be identical. *LTJ Diffusion SA v. Sadas Vertbaudet SA*[19] clarifies the application in relation to this issue. When confronted with the question of whether the sign ARTHUR ET FÉLICIE was identical to the mark ARTHUR (mark and sign written in the same way, but in the sign, additional material has been added), the European Court of Justice ruled that a sign is identical with the trade mark if it reproduces, without any modification or addition, all of the elements constituting the trade mark or if, viewed as a whole, it contains

[15] *Arsenal v. Reed* [2003] RPC 696, [2003] 2 CMLR 800.

[16] See *United Biscuits (UK) Ltd v. Asda Stores Ltd* [1997] RPC 513.

[17] *Origins Natural Resources Inc. v. Origin Clothing Ltd* [1995] FSR 280, repeated obiter in *British Sugar plc v. James Robertson & Sons Ltd* [1996] RPC 281.

[18] *Aktiebolaget Volvo v. Heritage (Leicester) Ltd* [2000] FSR 253. The fact that the defendant had, until recently, been an approved Volvo dealer was also a factor in this case; cf Case C-63/97 *BMW AG v. Ronald Deenik* [1999] ECR I-905, [1999] All ER (EC) 235.

[19] Case C-291/00 *LTJ Diffusion SA v. Sadas Vertbaudet SA* [2003] ECR I-2799.

differences so insignificant that they may go unnoticed by an average consumer.[20] In that sense, both aural and visual identity may be required. Additions and modification bring the case outside the scope of s. 10(1), which seems to be restricted merely to cases of blatant piracy. In the same way that ARTHUR ET FÉLICIE was not identical to ARTHUR, COMPASS LOGISTICS was held not to be identical to COMPASS.[21] The criterion of identity is therefore a very strict one, even if the use of the average consumer somewhat blurs the test.[22]

Use in relation to identical goods or services

Secondly, because the section requires use of the sign in relation to goods or services that are identical to those for which the mark has been registered, one must also determine whether the goods or services in relation to which the allegedly infringing sign is used fall within the specification contained in the trade mark registration.[23]

In the *Treat* case,[24] that meant answering the question of whether Robertson's product was a dessert sauce or a syrup. Jacob J adopted a pragmatic approach on this point. He argued that the words in a trade mark specification should be construed in a practical manner, taking into account how the product is regarded for the purposes of trade. A trade mark specification was, after all, concerned with use in trade. Robertson's spread would hardly be used on desserts; despite the comments on the label, it was marketed in a jam jar and supermarkets regarded it as a spread. The pragmatic conclusion had indeed to be that, for the purposes of trade, it was neither a dessert sauce nor a syrup. Isolated and rare use of the product as a dessert sauce could not change that conclusion. The product was not identical to the goods in relation to which the trade mark was registered and the infringement claim based on s. 10(1) failed.

An example

Section 10(1) can have consequences that may surprise at first glance. The trade mark badge is also reproduced faithfully when one produces a scale model of a car. In *Adam Opel AG v. Autec AG*,[25] Opel had also registered its trade mark for toys. When Autec affixed the mark to the scale model, it was held to be a straightforward infringement under s.10(1).

Section 10(2)

Section 10(2) of the 1994 Act resembles s. 10(1). The term 'sign' and the concept of 'use in the course of trade' are used in the same way here as they were in relation to s. 10(1); once more, the comparison that needs to be made is between the use of the claimant's trade mark in a normal and fair manner in relation to the goods for which it has been registered, and the way in which the defendant actually used its allegedly infringing sign, discounting added or surrounding[26] matter or circumstances.[27] The essential difference is that s. 10(2) deals either with a similar, rather than identical, sign that is used in relation to identical or similar goods or services, or with an identical sign, but this time in relation

[20] *Reed Executive plc v. Reed Business Information Ltd* [2004] RPC 767 (CA).
[21] *Compass Publishing BV v. Compass Logistics Ltd* [2004] RPC 809.
[22] *Reed Executive plc v. Reed Business Information Ltd* [2004] RPC 767 (CA).
[23] Ibid.; see also *Avnet Inc. v. Isoact Ltd* [1998] FSR 16.
[24] *British Sugar plc v. James Robertson & Sons Ltd* [1996] RPC 281.
[25] Case C-48/05 *Adam Opel AG v. Autec AG* [2007] ETMR 33.
[26] See *United Biscuits (UK) Ltd v. Asda Stores Ltd* [1997] RPC 513.
[27] *Origin Natural Resources Inc. v. Origin Clothing Ltd* [1995] FSR 280, repeated obiter in *British Sugar plc v. James Robertson & Sons Ltd* [1996] RPC 281.

to similar, rather than identical, goods or services. And the use of the allegedly infringing sign must give rise to a likelihood of confusion, because of the similarity.

If we restrict the analysis to s. 10(2)(a) in a first stage, it might be said that the section involves a three-point test:[28]

- is the sign used in the course of trade?
- are the goods or services for which the sign is used similar to those in relation to which the trade mark has been registered?
- is there a likelihood of confusion because of that similarity?

Similarity

The first point of the test requires no further comment; the question of similarity, however, needs some further analysis. That question is wholly independent of the particular mark or of the defendant's sign and similarity constitutes a separate issue that needs to be established independently before one considers the third point of likelihood of confusion. The category of similar goods needs to be defined narrowly, because the trade mark owner should, as a starting point, be encouraged to register the mark for all classes of goods for which he or she wants to use the mark. A comparison of the use, users, and physical nature of the claimant's and the defendant's goods or services, the way in which they were sold or offered, and the extent to which they were competitive were the relevant factors in considering similarity.

When applying these criteria in the *Treat* case,[29] Jacob J arrived at the conclusion that Robertson's spread was not similar to dessert sauces and syrups, because it was different in physical nature (hardly pourable and in need of spooning out, as opposed to pourable), because market research put it in a different sector, and because it was sold in another location in the supermarket. In another case, it was held that television programmes with an adult content were not similar to videotapes and video discs, which were the products in relation to which the claimant had registered his trade mark.[30] In that case, the products were distributed in a different way.

Overall, in assessing similarity, account must be taken of all of the relevant factors that characterize the relationship between the goods or services. Among these factors, one finds the nature, intended purpose, method of use of the goods or services, and whether they are in competition with each other or whether instead they are complementary.[31]

One should not forget, however, that, as a minimum, similarity between the goods or services must be established. Absence of similarity cannot be overcome for the purposes of s. 10(2), not even if the mark is virtually identical to a mark that is distinctive to a very high level. Glassware and wine were held not to be similar, and that meant that there could not be infringement, even if the mark 'Waterford' was used for both.[32]

Confusion

The third point of confusion has created grave difficulties; what is clear is that it can only been treated separately from similarity and once the latter has been established.[33]

---

[28] *British Sugar plc v. James Robertson & Sons Ltd* [1996] RPC 281.

[29] Ibid.

[30] *Baywatch Production Co. Inc. v. The Home Video Channel* [1997] FSR 22.

[31] Case C-39/97 *Canon Kabushiki Kaisha v. Metro-Goldwyn-Mayer Inc.* [1998] ECR I-5507 at [23]; Case T-169/03 *Sergio Rossi v. OHIM – Sissi Rossi* [2005] ECR II-685 at [54].

[32] Case T-105/05 *Assembled Investments (Proprietary) Ltd v. OHIM – Waterford Wedgwood plc*, judgment of the Court of First Instance of 12 June 2007, not yet reported, available online at curia.europa.eu.

[33] See *Baywatch Production Co. Inc. v. The Home Video Channel* [1997] FSR 22.

Otherwise, stronger marks would get protection for a greater range of goods or services than weaker marks, because the use of a strong mark in relation to dissimilar goods might create confusion in the mind of the consumer.

'Confusion' requires simply that the consumer will be confused. Traditionally, this has been interpreted as meaning that the consumer, when confronted with the similar goods or services that are labelled with the sign, is confused about the origin of these goods or services and thinks that they originate from the trade mark owner. The major problem that arises in relation to this traditional link between confusion and origin is created by the Benelux law-based addition in the 1994 Act that confusion must now include the likelihood of association with the trade mark. Laddie J ruled, in *Wagamama*,[34] that the traditional approach could remain unchanged and that the addition did not change anything in English trade mark law.

That conclusion must now be doubted, however, even though the practical outcome in the *Wagamama* case must be correct. The reason for the doubt is found in the European Court of Justice's decision on the confusion–association point in *Sabel v. Puma*.[35] That case concerned two bounding feline trade marks and the German *Bundesgerichtshof* (Supreme Court) asked the European Court of Justice to explain the relevant provisions of the Trade Mark Directive.[36]

Sabel v. Puma

A careful analysis of the *Sabel* case is required in an attempt to clarify the situation.

The new concept of confusion

Two views were put to the Court. Firstly, the Benelux countries argued that their concept of association had been incorporated into the wording of the Directive and should be followed.[37] That meant that, in an extreme case, the likelihood of association may arise *'where the public considers the sign to be similar to the mark and perception of the sign calls to mind the memory of the mark, although the two are not confused'*.[38] For example, the 'Sabel' mark would infringe if, when confronted with that mark, the public would associate it with the 'Puma' mark in the sense that the Puma mark would come to mind, without leading the public to confuse the two marks and think that it saw the Puma mark.

Sabel, the Commission, and the UK strongly opposed this view. They argued that the wording of the Directive excluded this interpretation. The Court agreed and argued that:

> it follows from th[e] wording[39] that the concept of likelihood of association is not an alternative to that of likelihood of confusion, but serves to define its scope[; t]he terms of the provision itself exclude its application where there is no likelihood of confusion on the part of the public.[40]

The Directive only uses the concept of 'association' to define the scope of the concept of 'confusion'. For the purposes of the Directive, there can be no likelihood of association

---

[34] *Wagamama Ltd v. City Centre Restaurants* [1995] FSR 713.

[35] See further P. Torremans, 'The likelihood of association of trade marks: an assessment in the light of the recent case law of the Court of Justice' [1998] IPQ 295–310.

[36] Council Directive 89/104 EEC to approximate the laws of the member States relating to trade marks (1989) OJ L 40/1.

[37] Case 251/95 *Sabel BV v. Puma AG* [1997] ECR I-6191, [1998] 1 CMLR 445 at [14] and [15].

[38] Ibid. at [16].

[39] Of TMA 1994, s. 10(2)—that is, *'there exists a likelihood of confusion on the part of the public, which includes the likelihood of association with the earlier trade mark'*.

[40] Case 251/95 *Sabel BV v. Puma AG* [1997] ECR I-6191, [1998] 1 CMLR 445 at [18].

if there is not at least a certain form of confusion.[41] Likelihood of association is not an alternative to, but a way to define the meaning of, likelihood of confusion.[42]

The Court backs its view up with a reference to the *'tenth recital in the preamble of the Directive, according to which "the likelihood of confusion…constitutes the specific condition for such protection"'*.[43] But two types of likelihood of confusion need to be distinguished.[44] Firstly, the straightforward type of direct consumer confusion—that is, confusion as to origin—arises in the situation in which the public sees the sign, and links the goods labelled with it to the trade mark and its owner. In the *Sabel v. Puma* example, such a situation would arise if the public was confronted with the Sabel mark, thought that it saw the Puma mark, and assumed that the Sabel goods originated from Puma.

The second type of likelihood of confusion is somewhat more sophisticated. In this situation, the public is not directly confused, but it makes a connection between the proprietors of the sign and those of the mark, and confuses them. This type of confusion can be described as indirect confusion or association, and it is here that the inclusion of the concept of association in the concept of confusion plays its widening role. An example would be the situation in which the public connects the Sabel mark with the Puma mark due to the similarity between the two marks and assumes that there is a link between the two trade mark owners. The public might unjustifiably suspect the existence of a licence or any other kind of business link between the two companies involved.[45]

A likelihood of confusion needs, however, to be demonstrated[46] and that assessment needs to be made at global level.[47] There is no ground for presuming the existence of confusion merely because a likelihood of pure association existed, even for highly distinctive marks. Neither is the mere fact that a risk or possibility that an association may give rise to confusion could not be excluded sufficient.[48]

It is submitted that both types of confusion are now covered by the Directive and the 1994 Act, because, whereas the prerequisite of the likelihood of confusion needs to be adhered to, the limitation of the concept of confusion to confusion in relation to the origin of the product or service can no longer be sustained: to do so would be to empty the concept of association of its content. The argument that European trade mark law must now include a finding of infringement in cases in which there is, strictly speaking, no confusion in relation to origin and therefore offers an increased level of protection to the trade mark owner is supported by a number of factors. Firstly, at no point does the Court's judgment refer to the notion of confusion in relation to origin, even if the Advocate-General

---

[41] Even the Benelux Court now recognizes that its previous views that were strictly based on association no longer apply under the Directive's regime. Consequently, on the one hand, the owner of a trade mark can oppose the use of a sign that resembles his or her own if the public is likely to be confused (in one way or the other); on the other hand, the possibility that the public may simply associate the two marks because they are worded similarly is, in itself, not enough for there to be infringement: *Val-Valvert*, Benelux Court, judgment of 2 October 2000 [2000] Ing-Cons 361.

[42] Case C-425/98 *Marca Mode CV v. Adidas AG* [2000] All ER (EC) 694, [2000] 2 CMLR 1061; Case C-39/97 *Canon Kabushiki Kaisha v. Metro-Goldwyn-Mayer Inc.* [1998] ECR I-5507, [1998] All ER (EC) 934.

[43] Case C-425/98 *Marca Mode CV v. Adidas AG* [2000] All ER (EC) 694, [2000] 2 CMLR 1061 at [19].

[44] Ibid. at [16] and [17].

[45] Case C-39/97 *Canon Kabushiki Kaisha v. Metro-Goldwyn-Mayer Inc.* [1998] ECR I-5507, [1998] All ER (EC) 934.

[46] Mere aural similarity between marks ('Lloyd' and 'Loint's'), for example, can create a likelihood of confusion: Case C-342/97 *Lloyd Schuhfabrik Meyer & Co. GmbH v. Klijsen Handel BV* [1999] ECR I-3819, [1999] All ER (EC) 587.

[47] *Reed Executive plc v. Reed Business Information Ltd* [2004] RPC 767 (CA).

[48] Case C-425/98 *Marca Mode CV v. Adidas AG* [2000] All ER (EC) 694, [2000] 2 CMLR 1061.

had made such a reference in his conclusion. Secondly, in a couple of recent cases,[49] the Court has given the trade mark owner a right under the trade mark to oppose shoddy advertising of his or her product or shoddy repackaging of it, even if no doubt is created in relation to origin. That must mean that trade mark law must protect more than the original function of the trade mark and that the quality guarantee function of the trade mark is now also protected. In turn, that means that the trade mark must be infringed by confusing associations that affect that guarantee of a certain level of quality.

Assessing the likelihood of confusion

A number of elements can be taken into account when determining whether or not there exists a likelihood of confusion. In *Sabel v. Puma*, the European Court of Justice elaborated on this point.[50] The Court lists, in a non-exhaustive way, a number of factors that are to be taken into account by the national courts in arriving at their decision on the point of likelihood of confusion, but adds that account must be taken of all factors that are relevant in the circumstances of each individual case. The degree of recognition of the trade mark on the market,[51] the degree of similarity between the sign and the trade mark, and between the goods and services that are labelled, as well as the possibilities to make associations with the registered trade mark are factors that the Court borrows from the Preamble to the Directive.

It is important to note that the assessment needs to take place at the moment at which the allegedly infringing sign starts to be use. The perception of the public at that stage, as a group of reasonably circumspect individuals, is the starting point.[52] What is assessed is whether there is a likelihood of confusion in that the public might believe that the goods or services originate from the same undertaking or from economically linked undertakings. That assessment must be undertaken in a comprehensive way, by reference to the perception of the relevant public of the goods or services and taking into account all relevant factors of the case that arise from the contact of the public with the sign, the mark, and the goods or services. Particular attention needs to be paid to the interdependence between the similarity of the sign and the mark, and that of the goods or services.[53] Accordingly, a lesser degree of similarity between the goods or services may be offset by a greater degree of similarity between the sign and the mark.[54]

One must also take into account the distinctive character of the earlier mark. In particular, its reputation must be taken into account when determining whether there is a likelihood of confusion.[55] The more distinctive the earlier mark, the higher will be the likelihood of confusion.[56] A good example is a case in which both the sign and the mark involved a cowhide and were used for milk goods.[57] There were, of course, conceptual similarities between the sign and the mark, but there were also strong visual differences. The goods were, of course, entirely similar. It was held that the cow-related nature of the

---

[49] Cases C-427/93, C-429/93, and C-436/93 *Bristol Myers Squibb v. Paranova* [1996] ECR I-3457, [1997] 1 CMLR 1151; Case C-337/95 *Parfums Christian Dior v. Evora* [1997] ECR I-6013, [1998] 1 CMLR 737.

[50] Case 251/95 *Sabel v. Puma* [1997] ECR I-6191, [1998] 1 CMLR 445 at [22]–[25] of the judgment.

[51] See also Case C-39/97 *Canon Kabushiki Kaisha v. Metro-Goldwyn-Mayer Inc.* [1998] ECR I-5507, [1989] All ER (EC) 934.

[52] Case C-145/05 *Levi Strauss & Co. v. Casucci SpA* [2006] ECR I-3703.

[53] Case T-162/01 *Laboratorios RTB v. OHIM – Giorgio Beverly Hills* [2003] ECR II-2821 at [29]–[33].

[54] Case C-171/06 P *T.I.M.E. Art Uluslararasi Saat Ticareti ve dis Ticaret AS* [2007] ETMR 38 at [13].

[55] Case C-39/97 *Canon Kabushiki Kaisha v. Metro-Goldwyn-Mayer Inc.* [1998] ECR I-5507, [1989] All ER (EC) 934 at [24].

[56] Case C-342/97 *Lloyd Schuhfabrik Meyer & Co. GmbH v. Klijsen Handel BV* [1999] ECR I-3819, [1999] All ER (EC) 587 at [20].

[57] Case T-153/03 *Inex SA v. OHIM* [2006] ECR II-1677.

sign and the mark made the similarity not very distinctive—that is, that the consumer expects something of that nature in that line of business. The mark was, however, not particularly distinctive. This led to the conclusion that there was no likelihood of confusion.

Another interesting scenario arises when a mark is combined by a third party with its company name in practice: for example, 'Life' and 'Thomson Life' respectively. If the mark still plays an independent distinctive role in the composite mark, and if the goods and services are identical, there can be a likelihood of confusion, even if the mark only has normal distinctiveness.[58]

It is indeed the case in this respect that the more similar the goods or services covered and the more distinctive the earlier mark, the greater will be the likelihood of confusion. And in determining the distinctive character of a mark and, accordingly, in assessing whether it is highly distinctive, it is necessary to make a global assessment of the greater or lesser capacity of the mark to identify the goods or services for which it has been registered as coming from a particular undertaking, and thus to distinguish those goods or services from those of other undertakings. In making that assessment, account is to be taken of all relevant factors and, in particular, of the inherent characteristics of the mark, including the fact that it does or does not contain an element that is descriptive of the goods or services for which it has been registered.[59] It is indeed recognized that, in the case of a largely descriptive mark, small differences may suffice to avoid confusion, because the consumer realizes that other traders are likely to rely on the same descriptive content.[60] The Court added in *Sabel* that the national court is to adopt the perspective of the average reasonably circumspect consumer and that the mark must be considered as a whole. It is clear that, in this perspective, a more distinctive mark will more easily give rise to a likelihood of confusion.[61] The Court specifically cited the German *Bundesgerichtshof* with approval on the point that the overall impression of a mark as a whole, while giving proper weight to special distinctive characteristics, must be the starting point of the analysis.

Section 10(2)(b)

That brings us back to s. 10(2) of the 1994 Act and, in particular, to s. 10(2)(b). Only the second point of the test changes here: the similarity test now applies to the sign and eventually also to the goods or services. Similarity in relation to the sign was held to be a question of degree; a degree of similarity is tolerable, provided that the mark and the sign were not confusingly similar.[62] Once more, all surrounding matter needs to be disregarded, both in relation to the mark and to the sign.[63]

There may also be cases in which the mark and the sign are visually different, but phonetically similar.[64] The aural effect of the mark is particularly relevant to the comparison in those cases, but nevertheless the claimant cannot rely on such an aural effect to disregard those distinctive features of its mark that could be seen, but not heard.[65] The assessment of

[58] Case C-120/04 *Medion AG v. Thomson Multimedia Sales Germany & Austria GmbH* [2005] ECR I-8551.

[59] Case C-342/97 *Lloyd Schuhfabrik Meyer & Co. GmbH v. Klijsen Handel BV* [1999] ECR I-3819, [1999] All ER (EC) 587.

[60] *Reed Executive plc v. Reed Business Information Ltd* [2004] RPC 767 (CA).

[61] Case C-39/97 *Canon Kabushiki Kaisha v. Metro-Goldwyn-Mayer Inc.* [1998] ECR I-5507, [1999] All ER (EC) 934.

[62] See the guidance given in *Conran v. Mean Fiddler Holdings Ltd* [1997] FSR 856.

[63] *United Biscuits (UK) Ltd v. Asda Stores Ltd* [1997] RPC 513 (the supermarket lookalike brands case).

[64] See *Conran v. Mean Fiddler Holdings Ltd* [1997] FSR 856 (zinc and the chemical symbol Zn).

[65] *European Ltd v. Economist Newspaper Ltd* [1998] FSR 283.

the visual, aural, or conceptual similarity between the sign and the mark is to be based on the overall impression that is given by them. In making that assessment, the distinctive and dominant component of the sign and the mark should be kept in mind.[66]

One also needs to remember that the consumer only rarely has the chance to make a direct comparison with both the sign and the mark in front of him or her.[67] Instead, the consumer relies on an imperfect recollection of them, and the reality is then that the dominant and distinctive features that are most easily remembered.[68] In assessing the overall impression, one is therefore not barred from assessing each of its components in order to identify the dominant features. That has led the European courts to decide, for example, that, in principle, there will be similarity between a sign and a mark if one consists of a word that has no conceptual meaning to the public and the second copies that word in combination with another word, which again has no conceptual meaning either alone or in combination, as long as the word found in both is identical, both visually and aurally.[69] But conceptual differences between sign and mark can be such as to counteract, to a large extent, the visual and aural similarities between them.[70]

Section 10(3)

Finally, we turn to s. 10(3) of the 1994 Act, which deals with use in relation to dissimilar goods or services—or so it seemed. The section will only apply when dissimilar goods or services are involved, but there are other requirements that need to be met for there to be infringement of the trade mark under this section.

Requirements

Firstly, the sign that is used in relation to the other goods or services must at least be similar to the trade mark. Obviously, the use of an identical sign will also be covered. It can be argued that the similarity of the mark must give rise to a likelihood of confusion on the part of the public; otherwise, the arguably illogical result that greater protection was granted in relation to dissimilar goods or services would be reached if, in comparison to s. 10(2), the confusion requirement were dropped.[71] But the requirement that likelihood of confusion is required was doubted by the Court of Appeal in the *One-in-a-Million* case[72] and has now effectively been ruled out by the European Court of Justice.[73]

Secondly, the mark must also have a reputation in the UK, meaning that not all marks can benefit under this section. The mark must be a strong mark—and this may also

---

[66] Case T-292/01 *Phillips-Van Heusen v. OHIM – Pash Textilvertrieb und Einzelhandel (BASS)* [2003] ECR II-4335 at [47].

[67] Case C-342/97 *Lloyd Schufabrik Meyer* [1999] ECR I-3819 at [26].

[68] Case T-104/01 *Oberhauser v. OHIM – Petit Libero (Fifties)* [2002] ECR II-4359 at [47] and [48].

[69] Case C-120/04 *Medion AG v. Thomson Multimedia Sales Germany & Austria GmbH* [2005] ECR I-8551; Case T-286/02 *Oriental Kitchen v. OHIM – Mou Dybfrost (KIAP MOU)* [2003] ECR II-4953 at [39]; Case T-22/04 *Reemark Gesellschaft für Markenkooperation mbH v. OHIM – Bluenet Ltd (Westlife)* [2005] II-1559 at [37]. Use of similar Internet domain names can also amount to an infringement: see *Tesco Stores Ltd v. Elogicom Ltd & anor* [2006] ETMR 91.

[70] Case C-171/06 P *T.I.M.E. Art Uluslararasi Saat Ticareti ve dis Ticaret AS* [2007] ETMR 38 at [13], approving of the Court of First Instance decision in the case and copying the reference to Case T-292/01 *Phillips-Van Heusen v. OHIM – Pash Textilvertrieb und Einzelhandel (BASS)* [2003] ECR II-4335 at [54].

[71] *Baywatch Production Co. Inc. v. Home Video Channel* [1997] FSR 22.

[72] *British Telecommunications plc v. One In A Million Ltd* [1998] 4 All ER 476, [1999] 1 WLR 903. Aldous LJ was prepared to accept that confusion is required for the purposes of this case.

[73] Case C-408/01 *Adidas-Salomon & Adidas Benelux BV v. Fitnessworld Trading Ltd* [2004] Ch 120, [2004] FSR 401, [2004] 1 CMLR 448.

explain why likelihood of confusion is not required and why that is not that illogical after all. Strong or famous marks may be entitled to a stronger protective regime. In order to enjoy this stronger protection extending to non-similar goods or services, the European Court of Justice has imposed the requirement that the registered mark must be known to a significant part of the public concerned by the products or services covered by the mark.[74] That significant part of the public can obviously be a significant part of the public in the country concerned, but it can also be a significant part of the public in a substantial part of the country concerned if the goods or services bearing the mark are specifically marketed (only) in that part of the country.[75]

Thirdly, the use of the sign must be without due cause. An example of use that is not without due cause might be found in the car repair business. An independent repairer may be entitled to use a sign that corresponds to the trade mark of a car manufacturer to indicate to the public that he or she specializes in repair work in relation to cars of that particular make. He or she may, for example, wish to describe him or herself as an 'independent Mercedes specialist'.[76]

Fourthly, that use of the sign must take advantage of, or must be detrimental to, the distinctive character or the repute of the mark.[77] This requirement effectively adds to the similarity requirement and can be seen as a more flexible alternative to the likelihood of confusion requirement. On the one hand, a negative example by means of which unfair advantage might be demonstrated arose when Daimler Chrysler sued a clothing retailer who used the name 'Merc' for his cloths.[78] The court acknowledged that the mark 'Merc' was commonly used as an abbreviation of the mark 'Mercedes', which had been registered by the claimant, but, in the light of the defendant's long-standing use of the mark and the claimant's recent entry in the clothing market, no unfair advantage or damage to reputation could be established. On the other hand, by way of a positive example, it was held, when cyberpirates registered domain names comprising the trade marks of well-known companies, that this use of a similar sign—for example, 'sainsburys.com'—did come under s. 10(3) and the use was held to be detrimental to the marks by damaging the claimant's exclusivity.[79] It was accepted that the domain names were registered to take advantage of the distinctive character and reputation of the mark, and that this was unfair and detrimental.[80] It was also held, in that case, that use in the course of trade meant use in the course of business, without requiring use of a trade mark. The use of a trade mark in the course of a business of a professional dealer for the purposes of making domain names

---

[74] Case C-375/97 *General Motors Corp. v. Yplon SA* [1999] ECR I-5421, [2000] RPC 572, applied by the third Board of Appeal of OHIM in Case R 551/1999–3 *Hollywood Partners* (unreported).

[75] Case C-375/97 *General Motors Corp. v. Yplon SA* [1999] ECR I-5421, [2000] RPC 572.

[76] Case C-63/97 *Bayerische Motorenwerke AG & BMW Nederland BV v. Ronald Karel Deenik* [1999] ECR I-905, [1999] All ER (EC) 235; see also the Opinion of Advocate-General Jacobs in this case of 2 April 1998 (unreported).

[77] *Baywatch Production Co. Inc. v. Home Video Channel* [1997] FSR 22; see also Jacob J's obiter comments in relation to s 10(3) in *British Sugar plc v. James Robertson & Sons Ltd* [1996] RPC 281.

[78] *Daimler Chrysler AG v. Alavi (t/a Merc)* [2001] RPC 813.

[79] *Tesco Stores Ltd v. Elogicom Ltd & anor* [2006] ETMR 91.

[80] The territorial nature of trade marks and the global scope of domain names often lead to clashes between trade marks and domain names. The World Intellectual Property Organization (WIPO) has established guidelines in this respect, and its Arbitration and Mediation Centre is very active in resolving these conflicts. The following two cases are examples in which actress Nicole Kidman and the city council of the city of Barcelona (Spain) were able to reclaim domain names that included their marks on the basis of the trade marks that they had registered in their respective names. The fact that the defendant attempted to take unfair advantage of famous names was an important factor in these cases: Case D2000–1415 *Nicole Kidman v. John Zuccarini, d/b/a Cupcake Party*; Case D2000–0505 *Excellentisimo Ayuntamiento de Barcelona v. Barcelona. com Inc.* (both available online at www.wipo.int).

more valuable through registration and extracting money from the trade mark owner before handing over the registration was clearly use in the course of trade.[81]

A wide approach in the courts

Another example of a case that would fit in well under s. 10(3) is the controversial Benelux case *Claeryn/Klarein*.[82] Because of their phonetic similarity in Dutch, these were similar signs and they were used in relation to gin and a toilet cleaner, respectively. That means that there was use in relation to dissimilar products. The finding of infringement in the case was primarily based on the fact that the strong mark was diluted and suffered detriment, because a sign once exclusively associated with gin would now also be associated with a toilet cleaner. Also, no due cause for the use of the sign could be established in this case.

The European Court of Justice has rendered a series of wide-ranging and remarkable judgments in this area. In order to understand these, as well as the new interpretation of the law in this area, a brief return to basics is warranted. Section 10(3) of the 1994 Act, based on Art. 5(2) of the Directive, contains an additional ground for infringement and member States were left to decide whether or not to implement this ground. Trade marks that have a reputation will get additional protection and they will also be infringed through the use of an identical or similar sign in relation to goods or services that are not similar to those in respect of which the mark has been registered. That additional protection is conditional upon the use of the sign being without due cause and taking unfair advantage of, or being detrimental to, the distinctive character or repute of the trade mark.

When the Directive was implemented in the Trade Marks Act 1994, it seemed clear that this was not an overall third layer of rights, but a special rule that dealt with an exceptional situation. First of all, it did not apply to all trade marks, but only to those trade marks with a reputation. The approach seemed to have a lot of similarities with the approach to famous trade marks in the historical Paris Convention for the Protection of Industrial Property 1883: it seemed to represent an equally narrow category. Additionally, there needed to be use of the similar or identical sign without due cause and that use needed to be detrimental to the distinctive character or repute of the trade mark, or it needed to take unfair advantage of that distinctive character or repute, which could be described as the dilution scenario. And, most importantly, the additional protection would only apply when the sign was used in relation to goods or services that were not similar to those for which the trade mark had been registered.

Or would it?

There is, of course, also the argument that the fact that a trade mark has a reputation—that is, that it is not your ordinary trade mark—entitles it to stronger protection. Its reputation gives it a special kind of goodwill, which is both important for the trade mark owner and for the public. Trade mark law should therefore not allow that goodwill to be diluted without due cause as a result of the use of an identical or similar sign over which the trade mark owner has no control. After all, the third party using the sign is free to pick another sign and does not necessarily lose out. Section 10(3) and Art. 5(2), respectively, seem to support this argument. If that is the case, then, why should there be a distinction between use in relation to goods or services that are not similar to those for which the trade mark

---

[81] *British Telecommunications plc v. One In A Million Ltd* [1998] 4 All ER 476, [1999] 1 WLR 903 (CA), in which the first instance decision was approved: *Marks & Spencer plc v. One In A Million, Ladbrokes plc v. One In A Million, J Sainsbury plc v. One In A Million, Virgin Enterprises Ltd v. One In A Million, British Telecommunications plc v. One In A Million* [1998] FSR 265.

[82] Benelux Court of Justice, 1 March 1975, [1975] NJ 472; see also Torremans [1998] and the comment made by Jacob J in *British Sugar plc v. James Robertson & Sons Ltd* [1996] RPC 281.

has been registered, on the one hand, and goods or services that are identical or similar, on the other? The negative impact of dilution is indeed even more likely to be felt, or to be felt more strongly, as a result of use of the sign in relation to identical or similar goods.

Davidoff

The potential problem could, of course, be defused or would not even exist if the concept of taking unfair advantage of, or of being detrimental to, the distinctive character of the repute of the trade mark were to be, in fact, based on the public being confused. The latter would then cover the use in relation to identical or similar goods or services, and s. 10(3) and Art. 5(2), respectively, would simply expand that same kind of protection for marks with a reputation to use in relation to goods or services that are not similar.

The European Court of Justice was confronted with this issue for the first time when it rendered its judgment in *Davidoff & Cie SA & Zino Davidoff SA v. Gofkid Ltd*.[83] Davidoff objected to the use of the sign 'Durffee' by Gofkid for goods that were similar. It alleged that the use of the similar sign, while not causing confusion, caused its 'Davidoff' mark to be diluted, without there being a good cause for Gofkid to use that sign.

The Court made it clear, first of all, that Art. 5(2)—and thus also s. 10(3) of the 1994 Act—is not based on the concept of confusion, but on a wider concept. In the words of the Court:

> where there is no likelihood of confusion, Article 5(1)(b) of the Directive could not be relied upon by the proprietor of a mark with a reputation to protect himself against impairment of the distinctive character or repute of the mark.[84]

But to the surprise of many, the Court went on to hold that:

> In those circumstances, . . . Articles 4(4)(a) and 5(2) of the Directive are to be interpreted as entitling the Member States to provide specific protection for registered trade marks with a reputation in cases where a later mark or sign, which is identical with or similar to the reg-istered mark, is intended to be used for goods or services identical with or similar to those covered by the registered mark.[85]

The Court accepted therefore that marks with a reputation deserve wider protection and that that logic exists not only in a case of use of the identical or similar sign in relation to goods or services that are not similar, but also in relation to similar or identical goods or services.

In *Davidoff & Cie SA & Zino Davidoff SA v. Gofkid Ltd*,[86] however, the Court seemed only to say member States are entitled to provide such a protection. Some of the points were barely spelled out and the exact width of the judgment was not clear, especially because questions could be asked about how this freedom for member States that seemed to go against the specific wording used in Art. 5(2)—that 'not similar' can hardly be said to mean 'identical, similar of not similar'—could be reconciled with the idea that the Directive would provide a complete harmonization on certain points such as this.

Adidas v. Fitnessworld

Of course, that sparked a lot of debate and there were far more questions than answers in terms of how far the Court really wanted to go—but the debate was fairly short-lived. Nine months after starting the debate in *Davidoff*, the Court handed down a much more

---

83 Case C-292/00 *Davidoff & Cie SA & Zino Davidoff SA v. Gofkid Ltd* [2003] ECR I-389, [2003] 1 WLR 1734.
84 Ibid. [2003] 1 WLR 1734 at 1735.
85 Ibid.
86 Ibid.

robust judgment in *Adidas-Salomon & Adidas Benelux BV v. Fitnessworld Trading Ltd.*[87] The case dealt with the use by Fitnessworld of a motif composed of two parallel stripes of equal width that contrast with the main colour of the item of clothing and which is applied to the side seams of the clothing. The clothing was sold under the name 'Perfetto'. Adidas considered this to amount to the use of a sign that was similar to its trade mark, which consisted of three, very striking, vertical stripes of equal width that run parallel. In the presence of a mark with a reputation and in the absence of confusion in the sense of s. 10(2), this was another case about the use of s. 10(3) in relation to similar goods or services.

Use in relation to identical, similar or non-similar goods or services
The Court made it, first of all, clear that, as a result of its decision in *Davidoff*, s. 10(3) could be used to offer anti-dilution-style protection in cases in which the goods or services were identical or similar, but not in cases in which the goods or services were not similar. It went on to add that:

> where the sign is used for identical or similar goods or services, a mark with a reputation must enjoy protection which is at least as extensive as where a sign is used for non-similar goods or services.[88]

It then concluded that:

> In the light of those findings, the Member State, if it transposes Article 5(2) of the Directive, must therefore grant protection which is at least as extensive for identical or similar goods or services as for non-similar goods or services. The Member State's option thus relates to the principle itself of granting greater protection to marks with a reputation, but not to the situations covered by that protection when the Member State grants it.[89]

In other words, the Court opts for a full purposive interpretation of Art. 5(2) and s. 10(3), respectively, even if it goes against the explicit language of the provision. In the Court's view, the logic of the overall scheme of trade mark protection prevails: what had seemed to be an option nine months earlier had now become an obligation for the member States.

Dilution instead of confusion
Once the principle established, the Court went on to clarify some of the concepts used—which was, indeed, much needed, because a lot of questions had remained unanswered in the aftermath of *Davidoff*.
   Firstly, the idea that confusion might be involved as a requirement was buried once and for all when the Court ruled that:

> it must be noted at the outset that, unlike Article 5(1)(b) of the Directive, which is designed to apply only if there exists a likelihood of confusion on the part of the public, Article 5(2) of the Directive establishes, for the benefit of trade marks with a reputation, a form of protection whose implementation does not require the existence of such a likelihood. Article 5(2) applies to situations in which the specific condition of the protection consists of a use of the sign in question without due cause which takes unfair advantage of, or is detrimental to, the distinctive character or the repute of the trade mark.[90]

---

[87] Case C-408/01 *Adidas-Salomon & Adidas Benelux BV v. Fitnessworld Trading Ltd* [2003] ECR I-12537, [2004] Ch 120, [2004] FSR 401, [2004] 1 CMLR 448.
   [88] Ibid. [2004] Ch 120 at 138.
   [89] Ibid.
   [90] Ibid. at 139.

A key point of difference with confusion is that the risk that the use without due cause of the mark will take unfair advantage of the distinctive character or the repute of the trade mark continues to exist when the consumer, without necessarily confusing the commercial origin of the product or service, is attracted by the mark for itself and will buy the product or service on the ground that it bears the mark, which is identical or similar to an earlier mark with a reputation.[91] There must, however, be an unfair advantage or detriment to the distinctive character or the repute of the trade mark; that is the essence of the dilution.

The owner of the earlier trade mark, meanwhile, is not required to demonstrate actual or present harm to his or her mark: all that needs to be shown is prima facie evidence of a future risk, which is not hypothetical, of unfair advantage or detriment.[92] The European Court of Justice has left it to the national court to determine whether or not an unfair advantage or detriment will exist, but the burden does not seem to be unduly high, because it was not ruled out that detriment could arise through the use of a trade mark for cars on scale models of those cars.[93]

A link

The crucial concept is, of course, that of 'dilution' and the interpretation that 'dilution' is to be given to the final section of Art. 5(2) and s. 10(3), respectively.

This is the definition put forward by the Court:

> The infringements referred to in Article 5(2) of the Directive, where they occur, are the consequence of a certain degree of similarity between the mark and the sign, by virtue of which the relevant section of the public makes a connection between the sign and the mark, that is to say, establishes a link between them even though it does not confuse them. The existence of such a link must, just like a likelihood of confusion in the context of Article 5(1)(b) of the Directive, be appreciated globally, taking into account all factors relevant to the circumstances of the case.[94]

One needs to be slightly careful with this typical association–dilution requirement in terms of there being a link. One needs to prove that the public makes the link between the sign and the trade mark, and while, until that point, the case seemed to be going Adidas' way, this proved to be its difficulty, because there was evidence that the public saw the Fitnessworld motif as an embellishment rather than as a mark, and did not make the link with the Adidas trade mark. Or, as the Court put it:

> The fact that a sign is viewed as an embellishment by the relevant section of the public is not, in itself, an obstacle to the protection conferred by Article 5(2) of the Directive where the degree of similarity is none the less such that the relevant section of the public establishes a link between the sign and the mark.
>
> By contrast, where, according to a finding of fact by the national court, the relevant section of the public views the sign purely as an embellishment, it necessarily does not establish any link with a registered mark. That therefore means that the degree of similarity between the sign and the mark is not sufficient for such a link to be established.[95]

---

[91] Case T-215/03 *Sigla SA v. OHIM* [2007] Bus LR D 53 at [42], judgment of 22 March 2007 available online at curia.europa.eu.

[92] Case T-67/04 *Spa Monopole v. OHIM & Spa-Finders Travel Arrangements* [2005] ECR II-1825, [2005] ETMR 9. See also Case T-215/03 *Sigla SA v. OHIM* [2007] Bus LR D 53 at [46], judgment of 22 March 2007, available online at curia.europa.eu.

[93] Case C-48/05 *Adam Opel AG v. Autec AG* [2007] ETMR 33 at [36].

[94] Case C-408/01 *Adidas-Salomon & Adidas Benelux BV v. Fitnessworld Trading Ltd* [2004] Ch 120 at 139.

[95] Ibid. at 140.

The establishment of such a link with the trade mark will then make the unfair advantage or the detriment possible. But the question remains open whether the presence of the link will automatically result in dilution and damage. The Court of First Instance's insistence on prima facie evidence of damage seems to suggest that damage will not be taken to result automatically. The Court of Appeal suggested, in a case concerned with imitation perfumes,[96] that, in those cases in which the imitation packaging managed to establish a link with the trade mark, an advantage for the imitator would follow automatically, but that it remained to be determined whether that would necessarily be an unfair advantage. The question what exactly was meant by an unfair advantage in such circumstances was referred to the European Court of Justice.

Due cause

The one point that the Court did not address was the concept of 'due cause'. Even if all of the other requirements are met, Art. 5(2) will only lead to a finding of infringement if the use of the sign was without due cause. There was clearly no due cause in *Adidas v. Fitnessworld*, but it is not always such a clear-cut case. In other words, it is important to know how strictly the requirement needs to be interpreted.

This is all the more important as a result of the relative ease with which a link can be demonstrated, which may bring rather a lot of cases within the scope of s. 10(3) when coupled with the low threshold for marks with a reputation that was set out by the Court in the *BMW* case.[97] The fact that the mark must be known to a significant part of the public concerned with the product of service to which the mark is applied is not going to be a major hurdle; the future will tell us whether this broad interpretation of s. 10(3) will effectively do away, in practice, with the careful approach and the restrictions that seemed to have been put in place in relation to association under s. 10(2). It will also make clear whether s. 10(3) will set the norm or whether the courts will tighten up the requirements for reputation, while widening the scope of the due cause exception.

Further examples and an extension of infringement rules

The 1994 Act goes on to give examples (non-inclusively) of the kind of acts that may equate to an infringement. The use of a sign on goods or on their packaging and the offer or sale of goods under the sign in question will both amount to an infringement; so too, potentially, will the import or export of goods under the sign and the use of the sign on any business papers or in advertising.[98] The provision of s. 10(2), whereby the use of a mark can still be capable of being an infringement even if the use is other than by a graphical representation, plugs a previous loophole and means that, unlike under the previous law, it will be an infringement to speak the name of a trade mark registered in its written form perhaps, as an example, in a radio advert criticizing a rival product.

It is clear from the careful matching of the phraseology of ss. 5 and 10 that the definitions of confusion, through similar marks or goods, and of reputation, in the case of dissimilar products, should be the same and the discussion of these points in the context of s. 5 need not be repeated here.

An extension to the normal infringement rules arises under s. 10(5). This extends the protection of the trade mark proprietor to include a right to act against anyone who applies

---

[96] *L'Oreal, Lancôme & Laboratoire Garnier v. Bellure, Malaika Investments (t/a Honeypot Cosmetic & Perfumery Sales) & Starion International* [2007] EWCA Civ 936 (CA).

[97] Case C-63/97 *Bayerische Motorenwerke AG & BMW Nederland BV v. Ronald Karel Deenik* [1999] ECR I-905.

[98] TMA 1994, s. 10(4). On the latter point, see also *Cheetah Trade Mark* [1993] FSR 263.

a trade mark to labels or packages of goods, business papers, or advertising material if that person knew, or had reason to believe, that the use of the mark was not authorized by its proprietor. Accordingly, it is now not only the person who makes the decision to infringe who will be liable: as an example, the printer who fails to act on his or her suspicions as to the unauthorized use of a trade mark will also be at risk of infringement litigation.

Comparative advertising

A final element of the law in this area is significant in that it offers liberalization of the approach to comparative advertising—that is, the practice of promoting one's own product with reference to its rivals and the alleged lack of quality in their goods.[99] As has been seen, the convoluted approach of the old law, as exemplified by *News Group Ltd v. Mirror Group Ltd*,[100] meant that the use of other marks in seemingly harmless comparative advertising activity could give rise to infringement actions.

Section 10(6)

Now, however, s. 10(6) specifically addresses this issue. Its primary objective is to allow comparative advertising:[101] it allows the use of a mark by anyone to take place without there being an infringement if the use is to identify any goods or services as being those of the proprietor of the mark.[102] So the use, as in the *News Group* case, of a rival paper's logo so as to emphasize the difference between the papers would now seem, as such, to be legitimate.[103] But the subsection has a proviso: such use will continue to be an infringement if it is not '*in accordance with honest practices in industrial or commercial matters*' and also if it takes unfair advantage of, or is detrimental to, the reputation of the mark.

To start with that proviso—because it is in this area that the problems are found—the owner of the registered trade mark has been given the onus to show that the factors indicated in it exist.[104] But as long as the use of the mark is honest, there is nothing wrong in telling the public of the relative merits of competing services and using trade marks to identify these competing services. Advanta was, in this sense, entitled to use Barclays Bank's Barclaycard trade mark to identify it as a competing service in a publicity leaflet in which a table comparing the features, and advantages and disadvantages, of the various credit cards—including the Barclaycard and its own card—were detailed.[105] There will therefore be no trade mark infringement unless the use of the registered trade mark is not in accordance with honest practices.[106]

The test that is applied in this respect is an objective one: would a reasonable man be likely to say, upon being given the full facts, that the advertisement is not honest?[107] Or would a reasonable trader have made the statement contained in the advertising based on the information he or she had at the time?[108] Obviously, a person who knowingly put

---

[99] See B. Mills, 'Comparative advertising: Should it be allowed?' [1995] 9 EIPR 417.
[100] [1989] FSR 126. See Chapter 24.
[101] *Barclays Bank plc v. RBS Advanta* [1996] RPC 307 at 315.
[102] See *Wolters Kluwer (UK) Ltd v. Reed Elsevier (UK) Ltd* [2006] FSR 28.
[103] See *MacMillan Magazines Ltd v. RCN Publishing Co. Ltd* [1998] FSR 9.
[104] *Barclays Bank plc v. RBS Advanta* [1996] RPC 307 at 315; see also *Vodafone Group plc v. Orange Personal Communications Services Ltd* [1997] FSR 34.
[105] *Barclays Bank plc v. RBS Advanta* [1996] RPC 307.
[106] Ibid. at 315.
[107] Ibid. at 315; see also *Vodafone Group plc v. Orange Personal Communications Services Ltd* [1997] FSR 34; *British Airways plc v. Ryanair Ltd* [2001] FSR 32.
[108] *Cable & Wireless plc v. British Telecommunications plc* [1998] FSR 383.

forward a false claim is not honest and his or her activity is not in accordance with honest practice.[109] A comparative advertisement is also not in accordance with honest practices if it is objectively misleading to a substantial proportion of the reasonable audience.[110] Statutory or industry codes of conduct, however, are not helpful in deciding whether or not the advertisement is honest.

Honesty also has to be gauged against the reasonable expectations of the relevant public in relation to advertisements for the particular type of goods or services.[111] These expectations of the public form the benchmarks in this area. It should be borne in mind, in this context, that the general public is well used to the ways of advertisers and that the public consequently expects to see hyperbole.[112] This leads, nevertheless, to the inevitable conclusion that an advertisement that is significantly misleading is not honest for the purposes of s. 10(6).[113] But in examining an advertisement, it should also be borne in mind that the public will not normally engage in a minute textual examination[114] and the advertisement must be considered as a whole.[115]

The second half of the proviso to s. 10(6) seems to introduce the additional requirement that the use of the trade mark in a comparative advertisement without due cause must take unfair advantage of, or must be detrimental to, the distinctive character or repute of the mark. It has been held that, in most cases, this adds nothing of significance to the first half of the proviso.[116] Any form of misleading comparative advertising and any dishonest use of the trade mark in this context must, almost by definition, be seen as detrimental to, or as taking unfair advantage of, the distinctive character or repute of the trade mark.

The *Advanta* case was concerned with comparative advertising practices in relation to credit cards, but most other recent cases deal with the battle for market shares in the telecommunications market. *Vodafone v. Orange*,[117] for example, was concerned with a campaign in which Orange claimed that its users saved, on average, £20 per month in comparison with someone that used the equivalent Vodafone tariffs. Obviously, in practice, not every user saved £20 per month and transfer costs to Orange had not fully been taken into account. Vodafone's claim for dishonest use of its trade mark was nevertheless rejected, because the ordinary man would expect some hyperbole in this type of market. He would have interpreted the slogan at face value and not literally; he would not have assumed that the saving would apply to every single customer, but only to an average customer. Looked at in that way, the claim of falsity and dishonesty had not been made out.

The Directive

The European Union (EU) has now also taken an interest in the issue of comparative advertising. A recent EU Directive[118] also accepts the principle that comparative

---

[109]　Ibid.

[110]　*Vodafone Group plc v. Orange Personal Communications Services Ltd* [1997] FSR 34. The 'one meaning rule' that is found in the law of malicious falsehood is not applicable in trade mark cases.

[111]　*Barclays Bank plc v. RBS Advanta* [1996] RPC 307, at 316.

[112]　Ibid. at 315; see also *Vodafone Group plc v. Orange Personal Communications Services Ltd* [1997] FSR 34.

[113]　*Barclays Bank plc v. RBS Advanta* [1996] RPC 307 at 316; see also *Vodafone Group plc v. Orange Personal Communications Services Ltd* [1997] FSR 34.

[114]　*British Telecommunications plc v. AT & T Communications (UK) Ltd* (18 December 1996, unreported), High Court.

[115]　*Barclays Bank plc v. RBS Advanta* [1996] RPC 307 at 316–18.

[116]　*Vodafone Group plc v. Orange Personal Communications Services Ltd* [1997] FSR 34.

[117]　Ibid.

[118]　Parliament and Council Directive 97/55/EC amending Directive 84/450/EEC concerning misleading advertising so as to include comparative advertising (1997) OJ L 290/18.

advertising should be allowed in principle. It defines comparative advertising as '*any advertising which explicitly or by implication identifies a competitor or goods or services offered by a competitor*'.[119]

As this definition already indicates, the European approach is wider in scope than only the use of a competitor's trade mark: for example, the use of an equipment manufacturer's identification numbers by a producer of alternative toner cartridges for the manufacturer's equipment in a catalogue of products can be a form of comparative advertising that objectively compares one or more material, relevant, verifiable, and representative features of the goods, and can thus be a permissible form of comparative advertising under the Directive's rules.[120] And in terms of the potential to take unfair advantage, the Court added that:

> where product numbers...of an equipment manufacturer are, as such, distinguishing marks..., their use in the catalogues of a competing supplier enables him to take unfair advantage of the reputation attached to those marks only if the effect of the reference to them is to create, in the mind of the persons at whom the advertising is directed, an association between the manufacturer whose products are identified and the competing supplier, in that those persons associate the reputation of the manufacturer's products with the products of the competing supplier. In order to determine whether that condition is satisfied, account should be taken of the overall presentation of the advertising at issue and the type of persons for whom the advertising is intended.[121]

The provisions of the Directive are, in general, also more detailed in nature and their implementation will probably require the introduction of additional legislation in the UK, even if the operation of s. 10(6) TMA has not been qualified.[122]

The interaction between the Directives concerning trade marks and comparative advertising is not straightforward, especially because, in the UK, part of the Directive on comparative advertising has been implemented in the Trade Marks Act 1994. The Court of Appeal has held that advertising that complies with the Comparative Advertising Directive must be covered by the exception in s. 11(2) of the 1994 Act and must meet the standard of 'honest practices' set out in that section.[123] What is not clear, however, is whether use of the mark must be indispensable: must there be a necessity of using the mark?[124] And if one uses the mark, does that also cover use of the mark not exactly as registered? For example, could one use the 'O2' trade mark of static images in a modified form as a background for a television advert for a competitor?

That was the question in the *O2* case,[125] in which all of these questions were referred to the European Court of Justice. The fundamental question that was also referred involved a definition of honest commercial practices, which leads on to the even more fundamental issue of whether use of the mark that does not affect the essential indication of origin function of the mark can infringe under s. 10 in the first place. If infringement is possible, what then is the role and scope of an honest practices defence, for example, if the use is

---

[119] Ibid., Art. 1.

[120] Case C-112/99 *Toshiba Europe GmbH v. Katun Germany GmbH* [2001] ECR I-7945. See also Case C-44/01 *Pippig Augenoptik GmbH & Co. KG v. Hartlauer Handelsgesellschaft mbH & Verlassenschaft Nach Dem Verstorbenen Franz Josef Hartlauer* [2003] ECR I-3095.

[121] Case C-112/99 *Toshiba Europe GmbH v. Katun Germany GmbH* [2001] ECR I-7945 at [60].

[122] *British Airways plc v. Ryanair Ltd* [2001] FSR 32.

[123] *O2 Holding Ltd v. Hutchinson 3G Ltd* [2007] ETMR 19 (CA).

[124] Case C-112/99 *Toshiba Europe GmbH v. Katun Germany GmbH* [2001] ECR I-7945 does not seem to require necessity.

[125] *O2 Holding Ltd v. Hutchinson 3G Ltd* [2007] ETMR 19 (CA).

purely for the purpose of comparing the merits of the goods or services?[126] And, in this way, we are returned neatly to the Comparative Advertising Directive and the question of the interaction of the Directives.

Exceptions to infringement

There are, of course, some exceptions to the foregoing in respect of which what would otherwise be an infringement is exempted. Section 11(1) of the 1994 Act refuses an infringement action to the owner of a mark that has also been registered. Obviously, in a properly functioning system of examination of trade marks, this situation should never arise; it is a second proprietor who will be in difficulty facing the prospect of revocation of his or her mark.[127]

Section 11(2) of the 1994 Act also removes the threat of an infringement action from a range of different situations, in each case subject to a proviso that the use that would otherwise be an infringement is a use that is, once again, '*in accordance with honest practices in industrial or commercial matters*'.[128] The test for honesty is to be judged by an objective standard.[129] This fits in well with s. 3(6), which, as has been seen, may prevent an application for a mark from succeeding if made in bad faith—although this would not prevent the possibility of a mark being registered in good faith and then being used in bad faith, in which case, infringement actions will still be available.

Section 11(2)(a)

The activities exempted by s. 11(2) include, firstly, the use by a person of his or her own name or address. This includes the use by a company of its own name.[130] The exception also covers trade mark use of the name.[131] Although this seems obvious and only fair, the use in trade of a sign including name and address is not an essential feature of many trades and may well therefore not be honest. If a Mr Ronald McDonald of Leicester were to want to open a burger bar, there are many burger-related names that would be more appropriate than his own name and the only reason for using it would be the less-than-honest desire to steal trade from his better known namesake; if a Mr Herbert Smith of Leicester wants to set up a solicitor's firm, this may be honest, given that a solicitor normally trades under his or her own name if a sole practitioner.

According to the European Court of Justice, the condition of 'honest practices' to which s. 11(2) is subject constitutes, in substance, the expression of a duty to act fairly in relation

---

[126] Similar questions and another reference to the European Court of Justice arose in *L'Oreal, Lancôme & Laboratoire Garnier v. Bellure, Malaika Investments (t/a Honeypot Cosmetic & Perfumery Sales) & Starion International* [2007] EWCA Civ 936 (CA).

[127] TMA 1994, s. 47(2).

[128] See *Philips Electronics NV v. Remington Consumer Products Ltd* [1998] RPC 283, *per* Jacob J. As seen above, the matter has now been referred to the European Court of Justice for further clarification: *O2 Holding Ltd v. Hutchinson 3G Ltd* [2007] ETMR 19 (CA); *L'Oreal, Lancôme & Laboratoire Garnier v. Bellure, Malaika Investments (t/a Honeypot Cosmetic & Perfumery Sales) & Starion International* [2007] EWCA Civ 936 (CA).

[129] *Aktiebolaget Volvo v. Heritage (Leicester) Ltd* [2000] FSR 253; see also *Cable & Wireless plc v. British Telecommunications plc* [1998] FSR 383.

[130] *Scandecor Developments AB v. Scandecor Marketing AB* [2001] 2 CMLR 30. The House of Lords nevertheless decided that this was not *acte clair*, and referred the issue for a preliminary ruling and further clarification to the European Court of Justice. The case has, however, been settled and withdrawn from the Register. See *Fields v. Klaus Kobec Ltd* [2006] EWHC 350, judgment of 2 March 2006; see also *Euromarket Designs Inc. v. Peters* [2001] FSR 20.

[131] *Premier Luggage & Bags Ltd v. Premier Co. (UK) Ltd* [2003] FSR 69 (CA); Case C-100/02 *Gerolsteiner Brunnen GmbH & Co. v. Putsch GmbH* [2004] RPC 761.

to the legitimate interests of the trade mark owner.[132] There must also be some degree of coexistence and some degree of confusion must therefore be tolerated. The extent of confusion that is to be tolerated is a matter of degree and infringement is only to be found if, objectively, the use of his or her name or address by the person concerned amounted to unfair competition. No doubt the Court will, in future, be called upon again to clarify this test further.[133]

Secondly, the subsection allows the honest use of all the descriptive matter that cannot be registered under s. 3(1), unless entirely factually distinctive prior to registration. Thus a trade mark granted on the basis of distinctive, but descriptive, words cannot be protected when the distinctiveness is lost by subsequent usage, as long as that use was honest.

Section 11(2)(b)

It is the purpose of s. 11(2)(b) of the 1994 Act to permit the fair use of the claimant's mark to indicate the characteristics of goods or services of the user of the sign.[134] That purpose does not extend to performing the dual function of indicating both the characteristics and the trade origin of the goods.[135] Use of a sign as a trade mark can, indeed, never constitute descriptive use that is authorized under s. 10(2)(b).[136] In *Philips v. Remington*,[137] Jacob J held that the use by Remington of the shaver mark was use as an indication of the kind, quality, etc. of the goods. Remington could therefore rely on the exception in s. 10(2)(b).

A somewhat exceptional set of facts arose in *Adam Opel AG v. Autec AG*.[138] This case deals with a trade mark, 'Opel', that had been registered both for motor vehicles and for toys. The question then arose whether the use of the trade mark on scale reproductions of these motor vehicles constituted trade mark infringement. The European Court of Justice held that if a trade mark is registered, inter alia, in respect of motor vehicles, the affixing by a third party of a sign identical to that mark to scale models of that make of vehicle, without the authorization of the proprietor of the trade mark, in order faithfully to reproduce those vehicles and the marketing of those scale models do not constitute use of an indication concerning a characteristic of those scale models, within the meaning of s. 11(2)(b).

Section 11(2)(c)

The third exception relates to the use of a mark to indicate the purpose of goods or services: for example, as spare parts or accessories. Thus if I am free to make spare parts for Ford cars, it will not be an infringement to use—as ever, honestly—the name, or even the mark, of Ford to indicate the suitability of my parts for Ford cars.

The European Court of Justice dealt with the lawfulness of use of the trade mark by a third party in *The Gillette Company & Gillette Group Finland Oy v. LA-Laboratories Ltd Oy*.[139] In this case, the defendant made replacement shaving knives that were compatible

---

[132] Case C-100/02 *Gerolsteiner Brunnen GmbH & Co. v. Putsch GmbH* [2004] RPC 761 at [24].

[133] *Reed Executive plc v. Reed Business Information Ltd* [2004] RPC 767 (CA). See also Case C-63/97 *BMW AG v. Ronald Deenik* [1999] ECR I-905; Case C-100/02 *Gerolsteiner Brunnen GmbH & Co. v. Putsch GmbH* [2004] RPC 761.

[134] See *D Green & Co. (Stoke Newington) & Plastico Ltd v. Regalzone Ltd* [2002] ETMR 241 (CA).

[135] *European Ltd v. Economist Newspaper Ltd* [1998] FSR 283, *per* Millett LJ.

[136] *British Sugar plc v. James Robertson & Sons Ltd* [1996] RPC 281.

[137] *Philips Electronics NV v. Remington Consumer Products Ltd* [1998] RPC 283, *per* Jacob J.

[138] Case C-48/05 *Adam Opel AG v. Autec AG* [2007] ETMR 33.

[139] Case C-228/03 *The Gillette Company & Gillette Group Finland Oy v. LA-Laboratories Ltd Oy*[2005] ECR I-2337, [2005] 2 CMLR 62.

with Gillette's originals. The Court held that, in these circumstances, the legitimacy of the use of the trade mark depended on whether that use was necessary to indicate the intended purpose of the product. This is the case, for example, if such use is the only means of providing the public with comprehensible and complete information on that intended purpose in order to preserve the undistorted system of competition in the market for that product; any other conclusion would lead to the use of the trade mark for anti-competitive purposes. The fact that the product involved is not a spare part of accessory, but could be described as the product itself—or, at the very least, the essential part of it—does not affect these findings. The use by the third party must, however, be honest use. The third party is therefore obliged to act fairly in relation to the legitimate interests of the trade mark owner. One should therefore not use the mark in such a way as to suggest a connection between the third party and the trade mark owner, or present one's own product as an imitation or replica of the original product. Neither should one discredit or denigrate the mark, or affect its value by taking unfair advantage of its distinctive character or repute.

Section 11(3)

A further area covered by these provisions that permit what would otherwise be infringements is created by s. 11(3) of the 1994 Act. This is a somewhat odd provision that protects the use in a particular locality of an earlier right applicable only in that locality. Such a right must be enjoyed continuously prior to the first use of the registration of the mark by its user. No assistance is given as to the definition of a 'locality' and, once again, the use of this provision should be infrequent, given that the earlier local mark should, in an effective system of examination, be unearthed and thus deprive the later mark of the necessary distinctiveness. Because of this, it is far from easy to think of an example of the operation of the provision, but a possible example may be if a trade mark is granted in respect of a Scotch named after an island and it is then discovered that a small local firm on the island has been brewing whisky for the locals using the island's name as part of the brand name.

Exhaustion

Section 12 of the 1994 Act creates an important and different restriction of the right to bring infringement actions. It brings into this area of the law the 'exhaustion of rights' principle that is familiar from other areas of intellectual property. In brief, this is the principle whereby goods that bear, in this case, a trade mark go beyond the control of the proprietor of the mark once they are put on the market—his or her rights in them are exhausted once the goods are in circulation and he or she cannot object to any use of them. This has a particular relevance in the European context, where the principle of the single market has obliged Community law to assert that the circulation of goods in any one member State equates to their circulation in all such States,[140] unless any of the standard objections to free movement principles apply, as exemplified by the *Hag II* case.[141]

The problem arises primarily in the context of parallel imports, in which case a company makes goods bearing a mark in both the UK, for example, and, more cheaply, through a subsidiary in Portugal. Ideally, such a company would prevent goods from Portugal being imported cheaply into the UK, thus undermining its home market, but the two principles of exhaustion and single market now combine to make this impossible.

---

[140] See, e.g., Case 78/70 *Deutsche Grammophon GmbH v. Metro-SB-Grossmärkte GmbH & Co. KG* [1971] ECR 487, [1971] CMLR 631.
[141] Case C-10/89 *CNL-Sucal NV SA v. HAG GF AG* [1990] ECR I-3711, [1990] 3 CMLR 571.

This situation is given effect in UK law by s. 12. This removes the right to bring an infringement action in relation to goods put on to the market anywhere in the European Economic Area (EEA) by the proprietor with his or her consent. But s. 12(2) goes on to remove this if the proprietor has legitimate reasons to oppose further dealings, such as a change in the conditions of the product, again reflecting the jurisprudence of the European Court of Justice.[142] Clearly, however, UK trade mark law can still be used to stop parallel imports from countries elsewhere in the world. This confirms the approach taken under the former law, as exemplified by *Colgate-Palmolive Ltd v. Markwell Finance Ltd*.[143] In that case, the US Colgate company operated through subsidiaries in both the UK and Brazil. Toothpaste from Brazil of an inferior quality was imported into the UK under the Colgate name, causing complaint and confusion, and both trade mark law and passing off combined to defeat the importer's appeal.

Consequences of trade mark infringement

The consequences of there being a trade mark infringement are far-reaching. The proprietor of the mark is entitled to bring infringement proceedings,[144] as is the exclusive licensee or, in certain cases, a non-exclusive licensee.[145] The only specific rule to note is that, in trade mark cases in which the infringement is innocent, damages can be awarded, but no account of profits may be ordered.[146] In addition to the usual remedies in the form of damages, injunctions, and accounts of profits, which are available in the usual manner, specific additional remedies are made available to the victim of trade mark infringement.

Under s. 15 of the 1994 Act, the court is given a discretionary power to order that the infringing sign be erased, removed, or obliterated from the offending goods. Naturally, this will not always be possible; if this is the case, the court can go to the next stage and order that the goods in question be destroyed. In the alternative, s. 16 enables the proprietor to request the court to order any person to deliver to him or her the infringing material, although this right is then lost if six years have elapsed since the infringing act took place—a period that may be extended if there has been concealed fraud or other such disability.[147] If goods are thus delivered up, then an order must be made by the court under the provisions of s. 19 of the Act. This may be for the destruction or forfeiture of those goods, or, alternatively, no order may be made, in which event the property will be returned to its source.

Regard must be had to the availability of other remedies in making such orders. This remedy appears to apply irrespective of the guilt or otherwise of the recipient of the order for delivery up, thus potentially affecting, for example, an innocent shopkeeper who was unaware that goods he or she obtained from a manufacturer infringe a trade mark. There seems to be no provision for the proprietor to take possession of the infringing goods himself.[148]

So what goods are infringing goods? Section 17 of the Act makes clear that goods, material, or items can all infringe and all are referred to in all of the remedies provisions. The section provides full definitions in this respect. Under s. 17(2), infringing goods must bear a sign that is identical or similar to the mark and must be either an infringement or

---

[142] Case C-3/78 *Centrafarm BV v. American Home Products Corp.* [1978] ECR 1823, [1979] 1 CMLR 326.
[143] [1989] RPC 497.
[144] TMA 1994, s. 14.
[145] See Chapter 25.
[146] *Gillette UK Ltd v. Edenwest Ltd* [1994] RPC 279.
[147] TMA 1994, s. 18.
[148] Ibid., ss. 16(3), 19(1) and (5).

be about to be imported, which would mean that they would then (subject to EC rules) infringe; finally, they may infringe in any other way—although it is far from clear what is achieved by this last part of the provision. Infringing material may include the labelling or packaging of goods, the use of the mark on business paper or in adverts; infringing items are those that are specifically designed or adapted for making copies of the mark or something similar to it, in relation to which the person in possession, custody, or control is, or should be, aware of its use in the process of infringement.

A new range of criminal offences concerning the unauthorized use of trade marks has also been created by s. 92 of the 1994 Act and other offences about false claims about registration are created by ss. 94 and 95. Also, goods, material, or items that may come into the possession of anyone in connection with the investigation or prosecution of these and related offences may be the subject of forfeiture if it appears to the court that such offences have been created.

Why are these extra remedies necessary in trade mark law? The answer is simple: the production of counterfeit goods has proceeded apace both in the UK and elsewhere. The value of the trade mark is under general threat from a tidal wave of counterfeit goods that, in order to succeed on the market, are very likely to infringe the trade marks on 'real' products. Wide-ranging measures, including those directed against importation and illicit manufacture, are thus necessary to protect the very real economic interests of the proprietors of trade marks.

The draconian nature of infringement proceedings means, however, that they represent a real threat to anyone innocently accused and thus also give a real motive to rivals to make groundless threats of infringement proceedings. Thus, for the first time, the 1994 Act makes provision for remedies for the victim of such groundless threats in relation to trade marks[149] as has been the case for some time in patent law.[150] This right is given only to what may be described as 'secondary infringers'—that is, not the person who actually applies the mark to the goods, or imports them, or supplies the infringing service, but rather those in the wholesale network, such as shop owners and distributors. Such claimants may seek redress in the form of declaration, injunction, and/or damages, and the onus is on the defendant to show that the claim of infringement is justified. This is useful, if limited, protection for innocent parties.

Revocation and invalidity

The grant of a trade mark lasts initially for ten years from the date of its registration[151] and this may be renewed for a seemingly indefinite number of further periods of ten years thereafter on payment of the appropriate fee[152]—currently £200 for a renewal in one class and £50 in any extra classes in relation to which the renewal of the registration is sought.[153] These are small prices to pay for the maintenance of a famous trade mark on the Register and thus the retention of a commercially valuable monopoly.

As ever, however, there is a problem: such rights may be lost in two ways—either by way of a successful application for the revocation of the trade mark or, alternatively, by way of a claim that the initial registration was invalid. Either of these routes will, if pursued

---

[149] Ibid., s. 21; see *Prince plc v. Prince Sports Group Inc.* [1998] FSR 21.
[150] Patents Act 1977, s. 70.
[151] TMA 1994, s. 42(1).
[152] Ibid., (2) and s. 43.
[153] Trade Marks (Fees) Rules 2000, SI 2000/137.

successfully, lead to the sudden end of the trade mark and the rights therein. The increasing use of opposition proceedings during which some of the grounds for revocation may have been raised brings about the question of estoppel for the purposes of the revocation proceedings. The Court of Appeal has held, however, that unsuccessfully raising an issue in the course of revocation proceedings does not mean that one is estopped from raising it again in the course of revocation proceedings, because the Act clearly created to different and parallel sets of provisions.[154]

Revocation

There are four grounds listed in s. 46(1) of the 1994 Act as being reasons for revocation. Firstly, five years of lack of genuine use of the mark in the UK[155] without cause can lead to revocation of the registration and it is for the proprietor to prove that there has been use.[156] It is not clear, however, whether the courts can revoke the trade mark in respect of part of the goods or services for which it has been registered on grounds of non-use in respect of that part of the registration. That matter has been referred to the European Court of Justice for a preliminary ruling, but it appears that the case has been settled and that no answer will therefore be forthcoming from the Court.[157]

Secondly, a suspension for the same period (after initial use) is a ground for revocation. A third ground is that, whether due to the acts or the inactivity of the proprietor, the mark has become the common name for the product in question in the trade. The main difficulty here is to determine the scope of the trade—that is, of the relevant circles in which the mark is now used as a common name for the product. This is a particularly difficult issue in those cases in which the product is not directly sold to the end user, but in which intermediaries are also involved. The European Court of Justice has provided the following guidance on that point:

> in cases where intermediaries participate in the distribution to the consumer or the end user of a product which is the subject of a registered trade mark, the relevant circles whose views fall to be taken into account in determining whether that trade mark has become the common name in the trade for the product in question comprise all consumers and end users and, depending on the features of the market concerned, all those in the trade who deal with that product commercially.[158]

Finally, revocation of a mark is also appropriate if it has been used in a misleading manner, especially as to the nature, quality, or origin of the goods or services in question. In effect, the first two grounds penalize non-use, while the latter two grounds are aimed at confusing use of a mark.

Genuine use

'Use' seems to be generously defined by the new law. Use by someone other than the proprietor—although with his or her consent—will suffice, which is an obvious corollary of the more relaxed approach to the licensing of trade marks. The grant of a trade mark licence on its own, however, was held not to be sufficient evidence of use of the trade mark;

[154] *Special Effects Ltd v. L'Oreal SA* [2007] RPC 15 (CA).

[155] See *United Biscuits (UK) Ltd v. Asda Stores Ltd* [1997] RPC 513.

[156] TMA 1994, s. 100.

[157] *Daimler Chrysler AG v. Alavi (t/a Merc)* [2001] RPC 813; see also *Decon Laboratories v. Fred Baker Scientific & Veltek Associates Ltd* [2001] RPC 293.

[158] Case C-371/02 *Björnekulla Fruktindustrier AB v. Procordia Food AB* [2004] ETMR 977 at [26].

real genuine use by the licensee was also required.[159] Similarly use of a mark that is not identical, but equally not different, in its essential character will count as use of the mark, as will the use of it in the UK solely for export purposes.[160]

A good example from the old law of the first type of revocation is provided by the facts of *Imperial Group Ltd v. Philip Morris & Co. Ltd,*[161] in which the word 'Nerit' was registered for cigarettes by the defendants, who were hoping in due course to launch the 'Merit' brand of cigarettes, which was, of course, unregistrable as a laudatory epithet, but the use of which by others could be blocked by the 'Nerit' mark. A tiny number of cigarettes were sold under the name, but the Court of Appeal saw through the subterfuge.[162] There was no genuine use of the mark and it was accordingly expunged from the Register. This case would appear to be one that would be decided similarly under the new law.

The question of what amounts to genuine use of the trade mark in this context was examined by the European Court of Justice in *Ansul v. Ajax.*[163] The Court ruled that there is 'genuine use' of a trade mark if the mark is used in accordance with its essential function—that is, to guarantee the identity of the origin of the goods or services for which it is registered—in order to create or preserve an outlet for those goods or services. Genuine use does not include token use for the sole purpose of preserving the rights conferred by the mark. When assessing whether use of the trade mark is genuine, regard must be had to all of the facts and circumstances that are relevant to establishing whether the commercial exploitation of the mark is real, particularly whether such use is viewed as warranted in the economic sector concerned to maintain or create a share in the market for the goods or services protected by the mark, the nature of the goods or services at issue, the characteristics of the market, and the scale and frequency of use of the mark. The fact that a mark that is not used for goods that are newly available on the market, but for goods that were sold in the past, does not mean that its use is not genuine if the proprietor makes actual use of the same mark for component parts that are integral to the make-up or structure of such goods, or for goods or services directly connected with the goods previously sold and intended to meet the needs of customers of those goods.

In the absence of genuine use, revocation can only be averted if there is a proper reason for the non-use. A proper reason must arise independently of the will of the trade mark owner, because any inference from the owner would enter into conflict with the basic premise that a trade mark registration carries with it a desire to exploit, rather than to block, opportunities for other competitors. The hurdle must also have a direct relationship with the mark. The potential to use the mark must depend on the hurdle being overcome successfully. Hurdles that are only indirectly related to the mark, but that, for example, make exploitation of the mark less profitable or more cumbersome than foreseen in the initial business plan will not be sufficient. On top of that, a hurdle that simply makes it more difficult to use the mark is not sufficient: the use must have become impossible or at least unreasonable. The appropriate use of the mark must have been jeopardized seriously. For example, a trade mark owner cannot seriously be required to sell its goods in the outlets of its competitors. In such a case, the use of the

---

[159] *Philosophy Inc. v. Ferretti Studio Srl* [2003] RPC 288 (CA) (the *'Philosophy di Alberta Ferretti' Trade Mark* case).

[160] TMA 1994, s. 46(2).

[161] [1982] FSR 72.

[162] See also *Bud & Budweiser Budbräu Trade Marks* [2003] RPC 477.

[163] Case C-40/01 *Ansul v. Ajax* [2003] ECR I-2349; see also *La Mer Technology Inc. v. Labratoires Goemar SA* [2005] FSR 29.

mark is not impossible, but it has become unreasonable. Or as the European Court of Justice summarized it:

> only obstacles having a sufficiently direct relationship with a trade mark making its use impossible or unreasonable, and which arise independently of the will of the proprietor of that mark, may be described as 'proper reasons for non-use' of that mark.[164]

Confusing use

The 'confusing use' grounds for revocation pose separate issues. The fact that the acts, in particular, of a proprietor lead to his or her trade mark becoming a household or generic name may be thought to be grounds for acclaim, rather than for the revocation of the mark. But the fact that this ground for revocation only arises from the acts or omissions of the proprietor is the explanation for the provision, the scope of which is quite narrow, and justifies its presence. If the public habitually refers to all vacuum cleaners as 'Hoovers', no ground for revocation arises; it is only if the proprietors cause the confusion—perhaps by failing to make clear that their use of 'Hoover' is as a trade mark—that this ground arises.

Misleading use is the most obvious ground for revocation, given that, if the intention was present at the time of registration, such a mark would never be allowed in the first place. Inactivity when a mark turns into a common name is also a risk: the mark 'spam-buster', for example, turned into a common name for computer programming services to prevent or combat spam. The right holder's inactivity then exposed it to the possibility of revocation on the basis of s. 46(1)(c) of the 1994 Act.[165]

The issue of whether use of a mark under a bare licence can render the mark deceptive and susceptible to revocation under s. 46(1)(d) remains an open and complex question. The Act clearly sees a mark as a sign that certain goods or services come from a single business source or undertaking[166] and it was therefore arguable that that function was still fulfilled as long as the goods came from one (or more) licensee(s)—but doubts are bound to arise if the licence involved is a bare licence that does not involve any cooperation or quality control.[167] As a matter of fact, it was even more likely that the public would be misled if, after the termination of a licence, two unrelated undertakings were allowed to continue the use of the same trade mark. The mark would then no longer be able to fulfil its function to distinguish and it would therefore fall to be revoked under s. 46(1)(d).[168]

Anyone can apply

Generally, the 1994 Act allows anyone to apply for revocation,[169] although the burden of proof is placed on the objector to overcome the presumption that the registration is valid.[170] The only restriction on this appears to be that five years of acquiescence in the use of a trade mark by the holder of an earlier right will debar such a person from objecting to the validity of the trade mark.

Section 46(1) of the 1994 Act provides that a trade mark may be revoked in any of the circumstances listed above, but the wording of Art. 12(2) of the Directive that the section

---

[164] Case C-246/05 *Armin Häupl v. Lidl Stiftung & Co. KG* [2007] ETMR 61 at [54].
[165] *Hormel Foods Corp. v. Antilles Landscape Investments NV* [2005] RPC 28.
[166] See, e.g., *Glaxo Group v. Dowelhurst Ltd* [2000] FSR 529.
[167] *Scandecor Developments AB v. Scandecor Marketing AB* [2001] 2 CMLR 30 (HL).
[168] Ibid. For another example on this point, see *Zakritoe Aktsionernoe Obchtechestvo 'Torgovy Dom Potomkov Postavechtchika Dvora Ego Imperatorskago Velitschestva Pa Smirnova' v. Diageo North America Inc.*, Ch D, judgment of 7 April 2003, [2003] EWHC 970.
[169] TMA 1994, s. 46(4).
[170] Ibid., s. 72.

implements is not clear on the point of whether revocation is mandatory or whether it involves a discretion for the court.[171]

Invalidity

Turning to removal of a trade mark from the Register on the grounds of its invalidity, it is s. 47 of the 1994 Act that provides the relevant rules. It is important to note that the key distinction between 'revocation' and 'invalidity' is that, in the latter case, the registration is deemed to have never been made and thus amounts to a complete legal nullity, except in relation to transactions that are past and closed.[172]

The grounds for claiming invalidity are straightforward and refer back to the rules on unregistrable marks created by ss. 3 and 5 of the Act. Any mark gained in contradiction to those provisions is an invalid mark. The sole exception to this is in relation to marks that should not have been registered on the grounds of non-distinctiveness, descriptiveness, or customary or generic use.[173] These will not lose their validity if, after registration, they acquire by their use the necessary distinctive character that, had it been present at the time of registration, would have, in any event, justified their valid registration at that time. Any person may once again object to the validity of a mark and, if registration has been obtained in bad faith, the Registrar may himself initiate the application for a declaration of invalidity.

In general, it is clear that the symbiotic relationship of infringement and revocation arguments has been well understood by the authors of the new trade mark legislation. The same basic ideas stemming from the basic notion of trade mark registrability run through both infringement and revocation provisions. This makes for a generally cogent piece of legislation, especially by contrast with its (much-amended) predecessor.

An overview

That the old law needed reform was undoubted: its convolutions and complexities were considerable, and became worse as amendment after amendment was made.

Radical changes were introduced in relation to trade mark infringement and the scope of trade mark protection. In these areas, the legal system now extends its protection beyond the origin function of the trade mark, even if the latter is still its primary function. This evolution is clearly based on the influence of the Directive; it is not always reflected clearly in the 1994 Act and the courts in this country do not necessarily readily accept it. Nevertheless, it clearly emerges from the case law of the European Court of Justice. *Sabel v. Puma*[174] provided a first indication in this respect and this has now been followed up by a ruling that confusion can exist if the public perceives the goods or services as being produced in different places and by economically linked undertakings, rather than necessarily by the same undertaking.[175] This clearly goes beyond the protection of the function of origin.[176] The trade mark owner also gets protection for some of the non-origin uses of its trade mark.

---

[171] *Scandecor Developments AB v. Scandecor Marketing AB* [2001] 2 CMLR 30.

[172] TMA 1994, s. 47(6) and (7).

[173] Ibid., s. 3(1).

[174] Case C-251/95 [1997] ECR I-6191, [1998] 1 CMLR 445.

[175] Case C-39/97 *Canon Kabushiki Kaisha v. Metro-Goldwyn-Mayer Inc.* [1998] ECR I-5507, [1998] All ER (EC) 934.

[176] P. Torremans 'The likelihood of association of trade marks: an assessment in the light of the recent case law of the Court of Justice' [1998] IPQ 295–310.

At one stage, one had the impression that things would stop there and that s. 10(3) of the 1994 Act would really remain reserved for exceptional cases. That has now all changed, and it seems easy for a mark to acquire a reputation and bring itself under the scope of that subsection. On top of that, the requirements contained in the subsection have been interpreted liberally and the impression is created that s. 10(3) will become the norm, and that s. 10(2) and its stricter norms will only apply to a limited number of cases. Such a move cannot be welcomed unreservedly and represents a massive expansion of the rights of the owners of trade marks.

Clearly, the legal debate has not yet reached a final conclusion in this area. But whatever the final outcome will turn out to be, the changes in this area will have been far more revolutionary than the initial cases tried to make us believe.

Further reading

CARBONI, A., 'Two stripes and you're out! Added protection for trade marks with a reputation' (2004) 26 EIPR 5, 229.

HARPER, S. and CURLEY, D., 'Bubble confusion: the O2 decision' (2006) 28 EIPR 9, 499.

KITCHIN, D., LLEWELYN, D., MELLOR, J., MEADE, R., MOODY-STUART, T. and KEELING, D. (2005) *Kerly's Law of Trade Marks and Trade Names*, 14th edn, London: Sweet and Maxwell, ch. 14.

SIMON, I., 'Embellishment: trade mark use triumph or decorative disaster' (2006) 28 EIPR 6, 321.

WÜRTENBERGER, G., 'Community trade mark law astray or back to the roots!' (2006) 28 EIPR 11, 549.

27

Trade marks—European and international aspects

International aspects—introduction

We have already noted that one of the reasons for a new law of trade marks in 1994 was the need for the UK to bring its system into accord with its various international and European obligations. It is Part II of the Trade Marks Act 1994 that seeks to do this by, in turn, making provision with regard to the European Union (EU) Community trade mark, the new Protocol to the 1891 Madrid Agreement concerning the International Registration of Marks, and the provisions of the Paris Convention for the Protection of Industrial Property 1883. The latter two are long-standing examples of the traditional incompatibility of aspects of the common lawyer's approach to trade marks with the general international approach.

The Community trade mark

The 1994 Act itself deals with each of these matters in an apparently cursory manner. Under s. 52 of that Act, the Secretary of State is simply given the power to make such regulations that he feels are appropriate in connection with the operation of the Community Trade Mark Regulation.[1] In particular, applying for a Community mark through the Patent Office, the interrelationship of domestic and Community marks, and jurisdictional issues are flagged up as particular issues in respect of which UK regulations may need to be made.[2]

But this low-key legislative approach should not be allowed to disguise the significance of the developments taking place under this heading: the Regulation establishing the new Community trade mark is, of course, binding in itself and this creates an entirely new trade mark system in parallel to that which operates in the UK, but the new system is not to be seen as a rival; rather, proprietors have a choice. If they are active across Europe, the Community trade mark will provide valuable comprehensive and consistent coverage from a single application. But for many applicants, only a domestic registration will be needed and this will be the (presumably) cheaper way forward that will be preferred by many.

The language of the Regulation is almost identical to that of the Harmonization Directive that, in turn, the 1994 Act implements, and the basic structure of the system and its key definitions are the same across the Regulation, the Directive, and the Act. It is not therefore proposed to go through the Regulation Article by Article, because to do so would simply be to repeat much of what has been said. It is, however, useful to refer to the overall structure of the Regulation for the sake of reference.

[1] Regulation 40/94 (1994) OJ L 11/1.
[2] Community Trade Mark Regulations 1996, SI 1996/1908.

Article 1 of the Regulation[3] establishes that the mark shall have a unitary character—that is, that it will be equally effective and be equally treated throughout the Community: a single mark in a single market. Article 4 gives the basic definition of a mark, which must be a sign that is capable of being represented graphically and of distinguishing goods or services from those of other traders. Article 7 provides the absolute grounds for non-registration, closely similar to those in s. 3 of the 1994 Act, while Art. 8 provides the so-called 'relative grounds for refusal of a mark', this approximating to s. 5 of the UK legislation. Article 29 creates a priority date system, and there is a full examination and search procedure.[4] The mark lasts for ten years and is renewable for further ten-year periods thereafter.[5]

There are, of course, some points of distinction between the Regulation and other trade mark legislation. The unitary nature of the Community trade mark is reinforced by the provision[6] that the grounds for absolute unregistrability apply across the whole Community even if they are applicable in only a part of the Community. So, if a UK company uses a mark that happens, in Greek, to be a word regarded as being against public morality, no Community mark can be granted and resort would thus have to be had to individual national registrations of the mark. Protection is given for prior rights even in unregistered marks, but only if they are '*of more than mere local significance*'.[7]

There is, unlike in the UK system, no need to file a declaration of use or bona fide intention to use the mark. Perhaps of more significance is that all of the relative grounds for not registering a mark apply only when they are raised in opposition proceedings.[8] The Office itself conducts a more limited official search: in essence, only formalities and absolute grounds for refusal are checked. A list of possibly conflicting marks and applications is also drawn up, and sent to the applicant and the right holders that are potentially affected by the application are informed of it. It is then up to them to follow the matter up via opposition proceedings. The number of opposition proceedings and of potential appeal to the European Courts of First Instance and, eventually, of Justice, is therefore rather high. There is a Community collective mark, but there is no provision for a Community certification mark. Once granted, a Community trade mark can only be dealt with as an entity—that is, it can only be assigned as a whole, etc.[9] Infringement proceedings are brought before national courts, but each member State has had to designate a small number of specialized Community trade mark courts, at both first instance and appeal levels.[10]

As soon as the new Community trade mark system came into being, the sceptics were proved to be wrong. The system has, in its first couple of years in operation, been highly successful. It has attracted more registrations than expected and it clearly has taken away business from the national trade mark registries. Its procedures are complex, but this is mainly due to the international nature of the whole operation and its fees are not unduly high, especially when compared to the fees of the European Patent Office in Munich as the other transnational intellectual property office. The Community Trade

---

[3] Community Trade Mark Regulation, Art 1(2).

[4] Ibid., Arts 36–39.

[5] Ibid., Arts 46–47.

[6] Ibid., Art 7(2).

[7] Ibid., Art 8(4).

[8] Ibid., Art. 8(1); cf TMA 1994, s. 8.

[9] Ibid., Art. 16.

[10] Ibid., Arts 91–92. These courts have exclusive jurisdiction to deal with infringement proceedings, actions for a declaration of non-infringement, actions for compensation for acts done during the application period, and counterclaims for revocation or for declarations of invalidity.

Mark Office will not make searches itself, but will depend on rivals to initiate opposition proceedings, thus alleviating the examination process and reducing it to purely administrative checks.

But the functioning of a system that has to consider the meaning and significance of words in all of the languages of an expanded Community is bound to be difficult; the fact that enforcement of rights conferred by Community trade marks is, to a large extent, left to national courts will surely hinder, rather than help, the creation of a unitary system. In any event, national registrations will continue and may well still have the effect of distorting the single market. More significantly, there is an alternative method of obtaining international registrations and it is to this that we now turn.

The international registration of marks

The second part of the 1994 Act with international repercussions concerns the international registration of marks. Once again, the legislation itself adopts a minimalist approach, s. 54 of the Act allowing the Secretary of State to make '*such provisions as he thinks fit*' for giving domestic effect to the provisions of the Madrid Protocol. Again, however, the significance of this is far-reaching.

There has long been an International Register of Trade Marks, maintained by the World Intellectual Property Organization (WIPO) and established under the Madrid Agreement. An international registration lasts for a period of 20 years, with provision for recurrent renewals for another period of the same duration. Only one application needs to be made nominating the signatory countries in relation to which the applicant wishes to be granted registration. If an international registration is secured, the national trade mark offices in the nominated countries must recognize it unless it falls foul of a domestic provision that would prevent a domestic registration. The effect is that a single application leads to a collection of domestic marks.

The Madrid Protocol of 1989 is designed to create a similar parallel system that enables many more countries to join the international system. The basis of an international registration may, under the Protocol, be a domestic application and not only, as hitherto, a domestic registration, and the periods of registration and renewal are reduced to ten years. The overall picture, however, is the same as that under the Agreement, in that a single international application should confer a collection of national trade marks.[11]

When provision was made under s. 54 of the 1994 Act,[12] two things were provided for: firstly, a UK application or registration was allowed to be directed onto the international level by establishing appropriate rules; secondly, provision was made for the recognition by the UK of an international registration that has originated in another jurisdiction— which will be known as an 'international trade mark (UK)'.[13]

The Madrid system and the Community trade mark

It is tempting to view the Madrid Protocol system and the Community trade mark as being rivals to each other, and this is indeed so for a business trading in a limited number

---

[11] For an excellent full account of the workings of the Madrid Protocol, see G. Kunze, 'The Madrid System for the international registration of marks as applied under the Protocol' (1994) 6 EIPR 223.

[12] The Trade Marks (International Registration) Order 1996, SI 1996/714. (The UK became a party to the Protocol to the Madrid Agreement on 1 December 1995 and the Protocol itself became operational on 1 April 1996. The UK is still not a party to the Madrid Agreement.)

[13] TMA 1994, s. 53.

of European countries, for example, France and the Benelux states. For a truly multinational company, however, it seems likely that both systems may be employed, with a Community application being made and this then forming the basis of an international registration (the Community trade mark will be recognized for this purpose) that allows a registration to be secured for non-EU states such as Switzerland and Norway. The only real advantage that the Madrid system enjoys is that, by establishing registration on a national, rather than an international, level, it avoids the problem that the unacceptability of a mark in one particular state would entirely prevent the registration of a Community trade mark and that it would simply allow registration to occur in all other states under the Madrid system.

The Paris Convention

The third and final area of the international aspects of trade mark law dealt with by the 1994 legislation concerns the changes made to the law in order to bring the UK into line with provisions of the Paris Convention 1883. The 1994 Act extends the protection of the law, as has been seen, to cover well-known trade marks held by nationals of, or businesses domiciled in, signatory countries, irrespective of whether there is business activity or goodwill in the UK.[14] This is the principal change, and has significant implications for both trade mark law and also for the tort of passing off, considered in the next chapter.

Additional provisions in the 1994 Act also clearly fulfil Paris Convention obligations: s. 57 protects flags and other state insignia of a signatory country, which shall not be registered without appropriate permission; similar protection is granted to any international organization of which one or more Paris signatories are members. Such emblems cannot be used as, or as a part of, trade marks if the use suggests a misleading connection between the organization and the trade mark. Thus entrepreneurs will not be able to sell WIPO sweatshirts, but WIPO apparently can.

A final Paris-related provision is found in s. 60 of the 1994 Act, which allows the holder of an overseas mark to render invalid a mark registered in respect of it in the UK by an agent or representative who has acted without the appropriate authority. An example of this under similar provisions of the old law is provided by *K Sabatier Trade Mark*,[15] in which a distributor had registered the mark of a French manufacturer of knives; this was expunged from the Register.

There is an obligation under the Paris Convention[16] to provide protection against unfair competition. Clearly, much of trade mark law and the tort of passing off has this effect, but the absence of any action for unfair competition as such is bound to raise a potential clash that may arise in the future.

Internationalization of both trade mark law and trade

The internationalization of the trade mark scene is an inevitable reflection of multinational companies and multinational trade. Clearly, such interests need protection as a

---

[14] Ibid., ss. 56, 6(1)(c).
[15] [1993] RPC 97.
[16] Article 10bis.

reflection of their commercial value—but there must be a slight note of caution. The pro-motion of image through trade marks is not an abstract exercise, but one that interacts with the citizen, who is being persuaded to buy a product or use a service. Individual perceptions vary from state to state and are nurtured in different ways by different lan-guages. International cooperation may be essential, but international conformity is not and may even be unwise. The permissive Madrid approach may be thought to reflect this more satisfactorily than the single Community trade mark, but more and more compa-nies do business across the EU and treat it as a single market in which they market their goods or services under a single trade mark. For them, the Community trade mark may be the ideal tool and they may use the Madrid system only to expand protection to certain non-EU member States.

Trade marks and the free movement of goods

We discussed, in relation to patents, how the provisions on free movement and competi-tion law in the Treaty of Rome apply to intellectual property rights. The principles we set out there obviously also apply to trade marks[17] and this section will only be concerned with the specific application of these principles.

Towards a definition of the specific subject matter and the essential function

Centrafarm v. Winthrop

The first case decided by the European Court of Justice is a parallel case to that of *Centrafarm v. Sterling Drug*[18] in relation to patents and is, in relation to trade marks, *Centrafarm v. Winthrop.*[19] As in the patent case, Centrafarm was buying drugs in the UK and importing them into the Netherlands for resale. In both countries, the drug was mar-keted under the trade mark 'Negram'. Winthrop, the Dutch subsidiary of Sterling, owned the trade mark in the Netherlands, and tried to exercise its rights under that right to block the importation into, and resale operation in, the Netherlands. Unfortunately, the Court did not spell out fully the essential function of a trade mark in this case, although it is fair to say that the approach taken is identical to that taken in relation to patents, because the Court went on to define the specific subject matter, which included a reference to the exhaustion doctrine.

The specific subject matter of a trade mark is:

> the guarantee that the owner of the trade mark has the exclusive right to use that mark, for
> the purpose of putting products protected by the trade mark into circulation for the first

---

[17] And along the same lines to geographical indications, appellations of origin, and designations for foodstuffs. The European Court of Justice held recently, for example, that 'Article 30 of the Treaty (now, after amendment, Article 28 EC) precludes a member state from applying to products imported from another mem-ber state, where they are lawfully produced and marketed, a national rule prohibiting the marketing of a cheese without rind under the designation "Emmenthal" in that member state'. The Court argued that consumers were not effectively being misled and that, even if they were, the measure would have been disproportion-ate; a bit of information added to the designation would have been sufficient: Case C-448/98 *Jean-Pierre Guimont* [2001] ETMR 14.

[18] Case 15/74 *Centrafarm BV v. Sterling Drug Inc.* [1974] ECR 1147, [1974] 2 CMLR 480.

[19] Case 16/74 *Centrafarm BV v. Winthrop BV* [1974] ECR 1183, [1974] 2 CMLR 480.

time, and is therefore intended to protect him against competitors wishing to take advantage of the status and reputation of the trade mark by selling products illegally bearing that mark.[20]

The owner of the trade mark has the exclusive right to use the trade mark for commercial purposes and can oppose infringement. He or she can exercise the right by putting products (or services) labelled with the trade mark on the market for the first time, but, afterwards, his or her rights are exhausted.

These are all rights available under parallel trade marks in the Community. The comments that we made in Chapter 4 in relation to the similar specific subject matter of a patent apply here as well. Any exercise of the trade mark that goes further will fall foul of Arts 28 and 30 of the EC Treaty. Obviously, the trade mark owner can put the products on the market him or herself, or he or she can allow a third party to exploit the trade mark with his or her consent. The option taken does not influence the application of the exhaustion doctrine: Winthrop could thus not be allowed to exercise its Dutch trade mark rights to block the importation and resale operation that Centrafarm was setting up for Negram, because the marketing in the UK had been done by the Sterling group, meeting the consent requirement, and had exhausted all rights under parallel trade marks in the Community. Such exercise of its trade mark rights by Winthrop would go beyond the specific subject matter of a trade mark, and it therefore falls foul of Arts 28 and 30. In the words of the Court:

> the exercise, by the owner of a trade mark, of the right which he enjoys under the legislation of a Member State to prohibit the sale, in that State, of a product which has been marketed under the trade mark in another Member State by the trade mark owner or with his consent is incompatible with the rules of the EEC Treaty concerning the free movement of goods within the Common Market.[21]

The fact that the product has been manufactured outside the EU, before it was put on the market inside the EU, is irrelevant as long as the product was put into circulation in the EU by, or with the consent of, the trade mark owner.[22]

The consent for the marketing within the EU is the crucial element. In its decision in *Peak Holding*,[23] the European Court of Justice clarified the concept of putting the goods on the market with the consent of the proprietor. In this case, the proprietor had imported the goods into the EEA and had offered them for sale in its own shops, but it had not actually sold them. The Court held that the goods had not been put on the market with the consent of the proprietor of the mark in the absence of a first sale of the goods; such a first sale would take place were the goods to be sold to another operator in the EEA even if the contract were to prohibit resale in the EEA. The onus to prove the consent—whether express or implied—of the proprietor of the trade mark lies with the parallel importer, but the standard of proof is the usual one in civil litigation—that is, the balance of probabilities. The Court has used the term 'unequivocal consent' simply to indicate that the consent must be clear and that proved acts that can be consistent with consent, but also with its absence, are not sufficient to demonstrate consent. That does not change the standard of proof.[24]

---

[20] Ibid. at 1194 and 5080.
[21] Ibid. at 1195 and 510.
[22] Case C-352/95 *Phytheron International SA v. Jean Bourdon* [1997] ECR I-1729.
[23] Case C-16/03 *Peak Holding AB v. Axolin-Elinor AB* [2005] ECR I-11313, [2005] Ch 261, [2005] 2 WLR 650.
[24] *Mastercigars Direct Ltd v. Hunters & Frankau Ltd* [2007] RPC 24, [2007] ETMR 44 (CA).

Hoffmann-La Roche v. Centrafarm

The essential function of the trade mark was spelled out in the next trade mark case to reach the European Court of Justice. In *Hoffmann-La Roche v. Centrafarm*,[25] the Court said that the essential function of a trade mark was:

> to guarantee the identity of the trade marked product to the consumer or ultimate user, by enabling him without any possibility of confusion to distinguish that product from products which have another origin.[26]

This has to be read in conjunction with the partial statement on the subject in *Centrafarm v. Winthrop*,[27] in which the protection of the goodwill of the owner of the trade mark was emphasized—but why this seemingly odd combination?

It is submitted that, in relation to trade marks, it is impossible to say that one function is more essential than the other as was the case in relation to patents. Goodwill is an essential element of a trade mark for its owner, but it will only exist if the consumer distinguishes the product or service labelled with the trade mark from other products or services. The guarantee for consumers or users that the product or service labelled with the trade mark is of a standard quality is essential in order for the goodwill—whether negative or positive—to be created. The combination of these two elements forms the essential function of a trade mark, which is fulfilled by the exercise of the rights within its specific subject matter.

It should also be remembered that this whole area of law is concerned with putting goods on the single market. The right holder can, in respect of lawfully manufactured goods, only act if the goods are to be put on the market. Lawfully manufactured goods that are in transit in order to be placed on a market outside the EU cannot be stopped and detained by customs authorities without infringing Art. 28 of the EC Treaty.[28]

The repackaging and relabelling saga

The starting point—repackaging in Hoffmann-La Roche

Further complications arose when certain trade marked drugs were sold in different packing formats in various member States. In the *Hoffmann-La Roche* case, the drug Valium was sold in packs containing a different number of pills in the UK and in Germany. Centrafarm bought the drugs in the UK, removed the outer packing and repacked the drug for the German market in packs containing the number of pills that was normal on the German market. It applied the Valium trade mark, which Hoffmann-La Roche owned all over Europe, to the packs destined for the German market. Hoffmann-La Roche wanted to rely on its German Valium trade mark to stop Centrafarm. It argued that it had not exhausted its rights in the trade mark, because it had not applied it to the repacked goods.

The European Court of Justice rejected the argument. Hoffmann-La Roche had marketed the drugs in the UK under the Valium trade mark and thereby exhausted its rights in all parallel trade marks. The way in which Hoffmann-La Roche wanted to use its trade mark went beyond its specific subject matter and fell foul of Arts 28 and 30. The interesting element in this case relates to the essential function of trade marks, because this needs

---

[25] Case 102/77 *Hoffmann-La Roche & Co. AG v. Centrafarm* [1978] ECR 1139, [1978] 3 CMLR 217.
[26] Ibid. at 1164 and 241.
[27] Case 16/74 *Centrafarm BV v. Winthrop BV* [1974] ECR 1183, [1974] 2 CMLR 480.
[28] Case C-115/02 *Administration des Douanes et Droits Indirects v. Rioglass SA & Transremar SL* [2004] ETMR 519.

to be fulfilled by the exercise of the rights under the specific subject matter of the trade mark. The goodwill of Hoffmann-La Roche and the interest of the consumers had therefore to be protected. This is the reason why the Court laid down additional requirements. It specified that there needs to be a guarantee that the repacking has no adverse effect on the original condition of the goods, because tampering with the goods would affect the goodwill of the owner of the trade mark and undermine the identity guarantee to which the consumer is entitled. The fact that the goods have been repacked means that the identity of the repacker should also figure on the repacked goods for the information of the consumer; the owner of the trade mark should be informed of the intention to repack the goods so that it can keep an eye on the market to safeguard its goodwill and act when that is threatened. If these conditions are met, the essential function of the trade mark is fulfilled and every exercise that goes beyond the specific subject matter of the trade mark will fall foul of Arts 28 and 30.[29]

The Court confirmed this approach in *Pfizer Inc. v. Eurim-Pharm GmbH*.[30]

The starting point—relabelling in American Home Products

It is not only repackaging that caused problems: a company could also use different trade marks for one product in different member States. This can, of course, be done for legitimate reasons, because it may not be possible to register the same trade mark in certain member States if a similar mark already exists or if the trade mark has a negative connotation in the language of that member State. The trade mark owner can, however, have less legitimate reasons. One trade mark per member State effectively partitions the single market: the owner of the trade marks can operate freely in each of the national markets from a dominant position. A challenger should be entitled to use the trade mark that the owner uses in that market in order to mount an effective challenge, and the owner will try to prevent this by relying on the trade mark and by alleging infringement.

This is what happened in *Centrafarm BV v. American Home Products Corp.*[31] American Home Products marketed the same drug in the UK under the trade mark 'Serenid', while using the trade mark 'Seresta' in the Benelux countries and Germany. Centrafarm bought the drug in the UK and sold it in the Netherlands, after changing the trade mark to Seresta, because Dutch consumers were familiar with this trade mark. American Home Products objected to this practice and argued that it infringed its Dutch Seresta trade mark. In this case, there was no legitimate reason to use a different trade mark in the Netherlands.[32] The goodwill of American Home Products was not affected and the interests of the consumers were unharmed, safeguarding the essential function of the trade mark. The rights conferred by the trade mark were exercised to serve one function—that is, to restrict the free movement of goods and to partition the single market. Therefore this exercise of the trade marks should fall foul of Arts 28 and 30, because it constitutes a disguised restriction of trade, and this was indeed what the Court decided.[33] To be precise, the specific subject matter of the trade mark as a description of what is allowed was preserved, because the trade mark owner still put all products concerned on the market for the first time.

This case has been criticized, because it introduces a subjective criterion by relying on the intent of the owner of the trade marks.[34] Subsequent developments in the case law of

---

[29] Case 102/77 *Hoffmann-La Roche & Co. AG v. Centrafarm* [1978] ECR 1139, [1978] 3 CMLR 217.

[30] Case 1/81 *Pfizer Inc. v. Eurim-Pharm GmbH* [1981] ECR 2913, [1982] 1 CMLR 406.

[31] Case 3/78 *Centrafarm BV v. American Home Products Corp.* [1978] ECR 1823, [1978] 1 CMLR 326.

[32] For an example of a case in which there was such a legitimate reason, see Case C-313/94 *Fratelli Graffione SNC v. Ditta Fransa* [1996] ECR I-6039, [1997] 1 CMLR 925.

[33] Case 3/78 *Centrafarm BV v. American Home Products Corp.* [1978] ECR 1823, [1978] 1 CMLR 326.

[34] C. H. Baden Fuller, 'Economic issues relating to property rights in trade marks' (1981) 6 Eur LR 162.

the European Court of Justice have shown that it never intended to introduce a subjective element: the parallel importer does not have to prove that the right holder set out to partition the market deliberately.

We now turn to the detailed analysis of these subsequent developments, which have clarified a number of points.

Article 7 of the Directive: mere codification?

This, then, was the position before the harmonization of national trade mark laws. The Court's case law dealt with the apparent clash between the national trade mark laws of the member States, and Arts 28 and 30 of the EC Treaty. The First Harmonization Directive changed that picture.[35] It deals with exhaustion in its Art. 7 and, on the basis of that Article, the pharmaceutical industry challenged the validity of the Court's case law.[36] The issue of whether *Hoffmann-La Roche v. Centrafarm*[37] was still good law was brought before the Court as a preliminary question on the interpretation of Art. 7 of the Directive after a series of cases had been brought in the national courts by pharmaceutical companies that objected to the repackaging activity of parallel importers.[38]

The Directive grants the trade mark owner the exclusive right to affix the trade mark to the product or its packaging,[39] subject to the impact of the exhaustion principle. That principle is said, in Art. 7(1), not to *entitle the proprietor to prohibit [the trade mark's] use in relation to goods which have been put on the market within the Community under that trade mark by the proprietor or with his consent'*. Article 7(2) adds that Art. 7(1) will not stop the trade mark owner from opposing the continued marketing of the goods if he or she does so on reasonable grounds. Obvious examples of such grounds are cases in which the goods have been impaired or altered after having been put on the market by the trade mark owner, or with his or her consent.

The pharmaceutical companies argued that Art. 7(1) should be interpreted in such a way that the goods are the goods in the format and the unit in which they have been put on the market. This would mean, for example, 20 tablets of the pharmaceutical product in a box with certain dimensions, colours, etc. The parallel importer would be free to buy these boxes in another member State and resell them as they are, but any repackaging and reaffixing of the trade mark would constitute an infringement of the trade mark. Article 7(2) would only operate, for example, to allow the trade mark owner to stop the marketing

---

[35] Council Directive 89/104/EEC to approximate the laws of the member States relating to trade marks (1989) OJ L 40/1.

[36] The real reason why parallel imports of pharmaceutical products are such a problem in the Community—and especially in the eyes of the main pharmaceutical companies—is the difference in prices between the different member States. This would not be such a problem if the different prices were determined entirely freely by the pharmaceutical companies that produce the drugs, but, in practice, there is also a lot of government regulation in the area. The circumvention of the absence of a harmonization in the national rules regulating the prices of pharmaceutical products and the perceived lack of political will to achieve it by breaching the rules on free movement is not, however, allowed. National trade mark law cannot be allowed to disregard Community law in this area: the purpose of trade marks is not to remedy the market distortions caused by the national price-regulating regimes; what needs to be done is harmonizing those different national regimes.

[37] Case 102/77 [1978] ECR 1139, [1978] 3 CMLR 217.

[38] Cases C-427, 429 and 436/93 *Bristol-Meyers Squibb, CH Boehringer Sohn, Boehringer Ingelheim KG, Boehringer Ingelheim A/S & Bayer AG, Bayer Danmark A/S v. Paranova A/S* [1996] ECR I-3457, [1997] 1 CMLR 1151; Cases C-71, 72, and 73/94 *Eurim-Pharm Arzneimittel GmbH v. Beiersdorf AG; Boehringer Ingelheim KG & Farmitalia Carlo Erba GmbH* [1996] ECR I-3603, [1997] 1 CMLR 1222; Case C-232/94 *MPA Pharma GmbH v. Rhone-Poulenc Pharma GmbH* [1996] ECR I-3671; see also P. Torremans, 'New repackaging under the Trade Mark Directive of well-established exhaustion principles' [1997] 11 EIPR 664.

[39] Article 5(3)(a) of the Directive.

of damaged products. The same result is achieved if one admits that Art. 7(1) results in the exhaustion of the trade mark as soon as the trade marked product has been put on the market in any form, while giving a broad interpretation to Art. 7(2) by including any change of the brand presentation—that is, any form of repackaging and/or reaffixing of the trade mark—as a reasonable ground on which to exclude the operation of the exhaustion principle in Art. 7(1).[40]

This would, of course, involve a radical change in the definition of the exhaustion principle and it would reverse the Court's case law. Can the Directive be interpreted in this way? Or should one stick to the interpretation that Art. 7(1) results in the exhaustion of the trade mark as soon as the trade marked product has been put on the market in any form, while the only reasonable ground on the basis of which the trade mark owner can object involves a change to the product that is actually consumed—that is, the tablets in our earlier example?

Article 7 of the Directive: a return to basics

Before jumping to any conclusion, one should start with the basics. The starting point of all Community law in this area is Arts 28 and 30 of the EC Treaty. Any secondary Community legislation can only apply and not change the Treaty, and should therefore be interpreted in a way that is in line and compatible with its provisions.[41] The provisions of the Directive must thus be interpreted in the light of Arts 28 and 30 of the EC Treaty. What is not under discussion is that Art. 30 only provides for a partial exemption of trade mark rights from the application of Art. 28 and its free movement rule; what is exempted is the specific subject matter of the trade mark. The trade mark can play its competition-enhancing role[42] in the economy, but any other use is caught by Art. 28.

What, then, is the essence of a trade mark? A trade mark is essentially an indication of origin. The trade mark guarantees the consumer that a certain product has been manufactured by, or under the control of, a certain company that bears responsibility for the fact that the product meets certain standards or expectations of quality. The trade mark is the means by which the product is identified. That identification by customers leads to the establishment of goodwill for the company that is able to bind the customers to itself.[43]

The next question that needs to be answered therefore is the origin of what is indicated by the trade mark. The obvious answer is that of the goods that are labelled with the trade mark—but this does not solve our problem if one considers that marketing experts might suggest that the whole trade dress of a carefully marketed product forms part of the goods. A return to the basic principles of trade mark law provides the solution to this problem: a trade mark is a sign to distinguish goods that is registered in relation to a certain category or certain categories of goods. This means that a trade mark is, for example, registered in relation to pharmaceutical products; no one will pretend that anything other than the product that is actually used for medicinal purposes is covered by this category.

[40] See K. Dyekjaer-Hansen, 'The Trade Mark Directive and the protection of brands and branding' [1996] 1 EIPR 62 at 63.

[41] See Case C-47/90 *Etablissements Delhaize Frères v. Promalvin* [1992] ECR I-3669 at [26]; Case C-315/92 *Verband Sozialer Wettbewerb* [1994] ECR I-317 at [12], referred to in Joined Cases C-427, 429 and 436/93 *Bristol-Meyers Squibb v. Paranova A/S* [1996] ECR I-3457 at [27].

[42] The Court explicitly recognized that trade mark rights (within the constraints of their specific subject matter) form an essential element of the system of free competition on the Common Market that the Treaty set out to establish: Joined Cases C-427, 429 and 436/93 *Bristol-Meyers Squibb v. Paranova A/S* [1996] ECR I-3457 at [43].

[43] Ibid. at [43], with reference to Case C-10/89 *CNL-SUCAL NV SA v. HAG GF AG (Hag II)* [1990] ECR I-3711 at [13] and Case C-9/93 *IHT Internationaler Heiztechnik GmbH & Danziger v. Ideal Standard GmbH* [1994] ECR I-2789 at [37] and [45].

The trade dress, meanwhile, is not part of the goods. The goods or products are, for example, the tablets, but they do not include the box in which they are packed by the manufacturer. This is the maximum coverage of trade mark law before the Treaty provisions interfere with it, which interference can only reduce the level of protection and the options offered to the trade mark owner due to the fact that Art. 28 rules out restrictions to the free movement and Art. 30 only partially alleviates that ban. The outcome of the process can therefore not be that trade dress is now included in the definition of the goods to which a trade mark is applied and in relation to which it creates certain exclusive rights.

Let us now turn to the Directive: it must be clear that the Directive, or any other piece of secondary Community legislation, cannot introduce quantitative restrictions if it can only apply the provisions of the Treaty. Any other conclusion would involve a violation of Arts 28 and 30[44]—and only a new Treaty can change these Articles.

The final step brings us to the national trade mark laws. These must obviously be interpreted along the lines of the Directive. Because the Directive was supposed to harmonize the trade mark laws of the member States and the protection of trade marks as allowed in the context of Art. 30, one should, first of all, turn to the Directive when the compatibility of a provision of national trade mark law with Community law is at issue.[45] The Directive is supposed to offer more detailed rules and guidance, which is fully in line with the provisions of the Treaty.

Article 7 of the Directive: practical implications

Where does all of this theory lead us in practical terms? The question of whether or not national trade mark law can allow a trade mark owner to oppose the repackaging of pharmaceutical products and/or the reaffixing of the trade mark needs to be answered on the basis of the provisions of the Directive.[46]

Article 7 deals with the exhaustion issue in a complete way. The trade mark owner can oppose the activities of the parallel importer if that Article does not exhaust his or her right to object to these activities. On the basis of the text of Art. 7(1), it could be suggested that the term 'goods' can be said to include the goods as packed. It has been shown above, however, that this would involve an unjustifiable expansion of trade mark protection and that such an interpretation of the Directive would not be in line with the Treaty provisions—which leaves us with the question of whether a change of packaging can be a reasonable ground under Art. 7(2) of the Directive. If so, no exhaustion would take place. Once more, the text of the Directive does not provide a conclusive answer. We have to turn to the provisions of the Treaty[47] and analyse whether such a wide interpretation of the reasonable ground concept is required to guarantee that the trade mark can fulfil its essential role.

It is submitted that the European Court of Justice rightly decided that this was not the case. The trade mark should function as an indication of origin. For the consumer, this means that he or she needs to be sure that, when buying the trade marked product, he or she is buying the original pharmaceutical product—for example, the tablets—produced by the trade mark owner or under his or her control. No other products should be marketed under the trade mark to achieve this aim. In the cases under discussion, there was

---

[44] See Case C-51/93 *Meyhui NV v. Schott Zwiesel Glaswerke AG* [1994] ECR I-3879 at [11], referred to in Joined Cases C-427, 429 and 436/93 *Bristol-Meyers Squibb v. Paranova A/S* [1996] ECR I-3457 at [35].

[45] See Case 5/77 *Tedeschi v. Denkavit Commerciale srl* [1977] ECR 1555 at [35]; Case 227/82 *Van Bennekom* [1983] ECR 3883 at [35]; Case C-37/92 *Vanacker & Lesage* [1993] ECR I-4947 at [9]; Case C-323/93 *Société Civile Agricole du Centre d'insémination de la Crespelle* [1994] ECR I-5077 at [31]; referred to in Joined Cases C-427, 429, and 436/93 *Bristol-Meyers Squibb v. Paranova A/S* [1996] ECR I-3457 at [25].

[46] Joined Cases C-427, 429, and 436/93 *Bristol-Meyers Squibb v. Paranova A/S* [1996] ECR I-3457 at [26].

[47] See ibid. at [40].

no evidence that the pharmaceutical products had been tampered with or that any product was passed off as the product of the trade mark owner. Indeed, in the one instance in which a vaporizer was added by the parallel importer,[48] that item did not bear the trade mark and it was made clear that the item had been added by, and under the sole responsibility of, the parallel importer.

The consumer should also be able to rely on the trade mark to be sure that the pharmaceutical product he or she buys is of a certain quality, which requirement is met as long as the original product is not tampered with. The trade mark owner should also be allowed to preserve the goodwill created by the trade mark. The indication of origin points indeed towards certain goods, of a certain quality, coming from one source, or at least with one party—the trade mark owner—controlling the system. This requirement is met as long as no other goods are labelled with the trade mark and as long as the goods are not tampered with.[49]

To guarantee this, further additional rules have been added. The packaging should clearly indicate who produced the goods, so as not to create the impression that the parallel importer or any third party has any right to the trade mark.[50] The parallel importer responsible for the repackaging needs also to be identified clearly on the packaging, in order to show that the third party, and not the trade mark owner, is responsible for the packaging. The straightforward way to do so is to print on the new packaging in a prominent way a message that 'X' manufactured the product, while 'Y', the parallel importer, imported and repacked the product.[51] Even so, the packaging should not be of a low standard, because that association with materials of a low quality would damage the high quality standard that is associated with pharmaceutical products.[52]

The trade mark owner should also be allowed to control the use of the trade mark and to prevent any damage to the goodwill associated with the trade mark that any inappropriate use of the trade mark could cause. This means that the trade mark owner should be advised in advance of any repackaging activity and should be given the opportunity to request a sample copy of the repacked product for inspection.[53] It is the responsibility of the parallel importer to give that notice and the right holder should at least be given 15 days in which to object.[54]

Under these conditions, the trade mark can fulfil its role as an indication of origin. Any further requirement goes beyond that role and would therefore be out of line with Art. 30 of the EC Treaty. A requirement, for example, that the fact that the repackaging took place without the consent of the trade mark owner should be mentioned explicitly on the packaging would create the impression that there might be something wrong with the product.[55]

Article 7 of the Directive: a mere codification!

Article 7(2) of the Directive is really only a way of restating the rule contained in Art. 30 of the EC Treaty.[56] The interpretation that the Court had previously given to that Article in a repackaging context remains good law; all that these new cases have added to it is the

---

[48] Ibid. at [61].

[49] Ibid. at [59]–[64].

[50] Joined Cases C-71, 72 and 73/94 *Eurim-Pharm v. Beiersdorf* [1996] ECR I-3603 at [64], with reference to Case 1/81 *Pfizer v. Eurim-Pharm* [1981] ECR 2913 at [11].

[51] Joined Cases C-427, 429 and 436/93 *Bristol-Meyers Squibb v. Paranova A/S* [1996] ECR I-3457 at [70].

[52] Ibid. at [65]–[66] and [75]–[76]. See also Case C-348/04 *Boehringer Ingelheim KG & ors v. Swingward Ltd & ors (No. 2)* [2007] 2 CMLR 52.

[53] Joined Cases C-427, 429 and 436/93 *Bristol-Meyers Squibb v. Paranova A/S* [1996] ECR I-3457 at [78].

[54] Case C-143/00 *Boehringer Ingelheim AG v. Swingward Ltd* [2002] ECR I-3759.

[55] Joined Cases C-427, 429, and 436/93 *Bristol-Meyers Squibb v. Paranova A/S* [1996] ECR I-3457 at [72].

[56] Ibid. at [40].

fact that the Court seized the opportunity to clarify the rule and to provide the national court with more detailed guidance.

The parallel importer of pharmaceutical products is not free to repack them in any circumstances. Repackaging only becomes an option if the product is de facto marketed in different quantities in different member States. The right of the trade mark owner to oppose repackaging is only exhausted if the repackaging is necessary for the product to be marketable in the country of importation:[57] for example, because health insurance legislation prescribes a standard size.[58] This can be seen as a prerequisite for any repackaging and reaffixing of trade mark operation.

There is, however, no need for the parallel importer to prove that the trade mark owner set out to partition the market deliberately by marketing the product in different quantities in different member States. It was therefore also held in a relabelling case that one has to assess whether all of the circumstances at the time of the marketing in the import state made it objectively necessary to use another mark to make marketing possible. In the absence of such objective necessity, there will be no artificial partitioning of the market, which is required to allow relabelling. By requiring an artificial partitioning of the market to be demonstrated before allowing the repackaging of products, the Court left open only the option of opposing the marketing of parallel imported products by the trade mark owner in those cases in which this is necessary to preserve the specific subject matter of the trade mark. A de facto use of different packaging sizes is all that the parallel importer needs to demonstrate initially to justify its activity.[59]

Necessity

This set of cases could create the false impression that the parallel importer has an almost absolute freedom to repack and relabel the products. The analysis above shows that this is not the case, and that the parallel importer's activity is restricted to what is required and necessary to allow parallel imports.

The necessity point has become a vital one. The European Court of Justice summarized it as follows:

> a trade mark proprietor may rely on its trade mark rights in order to prevent a parallel importer from repackaging pharmaceutical products unless the exercise of those rights contributes to artificial partitioning of the markets between Member States[60]

It continued, vitally, to state that:

> replacement packaging of pharmaceutical products is objectively necessary within the meaning of the Court's case-law if, without such repackaging, effective access to the market concerned, or to a substantial part of that market, must be considered to be hindered as the result of strong resistance from a significant proportion of consumers to relabelled pharmaceutical products.[61]

It is therefore clear that the necessity test applies to the act of repackaging, but the question of whether it also applies to the presentation of the repackaged product—that is,

---

[57] The fact that the product is, apart from the size in which it is bought by the parallel importer, also available in the country of exportation in the size in which it is repacked does not alter this conclusion: see ibid. at [54].

[58] Ibid. at [53]–[56].

[59] Ibid. at [57]; Case C-379/97 *Pharmacia & Upjohn SA v. Paranova A/S* [2000] 1 CMLR 51.

[60] Case C-143/00 *Boehringer Ingelheim AG v. Swingward Ltd* [2002] ECR I-3759.

[61] Case C-443/99 *Merck, Sharp & Dohme GmbH v. Paranova Pharmazeutika Handels GmbH* [2003] Ch 327, [2002] ETMR 923; Case C-143/00 *Boehringer Ingelheim AG v. Swingward Ltd* [2002] ECR I-3759.

should the parallel importer also show that it had done nothing more than what was necessary in the terms of the manner of repackaging?—needed to be answered. How broad exactly is the concept of necessity?

The Court clarified the point by holding that the condition that the repackaging of the pharmaceutical product—either by reboxing the product and reapplying the trade mark, or by applying a label to the packaging containing the product—be necessary for its further commercialization in the importing member State is directed solely at the fact of repackaging, and not at the manner and style of the repackaging. There is therefore no need to show that a particular manner and style of repackaging or relabelling were required.[62]

The *Ballantines* case[63] also illustrates the necessity point. The parallel importer was given a certain freedom to bring the labelling of the bottles of whisky in line with the requirements of each member State and to identify itself, but the Court did not approve of the removal of the identification numbers from the bottles.[64] The latter was not required to allow parallel import to take place. Obviously, the presence of these numbers would also allow the producer of the whisky to trace the suppliers of the parallel importer. The Court argued that competition law would provide a remedy in case the producer decided to take action against the supplier of the parallel importer in an attempt to stop the parallel importation.[65] This is, however, not necessarily a straightforward conclusion and the decision of the Court of First Instance to annul a Commission decision on this point is a stark reminder of the difficulties of applying competition law successfully on this point.[66]

Marketing authorization

It should also not be forgotten that the marketing of pharmaceutical products is subject to a marketing authorization and that the parallel import licence of the parallel importer makes reference to the marketing authorization of the original product.[67] Deliberately revoking the marketing authorization for the original product when bringing a newer version of the product on the market might therefore be a means for the producer of blocking parallel imports of the original product. The European Court of Justice held therefore that Arts 28 and 30 of the EC Treaty preclude national

[62] Case C-348/04 *Boehringer Ingelheim KG & ors v. Swingward Ltd & ors (No. 2)* [2007] 2 CMLR 52.
[63] Case C-349/95 *Frits Loendersloot v. George Ballantine & Son Ltd* [1997] ECR I-6227, [1998] 1 CMLR 1015.
[64] It has been held, along the same lines, by Belgian Courts that trade mark law allowed the trade mark owner to oppose acts of the parallel importer such as the deletion of bar codes, the deletion of the mention that the product is only sold through recommended distributors, and the cutting of the seal on the boxes of a perfume. It was held that these measures were not necessary to allow parallel import and that less invasive measures that did not affect the goodwill of the trade mark owner (such as mention on the shop window or shelves that, despite the impression created by the products, the parallel importer is not a recommended distributor) would have been sufficient. The cutting of the seals specifically could create the impression or the suspicion that the bottle in the box had been tampered with or had been replaced and this could seriously affect the goodwill of the trade mark owner: *Delhaize v. Dior*, Court of Appeal Liège, 13 April 1995, [1995] Ing-Cons 379; *SA Parfums Nina Ricci v. SA Best Sellers Belgium*, Commercial Court Liège, 18 October 1999, [2000] TBH 386.
[65] For further details see I. Stamatoudi, 'From drugs to spirits and from boxes to publicity: decided and undecided issues in relation to trade mark and copyright exhaustion' [1999] IPQ 95.
[66] Case T-41/96 *Bayer AG and EFPIA v. Commission & Bundesverband der Arneimittel-Importeure eV* [2000] ECR II-3383, [2001] All ER (EC) 1, [2001] 4 CMLR 4. Upheld by the Court of Justice on appeal (Cases C-2/01 P and C-3/01P) [2004] 4 CMLR 13.
[67] See also *Aventis Pharma Deutschland GmbH v. Kohlpharma GmbH & MTK Pharma Vertriebs-GmbH* [2002] 3 CMLR 659.

legislation under which the withdrawal, at the request of its holder, of the marketing authorization of reference of itself entails the withdrawal of the parallel import licence granted for the medicinal product in question. Restrictions on parallel imports of product are only allowed in such cases if there is, in fact, a risk to the health of humans as a result of the continued existence of that medicinal product on the market of the importing member State.[68]

A summary

The second *Boehringer Ingelheim v. Swingward* case[69] gave the European Court of Justice the opportunity to summarize the position on parallel imports of trade marked goods. The Court highlighted the following key points. The trade-mark owner may legitimately oppose further commercialization of a pharmaceutical product imported from another member State in its original internal and external packaging with an additional external label applied by the importer, unless:

- it is established that reliance on trade mark rights by the proprietor in order to oppose the marketing of the over-stickered product under that trade mark would contribute to the artificial partitioning of the markets between member States;
- the repackaging of the pharmaceutical product—either by reboxing the product and reapplying the trade mark, or by applying a label to the packaging containing the product—is necessary for its further commercialization in the importing member State, albeit that this condition is directed solely at the fact of repackaging, and not at the manner and style of the repackaging;
- it is shown that the new label cannot affect the original condition of the product inside the packaging;
- the packaging clearly states who over-stickered the product and the name of the manufacturer;
- the presentation of the over-stickered product is not likely to damage the reputation of the trade mark and of its proprietor—that is, the label must not be defective, of poor quality, or untidy;
- the importer gives notice to the trade mark proprietor before the over-stickered product is put on sale and, on demand, supplies the proprietor with a specimen of that product;
- the presentation of the pharmaceutical product after repackaging or relabelling is not such as to be liable to damage the reputation of the trade mark and of its proprietor. This condition is not limited to cases in which the repackaging is defective, of poor quality, or untidy. The standard usually applied in the trade is to be adhered to.

The question of whether the fact that a parallel importer responsible for any of the following is likely to damage the trade mark's reputation is a question of fact for the national court to decide in the light of the circumstances of each case:

- failure to affix the trade mark to the new exterior carton—that is, 'de-branding';
- application of either his or her own logo, house style, get-up, or a get-up used for a number of different products—that is, 'co-branding';

[68] Cases C-15/01 *Paranova v. Läkemedelsverket* [2003] 2 CMLR 856; C-175/00 *Ferring Arzneimittel GmbH v. Eurim-Pharm Arzneimittel GmbH* [2002] ECR I-6891.

[69] Case C-348/04 *Boehringer Ingelheim KG and ors v. Swingward Ltd and ors (No. 2)* [2007] 2 CMLR 52.

- positioning of the additional label so as wholly or partially to obscure the proprietor's trade mark;
- failure to state on the additional label that the trade mark in question belongs to the proprietor;
- printing of the name of the parallel importer in capital letters.

In terms of burden of proof, it is for the parallel importer to prove the existence of the conditions that:

- reliance on trade mark rights by the proprietor in order to oppose the marketing of repackaged products under that trade mark would contribute to the artificial partitioning of the markets between member States;
- the repackaging cannot affect the original condition of the product inside the packaging;
- the new packaging clearly states who repackaged the product and the name of the manufacturer;
- the presentation of the repackaged product is not such as to be liable to damage the reputation of the trade mark and of its proprietor;
- he or she has given notice to the trade mark proprietor before the repackaged product is put on sale and, on demand, supplied him or her with a specimen of the repackaged product. If a parallel importer has failed to give prior notice to the trade mark proprietor concerning a repackaged pharmaceutical product, he or she infringes that proprietor's rights on the occasion of any subsequent importation of that product, as long as he or she has not given the proprietor such notice.

As regards the condition that it must be shown that the repackaging cannot affect the original condition of the product inside the packaging, it is sufficient, however, that the parallel importer furnishes evidence that leads to the reasonable presumption that the condition has been fulfilled. This applies *a fortiori* also to the condition that the presentation of the repackaged product must not be such as to be liable to damage the reputation of the trade mark and of its proprietor. If the importer furnishes such initial evidence that the latter condition has been fulfilled, it will then be for the proprietor of the trade mark, who is best placed to assess whether the repackaging is liable to damage his or her reputation and that of the trade mark, to prove that they have been so damaged.[70]

Exhaustion covers publicity

Parallel importation can only work in practice if the parallel importer can sell the goods successfully. This requires that he or she can advertise the fact that the original product is now also available through his or her outlets and that his or her prices are lower. Can the parallel importer reproduce the trade mark for the purposes of this advertising?

The answer to this question can only be affirmative if the exhaustion of the trade mark by putting it on the market in the member State from which it was imported by the parallel importer also covered the trade mark's reproduction for advertising purposes. This should indeed be the case, because normal advertising practices will not damage the goodwill of the trade mark owner, if they only inform the public about the availability of the product. The consumer is not misled either, because the original product is

[70] Ibid.

advertised, rather than any similar product. The advertising does not normally create the impression that the parallel importer manufactures the product; on the contrary, the importer will try to emphasize that he or she is selling the 'real thing'—that is, the original product, from the original producer—but only at a lower price. That is his or her best strategy by which to maximize sales. This means that the essential function of the trade mark is fulfilled and that there is no need to allow the trade mark owner to use his or her trade mark to stop the advertising, because the goods concerned have been marketed with his or her consent.

The European Court of Justice approved this approach in the *Dior* case,[71] when it stopped Dior from relying on its trade marks to stop the parallel importer from advertising its goods by reproducing in its publicity the boxes in which the perfumes were sold. These boxes obviously carried the trade marks. The advertising took place in the format that was normally used by the parallel importer and others in the same type of trade. Dior argued that the form of advertising did not meet its high standards and could therefore affect the reputation of its trade marks in a negative way. The Court ruled that any form of advertising in the way and quality in which the parallel importer normally advertised its goods could not damage the goodwill of Dior.

The Court expressed this ruling as follows:

> The proprietor of a trade mark may not rely on Article 7(2) of Directive 89/104 to oppose the use of the trade mark, by a reseller who habitually markets articles of the same kind, but not necessarily of the same quality, as the trade-marked goods, in ways customary in the reseller's sector of trade, for the purpose of bringing to the public's attention the further commercialisation of those goods, unless it is established that, given the specific circumstances of the case, the use of the trade mark for this purpose seriously damages the reputation of the trade mark.[72]

The only reason why Dior could stop the use of its trade marks was the fact that its goodwill would be affected. This had to be demonstrated on the basis of the facts of the case. Advertising of a very low and sloppy quality, far below the normal standards of the type of business concerned, could be an example of such an exceptional case. In that case, the essential function of the trade mark could no longer be fulfilled, which justifies the use of the trade mark to stop such a practice.

International exhaustion

The concept of international exhaustion

The Agreement on the European Economic Area expanded the area in which exhaustion applies to the whole of the EEA, which means that, apart from the EU, it applies to Iceland, Liechtenstein, and Norway.[73] Until recently, however, it was unclear whether the EU would opt for the principle of international exhaustion or not.

In very simple terms, 'international exhaustion' means that all trade mark rights are exhausted once the product labelled with the trade mark has been put on the market anywhere in the world by, or with the consent of, the trade mark owner. Trade mark owners in the EU would no longer be able to stop parallel importation of their products from outside the EEA by relying on their parallel trade marks in the member States if the principle of international exhaustion were to apply.

---

[71] Case C-337/95 *Parfums Christian Dior SA & Parfums Christian Dior BV v. Evora BV* [1998] RPC 166.
[72] Ibid.; see Stamatoudi [1999].
[73] [1994] OJ L 1/3.

Traditionally, certain member States—such as Austria—had incorporated the principle of international exhaustion into their domestic trade mark system, but, recently, the majority of the member States and the Commission seemed to have abandoned the principle of international exhaustion. One could take a cynical view and argue that this was a symptom of the 'Fortress Europe' mentality and that they only wanted to protect themselves from cheap imports. The crucial issue was whether the Trade Mark Directive[74] had decided the issue or not.

Article 7 of the Directive deals with the issue of exhaustion and refers to goods that have been put on the market in the EEA. It is clear that this provision does not oblige the member States to operate an international exhaustion rule. In so far as it imposes a system of exhaustion, the provision restricts its scope to the EEA. Two conclusions seemed possible on this basis: firstly, it could be left to the member States to decide whether or not they wanted to adopt an international exhaustion rule, which argument sees Art. 7 as the minimum, but a minimum to which additions can be made; secondly, one could argue that Art. 7 is a restriction on the rights of trade mark owners and that the Directive does not allow the member States to add the further restrictions that an international exhaustion rule would necessarily carry with it.

Silhouette

The *Silhouette* case[75] gave the European Court of Justice the opportunity to decide the issue. Silhouette had sold a large number of its spectacle frames in Bulgaria and these had been re-imported into the EEA by Hartlauer, a parallel importer, for sale in the latter's outlets in Austria. Silhouette sued for infringement of its Austrian trade mark and the Austrian court asked the Court whether it could still operate an international exhaustion rule.

The Court argued that the Trade Mark Directive set out to harmonize fully all of those elements of trade mark law that may distort competition within, and the functioning in general of, the Common Market. The Court derives, from this starting point, the rule that 'Article 5 to 7 of the Directive must be construed as embodying a complete harmonization of the rules relating to the rights conferred by a trade mark'[76] and that member States can add only those rules that are included as optional provisions in this Article. Any other additions would destroy the aim of the Directive. Member States are therefore no longer free to operate a rule of international exhaustion, because such a rule was not included in the Directive as an option. The Court effectively declared international exhaustion dead under the existing legislation.[77]

Evaluation

This decision is, however, highly political and regrettable. There is nothing in the essential function of a trade mark that can justify the fact that exhaustion needs to stop at the borders of the EEA; on the contrary, the logic of the system is that the system of exhaustion should operate on all occasions when the original product is concerned and when that product has been marketed by, or with the consent of, the trade mark owner, irrespective of the place of first marketing. Exhaustion should only be put aside in exceptional cases, for example, if the product has been tampered with or if the quality of the parallel imported product is inferior to the product marketed under the same name by the

---

[74] [1989] OJ L 40/1.

[75] Case C-355/96 *Silhouette International Schmied GmbH & Co. KG v. Hartlauer Handelsgesellschaft mbH* [1998] All ER (EC) 769, [1998] 2 CMLR 953.

[76] Ibid. at [25].

[77] See also the confirmation of the approach in Case C-173/98 *Sebago & Maison Dubois* [1999] ECR I-4103.

original producer in the area into which parallel importation takes place. In those examples, the operation of the exhaustion rule would impinge on the goodwill of the producer and the interests of the consumers would be harmed. The essential function of the trade mark would be affected in these exceptional cases.

It is submitted that neither does the Directive rule out this radically different conclusion: the full harmonization in Art. 7 could be restricted to the operation of a EEA-wide exhaustion rule. All points that have not been decided by what is, after all, called a 'First' Harmonization Directive should be left to the discretion of the member States. Any such state would then be free to introduce an international exhaustion rule—and, arguably, any use of a trade mark to block parallel importation under the laws of a member State that had opted against international exhaustion would amount to an abusive use of the rights granted by a trade mark, because it would obstruct the operation of the Common Market.

Alternatively, the free circulation of the parallel imported goods that were first marketed outside the EEA could be restricted to the member State under the international exhaustion rule of which their importation took place, because they were not put on the market in the EEA by, or with the consent of, the trade mark owner. In either case, this solution would have fitted in much better with the current climate of worldwide free trade and the expectation for the latter that was created by the World Trade Organization (WTO) agreement signed in Marrakesh.

Davidoff *to no avail*

The European Court of Justice was yet again given an opportunity to reconsider its approach to the issue of international exhaustion when requests for a preliminary ruling were forwarded to the Court by the courts in the UK. Laddie J had ruled, in the *Davidoff* case,[78] that contract law had a role to play in this area and that, as a result, goods that had been put on the market outside the EEA with the consent of the trade mark owner could be parallel imported into the EEA if the trade mark owner had not used his or her right to include a reservation of title in the contract and to prohibit certain forms of re-exportation. In the absence of effective constraints, UK contract law allowed the conclusion that the trade mark owner had impliedly consented to the goods being re-exported and parallel imported into the EEA. It was argued that this approach could be adopted in parallel with the Court's ruling in *Silhouette* and that the latter remained unaffected.

The Court rejected this approach and ruled that the consent of a trade mark proprietor to the marketing within the EEA of products bearing that mark that have previously been placed on the market outside the EEA by that proprietor, or with his or her consent, may be implied—if that implied consent follows from facts and circumstances prior to, simultaneous with, or subsequent to the placing of the goods on the market outside the EEA that, in the view of the national court, unequivocally demonstrates that the proprietor has renounced his or her right to oppose placing of the goods on the market within the EEA.[79]

The need to demonstrate unequivocally that the right holder renounces his or her right to oppose marketing of the goods in the EEA had already slammed the brakes on

---

[78] *Zino Davidoff SA v. A&G Imports Ltd (No. 1)* [2000] Ch 127, [1999] 3 All ER 711. The Scottish courts adopted a slightly different approach: see *Zino Davidoff SA v. M&S Toiletries Ltd (No. 1)* [2000] 2 CMLR 735, 2000 SLT 683. See also P. Torremans and I. Stamatoudi, 'International exhaustion in the European Union in the light of *Zino Davidoff*: contract v. trade mark law?' [2000] 2 IIC 123.

[79] Joined Cases C-414/99 *Zino Davidoff SA v. A&G Imports Ltd*, C-415/99 *Levi Straus & Co. v. Tesco plc*, and C-416/99 *Levi Strauss & Co. v. Costco Wholesale UK Ltd* [2001] ECR I-1891, [2002] RPC 403 at 414.

Laddie J's approach, but the Court went on to really shut the door almost entirely when it added that:

Implied consent cannot be inferred:

- from the fact that the proprietor of the trade mark has not communicated to all subsequent purchasers of the goods placed on the market outside the European Economic Area his opposition to marketing within the European Economic Area;
- from the fact that the goods carry no warning of a prohibition of their being placed on the market within the European Economic Area;
- from the fact that the trade mark proprietor has transferred the ownership of the products bearing the trade mark without imposing any contractual reservations and that, according to the law governing the contract, the property right transferred includes, in the absence of such reservations, an unlimited right of resale or, at the very least, a right to market the goods subsequently within the European Economic Area.[80]

Ignorance on the side of the importer or failure by authorized retailers to re-impose the restrictions imposed originally by the right holder have also been excluded as grounds that could allow the parallel importation. The Court held in this respect that:

With regard to exhaustion of the trade mark proprietor's exclusive right, it is not relevant:

- that the importer of goods bearing the trade mark is not aware that the proprietor objects to their being placed on the market in the European Economic Area or sold there by traders other than authorised retailers, or
- that the authorised retailers and wholesalers have not imposed on their own purchasers contractual reservations setting out such opposition, even though they have been informed of it by the trade mark proprietor.[81]

This amounts to a very stringent approach that effectively blocks the door to parallel importation based on international exhaustion. The Court has squarely put the ball back in the camp of the legislator, but the latter is, at present, unable to reach any kind of agreement on this point.

The only slight comfort for the parallel importer in this context is to be derived from the fact that, where they would normally have to prove that they acquired the goods from a source that allows them to rely on Community exhaustion, they can argue that revealing their sources would bring with it a real risk of partitioning of the market. This would, for example, be the case if the right holder were to use an exclusive distribution system. The burden of proof then shifts to the right holder, who should demonstrate that the goods were originally marketed outside the EU. Proof of that point would require the parallel importer to prove the consent of the right holder to subsequent marketing of the goods in the EEA. Small as it may be, this is a welcome concession to the parallel importer, because revealing its sources may well get it off the hook, but it would, at the same time, make sure that the sources dried up quickly afterwards.[82]

The real context

Although the impression might be created that the interference of the Court and of European law in relation to trade marks is enormous, this is not correct and the whole

---

[80] Ibid. at 416.   [81] Ibid. at 417.

[82] Case C-244/00 *Van Doren+Q. GmbH v. Lifestyle sports + sportswear Handelsgesellschaft mbH & Michael Orth* [2003] ECR I-3051.

issue must be seen in its real context. Generally, the grant of trade marks and the right to take action against infringement are national (harmonized) competences. The Court will only interfere when these provisions are applied in a discriminatory manner.[83]

This was emphasized in the *Audi* case,[84] in which the Court verified whether the German requirements for trade mark protection were equally applied to trade marks of national and foreign origin, while leaving it to the German courts to decide whether, under German trade mark law, the use of the name 'Quadra' by Renault created confusion with Audi's 'Quattro' trade mark.[85] The Court merely focuses on the abusive exercise of trade mark rights.

The doctrine of common origin

The European Court of Justice set out the doctrine of common origin in the *Hag I* case,[86] which was a rather peculiar case. A German company, Hag AG, owned the trade mark 'Hag' in Germany, Belgium, and Luxembourg, but, after the war, its Belgian and Luxembourg property was sequestrated, and the trade mark was assigned to the Van Zuylen Frères company. Both companies produced coffee under the 'Hag' trade mark and a problem arose when Van Zuylen tried to rely on its Belgian trade mark to prevent Hag AG from importing coffee into Belgium. The argument was that Van Zuylen had not consented to the use of its trade mark, and had thus not exhausted its rights and could stop Hag AG from using the 'Hag' trade mark in Belgium.

This would have been the logical conclusion under the free movement rules as we discussed them above, but the Court arrived at a different conclusion by focusing on the common origin of the trade mark in the period before the war. The Court held that:

> one cannot allow the holder of a trade mark to rely upon the exclusiveness of a trade mark right—which may have the consequence of a territorial limitation of national markets—with a view to prohibiting the marketing in a member state of goods legally produced in another member state under an identical mark having the same origin.[87]

If the trade marks have a common origin, one cannot rely on the trade mark to prevent the other party from using it in the member State in which one owns the trade mark. Van Zuylen could not exercise any right under its 'Hag' trade mark to prevent its use in Belgium by Hag AG. The Court feared the partitioning of the single market—but this approach did not make sense, because it endangered the essential functions of the trade mark by putting both the goodwill of the trade mark owner and the interests of the consumers at risk: confusion would inevitably arise when two coffee producers started marketing their coffee 'Hag' in the same market.

The Court never used the doctrine in any other decisions until the *Hag II* case made its way to it. More than 15 years after the *Hag I* case had been decided, Van Zuylen had been acquired by Jacobs-Suchard and it intended to market the Belgian 'Hag' coffee in Germany. Under the doctrine of common origin, Hag AG could not object to this, because the trade marks had a common origin. The Court used the *Hag II* case[88] to admit that it

---

[83] See G. Würtenberger, 'Determination of risk of confusion in trade mark infringement proceedings in the European Union: the *Quattro* decision' [1994] 7 EIPR 302 at 304.

[84] Case C-317/91 *AG Deutsche Renault v. Audi AG* [1993] ECR I-6227, [1995] 1 CMLR 461.

[85] See Würtenberger [1994]; see also N. Reich, 'The "November Revolution" of the European Court of Justice: *Keck, Meng and Audi* revisited' (1994) 31 CMLR 459 at 463.

[86] Case 192/73 *Van Zuylen Frères v. Hag AG* [1974] ECR 731, [1974] 2 CMLR 127.

[87] Ibid. at 744 and 143–4 (different translations to the same effect).

[88] Case C-10/89 *CNL-Sucal NV SA v. HAG GF AG* [1990] ECR I-3711, [1990] 3 CMLR 571.

had made a mistake in *Hag I* and repealed the doctrine of common origin. Hag AG was consequently allowed to rely on its German trade mark, which had not been exhausted, to stop the importation into Germany of the Belgian coffee 'Hag'.

The Court expressed its decision as follows:

> Articles [28 and 30] of the EEC Treaty do not preclude national legislation from allowing an undertaking which is the holder of a trade mark in a member state from opposing the importation from another member state of similar products lawfully bearing an identical trade mark in the latter state or liable to confusion with the protected mark even though the mark under which the contested products are imported originally belonged to a subsidiary of the undertaking which opposes the importation and was acquired by a third undertaking as a result of the expropriation of that subsidiary.[89]

This created some doubt as to whether the doctrine of common origin had really been repealed or whether it might still apply in a case in which there was a common origin of the trade mark, followed by a voluntary assignment, rather than by a forced expropriation. This issue was solved in the *Ideal Standard* case,[90] in which the Court applied its dictum in *Hag II* to a case involving the voluntary assignment of a trade mark.

The doctrine of common origin is now legal history, because the dictum in *Hag I* has now been repealed fully by the combined effect of the *Hag II* and the *Ideal Standard* decisions.

Trade marks and competition law

Article 81

Trade mark licence agreements can restrict competition and are, in that respect, not different from patent licence agreements. The Commission will use its powers to enforce Art. 81 of the EC Treaty if an agreement has, as its effect or as its object, the restriction of competition and the partitioning of the single market.

The Commission's prime target is so-called 'absolute territorial protection'. It is based on the grant of a single exclusive trade mark licence per member State, coupled with an obligation for each exclusive licensee (and for the licensor) not to pursue any active or passive sales policy outside its licensed territory. Its aim is to produce full exclusivity, resulting in the product being available from a single source in each part of the single market, which is covered by an exclusive licence and which licence fully excludes parallel imports.

The Commission is not prepared to grant an exemption for this type of trade mark licence and, on two occasions, an appeal to the European Court of Justice on this point failed: in *Consten & Grundig v. Commission*[91] and in *Tepea BV v. Commission*.[92] The Commission is, however, prepared to grant an exemption if at least parallel imports remain possible even if the licence is exclusive, and licensees are prohibited to pursue an active sales policy outside their territory.[93] An exemption is also possible if the agreement has a positive effect on intra-brand competition and widens the consumer's choice.[94]

---

[89] Ibid. at [22] and [609] (different translations to same effect).

[90] Case C-9/93 *IHT International Heiztechnik GmbH v. Ideal Standard GmbH* [1995] FSR 59.

[91] Joined Cases 56 and 58/64 *Establissements Consten & Grundig v. EC Commission* [1966] ECR 299, [1966] CMLR 418.

[92] Case 28/77 *Tepea BV v. EC Commission* [1978] ECR 1391, [1978] 3 CMLR 392.

[93] *Re Davide Campari-Milano SpA Agreement* [1978] 2 CMLR 397, OJ L 70/69.

[94] *Moosehead/Whitbread* [1991] 4 CMLR 391, (1990) OJ L 100/32, which was a combined trade mark/ know-how case in which the trade mark aspect was clearly dominant.

Article 82

Certain ways of using a trade mark can amount to an abuse of a dominant position, but, in practice, few, if any, problems have arisen in this area up to now.[95]

An overview

Going beyond our national borders, trade mark law is based on the Paris Convention and the TRIPS Agreement, with the Madrid system offering an international registration system. Inside the EU, one can also register a single trade mark for the whole of the Community by means of the Community Trade Mark Regulation. The substantive provisions of the Regulation run parallel to those of the Directive that harmonized national trade mark laws.

Trade mark law also has a substantial interaction with the Treaty provisions on the free movement of goods. Parallel importation has given rise to a constant supply of challenging cases and heated debate. That debate focuses essentially on the relabelling and repackaging of parallel-traded goods. In *Boehringer Ingelheim v. Swingward*,[96] the European Court of Justice summarized the main points as follows.

The trade-mark owner may legitimately oppose further commercialisation of a pharmaceutical product imported from another Member State in its original internal and external packaging with an additional external label applied by the importer, unless:

- it is established that reliance on trade mark rights by the proprietor in order to oppose the marketing of the overstickered product under that trade mark would contribute to the artificial partitioning of the markets between Member States;
- the repackaging of the pharmaceutical product, either by reboxing the product and re-applying the trade mark or by applying a label to the packaging containing the product, is necessary for its further commercialisation in the importing Member State, albeit be it that this condition is directed solely at the fact of repackaging and not at the manner and style of the repackaging;
- it is shown that the new label cannot affect the original condition of the product inside the packaging;
- the packaging clearly states who overstickered the product and the name of the manufacturer;
- the presentation of the overstickered product is not such as to be liable to damage the reputation of the trade mark and of its proprietor; thus, the label must not be defective, of poor quality, or untidy;
- the importer gives notice to the trade-mark proprietor before the overstickered product is put on sale, and, on demand, supplies him with a specimen of that product;
- the presentation of the pharmaceutical product after repackaging or relabelling is such as to be liable to damage the reputation of the trade mark and of its proprietor. This condition is not limited to cases where the repackaging is defective, of poor quality, or untidy. The standard usually applied in the trade is to be adhered to.

---

[95] See *Chiquita/Fyffes plc*, Commission press release, 4 June 1992. The Commission invoked both Arts 81 and 82, although it seems this was more an Art. 81 case dealing with an agreement between the parties, whereby one of them would restrict the use of its trade mark in Continental Europe.

[96] Case C-348/04 *Boehringer Ingelheim KG & anor v. Swingward Ltd* [2007] 2 CMLR 1445 at 1488–90.

The Community does however limit exhaustion to the EEA sphere and international exhaustion has been ruled out. At one stage, a doctrine of common origin was also applied, but this has now been put to rest.

Competition law issues arise rather sparingly in relation to trade marks.

Further reading

DYRBERG, P., 'For EEA exhaustion to apply, who has to prove the marketing of the trade marked goods: the trade mark owner or the defendant?'[2004] EIPR 81.

MURPHY, G., 'Who's wearing the sunglasses now?' (2000) 21 Eur Comp LR 1.

STAMATOUDI, I., 'From drugs to spirits and from boxes to publicity: decided and undecided issues in relation to trade mark and copyright exhaustion' [1999] IPQ 95.

STAMATOUDI, I. and TORREMANS, P., 'International exhaustion in the European Union in the light of *Zino Davidoff*: contract versus trade mark law?' (2000) 31 IIC 123.

STOTHERS, C., 'Political exhaustion: the Eu Commission's Working [aper on possible abuses of trade mark rights within the EU in the context of Community exhaustion' [2003] EIPR 457.

28

Tortious protection of intellectual property rights

Now we move away from the creation of formal rights in intellectual property to consider the various ways in which the common law, in the form of the law of tort, creates rights of action, as opposed to proprietary rights, which have the effect of protecting activity in the area of intellectual property. Passing off and malicious falsehood will be the principal torts considered, although attention will also be paid to the ways in which defamation can assist. It must be emphasized that these rights are supplementary, and complementary, to the statutory formal rights. In particular, trade mark law and passing off closely overlap, although s. 2(2) of the Trade Marks Act 1994 preserves passing off as a separate cause of action. That said, the extensions to the range of protection afforded by the trade mark regime by the 1994 Act inevitably diminish the role of these tortious rights, especially in the absence of proprietary rights arising from them.[1]

Let us briefly look, in a little more detail, at the suggestion in the 1994 Act that the Act does not interfere with the law of passing off. Things are not as easy as this initial statement suggests, as became clear in *Inter Lotto (UK) Ltd v. Camelot Group plc*.[2] The claimant used the name 'Hotpick' as the unregistered mark for a lottery game sold in bars and pubs from 28 November 2001 onwards. The defendant filed an application for the registration of the name 'Hotpicks' for lottery games on 17 October 2001 and started using the mark in July 2002. The Court of Appeal was confronted with the question of which of the two marks took preference.

According to the claimant, s. 2(2) of the 1994 Act means that it has no impact on the tort of passing off and, in passing off, the relevant date on which to assess the goodwill of the claimant is the day of first use of the mark—that is, the moment of the first misrepresentation. At that moment, the claimant had developed goodwill in the name.

According to the defendant, reliance is instead to be placed on s. 5(4), which means that the relevant date for priority is the application date for the trade mark. Section 5(4) then deals with rights acquired under passing off before that date. Of course, in this scenario, the defendant wins.

In its judgment, the Court of Appeal recognized that the interaction between trade marks and passing off is far more complex than was suggested at first, but, in this case, it gave preference to s. 2(2). The Court argued that this section establishes the principle and that a specific rule, such as that in s. 5(4) on relative grounds for refusal, cannot deviate from that principle and can deal only with an additional point. Section 5(4) will therefore only apply once the question of passing off has been dealt with on its own terms in application of s. 2(2).

---

[1] See M. Ni Shuilleabhain, 'Common law protection of trade marks: the continuing relevance of the law of passing off' (2003) 34 IIC 722.

[2] [2003] 4 All ER 575, [2003] RPC 186.

Passing off

As will be clear to any student of patent law, some areas of the law of intellectual property appear, on the surface, to be deceptive in their simplicity; the tort of passing off, however, stands at the opposite end of the spectrum. Much heat and noise has been generated in the quest for definitions of the tort—but it is useful to assert at the outset that the essence of the tort is the protection of both consumers and other traders from the effect of confusion on their goodwill in trade. That confusion is generated by the activity of a trader in causing his or her goods or services and/or their presentation to become confused with those of the claimant, and that protection is afforded by the grant of a right of action to the trader whose economic interests and trading goodwill are harmed by the confusion.[3]

Historical development

The 'informal' protection of rights by the tort of passing off closely parallels the formal rights created by trade mark law. It is significant, however, that the tortious right came into existence long before the establishment of a trade mark system. It appears that the law first began to address the problem of trade confusion in the late sixteenth century: reference is made in *Southern v. How*[4] to a case arising the 1580s, in which an action was successfully maintained by a cloth manufacturer whose distinguishing mark was used by a rival trader on his greatly inferior cloth. The use of the term 'passing off' can be traced back to *Perry v. Truefitt*,[5] an unedifying dispute between two hair oil manufacturers, both selling their brands of 'Medicated Mexican Balm', in relation to which the claimant was refused an injunction, but not denied a legal right to protect his original use of the trade name in question.

A key point in the development of the tort appeared early in the twentieth century: *Spalding & Bros v. A W Gamage*[6] was a consideration by the House of Lords of a dispute between rival football sellers, the claimant manufacturer objecting to the sale of its balls by the defendants at a greatly reduced price in adverts that failed to disclose that the balls under offer were of an older and inferior design in comparison with the claimants' current model. Lord Parker emphasized, in finding for the claimants, that the essence of a passing off action was the protection of rights in the business and its goodwill, which may be harmed by the defendants' conduct. It was equally clear, however, that this right in goodwill was not a property right as such, but rather a right to seek a remedy during such period of time as the goodwill continues to exist. From this, the tort of passing off comes to exist in its modern form.

'Passing off' defined

Attempts to define 'passing off' have been, at times, confusing, particularly after the decision of the House of Lords in *Erven Warnink v. J Townend & Sons (Hull) Ltd*[7] offered two separate definitions.

---

[3] See, in general, C. Wadlow (2004) *The Law of Passing-Off: Unfair Competition by Misrepresentation*, 3rd edn, London: Sweet and Maxwell.

[4] (1618) Poph 143 at 144, 79 ER 1243.

[5] (1842) 6 Beav 66, 49 ER 749.

[6] (1915) 32 RPC 273.

[7] [1979] AC 731, [1979] 2 All ER 927.

That case is worth a moment's pause: the claimants produced Advocaat, a blend of spirit and eggs, while the defendants entered the market with 'Keeling's Old English Advocaat', a concoction of Cyprus sherry and egg powder. This attracted a lower rate of duty, being wine-based rather than spirit-based. It was found that this was a case of passing off, because, in so far as common ground could be found between the leading judgments, damage could be caused to the claimant's goodwill by the confusion engendered by the activities of the defendants. This analysis explains, if not defines, the essence of the action.

Various attempts were made to apply this case,[8] but a definitive answer has now been provided by the famous *Jif Lemon* case—*Reckitt & Colman Products Ltd v. Borden Inc.*[9]— aspects of which will be considered later in this chapter. In this case, Lord Oliver offered a clear and concise definition of the three elements that, in his view, were the essential ingredients of the tort:

> First, he must establish a goodwill or reputation attached to the goods or services which he supplies in the mind of the purchasing public by association with the identifying 'get-up' (whether it consists simply of a brand name or a trade description, or the individual features of labelling or packaging) under which his particular goods are offered to the public, such that the get-up is recognised by the public as distinctive specifically of the claimant's goods or services. Second, he must demonstrate a misrepresentation (whether or not intentional) leading or likely to lead the public to believe that goods or services offered by him are the goods or services of the claimant. Whether the public is aware of the claimant's identity as the manufacturer or supplier of the goods and services is immaterial, as long as they are identified with a particular source which is in fact the claimant. For example if the public is accustomed to rely upon a particular brand name in purchasing goods of a particular description, it matters not at all that there is little or no public awareness of the identity of the proprietor of the brand name. Third, he must demonstrate that he suffers or, in a *quia timet* action, that he is likely to suffer damage by reason of the erroneous belief engendered by the defendant's misrepresentation that the source of the defendant's goods or services is the same as the source of those offered by the claimant.[10]

The three requirements of goodwill, misrepresentation, and damage are the key test. But we have moved a long way from the oldest cases in which the tort was defined as a defendant passing his or her goods off as those of the claimant. The Court of Appeal recently even went as far as to argue obiter that the tort is perhaps now best referred to as unfair competition.[11]

What is really at the hearth of the tort is the fact that goodwill will be protected whenever someone engages in unfair competition or takes unfair advantage of the goodwill by making a misrepresentation. The latter is often noting more than a false association that is created, even involuntarily, in the minds of part of the public. The modern approach is illustrated well by the example Cross J gave more than three decades ago:

> A man who does not know where Champagne comes from can have not the slightest reason for thinking that a bottle labelled 'Spanish Champagne' contains a wine produced in France. But what he may very well think is that he is buying the genuine article—real Champagne— and that, I have no doubt, was the sort of deception which the judge had in mind. He

---

[8] See, e.g., *Anheuser-Busch Inc. v. Budejovicky Budvar Narodni Podnick* [1984] FSR 413 (and on this *Budweiser* litigation also *Re Bud Trade Mark* [1988] RPC 535); *Consorzio del Prosciutto di Parma v. Marks & Spencer plc* [1991] RPC 351, esp. at 386.

[9] [1990] 1 All ER 873, [1990] 1 WLR 491.

[10] Ibid. at 880 and 499.

[11] *Arsenal Football Club plc v. Reed* [2003] 3 All ER 865, [2003] RPC 696 (CA).

thought, as I read his judgment, that if people were allowed to call spar
duced in Champagne 'Champagne,' even though preceded by an adje
country of origin, the distinction between genuine Champagne and 'chai
produced elsewhere would become blurred; that the word 'Champagne' \
ally to mean no more than 'sparkling wine;' and that the part of the plainti
consisted in the name would be diluted and gradually destroyed. If I n
impertinence I agree entirely with the decision in the Spanish Champagne
it uncovered a piece of common law or equity which had till then escaped
a case there is not, in any ordinary sense, any representation that the gooc
are the goods of the plaintiffs, and evidence that no-one has been confused or deceived in
that way is quite beside the mark. In truth the decision went beyond the well-trodden paths
of passing-off into the unmapped area of 'unfair trading' or ' unlawful competition'.[12]

This is the starting point of the law as it stands now, which we will now analyse in further detail. Obviously, in so doing, reference will often be made to the case law developed in the area over the last century, not least because it shows the flexibility of the passing off action.[13]

Goodwill

The leading case of *Spalding & Bros v. A W Gamage*[14] identifies, as has been seen, the element of goodwill as being at the heart of an action in the tort of passing off. On its facts, it was clear that the footballs made by the claimants under the brand-name 'Orb' had been on the market from 1910 and that goodwill in the name was well established by August 1912, at which time the defendant began to market 'Orb' balls that were, in fact, discarded stock rejected by the claimants, and far below the standard (and price) of the improved balls that were now being produced by the claimants still under the 'Orb' name. This is a clear and straightforward case of passing off, but the question of goodwill is not always so easy to answer and will always ultimately hinge on factual considerations. The importance of the existence of goodwill should not be underestimated: in the absence of goodwill, no passing off can be established, even if the public is confused in relation to the source of the product.[15]

The Court of Appeal recently recommended Lord MacNaghten's definition of goodwill as the best one available in relation to passing off.[16] Accordingly, goodwill can be said to be:

the benefit and advantage of the good name, reputation, and connection of a business. It is the attractive force that brings in custom. It is the one thing which distinguishes an old-established from a new business at its first start. The goodwill of a business must emanate from a particular centre or source. However widely or extended or diffused its influence may

---

[12] *Vine Products Ltd v. Mackenzie & Co. Ltd* [1969] RPC 1 at 23, referring to the decision in *Bollinger J v. Costa Brava Wine Coy Ltd* [1960] RPC 16 and [1961] RPC 116, and cited with approval by Aldous LJ in *Arsenal Football Club plc v. Reed* [2003] RPC 696 at 715–16.

[13] Historically, the five-stage test that was put forward by Lord Diplock in the *Advocaat* case (*Erven Warnink v. v J Townend & Sons (Hull) Ltd* [1979] AC 731, [1979] 2 All ER 927) has also been important. The test involved (1) a misrepresentation (2) made by a trader in the course of trade (3) to prospective customers of his, or ultimate consumers of goods or services supplied by him, (4) which is calculated to injure the goodwill of another trader, and (5) which causes actual damage to a business or goodwill of the trader by whom the action is brought. It is submitted that this test is not substantially different from the three-stage *Jif Lemon* test and that the latter summarizes it in a more convenient way.

[14] (1915) 32 RPC 273.

[15] *HFC Bank v. Midland Bank* [2000] FSR 176 at 182–3.

[16] *Scandecor Development AB v. Scandecor Marketing AB* [1999] FSR 26 at 41.

goodwill is worth nothing unless it has power of attraction sufficient to bring customers home to the source from which it emanates. Goodwill is composed of a variety of elements. It differs in its composition in different trades and in different trades in the same trade. One element may preponderate here and another element there.[17]

One of the key elements in this definition refers back to the point made above that goodwill is the necessary starting point for any passing off action. As such, the goodwill must also be linked to the next elements and play an active role. In practice, the goodwill must be the reason why the consumer gives custom to the business. Customers must not be using the business for random reasons, but they must be giving it their custom as a result of the reputation that has been developed by the business.[18] But while goodwill must obviously be proven to exist, the requirements for it to exist are not unduly stringent and the Court of Appeal has held that the goodwill test is less demanding that that for distinctiveness in relation to trade marks.[19]

Duration of goodwill

When a business is started, as a question of fact, it is clear that it may take time to establish its goodwill. The courts appear reasonably generous in providing support for relatively new traders against their predatory rivals. This is shown by two contrasting cases in 1967. Firstly, in *Stannard v. Reay*,[20] both parties independently decided to establish a mobile fish-and-chip shop business in the Isle of Wight. Both hit upon the name 'Mr Chippy' as being appropriate for the venture, but the claimants had a head start of about five weeks. Once the rival operation began, the claimants sought an injunction and this was granted on an interlocutory basis by Buckley J, in the light of the fact that the evidence showed that the claimants had built up a substantial trade very quickly and could thus be said to have developed goodwill in the use of the name.

By contrast, in *Compatibility Research Ltd v. Computer Psyche Co. Ltd*,[21] two companies independently set up the then new business of running a computer dating agency. The claimants began one month earlier than the defendants and, with both companies using the biological male and female symbols in their publicity, the claimants sought to establish that their one-month head start had been sufficient to confer upon them goodwill in that pair of symbols. Their claim was rejected by Stamp J, who took the view that '*where a trader seeks to say that the name descriptive of his trade has become distinctive of his trade and no other, he assumes a heavy burden*'.[22]

It is clear, however, that, in deciding against the claimants, much emphasis was placed on their use of a commonplace and partly descriptive symbol that would make it much harder to develop goodwill than if they had thought up their own original logo that was then copied by a subsequent rival. It was not so much the short time for which they had traded, but the lack of a distinctive image that flawed their claim. The key element that emerges is that goodwill and reputation have to be demonstrated to exist at the time at which the defendant began the activities complained of; the protection of future goodwill, even if it can protect the logical and legitimate expansion of a growing business, does not come within the scope of passing off.[23]

---

[17] *IRC v. Muller & Co's Margarine* [1901] AC 217 at 224.
[18] *HFC Bank v. Midland Bank* [2000] FSR 176 at 183.
[19] *Phones 4U Ltd & anor v. Phone4u.co.uk Internet Ltd & ors* [2007] RPC 5 (CA).
[20] [1967] RPC 589.
[21] [1967] RPC 201.
[22] Ibid. at 207.
[23] *Cadbury Schweppes v. Pub Squash* [1981] RPC 429; *Teleworks Ltd v. Telework Group plc [2002] RPC 535.*

That these cases hinge on factual issues is well shown by the contrast between the *Compatibility* case and that of *BBC v. Talbot Motor Co. Ltd.*[24] The heavy launch publicity in the media arranged by Compatibility Research did not avail it in its goodwill argument, yet, in the *BBC* case, goodwill was found to exist for the 'Carfax' service of radio traffic information broadcasts from television and specialist press coverage, even though the service had not—and still has not—come into being. The BBC was thus held to be entitled to prevent the defendants from using the same name for their spare car part sales operation.

Clearly, in cases in which neither the project nor its preliminaries are under way, there is no chance that a passing off action can succeed. In *Marcus Publishing plc v. Hutton-Wild Communications Ltd*,[25] the two parties were rushing to be first into the market with identically named journals, but neither had yet reached the news-stands or, indeed, had gone beyond the stage of producing a pilot edition for advertisers. The Court of Appeal found that neither party had done enough to establish any goodwill, even for the purposes of an interlocutory injunction, although both parties had been planning their projects for the best part of a year.

Similar problems arise at the end of a business' life in assessing the time at which goodwill finally dissipates. In this respect, *Ad-lib Club Ltd v. Glanville*[26] is instructive. The Ad-Lib Club was a trendy London nightspot that operated from 1964 to early 1966, at which time it was closed due to complaints about noise and no substitute premises could be found. Late in 1970, the defendant proposed to open his own Ad-Lib Club and, in spite of the five-year gap, the claimants were held entitled to object to this. The issue was not the lapse of time, but rather whether the claimant's goodwill had lapsed. The fact that the press confused the two operations in stories concerning the 'reopening' of the famous club and the strong suspicion that the defendant's choice of name was quite deliberate were helpful factors in the claimants' case, but, ultimately, it was the retention of goodwill in their name and their right to exploit that, while it still lasted, was crucial to the success of the claim, even though they had no precise plans for reopening. Of course, the presence of such plans would always be helpful to a claimant, as evidenced by *Levey v. Henderson-Kenton (Holdings) Ltd*,[27] in which trade by the claimant under the name 'Kentons' was held to retain goodwill during a temporary closure caused by two fires and a compulsory purchase.

It is clear that goodwill cannot only survive the closing down of a business, but that it can also survive the death of a person. For example, the death of the composer who had released various recordings with his orchestra and toured the UK did not extinguish the goodwill held in his name.[28] Whether another person can benefit from that goodwill is another matter, however: inherited goodwill is not easy to prove and, in that case, the fact that the son of the composer had continued the business did not automatically mean that he had inherited the goodwill from his father; neither did the prolonged absence of the orchestra from the UK after the latest tour led by the composer himself help matters.

Geographical extent of goodwill

In relation to the question of the geographical area over which goodwill may be regarded as extending, the *Levey* case mentioned above provides a simple example. The claimant's

[24] [1981] FSR 228.
[25] [1990] RPC 576.
[26] [1972] RPC 673.
[27] [1974] RPC 617.
[28] *Riddle v. United Service Organisation Ltd*, Ch D, judgment of 26 April 2004, [2004] EWHC 1263, (2004) 27(7) IPD 27079.

shop was well known in Newcastle only, while the defendants were successfully trading under the same name, but primarily in the Midlands, with no store within 120 miles of Newcastle until the proposed opening of a store in Newcastle triggered off the claimant's action. The interlocutory injunction only extended to Newcastle and, if the claimant had sought to trade in the defendants' heartland in the Midlands, the claim would inevitably have been inverted.

This case may, however, be the exception rather than the rule in terms of how clear-cut is the geographical separation. A more complex—and perhaps more typical—set of facts arose in *Chelsea Man Menswear Ltd v. Chelsea Girl Ltd.*[29] The claimants sold clothes under the 'Chelsea Man' label in their shops in Leicester, Coventry, and London; the defendants proposed to extend their business from women's clothing to that for men and, naturally, also wanted to use 'Chelsea Man' in this venture. The defendants argued that any injunction against them should be confined to the areas of the claimants' pre-existing business, but this was rejected by the Court of Appeal, which allowed an injunction covering all of England and Wales, regard being paid to the fact that both people and goods move around the country, and also to the desire of the claimants themselves to extend their business in the future (although no specific plans appear to have been made). Nourse LJ noted[30] that the *Levey* case was the only reported case to have imposed a geographical limit and at only a pretrial stage. The desire of businesses to expand legitimately in the future may well make the *Chelsea Man* case the model for the future.

But there may still be circumstances in which local goodwill exists and in which a geographically limited injunction is appropriate. The *Daily Mail* recently relied successfully on its goodwill in London and the south-east of England to stop the publication of a London evening newspaper under the name *London Evening Mail.*[31]

International goodwill

Goodwill can, it seems, also transcend international boundaries. Many companies—such as, for example, the international oil companies—trade in dozens of countries and clearly have international goodwill. This area of the law needs to be considered in two different ways: firstly, the approach taken by the case law in recent years will be considered; secondly, it will be necessary to review the impact of the new protection of internationally well-known marks introduced into UK law for the first time by the 1994 Act.

The problem that has arisen in litigation is whether, in the absence of trade, goodwill can nevertheless be established within the jurisdiction. The case law suggests that this is possible, at least in some cases. The principal support for such a proposition comes from *Maxim's Ltd v. Dye,*[32] in which the owners of one of Paris' grandest and most prestigious restaurants succeeded in preventing the use of the name 'Maxim's' for a bistro in Norwich. Graham J refused to follow an earlier High Court decision[33] in which the owners of Paris' 'Crazy Horse Saloon' nightclub failed to stop the use of the same name on London premises, because, he insisted, goodwill could transcend frontiers and, indeed, was more likely so to do in an era of international integration, particularly within the Common Market.[34] In this case, there was ample evidence that the Paris restaurant was known in the UK, was patronized by its citizens, and—although no weight seems to have been attached to this factor—was owned by a UK-registered company. The judge also

---

[29] [1987] RPC 189.
[30] Ibid. at 208.
[31] *Associated Newspapers, Daily Mail & General Trust v. Express Newspapers* [2003] FSR 51.
[32] [1977] FSR 364.
[33] *Alain Bernardin et Cie v. Pavilion Properties Ltd* [1967] RPC 581.
[34] [1977] FSR 364 at 368.

considered that to fail to protect the goodwill enjoyed by a French company in the UK was discriminatory under the Treaty of Rome as being a disguised restriction on trade, a distortion of level competition, and a restriction on the free supply of services within the European Union (EU).[35] It seems that the goodwill of a company trading elsewhere within the EU will be treated henceforth on equal terms with that of a domestic business, with the factors noted above being relevant to the scope of the injunction awarded geographically.

But it is equally clear that *Maxim's* is not a door left wide open through which any foreign business can mount a passing off action in the UK: *Athletes Foot Marketing Associates Inc. v. Cobra Sports Ltd*[36] demonstrates this well. The claimants are a leading US business franchising a chain of sports shoe shops under the brand name 'The Athlete's Foot'—presumably the foot infection of that name bears a different appellation across the Atlantic. Beyond abortive discussions, no steps had been taken to develop the chain in England, so the defendants filled the gap by christening their London store 'Athlete's Foot Bargain Basement', a name apparently coined while watching a rugby match from the bar at Twickenham Rugby Stadium. After a full survey of the authorities, Walton J concluded that passing off does not confine its protection to those currently carrying on a business within the jurisdiction, as long as they have a reputation from which goodwill can arise. On these facts, however, the claimants did not even have a reputation, having provided no evidence of any transactions with UK citizens. It was consequently impossible to say that there was the necessary goodwill within the jurisdiction and this is a significant point of distinction from the *Maxim's* case.

A further twist is provided by *My Kinda Bones Ltd v. Dr Pepper's Stove Co. Ltd*.[37] This, on the face of it, looks like the *Athlete's Foot* case, with a US firm intending to open, for the first time, one of its now successful 'Chicago Rib Shack' restaurants in London, only to find, to its irritation, that the defendants were also proposing to operate a 'Rib Shack'. The claimants sued and the defendants sought to strike out the claim as giving no grounds for action, in the light of the *Athlete's Foot* case. Slade J refused to strike out the claim—which, of course, is not to say that he confirmed that it would succeed at trial. He simply felt that the lack of customers in the UK for the claimants' business could not be the sole test, because there was evidence that the claimants had begun to promote their new venture not least in their pre-existing chain of pizzerias. In the light of this, there was at least a triable issue under the principle established in *BBC v. Talbot*[38] that they had carried out enough preparation and interested enough people in their forthcoming product that goodwill had been created; it is hard to disagree with Slade J[39] that the claimants' prospects of success were, however, slender.

In summary, it seems clear that the starting point of the court in considering passing off will be to give protection across the whole of the relevant jurisdiction to anyone with a reputation within that jurisdiction. Such a reputation is most easily established by evidence of customers within that jurisdiction, so going a long way to show goodwill there. But, equally clearly, other acts such as self-promotion or work done preparatory to the product launch may also be helpful to showing goodwill within the jurisdiction.

The position at common law has, however, now been altered by s. 56 of the 1994 Act. This section brings into UK law, for the first time, the protection given by Article 6bis

---

[35] EC Treaty, Arts 30 and 49 respectively.
[36] [1980] RPC 343.
[37] [1984] FSR 289.
[38] [1981] FSR 228.
[39] [1984] FSR 289 at 303.

of the Paris Convention for the Protection of Intellectual Property 1883. This creates an obligation on signatory states to protect well-known marks belonging to any national of any Convention state. This allows such a person to act within this jurisdiction by obtaining an injunction against the use in the UK of a trade mark (or an essential part thereof) that is '*identical or similar to his mark, in relation to identical or similar goods or services, where the use is likely to cause confusion*'.[40] This right arises irrespective of whether the claimant has any business, or even any goodwill, in the UK, although the mark must be 'well known'.

The implications of this are far from clear. The key case to reconsider is *Athlete's Foot*. The claim there failed through lack of goodwill on the part of the claimants; this, in itself, would no longer bar them from opposing the use by their UK counterpart of the same name as a trade mark. But it seems that it would still be necessary to establish that theirs was a 'well-known' mark and it is not clear whether it is necessary to show that the mark is well known in the applicant's country or in the UK. Clearly, there is no problem in the former event, but if the latter is the case,[41] it will be an unusual mark indeed that has no goodwill but is nonetheless well known. It seems that s. 56 is therefore unlikely to make any great difference.

Goodwill in trading

In terms of the activities in respect of which goodwill may arise or be protected, just as in trade mark law, protection is not given universally, but rather only for the class, or classes, of activity in which trade is carried out. A parallel restriction therefore applies in passing off—but, first, a further parallel needs exploring: while in trade mark law there must be trade before any protection is conferred, so too, in a passing off action, there must be a recognizable trading activity.[42]

Professional bodies[43] and political parties are consequently unlikely to succeed in a passing off claim: it will not be easy for them to show that they are engaged in sufficient commercial activity. Charities, non-profit organizations, and certain unincorporated associations—such as, for example, the Countryside Alliance—may, however, find it easier to prove that they trade and that, as a result, they have acquired goodwill. They do not trade in a narrow sense, because they do not buy or sell goods or services, but, in achieving their aim of the promotion of the well-being of a section of the community, they engage is some commercial activity, even if it is only of secondary importance and aimed solely at raising funds. The concept of trade involved has to be interpreted in a wide sense.[44]

From here, it is appropriate to return to the question of what activities by a company or individual admittedly in trade are protected by the passing off action. To take an example, Butterworths—through its name and logo—has a reputation for, and consequent goodwill in, the production of leading legal tomes and could accordingly use the tort of passing off to prevent a newcomer to the field from using the name and logo, or anything close thereto. But if a new dairy products business were to decide to use the Butterworths name, it would be far from clear that any harm would be done, because confusion is unlikely

---

[40] TMA 1994, s. 56(2).

[41] R. Annand and H. Norman (1994) *Blackstone's Guide to the Trade Marks Act 1994*, Oxford: Blackstone, p. 31.

[42] *Erven Warnink v. v J Townend & Sons (Hull) Ltd* [1979] AC 731, [1979] 2 All ER 927, *per* Lord Diplock at 742 and 932.

[43] *British Association of Aesthetic Plastic Surgeons v. Cambright* [1987] RPC 549. Cf *Society of Incorporated Accountants v. Vincent* (1954) 71 RPC 325.

[44] *Burge & Armstrong v. Haycock* [2002] RPC 553 (CA). Cf *Kean v. McGivan* [1982] FSR 119, which must now effectively have been overturned by the decision of the Court of Appeal.

to arise, the publishers not being engaged in, and therefore enjoying no goodwill in, the dairy business. The way in which this has traditionally been considered is in the form of the need for a representation by the defendant to the customers of the claimant. If the customers are different, or are in entirely distinct areas of activity, then no goodwill is harmed and there will be no action in passing off; it is a common field of activity that is traditionally necessary.

A common field of activity

An easy example of this is shown by *Granada Group Ltd v. Ford Motor Co. Ltd.*[45] The claimants had a solid reputation in the television and cinema industry, and became concerned when they found out that the defendants were intending to christen their new luxury car the Ford 'Granada'. The claimants argued that the use of this well-known name would cause boundless confusion, but the defendants replied that the name had been chosen with regard to its Europe-wide effectiveness and that their business was in so different a field of activity that no impact on Granada's goodwill would be discernible. Graham J found for the defendants, refusing even an interlocutory injunction. No confusion would arise in the public mind between the very different companies and their very different products. Some of their customers may be the same, but there was no common field of activity to cause confusion even to those common customers.

Likewise, in *Wombles Ltd v. Wombles Skips Ltd*,[46] the claimants had the rights in the Wombles, fictitious furry creatures who, inter alia, were devoted to cleansing Wimbledon Common of litter and whose popularity meant that the claimants enjoyed the fruits of a successful merchandising programme. The defendants were a new company providing domestic rubbish skips and chose their name precisely because of both its popularity and its connotations of cleanliness. Walton J was clear that no injunction should be awarded, because there was no common field of activity and thus no common customers to be confused, as between toys and other merchandising items, on the one hand, and rubbish removal, on the other.

In considering whether there is a common field of activity and therefore a representation by the defendant to the customers of the claimant, some tenuous connections are sometimes made to assist the claimant's cause of action. In *BBC v. Talbot Motor Co. Ltd*,[47] the differences between the claimants' proposed 'Carfax' radio traffic information services and the defendants' 'Carfax' car parts appear to be obvious, yet Megarry V-C found the dangers of confusion to be real, because both operations were concerned with motor vehicles and confusion could particularly attend car radio purchases (although Talbot had offered in court to exclude car radios from its parts service).

In *Annabel's (Berkeley Square) Ltd v. Schock*,[48] the claimants were (and are) a top London nightspot frequented by the social elite. The defendant operated a business under the name 'Annabel's Escort Agency', providing young ladies to escort clients to dinner, dances, etc. The Court of Appeal, fortified by evidence of men ringing the nightclub in search of escorts and women arriving there seeking an escort job, found that there was a common field of activity in the field of night entertainment, that confusion could arise and had arisen, and that the public image of escort agencies was such that harm may be caused to the nightclub, and so an injunction was obtained in favour of the defendants.[49]

[45] [1973] RPC 49.
[46] [1977] RPC 99.
[47] [1981] FSR 228.
[48] [1972] RPC 838.
[49] For a similar decision, on less interesting facts, see *Walter v. Ashton* [1902] 2 Ch 282.

The courts have seemed more willing to uphold this type of case when the whiff of fraud is in the air: *Eastman Photographic Materials Co. Ltd v. John Griffiths Cycle Co. Ltd*[50] is such a case. Eastman made Kodak cameras while the defendants sought to sell a new brand of bicycle, the Kodak cycle. In the light of the fact that the claimants sold special 'Cycle Kodak' cameras specially adapted for use on bicycles and the deliberate conduct of the defendants, an injunction was awarded. Similarly, in *Harrods Ltd v. R Harrod Ltd*,[51] the claimant department store succeeded in preventing the defendants from using its name for a money lending business. The claimants did have a small banking section, but did not lend money; nonetheless, the Court of Appeal awarded an injunction, partly because of the closeness of the two businesses, partly because of evidence of customer confusion, and partly because of the fact that there was no legitimate reason for the defendants to use that name, no one called Harrod being in any way involved with the business.

Another *Harrods* case[52] was concerned with the use of the name 'Harrodian School' for a school that was unrelated to Harrods, but which was established in the buildings of the former 'Harrodian Club', membership of which had, at one stage, been restricted to employees of Harrods. Harrods alleged passing off, but, unlike the first case, this action failed. In relation to the common field of activity, it was held by the Court of Appeal that there was no requirement that the claimant should be carrying on a business that competed with that of the claimant or which would compete with any natural extension of the claimant's business. It was added, however, that the absence of a common field of activity was an important and highly relevant consideration in deciding whether there was a likelihood of confusion. Passing off will only protect goodwill against damage resulting from misrepresentations if there is a likelihood of confusion that makes damage to goodwill plausible. In this case, there was no common field of activity between the defendant, who was running a school, and the claimant, who was running a department store. The only question was whether there was a real risk that members of the public would be deceived into thinking that a school called 'Harrodian School' was owned or managed by Harrods or under Harrods' supervision or control. Did the public believe that the goods or services offered by the defendant were the goods or services of the claimant? Only if this was established could the claimant's reputation for excellence potentially suffer damage. This was a matter of fact and, in this case, no likelihood of confusion had been established.

Beyond the common field of activity

In summary, reasonably clear guidelines have been established to set the boundaries of goodwill created by trade. Firstly, there must be trade; secondly, there must be trade by both parties to the same customers and in the same, or at least broadly similar, fields of activity, with the level of broad similarity required being the area of greatest uncertainty or, if preferred, discretion.

But one significant decision appears to erode the clarity of the picture as far as the need for a common field of activity is concerned. In *Lego Systems Aktieselskab v. Lego M Lemelstrich Ltd*,[53] the claimants—well-known manufacturers of toy plastic bricks—took action against the sale by the defendants of 'Lego' brand water sprinklers and other such items of gardening irrigation equipment. Falconer J allowed an injunction to be granted. He rejected the argument that the common field of activity was essential here by pointing to the great fame of the 'Lego' name and the assumption that would be made by customers of Lego sprinklers

---

[50]   (1898) 15 RPC 105.
[51]   (1923) 41 RPC 74.
[52]   *Harrods Ltd v. Harrodian School Ltd* [1996] RPC 697.
[53]   [1983] FSR 155.

that they were buying products made by the Danish toy brick firm. In other words, Lego's goodwill is so great that it extends beyond its sole trading field into both related and, as here, unrelated areas of activity. People would be misled into thinking that any defect in the sprinklers was the fault of the toy firm and Lego would be prevented from using the goodwill in its name to diversify in the future into the garden sprinkler trade.

This is a bold decision that surely stretches the notion of goodwill in trade close to its breaking point. It goes far beyond cases in which there has been protection afforded by passing off for an active intention on the part of the claimant to diversify into related areas,[54] let alone those cases in which the courts have refused relief because the activities, although obviously related in a broad sense, have not amounted to a common field of activity: for example, ice lollies and bubble gum.[55] And yet it does not seem unacceptable: the phrase 'common field of activity' has never been part of the mainstream of the vocabulary of passing off,[56] and the approach now seems entirely compatible, in principle, with the language and approach of s. 5(3) of the 1994 Act.[57] The area in which the *Lego* decision still has a role, arguably, is when the threat of damage to the claimant's reputation is as vague (or illusory) as in the case itself, as opposed to the statute's requirement of detriment to the mark or its reputation, or, of course, if the claimant does not have trade mark protection.

The courts have now finally put to rest any remaining doubts concerning the requirement of a common field of activity in relation to passing off. Mr Justice Laddie held, in *Irvine v. Talksport Ltd*,[58] that it was the purpose of the law of passing off to vindicate the claimant's exclusive right to his goodwill and to protected it against damage. The law would therefore not allow others to use that goodwill so as to reduce, blur, or diminish its exclusivity. It followed from this that it was not necessary to show that the claimant and the defendant shared a common field of activity, or that the sales of products or services would be diminished either substantially or directly, at least in the short term. Instead, the essential point was to show a misrepresentation, because that element was required to enable the defendant to take advantage of the defendant's reputation. The unauthorized manipulation of a photograph of Mr Irvine, by means of which a Talksport Radio was put in his hand, and its subsequent use for publicity purposes amounted to such a misrepresentation, because it created the impression that Mr Irvine was endorsing Talksport Radio. This could affect Mr Irvine's goodwill and reputation, and the requirements for passing off were therefore met. The Court of Appeal upheld the decision on this point, while raising the amount of damages awarded to Mr Irvine.[59]

Meanwhile, some of the earlier case law may need rethinking: are not Granada and were not Wombles equally the possessors of the widest amount of goodwill? The first *Harrods* decision would now seem unduly cautious and narrow. Clearly, in the light of *Lego*, there is the potential for well-known brand names to establish broader goodwill than in the past if no longer confined to any type of common field of activity in bringing claims of passing off. But any *Lego*-based approach must be subject to one restriction: there must be a likelihood of confusion or deception and, in this respect, any indication of a common field of activity may still be a very relevant factor.[60]

---

[54] For example, *LRC International Ltd v. Lilla Edets Sales Co. Ltd* [1973] RPC 560.

[55] *Lyons Maid Ltd v. Trebor Ltd* [1967] RPC 222.

[56] *McCulloch v. Lewis A May Ltd* [1947] 2 All ER 845. See J. Phillips and A. Coleman, 'Passing-off and the "common field of activity"' (1985) 101 LQR 242.

[57] See Chapter 25.

[58] *Irvine v. Talksport Ltd* [2002] FSR 943, confirmed on appeal [2003] FSR 619.

[59] Ibid.

[60] *Nice & Safe Attitude Ltd v. Piers Flook (t/a 'Slaam! Clothing Company')* [1997] FSR 14; *Harrods Ltd v. Harrodian School Ltd* [1996] RPC 697.

Goodwill in real names

We have just seen in the *Harrods* decision that the unnecessary use of the name by another business amounted to passing off—but what would have happened if the proprietor of the rival business was indeed a 'Mr Harrod'? Clearly, just as much confusion and thus harm to goodwill may arise, but it may seem harsh to restrict the fictitious Mr Harrod from proudly using his own name for his business.

The courts do, however, seem prepared to so order. In *Baume & Co. Ltd v. A H Moore Ltd*,[61] the claimants sold watches under the trade mark 'Baume' and had done so for well over a century. The defendants began to import Swiss watches made by Baume and Mercier Ltd of Geneva, a fact marked both on the watches and their boxes. This was held to amount to passing off, although the use of the name was genuine in every respect (there had previously been a family connection between the two firms). The use of a real name could be actionable if it is used in such a way as to cause confusion with another's business and *'the defence of innocent and honest use of the manufacturers' name on the watches which the defendants have sold will not avail them as a defence if the other ingredients of passing off are established'*.[62] Confusion was likely given the similarity of both the name and the type of product.

If this seems harsh, it is worth reflecting that the importers of Baume and Mercier watches had taken no deliberate steps to distinguish them from the watches already on the market. This explains the opposite conclusion reached by Hoffmann J in *Anderson & Lembke Ltd v. Anderson & Lembke Inc.*[63] A specialist advertising agency in Sweden set up, and then sold off, international subsidiaries, including the parties to this litigation, based respectively in London and Connecticut. The US firm gained contracts in Europe and decided to open an office in London. The claimants' complaint was rejected; the defendants had taken steps to change the name under which they traded to 'A & L Europe' and then to 'Business Advertising Europe', and while there was reference in some documents to the connection with the US parent firm, this was regarded as inevitable and appropriate, and did not amount to passing off. It seems that honesty, although not a formal defence, is not unhelpful to a defendant's cause.

Another possible way of getting round *Baume* is to emphasize that the other ingredients of passing off need to be satisfied and it is far from clear that the defendants in that case had made any misrepresentation; they were, after all, selling watches made by Baume and Mercier, and it is customary for watches to bear the name of their manufacturer. It seems that the courts are more generous in allowing the honest use of a name for a business than for its products,[64] in relation to which greater care must be taken to distinguish one item from another.

In summary, if your name is McDonald and you want to open a burger bar, the tort of passing off will be reluctant to prevent the use of your name for your business—but if you invite McDonald to join your business just so as to be able to use his name, this is unlikely to be regarded as bona fide, after *Harrods*; in any event, it may be prudent to make your business as distinct as possible from that of your namesake, to avoid the problems of *Baume*. Likewise, use of the name or variants thereof on products rather than for the business at large is less likely to escape legal objection. In passing, use of the 'Mc' prefix seems to be regarded as a popular marketing weapon in the fast food trade; it would seem difficult, without more, for McDonalds to prevent this, unless other steps were taken to confuse customers.

---

[61] [1958] Ch 907, [1958] 2 All ER 113.
[62] Ibid., *per* Romer LJ at 917 and 117.
[63] [1989] RPC 124.
[64] *Marengo v. Daily Sketch & Sunday Graphic Ltd* (1948) 65 RPC 242, esp. *per* Lord Simonds at 251.

The Court of Appeal repeated recently that there can be goodwill in one's own name and that, after the name and the business have been sold, one can, in principle, use one's own name in connection with a competing business. But there is a risk: if the public perceives your activity as passing off the new business as that which you have sold—that is, if the three conditions for passing off have been met—the fact that you are using your own name will not be a valid defence.[65]

An unusual case in this area is the recent case of *Alan Clark v. Associated Newspapers*,[66] in which the distinguished—if controversial—politician succeeded in a complaint against the *Evening Standard* for a spoof column based on his diary-style of writing and using his name (although the columns were attributed to the journalist who wrote them). It was held that the prominent use of Alan Clark's name would be seen by the public as associating him with the articles and thus would amount to passing off.

Similar considerations are also found in the *Irvine* case,[67] in which a photograph of Mr Irvine was at the hearth of the matter, rather than his name, as such.

Goodwill in real words

Similar risks of granting an overgenerous monopoly arise in respect of the use of real words—especially those that are descriptive of a product. Clearly, the first person to make ice cream should not have a monopoly on those words that are descriptive of his or her product and this is reflected by the legal position.

County Sound plc v. Ocean Sound plc[68] is a good contemporary example. The parties are both local radio stations in southern England, broadcasting to adjacent, but overlapping, catchment areas. The claimants decided to launch a new service, broadcasting old records on their MW/AM frequency, which they christened 'The Gold AM'. Six months later, the defendants began to broadcast a similar service and used the same name. The Court of Appeal refused to grant an injunction against the defendants on the grounds that, although the claimants had had time to develop the necessary goodwill, no goodwill could develop around 'The Gold AM' because 'Gold' was, in the view of Nourse LJ,[69] a word '*descriptive of popular hits of the 1950s, 1960s, and 1970s and AM was simply the description of the frequency on which the service could be found*'. Descriptive words could only develop goodwill by the use of that name and no other for goods over a substantial period of time, as authority for which the old case of *Reddaway v. Banham*[70] was cited, in which more than a decade's usage of 'Camel Hair Belting' was held sufficient to generate the necessary goodwill. But this is clearly the exception, rather than the rule, and here, too, the question must arise as to whether there is anything in the nature of a misrepresentation in a subsequent use by another of purely descriptive wording.

The name 'Farm Fluids', a description of an agrichemical product has likewise been held to be unable to be used by a rival producer, because the name was known in the relevant market as synonymous with the claimant's business.[71]

Collective goodwill

In most of the cases so far examined, the claimant trader has generated, by his or her trading endeavours, his or her own goodwill and will therefore be its owner. This is not,

---

[65] *I N Newman Ltd v. Adlem* [2006] FSR 16 (CA).
[66] [1998] RPC 261. See also Chapter 31.
[67] *Irvine v. Talksport Ltd* [2002] FSR 943, confirmed on appeal [2003] FSR 619.
[68] [1991] FSR 367.
[69] Ibid. at 373.
[70] [1896] AC 199. This approach is now reflected in the proviso to TMA 1994, s. 3(1)(c).
[71] *Antec International Ltd v. South Western Chicks (Warren) Ltd* [1998] FSR 738.

however, a requirement of the tort of passing off; it is equally possible for the necessary goodwill to be generated by a group of traders collectively, as the group of cases colloquially known as the *Alcohol* cases clearly shows.

The first of these cases is *Bollinger v. Costa Brava Wine Co.*, heard first[72] on preliminary points of law and subsequently[73] as a full trial. The claimants were a group of French producers of champagne from that region of France and they were seeking to prevent the defendants from marketing their sparkling wine from Spain as 'Spanish champagne'. Obviously, no single producer has any sort of exclusive right to the word 'champagne', but the argument was that, together, the French manufacturers of the drink had developed a collective goodwill and reputation in the name. This then novel argument was successful. Danckwerts J[74] felt that the nature and purpose of passing off was to prevent unfair trading, and to control unfair competition, and that the necessary goodwill could just as easily be developed by, as here, a group of persons producing particular goods in a particular locality—although each of the claimants is separately entitled to bring his or her own legal action in respect of harm to his or her own share of the goodwill.[75] The decision represented both a substantial advance for the tort of passing off and a growing recognition of the potential that the tort has as a tool for regulating unfair trading—which latter aspect will be considered later in this chapter.

The lead given in *Bollinger* was followed in *Vine Products Ltd v. Mackenzie & Co. Ltd.*[76] This time, the drink in question was sherry—or, to be precise, British sherry—and the action was brought by a group of manufacturers seeking to establish their right to use the name 'sherry' against the objections of Spanish producers of the drink from the Jerez region from which traditional sherry originates. Cross J upheld the objections to a limited extent, in so far as the word 'sherry' itself was not to be used on its own on any drink other than that from Jerez; the long usage of 'British sherry' and other non-Spanish varieties, such as sherry from South Africa and Cyprus, was permitted to continue. In effect, then, 'British sherry is good' would be a permitted form of advert, but 'British sherry is good sherry' would not.

Cross J[77] appeared to regard *Bollinger* as creating a new tort of unfair competition, rather than as passing off, because the normal requirements of representation and confusion were absent. This appears to be an odd remark, because the drinks described as 'champagne' and 'sherry' were not from the relevant geographical areas, and this surely may amount to a misrepresentation and thus cause confusion. Nonetheless, these remarks were expressly adopted by Foster J in the third case in this group, *John Walker & Sons Ltd v. Henry Ost & Co. Ltd.*[78] In this case, the claimants were a group of Scotch whisky producers who were held able to prevent the name of Scotch whisky from being besmirched by its use on a blend of whiskey and cane spirit that was available in Ecuador.

The *Advocaat* case, however, restores the cases to the fold of passing off, albeit 'in an extended form'[79] and also bearing in mind that the larger a group claiming collective goodwill, the harder it will be to show the public recognition of distinctiveness that a word such as 'champagne' had attracted.[80] (One manufacturer only brought the action, so these comments are presumably obiter.)

---

[72] [1960] Ch 262, [1959] 3 All ER 800.

[73] *Bollinger v. Costa Brava Wine Co. Ltd (No. 2)* [1961] 1 All ER 561, [1961] 1 WLR 277.

[74] [1960] Ch 262, [1959] 3 All ER 800, at 284 and 811.

[75] [1961] 1 All ER 561, [1961] 1 WLR 277, at 563 and 281.

[76] [1969] RPC 1.

[77] Ibid. at 23 and 28.

[78] [1970] 2 All ER 106, [1970] 1 WLR 917.

[79] [1979] AC 731 at 739, [1979] 2 All ER 927, *per* Lord Diplock at 929.

[80] [1979] AC 731 at 744, [1979] 2 All ER 927, *per* Lord Diplock at 934.

The continuing relevance of this area of case law, and its continuing existence within the tort of passing off, is confirmed by a more recent case—on that is still concerned with alcohol. Once again, the highly litigious champagne industry came to the courts, this time to restrain the use of 'its' word in a non-alcoholic product made from elderflowers known as 'Elderflower champagne'. In *Taittinger v. Allbev Ltd*,[81] the Court of Appeal held that the industry could so restrain the use of 'champagne'. After consideration of mainstream passing off case law, the view was taken that there was a clear threat to the collective goodwill of the champagne industry if this cheap, non-alcoholic drink could continue to bear the hallowed name.

The claimants also sought and gained an injunction on the alternative ground that the defendants were in breach of EC Regulation 823/87 laying down special provisions relating to quality wines produced in specified regions.[82] These regulations insist on correct wine labelling, of which there was a clear breach in this respect, and so an injunction was appropriate in view of the fact that the purpose of the Regulation was to avoid the very confusion that the use by the defendants of the word 'champagne' had caused. Collective goodwill thus remains a valid method of satisfying the first requirement of the tort of passing off, but *Vine Products* reminds us that it may only receive limited protection by a restrictively drawn injunction, while the *Advocaat* case suggests that use of collective goodwill may not be widely available except in the clearest of cases.

The most recent example of this type of claim is the successful action by Swiss chocolatiers to prevent the UK-based Cadbury from using the name and image of Swiss chocolate in promoting what is doubtless a fine product—but which was made in Birmingham— through the use of the 'Chocosuisse' name.[83] This case illustrates the difficulties that surround the use of descriptive words as names in which collective goodwill is claimed to exist. The case makes it clear that a passing off action can only get off the ground if these descriptive words—here, the reference to Swiss chocolate—are taken by a significant part of the public to be used in relation to, and indicating a particular group of, products having a discrete reputation as a group. The requirement does not go as far as demanding that the goods which fall into the group and which are protected by the name must be distinguishable, in fact, from all competing goods. In the case at issue, the public clearly identified Swiss chocolate as a group of products with a separate reputation, despite the fact that it is not possible to point towards a particular recipe that is used for all Swiss chocolate and which is used nowhere else in the world.

The new collective trade mark, created by s. 49 of the 1994 Act, will, of course, meet many of these problems, but only if the claimants are part of a formal association of traders, rather than simply a group of rivals with, nonetheless, a common interest in seeing off outside competition. In many of these cases, the issue of who owns the goodwill and is therefore entitled to sue consequently arises. It may be difficult to argue that an unincorporated trade association that does not manufacture or sell any particular product can establish goodwill of its own, but its unincorporated status does not impede it from owning goodwill through its members if it does trade in one way or another, for example, by putting on trade exhibitions. In the latter case, a member of the association acting in a representative capacity could commence an action in passing off on the basis of that goodwill in trading.[84]

---

[81] [1994] 4 All ER 75, [1993] 2 CMLR 741.

[82] Incorporated into UK law by the Common Agricultural Policy (Wine) Regulations 1992, SI 1992/672, now, in the latest form, the Common Agricultural Policy (Wine) (England And Northern Ireland) Regulations 2001, SI 2001/686, as amended by SI 2007/1943.

[83] *Chocosuisse Union des Fabricants Suisse de Chocolat v. Cadbury Ltd* [1998] RPC 117.

[84] Ibid.; *Artistic Upholstery Ltd v. Art Forma (Furniture) Ltd* [1999] 4 All ER 277, [2000] FSR 311; see also *Consorzio del Prosciutto di Parma v. Marks & Spencer plc* [1991] RPC 351.

Range of goodwill protected

In most of the cases considered so far, the attack on the claimant's goodwill has been straightforwardly aimed at some feature at the heart of the claimant's business, such as brand name, company name, or distinctive product description. The question arises, however, of how broadly the notion of goodwill can extend towards more peripheral parts of the claimant's trading activity.

A notable extension of the range of goodwill protected by the tort of passing off has been provided by the Privy Council in *Cadbury Schweppes Pty Ltd v. Pub Squash Co. Pty Ltd*.[85] This litigation arose when the claimants and, subsequently, the defendants both entered the Australian drinks market with lemon-flavoured soft drinks. There was no doubt that the defendants were seeking to exploit the large market that the claimants' product, called 'Solo', had shown existed for this type of product, but the defendants chose a very different name, 'Pub Squash', for their product. The problem arose in the two firms' respective marketing campaigns: both used a broadly similar strategy; both tried to associate their drink with two separate themes—heroic masculine endeavour and nostalgia for tasty drinks in the past; both products were sold in a yellow can. The issue then was plain: would the tort of passing off extend to more general imagery associated with the product?

The answer given by Lord Scarman was clearly that passing off could so extend. The tort may have originated with the name and description of the product itself, but it was not in any way constrained to remain there. Rather, it was now capable of conferring protection on goodwill created by many other types of descriptive material:

> such as slogans or visual images, which radio, television or newspaper advertising campaigns can lead the market to associate with a claimant's product, provided that such material has become part of the goodwill of the product. And the test is whether the product has derived from the advertising a distinctive character which the market recognises.[86]

So, in allowing the protection of passing off to be thus extended, Lord Scarman is being doubly cautious. Not all advertising and other such imagery will be protected—only that which is part of the company's goodwill. So a standard advert of a contented family group or a sunny tropical isle will never attract the necessary goodwill, but an innovative advert or campaign in which unlikely concepts—such as rugged masculine endeavour—are linked with the product—here, lemonade—may do so. They also appear to fulfil Lord Scarman's second constraint—namely, that of distinctiveness. Only those brands are thus advertised and there is no inherent reason why they should be: creativity has been employed so as to establish distinctiveness.

After this, a successful conclusion to the claimants' claim may have been anticipated— but they were unable to restrain Pub Squash's use of their marketing material. As a matter of policy, Lord Scarman expressed concern that to allow the claim would be to blur the line between fair and unfair methods of competition: '*a defendant, however, does no wrong by entering a market created by another and there competing with its creator.*'[87] Passing off was not to be confused with a wider tort of unfair competition and, here, the defendants—although consciously trying to grab part of the claimants' market share— were not trying to make the public think that their product was that of the claimants: there was thus no deception, no misrepresentation, and no infringement of the rights of the claimants.

---

[85] [1981] 1 All ER 213, [1981] 1 WLR 193.
[86] Ibid. at 218 and 200.
[87] Ibid.

In spite of its outcome, *Cadbury Schweppes* is clearly a decision of potentially great significance. Its broadening out of the range of goodwill protected is a major advance on the previous position; its practical effect may well, however, be limited. After the initial expansion, Lord Scarman is cautious to dampen down expectations by emphasizing that only that material which is both distinctive and becomes part of goodwill is protected, and the need for fair competition to be preserved clearly also reduces the chance of claiming successfully. Indeed, arguments based on this expansion of goodwill have been notable only by their absence in ensuing years. A likely explanation of this is that goodwill in such cases is generated so far away from the product itself that no misrepresentation is likely.[88] The basic differences—for example, in the product name—far outweigh the broad similarities found in the marketing campaign.

Notwithstanding this, it is still appropriate to conclude the entire section on goodwill with such a case because it typifies, in its own way, the continuing development and expansion of the notion of goodwill that has been a common feature of many of the areas discussed. Granted that findings of fact can diminish their overall impact, it is significant that the concept of goodwill being contracted in only a few areas, while in many, it has expanded, is expanding, or, at the least, has the potential to expand.

Misrepresentation

The next vital element in any passing off action is that the defendant must represent his or her goods or services to be those of the claimant. The representation must create a false belief of connection between the two products in the mind of the consumer and, accordingly, it is appropriate to refer to it as a *mis*representation. The creation of an association is sufficient for there to be a misrepresentation:[89] to sell orange-flavoured cakes as 'Jaffa cakes' does not amount to passing off, because that is no more than a description of the product and does not create any form of confusion in the mind of the consumer—but to market the cakes in packs of similar design to that of the market leader may be actionable in passing off, because, by using that design, customers may be likely to confuse the two products. It may therefore be a misrepresentation so to do.[90]

In recent years, supermarket lookalike products have tried to resemble the original, but supermarkets have at least claimed[91] that they made every effort to avoid giving rise to confusion by making a misrepresentation. To put it another way, a true representation of a product, quite apart from being unlikely to attract goodwill, will not cause any confusion and will not therefore be actionable. The hallmark of the misrepresentation is that confusion is its result. Of course, not all confusion in trading is necessarily the result of a misrepresentation; confusion is inevitable whenever a monopoly is first broken. There must be a representation that the newcomer's goods are, or are connected with, those of the original seller.[92] A simple belief, for example, that the claimant had sponsored or given financial support to the defendant would not ordinarily give the public the impression that the claimant had made himself responsible for the quality of the defendant's goods

---

[88] Some authors have argued that a strict approach is the only correct approach and that the three traditional requirements should be adhered to strictly. Passing off should remain a misrepresentation tort. See, e.g., H. Carty, 'Passing off at the crossroads' [1996] 11 EIPR 629.

[89] *Sir Robert McAlpine Ltd v. Alfred McAlpine plc* [2004] RPC 711.

[90] See *United Biscuits (UK) Ltd v. Burton Biscuits Ltd* [1992] FSR 14.

[91] Asda did not succeed in this respect, although in *United Biscuits (UK) Ltd v. Asda Stores Ltd* [1997] RPC 513, it was held to have passed off its lookalike 'Puffin' biscuits as United Biscuits' 'Penguin' biscuits.

[92] *My Kinda Town Ltd v. Soll & Grunts Investments* [1983] RPC 407.

or services.[93] Such a connection would not constitute a misrepresentation, because there has to be deception; mere confusion or likelihood of confusion is not sufficient. A full misrepresentation must take place and such a misrepresentation is a necessary ingredient of a cause of action of passing off.[94]

The range of misrepresentations is very broad. They may relate to the nature of the product itself, as the cases on champagne noted above exemplify well. In many other cases, the get-up of the product—that is, its packaging and presentation—may be the source of confusion. It may be more remote: the *Cadbury Schweppes* case considered above shows that goodwill may extend to cover general aspects of the marketing campaign and thus misrepresentations may exist in that context too.

Misrepresentation by get-up

The most common category appears to be cases concerning the get-up of a product. The courts do not seem to object to essential similarities in appearance dictated, for example, by the function that a product has to perform. In *J B Williams Co. v. H Bronnley Co. Ltd*,[95] the separate brands of shaving stick were sold in similar containers. The Court of Appeal found that the claimants' container was not distinctive; all of its features were either dictated by the shape of the stick or were common to many other types of container in everyday use.

William Edge & Sons Ltd v. William Niccolls & Sons Ltd,[96] meanwhile, was a case in which the similarity was not necessary and therefore did amount to a misrepresentation. The claimant had long sold laundry blue, a type of dye, in bags with a wooden stick attached, to enable it to be lowered into a sink of washing without the hands of the user coming into contact with the water and dye. The defendants then began to sell a similar product of almost identical appearance. The House of Lords found that this amounted to passing off, because there was nothing essential about the size and shape of the stick—any stick would perform the same useful function—and so there was no justification for the defendants to have used the same type of get-up.

Jif Lemon

The principal case of this type is now *Reckitt & Colman Products Ltd v. Borden Inc.*[97] This concerns the sale of 'Jif Lemon' juice in lemon-shaped containers, which had been going on successfully and profitably for over thirty years. The defendants then decided to market their lemon juice in similar, although not identical, containers, different models of container being of a different size from that of Jif, or with a different coloured cap and/or label. None of these refinements detracted from the essential lemon shape and colour that was at the base of Borden's marketing strategy. Lord Oliver emphasized[98] that the key questions in a passing off action were always those of fact and the vital finding of fact made by the trial judge, Walton J, was that there was a likelihood of confusion in the marketplace if both firms sold their juice in similar containers. This conclusion was reached with regard to the way in which this particular product was purchased by a busy shopper rushing around a busy supermarket, making an occasional low-price purchase of an ordinary item; in such circumstances, no great care can be expected to be taken and confusion can readily ensue.

93 *Harrods Ltd v. Harrodian School Ltd* [1996] RPC 697.
94 *Barnsley Brewery Co. Ltd v. RBNB* [1997] FSR 462.
95 (1909) 26 RPC 765; see also *Scott v. Nice-Pak Products* [1989] FSR 100.
96 [1911] AC 693.
97 [1990] 1 All ER 873, [1990] 1 WLR 491.
98 Ibid. at 880 and 499.

Several points arise from the significant *Jif* case. Firstly, it shows the tort of passing off to be in good health, offering protection beyond that given by the trade mark registration that, at that time, did not extend to goods and/or containers following *Re Coca-Cola Co's Application*.[99] Secondly, it stands out as a rare instance of the House of Lords, in recent times, extending the scope of monopoly. Lord Oliver addressed this issue by asserting '*the principle that no man is entitled to steal another's trade by deceit is one of at least equal importance to the alleged need to curtail monopolies*'.[100] Lord Bridge, however, clearly regretted that the judge's findings of fact left him with no option but to grant an injunction in the case.[101]

Jif is also notable for its confirmation that the identity of likely customers is an element in the equation. Were great care taken habitually by lemon juice purchasers, no confusion would arise and no action would have succeeded, but Walton J confirms that, in practice, care is not taken in such a minor and routine transaction (incidentally, enabling Jif to be sold at a far higher unit price than bottled lemon juice). But if the differences are so great that the reasonable man will be able to discern them, the fact that a few still may get confused is not sufficient to ground an action. This was well illustrated by Foster J in *Morning Star Co-operative Society Ltd v. Express Newspapers Ltd*,[102] when he observed that the differences between the austere broadsheet *Morning Star* and the racy tabloid *Daily Star* were such that '*only a moron in a hurry would be misled*',[103] and thus no passing off had occurred. The knowledge—actual or imputed—of the customers is also relevant; separate firms trading as 'JSB Motor Policies at Lloyds' and 'BJS Motor Syndicate at Lloyds' did not generate any confusion, because the defendants only traded with insurance brokers whose expertise included knowledge of the separate nature of the two operations.[104]

The *Jif* case also highlights a most important practical point in passing off litigation—namely, how to obtain the all-important evidence that confusion has been, or is likely to be, engendered. This is particularly difficult in a case in which the offending new project is yet to be launched, so no members of the public have, as yet, been confused. The vital evidence in *Jif* itself came from tests carried out by the claimants, involving stopping shoppers in the street, offering them one of the defendants' lemons, holding interviews with shoppers, and displaying the defendants' lemon in a supermarket on Shrove Tuesday, when much lemon juice is sold for use on pancakes; each of these tests showed a great degree of confusion, with shoppers believing that the defendants' lemon was, in fact, a Jif lemon.

Evidence

Such unequivocal evidence is, however, rare: too often, survey evidence is not found to be convincing by the courts, because of flaws in the survey itself. Useful guidelines were set out by Whitford J in *Imperial Group plc v. Philip Morris Ltd*.[105] He insisted that, in order to be of any value in court, a survey should be of an adequately large size and be fairly conducted. Full details of results and methods should be made available to the defence. Care should be taken about the use of questions that lead, or otherwise direct, their target.

---

[99] [1986] 2 All ER 274, *sub nom In re Coca Cola Co.* [1986] 1 WLR 695; cf TMA 1994, s. 1(1). See Chapter 24.

[100] [1990] 1 All ER 873, [1990] 1 WLR 491, at 889 and 509.

[101] Ibid. at 877 and 495.

[102] [1979] FSR 113.

[103] Ibid. at 117.

[104] *John Hayter Motor Underwriting Agencies Ltd v. RBHS Agencies Ltd* [1977] FSR 285. The lack of confusion at the point of sale prevented a passing off claim in *Bostick Ltd v. Sellotape GB Ltd* [1994] RPC 556.

[105] [1984] RPC 293 at 302.

A good example of survey evidence failing this test is provided by *United Biscuits (UK) Ltd v. Burtons Biscuits Ltd*.[106] This was a dispute between rival brands of Jaffa cakes. A straw poll questionnaire and a survey were regarded as worthless by Vinelott J, as being ill defined and capable of misinterpretation, while a tachistoscope test, which tests the operator's recognition of a brand by quickly flashing an image of it, was also of no help, because the false recognition of the defendants' package as that of the claimants could be equally explained by the fact that the claimants were the clear brand leader.

Clearly, care needs to be taken by the parties in the collection of survey evidence and caution will be the hallmark of the courts in their use of it;[107] its dramatic impact in the *Jif* case shows, however, that, in an appropriate case, it will have great value. Equally, the courts are also unwilling to hear evidence from marketing 'experts' if the issue relates to potential confusion among the public at large.[108]

Other examples

A few other examples of passing off by confusing get-up may be helpful. In *Rizla Ltd v. Bryant & May Ltd*,[109] the claimants' long-standing business of selling packs of cigarette papers faced a serious threat of competition from the defendants. They proposed to market three different types of paper, as did the claimants, and were proposing to use the same colour as their rivals for each type of paper. There, however, the similarity ceased with the defendants' 'Swan' brand name being prominently displayed, preventing any confusion with the Rizla papers arising.

Likewise, the inclusion of a pink paper section for business news in the tabloid evening newspaper the *Evening Standard* was not thought likely to cause any confusion with the broadsheet morning pink paper newspaper the *Financial Times*.[110]

Nor too could the proprietor of the magazine *Gourmet* restrain the introduction of a new journal *BBC Gourmet Good Food* when its get-up was different and it would be typically purchased from a rack on the basis of that get-up, rather than orally purchased from behind the newsagent's counter.[111]

Low-cost airline Easyjet was, however, able to stop an unrelated defendant from trading as Easyrealestate. Passing off could be established in this case, despite the fact that Easyjet could not appropriate the word 'Easy', because the defendant had copied the four distinctive features of Easyjet's get-up on its website.[112]

Misrepresentation by name

In other cases, it is not the get-up of the goods, but the name being used that is the source of potential confusion. In *Newsweek Inc. v. BBC*,[113] the publishers of the international news magazine sought to prevent the use of *Newsweek* as the title of a current affairs television programme. The Court of Appeal rejected the claim, because the BBC would broadcast the programme with its usual logos, etc., and there would be no risk of confusing it with the claimants' magazine. The mere use of a name used by another trader does not necessarily create the impression that the businesses are in some way connected, it seems.

---

[106] [1992] FSR 14.
[107] See C. Morcom, 'Survey evidence in trade mark proceedings' [1984] 1 EIPR 6.
[108] *Dalgety Spillers Foods Ltd v. Food Brokers Ltd* [1994] FSR 504.
[109] [1986] RPC 389.
[110] *Financial Times Ltd v. Evening Standard Co. Ltd* [1991] FSR 7.
[111] *Advance Magazine Publishing Inc. v. Redwood Publishing Ltd* [1993] FSR 449.
[112] *Easyjet Airline Co. v. Tim Dainty (t/a Easyrealestate)* [2002] FSR 111.
[113] [1979] RPC 441.

But the use of the same name in a related field of activity is more likely to be restrained. In this respect, *Island Trading Co. v. Anchor Brewing Co.*[114] is instructive. The claimants sold 'Newquay Real Steam Bitter', with a steam theme used as part of its promotion. The defendants then began to import from California, for the first time, their 'Anchor Steam Beer' and the claimants feared that confusion would arise. Knox J found that the Newquay brand was often referred to by customers as 'Steam Beer', and he awarded an injunction against the sale of Anchor Steam Beer in kegs, but allowed it in bottles. The reasoning was that kegs of beer in pubs might well cause confusion when a drinker asks for a 'pint of Steam', but bottled beer sold from the shelves of off-licences would not give rise to such confusion, the bottles being very different in appearance, the customer being more likely to be sober, the sales staff being less under pressure, and the noise level being likely to be lower.

Recently, the famous luxury goods company Asprey and Garrard successfully brought a claim in passing off relying on the goodwill in its 'Asprey' name against another trader in luxury goods in the London area that wanted to include the word 'Asprey' in its trading name, William R Asprey Esquire. It was held that any use of the word 'Asprey' in such a context was likely to confuse, and was especially likely to confuse the high proportion of potential foreign customers of Asprey and Garrard.[115]

Much will, however, depend on the facts: in another case, the use of the words 'Arsenal' and 'Gunners', or other signs related to Arsenal football club, in relation to unlicensed memorabilia was not enough to establish passing off, because, in this case, the specific habit of marking licensed merchandise as 'original' meant that, in the absence of this mention on the merchandise at issue, the public would not be confused into thinking that they were offered 'official' Arsenal merchandise.[116]

A particular problem arises when the same name is used on two similar products in cases in which a real name is being used: can the use of your own name amount to a misrepresentation, given that goodwill may attach, as we have seen, to a person's name? Well-known families appear to be particularly susceptible to this kind of dispute. In *Tussaud v. Tussaud*,[117] the claimants ran the famous Madame Tussaud waxworks in London; this had been a family business, but had just been sold to an outsider. Young Louis Tussaud had worked in the family business, but was now intending to open his own rival waxworks as Louis Tussaud Ltd. An injunction was awarded to the claimants stopping the defendant from registering a company of that name, because of the confusion that would arise and also because Louis Tussaud was not in the process of incorporating a pre-existing business.

Similar decisions have been reached in other cases. *Parker-Knoll Ltd v. Knoll International Ltd*[118] saw a clash between the claimants, manufacturers of traditional furniture, and the defendants, who made more modern designs primarily for industrial use. The proprietor of the defendants was the wife of the nephew of the original Knoll who lent his name to the claimant firm. The House of Lords found, by a majority, that the defendants could be prevented by injunction from using their name because of the likelihood that they would be referred to as 'Knoll' and the confusion that would arise thereby. More recently, the Gucci family have also resorted to litigation. In *Guccio Gucci SpA v. Paolo Gucci*,[119] the defendant was also prevented from trading under his own name, because the

[114] [1989] RPC 287.

[115] *Asprey & Garrard Ltd v. WRA (Guns) Ltd (t/a William R Asprey Esquire)* [2002] FSR 477, upheld on appeal [2002] FSR 487.

[116] *Arsenal Football Club plc v. Matthew Reed* [2001] 2 CMLR 23, [2001] RPC 922.

[117] (1890) 44 Ch D 678.

[118] [1962] RPC 265.

[119] [1991] FSR 89.

evidence was that the buyers of designer label clothes might be confused by the use of the Gucci name by anyone other than the claimants. These decisions may appear harsh on defendants legitimately using their own name, but they are a reminder that the first in the field has the opportunity to develop a reputation and thus acquire goodwill, and that this inevitably confers on him an advantage over later entrants into the market who, after all, do not have to use their own name in their trading activities and only do so because of the cachet that their (well-known) name may confer.

The Court of Appeal recently held that, after the name and the business have been sold, one can, in principle, use one's own name in connection with a competing business—but there is a risk: if the public perceives your activity as passing off the new business as that which you have sold—for example, because you make comments indicating that you are the 'real' one or even because you do not correct a self-induced misapprehension by the public[120]—this will amount to a misrepresentation for the purposes of passing off.[121]

Cybersquatting

The development of the Internet has, in recent years, given rise to a new type of case in which misrepresentation by name takes place. 'Cyberpirates' have tried to register the names of famous companies as domain names in order to be able to sell them to the companies involved for a profit. Some would call it extortion, but actions in passing off have proved useful to stop this practice. The goodwill of the famous companies is not in doubt and it was held that the registration of the names by cyberpirates amounted to a misrepresentation. The least that could be said was that the registration amounted to the creation of an instrument of deception.[122]

This flexible approach to misrepresentation is, however, linked to one condition: what is complained of must inherently tell a lie in order for it to be an instrument of deception.[123]

Misrepresentation of the product itself

Another form of misrepresentation may arise when the product itself appears to be that of the claimants. This can particularly arise in cases of parallel imports, in relation to which goods made elsewhere by a multinational firm are imported and compete with their home-grown product, at a lower price, because of the cheaper manufacturing costs elsewhere.

In *Colgate-Palmolive Ltd v. Markwell Finance Ltd*,[124] the claimants made and sold toothpaste in the UK as a subsidiary of its US parent company. There was also a Brazilian subsidiary, which made toothpaste of poorer quality; it was not intended to compete in the markets of other members of the Colgate group, but the defendants succeeded in circumventing the restrictions that had been placed on the trading activity of the Brazilian firm. It was clear that confusion was caused—complaints were made to the claimants about

---

[120] *British Sky Broadcasting Group plc & ors v. Sky Home Services Ltd & ors* [2007] FSR 14.

[121] *I N Newman Ltd v. Adlem* [2006] FSR 16 (CA).

[122] *Marks & Spencer plc v. One in A Million Ltd, Ladbroke's plc v. One in A Million Ltd; J Sainsbury plc v. One in A Million Ltd, Virgin Enterprises Ltd v. One in A Million Ltd; British Telecommunications plc v. One in A Million Ltd* [1998] FSR 265 at 271, confirmed on appeal *British Telecommunications plc v. One in A Million Ltd* [1998] 4 All ER 476. See also *Phones 4U Ltd & anor v. Phone4u.co.uk Internet Ltd & ors* [2007] RPC 5 (CA). Other cases are concerned with the registration of company names in bad faith: *Glaxo plc v. Glaxowellcome Ltd* [1996] FSR 388; *Direct Line Group Ltd v. Direct Line Estate Agency Ltd* [1997] FSR 374.

[123] *L'Oréal SA, Lancôme Parfums et Beauté & Cie & Laboratoire Garnier & Cie v. Bellure NV, Malaika Investments (t/a Honeypot Cosmetic & Perfumery Sales) & Starion International Ltd* [2007] EWCA Civ 936 (CA).

[124] [1989] RPC 497.

what was, in fact, toothpaste from Brazil. The Court of Appeal found that this amounted to passing off, even though both types of Colgate product derived from a common origin: it was not the origin, but the quality, of the goods that was at issue and the use by the defendants of products bearing the 'Colgate' name amounted to a misrepresentation to their customers of the quality to be expected from those goods. A similar decision was reached much earlier in *Gillette Safety Razor Co. v. Franks*,[125] in which the defendant was prevented from selling second-hand imported Gillette razor blades in Gillette packaging as new blades.

Imitation products—such as perfumes with similar-sounding names, in similar-looking bottles, and with a similar smell—are another interesting case. The original perfumes may be well known and possess a lot of goodwill; the mere fact that someone is seeking to emulate them does not amount to a misrepresentation. This remains true as long as the public does not see the imitation as the genuine goods originating from the original producer and that also explains why the conclusion in *L'Oréal*[126] was different from that in *Colgate-Palmolive*.

Developments in misrepresentation

It is evident that the law is willing to recognize a variety of different ways in which trading activity can amount to a misrepresentation. In areas in which there is such flexibility, it is always open to litigants to try to exploit that flexibility by seeking gradually to extend the frontiers of liability. There is evidence, from two recent decisions, of this happening in respect of misrepresentations in passing off cases.

Bristol Conservatories Ltd v. Conservatories Custom Built Ltd[127] was a case of what may be described as reverse passing off. Usually, the representor seeks to establish that his or her goods are the goods of the claimant, but here the opposite was the case and the claim was that the goods of the claimant were, in fact, his. This arose in relation to the erection of ornamental conservatories as extensions to buildings. The claimants were engaged in this business when an employee left and joined the defendants' newly formed business. He then touted for business, showing prospective customers pictures of conservatories erected by the claimants, conveying the impression that they had been the work of the defendants.

The Court of Appeal ruled on a preliminary point that these facts disclosed a good cause of action. The basis of the decision is, in essence, that any confusion—however caused and even if indirect in origin—will be enough to ground a misrepresentation claim and, clearly, here customers would become confused as to the true origin of the conservatories. In fact, the defendants' salesman had been silent as to the basis of the pictures, so inferences drawn from a silence can also amount to a misrepresentation, which is a long way from traditional definitions of misrepresentation. Ralph Gibson LJ specifically endorsed[128] the view that the common law should seek to parallel the legislative trend towards ever higher standards of commercial integrity and this invitation, if taken up, will only strengthen the expansionist tone adopted in recent times by the tort of passing off.

More recently, the existence of this type of claim has been confirmed by the sale of 'Welsh Whiskey', which was, in fact, based on a blend of Scotch whisky and herbs. This

---

[125] (1924) 41 RPC 499.

[126] *L'Oréal SA, Lancôme Parfums et Beauté & Cie & Laboratoire Garnier & Cie v. Bellure NV, Malaika Investments (t/a Honeypot Cosmetic & Perfumery Sales) & Starion International Ltd* [2007] EWCA Civ 936 (CA).

[127] [1989] RPC 455, noted J. Holyoak 'Reverse passing off: a new liability' (1990) 106 LQR 564.

[128] [1989] RPC 455 at 466.

was found to be an abuse of the name and reputation of Scotch whisky by dressing it up as being Welsh.[129]

The other case that, again, shows a broad approach to misrepresentation is that of *Associated Newspapers plc v. Insert Media Ltd.*[130] The claimants, newspaper proprietors, sought to prevent the unauthorized insertion of advertising material into copies of their newspapers. Just as in *Bristol Conservatories*, the problem was that, in one sense, there was no misrepresentation, because nothing was said to the readers to indicate that the inserts were not by, or with the permission of, the proprietors.

The Court of Appeal found for the claimants. While accepting that the mere act of inserting copy into the papers may not, in itself, amount to a misrepresentation, it would do so if all of the surrounding circumstances suggested that the inserts were there with the permission of the proprietor and, in particular, if, as a result, the public is likely to be confused because of what has been done. On these facts, the defendant had himself, in his publicity, pointed to the link that would be made by people associating the insert and the product it promoted with the quality newspaper that accompanied it; thus confusion would be generated, with members of the public thinking that the publishers of the paper were responsible for the insertion. This was sufficient to lead to a finding that the conduct of the defendants amounted to a misrepresentation—and one that could cause harm to the reputation of the claimants in appropriate circumstances.

Unintentional misrepresentation

Throughout the entire discussion of misrepresentation in the tort of passing off, there is one common element that may be emphasized: in common law actions for misrepresentation, much depends on the state of the defendant's mind in making the statement, but that is not the case in passing off claims; rather it is merely necessary, as Lord Diplock put it in the *Advocaat* case,[131] that the misrepresentation is '*calculated to injure*' the goodwill of the other trader.

But even this formulation is prone to mislead, because 'calculating' is normally thought to involve some element of deliberate conduct, which is not the case here. The view has long been taken that all that is needed is to show that the misrepresentation is likely to harm the claimant's interests, and that this may be the case even if the defendant is innocent and does not intend to cause harm.[132] In a case in which the defendant becomes aware of a self-induced misapprehension on behalf of the public—that is, in which he or she played no active part—but if he or she then fails to react to eliminate the misapprehension, a finding that this amounts to a misrepresentation will be inevitable.[133]

The only exception to this clear rule arises when the misrepresentation occurs through the actions of a third party on facts such as those of *Bovril Ltd v. Bodega Co. Ltd.*[134] In this case, the defendant had served Oxo in response to requests for Bovril; clearly, in such a case, the innocence of the manufacturers of Oxo would count in their favour, although their goods were, in fact, being passed off as the goods of another. Perhaps the simplest way of explaining such a case is that Oxo made no representation at all. The innocent passer off may be at a slight advantage when remedies are considered; any account of profits may be limited to the time after which the defendant becomes aware of the

---

[129] *Matthew Gloag & Sons Ltd v. Welsh Distillers Ltd* [1998] FSR 718.
[130] [1991] 3 All ER 535, [1991] 1 WLR 571.
[131] [1979] AC 731, [1979] 2 All ER 927, at 742 and 933.
[132] See, e.g., *Baume & Co. v. A H Moore Ltd* [1958] Ch 907, [1958] 2 All ER 113, at 916 and 116.
[133] *British Sky Broadcasting Group plc & ors v. Sky Home Services Ltd & ors* [2007] FSR 14.
[134] (1916) 33 RPC 153.

situation and continues with the misrepresentation,[135] but there seems to be no ground for differentiating between innocent and other defendants in relation to the award of damages. This has been an area of controversy in the past,[136] but this view is now confirmed by the decision of Blackburne J in *Gillette UK Ltd v. Edenwest Ltd*.[137]

The failure to require any intention on the part of the defendant can lead to ironic results. On the one hand, the defendants in the *Cadbury Schweppes* case intentionally copied the marketing ideas of the claimants, but were not liable, because no one was deceived. On the other hand, in the *Jif* case, clear attempts were made to differentiate the products (although admittedly without abandoning the basic lemon shape), yet their failure to avoid confusion led to the defendants being found liable. The failure to provide a defence of innocence adds to the force of the tort of passing off, and shows that traders must be continually on their guard not to generate confusion between their product and that of another trader.

Damage

All of the various proferred definitions of the elements of the tort of passing off include the necessity of damage being incurred by the claimant or, in a case in which injunctive relief is sought, the likelihood of damage. Passing off is therefore not actionable per se and harm to goodwill resulting from the misrepresentation has to be proven.

Or does it?[138]

Isolated instances of case law show that the courts may be prepared to assume the existence of damage. In *Draper v. Trist & Tristbestos Brake Linings Ltd*,[139] the trial judge was only prepared to award nominal damages in the absence of proof that the passing off caused any specific damage. The Court of Appeal, however, substituted an award of £2,000. Sir Wilfrid Greene MR noted that:

> [the] right which is infringed in a passing-off case is one which was regarded at law as one the mere violation of which led to damage...it was not regarded at law as a case in which damage was of the gist of the action.[140]

Goddard LJ, meanwhile, commented that the law '*assumes... that if the goodwill of a man's business has been interfered with by the passing-off of goods, damage results therefrom*'.[141] Although the claimant could not show direct loss of trade from the passing off, he was able to show that this was a '*real business possibility*'[142] and thus succeeded.

This case was followed in *Procea Products Ltd v. Evans & Sons Ltd*,[143] in which the defendants were selling a type of loaf known as 'process bread', which the claimants thought would engender confusion with their product name. There was no evidence of actual loss of trade and only nominal damages were being sought. Roxburgh J followed the *Draper* decision and awarded £1 in damages. (This was an innocent misrepresentation and the judge was clearly troubled by the same doubt as noted above as to whether

---

[135] *Spalding & Bros v. A W Gamage Ltd* (1915) 32 RPC 273, *per* Lord Parker at 283.
[136] See, e.g., *Marengo v. Daily Sketch & Sunday Graphic Ltd* (1948) 65 RPC 242.
[137] [1994] RPC 279.
[138] It is at least not clear whether the claimant must identify some specific head of pecuniary loss in order to succeed: see *Law Society of England & Wales v. Society of Lawyers* [1996] FSR 739.
[139] (1939) 56 RPC 429.
[140] Ibid. at 435.
[141] Ibid. at 442.
[142] Ibid., *per* Sir Wilfrid Greene MR at 440.
[143] (1951) 68 RPC 210.

anything more than nominal damages should be awarded in a case of innocence—as has been seen, this has been resolved and full damages may now be awarded.)

The status of these two cases is somewhat hazy. They have not been the subject of attack or criticism, but may appear inconsistent with the demands that damage be proven. It is suggested that they can be reconciled. Clearly, a claimant has to show damage has occurred,[144] but the exact loss of trade is very often difficult to pinpoint. If a firm's business declines, a whole range of factors quite apart from passing off by rivals—poor product, high price, etc.—as well as legitimate, as opposed to illegitimate, forms of competition may be to blame. As a result of this, in a case such as *Draper*, the court is requiring proof of likely losses rather than actual losses and the assumption being made is not that any passing off always causes damage, but that the particular circumstances are such that damage of some kind is likely to occur.

A case such as *Procea* is different again: if no damage has (yet) been shown to occur, although some may be likely to result, nominal damages is clearly all that can be awarded (as well as the injunction that was granted). In deciding whether the facts show the likelihood of damage, the scope of the goodwill of the claimant and the way in which confusion may arise will be of importance to the court in deciding whether there is liability by inferring the risk of damage from those elements.[145] What is clear, though, is that the concept of damage cannot be restricted to loss of sales or directly provable losses and that the loss of goodwill can almost be presumed to lead to damage.[146]

A useful case demonstrating this process and showing that damage remains of importance is *Stringfellow v. McCain Foods (GB) Ltd*.[147] The claimant owned a top London nightclub, while the defendant named its new brand of long, thin, oven chip 'Stringfellows' and advertised it on television with a disco scene set in a domestic kitchen. Clearly, the claimant was possessed of goodwill, and it may be thought that the name and imagery suggested that the chips were, in some way, connected with the nightclub. The Court of Appeal rejected the claim. This was, in part, due to its view that there was no misrepresentation in the use of the name, but also because, even after the television adverts, which may have amounted to a misrepresentation, there was no actual evidence of goodwill being damaged. Although the claimant feared loss of goodwill, that was not enough: there was no evidence of trade declining and the argument that his future merchandising activity may be compromised was short-circuited by Stringfellow's admission that it was only this action that had alerted him to the possibility of merchandising. No damage was therefore found likely to occur and the claim was, as a result, found not to succeed.

The damage requirement also proved to be problematical when the tort was used to combat the practices of cyberpirates. The Court of Appeal was prepared to accept that the registration of a domain name that included the famous name would amount to an erosion of the exclusive goodwill in the name and it was assumed that damage was likely to result from the registration as such. Use of the registered name would definitely lead to damage and the Court was prepared to grant interlocutory relief to stop damage from occurring. Aldous LJ ruled that:

> In my view there be discerned from the case a jurisdiction to grant injunctive relief where a defendant is equipped with or is intending to equip another with an instrument of fraud.

---

[144] *Reckitt & Colman Products Ltd v. Borden Inc.* [1990] 1 All ER 873, [1990] 1 WLR 491, *per* Lord Oliver at 880 and 499.

[145] See, e.g., *Annabel's (Berkeley Square) Ltd v. Schock* [1972] RPC 838. Cf *Miss World (Jersey) Ltd v. James Street Productions Ltd* [1981] FSR 309.

[146] *Sir Robert McAlpine Ltd v. Alfred McAlpine plc* [2004] RPC 711.

[147] [1984] RPC 501.

Whether any name is an instrument of fraud will depend upon all the circumstances. A name which will, by reason of its similarity to the name of another, inherently lead to passing-off is such an instrument. If it would not inherently lead to passing-off, it does not follow that it is not an instrument of fraud. The Court should consider the similarity of the names, the intention of the defendant, the type of trade and all the surrounding circumstances. If it be the intention of the defendant to appropriate the goodwill of another or enable others to do so, I can see no reason why the Court should not infer that it will happen, even if there is a possibility that such an appropriation would not take place. If, taking all the circumstances into account the Court should conclude that the name was produced to enable passing-off, is adapted to be used for passing-off and, if used, is likely to be fraudulently used, an injunction will be appropriate.[148]

When can an action be brought?

The above ruling of the Court of Appeal is also helpful in another respect: it shows clearly in which different situations the passing off action can be used. Aldous LJ summarized it as follows:

It follows that the Court will intervene by way of injunction in passing-off cases in three types of case. First, where there is passing-off established or it is threatened. Second, where the defendant is a joint tortfeasor with another in passing-off, either actual or threatened. Third, where the defendant has equipped himself with or intends to equip another with an instrument of fraud. This third type is probably a mere quia timet action.[149]

It should be added, however, that merely providing assistance is not sufficient to become a joint tortfeasor.[150]

Remedies

There is little that needs to be said specifically about remedies in the context of passing off. Injunctive relief is often sought, particularly to prevent the alleged passing off from ever occurring given the speculative nature of the damage in fact caused by the passing off, as has just been noted. Alternatively, but unusually, the claimant may seek a declaration instead: for example, in cases in which the defendant has already ceased his or her wrongful trading.[151]

As far as monetary compensation is concerned, the claimant is faced with a choice of a claim for damages or an account of profits. The latter is, of course, discretionary and, as has been seen previously, not available in respect of innocent passing off. That said, if available to a claimant, it is clearly advantageous, because the account will be for profits from all sales of the offending product even if the passing off does not contribute to the sales in question.[152]

Damages are awarded on standard tortious principles to reflect the harm caused to the goodwill of the claimant with all of the attendant difficulties of deciding what harm is attributable to the conduct of the defendant. Perhaps as a response to that, an alternative approach has been canvassed in the case of *Dormeuil Frères SA v. Feraglow Ltd*,[153] in

---

[148] *British Telecommunications plc v. One in A Million Ltd* [1998] 4 All ER 476.

[149] Ibid.

[150] See *Crédit Lyonnais Bank Nederland NV v. Export Credit Guarantee Department* [1998] 1 Lloyd's Rep 19.

[151] For example, *Treasure Cot Co. Ltd v. Hamleys Bros Ltd* (1950) 67 RPC 89.

[152] *Lever v. Goodwin* (1887) 36 Ch D 1.

[153] [1990] RPC 449.

which the defendants had been quite extensively engaged in the manufacture of cloth that contained, and thus infringed, the trade mark of the claimants. The difficulty of assessing the losses of the claimant led to the argument that damages should be awarded on a royalty basis, as in patent cases, and that relevant licensing agreements could be examined to come up with an appropriate figure. Knox J reviewed the law in detail and concluded that it was possible, but not certain, that a royalty-based claim could be made and, because this was a preliminary hearing, it was not appropriate at this stage to create a new royalty-based approach. The key question is whether the analogy suggested with patent cases is appropriate; there, of course, it is the claimant's proprietary right that is being usurped by the defendant, whereas the rights created by the tort of passing off are not proprietary in character. It would therefore be something of a jump to allow passing off damages to be calculated in this manner and would enhance the protection of the claimant's goodwill considerably. This may be too big a leap for the tort to take, although equally it has not recently been noted for its timidity.

Passing off—an overview

In reviewing the contemporary role of this tort, several issues arise:

- why has it expanded in so many ways in recent years?
- will it still have a role in the light of the Trade Marks Act 1994?
- does it have the effect of being a tort of unfair competition?

The first question can easily be answered with reference to two factors. The most obvious is the shortcomings of the, at times, ill thought-out trade marks legislation at the time of the key developments in the tort's recent development. Most of the expansion of the tort has been in response to these difficulties; an analogy might be made with the way in which the tort of negligence, in its expansionist period, rushed in to fill some of the holes in contract law and public law.

The second factor to bear strongly in mind is that goodwill, although not a proprietary interest as such, is nevertheless a real and tradeable commodity. If, for example, I decide to sell my cruise ship, that will cost the buyer £X; if I decide to make available to the new owner of the ship the business that it has been operating, I would expect a further £Y to reflect the goodwill of that business. It is suggested that only passing off can protect that goodwill interest.

This all leads logically to our second question. Clearly, the broader scope of the new legislative approach reduces the role of the tort. As we have seen, several problems that were previously the exclusive province of passing off are now broadly, although not precisely, covered by the 1994 Act. Examples would include the *Bollinger* type of case (under s. 49) and the *Lego* type of case (under s. 5(3)).

But both of these examples have gaps and a provisional list of instances in relation to which the law of tort still has a role to play might be:

- cases of attack on general goodwill rather than on the mark itself, especially of no mark has been registered, in that area (as in *Lego*) or at all;

- cases of attack on general image, which is not capable of being protected by a trade mark, of which *Cadbury Schweppes* is the classic example.

- cases like *Bristol Conservatories*, in which it is not clear that the odd facts can be resolved in any way other than through the tort of passing off, unless a trade mark had been, on those facts, registered in the pictures of the conservatories, which seems unlikely.

We may add to this list the likelihood that a claim in passing off will continue to be co-pleaded with a trade mark action due to a combination of the uncertainties still attaching to the 1994 Act and the understandable conservatism in these matters of the legal professions.

In relation to the tort of unfair competition, the claims that there may be one in the *Alcohol* cases have been soundly and authoritatively refuted in *Cadbury Schweppes*. The absence of such an immediate remedy distinguishes the UK jurisdiction from that of many others, such as, for example, the broad approach of Australia's Trade Practices Act 1974. So, as so often in the common law, the question has to be whether the sundry elements of the law provide adequate protection for the parties. In *Arsenal v. Reed*,[154] there has been an obiter comment that passing off has effectively been turned into a tort of unfair competition; whatever may be in a name, the Court of Appeal has subsequently refused to invent a separate tort of unfair competition. The requirements for passing off remain the hurdles that a case must clear in order for there to be a legal remedy.[155]

Meanwhile, passing off clearly still has a role. As we have seen, it has a role—albeit a diminished one—in filling the gaps in trade mark law; it also stands out in the world of tort law as a protector of economic interests, directly, those of traders and, indirectly, those of consumers too. Also, as a tort created by the courts and developed by them, it has an inherent flexibility that is not a quality normally associated with statutory provisions. This tort will therefore not fade away.

Defamation and malicious falsehood

The law of defamation—that is, of libel and slander[156]—provides protection for the reputation of an individual, while malicious falsehood—which is also sometimes referred to as 'injurious falsehood' or 'slander of goods'—provides a parallel protection for the reputations of businesses. It is thus convenient to consider them in the same section.

Defamation

It is clear that, in its protection of an individual's reputation, the tort of defamation will extend its coverage to the professional or business aspects of that individual's life. The classic instance of this is provided by *Tolley v. JS Fry Ltd*,[157] in which the claimant, a (genuinely) amateur golfer, was appalled to discover that a likeness of him was appearing in the newspaper adverts for the defendants' chocolate bars, accompanied by a banal limerick comparing the excellence of Tolley's golf with that of the defendants' product. Tolley complained not on grounds of taste or with regard to the as-yet-unconceived notion of character merchandising, but because he felt that his status as an amateur would be hopelessly compromised in the minds of readers, because they would assume that, contrary to the then rules, he must have been paid to lend his name to the adverts. The House of Lords found that that was an appropriate conclusion for them to reach, and thus the adverts amounted to defamation by innuendo and were thus actionable.

---

[154] *Arsenal Football Club plc v. Reed (No. 2)* [2003] 3 All ER 865, [2003] RPC 696 (CA).

[155] *L'Oréal SA, Lancôme Parfums et Beauté & Cie & Laboratoire Garnier & Cie v. Bellure NV, Malaika Investments (t/a Honeypot Cosmetic & Perfumery Sales) & Starion International Ltd* [2007] EWCA Civ 936 (CA).

[156] See P. Milmo, W. V. H. Rogers, R. Parkes, C. Walker and G. Busuttil (2005) *Gatley on Libel and Slander*, 10th edn, London: Sweet and Maxwell.

[157] [1931] AC 333.

But the role of defamation in this field goes further than that.[158] There is also clear authority that a business can sue in defamation when its reputation is falsely impugned and this amounts to a backdoor method of protecting a trading reputation against false allegations. Cases of this nature have been few and far between, and have not always been accompanied by success, but it seems reasonably clear that such a cause of action exists.[159] In *South Hetton Coal Co. v. North-Eastern News Association Ltd*,[160] criticism was published of the insanitary state of the housing provided by the coal company for its employees. Lord Esher MR[161] was quite clear that the laws of libel gave a company the same rights as an ordinary person, but that this was not an actionable libel as being legitimate fair comment on a matter of public interest.

In *Lewis v. Daily Telegraph Ltd*,[162] a company and its chairman brought an action in libel against the defendants for a news story reporting that the police had raided the company's premises in a fraud inquiry. The House of Lords seemed to accept that a company could sue in libel without demur, but ruled that the stories were not libellous, because they only referred to the investigation of possible crimes and did not state or imply that actual crimes had been committed. The House of Lords also recently denied the availability of libel to a local authority,[163] but this was on the particular ground of the public interest in democratic free speech, cases in the *South Hetton* line of authority were approved, and it is difficult to see how public interest would act so compellingly to prevent any claim in libel by a company.[164]

Malicious falsehood

It is evident that the role of defamation in this field is peripheral and that most cases are more likely to be brought by companies within the more appropriate, but also more restrictive, tort of malicious falsehood. This is a classic example of an action on the case that evolved and developed a long way from its initial roots to the role that it now plays. It began to deal with wrongful allegations of unlawful claims to proprietary rights in land,[165] but now extends to cover the trading reputation of a business and its product. It is only in the latter part of the nineteenth century that the tort came to fulfil this type of need.

Two significant cases in its development at this time were *The Western Counties Manure Co. v. Lawes Chemical Manure Co.*[166] and *Riding v. Smith*.[167] In the *Manure* case, the defendants wrongly impugned the quality of the claimants' product and this attack on the goods was found to give a novel cause of action to the claimants; in *Riding*, it was the business itself that was the subject of criticism. In this enchanting case, the defendant alleged that the claimant's wife (who helped in his shop) had committed adultery in the shop with the new vicar. Whereas today the tabloids would encourage flocks of their readers to visit the shop, in those stern times there was evidence of a falling off in the trade of the claimant following the allegations and this too was held to represent a good cause of action.

---

[158] See, e.g., *McKenna v. MGN Ltd* (2006) 103 (33) LSG 23.
[159] See, e.g., *Berkoff v. Burchill* [1996] 4 All ER 1008, CA.
[160] [1894] 1 QB 133.
[161] Ibid. at 138.
[162] [1964] AC 234, [1963] 2 All ER 151.
[163] *Derbyshire County Council v. Times Newspapers Ltd* [1993] AC 534, [1993] 1 All ER 1011.
[164] Cf F. Patfield, 'Defamation, freedom of speech and corporations' [1993] Jur Rev 294.
[165] *Gerard v. Dickenson* (1590) 4 Co Rep 18a, 76 ER 903.
[166] (1874) LR 9 Exch 218.
[167] (1876) 1 Ex D 91.

The strands of this emergent tort were pulled together in *Ratcliffe v. Evans*,[168] in which the defendant falsely alleged that the claimant's business had ceased to exist. This was clearly harmful to the interests of the claimant, but was inaccurate, rather than defamatory. In spite of this, Bowen LJ found the statements to be actionable, stating that:

> an action will lie for written or oral falsehoods, not actionable *per se* nor even defamatory, where they are maliciously published, where they are calculated in the ordinary course of things to produce, and where they do produce, actual damage.[169]

The House of Lords confirmed that this was so in *White v. Mellin*,[170] but added that it was necessary for the claimant to establish that special damage had been suffered and, for this reason—and also for the reason that the facts did not reveal the necessary denigration of the claimant's goods (White sold Mellin's baby food, but put on the wrappers a notice stating that another brand in which he had an interest was more nutritious)—no action was found to exist on the facts as then found.

In the light of these cases, it can be established that several elements go to make up this tort and that all need to be established if a claim is to succeed. It is necessary to show that the defendant has made a false statement that is derogatory of the claimant's goods or business, that the statement has been made with malice, and that it has resulted in damage to the claimant.

It is also worth noting that, in recent years, an action in defamation in an intellectual property case has been brought in combination with an action for trade mark infringement.[171] A pattern similar to that in relation to passing off and trade marks is being established—but the wisdom of such an approach can be questioned and malicious falsehood is difficult to prove.[172]

Falsity

The requirement of falsity in relation to malicious falsehood is simple: as in relation to defamation, the statement must not be true. If the claimant cannot prove falsity, he or she will not succeed.[173] The action brought by British Airways against the Ryanair advertisements 'Expensive BA——DS' and 'Expensive BA' failed to clear this first hurdle, because the price comparisons contained in them were not false and apparently did not mislead the public. As a result, BA's action, as a whole, failed spectacularly.[174]

This contrasts with the position in mainstream defamation cases, in which it is for the defence to justify the truth of statements made. In determining the falsity of a statement, the 'one meaning rule' applies, meaning that the single natural and ordinary meaning of the words used must be determined.[175]

Denigration

For this tort, it is not sufficient that the statement be false; it must go further and damage the reputation of the goods or business by denigrating it—that is, by making derogatory statements that harm the reputation of the goods or business. As we have just seen, this

---

[168] [1892] 2 QB 524.

[169] Ibid. at 527.

[170] [1895] AC 154.

[171] See *Vodafone Group plc v. Orange Personal Communications Services Ltd* [1997] FSR 34; *Macmillan Magazines Ltd v. RCN Publishing Co. Ltd* [1998] FSR 9; *WebSphere Trade Mark* [2004] FSR 39.

[172] *British Airways plc v. Ryanair Ltd* [2001] FSR 32; *WebSphere Trade Mark* [2004] FSR 39.

[173] *Anderson v. Liebig's Extract of Meat Co. Ltd* (1881) 45 LT 757.

[174] *British Airways plc v. Ryanair Ltd* [2001] FSR 32.

[175] *Vodafone Group plc v. Orange Personal Communications Services Ltd* [1997] FSR 34.

was a problem in *White v. Mellin*, in which there was no derogatory comment about the claimant's product, but rather only a suggestion that that of the defendant was superior. It would have been different if it had been stated that White's product was in some way harmful to children.

The context in which the statement is made will be an important factor in deciding whether it is derogatory or not. *De Beers Abrasive Products Ltd v. International General Electric Co. of New York Ltd*[176] demonstrates this well. The defendants circulated to the trade results of tests that, in a highly technical manner that would only be comprehensible to people within the trade, purported to demonstrate that the defendants' synthetic diamond abrasive (used for cutting concrete) was of a superior quality to the natural diamond abrasive of the claimants. Walton J found that the defendants would be liable if the facts, as assumed at that stage of the proceedings, were proven and, in so doing, emphasized that the offending statements were not mere puffs, but detailed technical information aimed solely at people expert in the field who would understand it and its significance, and who would clearly see the alleged inferiority of the claimants' goods.

Statements that, on the face of it, are innocuous may come to be regarded as denigratory once placed in context. In *Lyne v. Nicholls*,[177] the defendant stated falsely that his newspaper's circulation was 20 times that of any local rival. This was found to denigrate rivals in potentially causing advertisers to switch away from other papers to that of the defendant. An odd case, however, is *Serville v. Constance*.[178] In this case, the claimant was the official welterweight boxing champion of Trinidad who, on arrival in London, discovered that the defendant was claiming that title. Harman J found that, had malice been proven, that would amount to a malicious falsehood against the claimant, presumably in suggesting that his claims to the title were false and that he was therefore a liar. Other more obvious examples of the tort are claims that a claimant had departed from the address used for his business[179] and claims by the defendant that the goods of the claimant were infringing a trade mark.[180]

A significant recent case showing how the denigration can arise indirectly and/or by conduct is *Kaye v. Robertson*.[181] The claimant, a well-known actor, suffered life-threatening head injuries in an accident during a gale, which blew a plank through the windscreen of his car. While lying in hospital, still very ill, representatives of the *Sunday Sport* newspaper broke in, took photographs of the actor, and recorded his delirious utterances, with a view to running a major feature in its next edition. An injunction was sought and granted to prevent publication. The Court of Appeal thought that the publication, with the implication that Kaye had consented to its tasteless content, would amount to defamation, but felt constrained from injuncting it on this basis, following a long line of authority restricting the use of injunctions in libel cases.[182] No such caution attended Kaye's alternative claim in malicious falsehood: by implying his consent, the proposed feature amounted to denigration of Kaye's trade as a celebrity.[183] He may have wished to publish his story of the incident himself and in a more salubrious forum, and this expectation was harmed by the conduct of the defendants. The case both shows the inherent flexibility of the tort and also the great ease with which injunctions can be obtained.

---

[176] [1975] 2 All ER 599, [1975] 1 WLR 972.
[177] (1906) 23 TLR 86.
[178] [1954] 1 All ER 662, [1954] 1 WLR 487.
[179] *Joyce v. Motor Services Ltd* [1948] Ch 252.
[180] *Greers Ltd v. Pearman & Corder* (1922) 39 RPC 406.
[181] [1991] FSR 62.
[182] From *William Coulson & Sons v. James Coulson & Co.* (1887) 3 TLR 846 onwards.
[183] See Chapter 31 on this aspect of the case.

Malice

The element of malice is at the core of this tort and, in insisting that the claimant proves this element, it greatly reduces the impact of the tort, because, in many cases, a defendant will be able to claim accidental mistake rather than deliberate malice as the reason for the false statement. This element also makes this tort stand out from its neighbours, passing off and defamation, in relation to each of which it is not a necessary element of the cause of action.[184]

Given the importance of malice, it is perhaps surprising that the courts have, over the years, had some difficulty in deciding how precisely to define it. In *Shapiro v. La Morta*,[185] the claimant musician lost her claim against the defendants, who had claimed wrongly that she would be performing at their music hall, because she could not prove malice, defined by Atkin LJ[186] as being an intentionally or recklessly made statement. Earlier, in one of the leading cases, *Royal Baking Powder Co. v. Wright, Crossley & Co.*,[187] Lord Bankes had defined 'malice' as meaning the absence of any 'just cause or excuse'[188]— clearly a much less rigorous definition, but one that seems not now to be followed,[189] thus adding to the burden placed on the claimant.

A more recent case to touch on this area is that of *McDonald's Hamburgers Ltd v. Burgerking (UK) Ltd*.[190] As we have already seen in the *De Beers* case,[191] this tort has great potential in cases of comparative advertising. In *McDonald's*, the defendants advertised their Whopper burger under the slogan 'It's Not Just Big, Mac' and went on to claim that their product was 100 per cent beef 'unlike some burgers'. The claimants saw this as an attack on their Big Mac burger, described memorably by Whitford J as the *'flagship of the McDonald's range, though not, I apprehend, with reference to the ease with which it can be sunk'*.[192] The claimants' claim in passing off was successful, because readers may have deduced from the overall appearance of the advert that Big Macs could be purchased from Burgerking outlets, but their claim in malicious falsehood that Big Macs were wrongly imputed to be less than 100 per cent beef did not succeed, partly because it required a sophisticated analysis of a kind not normally reserved for adverts in Underground trains to reach this conclusion and so was probably not denigratory, and also because there was no evidence of malice, which Whitford J regarded as, at the least, a reckless indifference as to whether harm may be caused to the interests of the claimant.[193]

The courts have now accepted that malice can be defined in four ways.

1. Malice will exist if one makes a false statement that one knows to be false.

2. It will also exist if one makes a false statement when one does not care whether it is true or false.

3. It will exist if one makes a false statement that one believes to be true, but when one makes the statement to give vent to one's personal spite or ill will.

---

[184] Many defamation cases fail because the claimant cannot prove the element of malice in a convincing way: see *Vodafone Group plc v. Orange Personal Communications Services Ltd* [1997] FSR 34.

[185] (1923) 40 TLR 201.

[186] Ibid. at 203.

[187] (1900) 18 RPC 95.

[188] Ibid. at 99.

[189] See, e.g., *Balden v. Shorter* [1933] Ch 427.

[190] [1986] FSR 45; rev'd [1987] FSR 112 (on another point).

[191] *De Beers Abrasive Products Ltd v. International General Electric Co. of New York Ltd* [1975] 2 All ER 599, [1975] 1 WLR 972.

[192] *McDonald's Hamburgers Ltd v. Burgerking (UK) Ltd* [1986] FSR 45 at 47.

[193] Ibid. at 61.

4. Malice will also exist if one makes a statement the purpose of which is to injure.

In each of these situations the requirement of malice will be satisfied.[194]

Damage

Traditionally, there has been the need for the claimant in actions based on this tort to have to prove special damage—that is, to bring distinct evidence of harm to their business. This requirement is, however, no longer present in most cases, following the Defamation Act 1952, s. 3(1). This section establishes, in respect of this tort, that special damage is not necessary if the words used are *'calculated to cause pecuniary damage to the* [claimant] *and are published in writing or other permanent form'* or alternatively are *'calculated to cause pecuniary damage to the* [claimant] *in respect of any office, profession, calling, trade or business'*. Given the requirement of malice and the way in which it is interpreted by the courts, it is most likely that cases of malicious falsehood will fall within this exception. The word 'calculated' should be interpreted as meaning 'likely' or 'probable' in an objective way; the simple fact that damage is possible, without further proof being added, is not sufficient.[195]

Guidance on quantum in such cases was provided in *Fielding v. Variety Inc.*,[196] in which the *Variety* newspaper singled out a musical promoted by the claimant as being a disastrous flop. This was not the case: it was, and continued to be, a great success. It was difficult to see what loss the claimant had suffered as a result of the falsehood and a nominal figure of £100 was awarded in respect of the malicious falsehood.

An overview

The impact of malicious falsehood on intellectual property law is limited, to a great degree, by the requirement of malice. It is, however, a notable recognition that businesses and products have reputations too, which the tort will, in its terms, protect, just as do the proprietors of businesses, whose personal reputation falls within the ambit of the tort of defamation. Clearly, however, the notion of a business' reputation overlaps extensively with the notion of its goodwill and much more effective protection is afforded by the tort of passing off, most significantly because of its focus on the likely consequences of words and acts, rather than on the intention of those making them. Trade mark law will also deal with most cases if the case is brought as one involving trade mark infringement. The question needs therefore to be asked whether a falsehood claim can really still add anything in most cases.[197]

It is true, however, that passing off requires there to be the all-important confusion between the goods or services of the parties, while malicious falsehood goes wider, to cover any attack on the quality of those goods or services. It may therefore remain that, together, the torts provide vital back-up to the proprietary intellectual property rights in covering the vague, but vital, areas of goodwill and repute.

---

[194] *WebSphere Trade Mark* [2004] FSR 39; *Horrocks v. Lowe* [1975] AC 139 (HL), *per* Lord Diplock at 149; *Spring v. Guardian Assurance plc* [1993] 2 All ER 273 (CA, overruled by the House of Lords on another point).

[195] *WebSphere Trade Mark* [2004] FSR 39.

[196] [1967] 2 QB 841.

[197] See *Cable & Wireless v. BT* [1998] FSR 383, *per* Jacob J at 385; *British Airways v. Ryanair* [2001] FSR 541, *per* Jacob J at 545–6.

Further reading

Carty, H., 'Advertising, publicity rights and English law' (2004) 3 IPQ 209.

Middlemiss, S. and Warner, S., 'Is there still a hole in this bucket? Confusion and misrepresentation in passing off' (2006) 1 JIPLP 2, 131.

Moscona, R., 'The sale of business goodwill and the seller's right to use his own name' (2006) 28 EIPR 2, 106.

Ni Shuilleabhain, M., 'Common law protection of trade marks: the continuing relevance of the law of passing off' (2003) 34 IIC 722.

Wadlow, C. (2004) *The Law of Passing Off: Unfair Competition by Misrepresentation*, 3rd edn, London: Sweet and Maxwell.

SECTION F

ISSUES IN
INTELLECTUAL
PROPERTY

This section merits a brief explanation. So far, we have been concerned with identifying the nature and scope of the individual rights that make up intellectual property law. In this section, however, we are concerned with some broader issues in intellectual property law and practice that can only be understood with reference to a wide range of different rights that, collectively, provide—or at least go some way towards providing—a resolution of these important issues.

29
Confidentiality and trade secrets

The laws protecting the confidentiality of information arise in a broad range of decided cases. It is inevitable that discussion of the current state of the law will reflect this fact, but it is important to assert at the outset that the remit of this chapter is to consider the use of actions for breach of confidence as a means of protecting intellectual and industrial property rights. The ramifications of the case law for personal privacy and governmental secrecy are matters on the periphery of the scope of this work, and will only receive passing attention.

It is also important from the outset to establish why this action is relevant, indeed vital, to an understanding of intellectual property law. A right of action for breach of confidence underpins and, in many cases, pre-dates a more formed intellectual property right. As an example, it is obvious that I have no copyright protection in my idea for a new film until the idea is translated into concrete form; if, however, I discuss the idea with you secretly and then discover subsequently that you have created a film using the same idea, then, in principle, an action for breach of confidence may arise. Equally, this area of law may protect the idea for a new invention long before I achieve a working, and thus patentable, model. In trade mark law too, discussions about marks prior to their registration, rough drafts, etc., may all give rise to an obligation on the part of anyone privy to such discussions.

A final preliminary point is important: in all of these actions, the claimant is seeking to restrict the propagation of information that is true. Clearly, the law has an interest in protecting both an individual victim and society more generally from falsity, and, for example, the various torts such as passing off and injurious falsehood exist to achieve this purpose. Where truth is concerned, however, the interest of the individual and that of society may part company. On the one hand, the individual will wish to keep information close to his or her chest, whether for commercial or personal reasons; society, on the other, may be thought to have an interest in the free availability of all true information.

Historical development and conceptual basis[1]

The law of breach of confidence took its modern form in the middle of the nineteenth century. Perhaps the leading case from this period is *Prince Albert v. Strange*.[2] This action—oddly foreshadowing the excesses of modern tabloid journalism—was an

---

[1] For a fuller discussion, see F. Gurry (1984) *Breach of Confidence*, Oxford: Clarendon Press.

[2] (1849) 2 De G & SM 652; aff'd (1849) 41 ER 1171.

action brought by the husband of the reigning monarch, Queen Victoria. It appeared that the royal couple had been in the habit of, privately, making drawings and etchings. Some of these works were sent away to be printed professionally and it seemed that this printer (Strange) made unauthorized copies, which he then intended to display for gain in a public exhibition. Strange claimed that such an event would add to the reputation of the royal couple by showing their 'eminent artistic talent'. The outcome of such a case was inevitably a finding in favour of the claimant, but the reasoning of the court is important too.

Clearly, the action against Strange was not an action based on any contract, for reasons of privity. The House of Lords, in the speech of Lord Cottenham LC,[3] seemed to take the view that the action arose as an aspect of the claimant's proprietary rights in the drawings, but he was keen to point out that the action was equally sustainable on grounds of equity, confidence, and (presumably as against the printer only) contract law. It should be noted that there have been attempts subsequently to use contract as the basis of breach of confidence actions[4] and, clearly, confidentiality will often arise, whether expressly or impliedly, as a term of a contract—but the leading *Spycatcher* case[5] has made clear that the obligation may arise independently of any contractual relationship.[6]

The nature of an action for breach of confidence was further considered in another of the pioneer cases—namely, *Morison v. Moat*.[7] The parties and families had jointly been involved in the development of a commercial medicine rejoicing in the name of 'Morison's Universal Medicine'. Subsequently, the partnership arrangements ended and the defendant continued to make the medicine. The claimant claimed that this was improperly using information gained during the period of the partnership and sought an injunction. This was granted, with the court accepting that the basis of the action was far from certain, but may well be based on trust or confidence creating an obligation on the defendant's conscience not to breach that confidence—a distinctly equitable tinge to the obligation. An important point was also made in this case: faced with the claim that to allow the claimants' claim would give him patent-style protection for non-patentable subject matter, it was made clear that the key distinction was that Morison was protected only against Moat and not against the world at large.

Returning to the precise basis of the obligation, *Robb v. Green*[8] is also instructive. In this case, the defendant secretly copied a customer list from his employer. The Court of Appeal found that this conduct was in breach of an implied contractual term, but the basis of that term was the good faith that must exist between employer and employee. Kay LJ[9] made clear that it was immaterial whether the action was founded on breach of trust or on breach of contract, because, in either event, an injunction should be granted.

The *Spycatcher* case[10] confirms this approach. In the words of Lord Keith: '[The obligation] *may exist independently of any contract on the basis of an independent equitable principle of confidence.*'[11] The equitable nature of the action appears to be an important part of its foundation, with obvious consequences for anyone seeking to bring an action who has him or herself behaved in an unconscionable manner.

---

[3] (1849) 1 Mac & G 25 at 44, 41 ER 1171 at 1178.
[4] For example, *Vokes v. Heather* (1945) 62 RPC 135.
[5] *A-G v. Guardian Newspapers (No. 2)* [1990] 1 AC 109, [1988] 3 All ER 545.
[6] Ibid., *per* Lord Keith at 255 and 639.
[7] (1851) 9 Hare 241, 68 ER 492.
[8] [1895] 2 QB 315.
[9] Ibid. at 319.
[10] *A-G v. Guardian Newspapers (No. 2)* [1990] 1 AC 109, [1988] 5 All ER 545.
[11] Ibid, *per* Lord Keith at 255 and 639.

Elements of the action

The leading modern case that formulated the ingredients of a successful action for breach of confidence is *Coco v. AN Clark (Engineers) Ltd*.[12] In this case, once again, what began as a cooperative venture between the parties, in respect of a new moped engine, ended in tears when the parties went their separate ways, the defendant allegedly then making use of confidential information acquired during the period of cooperation. In the High Court, Megarry J pointed to the absence of any formal contractual relationship and concluded that he was dealing with '*the pure equitable doctrine of confidence unaffected by contract*'.[13] He went on to state that there were three essential elements necessary in a claim for breach of confidence.[14]

1. The information must be, in itself, of a confidential character.
2. The imparting of the information must occur in circumstances or on an occasion of confidence.
3. The information must be used in an unauthorized way and so as to cause detriment to the claimant.

Clearly, the same principles will be applicable in a contractual context, subject, of course, to any contrary express terms of the contract.

Each of these elements will be considered in turn, but the *Coco* saga should first be concluded: Megarry J held that the claim should not succeed. Although the information was passed on an 'occasion of confidence', it was not clear that the nature of the (rather vague) information was confidential, nor could the claimant establish clear misuse of the information.

When is information confidential?

It is clear that a very wide range of different items of information may be regarded as confidential in character. Examples include items of considerable commercial significance, such as sales lists,[15] or information of a personal and private character.[16] What these, and many other, examples have in common is that people would generally recognize that such information was not intended for the public domain and that fact alone is sufficient to give the information in question the cachet of confidentiality.[17]

It is best regarded as an objective test, dependent upon the expectations of ordinary or reasonable men[18] who will, with an unerring instinct, be aware that commercially valuable lists of customers or the secrets of the boardroom should not be spread beyond those persons who have to know of the facts in question. A recent example is provided by the case in which the operator of a gossip website was held to be in breach of confidence when it gave more prominence to a third-party posting of the draft advice of counsel to a

---

[12] [1969] RPC 41.

[13] Ibid. at 46.

[14] Ibid. at 47.

[15] As in *Robb v. Green* [1895] 2 QB 315.

[16] For example, *Argyll v. Argyll* [1967] Ch 302, [1965] 1 All ER 611.

[17] For a negative example in which the confidential nature of the information was rejected, see *Cray Valley Ltd v. Deltech Europe Ltd, John Scanlan & Christopher Riley* [2003] EWHC 728.

[18] For an application in an employment context, see *Ocular Sciences Ltd v. Aspect Vision Care Ltd, Geoffrey Harrison Galley v. Ocular Sciences Ltd* [1997] RPC 289.

celebrity. It was held that the nature of the material would have made any reasonable man realize that it was confidential in nature.[19]

The cachet of confidentiality may, however, be bestowed upon the most trivial bit of information if it is not yet in the public domain. In such cases, it is sufficient that the reasonable man realizes (or is told about) the confidential character of the information.[20] In relation to information about the private life of a person, a duty of confidence will arise if the person subject to the duty is in a situation in which he or she knows, or ought to know, that the other person concerned can reasonably expect that privacy to be protected.[21]

A more subjective element is, however, imported into the equation by the decision of Megarry V-C in *Thomas Marshall (Exports) Ltd v. Guinle*.[22] In this case, a company's managing director set up rival operations in a similar field. Unsurprisingly, the company gained an injunction; it was observed that information in this type of case becomes confidential when the owner of the information believes that its release would be harmful to him or her and when he or she believes that it remains outside the public domain, in each case that belief being reasonable, with regard to the relevant area of activity and its practices. This simply suggests that the decision as to whether information is confidential or not will include the beliefs of the owner of that information, but the requirement that only reasonably held beliefs are considered means that it is not likely that the subjective views of the owner of the information are likely to contradict the objective view of the reasonable man.

The private or restricted nature of the information

It is clear that the private—or at least restricted—nature of information is an essential element if it is to become confidential. In *Woodward v. Hutchins*,[23] lurid revelations by a former employee of the management company of a group of pop stars under such headlines as 'Tom Jones, Superstud' could not be the subject of an injunction, because several of the incidents described took place in public: for example, on board an airliner.

Information may, however, go beyond its initial source to other people, while still remaining confidential, an example of which is provided by *Stephens v. Avery*.[24] In this case, the claimant sued in relation to a newspaper story telling of her lesbian relationship with the wife of a notorious criminal. She had revealed this to a friend, who unhelpfully passed on the information to the press. It was argued that, by telling her friend, she had removed the label of confidentiality, but this claim did not succeed. The High Court held that information could retain its secret character even while being passed on. In the words of Sir Nicolas Browne-Wilkinson V-C:

> the mere fact that two people know a secret does not mean that it is not confidential. If in fact information is secret, then in my judgment it is capable of being kept secret by the imposition of a duty of confidence on any person to whom it is communicated. Information only ceases to be capable of protection as confidential when it is in fact known to a substantial number of people.[25]

Further litigation has to be awaited to find out how 'substantial' this group must be.

---

[19] *Elton John v. Countess Joulebine* [2001] Masons CLR 91.
[20] See *PCR Ltd v. Dow Jones Telerate Ltd* [1998] FSR 170. Arguably, the claim based on breach of confidence also failed in this case, because the information had not been passed on during an occasion of confidence.
[21] *Campbell v. MGN Ltd* [2004] 2 All ER 995 (HL); see also *A v. B plc* [2002] EMLR 21.
[22] [1979] Ch 227, [1978] 3 All ER 193.
[23] [1977] 2 All ER 751, [1977] 1 WLR 760.
[24] [1988] Ch 449, [1988] 2 All ER 477.
[25] Ibid. at 454 and 481.

The springboard doctrine

One group of cases, now clarified by and large, appears to suggest that an action for breach of confidence may lie in respect of information that is in the public domain. This apparently contradictory notion first arose in *Terrapin Ltd v. Builders Supply Co. (Hayes) Ltd.*[26] The defendants made portable buildings designed by the claimants and, in due course, began to sell their own buildings made to a markedly similar design. The problem for a breach of confidence action was that these buildings were widely available and could be inspected by anyone who so desired. Nonetheless, at first instance, Roxburgh J found in Terrapin's favour. He stated that:

> the essence of this branch of the law is that a person who has obtained information in confidence is not allowed to use it as a spring-board for activities detrimental to the person who made the confidential communication.[27]

In this respect, the technical information disclosed while the parties were in collaboration would assist the defendants materially in making their own design of portable building. The Court of Appeal consequently upheld the trial judge's judgment.

Likewise, in *Cranleigh Precision Engineering Ltd v. Bryant*,[28] the defendant was the managing director of the claimant company, which made and sold a unique type of swimming pool, who set up his own business selling similar pools. These pools were made under an assigned Swiss patent that had been known to Bryant (but not his employer) for some years and which incorporated features of Cranleigh's pools. In spite of this information being, albeit obscurely, in the public domain, an injunction was awarded, because Bryant had gained his knowledge of the Swiss patent in his capacity as managing director of Cranleigh and thus it should be regarded as confidential information. In effect, Bryant had gained a springboard that put him in a uniquely advantageous position when he set up his own business.

Speed Seal Products Ltd v. Paddington[29] provides a further, more recent, example. The defendant had been employed by the claimants on the design of oil pipe couplings and had then set up his own company in the same trade. Paddington ran the defence that the information he had used was not confidential, in that it appeared in his publicity brochures and in a patent application that he had filed, and was thus known to the world. This did not succeed; the first disclosure was by the defendant and this could not prevent the claimants from taking action, with *Cranleigh* expressly followed.

This surprising trio of cases has now happily been reviewed by the House of Lords in the *Spycatcher* case.[30] Because it will be mentioned so often, it is appropriate here to recall the basic facts of *Spycatcher*. A former British spy, Wright, produced a book detailing clearly confidential information gleaned during his career. The British government, in this action, sought to prevent newspapers from printing extracts from it, but failed—basically, because the book was widely available in other jurisdictions and the information contained in the book had lost its confidential character as a result of its widespread availability. The defendant newspapers offered, as one of their defences, the fact that the information was no longer confidential, because it was widely available: for example, in the many countries in which the *Spycatcher* book was freely available in open sale.

[26] [1967] RPC 375 (HC), [1960] RPC 128 (CA).
[27] [1967] RPC 375 at 391.
[28] [1964] 3 All ER 289, [1965] 1 WLR 1263.
[29] [1986] 1 All ER 91, [1985] 1 WLR 1327.
[30] *A-G v. Guardian Newspapers (No. 2)* [1990] 1 AC 109, [1988] 3 All ER 545.

Lord Goff of Chievely addressed the issue directly.[31] He considered the *Cranleigh* decision to be merely an example of the 'springboard' principle derived from the earlier *Terrapin* decision. He refuses to allow the case to stand as a general principle and denies that there is any rule that disclosure by a third party releases the confidant from his or her obligations. It then follows that *Speed Seal*, based as it is on *Cranleigh*, cannot stand either. So it seems that, after all, information must remain private and outside the public domain if it is to be subject to the obligation of confidence. Lord Goff discussed at length whether this is tantamount to allowing the holder of confidential information to rid himself of the obligation of confidence by disclosure, but pointed to the existence of other remedies, such as copyright and criminal law. He reserved his position on the question left unanswered by his analysis of *Cranleigh*—namely, what is the scope of any 'springboard' type of obligation imposed on a confider who benefits from his or her destruction of a confidence.

This, added to the obiter character of Lord Goff's views and the failure of the other Law Lords to address the issue in detail given that they were of the view that the obligation of confidentiality was ongoing, means that a conclusive view of the law in this area cannot yet be reached.[32] The understandable reluctance of the courts to allow a confidant to benefit by breaching his or her confidence stands in the way of a clear unequivocal statement by the law that, as would seem sensible, information that is confidential cannot be public. The point that information that is supposed to be confidential cannot be public was, however, emphasized by Laddie J in a case in which the element of reluctance was almost absent due to the vexatious nature of the proceedings brought by the claimant and the oppressive way in which these proceedings had been conducted by the claimant.[33]

Encrypted information

Encrypted information presents an interesting problem: does encrypted information that is only in the public domain in its encrypted form possess the necessary quality of being confidential information? Jacob J was confronted with this issue in a case concerning discriminators for coin-receiving and coin-changing machines, and ruled that the information could not be confidential, because anyone with the necessary skill to decrypt had the possibility to have access to the information. The defendant, who had reverse engineered the piece of equipment in that way, was therefore not in breach of confidence.[34]

What is not—or is no longer—confidential information

One clear example does exist whereby confidential information ceases so to be—that is, when the confider himself discloses the information—and this arose in the 1928 case of *Mustad & Son v. Allcock & Co. Ltd & Dosen*.[35] In this case, an employer was held unable to sue an employee for breach of confidence once they had themselves applied for a patent, thus disclosing the relevant information.

Equally, it seems clear that lapse of time may cause there to be an erosion of the obligation of confidentiality, as in *A-G v. Jonathan Cape Ltd*,[36] a case arising from the publication of the diaries of the late Richard Crossman, written when he was a Cabinet

---

[31] Ibid. at 285–6 and 661–2.

[32] See the Law Commission's view, Cmnd 8388, para. 4.30. See also F. M. Patfield, 'Attorney-General v. The Observer Ltd; Attorney-General v. The Times Newspapers Ltd—The decision of the House of Lords in the *Spycatcher* litigation' [1989] EIPR 27.

[33] *Ocular Sciences Ltd v. Aspect Vision Care Ltd, Geoffrey Harrison Galley v. Ocular Sciences Ltd* [1997] RPC 289 at 368 and 373–5.

[34] *Mars v. Teknowledge* [2000] FSR 138.

[35] [1963] 3 All ER 416, [1964] 1 WLR 109 NOTE.

[36] [1976] QB 752, [1975] 3 All ER 484.

Minister a decade previously. The information contained in them was held to have lost its confidentiality simply because of the years that had passed, although with due regard also paid to the nature of the information and its likely effect. Crossman's chronicling of political gossip had long lost the chance of causing any serious harm.

Finally, in looking at what is not confidential information, it is worth recording the comment of Megarry J in *Coco v. Clark*[37] that it is not appropriate for protection to be given to 'trivial tittle-tattle': such matters of little consequence do not deserve the mighty protection of equity. Whether this should raise a question about the role of confidence in cases involving lesbian relationships with prisoners' wives[38] or the active sex life of an arms dealer's wife[39] is not, it seems, the point, because, in these cases, no such objection has been taken. In any event, information that is of commercial significance is hardly likely to fall within the category of 'tittle-tattle'.

The public interest exception

A major gap—but one that is justifiable—is opened up in the law's protection of confidential information by the exception created to allow the dissemination of information in cases in which that dissemination is seen as being in the public interest. Thus the truth will come out in an appropriate case. One of the earliest cases to use this approach was *Gartside v. Outram*,[40] in which a firm of wool-brokers sought to prevent their former sales clerk from using customer information gained by him during his period of employment, while he, in turn, alleged that their business was conducted in a fraudulent manner. It was held that, if proven, these allegations would wipe out any obligation of confidence, because 'there is no confidence in the disclosure of an iniquity'.[41]

What is covered by the exception?

Over the years, a wide range of differing instances have been found to fall within this exception. Sometimes, the exception is used if upholding confidence would have the effect of concealing evidence of wrongdoing. A classic example is provided by *Lion Laboratories Ltd v. Evans*.[42] The claimants in this case were the manufacturers of the intoximeter device used by the police for measuring alcohol consumption by road users. The defendants were ex-employees of the firm, who revealed to the press documents obtained while they were employees, which indicated that the devices were erratic and unreliable. An action against them for breach of confidence failed, on the grounds that the faulty intoximeters represented a serious threat to the fair administration of justice and that it was essential to ventilate public disquiet about the accuracy of the evidence provided by the machines.

W v. Egdell[43] also illustrates this area well. W was a mental patient who had been convicted of multiple manslaughter and who had been examined by the defendant. His concern at W's condition was such that he sent a copy of his report to the Home Secretary. W sued, alleging breach of confidence, the doctor–patient relationship clearly being one in which an obligation of confidence can normally be expected to arise. But the Court of Appeal found that, exceptionally, the interests of the public outweighed the interests

[37] [1969] RPC 41 at 48.

[38] See *Stephens v. Avery* [1988] 2 All ER 477. Sir Nicolas Browne-Wilkinson V-C said that the question could only arise at the trial and not at the interlocutory injunction stage.

[39] See *Khashoggi v. Smith* (1980) 124 Sol Jo 149.

[40] (1856) 26 LJ Ch 113.

[41] Ibid., *per* Wood V-C at 114.

[42] [1985] QB 526, [1984] 2 All ER 417.

[43] [1990] Ch 359, [1989] 1 All ER 1089.

of the patient and the doctor was justified in disclosing the report, so as to minimize the chances of W being freed and thus the public being put at risk of further attacks.[44]

This case followed on from *X v. Y*,[45] although in this case a different answer was reached. In this case, two doctors were revealed in the press as suffering from AIDS, the story being based on internal health authority documents. The paper's argument that the public had an interest in knowing of these facts was not enough to overturn the vital confidentiality of patient records and an injunction was granted to restrain the information from being published. The same vital confidentiality exists in the relationship between the police and the accused in relation to statements made by the accused under caution to the police. The information contained in those statements could only be used for the purposes for which it was provided and not for extraneous purposes.[46] It is likely therefore that *W v. Egdell* and its extreme facts will be the exception, rather than the rule.

In other cases, the harm cited to justify the breach of confidence may be less tangible. In *Hubbard v. Vosper*,[47] the defendant left the Scientology movement and subsequently wrote a book denouncing it, which drew heavily on material issued by the movement itself. The Court of Appeal found that the disclosures were justified as revealing what Lord Denning MR described as '*medical quackeries of a sort which may be dangerous if practised behind closed doors*',[48] while Megaw LJ highlighted evidence that the movement was prepared to use violence against those who had criticized it.[49]

An attractive, if simplistic, argument that has the effect of widening the likely scope of this exception was proposed in *Woodward v. Hutchins*.[50] An ex-employee was selling stories about the private lives of rock stars, clearly in prima facie breach of his obligations of confidence. Nevertheless, the Court of Appeal found that no injunction should be granted, because of the fact that the stars were keen to manage and manipulate their own images so as to appear in the best possible light, and therefore they could not object if what were presumed to be true, but less flattering, tales about them were released. In the words of Lord Denning MR, just as there should be '*truth in advertising*', so there should be '*truth in publicity*';[51] Bridge LJ sternly warned:

> it seems to me that those who seek and welcome publicity of every kind bearing on their private lives so long as it shows them in a favourable light are in no position to complain of an invasion of their privacy by publicity which shows them in an unfavourable light. [52]

While not normally sympathetic to people such as the claimants in this case, it may be thought harsh to offer less protection against breaches of confidence to those who are most likely to be the subject of such breaches.

---

[44] This approach was confirmed in *R v. Chief Constable of the North Wales Police, ex p AB* [1998] 3 All ER 310, [1998] 3 WLR 57, in which the Court of Appeal accepted that confidential police information concerning paedophiles who had served their sentences could be released to the owner of a campsite in order to allow him to take precautionary measures to safeguard the children that were to arrive on the campsite over the Easter holidays. Once more, the interests of the public prevailed over the obligation of confidence.

[45] [1988] 2 All ER 648.

[46] *Bunn v. BBC* [1998] 3 All ER 552, but the action for breach of confidence failed in this case and no injunctive relief was granted, because the information had been read out in open court and it had also been published in a book, of which 2,000 copies had already been distributed. These facts had brought the obligation of confidence to an end.

[47] [1972] 2 QB 84, [1972] 1 All ER 1023.

[48] Ibid. at 96 and 1029.

[49] Ibid. at 100–1 and 103.

[50] [1977] 2 All ER 751, [1977] 1 WLR 760; see also *Lennon v. News Group Newspapers Ltd* [1978] FSR 573.

[51] Ibid. at 754 and 764.

[52] Ibid. at 755 and 765.

There seems to be no reason, in principle, why this argument should not also be used to justify breaches of confidence about heavily advertised goods or services, although it is fair to note that the approach in *Woodward* has not been expressly adopted in subsequent cases. On the contrary, the courts have taken away some of the sharper edges and the potential for a broad application. It has, for example, been held that public figures who have been tolerant of, or welcoming to publicity, on other occasions have no less a right to complain of unwanted intrusion in relation to events that they wanted to keep private.[53] The court contrasted this with the situation in which the claimant has fostered an image that is not true[54] or has behaved in a way that is contrary to the image that he or she portrays publicly.[55] In that latter case, there is still a prevailing public interest in correcting the fostered and portrayed information that is out of line with reality.

Limits of the public interest exception

Just as the breach of confidence action does not extend to protect lightweight gossip, so also the public interest exception is curtailed. In *Beloff v. Pressdram Ltd*,[56] the claimant was a senior journalist who had sent a memo to her colleagues concerning a senior government Minister and allegations of possible misconduct. This memo subsequently was reprinted in the satirical magazine *Private Eye*. The action was framed in breach of copyright, but the principle of public interest applies there too. Ungoed-Thomas J found that the exception did not apply. This was not a case involving grave misdeeds, but was rather only the retelling of current political gossip and, as such, did not attract the public interest exception.

Naturally, as time goes by, so do public perceptions of conduct change. This reflects itself when a court has to decide what amounts to 'iniquity'. In *Stephens v. Avery*,[57] the court was faced with an attempt to use confidence to protect a story of a lesbian relationship. Sir Nicolas Browne-Wilkinson V-C took the view that there was no widespread view within society that sexual activity, even homosexual acts, between consenting adults was grossly immoral and thus appears to suggest that only universally deplored activity—on grounds of it being immoral, scandalous, or contrary to family life[58]—would count as being iniquitous for the purposes of the public interest exception.

Ironically, perhaps, *Stephens* suggests that the heart of the public interest exception—namely, claims of iniquity—is diminishing in importance just as the broader exception seems to expand into an ever-increasing range of different instances. The courts seem willing to subordinate confidentiality to the public interest in a wide range of cases, with perhaps *W v. Egdell*[59] the clearest indication that the rights of the public can take priority over one of the longest established relationships of confidence: that between doctor and patient. The inherent flexibility of the public interest immunity is an obvious asset in aiding its sensible and flexible use. The purpose for which the confidential information may be used will be relevant: in *Lion Laboratories*,[60] for example, the defendants were

---

[53] *Douglas v. Hello! Ltd (No. 5)* [2003] 3 All ER 996.
[54] See *Campbell v. MGN Ltd* [2004] 2 All ER 995, even if restrictions were imposed on what could be done in the public interest.
[55] *Woodward v. Hutchins* [1977] 2 All ER 751, [1977] 1 WLR 760, referred to in *Douglas v. Hello! Ltd (No. 5)* [2003] 3 All ER 996.
[56] [1973] 1 All ER 241.
[57] [1988] Ch 449, [1988] 2 All ER 477.
[58] See *A v. B* [2000] EMLR 1007, in which the content of pages of a wife's diary were held not come within any of these categories, which would have justified the refusal to enforce the confidence in them.
[59] [1990] Ch 359, [1989] 1 All ER 1089.
[60] *Lion Laboratories Ltd v. Evans* [1985] QB 526, [1984] 2 All ER 417.

motivated by a sense of civic responsibility and the decision may well have been different had they simply been seeking to sell the information for a personal profit.

A clash between different interests

The clash between the interests of the owner of the information in keeping it confidential and the interests of society in making it accessible in the interests of the general public may be seen as a clash between private and public interests. A case such as *W v. Egdell*, however, adopts the view that both of the conflicting interests are public: the interest of W in keeping his medical record to himself and his doctor is part of the general public interest in knowing that private information is able to retain its confidentiality. The decision in the case merely reflected that one aspect of public interest in the freedom from threats of attack by W was so important that it should take priority over the confidentiality of the relationship.

All cases in which this exception comes into play have in them this inherent clash. The facts of the *Spycatcher*[61] case illustrate it well. As a society, it may be argued that we have an interest in having a secret service that is just that, so we can argue that its working should be protected by confidentiality, but, equally, in a democratic society, we want openness so that we can learn and act upon information that the intelligence community is acting (or threatening to act) against the elected government of the country. In resolving this difficult choice, the House of Lords made one important pro-disclosure point in following the High Court of Australia in *Commonwealth of Australia v. John Fairfax & Sons Ltd*[62] by ruling that a government must prove that any disclosure is harmful to the public interest. The force of this is, however, reduced by the assertions—particularly of Lord Keith[63]—that wholesale disclosure of information about the workings of the secret service was obviously against the public interest and far more significant than that small part of the book that suggested that there had been improprieties.

Perhaps the most pointed of clashes comes when use is sought to be made in legal proceedings of information that the law would normally regard as being confidential in character. The leading case on this is now *R v. Licensing Authority, ex p Smith, Kline & French Laboratories Ltd*.[64] The statutory function of the authority is to award product licences for drugs that have been appropriately tested and proven to be safe. Smith, Kline & French had secured a licence for the drug Cimetidine and, in the course of its application, had revealed various items of confidential information to the authority. It was concerned that rival firms were now seeking product licences for generic versions of the same drug and that the authority would make use of, and thus possibly reveal, the information provided earlier, and so it brought an action against the authority.

The claim did not succeed. The House of Lords held that the statutory duty of the authority should take priority, and that it had both the right and the duty to make whatever use it saw fit of all information that was available to it. This was, it must be said, not a particularly meritorious claim by Smith, Kline & French, which, by making objections to the grant of licences for generic counterparts of its drug, was effectively seeking to extend the lifespan of its own patent monopoly. That the interests of justice and the merits of the claim thus came together to defeat the company's claims is a pleasing coincidence.

[61] *A-G v. Guardian Newspapers (No. 2)* [1990] 1 AC 109, [1988] 3 All ER 545.
[62] (1980) 147 CLR 39.
[63] [1990] 1 AC 109, [1988] 3 All ER 545, at 259 and 642.
[64] [1990] 1 AC 64, *sub nom Smith Kline & French Laboratories Ltd v. Licensing Authority* [1989] 1 All ER 578.

The use of confidential information in court proceedings

The use of confidential information in court proceedings themselves has been at the heart of two recent cases. In *Marcel v. Metropolitan Police Comr*,[65] the police had obtained documents from the claimants under the powers of the Police and Criminal Evidence Act 1984. The claimants then found that the defendants in a civil fraud case in which they were also claimants subpoenaed the police to give evidence from the documents in question. The Court of Appeal held that the claimants could not succeed in an action claiming that the documents contained confidential information and that they therefore should not be used. While accepting that an obligation of confidentiality was imposed on the police in respect of evidence obtained pretrial,[66] except in so far as disclosure was intended to occur for the purpose of the statute, that obligation was overcome by the subpoena issued to the police and which, equally, could have been issued against the claimants if still in possession of the documents themselves. In *Hoechst UK Ltd v. Chemiculture Ltd*,[67] these principles were applied when information supplied to the Health & Safety Executive was given to Hoechst, who promptly used it as the basis of an Anton Piller order (now the search order) in trade mark and passing off litigation against the defendants. Morritt J found that disclosure of this information, which related to use of an unauthorized pesticide, was not in breach of confidence as being within the purposes envisaged by the relevant legislation: the Food and Environment Protection Act 1985.

Thus disclosure of information that is otherwise confidential is quite likely to occur in legal and related proceedings. The statute may authorize disclosure for all or, more likely, limited purposes; the duty of the court or other agency may be to make the fullest use of all information before it and, finally, a subpoena will take priority.

Generally, the public interest exception is vital to the health of the action for breach of confidence. It recognizes that simple assertions of secrecy or privacy do not do enough to resolve the inexorable contradiction between one person's right to confidentiality and one person's right to knowledge.

Privacy

The outline of the exception is to try to split situations up between the genuinely private, which can be kept secret, and the increasingly wide range of cases in which the public has interests and rights too, and in which confidentiality has to be curtailed. To assess whether the balance is right is not easy and risks trespassing into the domain of the right of privacy debate. But no one can deny that the public has rights too, and has an interest in the outing of truth and, to the extent that that right or interest is recognized, it is recognized by this exception. The balancing of the interests involved is also reflected in the provisions of the European Convention on Human Rights, which is now fully part of English law as a result of the Human Rights Act 1998. On the one hand, Art. 8 seeks to guarantee a right of respect for an individual's private and family life, his or her home, and his or her private correspondence; on the other hand, there are clearly limitations to this right, as evidenced by the text of the Article itself and, for example, by the freedom of expression that is guaranteed by Art. 10 of the Convention. The courts have made it clear that, in their view, English law still has no right of privacy and that to create one would be a matter for Parliament—but they have accepted that an action for breach of confidence can have a person's right to protect his or her privacy at its heart. In other words, while

---

[65] [1992] Ch 225, [1992] 1 All ER 72.

[66] For the position in relation to statements made to the police during an interview under caution, see *Bunn v. BBC* [1998] 3 All ER 552.

[67] [1993] FSR 270.

there is no special right of privacy with a specific action linked to it, breach of confidence will cover the area and it is hence appropriate for us to deal with the matter here.[68]

Douglas v. Hello

The important legal developments in this area after the Human Rights Act 1998 were put in motion by the litigation brought by Michael Douglas and Catherine Zeta-Jones against *Hello!* magazine to stop the publication of unauthorized photographs of their wedding. While accepting the principle of a right of privacy for citizens as a result of Art. 8 of the Convention, the Court of Appeal discharged the injunction prohibiting publication of the pictures. It was held that the wedding was by no means a fully private affair and that the right of privacy had to be balanced with the right of freedom of expression. The limited amount of privacy left could, at the trial stage, be compensated by the award of damages.[69] At the full trial, the Court built upon this limited first step.

The case then moved on to the House of Lords, which allowed the appeal in *Douglas v. Hello.*[70] Although information about the wedding generally was information that anyone was free to communicate, the photographic images of the wedding were not publicly available and were therefore confidential information. From that starting point, the majority in the House of Lords derived that there was no conceptual reason why the obligation of confidence should not be imposed only in respect of the photographs if the third claimants were willing to pay for the right to be the only source of that particular form of information and that it did not mind that others were free to communicate other information about the wedding. The photographs of the wedding constituted information of commercial value over which the claimants had sufficient control to enable them to impose an obligation of confidence and there was no public policy reason why the law of confidence should not protect that obligation. The journal, having bought the benefit of the obligation of confidence imposed by the claimants on those present at the wedding, was entitled to protect the right to that benefit against any third party who intentionally destroyed it. The duty of confidence imposed was binding upon the unauthorized photographer and, by reason of the circumstances in which the defendant had acquired the photographs, the duty of confidentiality had also been binding upon it. Publication of the authorized photographs before the defendants had published the unauthorized photographs did not necessarily mean that the photographic images were by then in the public domain so that they could no longer be the subject of confidence; whether information was in the public domain and whether there was still any point in enforcing the obligation of confidence thereafter depended on the nature of the information and the facts of the case. Breach of confidence had therefore been established.

Turning to the issue of the right of freedom of expression, the series of judgments in this case demonstrate that, as such, the right of freedom of expression cannot justify such an intrusion. It is indeed necessary to strike a balance between Arts 8 and 10 of the European Convention on Human Rights. In a sense, that balance is already found in Art. 10 itself: the right to freedom of expression in Art. 8(1) is made subject in Art. 8(2) to the right to respect for private and family life contained in Art. 8, but that it is also made subject to rights recognized by the law as to confidence even outside the rights contained in the Convention.[71]

What remains outstanding, however, is the influence of the test in *Coco v. Clark* on the issue of relief. The first limb of the test in *Coco v. Clark* deals only with the issue of whether

---

[68] *Campbell v. MGN Ltd* [2004] 2 All ER 995.
[69] *Douglas v. Hello! Ltd* [2001] QB 967, [2001] 2 All ER 289, [2001] 2 WLR 992 (CA).
[70] *Douglas & ors v. Hello! Ltd & ors (No. 3)*[2007] 2 WLR 920, [2007] EMLR 12 (HL).
[71] Ibid.; see also *Venables v. News Group Newspapers Ltd* [2001] EMLR 10; *A v. B plc* [2002] EMLR 21.

the information is already public property and public knowledge; the issue of whether the information is private, in the sense that its disclosure would be significantly harmful, does not arise at that stage. The degree of offensiveness and its propensity to injure only comes into play once all requirements under the test have been met and the issue of relief is addressed. Substantive relief is not a foregone conclusion. Confidence in an inequity would not be protected, for example, and, at this stage, the balance between confidentiality and freedom of expression should be taken into account.[72]

Campbell v. MGN

This approach involving the balancing of rights, but offering protection for a person's privacy by means of an action for breach of confidence, has now been approved by the House of Lords in the *Naomi Campbell* case.[73] *The Mirror* newspaper published two articles revealing that, contrary to her previous false assertions, Naomi Campbell, the internationally known fashion model and celebrity, was a drug addict and that she was attending meetings of Narcotics Anonymous (NA) in order to overcome her addiction. The articles were accompanied by covertly taken photographs of Naomi Campbell leaving a meeting of NA. The newspaper had been tipped off about the fact that the claimant was attending NA meetings by an unknown source.

Naomi Campbell brought proceedings seeking damages for breach of confidence. She accepted that, because of her previous false statements, *The Mirror* was entitled to publish the fact of her addiction and the fact that she was seeking treatment for it, but she contended that the fact that she was receiving treatment at NA, the details of the treatment, and her appearance leaving a meeting were private and confidential matters, and that there was no overriding public interest justifying their publication. *The Mirror* argued that it was entitled to publish the articles in the exercise of its right to freedom of expression.

The House of Lords[74] ruled, with a three-to-two majority, that a duty of confidence arises whenever the person subject to the duty is in a situation in which he or she knew, or ought to know, that the other person could reasonably expect his or her privacy to be protected. In considering whether there is a reasonable expectation that privacy would be protected, it is important to bear in mind that, if the information in question was obviously private, there would normally be no need to ask whether it would be highly offensive for it to be published.[75] The details of Naomi Campbell's attendance at the NA meetings were, according to the House of Lords, to be considered as private information that imported a duty of confidence and the private nature of the meetings encouraged addicts to attend in the belief that they could do so anonymously. The assurance of privacy was an essential part of the exercise. The therapy was at risk of being damaged if the duty of confidence that participants owed to each other was breached by making details of the therapy public. Accordingly, those details were obviously private.

The right to privacy interest had, on the other hand, to be balanced with the interest of *The Mirror* in the right of freedom of information. The House of Lords argued that the conclusion that the details of the claimant's treatment were private meant that the protection of the claimant's right to respect for her private life was sufficiently important to justify limiting the right to freedom of expression of the press, provided that the limitation

---

[72] *Douglas v. Hello! Ltd (No. 5)* [2003] 3 All ER 996, [2003] EMLR 641; see also *A-G v. Guardian Newspapers Ltd (No. 2)* [1990] 1 AC 109.

[73] *Campbell v. MGN Ltd* [2004] 2 All ER 995.

[74] Ibid.

[75] In other cases, the correct test was to ask whether publication of the information would be highly offensive to a reasonable person of ordinary sensibilities if he or she were in the same position as the claimant.

was rational, fair, and not arbitrary, and did not impair the right more than necessary. It was, in this respect, important to note that the right of the public to receive information about the details of Naomi Campbell's treatment was of a much lower order than its undoubted right to know that she was misleading the public when she said that she did not take drugs. And it should be taken into account by the court that publication of the details of the treatment had the potential to cause harm to Naomi Campbell.[76]

On the basis of the facts of the case, the House of Lords concluded therefore that the reasonable person of ordinary sensibilities would regard publication of the photographs, and the way in which they were linked to the text, as adding greatly to the intrusion that the article as a whole made into Naomi Cambell's private life. The taking of photographs in a public street should be taken as one of the incidents of living in a free community, but the real question was whether publicizing the content of the photographs was offensive. Naomi Campbell could therefore not have complained if the photographs had been taken to show the scene in the street by a passer-by and later published as street scenes— but the photographs published by *The Mirror* had been taken deliberately, in secret, and with a view to their publication in conjunction with the articles. The argument that the photographs added credibility to the story had little weight, because they were not self-explanatory and neither the place, nor the person was instantly recognizable.

In conclusion, the publication of the fact that Naomi Campbell was receiving treatment at NA, the details of the treatment, and her appearance leaving a meeting as part of the articles was an infringement of her right to privacy that could not be justified.[77] This endorsement at the highest level of the approach developed in relation to privacy and of the role of the action for breach of confidence in this respect is a welcome development. It greatly enhances the protection available to a private person against unwanted intrusions of his or her privacy, while at the same time safeguarding the interests of the right of freedom of expression.

Privacy—a brief summary

The Human Rights Act 1998 has brought significant changes to the action for breach of confidence in relation to personal or private information, as we have just seen. When the conflict between privacy and freedom of expression is played out, the requirement of a relation of confidence seems to disappear and the emphasis shifts towards the private, rather than the confidential, nature of the information.[78]

The balancing act between privacy and freedom of expression can briefly be summarized as follows. In cases about the wrongful publication of private information, the court has to decide, first, whether the information was private in the sense of Art. 8 of the Convention. If that is the case, the court then has to decide whether, in all of the circumstances, the interests of the owner of the private information has to yield to the right of freedom of expression in the sense of Art. 10 of the Convention.[79] In cases in which a duty of confidence can be shown, the test to be applied in relation to whether it was necessary to restrict the freedom of expression in order to prevent disclosure of information received in confidence is not simply whether the information is a matter of public interest, but whether, in all of the circumstances, it is in the public interest that the duty of confidence should be breached. In applying the test of proportionality, the nature of the relationship that gave rise to the duty of confidentiality might be important.[80]

---

[76] *Campbell v. MGN Ltd* [2004] 2 All ER 995.

[77] Ibid.

[78] See T. Aplin, 'The development of the action for breach of confidence in a post-HRA era' [2007] IPQ 19.

[79] *McKennitt v. Ash* [2007] 3 WLR 194, [2007] EMLR 4 (CA).

[80] *HRH Prince of Wales v. Associated Newspapers Ltd* [2007] 3 WLR 222, [2007] 2 All ER 139 (CA).

Moving away from private persons

Let us end this discussion with a reminder that these points about privacy are not solely relevant in relation to private persons: equally, this area is important in reminding commercial interests that their private activity may have public interest implications. Firms, such as drug or food companies, may wish to keep their manufacturing problems secret, but the public may need to know about those problems—and any attempt to conceal the problems behind a cloak of confidentiality may, in turn, be overcome by an allegation of iniquity, as the *Lion Intoximeters* case has vividly shown.

The obligation of confidence

The second element in the action, as defined by Megarry J in *Coco v. Clark*,[81] is the issue of what circumstances give rise to an obligation of confidentiality. This question focuses not on the nature of the information itself, but on the relationship between the parties and, in particular, whether the relationship is one that should give rise to the obligation of confidentiality.[82] Megarry J makes it quite clear that the test is an objective one, with the ever-popular judicial device of the reasonable man being employed to encapsulate the appropriate tests:

> it seems to me that if the circumstances are such that any reasonable man standing in the shoes of the recipient of the information would have realised that upon reasonable grounds the information was being given to him in confidence, then this should suffice to impose upon him the equitable obligation of confidence.[83]

The judge also emphasizes the independence of this element from the confidentiality of the information itself:

> However secret and confidential the information, there can be no binding obligation of confidence if that information is blurted out in public or is communicated in other circumstances which negative any duty of holding it confidential.[84]

Equally, if the circumstances do support the existence of a duty of confidentiality, it will be hard for the recipient of information to deny the existence of the obligation; the type of case in this category envisaged by Megarry J is that in which information is of commercial value and is passed on in a business context, such as a joint venture.[85]

Many different types of relationship may give rise to the obligation of confidence. On the one hand, as has just been noted, business dealings will often create obligations of confidentiality even when no contract is ultimately concluded, as in *Coco v. Clark* itself.[86] On the other hand, private and personal relationships such as marriage may also create an obligation not to divulge confidences, as in *Argyll v. Argyll*,[87] in which the claimant Duchess was able to prevent her ex-husband from revealing personal matters in the tabloid press, doubtless to the regret of millions.

In relation to privacy, the House of Lords has held that a duty of confidence will arise whenever the person subject to the duty was in a situation in which he or she knew, or

---

[81] [1969] RPC 41.

[82] For a negative example, see *Cray Valley Ltd v. Deltech Europe Ltd, John Scanlan & Christopher Riley* [2003] EWHC 728.

[83] [1969] RPC 41 at 48.

[84] Ibid. at 47–8.

[85] Ibid. at 48.

[86] Ibid.

[87] [1967] Ch 302, [1965] 1 All ER 611.

ought to have known, that the other person would reasonably expect his or her privacy to be respected. That reasonable expectation would normally be determined on the basis of a test asking whether publication of the information would be highly offensive to a reasonable person of ordinary sensibilities if he or she were to be in the same position as the claimant. That test should not, however, be applied if the information was obviously private. In those cases, the reasonable expectation can be presumed.[88]

It is obviously not sensible to list every possible relationship in which the reasonable man may decree that an obligation of confidence is created, but certain types of case have given rise to frequent litigation and it is therefore appropriate to proceed by giving detailed consideration to cases arising from fiduciary relationships, contractual relationships (especially in the context of employment), and third-party relationships in which parties outside the initial bond of confidence are nonetheless caught up in its obligations.

Fiduciary relationships

The essence of a fiduciary relationship is that equity imposes a strong obligation on the trustee to act not in his or her own interests, but in those of the beneficiary. The close relationship between the parties is inevitably one in which information will pass between the parties and this information is likely to be regarded as confidential. The obligation can arise in a range of different cases: company directors and top managers owe a fiduciary duty to their companies; professionals, such as accountants and lawyers, may owe fiduciary duties to their clients. A useful example is provided by *Jarman & Platt Ltd v. I Barget Ltd*,[89] in which the claimant company, engaged in the reproduction furniture trade, commissioned a report on its somewhat parlous financial condition. One of the defendants, Hutchins, then the sales manager of the claimants, appears to have taken the report from the desk and then circulated it to other sales representatives of the company, seemingly so as to lure them to a rival firm that Hutchins was intending to join. This was held to be a clear breach of confidence by a senior employee and was accordingly held to be actionable.

Not every fiduciary duty necessarily gives rise to liability for breach of confidence. A simple example of this is *Baker v. Gibbons*,[90] in which a director of a cavity wall insulation firm set up a rival operation and solicited some of the company's agents in the hope of persuading them to transfer their allegiance to him. This was clearly contrary to his fiduciary obligations towards the company, but the action did not succeed for the simple reason that the name and addresses of the agents concerned were in the public domain, and thus did not represent confidential information.

Contractual relationships

Parties to contracts are naturally free to make whatever provision is felt to be appropriate in relation to information passing as a result of the contractual nexus. It is common to stipulate expressly that information is not to be passed beyond the parameters of the contract; *Exchange Telegraph Co. v. Gregory & Co.*[91] provides a good example of the potential effect of this. The claimants operated a news agency service providing up-to-date share price information to its subscribers. The defendants were originally subscribers, but the claimants did not renew the contract, because the London Stock Exchange—the source of the information—did not want the service offered to parties such as the defendants

---

[88] *Campbell v. MGN Ltd* [2004] 2 All ER 995 (HL).
[89] [1977] FSR 260.
[90] [1972] 2 All ER 759, [1972] 1 WLR 693.
[91] [1896] 1 QB 147.

who were 'outside brokers', not subject to its rules. In pique, the defendants arranged to obtain the information service from another subscriber and then sold it on to their own subscribers. The terms of the claimants' subscription contract included a provision that information was not to be passed on to non-subscribers. Clearly, had they been identified, the subscriber who was prepared to allow the defendants access to the service would have been liable directly for breach of contract; the defendants, as past subscribers, knew of the terms of the agreement and so knew of the confidentiality obligation—and, accordingly, were held to be liable for infringing the claimants' rights of confidentiality.

In many other cases, it will be an implied term rather than an express one that is relied upon, because many contracts will only be workable if information passed under their arrangements remains confidential: for example, as between doctor and patient, or between the manufacturer of a new product and its advertising agency. A clear illustration is provided by *Tournier v. National Provincial & Union Bank of England*,[92] in which the claimant banked with the defendants and was overdrawn. The bank kept a careful eye on Tournier's affairs and noted that he had endorsed a cheque payable to his account over to someone else's account, this party being a bookmaker. The bank accordingly rang his employer and revealed this nugget of information, resulting in his dismissal. The Court of Appeal found for Tournier; it was an implied term in the banker–customer relationship that the bank should not disclose information derived from that contract, unless the law compels such a disclosure.

Just as a contract can create an obligation of confidence, so, of course, it can deny that obligation, as the claimant in *Fraser v. Evans*[93] discovered. He wrote a report for the Greek government (then a military junta) on its public relations. A copy of the report found its way back to Britain, and the *Sunday Times* proposed to write an article featuring the report and making criticisms of Fraser, who objected that it was a confidential report. On examination of the contract under the terms of which the report had been written, the Court of Appeal found that, while Fraser was expressly bound by an obligation of confidentiality, there was no such obligation placed on the government of Greece. In effect, it had bought the information from Fraser and was free to use it as it saw fit; if the disclosure had been unauthorized, then the Greek government would be able to restrain publication, but it had taken no steps to do so.

The employment relationship

Particular problems arise in relation to the inevitably large amount of information of a confidential character that passes between employer and employee—information about working methods, manufacturing processes, etc. Express terms may frequently be used,[94] but it is clear that the courts, in any event, regard the employee as being under a duty of fidelity towards his or her employer and will use this to enforce the obligation of confidentiality.

The basic duty of fidelity arises throughout the course of the employment relationship and can be far-reaching in its effect. The leading case is *Hivac Ltd v. Park Royal Scientific Instruments Ltd*.[95] The claimants employed Mr and Mrs Davis as production engineer and forewoman, respectively, at their plant, which made the midget valves that were in great demand during the war. The defendants started a business nearby, also making midget valves, and the evidence was clear that Mr Davis had been involved in the foundation

---

[92] [1924] 1 KB 461.
[93] [1969] 1 QB 349, [1969] 1 All ER 8.
[94] For example, *Bents Brewery v. Hogan* [1945] 2 All ER 570.
[95] [1946] Ch 169, [1946] 1 All ER 350.

of the business, albeit only in his spare time, and that Mrs Davis, who had left Hivac on health grounds, was soon well enough to work for Park Royal. They also encouraged several of their colleagues to join them in their 'moonlighting'. Hivac sought an injunction to prevent the Davis couple from working for the rival firm.

The trial judge found as a fact, perhaps surprisingly, that no confidential information had been used in setting up and operating Park Royal, although it was clear that there was an ongoing risk that this would happen: for example, if Hivac were to improve its process, there would be an obvious temptation for that improvement also to be made at Park Royal. In the light of this, the Court of Appeal was prepared to award an interlocutory injunction, having additional regard to several other factors. The duty of fidelity owed by an employee was said to be variable depending on the status of the employee, with Morton LJ noting that these were skilled employees;[96] it was also relevant that their activities—even without (yet) breaking confidences—were clearly harmful to their employers, putting at risk the lucrative monopoly that they had enjoyed, and the fact that those activities were carried out in a highly secretive manner was a further factor militating against the defendants.

This important decision is ultimately resolved with close reference to the specific facts of the case—but it does seem to imply that any employee who discloses confidential information is in breach of his or her obligations, given that an injunction was awarded with reference to what was merely a risk of future disclosure, albeit a significant risk. This is illustrated too by *Printers & Finishers Ltd v. Holloway*,[97] in which the defendant was dismissed for inviting an employee of a rival firm to inspect a testing room; indeed, that employee was also the subject of an injunction preventing him from using any confidential information that he may have gleaned while there.

Clearly, the more senior the employee, the greater and more onerous the duty that is imposed upon him or her; indeed, at the more senior end of the scale, the duty is probably best regarded as fiduciary in character.[98] More lowly employees are less likely to be affected, as illustrated by *Nova Plastics v. Froggatt*,[99] in which an 'odd-job man' was allowed to work for a rival in his spare time, given that there was no evidence of any harm to his main employer having occurred or even being likely. More questionable is the decision in *Laughton v. Bapp Industrial Supplies Ltd*,[100] in which a warehouse manager and a driver used their knowledge of the company's suppliers to write to them requesting price lists and other information, with a view to setting up their own competing business. It was held that their dismissals were unfair, in circumstances under which they had acted in their own time and not that of the firm, and under which there was no clear evidence of their present or future breach of confidence. This seems a generous decision in the light of the status of the warehouse manager within the firm and in the light of the fate of the employees in *Hivac*.

But it is clear that subsequent cases are prepared to make use of the *Laughton* decision, albeit on rather different facts. In *Balston Ltd v. Headline Filters Ltd*,[101] an employee-director gave notice in March 1986 that he would leave in that July. He had already agreed to lease his own premises. In fact, he resigned as director and ceased work in April 1986, and then moved quickly, making contact with his former employer's customers and workforce with a view to establishing a rival business. Falconer J held that there was no breach

96 Ibid. at 181 and 356.
97 [1964] 3 All ER 731, [1965] 1 WLR 1.
98 *Boardman v. Phipps* [1967] 2 AC 46, [1966] 3 All ER 721.
99 [1982] IRLR 146.
100 [1986] ICR 634.
101 [1990] FSR 385.

of his duties as both director and employee in respect of the minimal acts carried out prior to his resignation as a director, but that he was in breach of his employee's duty of fidelity in actively competing with the claimants while still on their payroll, even though not actually working for them. *Laughton* was used as the basis of this decision and also that of *Marshall v. Industrial Systems & Control Ltd*,[102] in which a managing director, while still in his post, made active plans to set up a rival business, and contacted employees and customers of his firm to that end. His status and his actions were both the opposite of the facts of *Laughton*, which was duly distinguished, and Marshall was held to be fairly dismissed. This decision is in line with the earlier case of *Sanders v. Parry*,[103] in which an assistant solicitor negotiated a deal with one of the law firm's main clients, whereby he was to set up on his own firm and handle all of the client's legal work in his own right. By doing this while still employed by the firm, he was held to be clearly in breach of his implied duties of good faith and fidelity.

Taken together, these cases show an awareness that the company's whole business—its plans, its customers, its employees—is given clear protection by the law. An action for breach of confidence or the broader *Hivac*-type action for breach of fidelity duty almost has the effect of protecting the current trading activity of the business in the same way as the tort of passing off protects its business goodwill, and it will be interesting to see whether there grows a clearer conception of what is 'protectable trading activity', the use of which is improper, and what is 'just fair competition' as in *Laughton* itself. Meanwhile, the courts provide further support for the protection of trading activity by restricting the use that can be made by former employees of information gained during the period of employment.

In general, it is arguable that a duty of confidence that has been assumed expressly under a contract carries more weight, when balanced, for example, against the right of freedom of expression, than a duty of confidentiality that was not buttressed by an express agreement. While this starting point has an obvious impact on the position in relation to former employees, it is not clear what the effect of a wrongful repudiation of the contract will be on such an obligation of confidentiality agreed by contract.[104]

The former employee's obligations

Once an employee has left, his or her duties in relation to confidential information diminish, but do not disappear. It may well be that the contract itself has laid down stipulations as to future conduct, perhaps restricting the nature and location of subsequent work to avoid the risk of prejudicial competition, or limiting the use that may be made of information learnt during the period of employment. In imposing such terms, however, great care needs to be taken by the employer, because there is a clear risk that a court will strike them down as being void for restraint of trade.

This is a complex issue of contract law, but, in short, the courts will uphold clauses that are seen as being legitimately necessary to protect the employer's interests, while seeking to preserve, as far as possible, free and fair competition. Two recent examples can illustrate the point. In *International Consulting Services UK Ltd v. Hart*,[105] the court upheld a restrictive covenant that prevented the former employee from canvassing existing and potential clients of his former employers for a period of 12 months from the termination of his employment, because this looked reasonable in the circumstances. But in *Barry*

---

[102] [1992] IRLR 294.
[103] [1967] 2 All ER 803, [1967] 1 WLR 753.
[104] *Campbell v. Frisbee* [2003] EMLR 3 (CA).
[105] [2000] IRLR 227.

Allsuch & Co. v. Jonathan Harris,[106] a covenant that restricted the former employee from working in a defined area for two years was rejected as unreasonably long in terms of its duration, especially because there seemed to be very little confidential information worth protecting involved in the case.

Quite irrespective of any contractual stipulations, however, the law of confidence may also be prepared to intervene; the leading case in this area is now *Faccenda Chicken Ltd v. Fowler*.[107] Fowler was the company's sales manager and established a surprisingly successful aspect of the company's operation, running a fleet of vans around the streets selling fresh chickens. On leaving the firm—he resigned after being charged with stealing company property, of which he was later acquitted—he set up his own business, which also was to sell fresh chickens from vans in the same area. Clearly, Fowler was aided by his prior knowledge of the identity and requirements of regular chicken customers, and he also recruited his staff from among Faccenda's employees.

At first instance,[108] Goulding J categorized information that an employee may acquire into three types.

1. Some information will not be regarded as confidential at all, given its easy accessibility from the public domain, and the employee is always free to disclose this—the logos used by the company would be a good example.

2. Some information is confidential during the period of employment, but not after the employment has ceased, when the ex-employee is entitled to use it as part of the package of skills that he or she brings to the workplace—examples including the basic manufacturing processes used, or customer information remembered, by the ex-employee after he or she has finished employment (although this does not extend to lists deliberately copied during employment).[109]

3. Some information is best described as a 'trade secret'—such as secret manufacturing processes—and this information remains confidential even after employment has ceased.

Both Goulding J and, subsequently, the Court of Appeal ruled that Fowler had only used information in the second category and, no longer being in Faccenda's employment, was therefore at liberty to make use of it, there being no express stipulation in his contract of employment.

The Court of Appeal provided some useful guidance as to what should be regarded as a trade secret. Consideration should be given, according to Neill LJ,[110] to the nature of the employment—habitual handling of confidential information giving rise to a higher burden on the employee, because its importance is more likely to be realized—the nature of the information and the aura of secrecy (or otherwise) that surrounds it, whether the employer has stressed the secret nature of the information, and whether the information is separate or whether it forms an inevitable part of the employee's package of skills that he or she is entitled to take to a new post. On this latter matter, the Court of Appeal left open the question of whether the answer would be different had Fowler not been legitimately using his skills, but simply selling the customer information to another for profit.

It is clear from *Faccenda* that the number of instances in which an obligation of confidence will survive will be significantly limited and this represents a stark contrast with

---

[106] QB D, judgment of 4 May 2001, unreported (2001 WC 720358).
[107] [1987] Ch 117, [1986] 1 All ER 617.
[108] [1984] ICR 589.
[109] *Robb v. Green* [1895] 2 QB 315.
[110] [1987] Ch 117, [1986] 1 All ER 617, at 137–8 and 626–7.

the wide-ranging character of the duty of fidelity while the course of the employment continues. Subsequent case law indicates that the courts appear to be reluctant to characterize information as being in the trade secret category. In *Roger Bullivant Ltd v. Ellis*,[111] a company's managing director left and set up in competition using a copy of the firm's customer card index. This was regarded as being confidential only during employment, but this was when he had misappropriated it, so it might be expected that an injunction might be awarded against him. The trial judge did so award, and the Court of Appeal agreed that this was right and rejected Ellis's argument that much of the information in the index was also in his memory. The injunction was, however, discharged solely on the grounds that the benefit of the information was short-lived, providing no more than a quick bounce on the springboard.

This type of case makes the important point that trade secrets are not restricted to secret formulae, but might also include highly confidential information of a non-technical nature, such as lists of names of customers that, if disclosed to a competitor, could cause real and significant harm.[112] In *Berkeley Administration Inc. v. McClelland*,[113] use by former employees of figures in a company's business plan was not grounds for an injunction; the information was really little more than assumptions made in the plan, and the figures were not accurate figures of turnover and profitability, and did not attain any level of protection. Some figures were in the public domain; others represented the kind of guess that anyone in the relevant trade—that is, a currency exchange bureaux—would know as part of his or her ordinary experience of that trade. Similarly, in a case concerning contact lenses,[114] it was held that the use by the former employees-defendants of formulations within the ranges of the target figures of the claimant's master formulae was not a breach of confidence. This was so because every skilled man in the area would have spent a significant part of his working life working with the specific class of polymers concerned and would know how to adjust the mix of reagents in order to make the various polymers differing in their water-absorbing qualities. These things could easily be worked out on the basis of details that were in the public domain. In *Mainmet Holdings v. Austin*[115] too, the information used by the defendant, documenting defects in his former employer's products, was not even confidential information.

In reviewing these cases, two things are clear. Firstly, the courts seem to be reluctant to hold that information is in the second category of confidentiality during the period of employment, let alone that it amounts to being a trade secret and is thus protectable beyond the period of employment. This is good news for ex-employees, who will often be free to transfer their skills, knowledge, and experience to other firms without fear of legal redress, and thus good news for those enthused by free competition. The law, however, does not provide any great protection for the original employer unless he or she goes out of his or her way expressly to declare matters to be confidential in nature, thus helping them to become trade secrets. The second point is very different: several of the cases in this area of the law are notable for the length of the hearings involved, which may suggest that the courts are finding this area difficult to apply, perhaps because of the evidential difficulties of deciding in what category each item of information belongs and in seeing what advantage, if any, has been gained by its use.

---

[111] [1987] FSR 172.

[112] *Intelsec Systems Ltd v. Grech Cini* [1999] 4 All ER 11, [2000] 1 WLR 1190.

[113] [1990] FSR 505.

[114] *Ocular Sciences Ltd v. Aspect Vision Care Ltd, Geoffrey Harrison Galley v. Ocular Sciences Ltd* [1997] RPC 289 at 385–6.

[115] [1991] FSR 538.

In determining whether a certain piece of information should be classified as a trade secret, the courts seem to use a variant of the objective test that is generally used in relation to breach of confidence. The notional reasonable man reappears, to assess what forms the part of the employee's acquired general skill and knowledge that he is free to use, and to distinguish that part of the information that is a trade secret. The test is whether:

> the information in question can fairly be regarded as a separate part of the employee's stock of knowledge which a man of ordinary honesty and intelligence would recognise to be the property of his employer, and not his own to do as he likes with.[116]

Restricted as the idea of the trade secret has become, it is still important to assert its value in what may be described as its 'core' area—namely, that in which the employer has gone out of his or her way to establish that secrecy of work is vital. A classic example of this is during the development work pre-dating a patent application. Key employees will know of the vital need for secrecy even without any added reminders from the management. The employee who leaves with information that is vital to the proposed patent and who prevents its registration by giving or, worse, selling such information to a rival, thus disclosing it, is an obvious example in relation to whom the use of trade secrets will be grounds for an injunction. Equally, the example shows the vital importance of trade secret law in protecting the steps taken prior to the application for a patent.

Third-party relationships

If I tell you some information in confidence, you will be bound by that confidence—but what if you tell someone else? Can the obligation of confidentiality extend onwards to third parties?

The short answer to this question is 'Yes' and the leading case is *Saltman v. Campbell*.[117] This was a 1948 decision[118] in which the claimants were the owners of drawings of a type of tool used for making leather punches. They instructed another linked company, Monarch, to arrange with the defendants to manufacture tools from the drawings and the defendants did this, but also retained the drawings for their own use. In finding that there had been a breach of confidence, the Court of Appeal ruled that it made no difference that the parties had not been in a direct contractual nexus, because the confidentiality of the drawings and the rights of Saltman in their respect were obvious to the defendants.

Cases involving disclosure to newspapers also illustrate the proposition. In *Argyll v. Argyll*,[119] what the Duchess told the Duke, the Duke was now telling to the Sunday papers, but, clearly, the papers were aware from the nature of the information that it was of a private and confidential character, and thus they too were restrained by the confidentiality. The *Spycatcher* case[120] can be analysed in similar terms, although, of course, the element of confidentiality had been lost by the time of the hearing: were this the first disclosure of such information, its nature would have been such as to render it obviously confidential in character.

It must be emphasized that the third party only enters the liability picture when the information is not only known, but is also known to be of a confidential nature. *Fraser v. Thames Television Ltd*[121] shows this well: the claimants had the idea for a television drama

---

[116] *Ocular Sciences Ltd v. Aspect Vision Care Ltd, Geoffrey Harrison Galley v. Ocular Sciences Ltd* [1997] RPC 289 at 371; applying *Printers & Finishers Ltd v. Holloway* [1965] 1 WLR 1, [1965] RPC 239.
[117] [1963] 3 All ER 413 NOTE.
[118] Contemporaneously reported at (1948) 65 RPC 203.
[119] [1967] Ch 302, [1965] 1 All ER 611.
[120] *A-G v. Guardian Newspapers (No. 2)* [1990] 1 AC 109, [1988] 3 All ER 545.
[121] [1984] QB 44, [1983] 2 All ER 101.

series concerning the exploits of an all-female rock group and this was discussed confidentially with a scriptwriter, who discussed it with a producer, and Thames itself was fully aware of these discussions. The project did not proceed, but, shortly afterwards, the producer, scriptwriter, and Thames collaborated on a series called *Rock Follies*, which closely resembled the claimants' original proposal. All were held liable for breach of confidence, because, at every stage, both the identity of the originators of the proposal and the need for confidentiality were clearly known, and therefore all of the defendants were aware of those matters and thus in breach of their obligations. The case is also a useful reminder of a point made at the outset of this chapter: no final scripts were ever produced by the claimants, being still at the ideas stage, so no copyright protection could exist; the ideas stage was protectable by an action for breach of confidence.

Particular difficulty is caused by unauthorized acquisition of confidential information by a third party: the two main cases involve information gained by the use of unauthorized telephone tapping and do not appear to tell a consistent tale, so consideration must be given to both *Malone v. Metropolitan Police Comr*[122] and *Francome v. Mirror Group Newspapers*.[123]

In *Malone*, the prosecution in a handling stolen goods case made use of authorized phone taps by the police and the claimant applied to the courts for a declaration that use of the taps was unlawful. Megarry V-C refused to give this: in discussing whether a breach of confidence had occurred, he stated that, in any situation, a speaker recognizes that there is a risk of an unknown person overhearing the conversation and that, in the case of telephone calls, there is always the risk of being overheard by a crossed line or by a deliberate tapping of the telephone.[124] In such cases, the speaker takes the risk that any confidences that he or she divulges may be intercepted and no obligation of confidence is created on that third party. In any event, in such a case as *Malone*, it may well be that the public interest in the revelation of iniquity would, in any event, overcome the obligation of confidentiality.

In *Francome*, the facts were rather different. The claimant was a well-known jockey, whose phone was tapped by an unknown party. The tap appeared to reveal evidence that Francome was breaching various rules of the racing business and the recordings were made available to the *Daily Mirror*, with a view to its making their contents public. This time, an interlocutory injunction was granted, restraining publication of the recordings on the grounds that there appeared to be a breach of confidence and any suggestion that the public interest defence was relevant could be dealt with at a subsequent full trial.

It is possible to reconcile these two decisions, either by pointing to *Francome* as being purely an interlocutory proceeding and thus easy to distinguish, or to *Malone* as hinging on a remedies point (as discussed later in this chapter), or, more satisfactorily, by emphasizing, as it was in *Francome*, the words of Megarry V-C in *Malone*[125] that he was only seeking to lay down principles to govern the use of authorized police phone taps in criminal proceedings and did not purport to be dealing with other categories of cases.

This is a convenient let-out, but it is surely not satisfactory. The basis of *Malone* is clearly flawed. While it is acceptable to argue that there is a risk of any conversation being overheard, it does not, in any way, follow logically from this that any hearer should be freed automatically from an obligation to help the information gleaned stay confidential.

---

122 [1979] Ch 344, *sub nom Malone v. Metropolitan Police Comr (No. 2)* [1979] 2 All ER 620.

123 [1984] 2 All ER 408, [1984] 1 WLR 892.

124 [1979] Ch 344, [1979] 2 All ER 620, at 376 and 633–4. There are significant differences between the two reports.

125 Ibid. at 384 and 651.

The basic approach in cases of third parties, from *Saltman v. Campbell*[126] onwards, is that a third party is bound if he or she receives confidential information in circumstances under which he is aware of that confidentiality. If you overhear my counsellor and me discussing my private sexual problems, you will realize that this is confidential information and will become enveloped in the web of confidence that already binds my counsellor and me. It surely makes matters worse, not better, for the third party if the information is gained not by an inadvertent overhearing, but by a deliberate telephone tap. And this is not a charter for criminals: if my statements include confessions of criminal behaviour, it is clear that the defence of iniquity will act to justify the breach of confidence, as shown by the practice of reputable film developers of disclosing to the police photographs that they develop that appear to show evidence of illegal conduct. *Malone* does not sit within the general principles of third-party confidentiality, provides a quite unnecessary breach in the web of confidence that protects individuals, and should thus be regarded as incorrectly decided.

When an occasion is one of confidence, an obligation is created. Overall, the law has developed clear guidelines to deal with the principal examples of such an occasion and the attempts to balance free access to, and use of, information that have clearly been made by the law have generally reached an acceptable compromise. But it should always be borne in mind that these are merely examples of the general principle and that the judicial cypher of the reasonable man is always at hand to vary the balance, particularly in novel situations.

Unauthorized use of confidential information

Use of the information

Several elements come together at this stage of the definition. Firstly, and obviously, there has to be use of the information, but it is clear that not every use will be sufficient. In *Amber Size & Chemical Co. Ltd v. Menzel*,[127] the defendant was an ex-employee who had been misusing a trade secret in his subsequent employment. The trade secret in question was a scientific process involving various materials, the proportions between them, the density of the ensuing mixture, and the timing of the operation. Menzel knew which materials were involved, but did not know the proportions and density precisely. He knew, however, that the claimants used a particular type of hydrometer in the process and this, coupled with his knowledge of the materials and the timing, was brought to bear in his new employment. The High Court found that this was enough to ground a breach of confidence action: Menzel had been aware of the principal features of the process, and he and his new employers were expecting him to be able to recreate the process from his stolen knowledge, even though not all the details were known to him.

It seems to follow from this that use of a minor or unimportant part of the information may not ground a breach of confidence action, but that might seem to dent the protection afforded by the law to confidentiality. A better view may be to assume that the approach in *Amber Size* was calculated to consider merely whether it was usable information that the claimant had acquired. On this basis, too, *Fraser v. Thames Television Ltd*[128] is also explicable: the mere idea of a drama series about a female rock group may not have been usable as such, but considerable plot and character development had taken place, and this was directly used in the subsequent unauthorized (by the claimants) programme.

---

[126] [1963] 3 All ER 413 NOTE.
[127] [1913] 2 Ch 239.
[128] [1984] QB 44, [1983] 2 All ER 101.

Deliberate and innocent use

Next, it is important to note that the law does not seek to concern itself with the way in which the information is used and, in particular, with the state of mind of the person using, or rather *mis*using, the information. In other words, the law will intervene to protect not only deliberate, but also innocent, uses of confidential information. This is important because, often, it will be tempting for the user to claim that the use of information is subconscious or coincidental. To adapt the facts of *Fraser v. Thames*, it would be easy for someone in the position of the defendants to say, 'Yes, now you mention it I do recall a conversation about a female rock group series; it must have been lurking at the back of my mind all this time', but the law will still act to control such apparently innocent uses of confidential information.

The clearest example of this is provided by the decision of the Court of Appeal in *Seager v. Copydex Ltd (No. 1)*,[129] when scandal and intrigue rocked the world of stair carpet grip manufacture. Seager designed a new type of stair carpet grip, and he and the defendants discussed its possible manufacture to no avail. Soon after this, the defendant company produced a new type of stair carpet grip, which embodied the key design features of Seager's grip, although not so far as to infringe Seager's patent. The name used, 'Invisigrip', had also been suggested by Seager; the company claimed that it was all its own work. The court took the view that this was subconscious copying and so found in Seager's favour, awarding him damages.

The latter aspect is not entirely compatible with the case of *Nichrotherm Electrical Company Ltd v. Percy*.[130] This was a dispute about a machine for artificially rearing pigs. It was a notably unsuccessful machine, but this was no bar to—it may even have been the cause of—litigation. The defendant was found to have misused the claimants' confidential information in making his own rival, and equally unsuccessful, pig-rearing machine, but the problem arose that the second defendants gave Percy the claimants' plans for the machine, apparently in innocence, having received them from the claimants, with a view to their involvement in the manufacture of the devices. In the view of Harman J at first instance, the second defendants were liable in breach of confidence, but their innocence should mean that they were not obliged to pay damages, thus presumably suggesting that an innocent breach of confidence is only remediable by an injunction if appropriate.[131] Because only Percy appealed, the Court of Appeal gave no consideration to the position of the second defendant.

Nichrotherm was not considered in *Seager* and the latter case bears the stamp of the Court of Appeal's authority. It may also be suggested that *Nichrotherm* is not entirely compatible with the provisions in Lord Cairns' Act 1858, which allows a court to award damages in its equitable jurisdiction '*in lieu of or in addition to*' an injunction; at best Harman J was not willing to exercise this discretion. In any event, the fact that Harman J nevertheless ordered an inquiry into damages against both defendants suggests that there was some confusion present and it is suggested that *Seager* is the more reliable authority, at least in relation to cases in which there has been a change of position following the innocent use of the confidential information.

Authorization

Sometimes, an issue arises as to whether the use of the confidential material is unauthorized. This happens particularly if the confidential information is the result of a joint effort

---

[129] [1967] 2 All ER 415, [1967] 1 WLR 923.
[130] [1956] RPC 272 (HC); aff'd [1957] RPC 207 (CA).
[131] Such an injunction was awarded by Cross J in *National Broach & Machine Co. v. Churchill Gear Machines Ltd* [1965] RPC 61.

and one or more members of the team that put in the joint effort commit(s) the alleged breach of confidence. Typically, the claimant is a member of the team that did not authorize the use that was made of the information.

Murray v. Yorkshire Fund Managers Ltd[132] was such a case. Mr Murray had contributed a vital section on marketing to a business plan that was drafted by a team of people seeking to take over a company. At a later stage, Mr Murray had been excluded from the team. Nevertheless, the takeover went ahead on the basis of the business plan and Mr Murray sued for breach of confidence. He argued that his section on marketing was protected by an obligation of confidence and that unauthorized use had been made of the information. The action failed in the Court of Appeal, because the Court ruled that there had been no unauthorized use of the information. Nourse LJ relied on a dictum of Kekewich J in *HeylDia v. Edmunds*[133] when he considered that, when a team of people had collaborated in the production of confidential information, they were co-owners of it and, in the absence of any contractual restraint, each co-owner was free to deal with the information.[134] In this case, this meant that Mr Murray's former partners were free to use all of the confidential information when they took over the company, because they were the co-owners of the property right in the information.

This outcome is perfectly acceptable in the sense that a single person should not be given a veto over the use of the confidential information in such a situation; that would be an abusive use of the law of confidence. Such a person should rather pursue an action in restitution for the value of his contribution. But the outcome does raise some questions concerning the nature of the action for breach of confidence. The Court of Appeal treated information as property, and drew parallels with co-ownership cases concerning patents and the proprietary aspects of the latter. This may have provided a neat solution in this case, but, clearly, one cannot simply ignore the equitable nature of the action for breach of confidence. It is hard to see how, on this point, *Murray v. Yorkshire Fund Managers Ltd* could have provided the final and conclusive answer.

Detriment

The final element that makes up this head of the law of confidentiality is the question of whether the claimant has to suffer a detriment as a result of the breach of confidence. Clearly, the presence of such detriment is of great assistance in a case in which damages are sought and its presence will strengthen the case for an injunction—but is it essential? Certainly, in *Coco v. AN Clark Engineers Ltd*,[135] Megarry J referred to detriment as being part of the definition of the breach of confidence action, although he accepted that there may be arguments for a broader approach to the action without the requirement of detriment and the issue has been discussed in two significant recent cases.

In *X v. Y*,[136] discussion on the point was obiter, because the doctors who were the subjects of the newspaper story about doctors with AIDS did suffer detriment, in the form of distress caused by the unwarranted intrusion into their lives of reporters in hot pursuit of the story. Nonetheless, Rose J addressed the issue and concluded that detriment in the use of the information was unnecessary, and that an injunction, at least, could be awarded if there was no actual or likely detriment. He emphasized that the cause of action related to the initial disclosure and not the subsequent publication, which was the effective cause of the distress suffered.[137]

---

[132] [1998] 2 All ER 1015.   [133] (1899) 81 LT 579 at 580.

[134] *Murray v. Yorkshire Fund Managers Ltd* [1998] 2 All ER 1015.

[135] [1969] RPC 41 at 48.   [136] [1988] 2 All ER 648.

[137] Ibid. at 658.

In *Spycatcher*[138] too, the issue is considered, but a less-than-clear picture emerges. The failure of the government to restrain the publication of extracts from the book could be seen as reflecting the lack of detriment, due to the pre-existing wide knowledge of the book and its contents. But this factor simultaneously removed the confidentiality of the information itself and it is not therefore clear evidence for the essential role of detriment. Lord Keith[139] took the view that the disclosure of that which was intended to be kept a secret was itself a detriment, so there would thus always be a detriment present and neatly sidestepping the question, although he adds that, in a case brought by the government, harm to the public interest must be demonstrated anyway. Lord Griffiths adopted[140] the *Coco* test as his basic definition and thus appeared to embrace detriment as being essential, agreeing with Lord Keith on the special position in claims by government. Lord Goff, meanwhile, felt that it was still an open question.[141]

In attempting to resolve this conundrum, the first thing to reiterate is the value of detriment in strengthening a claim, whether for damages or for an injunction. Beyond this, it is tempting to follow Rose J and deny the vital nature of detriment in a breach of confidence action. This would help in cases in which confidential information about two people is to be leaked, in which it would disclose negative information about one, who may therefore be reluctant to take the public action of litigation, but which would still permit the other to take action. If a police document is about to be leaked, revealing that A and B have been questioned about a murder, and that A's answers were satisfactory and B's were not, A suffers no detriment by its disclosure, yet clearly still ought to have a right of action.

The same conclusion can, of course, be reached courtesy of Lord Keith's intellectual acrobatics and the tentative conclusion is offered that no detriment beyond that created by the fact of disclosure per se is necessary to be proven in bringing a breach of confidence action and that, in particular, this should justify injunctive relief with substantial damages available if greater harm ensues.

Remedies for breach of confidence

Injunctions

Little needs to be said here about injunctive relief; the law and practice in relation to breach of confidence is, in most ways, no different from that in other areas of intellectual property and the general coverage of remedies in Chapter 33 is fully relevant here. In *Coco v. Clark*,[142] however, Megarry J laid down some guidelines as to factors that may be relevant in exercising the discretion whether or not to issue an injunction in actions of this type and suggests that damages alone may suffice in a case of subconscious copying (as in *Seager*, two years earlier). He also suggests that the use made by the defendant in reliance on the information may make an injunction to restore the status quo difficult (if not impossible) to award. Clearly, in business-related cases, it may be relatively easier to award damages rather than an injunction, because the damage may be readily quantifiable if, for example, business has been lost, as opposed to cases involving personally

---

138 *A-G v. Guardian Newspapers (No. 2)* [1990] 1 AC 109, [1988] 3 All ER 545.
139 Ibid. at 256 and 640.
140 Ibid. at 269–70 and 650–1.
141 Ibid. at 282 and 659.
142 [1969] RPC 41 at 49 and 50.

confidential matter, in which the distress caused by the disclosure will be far harder to quantify and injunctive relief thus more appropriate. Nevertheless, injunctive relief may still be an appropriate remedy in commercial cases, especially if pre-empting the defendants (often former employees in this case) from disclosing the confidential information is the vital aim of the case.[143]

Damages

In considering the award of damages in an action for breach of confidence, the first question to consider is what is the precise nature of the action. If the breach of confidence is also a breach of an express or implied term of a contract, an award of damages is appropriate and should be based on the standard contractual principles on which those damages are assessed, as in *Nichrotherm Electrical Company Ltd v. Percy*.[144] If the action is not based on contract, but on the more general equitable principle of confidence, it is clear that damages may also be awarded under the modern successor to Lord Cairns' Act, s. 50 of the Supreme Court Act 1981. This permits the court to award damages '*in addition to, or in substitution for, an injunction*' in any cases in which the court has the '*jurisdiction to entertain an application for an injunction*' and leaves no doubt that damages can be awarded in any case: there is no need for any injunction claim to succeed; it must merely fall within the jurisdiction of the court.[145]

This then raises the question of the way in which these non-contractual damages will be awarded. An answer is provided by a return to the torrid world of stair carpet grip manufacture in *Seager v. Copydex (No. 2)*.[146] This hearing followed the first case in which it was held that damages should be paid for unconscious copying, because the parties could not agree on an appropriate measure. Lord Denning MR[147] drew an analogy with damages for conversion, under which damages are paid reflecting the value of the goods stolen. Here, too, information has effectively been stolen and so the court has to place a value on it. This can be done in one of two alternative ways: if the information is ordinary confidential information that might be obtained by the use of the services of an expert consultant, then the measure of damages should be the cost of using such a consultant, because that is, in effect, the cost of the information; if, however, the information has a special character and was so inventive or otherwise unusual that no consultant would be likely to be able to provide such information, its value is what it would receive if sold on the open market between a willing seller and a willing buyer,[148] or, perhaps, might be based on what royalties may be gained by exploitation of the information, although this would have the side-effect of legitimizing the acquisition of the information by the defendant.

This approach is not without its problems. While claiming to be tortious in approach, the focus seems to be not so much on the claimant's loss, as is usual in tort, but on the defendant's gain, making the claim more quasi-contractual in character.[149] The *de jure* approval of the defendant's de facto acquisition of the information may also be harsh

---

[143] See *Ocular Sciences Ltd v. Aspect Vision Care Ltd, Geoffrey Harrison Galley v. Ocular Sciences Ltd* [1997] RPC 289 at 409.

[144] [1957] RPC 207.

[145] Megarry V-C in *Malone v. Metropolitan Police Comr* [1979] Ch 344 at 360, *sub nom Malone v. Metropolitan Police Comr (No. 2)* [1979] 2 All ER 620 at 633.

[146] [1969] 2 All ER 718, [1969] 1 WLR 809.

[147] Ibid. at 719 and 813.

[148] See *Gorne v. Scales* [2006] EWCA Civ 311.

[149] See N. Jones, 'Restitution of benefits obtained in breach of another's confidence' (1970) 86 LQR 463.

on a claimant who may still want to exploit the information him or herself. The fact that the Court of Appeal remitted the application of these principles back to the court of first instance is not helpful to understanding their precise operation.

A particular problem in assessing damages in breach of confidence actions arises in cases in which it is not clear what proportion of the defendant's subsequent trade is due to the misuse of the information and what is due to other factors, such as his or her own efforts, contract, reputation, etc. This was the problem in *Universal Thermosensors Ltd v. Hibben*.[150] The defendants left their employment with the claimants to set up a rival business. They took customer information and other documents away with them. This was clearly in breach of their obligations of confidentiality, but because there was no contractual bar on their setting up a rival business, because they were not using any trade secrets, and given that they were free to use contacts and other information within their own memories, the rest of their activity was legal. The claimants argued, however, that all of the business of the defendants was irrebuttably presumed to be due to the misuse of the confidential information.

Sir Donald Nicholls V-C did not accept this: each item of business was to be looked at separately to see whether the profits were gained by use of the information. The use of common sense might suggest that it was more likely that contacts were made through use of a list of customers deliberately stolen for that purpose than through memory—why else steal the list?—and, generally, doubts would tend to be resolved in the claimant's favour. But applying these principles to the facts, the judge found that only one minor contract was due to misuse of the secret information and the claimant's claim for over £36,000 in damages was reduced finally to £18,610—scant reward for five weeks in court, and a reflection of the fact that the claimant had to show both that the defendants had made contracts using the claimant's information *and* that they would not otherwise have gained the contracts themselves.[151]

Other equitable remedies

The equitable character of the breach of confidence action means that the range of equitable remedies is also available to the claimant. Most significant among these is the action for an account of profits, whereby the claimants can simply demand that the profits made by the defendant after the acquisition of the confidential information are handed over. This is the essence of the claim in *Peter Pan Manufacturing Corp. v. Corsets Silhouette Ltd*.[152] Peter Pan licensed Silhouette to make, on its behalf, a then new design of women's brassieres. After a while, Silhouette used diagrams and examples provided under the licensing agreement to make similar garments to its own account. The obvious problem is, again, to what extent did the breach of confidence contribute to the profits made by Silhouette? Pennycuick J accepted the principle that the account should only be of that proportion of the profits attributable to the breach of confidence, but, on the facts of the case, he found that the manufacture of the garments by Silhouette would have been entirely impossible without the information, reflecting presumably the quantum leap forward that Peter Pan had taken with this new type of garment, and that, in the light of this, the entire profits made on the products in question should be passed to Peter Pan.

---

[150] [1992] 3 All ER 257, [1992] 1 WLR 840.

[151] The defendants successfully counterclaimed for £20,000 for losses they had suffered due to the excessive breadth of the interlocutory injunction awarded to the claimants and the consequent harm to their business.

[152] [1963] 3 All ER 402, [1964] 1 WLR 96.

In *Spycatcher*,[153] an account of profits was allowed by the House of Lords in favour of the government, as owner of the information, against the *Sunday Times*, which ran extracts from the offending book—but this award begs the kind of questions just raised. Fearing an injunction, no prior publicity was given to the fact that the extracts were to be published; indeed, the first edition did not include them, in case an injunction was promptly obtained. It is far from easy to calculate what proportion, if any at all, of the profits of that edition—which, of course, carried hundreds of articles and advertisements—was due to the unlawful publication of the confidential information.

The House of Lords has now added that an account of profits is only to be awarded as a remedy in those exceptional cases in which the normal remedies, such as damages and injunctions, are inadequate compensation for the breach of the contractual obligation of confidence. The profits of an autobiography that a spy wrote in breach of his obligation of confidence therefore had to be paid to the Attorney-General, because this was the only effective way of stopping the former secret agent from benefiting from his breach of confidence and of securing the proper functioning of the secret service. An injunction that simply froze the payment of royalties to the author until he returned to stand trial, which was an unrealistic prospect, was not an effective remedy and had no basis in law, because it de facto amounted to a confiscatory order.[154]

It is worthwhile noting that other possible remedies that may be available include orders for delivery up and/or destruction of goods that have been made by virtue of unauthorized confidential information.[155] Such orders were appropriately made in the *Peter Pan* case, but, again, this must hinge on the fact that no such manufacture could possibly have taken place but for the misuse of the claimant's confidential information.[156]

Information—the international dimension

This whole area of confidential information has been regarded as very much the creation of the common law or, rather, of equity. But in this respect, too, the internationalization of the law of intellectual property is now having its impact. Two separate developments need to be noted. Firstly, the problems of patent licensing in EU law, discussed earlier, spill over to information, which is not in itself patentable, but which may be essential to the operation of the patented product or process, or for the most economical manner for using a patented process. Examples might be the instructions for the best possible use of a patented machine. A block exemption on such know-how was created, alongside the block exemption on patent licensing[157] and these have now been fused together into the technology transfer block exemption discussed previously.[158] It is important to note that 'know-how'-type information and the patented product or process are inherently

[153] *A-G v. Guardian Newspapers (No. 2)* [1990] 1 AC 109, [1988] 3 All ER 545.

[154] *A-G v. Blake (Jonathan Cape Ltd third party)* [2001] 1 AC 268, [2000] 4 All ER 385.

[155] *Ocular Sciences Ltd v. Aspect Vision Care Ltd, Geoffrey Harrison Galley v. Ocular Sciences Ltd* [1997] RPC 289 at 410.

[156] Ibid. But that case also illustrates the point that all legitimate interests of all parties will need to be balanced carefully before these remedies are awarded in all cases in which the defendant's activity is not, in every single detail, based on misuse of the confidential information.

[157] Regulation 2349/84 on the application of Art. 85(3) of the Treaty to certain categories of patent licensing agreements (1984) OJ 219/15, as amended; Regulation 556/89 on the application of Art. 85(3) of the Treaty to certain categories of know-how licensing agreements (1989) OJ L 61/1, as amended.

[158] Commission Regulation (EEC) 240/96 on the application of Art. 85(3) to certain categories of technology transfer agreements (1996) OJ L 31/2; see Chapter 5.

distinct legal notions—but, that said, the controls on their use and dissemination are now the same.

The second development that needs noting is that the TRIPS agreement also extends to cover 'trade secrets',[159] this phrase not equating to the same words in the UK law, but rather relating to the know-how type of information. Signatory states have to ensure that such information is given an appropriate level of legal protection.

Further problems arise due to the fact that confidential information is protected in different national ways in each country: no international level of protection exists. Nonetheless, the use of international communication networks, such as the Internet, has substantially facilitated and increased the international and cross-border flow of (confidential) information. Which court will have jurisdiction to deal with actions concerning breach of confidence or any equivalent action, and which law will be applied by that court? These formidable questions of private international law remain to be answered and a solution is urgently needed.[160]

An overview

Information is not property,[161] at least for the purposes of the criminal law. Nonetheless, the law of breach of confidence has, as it has developed, gone forward to construct a network of rights and duties that protects information and its owners. Once the information crosses the threshold of confidentiality and is transmitted on what we have described as an occasion of confidence, that protection is attained. In defining what is confidential, the law is defining the boundaries of truth that is protected from revelation, and, in drawing this line, it is setting out the balance between the right of the individual or firm to keep a secret and the right of the public at large. Whether this balance is correctly drawn is, ultimately, a matter for the individual reader, but the existence and importance of the public interest defence is of significance in relation to the public's right to know, which is vital in an open and democratic society. If information does not fall within this exception, then it has almost tangible form in the range of rights and remedies open to its owner against those who abuse its confidential character.

The employment cases create variants on this information right. Trade secrets are the subject of strong protection and increasingly appear to be part of a company's property, but cases such as *Hivac Ltd v. Park Royal Scientific Instruments*[162] show a broader legal recognition and protection of a wider range of trading activity. In non-trade-secret cases, meanwhile, it seems that it is the employee who is allowed to transfer skills and knowledge from one job to the next as part of his or her repertoire, and his or her former employer cannot restrain him or her from doing so. So the employee, too, gains new intangible rights from the developing law of breach of confidence and of all these rights have the potential to grow into more tangible forms in years to come, if that is the way in which the law wishes to progress.

Legal history shows that such rights can develop slowly, but inexorably, if there is a perceived need for them so to do. As more and more information becomes available, through the evolution of time and the revolution of technology, it may be that such a

---

[159] See further J. J. Fawcett and P. Torremans (1998) *Intellectual Property and Private International Law*, Oxford: Clarendon Press.

[160] Part II, Ch. 7, Art. 39 of the TRIPS Agreement [1994] 25 11C 209–37 at 224.

[161] *Oxford v. Moss* (1978) 68 Cr App Rep 183.

[162] [1946] Ch 169, [1946] 1 All ER 350.

need will be perceived—which is not a prediction so much as an awareness of future potential of what may lie at the end of the information superhighway down which we presently inexorably surf.

It may be that trade secrets and confidentiality law will evolve into some form of 'right in information'.[163] It will be encouraged to do this while a common law action can arise without the need to resort to expensive, yet limited term, patent or trade mark protection, but can protect the essential secrets underlying those property rights. It seems an obvious area for the potential development of a yet stronger new right in due course.

Meanwhile, actions for breach of confidence can already be clearly seen to be filling the gaps between longstanding rights. Copyright could not protect the idea for *Rock Follies*, but confidence could. Patent law could not protect Nichrotherm's hopeless pig-rearing machine, but confidence could. In these and many other cases, it is at the difficult early stages of a project—when a formal intellectual property right is a target, but one that has yet to be achieved—that rights in confidential information may have their most valuable role to play.

Further reading

APLIN, T., 'The development of the action for breach of confidence in a post-HRA era' [2007] IPQ 19.

DEAZLEY, R., 'Introducing publicity rights? Breach of confidence, the photograph and commodifying the image' (2003) 54 NILQ 99.

PHILLIPSON, G., 'Transforming breach of confidence? Towards a common law right of privacy under the Human Rights Act' (2003) 66 MLR 726.

SCHREIBER, A., 'Confidence crisis, privacy phobia: why invasion of privacy should be independently recognised in English law' [2006] IPQ 160.

SIMS, A., '"A shift in the centre of gravity": the dangers of protecting privacy through breach of confidence' [2005] IPQ 27.

---

[163] See J. Reichman, 'Legal hybrids between the patent and copyright paradigms' (1994) 94 Col LR 2432; see also critiques thereof (1994) 94 Col LR 2559 *et seq*.

30
Computer technology and intellectual property

The relationship between computer technology and intellectual property is a complicated issue, and a huge number of theoretical and practical problems arise in relation to it. It is not our intention to go into much detail here.[1] Our analysis will focus on the headlines and we will accordingly discuss five issues:

- the availability of patent protection for computer hardware and for computer software (computer programs);
- copyright in computer software;
- databases and the *sui generis* right;
- the Internet;
- semiconductor chip protection.

It should be emphasized that the protection for databases also involves copyright. That aspect was already referred to in the chapters on copyright and not all of the details will be restated here. Most databases are, nowadays, in electronic form—hence our decision to discuss them in the computer technology chapter—but the regime of protection for databases also extends to non-electronic databases—that is, those based on paper supports.

Patent protection for computer technology

Hardware

It is obvious, but nevertheless important to note, that the normal requirements of patent law will apply in relation to computer technology. In other words, any piece of computer equipment must be new, must involve an inventive step, and must be capable of industrial application if it is to attract patent protection. This does not create specific problems, although the number of patents granted is, in relative terms, rather low, because most developments in computer hardware are constant minor improvements of existing technology, which, although new, do not involve an inventive step and are obvious.

---

[1] We refer the reader to the specialized works on computer law and information technology law.

Software[2]

More difficulties arise when one attempts to determine whether a computer program can attract patent protection. The starting point seems rather easy, because s. 1(2)(c) of the Patents Act 1977 explicitly excludes computer programs—but it is not entirely correct to conclude that a computer program will never be patentable, because the exclusion is restricted to a computer program 'as such'. This means that patents cannot be granted for the computer program alone and this rule applies irrespective of the content of the program. For patentability purposes, the invention must comprise something other than the computer program: it must be a computer-related invention.

Various attempts were made to patent software incorporated in a ROM chip,[3] as a piece of hardware, or recorded on any other carrier, such as a floppy disk. All were unsuccessful on the grounds that the applications involved nothing other than the computer program as such: *'The disc or ROM is no more than an established type of artefact in which the instructions are physically embedded. It is merely the vehicle used for carrying them.'*[4]

It would indeed make no sense at all to exclude a computer program from the scope of patent law and allow it back in the form of a floppy disk containing the very same program.[5] The same conclusion is normally reached when a computer program is loaded into a computer, because it would deprive the computer software exclusion of any practical sense if a non-patentable program, the only conceivable use of which is to run it on a computer, would become patentable if the claims made reference to conventional hardware elements.[6]

Computer-related inventions are not excluded from the scope of patentability.[7] This category is extremely wide in scope, because more and more new inventions involve the use of some software that is incorporated in the device. For example, production line robots are instructed through the use of a computer program and all kinds of engines— from that in your car, to those that move the lens and the film in your camera—are controlled by computer software. As long as a technical effect is produced and a technical problem is solved, the exclusion of a computer program as such no longer applies and the invention might be patentable. An example of this approach is found in the *Vicom* case,[8] in which the patent application was concerned with a method and apparatus for improving the quality of pictures and speeding up their processing. A computer program guided all of this, but the technical invention produced a technical effect on the pictures and was thus patentable. One should look at the invention as a whole[9] in assessing whether a technical effect occurs, and it is the question of whether the whole invention as a combination

---

[2] For a detailed analysis, see I. Lloyd (2004) *Information Technology Law*, 4th edn, Oxford: Oxford University Press, ch. 18; G. Dworkin (1993) 'The patentability of computer software', in C. Reed (ed.) *Computer Law*, 2nd edn, Oxford: Blackstone, ch. 5. See also C. Reed and J. Angel (eds) (2007) *Computer Law*, 6th edn, Oxford: Oxford University Press; D. Booton, 'The patentability of computer-implemented inventions in Europe' (2007) 1 IPQ 92.

[3] *Gale's Application* [1991] RPC 305.

[4] Ibid., *per* Nicholls LJ at 325.

[5] See *Genentech Inc's Patent* [1989] RPC 147, *per* Dillon LJ.

[6] See *IBM/Documents abstracting and retrieving* (T-22/85) [1990] EPOR 98; *IBM/Text processing* (T-65/86) [1990] EPOR 181.

[7] The EU tried to agree a Directive on the patentability of computer-implemented inventions in an attempt to harmonize the different national approaches, but the Council and the Parliament disagreed fundamentally, and, in the end, the project was shelved. See EC Commission (2002) *Proposal for a Directive of the European Parliament and of the Council on the Patentability of Computer-Implemented Inventions*, COM (2002) 92 final, available online at eur-lex.europa.eu/LexUriServ/site/en/com/2002/com2002_0092en01.pdf.

[8] *Vicom Systems Inc's Application* (T-208/84) [1987] 2 EPOR 74.

[9] *Koch & Sterzel/X-ray apparatus* (T-26/86) [1988] EPOR 72; *Merrill Lynch's Application* [1988] RPC 1.

between a computer program and all other elements is patentable that is at issue. It is also not relevant when the technical effect occurs and there is no need to balance the technical features of the invention against its non-technical features. If these requirements are met, a software-related invention may be patentable if it meets the other standard requirements for patentability.[10] The focus of all attention is therefore placed on what the claimed invention achieves, rather than on the manner in which it achieves it.

It must be emphasized, however, that the courts seem to apply the exclusion test twice. The exclusion also applies if a technical effect is produced, but only if that effect or result is itself caught by the exclusion. This means that what is produced is a prohibited item under s. 1(2) of the 1977 Act. A clear illustration is found in Merrill Lynch's application for a patent for a business system and, specifically, for an improved data processing system for implementing an automated trading market for securities. It was said that:

> whatever the technical advance may be, is simply the production of a trading system. It is a data processing system for doing a specific business, that is to say making a trading market in securities. The end result, therefore, is simply 'a method...of doing business', and is excluded by section 1(2)(c)...A data processing system operating to produce a novel technical result would normally be patentable. But it cannot, it seems to me, be patentable if the result itself is a prohibited item under s 1(2). In the present case it is such a prohibited item.[11]

Merill Lynch's application failed on the second application of the test, even though there was a technical effect.

The position on the issue of patents for software was subsequently summarized neatly in the case of *Fujitsu's Application*.[12] The patent application concerned crystal structures that could be depicted and manipulated on a computer screen by chemists through the use of virtual reality, replacing the use of three-dimensional lattices. The application was turned down for lack of a technical effect. Laddie J summarized the general position as follows at first instance:

1. The types of subject-matter referred to in s 1(2) are excluded from patentability as a matter of policy. This is so whether the matter is technical or not.

2. The exclusion from patentability is a matter of substance, not form. Therefore the exclusion under section 1(2) extends to any form of passive carrier or recording of excluded subject matter. Thus, merely because a piece of paper is in principle patentable (safe to the extent that it lacks novelty), it is not permissible, for example, to record a literary work (s 1(2)(b)) or a computer program (s 1(2)(c)) on a piece of paper and then seek patent monopoly for the paper bearing the recorded work. Similarly, it is not permissible, without more, to seek protection for a computer program when it is stored on a magnetic medium or when merely loaded into a computer.

3. Prima facie a computer running under the control of one program is a different piece of apparatus from the same computer when running under the control of another program. It follows that a claim to a computer when controlled by a program or to a method of controlling a computer by a program or to a method of carrying out a process by use of a computer so controlled can be the subject of patent protection. However, because the court is concerned with substance, not form, it is not enough for the designer of a new program to seek protection for his creation merely by framing it in one of these terms. The court or patent office has to direct its intention not to the fact that the program is controlling the computer, but to what the computer, so controlled, is doing.

10 See G. Kolle, 'Patentability of software-related inventions' (1991) 22 IIC 660.
11 *Merrill Lynch's Application* [1989] RPC 561 at 569.
12 [1996] RPC 511 (HC); confirmed on appeal [1997] RPC 608 (CA).

4. Therefore, a data processing system operating to produce a novel result would not be deprived of protection on the ground that it was a program as such. On the other hand, even if the effect of the program is to make the computer perform in a novel way, it is still necessary to look at precisely what a computer is doing, ie at the nature of the process being carried out. If all that is being done, as a matter of substance, is the performance of one of the activities defined under s 1(2) as unprotectable, then it is still unprotectable.[13]

The approach set out in *Fujitsu*[14] was subsequently confirmed in *Crawford's Application*.[15] The patent application at issue described a display system for buses, which could be used to indicate in which of two modes the bus was operating. If the bus were operating in boarding mode, then it would both pick up and drop off passengers; if it were operating only in exit mode, then it would only drop off passengers. The object of the invention was to provide a means of preventing 'bus bunching'—that is, the phenomenon whereby buses arrive in groups rather than at regular intervals. This object was achieved by allowing the bus at the front of a queue to switch into exit mode when it was considered necessary to increase the separation between it and the following buses. When sufficient separation had been achieved, the front bus reverted to a normal mode of operation and the display was switched accordingly. The application for what would effectively have been a business model patent was turned down, because it was the mere presentation of information or a method of doing business. The absence of a technical effect meant it fell under the exclusion from patentability.

The English courts are therefore bound to check whether the invention as defined in the claims made a technical contribution to the known art.[16] If it does not, the exclusion in s. 1(2) of the 1977 Act or its equivalent in Art. 52(2) of the European Patent Convention (EPC) applies. Different approaches have been around though and the approach of the European Patent Office (EPO) has not been consistent. The Court of Appeal identified the different approaches in *Aerotel v. Telco & Marcossan's Application*[17] and suggested that the EPO convene an Enlarged Board of Appeal to arrive at a uniform approach.[18]

The Court described the different approaches as follows:[19]

(1) The contribution approach

Ask whether the inventive step resides only in the contribution of excluded matter—if yes, Art. 52(2) applies. This approach was supported by Falconer J. in *Merrill Lynch*[20] but expressly rejected by this Court.

(2) The technical effect approach

Ask whether the invention as defined in the claim makes a technical contribution to the known art—if no, Art. 52(2) applies. A possible clarification (at least by way of exclusion) of this approach is to add the rider that novel or inventive purely excluded matter does not count as a 'technical contribution'. This is the approach (with the rider) adopted by this Court in *Merrill Lynch*.[21] It has been followed in the subsequent decisions of this Court, *Gale*[22] and *Fujitsu*.[23] The approach (without the rider as an express caution) was that first adopted by

13 Ibid. (HC) at 530.
14 *Fujitsu's Application* [1997] RPC 608 (CA).
15 *Crawford's Application* [2006] RPC 11.
16 *Aerotel v. Telco & Marcossan's Application*[2007] 1 All ER 225, [2007] RPC 7 (CA), at [38].
17 Ibid.   18 Ibid., at [75].
19 Ibid., *per* Jacob LJ at [26].
20 *Merrill Lynch's Application* [1988] RPC 1.
21 *Merrill Lynch's Application* [1989] RPC 561 (CA).
22 *Gale's Application* [1991] RPC 305 (CA).
23 *Fujitsu's Application* [1997] RPC 608 (CA).

the EPO Boards of Appeal, see *Vicom*,[24] *IBM/Text processing*[25] and *IBM/Data processor network*.[26]

(3) The 'any hardware' approach

Ask whether the claim involves the use of or is to a piece of physical hardware, however mundane (whether a computer or a pencil and paper). If yes, Art. 52(2) does not apply. This approach was adopted in three cases, *Pension Benefits*,[27] *Hitachi*[28] and *Microsoft/Data transfer*[29] (the 'trio'). It was specifically rejected by this Court in *Gale*.[30]

However there are variants of the 'any hardware' approach:

(3)(i) Where a claim is to a method which consists of an excluded category, it is excluded by Art. 52(2) even if hardware is used to carry out the method. But a claim to the apparatus itself, being 'concrete' is not so excluded. The apparatus claim is nonetheless bad for obviousness because the notional skilled man must be taken to know about the improved, excluded, method. This is the *Pension Benefits* approach.

(3)(ii) A claim to hardware necessarily is not caught by Art. 52(2). A claim to a method of using that hardware is likewise not excluded even if that method as such is excluded matter. Either type of claim is nonetheless bad for obviousness for the same reason as above. This is *Hitachi*, expressly disagreeing with *Pensions Benefits* about method claims.

(3)(iii) Simply ask whether there is a claim to something 'concrete', e.g. an apparatus. If yes, Art. 52(2) does not apply. Then examine for patentability on conventional grounds—do not treat the notional skilled man as knowing about any improved excluded method. This is *Microsoft/Data Transfer*.

Because there is no immediate prospect of the EPO arriving at a uniform approach, the Court suggested that the courts, in applying the UK test, should apply the following structured approach when looking for a technical effect:

(1) properly construe the claim;

(2) identify the actual contribution;

(3) ask whether it falls solely within the excluded subject matter;

(4) check whether the actual or alleged contribution is actually technical in nature.[31]

Copyright protection for computer software

Preliminary issues

The drafters of the Copyright, Designs and Patents Act 1988 included computer programs in the category of literary works.[32] We outlined the provisions of the 1988 Act that apply to literary works in Chapter 10 and we do not intend to repeat them here. These normal

---

24 *Vicom Systems Inc's Application* (T-208/84) [1987] 2 EPOR 74.

25 *IBM/ Text processing* (T-65/86) [1990] EPOR 181.

26 *IBM/Data Processor Network* (T-6/83) [1990] EPOR 91.

27 *Pension Benefits* (T-931/95) [2002] EPOR 52.

28 *Hitachi* (T-258/03) [2004] EPOR 55.

29 *Microsoft/Data Transfer* (T-424/05) [2006] EPOR 52.

30 *Gale's Application* [1991] RPC 305 (CA).

31 *Aerotel v. Telco & Marcossan's Application* [2007] 1 All ER 225, [2007] RPC 7 (CA), at [48]–[49].

32 CDPA 1988, ss. 1(1)(a) and 3(1)(b); preparatory design materials for a computer program is also protected as literary work: CDPA 1988, s. 3(1)(c).

copyright rules apply simply to computer programs; we will highlight only specific provisions and the troublesome application of some copyright provisions in relation to computer programs.

The 1988 Act does not define computer programs. This allows for the necessary amount of flexibility in a fast-developing area, in which technological evolutions outdate definitions rapidly. In general terms, it can be said that a computer program is a series of coded instructions that are intended to bring about a particular result when used in a computer.[33] Most computer programs are first written in high-level programming languages, such as COBOL, which bear a fair amount of similarity with normal languages, before they are compiled into machine code in order to allow the computer to run them. This machine code is in binary form—the well-known collection of '0's and '1's.

The 1988 Act protects computer programs; it does not protect, as such, individual files or parts of a program, in the same way as it protects, for example, a novel as a literary work rather than each individual chapter of the novel. It is submitted that the distinction is vital in infringement cases in order to determine whether or not substantial copying has taken place. The program must be taken as a whole when analysing whether infringement has taken place. This seems logical in relation to a novel, for which the test is whether there has been 'substantial' copying of the novel, rather than copying of a paragraph or sentence. This applies *mutatis mutandis* to computer programs. Separate programs can, of course, afterwards be combined in one program, which would, in copyright terms, be treated as a compilation.[34]

A number of authors and practitioners have relied heavily, in this area, on US case law. We do not intend to follow that approach, because there is an important difference between US copyright law and UK copyright law in that the US courts have systematically excluded functional works from the scope of copyright. This has had a profound influence on the case law in relation to computer programs and we will therefore not take this case law as the starting point of our analysis. Although we may have to come back to some of the US cases, we agree with Jacob J that the provisions of the 1988 Act must be the starting point of the analysis.[35]

Computer programs as literary works in copyright

Originality

Only original literary works attract copyright protection and a computer program must thus be original if it is to attract copyright. The 1988 Act does not, however, define originality. In the UK, we have traditionally used the minimalist definition of originality, which required only that the work was not copied and that a sufficient amount of skill, judgment, and labour had been invested in it. In the copyright chapters, we drew the reader's attention to the marginally higher threshold in the European Copyright Directives and, because the computer program is one of the areas in which the provisions inserted in the 1988 Act find their origin and raison d'être in the Computer Software Directive,[36] it is crucial to interpret the originality requirement for computer programs in a European

---

[33] See Lloyd (2000) ch. 20.

[34] It is not clear from the report in FSR whether this distinction was really made in *Ibcos Computers Ltd v. Barclays Mercantile Highland Finance Ltd* [1994] FSR 275.

[35] *Ibcos Computers Ltd v. Barclays Mercantile Highland Finance Ltd* [1994] FSR 275 at 302.

[36] EC Council Directive on the legal protection of computer programs (1991) OJ L 122/42; the modifications were introduced in the CDPA 1988 by the Copyright (Computer Programs) Regulations 1992, SI 1992/3233.

sense, which requires the program to be the author's own intellectual creation
a definition of the concept of originality in the 1988 Act enables us to adopt th
approach for computer programs and we are bound to accept it, because o
would be in breach of our duty to implement the Directive.

A major part of the originality of traditional literary works such as novel
found in the plot. The issue is more complex when software is concerned, b
argued that the alternative for the plot is in such a case the algorithms or the operational
sequences and that the required originality is to be found there, as well as potentially in
the architecture of the program if a lot of work and expertise had gone into creating the
latter.[37]

Idea and expression

Copyright only protects expression and does not protect ideas. This statement, which was
qualified in the copyright chapter, must now be applied to computer programs: so what is
an idea? Clearly, the starting point and the reason for which a computer program is written come within this category. In the famous US *Whelan* case,[38] a program was written to
manage a dentistry laboratory. This was clearly part of the idea, as was the list of functions
that the program should be able to perform and the targets it should meet; how all of this
was to be achieved in practice forms part of the expression of that idea and this not only
includes the code lines of the program, but also its structure. The latter refers to the way in
which the various parts and files are organized.[39] But the precise borderline between idea
and expression cannot be drawn in theory. As Judge Learned Hand said, already more
than half a century ago: '*Nobody has ever been able to fix that boundary and nobody ever
can.*'[40] It has to be fixed in each individual case on the basis of the facts of that case.

In a case that was concerned with computer games, the Court of Appeal held that the
mere 'idea' as to what the program should do was not protected by copyright, because it
had nothing to do with the nature of the work. The nature of the work was instead a computer program that had all of the necessary coding to function. That expression would
be a copyright work. The general idea was only faintly related to that.[41] Similarly, it was
held in a case concerning booking software for airlines that, while the computer program
as such could be protected, it would be an unjustifiable extension of copyright to include
the protection of mere ideas if copyright were to be granted to the business logic of the
program on its own.[42]

Fixation

The obvious way that comes to mind of recording a computer program is the written draft
version of the source code of a program. It is indeed reasonable to expect that many software developers would write the source code down, and develop flow-charts and other
similar things, when developing a new computer program. In this scenario, the machine
code version of the program could be seen to be an adaptation of the work. But it is possible that the program never existed in such form and this does not deny it copyright

---

[37] *Cantor Fitzgerald International v. Tradition (UK) Ltd* [2000] RPC 95.

[38] *Whelan Associates Inc. v. Jaslow Dental Laboratory Inc.* [1987] FSR 1.

[39] Jacob J rejects the idea–expression dichotomy in *Ibcos Computers Ltd v. Barclays Mercantile Highland
Finance Ltd* [1994] FSR 275 at 291, but reintroduces it as the general–detailed idea dichotomy. It is submitted
that there is no difference on substance between his concept and ours.

[40] *Nichols v. Universal Pictures Corp.* 45 F 2d 119 (1930).

[41] *Nova Productions Ltd v. Mazooma Games Ltd, Nova Productions Ltd v. Bell Fruit Games Ltd* [2007]
RPC 25, [2007] ECC 21 (CA).

[42] *Navitaire Inc. v. Easyjet Airline Co. Ltd* [2005] ECDR 17, [2006] RPC 3.

protection. Section 3(2) of the 1988 Act allows the work to be recorded 'in writing or otherwise' and what is really required is a fixation of the work with a certain degree of permanency. Fixation on the hard disk or on a floppy disk clearly meets this requirement.

A program can also be permanently hard-wired in a microprocessor in the form of 'microcode' or 'microprograms'.[43] The RAM memory of a computer constitutes a difficult problem. A program that exists only in the RAM memory of the computer exists only in the form of electrical currency and, when the power supply is interrupted, the program disappears. At first sight, this does not involve the required degree of permanency, but the conclusion may be different if such a program lives in the RAM or a similar memory of a computer network[44] and if it is quite unreasonable to expect the network to be shut down in the foreseeable future.[45] The example of software made available via the various bulletin boards of the Internet comes to mind.

So what is really protected?

In a computer program, the expression is protected. We hold this to include the code lines and the structure of the program. But this expression is only protected in so far as it meets the originality requirement: it must be the author's own intellectual creation. This implies that there is more than one way to express the idea, otherwise the one possible way of doing so cannot be the author's own intellectual creation or his or her particular way of expressing the idea. This leads us to the conclusion that those parts of the computer program that can only be expressed in one way if a certain result is to be achieved, due to technical restrictions, are not original and do not attract copyright.[46] These parts of the program can be copied freely; to hold otherwise would bring the development of new software and the whole software industry to a standstill.

It can be seen here why the European interpretation of the originality requirement is vital in this context. It fulfils an essential role in the system set up by the Directive and implemented in UK law. It also allows the UK to avoid the need to rely on the US case law[47] and its principle that functional works do not attract protection for which there is no legal basis at all in UK copyright law.

Infringement

Infringement can take various forms, but the most obvious is copying. It is important to keep in mind that, in relation to copying, a three-stage test has to be applied.

1. Does the work attract copyright protection?
2. Has there been copying of the elements protected by copyright?
3. Was the copying substantial?[48]

---

[43] Programs stored in the ROM (read-only memory) of the computer are still literary works in the copyright sense, because the mode of storage does not affect the nature of the program: see the US case *NEC Corp. v. Intel Corp.* 645 F Supp 1485 (D Minn 1985).

[44] See *TriadSystems Corp. v. Southeastern Express Co.*, US District Court for the Northern District of California 31 USPQ 2D 1239; *Mai Systems Corp. v. Peak Computer Inc., Vincent Chiechi & Eric Francis*, US Court of Appeals for the ninth Circuit 991 F 2d 511, 26 USPQ 2D 1458.

[45] Especially because other electromagnetic ways of storing works—such as audio cassettes—will also only last for a number of years.

[46] *Total Information Processing Systems v. Daman* [1992] FSR 171.

[47] *Whelan Associates Inc. v. Jaslow Dental Laboratory Inc.* [1987] FSR 1 uses the phrase that the task dictates the form, while *Computer Associates v. Altai* 982 F 2d 693 (1992) (2nd Cir) refers to elements dictated by efficiency.

[48] Compare *Ibcos Computers Ltd v. Barclays Mercantile Highland Finance Ltd* [1994] FSR 275.

If copying took place, the next issue to consider is whether a defence was available, but let us first turn to infringement and, more specifically, to the various forms of copying.

Literal copying

The literal copying of a computer program, in which parts of code lines are copied and both programs are written in the same programming language, was discussed at length by Jacob J in *Ibcos Computers v. Barclays Mercantile Highland Finance*.[49] Having established that copyright existed in the program that was allegedly copied, the judge turned his attention to the question of whether there had been copying. He stated that:

> For infringement there must be copying. Whether there was or not is a question of fact. To prove copying the plaintiff can normally do no more than point to bits of his work and the claimant's work which are the same and prove an opportunity of access to his work. If the resemblance is sufficiently great then the court will draw an inference of copying. It may then be possible for the claimant to rebut the inference—to explain the similarities in some other way. For instance he may be able to show both parties derived similar bits from some third party or material in the public domain. Or he may be able to show that the similarities arise out of a functional necessity—that anyone doing this particular job would be likely to come up with similar bits.[50]

He went on to clarify that '*at this stage . . . both the important and the unimportant bits of the works being compared count*'.[51]

In the case before him, Jacob J found that there was plenty of evidence of copying. There were common spelling mistakes, similar headings, redundant and unexplained bits of code that appeared in both programs, and the allegedly infringing program contained a part of the original program in its source code even though it did not use this part.[52] All of these items are good examples of the kind of evidence for which the plaintiff is looking and with which the claimant will have great difficulties if he or she is to explain away the similarities.

The next issue is whether that copying amounts to the copying of a substantial part of the copyright protected work. It should be remembered that a purely quantitative approach is not appropriate here and that qualitative issues are predominant. Jacob J suggested that it comes down to:

> a question of degree where a good guide is the notion of overborrowing of the skill, labour and judgment which went into the copyright work. . . . In the end the matter must be left to the value judgment of the court.[53]

He agreed with the statement of Ferris J in the *John Richardson* case[54] that '*Consideration is not restricted to the text of the code*',[55] while adding that:

> That must be right: most literary copyright works involve both literal matter (the exact words of a novel or computer program) and varying levels of abstraction (plot, more or less detailed of a novel, general structure of a computer program). I therefore think it right to have regard in this case not only to . . . 'literal similarities' but also to . . . 'program features' and 'design features'.[56]

---

49 Ibid.; see also *Cantor Fitzgerald International v. Tradition (UK) Ltd* [2000] RPC 95.

50 *Ibcos Computers Ltd v. Barclays Mercantile Highland Finance Ltd* [1994] FSR 275 at 296–7.

51 Ibid. at 297.

52 Ibid. at 297–301.

53 Ibid. at 302.

54 *John Richardson Computers Ltd v. Flanders* [1993] FSR 497.

55 Ibid. at 526.

56 *Ibcos Computers Ltd v. Barclays Mercantile Highland Finance Ltd* [1994] FSR 275, *per* Jacob J at 302.

In the *Ibcos Computers* case, substantial copying had clearly taken place. Reference was, in this respect, made to the program structure, to an extremely long list of individual parts of the program, and to the file transfer programs.[57]

Non-literal copying

It flows from our discussion of what is the expression that is protected by copyright in the context of computer programs that non-literal copying can also infringe the copyright in a computer program. Examples are the copying of the structure of the program and the copying of parts of the program, while translating it in another programming language. The test we described in the previous section also applies to cases of indirect copying, but it will, in practice, be more difficult to determine what exactly has been copied and whether that copying is substantial.

Ferris J was confronted with a case of indirect copying in the *John Richardson* case.[58] In this case, the original program was written in BASIC, for use on a Tandy computer, and aimed to assist pharmacists in controlling their stock and in producing labels for prescriptions. A former employee produced the allegedly infringing version, which was written in QuickBasic, for use on an IBM personal computer. Due to the use of different programming languages, the judge found no literal copying, but, when looking at the structure and the sequence of the programs, the input and output routines, the formats, the menus, the options, and facilities of the programs, he found 17 objective similarities that could not readily be justified by the claimant.

Ferris J then considered and applied the test established by the US case of *Computer Associates v. Altai*.[59] He stated that:

> In the test propounded in *Computer Associates* the discovery of a program's abstraction is the first step. The second step is to filter these abstractions in order to discover a 'core of protectable material'. In the process of filtration there are to be excluded from consideration (a) elements dictated by efficiency; (b) elements dictated by external factors and (c) elements taken from the public domain.[60]

We agree with Jacob J's comment in *Ibcos Computers* that this approach is neither appropriate nor helpful.[61] In any case, Ferris J found it difficult to apply the test to the facts of the case that he had in front of him and his application was criticized for not carrying out the second stage of the test.

We submit that a proper application of the originality criterion, as explained above, will result in the elements that the *Computer Associates* test sets out to eliminate to arrive at the core of protectable elements not being protected by copyright in the first place. At the infringement stage, it is then only necessary to consider those parts that are protected by copyright, and to determine which of them have been copied and whether that copying is substantial. This is also the core of the approach taken by Jacob J in *Ibcos Computers*. Although that was a case involving literal copying, he seemed to suggest that his approach was also valid in non-literal copying cases.[62]

That focus on what is protected by copyright and on whether a substantial part of the protected work has been copied is also found in *Nova v. Mazooma*.[63] The Court of

---

[57] Ibid. at 304–14.   [58] *John Richardson Computers Ltd v. Flanders* [1993] FSR 497.

[59] *American Computer Associates v. Altai* 982 F 2d 693 (1992).   [60] Ibid. at 526.

[61] *Ibcos Computers Ltd v. Barclays Mercantile Highland Finance Ltd* [1994] FSR 275 at 302.

[62] Ibid.; see L. Jacobs, 'Demystifying copyright infringement of computer software: *Ibcos Computers v. Barclays Mercantile*' [1994] 5 EIPR 206 at 208–9.

[63] *Nova Productions Ltd v. Mazooma Games Ltd, Nova Productions Ltd v. Bell Fruit Games Ltd* [2007] RPC 25, [2007] ECC 21 (CA).

Appeal in that case also helpfully restated the principle that not every non-literal simi-larity means that there is infringement and, indeed, that merely making a program that emulated another program without copying any of the code or graphics is legitimate, and does not amount to an infringement.[64]

Navitaire Inc. v. Easyjet Airline Co. & Bulletproof Technologies Inc.[65] dealt with copy-right in software and while it is, in essence, an infringement case, it also neatly summa-rizes a couple of other points concerning the scope of copyright in relation to software. Navitaire brought an infringement action against easyJet and BulletProof software developers. In the past, easyJet had taken a licence from Navitaire's predecessor in title for an airline booking system, OpenRes, for use in so-called 'ticketless' flight reservation transactions. Under the licence agreement, Navitaire also supplied easyJet with a pro-gram, TakeFlight, that provided an interface to OpenRes that enabled it to be used on the Internet. Subsequently, easyJet used another web interface. BulletProof, in consultation with easyJet's information technology department, wrote the code for a booking system, eRes, which allegedly breached the terms of the licence and infringed Navitaire's copy-right in various works that contributed to the source code of OpenRes.

Navitaire maintained that the 'business logic' of the OpenRes system had been appro-priated by easyJet's new system, which possessed a user interface that was substantially indistinguishable from the OpenRes system. Navitaire claimed that the copyright in OpenRes had been infringed by, among other things, 'non-textual copying'. It is impor-tant to note that the parties agreed that none of the underlying software in any way resem-bled that of the other. The similarity was limited to the fact that the software acted upon identical, or very similar, inputs and that it produced very similar results. The non-textual copying allegations focused on command names and screen displays.

Navitaire submitted, among other things, that:

(i)   each individual computer command name was a copyright work in its own right or that each complex group of commands was a work in its own right;

(ii) the collection of commands as a whole was entitled to copyright protection as an original literary work in that it was a 'compilation';

(iii) the template of certain of the screen displays was a copyright work in respect of each display derived from it.

Pumfrey J held that neither individual command names nor collections of complex com-mands had the necessary qualities of a literary work for them to be regarded as being protectable by copyright. The source code of Navitaire's program recorded the complex commands, in the sense that it was possible to analyse the code to ascertain that a compu-ter, operating according to that code, would recognize the command. The 'syntax' of com-mands was, however, recorded without being stated and, although a computer program controlled a machine, the result of that control might not appear from the program at all. A defined user command interface did, in fact, amount to an ad hoc computer language and the Software Directive[66] made it clear that computer languages were not protected.

Screen displays comprised of characters were properly to be viewed as 'tables' under s. 3 of the 1988 Act. They were therefore literary works for the purposes of copyright protection. They provided a static framework for the display of dynamic data that it was the task of the software to produce. But when the court turned to the facts of the case, it ruled that, on

---

[64] In the process, the Court of Appeal referred to *Navitaire Inc. v. Easyjet Airline Co. Ltd* [2005] ECDR 17, [2006] RPC 3 with approval.

[65] Ibid.

[66] EC Council Directive on the legal protection of computer programs (1991) OJ L 122/42, Recitals 13–15.

consideration of display aspects of OpenRes and eRes, there had been no infringement of the character-based screen displays. Navitaire's action accordingly failed in their respect.[67]

Screen layouts comprised of material other than characters may, in the view of the court, be protected under copyright as artistic works. Although Navitaire's visual screen displays were recorded as such only in the complex code that displayed them, this form of recording was strictly analogous to simpler digital representations of graphic works and, in that respect, sufficient skill and labour had been utilized. There had been infringement of that copyright and Navitaire's action therefore succeeded in respect of those screens.[68]

The court also found that a sufficient degree of skill and labour had gone into the drawings of icons appearing in Navitaire's software for them to be protected by copyright, and that these had been copied exactly by easyJet and BulletProof. There had therefore been copyright infringement in this respect.[69]

Adaptations

Copyright can also be infringed by making an adaptation of a protected work; this also applies to computer programs.[70] In this context, an adaptation of a computer program is made whenever the source code, which is written in a high-level programming language, is compiled into machine code (also referred to as 'object code') in binary. An adaptation is also made when the binary machine code is disassembled into a low-level assembly language. This process is used to reveal the ideas and the techniques that are contained in the program, and which are not identifiable in an endless binary sequence. The reverse process is called assembling and also involves, obviously, an adaptation of the program.

Defences

Copyright contains a long list of defences against alleged copyright infringement. We will refer here only to defences that are available only in relation to computer programs.

Reverse engineering

It is a common practice in the software industry to reverse engineer a computer program. This means that the object code version of the program is converted into a more readily understandable version, such as the source code. This allows the programmer to discover how the program works and this knowledge will then be used to develop a new program. This new program can eventually be a competing program, although, in most cases, the main objective of the process of reverse engineering is to discover the interfaces of the program, which are to be copied in the new program if it is to be compatible with the existing program. The latter technique is known as decompilation for interoperability purposes and the European Software Directive[71] has introduced it into copyright as a defence against the copying that necessarily forms part of the technique. It has to be emphasized that copyright only allows the reverse engineering decompilation technique to be used for the purposes of achieving interoperability.

The decompilation right makes it lawful to convert a computer program that is expressed in a low-level language into a version in a higher level language[72] and to copy

---

[67] *Navitaire Inc. v. Easyjet Airline Co. Ltd* [2005] ECDR 17, [2006] RPC 3.
[68] Ibid.
[69] Ibid.
[70] See CDPA 1988, s. 21(3) and (4).
[71] (1991) OJ L 122/42, Art. 6.
[72] CDPA 1988, s. 50B(1)(a).

the program incidentally in the course of converting it.[73] A number of conditions apply to this decompilation right. Firstly, it must be necessary to decompile the program to obtain the information necessary to create an independent program that can be operated with the program decompiled or with another program.[74] Secondly, the information that is obtained is not to be used for any purpose other than the objective that is outlined in the first condition.[75] The decompilation right does not exist if the potential decompiler has ready access to the information that he or she needs to obtain interoperability.[76] This will obviously be the case if, for example, the interfaces are described in the user manual or are available from the producer of the program upon simple request. The right also no longer exempts any infringement if the information obtained is communicated to third persons when this is not necessary to achieve interoperability,[77] or when the information obtained is used to create a program that is similar in its expression.[78] Other acts that are restricted by copyright cannot be defended by invoking the decompilation defence, which means that the decompiler's activity is restricted to those acts that are necessary to get access to the information concerning the interfaces.[79]

The defence will make it possible to gain access to the technical details of, for example, an operating program such as Microsoft Windows, should Microsoft not make that information available itself. Because it is vital for independent producers of application software that their program can be run under Windows—the world's most popular operating program—in order to make their potential market as large as possible, they need to know these interfaces and incorporate them into their program. The defence thus plays an important role in the software industry and enhances competition, while not permitting the outright copying of other parts of a computer program. To make sure that it fulfils this role adequately, it cannot be restricted or prohibited by contract.[80]

Having excluded the matter from the scope of the fair dealing provisions, the Copyright and Related Rights Regulations 2003 have added a s. 50BA to the 1988 Act.[81] According to that new section:

(1) It is not an infringement of copyright for a lawful user of a copy of a computer program to observe, study or test the functioning of the program in order to determine the ideas and principles which underlie any element of the program if he does so while performing any of the acts of loading, displaying, running, transmitting or storing the program which he is entitled to do.

(2) Where an act is permitted under this section, it is irrelevant whether or not there exists any term or condition in an agreement which purports to prohibit or restrict the act.

An important restrictive condition that applies to the decompilation right, as well as to any of the other computer software specific defences that we will discuss in the next two sections, is that the defences can only be invoked by a person described in the 1988 Act as a 'lawful user'.[82] This is a person who has the right to use the computer program and who has obtained this right under a licence or otherwise. Licensees and persons who act for them, such as their employees, are clearly lawful users, but it is submitted that the category also includes independent consultants and agents working for the licensee, and all persons who need to use and eventually copy the program if they are to exercise their legal

[73] Ibid., (b).   [74] Ibid., (2)(a).
[75] Ibid., (b).   [76] Ibid., (3)(a).
[77] Ibid., (c).   [78] Ibid., (d).
[79] Ibid., (b).   [80] Ibid., (4).
[81] Regulations 9 and 15, respectively.
[82] CDPA 1988, s. 50A(2).

duties, such as receivers, auditors or solicitors executing a search order.[83] It also includes persons who obtained a copy of the program through rental or loan.

Back-up copies, adapting a program, and error correction

The lawful user of a computer program is allowed to make a back-up copy of the computer program if he or she needs to have such a copy for the lawful use of the program[84] and this right cannot be restricted or prohibited by contract.[85] The lawful user can also adapt the program or copy it if this is necessary for the lawful use of the program—for example, to adapt the standard program slightly to meet the specific needs of the lawful user— but this facility can be prohibited by the terms of the contract under which the lawful user is using the computer program.[86]

The lawful user always has the right to correct errors in the program;[87] to hold otherwise would deprive the lawful user of the full use of the program and of some of his or her contractual rights, because it must be an implied term of each contract by which a computer program and the lawful right to use it is acquired that the program is supplied for error-free use.

Databases

The UK has implemented the EU Database Directive[88] and the discussion that follows is therefore primarily based on the Copyright and Rights in Databases Regulations 1997.[89] The regime[90] came into force on 1 January 1998.

A database

The term 'database' has been defined as a collection of independent works, data, or other materials, which are arranged in a systematic or methodical way, and are individually accessible by electronic or other means.[91] This definition can be summarized by means of a number of points, as follows.

1. A database has to be a collection of independent material. In practice, this means that separate items that do not interact with each other are stored in a database. The non-interaction rule excludes items such as film, in which the script, music, etc., interact to form the final work.

2. The works in a database can be works that are protected by copyright, as well as non-copyrightable data or any other materials. Copyright protection for these items, as such, is not required and a database can contain a mixture of different items: for example, a combination of copyright works and other data.

---

[83]   See Chapter 33 on remedies for more details.
[84]   CDPA 1988, s. 50A(1).
[85]   Ibid., (3).
[86]   Ibid., s. 50C(1).
[87]   Ibid., s. 50C(2).
[88]   European Parliament and Council Directive on the protection of databases [1996] OJ L 77/20.
[89]   SI 1997/3032.
[90]   See J. N. Adams, '"Small earthquake in Venezuela": the Database Regulations 1997' [1998] EIPR 129.
[91]   CDPA 1988, s. 3A(1); the European Court of Justice ruled that a database is '*any collection of works, data, or other materials, separable from one another without the value of their contents being affected, including a method or system…for the retrieval of each of its constituent material*' in Case C-444/02 *Fixtures Marketing v. OPAP* [2004] ECR I-10549.

3. The items in a database must be accessible on an individual basis—that is, one must be able to retrieve them individually. This excludes numerous multimedia works in which the user necessarily gets access to a combination of works in different media at any one time during the use of the work.

4. Both electronic and non-electronic collections or databases are included in the scope of the definition.

5. The independent works, etc., must be arranged in a systematic or methodical way. Putting random information and items in a box will therefore not create a database— but it can be argued that a newspaper is a database, because the articles in it (which are independent and individually accessible works) are arranged in a systematical way (grouped by home news pages, overseas news pages, etc.).

This final requirement creates specific problems in relation to electronic databases. Often, the information is fed into the system in a random way, while the software of the database[92] organizes the information afterwards. The physical storage of the information in the memory of the computer (or on floppy disk, CD-ROM, etc.) is not even necessarily in the same or another systematic way.

It is submitted that these collections nevertheless meet the arrangement criterion. A systematic or methodical arrangement exists and it is provided by an element of the database itself. The technical way in which this is achieved is irrelevant in this context. The conclusion must be different when the arrangement is provided by an element outside the database itself. A clear example is the Internet, which forms a collection of independent and individually accessible materials. A systematic arrangement is missing, however, and the presence of search engines[93] cannot change that. These search engines are external to the collection of materials and so is the arrangement of the materials that they provide. A collection such as the Internet is therefore not a database.

Copyright protection for a database

A database is a complex product or work, in relation to which copyright can be involved at many stages. A first distinction needs to be drawn between the computer program,[94] which allows the database to be set up and which organizes the data, and provides the search facilities, etc. and the contents of the database. The special regime of protection for the database does not affect either of these. The computer program will potentially be protected by copyright as a computer program, under the provisions that implement the Software Directive, if it meets the standard requirements for computer programs. Those items that are included in a database and which were works protected by copyright will continue to benefit from the protection afforded to them in that way. The rights of the owner of the copyright in these works will not change and neither will the ownership of that copyright. Unprotected works, data, and other materials will not attract copyright through their inclusion in a database.

Secondly, the contents and the computer programs, and the copyright in them, need to be distinguished from the database and any potential copyright in the database. Any copyright in a database will have to be independent from the rights in the contents, etc., and will come on top of the existing rights; it may also be awarded to different owners. What is left apart from the contents, etc., resembles a compilation. Prior to the

---

[92] Which forms part of the database as a product and is sold, or made available, as an integral part of it.
[93] These pieces of software can be protected by copyright as computer programs.
[94] See Art. 1(3) of the Directive.

implementation of the Database Directive, many databases could indeed be protected and the new regime makes it clear that the category of compilations now excludes any work that is a database.[95]

Copyright in a database is thus confined to the selection and arrangement or structure of the materials that are contained in it. As a work, a database has been categorized as a form of literary work.[96] The originality criterion that applies to databases is the slightly higher originality criterion that is found in all European Directives:

> a literary work consisting of a database is original if, and only if, by reason of the selection or arrangement of the contents of the database the database constitutes the author's own intellectual creation.[97]

This 'author's own intellectual creation' criterion has now been copied *expressis verbis* into UK legislation in relation to databases. In so far as this implies that it only applies to databases, the UK is flagrantly in breach of the Software Directive, because, as we saw above, the slightly higher criterion should apply there too. The new originality criterion means that some intellectual judgment that is the author's own must have gone into the selection of the materials or into the method of their arrangement.[98] This approach will deny copyright protection to most modern databases: for example, because they aim at a complete coverage of a certain topic, rather than at selecting material, or because they arrange their materials in an alphabetical or other standard way, rather than in an original way. This approach must be applauded, because the alternative would have involved the grant of multiple copyrights in standard and commonplace structures, and such a multitude of exclusive rights could have stifled competition in this area.

As a form of literary work, a database is subject to the normal copyright regime. For example, copying the selection of the materials or the structure of the database, or a substantial part of them, will be an infringement of the copyright in the database. A few special provisions do, however, exist. Making an adaptation or doing a restricted act in relation to an adaptation of a database will still be an infringement of the copyright in the database, but the term 'adaptation' has been redefined to mean an *'arrangement or altered version of the database or a translation of it'* in relation to a database and a database has been excluded from the list of works to which the normal definition of an adaptation applies.[99] Fair dealing for the purposes of research and private study defence does not apply to databases in its normal form either. The special rule stipulates that *'fair dealing with a database for the purposes of research or private study does not infringe any copyright in the database provided that the source is indicated'* and it has been added that *'doing anything ... for the purposes of research for a commercial purpose is not fair dealing with the database'*.[100] Additionally, a legitimate user of a database is allowed to do anything that is necessary for the purposes of gaining access to the database and for the use of the contents of the database. That latter right cannot be restricted by agreement.[101]

---

[95] CDPA 1988, s. 3(1).
[96] Ibid.
[97] Ibid., s. 3A(2).
[98] Compare the US approach in *Feist Publications v. Rural Telephone* 499 US 330 (1991) (Supreme Court). In the UK case *Waterlow Directories Ltd v. Reed Information Services Ltd* [1992] FSR 409, the opportunity to address this issue was missed.
[99] CDPA 1988, s. 21(3).
[100] Ibid., s. 29(1A) and (5).
[101] Ibid., s. 50D.

The database right

A new *sui generis* right to protect databases has been created and that right operates irrespective of whether the database, or any of its contents, attracts copyright protection.[102] The creation of this right was necessary because copyright was not the appropriate instrument to protect non-original databases, which are nevertheless valuable and have required a substantial investment. Electronic databases especially are, in such a situation, extremely vulnerable and it was felt that some form of protection was needed to protect the valuable investment in these databases.

The new right

The new database right has been defined as a property right and it is granted '*if there has been a substantial investment in obtaining, verifying or presenting the contents of the database*'.[103] Once again, this right does not interfere with any of the existing materials and the rights in them. As a right in the database, it comes on top of any existing rights and its existence rewards, and is conditional on, a substantial or sizeable investment either in collecting, in verifying, or in presenting the contents of the database. For example, the substantial investment requirement will not be met by simply putting different works together on a single support; such a collection will not be protected by the database right.[104]

The European Court of Justice held that 'obtaining' must be interpreted as referring to the resources used to seek out existing independent materials and to collect them in the database. The resources used for the creation of materials that make up the contents of the database are not covered. 'Verification', however, refers to the resources used with a view to ensuring the reliability of the information contained in the database, to monitor the accuracy of the material originally collected, as well as later on. Resources used to verify materials that are created for the database are not covered.[105] It follows that investment in common data will not trigger the *sui generis* right. Databases that consist of created data, such as television listings or dates of sports fixtures, will thus remain unprotected.[106] The *British Horseracing* case[107] offers the example of lists of riders and runners that were intending to run in a certain race. Without further verification as to who would actually be running, etc., there could not be a database right in simply listing existing independent material.

The first owner of the database right has been identified as the maker of the database.[108] The maker of the database is, in turn, '*the person who takes the initiative in obtaining, verifying, or presenting the contents of the database and assumes the risk of investing in that obtaining, verification or presentation*'.[109] Making a database may involve more than one person. If several people act together in relation to the activities that have to be undertaken by the maker, they will be the joint makers of the database and the joint first owners

---

[102] Copyright and Rights in Databases Regulations 1997, reg. 13(2).

[103] Ibid., reg. 13(1).

[104] See E. Derclaye, 'Database *sui generis* right: what is a substantial investment? A tentative definition' (2005) 36 Int Rev IP & Comp L 1, 2.

[105] Case C-203/02 *The British Horseracing Board Ltd & ors v. William Hill Organisation Ltd* [2004] ECR I-10425, [2005] 1 CMLR 15, [2005] RPC 13.

[106] See E. Derclaye, 'The Court of Justice interprets the database *sui generis* right for the first time' (2005) 30 Eur LR 3, 420.

[107] *British Horseracing Board Limited & ors v. William Hill Organisation Ltd* [2005] RPC 35, [2005] ECDR 28.

[108] Copyright and Rights in Databases Regulations 1997, reg. 15.

[109] Ibid., reg. 14(1).

of the right.[110] A database made by an employee in the course of his or her employment will be considered to have been made by the employer, subject to any agreement to the contrary.[111]

The database right exists for a 15-year term. That term starts running from the end of the calendar year in which the database was completed, but that rule is displaced if the database is made available to the public before the end of that period. In that case, the right expires 15 years from the end of the calendar year in which the database was first made available to the public.[112] A substantial change to the contents of the database that can be considered to be a substantial new investment will lead to the grant of a new 15-year term of protection. Such a change may be the result of the 'accumulation of successive additions, deletions or alterations' to the database.[113] Any sustained effort and investment to keep the database up to date will therefore automatically lead to permanent protection through the ever-renewed database right in the latest version of the database. This is the case because the concept of 'substantial change' to the contents of a database, which qualifies the database for its own term of protection, entails that the resulting database must be considered to be a new, separate database.[114]

Infringement of the right

The owner of the database right is granted the right to object to the extraction or reutilization of all, or a substantial part, of the contents of the database. The right in the investment clearly covers the use of the contents of the database. The right will be infringed by the unauthorized extraction or reutilization of all, or a substantial part, of the contents of the database.[115] The threshold of a substantial part of the contents of the database can be passed through the repeated and systematic extraction or reutilization of insubstantial parts of these contents.[116] A typical example of an infringement would consist of the taking out of a substantial part of the contents of the database and their reorganization by computer into a prima facie different database.[117]

In the first case to arise before an English court on this issue, Laddie J had to deal with an issue involving information related to horseracing, which was originally contained in the British Horseracing Board's database, emerging on the website of the Internet betting service of William Hill Organisation.[118] The judgment was appealed and the Court of Appeal decided to request a preliminary opinion from the European Court of Justice. That Court rendered its judgment on 9 November 2004, but we will also need to look at the very complete opinion of the Advocate-General.[119] The domestic proceedings were then finalized in the Court of Appeal.[120]

---

[110] Ibid., (5).

[111] Ibid., (2); provisions on Crown rights are contained in reg. 14(3) and (4).

[112] Ibid., reg. 17(1) and (2).

[113] Ibid., (3).

[114] Opinion of Advocate-General Stix-Hackl in Case C-203/02 *The British Horseracing Board Ltd & ors v. William Hill Organisation Ltd* [2005] RPC 13.

[115] Copyright and Rights in Databases Regulations 1997, reg. 16(1).

[116] Ibid., (2).

[117] Such a case could have been problematical under a 100 per cent copyright system.

[118] *British Horseracing Board Limited & ors v. William Hill Organisation Ltd* [2001] 2 CMLR 12.

[119] Opinion of Advocate-General Stix-Hackl in Case C-203/02 *The British Horseracing Board Ltd & ors v. William Hill Organisation Ltd* [2005] RPC 13.

[120] *British Horseracing Board Limited & ors v. William Hill Organisation Ltd* [2005] RPC 35, [2005] ECDR 28.

In this case, the information had been supplied to the claimant by an intermediary, but it was virtually certain that it had been derived from the claimant's website. The first essential point that arose was whether extraction and/or reutilization of a substantial part of the database had taken place. The judge rightfully pointed out that, while a systematic and methodical organization of the information was required for a database right to exist, extraction and reutilization as forms of infringement of such a database right were not linked to the arrangement of the database being used by the alleged infringer. Extraction and/or reutilization of the data as such was sufficient for there to be infringement of the database right.[121]

The European Court of Justice has now ruled that the terms 'extraction' and 'reutilization' must be interpreted as referring to an unauthorized act of appropriation and distribution to the public of the whole, or part, of the contents of a database. In the view of the Court, direct access to the database is not implied in this definition; the fact that the contents of the database were made accessible to the public by the maker of the database or with its consent has no impact on the right of the make of the database to prevent acts of extraction and/or reutilization of the whole, or a substantial part, of the contents of its database.[122] It is therefore fairly certain that the question of whether the works, data, or other materials derived from the database have the same systematic or methodical arrangement and individual accessibility as in the original database is not relevant to the interpretation of the expressions 'a substantial part... of the contents of that database' or 'insubstantial parts of the contents of the database'.[123] Extraction of data from a database did NOT, according to Laddie J (and the Advocate-General), need to involve data being taken away from the database. Mere copying of data and its transfer to a new medium were sufficient,[124] in so far as a substantial part of the database had been extracted.

The latter question depends, in essence, on a comparison between what has been taken (or used) with what was left in the claimant's database, but the importance of the data that had been extracted to the claimant also had to be taken into account. Additionally, account has to be taken of the protection that the Directive affords for the investment made by the database owner in obtaining, verifying, and presenting the contents of the database. A substantial part can therefore be extracted and/or reutilized if the claimant relies upon, and takes advantage of, the completeness and accuracy of the information in the database. Qualitative considerations are therefore also to be taken into account.[125]

In the view of the European Court of Justice, the term 'substantial part' refers to the volume of data extracted from the database and/or reutilized. It must be assessed in relation to the total volume of the contents of the database. The scale of the investment in obtaining, verifying, and presenting of the content of the subject of the act of extraction and/or reutilization is to be taken into consideration as an important factor, irrespective of whether that subject represents a quantitatively substantial part of the contents of the database. An 'insubstantial part' of the database is simply defined by the Court as any part that does not fulfil the definition of a substantial part, evaluated both quantitatively and qualitatively.[126]

[121] *British Horseracing Board Limited & ors v. William Hill Organisation Ltd* [2001] 2 CMLR 12 at 232–5.
[122] Case C-203/02 *The British Horseracing Board Ltd & ors v. William Hill Organisation Ltd* [2004] ECR I-10425, [2005] 1 CMLR 15, [2005] RPC 13.
[123] Ibid.
[124] *British Horseracing Board Limited & ors v. William Hill Organisation Ltd* [2001] 2 CMLR 12 at 236–8.
[125] Ibid. at 235–6.
[126] Opinion of Advocate-General Stix-Hackl in Case C-203/02 *The British Horseracing Board Ltd & ors v. William Hill Organisation Ltd* [2005] RPC 13.

Having concluded that a substantial part of the database had been extracted along the lines of his analysis, Laddie J moved on to consider the reutilization point. He ruled that any use by the defendant of a database through which the extracted data was transmitted or made available to the public amounted to reutilization, and that this included loading the information concerned onto the defendant's computers for the purpose of making it available on its website. The fact that some of the information was also available from another source was entirely irrelevant in this respect.[127]

The second essential point that arose was whether the defendant had engaged in repeated and systematic extraction or reutilization of the contents of the database. The defendant's database was in constant evolution and was updated on a day-to-day basis. The defendant took information from it on a daily basis and this prejudiced the legitimate interests of the claimant, and amounted to repeated and systematic extraction or reutilization of the contents of the database.[128]

It should be remembered, too, that the threshold of a substantial part of the contents of the database can be passed through the repeated and systematic extraction or reutilization of insubstantial parts of these contents. In this respect, the Court held that the prohibition contained in Art. 7(5) of the Database Directive refers to unauthorized acts of extraction or reutilization that have, as their cumulative effect, the reconstitution or the making available to the public of the whole or a substantial part of the contents of the database, in the absence of any prior authorization by the maker of the database. In being made available in this way, they seriously prejudice the investment of the maker of the database.[129]

Exceptions to the right

The exceptions to the database right are not numerous and they are also narrower in scope than those of their copyright counterparts. Some form of fair dealing exception exists, but not for the purpose of criticism, review, or news reporting, and the library exceptions are also missing. Regulation 20 of the Copyright and Rights in Databases Regulations 1997 contains the narrow exception that:

(1) Database right in a database which has been made available to the public in any manner is not infringed by fair dealing with a substantial part of its content if—

   (a) that part is extracted from the database by a person who is apart from this paragraph a lawful user of the database,

   (b) it is extracted for the purpose of illustration for teaching or research and not for any commercial purpose, and

   (c) the source is indicated.

(2) The provisions of Schedule 1 specify other acts which may be done in relation to a database notwithstanding the existence of database right.

Qualification

There is also a qualification requirement that has to be met before the database right can be granted. The main principle of this is that an attempt has been made to require reciprocity

---

[127] *British Horseracing Board Limited & ors v. William Hill Organisation Ltd* [2001] 2 CMLR 12, at 238–9.

[128] Ibid. at 239–43. There are also indications in other member States that deep-linking on the Internet to another website containing a database and thereby skipping the front page of the latter, giving the user the impression that both databases are one and the same amounts to reutilizing a substantial part of a database: See A. Bennett, 'Euro copyright law used to block link to web site' Yahoo News, 22 January 2001, available online at news.yahoo.com.

[129] Case C-203/02 *The British Horseracing Board Ltd & ors v. William Hill Organisation Ltd* [2004] ECR I-10425, [2005] 1 CMLR 15, [2005] RPC 13.

in the sense that non-European Economic Area (EEA) persons will only be granted the right if their country offers a similar level of protection to that of the European makers of databases. Qualification is made dependent on the fact that at least one of the makers of the database was, at the material time at which the database was made:

(a) an individual who was a national of an EEA State or habitually resident within the EEA,

(b) a body which was incorporated under the law of an EEA state and which, at that time, satisfied one of the conditions in paragraph (2), or

(c) a partnership or other unincorporated body which was formed under the law of an EEA state and which, at that time, satisfied the condition in paragraph (2)(a).[130]

These conditions are:

(a) that the body has its central administration or principal place of business within the EEA, or

(b) that the body has its registered office within the EEA and the body's operations are linked on an ongoing basis with the economy of an EEA State.[131]

Outstanding questions and the risk of abuse

These rather vague provisions will undoubtedly give rise to a whole series of disputes before the courts.

The database right presents the inherent danger that it will grant a monopoly right over major sources of (statistical or other) information and that this right will be owned by a single right holder (either the producer of the information or the holder of the sources). Any abuse of the database right will be restrained through the use of Art. 82, but there are no special provisions available to counter this threat, apart from the *Magill*[132]-style action against the abuse of a dominant position.

The Internet

It would lead too far to discuss all intellectual property-related aspects of the Internet in this chapter; we will consequently restrict our comments to some copyright-related issues.[133] Three major questions will be addressed:

- is material found on the Internet protected by copyright and, if so, how?

- what amounts to copyright infringement in an Internet context?

- how do the defences to copyright infringement apply to alleged infringement on the Internet?

Two preliminary points also need to be addressed. The first of these is that the Internet and the use of works on it do not change copyright: works that are protected, as such, do not lose this status when they appear on the Internet. The situation in this respect is identical to that we described in relation to copyright in databases. Equally, copyright applies to Internet-related issues. Up to now, there has been no change to the provisions

---

[130] Ibid., reg. 18(1).

[131] Ibid., (2).

[132] See Case C-241/91 P *Radio Telefís Éireann v Commission of the European Communities* [1995] ECR I-743.

[133] See H. MacQueen (1997) 'Copyright and the Internet', in C. Waelde and L. Evans (eds) *Law and the Internet: Regulating Cyberspace*, Oxford: Hart, p. 67.

of copyright: we simply need to apply the existing rules to the Internet—but our comment will highlight some of the problems that arise through that application.

The second preliminary point flows naturally from the borderless and international nature of the Internet. Works cross borders on the Internet as a way of life. The contrast with the national nature of the UK copyright legislation gives rise to numerous issues of private international law. Examples are in plentiful supply, but the most obvious relates to the copying of a work: where does the copying take place? Does it take place on the server on which the work is stored, on the foreign terminal on which the user views the work and from which he or she prints a copy of it, or in any of the countries through which the work passes on its way from the server to the user's computer? Which national court will have jurisdiction to decide the issue? And under which law will the issue be decided? These issues come on top of the discussion that follows and in which we will describe the UK's substantial provisions. The private international law issues are highly complex and we refer the reader to Fawcett and Torremans (1998) for further details.

Existence of copyright and classification

A lot of websites contain text, music, and artistic works, such as photographs and drawings. These works will be protected as literary, musical, or artistic works as long as they meet the normal copyright requirements. Copyright in the works that are specifically created by the creator of the website for that purpose will be owned by that creator, subject to the employer–employee rule. Collaborative efforts may give rise to joint authorship and joint ownership. Sound recordings, films, and broadcasts also maintain their copyright status when they are put on the Internet.

But can a website, as such, be classified as a work that attracts copyright protection? The arrangement of a website can be protected by means of the copyright that is available in a typographical arrangement. This conclusion is reached through the interpretation of the concept of 'publication'. The website is published, because copies are made available to the public by means of an electronic retrieval system.[134] The Internet fits in with that requirement, which means that the author of the arrangement of a website has a typographical arrangement copyright in that arrangement.

The Scottish *Shetland Times* case[135] suggested that a website was a cable programme service or a cable programme, as these were defined in the original text of the 1988 Act. A cable programme was any item that was included in a cable programme service under the original text of that Act. Such a service was defined as:

> a service which consists wholly or mainly in sending visual images, sounds or other information by means of a telecommunication system, otherwise than by wireless telegraphy, for reception at two or more places [whether or not simultaneously], or for presentation to members of the public.[136]

Two-way or interactive communication systems were excluded.[137]

Lord Hamilton came to the conclusion that a website came within this definition by rejecting the argument that the public accessed information, rather than being sent information, and the argument that a website was an interactive system. One could indeed

---

[134] CDPA 1988, s. 175(1).

[135] *Shetland Times v. Wills* 1997 SLT 669, 1997 SCLR 160; see also *British Telecommunications plc v. One in a Million* [1998] 4 All ER 476, [1999] 1 WLR 903.

[136] CDPA 1988, s. 7(1).

[137] Ibid., (2).

argue that the information is sent by the owner of the website when the request of the user arrives, or at least that the Act allows for the word 'sending' to include the concept of ena-bling the information to be sent. The interactivity exists because the user can send email messages to the operator of the website and is even invited to do so, but for the exclusion to apply, the interactivity—or the potential for interactivity—must be an essential feature of the service. The definition that is given to the word 'essential' is clearly the crucial point. Sites that are mainly there to provide information in a passive way—such as the websites of a newspaper—may well have escaped the exclusion, but it was hard to see how a website that was accessed for the purposes of interactivity—such as the catalogues of mail order shops or the Internet ticket reservation sites of airlines—could escape the exclusion.

Clearly, the *Shetland Times* case did not provided the definitive answer; it merely got the discussion started. The category of cable programs has now been included in the broad category of broadcasts, but most websites have been excluded specifically by the new s. 6(1A) of the 1988 Act, which states:

Excepted from the definition of 'broadcast' is any internet transmission unless it is—

(a) a transmission taking place simultaneously on the internet and by other means,

(b) a concurrent transmission of a live event, or

(c) a transmission of recorded moving images or sounds forming part of a programme service offered by the person responsible for making the transmission, being a service in which programmes are transmitted at scheduled times determined by that person.

Those websites that are excluded from the category of broadcasts may still attract protec-tion, however—for example, as databases, literary works, or artistic works—but a single categorization is no longer possible. One should also not forget that the issue of the pro-tection of the website as such as a copyright work does not affect the fact that copyright may subsist in the various works contained in the website.

Infringement issues

Reproduction

Browsing the Internet involves storing material in the RAM memory of the computer: does this amount to copying? Copying is defined as '*reproducing the work in any material form*' in as far as literary, dramatic, musical, and artistic works are concerned.[138] Such a reproduction may be made through the storage of the work in any medium by electronic means;[139] transient or incidental copies are also included.[140] Loading software or the con-tents of a page of a website into the RAM memory of a computer must thus involve an act of copying. Laddie J indeed held that it did and that the fact that the material was only present for a limited time was irrelevant.[141]

When material is downloaded, things become even clearer. Printouts and copies on the hard disk or on floppy disk are clearly copies. The typographical arrangement copyright in the site is also copied on each occasion and, if a website is held to be a cable programme, the acts named above will also involve copying through the making of a photograph of

---

[138] Ibid., s. 17(2).

[139] Ibid.

[140] Ibid., (6). See also European Parliament and Council Directive 2001/29/EC on the harmonization of certain aspects of copyright and related rights in the information society [2001] OJ L 167/10, Art. 2.

[141] *Kabushiki Kaisha Sony Computer Entertainment Inc. (also t/a Sony Computer Entertainment Inc.), Sony Computer Entertainment Europe Ltd & Sony Computer Entertainment UK Ltd v. Gaynor David Ball & ors* [2004] ECDR 323.

the whole, or a substantial part, of any image that forms part of the cable programme.[142] As with software, there may also be a case of non-literal copying when (only) the design and the structure of the website are copied.[143]

Public performance and communication to the public

The copyright in literary, dramatic, or musical works can also be infringed through their public performance, showing, or playing.[144] That might easily be accomplished by displaying them on a computer screen or by playing them over the computer's audio system. The only problematical point is the fact that the performance, etc., needs to take place in public.

The latter concept no longer requires that there be a group of paying people forming an audience for whom the work is performed; neither is there a need for a gathering of people in one place. 'In public' rather seems to mean that there must be an audience, from whom the author is entitled to expect remuneration for the enjoyment of his or her work. Recent foreign decisions have shown that such an audience exists in cases in which several people listen at different times to recorded music when their call is put on hold when they use their mobile phones[145] or when several people watch non-simultaneous television and video broadcasts in individual hotel rooms.[146]

The European Court of Justice has now also confirmed the latter point.[147] As a result of the implementation of the Information Society Directive[148] the point has now be solved definitively, and the right of communication to the public and the right of making available to the public will also apply to situations in which members of the public may gain access from a place and time individually chosen by them. The incorporation of copyright works, without owning the rights in them or without authorization, into a website for it to be accessed by Internet users will infringe the copyright in these works, because it amounts to communicating the work to the public. Disseminating live broadcasts of Champions League football matches via a website was therefore also an infringement as an unauthorized communication to the public.[149]

Hypertext links

Hypertext links to other websites or other copyright works could be seen as making the work available and therefore they could be seen as amounting to an infringement under s. 20 of the 1988 Act. Indeed, through the link, the work becomes available to different audiences. But, arguably, most hypertext links are more akin to endnotes, bibliographies, or hints for further reading: they make it easier to locate and access works that are already available to the public. They refer to the other sites, but they do not include the sites themselves in the site of the alleged infringer. It is therefore submitted that the better view is that hyperlinks do not amount to infringement through reproduction or communication to the public.

---

[142] CDPA 1988, s. 17(4) and (5).

[143] See MacQueen (1997) p. 81.

[144] CDPA 1988, s. 19.

[145] *Australasian Performing Right Association Ltd v. Telstra Corp. Ltd* [1997] IIC 136 (Federal Court of Australia, 23 August 1995).

[146] *SGAE v. Hotel Blanco Don J SA* [1997] 1 EIPR D-21 Supreme Court of Spain, 11 March 1996.

[147] Case C-306/05 *SGAE v. Rafael Hoteles SA* [2007] ECDR 2.

[148] Article 3. This applies to all kinds of original copyright works, as well as to performances, phonograms, films, and broadcasts: see the new CDPA 1988, s. 20(2). Performers have a similar right to object to their works being made available to the public without their prior consent: see CDPA 1988, s. 182CA.

[149] *Union des Associations Européennes de Football v. Briscomb* (2006) 150 SJLB 670.

It is submitted, however, that such a conclusion is no longer valid if the alleged infringer organizes the links in such a way that the other sites will be shown inside the frame of the alleged infringer's site. Such a link is stronger and should be seen as inclusion, especially because the alleged infringer sets out to derive an economic benefit from the contents of the other site.[150]

Authorization

Copyright infringement by authorizing someone else to commit certain acts[151] is less of a problem in relation to the Internet. It is true that those who provide end users with access to the Internet—for example, universities or cybercafes that make networked terminals available—provide these users with the means to copy, etc. But all of that equipment can also be used for the lawful use of the Internet and that is sufficient to counter the threat of infringement liability.[152]

Service providers that participate in the infringing activities of the users—for example, by providing road maps to items that can be downloaded—may not escape liability, but temporary acts of reproduction that are transient or incidental and an integral part of a technical process, and the sole purpose of which is to enable a transmission in a network between parties or a lawful use of a work have been exempted specifically from the right of reproduction, if the copies made have no independent economic significance.[153] This provision is vital for the functioning of the Internet.

Peer-to-peer

Peer-to-peer file sharing over the Internet gives rise to a whole range of issues. There is no doubt about the fact that the actual act of sharing involves, at the very least, reproducing the material. The individuals involved are therefore infringing copyright if the material shared is protected by copyright. Innocence or ignorance is not a defence, and simply connecting a computer containing the material and making it available to download will be sufficient.[154] It might, however, be rather impractical for the copyright holder to sue all of the individual users of peer-to-peer software. But might it be argued that the Internet service providers, and the designers and suppliers of the software, also commit an infringement?

Service providers do not normally engage in making the copy and they escape liability unless they can be seen to authorize the making of the copy. If they do nothing more than offer the Internet service, however, it is hard to see how that can be fitted into the concept of authorizing the user to copy: authorization requires more than mere enabling. Peer-to-peer software suppliers that operated a central server, such as the old Napster, were much easier targets. At least under US copyright law, they could be seen to contribute to copyright infringement. The old Napster had, at least, knowledge of what was going on on its service and could act by cutting off copyright infringers.[155] Newer peer-to-peer software is more sophisticated and works without a central server. The software is supplied to individual users and the suppliers have no further control over its use. Importantly, from a US copyright law point of view, there is an opportunity for substantial non-infringing use to be made of the software and it was at least arguable that, in those circumstances,

[150] Cf MacQueen (1997) p. 84.

[151] CDPA 1988, s. 16(2).

[152] See *CBS Inc. v. Ames Records & Tapes Ltd* [1982] Ch 91, [1981] 2 All ER 812; *CBS Songs Ltd v. Amstrad Consumer Electronics plc* [1988] AC 1013, [1988] 2 All ER 484.

[153] CDPA 1988, s. 28A, which implements Art. 5(1) of the Information Society Directive into UK law.

[154] *Polydor Ltd v. Brown* [2005] EWHC 3191, (2006) 29(3) IPD 29021.

[155] 239 F.3d at 1027.

contributory liability presupposes that the defendant had reasonable knowledge of specific infringing files and had failed to act on that knowledge to prevent infringement.

In the *Grokster* case,[156] that debate went all the way up to the Supreme Court. The final ruling held that the providers of software that is designed to enable the file sharing of copyright works may be held liable for copyright infringement that takes place through use of the software by users. In the Court's words:

> one who distributes a device with the object of promoting its use to infringe copyright, as shown by clear expression or other affirmative steps to foster infringement, is liable for the resulting acts of infringement by third parties.[157]

The only peer-to-peer software that escapes this ruling is that which has genuine dual non-infringing use and does not promote infringement or take affirmative steps to foster it.

Defences that may come to the rescue

Consent

There are no doubt a whole host of reasons that motivate people to set up their own website and home pages, and to make material available on them. One of these reasons must be that other users may access their material and that they feel they have something to say or to offer to these other users. The whole concept of an Internet, or any other network, is that a connection will be made with other people, with whom content will be shared.

From a legal point of view, this must mean that whoever makes material available on the Internet consents to the fact that others will access that material: there must be some kind of implied licence to do certain acts that are necessary to access the material. Such a licence must be non-exclusive in nature, because it is given on equal terms to all potential accessors of the material. Copyright law finds no problem with such a non-exclusive implied licence, because there is no ban on them and no written instrument is required for this type of licence. The licence can be implied from the way in which the dealings between the parties have been set up. In this respect, the whole set-up of the Internet points towards the conclusion that an implied licence must exist.[158]

The remaining problem is that it is not necessarily clear what can be done under such an implied licence. The starting point seems uncontroversial: it must be a licence for any Internet user to access the material on the site and to perform all acts of copying that are necessary to gain access. Any intermediary provider of services must be allowed to transmit the material and to make transient copies, in so far as this is required from a technical point of view. It is less clear whether the user can download the accessed material onto any hard disk, CD, etc., whether he or she can print it, and whether he or she can make any further use of the material. It is submitted that this depends on the type of material that is accessed and the type of site on which it is found.

The starting point must be that the Internet medium does not change the basic rules of copyright. Any material that qualifies for copyright protection will still be protected when it is made available on the Internet. Users are licensed to access the site on which the material is contained in the same way as they are licensed to read a book, or to play a CD or videotape. Copying or any other restricted act requires a further licence. That further licence can only be implied if it is clear, from the type of material or from the type

---

[156] *MGM v. Grokster* 545 US 913 (2005), Supreme Court, 27 June 2005, overruling *MGM & ors v. Grokster & Streamcast*, US Court of Appeals for the Ninth Circuit, judgment of 19 August 2004.

[157] Ibid. at 10–24.

[158] Compare MacQueen (1997) pp. 89–90.

of site, that further use is intended, or at least authorized. That can be derived from the fact that the material on the site has no use through access only and that further potentially infringing acts are required for its use. For example, pieces of software are clearly not intended to be read on a computer screen, and must therefore come with an implied licence to download and to use, while poetry or other texts can be read on the screen and need not be downloaded before proper access to them can be gained. Sites that are labelled 'shareware' clearly come with an implied licence to copy the material on them and to make further use of the material. The only limitation on such further use may be that the product can only be used as such and in its entirety under the implied licence: maybe it is only a licence to share the original product with other interested users, even if that sharing can be undertaken on a commercial basis.[159]

Notices

It is submitted that notices on sites can obviously change the pattern. The site owner can license any other users to make use of the material in a particular way and that may even take the form of a blanket licence to do anything with the material. Obviously, a site owner can only waive rights through such a licence in so far as he or she possesses these rights him or herself. For example, he or she cannot waive copyright in material on a site in which he or she does not own the copyright, unless he or she is authorized by the right owner to do so. Alternatively, certain, or all, types of use may explicitly be prohibited or made subject to a further authorization. A clear notice that certain materials or certain rights in them are for sale, or the presentation of the site as a commercial trade catalogue must be seen as an example of the latter reservation of rights. Certainly, the use of notices on sites would provide a far greater degree of transparency and clarity than that which is currently available on the Internet.

Addresses and search engines

The copying of site addresses and the use of search engines raises further issues. Sites are created in order for access to them to be gained: this must mean that an implied licence is given to any user to copy the address of the site onto the hard disk of his or her computer, in order to gain easy access to that site on a future occasion. Copying undertaken by search engines must also be allowed under an implied licence, in so far as it is necessary to facilitate access to the site. The access aim of the creator of the site can only be realized through the use of search engines, due to the untransparent technical structure of the Internet.

Hypertext links to other sites are covered by the implied licence for the same reason that any facilitation of access needs to have been intended. Obviously, this only covers the pure signposting function: all that is covered is the provision of access to the other site as such. The implied licence does not allow any site owner to put in place a system that allows access to other sites, while the frames of the first site are retained. It must be access to the other site as it is, and in its complete and original form. All the aspects of the implied licence that have been described in this paragraph apply only to addresses and titles, in so far as the latter are protected by copyright in the first place for obvious reasons.[160]

Fair dealing

The fair dealing defence to copyright infringement[161] may also be used in an Internet context. It may be fair dealing for the purposes of research and private study to make

---

[159] See the Australian case *Trumpet Software Pty Ltd v. OzEmail Pty Ltd* [1996] 12 EIPR 69.

[160] See, e.g., *Exxon Corp. v. Exxon Insurance Consultants International* [1982] Ch 119; aff'd [1982] RPC 81.

[161] CDPA 1988, ss. 29 and 30.

hard or electronic copies of a certain part of the material that the user accesses on the Internet, but the constraints of the defence apply here, as in any other copyright context. It must, for example, be the user's own research and private study that is facilitated, and it may be difficult to justify the copying of whole works. Copying materials from other websites to put them on your own site is clearly something that is not exempted by this defence.

Fair dealing for the purposes of review and criticism can also be used as a defence, but, in this respect, a fair level of review and criticism is required. The amount of copying must be justifiable in comparison with the amount of commentary.

Time shifting

The 1988 Act also allows a broadcast to be viewed at a time that is more convenient to the viewer.[162] This 'time shifting' exception might be pleaded by the users of a website who copied its contents, but only in those now-very-limited cases in which the site comes within the definition of a broadcast.

Technical protection measures (TPMs)

The Information Society Directive also put in place new measures concerning technical measures and rights management information,[163] which are intended to reinforce copyright and related rights protection in the electronic and digital environment. The implementation of these measures into English law has already been discussed in the chapters on copyright and related rights, and will not be repeated here.[164]

Semiconductor chip protection

Introduction

Semiconductor chips are integrated circuits, usually made out of layers of materials that are conductive to a different extent. In most cases, some layers are not conductive at all, while other layers are made out of semiconductive materials, such as silicon. The production of these chips involves an etching process, whereby photographically made masks are used; these masks determine the final wiring of the chip.

It was not immediately clear which intellectual property right should be used for the protection of semiconductor chips and what exactly would be the subject of protection. The latter issue was solved when it was decided to protect the topography of the integrated circuit, rather than the chip itself. Because it was dissatisfied with the protection offered by the conventional intellectual property rights and after intense lobbying by the chip industry, the USA became the first country to enact a statute that provides a *sui generis* intellectual property right that covers semiconductor chips.[165] The European Community followed suit and a Directive[166] obliged the member States to introduce protection for

---

[162] Ibid., s. 70.

[163] Articles 6 and 7 of the Information Society Directive.

[164] See also *Kabushiki Kaisha Sony Computer Entertainment Inc. (also t/a Sony Computer Entertainment Inc.), Sony Computer Entertainment Europe Ltd & Sony Computer Entertainment UK Ltd v. Gaynor David Ball & ors* [2004] ECDR 323.

[165] Semiconductor Chip Protection Act of 1984, Pub L No 98–620, Title III, Stat 3347 (codified at 17 USC 901–914, Supp II 1984).

[166] EC Council Directive on the legal protection of topographies of semiconductor products (1987) OJ L 24/36.

topographies of integrated circuits. Most member States created a *sui generis* right, while the UK decided to offer protection via the design right.

The Design Right (Semiconductor) Regulations 1989[167]

The Design Right (Semiconductor) Regulations 1989 rely upon the provisions in the 1988 Act for the design right and add a number of special provisions to them to protect semiconductor topographies. A design is further defined as:

(a) the pattern fixed, or intended to be fixed, in or upon—

    (i) a layer of a semiconductor product, or

    (ii) a layer of material in the course of and for the purpose of the manufacture of a semiconductor product, or

(b) the arrangement of the patterns fixed, or intended to be fixed, in or upon the layers of a semiconductor product in relation to one another.[168]

A semiconductor product is, in turn, defined as:

an article the purpose, or one of the purposes, of which is the performance of an electronic function and which consists of two or more layers, at least one of which is composed of semiconducting material and in or upon one or more of which is fixed a pattern appertaining to that or another function.[169]

A semiconductor topography that forms such a design is only protected if it is original and, as is usual for designs, it will not be original if it is commonplace in the relevant design field at the time of its creation. There is also a qualification requirement.[170] Its only noticeable difference with that for designs is that any sale or hire, or any offer or exposure for sale or hire, that is subject to an obligation of confidence[171] is to be taken into account when qualification through first marketing is examined.

A semiconductor topography design that satisfies these requirements is owned in the same way as any other design right, apart from the fact that commissioners and employers do not have to be qualifying persons.[172] The term of protection normally expires ten years after the end of the year in which the design was first commercially exploited anywhere in the world. Exceptionally, the design right expires 15 years from the time at which the topography was first recorded in a design document or from the time at which an item was made to the design, whichever is the earliest. This rule will apply in cases in which the design is not exploited within 15 years of the creation of the topography.[173]

In general, the provisions on primary and secondary infringement are similar to those that generally apply to design rights, but the Regulations introduce some particular provisions. Anyone can freely reproduce the design privately for non-commercial purposes[174] and '*the reproduction of a design for the purpose of analysing or evaluating the design or analysing, evaluating or teaching the concepts, processes, systems or techniques embodied in it*'[175] will not infringe the design right in the topography. But the most interesting departure from the traditional design rules is the introduction of a provision that allows for the reverse engineering of a semiconductor design right. Regulation 8(4) states that it is not an infringement of the semiconductor design right to create another original

---

[167] The Design Right (Semiconductor Regulations) 1989, SI 1989/1100.
[168] Ibid., reg. 2(1).   [169] Ibid.
[170] Ibid., reg. 4.   [171] Ibid., reg. 7.
[172] Ibid., regs 4 and 5.   [173] Ibid., reg. 6.
[174] Ibid., reg. 8(1).   [175] Ibid.

topography on the basis of the outcome of the reverse analysis and evaluation of an exist-ing semiconductor design. This exception even includes the making of a copy of that existing semiconductor design.[176] This exception is, however, narrow in scope, because it will only apply if the new design meets the originality requirement.

Two minor provisions should also be mentioned here. The exhaustion doctrine is appli-cable in relation to semiconductor designs,[177] while licences of right, which are normally available during the last five years of the term of design protection, are not available in relation to semiconductor designs.[178]

An overview

The presence of several pages dealing with the issue of how computer technology can be brought under the intellectual property umbrella can be explained in two ways. The first, easy explanation is that computer technology is not easy to understand and that it is appropriate to give more detail in relation to how it fits in with intellectual property. A difficult example simply needs more explanation.

The second explanation is that computer technology does not fit into any of the existing intellectual property rights and that all attempts to make it fit distort the existing catego-ries of intellectual property rules. From this point of view, *sui generis* regimes need to be created for the various aspects of computer technology if the long-term effectiveness and viability of intellectual property is not to be undermined.

The relatively smooth interaction between copyright and software seems to support the first explanation, while the *sui generis* approach taken in relation to databases and semiconductor chips seems to support the second. It is, indeed, not possible to regard the semiconductor design right as a 100 per cent normal design right; it is submitted that it is, at present, not possible to choose between both explanations. But it is clear that computer technology raises a series of complex and challenging questions in relation to intellectual property.

Further reading

BOOTON, D., 'The patentability of computer-implemented inventions in Europe' (2007) 1 IPQ 92.

DERCLAYE, E., 'Database *sui generis* right: what is a substantial investment? A tentative def-inition' (2005) 36 Int Rev IP & Comp L 1, 2.

DERCLAYE, E., 'The Court of Justice interprets the database *sui generis* right for the first time' (2005) 30 Eur LR 3, 420.

FAWCETT, J. and TORREMANS, P. (1998) *Intellectual Property and Private International Law*, Oxford: Clarendon Press.

FLINT, D., 'Computers and Internet: making the news' (2007) 28 Bus LR 2, 34.

LLOYD, I. (2004) *Information Technology Law*, 4th edn, Oxford: Oxford University Press.

REED, C. and ANGEL, J. (eds) (2007) *Computer Law*, 6th edn, Oxford: Oxford University Press.

---

[176] Ibid., (4).   [177] Ibid., (2).   [178] Ibid., reg. 9.

31
Character merchandising

The topic of character merchandising is one of great commercial significance, but one that, as yet, has received only limited legal recognition in the UK.[1] We are concerned with rights in 'character'—another vague concept that the law has to struggle to turn into something tangible[2]—and such rights can take two forms. A right in character might be seen as the private right of an individual to develop and protect his or her own character, which is really an issue that falls within the ambit of any tortious protection of privacy, a topic on which tort lawyers wail endlessly and, so far, fruitlessly. It falls outside the ambit of a work such as this, unlike the other forms of character right, which relate to the commercial exploitation of a character and its attributes.

The commercial exploitation of character is the antithesis of privacy. Far from wishing to keep quiet about one's character, the character merchandising industry is devoted to its, at times, ruthless exposure. No self-respecting rock star would nowadays dream of giving a concert without ensuring the supply at the venue of T-shirts and other souvenirs; a celebrity can command fees for showing his or her home to the excited readers of *Hello!* magazine or for telling amusing tales of past antics to a talk show host. The entire Disney industry shows the value of successful character merchandising activity.

As a broad generalization, it may be argued that the whole development of intellectual property law has been as a response to commercially important activity that has merited legal protection. Thus patent law grew as a response to growing industrialization, while copyright's expansion has reflected the growing importance of, and differing forms of, mass media. As yet, however, character merchandising does not have much in the way of specific recognition in UK law in spite of the eloquent arguments of Frazer[3] that there should be a statutory tort giving a right of protection to a victim of the unlawful appropriation for commercial purposes of aspects of character, such as name, image, or voice. Indeed, the recent review of the law on trade marks, faced with the opportunity of creating a form of character right, declined so to do, claiming that so to do would create '*legal or administrative difficulties disproportionate to any problems that it would obviate*'.[4]

Faced with this refusal to address their concerns directly, the character merchandising industry—because it is an industry—has to seek legal protection in the form of the adaptation of other intellectual property rights and their application to the merchandising

---

[1] See T. Frazer, 'Appropriation of personality: a new tort?' (1983) 99 LQR 281; J. Holyoak, 'UK character rights and merchandising rights today' [1993] JBL 444; H. Carty, 'Character merchandising and the limits of passing off' [1993] LS 289.

[2] See J. Adams (2007) *Merchandising Intellectual Property*, 3rd edn, Haywards Heath: Tottel; H. Ruijsenaars (2003) *Character Merchandising in Europe*, New York: Aspen.

[3] (1983) 99 LQR 281.

[4] Cm 1203, para. 4.43.

field. It may be that statutory protection would be a simpler approach, but, equally, it will be seen that, taken overall, a fair range of protection is provided and we are now at a stage where the number of worthy cases that will slip between the gaps between the various intellectual property rights that may be relevant to a character merchandising situation will be few indeed.

In assessing the way in which copyright, trade mark law, and various torts combine to confer legal protection on character merchandising, it is important at the outset to point to an important distinction between two types of character. Merchandising may take place in relation to either a real character (or characters)—Madonna or Take That, for example—or in relation to a fictitious character—such as Noddy or Superman—but the key distinction is that copyright is only relevant to the latter category. It is thus sensible to look at ways in which the law can protect *any* type of character merchandising before returning to the specific issue of fictitious characters.

Trade mark law

Clearly, many characters will be associated with an image and this, if distinctive, may very well form part of the character merchandising activity. If de facto distinctive, then, of course, that image will be able to attract the protection of registration as a trade mark under the Trade Marks Act 1994. Pictures of celebrities, their real names or nicknames, their caricatures, or representations of objects associated with them—such as Dame Edna Everage's spectacles—could all be protected in this way.

Hurdles of the past

In the past, however, relatively little use was made of trade marks in this way. The likely reason for this was the prohibition, by s. 28(6) of the Trade Marks Act 1938, of trafficking in trade marks by disallowing the registration of any mark used for trafficking. This was considered by the House of Lords in *Re Hollie Hobby Trade Mark*,[5] in which the image of a winsome small girl, originally in use on greeting cards, was the subject of considerable licensing activity with other traders so that goods, such as toys and toiletries, could be made featuring the girl's image. Unfortunately, this perfectly legitimate commercial activity could not be protected by trade mark law. The House of Lords was clear that, to its regret, this was trafficking, described by Lord Brightman as:

> dealing in a trade mark primarily as a commodity in its own right and not primarily for the purpose of identifying or promoting merchandise in which the proprietor of the mark is interested.[6]

Most characters do not want to get their hands dirty in making the merchandise themselves, and it is normal and sensible for the exploitation to be carried out by others under licence. The *Hollie Hobby* case denied the protection of trade mark registration to this typical example of valuable commercial activity. This was unacceptable, so the White Paper on *Trade Mark Reform* that presaged the 1994 Act recommended that s. 28(6) should be repealed. The 1994 Act contains no reference to the problem of trafficking and a simplified licensing system now applies to trade marks.[7]

---

[5] [1984] RPC 329.
[6] Ibid. at 356.
[7] Trade Marks Act 1994, ss. 28–31.

A bright future?

The future of the trade mark approach to character merchandising thus looks promising, at least from the viewpoint of the celebrity who is actively engaging in merchandising activity. The emphasis in the 1994 Act on distinctiveness accords with the desire of the marketing expert to accentuate the distinctive. It seems likely that many other celebrities will follow—for example, Paul 'Gazza' Gascoigne may obtain trade mark registration, in that case for his nickname, to help with lucrative merchandising activity. Others who may seek to register the character as a mark will be likely to fall foul of the provisions in s. 3(3) and (6) preventing deceptive marks and marks sought in bad faith from being registered.

But such non-authorized use may prevent the character him or herself from registering a descriptive type of mark as being not distinctive enough for the purposes of the proviso to s. 3(1)(c) of the 1994 Act, if personal origin is regarded as within that subsection. Geographical origin is seen as descriptive as are 'other characteristics' and it must at least be arguable that personal origin is a factor belonging in this subsection. This could mean that earlier unauthorized use could prevent the registration of a trade mark in legitimate character merchandising activity.

Hurdles of the future

The requirement of distinctiveness could prove to be the major hurdle. This was already clear in the *Elvis Presley* case,[8] even though that case was still decided under the 1938 Act. Laddie J emphasized that distinctiveness means that the trade mark must enable the consumer to distinguish the goods of one trader from the similar goods of another trader. In his view, the use of the names 'Elvis' and 'Elvis Presley' did not provide the consumer with an indication concerning the origin of the product; the name of the celebrity was rather the subject matter of the goods. Laddie J did not accept that the consumer would expect that a product bearing either of the marks originated from Elvis Presley Enterprises Inc., the company that had applied to register the marks. Most people would buy the product because it had the name of the celebrity on it and would not bother about the origin of the product. That conclusion was reinforced by the fact that other manufacturers did de facto manufacture and sell Elvis Presley memorabilia, without there being any indication that the consumer believed that these products originated from Elvis Presley Enterprises. The judgment indicates that similar problems would arise in relation to the registration of the Elvis Presley signature as a trade mark. It is also clear from the emphasis on distinctiveness that the approach taken in this case will also apply under the 1994 Act.

The judgment in the *Elvis Presley* case can be criticized for its refusal to accept that the public is aware of these merchandising activities. One could, indeed, argue that the public may, in certain circumstances, believe that a product that is labelled with the name of a celebrity originates from a producer that has been approved by the celebrity.[9] The celebrity's name could then distinguish these products from similar products (not featuring the name) made by other traders. In those cases, the application to register the celebrity's name as a trade mark may be able to pass the distinctiveness hurdle, but the facts of the *Elvis Presley* case make it clear that the situation was quite different in that case.

---

[8] *Re Elvis Presley Trade Mark* [1997] RPC 543, affirmed on appeal *Elvis Presley Enterprises Inc. v. Sid Shaw Elvisly Yours* [1999] RPC 567.

[9] See, indirectly, *Re Anne Frank Trade Mark* [1998] RPC 379 (a Trade Mark Registry case).

Laddie J did accept that someone might be able to build up a reputation and goodwill in a celebrity name in the course of trade. But that will not be easy: a very famous name—such as Diana, Princess of Wales, or Jane Austen—was held to trigger such a strong reference to the celebrity involved that it would, in normal circumstances, outweigh any acquired distinctiveness in relation to merchandise sold under that name. Any trade mark registration will therefore depend on evidence being provided that the name now (also) fulfilled the function, in the eyes of the public, of guaranteeing that items bearing it had originated under the control of a single undertaking responsible for their quality; otherwise, any use of the name to endorse a product would not be a trademark use.[10] Or as Lord Justice Simon Brown put it in the *Elvis Presley* case:

> there should be no a priori assumption that only a celebrity of his successors may ever market (or licence the marketing of) his own character. Monopolies should not be so readily created.[11]

Evidence that the character works as a proper trade mark in terms of distinctiveness as to origin will need to be provided, including proof that the celebrity aspect does not take the upper hand. In any case, a name of character cannot be registered if the goods are seen to be 'mere image carriers'. What is being sold then is, in essence, the name or the character and any trade mark would then not be a mark, but would instead refer to the goods themselves in a descriptive way. It must therefore fail by lack of distinctiveness.[12]

Even if a trade mark is eventually secured, the celebrity aspect may still pose a risk. The European Court of Justice argued, in the *Picasso* case,[13] that, because the name Picasso was so famous, the public would recognize it immediately—but they would also immediately notice the difference with a slightly different sign, here 'Picaro'. The Picasso trade mark could therefore not oppose the registration of the Picaro mark. The more well-known the name is, therefore, the narrower the scope of the trade mark protection will be as against similar marks. This comes on top of the already lower distinguishing capacity in relation to the goods for which it is registered in those circumstances.

Assigning trade marks that consist of the names of well-known individuals is, however, well accepted. The public does not expect the famous person to be involved with any aspect of the business or to stay involved indefinitely. The mark can be assigned with the business to a third party without there necessarily being a risk of revocation, because the public is being misled even in those circumstances in which the celebrity whose name is used as a trade mark (for example, a fashion designer) is no longer involved.[14]

Design law

In some cases, the two design rights may be appropriately used to protect character merchandising. Under the Registered Designs Act 1949, a design can be registered for the appearance of the whole, or a part, of a product resulting from the features of, in particular, the lines, contours, colours, shape, texture, or materials of the product, or its ornamentation.[15] The production of a coffee mug shaped so as to depict the facial

---

[10] *Diana, Princess of Wales Trade Mark* [2001] ETMR 25; *Jane Austen Trade Mark* [2000] RPC 879 (two Trade Mark Registry cases).

[11] *Elvis Presley Enterprises Inc. v. Sid Shaw Elvisly Yours* [1999] RPC 567, at 597.

[12] See also *Linkin Park LLC's Application* [2005] ETMR 17.

[13] Case C361/04 P *Ruiz-Picasso v. OHIM* [2006] ECR I-643, [2006] ETMR 29.

[14] Case C259/04 *Elizabeth Emanuel v. Continental Shelf 128 Ltd* [2006] ECR I-3089, [2006] ETMR 56.

[15] RDA 1949, s. 1.

feature of a well-known personality would fit easily within this definition. Similarly, such an object could fall within the newer unregistered design right created by s. 213 of the Copyright, Designs and Patents Act 1988—but this expressly excludes surface decoration, so a mug bearing only a picture of a celebrity would not qualify for this right, although it would appear to be within the registered design right. A mug shaped in the form of the face of a celebrity could also be the subject of an unregistered design right. In each case, it is an item, or features thereof, that are the subject of the right and this obviously limits the use of these rights to a small proportion of merchandising activities.

Tort

Passing off

Prior to the passage of the new trade marks legislation, it was the tort of passing off that did most to protect the commercial exploitation of character by merchandising. It seems likely that this tort will continue to function in this area, although, in the future, it will be overshadowed more by trade mark law. It is nonetheless only relatively recently that the tort of passing off has come to play a role in this field, having been held back for some time.

The common field of activity hurdle

The problem previously was that it was generally thought that, for liability to exist, the parties must be working in a common field of activity. So an action would be between two rival clothing manufacturers, but not between a celebrity and a clothing manufacturer, even if the celebrity wanted to engage in merchandising activity involving clothing.

This was used to prevent a claim from succeeding in respect of authorized character merchandising as long ago as 1947. In *McCulloch v. Lewis A May (Produce Distributors)*,[16] the claimant was a well-known children's broadcaster, known as 'Uncle Mac'. As a BBC employee at that time, involvement with anything so sordid as commerce was out of the question, so he was doubly appalled when the defendant began selling 'Uncle Mac's Puffed Wheat' without permission. The breakfast cereal was advertised in such a way as to associate closely the product and the celebrity. Wynn-Parry J found against the claimant: he was a broadcaster, not a cereal manufacturer, and there was thus no common field of activity and no passing off claim.

This approach was resolutely adhered to by the UK courts. In *Lyngstad v. Anabas Products*,[17] an attempt to prevent the sale of unauthorized Abba merchandise was unsuccessful on this ground, in spite of the fact that Abba had developed a sizeable merchandising trade alongside their musical activities. Similarly, in *Tavener Rutledge Ltd v. Trexapalm Ltd*,[18] the supposed lack of common field of activity was enough to defeat an attempt to prevent the sale of 'Kojakpops' lollipops designed to evoke the image of Kojak, a popular, lollipop-sucking, television detective. This was especially ironic, because, by being first in the field, the unauthorized trader was able to prevent a properly licensed manufacturer from putting 'Kojak lollies' on the market. Law and commercial reality were not working hand in hand at this stage of the law's development.

[16] [1947] 2 All ER 845.
[17] [1977] FSR 62.
[18] [1977] RPC 275.

A way forward emerges

The Australian courts soon showed the way forward. In *Henderson v. Radio Corp. Pty Ltd*,[19] the High Court of New South Wales rejected the *McCulloch* approach and allowed two well-known dancers to prevent the unauthorized use of their picture on the cover of a record of dance music. Particularly instructive is *Children's Television Workshop Inc. v. Woolworths (NSW) Ltd*.[20] In this case, the claimants had rights in the characters from *The Muppet Show* and they were able to prevent the sale by the defendants of unauthorized Muppet memorabilia by demonstrating that they had their own merchandising operation, and that, although it was conducted on a licensed basis, they continued to exercise close quality control over it. It was also relevant that the public were aware of the merchandising link and, in particular, of the existence of quality control.

Slowly, then, the UK courts have come to grips with the phenomenon of character merchandising. An important first stage was recognition of the practice and, with it, recognition that of public awareness. This came in *IPC Magazines Ltd v. Black & White Music Corp. Ltd*,[21] in which the proprietors of a magazine featuring the exploits of Judge Dredd sought protection against the release of a pop record featuring the fabled jurist. Although no injunction was awarded (damages at full trial being thought to be an adequate remedy), Goulding J was prepared to recognize that the public would assume that the claimants had, in some way, authorized the record. In other words, once it is realized that character merchandising does go on and that the public have realized that, for example, not every Abba sweatshirt was personally knitted by one or other of the Swedish superstars, but that Abba are nevertheless trading in sweatshirts as well as songs, the celebrity has goodwill that the tort of passing off can protect in not only songs and records, but also in sweatshirts. This reflects the modern reality that many films, shows, or items are nowadays launched as a package in which the revenue from merchandising activity is as important as that derived from the entertainment performances. There is no point launching, for example, a new pop group into the world to great acclaim if you have no souvenirs to sell to their excited fans and, in practice, these will be already in the warehouse.

Recognition of a role for passing off

The recognition of broader ideas of goodwill in these claims and the more general renewed emphasis on goodwill in the *Jif Lemon* case[22] all help the use of the tort of passing off in character merchandising situations, but formal recognition of its role at last transpired in *Mirage Studios v. Counter Feat Clothing Co.*,[23] in which the use of images of the Teenage Mutant Ninja Turtles on clothing was at issue. The launch of the Turtles was a classic example of the development of an overall product in relation to which sales of merchandise were as significant as sales of the television programmes. It was thus clear that the claimants enjoyed goodwill in the clothing trade, as well as in the entertainment business. The knowledge of the buying public that properly licensed merchandising activity is common meant that there was a misrepresentation in the form of the unauthorized sales and that obvious damage could be envisaged to the trade of the claimants. Thus the elements of passing off were satisfied and an injunction granted. The earlier Australian cases were approved and the earlier English cases distinguished as being inappropriate to cases in which the claimant has copyright in the character and is already in the business

---

[19] [1969] RPC 218.
[20] [1981] RPC 187.
[21] [1983] FSR 348.
[22] *Reckitt & Colman Products Ltd v. Border Inc.* [1990] 1 All ER 873, [1990] 1 WLR 491.
[23] [1991] FSR 145.

of merchandising. In reality, it is unlikely that the 'no common field of activity' argument has any life in it.

Meanwhile, the Federal Court of Australia has gone yet further in the protection of character merchandising in *Pacific Dunlop Ltd v. Hogan*.[24] Paul Hogan, actor, comedian, and star of the film *Crocodile Dundee*, successfully brought an action against an advert for shoes that mimicked one particular scene in the film; the Hogan character in the advert wore similar clothes to those worn by Hogan in the film. It was held that Hogan, who himself appeared in many adverts and always in the role of 'a good-natured larrikin'[25] had a right to be protected against the unauthorized use of his character, because it would harm his own marketing opportunities. Hogan was trading not only as an actor and comedian, but as a general all-round celebrity and thus any activity deriving from his fame would be protected by the tort of passing off.

One further development in passing off is also relevant and perhaps accords with the *Hogan* case. As we have seen in an earlier chapter, the case of *Lego System Aktieselkab v. Lego M Lemelstrich Ltd*[26] allowed Lego to use the tort of passing off against another, but totally unrelated, user of the Lego name on the basis that the fame of Lego is such that anyone seeing the name would automatically assume, whatever the context, that it was the name of the renowned Danish toy brick manufacturer and any defects would be assumed to be its fault, thus risking harm to its reputation. This fits well into the character merchandising field. For example, an unauthorized dealer sells a Gordon Brown pen that often leaks; the public knows of the practice of character merchandising and thus blames Gordon Brown for the leaks. This would harm his current merchandising activity, if there were any, but, after *Lego*, the possible harm to any future merchandising activity will also be enough to sustain an action in passing off.

We have argued earlier that this is a tort bursting with vigour in recent years. Its application to character merchandising shows this well, if perhaps belatedly. The flexibility and adaptability of the common law afforded protection comparable to that which legislation might be expected to provide. Recently, however, fresh doubt was cast over the fact that the public is now aware of the practice of character merchandising—but, at the same time, Laddie J seemed to recognize in the *Elvis Presley trade mark* case[27] that it must be possible to use the name of a celebrity to market a product, and to build up a reputation and goodwill in that name in the course of trade.

This point receives additional support from the judgment in the *Alan Clark* case.[28] It was readily accepted in the latter case that Mr Clark had goodwill in his name, and that the passing off of the spoof diaries in the *Evening Standard* newspaper through the false attribution of authorship could lead to substantial damage to his reputation (and earnings) as a columnist and diarist. But Mr Clark had the advantage of a reputation as a writer and not only as a celebrity: it is no doubt still easier to succeed in an action in passing off if the goodwill relates specifically to the merchandising activity or to any other commercial activity, rather than only to the general reputation and goodwill that one acquires as a celebrity.

But the latter is also possible following the *Eddie Irvine* case,[29] in which Laddie J held that it was the purpose of the law of passing off to vindicate the claimant's exclusive right

---

[24]   (1989) 14 IPR 398.

[25]   Ibid. at 400.

[26]   [1983] FSR 155.

[27]   *Re Elvis Presley Trade Marks* [1997] RPC 543.

[28]   *Clark v. Associated Newspapers Ltd* [1998] 1 All ER 959.

[29]   *Irvine v. Talksport Ltd* [2002] FSR 943, upheld (while raising the amount of the damages) by the Court of Appeal [2003] 2 All ER 881.

to his goodwill and to protect it against damage. The law would therefore not allow others to use that goodwill so as to reduce, blur, or diminish its exclusivity. It followed from this that it was not necessary to show that the claimant and the defendant shared a common field of activity, or that the sales of products or services would be diminished either substantially or directly, at least in the short term. Instead, the essential point was to show a misrepresentation, because that element was required to enable the defendant to take advantage of the defendant's reputation. The unauthorized manipulation of a photograph of Mr Irvine, by means of which a Talksport Radio was put in his hand, and its subsequent use for publicity purposes amounted to such a misrepresentation, because it created the impression that Mr Irvine was endorsing Talksport Radio. This could affect Mr Irvine's goodwill and reputation, and the requirements for passing off were therefore met.

Defamation

We have, elsewhere in this book, noted the decision in *Tolley v. J S Fry Ltd*[30] that an amateur golfer could sue in defamation for the unauthorized use of his character in an advert that carried the implication that he had compromised his amateur status. This is clearly applicable to protect character merchandising activity, but its use is limited to those cases in which reputation is lowered. So it would be defamatory to create a false quote from the dean of the law faculty of a prestigious university apparently endorsing a pornographic magazine, but it was not appropriate for David Frost to use defamation law against a hotel that falsely claimed his endorsement, because no harm was done to his reputation thereby.[31]

Malicious falsehood

If character merchandising activity is already under way, it is easy to see how the unauthorized merchandising of poor quality goods could be seen by customers as being an attack on that activity by implication and, if false and denigratory, thus actionable in the tort of malicious falsehood. The use of this tort has, however, been considerably enhanced in the context of character merchandising by the notable decision in *Kaye v. Robertson*,[32] in which an injured actor was able to use the tort to prevent the publication of a true story about his condition in hospital after a serious accident. The basis of the decision was that publication would imply that the actor had consented; the tawdry context of the publication would be harmful to his image as a celebrity, but, more particularly, it would harm his own right to sell his story on his own terms for his own gain on his recovery. This loss then forms the necessary damage to complete the grounds for a claim.

The easier availability of injunctive relief was a key to Kaye's success in malicious falsehood rather than defamation. Another reason for preferring to use malicious falsehood is that, unlike in defamation, it is possible to obtain legal aid for it, a point highlighted in *Joyce v. Sengupta*.[33] A newspaper alleged that the claimant, Princess Anne's maid, had stolen embarrassing royal correspondence, but this was false. She was allowed to frame her claim in malicious falsehood in view of the obvious harm to her trade as royal servant caused by the inaccurate story.

These two cases show that malicious falsehood can be used against any falsity that may have the effect of harming the victim's trade and that, after *Kaye*, if the victim is a

[30] [1931] AC 333.
[31] Example cited in R. Wacks (1980) *The Protection of Privacy*, London: Butterworths, p. 167.
[32] [1991] FSR 62.
[33] [1993] 1 All ER 897, [1993] 1 WLR 337.

celebrity, it will be assumed that he or she is trading not only as, in that case, an actor, but also as a celebrity. This notion neatly parallels that in the *Crocodile Dundee* case. There remain, however, limits on the use of this tort. A celebrity who does not trade as such may have difficulty establishing that there is damage; the exception to this requirement, under s. 3 of the Defamation Act 1952, in cases of words calculated to cause pecuniary damage is also of no assistance to a claimant who is not using his or her celebrity status as the base of merchandising activity.

More seriously, there is a need to prove malice and this may be difficult if a trader honestly, but without authorization, puts good quality character merchandise on the market. In *Kaye*, however, it was asserted by Glidewell LJ that:

> malice will be inferred if it be proved that the words were calculated to cause damage and that the defendant knew when he published the words that they were false or were reckless as to whether they were false or not.[34]

False words may be equated to the act of merchandising goods falsely, attributing them as being authorized by the character in question, and, on this basis, it would seem that malice will be found to be present at least if the claimant is him or herself engaged in merchandising activity.

Copyright

Can traditional copyright concepts apply?

If we now confine our attention to fictitious characters, it is evident that copyright protection for artistic or literary works will be available. An unauthorized drawing of Donald Duck on a T-shirt will soon be met with a writ from the Disney organization; the creation of a character in the words of a book is the result of much literary effort, whether in putting together the stunts and wit that are Ian Fleming's James Bond, or the more refined characteristics that make up Agatha Christie's Miss Marple. The principal authority in this field is the decision of the House of Lords in *King Features Syndicate Inc. v. Kleeman*,[35] in which unauthorized merchandise was being sold exploiting the popular newspaper cartoon figure of Popeye. This merchandise was held to infringe the copyright in the Popeye character.

The case is particularly significant in so far as the drawings of Popeye were made by the defendant and were not direct copies of any of the claimants' drawings. Of course, they used the distinctive features of Popeye to ensure the necessary recognition essential for sales. The problems of using copyright in cases of imprecise copying were referred to in *Mirage Studios v. Counter Feat Clothing Ltd*,[36] in which the drawings of humanoid turtles were again not directly copied by the defendants. Although an interlocutory injunction was granted, it was by no means clear that, at trial, there would be no problem in saying that drawings of the concept of a humanoid turtle infringed copyright in the claimant's specific drawings. This is a classic example of the problems posed by the way in which copyright law will protect the expression of ideas, but not the ideas themselves.

Further problems arise in cases relating to the use of a fictitious name. Copyright is only granted to those who have exercised some degree of creative energy. Thus in *Exxon*

---

[34] [1991] FSR 62 at 67. Cf P. Milmo, W. V. H. Rogers, R. Parkes, C. Walker and G. Busuttil (2005) *Gatley on Libel and Slander*, 10th edn, London: Sweet and Maxwell, pp. 303 and 323.

[35] [1941] AC 417.

[36] [1991] FSR 145.

Corp. v. Exxon Insurance Consultants International Ltd,[37] the invented name 'Exxon' was not capable of copyright protection as being a highly artificial word that was not the product of creative endeavour, but it was conceded by Graham J at first instance[38] that a title could be registered for copyright if it has qualities or characteristics in itself. Lewis Carroll's 'Jabberwocky' is cited as an example in relation to which the name, coupled with the literary work in which it appears and the images evoked by it, is enough to justify the grant of copyright protection. In *Mirage Studios*, however, the name 'Ninja Turtles' alone was held not to be capable of copyright protection, so doubt remains as to the precise boundary of copyright protection of names. The general rule remains that there will be no copyright in a name as such, or in a signature.[39]

The image of a celebrity is also probably not capable of protection by copyright. The pop star Adam Ant used to wear distinctive face make-up, but this was not regarded as an artistic work for copyright purposes in *Merchandising Corp. of America Inc. v. Harpbond*.[40] Maybe a more permanent form of decoration would provide a different decision and it is clear, in general, that copyright provides a useful protection against the unauthorized merchandising of fictitious characters, particularly given the length of protection afforded.

False attribution

The moral right to object to the false attribution of authorship[41] may also assist celebrities, albeit in a defensive way. It can be used to stop the unauthorized use of the celebrity's name to suggest that he or she is the author of work with which no such link exists in reality. The successful use of this right by Alan Clark to stop the attribution to him—or at least that belief in the eyes of a substantial number of readers—of the spoof diaries that appeared without his authorization in the London *Evening Standard* newspaper demonstrates this point clearly.[42] The right cannot, however, be used positively to protect any form of merchandising activity.

An overview

Although no specific character protection right has been developed in the UK, this does not of itself dent the initial suggestion in this chapter that intellectual property rights develop in response to the need to protect commercially significant activity. As recently as when Frazer argued[43] that a new character right was needed, such an argument had more force than it does now. Since then, the law of trade marks has been amended to remove a key block to character merchandising activity's protection in law, while passing off has learnt to recognize the existence and importance of such activity in the *IPC* and *Mirage Studios* cases that, when coupled with the broad sweep of the *Lego* decision, give a far broader degree of protection than seemed likely a decade or so ago. Meanwhile,

---

[37] [1982] Ch 119; aff'd [1981] 3 All ER 241.
[38] [1982] Ch 119 at 131, [1981] 2 All ER 495 at 504. The decision was upheld by the Court of Appeal and nothing said there contradicts the approach of Graham J at first instance.
[39] *Re Anne Frank Trade Mark* [1998] RPC 379 (a Trade Mark Registry case); see also *Re Elvis Presley Trade Marks* [1997] RPC 543.
[40] [1983] FSR 32.
[41] CDPA 1988, s. 84.
[42] *Clark v. Associated Newspapers Ltd* [1998] 1 All ER 959.
[43] Frazer (1983).

the recognition that one can trade as a celebrity, in *Kaye*, gives further protection to the famous.

It may be argued that this patchwork of remedies is fine for the famous, but does not protect ordinary citizens from exploitation. The answer to this, once again, is the law's reflection of commercially important activity and the fact that there is no such commercial need for legal intervention. There is no need to protect Holyoak and Torremans from the unauthorized use of their names on T-shirts, because such a use has no commercial value (yet). There may be reasons related to personal privacy to extend protection, but these we leave to civil libertarians to debate. From our commercial standpoint, we would assert the need to take care in the formulation of any new law. It would be absurd if, for example, everyone on board a crowded paddle steamer had any right to prevent the sale, or demand a royalty from, a postcard showing the vessel heading into port.

It may be that a simple statutory move to create a character right would be beneficial in terms of simplicity and legal elegance—but the developments of the last two decades show that the law has become seized of the legal and commercial importance of character merchandising activity, and has moved to protect it in an entirely adequate manner.

Further reading

ADAMS, J. (2007) *Merchandising Intellectual Property*, 3rd edn, Haywards Heath: Tottel.

BEVERLEY-SMITH, H. (2002) *The Commercial Appropriation of Personality*, Cambridge: Cambridge University Press.

BEVERLEY-SMITH, H., OHLY, A. and LUCAS-SCHLOETTER, A. (2005) *Privacy, Property and Personality: Civil Law Perspectives on Commercial Appropriation*, Cambridge: Cambridge University Press.

MACLEOD, C. and WOOD, A., 'The *Picasso* case, famous names and branding celebrity' (2006) 17 Ent LR 1, 44.

RUIJSENAARS, H. (2003) *Character Merchandising in Europe*, New York: Aspen.

32

Franchising and intellectual property

The concept of 'franchising'

Franchising is typically a business situation in which a franchisee pays a franchisor for the use of the latter's name, reputation, and get-up, the exploitation of which will normally remain under the franchisor's control and supervision. 'Normally' is an important word here: there is no specific legal definition of a franchise; rather, it is up to the (presumably) freely contracting parties to define the nature and extent of their relationship.

In the most common situation, a common business format is developed by the franchisor. A series of intellectual property rights may substantially increase the value of this format: trade marks, know-how, copyrights, and, sometimes, even patents. This results in a package of rights, which is licensed by the franchisor, who wishes to establish a franchise network in which the franchisees trade under a common name in order to obtain an optimal return from the business format developed. Apart from paying a fee for the use of the common business format and the associated intellectual property rights, the franchisee undertakes to maintain and preserve the character of the franchise.

This system presents a major advantage to undertakings that lack the capital and/or the skills to undertake the eventually worldwide exploitation themselves: they become franchisors and their franchisees undertake the exploitation. But from the franchisee's point of view, the franchise system presents the advantage that it becomes possible to enter the market without having to invest in the creation of a business format and a name. The existing package and the business reputation of the franchise network reduce the risks for the franchisee. If the system operates properly, the market sees the beneficial arrival of new independent operators, who, in a sense, run their own business, while the control system put in place by the franchisor allows the consumer to get the same product with a standard quality level from each of these operators.[1] Recognition of trade names and a quality level guarantee are surely advantageous for the consumer, which means that a properly operated franchise system can be beneficial to all parties involved.

No one can deny the importance of franchising today. The 2007 NatWest/BFA Franchise Survey reveals that franchising is currently a £10.8bn industry in the UK which continues to expand. It is also likely that the sharing of capital burdens between the two sides of the agreement and the motivation of the often newly self-employed franchisee will combine to give the business a fighting chance in stormy economic times.

An enormous range of businesses are operated on a franchise basis. These may be large business ventures necessitating considerable investments: the Holiday Inn chain of international hotels is a franchise operation, as are the hundred or more Clarks shoe shops

---

[1] See R. Whish (1993) *Competition Law*, 3rd edn, London: Butterworths, p. 544.

around the UK. Many smaller operations, such as various domestic cleaning firms, are also run in this way. The provisions of the Business Names Act 1985[2] enable readers who wish to become franchise-spotters to track down their prey by insisting, inter alia, that premises operated by a business under a different name from that of the actual owner must identify the actual owner 'in a prominent position'. Thus, if I were to become the franchisee of a national fast-food chain, marketing my goods with reference to its name, I would need to identify my name, or that of my company, on the premises so used.

Franchising is a little-investigated area of the law.[3] This may, in part, be due to the relatively recent growth in its importance, but may also be due to the fact that the relevant legal rules emanate from a range of different sources.[4] As already indicated, contract law is of direct relevance to the creation and content of a franchising agreement, and particular care must be taken to avoid an agreement becoming void as being in restraint of trade. Similarly, the perils of the laws—both domestic and European—that exist to promote free competition must be borne in mind, because the interests of the parties to a franchising agreement will often lie in creating a monopoly. Last, but not least, the use of images, logos, and other marketing material as part of the franchisor–franchisee relationship gives rise to significant difficulties in intellectual property law and it is these issues, rather than those in other areas of law (in so far as they can be treated separately), with which we are concerned in this chapter.

Franchises and trade mark law

The starting point

How do the basic provisions of trade mark law, as outlined earlier in this book, help or hinder the franchisor and franchisee? The law in this area is equally applicable to services since the entry into force of the Trade Marks (Amendment) Act 1984. The first problem is the difficult question of who is the proprietor of the mark, given that the franchisor has created the trade marks that characterize the business—the logos of Colonel Sanders that haunt the shops of the Kentucky Fried Chicken chain worldwide are a good example to consider—while the franchisee, not the franchisor, is the person actually responsible for delivering the product and service. The mark is defined as '*any sign capable of being represented graphically which is capable of distinguishing goods or services of one undertaking from those of other undertakings*'.[5] The goods or services that are distinguished from those of other undertakings are the goods and services of the franchise chain, not those of the individual franchisee. Therefore the franchisor should apply for trade mark registration and become the proprietor of the trade mark.

Assignments

The simplest way forward is to assign the mark to the franchisee and this is perfectly permissible.[6] The problem here is clear, however: the franchisor who fully assigns the

[2] Section 4(1)(b).
[3] Although it is served well by: J. Adams and K. Prichard-Jones (2006) *Franchising*, 5th edn, Haywards Heath: Tottel; M. Abell (1989) *The Franchise Option*, London: Waterlow. See also M. Mendelsohn (2003) *International Encyclopedia of Franchising Law*, Richmond: Richmond Law and Tax.
[4] See, e.g., *Six Continents Hotels Inc. v. Event Hotels GmbH* (2006) 150 SJLB 1251.
[5] TMA 1994, s. 1(1).
[6] Ibid., s. 24.

mark assigns all of the rights associated with it and thus loses any rights in connection with it.[7] Under the Trade Marks Act 1938, the proprietor who did not use the mark him or herself could find that he or she was the victim of an action to strike out the mark on the grounds of non-use,[8] although, in the absence of any direct authority on the point in terms of franchising law, it seemed strongly arguable that use in the sense of being the basis of a franchising operation is still 'use in relation to goods' (albeit an indirect use) and therefore not attackable by these provisions. Successful non-use cases were typically those in which there was no current intention to trade[9] or to trade commercially.[10]

The new Trade Marks Act 1994 removes all doubt. Revocation of the trade mark is not possible if the trade mark has been used genuinely by the proprietor of the mark or with his or her consent.[11] The latter provision clearly applies to a franchising operation.

Licences

Trade mark legislation, however, offers a more specific method of protecting franchise operations. Under ss. 28 and 29 of the 1994 Act, it is possible to grant a licence, including an exclusive licence, to use a trade mark. This does not involve a transfer of the ownership of the trade mark, but it does normally result in use of the trade mark with the consent of the proprietor and thus steers clear of the sanction of s. 46. Such a transaction can be registered[12] and a licensee registered as such will obtain certain rights. The complicated provisions of s. 30 can be summarized as allowing the registered user to require the proprietor to act in relation to any infringement of the mark and allowing the user to institute, in default, an action him or herself. Exclusive licensees get the rights of an assignee and can therefore independently bring an infringement action.[13]

Trafficking

One hazard that need no longer be considered here is the issue of trafficking. Whereas the use of a trade mark purely as an item in its own right was not permissible under the provisions of the 1938 Act, the Trade Marks Act 1994 has repealed that provision and no longer refers to the issue.

Summary

In summary, it can be seen that the most appropriate way forward to protect a franchise agreement is to grant a licence to use the trade mark to the franchisee and to register that transaction, thus enabling the franchisee-licensee to share the protection already enjoyed by the franchisor against the outside world. The franchisee is not protected against the activities of the franchisor by this method and will have to look at the terms of the contract agreed between the parties for assistance in that respect. An exclusive license clearly offers more protection in this area, because it also excludes the use by the licensor-franchisor of

---

[7] But all kinds of partial assignments are possible: ibid., (2).
[8] TMA 1938, s. 26.
[9] For example, *Pussy Galore Trade Mark* [1967] RPC 265.
[10] For example, *Imperial Group Ltd v. Philip Morris* [1982] FSR 72.
[11] TMA 1994, s. 46(1).
[12] Ibid., s. 25.
[13] Ibid., s. 31.

the trade mark in the manner authorized by the licence.[14] In exceptional cases, it may be that a franchise operation will fall within the category of certification trade marks,[15] but this would not be common given the infrequency with which this type of mark is used in any situation, let alone a franchising situation.

It must be emphasized that failure by the franchisor to use either the assignment or licensing routes will leave the franchisee unprotected, because his or her use of the mark with the consent of the franchisor justifies the award of the mark to the franchisor[16] and not to the franchisee. A franchisee who has to face competition from a third party and who fails to gain the support of the franchisor to take action against that third party is unprotected by trade mark law, and will only find a remedy at common law.

Franchising and passing off

At the heart of any franchise relationship lies the concept of goodwill: the franchisee wishes to attract some of the goodwill created by the franchisor; likewise, the franchisor will wish to see his or her goodwill extended, and certainly not harmed, by the activities of the franchisee. In cases in which goodwill is mentioned, inevitably, the tort of passing off—the function of which is to protect goodwill—will become involved. But the key question is whose goodwill is at stake?

The position of the franchisor

The creator of the franchise is the most obvious candidate to be the owner of the goodwill and thus the claimant in a passing off action. That this is so is confirmed by the decision of the Privy Council in *J H Coles Pty Ltd v. Need*,[17] an appeal from Australia. Coles was a chain of stores, one of which was operated on a franchise basis by Need. The business relationship failed to endure and, eventually, Coles went into liquidation, while Need, now without authority, continued trading under the 'Coles' banner.

In his speech, Lord Wright identified the ability of Need to use the 'Coles' trading name as being a revocable licence to use the name as long as the business arrangement continued.[18] Given that the relevant licence had been revoked unequivocally by Coles, it was therefore clear that Need was now unlawfully passing himself off as being authorized to use the Coles name, and that this deception would prejudice Coles' reputation and goodwill. In passing, it is by no means obvious that Coles, being in liquidation, still enjoyed such reputation and goodwill, but the decision can be explained by reference to the fact that Coles's initial complaint was made prior to the sad demise of the business.

If the franchisor's goodwill is protected against the franchisee, it seems to follow inexorably that he or she will also be protected against outsiders. Protection by the tort of passing off is valuable to a franchisor, given the currently vigorous and expansionist nature of the action that, as we have seen,[19] is capable of extending its net to capture similar advertising campaigns and 'get-up' of goods by rival traders, and also will cover future trading areas by well-known names. All of these points may be of particular relevance in a franchise environment.

[14] Ibid., s. 29(1).   [15] Ibid., s. 50.
[16] Ibid., s. 32(3).   [17] [1934] AC 82.
[18] Ibid. at 87.   [19] See Chapter 28.

The position of the franchisee

A more problematic question is whether all of these benefits of a passing off action can also be enjoyed by the franchisee. Consider a far from implausible scenario: the Kentucky Fried Chicken fast-food store outlet in Leicester suddenly finds its business in serious decline, because a rival operation has started trading selling similar products, and using logos and other promotional material sufficiently similar to that of the Kentucky firm that an action in passing off appears viable. We have just seen that the franchisor is protected, but the loss is more likely to fall on the franchisee, whose immediate income will be reduced, but who may, depending on the precise terms of the franchise agreement, still have to pay fixed sums, perhaps based on pre-agreed turnover calculations for the franchise. In an ideal world, the contract between the parties may incorporate an appropriate term forcing the franchisor to act and providing for the franchisee to benefit from the fruits of that action—but such clauses do not appear to be in regular use.

Authority on the specific issue of franchisees' rights of action in passing off appears non-existent. The problem arises in the way in which the public recognizes and responds to the goodwill and reputation of the franchisor, from which the unknown (to the public) franchisee then indirectly benefits. It is clear, however, that there is no reason for an action in passing off to hinge on the identity of the victim of the tort.

In *Birmingham Vinegar Brewery Co. v. Powell*,[20] a dispute concerning two rival versions of a sauce called 'Yorkshire Relish', it was asserted that the failure of the defendant to identify himself as the manufacturer of the sauce was no bar to a successful action even though *'the customer does not know or care who the manufacturer is, but it is a particular manufacture that he desires'*.[21] It seems sensible to adopt a similar approach if the source of the claimant's goods or services is similarly confused, between franchisor and franchisee. It also seems compatible with the general approach of the courts that permits a passing off action by someone with only an indirect or partial involvement with the goods or services in question, and the solution suggested also appears to accord with good policy given the difficulties the franchisee may otherwise face.

In summary, that passing off protects the franchisor is undoubted; for the franchisee, the tort, in its currently vigorous form, appears capable of providing the necessary protection and it is clear that, to protect the financial and personal commitment of the franchisee, it should do so.

Franchising and other areas of intellectual property law

A franchising operation will often give rise to many of a wide range of intellectual property issues. The purpose of this section is to do little more than identify those areas, because, unlike in the previous sections of this chapter, we feel that there are no unique features that arise only in franchising situations. Most obviously, the creation of the identity of the franchise will often give rise to the possibility of copyright protection for the original work of the franchisor. This may cover logos, as artistic works, or advertisement copy, as a literary work, or promotional photographs or drawings. Of course, there would be no

---

[20] [1897] AC 710.
[21] Ibid., *per* Lord Halsbury LC at 713.

problem within a properly established franchise, because authorized use of copyright material by a licensed user does not amount to infringement.[22] Clearly, however, unauthorized use—even by a franchisee acting beyond his or her remit—would be an infringement. The various provisions protecting designs, as discussed in Chapters 21 and 22, are also potentially relevant on a similar basis.

Patent law may also provide an essential element in a franchising operation: I may invent a wonderful new type of dishwasher that can be taken from door to door to clean up after wild parties, but I may not have the energy or ability to set up a business to exploit this new wonder properly; I may well wish to set up a franchise operation so to do, which would be based, at its heart, on the franchisees being granted licences to operate the patented invention.

Finally, and briefly, much know-how and trade information will inevitably pass between franchisor and franchisee, and, subject to any specific contractual provision, obligations of confidentiality are inevitably likely to arise between them.

Franchising and competition law

It is inevitable that franchisees will seek some form of monopoly. There is no point in spending time and effort developing the franchise business if the franchisor has also contracted with your next-door neighbour, or another resident of the same town, region, or even country, depending upon the scale and type of business in question. Likewise, a franchisor will be keen to ensure that the franchisee will loyally devote him or herself to selling the franchisor's goods and services, and will not dilute the value of the franchise by also selling the goods and services of commercial rivals of the franchisor.[23] Terms to cover these sorts of problems are common in franchise agreements,[24] but are immediately confronted by UK and EU competition law, which seeks to limit anti-competitive monopolies.

The Treaty provisions

The Competition Act 1998 has remodelled UK competition law on the basis of the European Union's rules on competition, and it is therefore to Art. 81 of the EC Treaty and its application to franchise agreements that we now turn.

It is obvious that Art. 81 is relevant, because a franchise agreement can be an agreement that may affect trade between member States and has as its object or effect the prevention, restriction, or distortion of competition within the EU. The provisions of Art. 81 were first applied to a franchise agreement by the European Court of Justice in *Pronuptia de Paris v. Schillgalis*.[25] As is so often the case, the Article was invoked as a defence in contractual proceedings. Pronuptia de Paris—the franchisor—sued Mrs Schillgalis—the franchisee for Hamburg, Oldenburg, and Hanover in Germany—on the basis that her royalty payments were insufficient as compared to the royalty provisions of the franchise agreement.

---

[22] CDPA 1988, ss. 16(2) and 90.

[23] There may, however, be circumstances in which the franchisee will legitimately be pursuing another part of its business alongside the franchise: see *Fleet Mobile Tyres Ltd v. Stone* (2006) 150 SJLB 1150 (CA).

[24] Restrictive covenants limiting the freedom of activity of a former franchisee are common and also give rise to problems: see *Dyno-Rod plc v. Reeve* [1999] FSR 148; *Convenience Co. Ltd v. Roberts* [2001] FSR 625.

[25] Case 161/84 [1986] ECR 353, [1986] 1 CMLR 414; see J. Venit, '*Pronuptia*: ancillary restraints or unholy alliances' (1986) 11 Eur L Rev 213.

Mrs Schillgalis argued that Pronuptia could not rely on the franchise agreement, because that agreement was void as contravening Art. 81.

Firstly, the Court analysed the specific nature of a franchise agreement. In the Court's analysis, the transfer of intellectual property rights from the franchisor to the franchisee is not only relevant to distinguish a franchise agreement from more conventional distribution systems, but it is a vital element if a franchise agreement is to realize its main aim, which is to allow the franchisee to operate as an independent business that is using the franchisor's name and know-how. This implies that certain restrictions need to be imposed regarding the maintenance of the common standards of the franchise and regarding the protection of the intellectual property rights involved. The franchisor should, indeed, be able to impose common standards on all franchisees if the franchise system is to work effectively and to benefit from its main asset: the common business format, which is recognizable by the consumers and attracts them, because they are entitled to expect the same quality standards from each outlet. The protection of the intellectual property rights involved is equally essential, which requires the franchisor to impose certain restrictions upon the franchisee on top of the fee that is already paid by the franchisee for the use of the franchisor's know-how, trade mark, design, logo, and other intellectual property rights. As a result of its analysis, the Court reached the conclusion that these restrictions, which are imposed to maintain common standards and to protect intellectual property rights, did not fall within the scope of Art. 81(1). The Court indicated that these essential elements of a franchise agreement did not restrict competition at all.

In a second part of the judgment, the Court made it clear that only the essential elements described above fall outside the scope of Art. 81(1); restrictions that are able to partition the Common Market on a territorial basis are caught by Art. 81(1). Eventually, they may be granted exemption under Art. 81(3), but such an exemption is not available for restrictions imposing resale price maintenance. The latter restrictions are caught by Art. 81(1) and will not be granted an exemption on the basis of Art. 81(1).

We think this fairly favourable treatment of franchise agreements by the European Court of Justice can be explained by the high degree of integration that characterizes franchise agreements. Indeed, the commercial policy of the franchise network is essentially determined by the franchisor, as if it were one single business, although all franchisees run an independent business from a legal point of view. The Court clearly had in mind that one cannot compare a franchise network with its restrictions on competition to a series of independent businesses in free competition without taking into account that the alternative to the franchise network would probably be one single business with a whole series of outlets. Employees of the producer-franchisor would then simply replace independent franchisees and there would be no competition at all.

Individual exemptions

It is worth mentioning a number of individual decisions published by the Commission of the European Communities in which the Commission brought the main principles of the Court's ruling in the *Pronuptia* case into practice.[26] These decisions deal with territorial restrictions. The type of franchise agreements under which the franchisor manufactures or selects the goods that are sold by the franchisee was at the heart of the

---

[26] See Whish (1993) 598.

Pronuptia[27] and *Yves Rocher*[28] cases. In *Computerland*,[29] the Commission applied the principles laid down by the Court to a franchise agreement that provided only a distribution method and left the franchisee free to buy microcomputers wherever it wished.

The Commission was confronted, for the first time, with a service franchise in the *ServiceMaster* case.[30] Such franchises provide a common business format for the provision of services, rather than for the distribution of goods. In this case, services provided by the franchisee to commercial and domestic customers were related to housekeeping, cleaning, and maintenance. The Commission indicated that the same principles could be applied to this slightly different type of franchising agreement and granted an individual exemption.

The block exemption

Based on these individual decisions, the Commission drafted a block exemption for certain types of franchise agreement in 1988,[31] which remained in force until 31 May 2000. From 1 June onwards, franchising agreements were covered by the new wider Regulation dealing with vertical agreements.[32]

Franchise agreements are vertical in nature, because the franchisor and franchisee operate at different levels, and can therefore be described as 'suppliers' and 'buyers' in terms of the Regulation. It is therefore to the provisions of the Regulation that we now turn.

The Vertical Agreements Regulation 1999

The starting point is a very simple one. Regulation 2(1) exempts from the application of Art. 81(1) of the Treaty:

> agreements or concerted practices entered into between two or more undertakings each of which operates, for the purposes of the agreement, at a different level of the production or distribution chain, and relating to the conditions under which the parties may purchase, sell or resell certain goods or services.

This clearly covers most franchise agreements.[33]

Franchise agreements are additionally complicated by the fact that they involve, generally, a transfer of intellectual property rights to the franchisee. The Regulation exempts such transfers of or rights to use intellectual property rights, provided that they do not constitute the primary aim of the agreement and provided that they are directly related to the sale of goods or provision of services that forms the object of the franchise agreement. Any restrictions that are excluded under the Regulation can also not be brought back in via the exemption for intellectual property rights.[34]

---

[27] [1989] 4 CMLR 355, [1989] FSR 416.

[28] [1988] 4 CMLR 592, (1987) OJ L 8/49.

[29] [1989] 4 CMLR 259, (1987) OJ L 222/12.

[30] [1989] 4 CMLR 581, (1988) OJ L 332/38.

[31] Regulation 4087/88 (1988) OJ L 359/46, [1988] 4 CMLR 387 (with annotations by V. Korah). For a detailed analysis, see Chapter 28 of the second edition of this book.

[32] Commission Regulation (EC) 2790/1999 on the application of Art. 1(3) of the Treaty to categories of vertical agreements and concerted practices [1999] OJ L 336/21, reg. 12.The Regulation will remain in force until 31 May 2010: reg. 13.

[33] See also the special rules in reg. 2(4) for agreements entered into by competing undertakings.

[34] Regulation 2(3).

In its own guidelines on vertical restraints,[35] the Commission summarized the position as follows:

> The Block Exemption Regulation applies to vertical agreements containing IPR provisions when five conditions are fulfilled:
>
> - the IPR provisions must be part of a vertical agreement, ie an agreement with conditions under which the parties may purchase, sell or resell certain goods or services;
>
> - the IPRs must be assigned to, or for use by, the buyer [franchisee];
>
> - the IPR provisions must not constitute the primary object of the agreement;
>
> - the IPR provisions must be directly related to the use, sale or resale of goods or services by the buyer or his customers. In the case of franchising where marketing forms the object of the exploitation of IPRs, the goods or services are distributed by the master franchisee or the franchisees;
>
> - the IPR provisions, in relation to the contract goods or services, must not contain restrictions having the same object or effect as vertical restraints which are not exempted under the Block Exemption Regulation.[36]

In this way, the intellectual property rights involved are confined to playing the positive role of enhancing the operation of the franchise, and the distribution of goods and services that forms its aim.

The exemption has one major limitation: the market share of the supplier—that is, the franchisor or the supplier designated by the franchisor—cannot exceed 30 per cent of the relevant market on which the contract goods or services are sold.[37] The exemption does not apply above that threshold. Underneath the threshold, vertical restraints on the purchase, sale and resale of the goods and services within a franchising agreement—such as selective distribution, 'non-compete', or exclusive distribution—are exempted.[38]

Additionally, the exemption shall not apply to vertical agreements that, directly or indirectly, in isolation or in combination with other factors under the control of the parties, have certain restrictions as their object.[39] The first two of these have as their object the restriction of the franchisee's determining its prices freely, or the restriction of the territory into which, or the customers to whom, the franchisee may sell the contract goods or services. But the strictness of these provisions is relaxed somewhat: the franchisor-supplier is allowed to recommend a sale price or to impose a maximum sale price as long as this does not result in a fixed or a minimum sale price as a result of pressures or incentives from any of the parties. The territorial restriction, meanwhile, can be allowed in certain circumstances: a franchisee can be restricted in terms of active sales to its exclusive territory or customer group, as long as its customers are free to sell the goods on. A franchisee operating at the wholesale level can also be stopped contractually from selling to end users and sales by members of a selective distribution system to unauthorized distributors can also be ruled out.

Further restrictions have as their object the restriction of active or passive sales to end users by members of a selective distribution system that operates at retail level. Such vertical agreements are not exempted, but members of such a distribution system can be obliged to operate at approved places of establishment.

---

[35] Commission Notice, *Guidelines on Vertical Restraints* [2000] OJ C 291/1.
[36] Ibid., para. 30.
[37] Regulation 3.
[38] Guidelines, para. 200.
[39] Regulation 4.

Finally, restrictions that exclude cross-supplies between distributors within a selective distribution system will also place the vertical agreement outside the scope of the exemption.

Article 5 of the Regulation does not place vertical agreements as a whole outside the scope of the Regulation, but limits itself to specific obligations in such agreements that will not be allowed to benefit from the exemption. The main result of this provision in relation to franchise agreements is that non-compete obligations on the goods or services purchased by the franchisee will only be exempted when such an obligation is necessary to maintain the common identity and reputation of the franchised network. In such cases, there will also be no restriction on the duration of the non-compete obligation, as long as it does not exceed the duration of the franchise agreement itself.[40] The protection of the franchisee's know-how can also be allowed to impose further restrictions on the franchisee or ex-franchisee, but such restrictions need to be indispensable for that purpose and they can normally only run until one year after the franchise agreement has expired. The use and disclosure of know-how that is still secret and has not yet entered the public domain can, however, be restricted indefinitely.[41]

As is the case with the benefit of each of the block exemptions, the benefit of this Regulation can be withdrawn if a franchise agreement or any other vertical agreement would unduly restrict competition, even though it met the requirements of the Regulation. If the undue restrictions happen at Community level, it will be up to the Commission to withdraw the benefit of the Regulation from a specific agreement[42] and, if the undue restrictions occur at national level, that task and power will be left to the competent (competition) authority of the member State concerned.[43]

An overview

It is clear that franchise agreements can restrict competition and that competition law interferes with this type of agreement. Nevertheless, one can say that franchising is generally seen as a beneficial commercial system and that competition law only tries to stop the undue restrictions to competition that are not the rule, but clearly the exception. Trade marks are clearly at the heart of many franchising agreements. The Trade Marks Act 1994 facilitates the use of trade marks in this context and the law of passing off may still provide valuable assistance. Intellectual property law now offers adequate protection to what are often the most valuable assets of a franchising operation: its mark and the reputation linked to it. Any franchise agreement will, however, have to take account of competition rules and particularly of the Vertical Agreements Regulation.

Further reading

ABELL, M. (1989) *The Franchise Option*, London: Waterlow.

ADAMS, J. and PRICHARD-JONES, K. (2006) *Franchising*, 5th edn, Haywards Heath: Tottel.

MENDELSOHN, M. (2004) *International Encyclopedia of Franchising Law*, 2nd edn, Richmond: Richmond Law and Tax.

WIJCKMANS, F., TUYTSCHAEVER, F. and VANDERELST, A. (2006) *Vertical Agreements and the EC Competition Rules*, Oxford: Oxford University Press.

---

[40] Regulation 5(a); Guidelines, para. 200.   [41] Regulation 5(b).
[42] Regulation 6.   [43] Regulation 7.

33

Remedies in intellectual property litigation

Throughout this book, we have been pointing out the ways in which the various legal remedies can be used in relation to the various different intellectual property rights. In this chapter, we will give a relatively brief overview of the enforcement procedures that are used in relation to intellectual property rights, of the civil remedies that apply, and of some issues that arise in relation to the gathering of evidence in intellectual property cases.

Intellectual property rights are often applied for in many countries. In such cases, many of these rights may be involved in a single infringement action or similar infringing acts may have been committed in the various jurisdictions. Intellectual property rights are also increasingly exploited internationally; that exploitation may also give rise to transnational litigation. The interaction between intellectual property and private international law gives rise to complex issues, both at the jurisdictional level (which court will decide the case) and at the choice-of-law level (which law will that court apply). A full discussion of these issues would lead too far and we refer the reader to the full discussion of these issues that can be found in Fawcett and Torremans (1998).

Enforcement issues

Intellectual property rights can be enforced in four ways: civil actions are used most commonly; criminal proceedings, administrative proceedings, and measures of self-help complete the picture.

Civil actions

Despite a slight reservation for breach of confidence, most intellectual property rights can be characterized as property rights. The way in which that property right is affected in cases of infringement can consequently be described as tortious in nature. Essentially, what we are dealing with are torts committed against property. On top of that come the actions between assignors and assignees, and between licensors and licensees, some of which are contractual in nature, because the claim is not based on the infringement of the intellectual property right involved, but on a breach of the contractual provisions that had been agreed. This can lead to actions for breach of contract.

Infringing acts may also give reason for concern to licensees of intellectual property. But while it is obvious that the owner of the right is entitled to bring an action against the alleged infringer, the same cannot be said about the licensee. The starting point is that a licensee cannot sue for infringement and must rely on the owner of the intellectual property right to bring the action. Exceptionally, an exclusive licensee can bring the action. This possibility is subject to a number of restrictions.

1. It has only been made possible in relation to exclusive patent,[1] trade mark,[2] copyright,[3] and unregistered design[4] licences. Registered design licences and know-how licences, etc., are not covered by it.

2. The exclusive licence must be fully exclusive, in the sense that even the licensor cannot exploit the right in the area that has been allocated to the licensee.[5]

3. The licensor has to be joined as a party to the proceedings, normally as a claimant, or alternatively as a defendant.[6]

On the defendant's side one finds the alleged infringer: this is normally the person who performed the restricted act. Anyone who collaborates with that person in common design can be sued as joint tortfeasor.[7] An employer, but not someone who commissions a work, is vicariously liable for the infringement of intellectual property that an employee committed in the course of his or her employment, just as this is the case for any other tort. Such an employer is quite often a company, but also the real person behind the company, such as a company director, can be personally liable for torts committed on behalf of the company if he or she has ordered or procured their commission.[8]

All of these civil actions are normally brought before the Chancery Division of the High Court of England and Wales,[9] or before the Outer House of the Court of Session in Scotland. Actions that involve lower amounts of money can also be brought in the county court and there is now, in London, also a specialized patents county court.

This is primarily an area of domestic law—but the TRIPS Agreement imposes minimum standards on all contracting states and, now, the European Union (EU) has decided to harmonize this area of intellectual property law by means of an Enforcement Directive.[10] This move has been criticized,[11] but when the scope of the Directive was reduced, the changes to domestic law turned out to be minimal.[12]

Criminal proceedings

Criminal proceedings do not play an important role in the area of intellectual property. Some offences do, however, exist and these types of proceedings are specifically concerned with cases of infringement that are seen as particularly serious from a public policy point of view. Obvious examples are actions against copyright or trade mark pirates.

---

[1] Patents Act 1977, s. 67.

[2] TMA 1994, s. 31.

[3] CDPA 1988, s. 101.

[4] Ibid., s. 234.

[5] And it must exist when the writ is issued: *Procter & Gamble v. Peaudouce* [1989] FSR 180.

[6] See, e.g., CDPA 1988, ss. 102 and 235.

[7] See *Mölnlycke AB v. Procter & Gamble Ltd* [1992] RPC 21 at 29; *Unilever plc v. Gillette (UK) Ltd* [1989] RPC 583 at 608.

[8] *MCA Records v. Charly Records* [2002] FSR 401, [2002] EMLR 1 (CA).

[9] Within the Chancery Division of the High Court, the Patents Court deals with patent matters.

[10] European Parliament and Council Directive 2004/48/EC on the enforcement of intellectual property rights [2004] OJ L 195/16.

[11] W. R. Cornish, J. Drexl, R. Hilty, and A. Kur, 'Procedures and remedies for enforcing IPRS: the European Commission's proposed Directive' [2003] EIPR 447.

[12] The Intellectual Property (Enforcement, etc.) Regulations 2006, SI 2006/1027.

The commission of the kind of acts that amount to secondary infringement of copyright now also leads to criminal liability in the circumstances that are described in s. 107 of the Copyright, Designs and Patents Act 1988. The Act also makes provision for orders for delivery up[13] and for search orders[14] in this context. Infringing goods can be disposed of[15] and can be forfeited.[16]

In those cases in which both criminal and civil proceedings can be brought, the court cannot express a preference or make a choice. The right owner makes his or her choice when bringing the case either via civil or via criminal proceedings.[17] These offences can, in serious instances, be prosecuted summarily or on indictment.[18]

Counterfeiting of registered trade marks can also give rise to criminal liability. This will, for example, be the case if the trade mark, or a similar and confusing mark, is applied to goods or their packaging, if such goods are sold or offered for sale, or if such a sign is applied to packaging or labelling material.[19] The goods to which the mark is applied can obviously be goods within the class for which the mark has been registered, but other goods are also covered in cases of improper dilution.[20]

Other offences exist in relation to intellectual property registers. It is an offence to make, or cause to be made, false entries in the Trade Marks Register;[21] another offence covers the act of falsely representing a trade mark as registered.[22] Both of these types of offence also exist in relation to patents[23] and registered designs.[24]

In more general terms, the crime of conspiracy to defraud can also be committed in relation to intellectual property. This could, for example, be the case for those agreeing to try to bribe cinema employees into handing over copies of films that would subsequently be copied and released on video in an unauthorized way, because the conspirers seek to obtain a pecuniary advantage and they try to make others act contrary to their duties.[25] The crime also applies to cases in which the conspirers are proposing to acquire property, which could include intellectual property, dishonestly. The outcome of the attempt to obtain an advantage, or to make others act against their duties, or to acquire property is not particularly relevant, because it is the conspiracy element that counts, and neither is the fact that the infringement of the right amounts to an offence as such.

These criminal offences are hard to prove: the defendant must be shown to be guilty 'beyond reasonable doubt', rather than 'on the balance of probabilities' as is the case in most civil cases, and the type of *mens rea* must be that the defendant knew, or had reason to believe, that he or she was committing an infringing act or another offence.

---

13   CDPA 1988, s. 108.

14   Ibid., s. 109, as amended by Copyright, etc. and Trade Marks (Offences and Enforcement) Act 2002, s. 2. The latter Act also expanded the search order system to unauthorized decoders by inserting s. 297B into the CDPA 1988.

15   CDPA 1988, ss. 114 and 204 in relation to illicit recordings.

16   CDPA 1988, ss. 114A (infringing copies), 204A (illicit recordings), and 297C (unauthorized decoders)m inserted by Copyright etc. and Trade Marks (Offences and Enforcement) Act 2002, ss. 3–5.

17   *Thames & Hudson Ltd v. Designs & Artists Copyright Society Ltd* [1995] FSR 153.

18   CDPA 1988, ss. 107–110.

19   TMA 1994, ss. 92 and 93. The system of search warrants has also been added here as s. 92A by Copyright etc. and Trade Marks (Offences and Enforcement) Act 2002, s. 6. Section 92 does, however, require use of the mark as a trade mark; descriptive use is not covered: see *R v. Johnstone* [2003] FSR 748, [2003] 3 All ER 884 (HL).

20   TMA 1994, s. 92(4).

21   Ibid., s. 94.

22   Ibid., s. 95.

23   Patents Act 1977, ss. 109 and 110; see also s. 111.

24   Registered Designs Act 1949, ss. 34 and 35.

25   See *Scott v. Metropolitan Police Comr* [1975] AC 819.

Administrative procedures

Customs officers, trading standards authorities, advertising standards authorities, the Radio Authority, and the Independent Television Commission play an ancillary role in the enforcement of intellectual property rights. Only the role played by customs officers is really of great significance in relation to the main intellectual property rights.

At the request of the right holder, customs officers may arrest infringing imports at their point of entry. These infringing imports must either be infringing copies of literary, dramatic, or musical works, of sound recordings or of films,[26] or, in the case of trade marks, goods in relation to which the use of the trade mark would amount to an infringement.[27] These measures operate together with an EU Regulation to stop the release into free circulation of counterfeit goods.[28]

All of these procedures are based on an application by the owner of the right—that is, a 'tip-off', including a description of the goods[29]—and involve indemnification provisions. The EU Regulation gives the right holder ten days from notification of seizure to start full-scale infringement proceedings[30] and counterfeit goods are normally destroyed.[31]

Self-help

The 1988 Act gives the copyright owner an additional right that can be used as a self-help remedy. This is the only example of self-help in the intellectual property area and no equivalent to the general right of recaption for those that are entitled to the possession of chattels (tangible property) exists.

Section 100 of the 1988 Act enables the copyright owner or his agent to seize and detain infringing copies. A series of restraints quite rightly applies to this far-reaching right.

1. The infringing copy must be exposed, or otherwise immediately available, for sale or hire.[32]

2. No force may be used, and advance notice of the time and place of the proposed seizure must be given to a local police station.[33]

3. In any event, nothing may be seized from what appears to be a regular place of business and only premises to which the public[34] has access may be entered in the exercise of this right. While it may appear clear that stalls outside pop concerts are not regular places of business, it will depend on the circumstances whether market stalls are permanent, or at least regular, places of business.[35] It should also be emphasized that the term 'premises' is given a wide definition and includes vehicles, vessels, aircraft, and hovercraft, apart from land, buildings, and moveable structures.[36]

---

[26] CDPA 1988, ss. 111 and 112.

[27] TMA 1994, ss. 89–91.

[28] Council Regulation 3295/94 laying down measures to prohibit the release for free circulation, export, re-export or entry for a suspensive procedure of counterfeit and pirated goods [1994] OJ L 341/8, as amended.

[29] See, e.g., reg. 3.

[30] Regulation 7.

[31] Regulation 8.

[32] CDPA 1988, s. 100(1).

[33] Ibid., (2) and (3).

[34] Ibid., (3).

[35] See J. Phillips, R. Durie, and I. Karet (1993) *Whale on Copyright*, 4th edn, London: Sweet & Maxwell, p. 89.

[36] CDPA 1988, s. 100(5).

4. A notice in a form prescribed by the Copyright and Rights in Performances (Notice of Seizure) Order[37] must be left behind when anything is seized. This notice should mention the grounds on which the seizure took place and the identity of the copyright owner.[38]

The seizure is normally followed by an application for an order for forfeiture or destruction of the infringing goods.[39]

The remainder of this chapter will be concerned with civil actions, and the remedies and evidence issues that relate to them.

Civil remedies[40]

Injunctions

The right holder's first concern in cases of infringement is that the infringement of his or her right stops: the sooner this happens, the easier it will be to limit the damages to his or her trade, rights, and reputation. As an order of the court that directs a party—here, the alleged infringer—to do an act or to refrain from doing an act, the injunction is an excellent tool and remedy for that purpose, hence its frequent use in intellectual property cases. The injunction will almost necessarily be prohibitory and will either stop the threatened commission[41] of infringing acts or the continuation of infringing activities. The order is normally highly effective, partly because wilful non-compliance will amount to contempt of court and contempt is punishable by fine, imprisonment, or sequestration of assets.[42]

Interlocutory injunctions[43]
If you discover that a rival trader is seeking to attack your market share by flooding the shops with counterfeit clothing, bootleg records, or stair carpet grips made in breach of confidence, there is no time to waste. Allowing this trade to develop will obviously be harmful to you, yet the losses will be difficult to calculate precisely in a competitive capitalist society. So immediate action is necessary and the obvious legal route to take is to seek an injunction to prevent the allegedly illegal trade that is about to develop. In this respect, the usual delays of the civil justice system are not helpful and it is therefore necessary to expedite matters with the use of an interlocutory injunction in a quest to freeze the situation before damage can start to occur, pending a subsequent trial on the merits. Of course, the reality, in many cases, is that proceedings are subsequently abandoned or settled and thus the interlocutory stage is the only formal litigation that is ever recorded. This means that the basis of such proceedings must be examined closely.

---

[37] Copyright and Rights in Performances (Notice of Seizure) Order 1989, SI 1989/1006.

[38] CDPA 1988, s. 100(4).

[39] Ibid., s. 114.

[40] Note that the action for breach of confidence forms a special case. The comments underneath apply in general terms to all other intellectual property rights.

[41] The *quia timet* injunction.

[42] See *A-G v. Newspaper Publishing plc* [1988] Ch 333, [1987] 3 All ER 276; *Director General of Fair Trading v. Smith's Concrete* [1991] 4 All ER 150.

[43] Civil Procedure Rules, r. 25.1(a); see also Art. 9 of the Enforcement Directive.

Two basic points

In order to obtain any injunction, two basic points need to be established.

1. It must be clear that damages will not be an adequate remedy,[44] although this, as just explained, should not be too frequent a problem in an intellectual property case. The matter must be urgent or the granting of an injunction must otherwise be desirable in the interests of justice.[45]

2. It is important to remember that an injunction is an equitable right and is thus subject to equity's ever-present requirement of conscionability.[46]

American Cyanamid

The leading case on interlocutory injunctions remains the decision of the House of Lords in *American Cyanamid Co. v. Ethicon Ltd.*[47] In this case, the claimants were the holders of a patent for absorbable surgical sutures and they were displeased to discover that the defendants were proposing to put on to the market a similar, and allegedly infringing, product. The House of Lords agreed with the judgment of the court of first instance and allowed the claimants an interlocutory injunction preventing Ethicon from proceeding with its plans.

The House of Lords, in the sole speech of Lord Diplock, took the opportunity to clarify the general approach to interlocutory injunctions.[48] Lord Diplock pointed out that the general practice was to require the claimant to undertake to compensate the defendants for any losses incurred by them if the claimant failed to prove the case at full trial.[49] This appeared to justify a generous approach to the award of interlocutory injunctions. It was necessary merely to show that there was a 'serious question to be tried'[50] and that the balance of convenience as between the parties, having regard to the utility or otherwise of an award of damages to the claimant or an indemnity by the claimant, should then be considered.[51] Both of these factors were found to be favourable to the claimants.

It should be noted therefore that there is not really, in most cases, an enquiry into the merits of a dispute, but rather simply a finding that there is a genuine issue at stake. This therefore carries a vitally important implication that has been alluded to frequently, but which needs to be spelt out clearly at this juncture. The decision to award an interlocutory injunction in, for example, a case of alleged passing off does not mean that a right has been infringed, but merely that one might have been; there is a serious issue to be tried, in theory, at a future date. So, on the one hand, the court is answering 'maybe', rather than 'yes', to the question of whether a right exists. On the other hand, a refusal to award an interlocutory injunction is really rather damning: not only is an injunction refused, but the basis of the claimant's entire argument is regarded as quite unsustainable.

It is, however, more appropriate to examine the merits of the claims more closely in cases in which, as in those typical of passing off or trade mark infringement, the interlocutory stage is likely, in fact, to be the only stage of the proceedings. The evident strength

---

[44] *London & Blackwall Rly v. Cross* (1886) 31 Ch D 354, *per* Lindley LJ at 369.

[45] Civil Procedure Rules, r. 25.2(2)(b).

[46] See, e.g., *Leather Cloth Co. Ltd v. American Leather Cloth Co. Ltd* (1863) 4 De G J & Sm 137; aff'd 11 HL Cas 523.

[47] [1975] AC 396, [1975] 1 All ER 504.

[48] This approach was again confirmed by the Court of Appeal in *Dyrlund A/S v. Turberville Smith Ltd* [1998] FSR 774.

[49] Ibid. at 406 and 509.

[50] Ibid. at 407 and 510.

[51] Ibid. at 408 and 511.

of the claimant's claim may assist in gaining injunctive relief[52] and this is a justifiable consideration if it is the only stage in the proceedings; the courts are prepared to make a preliminary assessment of the evidence in deciding whether the grant of an injunction is justified or not.[53]

Applications

Plenty of examples can be found of courts endeavouring to apply these general principles. In *BBC v. Precord Ltd*,[54] the defendants proposed to make a rap record featuring illicitly obtained extracts from an unbroadcast interview in which the then Opposition leader had famously lost his temper. This was an appropriate case for interlocutory relief. Although a delay to the record might harm its sales at the peak Christmas season and there were arguable defences, the key point was that a clear property right had been infringed and this was the fundamental issue that merited protection.

In *Mothercare UK Ltd v. Penguin Books Ltd*,[55] meanwhile, the complete lack of likely confusion meant that no interlocutory relief was permitted in the passing off claim and that the defendants were allowed to continue publishing a serious sociological study entitled *Mother Care/Other Care*. Likewise, the small and quantifiable harm to an established claimant, as compared with the very disruptive effects of an interlocutory injunction on a new magazine with a similar title that was just in the process of being launched, meant that no injunction was awarded in *Emap Pursuit Publishing v. Clive (t/a Matchday)*.[56]

The courts do seem prepared to look very carefully at where the balance of convenience lies and should '*take whichever course appears to carry the lower risk of injustice if it should turn out to have been "wrong"*'.[57] Thus in *Neutrogena Corp. & Neutrogena (UK) Ltd v. Golden Ltd & L'Oréal (UK) Ltd*,[58] a dispute concerning possible passing off of the claimants' product 'Neutrogena' by the defendants' new 'Neutralia', Ferris J considered that an injunction would cause loss to the defendant through loss of sales, wasted preliminary expenditure, loss through having to compensate others, loss of opportunity to enter the market, and general disruption, and so, in the light of these factors, refused interlocutory relief. This case and the *Emap* case both show that the time of the actual launch of a rival product may well be too late to gain injunctive relief, given the commitments entered into by the defendant and the resultant shift in the balance of convenience.

Overall, the post-*Cyanamid* approach to the award of interlocutory injunctions[59] shows the courts able to invoke a range of potentially contradictory factors in a generally sensible way. In any event, the more cautious approach to their use in cases in which they may well be the final solution rather than a mere preliminary,[60] which will be the case in many intellectual property examples, goes some way to cushion the impact of *Cyanamid* in this particular area. They will thus remain a significant way of resolving intellectual property disputes.

---

[52] *Quaker Oats Co. v. Alltrades Distributors Ltd* [1981] FSR 9.

[53] See, e.g., *Rizla Ltd v. Bryant & May Ltd* [1986] RPC 389.

[54] [1992] 3 EIPR D-52.

[55] [1988] RPC 113. Cf *Games Workshop Ltd v. Transworld Publishers Ltd* [1993] 9 EIPR D-221.

[56] [1993] 2 EIPR D-40.

[57] *Films Rover International Ltd v. Cannon Film Sales Ltd* [1986] 3 All ER 772, [1987] 1 WLR 670, *per* Hoffmann J at 781 and 680; see also *Dalgety Spillers Foods Ltd v. Food Brokers Ltd* [1994] FSR 504.

[58] [1994] 6 EIPR D-157; see also *Vollers The Corset Company Ltd v. Cook & ors* [2004] ECDR 288.

[59] The court now also has to take certain human rights aspects into account and, in cases in which the injunction may have an effect on the right to freedom of expression, no relief that restrains publication prior to trial is to be granted '*unless the court is satisfied that the applicant is likely to establish that publication should not be allowed*': Human Rights Act 1998, s. 12(3).

[60] For example, an injunction cannot be used as protection against irrecoverable losses, or to avoid damages that would be too remote, if suffered: see *Peaudouce SA v. Kimberly-Clark Ltd* [1996] FSR 680.

An attempt to summarize matters

A lot of factors need to be considered and an attempt was made in *Series 5 Software Ltd v. Clarke*[61] to summarize the matters that the court should take into account when considering whether or not to grant an interim injunction:[62]

- the grant of an interim injunction is a matter of discretion and depends on all the facts of the case;
- there are no fixed rules as to when an injunction should or should not be granted— the relief must be kept flexible;
- because of the practice adopted on the hearing of applications for interlocutory injunctions, the court should rarely attempt to resolve complex issues of disputed fact or law.

Major factors that the court can bear in mind are:

(a) the extent to which damages are likely to be an adequate remedy for each party and the ability of the other party to pay;

(b) the balance of convenience;

(c) the maintenance of the status quo;

(d) any clear view that the court may reach as to the relevant strength of the parties' cases.

Helpful as it may be, it should, of course, be kept in mind that this summary stems from a first instance decision that is yet to be affirmed by a higher court.

Final injunctions[63]

A final injunction can be granted as a remedy after a trial in which the infringement of the claimant's right was established. The injunction is, at that stage, granted to protect the proprietary right or interest of the claimant, but the Court retains its discretion. An injunction is readily[64] granted against the proven infringement of patents, designs, trade marks, and copyright; Otherwise the claimant would be unable to stop the continuation of the infringement and would be compelled to grant a de facto licence.

Delivery up

An injunction may stop any further infringement, but the defendant may consequently be left with a supply of infringing goods. The pile of illegally copied tapes or the T-shirts illegally labelled with a famous trade mark may still be sitting in a warehouse. An order for delivery up of all infringing items is the ideal tool with which to solve this problem. Under a 'delivery up' order, the defendant is ordered to hand over all infringing items or documents and these will normally be destroyed. Exceptionally, the defendant can also be authorized to destroy them under oath or the erasure of the trade mark can be ordered.

All of these measures will effectively remove the infringing goods or documents—or at least their infringing element—from circulation.[65] In relation to trade marks, this power

---

[61] *Series 5 Software v. Clarke* [1996] 1 All ER 853, [1996] FSR 273.

[62] See J. Adams (2007) *Merchandising Intellectual Property*, 3rd edn, Haywards Heath: Tottel, pp. 205–6.

[63] See also Art. 11 of the Enforcement Directive.

[64] Unless the defendant comes with unclean hands or if any repetition of the infringement is not likely. Other special circumstances may also change the situation and the defendant can obviously decline to seek an injunction.

[65] See, e.g., *Peter Pan Manufacturing Corp. v. Corsets Silhouette Ltd* [1963] 3 All ER 402, [1964] 1 WLR 96.

for the court to make an order for delivery up has now been incorporated in the Trade Marks Act 1994.[66] The Copyright, Designs and Patents Act 1988 adds to this general power of the courts through special provisions in relation to copyright and (unregistered) designs. Orders for delivery up for destruction are still possible under these special provisions, but the infringing copies, item, and apparatus may, at the discretion of the court, be forfeited to the right holder in order to compensate him or her for the loss suffered as a result of the infringement.[67]

Damages

Damages are awarded with the aim of undoing the effects of the defendant's breach of contract or commission of a tort.[68] The claimant is compensated for the harm that is caused by the tort or the breach of contract, but losses that are unforeseeably remote are excluded. Exemplary damages that exceed the amount needed for the compensation of the harm suffered may only be awarded in exceptional cases in which the defendant's conduct was calculated to make a profit that would exceed the damages that would have to be paid to the claimant.[69]

The assessment of damages

There is no standard rule for the assessment of damages in intellectual property cases. In a first scenario, the claimant and the defendant may be competitors. If the claimant would have been willing to grant a licence if only the defendant had applied for one, the amount of damages will normally be calculated on the basis of the royalties and other costs that would have been payable under the licence.[70] If the claimant would not have been willing to grant a licence, the amount of damages is normally calculated on the basis of the losses suffered by the claimant through the defendant's competition. Lost profits, lost opportunities, and competitive position acquired by the defendant may all be taken into account.[71]

In a second scenario, the parties do not find themselves in a competitive relationship. Damages are then calculated on the basis of a reasonable royalty for a licence for non-competing use. If neither of these scenarios suggests itself as the most appropriate way forward, the claimant is left the choice between damages calculated on the basis of lost profits or damages calculated on a royalty basis. Even a combination of both can be envisaged in appropriate cases.[72]

The grounds on which damages need to be assessed have now been set out in the course of the implementation of the Enforcement Directive in reg. 3 of the Intellectual Property (Enforcement, etc.) Regulations 2006,[73] in which it is stipulated that:

(1) Where in an action for infringement of an intellectual property right the defendant knew, or had reasonable grounds to know, that he engaged in infringing activity, the damages awarded to the claimant shall be appropriate to the actual prejudice he suffered as a result of the infringement.

---

[66]   TMA 1994, ss. 15–19.
[67]   CDPA 1988, ss. 99 and 230.
[68]   See also Art. 13 of the Enforcement Directive.
[69]   See *Rookes v. Barnard* [1964] AC 1129 at 1220–31.
[70]   *General Tire & Rubber Co. v. Firestone Tyre & Rubber Co.* [1976] RPC 197 at 212.
[71]   See *Gerber Garment Technology Inc. v. Lectra Systems Ltd* [1995] RPC 383.
[72]   *Gerber Garment Technology Inc. v. Lectra Systems Ltd* [1997] RPC 443 at 486, CA.
[73]   SI 2006/1027.

(2) When awarding such damages—

    (a) all appropriate aspects shall be taken into account, including in particular—

        (i) the negative economic consequences, including any lost profits, which the claimant has suffered, and any unfair profits made by the defendant; and

        (ii) elements other than economic factors, including the moral prejudice caused to the claimant by the infringement; or

    (b) where appropriate, they may be awarded on the basis of the royalties or fees which would have been due had the defendant obtained a licence.

Innocent infringement

Damages are also payable for the innocent infringement of a trade mark,[74] but the same rule does not apply to copyright, registered designs, designs, and patents. In these cases, Parliament felt that it would have been rather harsh to oblige an innocent infringer to pay damages. The concept of 'innocence' is defined in a narrow way and the alleged infringer must show that he or she made reasonable enquiries to check whether his or her activities would infringe any existing rights. The defendant will only be innocent if he or she did not know, and had no reason to believe, that the rights that he or she infringed existed.[75]

Additional damages

The Copyright, Designs and Patents Act 1988 introduced the concept of additional damages for the infringement of copyright and (unregistered) design rights. These additional damages come on top of the normal damages[76] and are awarded in flagrant cases of infringement. The court will determine the amount on the basis that justice must be done in each case, and will take the flagrancy of the infringement and the benefit accruing to the defendant by reason of the infringement into account when deciding whether or not to award additional damages.[77]

Account of profits

The claimant is entitled to reclaim the amount earned by the defendant by way of unjust enrichment through the infringement of the claimant's intellectual property right. To achieve this, the claimant can use the remedy of an account of profits, which is restitutionary and equitable[78] in nature. Rather than be compensated by damages, the claimant may opt to investigate the actual accounts of the defendant and to require that any profit that was made as a result of the infringement be handed over.[79] That profit may be the profit on each item that is sold and in which the protected subject matter is included,[80] or

---

[74] *Gillette (UK) Ltd v. Edenwest Ltd* [1994] RPC 279.

[75] Registered Designs Act 1949, s. 9(1); Patents Act 1977, s. 62(1); CDPA 1988, ss. 97(1) and 233.

[76] They can only be awarded if damages are the other remedy that is awarded: *Redrow Homes Ltd v. Bett Bros plc* [1998] 1 All ER 385, [1998] 2 WLR 198, overruling *Cala Homes (South) Ltd v. Alfred McAlpine Homes East Ltd (No. 2)* [1996] FSR 36.

[77] CDPA 1988, ss. 97(2) and 229(3).

[78] The court therefore has a discretion whether or not to grant this remedy: see *Sir Terence Conran v. Mean Fiddlers Holding* [1997] FSR 856, in which an account of profits was refused in relation to a case in which the trade mark infringement was innocent, and in which the causal link between the profits and the infringement was hard to establish.

[79] See Patents Act 1977, s. 61(2); CDPA 1988, s. 96(2).

[80] *Peter Pan Manufacturing Corp. v. Corsets Silhouette Ltd* [1963] 3 All ER 402.

the increase in the defendant's profit made through the use, other than by inclusion in the defendant's products, of the protected subject matter.[81]

In practice, it is often difficult to calculate the profit that is caused by the infringement, because the latter is often not the single cause of the profit. Often, only a part of a product is an infringement and, in all of these cases, the courts face the difficult task of determining what part of the profit has been caused by the infringing acts.[82] This remedy is therefore not used often, because it involves a lot of work and an expensive accounting procedure. The decision by the House of Lords that additional damages cannot be awarded in copyright or unregistered design cases in which the claimant opted for an account of profits is bound to make it an even less popular remedy.[83] Nevertheless, the claimant could be well advised to consider the use of this remedy in those cases in which he or she could never have made the profits that were made by the defendant, because it may enable the claimant to obtain a higher amount by way of compensation.

The gathering of evidence

The gathering of evidence is often a crucial issue in intellectual property cases. In this part of the chapter, we will highlight the instruments that are used most often; an overview of all of the relevant aspects of the law of civil procedure is not envisaged. The Enforcement Directive also addresses the issues surrounding evidence.[84]

Search orders

The origin of the order

The success of infringement actions and the effectiveness of remedies depend on the availability at the trial stage of evidence relating to the alleged infringement. It is vital that the claimant is given the opportunity to discover this evidence. It is relatively easy for a mala fide defendant to alter or to destroy incriminating documents, to move goods, or to hide machinery and raw materials, once he or she has been served with a writ. The production of infringing copies of audio cassettes provides a good example: all that is needed is a number of cassette players and tapes, plus some labels; all of this can be moved within a few hours and it can be hidden in any spare room or shed.

What is required, then, is a tool that would allow the claimant to discover the evidence without any advance warning being given to the defendant. This tool would involve an *ex parte* application to the court, which would then authorize the claimant and his or her solicitors to enter the defendant's premises, so as to discover the evidence and to seize or copy any relevant information. It would be a kind of civil search warrant.

Such a tool was introduced by the Court of Appeal[85] in *Anton Piller KG v. Manufacturing Processes Ltd*[86] and consequently became known as the 'Anton Piller order'. Recent

---

[81] *United Horse Shoe v. Stewart* (1888) 13 App 401, 3 RPC 139 at 266–7.

[82] See *Celanese International v. BP Chemicals* [1999] RPC 203.

[83] *Redrow Homes Ltd v. Bett Bros plc & Nail Co.* [1999] 1 AC 197, [1998] 1 All ER 385, overruling *Cala Homes (South) Ltd v. Alfred McAlpine Homes East Ltd (No. 2)* [1996] FSR 36.

[84] Articles 6 and 7 of the Enforcement Directive.

[85] On the basis of a limited previous practice in the Chancery Division: see *EMI v. Pandit* [1975] 1 All ER 418, [1975] 1 WLR 302.

[86] [1976] Ch 55, [1976] 1 All ER 779.

changes in the wake of the Civil Procedure Act 1997 led to that order being renamed the 'search order'.[87]

Lord Denning MR has described the order as follows:

> Let me say at once that no court in this land has any power to issue a search warrant to enter a man's house so as to see if there are papers or documents there which are of an incriminating nature. But the order sought in this case is not a search warrant. It does not authorise the claimant's solicitors or anyone else to enter the defendants' premises against their will. It only authorises entry and inspection by the permission of the defendants. It does more, it actually orders them to give permission—with, I suppose, the result that if they do not give permission they are guilty of contempt of court.[88]

Applications for a search order are to be made *ex parte* to a patents judge in the High Court or to the patents county court. They can eventually also be made to a Chancery judge.[89]

The order and its expansion

The essential prerequisites for making such an order were set out by Ormerod LJ:

> First, there must be an extremely strong prima facie case. Second, the damage, potential or actual, must be very serious for the applicant. Third, there must be clear evidence that the defendants have in their possession incriminating documents or things, and that there is a real possibility that they may destroy such material before any application inter partes can be made.[90]

The claimant's solicitor will be authorized to carry out the order as an officer of the court and the defendant is obliged to permit the inspection, otherwise he or she will face proceedings for contempt of court.[91] This does not, however, deprive the defendant completely of the possibility to refuse to permit the inspection, but this option becomes very risky and needs to be combined with a swift application for discharge of the order. The applicant has a duty of full and frank disclosure of all relevant elements to the court, and the granting of the order is subject to the applicant making a cross-undertaking in damages.

It is the basis of the search order to preserve evidence that may otherwise be destroyed by the defendant. The real need meant that the order became an instant success, rather than the exceptional measure it was supposed to be. One of the first cases to extend the order slightly was *EMI Ltd v. Sarwar & Haidar*,[92] in which the defendants were also ordered:

> to disclose to the person serving the order, the names and addresses of the persons or companies responsible for supplying the defendants and to place into custody all invoices, books of sale, order books, and all other documents in their possession, power, custody or control relating to the acquisition, disposal or distribution of the infringing tape recordings.[93]

This will enable the defendant to obtain full evidence regarding anyone involved in an infringement network on the basis of a single search order and increases the value of the

[87] Section 7; Civil Procedure Rules, r. 25; Practice Direction, para. 25.
[88] *Anton Piller KG v. Manufacturing Processes Ltd* [1976] Ch 55 at 58.
[89] Civil Procedure Rules, r. 25A; Practice Direction, para. 8.5.
[90] *Anton Piller KG v. Manufacturing Processes Ltd* [1976] Ch 55 at 62; see also *Thermax Ltd v. Schott Industrial Glass Ltd* [1981] FSR 289; *Columbia Picture Industries v. Robinson* [1987] Ch 38, [1986] 3 All ER 338.
[91] On the issue of failure to comply, see *Wardle Fabrics v. Myristis* [1984] FSR 263.
[92] [1977] FSR 146.
[93] Ibid. at 147.

order substantially. It also became possible to obtain an order against a represented class of persons if there is a sufficient amount of identity of interest among the members of such a class. This extension allowed EMI Records to act against all persons dealing in a certain type of pirated audio cassettes with one search order, because they all had an interest in preventing EMI from tracing the source of these pirated cassettes.

The expansion of the search order and its growing effectiveness came under threat when the House of Lords decided that orders requiring the defendant to make a disclosure that could be self-incriminating were contrary to the principle of privilege against self-incrimination.[94] The possibility for the defendant to withhold information on the basis that he or she would otherwise be incriminating themselves reduces the potential and value of the order substantially. This conclusion, which had been reached by a reluctant House of Lords, was reversed by s. 72 of the Supreme Court Act 1981 when the legislature stepped in to preserve the order. The self-incrimination defence will now no longer be available against the implementation of a search order,[95] although the statements or admissions made at that stage will not be admissible as evidence in relation to any related offence.

Abuse of the order and its redress

Abuse

Not only did search orders become a frequently used tool, they also gave rise to abuses,[96] of which two forms can be identified. Firstly, the courts became too flexible in granting the order[97] and it became fashionable to use them to go on a 'fishing expedition'. An order was, in such cases, granted on the basis of a mere suspicion of infringement, rather than on the basis of a very strong prima facie case, and was used simply to establish whether the infringement took place.[98] Often, the applicant also obtained very valuable commercial information on a competitor.

Secondly, the execution of the order was not always impeccable. The limits and restrictions imposed in the order were often exceeded, documents disappeared,[99] etc., and the orders were also used to harass the defendant and to drive him or her out of business.[100] Orders were executed at impossible times[101] or with a great deal of publicity. So much material was taken that the defendant could no longer operate properly and meet his or her contractual obligations[102] or improper publicity surrounding the order scared customers away from further dealings with the defendant.[103]

Towards a solution

The urgent need to weed out these abuses, while at the same time preserving the search order as an extremely useful tool in certain circumstances, became clear and Sir Donald Nicholls V-C suggested a way to achieve this double goal in *Universal Thermosensors v.*

---

[94] *Rank Film Distributors Ltd v. Video Information Centre* [1982] AC 380, aff'd [1981] 2 All ER 76.

[95] See *Universal City Studios Inc. v. Hubbard* [1984] Ch 225, [1984] 1 All ER 661.

[96] See, e.g., *TRP v. Thorley* [1993] Court of Appeal, unreported, Lexis transcript available; *Lock International Plc v. Beswick* [1989] 3 All ER 373, [1989] 1 WLR 1268, *per* Hoffmann J.

[97] See the remarks in this sense by Whitford J in *Systematica Ltd v. London Computer Centre Ltd* [1983] FSR 313.

[98] Ibid.

[99] *Universal Thermosensors v. Hibben* [1992] 1 WLR 840, [1992] FSR 361.

[100] *Columbia Picture Industries v. Robinson* [1987] Ch 38, [1986] 3 All ER 338.

[101] *Universal Thermosensors v. Hibben* [1992] 1 WLR 840, [1992] FSR 361.

[102] *Columbia Picture Industries v. Robinson* [1987] Ch 38, [1986] 3 All ER 338.

[103] *BUPA v. First Choice Health Care* [1993] 4 EIPR 87.

Hibben.[104] Most points of his advice were then incorporated in a new Practice Direction[105] and further refinement followed in the wake of the Civil Procedure Act 1997.

Search orders will now only be given if the matter is urgent or if the order is otherwise desirable in the interest of justice.[106] Search orders should also only be executed on working days in office hours and not during weekends, or early in the morning, or late at night.[107] This implies that the defendant should be in a position to use effectively his or her right to consult a solicitor and to obtain legal advice at the very moment that he or she is presented with an order before complying with it, without running the risk of being in contempt of court by delaying the execution of the order.[108] A woman should also be present when the order is to be executed by a male solicitor at premises that are likely to be occupied by an unaccompanied woman.[109] Additionally, when the nature of the items that are removed makes this necessary, the applicant should insure them.[110]

The Practice Direction contains a further range of provisions and also allows the judge more time to consider the application more in depth,[111] but by far the most important change is that the claimant's solicitor should now no longer execute a search order. The role of the claimant's solicitor is reduced to securing the grant of the order and, afterwards, the execution is entrusted to a solicitor who does not act for the applicant.[112] This *'supervising solicitor should be an experienced solicitor, having some familiarity with the operation of* [search] *orders, who is not a member or employee of the firm acting for the applicant'.*[113] The supervising solicitor must also explain the terms of the search order to the respondents in plain English and he or she must advise them of their rights.[114]

In the old situation, the claimant's solicitor was torn between the interests of his or her client, who was also footing the bill, and his or her neutral role as an officer of the court. This will now no longer be the case, although the risk of bias remains at the application stage due to the *ex parte* nature of the proceedings.[115] The Practice Direction and the Civil Procedure Rules are also unsuccessful in solving the difficult problem of who may consent to entry to the premises, to the searching of these premises, and to seizure. In the absence of the obvious defendant, the Practice Direction gives this power to *'a responsible employee of the defendant'* as well as to the more established category of *'person(s) appearing to be in charge of the premises'.*[116] The precise definition of these categories is bound to cause confusion, which may lead to incidents when a search order is executed under these circumstances.[117]

104 *Universal Thermosensors Ltd v. Hibben* [1992] 1 WLR 840 at 860–1.
105 Practice Direction [1994] 4 All ER 52, [1994] RPC 617.
106 Civil Procedure Rules, r. 25.2(2)(b).
107 Practice Direction [1994] 4 All ER 52 at 54, Annex 1; *Universal Thermosensors Ltd v. Hibben* [1992] 1 WLR 840, *per* Sir Donald Nicholls V-C at 860.
108 *Universal Thermosensors Ltd v. Hibben* [1992] 1 WLR 840, *per* Sir Donald Nicholls V-C at 860.
109 Practice Direction [1994] 4 All ER 52 at 53; CDPA 1988, s. 3B(2); *Universal Thermosensors Ltd v. Hibben* [1992] 1 WLR 840, *per* Sir Donald Nicholls V-C at 860. See now Civil Procedure Rules, r. 25A; Practice Direction, para. 7.4(5).
110 Practice Direction [1994] 4 All ER 52 at 53; CDPA 1988, s. 3B(3).
111 Practice Direction [1994] 4 All ER 52 at 53; CDPA 1988, ss. 3A(1) and 3B(5).
112 See also *Universal Thermosensors Ltd v. Hibben* [1992] 1 WLR 840, *per* Sir Donald Nicholls V-C at 861.
113 Practice Direction [1994] 4 All ER 52 at 53; CDPA 1988, s. 3B(1)(a).
114 Civil Procedure Rules, r. 25A; Practice Direction, para. 7.4.
115 M. Davies, 'Anton Pillers after the Practice Direction' [1996] 15 CJQ 17.
116 Practice Direction [1994] 4 All ER 52 at 54–5, Annex 1.
117 Davies [1996].

It is nevertheless submitted that the Practice Direction and the new Civil Procedure Rules will be successful in eliminating the abuse, and in securing the survival, of the search order. In the new system, claimants who:

> wish to take advantage of this truly draconian type of order…must be prepared to pay for the safeguards experience has shown are necessary if the interests of defendants are fairly to be protected.[118]

Freezing orders

Derived from the name of one of the parties in the oldest case in this area, *Mareva Cia Naviera SA v. International Bulk Carriers SA*,[119] the so-called 'Mareva injunction' was often called a 'freezing injunction', because this *ex parte* injunction freezes the assets of a party by restraining that party from removing them from the jurisdiction. In the wake of the Civil Procedure Act 1997, the order has now been renamed the 'freezing order'.

Lord Denning MR laid down the following guidelines in *Third Chandris Shipping Corp. v. Unimarine SA*.[120]

1. The claimant must make full and frank disclosure of all relevant information and materials.

2. He or she must set out his or her claim and the grounds for it, as well as the arguments raised against this claim by the defendant. He must also give indications that the defendant has assets within the jurisdiction and that there is a risk that the assets will be removed from the jurisdiction.

3. The claimant must give an undertaking in damages.

These guidelines were later supplemented by two further guidelines.[121]

4. The claimant must show that his or her case has a certain strength.

5. That strength needs to be balanced against all other relevant factors before the judge uses the discretion to grant a freezing order.

Banks and other third parties can be bound by a freezing order,[122] which therefore becomes another useful tool in the war against untrustworthy defendants in intellectual property infringement cases.[123] Quite often, a search order is combined with a freezing order[124] and, while this offers a great deal of relief to the claimant, it must be clear that this can also be used quite effectively to put a defendant out of business.[125] This risk is especially present in cases brought by commercially powerful claimants against small innovative competitors, because the latter may go out of business before the case is fully argued in court. It can even be said that, on certain occasions, that has been the purpose of the claimants, because it has

---

[118] *Universal Thermosensors Ltd v. Hibben* [1992] 1 WLR 840, *per* Sir Donald Nicholls V-C at 861.

[119] [1980] 1 All ER 213, [1975] 2 Lloyd's Rep 509.

[120] *Third Chandris Shipping Corp. v. Unimarine SA* [1979] QB 645, *sub nom Third Chandris v Unimarine* [1979] 2 All ER 972.

[121] *Ninemia Maritime Corp. v. Trane Schiffarhtsgesellschaft mbH und Co. KG (The Niedersachsen)* [1984] 1 All ER 398.

[122] See *Z Ltd v. A-Z & AA-LL* [1982] QB 558, [1982] 1 All ER 556.

[123] Third parties, such as banks, may be liable for contempt of court if the order is not implemented correctly, but they do not own a duty of care towards the third party that obtained the order: *Customs & Excise Comrs v. Barclays Bank plc* [2007] 1 AC 181 (HL).

[124] Civil Procedure Rules, r .25(f); see, e.g., *McDonald v. Graham* [1994] RPC 407.

[125] See *CBS United Kingdom Ltd v. Lambert* [1983] Ch 37, [1982] 3 All ER 237.

been quite clear, on these occasions, that no infringement would eventually be found, and yet an application for a search order and a freezing order was nevertheless brought.

The *Norwich Pharmacal* order

Infringement actions often start when the owner of an intellectual property right finds an infringing product at the end of the distribution chain; the goods may alternatively be in transit. It is vital for the right owner that he or she is able to trace the source of the infringing product in order to be able to stop the infringement at its roots, because the person in whose hands the product is found may not even know that the product is a copy or an infringing product and may not be infringing him or herself. The person may also be unaware of the fact that others must have infringed any intellectual property right. The only way for the right owner to proceed successfully in such a case is to get hold of the names and addresses of any consignors or consignees, and to track the infringing product all the way up to its manufacturers.

The *Norwich Pharmacal* order has the same aim and such an order obliges the party against whom it is made to reveal these names and addresses.[126] In the original case,[127] from which the name of this disclosure order is derived, the Commissioner of Customs and Excise was obliged to reveal the names of the importers of a patented drug. Later cases obliged telephone operators, for example, to reveal the names of mobile phone users that were allegedly involved in passing off.[128]

The order is discretionary in nature and will normally only be granted if it is the only way in which the claimant can get hold of the information and if it is demonstrated that the person against whom it is made is (unwittingly) facilitating the infringement or any other wrongful act. The order may be extended to cover also a prohibition to remove the infringing goods.

The *Norwich Pharmacal* order is often applied in tort—that is, infringement—cases, but it is not confined to tort. It can, for example, also arise in the context of breach of contract, such as breach of a licence contract, and in the context of breach of confidence.[129]

An overview

Three elements are really important in the relationship between intellectual property rights and remedies. Firstly, there are the traditional remedies headed by damages that are normally granted at the trial and which we discussed in the various chapters concerned with each of the substantive intellectual property rights. Secondly, intellectual property infringement often requires immediate action or a pre-emptive strike. This is the area in which interlocutory injunctions play an important role. Finally, gathering evidence that is vital for the full trial is not always easy, but it would not be just to allow infringers to 'get away with it' simply because the right owner did not have the means of discovering the evidence needed in an infringement case. Search orders address this problem.

---

[126] Civil Procedure Rules, r. 31.

[127] *Norwich Pharmacal v. Comr of Customs & Excise* [1974] AC 133; rev'd [1974] RPC 101; see also *British Steel Corp. v. Granada Television Ltd* [1981] AC 1096, [1981] 1 All ER 417, a case that shows the potential of the order in a wider context.

[128] *Coca-Cola Co. v. British Telecommunications* [1999] FSR 518.

[129] *Ashworth Hospital Authority v. MGN Ltd* [2003] FSR 311 (HL); see also *Interbrew v. Financial Times* [2002] EMLR 446.

Further reading

CORNISH, W. R., DREXL, J., HILTY, R. and KUR, A., 'Procedures and remedies for enforcing IPRS: the European Commission's Proposed Directive' [2003] EIPR 447.

FAWCETT, J. and TORREMANS, P. (1998) *Intellectual Property and Private International Law*, Oxford: Clarendon Press.

GARNETT, K., DAVIES, G. and HARBOTTLE, G. (2005) *Copinger and Skone James on Copyright*, 15th edn, London: Sweet and Maxwell, ch. 22.

HUNIAR, K., 'The Enforcement Directive: its effects on UK law' [2006] EIPR 92.

KITCHIN, D., LLEWELYN, D., MELLOR, J., MEADE, R., MOODY-STUART, T. and KEELING, D. (2005) *Kerly's Law of Trade Marks and Trade Names*, 14th edn, London: Sweet and Maxwell. ch. 19.

THORLEY, S., MILLER, R., BURKILL, G. and BIRSS, C. (eds) (2006) *Terrell on the Law of Patents*, 16th edn, London: Sweet and Maxwell, ch. 13.

TREACY, P. and WRAY, A., 'IP Crimes: the prospect for EU-wide criminal sanctions—a long road ahead?' [2006] EIPR 1.

Postscript

Though each of the three main proprietary intellectual property rights has been with us for a long time, it is significant that all three—patents, copyright, and trade marks—have needed to be completely rewritten by Parliament within the space of the last four decades. This is no surprise, reflecting as it does simultaneously the growth of European and international obligations, which are so important when the law of intellectual property has to try and operate on a global basis, and also the growth of new technologies. While these forces of change continue to exert their influence it is a safe prediction that the law of intellectual property will continue to be reformed to reflect the changing conditions.

Some hundreds of pages ago we began by considering the range of potential intellectual property rights that might arise from a great operatic performance. Had this scenario been devised 20 years earlier, it would have been far shorter. Even at what seems a date in modern history the reader would have had no notion of compact disc players, satellite television, and much of contemporary computer and Internet technology. Intellectual property law is forced to keep pace with the pace of technological development and a legitimate method of critique of the law is to ask whether it has always succeeded in protecting the full range of commercially valuable activity that has continued constantly to evolve. Equally if we look forward 20 years it may be confidently predicted that the position will have dramatically changed yet again. Opera fans may access the performance along their fibre optic cables along with thousands of other choices of entertainments; biotechnology may have produced a new race of Italian super-tenors. In whatever event, the law will be requested to adapt and evolve to meet the evolution of technological achievement.

Equally the law has had to take on new responsibilities for the protection of other intangible but commercially important interests and has had to add to the range of protected interests, goodwill, information and character, for example. It may be that these areas will benefit from a codification in future years, especially if the inherent vagaries of the common law are thought to be inappropriate in addressing rights which, like their older counterparts, inevitably operate on a global basis. Information, in particular, seems a potential candidate for reform; literary copyright and common law or equitable rules of confidentiality hardly seem the best approaches to the protection of the ever growing flood of electronic data encircling the world. Likewise the law's lack of quality control—for instance copyright protection is afforded equally to grand opera and radio jingles—will have to be addressed at some stage.

It seems likely therefore that the law that we have set out to illuminate will continue its evolutionary, and occasionally revolutionary, path into the future. At present, though, we express the hope that we have helped in some way to bring to wider attention issues we believe to be of great legal and national interest and importance, and which have in the past been confined to the somewhat closed world of the specialist lawyers and law reports. In doing so that should result in a larger audience for wherever we are taken by the next steps in the evolution of intellectual property.

Index